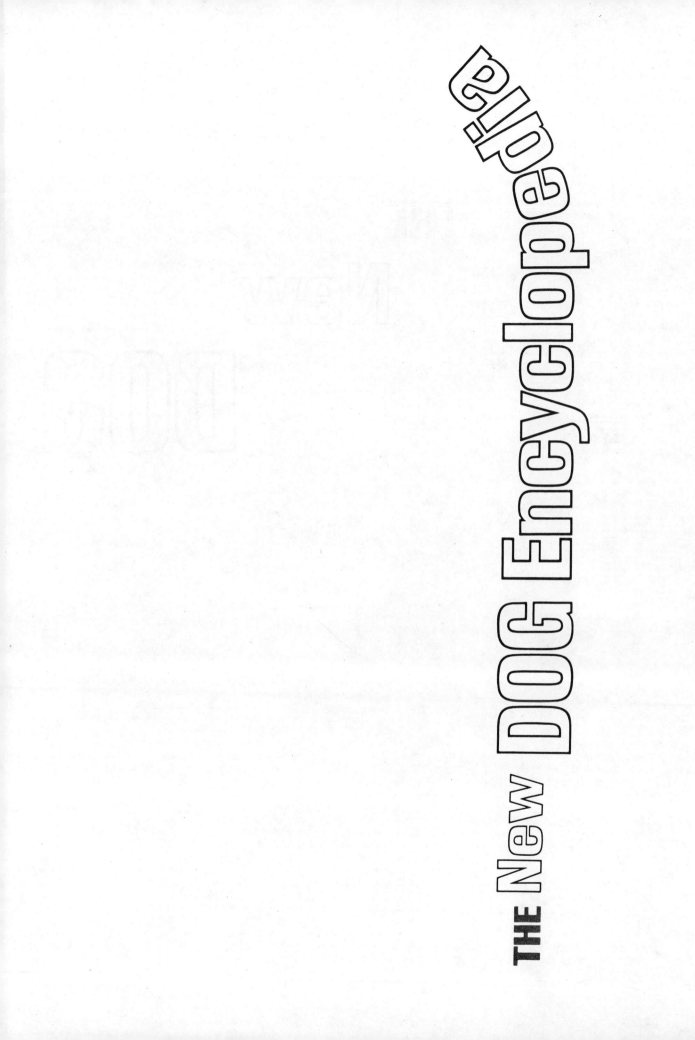

THE New DOG

Encyclopedia

completely revised and expanded updating
of the HENRY P. DAVIS classic
Modern Dog Encyclopedia

GALAHAD BOOKS · NEW YORK

Reprinted in 1982 by
Galahad Books
95 Madison Avenue
New York, NY 10016

Published by arrangement with Stackpole Books

Manufactured in the United States of America

10 9 8 7 6 5 4 3 2 1

Library of Congress Catalog Card Number 74-82433

ISBN 0-88365-215-3

FOREWORD

THE NEW DOG ENCYCLOPEDIA is an expanded, amplified version of that hefty predecessor known as *The Modern Dog Encyclopedia* which, in its time, exhausted six printings and, as to its place among all other dog books, was rated by some American reviewers as second only in quality of information and importance to England's large three-volume Hutchinson's dog encyclopedia, the latter recognized as the largest book in the world devoted exclusively to dogs.

Several years under preparation, THE NEW DOG ENCYCLOPEDIA offers expanded and updated treatment on many of the topics the encyclopedia formerly covered and, in addition, offers much new material on dog-related topics not in the earlier volumes.

To understand the scope of this new encyclopedia, one must first know something of the coverage of its predecessors. The original was a remarkable collection of authoritative, extensive articles dealing with dogs from virtually every standpoint: Selecting a dog, various American and foreign classifications of dogs, the dog as man's ally—as hunter, guard, soldier, companion, worker, aid to the blind; dogs of the Presidents, dogs in the movies, dogs in sport, in field trials, sheepdog trials, in coursing and racing, and so forth.

Featured before and amplified in this edition with appropriate correction or updating are the histories, descriptions and listings of the standards of each of the breeds recognized by AKC. This covers, alone, of course, more than one hundred separate breeds.

The encyclopedia also featured extensive articles about the dog's anatomy and physiology, first aid, health care, how to give medicine, breeding, general care, dog nutrition, kenneling, and even the psychology of the dog. There were several articles on dog

training, whether the case of simple training for a puppy or as to training a dog for field or shows.

Included also was much information on conditioning a dog for bench and field, details on proper trimming and plucking of the various breeds. Also historical and current information on the more prominent kennel clubs such as AKC, the Canadian Kennel Club, the Kennel Club of England, and the various dog registers and stud books. Even the rules for various trials and events were included such as those for sheepdog trials, the rules of the Amateur Field Trial Clubs of America, the AKC, and listings of important field trial winners.

All of these topics are covered here also, but with necessary revision and updating—in a number of cases with considerable text expansion to cover new information or aspects not earlier treated.

Entirely *new text* has been added dealing with:
Your Dog and the Law
Guide to Dog Nutrition
Kenneling
Suggestions on Transporting Your Dog (This includes information about quarantine, immunization, etc., requirements applicable when dogs are to be shipped to various foreign countries and covers as well the requirements of the various states together with suggestions on air shipments.)
The New Knowledge of Dog Behavior (Findings from the studies of Pfaffenberger and others.)
World Dog Show Systems
The Art of Showing Dogs
The Art of Judging Dogs
Dog Ailments and First Aid (This text, sometimes referred to as "the veterinarian's section", has been extensively expanded to include more health

problems than ever before and reflects the thoughtful work of several thoroughly competent veterinarians.)

Puppy Production (Text based on experience gained at the Purina Dog Care Center.)

The Dog as an Aid to the Blind (Now descriptively covers the operations of all known U.S. organizations training dogs as aids to the blind.)

The Dog as a Guard

The Dog as a Soldier

Training the Hunting Dog (Includes information on Electronic Training Aids.)

The latest Amateur Championship Stakes and Running Rules of the Amateur Field Trial Clubs of America have been included, and the listings of important field trial winners has been updated.

The text concerning dog classifications has been much expanded with new material. It contains much new information—reference material, etc. about the Bermuda Kennel Club, F.C.I. and other foreign breed classifications.

The text on Famous Dogs has been expanded respecting the dogs of our Presidents and the dogs today prominent in movies and t.v.

Never before published but now included in the text on kennel clubs is the history of U.K.C., Inc., together with supplementary information on this organization's official rules for its Official Nite Hunt and Licensed Water Race events. There is included also a list of the breeds recognized and registered by UKC.

Those who may wish to look up various sections of the American Kennel Club rules will find a complete listing of regulations. For those who may wish to enter dogs in any of the Bermuda Shows there are also many helpful details and important rules information and suggestions on the shipment of entries to Bermuda, together with helpful information for those who may wish to combine a Bermuda vacation with show activities.

The historical background and growth of the Humane Movement is also the topic of a new and extensive write-up.

Finally, the Appendices include a general glossary, a reference listing of the seven *other* special-interest glossaries elsewhere in the book, information on dog publications, the *"American Field,"* and a listing of stud books and registers. Those wishing to write abroad to contact some of the more prominent foreign kennel clubs will find useful references and addresses.

There are hundreds of new illustrations throughout the volume.

It is difficult, indeed, to visualize the dog owner, breeder, fancier, trainer, trial or show enthusiast or handler, veterinarian or pet shop owner today who would not find somewhere within these pages something of strong interest, of reference value or other usefulness, reliable and authoritative information respecting almost any question one could think to ask about dogs, whether it be from the standpoint of their feeding and handling, their health and training, their care or welfare.

For educational use also, here in one volume has been collected an enormous amount of information useful for the student, the researcher, the counselor, or the teacher.

Every effort has been directed towards offering the reader the latest and best information. Such things as the names of individuals, firms, etc., and their addresses, rules and regulations of various kennel clubs and breed standards are vulnerable, however, to occasional change with the passage of time. To the extent this may sometimes pose a problem to the reader, it poses no less a problem to the publisher, and is one for which there appears to be no better solution than to counsel patience and follow-up. In such a case, try writing for the needed new address or rule to any of several reference sources such as the AKC or UKC, or—in some instances, perhaps—to the publisher of a dog magazine. These are all points where considerate treatment of inquiries is usually the rule. Very often they are able to provide a ready suggestion or such new address as may be needed.

ACKNOWLEDGMENTS

SPECIAL THANKS and appreciation are extended to the following who, frequently beyond the contributions here noted, gave the helpful information and assistance which made this expanded revision possible:

Mrs. Dana I. Alvi, President and one of the founders of The Kuvasz Club of America, also owner of Kuvasz Hamralvi Kennels, for assistance with material relevant the Kuvasz.

Mr. Jack Baird, well-known obedience trial judge, for "Obedience Trials."

Dr. Frank A. Beach, noted psychologist of Yale University, for "Psychology of the Dog."

Dr. Francisco Beltram of Puebla Mexico, for breed histories of the Chihuahua.

Mr. Carl H. Bradford, breeder and trainer of Working Border Collies, for "History of the Working Border Collie."

Mrs. Jo Brandenburg, The Chase Publishing Co., Inc., Editor, The Chase, for various details relative foxhound trials.

Mr. Bill Brown, Editor, The American Field, for his assistance in reviewing several portions of the manuscript and furnishing statistics and data on various field trial winners.

Dr. William A. Bruette, famous dog authority and author, for making available library facilities and providing other valued assistance.

Mr. Roy H. Carlberg, Secretary, AKC, for helpfulness in several areas of the text concerning the AKC and AKC rules.

Mr. Joseph E. Carney, Sr., for assistance on the text dealing with greyhound racing.

Mrs. L. Chiverton of The Kennel Club, London, England, for making available general information relative her club's rules and the breeds recognized.

Dr. Edwin H. Colbert, curator of fossil animals and reptiles, American Museum of Natural History, for assistance on "The Origin of the Dog."

Dr. James Corbin, Ph.D., Purina Dog Care Center, for information relative dog food research and for several writings relative feeding, puppy raising, etc. as gained from the Center's experience.

Mrs. Francis V. Crane, for preparation of the breed history of the Great Pyrenees.

Mr. David Michael Duffey of Outdoor Life magazine, for review and assistance with certain portions involving hunting dogs, including beagle training.

Mr. Ernest Eberhard, noted breeder of Bull Terriers, for breed history of same.

Mr. A-Ch. Fahlstedt, staff member of Svenska Kennelklubben, for helpful information regarding breeds recognized by that organization.

Mr. Jeff Fellows of Walt Disney Productions, for helpful information relative movie and t.v. dogs.

Mrs. Edward Flieger, Show Secretary, The Bermuda Kennel Club, Inc., for information relative the program and rules of her club.

Dr. E. G. Fuhrman, President, U.K.C., Inc., for much previously unpublished information, reference material and facts relative the history of U.K.C. and its program.

M. Charles Gendebien, Secretary General, F.C.I., for information relative breeds recognized by this organization.

Diana Henley, ASPCA, for information relative dog travel, the shipment of pets by air, and quarantine and other requirements of various foreign countries as reflected in booklets of her organization.

Mr. R. A. E. Herbhold, for assistance with the history of Borzois.

Mr. John Kelley, authority on dog racing, for much of the information on Coursing and Racing.

Evelyn Lincoln, secretary to Former President Kennedy, for details relevant dogs of the White House during JFK's tenure.

Mrs. Alva McColl, for text and historical notes on The Canadian Kennel Club.

Lequita J. McKay, Executive Director, Eye Dog Foundation, for details on the program of that organization.

Mr. Noble M. Melencamp, staff assistant to President Nixon, for details on the President's dogs.

Mr. A. Raymond Miller of the Shetland Sheepdog Club of America, for historical notes on the Shetland Sheepdog.

Mr. Harry Miller of the Gaines Dog Research Center, for material relevant dog nutrition.

Evelyn Monte, Associate Director, Gaines Dog Research Center, and authority and writer on dogs. Author of The Dog in Religion, The Dog in Ancient Myth and Legend, The Dog as a Companion, and a contributor in many other ways of valued assistance in the development of this volume.

Dr. Todd O. Munson, veterinarian, for assistance with the text on Suggestions on Feeding Growing Dogs.

Mr. Edwin J. Myers of Arden Hills Kennel, for the breed history of the Collie.

Mr. John C. Neff of The American Kennel Club for text relative Bench Shows and the history of The American Kennel Club.

Mrs. Ross Obenauer, for the breed history of the Cairn Terrier.

Mr. Hans Oberhammer, noted architect and bench show judge, for much of the text relative Kenneling.

Mr. George J. O'Leary, for the text relative The Master Eye Foundation.

Margaret Peck, for assistance with the breed history on the Borzois.

Mr. Clarence J. Pfaffenberger, outstanding researcher on dog behavior and author, for his article on The New Knowledge of Dog Behavior, and other helpful material. (It is with much regret that the publisher learned only recently this writer's death occurred within the past year or two.)

Mrs. Catherine Quereaux of the Samoyed Club of America, for the breed history of the Samoyed.

Mr. Maxwell Riddle, noted dog judge, authority, and associate editor of the Cleveland Press. He has judged dog shows in South Africa, Australia, Japan, China, India, Cuba, Bermuda, and many European countries. To him is extended credit for the text on World Dog Show Systems, The Art of Judging Dogs, and Dogs of the World. Mr. Riddle's assistance with a number of breed histories in AKC's Working Group and the Toys is also gratefully acknowledged.

Mr. Ed Ring of Filmways T.V., for helpful information on dogs seen on t.v.

Mrs. Phyllis Robson of Dog World magazine, London, England, for much information on The Kennel Club of England.

Miss Anne Hone Rogers, top dog show handler, for The Art of Showing Dogs.

Mrs. Horace B. Sodt, for helpful material relative dog heroes and the American Humane Association.

Mr. Ivan Swedrup, Secretary General, Svenska Kennelklubben, who not only supplied the list of breeds recognized by that organization, but as a special courtesy also arranged for English translation of the listing.

Mrs. Willie Day Taylor, assistant to Former President Johnson, who provided details relevant the dogs in the White House during LBJ's tenure.

Mrs. Margaret Underhill, for the Seeing Eye text.

Mr. Gerald F. White of The Briard Fellowship, for the breed history of the Briard.

Dr. Leon Whitney, outstanding veterinarian of Orange, Connecticut, for text relative Bloodhounds, Anatomy and Physiology of the Dog, Breeding, Common Ailments and Diseases, and First Aid.

Grateful mention and full credit for valued assistance with many other portions of the text is also due the following individuals and organizations:

Mr. Hank Babbitt, outdoor writer, of Michigan.

The Canadian Kennel Club.

Mrs. Anne Rogers Clark, noted bench show handler.

Dr. James E. Greene, Dean, School of Veterinary Medicine, Auburn University, Auburn, Alabama.

Mr. Jeff Griffen, author and authority on dogs.

Dr. B. F. Horlein, Head, Small Animal Surgery and Medicine, Auburn University, Auburn, Alabama.

Dr. Robert Horne, staff member, School of Veterinary Medicine, Auburn University, Auburn, Alabama.

Marianna Jacobs, of Jetco Electronic Industries, Inc.

Dr. William P. Ramsey, practicing veterinarian, Camp Hill, Pennsylvania.

Mr. Lewis Sharpley, Past President, Dog Writers Association of America and member of the news department, The Louisville Times, Louisville, Kentucky.

Staff personnel of Verband für das Deusche Hundewesen, who supplied listings of breeds recognized by that organization.

Photographic credits, wherever special credit is due, appear throughout the text in appropriate credit lines.

Inasmuch as the production of a volume of this size involves the assistance of many individuals, firms, and organizations, there is always the possibility that more names could have been added to these acknowledgments. Nevertheless, reasonable diligence has been exercised to make this listing as complete as possible.

Last, but by no means least, grateful thanks are extended to Mr. James D. Leffel for certain art work used, and to Miss Jemma Veckerelli for her very extensive secretarial assistance.

CONTENTS

PART III   UNDERSTANDING YOUR DOG

PART IV   STARTING YOUR DOG'S TRAINING

PART V   DOG SHOWS—HOW TO TRAIN AND SHOW YOUR DOG

PART VI   DOG AILMENTS AND FIRST AID

PART VII   DOG BREEDING

PART VIII   THE DOG ON DUTY

PART IX   THE DOG IN COURSING AND RACING

PART X   DOGS IN HARNESS AND HERDING WORK

PART XI   THE DOG IN HUNTING

PART XII   TRAINING THE HUNTING DOG

PART XIII   THE DOG IN FIELD TRIALS

PART XIV   DOGS IN THE PRIMITIVE WORLD

PART XV   DOG'S EARLY ASSOCIATION WITH MAN

PART XVI   DOG CLASSIFICATIONS

PART XVII   DOGS AROUND THE WORLD

PART XVIII   KENNEL CLUBS

PART XIX   BREEDS RECOGNIZED BY THE AMERICAN KENNEL CLUB

CONTENTS

PART XX   THE HUMANE MOVEMENT

PART XXI REFERENCE MATERIAL

Part I

CHOOSING A DOG

Dogs are versatile animals. They have proved their ability to adapt themselves to almost any sort of living conditions mankind has imposed upon them. And by instinct and use through many generations, every breed has a definite place in some part of the scheme of present-day social life. Yet, despite the claims of the proponents of some breeds, there is no real "jack-of-all-trades" in dogdom. There is a dog for almost every purpose but no dog for all purposes.

——Choosing a Dog for the City——

AS TO popular breeds, one newspaper recently reported the French Poodle as the most popular in the U.S.A., the Beagle in second place, and the German Shepherd third. But breed popularities are a variable thing and few people may acquire a certain breed simply because it rides such a wave.

Regardless of the breed you choose and the purpose for which he is chosen, be sure he is a pure-bred dog. It costs no more to keep a pure-bred dog than to keep a mongrel, and the advantages are many. True, some of the smartest dogs known have been and are mongrels, but they were indeed exceptional individuals and unable to reproduce their own kind.

People are sometimes judged by the kind of dogs they own, and the owner of a mongrel can seldom be properly proud of the dog he owns. There is no set standard among mongrel dogs. Rather, as C. E. Harbison, noted authority, expressed it, the mongrel is somewhat like a second-hand car made out of the parts of a variety of makes. The pure-bred dog has the advantages of many years of careful, selective breeding, proper rearing and, generally, training, all of which have been pointed toward the virtues of type and utility. Most pure-bred breeds have been developed for specific purposes. The mongrel, while he may be intelligent, is seldom fitted by instinct or conformation for any particular job, although many, given proper training, have proved serviceable in a high degree.

Our purpose, however, is to discuss the choice of a dog for city living. First, one should carefully consider his own family and home situation. How many members in the family? How many children and of what temperament? How large is the home or apartment? How much time can members of the family devote to the dog? For what purpose do you desire a dog?

It is obvious that the larger breeds such as the St. Bernard, Newfoundland, Great Dane, Irish Wolfhound, Great Pyrenees and others are rather out of place in a city apartment. Perhaps one of these breeds is your favorite, but, out of consideration for the dog, as well as for yourself, you should look elsewhere. These large dogs require room and a lot of it.

On the other hand, many large dogs living in the country actually have less room to run than do their city cousins, especially under kennel conditions. Large dogs need considerable exercise if they are to remain in good health, and an occasional romp in the park is insufficient. Yet, if you are willing to invest the time, a large dog in the city is just as rewarding a pet and companion as he would be if you both lived in the country.

For all concerned, however, it may be best that you confine your selection to the smaller breeds. In choosing one of these, first consider your own needs and desires. Then attend a dog show and see all the various breeds in action and repose. Almost every large city has several dog shows annually and here you can size up the breeds which might fit into your picture, see them first hand, and obtain considerable information concerning them from their owners or handlers.

Any of the smaller dogs make good city dogs. The terriers are generally the most active of the lot, yet several of the terrier breeds are rather placid in disposition and at the same time alert to all that transpires.

The Scottie, the Cairn, the West Highland White, and the Sealyham are all terriers in demand as house dogs. But it must always be borne in mind that all terriers are active little dogs that like the outdoors, and most of them like to dig in the ground.

Almost all breeds have a rather well-developed instinct to protect their master's person and property.

The responsibility of caring for a dog is fine training for any youngster. Photo by Georgia Engelhard.

agree to a sale with a built-in trial arrangement. This gives you the opportunity to "try on" the dog, so to speak, and to verify his health with a veterinarian. Trial arrangements are especially common in dealings that involve the hunting breeds. Give the new dog every opportunity to become acquainted with his surroundings and to get his bearings. Do not try to force your attentions on him too quickly.

Do not look for a bargain. There are none. Expect to pay for what you get, and if you are buying from a reputable dealer or breeder, you will get just that. "Cheap" or "bargain" dogs are, in the long run, expensive, for they generally possess some fault which may not be immediately obvious to you. If you will explain just what you want to a reliable dealer, you may be sure that he will do his best to fill your requirements.

"Which is the best dog to buy, a male or a female?" is a question often asked by the novice. The female has much in her favor and only one thing against her—her mating seasons may be expected about every 26 weeks. During these periods (which last about 22 days each, during about 12 of which she can be bred) she must be confined or otherwise protected against misalliance. Today, there are sprays which make a female less attractive to neighborhood

The terriers are especially alert in this regard, but if the dog is especially desired as a guard, it will be well to give full consideration to some of the larger breeds, such as the Airedale and the Kerry Blue.

But make up your own mind. Weigh all factors carefully and then make the decision yourself. Dog fanciers are quite free with their advice but are, also, generally somewhat biased in their opinions. The inquiring novice will be told that this breed is nervous and high-strung, another is quite dull and unambitious, still another too vicious to be trusted around children; this breed too hard to raise, that one exceedingly fond of children, and this one (generally the Poodle or the mongrel) the smartest. While it is true that certain breeds have certain characteristics, no really truthful blanket statement similar to the above can be made about any breed. Dogs are individuals and all possess individual temperaments. Most of the members of some breeds show boldness to some degree, yet some timid individuals can be found in all breeds, particularly where strangers are concerned. And improper handling or treatment can develop timidness in almost any individual.

When you have made up your mind concerning the breed you desire, then look for the proper individual. Deal with a reliable and established breeder or a dealer of good reputation. If possible, look the prospect over carefully before you buy. Make sure that he is healthy, free from external parasites, and is not timid. Most reputable dog breeders would readily

Considerably dwarfing his Pomeranian friend this St. Bernard may seem too large to be a good city dog, but size alone is not always a critical factor. Photo by Evelyn M. Shafer

Highly popular, the French Poodle comes in three sizes and, since he does not shed, is a good choice for many city families. Photo by Ventzle Ruml III.

ral functions, and often they become better dogs after they have had a litter of puppies. Spayed females have a tendency toward obesity, and require a carefully supervised diet and extra exercise to prevent their becoming overweight and listless. A further consideration on spaying is that, if your puppy is a female, there may come a day when you will want to have puppies from her; that, of course, won't be possible if she has been spayed.

males, and there are pills that help accomplish the same thing. There are also "birth control" pills for dogs and there are medications available through your veterinarian that will remedy a misalliance, but only if you act within 48 hours of its occurrence.

On the other hand, the male is constantly "in season", which explains the fact that almost every male dog of any breed is a roamer, if permitted to be.

The female is mentally quick, usually a good watchdog, and generally affectionate to a high degree. In the house, the female is generally cleaner, quieter and more devoted. As a rule, she is more tolerant of the sometimes rough tactics of children, although generally the male is more inclined to engage in rough-and-tumble play.

The periods of season can, of course, be eliminated by spaying, but this is generally not recommended. All females should be allowed to exercise their natu-

Small dogs often make outstanding watchdogs. Regardless of breed, the good home watchdog will have an aggressive nature—a quality which varies among individual dogs. Also, if he is raised in the home and in the process not frightened or cowed or his barking unduly discouraged, he will usually take naturally to giving warning when strangers come near.

Before you bring a dog into your home, prepare a place for him. Teach him to recognize it as his own. But at the same time, be prepared to open up your heart to him and make him a member of the family. Before you realize it, he will have won his way into your affections.

——Choosing a Dog for the Farm——

TIME WAS when the average American farmer owned one or more dogs of mongrel type, some of which were quite serviceable in a number of ways. Others were "just dogs" and were treated as such. This situation still exists among many farmers, but today's progressive agriculturist has developed into a "specialist" and his dogs are generally kept for specific purposes.

As stock tending has long been the task of dogs the world over, the stock raiser of today can choose from a number of pure-bred dogs developed with the idea of utility as the primary consideration. Not all farms today raise stock in appreciable numbers, but any of

these dogs can fit in well with farm life and the multitude of chores which accompany it.

One favorite with the American stock farmer is the Working Border Collie. This rugged little dog, generally black and white in color, has been developed not so much for type as for his general all-around usefulness on the farm and his outstanding proficiency at handling stock. The breed is discussed at considerable length elsewhere.

Many farmers want dogs as protectors of premises and property, whether it be home, livestock or stored grain and other valuables. The German Shepherd makes a very fine dog for this purpose for he is alert,

Any of the terriers make fine assets to any farm, and their ability as ratters around barn, granary, and utility buildings make them especially valuable. They also make good rabbit and squirrel dogs, but the wise hunting farmer will choose a Beagle for his daytime small game hunting, one of the larger hound breeds for night hunting, and one or more of the pointing breeds for upland game birds. Probably the nearest approach to the ideal single all-around farm dog is the Airedale, but, on the average, he is neither as good a stock dog as the Collie and other "sheep dog" breeds nor as good a hunter as the hounds or bird dogs.

While the mongrel still far outnumbers the purebreds in America's rural life, farmers are rapidly coming to realize the general superiority of breeds developed for the specific purpose of lightening the farmer's work and making his domain a more enjoyable place on which to live.

Many a country boy has a mixed-breed dog, sometimes like this "Shaggy"—one time the canine star of a Paramount movie by the same name. Photo by Bud Fraker.

"If you can't drive them, lead 'em!" apparently is the philosophy being tested by this little farm dog, for certainly not all farm dogs are Collies or Shetlands.

aggressive, and loyal. The Collie is especially adaptable to farm use, having been developed for herding purposes, and for many generations the old fashioned Shepherd was a fixture on many American farms.

Hunting dogs seldom make good stock dogs, although the Airedale Terrier can be easily trained to serve both purposes. This is a rugged, hardy breed that thrives on outdoor life and a better general all-around farm dog would be hard to find. He makes an excellent guard dog, has a splendid nose, possesses the varmint hunting instincts of the terriers, is intelligent, tractable, affectionate, and extremely loyal. With a Working Border Collie for work with stock and an Airedale for general all-around use, the average farmer would have just about all the dogs needed.

Choosing a Dog for
——the Suburbs or Town——

PEOPLE WHO live in suburban or small town homes have the advantage of a wider choice in dogs as companions, pets or guards than those who live in the city, as they generally have more room and easier access to the out-of-doors.

With these advantages the suburbanite or small-town citizen may indulge his fancy with greater latitude. A backyard kennel can be provided and it is not necessary that the dog become a permanent resident of the owner's house. Consequently the larger breeds that need more exercise will fit into the picture very nicely. This is by no means any indication that the smaller breeds should be bypassed in consideration of a choice, for very few of them are strictly indoor dogs. It is only to state that a satisfactory choice can be made from a larger circle of breeds.

In 1966, Hero, an aptly named blue-merle Collie owned by Shawn —lley of Priest River, Idaho, saved his young master from the attack a beserk horse.

Again close attention should be given to the conditions which surround the home and full consideration should be given to the neighbors, for community harmony must be preserved. The neighbors have children who may or may not get along well with your dog. They have lawns and flower gardens, too, and any transgression against these will be met with keen displeasure. It is up to you, as the owner, to see that your dog, whatever the breed, takes his place in neighborhood life with calm, quiet demeanor and gentlemanly conduct. Practically all breeds will thrive happily in suburban life. The choice of breed is mostly up to your own preference or that of your family. And if you are careful to see that your dog is properly behaved around your neighbor, his children and his property, you will find him a welcome addition to the community.

Children, as a rule, love dogs. And dogs, as a rule, love children. To own a real, live dog gives every child a feeling of importance, but as the owner, he should be given to understand that he is responsible for the care, well-being, and behavior of his dog.

Most all dogs become greatly attached to their child owners and seem to feel a sense of responsibility for their safety, carefully watching over them with genuine guardianship. If you want a dog for your child, the best combination is reached when you match the dog's disposition with that of the child. A lively, outdoorsy boy or girl, always ready for a romp or game, should have a lively dog that is willing to engage his owner in play. Children of a more placid

No matter where she lives, this girl and her Afghan are a winning combination.

nature should have dogs that are content to accompany them on their walks or remain quietly watching when games requiring little action are engaged in.

For the active child, a Brittany Spaniel or a Beagle would make an ideal pet. Both are alert and every ready for a romp. They are not as quarrelsome as some of the terriers, yet are more active than many breeds. Speaking of terriers, these dogs, too, make fine pets for active children, especially if their sparky nature is appreciated.

For the child of a quiet disposition it is hard to find a better pet than a Collie or Shetland Sheepdog. Both are beautiful animals and exceedingly loyal.

The Poodle is *the* dog to all who own him. Friendly of disposition, often of outstanding intelligence, this "Fancy Dan" seems to be enjoying himself most when he is pleasing his master or his master's

Of combinations such as this a frequent question is "Who's having —e most fun, the boy or the dog?" Photo by Harold M. Lambert.

family. An excellent house dog, he is also an outdoorsman to the core, for he was originally used for sporting purposes and makes an excellent retriever today. The problem of keeping his coat trimmed in "style" presents itself, but, if kept properly combed and brushed, his coat should present no serious problem even if left untrimmed.

Another good all-around family dog is the English Springer Spaniel. Not only is he an affectionate pet for children, a mannerly dog around the house and an ornament indoors and out, but he has the added advantage of providing Dad or Junior a good day's sport afield if either or both are sportsmen.

The setters, English, Irish, and Gordon, all make good family dogs, as do most of the retrievers, but the Pointer is happiest when he is hunting and will become a roamer if allowed considerable freedom.

The larger breeds, such as the Great Dane, Greyhound, Mastiff, and Wolfhounds, are better fitted for large estates where exercise facilities are not at such a premium. They are not to be especially recommended for small areas and small children can hardly be expected to handle them properly.

If you want a dog for a specific purpose, carefully study the breeds which seem to fill those requirements best. Even if you "just want a dog", appraise your local situation thoroughly and see what breeds best fit into the picture. When you have decided upon a breed, then go slow in picking the proper individual, remembering that, while different breeds

Pool-side cocktail!

have different characteristics, all dogs are individuals and individuals vary considerably in temperament and willingness to learn.

Then when you have found the individual you want, see to it that he is trained in good behavior and will so conduct himself as to provide pleasure for you and secure friendly acceptance from your neighbors. Owning a dog of this nature, no matter what breed, is a joy indeed.

—Your Dog and the Law—

THE DOG was highly prized, frequently protected by law and sometimes even exalted to godhood in ancient times; suffered comparative neglect for thousands of years, but has won new legal rights in the last half of the 20th Century.

In the U.S., the year 1966 saw the passage of the first nationwide law for the protection of dogs. The year also was marked by the passage of the first state law establishing the right of breeders to raise and keep dogs for use in hunting, guard duty, field or obedience trials, conformation shows or similar exhibitions, free of any and all zoning restrictions.

Significantly, this state law was enacted in Kentucky, where dogs and horses always have been greatly beloved, but where the statutory rights of dogs were long below par. Movements were under way in a number of states seeking the enactment of laws similar to Kentucky's, to foster noncommercial kennels and/or to back up enforcement of the Federal "anti-dognapping" law by closing possible local loopholes.

THE DOG AND EARLY LAWS

The world's first dog laws undoubtedly were tribal customs (common law) which developed in the Stone Age after man learned the value of the dog as a hunting companion.

The first formal dog laws were promulgated in Egypt in the time of the early Pharaohs, around 5000 B.C. Even prior to that, Egyptian tablets carved around 6000 B.C. show that dogs had won a common-law status as valuable pets and hunters and occasionally as objects of reverence. In the early dynasties, decrees by the Pharaoh were not written, but were committed to memory by court officials and handed on by word of mouth. In later periods, the royal edicts were carved in stone, and centuries later, were written on papyrus. The texts of all these ancient laws are now dust, but historians know much of the rights guaranteed by several ancient nations to man's best friend.

Over two thousand years ago, in Imperial China,

the Lion Dog (forerunner of the Pekingese) acquired preeminent legal status after the introduction of Buddhism from India. Because the lion was Buddha's symbol, it was a great day when someone noticed that the Emperor's dog of Fu (guard dog) resembled the King of Beasts. While Chinese peasants sometimes ate other breeds, the imperial hunting dogs and the smaller dogs prized as court favorites were protected by law. They held mandarin rank and sometimes were created dukes or princes. The horrible "death by ten thousand slices" was provided by law for anyone removing one of these dogs from the Chinese Imperial Palace. If such an offender were lucky, he was merely stoned to death.

Around 2100 B.C.—before the time that dogs were achieving legal protection in China, there came a similar recognition in Babylon. The Babylonians esteemed dogs chiefly for use in hunting and making war. The Code of Hammurabi protected dogs as important property.

While the ancient Israelites abhorred dogs, it is interesting to note that derogatory use of the word "dog" in the Old Testament becomes less frequent after the Jewish nation's captivity in Babylon. Evidently the Babylonians taught the Jews to regard dogs as something more than pariah street scavengers.

In ancient Ethiopia, tribesmen once crowned a dog as King. The canine ruler held judicial power over human subjects. If the dog King licked your hand, honors were bestowed. If the King growled, off went your head.

In medieval times in Europe, the ordinary dog had few legal rights, but a nobleman's hunting hound or armored war dog was well protected by feudal law. Early in the 19th Century, Napoleon I, Emperor of France and conqueror of most of Europe, decreed protection for dogs needed by his armies.

Most of the early modern laws protecting dogs from cruelty or property owners from roving dogs were enacted in Great Britain and the United States. The growth of urban and suburban populations brought licensing and other restrictions to an animal historically free to roam.

LAWS FOR RABIES CONTROL

Early in the 19th Century, the Scandinavian countries enacted rabies-control laws which included provisions for the destruction of strays and the quarantine of suspected animals, premises and areas. By 1826, Norway, Sweden and Denmark were declared free of rabies—decades before Louis Pasteur found the actual cause and developed the celebrated serum in France in 1884.

By 1903, through similar quarantine measures, Great Britain was declared free of rabies and remains so to this day.

In America, rabies was recorded in the colony of Virginia as early as 1753 and in New England in 1785, but legal preventive steps came much later. The first anti-rabies inoculation serum deemed by the veterinary profession to be practical for general use on dogs was not developed until the early 1920's.

The first law for the compulsory vaccination of dogs was passed in North Carolina in 1935. Since then many states have followed suit, although some still rely upon education and persuasion. With the increased emphasis on public health work and preventive medicine, the average citizen who owns a dog is constrained to have it inoculated, much the same as he would have a child immunized against smallpox or diphtheria. The owner of a rabid dog is assuming a great liability; although inoculation is not 100 percent effective, it is safest and hence advisable.

LAWS AGAINST CRUELTY TO DOGS

Laws against cruelty to dogs go back to the time of the ancient Medes and Persians, who held dogs in high esteem. Depending on the type of dog, a punishment of 500 to 1,000 stripes with a scourge was dealt to the killer of a dog. Giving a dog bad food was penalized with 50 to 200 stripes, depending on the importance of the dog.

In the United States, the early legal proceedings to protect dogs against cruelty were taken under the common law. Convictions were difficult to obtain. In 1856, New York State's legislature passed a strengthened anti-cruelty law which included a provision for the arrest and punishment of any person promoting a dog fight. Ten years later the legislature also outlawed the malicious killing of a dog or any other animal belonging to another person.

In 1867 the New York legislature passed a still stronger statute requiring that dogs used in drawing carts or any other vehicles for business purposes must be licensed and properly fed and watered.

The first Federal dog legislation occurred in 1870 —an anti-cruelty law for the District of Columbia. The District's first dog-licensing law was passed by Congress in 1878. This law was amended in 1945 to increase the license fee from $2 to $3.

Left outside to their own devices without collars or tags, these pups may stray too far exploring and be picked up in violation of some local ordinance. Photo by Kaufmann (Chicago).

The advent of motor vehicles increased legal problems in relation to dogs. A motorist whose car strikes and injures a dog may not simply drive off, but must, in many states, stop, render aid, ascertain the dog's injuries, perhaps face suit.

TODAY'S LAWS AND THE ZONING PROBLEM

On August 24, 1966, President Lyndon B. Johnson signed Public Law 89-544, an act to require humane care and housing of dogs and other animals used in research, and to prevent the theft of dogs and cats for sale to scientific institutions. The passage of this law was the culmination of many years' work by many humane organizations.

The law authorizes the U.S. Department of Agriculture "to regulate the transportation, sale and handling of dogs, cats, and certain other animals intended to be used for purposes of research or experimentation and for other purposes." Under the law, the Secretary of Agriculture licenses such dealers supplying dogs and other animals for research as "shall have demonstrated that his facilities comply with the standards promulgated by the Secretary . . ."

Section 4 provides: "No dealer shall sell or offer to sell or transport or offer for transportation to any research facility any dog or cat, or buy, sell, offer to buy or sell or transport . . . to or from another dealer under this Act any dog or cat, unless or until such dealer shall have obtained a license from the Secretary and such license shall not have been suspended or revoked."

Research facilities are forbidden to buy a dog except from a licensed dealer. The same restriction is applied to purchases made for the use of any Federal agency or instrumentality.

Complete records are required and: "All dogs . . . sold in commerce by any dealer shall be marked or identified at such time and in such humane manner as the Secretary may prescribe."

Investigations and inspections are provided for. The Secretary of Agriculture was empowered to issue cease-and-desist orders to research facilities accused of failing to comply with the standards set by the Department. Any facility defying such an order would be subject to a fine of $500 a day as long as it failed to comply. Violators assessed such penalties either will have to pay up or appeal to a U.S. District Court for a review of the Department of Agriculture's action.

Aroused by a number of flagrant dognapping incidents, officials in a number of states have prosecuted dog dealers and truckers under state anti-cruelty laws. Convictions have been obtained in Tennessee, Kentucky, Ohio, Pennsylvania and other states.

Dog laws vary from state to state and from city to city. Most state dog laws merely provide for licensing and anti-rabies vaccination. Many also provide for the use of dog-tag revenues as a fund from which the owners of livestock killed or injured by roving dogs may be recompensed.

Kentucky's 1954 law (amended in 1956) includes all three provisions, but the law passed in 1966 by its General Assembly forbids any city or county to impose any zoning restrictions on non-commercial kennels. A liberal definition is provided for such kennels and the occasional raising and sale of puppies is permitted without losing non-commercial status.

The Miller Act, sponsored by the Kentucky Association of Dog Clubs, frankly is intended to encourage the breeding of pure-bred dogs, as an asset to the state's economy. The law, passed with overwhelming bipartisan support in both houses of the Assembly, is brief but to the point. Here is the full text:

"The maintenance and operation of a non-commercial kennel upon any lot or other premises occupied by the owner or tenant as a dwellinghouse does not constitute a nonconforming use of land zoned for residential purposes, in violation of the zoning regulations of any city or county.

"As used herein a non-commercial kennel means a kennel at, in or adjoining a private residence where hunting or other dogs are kept for the hobby of the householder, in using them for hunting or practice tracking or for exhibiting them in dog shows or field or obedience trials or for guarding or protecting the householder's property.

"The occasional raising of a litter of puppies at the kennel and occasional sale of puppies by the keeper of a non-commercial kennel does not change the character of residential property."

Dog-club officials who sponsored the law pointed out that it does not interfere in any way with the protection afforded other members of the community under the health and nuisance laws, against any kennel-keeper who abuses the privilege.

A number of states have passed laws requiring that access be given to public accommodations, such as hotels, motels, theaters or restaurants, for any blind person accompanied by a trained guide dog.

A number of states also have increased the penalties in their anti-cruelty laws. In Kentucky, for example, the Assembly raised the fine from "up to $100" to a range from $100 to $1,000 and added "a jail term of not more than 12 months," or both.

Zoning laws have become a nationwide bugaboo for dog breeders and fanciers. Owners with thousands of dollars invested in fine homes adjoining or near kennels which also cost thousands suddenly find that rapidly expanding cities have reached their doorsteps. New residents, either unfriendly to dogs or justly aroused by a few kennel owners who are not good neighbors, demand zoning regulations which jeopardize kennel investments totaling into the millions of dollars.

Dog-owning New Yorkers who took refuge in California soon found out that they were worse off than before, as the population explosion put legal heat on kennels near or in residential areas. Some town councils or township governing bodies in New Jersey, New York State, Missouri, California and elsewhere, acting more on the basis of hysteria than anything else, have enacted ordinances forbidding more than three, two or even one dog at any one address.

In some localities the zoning laws and regulations have developed into a sizable racket, with corrupt officials or inspectors and fee-hungry lawyers reaping thousands of dollars.

Ohio's legislature passed the strictest leash law in the United States as a result of a campaign spearheaded by the Youngstown All-Breed Training Club in 1965. The Club acted as the result of an appeal from Mrs. Peggy Turner, whose 9-year-old daughter, Beth, was severely bitten on the leg while at play during a recess at her school. Investigation showed that a roving dog that had bitten six other children was also the one that attacked Beth.

Mrs. Turner wrote to Gov. James A. Rhodes, who suggested how she and her friends might start a campaign, working through their legislators. It had been 21 years since a bill dealing with dogs had gotten out of committee in the Ohio legislature, but House Bill 388 became law on Sept. 3, 1965. It provides:

"It shall be unlawful for the owner, keeper or harborer of any female dog to permit such a dog to go beyond the premises of such owner or keeper at any time such dog is in heat, unless such dog is properly in leash.

"The owner or keeper of every dog shall at all times keep such dog either confined upon the premises of the owner or firmly secured by means of a collar and chain or other device so that it cannot stray beyond the premises of the owner or keeper, or it shall be kept under reasonable control of some person, except when lawfully engaged in hunting, accompanied by an owner or handler."

An increasing number of cities and counties have leash laws. Most states and municipalities require that every dog be licensed after the age of six months and that the dog tag be kept on the dog's collar.

For example, the owner of a dog in Arkansas, Arizona, Connecticut or Virginia, or an owner in Philadelphia, Des Moines, Iowa, or Walla Walla, Wash., can wait until the dog is six months old before buying it a license.

The deadline is the age of four months in Hawaii, in Baltimore County, Maryland, in most Michigan cities, and in cities such as Charlotte, N.C., and Seattle, Wash. Puppies must be licensed at the age of three months in Minneapolis, Minn., or Idaho Falls, Idaho; at the age of two months in Salt Lake City, Utah, and immediately after being weaned if they are domiciled in Omaha, Nebraska.

Some cities, such as Norfolk, Va., Billings, Mont., and Santa Barbara, Calif., require proof that a dog has been vaccinated against rabies before a license may be issued. There is a wide variation sometimes within the same state. Any dog whose owner lives north of the Chesapeake and Delaware Canal in Delaware must undergo rabies inoculation before it can be licensed; south of the canal, no.

A city-resident dog in Delaware need not be licensed until it is six months old; a country dog must be licensed at four months.

Weimaraner puppies. Breeders today must be well acquainted with zoning laws, ordinances, and local regulations affecting their puppy production enterprises. Photo by E & E Deal.

In states and cities where rabies vaccination is required by law, the effective age is usually six months. Examples: Mississippi, Kentucky; Miami, Fla., Fort Smith, Ark. However, Los Angeles, St. Louis and Norfolk specify inoculation at the age of four months and cities such as Atlanta and Colorado Springs, Colo., require it at three months.

Most states require that any dog being shipped into the state be accompanied by a health certificate. Usually, as part of the certificate, there must be a statement either that the shipment originated from a rabies-free area or that the dog has been recently inoculated against rabies.

DOGS AS PROPERTY

Dogs are valuable property, but the law has been slow to recognize this. In the reign of William the Conqueror (1066-1087), the theft of anything valued at one shilling or more was grand larceny under the law of England. Grand larceny was punishable by death. For the theft of a trained falcon, a man could pay with his life.

However, under the English common law of that day, the theft of a dog was not larceny in most cases. Justice Edward Coke (1552-1634) commented: "It was not fit that a person should die for them."

Another eminent English jurist, Sir William Blackstone (1723-80), mentioned the "olden" practice of considering that certain animals "have no intrinsic value, as dogs of all sorts, and other creatures kept for whim and pleasure." Even in Blackstone's day it was considered impossible, in most cases, to maintain a successful lawsuit over the loss of a dog.

However, there was a growing public appreciation of the value of dogs, and Blackstone was forced to the conclusion that dogs were "of such estimation that the crime of stealing them amounts to larceny."

Famous achievements by dogs helped dispel lingering judicial notions that they could not truly rank as property. In a 19th Century case, Justice Robert Earl of the New York Supreme Court referred to the St. Bernards' rescues of lost travelers and the historic story of the pet spaniel that awakened and saved the life of Prince William of Orange when a large Spanish force infiltrated his camp at the Siege of Mons (1572). Mr. Justice Earl concluded: "The claim that the nature of a dog is essentially base . . . will not now receive ready assent."

Since dogs have been recognized by modern man as actual property, legislation authorizing the killing of all unlicensed dogs (not wearing tags) has been held invalid. Such laws were ruled void, as an arbitrary and unreasonable exercise of the state's police power (Aldrich v. Reichert, 151 N.E. 608, 321 Ill. 123; Kasch v. Anders, 149 N.E. 275, 318 Ill. 272).

In general, no one but the owner of a dog has the right to kill it. In most states a dog trespassing on someone's land may not be injured or killed except in defense of life or property. However, a vicious dog that has become a public nuisance and a common enemy may be lawfully killed—in some states the right to such killing is restricted to dog wardens or peace officers; in many states, any citizen, in the face of neighborhood danger, may act.

DOGS THAT BITE OR DAMAGE

The old saying that "Every dog is entitled to one bite" finds little support in the law. One bite does not prove that the dog is vicious, but a previous bite is not necessary in order that the animal's owner should have recognized it to have a vicious or dangerous tendency.

"Yes," ruled the judge who heard the case of Carrow v. Haney (219 S.W. 710; 203 Mo. App.485), "the dog is entitled to his first bite, provided he conceals his intention and makes no manifestation of his purpose in such a manner as to impart notice to his owner or keeper, but if the dog's vicious propensities be shown, or his inclinations to want to bite be manifested, then he is not permitted to carry out his designs before being recognized as a dangerous, vicious or ferocious animal."

If it can be shown that the owner knew of his pet's vicious tendency, he can be held liable for damages —regardless of another false saying to the effect that "Barking dogs never bite."

The courts generally recognize that teasing or sudden pain or fright may cause a dog to bite. Thus, a person who teases a dog, or carelessly treads on a tail or paw, then being bitten, would not have a just complaint at law, since he was guilty of contributory negligence.

However, most evidence, merely tending in general to show what made a dog savage, is not admissible. Still, every accused dog may be taken into court so a jury can observe its temper and disposition.

In the Middle Ages, dogs belonging to criminals or to persons accused of witchcraft or heresy sometimes were tried, along with their owners. Legend has it that a dog was hanged as a witch in Salem, Mass. Cotton Mather records the case of a man executed at New Haven, Conn. for bestiality after he himself had hanged the accused dog.

Records of the trials of dogs in France, England, Scotland and Italy range from 1525 to 1845. As late as 1906, in Switzerland, two men and a dog were tried together on charges of murder and robbery. The two men were sentenced to life imprisonment. The dog was executed.

In modern courtrooms a human defendant may escape prosecution by successfully pleading insanity, yet a mad dog is executed without argument. It is interesting to recall that in ancient Mesopotamia, the Code of Eshnunna provided that the owner of a mad dog had to confine it for observation. If the dog had bitten someone and death resulted, the owner was liable for a large fine. Although these regulations may have had to do with ferocious dogs rather than rabid ones, no executions are mentioned.

Nowadays, in many instances a property owner may have a destructive dog impounded pending adjudication of damages. The seller or donor of a dog is sometimes liable for harm or damage done to the person or property of the recipient. But there is no liability if the harm or damage occurs as a result of the ordinary behavior of that type of dog.

A dog owner is usually liable for damages if he knew that the offending dog had a history of past offensive acts, then failed to keep the animal in suitable confinement.

Two other occasions for liability on the part of a dog owner are: (1) if an offending dog is wrongfully in some place where an injury or damage is done, or (2) even though the dog was previously of mild disposition, if the owner allows him to rove.

The prudent dog owner informs himself concerning local, state and possibly Federal rights and regulations. Regulations and responsibilities in this field are increasing. However, there is also a definite swing toward more rights for the conscientious breeder; there is full protection for the pet owner who is a good neighbor, and there are more safeguards today for dogs in general.

Part II

HOW TO FEED, HOUSE, & CARE FOR YOUR DOG

Whatever the dog's primitive diet may have been, it certainly wasn't all steaks and chops, and it did include a great deal more bulk and had an entirely different balance from an all-muscle-meat diet. Nor was it the sort of diet you would want to feed your dog today if you could. For finding the nutritional needs and planning the feeding of present-day dogs, scientists use the more practical and accurate method of analyzing foods, feeding them to dogs, and studying the effects. Such research has been carried on for more than a century now, and through it a great deal has been learned about nutrition in general, as well as about the best feeding programs for dogs.

—Guide to Dog Feeding and Nutrition—

FROM THE time of conception until death, the well-nourished dog requires at least 43 nutrients for maximum well-being. Nutrients are provided initially through the mother's blood directly, through an exchange mechanism into the young developing fetuses. After birth, milk provides nutrients for the nursing young; after weaning, the puppy receives these nutrients from its solid diet.

FORTY-THREE NUTRIENTS NEEDED

The 43 nutrients known to be needed by dogs can be derived from many sources. For example, we know that dogs can be fed table scraps and supplements, or chemicals, or whole animals such as rabbits, or commercial dog foods. When each of these is fed under the proper conditions, we can expect satisfactory results. Here we will discuss optimum nutrition and also some of the commonly practiced folk-lore concerned with nutrition.

There is a tendency, when discussing the nutrition of animals, to select some nutrients that are better known than others and call these "most valuable." All 43 nutrients needed by dogs must be in optimum or balanced ratios if one is to expect maximum performance. Not a single nutrient can be left out of the ration or added at inadequate levels and satisfactory performance still be obtained. Nutrients must be in relative ratios to each other; that is, if a large excess of one nutrient occurs, then the quantities of other nutrients in the ration must be increased since a deficiency of some of the nutrients might otherwise exist. One good example of this is fat. If the fat in the diet is increased to high levels, then this fat can satisfy the energy requirement of the dog before the requirement for the other nutrients are met with the result that a nutritional imbalance may occur. High levels of fat also increase requirements of other nutrients, such as Vitamin B12. With this as a background, let's review some of the various nutrients needed by dogs and see how they function.

Protein. Protein is a nitrogenous body-building material generally associated with lean meat, soybeans, fish, cottage cheese and other nitrogen-rich foodstuffs. Proteins are found in every part of the body with the largest concentration in lean tissues, but they are also found in enzymes, in the blood, in the bones, and all other parts of the body. Some proteins in the ration can be utilized very efficiently by the dog to supply protein for his body needs that other proteins cannot. For example, hair is almost a pure protein, but it is of poor quality which cannot be digested and utilized efficiently by the dog. Other proteins, such as lean meat and cooked soybean meal protein, can be digested by the dog and utilized efficiently.

Proteins include some 23 different amino acids that occur naturally in nature. These amino acids are the so-called building blocks that help make the protein structure. Ten of these amino acids must be in the diet of dogs in ample quantitites to satisfy his nutritional requirements. These are called "essential amino acids." Some of the other amino acids are required, but the other amino acids can be made by breaking down the 10 essential amino acids.

Amino acids are important in the ration and can be limiting dietary factors under some conditions. For example, if a ration is overheated, one of the amino acids needed by the dog—lysine—is tied up or destroyed. This will result in poor dog growth. When a protein is slightly overheated so that the lysine is destroyed, the protein value can be retained only by adding lysine to the ration. There are other amino acids that can be tied up or destroyed also by heating, chemicals, or other antiprotein activity. For this reason the preparation of protein for dog rations is extremely important.

Proteins are needed by the dog for growth, blood formation, antibody formation against disease, for tissue repair, hair growth, and for many other purposes. The dog cannot get along without protein.

Growing dogs require at least 17% protein in the ration, (dry matter basis), and for optimum antibody formation more than this amount of protein is desirable. If a large excess of protein is fed, the extra protein will be "worked on" by the liver and the nitrogen split off and excreted. The remaining portion of the protein molecule will be used as energy within the dog's body. A large excess of protein can be detrimental since the nitrogen split off from the protein in the liver must be discarded. This can place a very severe strain on the liver and kidneys of the dog. For the normal dog, a large excess of protein can be tolerated for several years; however, in old age the strain on the kidneys and the liver becomes noticeably great or even intolerable, and excess nitrogen can accumulate in the blood. For dogs that have had distemper, leptospirosis or hepatitis, the quantity of protein is extremely important since their liver and kidneys may have been damaged and the ability to function impaired. This means that they cannot dispose of excessively large quantities of protein easily. For this reason it is important to feed the right level of protein, with neither a large excess nor deficiency.

Fat. Fat in the dog's diet provides energy or calories and in addition provides fatty acids needed for normal dog nutrition and growth. A deficiency of fatty acids in the dog will result in dry skin, poor growth, and a severe deficiency will often result in death. There are many different kinds of fatty acids available; however, highly unsaturated fatty acids at low levels are necessary for optimum skin condition in dogs. Fat is a concentrated source of energy and contains about $2\frac{1}{4}$ times as much energy as pure carbohydrates, such as sugar or starch.

Fat absorption by the dog is sometimes impaired if the dog has had distemper or hepatitis or some other disease that may have adversely influenced the pancreas. The pancreas secretes enzymes that help digest fat in the intestinal tract and promotes its absorption through the intestinal wall into the blood stream. If the pancreas has been damaged, very little fat may be absorbed from the intestinal tract with the result that a dog will frequently have a deficiency in fatty acids even though the rations he consumes contains ample fat for normal dogs. Frequently the observation of voluminous stools, especially those that contain a lot of slimy fat, is an indication that the dog has pancreatic problems.

Normally, these dogs will eat large quantities of food but fail to digest the food advantageously. When this circumstance is observed, the veterinarian can supply pancreatic materials which can be fed along with the ration to make the fat available to the dog, or the dog owner can add extra unsaturated fat, such as corn oil to the diet. In this way the fatty acids needed by the dog deficient in pancreatic activity can be supplied.

Carbohydrates. Carbohydrates also supply energy to the dog. Generally, carbohydrates are a much less expensive source of energy than are the fats. Carbohydrates are found in many feed ingredients, especially those of grain origin. The carbohydrate content of meat is extremely low, while the carbohydrate content of grains, such as corn and rice is quite high. Cooked carbohydrates can be used very efficiently by the dog to supply the energy required for lactation, growth, and heavy work.

Some carbohydrates, such as lactose, the carbohydrate of milk, may be poorly utilized by dogs. Generally, the puppy soon after birth can tolerate relatively large quantities of milk, even cow's milk; but, as the puppy grows older, this tolerance to cow's milk or the lactose (milk sugar) in cow's milk tends to decrease. Many puppies produce very low levels of lactase, the enzyme which permits the use of lactose in cow's milk. When this enzyme production decreases as the puppy matures, the lactose fed to the dog, instead of being digested and absorbed, tends to ferment in the digestive tract with the result that acid and diarrhea are produced from this fermentation. This also happens in many men, especially those reaching middle age. Their lactase production slows dramatically and many men consuming milk for ulcers will actually have the milk fermenting in the digestive tract, which produces acids and further aggravates the ulcers

Their ears as yet uncropped and only about eight weeks old, these Miniature Schnauzer pups will thrive and grow with a feeding program employing only commercial dog foods. Photo by Jonaire Kennels.

rather than curing or helping them. Bitch's milk contains approximately a third as much lactose as cow's milk. This is one reason that bitch's milk is much more satisfactory for dogs than cow's milk.

Supplementation of rations with milk is generally not necessary. If you insist on supplementing and then observe diarrhea from dogs after milk feeding, the complete cessation of milk supplementation will often curb the diarrhea.

Vitamins. Since vitamins are required in such small quantities many dog owners feel that vitamins are of little use in the dog's ration, while other dog owners believe that large quantities of vitamins should be added. Excessive vitamins, or a deficiency of vitamins, can both cause problems.

Vitamins are generally divided into two different groups based on their solubility. One group is called the "water-soluble vitamins" and includes the vitamins riboflavin, niacin, choline, pantothenic acid, Vitamin B-12, folic acid and others. The second group consists of vitamins that are soluble in fats or oils—these are called "fat-soluble vitamins" and include Vitamins A, D, E, and K. Knowing that the vitamins fall into these two groups can help tremendously in the nutrition of dogs. For example, the water-soluble vitamins are generally found in fresh meats, lean tissues especially, the glandular organs of animals, such as liver, pancreas, and similar organs. The fat-soluble vitamins are generally associated with the fatty tissues of animals and this provides a clue to the source and use of the fat-soluble vitamins by dogs. Fat-soluble vitamins tend to oxidize or become tied up or destroyed fairly easily. This means that fats becoming rancid, or oxidizing excessively, may be void of these vitamins. This is why fats in the process of becoming rancid should not be fed to dogs.

There has been a tendency in the past to select specific vitamins, such as pantothenic acid, and indicate that pantothenic acid deficiencies tend to produce gray hair . . . and then to leave their nutritional role at this point.

PUPPY NUTRITION

Nutrition Of The Prenatal Puppies. At the time of conception, the instant when the egg of the female is fertilized by sperm from the male, the nutrition of this developing egg is supplied by body fluid associated in the uterus of the female. After a few hours the developing egg becomes attached to the wall of the uterus. Soon thereafter, the developing embryo forms its own circulatory system and through an exchange with the mother supplies nutrients taken from the mother's blood to the developing embryo. As the embryo continues to develop through the average 63-day gestation period, the young fetal circulatory system becomes much more advanced and reaches a point where a very efficient network of veins and arteries from the fetus exchanges gasses in solution and waste materials with the mother's blood. There is no direct connection between the blood flow of the mother and the blood flow of the developing puppy. All of this nutrient exchange takes place through a band around the young developing puppy.

It is easy to see that the nutrients supplied to the bitch influence the quantity of nutrients deposited in the developing fetus. If the bitch's ration is deficient in nutrients, or contains a huge excess, then the chemical composition of the developing fetus can be influenced. Improper nutrition during gestation can influence litter size, stamina of the young pups, and puppy mortality.

Nutrition After Birth. After birth, the young puppy begins to obtain his nutrients from the bitch through milk secreted by the bitch's mammary glands. In some instances, milk is either not available or perhaps is contaminated through bacterial congestion in the bitch's udder. At this point the nutrients must be supplied from some other source. This may be a commercial bitch milk replacement or it may include some other bitch that can be used as a nursemaid. This is fairly common.

Feeding The Orphan Puppy. Sometimes the bitch is incapable of producing milk, or it is so heavily contaminated with bacteria that a bitch milk replacement must be fed. The bitch milk substitute, such as Esbilac or any of several other good ones on the market, can be fed immediately to the puppy and can be continued until he is consuming ample dry rations to meet his nutritional requirements. If, for any reason, you cannot obtain a commercial bitch milk substitute, you can make a temporary formula of: 1 cup evaporated milk, 1 cup water, 1 egg yolk (no white), one tablespoon corn oil, and a pinch of salt. Extra vitamins, preferably in the form of prepared soluble supplements, should also be provided.

Orphan puppies require feeding at least every eight hours for the first three weeks (every six hours for especially weak or small puppies) and then every twelve hours until they are consuming enough solid food to maintain normal growth. The feeding of newly born puppies can be relatively simple, or it can be quite complex. One of the simplest ways of feeding one or two orphaned puppies is to use a bottle designed for premature infants. For more than two puppies, you'll want to check with your veterinarian for instructions on a new, catheterized form of force feeding that saves you considerable time and insures a higher survival rate for the litter.

When feeding the young pup, its body should be held in a horizontal position so milk will not enter its lungs. Orphaned puppies during the first 10 or 12 days must be massaged to stimulate urination and defecation. Otherwise the urine and fecal matter would accumulate in the body and could lead to pneumonia. In normal bitch-nursed puppies, the bitch licks them for the first 10 days and removes the fluids through stimulation of their urinary and fecal excretory areas.

Feeding The Growing Pup. Most pups start nibbling on solid food by the time they are three or four weeks of age. This food can be the same ration the dam is receiving. Pups of medium sized breeds (pointers and setters) at 5-6 weeks of age consume approximately 3½ percent of their body weight as air-dry food in addition to whatever milk they receive from the dam. Pups are usually weaned at about six weeks of age and at that time can be fed the same regular dog food that they were given prior to weaning. At this time, they can have all of the food they want and no supplementation with cereal, cottage cheese, eggs, etc., is needed.

The weaned pup can be fed good commercial dog foods, dry or moistened. Normally the pup will more readily consume a dry ration if it is fed moistened. If fed dry in a self-feeder, the pups can have access to the ration at all times.

If the food is fed moistened, the pup should be fed three times daily until 3-4 months of age, then twice daily is adequate until he is 8-9 months of age. Feed all the moistened ration the pup will clean up at each feeding. It is entirely acceptable to feed a puppy once daily providing all of the ration that will be consumed through the 24 hour period.

The period from weaning to approximately 20 weeks of age is the time when a pup grows fastest. During this period of rapid growth, a pup of a medium-sized breed, such as a pointer or setter, requires approximately 3½ pounds of air-dry food to gain one pound of body weight.

Most larger breeds require slightly less, most smaller breeds slightly more food per pound of gain. If canned dog foods are fed, three times as much canned food will normally be needed. Sometimes a pup can't consume adequate canned ration to enable him to grow normally. This is due to the high moisture content of the canned rations. Until a pup is about 8 months old, he should have all the food he wants.

When the pup is approximately 8 to 10 weeks of age, he will consume a higher level of feed in proportion to his body weight than at any other time in his life. (An exception to this is a lactating bitch.) As the dog becomes older and gains weight, the amount of feed intake in proportion to body weight gradually decreases and levels off at maturity. If at any time during the growing period the dog tends to become overweight, then his feed intake should be reduced.

At the Purina Dog Care Center over 600 pups are whelped annually. Of those whelped alive, approximately 90% were weaned. All of these pups received only the dam's milk plus dry dog food and water until they were weaned. At weaning time they go on test and receive only good commercial rations or experimental rations and water. Growth in all breeds from Chihuahuas to Great Danes is normal and the dogs maintain good body condition. Good commercial rations contain all of the nutrients including the essential vitamins, minerals and amino acids that young growing puppies need in an economical form.

MAINTENANCE FEEDING —THE ADULT DOG

Upon reaching maturity most field dogs require only a maintenance ration. This is especially true if they are house pets and are hunted or exercised only once a week. During the maintenance period sporting dogs require about ½ ounce (air-dry) of a good dry dog food per pound of body weight. Larger dogs usually require slightly less—smaller dogs slightly more in order to maintain good body condition. This means that a 50-pound pointer or setter not working hard will require approximately 1½ pounds of dry ration daily.

It is important that the mature dog receive a good nutritious diet. Inadequate or deficient diets fed to adult dogs can cause poor body condition, rough hair coat, and lower the body's resistance to disease. Feeding once a day is usually sufficient for adult dogs. It is generally desirable to feed at about the same time, usually in the evening since this tends to help keep the dog quiet during the night. Dry self-feeding is an easy and convenient way to feed mature dogs. This is done by many dog owners and most dogs will not overeat with this feeding method. Fresh water should be available at all times.

Overweight Problems. One of the problems that frequently occurs in feeding mature dogs is that they may overeat and consequently become overweight. Overweight dogs not only present a poor appearance, but excess weight can shorten their life expectancy. Usually a dog that is fed all he will eat at each feeding without becoming excessively lean or fat is receiving an ample amount. This is probably the best way to gauge whether or not the dog owner is feeding enough, rather than using a set pattern of feeding a certain amount. If a dog tends to become overweight, he should be placed on limited feed intake to maintain normal weight. Many dog owners know that the weight of adult dogs depends on the size of the body framework. Unless a dog is being used for show purposes, he should be kept slightly lean. In this way, he will be most active and will normally tend to lead a longer, healthier life.

What About Variety In Feeding? Many people feel that their dogs need a variety of food, such as a regular change in the commerical dog food they buy or the addition of a large amount of table scraps. Actually, dogs can do very well on one ration during their lifetime and do not need a change. This has been proven by many kennel and pet dog owners as well.

Occasionally a dog owner will say that his dog will not eat dry dog food or is a finicky eater. It is usually found that he is feeding table scraps or cooking meat and broth for his dog, which dogs prefer, and therefore they refuse to eat the regular commercial dog foods. A dog fed in this way is not getting the balanced diet he would be receiving if a good commercial dog ration was being fed.

It is not unusual for dogs to go off feed for a day or two and refuse to eat any food, or very little. This condition is quite natural and unless it persists, there is nothing to become alarmed about since dogs vary widely in their food requirements depending on age, size and activity. Feeding according to body condition is a good sound method.

FEEDING BREEDING STOCK

Feeding the breeding stock, especially brood bitches, a well-balanced ration in the correct amount is important. Brood stock in poor body condition receiving an inadequate diet during gestation and lactation will have small pups and a low-milk supply.

A brood female not hunting or being worked in other ways can be maintained on a maintenance ration between litters. She should not be overweight at any time. An overweight female will usually have whelping problems and produce small litters. During the last two to three weeks of the gestation period, her feed consumption tends to increase as much as 20% as compared to the amount she was eating during the maintenance period. Generally if the female is fed on a maintenance level of ½ ounce of feed per pound of body weight, her increased body weight gain will increase feed consumption adequately during the gestation period. If she is somewhat thin, increase her food intake by 20-30% during the final 4 weeks of the gestation period.

During the lactation period a bitch may consume 2½ to 3 times the normal maintenance level by the

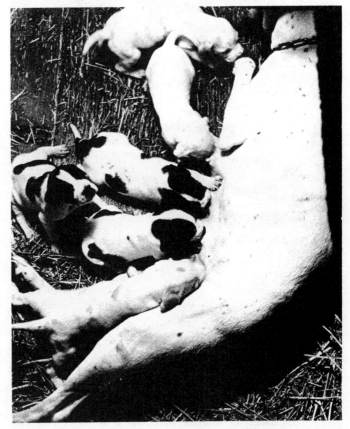

Chow time for a litter of very young Pointer pups.

time the pups are three to four weeks of age. She should have all she wants to eat for the increased food intake necessary to meet the heavy milk production. Since pups start to consume solid food by the time they are three to four weeks of age, their feed consumption will increase while the dam's feed consumption will decrease. The dog food the dam receives should also be available to her pups.

WEANING

On the day of weaning, the dam should not be fed any food but should have water available. The second day feed ¼th the normal maintenance level, on the third day ½, on the fourth day ¾th, and on the fifth day the amount of food offered is brought up to the normal maintenance level. Cutting back on her food intake and then increasing it gradually helps decrease milk production and aids in the maintenance of a healthy mammary gland.

Many dog breeders believe that the brood bitch cannot be maintained on a diet of dry dog food alone, without supplementation. All of the brood females (about 70 of them) at the Purina Dog Care Center receive good commercial dog rations or experimental rations and water during their lifetime. This is true regardless of whether they are Chihuahuas, sporting dogs, or Great Danes. At this writing there are three English Setters at the Purina Dog Center

The Ralston Purina Pet Care Center, St. Louis, Missouri. Purina photo.

that have had over 100 puppies; one has had 107 pups, another 110, and another 126. All of these setters received only dog food and water during their lifetime.

DOG FOOD—CANNED VS. DRY

A stud dog should be kept in good body condition without being overweight. He usually requires only a maintenance level of ration.

A point to keep in mind when feeding dogs, regardless of whether they are on a maintenance or growing ration, is that it takes three pounds of a complete canned dog food to be equivalent to one pound of a dry dog food. Using a canned dog food can increase feeding costs.

The new, and very convenient, soft-moist dog foods are also excellent rations, but again are rather high in price. These generally contain the same basic nutrients found in dry dog foods, with the addition of moisture, often in the form of broths or dehydrolized fatty material. They are easy to store, need no refrigeration and are relished by most dogs . . . but provide no more food value than any good dry dog food.

Good nutrition is not the only factor in producing and raising large healthy litters. Good breeding stock, proper sanitation procedures, and good management of the newborn puppies all go together to produce quality litters. The best dog food in the world will not make up for poor sanitation and a cold, damp kennel.

FEEDING HARD-WORKING DOGS

Working dogs use a lot of energy. To replace this energy a large amount of high quality, nutritious food is required. These dogs should be offered all of the dog food they want, unless they begin to become overweight.

Feeding once a day is ample, unless weight is a problem, and the dog is thin. Then feeding twice a day may be necessary. Usually the best time to feed is in the evening although dogs should not be fed just prior to being worked. Feed all of the food the dog will clean up—if fed moistened. If the dogs are self-fed dry, then a constant supply of dry food can be left in front of them at all times. If the dog is not maintaining good condition on dry feeding, then he should be switched to moistened dry dog food, since a moistened ration is usually much more acceptable than the same ration fed dry and most dogs will consume more.

If a hard-working dog still does not stay in good body condition using a regular moistened dry dog food, then it is recommended that up to 20% meat be added. The meat does not increase the nutritional balance of a good dry dog food, but in most cases will increase the palatability and thus increase the food intake. During the period when the dog is not working, care should be taken not to create a weight problem by overfeeding.

Feeding a dense dog food with a high bushel weight will enable the hard-working dog to have a higher feed intake than if a low bushel weight product is fed. That is why dense, high-protein-high-fat rations are recommended for hard-working dogs with high-energy needs.

DOG FOOD SUPPLEMENTS

Many dog owners still refuse to believe that good commercial dog foods contain all of the nutrients needed by normal dogs for all phases of their lives. Occasionally an individual dog may have a higher-than-average requirement for a particular nutrient, but this is exceptional and is usually the result of a metabolic abnormality. Supplementation is costly, unnecessary, and may cause nutritionally-induced health problems. How can this happen?

Eggs. Adding raw whole eggs to rations for puppies or even mature dogs is not uncommon. Raw egg white contains an enzyme, avidin, which ties up the vitamin biotin, and if fed continuously a biotin deficiency can occur. Raw egg whites are used to produce biotin deficiencies experimentally. Symptoms include dermatitis, loss of hair, and poor growth. Although it is not necessary to add eggs to the diet, the addition of cooked eggs will not cause a destruction of biotin.

Calcium. Adding supplemental minerals, such as calcium pills, to a regular diet can also be detrimental. It is known that both calcium and phosphorus must be present in the diet in ample quantities and in the proper ratio for normal bone development. In dogs, a calcium phosphorus ratio of 1.2:1 promotes maximum calcification. If additional calcium is added to push this ratio even further apart, for example 5:1, there would be an inefficient assimilation of these two minerals even though the phosphorus was present in the correct amount. Rickets is one sign of a deficiency or imbalance of either of these two minerals in the ration of growing dogs.

Vitamins D and E. Cod-liver oil and wheat germ oil are sources of vitamins D and E. Adding excessive cod-liver oil can supply more vitamin D than is actually needed. Vitamin D must also be given in the proper proportion along with calcium and phosphorus for good bone and teeth formation.

If either of these two oils are in the process of becoming rancid, or if a rancid fat is added, this can destroy the Vitamin E. In fact, low levels of rancid fish oil are often used to produce a vitamin E deficiency in experimental work. Vitamin E is necessary for normal growth, reproduction and lactation. All of the vitamins known to be needed by normal dogs are added in sufficient amounts to most good commercial dog foods. These vitamins are in stable forms that can withstand the heat and pressure that might occur during manufacturing and possible long periods of warehouse storage.

Unnecessary Special Foods for Pups. Many young puppies, especially prior to weaning, are fed a mixture of milk, baby cereal, vitamins, eggs, and meat. Besides being expensive, the preparation of a diet of this type is time-consuming and difficult. A good commercial dry dog food that has been moistened with water or milk is highly palatable for pups and will supply them with the balanced nutrition that cannot be furnished by many home-mixes.

Charcoal. Occasionally, charcoal is added to the diet. Unless fed in excessive amounts this ingredient is usually considered to be nonharmful, but there is no real advantage in feeding it. It is relatively indigestible and absorbs some vitamins in the digestive tract and carries them out of the dog's body, thus making these nutrients unavailable to the dog.

Raw Meat. Hard-working dogs, such as field trial dogs hunted and trained heavily, require a high level of feed intake to meet their high-energy requirements. It is very important that they receive a highly palatable ration so they will consume a high caloric intake. Many trainers add up to 20-25% raw meat to the diet; this does not improve the nutritional balance of the ration, but usually increases acceptance. Meat fed at this level should not cause any problems.

Major Danger in "All Meat" Diet. Often dog owners are led to believe that an "all meat" diet would be the best thing they could provide for their pet. The logic fostered here is that in the wild, dogs would eat an all meat diet and that most commercial dog foods contain a high percentage of cereal matter. The latter part of this theory is true, most commercial dog foods have some vegetable content, but this is not a trick being played on the consumer by the manufacturer.

Adult dogs require 120 milligrams of calcium per pound of body weight per day. They also require 100 milligrams of phosphorus per pound per day. Meat contains approximately 50 milligrams of calcium per pound and approximately 1,000 milligrams of phosphorus per pound. Projecting these figures, a 35-pound dog would require 4,200 milligrams of calcium

per day—and would have to eat 84 pounds of meat to obtain it! Further, instead of the proportionate 3,500 milligrams of phosphorus (the daily requirement), the dog would then be ingesting 84,000 milligrams per day.

Obviously, a 35-pound dog is not going to eat over 80 pounds of meat per day, so the body's calcium content is rapidly depleted. A puppy weaned onto an all-meat diet will have a store of calcium acquired during the weeks of nursing but this will soon almost vanish. A condition called nutritional secondary hyperparathyroidism will manifest itself in the form of rickets, usually within three or four weeks. With adult dogs, a change to an all-meat diet will rapidly lead to the so-called "paper bones," where the dog's skeletal system is weakened to the extent that easily broken bones which will not heal often result in the dog being euthanized.

When a dog's diet is too high in meat content, even though it is not an all-meat diet, nutritional secondary hyperparathyroidism shows up in puppies with poorly developing teeth, and in adult dogs will first show itself in loosening teeth. Since nutritional secondary hyperparathyroidism is a condition and not a disease, it can often be corrected if appropriate steps are taken in time. A properly balanced diet, sometimes with a veterinarian-prescribed calcium supplement, will soon restore the dog to good health. In puppies, the change is often remarkable, with a complete "cure" being seen in a matter of weeks.

What about the "natural" all-meat diet of carnivores? This, too, is a fallacy. In the wild, wolves and coyotes—and wild-dogs as well—actually fight each other for the stomachs and intestines of their kills. This, in addition to bones, skin, and plant matter eaten as a normal thing, helps round out the balanced diet for carnivores.

When a dog is receiving a well-balanced diet, supplementation is unnecessary and may even prove to be detrimental at times. More and more dog owners are finding that supplementing good commercial dry dog foods offer no advantages for their dogs. This has been proven time and time again by the many thousands of dogs self-fed dry rations and water with excellent results. Excess vitamin and mineral supplementation can aggravate hip problems, heart problems, and impair dog health.

EXCESSIVE CHEWING/EATING

Quite often dogs will just chew on almost anything in sight, and some have a bad habit of eating dirt, grass or even their own or other dogs' droppings. This latter activity is called "coprophagy."

The problem of dogs chewing on "things" is especially prevalent in young, teething puppies but is usually outgrown by 8-10 months of age. Puppies will chew on wood, toys, articles of clothing, or anything they can pick up or reach.

Several methods can be used to curb or prevent excessive chewing. If possible, items that pups like to chew on should not be left in an area where they

Time for the day's speculation's—four handsome and splendidly trained German Shepherds. Grafmar Kennels photo.

might be tempted. Discipline in the form of a swat with a rolled-up newspaper can also put the point across in many instances. Since chewing is a natural tendency of the pup, and most pups are quite active, it may be advisable to give him a plaything or something of his own to chew on. This can be an old shoe or a toy (not plastic) made especially for dogs. Bones can be used, but they should be the large round beef bones or oxtails and not pork or chicken bones.

The problem of dogs eating dirt, wood, sand, their own droppings or other items is thought to be caused by several factors including confinement and boredom. This is not unusual, especially in confined dogs and dogs will not only chew on these items but may actually eat them. Again, the main causes of dogs eating undesirable items often seems to be confinement and boredom. This occurs at all ages and in any breed, although it appears to be more prevalent in the working and hunting breeds. Currently we do not know how to produce this habit nutritionally and have no evidence to indicate that it is related to nutrition. It can occur on any commercial dog food, as well as on home-made rations.

Here again, providing something for the dog to play with or chew on, such as green hardwood limbs, old shoes or rubber toys made for dogs, may be helpful. It may also be beneficial to give the dogs more exercise or a larger area in which to run. As the dog owner has probably noticed, when he is playing with

or exercising his dog, the problem of eating undesirable items does not occur.

Quite often this problem starts in winter in northern areas when the droppings are frozen. Dogs on a limited feed intake or those not receiving enough food may develop this habit. Once a dog starts chewing on items, including droppings, it seems to become a habit. One dog seeing another consuming droppings often acquires the habit.

There is no specific remedy that can be used to prevent dogs from doing this. Disciplining the dog, removal of the various items from the area, if possible, or giving the dog more exercise or something to play with may be helpful. As far as stopping dogs from eating their droppings, we know of no specific remedy. Some people have used a product called "Ectoral," which is given to control external parasites. When this product is fed at a low level for a few days, it apparently gives the droppings a bad taste. Ectoral can be obtained from your veterinarian. The coprophagic dog should also be checked for parasites and any disease problem that might be present. Some people feel that these factors contribute to coprophagy.

If the dogs are looking for something to chew on or eat, keep dry dog food available in a self-feeder or pan where they can reach it at all times to provide them with something to do. In addition, give him a

. . . And a little "togetherness"—the same foursome as on the opposite page (Rear view). Grafmar Kennels photo.

green limb about 1″ in diameter and 12″ long so he can chew on it.

NUTRITION AND CARE OF THE AGING DOG

As a dog owner you have an obligation to your dog and can tremendously influence his biological status during aging. The geriatric dog reflects the care and treatment received during growth, and maintenance, starting soon after birth. The pattern for geriatric response by your dog is set during the time when he first starts eating solid foods.

Like everyone else, dog owners often feel that developing puppies must be the cutest, fattest, largest and most advanced for their age. This philosophy causes the dog owner to keep his puppy stuffed with food, usually including those tidbits that are highly unbalanced nutritionally, with the result that the pup is forced towards a state of nutritional obesity from which he does not recover during his adult life.

Why are more dogs living longer?

1. Improved pediatric care.
2. More effective biologicals for the control of infectious diseases.
3. Superior anthelmintics, insecticides, fungicides and miticides.
4. More skill and knowledge by the veterinarian.
5. Confinement.
6. Education of dog owners.
7. Improved diagnostic procedures.
8. Genetic selectivity.
9. Superior nutrition in modern dog foods.

The aging process is apparently initiated during conception and continues until death. Aging of specific tissues proceeds at a differential rate within an animal during various phases of growth, maturity, reproduction, diseases, and is not confined to the terminal state. Nutrition of the aging dog is exceedingly complex and must take into account the dog's environment, breed, sex, age, weight, activity, previous treatment, and must include an accurate clinical and laboratory evaluation of the dog's current physiological and pathological condition.

At mating it is possible to make many predictions about the expected progeny. If the bitch is fat when conception occurs, it is likely to produce a small litter. Obese females tend to shed fewer ova than females in normal flesh and implantation may be impaired.

Small litters tend to have heavier individual puppies than do larger litters; the chances for survival are greater in smaller litters. The offspring from the obese females, since it is from a smaller litter and has a heavier birth weight has less competition at the "dinner plate" during nursing and can be expected to develop into heavier pups later on. These observations have been confirmed by tests at leading research centers.

Cholesterol and Fats. A group of 160 pet dogs was cared for in two animal hospitals while their owners were vacationing, and were compared with 156 adult dogs held in the animal research quarters of two teaching hospitals. Most of the pets were fed commercial diets plus added cottage cheese, eggs, milk and meat, while the dogs in the teaching hospitals received commercial rations plus horse meat once or twice each week. The dogs in the teaching hospitals had serum cholesterol levels ranging from 56-260 mg/100 ml. with an average of 133 mg/100 ml; only 6 dogs had cholesterol values in excess of 200 mg/100 ml. The pet dogs had an average cholesterol value of 225 mg/100 ml. with a range of 95-973 mg/100 ml. Fifty-one percent had cholesterol levels over 200 mg/100 ml.

Nutrition and management probably offer the most immediate potential for increased canine life span. The startling results with mouse liveability might offer a starting place and an indication of what could be expected with dogs. Researchers working with an obese strain of mice found that those fed *ad libitum* from 6 weeks of age had a mean life span of 457 days while those fed a limited intake lived 795 days. Put another way, all of the mice fed *ad libitum* were dead by the 667th day, while 81% of those fed restricted amounts were alive at 730 days. Others using dystrophic mice found that one commercial mouse diet would produce a liveability in males 139% longer than in males on another commercial diet. The increase in life span in the females was 79%. Controlled feed intake as just demonstrated is not the complete answer; nutritional formulation also influences liveability.

Others found that high fat diets increased the longevity of mice 18% as compared with a diet without 25% added lard. This may lend support to the theory that high-fat intakes may actually limit total caloric intake. In these tests the controls and high-fat groups lived significantly longer than the limited-fed groups. With different levels of the same ration, however, it was found that restricting total intake significantly increased life span in the mice.

Caloric restriction in rats increased longevity to 971 days as compared with 680 days for rats receiving unlimited feed.

Other Considerations. The reaction of the geriatric dog to a beneficial nutritional program depends on the previous nutrition, individual metabolic response, and the current physical and physiological status. Dogs restricted to a caloric intake that will avoid obesity are those least likely to present disease signs associated with aging.

Feeding Programs for the Aging Dog. Normal aging dogs not tending towards obesity can be self-fed a good commercial dry dog ration and water. The dry ration can be self-fed to most dogs. Those with a tendency to become overweight should be restricted to one feeding daily with the amount offered just enough to keep a desirable lean healthy condition. As a guide, ½ ounce of dry food per pound of body weight will maintain most dogs in a desirable body condition. Some dogs will require only half this amount while others will need more. Usually castrated males and spayed females will need less food that intact female dogs, who in turn usually require less food than intact males.

Heart problems can be expected to produce excess fluids that are retained in the body, unless low-sodium diets are fed, and again the intake must be controlled to alleviate the stress of excess body weight. Good commercial low-sodium canned rations are available for dogs with cardiac stress. In some cases where these rations are not available, satisfactory nutrition can be supplied by a mixture of 40% by weight of a dry corn meal and 60% dry commercial ration. The corn meal should be cooked with water and boiled for 5 minutes and the dry dog food added after the corn meal mush has cooled. Home softeners using ion exchange resins to remove the calcium often supply all of the sodium needed by normal men and dogs. If the sodium in softened water is added to that of a normal diet of these stressed cardiac insufficiency cases, it is easy to see that the problem is compounded.

Nephritic low-protein diets are available that in some instances are completely satisfactory; under other conditions a high-protein diet aids in lessening this stress. Again when the low-protein nephritic diets are not available, a good diet for the interstitial nephritic dog can be made by combining the corn meal and the dry food in the manner described.

Obesity is a direct function of caloric intake even though energy expenditures may be influenced by hormonally controlled mechanisms. The only logical permanent management of obesity is through the regulation of caloric intake. In most cases this involves convincing the dog owner that his dog is dangerously fat and teaching him how to regulate his dog's caloric (energy) intake through feed control. In some instances the elimination of table scraps and tidbits is enough for weight reduction. Since dogs consume approximately 20% more dry food that is offered moistened than that fed dry, this may be one way to reduce food intake. Many dogs roam neighborhoods and raid the garbage cans. Restricting caloric intake increases the tendency of the aging dog to search for food on the outside and increases the propensity of the younger dogs towards coprophagy.

Scurvy. Scurvy is more common in aging pets than is usually recognized. The painful muscular movements observed in dogs that have been still for one or two hours and then suddenly roused with reactions of pain and stiffness, often respond to ascorbic acid therapy. Fifty mg. of ascorbic acid for small dogs (15-20 lbs.) and 100 mg. of ascorbic acid for large dogs (60-70 lbs.) is usually sufficient. Normally dogs "manufacture" ample vitamin C in their bodies.

Diabetes. Diabetes in dogs is usually diagnosed after noting that the dog drinks excessive quantities of water. The veterinarian will generally confirm diabetes if a urine assay following a high-sugar meal indicates excess sugar. Dietary control can effectively support medication. A ration of ⅓ animal fat and ⅔ dry dog food usually helps with a lessening of the insulin deficiency stress by decreasing the ration energy derived from the carbohydrates.

Arthritis. Arthritic conditions in sporting dogs can be managed by a combination of corticosteroids and high phosphorus diets which help remove calcium. Those arthritic conditions which almost always accompany hip dysplasia can be made less painful by the additional phosphorus added in the form of raw meat; for the severely arthritic dog, a combination of ½ by weight of a good commercial dry dog food and ½ raw meat offered in limited amounts is indicated. Again, weight control is imperative to lessen irritation and accompany joint edema. For each pound of body weight, ¾ ounce of this combination diet is usually ample for maintenance. Supplementation with vitamin D and added calcium tends to increase calcium deposits in soft tissues and such supplementation is most undesirable in arthritic conditions.

Constipation and Diarrhea. Chronic constipation can be managed satisfactorily by the use of rations containing a low level of an absorbent, like beet pulp. The small amount of beet pulp will act like thousands of tiny sponges in the digestive tract and pick up enough water to keep the senile digestive tract in good muscle tone. Excess lean raw meat and bones will contribute to constipation and must be avoided.

Chronic diarrhea can be caused by many factors including pancreatitis, malnutrition, and coccidiosis. Pancreatitis usually causes an increased water intake, steatorrhea and diarrhea. This can be easily checked by adding dried pancreatic tissue to the diet of the dog for two days; a return to normalcy will confirm pancreatitis. Your veternarian can do this for you.

Pancreatic Insufficiency. Pancreatic insufficiency is easily pinpointed and may progress from fat in the droppings and a ravenous appetite with no weight gain to gradual debilitation. A reduction or cessation of fat absorption can limit the fatty acid, vitamin A, vitamin E and vitamin D utilization by the dog. The debilitated dog may be reflecting the avitaminosis. A simple, convincing test of pancreatic insufficiency consists of a 5 ml. blood sample from a dog fasted overnight. Then feed 1½ ml. of corn oil per pound of body weight in the amount of dog food that the dog will consume immediately. Two hours later the veterinarian takes another 5 ml. and spins both samples in the centrifuge. A normal dog shows a heavy "cream line" on the 2-hour sample while the pancreatic-deficient dog will show very little more than in the overnight control sample.

Coccidia. Coccidiosis causes most diarrhea and with care can be identified from fecal smears or by the flotation process. Coccidia can be controlled with sulfas or nitrofurans.

Flatulence. Flatulence or intestinal gas is common in the aging dog. Aging is accompanied by diminished intestinal motility, less body activity, decreased cellular and fluid metabolism, and longer food retention in the intestinal tract. This means longer exposure to the putrifying and fermenting activity of bacteria. Reduced respiratory gaseous exchange doesn't effectively eliminate the intestinal gasses of the old, inactive, overfed dog. As a result, his company on a winter's evening before the fire or in a closed car is often almost unbearable. Flatulence usually increases in proportion to the level of meat in the diet. The reduction of supplementary meat and total food intake along with increased exercise is the easiest way to control flatulence.

PROPER NUTRITION AND COMMERCIAL FOODS

With the research available on the requirements of dogs, it is easy to understand why it is thought that American dogs fed good commercial dog rations are fed better than America's human population. America's leading dog foods contain less bacteria than milk purchased in the same supermarket for human consumption.

The aging pet offers many challenges in its nutrition, care and medication. Nutrition of the aging animal is exceedingly complex; however, the nutritional research and technology has continued to progress at a rate that exceeds that of man. Hence you certainly can help your dog live an extended useful life through proper feeding.

Generally speaking, you will find that the instructions accompanying most good commercial dog foods will help you properly feed your dog. Do not blindly follow any tables or other such directions, however. If the evidence before you indicates your dog is gaining too much weight, adjust his food accordingly. If the dog has an adequate food intake and is losing weight, look for problems elsewhere.

Remember, commercial dog foods vary considerably in density. The directions for feeding one brand may not apply for another brand.

Any pup will grow and thrive when given a commercial dog food and fed in accordance with the manufacturer's instructions. Photo by Hank Babbitt.

—Kennels and Kenneling—

KENNEL FACILITIES are adaptable to the breed, size, and number of dogs housed, the climate, and the pocketbook and wishes of the owner. There are two basic types of kennels: the individual or dual dog house, surrounded by an enclosure or pen, and the multi-dog kennel building, which may range from a converted poultry house or barn to an elaborate manor house of brick or stone. Chief advantage of the former is minimum expense in a natural surrounding. Convenience and efficiency in operation are the advantages of the more centralized kennel building.

Existing buildings may often be modified into successful kennels. Most people raise dogs as a hobby or sideline, and start with an individual pet, gradually enlarging their operation. Care must be taken to provide adequate light and air when making an existing building into a kennel. The cellar or barn, most often used, is notably lacking in both, to start with.

MULTI-DOG KENNEL BUILDINGS

The usual plan for a multi-dog kennel building, whether large or small, consists of a central services section with wings going out on both sides or to the back. The central section comprises office, feeding, grooming, and special care units, such as whelping and puppy pens, separate quarters for sick dogs, etc. The wings consist of a center hall with individual inside stalls on both sides, connecting with individual outdoor runs.

Multi-dog kennel building, part of the Gunsmoke Kennels complex, Springfield, Illinois. Photo by Gunsmoke Kennels.

Barrel housing facilities at Elhew Kennels, Scottsville, N.Y. Photo by Jack Hanna.

Dogs like to sun themselves on top of all-weather wood box do protectors in concrete runs. Torgerson Photos.

General Features. This type of building requires maximum outlay in building and fencing for each dog, but gives them as much access to exercise and the outdoors as is possible within a restricted but secure environment. In such a kennel the partitions may be solid or wire, or a combination, with solid stall divisions up to waist height, with wire above. Wire fronts will keep the dogs from feeling "closed in" and allow passage of light and air. There should be windows above the doors to the outside runs, to let in plenty of sunlight and air, necessary for the health and well-being of kenneled dogs.

Crates, Cages or Pens. Another way of kenneling dogs in a central building is to use crates or cages, usually in banks against the wall. These pens may be homemade of the same materials as stalls, or crates of the type used for shipping dogs, although they should be larger than the minimum size required to hold a dog comfortably. Veterinary hospitals often use cages of stainless steel for ease in cleaning and disinfecting. These represent a large initial investment, but they will last virtually forever, while substances like wood may be chewed wherever a dog can find an unprotected edge. Tile is also sanitary, but expensive. Smooth-finish plywood or hardboard, with no edges within reach of a dog's teeth, are the generally used and satisfactory components.

For small breeds which tend to be easily excited, the crating system promotes quiet, although diversions should be provided to prevent boredom. Exercise in spacious runs at least twice a day is a necessity. Several congenial dogs may run together, allowing maximum use of available space.

Planning Factors. Important factors to consider in planning a kennel are heat and cooling, light, ventilation and plumbing. A longhaired, hardy breed may need no heat at all even in the coldest climate, but some warmth must be provided for whelping bitches and young puppies. If there is no central furnace for the entire kennel, electric space heaters, infra-red bulbs, plug-in radiators or radiant heating may be the best solution to warm a small area. Room temperature immediately surrounding a new litter must be above 70° to 80° if the puppies are without their dam for any reason.

Air-conditioning. Air-conditioning is also important for the comfort of boarders accustomed to air-conditioned homes in the South or during warm-weather months, and for the kennel operator and help. It may also be worthwhile for the breeding kennel with show dogs, to prevent skin disorders, to promote coat growth and add to their comfort.

Lighting. Light is an essential for dogs' health and provision must be made for windows to let it in, particular in the puppies' area if cold weather prevents them from being outside for at least a short time each day. Ventilation by means of circulating fans and roof outlets will be necessary in the large kennel. Because considerable water is used for cleaning around a kennel, either steam-cleaning floors or washing them down, there must be evaporation or the dogs will live in an overhumid atmosphere, which is most unhealthy. Odors are also a kennel problem which good ventilation, combined with good sanitation practices, will keep under control. There should be no drafts, but the air should be changed frequently.

Adequate lighting fixtures should be provided for night kennel work or checking and outlets for clippers, driers or any other necessary appliances in the work area. If the kitchen does not include complete facilities, freezer for meat storage, refrigerator for food and drugs, stove for cooking, an electric plug-in burner at least will probably be needed. Many kennel owners find that the noise from a radio keeps dogs happy, as well as accustoming puppies to background

A well planned sporting dog kennel.

noise before they are exposed to the busy world outside the kennel.

Plumbing. Plumbing is one of the most expensive elements in building, whether it is for kennel or home. Keeping the fixtures in a central core will keep costs to a minimum. The washing room, kitchen and lavatory facilities should be adjoining, with fixtures kept away from outside walls in cold climates. Carrying water to dogs is expensive in terms of labor, so it may be worthwhile to install automatic watering devices on a water line to the ends of the housing wings. Electric heating tape will protect these from freezing if the section is not heated.

Grooming and Show Room Accommodations. Facilities for bathing, which all kennels need sooner or later, may be combined with the grooming room, kitchen or, in the smaller kennel, an all-purpose workroom. A tub for bathing should be set up so that the person doing the job does not have to bend over too far to work comfortably. The grooming area must also include facilities for handling dogs, whether clipping and trimming is done professionally, or it is

Tie-out boxes are spaced evenly on gravel beds that slope from the center of the area to facilitate drainage. Gunsmoke Kennels photo.

Close-up of barrel housing at Elhew Kennels. Photo by Jack Hanna.

KENNELING THE INDIVIDUAL DOG

The traditional barrel still makes a good individual dog house. Architectural styles also vary from the A-frame to "bird house" kennels. The latter are flat-topped square houses atop a solid post, used by the Air Force to kennel sentry dogs individually. The dog may be fenced in or chained to a ring around the post which allows him 360° of freedom within the range of his tether.

In colder climates the door to an individual dog house should be small compared to the size of the dog and the building, protected by a porch or ell which will keep out wind and rain. The house should also be faced away from the prevailing wind. A hinged top will make it easy to clean out soiled or damp bedding, and the house should be built with the floor up off the ground for warmth. In hot climates ventilation is necessary. There should be an opening under the roof or sufficient height to allow air circulation. If the dog is confined in a run or tied to his house, shade should also be provided. If there is no natural cover such as trees or large shrubs, a canvas awning or fiberglass across the top of the run will provide needed protection from the sun. Even a wire hammock covered with brush will serve this purpose.

RUNS

Some breeders report on raising puppies successfully on wire. Fine mesh must be used, which allows urine

only the owner's dogs that are groomed before shows, etc. A rotating table with post to hold the dog's head by a collar is a help in the larger operation. A regular crate or table with non-slip surface, preferably with a grooming post, will suffice for a few dogs.

A showroom, with display of ribbons and trophies, and to exhibit puppies for sale without allowing visitors to wander through the main kennel, may be combined with the office where records are kept, correspondence answered, and other activities connected with the dogs carried out.

Floors. Flooring throughout the kennel is an important item in care and maintenance. In work spaces and office, linoleum or vinyl is easily mopped and cleaned. Wood may be used, but it is harder to clean and use of water should be avoided. Concrete is most satisfactory for the dogs' living areas and corridors. A sealer to prevent porosity is necessary; the new epoxy paints or similar surfaces are sanitary and wear well. Sleeping boxes or benches should be provided to keep the dogs off cold or damp concrete.

Bedding. Bedding may be of fragrant cedar shavings, washable rugs (which puppies will carry outside and play with, if given the chance, eventually tearing them to shreds), or newspapers. Shredded papers make excellent bedding and flat sheets of paper are fine for liners. These cost nothing and can be easily disposed of in an incinerator when replaced. A local newspaper or printer will usually sell or give away the ends of newsprint rolls. This fresh, unprinted paper may be cut to fit the pens and light-colored dogs will not be discolored by ink, as they may be with printed papers. Occasionally, puppies will develop sores on their tender bellies and these can often be traced to the use of printed newspapers as bedding.

Elevated tie-out boxes help keep dogs clean and dry. Metal corner strips protect wood from chewing. Torgerson Photos.

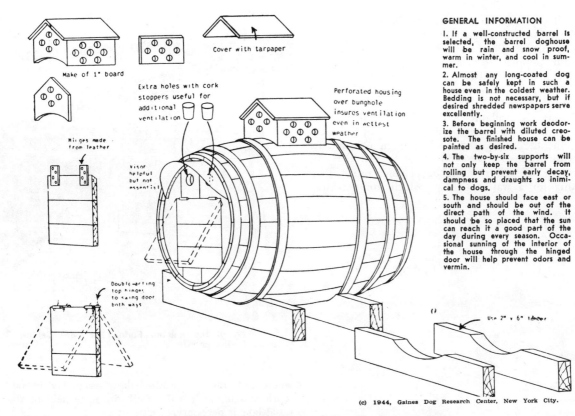

Make of 1" board

Cover with tarpaper

Extra holes with cork stoppers useful for additional ventilation

Perforated housing over bunghole insures ventilation even in wettest weather

Hinges made from leather

Visor helpful but not essential

Double-acting top hinges to swing door both ways

Use 2" x 6" lumber

(c) 1944, Gaines Dog Research Center, New York City.

Plan for building a barrel doghouse. Gaines Dog Research Center.

GENERAL INFORMATION

1. If a well-constructed barrel is selected, the barrel doghouse will be rain and snow proof, warm in winter, and cool in summer.

2. Almost any long-coated dog can be safely kept in such a house even in the coldest weather. Bedding is not necessary, but if desired shredded newspapers serve excellently.

3. Before beginning work deodorize the barrel with diluted creosote. The finished house can be painted as desired.

4. The two-by-six supports will not only keep the barrel from rolling but prevent early decay, dampness and draughts so inimical to dogs.

5. The house should face east or south and should be out of the direct path of the wind. It should be so placed that the sun can reach it a good part of the day during every season. Occasional sunning of the interior of the house through the hinged door will help prevent odors and vermin.

and feces to go through, but does not risk a puppy's getting his toe caught. These pens may be moved occasionally to fresh ground, or placed over a concrete foundation which can be washed down and disinfected. Where the type of soil makes internal parasites a major problem, wire flooring may be a good idea.

Nothing compares with grass for a puppy run, however, and if the pups are confined to a small pen, allow them to run loose on the lawn, or keep them in a portable wire-enclosed run which may be moved from one area to another of clean ground which will prevent damage to the grass. Young puppies that are still indoors at night may be put out in semi-shade in such a portable run for exercise and for the vitamins they will derive from sunlight.

Fencing and Run Separations. Chain link fencing is the best long-range investment for runs. If it is not to be permanent, this type of fence may be purchased in sections that can be moved to another location. Fencing should be high enough to be escape-proof, "digproof" and with secure latches, but accidents can still happen. For a boarding kennel, an outside fence enclosing the entire area beyond the individual runs, is a necessity. If there is an enclosure beyond the run, the loose dog will not be able to go beyond the property and he can be returned quickly to where he belongs. Nothing is so time-consuming and exasperating as chasing a dog which has escaped from its pen.

If the noise is a problem due to neighbors or traffic,

outside fencing should be solid. It may be of rough, stained or painted boards.

While chain link fencing has the advantage of durability and neat appearance, and being escape-proof, virtually unclimbable, welded wire in rectangular mesh is often used satisfactorily, and is a good deal less expensive. Latches must be paw-and chew-proof. All gates should open in, to make it harder for a dog to slip by anyone going in or out to clean, feed, water, etc.

Many boarding kennels have gone to using low cinderblock walls between the runs, with fencing extended upward from the tops of these walls. This helps prevent the spread of any disease from one run to the next and stems any tendency of the dogs to fight. For the first part, waste matter is washed out the end of the run to a common drain system; this prevents contamination of one run with any matter from another. Fighting dogs find it difficult to be effectively aggressive when they have to stand on their hind legs to do battle.

Dogs That Dig or Climb Out. The best way to prevent dogs from digging out of a dirt-surfaced run, is to set fence posts and bottom of the wire in concrete. Failing this, the fence may be buried in the ground to start, or heavy wood, such as 4 x 4s, used at the bottom, fastened from one post to the next. Breeds and individuals vary in digging ability, so if you have one problem digger, he should be placed in a center run which has concrete on all sides, so that he will not lead other dogs astray.

If all your runs are not concrete-surfaced, digging will not hurt the dogs, but make sure they do not make pools for stagnant water, or eat dirt and gravel. If your puppies are constant diggers, mixing the gravel on top with dirt, it may be simpler to resurface their run with concrete, except in a large exercise run.

If space is available, a grass area from 100 feet square up to as much as an acre is an excellent investment. Fencing need not be as high as in smaller individual runs, because dogs will be out here for short periods and running or playing, rather than looking for a way out. Dogs which are persistent

A section of the Ralston Purina Pet Care Center, St. Louis, Missouri. Purina photo.

where runs must be washed down each day, a good septic system, with a dry well, drainage field or disposal lake is necessary.

Packed cinders or slag, or crushed rock are also used as run surfaces by many kennel operators. Grass will quickly become dirt, and then dust or mud, unless there is a lot of ground available for relatively few dogs, and unless runs can be rotated. Paths will still be worn and will have to be covered with hay, wood chips or similar mulch to prevent mud.

THE KENNEL BUSINESS

While most people who raise, show or train dogs do it as a hobby or sideline, there are many full-time

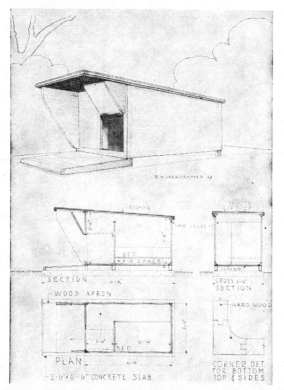

Kennel for dogs, 40 to 60 lbs. Corner detail explains construction principle. Corners, bottom and top rail to be cut from 2" x 2" hardwood stock; use either ¾" tongue and groove hardwood flooring or ¾" waterproof plywood (birch or maple finish). Bottom sealed with mastic. Roofing drawn over top and tacked at sides with ⅜" x ⅜" wood batten. Top overlapping to lift up with hinges at one side. Set on concrete slab, stone, or bed made up with brick. For maintenance, do not paint. Any clear oil base will do for maintaining and preserving the natural color of hardwood.

jumpers or scalers will have to forego this pleasure, but the others will be in better, more sound condition, fit and happier, because of the chance to stretch their legs.

Run Surfacing. Runs may be surfaced with concrete, crushed cinders or rock, or dirt. Concrete is generally most satisfactory for the commercial kennel, being easy to clean, except in very cold weather. The steam cleaner which is used to advantage inside will solve that problem, also. Runs, like floors, should be sloped for drainage, with gutters at the bottom to the septic tank or other endpoint. In the boarding kennel

Main kennel stalls should be checked daily. Self-feed boxes mounted on walls are easily serviced. Here Ron Kayser makes one of his frequent rounds at Gunsmoke Kennels. Photo by Gunsmoke Kennels.

professionals in the various fields connected with dogs. The pet shop owner or dog dealer, the person who runs a grooming and trimming salon or sells pet accessories, food, etc., and the professional trainer and handler all make a livelihood from dogs. It is no way to get rick quick, and it demands experience and knowledge, but for those who like to work hard and really love dogs, it is a satisfying way of life.

While there is considerable outlay for suitable kennels, most persons making a living from dogs have boarding facilities. They may raise and train their own dogs, and be successful as show or field trial breeders and exhibitors, but luck as well as skill are necessary to make money from breeding dogs alone. A steady boarding clientele is more dependable. Additional services including pick-up and delivery, grooming and bathing, specializing in poodle clipping or terrier stripping, all bring in good wages in these days of affluence when the dog is considered an important member of the family.

Outside paid help will usually be necessary in the boarding kennel, but often young people who are interested in a career in dogs are available, and dependable help makes it possible for the owner to go on show trips or to take a needed vacation. In planning to operate a boarding kennel, factors such as nearness to a metropolitan center or the demand for facilities must be considered. Also, a suitable location, zoned for commercial business, is necessary, while in many localities breeding dogs alone will

A thriving kennel business requires a sizable investment in land as well as buildings. This is an aerial view of Gunsmoke Kennels, Springfield, Illinois, owned by Mr. Herbert N. Holmes. Photo by Gunsmoke Kennels.

qualify for a home enterprise or under farming-residential requirements.

There is no reason why the well-run breeding kennel cannot break even if showing and advertising are kept in proportion to sales and stud fees earned by the dogs, and quality stock is kept, commanding premium prices. However, this is not enough for a living in most cases and, in the long run, the money in dogs is in offering additional services.

—General Care—

DOGS ARE very much like human beings in many respects. While proper food, shelter, exercise, and sanitation are all very essential to the health and good temperament of a dog, attention, companionship, and affection also play an important part in his well-being. With the exception of some of the very small breeds which require extra care, dogs are generally hardy individuals, able to adapt themselves to almost any climate or living conditions. Pampering is unnecessary and should, for the dog's own sake, be avoided, but he is entitled to the attention and affection of his master.

"Never make a pet of your hunting dog" is a fallacy which persists despite the fact that it has been disproved many, many times. Complete understanding between master and dog exists only when mutual confidence, trust, and affection are present.

Every dog owner should spend at least a little time every day with his dog, in addition to looking after his necessities such as feed, water, proper shelter, and sanitation. Of course, if the dog is kept in the house he sees much of the family and becomes a part of it. But if he is kept in an outside kennel, he should be removed from his confines at least once daily, given a

period of exercise on a leash or, if possible, a good romp in some open space where he is not likely to get into mischief. These periods can be employed to good advantage in training the dog in the niceties of behavior. They allow time for a good brisk grooming so essential to the development and maintenance of a healthy coat and skin, and these attention-training periods will be eagerly looked forward to by the dog.

Fresh water should be available to the dog at all times, regardless of where he is kenneled. He should be kept free of both external and internal parasites and prompt attention should be paid to the physical ills to which he may be subjected.

Bathing and Grooming. Occasional bathing is an aid to good health and cleanliness. But it can be overdone to the detriment of the coat and skin. The dog should not be bathed oftener than every two or three weeks unless an emergency arises. In cold weather the bath should be given in a warm room and the dog kept indoors for several hours after thoroughly drying. Any good germicidal soap is satisfactory but care should be taken to keep the soapy water out of the dog's eyes and ears, and the skin and coat should

To find the puppy you want, try visiting a dog show. Here the Jonaire Kennels offers Miniature Schnauzers at its bench in an Elmira, New York show. Photo by Jonaire Kennels.

be cleared of every particle of the soap by rinsing as often as necessary. The dog should be rubbed thoroughly dry with rough towels or clean, dry gunny sacks, and particular care should be taken to dry the ears and feet.

Frequent brushing is much more important than bathing, especially in cold weather when the risk of respiratory infection exists. Brushing with a stiff brush cleans the coat of foreign matter, dirt, and filth and stimulates the flow of oil in the skin, promoting the growth of healthy hair that has a pleasing sheen.

Eye Care. The eyes should be watched carefully. After each romp into high grass or cover, weed seeds and foreign matter should be washed out with a boric acid solution, for the presence of such material is exceedingly irritating and may cause serious damage.

Ear Care. The ears of a dog are very sensitive and extreme care should be taken not to irritate them. Never wash out a dog's ear with soap and water. If it becomes necessary to clean the ear, swab it out with cotton and peroxide, or cotton with a little olive or sweet oil. Be gentle in this swabbing and do not probe deeper than you can see.

Care of the Feet. Examine the feet carefully after each run. Prompt attention should be given to any cut on the pads. If the nails are kept trimmed or the dog given enough exercise on hard surfaces to keep them worn down to proper length, there is little danger of trouble from this source, but if allowed to grow, they may break off. A broken nail can cause severe pain and should be promptly treated and, if necessary, removed. Tar and gum may be removed

from the pads and hair of the dog's feet with ether. If that isn't practical, nail-polish remover will serve.

In trimming the nails, care should be taken to avoid cutting into the "quick," the sensitive, blood-filled core of the nail. If the dog has clear nails, the "quick" can be seen and avoided easily. If the dog has some clear nails, you can judge the opaque nails by the length of quick in the clear nails. If the dog's nails have been neglected, it may be necessary to trim the nails back almost to the quick and then to wait for several days. The quick line will recede and then the nails may be trimmed again. There are many good nail clippers for dogs on the market; if you cannot get one, a pair of diagonal wire cutters will suffice. A small, sharp mill file is handy for smoothing the edges of the dog's nails after they have been trimmed, or even for the actual trimming.

TUG-A-CIZER®—A device which gives fun and needed exercise fo dogs of all ages and sizes. Quickly mounted indoors or out, dog find Dog-Lure special scent irresistible, play for hours. (For informa tion, write Canine Behavior Institute, 11927 Montana Ave., Lo Angeles, Calif. 90049.) Courtesy, Canine Behavior Institute.

Care of the Teeth. Dogs do not need bones to keep their teeth clean. Actually, of course, many dogs may safely be given bones to chew and there may never be any problem, but there is always the possibility of a dog breaking a tooth on a bone. Dogs do enjoy chewing, however, and now there are many satisfactory products, such as nylon bones, that may be given to the dog. Never give your dog bones from any bird (chicken, turkey, etc.) or pork bones; these are often splintered when the dog chews them and the shards of bone may create serious problems.

The dog's teeth should be checked periodically. Any accumulation of tartar at the base of the teeth can be scraped off with an orange stick, as used for manicuring, or a similar, sharp stick. Avoid cutting the gums.

—Conditioning for Bench and Field—

CONDITIONING THE dog for bench or field work simply means bringing his body into as near as possible a state of ideal muscular and physical perfection for the job at hand. For the show ring this means coat, eyes, teeth, feet, and contour. For the field this means, in addition, a hard, muscular body, toughened pads, and a healthy interior, the combination of which is necessary to carry him through on the long chase or allow him to keep forging through difficult cover and over rough terrain in a day afield in front of the gun. In either event, regular exercise is one of the most important factors in building "condition." Exercise, proper feeding, and careful attention to all the dog's needs, are essential in creating that state of well-being, proper condition, that reflects itself in the dog's manner, carriage, and disposition.

Particular attention must be paid to the bench show dog's nails as he does not have the advantage, generally, of wearing them down to proper length through field or hunting exercise. Long nails are really a menace. Not only is there danger that they may become torn, causing lameness and possible infection, but they give a compact foot the appearance of greater length, they spread the toes and throw the foot back on the pastern. Clipping the nails is not as simple as it sounds. They must be cut very carefully. Regular dog nail clippers should be used and the nails cut back only to the quick, the fleshy part that nourishes the nail. This is not painful and no bleeding will occur if the quick is untouched. Once they are shortened to the proper length, filing with a dog nail file will keep them that way, although regular exercise on hard, rough surfaces will keep them in proper shape.

The teeth should be brushed regularly with a hard brush and table salt. Powdered pumice is also good. If the tartar film is heavy, a thorough cleaning should be administered by a competent veterinarian.

Assuming that the owner realizes the necessity for excellent coats on his bench show dogs and has so conditioned and groomed his dogs to bring this happy state about, the matter of trimming or plucking the coat to accent for proper conformation is one for important consideration. There are several related reasons for trimming. These are neatness, the accentuation of certain lines, the bringing out of good features and, in some instances as that of the Poodle, to conform with accepted style or to follow tradition.

It is no simple or easy matter to give a number of breeds the proper hair-trim. First, one must be fully acquainted with the effect he desires to accomplish. Then he must possess no little amount of skill to bring it about. The amateur should turn his bench show contender over to a professional or some experienced person for the first hair trim, for trimming is really an art in which efficiency comes only through practice. By carefully watching the professional and then intently studying the trimming charts one may,

with practice, turn out an acceptable job and master the art.

Conditioning the hunting or working dog is not done overnight. A field dog is only as good as his feet and particular care must be taken of them. If he is given too much field work at one time over rough territory his pads become worn or even torn, which may mean a period of enforced rest. Watch his feet carefully. At the first signs of tenderness or the pads' wearing through, coat them with Friar's Balsam, or tincture of benzoin. A coating of fullers earth and pine tar, mixed to the consistency of paste, or a mixture of pine tar and tannic acid, is most helpful. There are several commercial mixtures on the market which are worth a trial. Many hounds and bird dogs will continue to hunt, if allowed to do so, when their pads are torn and bleeding. This most certainly should not be allowed.

Don't expect your dog to turn in a good day's hunt for you on Opening Day unless he is in proper physical condition. Long before the curtain goes up on the hunting season, every hunting dog should be given regular exercise, starting with short periods daily and gradually increasing the length of them.

Actual field work is the best way in which to bring this about, but if that is not practical, pacing the dog on a quiet road from a bicycle, or even a car, will serve. Road work on a leash will harden his muscles, especially if he will pull against the leash. In that event, equip him with a harness. This will allow him to pull against his shoulders and push with his hind quarters and at the same time his breathing apparatus will be unhampered.

Remember that the working or field dog burns up more energy than the inactive dog and should be fed accordingly. Increase his feed as you increase his exercise. By watching his weight and his appetite the proper amount of feed can be determined. Give him almost all he'll eat, but keep him on the eager side.

Treadmills are sometimes employed to develop muscle and some show dog breeders keep triangular ramps in their runs over which the dogs must climb.

Above all things, take it easy. Don't work the dog too hard or else his muscles will become sore and stiff.

Exercising a group of dogs, all at one time, by use of a mechanical "Run-Around." Photo by Gunsmoke Kennels.

──Trimming and Plucking──

THERE ARE a number of reasons why the trimming and plucking of the coats of many breeds of dogs is desirable, particularly if the individual dog is to be entered in bench show competition. If the coats of some terriers were left untended for any length of time, many of those individuals would take on a rather grotesque appearance quite different from that of their well-groomed brothers.

Dogs are trimmed and plucked for neatness, to accent type, to uncover and emphasize good features and, in the case of the Poodle, to follow tradition or a certain style.

Hair, growing awry as it often does, can mar the natural beauty of many dogs. Too much hair on the skull would give it a rather coarse appearance, rather than the delicate moulding the trimming will reveal. Too much hair can make a shapely neck look too thick. Top-lines may be ruined by bunched hair in wrong places. Excessive feather may give an "out in elbow" effect to a naturally straight front. A dog that has been properly trimmed and plucked to accentuate his good points has the advantage of one which goes in the show ring with some of his good points marred by too much hair.

Dog trimming for the show ring is something of an art. Proficiency comes only with practice. The novice should watch the professional carefully before he undertakes the first job himself. For his first show, the aspirant for bench show honors had best be placed in the hands of a professional for debut grooming. The trimming charts, shown here through the courtesy of the Durham Duplex Company, are guides by which the owner may keep his dog in neat appearance. With practice he may acquire the knack of fine canine barbering. Care must be exercised not to overdo the trimming and plucking job, else an "unnatural" effect will be obtained.

AIREDALE TERRIER

1. Trim neck closely and evenly down into back.
2. Trim back level but not as closely as the neck.
3. Front part of neck and brisket to be trimmed very closely with just a shade more hair left on as one works down to where the front legs join the body.
4. The shoulders to be trimmed evenly and closely.
5. The front legs should be merely trimmed to straightness. Trim principally from rear line. Take out a few hairs from the front and outside of the front legs where they join the shoulder to give a straight line from the top of the shoulder to the feet and from the brisket to the tips of the toes. Trim superfluous hair from edges of feet and between toes with scissors. Shape feet to roundness.
6. Shape ribs to follow the body conformation, working hair evenly from a closely trimmed back to a fairly heavy coat on the under part of the ribs and chest. On the under part of the chest only remove those hairs necessary to prevent shagginess. Trim under line of chest to follow the body line.
7. Take out loin closer than chest but not too fine. The under line is trimmed closely to emphasize tuck up.
8. Do not take all the hair off the belly but only those that are snarled or shaggy.

9. In this area trim from a fine back to a fairly heavily coated thigh.
10. From middle of thigh to hock trim only those hairs that are shaggy.
11. Trim back line of hock straight. Trim superfluous hairs from edges of feet and between toes. Shape to roundness.
12. Trim insides of back legs clean, taking care to give a clean, even line to the hind legs from the rear view.
13. Trim tail closely to a tip toward the head, take out very fine in rear where it joins the stern.
14. Trim stern very closely where it is joined by tail, working it heavier toward the hind legs.
15. Trim skull very closely. Leave eyebrows fairly heavy over the inside corner of the eye. Leave very little over the outside corner. Trim eyebrows evenly and closely at the outside corner of the eye with plenty of length over inside corner.
16. Trim cheeks closely from the outside corner of the eye to the corner of the mouth.
17. Trim very slightly from inside corner of eye downward to corner of mouth to give proper expression.
18. Trim hairs on top of muzzle from slightly between eyebrows to nose to give straight line from top of skull.
19. Leave chin whiskers, brush forward, but clean under jaw from corner of mouth back to neck.
20. Clean off ears closely inside and out. Straighten edges with scissors.

BEDLINGTON TERRIER

The Bedlington in his rough state grows a hard, wiry outer coat which is usually quite sparse. Before the trimming actually begins this should be plucked out entirely. After this has been accomplished proceed to work out the undercoat.

The Head

The sheep-like appearance of the Bedlington's head is largely obtained by the correct trimming of his pompadour or top-knot. This pompadour should start at the tip of the nose, be slightly and ever increasingly raised as it travels up the top of the muzzle and extravagantly domed on the top of the head, then evenly decreased until it works into the back of the neck slightly below the point where the skull joins the neck.

The flews of the lips, the under part of the jaw and the cheeks should be trimmed very closely.

The pompadour must be worked into the very closely trimmed muzzle and cheeks very evenly. The actual dividing line between the built up area and the closely trimmed area being from the direct sides of the nostril to very slightly below the outside corner of the eye, to very slightly below the point where the ear joins the head and from there very closely back into the neck.

1. The hair is cleaned closely from the insides and outsides of the ears, but quite a long and ragged but smooth tassel is left on the tip of the ears.

2. Trim back and sides of neck evenly into the back.

3. Trim under part of neck very closely, leaving slightly more hair as you work down toward the brisket.

4. Trim the back not quite as closely as the neck and try to emphasize the roached appearance of the back over the loin.

5. The sides of the chest and shoulders should be trimmed very closely and flat.

6. As much hair as possible is left on the under part of chest to emphasize its depth. The shaggy hairs on this area may be trimmed to follow the desired contour.

7. The loin is trimmed very closely and fine.

8. Trim the very shaggy hairs from the front legs. Trim any hairs from the top outside of the front legs that detract from the dog's straight and narrow appearance when viewed from the front. In trimming around the feet, follow the natural hare foot contour.

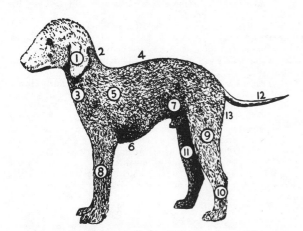

9. The rear legs should be trimmed evenly, leaving slightly more hair as you work towards the hocks.

10. Trim only the very shaggy hairs from the hocks.

11. Trim the insides of hind legs closely down to hocks.

12. Trim tail extremely close on under part and sides. Leave a slight amount of hair on top of tail for half its length, the rest of top is trimmed closely.

13. Trim the stern, under the tail, very close and evenly.

CAIRN TERRIER

Stripping is necessary for the Cairn in order to keep his coat in good healthy condition and emphasize the alert gamey appearance of this breed. His shagginess should be preserved but not to the degree that it hides his virtues and emphasizes his faults.

1. Pluck dead hairs from the neck and trim the new ones slightly. Take off more if your dog is inclined to be heavy or coarse through the neck.

2. Pluck dead hairs and trim the new coat—not closely, but enough to give a level back line.

3. Trim neck and brisket slightly. Too much hair in this area detracts from the dog's quick, active appearance.

4. Trim shoulders of bumpy or patchy places. Leave somewhat shaggy but not profuse.

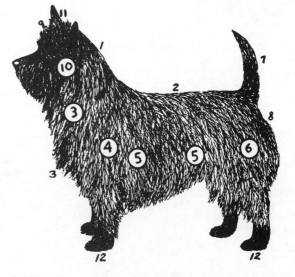

5. Trim sides of body to follow body conformation.

6. Trim upper parts of thigh slightly. Leave hair longer and shaggier on lower part, just above the hock joint.

7. The tail should be bushy but not too shaggy. Trim hair, leaving somewhat thick at base and working it slightly finer toward tip. Do not leave any hairs that make the tail appear longer than it is.

8. Trim those hairs from the stern that give a bunchy appearance, but do not remove fringe. Take the hair out closest where the tail joins the stern.

9. Enough hair should be trimmed from the skull so that about one half of the ear stands clear.

10. Hair around cheek should be trimmed slightly to follow the conformation of the head.

11. The backs and sides of the ears should be trimmed absolutely free of long hair. Straighten edges with scissors.

12. Feet should be shaped to roundness with scissors.

IRISH TERRIER

1. Trim neck very closely and evenly into back.

2. Trim back evenly but not as closely as the neck.

3. Front part of neck and brisket to be trimmed closely, with just a shade more hair left on as one works down to where the front legs join the body.

4. The front shoulders to be trimmed evenly and closely.

5. Front legs should be slightly trimmed to straighten lines. Trim principally on back line; trim superfluous hair from edges of feet and between toes, shaping to roundness.

6. Shape ribs to follow body conformation from a finely

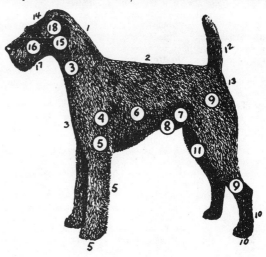

trimmed back to a fuller coat on the under part of ribs and chest, but do not leave any on sides or under chest that are in any way shaggy.

7. Trim loin but do not emphasize tuck up.

8. Trim only shaggy or snarled hair from belly.

9. Trim thighs from back line to hock, taking off sufficient hair to show a definite outline of leg.

10. Straighten back line of hock and trim superfluous hair from edges of feet and between toes, shape to roundness.

11. Trim inside of hind legs down to hock joint.

12. Trim tail evenly, but not too closely, to a tip towards head.

13. Trim stern closely and evenly.

14. Trim skull very closely. Leave eyebrows but not too heavy. Leave slightly more over inside corner of eye than outside corner.

15. Trim cheeks clean back from corner of mouth.

16. Trim under eyes to emphasize expression.

17. Clean under jaw from corner of mouth back to neck. Leave chin whiskers and brush forward.

18. Clean off ears inside and out, straighten edges with scissors.

KERRY BLUE TERRIER

1. Trim neck evenly down into back.

2. Trim back evenly and level top line.

3. Trim under part of neck and brisket closely, leaving a shade more hair on as one approaches the lower part of the brisket, where the front legs join the body.

4. Trim shoulders evenly down into front legs.

5 Leave hair on front legs except for a slight trimming to straighten. Trim on the back line of legs to get the desired effect. It is sometimes necessary to remove a few hairs from the front and sides of the front legs, where they join the body, to give the necessary straight line from the shoulder to the ground and from the brisket to the tips of the toes. Clean hair from between pads and shape foot to roundness.

6. Trim sides from a fairly closely trimmed back to an almost full coat on the under part of the ribs and chest. Trim underline of chest evenly to follow body line.

7. Trim loin sufficiently to show tuck up.

8. Trim from back to middle of thigh evenly, working the hair heavier on the leg.

9. From middle of thigh to hock joint remove only those hairs necessary to avoid excessive shagginess.

10. Trim backline of hock evenly with scissors. Trim hair from between toes and shape feet to roundness.

11. Trim tail evenly but not too closely. Remove all hairs that appear to make the tail look longer than it is.

12. Trim stern of shaggy hairs. Strip closest where the tail

joins the body, working the hair slightly heavier toward the bottom of stern and rear of legs.

13. Trim top of skull very closely leaving plenty of eyebrow. Do not trim between eyebrows as with most other terriers.

14. Trim cheeks leaving hair slightly longer than on the skull. Work evenly but quickly into a heavy beard on the foreface.

15. Trim slightly under the eyes to slightly behind the corner of the mouth.

16. Trim ears closely, inside and out. Straighten edges with scissors.

SCHNAUZER
(Miniature, Standard, and Giant)

1. Trim neck evenly into back.

2. Sometimes the hair grows against the grain and is unruly on the back, so trimming must be done carefully to obtain the desired results. Trim hairs to even length but not too closely. Avoid a shaggy appearance and make the back line even.

3. Trim neck and brisket closely, leaving a shade more hair as one works down to where the front legs join the body.

4. Trim shoulders closely down into front legs.

5. Trim front legs to straightness. Work principally on the back line. It is sometimes necessary to remove a few hairs from the front and sides of the front legs, where they join the body, to give a clean even line from the shoulder to the sides of the feet and from the brisket to the tips of the toes. Trim superfluous hair from the sides of the feet and between the toes.

6. Trim from back down the ribs, working the hair slightly longer and heavier on the under part of the ribs and chest. Trim under line of chest to follow body line.

7. Trim loin closer than chest and trim under line to emphasize tuck up.

8. Trim back legs from back to middle of thigh fairly closely.

9. From middle of thigh to hock trim out all shaggy hairs but not too closely.

10. Trim rear line of hock to straightness with scissors. Trim superfluous hairs from sides of feet and between toes.

11. Trim insides of rear legs clean.

12. Trim tail of shaggy hairs, but not too closely.

13. Trim stern fairly closely and evenly.

14. Trim skull closely leaving fairly heavy eyebrows. Leave more eyebrow over the inside corner of eye than the outside corner.

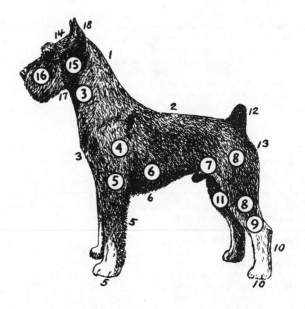

15. Trim cheeks closely from slightly in back of the eye and slightly behind the corner of the mouth.

16. Very little trimming is done on muzzle or chin whiskers except to shorten a few hairs to blend them slightly with the cleanly trimmed cheek.

17. Clean under jaw from slightly behind corner of mouth back into neck.

18. Trim ears clean inside and out. Straighten edges of ears with scissors.

SCOTTISH TERRIER

1. Trim neck and back evenly.

2. Trim back level but not too fine.

3. Trim front of neck closely, but as one works down to brisket, leave hairs long but not shaggy. Never shorten any hairs that would detract from the appearance that the dog is built close to the ground.

4. The shoulders to be trimmed enough to blend the body of the dog to the front legs with a clean even line.

5. Front legs should not be trimmed. Although they are somewhat bent, the hair should be combed to make them appear straight from either front or side view. Trim superfluous hair from feet and between toes and shape to roundness.

6. Trim hair evenly from finely trimmed back to an absolutely full coat on the under part of the ribs and chest. From the front view the dog should not bulge or look shaggy, but do

not take so much off as to detract from the appearance of breadth and substance.

7. Only shaggy hair should be taken off thighs. Trim back line of hock straight. Superfluous hair should be trimmed from edges of feet and between toes. Shape feet to roundness with scissors.

8. Trim tail to a point, leaving fairly heavy at base.

9. Stern should be trimmed fairly close where the tail joins but quickly worked into the long hair that helps to make the rear view of the dog heavy and low to the ground.

10. Trim skull very closely, leaving considerable eyebrows.

11. Trim cheeks outside corner of eye to corner of mouth.

12. Trim very slightly from inside corner of eye to corner of mouth to give expression.

13. Trim backs and edges of ears fine. Leave hair on insides of ears to blend into skull.

14. Trim between eyebrows and part hair over muzzle and comb downward and forward.

15. Leave chin whiskers, but clean hair off under part of jaw from the corner of the mouth back into the neck.

THE SETTERS
(English, Gordon, and Irish)

1. The muzzle should be trimmed of feelers and rasped to perfect smoothness.

2. The skull and cheeks should be smoothed closely and hair taken out where the ear joins the skull. The object is to make the ear appear to be set as far back on the skull and as low as possible.

3. Trim outside of ears slightly where they join the skull, leaving more hair toward the bottom. Trim insides of ears and the part of the neck which they cover closely to enable the ear to lay closely to the head. Trim edges with scissors, rounding them slightly on the bottom.

4. Clean hair from under part of jaw down the neck evenly.

5. Take sufficient hair from the brisket to avoid bushiness. When the hair is combed down straight it should fall evenly to make a graceful line from the neck into the front legs.

6. Straighten feathering on front legs and very slightly even the hairs growing out over the toes.

7. Clean shoulders sparingly when necessary.

8. Trim a few hairs from loin to show some tuck up but do not emphasize.

9. Trim the fringe on the hocks even.

10. Trim feathering on tail to a graceful even curve tapering to a point toward tip. The tail should never appear bushy. If hair grows too thick it should be thinned out with the stripping knife.

For Field Work. The general procedure for trimming the setter for field work is the same as for the home or show bench, except that some practical hunters find it more comfortable for their dogs and easier for themselves if the long hair on the brisket, ears, legs and under parts of the body is taken off closely, to avoid its being ripped out by the undergrowth and also being tangled and snarled beyond repair by the burrs and ticks.

THE SPANIELS
(Clumber, Cocker, and Springer)

The spaniel should carry a very dense coat, but in a few cases too abundant a coat is found. When this is true it is necessary to strip out the excess coat over the entire body. This should be done enough so that the coat lays smoothly to the body outline and does not appear bushy or bunchy at any place. After this general thinning process, trim the dog to the correct finish according to the following instructions:

1. Trim muzzle of feelers (long coarse hairs) and rasp to smoothness. Also trim feelers from above the eyes.

2. The skull and cheeks should be smoothed closely, the hair taken out finely where the ears join the skull. The object is to make the ears appear to be set as far back and as low on the skull as possible.

3. Trim outside of the ear slightly at the top where it joins the skull, leaving more hair at the bottom of the ear. Trim the inside of the ear and that part of the neck which covers fairly close to enable the ear to hang flat and close. Trim the edge of ear evenly with scissors.

4. Trim hair from the under part of the jaw and down the neck evenly.

5. Trim brisket slightly to avoid a bushy effect.

6. Straighten feathering on front legs with scissors.

7. Clean shoulders if the coat is patchy, bumpy or profuse over this area.

8. Clean feathering from the hocks.

9. Clean feathering from the tail but not too closely.

10. Trim hair to shape of foot, but leave long enough to cover the nails. Do not take any hair from between the toes but trim the excess hair from the bottom of the pads. The effect should be that of a hard, round, compact paw.

For Field Work. The general procedure for trimming the spaniel for field work is the same as for the home or the show, except that most hunters find it more comfortable for their dogs and easier for themselves if the long hair on the brisket, ears, legs and the under parts of the body is taken off closely, to avoid its being ripped out by the undergrowth and also being tangled and snarled by burrs and ticks.

Grooming. Daily brushing with a stiff, long bristle brush (not a wire brush) will greatly improve the appearance of the spaniel's coat. Always brush in the direction the hair grows as a fairly flat, slightly wavy coat is desired. A nice sheen can be obtained by finishing off with either a hand rub or by rubbing with a soft towel.

Ears. Spaniel ears being long and heavily coated, cover the aural opening most of the time. This lack of ventilation encourages dirt to collect in the ear and if not cleaned can cause ear canker. It is wise to clean the ears every week or so with cotton slightly moistened with alcohol. As it is never wise to allow water to get down into the ear, avoid using it in cleaning.

SEALYHAM TERRIER

1. Trim neck from behind ears to back, take out particularly closely at withers.

2. Trim back fine and level.

3. Trim front of neck closely but as one works down to the brisket leave hairs long but not shaggy or bunchy. Never shorten any hairs that would detract from the appearance that the dog is built close to the ground.

4. The shoulders to be trimmed enough to blend the body of the dog to the front legs with a clean, even line.

5. Front legs should not be trimmed. Although they are bent, the hair should be combed smooth to make them appear straight from front or side view. Trim superfluous hair from edges of feet and between toes and shape to roundness.

6. Trim hair evenly from a finely trimmed back to an absolutely full coat on the under part of the ribs and chest. From front view the dog should not bulge or look shaggy, but do not take so much off sides as to detract from the appearance of breadth and substance.

7. Only shaggy hairs should be taken off thighs. Trim back line of hock straight. Superfluous hair should be trimmed from edges of feet and between toes. Shape feet to roundness with scissors.

8. Trim tail fine and shape to point tipped toward head.

9. Stern should be trimmed close where it is joined by tail but quickly worked into the long hairs that help to make the rear view of the dog heavy and close to the ground.

10. Trim skull cleanly leaving considerable eyebrows.

11. Trim cheeks fine from outside corner of eye to just back of the corner of the mouth. Carefully blend the long hairs of the whiskers to the entirely cleaned cheek.

12. Trim ears fine outside and inside. Trim edges with scissors.

13. Trim only the very shaggiest hairs from the eyebrows and top of muzzle.

14. Leave chin whiskers, but clean hair closely from slightly behind corner of mouth into the neck.

WELSH TERRIER

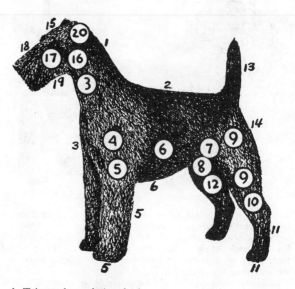

1. Trim neck evenly into back.

2. Trim back level but not as closely as the neck.

3. Front part of neck and brisket to be trimmed closely with just a shade more hair left on as one works down to where the front legs join the body.

4. Trim front shoulders evenly and closely.

5. Front legs should be merely trimmed to straightness. Trim principally on the back line. It is often necessary to take out a few hairs from the front and outsides of the front legs where they join the body to give the effect of a straight line from the top of the shoulder to the feet and from the brisket to the tips of the toes. Do not leave any superfluous hair on edges of feet or between toes. Shape to roundness.

6. Shape ribs to follow the body conformation, working hair evenly from a closely trimmed back to a fairly heavy coat on the under parts of the ribs and chest. On the under parts of the ribs and chest remove only those hairs necessary to prevent shagginess. Trim chest to follow body line.

7. Loin is taken out cleaner than chest but not too fine

and the under line is trimmed closely with scissors to emphasize tuck up.

8. Do not take all the hair off belly, but only those that are shaggy or snarled.

9. In this area trim from finely trimmed back line to fairly heavily coated thigh.

10. From middle of hock to thigh, trim only those hairs that are shaggy.

11. Trim back line of hock straight. Trim off superfluous hairs from edges of feet and between toes and shape to roundness.

12. Trim insides of hind legs clean down to the hock joint. Take care to give a clean even line to the hind legs from rear view.

13. Trim tail evenly but not too closely to a tip toward the head. Take out fine in rear where it joins stern.

14. Trim stern very closely where it is joined by tail working the coat heavier toward the hind legs.

15. Trim skull very closely. Leave eyebrows fairly heavy over inside corner of eye. Leave very little over outside corner. Trim eyebrows evenly and closely over the outside corner, with plenty of length over the inside corner.

16. Trim cheeks closely from outside corner of eye to corner of mouth.

17. Trim slightly from in front of eye to corner of mouth.

18. Trim top of muzzle from slightly in between eyebrows to nose to give a straight line from top of skull.

19. Leave chin whiskers, but clean under jaw from corner of mouth back to neck.

20. Clean ears closely inside and out. Straighten edges.

WIRE-HAIRED FOX TERRIER

1. Trim neck closely and evenly down into the back.
2. Trim back level and fine, but not as closely as neck.
3. Front part of neck and brisket to be trimmed very closely, with just a shade more hair left on as one works down to where the front legs join the body.
4. Trim front shoulders evenly and closely.
5. Front legs should be trimmed to straightness. Trim principally on back line. It is often necessary to take out a few hairs on the front and outsides of front legs, where they join the shoulder, to give effect of a straight line from the top of the shoulder down to the feet, from the brisket to the tips of the toes. Trim superfluous hair from edges of feet and between toes, shape feet to roundness.
6. Shape ribs to follow the body conformation, working the hair evenly from a closely trimmed back to a fairly heavy coat on the under part of the chest and ribs. On the under part of

the chest only remove those hairs necessary to prevent shagginess. Trim under line of chest to follow body line.

7. Loin is taken out closer than chest but not too fine. Trim under line closely to emphasize tuck up.

8. Do not take all hair off belly, but only those that are snarled or shaggy.

9. In this area trim from a fine back to a fairly heavy coated thigh.

10. From middle of thigh to hock, trim only those hairs that are shaggy.

11. Trim back line of hock straight. Take superfluous hair from feet and between toes, shape to roundness.

12. Trim insides of hind legs clean down to hock joint, taking care to give a clean even line to the hind legs from the rear view.

13. Trim tail evenly but not too closely to a tip toward head. Take out fine in rear where it joins stern.

14. Trim stern very closely where it is joined by the tail, working it heavier toward the hind legs.

15. Trim skull very closely. Leave eyebrows fairly heavy over the inside corner of the eyes. Leave very little over the outside corner. Trim eyebrows evenly and closely over the outside corner of the eye with plenty of length over inside corner.

16. Trim cheeks closely from outside corner of eye to the corner of the mouth to give proper expression.

17. Trim slightly from inside corner of the eyes downward to corner of mouth to give proper expression.

18. Trim top of muzzle from slightly in between eyebrows to nose to give a straight line from top of skull.

19. Leave chin whiskers and brush forward, but clean under jaw from corners of mouth back to neck.

20. Clean ears closely inside and out. Straighten edges.

CLIPPING THE POODLE

To properly clip a Poodle in any one of the several accepted "styles" one must have full knowledge of the effect, or "pattern", he wishes to accomplish, the right barber equipment, some degree of barbering skill, and infinite patience. In clipping, mistakes made cannot be erased, so the work must be undertaken with utmost care.

The uninitiated may look with some misgiving upon the first Poodle he sees with full-bloom coat clipped in the height of "fashion", but this is a long-time practice which is neither a fad nor impractical. It has certainly enhanced the dog's looks and has in no way affected his character or abilities.

The chart depicts the English trim. In the Continental trim the scissored saddle is not retained and the rear part of the dog is clipped bare except for rosettes on the hips. Many Poodle owners clip the rear part of the dog bare in the summer time, except for a tuft at the end of the tail.

Barber equipment needed are electric clippers, coarse and medium combs, moderately stiff brush, barber scissors, nail

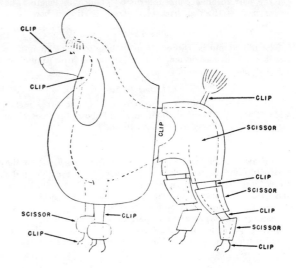

clippers and file, and grooming table. Teach the dog to lie down on the grooming table while the feet are being trimmed.

The parts of the Poodle pattern are: Ruff . . . main coat on the forepart of the dog. This is left long; saddle . . . the short scissored coat on the hind quarters; bracelets . . . longer scissored strips on the hind legs puffs . . . scissored strips on the fore legs; clipped sections on legs.

The Feet

Clip the foot in its entirety, on top, underneath and between the toes. Start the lower bracelet at about an inch above the toes.

The First Bracelet

At a point just above the hock, clip a band completely around the leg and about an inch or two wide. In the width, be guided by the size of the dog and your own personal preference. This band or line must be parallel to the lower line or band above the toes and at right angle with the leg. This completes the first bracelet and forms the lower line for the second bracelet.

The Second Bracelet

This bracelet should extent to the first thigh joint. At this point clip a horizontal band or line at the desired width.

The Second Band

Clip all the way around the leg upward to the upper thigh joint. Both upper and lower lines must be parallel. The inside of the leg should also be clipped.

The Rear Coat

With the bracelets finished, the lower line of the saddle or "pants" has been formed. This should extend about an inch or an inch and a half below the crotch. Before the saddle is blocked out, the remaining rear coat should be cut with scissors to about one inch in length, trimming forward to the second or third from the last rib. If the dog has a long back, leave more ruff.

The Saddle

Begin the saddle point at the center of the spine, about an inch or a little more back of the ruff. In clipping follow the illustration, going back and downward. Miss the hip bone by about an inch. Move forward and downward toward the brisket to a point just back of the ruff, tapering as you go. Square this sharply, clipping a band parallel with the ruff, and carrying this strip underneath the body. Square the point at the center of the back, making it about an inch in width. Clip the other side the same, making sure that both sides are even. Go slow on this, making sure your design is correct.

It will be necessary to square off the lower edge of the "pants" with the scissors. Use the scissors on the saddle to get the hair to about three-fourths of an inch in length. The under part of the dog, back of the ruff, is clipped bare.

The Tail

The tail should be clipped from its base so that a pom-pom about three inches in length remains at the tip. Round off the pom-pom.

The Front Puffs

These should consist of a strip of coat about three inches wide. They should start about an inch above the toes. The legs should be clipped close above the puff.

The Head

Clip away from the eyes, not toward them. Clip out to the end of the muzzle from the inner corner of the eye. Clean the cheeks well, clipping all intervening space. Clip an arc downward from the base of the ear to the center of the neck, about four or five inches below the lower jaw. Be sure to get both sides even. Clip under jaw and the part of the throat desired.

The finishing touches add much to the neatness of the job. The bracelets and puffs should be scissored to about two inches in length. With comb and scissors square them where they appear to need it to follow the natural lines of the leg structure. It is in the finishing touches that the artistry of the trimmer is evidenced.

SHIH TZU

For proper grooming, tie the front locks into a single curl on top of the head. Mustaches are also vogue for this breed, with the eyes barely visible behind all the hair.

FILING AND CLIPPING A DOG'S NAILS

Few dogs wear their nails down sufficiently to avoid the necessity of having them cut and filed. The average dog's nails need attention about once a month, for if they are allowed to grow too long they force a dog to walk flatfooted, thereby pushing the weight way back over the pastern; also, the pounding of long nails on the hard pavements and roads is extremely painful and one of the most prevalent causes of lameness. Nails that are allowed to grow beyond the point where they are nourished by the quick become dead and brittle and are apt to fracture and tear off.

The important point to watch when attending to the dog's nails is not to cut into the quick, which is the live pink flesh within the nail. This is easily seen from any position in white nails, but in those nails which are black or dark in color it is more easily located from the underneath part of the nail where it has a soft, spongy appearance in contrast to the hard brittleness of the nail matter itself.

Thorough and proper nail shortening is accomplished by the use of two instruments, nail clipper and a heavy, fairly coarse file, although the latter, except in the cases of show dogs, is not essential.

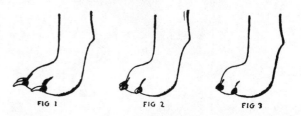

FIG 1   FIG 2   FIG 3

FIGURE 1: The average nail before cutting, showing the extension of the nail beyond the quick.

FIGURE 2: Showing how closely the nail should be cut to the quick. If the nail is left like this it will wear down evenly in a few days.

FIGURE 3: The nail after filing, with just a thin layer of protecting shell left to shield the tender quick.

N.B.—When using a file, it should be drawn only in one direction, i.e., from the top of the nail downward in a round stroke to the end of the nail or underneath. Considerable pressure is needed for the first few strokes in order to break through the hard polished surface of the nail. After the first few strokes the filing is easily accomplished.

NECESSARY TOOLS AND HOW TO USE THEM

A comb, a brush, a hound glove, and a stripping knife are essential in the proper care of a dog's coat. A steel comb is always preferable, but it should not have sharp teeth.

Dogs carrying a profuse coat and those having long feathering require a comb with heavy teeth set wide apart, while a finer tooth comb is more efficient for dogs having a short coat. Never comb a long-coated dog while the hair is wet, as the comb will tear out live hairs.

The length of bristle on the brush should vary with the length and density of the dog's coat, the long-coated dogs naturally requiring the deeper brush. For those animals carrying a profuse or wire coat, the bristles should be as stiff as it is possible to obtain, while the short-haired or lightly coated dogs may be advantageously groomed with a brush but slightly stiffer than the ordinary human hair brush.

The hound glove gives an incomparable finish where a coat is required to lay flat to the body. It is to be particularly recommended for use on all terriers, setters, spaniels, and smooth-coated dogs. It not only lays the hair in place, but adds greatly to the lustre of the coat.

The stripping knife, or dog dresser, is for the removal of the dead hairs and the trimming of the new ones, to give the finish that conforms with the standard of the breed of dog on which you are working. Hold the handle of the knife in the palm of the hand—the end resting against the heel of the hand and the first finger wrapped around the shank. The hair that is to be removed should be pressed against the knife with the thumb. A slight upward twist of the wrist brings the stripping edge in contact with the hair. Best results can be obtained by removing only a few hairs at a time.

Chalk is advantageously used on any dogs having principally a white coat, more especially on the terriers. It should be rubbed in before the dog is stripped, as it prevents the hairs from slipping through the operator's fingers during the stripping. In addition to cleaning and whitening the coat it improves the texture, particularly on those breeds where a hard coat is required.

Dull-pointed scissors are of great assistance in trimming and straightening the lines of the ears, the legs, and the belly; also for trimming the feet and between the toes.

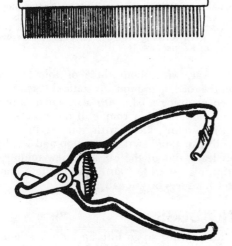

Necessary tools for grooming.

Suggestions on
—Transporting Your Dog—

TRANSPORTING YOUR dog should never become a problem, if you and the dog start out properly. Initially, the young dog should be introduced to riding in automobiles by taking him on short trips under ideal conditions. Confine the young dog in a carton, or box. Never start on a ride just after the dog has been fed. Try to have a passenger along to soothe and comfort the dog if he becomes anxious. Keep the first rides short.

All dogs should be accustomed to riding in automobiles, if for no other reason than that they must usually make at least one trip a year to the veterinarian. A well-trained dog will "Down" on the floor of either the front or back seat and will probably stay there, though wide-eyed and frightened, even if he becomes sick. There is little reason for this, however, if the dog has been properly introduced to riding in the car.

Hunting dogs must be so acclimated. Show dogs must be acclimated. Since dogs in these two categories are more often acquired at a later age than are most pets, you are more likely to have a dog that has not been acquainted with car riding . . . and that may present more of a problem than you would face with a very young and very trusting puppy. Since a full stomach will almost guarantee car sickness, don't feed your dog, or allow him to drink much water, for at least two hours before starting a trip.

One of the newly-recognized causes of persistent car sickness may be static electricity upsetting the dog's system. If you cannot find any other explanation for persistent car sickness, try fastening a short length of

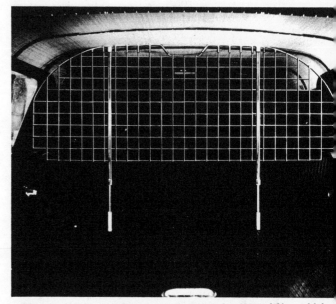

The Barrie-Aire partition manufactured by Kennel-Aire which available for virtually all station wagons and prevents dogs from annoying the driver and other passengers during travel. (Kennel-Aire Mfg. Co., 725 North Snelling Avenue, St. Paul, Minnesota 55104 Photo courtesy of Kennel-Aire.

chain to the car, with about three or four inches dragging on the road, to ground any static charge.

Even when planning a trip with a seasoned canine traveler, you should have a couple of old rags, or a roll of paper toweling, along with you. At the first sign of drooling or rapid swallowing, stop and let the dog, on his leash, out of the car for a few minutes. On long trips, plan stops so your dog can relieve himself and stretch his legs occasionally.

HUNTING DOGS

Getting a hunting dog to go into an auto is seldom much of a problem. Once the dog understands that a trip with his canvas-clothed master means a hunt is in the offing, the problem is more often how to keep the dog out of the car whenever an open door is presented. Controlling the dog in the car may be another matter.

First of all, dogs should not be transported in the automobile trunk, at least not in an unmodified trunk. There are devices available for supplying ventilation to a dog in an auto trunk, either through the trunk itself or through a vent inside the car, but these are not an ultimate answer. Tying down the trunk lid, leaving a gap for ventilation, is an even worse answer, because of the invitation this provides

Station-wagons are popular vehicles for transporting dogs. These six Dalmatians may ride leashed as they are satisfactorily on very short trips, but for the long ones, the leashes are apt to become badly entangled. Screening or partitioning between front and back seats is preferred by many owners. Photo by Evelyn M. Shafer.

for carbon monoxide in the auto exhaust fumes to enter the trunk. Considered from a purely selfish aspect, even a small whiff of carbon monoxide can destroy the dog's scenting abilities for hours; prolonged exposure to carbon monoxide fumes can cause irreparable brain damage to the dog, and even his death.

Further, the dog locked up in an automobile trunk is being exposed to the dangers of suffocation every time the car is stopped for more than a few moments; the soaring temperature in a closed trunk of a stopped auto is, at the least, extremely uncomfortable for the dog. Even on cool or cold days, sunshine can transform an auto trunk into an oven.

If your dog has been trained in basic obedience, he will probably ride quite well on the floor of the back seat, or on the seat itself. On muddy days, or when the dog is shedding, an old blanket on the seat will help protect it. If the dog is more the unruly, rowdy type, you may want to confine him to a crate, or kennel box. For station wagons, these are an excellent answer, for they not only restrict the dog's movement without causing him any discomfort, they also prevent the dog from sliding around—and perhaps injuring himself—in the event of a sudden stop. If the kennel box is securely attached to the flooring of the wagon, it won't crash into the driver of the car, if he should have to slam on the brakes. Professional dog handlers, who constantly travel with a number of dogs, are especially aware of this danger.

Many hunters rig trailers for transporting large numbers of dogs. A small unit can transport a dozen dogs in comfort and style, affording protection, preventing scraps among the dogs, and offering the driver almost complete freedom from worry or concern. The two major considerations in constructing or altering a trailer for this purpose are (1) Providing adequate ventilation without creating excessive drafts, and (2) Avoiding auto exhaust fumes. Ventilators in

Most campers are aware of the restrictions imposed upon pet owners by various camping grounds and the Federal and state parks. Portable pet pens as in this photo allow the camping family to enjoy the company of their pets while traveling, especially when they expect to stay several days at one location. Hank Babbitt photo.

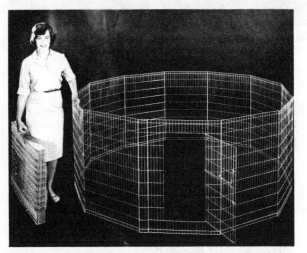

Folding portable dog pen manufactured by Kennel-Aire. These enclosures take up little vehicle space when traveling and are easily set up at stops so that dogs may exercise now and then. They have many other applications, of course, as even in a suburban backyard they may be easily moved about the yard. Photo courtesy of Kennel-Aire.

the roof of each partition, preferably covered and facing toward the rear, in conjunction with vent holes in the doors of each section, answer both of these needs.

Bedding in the trailer unit may range from straw or shredded newspaper to plastic-covered foam padding. The only thing to keep in mind is that it should be easily replaced or cleaned, as the need arises.

SHOW DOGS

Generally speaking, show dogs fall into one of two broad categories; they are either family pets, shown on occasions when sanctioned events are within an easy drive of home or they are being shown with a high degree of determination, i.e., with every intent of earning a breed championship and gaining the attendant honors. The former, family pets, usually travel as just that—family pets. Little extra provision is required and little is provided. For the latter, handlers or owners who travel with their dogs almost every weekend, sometimes many hundreds of miles in

For dogs that will travel quite a bit by station wagon, the best arrangement is that each dog have his own enclosure. Shown here re the Supreme Kennel-Aires, travel crates manufactured by Kennel-ire Mfg. Co., 725 North Snelling Avenue, St. Paul, Minnesota 55104. Write manufacturer direct for details.) Photo courtesy of Kennel-Aire.

Travel is a natural way of life for those in show business. This is Ernest Pressley and his troupe of performing dogs. Hank Babbit photo.

quest of the ribbons and trophies—and championship points—usually wind up transporting their dogs in crates or kennel boxes. This not only restricts and protects the dog in transit, it also gives the owner or handler a place to keep the dog, a place the dog knows and recognizes as a secure "home away from home" and a place to stay between judgings at the unbenched dog shows. The tops of these crates may also serve as grooming benches, so the handler will have a convenient place to spruce up his dog at the last minute before entering the show ring.

A survey would probably show that most dog handlers, and their dogs, travel by station wagon. These vehicles seem almost to have been designed with this sort of thing in mind. The back of a station wagon provides a smooth, stable platform for kennel boxes, there is plenty of room and light, ventilation is hardly ever a problem, heat can be supplied in adequate quantity, and the wagon can go anyplace an automobile may; this last is a condition not always applicable to trucks, even the smallest of trucks.

ADDITIONAL TRAVEL TIPS (ASPCA)

The American Society for the Prevention of Cruelty to Animals publishes a booklet entitled TRAVELING WITH YOUR PET which contains extensive and valuable information for those wishing to take their dog with them, whether to other states or abroad. The booklet is available from ASPCA at a very nominal price. Here are some of ASPCA's tips on traveling with your dog (extracted by permission).

Most dogs enjoy automobile trips. If possible, start the dog out on short drives when he's still a puppy. Gradually get him used to the motion of the car. Don't give up too quickly. Practice taking your dog for short rides near home before vacation time rolls around.

If the dog suffers from motion sickness, ask your veterinarian to prescribe a motion sickness pill or a sedative.

For the safety of everyone, don't let him jump around in the car. He should sit or lie quietly and not annoy the driver. Don't let him hang his head out the window. The dog may get something in his eye, and his nose and eyes may become inflamed from the wind.

Don't feed him for several hours before any trip. Carry a container of drinking water in the car, especially in hot weather. Stop frequently to let the pet drink. Dogs should be exercised.

If you must leave the pet in a parked car, lock the car, but leave windows rolled down two inches on all sides for ventilation. The heat in a closed car can reach well over 120 degrees. Even if your car is parked in the shade, don't forget that the sun may shift before you get back.

Take along familiar toys and feeding dishes, and the pet's own blanket or bed to give him a touch of home no matter where you are. The dog or cat will feel more at home on his own bedding, and he will have an added feeling of security from using his regular bowl.

Requirements for taking dogs and cats on trips—in the United States and to foreign countries

TRAVELING WITH YOUR PET

compiled as a service for travelers by THE AMERICAN SOCIETY FOR THE PREVENTION OF CRUELTY TO ANIMALS

SHIPPING YOUR DOG

When the occasion arises where you must have your dog transported by common carrier, be sure to check on state and municipal laws *at the destination.* Write to the department of health in the city the dog will be shipped to or, if it is a rural area, to the state capital. Inquire specifically about statutes regulating the importation of dogs. Most states require a certificate of health, signed by a veterinarian within a certain number of days prior to the importation of the dog. This certificate should accompany or be attached to the outside of the crate or kennel box in which the dog is shipped.

Most common carriers are very strict about observing such regulations and having the required certifications, or other papers, will smooth the transfer of the dog from the common carrier to the intended receiver. Without the papers, the dog could wind up

```
┌─────────────────────────────────────────────────┐
│        VETERINARY HEALTH CERTIFICATE              │
│ ─────────────────────────────────────────────    │
│ Owner                                             │
│ ─────────────────────────────────────────────    │
│ Address                                           │
│ ─────────────────────────────────────────────    │
│ Animal                      Rabies vaccination    │
│ ─────────────────────────────────────────────    │
│ Species      Breed       Sex        Age           │
│ ─────────────────────────────────────────────    │
│ Color        Date            Tag no.              │
│ ─────────────────────────────────────────────    │
│ Distemper vaccine                                 │
│ ─────────────────────────────────────────────    │
│ Date                                              │
│ ─────────────────────────────────────────────    │
│ I hereby certify that I have examined the above   │
│ described animal and, to the best of my knowledge,│
│ find same to be free of any communicable disease  │
│ or contact therewith except as noted in remarks.  │
│ This animal has (not) been permanently immunized  │
│ against distemper.                                │
│                                                   │
│  ──────────────        ──────────────             │
│     (Place)               (Date)                  │
│                                                   │
│  ────────────────────────────────────            │
│  (Signature of official veterinarian)             │
└─────────────────────────────────────────────────┘
```

being quarantined for as long as 90 days in some states. This verification of statutes is even more important if the dog is being shipped to another country.

If the dog is to be returned by common carrier, be sure you know your own local regulations. It would be entirely possible to have a dog shipped out, to be bred or shown, for instance, and then to have it wind up quarantined upon its return.

In shipping dogs, air transportation is undoubtedly the best method available, considering all aspects. It is fast and at least as certain as any other mode. There is sometimes a little more immediate discomfort for the dog, in the form of jostling and confusion, but the discomfort lasts for a relatively short period of time. There are commercially-served airports within a couple of hours drive of almost any point in the country. Since most airlines supply an appropriate-size crate for the dog, the only thing required (or at least suggested) is an old blanket or chew-toy with which the dog is familiar. This will help him feel more secure during the trip.

The old, evil days of air travel for dogs are part of history now. There was a time when a dog (in his crate) was handled as any other item of baggage. This sometimes meant the dog was subjected to extreme cold and great drafts, and sometimes high altitudes without the benefit of compartment pressurization. Dogs occasionally arrived in very poor health, dead or deaf (from altitude exposure) and air travel

for dogs had, deservedly, a very bad reputation. Today, all the major airlines are well aware of the value of show dogs and pet dogs and go out of their way to make the dog's trip an easy one. If you should ever have occasion to ship your dog by a small, unscheduled airline, however, you might want to keep some of these things in mind . . . and to ask specifically before the dog is turned over to the airline agent.

Reminders re Cross-Country Dog Travel or Shipment.

Keep cleanup materials at hand on any auto trip.

Try to keep the dog relatively confined, either by cage or command, for his sake and for yours.

An old blanket or rug will help protect auto upholstery on a trip.

Never allow the dog to ride with his head out of the car window. Most dogs enjoy keeping their "noses into the wind" on a trip but this can lead to respiratory ailments, eye irritation, injury from insects or odd pieces of flying debris, ear problems, etc.

Be sure the dog is adequately identified, that is, has a strong collar to which is attached a tag with your name, full address and telephone number. Dogs sometimes become disturbed or confused on trips and, if they slip away from you, may be lost for good if they are not fully identified. Further, it is sometimes difficult to establish ownership of a dog that has escaped, even when you know the dog being held by a stranger belongs to you. Identification tags (and sometimes tatoo marks) will help.

Take along health certificates, inoculation records and registration papers, especially on trips that involve crossing state lines. All these papers will fit into a single envelope and could save you much grief.

Always verify statutes at the destination, especially if the dog is being shipped by common carrier.

Never feed a dog heavily, or allow him very much water, within two hours of starting a journey.

WHEN YOUR DOG TRAVELS BY AIR OR GOES ABROAD (ASPCA)

The following information (by permission) is from the ASPCA pamphlet TRAVELING WITH YOUR PET, For data on countries other than those listed here and for data updated from time to time in booklet revisions, order your personal copy of the pamphlet from ASPCA, 441 East 92nd St., New York, N.Y. 10028. (Price, approximately 30¢.)

Each year thousands of American travelers take their pets along when they travel in the United States or go overseas. And the United States welcomes visitors from abroad who arrive with their pets or ship them ahead. Travel regulations for pets vary widely from country to country. Some countries require rabies certificates. Others ask for health certificates. Still others have quarantine rules.

As a service to travelers The American Society for the Prevention of Cruelty to Animals has compiled this list of regulations for dogs and cats traveling to the United States and foreign countries. . .

The material was compiled from information supplied by the various states and countries. Because regulations are subject to change, the ASPCA suggests travelers check with the state agriculture or health department or the country's nearest consulate or the Embassy in Washington, D.C., for most recent changes, if any.

Tips on Shipping a Pet by Air. A health certificate and rabies inoculation are recommended. Most foreign countries and states in the United States require them. Distemper and hepatitis inoculations are also recommended.

Plan the trip with a minimum of stops and transfers en route.

Provide a sturdy crate with a leakproof bottom. It should be large enough for the pet to stand, lie down or turn around. Let him get used to the crate well before the trip.

On the outside of the crate print clearly your name and address and the pet's destination. Add the pet's "call" name so that attendants can talk to him. This will make him feel less lonesome. If he bites, indicate that, too.

Attach a tag with the owner's name and address and the pet's destination to a collar around the dog's neck, so that if he should escape his crate he can be identified.

Put a comfortable pad and a few favorite toys in the crate.

Exercise a dog before shipment.

Feed a light meal six hours before shipping.

Don't give water within two hours of shipping, except on a very hot day.

Provide a water dish so that attendants can give the pet water at stopovers. Attach the dish so attendants can reach it without being bitten or the pet escaping. Do not leave water in the dish during flight. It may spill and wet the crate.

If the trip will take over 24 hours, send some food along—dry food is best. If canned food is sent, provide a can opener and a dish. Attach them to the outside of the crate in a cloth or mesh bag. Feeding instructions can be attached to the top of the crate.

Your Pet Will Love Being in the Dog House. Flight kennels for dogs and cats come in custom sizes . . . just to make sure your pet is as comfortable as he can be. The kennel should be large enough for the pet to stand, turn around and lie down. You may use your own or buy one. Here are four of the most popular sizes.

22″ long x 12″ wide x 15″ high . . . good for small cats and toy breeds of dogs. Weight: 12 lbs.

26″ long x 18″ wide x 19″ high . . . ideal for Beagles, Cockers, Fox Terriers, Miniature Poodles, cats and other smallish pets with shoulder heights up to 15 inches. Weight: 20 lbs.

36″ long x 22″ wide x 26″ high . . . perfect for Dalmatians, Standard Poodles, Springer Spaniels and other breeds with shoulder heights up to 22 inches. Weight 35 lbs.

43″ long x 25″ wide x 30″ high . . . provides plenty of room for Collies, Dobermans, retrievers and other pets with a maximum shoulder height of 25 inches. Weight: 45 lbs.

Weights and sizes shown are approximate and are subject to change.

Ship Your Pet Via the ASPCA Animalport. If your pet arrives in New York before your plane does, or if his plane leaves after yours, he can relax in the modern ASPCA Animalport in the Cargo Area at Kennedy Airport while waiting to be picked up. The two-story beige brick building is especially handy if there is a stopover between domestic and foreign flights.

Your pet will be fed, exercised in outdoor runs and given veterinary care if necessary. He can stay a few hours, overnight or a few days.

Here are some sample rates per day or part of a day:

Cats $2.00
Dogs
    Average size, such as Beagles, Cocker
      Spaniels and terriers 2.00
    Large, such as Boxers and Shepherds 2.50
    Extra large, such as St. Bernards and
      Great Danes 3.50

Special diets and veterinary care extra.

When you make flight arrangements, consign your pet care of the ASPCA Animalport, Kennedy International Airport, New York.

Requirements for Taking Pets into Foreign Countries

Argentina

Health certificate and rabies inoculations. Both must be validated by the senior U.S. Department of Agriculture veterinarian in the state of origin, usually located in the state capital, and legalized by the Argentine consulate. The legalization fee is $8.48.

Australia

Dogs and cats may not enter except for those arriving from Britain, Ireland or New Zealand. Animals from the United States must be taken to Great Britain or Ireland to undergo a six-month quarantine there. The animal must then he brought to Australia by sea and not by air. After arrival in Australia the animal must remain in quarantine for 120 days, after which it will be released if it is in good health. If certain conditions of isolation are observed on the sea voyage to Australia, the quarantine may be reduced to 60 days. Animals that do not comply with these regulations will be destroyed on arrival.

See New Zealand for pets that will enter Australia through New Zealand.

Austria

No restrictions on adult travelers taking not more than two dogs or two cats into Austria. In other cases specific authorization is needed from the Federal Ministry of Agriculture and Forestry in Vienna.

Bahamas

Rabies vaccination not less than 10 days nor more than nine months before departure for the Bahamas. Health certificate signed by a veterinarian not more than 24 hours before departure. Dogs and cats under six months of age are admitted only if the owner has obtained a permit from the Bahamas Ministry of Out Island Affairs, Agriculture and Fisheries at Nassau.

Belgium

Rabies vaccination 30 days before entry. Health certificate filled out on a special form and signed by a licensed veterinarian and legalized by the senior U.S. Department of Agriculture veterinarian in the state of origin, usually located in the state capital.

Bermuda

For those transporting dogs for entry in shows sponsored

by The Bermuda Kennel Club, Inc., see text relative Bermuda Kennel Club, Part XVIII.

Import permit must be obtained from the Director of the Department of Agriculture and Fisheries, Point Finger Road, Paget, Bermuda. Applications must be received at least 10 days before the intended date of arrival. Animals without permit will be refused entry. Application forms (not permits) may also be obtained from the Bermuda offices in New York, Chicago, Toronto and London.

Animals must be accompanied by

(1) a veterinary certificate stating that the animal is free from all infectious and contagious disease,

(2) a certificate stating that the area within a radius of 50 miles from the place where the pet has been kept during the six months before shipment has been free of rabies for at least one year.

(3) a certificate stating the animal has been vaccinated against rabies within one year prior to arrival.

> Most hotels and guest houses do not permit dogs and cats. Those that do, accept only small, well-trained pets, and permission must be requested in advance.

Small dogs accompanying air passengers may be carried as excess baggage. Permission must be requested well in advance and may be impossible to grant. Animals must be in sturdy, leak-proof crates.

Cunard Line ships carry pets one way, only if accompanied by the owner. Pets are not accepted on round-trip cruises. Animals are not allowed in passenger's staterooms or public rooms. Kennels are available, and an attendent will feed them. Unaccompanied dogs are accepted as freight on the Amerind Line.

Bolivia

Health and rabies certificates, stamped by the Bolivian Consulate.

Brazil

Rabies vaccination and health certificate issued by a

Samples of modern crates available for transporting dogs. Above is the KD collapsible crate; upper right, the low-profile station wagon crate; and, lower right, the KD standard crate. (For information, write KD Kennel Products, 1741 North Broadway, Wichita, Kansas 67214.)

licensed veterinarian. Certificates must be certified by the Brazilian Consulate.

Canada

No restrictions for cats. Dogs must be accompanied by a certificate signed by a licensed veterinarian certifying that the dog has been vaccinated against rabies during the preceding 12 months. The certificate must carry an adequate and legible description of the dog and date of vaccination and be initialed by the inspecting official at the Customs port of entry. Performing and guide dogs for the blind entered temporarily and kept under direct control are exempt from these requirements.

Chile

Rabies inoculations and health certificate authenticated by the senior U.S. Department of Agriculture veterinarian in the state of origin, usually located in the state capital. The certificate must be legalized by the Chilean Consulate at a cost of $9.

Colombia

Rabies and distemper inoculations. Health certificates stating that the dog is free of hepatitis, internal and external parasites and is in general good health. The certificate should include a brief description of the dog, including color, breed, name, sex, and should be issued by the senior U.S. Department of Agriculture veterinarian in the state of origin usually located in the state capital. The Colombian Consulate must authenticate the signature of the United States official at a cost of $5.

Costa Rica

Animal must be accompanied by
(1) entrance permit signed by the Chief of the Veterinary Department of Health before arrival.
(2) a certificate not more than 30 days old, signed by the senior U.S. Department of Agriculture veterinarian in the state of origin, usually located in the state capital. The certificate must state that the animal is in good health and free of contagious diseases,
(3) official certificate of stool test not more than 30 days old, stating that the dog is free of Taenia Equinococcus,
(4) certificate of rabies vaccination with a vaccine of avianizada, not less than one month and no more than three years before application.
Six-month quarantine at the owner's expense if the animal comes from a country where rabies prevail.

Denmark

Danish law prohibits importing live animals. However, permission may be granted to bring an animal in on application to Veterinaerdirektoratet, Nyropsgage 37, Copenhagen, Denmark. In writing, mention whether the dog is being taken in by car, ship, train or plane. If permission is granted, the dog must be vaccinated against rabies upon arrival in Denmark and quarantined for six weeks in a veterinary hospital at the owner's expense.

Dominican Republic

A certificate of health signed by a veterinarian, a public notary and the county clerk. The Dominican Consulate must then legalize it. The charge is $13.

Ecuador

No dogs admitted until further notice.

El Salvador

Certificate of good health and inoculation against rabies.

France

Vaccination against rabies more than one month and less than six months before entry. Or a certificate of health delivered no more than three days before departure, stating the animal comes from a country free of rabies for at least three years and has lived in the country for the last six months (or since birth). Other carnivorous animals must be cleared with the Ministry of Agriculture in Paris.

Germany (West Germany and West Berlin)

No restrictions for cats. For dogs a special permit must be obtained in advance from the one of the ten states of West Germany in which the point of entry is located. (List of states is available from the German Consulate.) The permit requires submission of a certificate at the point of entry issued by a licensed veterinarian of the area in the United States where the dog normally lives. The certificate, which must be in German or with a certified German translation attached, must state that the dog is in good health and free from rabies or suspicion of rabies and that within three months prior to issuance of the certificate no case of rabies occurred in the place of origin or within 20 kilometers (about 12 miles). The certificate must not be issued earlier than eight days before departure from the United States. There may be an examination and fee at point of entry. No birds admitted.

Great Britain

Quarantine of six calendar months in approved kennels. Accommodations must be secured at one of the approved quarantine kennels and an authorized carrying agent must be engaged to meet the animal, clear it through customs and deliver it to the quarantine kennels.

After written confirmation from kennel and carrier are received, Form ID, 1 must be completed and sent to: Ministry of Agriculture, Fisheries and Food, Hook Rise South, Tolworth, Surrey, England. In Scotland mail to Department of Agriculture and Fisheries for Scotland, 6, St. Colme Street, Edinburgh 3, Scotland.

Lists of approved quarantine kennels and carrying agents may be obtained by writing to these addresses. Blind travelers can get a temporary guide dog for the six months by writing to the London Association for the Blind, 90 Peckham Road, London, S. E. 15.

Greece

Certificate of health and rabies inoculation, certified by the senior U.S. Department of Agriculture veterinarian in the state of origin, usually located in the state capital. Certificate must also be certified by the Greek Consulate (fee $2.52).

Guatemala

Certificate of health and rabies vaccination, legalized by the Guatemalan Consulate. If the animal is pedigreed, the pedigree should be submitted.

Honduras

Health certificate must be obtained from the Ministry of Natural Resources. That department takes charge of inoculation at every port of entry and applies quarantine measures according to existing regulations.

India

A health certificate from a veterinarian stating that the dog is free from Aujossk's disease, distemper, rabies, leishmaniasis and leptospirosis, and in the case of cats from rabies and distemper. Rabies vaccination more than one month, but within 12 months before actual embarkation with nervous tissue vaccine or within 36 months of embarkation with chicken embryo vaccine, both the vaccines having previously passed satisfactory potency tests. A certificate must contain a record of the vaccination, the vaccine used, brew of the vaccine and the name of the laboratory.

Ireland

Six-month quarantine at an approved quarantine kennel. Animal must be transported from the port of entry to the quarantine kennel by an approved carrying agent. Approved quarantine kennel for dogs is Wheatfield, Malahide, Co. Dublin. For cats Warren Villa, Sutton, Co. Dublin. Approved carrying agents are: For Dublin—Coras Iompair Eireann, Transport House, Bachelor's Walk, Dublin 1. For Cork—Coras Iompair Eireann, Glanmire Station, Cork.

Write to kennel and carrying agents for confirmation of accommodations. Then send application for an import license to Secretary, Department of Agriculture (Veterinary Section), Upper Merrion Street, Dublin 2.

Israel

Rabies inoculation and health certificate signed by a veterinarian.

Italy

Certificate of origin and health signed by a veterinarian stating that the animal comes from a locality free of rabies for six months. Animal will be examined on entry.

Jamaica

No dogs or cats admitted, except for animals coming directly from Great Britain, Northern Ireland or the Republic of Eire.

Japan

Dogs: Two-week quarantine. Health certificate and rabies inoculation certificate (at least one month old, but not older than 150 days). Both certificates must be endorsed by the senior U.S. Department of Agriculture veterinarian in the state of origin, usually located in the state capital.

Mexico

Inoculation against rabies and distemper. Health certificate in duplicate must be dated, bear the owner's name and address, a full description of the animal and tag number, and attest that it has been examined (giving date) and found free of any contagious disease as well as immunized (giving date). The veterinarian's signature must be handwritten in ink. If it is illegible the name must be typed under the signature. The certificate must be certified by the Mexican Consulate. The fee for certification is $4.

Netherlands

Inoculation against rabies using either the inactivated nerve tissue vaccine or the vaccine of the Flury type (low egg passage strain for dogs over three months old and high egg passage for cats and dogs less than three months old).

Inoculation must be done at least 30 days, but no more than three months before entry if high egg passage strain is used, and at least 30 days but no more than one year before entry if the other vaccines are used. Inoculation certificate must show date of inoculation, type of vaccine used, name of the manufacturer and the manufacturing serial number; a description of the animal, including sex, age, breed, color and type of hair and markings; the name of the owner; and must be signed by a veterinarian and legalized by the senior U.S. Department of Agriculture veterinarian in the state of origin, usually located in the state capital.

New Zealand

Entry prohibited, unless the animal has first spent nine months in the United Kingdom or Ireland before shipment and travel by sea.

Nicaragua

Permit issued by the Nicaraguan Ministry of Agriculture and Livestock. A rabies vaccination not less than 30 days or more than one year before shipment.

A veterinary certificate stating that the animal was born in the United States and is free of contagious disease. The certificate must also give a complete description of the animal, date of vaccination, kind of vaccine used, lot number, and name and address of manufacturer.

Norway

Entry prohibited, but exceptions may be granted on application to the Royal Ministry of Agriculture, Veterinaerdirektoratet, Oslo, Norway. Applications must contain the name and address of the owner, kind and number of animals, means of transportation, and place and approximate time of arrival. If an import license is granted, a health certificate from a veterinarian is required, plus inspection by veterinary authorities on arrival in Norway. Six-month quarantine after arrival.

Okinawa

Examination by a licensed veterinarian no more than 10 days before shipment. Immunization against rabies by a licensed veterinarian more than one month, but not more than 12 months, before arrival in Okinawa, if a nervous-tissue vaccine is used; or more than one month, but not more than 36 months before arrival, if chicken-embryo vaccine is used. A valid health certificate and a valid rabies vaccination certificate, both in triplicate, must accompany each animal.

Limit two pets to a family. Animals must be older than two months. Pets under three months will be confined.

Philippines

Health certificate issued shortly before shipment by the senior U.S. Department of Agriculture veterinarian in the state of origin, usually located in the state capital. The certificate should state that the animal is free from, and has not recently been exposed to, any dangerous and communicable disease. If there is no health certificate, the Director of Animal Industry may place the animal in 10-day quarantine. If a disease appears in one or more of the animals, they must all be held in quarantine until 10 days after the disease has disappeared.

Rabies vaccination immediately before shipment.

Portugal

Certificate of health and rabies vaccination (stating date and type of vaccine) issued by a qualified veterinarian and legalized by the Portuguese Consulate.

Veterinarian's signature must be notarized and notary's signature certified by county clerk.

Puerto Rico

Health certificate, dated not more than 10 days before departure, stating animal is free of disease. Rabies vaccination certificate dated not more than 30 days before departure. Statement that rabies has not been reported in the last six months within 50 miles of point of origin. Certificates must be legalized by the senior U.S. Department of Agriculture veterinarian in the state of origin, usually located in the state capital.

South Africa

Entry permit must be obtained by writing to the Director of Veterinary Services, Private Bag 138, Pretoria, Republic of South Africa. If the permit is issued, the animal may be admitted under the following conditions:

It must be accompanied by the permit and a certificate from a licensed veterinarian dated not earlier than 21 days before departure, stating that:

1. He examined the animal prior to departure and that he found it to be in good health, free from external parasites and all contagious and infectious diseases.

2. The animal was subjected to the Histoplasmin test for Histoplasmosis with negative results within 14 days before departure (for dogs).

3. To the best of his knowledge the animal has not been in contact with rabies-infected animals.

There is a 180-day quarantine in a government quarantine station at the owner's expense, unless the animal is accompanied by a certificate from a licensed veterinarian stating that it was vaccinated with the Flury strain (Lederle) of chick embryo anti-rabies vaccine, potency tested and fully viable at the time of injection at least six months but not longer than 36 months (not longer than 12 months in the case of cats) before introduction into South Africa. The following vaccines are also recognized: Kelev, Pasteur, Vom and Pitman Moore. However, animals vaccinated with the Pitman Moore must be revaccinated with the Flury strain on arrival.

The vaccination certificate should be issued on the special forms provided by the laboratories that produce the vaccine. It must be signed or countersigned by and bear the official stamp of the senior U.S. Department of Agriculture veterinarian in the state of origin, usually located in the state capital. The age of the animal, date of vaccination and batch number of the vaccine must also be indicated.

If the animal was inoculated less than six months before, it will be quarantined until the six months are up. Animals vaccinated before six months of age must be revaccinated before reaching 12 months.

Dogs from the United States must be free from histoplasmosis.

Animals entering by air or ship must be crated and must not leave the airport or any port en route. The plane captain or shipmaster must certify to this and that the animal did not come in contact with any other animals during the trip.

Animals will be examined by a South African government veterinary officer at port of entry. Unvaccinated dogs will be vaccinated at a government quarantine station at the airport.

Notify the Sub-Director of Veterinary Services, P.O. Box 397, Pietermaritzburg, or P.O. Box 168, Cape Town, or Private Bag 138, Pretoria (telegraphic address Veterimus in all cases) well in advance of the approximate time of arrival.

Spain

Health and rabies certificates legalized by the Consulate General of Spain. The consular fee is $5.45.

Office hours 9 a.m. to 1 p.m. Waiting time 24 hours.

Sweden

Obtain import permit from National Swedish Veterinary Board, Fack, Stockholm 3, Sweden. The original copy must be shown to the Frontier Veterinary Surgeon and the customs officer. It will state the date before which the dog may enter.

Affidavit submitted to customs officer must state that dog is in good health with no signs of contagious disease and that it has undergone a blood test for leptospirae (spirochaete) within 10 days of departure. Signature of the examining veterinarian must be legalized by the senior U.S. Department of Agriculture veterinarian in the state of origin, usually located in the state capital, or by a Swedish diplomatic or consular mission (at a $3 fee).

Dog must be quarantined for four months at a quarantine station. Book space well in advance. Not later than one day before arrival notify the Frontier Veterinary Surgeon at the import station of the arrival and on what ship, train or plane. At import station the dog will be examined and transferred to quarantine in a basket or transport cage, sealed by a customs officer, or under the supervision of the Frontier Veterinary Surgeon.

In a blood test made right after the dog is admitted it must be found serologically free from leptospirosis. If the disease or other contagious disease shows up, the dog will be destroyed immediately or deported—unless the National Veterinary Board decides otherwise—or unless the dog has rabies. All costs are borne by the owner.

No permit is required for dogs in transit. The Frontier Veterinary Surgeon will decide on the procedure in such cases.

Switzerland

Rabies vaccination not less than 30 days or more than one year before entry. Rabies certificate must contain name and address of owner, description of animal (breed, sex, age, color), date of vaccination, type of vaccine, name of manufacturer and serial number. The certificate, signed and stamped by a veterinarian, must state that the animal was clinically examined by the veterinarian before vaccination and found to be healthy.

These requirements are waived for animals passing through Switzerland by rail or air without staying.

United States

Must be inspected by a quarantine officer at the port of arrival. Animals that do not appear to be in good health may be detained at facilities provided for and paid for by the owner. A healthy animal exposed to sick or dead animal will be admitted only after tests or examinations show the animal is free of communicable disease. The quarantine officer will not admit animals in insanitary containers until the containers are cleaned.

Dogs require a rabies vaccination with nerve-tissue vaccine more than one month, but not more than 12 months, before the dog's arrival, or with chicken embryo vaccine more than one month, but not more than 36 months, before arrival. If a dog arrives without a valid certificate of vaccination, it will be vaccinated on admission and confined for at least 30 days.*

If the vaccination was done less than one month before arrival, the dog will be confined until at least 30 days have elapsed since vaccination. Vaccination will not be recognized if performed on a dog less than three months of age. Such dogs will be confined, and the owner must certify that the dog will be vaccinated at three months of age and held in confinement for at least one month following vaccination.

The rabies vaccination requirement is waived for dogs that for six months have been only in a country determined by the Public Health Service to be rabies-free. A current list of such countries may be obtained from the Chief, Foreign Quarantine Program, National Communicable Disease Center, U.S. Public Health Service, Atlanta, Georgia 30333, or from Public Health Quarantine Stations at United States ports.

If a dog or cat comes from a locality with a high incidence of rabies or under conditions indicating that a special hazard of rabies introduction is present, the medical officer in charge may take additional steps to prevent the introduction of rabies.

However, any such dog that has been vaccinated after the age of three months will be admitted after 30 days have elapsed since vaccination, if inspection of the ani-

---

* Confinement means restriction of an animal by the owner in a building or other enclosure isolated from other animals and people, except for contact necessary for its care. If it is allowed out of the enclosure, it must be muzzled and on leash.

mal after this period reveals no evidence of communicable disease.

Collie, Shepherd and other dogs imported from any part of the world except Canada, Mexico and countries of Central America and the West Indies must be quarantined at the port of entry if they are to be used for handling livestock. Such dogs will be detained for a sufficient period of time to determine their freedom from the tapeworm *Taneia Coenurus*. If found to be infested, they will be treated under the supervision of a veterinary inspector at the port of entry until they are free from infestation.

Uruguay

Health certificate signed by a veterinarian. The veterinarian's signature must be authenticated by the senior U.S. Department of Agriculture veterinarian in the state of origin, usually located in the state capital. Certificate must be legalized by the Uruguay Consulate for a $10.50 fee.

Venezuela

Health, distemper and rabies certificates for a dog. Certificates must be stamped and signed by the Venezuelan Consul.

Virgin Islands

Health certificate signed by a veterinarian stating that the animal is free from symptoms of infectious, contagious or communicable disease and did not originate in an area under quarantine for rabies. Dogs and cats more than eight weeks of age must have been vaccinated against rabies within six months or not less than two weeks before shipment and must arrive with proper identification tag and certificate of rabies vaccination.

Health certificate must be prepared on the official interstate health certificate forms of the state of origin and must include the name and address of the consignor, the origin of the animal and the consignee's name and address with an accurate description of the animal. The health certificate must indicate the health status of the animal, including the results of required tests and dates of vaccination. Health certificates will be void 30 days after inspection and issuance.

State Requirements, U.S.A.

For vaccination and other requirements of various states in the U.S.A., see page 714.

Part III

UNDERSTANDING YOUR DOG

The "Psychology" of any species consists of its bahavior. Human psychology is human behavior. Canine psychology is canine behavior. Behavior is never uncaused. It always occurs in response to some kind of stimulation. We do not as yet know all of the stimuli responsible for many complex forms of behavior, but in some instances one or two kinds of stimulation play a leading role.

—Dog Psychology—

MALE DOGS sometimes travel a long way to join a female that is in heat. One stimulus to which the male is responding is the odor a bitch emits during the period of sexual receptivity. When a dog chases a fleeing cat, the important stimuli are visual. He sees the cat bound away and reacts by pursuing. Hearing controls many responses. The dog who comes running at the sound of his master's voice is reacting to auditory stimulation.

Sights, sounds, tastes, smells, and "feels" are signals from the environment. The things an animal does in response to these signals go to make up its behavior. If we wish to understand the behavior of a dog or any other animal, we must study its ability to receive and interpret sensory messages from the world in which it lives.

THE SENSE OF SMELL

The olfactory sense of the dog is superior to that of human beings in several respects. There are, of course, differences between breeds; but compared with our own, the dullest canine nose is exquisitely sensitive.

There is nothing particularly mysterious about this superiority. The nerve cells responsible for olfactory sensations are embedded in a patch of mucous membrane which in man is confined to a small space in the upper regions of the nasal cavity. The dog possesses a much larger area of olfactory mucous membrane bearing many more smell receptors. Furthermore, the turbinal bones of the human nose act as a series of baffles which deflect and reduce the flow of air over the critical nerve cells. When he breathes

gently and quietly man does not smell much, for the air around the olfactory membrane is relatively stationary. The dog, in contrast, has turbinal bones that provide a quite different sort of air flow. In every inhalation and exhalation all of the air passes directly over the nerves of smell.

As a result of their more efficient receptor machinery, dogs can detect odors so faint that they are imperceptible to us. A dog which has been trained to do so can smell the difference between pure and salt water even though there is only one teaspoon of salt in 13 gallons of liquid. Dogs are even more sensitive to the acids of certain organic salts. It is acetic acid which gives vinegar a distinctive smell. If one teaspoon of this substance is mixed in 1300 gallons of distilled water, a dog can recognize the presence of the acid. This mixture represents a ratio of 1 to 1,000,000 and is far too dilute to arouse any sensations in human beings. The dog is even more sensitive to sulphuric acid. He can smell this substance in concentrations of one part of acid to 10,000,000 parts of pure water.

Another indication of the dog's excellent olfactory acuity is reflected in his ability to discriminate between certain mixtures which smell the same to a man. A dog can tell the difference between artificial musk and the genuine product, although to the human nose the odors are indistinguishable.

After a certain amount of training dogs can analyze complex mixtures of different odors. Nitrobenzol has the odor of bitter almonds. If this substance is mixed with four or five other chemical substances the dog is still able to detect its presence; but for human beings the original odor is completely masked by conflicting

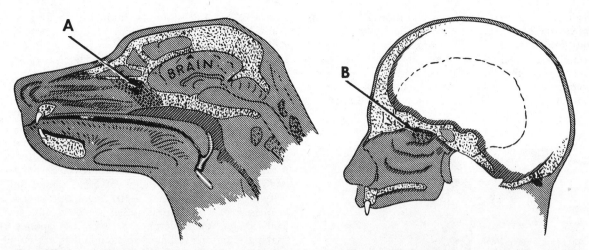

A. —Olfactory mucous membrane in the dog. B. —Same in man. The flow of air through the nose passes straight over or around the olfactory mucous (black dots) in the dog. In man the turbinal bones "baffle" the air flow and divert a good deal of it from the small receptors. In absolute size, the area of nerve receptors is greater in dog than in man.

smells. It is this analytical capacity which permits the dog to identify people on the basis of body odor. Any dog can do this to some degree but the ability is greatly increased by training. A trained dog can retrieve from a pile of 20 or 30 wooden sticks the one which was handled by his master. The man need hold the stick for only a second or touch it with a finger tip, thus transferring to the wood his individual odor. If several men throw similar sticks toward the same target, the dog is able to seek out and bring back the one which his master handled.

It is clear that dogs can learn and remember the odor of persons with whom they are regularly in contact, but it is much less certain that strangers can be differentiated on this basis. Bloodhounds are reputed to follow a man's trail after a single exposure to some object which he has worn or handled. A properly-handled hound unquestionably often aids in trailing a fugitive or a lost child, but usually the handler has a lot to do with the eventual success of the chase.

Several factors normally assist the trailing dog. Most important is the odor left by the shoes or boots of the "trailee." Body odor itself is less important. A dog will trail a stranger who wears his master's footgear. On the other hand the animal may have trouble following the trail of the master who wraps heavy paper around his shoes. When trailing in the country the dog depends in part upon the odors of crushed vegetation and disturbed earth that mark a man's footsteps. But these smells are minor aids only.

It is sometimes supposed that as he passes, a man leaves in the air odoriferous traces which a dog can detect. This is improbable. Police tests have shown that a man must continue to make contact with the ground if the dog is to follow. When men climbed into a suspended seat and were moved along several feet above the ground, the dogs lost the scent and started to backtrack. This throws doubt on accounts of dogs which have trailed a criminal even after he got into a car and drove away.

There are differences in the attractiveness which various scents hold for the dog. Odors of animal origin have especially strong stimulative value, and dogs which have no special training detect the smell of meat or urine in concentrations far below those to which men are sensitive. The smell of flowers or perfume is less significant as far as the dog's daily life is concerned. Without training he pays little attention to them. If he is properly taught, however, the dog is capable of following a trail laid with heliotrope or rose water.

Hunters refer to the "scent cone" to which dogs respond. For a "cone" to form three things are necessary. There must be a moderately strong source of gaseous particles which are the scent carriers. The gas must be as light or lighter than air. A fairly strong, steady breeze must be blowing. Given these conditions the distribution of the odorous particles will be approximately as indicated in the accompanying Plate.

This pattern of distribution of particles is nicely calculated to lead the dog to the point from which the odor emanates. Two "gradients" are in operation. One is indicated by the line AB. The concentration of gaseous particles is greatest at A and decreases progressively with movement toward B. The second gradient is indicated by the line CDE. Here the maximal concentration is at D. Strength of odor falls off as we move toward either C or E. Comparable gradients exist along any imaginary line parallel to AB or to CDE.

Now, well-trained hunting dogs tend to move always in the direction of increasing stimulation—in the direction from which the odor is strongest. Regardless of the angle from which he enters the "cone", a dog will inevitably be led to the source of the scent if he adjusts his line of approach so as to move toward areas of greater and greater stimulation.

Now turn to the case of a dog entering the "scent cone" at point B. Obeying his instinct to select regions of greatest odor concentration he starts to move toward A. If, as he moves along the line AB, the animal wavers to the right or to the left, the scent grows weaker. When he gets a yard or two to the left of the line the dog finds that the scent coming from the right is stronger than that from the left. Readjusting his line of movement, the animal

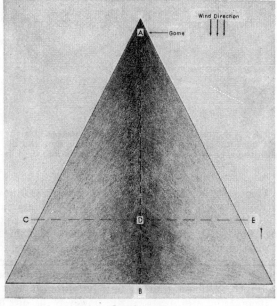

Scent cone.

goes toward the side of strongest stimulation and this automatically brings him back to some point on AB. If he overshoots, the same mechanism will operate to correct his error.

This interpretation is greatly oversimplified. No dog will move in straight lines, set at right angles to each other. Rarely are field conditions exactly right for the occurrence of a perfectly symmetrical distribution of odor particles. Nevertheless the general principles outlined here are sound. And this explanation of the dog's ability to find the source of the scent is valid.

THE SENSE OF HEARING

The dog's sense of hearing excels that of man in three respects. He can hear higher tones. He can hear fainter sounds. He is, save in one respect, more accurate in localizing the point in space from which a sound has come. Human hearing is better than that of the dog in that man can discriminate different pitches more precisely and can estimate more accurately the distance over which a sound has travelled.

Vibrations of 20 to 20,000 cycles per second are heard as sounds by the human ear. Our hearing is most acute between 1,000 and 3,000 cycles, and most of the tones in human speech range around 2,000. Middle C in the musical scale is 256 cycles.

There is no indication that dogs can hear lower tones than we, but the upper limit of their range certainly exceeds human audibility. Russian scientists claim to have obtained evidence for hearing at 70,000 and even 100,000 cycles. This is five times as high as any human ear could reach, but other experimenters have not been able to substantiate these results. Thirty-thousand cycles is a more conservative estimate, which still surpasses our own range.

The evidence concerning intensity discrimination is much more satisfactory. With very low tones there is no difference in the human and canine ability to hear. But as the pitch is raised the efficiency of the dog's ear becomes increasingly apparent. Some superiority is evident with tones of 500 cycles, but when the frequency of vibration is raised to 2,000 and then 8,000 cycles, the difference between the species is striking. The dog responds to sounds that are imperceptible to the most sensitive human listener. The dog's hearing is most acute at about 4,000 cycles, whereas man's auditory sensitivity is greatest in the region of 2,000 vibrations per second.

The delicacy of the dog's hearing can be illustrated with a simple experiment. If a small steel ball is dropped from a height of one inch and allowed to strike a metal plate it will produce a sharp "click." A man with normal hearing can detect this sound when he is standing 20 feet away. But a dog hears the same sound from a distance of 80 feet.

Almost all human beings can tell the difference between two musical notes ¼ to ½ of a tone apart on the scale. Dogs are less gifted in this respect. They cannot discriminate pitch differences of less than a whole tone.

The dog is especially adept at localizing the sources of sounds. This ability is tested by determining how far apart two equi-distant sound sources must be in order for the animal to discriminate between them. First a T is marked off on the ground. Then the dog is placed at some point along the upright of the T. Two small screens are put on the top of the T at equal distances from the center. Now the distance from the dog's head to either screen is the same. Behind each screen is a small buzzer. Only one buzzer is sounded at a time and the dog's task is to tell which one it is. By moving the screens closer together or farther apart, it is possible to increase or decrease the difficulty of the problem.

When dogs are 16 feet from the top of the T they pick the right buzzer if the screens are only 18 inches apart. If the animal is 60 feet away the screens must be separated by 54 inches. In this test men are markedly inferior to dogs.

Dogs also exceed human beings when it comes to deciding whether one source of sound is higher or lower in space than another. The only type of localization in which the dog cannot equal man is that involving distance. When three buzzers are placed in a straight line, and the man or dog stands on this line, the man can tell whether the nearest, the farthest or the middle buzzer is sounded. Dogs are less accurate.

THE SENSE OF SIGHT

Occasionally a baby is born with cataracts in both eyes which are so large that they produce complete blindness. If these obstructions are not removed until the individual has grown up, blindness persists for several months or even years after the operation. Perhaps "blindness" is the wrong term. As soon as the bandages are removed, the patient shows most of the usual visual reflexes. The pupils contract and expand according to the amount of light falling on the eye. Differences between colors are almost immediately perceived. Obstacles are easily seen and avoided.

But there are a number of peculiar symptoms. The individual cannot tell the difference between a square and a circle unless he traces the outline with his fingers. After months of conferences with two doctors, the patient is unable to tell them apart simply by looking at their faces. Abilities of this sort are gained slowly through laborious learning. We are apt to take them for granted because we overlook the fact that every baby has to learn to use its eyes. Practice and experience are all-important.

Casual observation suggests that the dog's eyesight is much less keen than that of human beings. However, a large part of this difference may be due to the fact that the dog, like the patients just described, has not learned to interpret complex visual sensations. The eye of the dog is not structurally inferior to the human eye. There are differences, of course, but they are not pronounced. Nevertheless, under ordinary circumstances the dog's use of vision is distinctly limited. This fact has been brought out clearly in the course of laboratory experiments on learning.

Dogs have learned to solve various sorts of problems such as opening a box by pressing on a lever. After the trick has been mastered the dog is completely baffled if the box is turned around so that the lever is in a new position. Even though it is clearly visible, the lever is neglected while the animal makes pressing motions in the air at the spot where it used to be. A dog can solve this sort of problem almost as well in total darkness as in a well-lighted room.

Results of this type tell us merely that dogs do not rely on vision in circumstances where a man would employ it. They definitely do not prove that the animal's eyesight is inherently inferior. As a matter of fact there are situations in which excellent visual acuity is demonstrated.

Sensitivity to movement is highly developed. The Borzoi, Greyhound and some other breeds hunt almost entirely on the basis of vision. They must keep their prey in sight or give up the chase, and it is the motion rather than the actual appearance of the prey which stimulates the dog. One study of 14 police dogs showed that they could learn to respond to a motionless target at a distance of 600 yards, but a moving one was effective at 900 yards.

In certain "intelligence tests" to be described later, dogs have demonstrated what appeared to be superhuman powers. Careful investigation revealed that the animals were responding to very slight movements made unconsciously by the human experimenter.

The dog is at least equal to man in detecting differences in brightness. This fact has been established by teaching animals to choose the brighter of two pieces of grey paper. When the method has been learned the brightness difference between the papers is gradually reduced, and the point at which the ability to discriminate breaks down is called the "threshold." If dogs and men are tested under similar circumstances the dog's threshold turns out to be slightly lower than man's.

Another superior feature of canine vision is the size of the visual field. By virtue of the placement of the eyes in the head, some animals can see above and behind them as well as straight ahead. Man's visual field is about 180 degrees when the eyes are at rest. The visual field of the dog is approximately 250 degrees, which means that he receives impressions from the side and even to the rear without turning his head or rolling his eyes.

Man, however, is endowed with a larger binocular field. This refers to that portion of the visual field which is seen by both eyes simultaneously. In dogs this region encompasses less than 100 degrees but in man it amounts to 140 degrees. Binocular vision is superior because it is stereoscopic, or three-dimensional, and assists in the perception of depth or distance.

Perhaps the most surprising feature of the dog's visual capacities is the absence of color vision. Many insects, fishes, amphibians, reptiles, and birds can see colors, but all of the lower mammals are color blind or nearly so. Only in monkeys, apes, and human beings does the color sense reappear.

The majority of dog owners are so reluctant to accept this statement that it will be well to give the proof. It should be stated at the outset that the presence or absence of color vision cannot be determined on the basis of casual observations. Carefully controlled tests are essential.

The first step is to teach the dog to go toward a card or lighted panel of one color and to avoid another. Assume that red and green are the colors used. The animal will learn to go to the green card and avoid the red if he is rewarded with food each time he makes the correct choice. However, green is generally brighter than red and the dog actually is responding to the brighter card and paying no attention to its color.

This is easily demonstrated. By gradual steps we reduce the brightness of the green and increase that of the red. The actual colors are not changed. Eventually, at some stage in the series the animal's discriminatory ability breaks down. This is the point at which, for his eye, the red and green are of equal brightness. No matter how long training is continued, he will never be able to tell these colors apart.

Under normal circumstances the various colors we encounter are never exactly matched for brightness. Accordingly a smart dog may learn to "Fetch the red shoe," or, "Go to the blue chair." He is, nevertheless, reacting to differences in brightness and not to hue or color *per se*.

REFLEXES

Having surveyed the dog's ability to receive and interpret stimuli from the surrounding environment, we are now in a position to examine the characteristic types of behavior which these sensory messages call forth. For the purposes of description it is possible to divide behavior into three broad classes: reflexes, instincts, and learned responses. One should realize, however, that separate types of behavior do not normally occur in pure form. Furthermore, all complex patterns of activity involve some reflexive, some instinctive, and some learned elements.

To list all of the common reflexes would be a tedious and pointless task. But an account of the psychology of any kind of animal would be incomplete without some mention of its reflexive behavior. Our aim is merely to point out the existence of numerous reflexes and to emphasize the extremely important role they play in the dog's adjustment to its environment.

A reflex consists of a simple response to a simple stimulus. Usually it involves activity in a restricted part of the organism, such as contraction of the throat muscles in swallowing or secretion by the tear glands when dust irritates the eyeball. Reflexes are not dependent upon previous experience. They are not guided by rational decisions. Frequently reflexes occur without the animal being aware of their existence. They depend upon "built in" connections within the nervous system and the muscles and glands.

Good examples of reflexive activity are seen in sneezing, coughing, blinking, and moving a limb away from painful stimulation. The newborn puppy's nursing behavior is primarily reflexive. Light touch stimulation on the lips calls forth reflexing opening of the mouth. If the stimulating object is soft and warm, as is the nipple, the lips and gums are closed over it. This is another reflex. Then when any object is present in the mouth the sucking reflex is elicited. If the object is a nipple, milk flows into the baby's mouth. Presence of fluid in the mouth stimulates still another reflex, namely swallowing. Thus the entire procedure of obtaining nourishment rests squarely and, in the beginning, almost exclusively upon the operation of a chain of reflexes. Each simple reaction gives rise to a new kind of stimulation which in turn evokes the next response. No intelligence, no thought is necessary.

In the main the reflexes of the dog are quite similar to those found in human beings. In fact a great deal of the behavior of both species is carried on at a reflexive level; and much of this behavior is vital. Death follows failure of the basic reflexes involved in respiration, circulation or digestion.

Some of the reflexive adjustments seen in dogs have been lost or greatly reduced in the course of human evolution. The pinna reflex depends upon contraction of muscles which elevate the external ear. It is well developed in the dog, and occurs in response to auditory stimulation. Most of the muscles responsible for this reflex are present in man but the reflex is absent, although some people are capable of voluntary ear movements.

Pilo-erection reflexes cause the hair of the dog's back to stand up. The same reflex occurs in man, but it takes the form of "goose flesh." The tiny skin muscles involved in this response are not as powerful in man as in the dog and there is less hair to be erected. The stimulus calling forth pilo-erection is variable and complex. In most instances it is an emotional condition such as anger or fear.

INSTINCTS

The difference between reflexes and instincts is chiefly one of relative complexity. A reflex consists of the reactions of a certain gland or a particular set of muscles. Instincts, in contrast, consist of more complex behavior involving the animal as a whole. Both reflexes and instincts are inborn. They depend upon heredity rather than learning or experience.

The identification of instinctive behavior is difficult. To prove that a particular response is instinctive, one must be able to show that it appears in individuals who have had no opportunity to learn it.

No one could describe all of the instincts that dogs possess. In many instances the essential information is lacking. In some cases, however, adequate evidence is available. A few examples will suffice to illustrate the nature of instinctive reactions, the functions they serve, and the means by which they are studied.

Trail Barking. The dog's tendency to vocalize on the trail does not depend upon training. Such behavior appears the first time a dog follows an animal track and its occurrence or non-occurrence depends largely upon heredity. Two pure-bred hounds almost never produce mute trailing pups. Pure-bred mute breeds almost never produce open trailers. In order to study the heredity of this behavior various breeds have been crossed and the trailing responses of the second generation have been recorded.

Open trailers were crossed with mute trailers in the combinations shown in the following table:

Open-trailing parent	Mute-trailing parent
Bloodhound	Airdale
Bloodhound	Norwegian
Springer	English Setter
Beagle	Cocker
Dachshund	Fox Terrier
Foxhound	Airedale
Foxhound	Collie

In every case the pups resulting from these crosses proved to be open trailers. This indicates that the hereditary factors responsible for open trailing are dominant over those causing muteness. The tendency to bark or remain mute on the trail is plainly instinctive.

It is interesting to note, however, that the type of

Dapple Dachshunds, short-haired. Photo by Romaine.

sound produced depends upon the physical structure of the vocal apparatus. This also is inherited, but may resemble that of the mute-trailing parent. For example, although they vocalize while trailing, the offspring of a Collie-Hound cross produce the yapping voice of the Collie rather than the full note of the Hound.

Micturition Behavior. The dog's behavior during urination is another example of instinctive activity. It is a particularly good illustration because it depends upon inherited physiological characteristics, because it differs in the two sexes, and because it plays an important role in the animal's daily life.

Almost as soon as they are able to stand young puppies of both sexes assume a squatting position to urinate. In the bitch this pattern of behavior persists throughout life, but the male's response changes at the time of puberty. At the age of sexual maturity young males begin to lift one hind leg and to direct the urine against some object in the environment. At the same time there appears a tendency to urinate more frequently and to expel only part of the bladder contents at any one time. The result is that urine is distributed over a larger geographical area.

This change in the male's behavior appears in small breeds at about 21 weeks of age. It depends upon male sex hormone which is produced by the testis. If synthetic male hormone is injected into very young pups the adult urination pattern is adopted as early as eight weeks after birth. Males that are castrated in infancy continue to display the feminine type of behavior throughout life because the essential hormones are lacking.

Occasionally an old bitch or one which has been spayed will urinate in masculine fashion. Presumably this inversion reflects some abnormality in the hormonal constitution of the individual. If females are injected with large amounts of male hormone they sometimes shift to the masculine type of micturition behavior.

The instinct to deposit urine on conspicuous objects in the environment leads the dog to leave a trail wherever he goes. It also serves to mark the boundaries of his territory. In wild animals territory markers probably inform any wandering stranger that a particular region is occupied. It is sometimes asserted that dogs can identify other individuals of their species on the basis of urine odors but this belief has never been satisfactorily proved. It is extremely likely, however, that dogs can and do differentiate between the odor of masculine and feminine urine. They also smell a difference between urine left by females in heat and those not in heat.

Territorial Defense. The instinct to establish control over a given geographical area and to defend it against intrusion is well developed in most canine species. Wolves often live in small bands of five to ten individuals. The region surrounding the home den is hunted regularly, and if a strange wolf is encountered within the confines of the group territory, it is attacked by all resident members.

Domestic dogs retain this instinct to a limited degree. There are, of course, marked individual differences, but most dogs resent and act against any strange dog who invades the yard in which they live. If several dogs occupy the same neighborhood they may play amiably together and join in concerted attack upon a newcomer.

This sort of territoriality is quite evident in the Eskimo dogs of East Greenland. The dogs of a particular village associate in small groups, and each group establishes sovereignty over a different part of the village. Members of one group are savagely attacked if they venture into territory owned by another band.

The tendency to defend a territory is instinctive, but the limits of the group possessions must be learned by each member of the band. At first the young pup is likely to trespass several times each day, but he quickly learns where he can and cannot move in peace.

This particular instinct depends in part upon hormones. Prior to sexual maturity the Eskimo dogs show very little territorial behavior. But active fighting in defense of territory rather suddenly appears at adolescence.

Mating Behavior. The dog's sexual behavior can safely be classified as instinctive. Individuals that have been reared away from others of the opposite sex are capable of mating effectively the first time they are given a chance. This is not to say that sexual behavior is unmodifiable. Various kinds of experience can change a dog's willingness and even its ability to mate. The essential point is that no specific practice is necessary before fertile mating can occur.

Maternal Behavior. The tendency of the bitch to nurse and protect her pups is a form of instinctive behavior. It depends largely upon inheritance. If inheritance is altered as a consequence of selective breeding the maternal efficiency may be changed. In selecting for certain body types and other physical features some specialists have unwittingly bred against the maternal factor, and there are some breeds in which the lactating female is not strongly maternal.

Females which possess a normal degree of maternal drive are able to care for their first litter without the benefit of previous experience. The newborn pup is cleaned of fetal fluids while the mother licks it. This is an eating response stimulated by the saline content of the fluids rather than an intentional attempt at aiding the young. The female just as avidly licks up those fluids which have spilled on the floor.

The tendency to suckle the young is also based in part on "selfish" motives. As the pups suck, milk is withdrawn from the swollen dugs. The resulting relief from discomfort leads the mother to encourage nursing on the part of her litter.

Retrieving pups to the nest also is not a "learned" characteristic. And so, too, with the later habit of disgorging food during the final stages of lactation. If the bitch is fed at some distance from the nest box she will eat her own meal, then ingest additional food and return to the nest. There she disgorges it before the pups. This disgorged material is devoured by the litter but is not touched by the mother. The stimulus to disgorge is provided by the pups themselves. A female whose litter is removed while she is away will not disgorge in the empty nest, but as soon as the young are returned disgorging occurs.

This way of supplying food provides a natural transition from mammary feeding to a solid diet. It is thought to be dependent upon hormonal changes which take place in the female toward the end of the lactation period.

Pointing and Retrieving. The tendency to point game and to retrieve is present to some degree in most dogs. There is a firm instinctive basis for this sort of behavior. As a result of selective breeding, these abilities are more highly developed in some strains than in others. Even within the same litter there may be pronounced individual differences.

Experiments with German Shepherds have shown that in both breeds some individuals carry objects in their teeth without training whereas others failed to show this behavior. Cross breeding the different types of animals revealed that the "carrying tendency" is inherited. Dogs which do not inherit it can be trained to retrieve, but animals with the inborn tendency retrieve much more quickly and easily.

Essentially the same situation obtains with respect to pointing. Highly bred bird dogs will point in puppyhood without any training whatsoever. Nevertheless some are more strongly inclined to do so than others, and even the most sensitive animal must be trained to point particular species of birds, to ignore others, and to hold point under appropriate conditions. The inherited tendencies or instinctive leanings thus provide the raw material which can be shaped and modified by individual experience and learning.

EMOTIONAL BEHAVIOR

The emotional behavior of dogs resembles that of human beings in several important respects. Note that we refer to emotional behavior rather than emotions *per se*. The inner feelings of animals are not open to direct inspection. We may infer from its behavior that a dog is angry, frightened, jealous or pleased. But this inference really constitutes an interpretation of the observed facts and should always be recognized as such. One must always be careful to avoid "reading into" an animal's behavior feelings and motives which do not actually exist. We should not, in other words, project our own complex emotions into the dog.

Confining ourselves to an objective description of the facts it is plain that canine behavior includes counterparts of human anger, fear, love, joy, jealousy, and shame. Finer shadings of these fundamental patterns may be detectable in some cases, and perhaps still other items such as pride and embarrassment might be added. Now in using such terms we imply nothing more than a gross similarity to human behavior. In saying that a dog displays jealousy, all that is meant is that the animal's behavior resembles that of a jealous man or woman. We cannot be sure and should never imply that the dog's sensations are identical or even closely similar to our own. In the interests of accuracy and scientific verification any description of animal emotions must be confined to the observable facts of behavior.

Temperamental Differences. Dogs often differ grossly from one another in emotional temperament. Some are highly excitable, easily upset, and generally unstable. Others tend to be phlegmatic, stolid, and resistant to serious emotional disturbances. Differences of this sort often can be observed between individual dogs of the same strain, but they are particularly obvious when different breeds are compared. Some of the terrier breeds contain a high proportion of very emotional individuals. Nor are terriers unique. The Saluki and German Shepherd are of the same general type. In contrast, many of the hound breeds are more stable in their emotional make-up.

It is always important to remember that individual differences exist. We are here dealing with general trends. Within any emotional strain there may be found an occasional animal in whom the characteristics of the strain are lacking. But in general the temperamental traits of a particular breed are deeply ingrained and present in the vast majority of its members. This is because such traits are hereditary.

Timidity, aggressiveness, and similar emotional characteristics may depend in part upon the experience of the individual. But in large measure they are founded upon inherited physiological factors. Anatomical studies show that dogs from highly-emotional breeds possess larger thyroid and adrenal glands than non-emotional animals. In human beings excess of thyroid hormone frequently is accompanied by a hyper-excitable condition and a pronounced degree of emotional instability. Adrenalin, a hormone from the adrenal glands, also is involved in acute emotional states.

It appears highly probable that wide and lasting differences in temperament eventually will be traced to differences of glandular constitution plus other hereditary differences such as the general level of responsiveness of the central and autonomic nervous systems. That these factors are hereditary is of great practical importance. Genetically-controlled characters often are transmitted in bundles, so to speak. Several may be linked together and inherited as a group.

The groupings or linkages need not consist of similar or logically related characters. A gene for curly hair may be linked with one which carries a tendency for nervous disposition. This means that when we breed for a certain set of physical characteristics we may be unwittingly selecting in favor of equally distinct temperamental traits. If these are desirable no harm is done. But sometimes they are not, and the strain becomes so nervous and unmanageable that it has to be discontinued.

Neurotic Behavior. Some extremely sensitive dogs develop symptoms similar to those of the neurotic human patient. Usually these abnormal forms of behavior first appear when the animal is under severe emotional stress.

Gunshyness is a well-known example. It is, in all probability, based upon an inherited instability which manifests itself in many ways. Examined in the laboratory, gunshy dogs often prove to be poor learners. Even the mild pressure of a learning test raises emotional barriers to mental progress. Such animals overreact to the faintest auditory stimulus. When required to make a choice between two stimuli they show nervous panting, irregular respiration, and a very rapid heart rate. To view gunshyness as a simple affliction is incorrect. The condition is actually one

symptom of a pervasive and deep-rooted emotional dysfunction that affects many aspects of the dog's behavior.

Less extreme forms of neurotic behavior may appear. Many dogs are capable of adequate adjustment to normal life situations but break down if unusually difficult problems are encountered. Interestingly enough it is not always the emotional type that gives way under pressure. Animals that have succeeded in passing various psychological tests may show distress when the task is made more difficult. In one instance a dog suddenly became extremely distressed, whining and panting, and refusing to continue the test. Not only did she fail the difficult parts; she became completely incapable of repeating her earlier success on simpler tests.

Dogs that become neurotic as a result of a particular experience sometimes develop abnormal fears and peculiar inhibitions. In one experiment an individual dog suddenly and for no obvious reason became violently disturbed by a test in which he was supposed to respond to the louder of two tones. From the moment of the original breakdown the animal showed a persistent antipathy to the experimental room. If placed in the room he showed little or no response to any of his surroundings. When a bitch in heat was led into the room the dog disregarded her. But in the paddock a few minutes later he mated readily and his behavior was entirely normal.

When he responded correctly in the experimental tests the dog had been rewarded with a certain kind of dog biscuit. After his breakdown this food was consistently refused, no matter how hungry the animal might be. In an attempt to cure the neurotic condition the dog was placed on a farm where he could live a relatively free existence. After many months the original food was put before the animal. Although he had not seen it in the meantime, the dog promptly backed away from the biscuit and exhibited all the signs of his original emotional upheaval.

Under conditions of chronic anxiety some dogs develop symptoms comparable to men with peptic ulcer. The acidity of the stomach becomes abnormally high. Digestion is interfered with and passage of food through the stomach is unduly delayed. When the source of anxiety is removed, the physiological symptoms disappear.

These findings are reminiscent of accounts of dogs which refuse to eat when separated from their masters. It seems entirely possible that the extreme anxiety occasioned by an enforced separation might produce severe physiological symptoms. And among these we would expect to find disorders of the digestive system—disorders which would upset the appetite and preclude the assimilation of nourishment.

Emotional Interaction With Other Dogs. We have previously discussed courtship and mating, care of the young, and territory defense. These are forms of emotional behavior. They depend upon physiological changes similar to those associated with human emotions.

The irritability of some females during late pregnancy and throughout lactation is due in part to a deficiency of calcium. The developing fetus needs large amounts of calcium for formation of the skeleton. This material must be drawn from the blood of the mother. Now under conditions of hypocalcaemia (abnormally low calcium level), the nervous system becomes extremely sensitive to stimulation. The faintest noise, the lightest touch is apt to evoke a burst of nervous activity.

Thus the hyper-sensitivity of the pregnant bitch is seen as a product of blood chemistry. Non-pregnant animals show hypocalcaemia when treated with certain drugs. And until the calcium is replaced these dogs are irritable and easily upset just like the pregnant or nursing female.

Aggressive behavior such as that involved in territory defense and other forms of fighting is known to depend in part upon male hormone secreted by the sex glands. The sudden appearance of territoriality in Eskimo dogs at adolescence is correlated with a pronounced increase in this hormone.

We have not yet studied in sufficient detail the role of individual experience in emotional behavior. But it is clear that the emotional responses of one dog toward another are heavily conditioned by physiological factors such as chemical constitution of the blood and general responsiveness of the nervous system. The same influences operate to determine emotional behavior in human beings, although here the picture is complicated by social control and previous learning.

Relations With Human Beings. Here we see the widest range of emotional reactions of which the dog is capable. The species is unique in its capacity for attachment to human companions. From the psychological point of view the dog's relation to man is essentially one of emotional dependence.

The evolutionary roots for this form of association are generally said to lie in the animal's highly developed social tendencies. It is true that wild canines live in packs and form some crude sort of social structure within their groups. However there are many other social species which have been domesticated. And none of these exhibit the intense emotional response which dogs show toward human friends and masters.

So strong is this attachment that it deserves to be classified as a powerful, biological drive. Although we know nothing of its physiological basis it has been established that praise or criticism by human companions serve as strong stimuli to action on the part of the dog. This is not true to any such degree in other domestic species. Even the highly intelligent monkey or ape lacks this sort of psychological bond with our own species.

"INTELLIGENCE"

The heading of this section has been set in quotation marks because there is a great deal of misunderstanding with respect to the meaning of "intelligence." Widespread confusion exists regarding the "intelligence of the dog."

Criteria and Definitions of Intelligence. Vague statements about the "intelligence" of a given species are meaningless. Mankind cannot sensibly be called "intelligent" or "stupid." Some human beings are more intelligent than others and the same is surely true for dogs as well. We have at present no satisfactory method of striking an average for all dogs or for all men. If the term is to have any real significance it must be more sharply defined. Psychologists are not in complete agreement as to the nature of intelligence within our own species. Some authorities believe in a general kind of intelligence which affects all behavior. Other equally eminent writers insist that there are several kinds of intelligence; and an individual may be highly endowed with one kind without being especially gifted with others. Until there is general agreement with respect to the nature of intelligence in human beings and the ways in which it is manifested, comparison with other species will continue to be difficult if not pointless.

In an attempt to circumvent this difficulty it is customary to avoid any reference to intelligence *per se*, and to deal instead with behavior as it is observed. It is then possible to differentiate between behavior which is intelligent and that which is not. To be classified as "intelligent," behavior must be adaptive. It must benefit the animal in some fashion. It must not adversely affect the welfare of the individual.

Not all adaptive behavior is intelligent. Most reflexes and instincts are highly adaptive but they are not controlled by intelligence. Intelligent behavior involves adaptation which occurs as a result of the personal experience of the individual. Intelligence thus comes to be identified with ability to learn, to solve problems, and to employ reasoning. Adopting this point of view, scientists have attempted to assess the intelligence of various species by measuring their performance in tests which measure these abilities.

Tests of Learning Ability. A common type of test employs the maze as a measure of learning. Animals are required to go from the starting point to a goal box through a series of connecting passageways. There are many blind alleys, and entrance into one of these is scored as an error. In successive runs through the maze the number of errors decreases. Simultaneously the time necessary to go from the start to goal box becomes progressively shorter.

Animals are encouraged to learn mazes by allowing them to become mildly hungry before each test and then rewarding them with food after they reach the goal box. When human beings and animals are tested in comparable mazes there seems to be little difference in learning ability. Rats and people make about the same number of errors and improve at approximately the same rate. Dogs have not been tested extensively in the maze, but such evidence as is available indicates that they are neither inferior nor superior to other mammals.

Dogs that learn to open doors or to operate simple mechanical devices often are credited with reasoning ability. Laboratory tests show that this sort of behavior need not involve reasoning. Instead it is a product of simple trial-and-error learning.

In one experiment a number of dogs were required to press down on a lever which lifted the lid of their food box. This act was learned slowly and laboriously. The first responses consisted of random and inappropriate behavior. Dogs chewed, pawed, and pushed at all parts of the box. Eventually, quite by chance, they happened to depress the lever and the food box automatically opened.

One might raise the legitimate objection that this was an unfair test since the dogs had no previous experience in operating mechanical devices. However, their behavior after having once opened the box was such as to raise doubts concerning any insight into the problem. Tested immediately after their initial success, none of the animals proceeded directly to push the lever. Instead the usual random behavior appeared and led eventually to depression of the lever. Only gradually did the dogs begin to concentrate more and more upon the lever. Eventually their behavior became simple and effective. As soon as they were permitted to do so they approached the lever, pushed on it with one paw, and took their reward from the food box.

In its final form the behavior looked as though it were a product of reasoning. But anyone who had watched the entire learning process could recognize the eventual efficiency as a product of slow and difficult learning. Many of the acts we perform every day have been learned by exactly this sort of "unreasoning" trial-and-error method. The child who learns how to roller skate or to ride a bicycle does so in this fashion. There are many achievements in which reasoning is of little assistance.

Another series of experiments provides additional insight into the dog's learning ability. Twelve dogs were fed regularly at a special vending machine. The experimenter pushed a button and a dog biscuit slid down into the feeding tray. After the animals had learned to associate the apparatus with food, the next step was to teach them to operate the machine themselves.

To do this it was necessary to drop a sponge rubber ball into a hole in the vending machine. A ball was forced into the dog's mouth while its head was held over the hole. Then the animal was allowed to spit the ball out. It fell into the machine, tripped a lever, and a biscuit was automatically delivered into the food tray.

The first indication of learning appeared when a dog voluntarily opened its mouth to receive the ball. Some animals began to do this after 25 repetitions and others took 280 trials. The wide difference between individuals is important. Some dogs are, obviously, much better learners than others. The second phase of learning occurred when dogs began spontaneously to pick up a ball from a tray beside the machine and drop it in the hole. The best learners showed this response very quickly and others needed as many as 290 additional trials.

Next the tray containing the balls was moved 8 inches away from the vending machine. This made the problem much more difficult. Different individuals required from 63 to 249 additional trials before they became proficient at carrying the ball to the machine and depositing it in the hole. After this response was perfected, the tray was moved even farther away. Now some animals carried the ball precisely 8 inches toward the machine, dropped it in the air and hurried to the food chute as if expecting their reward. It was obvious that they failed to appreciate the connection between their own behavior and the appearance of food in the machine.

Eventually the dogs became able to retrieve the ball from any place in the experimental room and run directly to drop it in the hole of the vending apparatus. But this took a long time. There were no indications of reasoning or insight. Simple learning was sufficient to account for all of the behavior.

A simple analogy to human behavior is seen in the way most of us solve mechanical puzzles. Disentangling the two parts of metal puzzles usually is achieved as a result of trial-and-error learning. Reasoning plays no part in the process. Often we find the two parts separate in our hands without knowing how success was achieved. Only by performing the solution again and again do we finally arrive at the point where it can be performed quickly and with no mistakes.

Tests for "Mental Images" and "Reasoning." Various tests have been devised to determine whether dogs have mental images. At first the animal learns to go through one of three doors behind which he will find food. The correct door is the one over which a light is turned on. Above the other two doors there is no light and behind them no food. Different doors are "correct" on successive trials.

Actress Cheryl Miller of the "Daktari" CBS television series and her Afghan pal. Photo courtesy Walt Disney Productions.

Once this has been learned the dog is restrained in a special compartment several feet away from the three doors. From this position he can see the doors and the lights, and while he is looking the light over one of the doors is turned on. However, it is turned off before the animal is released. If the dog continues to go to the correct door under these circumstances it is assumed that he has retained a "mental image" of the light.

This test proves difficult for most animals. The majority of dogs fail to select the correct door if they have to wait for more than half a minute after the light is extinguished. The exact length of time over which an animal can "delay" successfully varies with the method of training, but in no instance do dogs approach the ability of human beings in the same test.

One test of "reasoning" is based upon choice of four doorways as a means of access to food. Upon each trial three doors are locked and one is unlatched so that it can be pushed open by the dog. The only rule that can be learned is that the door which was unlocked on one trial is certain to be locked upon the next one. The most intelligent behavior consists of trying three doors and avoiding the one which was unlocked on the preceding trial. On this test dogs made better scores than rats, cats or horses, but were inferior to monkeys and human beings.

Behavior in Life Situations. The inherent difficulties and limitations of the method will by this time have become obvious. The situations under which animals have been tested are not directly comparable to anything in their everyday lives. It is not at all certain that they have been given a "fair trial." Certainly we have here no measure of the upper limits of the dog's ability.

But one should not be too eager to discount the findings of the laboratory scientist. He does not pretend to have done more than make a start toward studying learning in the dog. A great deal of important information has come out of his investigations. They provide the necessary checks against totally unscientific, emotionally biased claims which greatly exaggerate the reaches of the canine intellect.

Uncontrolled observation of an animal's behavior under natural conditions is unlikely to yield a fair estimate of its intelligence. Most behavior patterns are complex. Viewing them in their final form it is impossible to decide how much is due to instinct, how much to learning, and how much to higher forms of mental activity. On the other hand free-living animals show many forms of behavior which rarely or never appear under artificial laboratory conditions. Occasionally dogs perform acts which are obviously more intelligent than anything yet evoked in an experimental setting.

The final decision as to the dimensions of the dog's mind must await the collection of additional evidence. The crucial data will come not from the laboratory nor from the kennel and field, but from a combination of both.

The New Knowledge of Dog Behavior

"Because we inherit every physical, mental, temperamental, and emotional trait from our parents, we find it very important to know everything we can learn about each parent. Everything we were born with was inherited from our parents; nothing that ever happens in our life will add to or take away from what we inherited.

"Despite the fact that environment has a profound effect on every living thing and modifies the manner in which inherited traits are used, only what we inherit determines what we can do. Environment has never made a man, animal, or plant any better than the genes he or it inherited." *

ALTHOUGH THERE has been much known about genetics for nearly 100 years, there has been more useful information gathered, especially about dogs, in the last 25 years than had been in a long, long time; probably as much on genetics as had been learned in the entire 10,000 years or so that men and dogs have been known to have been companions.

While the new knowledge of dog genetics has been a revelation, what is new about the effects of environment upon dogs and at what time different environments have their most effect upon dog behavior have opened up an entirely new approach to rearing and teaching dogs.

CRITICAL PERIODS IN THE LIFE OF A PUPPY

The most significant of these discoveries was made by Dr. J. Paul Scott, senior scientist and Director of The Animal Behavior Research Program at Hamilton Station near Bar Harbor, Maine. (Hamilton Station is the Behavior section of the world-renowned Roscoe B. Jackson Memorial Laboratory, a philanthropic institution for the study of the non-contagious diseases such as cancer, heart trouble and diabetes. Here scientists from all over the world gather to try to find ways to cure these diseases of mankind.)

While Dr. Scott's work has been with animals, the purpose was also to benefit man. He and his associates made one discovery that is very significant and which he named the "Critical Periods in the Life of a Puppy." It is this new information which is of great value to dog trainers and organizations who depend upon the reliable service of dogs.

It was during 1948 that Dr. Scott, working at Bar Harbor, discovered when a puppy can start to learn, how long it needs its mother's care, when its brain reaches adult maturity so that it can start learning with near-adult efficiency, and when a behavior pattern has been formed that will govern the behavior of each individual throughout its life.

It was patient observation that brought about Dr. Scott's discovery. Each morning he and his assistants

The New Knowledge of Dog Behavior by Clarence J. Pfaffenberger, published by Howell Book House Inc., New York, 1963.

went to the puppy nursery and watched each litter, writing down everything the puppies did. When he began to put this information together, it suddenly began to make sense. The puppy's life was divided up into definite periods, and some of these appeared much more important than others. Especially important was the period beginning at about 3 weeks of age, when the puppy begins to form social attachments which will determine his close social relations for the rest of his life with both humans and dogs.

All sorts of interesting changes turned up just before the critical period. One morning Dr. Scott left the nursery and met Dr. John L. Fuller, who has been his associate in all his behavior studies since 1946.

"I can't see that a puppy learns anything during the first two or three weeks of life," he told Dr. Fuller. "He is still behaving exactly like a newborn pup at two weeks when his eyes open, and even after that he doesn't seem to learn by experience."

Dr. Fuller is a most unperturbable scientist, but Dr. Scott's remark stopped him in his tracks.

"I simply could not believe that anything could live to the age of three weeks without being affected in some way by its environment," he told Dr. Scott later. Dr. Fuller's special field at the laboratory is the establishment of the relationship between the dog's physical development and its emotional and intellectual development. He says, "I offered to set up an experiment that would show that Dr. Scott's conclusions were wrong."

Puppies—Their Age of Awakening. Out of this experiment came the discovery that while the newborn puppy can learn certain things slowly and imperfectly, just before three weeks of age, it suddenly, at approximately three weeks, becomes able to learn as quickly and efficiently as an adult. For the first time, it can quickly learn to tell one individual

Part of Hamilton Station, Animal Behavior Research Laboratory, part of the Roscoe B. Jackson Memorial Laboratory at Bar Harbor, Maine.

By 19 to 21 days of age, a puppy sees, hears and smells. These are Norwegian Elkhound puppies, three weeks old.

from another, an ability which is very important in forming new social attachments.

Other changes add to this new power. The newborn puppy is not only blind but deaf at birth. The average pup's eyes are completely open at 13 days, but vision develops only gradually, reaching near-adult levels by 4 weeks. The first clear-cut response to sound comes at about 19 days. Some time between two and three weeks of age, the pup begins to walk, cuts its first tooth, and begins to wag its tail. There is a pronounced change in the electrical activity of the brain as measured with the electroencephalograph. Within the space of a week the puppy has been transformed from a baby into a small dog, ready to enter the most important critical period.

Next an anatomical study of puppy brains was made by the late Dr. Pickney Harmon, 2nd, professor of anatomy in the College of Medicine at the University of New York and associate scientist at Jackson Laboratory.

His study revealed that the physical growth of the brain and nervous system paralleled the emotional and intellectual growth of the puppy. To a layman, this is like the telephone lines where the power and the switchboard were not properly hooked up. The nerves and their connections with the sense organs and the brain were not complete enough to function properly until the puppy was approximately three weeks old. Then, suddenly the whole world was revealed to the little dog and he started to live.

All that has been found in the critical period discoveries at Bar Harbor has been used in a practical manner in producing better Guide Dogs at San Rafael, California. Not one of the steps in the development has proven different than the Scott findings showed.

Findings. Dr. Scott found that the puppy needs the mother love and discipline until it is seven weeks of age. He found that this is the best time to wean a puppy and that now it needs a definite regular social adjustment with people, especially with the same people. He found that at seven weeks its brain is able to start to learn anything that can be taught in simple small lessons. He found that what the puppy is not taught between 3 and 16 weeks of age and

especially any neglect in socializing a puppy with people during this period will handicap it so severely for the remainder of its life that nothing can ever be done to completely remedy this neglect.

STUDIES BY GUIDE DOGS FOR THE BLIND, INC.

Guide Dogs for the Blind, Inc., first started trying to record the puppy's behavior once a week at 4 weeks of age. They also continued their tests until the puppy was 16 weeks old. Experience has caused them to shorten this program. Now puppy socialization starts at 6 weeks of age, when each puppy is taken entirely away from its mother and litter mates and given 5 minutes of a tester's time and affection playing on the lawn. Each puppy gets this human socialization at 6 weeks of age and at 7 weeks of age. On the 8th week they start puppy tests which altogether take about 30 minutes for each pup as it passes through different tests. Four of the tests are to see how well the puppy will learn under this once a week tutelage. They include: to heel on leash, to sit on command, to come on command, and to fetch a ball thrown in the testing room, directly to the person who threw it. On each Thursday for 4 weeks there are 4 tests given to find out by new experiences how a puppy will react to a different pain, new sounds, strange surroundings, and unexperienced opportunities. On the 12th week of age a puppy's reactions to a moving vehicle, changes in footing, an overhanging obstruction, a complete obstruction across a walk, and a pedestrian, whom it meets, are recorded.

From the first, the adaptable puppies showed up

By age 12 weeks, a good puppy will readily retrieve small object to its tester. Photo by Jon Brenneis.

well in the tests, and for the years when "controls" have been used, the puppies who failed the tests have failed in training to a much greater degree than those who passed the tests. ("Controls" were puppies who failed the tests but who were raised in homes and trained by the trainers.) Neither puppy raisers nor trainers knew that the puppies had failed their test. Thus, they were given an equal chance to succeed with the puppies who has passed.

And so two organizations, which had come into being on opposite sides of the country for very different purposes, each for the benefit of mankind, found that each might provide valuable information for the other in June, 1946.

Guide Dogs for the Blind, Inc., by then 4 years old, was suffering growing pains and looking for advice which would help it to breed and to rear dogs suitable for its work. This offered what could well be a study of dogs from the cradle to the grave. Hamilton Station, founded in 1945, was just beginning to get encouragment from its early findings. There were some advantages in working with a practical dog operation, if the practical people followed carefully planned research programs and kept significant records. There was also the advantage of using, in a practical way, laboratory tests which had given significant results with five small breeds, upon larger breeds from both Working Dog and Sporting Dog groups.

The Need For Better Guide Dog Stock. Guide Dogs for the Blind, Inc., was organized by a small group of public spirited and patriotic San Francisco women in May, 1942 as a private philanthropy to supply guide dogs to the returning Servicemen and women who had lost their sight in World War II.

Using dogs which were donated and, later, those which were bred by the organization, it was found that only about 1 in 10 of these dogs could be trained well enough to be reliable guides for the blind people.

THE PFAFFENBERGER PROJECTS

When Clarence Pfaffenberger was to go East in 1946 to serve on the American Kennel Club's Rules Committee for Obedience Trials, fellow members of the Guide Dogs for the Blind, Inc.'s board of directors asked him to try to find a system of puppy testing which would help to select dogs for Guide Dogs' breeding program and to raise dogs with greater potential for guide dog work. His search led him to Beltsville, Maryland; Morristown, New Jersey; Orange, Connecticut; and eventually to Bar Harbor, Maine.

It was at the Roscoe B. Jackson Memorial Laboratory, Hamilton Station Behavior Studies Department, near Bar Harbor that he got his first clues from Dr. J. Paul Scott as to how Guide Dogs for the Blind, Inc. could start to solve their problems. Dr. Scott, a young Rhodes Scholar and social psychologist, had been chosen to direct the research sponsored by the Rockefeller Foundation for a ten-year period in the

During the first two weeks of a puppy's life he does not see, hear, or smell.

behavior of animals, especially dogs, and to learn if possible why there is so much mental illness and unnatural behavior in the modern human beings.

The Effects of Heredity and Environment. Naturally a study of this kind took into consideration both heredity and environment. On the hereditary side a small colony of closely related dogs, in each of five breeds, had been acquired. Small breeds representative of the five principal groups of dogs, based upon natural inherited traits and the manner in which they serve mankind, had been selected. The breeds were Wire-haired Fox Terrier for earth-going dogs; Cocker Spaniels, for sporting breeds; Shetland Sheepdogs for working dogs; Beagles for scent-hounds; and Basenji for sight-hounds. The closely related dogs within a breed gave them genes quite similar so they would have much the same characteristics, while these five breeds offered a wide variety of the inherited traits found in the more than 100 recognized dog breeds.

Among the different environments set up for the study were sunny puppy nurseries where a regular routine of care and socialization would be conducted by certain selected persons who would care for the mothers and handle the puppies every day in a prescribed manner, and a group of one acre grassy fields each surrounded by a six-foot board fence and supplied with a medium-sized dog house which was well out in the field. Only one attendant ever entered these acre fields, and he only took food and water to the mother, or mother and father, and later the puppies, but never spoke to them or in any way socialized with them. The dogs and their puppies in the field were studied from a tree house situated well back in the woods, by means of binoculars, so that the dogs in the fields would live as nearly natural lives, uninfluenced by human associations, as possible.

It was as much like a natural wildlife situation as could be artificially created. Dr. Scott had assigned an associate to study the puppies in the field while he concentrated on the puppies in the nursery, trying to teach each puppy certain things as soon as it would learn.

Development of Puppy Testing Methods. Mr. Pfaffenberger was encouraged to set up tests for the puppies Guide Dogs were breeding. The nature of the tests, it was thought, should be similar to what they would do as guide dogs when they were grown. Tests which might reveal the puppies' inherited natural traits, which would make them especially suited for guide dogs, were also believed to be important.

At Hamilton Station the puppies in the field had not been observed much before 4 weeks of age, which indicated they did not naturally leave their nests at all until about that age. Dr. Scott had not been encouraged by what his puppies were learning during the first few weeks, so it was suggested that the tests at Guide Dogs for the Blind, Inc. could best start at about 4 weeks of age.

When Mr. Pfaffenberger returned to California, a group was formed to study the various types of personnel tests which were being used in the Services and business and industry. It seemed the type such as used for pilots in the Air Force was near to what was needed, for it simulated the things that would be expected of the one taking the test when he was actually doing his work. So the tests were set up based on what a Guide Dog should do. By March, 1947, the tests were ready to try out and there were young puppies to be tested at San Rafael, where the school had purchased an 11-acre campus.

In February, 1948 Mr. Pfaffenberger got together with Dr. Clarence Cook Little, Director of the Jackson Laboratory, to discuss with him the results of the first year of puppy testing at San Rafael. Dr. Little was very encouraging and made most helpful suggestions about the tests and their correlation with the records kept by the trainers. He also outlined how to breed the best dogs, as determined by the tests, to produce more good dogs.

In 1953 and 1954, Mr. Pfaffenberger, honored by a Guggenheim Fellowship and its extension, continued his study, especially at Bar Harbor with Drs. Scott and Fuller.

Findings—Puppy Testing. The first thing he discovered was that the tests did have value. The records had been kept so that they could be well analyzed. The puppy who failed the tests had little chance of becoming a Guide Dog. It was also found that not enough attention had been given to two of the tests:

1. *Fetch:* If a puppy would not pick up a ball and bring it to his trainer by the end of the five once-a-week lessons, he had practically no chance of making a Guide Dog. This turned out to mean that he did not naturally wish to do things for people.

2. *Moving Vehicle:* If a puppy actually panicked when he met a two wheeled cart being pushed toward him on the sidewalk at a normal walking gait he was almost sure to panic when confronted with new and strange experiences even after he was trained to be a Guide Dog.

There was another important thing which tied in with Dr. Scott's critical periods and socialization more than anyone suspected. A Guide Dog has to make decisions. It must decide when it is safe to follow the course the blind person instructs him to follow and when it is unsafe. This applies to crossing a street in traffic or passing an open manhole or a leaning tree. This is called "taking responsibility."

When the great number of dogs who failed because they would not take responsibility were carefully analyzed it was found that almost all of them had suffered the indignity of having been suddenly denied the attention and praise that they had become accustomed to have showered upon them every Thursday at puppy tests. Before 1954, homes might not be available for weeks, even months after the puppy tests had been completed. These Guide Dog puppies, having become socialized with people during the puppy tests and having come to expect to be a part of some activity, suddenly found themselves to be just kennel dogs. They were fed, watered, but little attention was given them.

A study of the effect of this break in socialization revealed that the puppy who passed the puppy test had a 90% chance of succeeding if he was placed in a good home within one week after he had finished his tests, while if he was kept in the kennel for 3 weeks or more, after finishing the tests and before being placed in a home, his chance of success was only 30%.

Mr. Pfaffenberger, having found that the dogs who failed the training because they would not take responsibility had had longer than one week break in socialization, made a more detailed study of a group of 154 puppies. The results of the study appear in the accompanying table.

When Placed In Homes After Tests	These Became Guide Dogs	These Failed In Training
(First: the 124 puppies who had passed their tests)		
40 within 1 week	36 = 90%	4 = 10%
22 within 2 weeks	19 = 86+%	3 = 13+%
19 within 3 weeks	11 = 57+%	8 = 42+%
43 placed after 3 weeks	13 = 30%	30 = 70%
Total Number	79 = 63+%	45 = 36+%
(Here are the 30 puppies placed in homes as controls of the 64 who failed tests)		
6 within 1 week	1 = 16⅔%	5 = 83⅓%
2 within 2 weeks	0 = 0%	2 = 100%
9 within 3 weeks	4 = 44⁴⁄₉%	5 = 55⁵⁄₉%
13 placed after 3 weeks	0 = 0%	13 = 100%
Total Number	5 = 16⅔%	25 = 83⅓%

A careful study of the dogs who failed to take responsibility showed that almost every one of them had a sharp break in socialization sometime in their puppyhood between 12 and 16 weeks of age.

In the group which were sent out as controls and who had failed their puppy tests there were three whose testing records showed that they had run a temperature during all or most of the tests. It had been recorded by the testers that these puppies' failure was in their opinion due to illness. It is significant that these three were among the five who became Guide Dogs from the control group.

It is believed the reason they would not take the responsibility, "of refusing to obey" when danger lay ahead, was related to their frustrating experience, which shook their confidence in themselves, at an age when their character was being formed (3 to 16 weeks old). Practically every dog which had refused to take responsibility up to 1954 had had a break in socialization. All dogs on the record who had had a break in socialization at this time showed some emotional disturbance. Some of the comments on these by the trainers are: "11 frightened by people and awnings"; "3 will not train"; and "3 nervous, wetting and defecating."

Discoveries On Socialization. The Journal of Genetic Psychology, 1959 Vol. 95, pages 145-155, published a study of this discovery as reported by C. J. Pfaffenberger and J. P. Scott, Guide Dogs for the Blind and Roscoe B. Jackson Memorial Laboratory, under the title *The Relationship Between Delayed Socialization and Trainability in Guide Dogs.*

In using this new knowledge to improve the chances of the puppies being raised by 4-H children to become Guide Dogs it was discovered that it was also important for the child to know what the puppy had already learned and to continue to give the puppy exercises daily in the things it knew. That this continued training should start at once was found to be important also. If the puppy were placed in a home and for some reason its socialization through training exercises were neglected for as much as two weeks the puppy had less likelihood of success than if the child carried on. This discovery resulted in puppy classes being formed with qualified instructors in the counties where 4-H Guide Dog puppy raising projects were being conducted.

The teachers of these classes instructed the 4-H children in the care of the puppy, house breaking, and the immediate continuance of the heel, sit, come, and fetch exercises.

Some things which came to light from this program that are of interest and need more investigation, but show up often enough to warrant careful consideration are: that a puppy not allowed his mother's love and discipline and contact with other puppies up to seven weeks of age does not usually adjust to other dogs (even on the street he is inclined to start a fight when he meets a strange dog); puppies raised without their mother have almost never become Guide Dogs; of two puppies from the same litter raised

These are some of the disaster and relief dogs that were trained in San Francisco by their owners under instruction of a Dogs For Defense class.

together in the same home, one usually makes a Guide, but never both; and puppies who are tied outside on a chain instead of having a woven wire run built for them, have all failed.

Most people know that a child needs a puppy to grow up with, but these studies indicate that a puppy needs a child to develop his best possible potential. Puppies in the same neighborhood and raised under identical conditions by adults with no children in the home, have been less successful than puppies raised with children.

Findings Relative Breeding Programs. Also at Bar Harbor was Dr. Benson E. Ginsburg, professor of biology, University of Chicago, an associate scientist at Jackson Laboratory. He was a special student of dogs and their origin and their inherited traits, including their ancestors, the wolves. A few years later, while Dr. Ginsburg was at the Center of Advanced Sciences in Palo Alto, California, he and Mr. Pfaffenberger got together with a study that Mr. Pfaffenberger, Dr. Scott and Dr. Fuller had started at Bar Harbor. It revealed that by choosing outstanding dogs and inbreeding intensively the good traits can be preserved for many generations and the inbred dogs are better than the original if the breeding stock is carefully selected in each generation.

At Guide Dogs for the Blind from 1942 to 1952 there had been many German Shepherd dogs raised. All told, there had been 62 individual bitches who had whelped, in that period, 730 puppies. There had been 50 males used in producing these 730 puppies. Yet, from all of these, although a great many were set aside for breeding, at the end of these first ten years of breeding there were to emerge only five bitches and two studs who produced dogs good enough to keep for breeding. By 1962 every German Shepherd dog in the breeding program had been selected for its excellence. At that time approximately 200 puppies were being raised a year. About half of these were German Shepherd dogs. All traced their ancestry back to these five females and two males and to no other dog.

It was found that by using great care in selecting away from common faults that the exceptionally good sire who was bred to a daughter or a granddaughter produced the most puppies in a litter who could be trained as Guide Dogs and that these line-bred litters produced the best breeding stock because they had been bred and selected for this type of work. They carried similar genes or in some cases many genes that were identical and, thus, produced uniform physical and behavioral traits.

No indication of serious bad effects were found as long as care was taken to not breed the same faults in both parents.

If an Indian corn plant is protected so that no pollen except that from its tassel can reach its silk, the grains of corn will have the same parent. This would be known as an inbred coefficient of .50. At Guide Dogs there were bred dogs of inbred coefficient of .50 with excellent results. Because very special types of dogs with very special physical and behavioral traits were needed for this work, this was tried and the results were very desirable.

WOLF, MAN, DOG RELATIONSHIPS

To the Guide Dogs study Dr. Ginsburg brought his insight into the nature of dogs' ancestor, the wolf. This added a look at canine behavior little known. In his studies of the wolf, Dr. Ginsburg found that it has many of the same characteristics as the dog, but it also has character traits that have been lost in domestication or in the association of the dog with mankind.

Wolves Can Be Socialized. Dr. Ginsburg found he could socialize the young wolves in much the same way that puppies are socialized. Others who have tried this have made highly useful and enjoyable companions of wolf puppies reared in good socialized conditions. He was also able to socialize grown wolves, who had been trapped, to where they showed great joy in his company and accepted him much as one wolf accepts another wolf with which it is friendly.

On the other hand, it is interesting to note that all of Dr. Scott's puppies reared in the acre fields, simulating a wild condition and by mothers who were highly socialized to human beings, never adjusted to people well enough to be even tolerable pets if they were not handled until they were 16 weeks of age.

It is the similarity of man and dog which makes them so socially compatible and it is their different abilities which makes them such valuable companions for each other, as in the field, the dog can smell the game which the hunter can neither see nor smell. The dog also has a very different eye from a man so that when game is shot he can mark down the fall very accurately and with his superb sense of smell he can locate and retrieve to hand what his human partner has brought down.

That man and dog have been closely associated for at least 8,000 years and probably more than 10,000 years is quite definitely established by the skeletons of the two found together in the sites of ancient civilization excavated in the Near-East and in Denmark.

The fact that most dog varieties have originated in the continents of Europe, Asia and North America and that all dogs have been widely used in these areas as compared to the more primitive use of dogs in Africa and South America invites thought respecting the possibility that dogs are all descended from wolves.

Wolves' habits are very dog-like, their skeletons are more similar to those of dogs than any other animal and so similar to some breeds that it is impossible to say for sure which is dog and which is wolf. Wolves will mate with dogs and their offspring can be bred together or to either a wolf or a dog and produce normal puppies.

(*See also* Part XIV, Dogs in the Primitive World.)

The dog has traits in behavior more like the wolf. The wolf runs in packs. The pack in the wild is the wolf and his family; sometimes maybe a friend is added. The entire pack is responsible for each other, including the baby wolves, with whom grandpa may baby-sit while mamma takes a run and hunts for herself. This tendency to pack is similar to the tendency of the family and the clan in the human race.

DOGS AND SCIENTIFIC STUDY

It has only been since 1945 that enough dogs have been studied by enough capable scientists and dog breeders under well enough controlled conditions to give reliable behavior statistics. It is only recently that the computer could analyze the vast amounts of data necessary to make sure that the conclusions are valid.

And so while man was learning much about dogs in the 10,000 years or so in which they have lived and worked together, it has been in the last one hundred years that organized types of study have begun to reveal many interesting facts. This started with organized clubs for various sports with dogs such as the American Spaniel Club, the American Kennel Club, fox hunting clubs, field trial clubs, dog show clubs and, in more recent years, the obedience clubs.

Even in Great Britain and Central Europe, which are very dog-minded, kennel clubs and public registration of dog breeds and club stud-books and standards for breeds, set by interested parent clubs, are matters of the last century.

Throughout the ages dogs have become so much the part of the human family and seemed to prefer man to his own kind, to the extent that it seemed as though the family knew all there was to know about the family dog. It never occurred to most people that the dog should be scientifically studied any more than they thought of running a scientific laboratory study on grandma.

It was only when certain things happened in the use of the dog, such as his use in armies and his use in leading the blind, that many people in different parts of the world began to ask questions about why dogs do things the way they do and what can be done to make them better.

DOGS IN WORLD WAR II

When World War II exploded as an American concern with the bombing of Pearl Harbor there were two ways that American dogs could be affected. One was that they could be thinned down to the minimum, to save food, as they were in some European countries. The other was that they could serve the country in many capacities of leading the blind who came back from the war, that they could help search out those trapped in bombed-out buildings, and especially that they could be trained to work at home and guard military supply depots, fuel storage areas, the coast lines, prison camps, airfields, and strategic areas.

That they would be especially helpful in the island-hopping under General MacArthur was not realized too well, at first, but here they proved superb.

As each of these services became better known and understood there were literally thousands of dogs trained for war services and hundreds of soldiers, Coast Guardsmen and Marines trained to use them.

This is important because up to 1942 there was little interest in almost all dog problems. Many veterinary schools had to teach their courses in dog care almost sub-rosa, because state and Federal governments were supporting other loads. They would not vote money for a course in medicine which they considered pet-practice. Although the dog had been a part of the human family for 10,000 years dog owners still felt they had to say, "I bought the dog for the kid."

At the entry of the United States in World War II, alarmists pointed out how much food the dogs of the country were eating. There were even a number of people who advocated that the population of dogs must be drastically reduced. Had the alarmists had their way, the new knowledge about dogs and even human behavior would have been less likely.

It was fortunate that Dogs for Defense, Inc. came into being at this critical time and, by serving the country, saved her dogs.

Fortunately, intelligent dog people in the United States not only offered the facilities of the dog organizations and the best talent of men and women who had most nearly the type of training and experience that would be needed for dogs in the Armed Services, but insisted that the Armed Services try the use of dogs seriously.

Over the country there were a number of groups with ideas of being useful, including a field trial group near Cleveland, Ohio, and the Northern California Field Trial Club, in San Francisco, California. The latter started in the spring of 1941 to train Cocker and Springer Spaniels to search for casualties from a bombing. They were at first trained under the guidance of a member, Evan George, then later by Clarence Pfaffenberger. School athletic fields were obtained for practice, using the stands as places to hide the simulated victims. More than 100 dogs were trained from 1941 through 1945, twenty served with disaster-rescue and relief units in San Francisco, and

with police. and fire departments. The group was recognized by the Dogs for Defense national organization then being formed, and made a part of its program.

Dogs for Defense. Dogs for Defense had the backing of the American Kennel Club, *American Field,* all the obedience clubs, and many of the various field trial clubs in all parts of the United States. Dogs were at first trained by members of these clubs and offered to the Armed Forces. The War Department was given a clear picture of how much dogs could do to help. Then the organization of Dogs for Defense made an offer to borrow from dog owners young dogs suitable for the Services.

As soon as the War Department realized the important roles dogs might play in the conflict it authorized both the Marine Corps and the Army to set up large War Dog Training Centers throughout the country and the Dogs for Defense organization established procurement offices where the dogs loaned by individual owners "for the duration" were screened. In San Francisco, the Dogs for Defense Office, under Mr. Pfaffenberger as regional director, was manned exclusively by the volunteers, many from the previously organized rescue-dog unit, which was then a part of Dogs for Defense. This group supplied more than 1,800 dogs trainable for war duty. It also supplied many dogs to Seeing Eye in Morristown, New Jersey and to Guide Dogs for the Blind, Inc., then located at Los Gatos, California.

A completely equipped office and shipping and testing area were loaned to Dogs for Defense by the San Francisco Public School Department along with the services of Mr. Pfaffenberger.

(*See also* The Dog As A Soldier, Part VIII.)

DEVELOPMENT OF TESTING AND BREEDING PROGRAMS

In 1946, when Guide Dog's puppy-testing study class was set up, it had the approval of the California State Department of Education and was organized in the Adult Department of San Francisco Schools with Mr. Pfaffenberger as instructor. The Dogs for Defense Office and the rescue-dogs program were demobilized and from the group of volunteers in both came eager students to study all the available materials concerning both animal and human behavior and to set up the program which has been in use to test puppies at Guide Dogs for the Blind, Inc. ever since. To this group a number of Junior Leaguers were recruited. The more experienced members have carefully trained new volunteers as personnel replacements, but for more than 20 years the original group has maintained great interest in the testing program. Six of the original testers were still a part of the group of thirty active members at the end of 15 years and two were still active at the end of 20 years.

It is important to know who did the testing of the puppies and their qualifications in order to evaluate the acceptability of the results they reported. This group is so careful to follow all known means of getting maximum results in testing that no changes are made without careful consultation with scientific advisors. They are so devoted to the volunteer work they are doing that they arrange their family and social life so that one day a week is free for them to come to Guide Dogs for the Blind and test puppies. Promptly at 10 a.m., usually every Thursday, the tests begin. A tester who has started a litter will be on hand for every test so as not to change the puppy's environment in the tests or the manner of testing, which may vary slightly between individuals.

When the puppies have completed their tests they are rushed to the 4-H homes. Mr. and Mrs. Pfaffenberger, as volunteers, spent eight years, from November 1954 to November 1962, delivering the puppies to their raisers in five Western states and organizing classes with the aid of competent dog people as liaison representatives and leaders.

The Role of Liaison Representatives. In this way the organization developed a uniform puppy-raising program set up under the use of a manual which details the things that need to be done and those that need to be avoided. The liaison representatives, working with the local farm advisors, go to the homes in advance and explain in detail what is expected and the expenses involved. They also make it clear that any home in which there is one person who is opposed to the puppy being accepted, is undesirable, because such a person can create an environmental situation which will develop patterns of behavior which will make even a good puppy unsuitable for a Guide Dog. The family dog is also given a careful look by the liaison representative, because it has been found that a shy or overly aggressive dog will affect adversely the behavior of the puppy raised in its company.

Since the puppies have been delivered within one week after their tests ended, and since the puppy classes have been organized and the liaison representative has been able to standardize the raising of the puppy in homes, the production of Guide Dogs has become much more uniform.

Hamilton Station and San Rafael Programs Compared. It is remarkable that so much was found in common between the two organizations. There are many extreme contrasts in the Hamilton Station program and the one at San Rafael. These add to the validity of the findings because they show several things: 1. That the critical periods apply to all breeds of dogs in almost exactly the same way; 2. That environment can completely ruin a very good puppy. Examples: (a) The one acre field-raised puppies who had no human socialization until 16 weeks of age; (b) The puppies who had a break in socialization after the puppy tests at Guide Dogs; (c) A person who dislikes a puppy can have an adverse effect on its development just by living in the same family with a puppy; (d) Association with well adjusted dogs away

from any association with people, as in the acre fields, does not give the puppy confidence in people; (e) Association with an overly aggressive or overly shy dog, even when the human factors are all good, can cause an otherwise good puppy to be an aggressive or shy dog.

These all tie in together, even though the dogs at Guide Dogs for the Blind are reared and housed entirely differently from those at Hamilton Station, are different breeds, and are tested differently by people who have an entirely different background. It is not only that all these things are different, but that they are so different as to be almost exactly the opposite in many ways!

At Hamilton Station, a "closed colony" to which no new strains have been added since 1945 consists of five breeds: (a) Cocker Spaniels from an era when Cockers were being hunted and run in field trials. The dogs at Hamilton Station are from Dual Champion Miller's Esquire C.D.X. and related Cockers; (b) Beagles, coming from dogs of the standards and behavioral traits of 1945 (both the Cockers and Beagles are very stable and social); (c) Shetland Sheepdogs of 1945. This breed was being stabilized for conformation of the Collie type at this time and some rather un-Shetland-looking dogs resulted from these matings; (d) Wire Fox Terriers, in 1945 quite popular and very aggressive. In the show ring, judges expected Wires to start serious fights. At Hamilton Station they have never been able to rear more than three Wire Fox Terriers together until one year of

The late Clarence J. Pfaffenberger, Former Vice President, Guide Dogs for the Blind, San Rafael, California, with Golden Retriever puppy.

age. All others were destroyed by their littermates; (e) Basenjis, dogs from England which only one or two generations previously had been owned by natives in the African bush. These have never shown much interest in socialization. They are indifferent to the people who work with them; they seldom show a desire to please in any training exercise.

It is important to know what the characteristics of a closed population like this was when the colony was formed, especially since all stock is descended from the original stock, and since the original stock is not necessarily very similar to dogs of the same breeds today.

All these breeds have been kept under almost a quarantine rearing and care condition. No other dogs are allowed on the premises to avoid the transmitting of disease. All dogs are reared entirely at Hamilton Station, reared in groups of three to six in large runs with a common dog house for the group, and food and water available at all times. The groups are usually littermates (a study of dominance is important at the laboratory). The personnel who handle the dogs in their tests are the same only for the same tests, but dogs may be moved from one tester to another when tests are changed or are added as a parallel course. The staff is a paid, trained group especially selected for this work. Visitors are not encouraged to go near the dogs.

At San Rafael the dogs have evolved from a very large group of breeding stock over the last 25 years, but have been selected. In the case of the German Shepherd Dogs the selection resulted in a closely related lot. This came about by selection of the best pups from the most successful producers through the puppy tests. All the breeding stock is kept in private homes and is brought in to be bred, for whelping, and for raising the puppies to seven weeks of age. All the puppies, after five weeks of age, are in runs outside with their littermates and, until seven weeks of age, with their mother. These are seen by thousands of visitors. These puppies, from six weeks on, are handled by testers. The working dogs, those in training, are taken into San Rafael or San Francisco daily and worked on the public streets and roads. All three of the above conditions make the exposure of the Guide Dog puppies about as complete as it can be. After the five weeks testing, the puppies are taken to private homes to be raised by 4-H children and to be taken to class, into town and anywhere the child may wish to go and take the puppy, even to class at school. The breeds now used at Guide Dogs are German Shepherd Dogs, Golden Retrievers and Labrador Retrievers.

One thing in common is that both Hamilton Station and Guide Dogs for the Blind breed all their own dogs from their own stock.

The amount of trust that can be put in the results of the studies done at Guide Dogs and at Hamilton Station becomes clear since the same results have been found at both places under such opposite rearing conditions and with such different personnel. The 4-H puppy raiser is not only a volunteer, but pays out of pocket about $100 in food and other expenses to raise a puppy. The testers and liaison people are all volunteers giving time and money to produce the Guide Dogs. Uniform results were obtained even from such different breeds of dogs.

Problems In the Breeding Program. At Guide Dogs, the knowledge that closely line-bred stock from selected parents was so important in the fixing of inheritance of good traits, came, unfortunately, after most of the great producing dogs had died of old age. If they could have been bred scientifically to establish breeding stock with the desired characteristics at Guide Dogs for the Blind, better dogs would have resulted.

The best that could be done was to select such of the get which was yet available and which had the most genes of the dogs and bitches whose records were the best. There are unfortunate things which sometime happen in a breeding program like that at Guide Dogs. The selected young breeding stock may not become, in fact, breeding stock: (a) Great need for dogs to train at the time such stock has matured may bring on such pressure for Guide Dogs that this stock is used for Guides. (Guide Dogs are spayed or castrated, a California legal requirement). (b) If placed in a home, things can go wrong, too. Examples: One valuable line-bred stud left tied on a back porch with a slipchain collar hanged himself; one similar dog was stolen; another as valuable was poisoned. Where there are no more dogs like them, the breeding program is hurt.

When an attempt was made to salvage some good breeding stock by breeding the old bitches who had been the very best producers, a new thing was learned. Not only did the older bitches have smaller litters, they had weaker, inferior puppies. From 12 months of age to 60 months (five years), all bitches produced more Guide Dogs out of each litter and dogs with better training records than the same bitches produced after five years of age. From 60 months of age the production of usable dogs deteriorated. At seven and eight years of age only two of these 20 bitches whelped any puppies at all. They had been producing 100% litters of Guide Dogs.

During their seventh year of age the two of them had eight puppies between them. During the eighth year they had seven. During their seventh year of age, four of the eight puppies became Guide Dogs. To everyone's surprise, all seven in the eighth year became Guides. But these puppies all came from the two Shepherd bitches with the best production record ever set at Guide Dogs for the Blind.

Geneticists shake their heads at this. "It is not true genetically," they say, but several geneticists have studied these records and none has, as yet, shown how this can be interpreted any other way. "Nutrition deficiency" has been suggested by those who have not studied the records.

It was also found that young bitches from the older mothers were not uniformly good breeding stock.

Inbreeding was done with the best stock available,

On the first Thursday in August of each year, the 4-H puppy raisers bring the puppies (potential guide dogs) to San Rafael for a field day and to compete in classes.

but this was not among the top ranking stock of the earlier inbred litters that had been most successful. As a result, it was shown definitely that there was a certain amount of improvement by selective inbreeding and no deteriorating effect came even when the inbreeding was carried well beyond what it had ever been done scientifically anywhere before.

GENERAL RESEARCH CONCLUSIONS

The general conclusions from some 20 years of research are:

1. Behavior traits are inherited just as physical traits are.

2. Good environment cannot make a good dog of a poor puppy, but it can make as good a dog of him as his inheritance permits.

3. Bad environment can spoil a good puppy.

4. Occasionally inheritance is so good that bad environment has minimal bad effects, but such strength of genetic quality is rare.

5. Critical periods in the life of a puppy apply almost equally to all breeds.

6. Knowledge of the critical periods and their effects can be used by dog breeders to get the maximum potential from their puppies.

7. By observing the times when a puppy needs canine socialization and the times when he needs human socializing the owner can mold his dog to the kind he wants him to be.

8. Once progeny tests establish that mating of certain pairs of dogs gives the results the breeder is looking for, he can continue this quality by using the get of this mating to select the best young stock and mate them with their parents. The best litters of Guide Dogs came from father-daughter matings. The best line of brood bitches at Guide Dogs came from a son-mother mating. The purpose of inbreeding is to establish a gene bank so the good genes are preserved where they can be used together.

Because of the many things which have come to light during the last 25 years of scientific research by social-psychologists it is now possible to breed, select, rear and educate the very best Guide Dogs that have ever been known. Through the faith of thousands of people in this program it is possible for these dogs to be given to any deserving blind person who can use one and who will come to San Rafael and train for four weeks, the cost free to himself.

Other Guide Dog schools in the United States do excellent work with blind people, supplying them with guides in their parts of the country.

California requires instructors at Guide Dog schools to serve a four-year apprenticeship in learning to train Guide Dogs and in educating blind people in their use. The apprentice must then take a very rugged State Board examination to be licensed.

No other organization of the type of Guide Dogs for the Blind, Inc., has set up its own *complete* breeding program nor made such a *complete research study* of what makes it click.

Only the San Rafael organization has its own puppy-testing program conducted by volunteers; a 4-H Club puppy-raising program where the club member assumes the financial as well as the raising responsibility, a liaison representative group who keeps the raising standards high.

By the puppy learning useful things from the time it is capable of learning, the very best possible dogs are turned out to take full responsibility for their blind masters and mistresses.

It takes good, well-trained, dedicated people to turn out the finished product. The better the material they have to work with, the better such dedication is rewarded.

Part IV

STARTING YOUR DOG'S TRAINING

In training any breed of dog to do anything there are certain fundamentals which must be constantly borne in mind. These are the three great P's of dog training: Patience, Persistence, and Practical Knowledge of the job at hand. Patience (which includes that priceless quality, self-control) carefully and painstakingly to teach the necessary lessons even in the face of discouraging resistance on the part of the pupil day after day; Persistence in the application of proper training methods until the pupil is letter-perfect in his lessons; and Practical Knowledge of the job at hand in order to know when and how to act, and when and why not to act.

——Fundamentals of Dog Training——

THE FIRST lesson in dog training is the one the trainer himself must learn. That is self-control. The work of hours and even days of patient training can be wholly undone and the dog's confidence in his trainer entirely shattered in one foolish burst of temper. It is naturally exceedingly trying for the beginner to see his young pupil disregard all his apparently well-learned lessons on occasion, but experienced trainers know that such happenings are bound to occur and take them as a matter of course. In fact, when the pupil goes stale in his training, it is sometimes best to allow him more latitude for a while.

Patience is the first virtue in dog training, and the failure of most spoiled dogs may be traced to the lack of this quality in the make-up of the trainer. Remember that a light hand, a soft voice, and a high heart are part of the equipment of the successful trainer.

The trainer must also possess or develop a high degree of persistence. Persistence to try and teach the same lessons day in and day out, over and over again until they are thoroughly understood by the pupil. Persistence to correct errors at the right time and in the right manner without show of temper, and persistence in acknowledging, by rewards of tidbits or caresses, work well done.

A practical knowledge of the job at hand is most essential if the best results are to be obtained. Know exactly what you want to accomplish. Study your pupil carefully. Adopt methods best suited for his temperament. Then put them into effect through patience and persistence. By proceeding carefully and slowly, exercising self-control at all times, there is no reason why any intelligent person, given a young dog of average intelligence and considerable boldness, cannot accomplish any reasonable end desired in dog training.

——Simple Dog Training——

THE DOG is an animal of intelligence, capable of being taught many things. There is no reason why he should not be well-mannered. Some individuals are more precocious than others, but with patience and perseverance almost any owner can teach his dog certain little accomplishments which make of him a better companion and improve his status among the neighbors with whom he comes in contact. In fact, these accomplishments are necessary if the chances of his becoming an occasional nuisance are to be reduced to the minimum.

While the dog is generally intelligent, one must remember that he has his limitations, can absorb just so much at a time, and must not be forced in his training. If his training can be made to seem a part of a game, so much the better and faster progress will be made. But at the same time, the dog must be brought to realize that his owner, or trainer, is the boss and must be obeyed. Care must be taken not to intimidate the pupil, but no lesson should end on a sour note. And lessons in any one phase should be confined to about 15 minutes.

The age at which training should be started depends on a number of factors. Some dogs develop slowly and still seem to be puppies when they have reached the age of one year. Others take to training at an early age, but lessons are better retained when given after the dog has had a chance to develop mentally.

If the dog is going to be given every chance to develop his abilities to the utmost, familiarization with humans must start in his second month. A short period of play with humans each day will lay the groundwork for greater responsiveness later. Actual training, the teaching of the dog to obey commands, should start when the puppy is about seven weeks of age. Years of experimentation indicate quite clearly that, just as there are physiological changes that occur at definite ages, so are there psychological changes; a dog becomes receptive to learning commands at about the fiftieth day, that is, at about seven weeks of age. Time beyond that day not spent in training, is time being wasted.

Actual maturity, of course, is another matter. Some of the larger breeds of dog do not become truly mature, and therefore their behavior is not truly dependable until they are as much as two years of age. Hunting dogs compete in what are called "puppy stakes" until they are 18 months old. The smaller breeds, particularly the toy breeds, are often mature in every way by the time they are eight or ten months old. Regardless of the breed, the puppy will be open to training at about seven weeks of age and there are some things which should be taught the dog soon after he comes into his permanent home.

THE NEW PUPPY

For the purpose of this discussion, it may be best to assume the reader has just acquired a healthy puppy with the intention of keeping him in the home as a companion. The puppy is just a baby and has spent his short life playing with his brothers and sisters in the kennel of his birth. He comes into your home as a complete stranger and is unaccustomed to the attention that is showered upon him.

It is best to bring him into your home in the daytime, the earlier the better. This will give him a chance to become at least partially acquainted with his new surroundings before facing the ordeal of the first night away from his family. Almost all puppies are of an inquisitive nature and unless this fellow is over-awed by the strangeness of the surroundings, he will want to look around and explore things. At any rate, leave him to his own devices for a while. Let him look into every nook and cranny and take every

precaution possible against his becoming frightened severely. Show him that he is welcome and has nothing to fear. Watch him carefully and at the first signs of restlessness take him outdoors or provide a newspaper on which he can relieve himself. The chances are that his nervousness will cause a few mishaps that you cannot prevent, but under no circumstances should he be punished at this stage. Time enough for that after he has become accustomed to his new locale.

Puppies sleep a good deal and this little fellow will probably grow tired fairly quickly, what with all the excitement. You have already provided a place for him to sleep, probably in the kitchen where there are no rugs for him to spoil. At the first signs of drowsiness place him in his box or on his mat and encourage him to take his nap. As soon as he wakens, he should be taken outdoors where he can attend to his needs or be placed in his sand-box which you have provided for the purpose on the back porch. If no back porch is available, torn-up newspaper in the kitchen corner will serve.

Settling Down for the Night. You make your new puppy comfortable for the night by placing him in his bed, providing him with a vessel of fresh water, and perhaps giving him some rubber toy with which to occupy himself. All goes well . . . until you, yourself, have settled down for the night. Then your new acquisition begins to miss his own family and naturally makes his loneliness known. It is hard to resist the temptation to go downstairs and soothe the sorrowing little fellow. You may succumb and bring him into your own bedroom. But the puppy must be taught his proper place and the sooner you accomplish this task the better for both of you. If you leave him alone, natural fatigue will take control and he'll go to sleep. This lonely howling may continue for several nights and if it persists you may scold the puppy severely and put him back in his box, making sure that your punishment is by voice only. If you relent and take him into your own room, you merely throw away the progress you have made. A ticking alarm clock placed in his bed, or a hot water bottle wrapped in an old towel, will sometimes work wonders.

Housebreaking. Dogs are naturally clean animals. They are loath to soil their own beds, but puppies have frequent calls of Nature and must respond. They do not know the difference between a Persian carpet and a rag rug, and must be taught. Remember your puppy is still a baby and intends no harm, he simply doesn't know better and should not be punished for unintentional misdeeds.

Housebreaking should begin at an early age. This should be accomplished in from four to eight weeks but you may expect occasional lapses in manners. Your puppy will usually relieve himself soon after eating. Adopt a definite feeding schedule and stick to it. He will soon learn to anticipate these times.

About ten minutes after feeding, take him outdoors for a walk. Use the same route every time. He may be

By now this Alaskan Malamute pup knows his name, is accustomed to being led on a leash, and much of the time will come when his young owner calls him. Hank Babbitt photo.

attracted to a patch of grass or a pile of ashes and attend to his duty there. If he does, take him to that spot every time. Dogs usually like to relieve themselves on the ground. Some will go for blocks on a leash without this relief, but allowed freedom, will attend to this necessity promptly. If possible, walk your puppy with an older dog. He learns much by imitating other dogs.

Puppies from three to six months of age should be taken outdoors at least five times a day; six to nine months, four times a day; older dogs three times a day.

When your puppy commits an error on your carpet or best rug (and he will), go to him promptly and by the tone of your voice make it plain to him that he has made a grievous mistake. Scold him severely, place his nose in close proximity to the spot of the "crime," shame him, and then take him outside promptly. It will be too late, but he will eventually get the idea. If he continues to make these errors, repeat these proceedings and give him a slap across the rump with a folded newspaper.

After a while the puppy will come to associate the outside walks with doing his duty and your troubles are almost over. Always praise him when he attends to this necessity promptly.

It is usually best to try keeping the puppy confined to one room at first, preferably the kitchen or some smooth or linoleum-floored room. Since it will not be possible to take him out every time he desires, you can start the training process by covering the entire floor with newspapers. When he has made a mistake in the house, and has had his error pointed out to him, the soiled papers can be removed and fresh papers put down. (It often helps the puppy focus his attention on one particular spot if a small piece of the soiled paper is left.) Gradually, over a period of several days, reduce the area of floor covered with the newspaper. Before long, the puppy will find only one place in the room where he can relieve himself— and there will be only one place for you to clean up. After this sort of conditioning, removal of the newspaper altogether will perplex the puppy and will stimulate his insistence on being let out; the job is accomplished.

Regular feedings and regular walks after feedings, immediate removal to the outdoors upon committing an error, will all bring about the realization desired, but your watchfulness must not be relaxed for some time. Patience and perseverance will have their rewards, but always remember that the puppy is still just a puppy and should never be severely punished.

Learning His Name. The first thing a puppy should be taught is to know his name. This can be accomplished during the housebreaking period. Select a short name for him and use it every time you address him. Whatever name you select, make sure it is one that will carry well if you later have to shout it at the top of your voice—a possibility, sooner or later. He will soon learn to recognize it. When he responds to the name and comes to you, reward him with a caress or a tidbit. In the early stages of his training call him by name frequently. Always reward him when he responds.

Choosing a name for a dog is not ordinarily thought of as a complicated matter, however, the name for a dog which may someday be registered with the Kennel Club of England ought to be chosen with due consideration. Rules of the Kennel Club of England prohibit some names from use and also limit the frequency of changing a dog's registered name. As an example, this Club advises against using the names of notable persons, places, kennels, countries, cities, common names, colors, and numbers (either in figures or words). It also prohibits the use of certain prefixes and affixes and allows a change of registered name no oftener than once during the dog's lifetime. (See paragraphs 15 through 19 of the extracted Kennel Club (of England) Regulations appearing in Part XVIII of this volume.)

To Lead. The next step is to accustom him to the leash. Teaching the dog to lead is a simple matter, but before you start, let him become familiar with a collar and leash. If you have more than one puppy, put collars on all of them. After they have become used to the collars, tie short pieces of rag to the collars. The puppies will tug against these streamers in play. This aids in accustoming the puppy to an attachment to his neck.

The collar should be loose enough that you can slip three or four fingers under it, yet tight enough so that it won't slide off over the puppy's head. Be sure to check the collar occasionally; puppies grow at a rapid rate and a collar that was all right ten days ago may be too tight now.

After he has become used to his collar, see that it is tight enough not to slip over his head and tie or chain him in a comfortable place where he cannot become tangled up or choke himself. Leave him to his own devices for a short period several times a day. He will soon stop his efforts to break away and come to realize that the leash or chain means that he no longer has his liberty.

After a few days of this, attach a leash to his collar, call him to your side and start for a stroll. He may desire to remain behind and will pull or plunge against the lead. Continue your walk, however, pulling him along with you and he will soon learn it is useless to struggle and more comfortable to come along than to be dragged. When he ceases to struggle, pet him and reward him. If he becomes frightened, reassure him, call him to you and reward him with a tidbit. Avoid taking him into strange surroundings for a while, and as you walk along, talk to him in a low, kindly tone, frequently petting him. Soon he will come to like these strolls and associate the leash with them.

To Come When Called. Learning to come when called by voice or whistle is next. Do not expect your young puppy to pick up this accomplishment immediately. He is still a playful, inquisitive youngster and should be allowed to develop naturally. If you crowd him too much, you may break his spirit. True, he has learned his name and will come to you when called ... provided he wants to and is not too interested in doing something else. Your object is to have him come to you when he doesn't want to. This lesson may well be postponed until the dog has reached the age of eight or nine months, or even older.

Take the young dog outside. Attach to his collar a light check cord 20 to 30 feet long. Sash cord from the hardware store, or light nylon parachute cord is ideal. Allow him to have a short romp. When his attention is attracted to something, *call him by name* and give the command "Come." If he responds, pat him, praise him, and allow him to continue his romp. Repeat this two or three times.

Presently he will become tired of having his pleasure interfered with and will refuse to come when ordered. Grasp the end of the check cord, repeat the command "Come", and give the cord a sharp jerk. He will probably try to resist, but keep giving the command, and a few sharp jerks will probably bring

him in to you. If he does not come, pull him in to you. Reward him with a tidbit and caresses. Repeat this several times and stop the lesson.

Do not allow a lesson to last too long. This can be repeated several times a day, but having him come to you three or four times in one session is sufficient. If he should sulk and remain with you, do not become discouraged. In such event, place him in his kennel or box. He will probably welcome the return as he wants to get away from you. Leave the kennel door or gate open and allow him to settle in his bunk. Then call his name, giving the command "Come."

HI-FIDO, a unique, patented teaching tool for dog owners, is a small special chain weighing less than four ounces and containing a built-in tuning fork, producing a sound just above the dog's conscious hearing range—at the subliminal level. Its producer describes the device as extremely effective both for stopping a dog's nuisance habits and teaching him various obedience commands. (For full information, write to Canine Behavior Institute, 11927 Montana Ave., Los Angeles, Calif., 90049.) Photo courtesy, Canine Behavior Institute.

When he fails to respond, jerk sharply on the cord and bring him to you, rewarding him as usual. With patience he will soon learn that he *must* come when his name is called. Never, under any circumstances, punish a dog after he comes to you. If punishment is necessary, take it to him. Never administer it when he has come to you voluntarily.

After a while, the whistle can be substituted for the voice, if you desire. The main advantage of introducing the dog to whistle commands is that he can then be controlled from a far greater distance. This is especially valuable when working with a hunting dog.

To Sit. This lesson, like all others, should be given in some quiet place where there are no distracting influences. And, like others, it should not be given until the dog is old enough to understand what you want him to do.

With the dog standing in front of you or by your side, hold the leash in your right hand and give the command "Sit" or "Hup," as you prefer. At the same time lean over and with your left hand press down steadily on his rump until he is in a sitting position. He may want to lie down or flop over on his side. Straighten him up with your left hand on his flank, or pull him up with the leash. As soon as he is in proper sitting position, slip a tidbit in his mouth and praise him. Do not keep him in this position long at first, but cluck to him and when he rises pet him again. Repeat this ritual several times, using the same command and pressing down on his rump. Always reward him at the right time. Soon he will associate the command with the pressure and anticipate it by sitting without being touched. You can then begin keeping him in a sitting position for longer periods of time. Never make this lesson too long. It can be practiced several times a day, however.

After a while the dog will instantly respond to the command and you can begin substituting the raising of a warning finger for the word "Sit." If desired, a short whistle can also be substituted.

When the dog has learned to "Sit," you may teach him to "stay" by placing him in the sitting position and gradually backing away from him, giving the command "Stay." He will probably try to move with you, but you must patiently replace him in the "Sit" position in the original place, repeating the command "Stay." This lesson is learned fairly easily after the dog knows what you want him to do, for generally he is anxious to please.

Finally, after considerable drilling, the dog may be taught to remain sitting for long periods of time and even after you have passed from sight.

Down. After you have taught him to "Sit," it is not difficult to teach him what "down" means. With one hand, hold the dog by the collar, give the command "Down," and press down on his rump with the other. When he is sitting, use the right hand to pull his front feet out from under him while you still press down on him with your left hand. Another way is to hold the leash taut with your right hand and press

down on the dog's shoulder with the left hand, as you give the command "Down." Give the command "Up" when you allow him to rise.

Repetition of this practice will soon teach the dog to drop to the ground at the command "Down" and then you may raise the hand when giving the command. Finally, all that is needed to cause the dog to drop is to bring the hand into an upraised position. The dog should then be taught to remain in the "Down" position for lengthened periods of time.

The accomplishments "Sit" and "Down" are especially valuable when you are in the presence of others who are not familiar with dogs. These niceties are easy to teach and no dog is really well-mannered without them.

To Heel. A dog that has been taught to walk directly behind you at "heel" or at your side, preferably, has an accomplishment that will be quite useful in taking him along city streets or through crowded areas. Place the dog on a short lead. Having him walk with his head near your left knee is preferred as your right side is free and you have him under continual observance. Walk along, and as he tries to go in front of you, tap him lightly on the nose with a limber switch or a folded newspaper and give the command "Heel." Repeat this every time he tries to pass you and he will soon learn that he must walk at your side or directly behind you at the command "Heel." Most dogs learn this accomplishment fairly easily, but do not expect to perfect your dog in this accomplishment without much practice. Postpone these lessons until your puppy has lost some of his puppy ways, for too much restraint is not good for any young dog.

Jumping Up. Most young puppies like to jump up on their masters and many masters erroneously encourage this. After the dog has passed his puppy stage and is approaching maturity, he must be discouraged from this enthusiastic display of affection; no one likes a dog's muddy feet smearing clean clothing and such a practice will become a source of

Teaching the dog to "come." Photo by Evelyn M. Shafer.

Teaching the dog to "drop" or "down." Photo by Evelyn M. Shafer.

embarrassment to you. Many try to stop the dog from doing this by treading lightly on his hind feet. Often this is successful, but sometimes it is not. A more direct method is to bring your knee sharply up against the dog's chest as he tries to rear up on you. This gives him a sharp, disturbing blow which will discourage him or throw him off balance without hurting him and he soon learns to keep all feet on the ground when he is around people.

It should be pointed out that neither of these methods will be necessary if the basic groundwork for training has been laid. The dog under control will hesitate in whatever he is doing, even if it is jumping up to greet his master, if the word "No" is given sharply. This admonition, followed by the command "Down" will keep the trained dog on the ground.

Barking. This habit (and it can become just that) often becomes annoying to both owner and neighbors. It reflects on the owner as well as the dog. The chronic barker presents quite a problem. If the dog has a habit of barking needlessly at night, give him his big meal in the evening, as feeding often has a quieting effect.

If he persists in barking at strangers, he cannot be entirely condemned for this as it is his nature to warn of intruders. He should be cautioned in a kind voice and reassured. If the owner is present, the bark can be anticipated and the dog cautioned to be quiet before he becomes noisy.

If the dog barks needlessly in the kennel, the provision of a kennel mate may stop this. Barking, however, sometimes seems to be contagious. If repeated reprimands fail to cause a cessation, dousing the dog with water generally will, and many kennel owners keep a pail of water handy for just this purpose. Others run a wire or rope from the kennel to the house, arranging it so that a pull on the rope rings a bell or causes a piece of iron to bang against the kennel house. Occasionally, an owner finds it necessary to install a loud speaker in the kennel so that he can reprimand his dogs without leaving his bedroom.

If you have a friend from whom you can borrow a remote-controlled shock collar, you may find it worthwhile to resort to this device. Expense, however, seldom makes it reasonable to invest in one for the training of a single dog. When the dog begins his senseless, objectionable barking, you can deliver an unpleasant electrical shock by pressing the button on the transmitter unit. With many dogs, one or two shocks at the appropriate times will cure the problem; with others, it should be noted, the electrical shock itself may instead bring on a worse paroxysm of unrestrained barking.

As a last resort, a muzzle made from a leather strap buckled around his muzzle and attached to his collar may be used to stop the barking dog. It can be so attached as to allow him to drink and breathe freely. A few applications of this frequently teaches the dog to refrain from needless barking.

The problem is never an easy one to solve and various methods often must be tried before a cure is effected. Some dogs are highly nervous, and are persistent barkers. Out of consideration for their neighbors, owners of such dogs must either eventually replace them or never allow them to be left alone.

Chasing. Almost any dog, allowed to run loose, will take to chasing something. In the city, this is usually automobiles or neighborhood children. In rural areas, dogs often chase cars or take up hunting by themselves. Since most communities today have "leash laws" requiring that dogs be kept either in an enclosed yard or on a lead, you may be in violation of the law if you allow your dog to run free. In addition, you are endangering your pet's life and certainly not endearing yourself with neighbors. In the country, most states empower their conservation officers to kill any dog seen harassing game animals. The most certain cure for a dog that chases cars, children or animals, is to keep the dog confined or controlled.

As to dogs chasing cars, their mortality rate is a lot higher than most owners may realize for a great many dogs are killed every year this way accidentally. Dogs that chase bicycles, as for example those belonging to neighborhood children, are not only a hazard to the youngsters, but will in all likelihood as quickly chase cars. Here again, the electronic shock collar is a valuable and quick way of breaking the habit, but you must be able to catch the dog in the act when using it.

There are other methods, but what works well with one offender does not always work equally well on another. Tying a long rope around the body of a notorious car chaser so it will bring him to an abrupt and inglorious halt short of the street or road is one method, the other rope end being either held ready by the owner, staked to the ground, or tied to a tree. In other cases, hampering the dog's running by suspending a T-shaped piece of lead pipe from his collar in front of him where it will strike his legs may eventually discourage him. Another method, seldom mentioned, involves having a friend deliberately ride by in a car somewhat in a "decoy" role, and equipped so that he can give the dog's face a strong blast of liquid ammonia as he comes charging forth. This may cure the habit. Other owners merely rely on punishing the dog as quickly as possible with some whipping and scolding, followed immediately by confinement for a time. Repeated enough, the dog eventually realizes his error. The "decoy" system can be worked with this method, too, *sans* ammonia.

Regrettably, however, it may also be noted that a good many dogs run over while chasing cars prove to be dogs that were originally tied up, but by means of an insufficiently stout rope or chain which broke or gave way.

Yet where the dog is kept confined or tied up securely against such temptations, about the worst he can do is bark. Still, in summary, let us not forget that nuisance behavior of this kind in a dog is a sign that he has received actually very little basic obedience training, probably, and this the owner should rectify.

Part V

DOG SHOWS—HOW TO TRAIN AND SHOW YOUR DOG

Breeding and exhibiting pure-bred dogs has become a worldwide sport. In general, it can be said that dog shows are being held in all nations except some of the newly-created African states, and those of the Communist persuasion, where dogs are a prohibited status symbol.

—World Dog Show Systems—

IN THE Western Hemisphere, dog shows are being held as far north as Fairbanks, Alaska, just below the Arctic Circle, and as far south as Buenos Aires, Argentina, and Montevideo, Uruguay. Dog shows are also given in Norway and Sweden, in Rhodesia and South Africa, in Japan, Hong Kong, India and Ceylon, and in Australia, Tasmania, and New Zealand.

SHOWS IN ENGLISH-SPEAKING COUNTRIES

Dog show procedures vary from country to country. This is true both of the classes offered, and in the systems of awarding championship points. Some countries permit bitches with nursing litters to be entered and judged. Some permit puppies as young as two months to be entered. Still others follow the American system which permits only puppies which are six months old or older.

Canada. The system of awarding championship points in Canada is very similar to the method used in the United States. In Canada, championship points are awarded on the basis of the number of dogs of each sex entered. And this is, in turn, based upon the popularity of the breeds. That is, the number of dogs competing must be measurably greater in popular breeds than in less popular ones.

Thus, it might require an entry of 25 males competing in order that the winner's dog be given five championship points, whereas only seven or eight competitors would be required in a relatively rare breed.

In Canada, a dog must win ten championship points to become a champion, whereas 15 points are required in the United States. A dog must win at least two shows with a rating of three points or better. These are called "majors," and they must be won under different judges.

Canadian rules require best-of breed winners to compete in the variety groups. The penalty for not doing so is the loss of ratings won earlier.

Bermuda. In recent years, shows in Bermuda have become very popular. These are usually a series of three or more shows, all held within a period of one week. They are held during November, and they draw dogs from both the United States and Canada as well as European entries.

Bermuda shows are held under Bermuda Kennel Club rules, and Bermudan championships are awarded. (See text, Part XVIII, re Bermuda Kennel Club.)

Nassau, The Bahamas, is also hosting a series of shows annually. The procedure is basically that used in the United States.

Great Britain. Dog shows in Great Britain are on the average the largest in the world. Among the reasons for this is the fact that the English have excelled for centuries as animal breeders and hobbyists. Another is the large population concentrated in a relatively small area. This means that there dog shows are more easily reached than they are in some other countries.

The Cruft's Show, which is held annually in London in February, is the world's largest dog show. It is a two-day event with an entry exceeding 7,000 individual dogs. Roughly half of these are shown each day.

The English system of awarding championships is more widely copied than any other. It is based upon the awarding of challenge certificates. To become a champion, a dog must win three of these. These can be awarded regardless of the number of dogs competing. However, challenge certificates cannot be awarded automatically at championship shows.

There are only 23 General Championship Shows annually in Great Britain. Other all-breed shows are called Open Shows. Besides the General Championship Shows, there is one for all hounds, and another for all terriers.

In addition, the more popular breeds are permitted to hold Specialist Club Championship Shows. These are based on breed registrations for the previous year. Highest number of Specialist Club Championship Shows is given to Miniature and Toy Poodles, with ten each. German Shepherds (called Alsatians in Great Britain) and English Cocker Spaniels are permitted nine each.

Most of those breeds which are allowed any Specialist Club Championship Shows at all, are permitted only two or three. About half the breeds get none.

Challenge certificates are not automatically available at all 23 General Championship Shows. The number of sets of challenge certificates (one for dogs and one for bitches) is worked out on the basis of registrations for the previous year.

Because of their immense popularity, Miniature and Toy Poodles receive challenge certificates at all 23 General Championship Shows, plus ten sets at their Specialist Club shows.

Reasonably popular breeds might receive 14 sets of challenge certificates, and would not be permitted Specialist shows. Less popular breeds might be permitted only four sets of challenge certificates. And the very rare breeds would get none.

This means that breeds which are rare in Great Britain, such as the Belgian Sheepdog, Siberian Husky, or American Cocker Spaniel, could never produce a champion in Great Britain. Such breeds are not considered sufficiently strong to deserve one.

At shows held under the American system, champions can usually enter in the open class, but they seldom do, since it is usually considered unsporting to "rob another dog" of points. So champions enter a special class for champions, usually called "Specials Only." This means they are competing for special awards only. That is, for best-of-breed and higher honors.

But this is not the case at shows held in Great Britain. Champions and non-champions must there compete together. Thus, the winner of the challenge certificate may have to defeat a dozen champions at that show.

SHOWS IN CONTINENTAL EUROPE

Continental European shows vary widely in procedure. Some twenty nations give more or less regular shows. Two types of championships are awarded. The first is a national championship. It requires the winning of four challenge certificates. There is no requirement for competition.

The award of a C.C. is almost automatic, since continental judges seldom withhold a C.C. for lack of merit. Thus, the winning of a "national" championship is not necessarily a great honor. In this sense, "national" means only a local championship in a given country.

Of far greater importance is the winning of an "International Championship." Such awards can be earned at shows approved for this purpose by the Federation Canine International.

This organization issues a type of challenge certificate called the C.A.C.I.B., which is simply called the CACIB. To become an international champion, a dog must win four CACIB's under four different approved judges.

The Federation Canine International can license a show to award CACIBs in all breeds, and even in some cases, in breeds not recognized by the Federation.

A judge need not award a CACIB if he feels the dog lacks sufficient merit. But in practice, Continen-

Am. Ch. Quaker Acres Eventide, going Best in Show at Bogota, Colombia, South America, 1967, handled by Senora Yolanda Vargas.

tal judges appear less likely to withhold awards than may, say, English judges.

Nevertheless, in the major breeds, competition is severe, and the dogs which win championships are truly deserving of them.

It should be pointed out here that a dog cannot rightly be called an international champion unless he has won the four CACIBs. It would not be correct, therefore, to call a dog an international champion which has won Canadian and American championships. The term "international champion" is the property of the Federation Canine International.

SHOWS PATTERNED ON THE ENGLISH SYSTEM

In general, it can be said that countries of the former British Empire follow the system set up for dog shows in Great Britain. To a certain extent, they will have followed Great Britain in the variety and popularity of the dogs. British terrier interest has always been high. It generally remains so in the former colonies, except where climate plays a heavy influence.

The most popular breeds in Great Britain are the Miniature and Toy Poodles, the English Cocker Spaniel, and the German Shepherd. Climate affects coat, and consequently Poodle popularity will be less in some of the tropical countries. German Shepherds and Boxers are universally popular.

Countries and colonies using the English system are South Africa, East Africa, Rhodesia, Ceylon, India, Hong Kong, Singapore, Malaysia, and perhaps a few others.

Almost all countries using the English system have, however, varied the procedures to suit their local requirements.

Australia. The separate Australian states have control councils which govern dog activities in their respective states. In an effort to achieve uniformity, each council is now sending delegates to a national body.

Victoria, for example, elects 40 delegates to its Kennel Control Council. This Council licenses shows, governs the procedure of shows, and licenses judges. Classes, up to five, are allotted according to the popularity of the breed.

These are 6 to 9 months and 9 to 12 months' puppies, graduate, junior, and open. A popular breed would have five classes.

Formerly a dog had to win four challenge certificates under four different judges. But now a dog must win 100 points. These are based upon challenge certificates, with the best dog and bitch each receiving one.

A challenge certificate carries a basic rating of ten points. The winner of the certificate is then allowed one point for each dog in competition, but including the basic ten. However, a maximum of 25 points is allowed at any given show. There are no separate classes for champions.

A club is allowed one championship show a year. In addition, specialty and semi-specialty clubs may be

The Sporting Dog Group, Club Canino Colombiano, Bogota, Colombia, South America. Photo by Alemana.

licensed to give a championship show, and so may be the agricultural societies.

In Victoria alone there are between 130 and 140 clubs affiliated with the Kennel Control Council. Australia's two largest shows are the Melbourne and Sydney Royals, which are held with their respective Royal Agricultural Fairs.

The two shows last for roughly a week, and vie for entry leadership with some 3,500 dogs each. Other shows vary in entries from 200 to 1,000 and may be one or two-day events.

New Zealand and Tasmania. New Zealand and Tasmania follow systems roughly the same as those used by the Australian states.

JAPAN AND SOUTH AMERICA

As early as 1920, Japan began to import German Shepherds on a large scale. These were trained for police and war work. To a certain extent, Boxers, Doberman Pinschers, Collies, and Airedales were imported and trained for the same purposes. All these breeds have been recognized and used for these purposes by the Nippon Police Dog Association.

It was not until the end of World War II, however, that Japan became a major fancier of show dogs. American occupation forces brought in a variety of dogs. And suddenly the Japanese, always artisans and fanciers of the highest class, became passionately interested in the sport.

They began again to import German Shepherds from Germany. They brought in large numbers of terriers from England, plus Airedales from the United States. And then they began to import large numbers of Boxers, Doberman Pinschers, Poodles, and sporting dogs from the United States.

Japan's own national breed, the Akita, has gained such popularity that it is now being imported into the United States. Akitas, in three sizes, each resembling the more-familiar Husky, are presently being shown in the U.S. as a Miscellaneous Breed.

Japanese dog shows are based primarily on the

American system. It is not unusual to find four or five American champions entered for competition in a single breed.

The importation of German Shepherds into Australia was prohibited about 1935. In most other areas of the world today, the German Shepherd has become the most popular breed. This is true in South America. In Brazil, for example, one may see up to 200 German Shepherds at a single show.

The South American countries are the most highly individual in their variations on dog show procedures. They may follow either the English or the American-Canadian systems, or they may use combinations of both.

Brazil. The Brazilian system is of most interest. Classes vary according to age. Dogs are rated Excellent, Very Good, Good, or Sufficient.

If the judge wishes, he may give a rating of Excellent to more than one dog. But in that case, he must place the dogs Excellent-one, Excellent-two, etc. Gold and silver medals are also awarded.

An Excellent-one, gold medal, is usually equivalent to a challenge certificate. To become a champion, a dog needs to win four challenge certificates under different judges.

The dog can be given a challenge certificate even if he gets an Excellent-two rating. But to become a champion, he would have to win at least one Excellent-one, gold medal.

As a rule, champions would always receive an Excellent rating. But the judge must judge them as a class. And he would therefore have to place them one, two, three, and four. And, conceivably, he could give a champion a lower rating, such as Very Good, or Good.

The American system of groups and best-in-show is used.

Venezuela. Venezuela uses a modified American system, which was also used in Cuba before Castro ended dog shows there. Under this system, in rare breeds, or in one in which competition is not great, the judge can award not more than three championship points.

This works out in the following way.

A point system, based on registrations and upon show entries is worked out on a similar system to that used in the United States.

Under it, a breed might require ten males for a three-point major win. But only three males are entered. The judge might then say that the dog is worth three points. And he could then award three points.

However, the dog, to become a champion, would have to win at least one show in which he defeated an entry making up three points or better.

Colombia. Colombia, which has perhaps the widest variety of good dogs of any of the South American countries, uses a system very close to that of the United States and Canada. The major variation is in the classes themselves.

Other South American Shows. Dog shows are also being held in Argentina, Uruguay, Chile, and Peru. The Island of Trinidad also conducts shows. All these countries import dogs from the United States, Canada, England, and Germany.

—Bench Shows—

DOG SHOWS in the United States, starting as a scattered half-dozen poorly regulated events in the 1870's, have grown to a place of importance in the national sports world.

There are approximately 1,000 championship point shows held in the United States and possessions each year and, in addition, well over 700 "match" shows. Participating in these events are approximately one-third of a million dogs, about 5,500 dog show judges and 7,000 professional handlers who look to this sport as a major source of income.

HISTORICAL NOTES

The history of this sport or hobby has been, in effect, the history of the American Kennel Club, an association of several hundred clubs under whose rules a system of organized dog shows was started in this country.

This organization, through its delegates, representing show-giving member clubs, has evolved an extensive set of rules which regulate all American Kennel Club shows. From time to time, these rules and regulations are amended by the delegates to meet changing conditions. The present American system of dog shows is unique and was created by the fanciers themselves through their membership in accredited show-giving clubs.

The oldest club in the United States with a continuous record of annual dog shows is the Westminster Kennel Club of New York City. Its first event was held in 1877 and American Kennel Club records say that a show was also held in Philadelphia that year. The following year shows were held in Baltimore, Boston, and New York. While the sport grew continuously, it has experienced a greater growth during the last twenty years than it did during the first fifty years of American Kennel Club records. In fact, as recently as 1918, there were but seventy championship shows held in the country.

SHOWS AND BREED IMPROVEMENT

Like horse racing, the primary purpose of dog shows is "for the improvement of the breed." While today's average exhibitor doubtless is more moved by the profit or prestige motive of an important win than by this lofty purpose, the fact remains that the more than 100 breeds of dogs which are recognized by the American Kennel Club have undergone remarkable improvement in type, conformation, and temperament. The almost constant presence of America's breeding stock before the eye of critical dog-show judges and discriminating fanciers has achieved amazing effects. A comparison of photographs of top-winning dogs of any breed 35 years ago with todays' winners dramatically proves that dog-show competition has produced gratifying results.

The American Kennel Club publishes a standard of perfection for each breed which it recognizes, and serious breeders constantly strive to meet this standard. It is through competition in the show ring that breeders learn how well they are succeeding in their effort.

AKC SHOWS

All American Kennel Club shows fall into one of two main classes, so-called "point" shows and match shows. Point shows may be undertaken by a club only after it has satisfactorily conducted a series of match shows. The latter are generally quite informal and are designed primarily for the pleasure of local club members and exhibitors. Young dogs frequently receive their first show experience at match shows.

Each member club in the American Kennel Club organization is entitled to conduct at least one "point" show each year. Such shows are known as member shows. Non-member clubs which can qualify may obtain a license from the American Kennel Club to offer a show of the same type. Such shows are designated licensed shows.

It is at these member or licensed shows that the real competition occurs. Entries are accepted at most of these shows from any of the AKC-recognized breeds. Specialty clubs, devoted to a single breed, offer shows only for the breed they represent.

The scheduling of many hundreds of shows so as to avoid conflicts is the responsibility of the American Kennel Club. A complete set of regulations guides the show-giving club in laying out its program. Its premium list and entry blank (the forms upon which exhibitors enter their dogs for a show) are of a prescribed form, and must contain certain American Kennel Club rules, as well as rules which may be adopted by the show-giving club. The premium list constitutes the contract between the exhibitor and the show. As we shall see later, this is an important point in the regulatory system of the American Kennel Club.

Catalogues, which are sold at the show and which identify each dog as to ownership, breeding, age, and description, also are of a form prescribed by the American Kennel Club.

In Hope of Championship Credits. Though certain of the larger shows offer very attractive cash and trophy prizes, a consistent exhibitor does not expect his prize rewards to go very far toward covering the expense of exhibiting dogs. At present, the fee for entering a dog in one class at a show ranges from $5 to $8. In addition, there is a small recording fee which is remitted by the show-giving club to the American Kennel Club. This fee is used to help defray the expense of recording in the American Kennel Club's permanent files the exact win of each dog in the show.

It is the building up of such a record of important wins for a dog, rather than the prize lure, that causes exhibitors to "campaign" dogs at show after show. Frequently, it is to the advantage of an owner to turn his promising dog or dogs over to a professional handler who devotes his full time to the conditioning and showing of dogs at American Kennel Club shows. As has been mentioned, this sport of showing dogs is so extensive as to provide chief support for several thousand professional handlers. Even so, most show dogs are handled by owners.

The present policy of the American Kennel Club in the licensing of shows does not permit two clubs which are less than 200 miles apart to schedule their shows on the same day. However, neighboring clubs frequently do arrange their plans so as to share a weekend, one club holding a show on Saturday and a nearby club offering its show on Sunday. These have become known as weekend doubles and they occur frequently. Thus, an exhibitor or professional handler who is following the sport to the limit may enter in almost 100 shows in a year.

Before attempting to describe a dog show, it may be well to point out that the urge which sends thousands of exhibitors to dog shows week after week is not the hope of winning a blue ribbon! True, a blue ribbon, for first prize, is highly valued and may possi-

High point of a show for this youngster and his dog. Hank Babbit photo.

bly represent a very high distinction. But, that which is most avidly sought is credit toward a championship.

To earn the championship title, the "Ch." which is frequently shown as a prefix with a dog's name, it must prove its superiority over a certain number of other dogs, under different judges, at a number of shows. The title can be gained through wins at three shows; more often it requires thirteen tries; sometimes thirty—or even twice that number. Thus, there are two kinds of champions; those which are so superior as to complete their title promptly, and those which earn it the hard way.

This system of awarding championships has been discussed, pro and con, for years and years and, despite its obvious shortcomings, the fancy seems to consider it the most satisfactory system yet devised. It is true that a fairly good dog exhibited by a determined owner can earn the coveted title "Champion" through persistence. Such a dog then enjoys the same

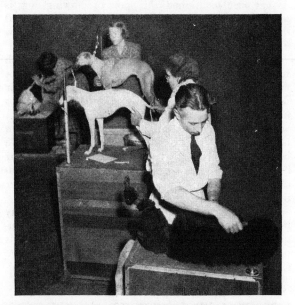

A typical scene in the grooming corner of a bench show where owners and handlers make final preparations for the show ring.

rank as one which has gone to three large shows and defeated every dog of its breed.

But breeders, exhibitors, and followers of the sport have a way of remembering where and how these championships were made and dogs become known as "quick champions," "easy champions" and "circuit champions" (dogs taken on tour, from show to show, until they have earned the required points).

Visiting A Typical Show. You go to your first show. There is noise and confusion. People are rushing hither and yon with dogs. Others are sitting in little groups visiting as quietly as they might in a restful corner of the park. One group seems excited and incensed over some disappointment. It all seems puzzling. Dogs are sitting and lying on benches, hurrying

down the aisles with their handlers, standing on their shipping crates being groomed in preparation for showing, others already in the judging ring being posed, gaited, examined—all this is part of the dog show; but the system which makes it work isn't so apparent.

To get a good understanding of the sport, let's choose just one of the scores of breeds at this show and spend our day with it. Let's spend the day with the Irish Setters, a great favorite with the public. We buy a catalog and in the index note that there are 50 representatives of this breed entered. We also see that the breed is to be judged at 11 o'clock, so we have plenty of time to stroll around and examine the dogs.

Going to the benches which may be in a room apart from the arena in which dogs are being judged or may be arranged along the walls of the arena room, we find a section marked "Irish Setters." Near this section we also see the Pointers, English Setters, Spaniels, Retrievers, and other breeds which are defined by the American Kennel Club as Sporting Dogs. Row upon row of proud red dogs greet us as we pass them sitting or lying in their stalls.

Some are being brushed in preparation for an early appearance in the ring; others are eagerly watching all who pass while their owners sit nearby; still others, the seasoned campaigners, are stretched out in peaceful slumber with the knowledge that there need be no excitement—that in due time they'll be prepared for their big moment in the ring.

Here is a dog being led away from its bench and we decide to follow. We arrive at a corner of the building where perhaps a hundred dog crates are arranged in neat rows and atop almost every crate is a dog being brushed and groomed. This is the professional handlers' corner. Each of them has arrived by car, station wagon or by truck with from several to a couple dozen dogs.

For the comfort of the dogs and to permit their being handled in large numbers, handlers almost invariably transport their charges in especially built crates. The rules of the show require that all dogs be kept on their benches except when being exhibited or when being exercised or prepared for the rings. Nearby are two exercise rings, one for each sex, where the dogs may relieve themselves.

After watching the handlers brush and comb and do some last minute trimming, we find a seat and give our catalog some further study. We find a chapter devoted to our favorite breed and there are listed all the particulars on the 50 dogs which we expect to see.

The dogs are listed under eleven different class headings and each dog is assigned a catalog number. In the class headings, the term "dog" refers only to the males. There is a class for puppies (often divided into two classes for puppies from six to nine months and puppies from nine to twelve months of age), another class for novice dogs, one for American-bred dogs, another for bred-by-exhibitor dogs, and a class for open dogs. We find there are similar classes for the bitches, that is, puppy bitches, novice bitches, and so on. Finally, there is an eleventh class called "Specials for Best of Breed."

Immediately following the male classes, there is a line entitled "Winners Dog," with a space in which we may mark the number of the dog so designated. Upon inquiry, we learn that after the male classes are judged, the first prize winners in each class excepting those which may have been defeated in another class, are brought together in the Winners class and best of these blue-ribbon winners is chosen. That dog is known as the "Winners Dog."

And, that dog wins credit toward its championship!

There are strict requirements and conditions governing a dog's eligibility to compete in each of these five regular classes. It is not uncommon for an exhibitor to make an improper entry. If a dog should win the Winners class after having been improperly entered, the American Kennel Club will catch the error when auditing the report of the show and the win will be cancelled.

To cover that contingency, another dog is designated "Reserve Winners Dog" by the judge. If the winner is disqualified, the Reserve dog is advanced to the position of Winner.

After the Winners dog has been chosen, the judge selects his Reserve Winner from among the remaining blue ribbon dogs plus such other dog as has been defeated only by the Winners dog (the dog which was second to the Winners dog when it won its blue ribbon).

If a dog is improperly entered or is in any way ineligible to compete as entered, any win which the dog makes at that show is automatically cancelled by the American Kennel Club; and all dogs which have been placed below the disqualified dog are advanced one position in their wins.

Complete reports of all shows are filed with the American Kennel Club within seven days after the show and the full results, after auditing and corrections, are published in the club's official magazine, *The American Kennel Gazette,* within about 90 days.

When a win is disallowed, all exhibitors who are affected by it are notified by the American Kennel Club and they are required to surrender their ribbons, trophies, and prizes so that proper allocations may be made.

Returning now to our ringside seat, we will observe the judging of the first class, the puppy dog class. Sitting at a table inside the ring is the judge. He has applied to the American Kennel Club for a license to judge this breed. After investigation of his knowledge and character, the license was granted to him. A complete record of his judging activity is on file at the American Kennel Club, and before he was approved to judge this particular show it was determined that he was not scheduled to judge this breed within 200 miles of this location during the preceding or succeeding thirty-day period.

This safeguard is an obvious one. If he were permitted to judge the breed in one locality week after

week, the succeeding results of each show would be almost foregone conclusions, as judges do take rightful pride in being consistent.

The American Kennel Club does not select or engage judges for shows. Each show-giving club makes its own selection from among the thousands licensed by the American Kennel Club.

On the table beside the judge are envelopes containing ribbons and, sometimes, prize money for each of the classes which he is to pass upon. There is also a judge's book, especially prepared by the superintendent or the show secretary. In this book appear the catalog numbers of each dog which is to be brought before the judge. The pages are in triplicate; one copy being the American Kennel Club's, one copy for the judge, and the third copy for the show-giving club.

The second person in the ring is the steward. Like the judge, he wears a badge designating his duty. He is the judge's assistant, though he is not permitted to discuss the dogs with the judge. It is his responsibility to see that the proper dogs come into the ring when the judge is ready for them. He is supplied with a catalog so that he may identify dogs by name and by owner and, as the judge knows the dogs only by number, it is the steward's responsibility to see that each dog which enters is shown under the proper number. Arm bands bearing the catalog number of each entry are given to each handler as he enters the ring.

It is also the steward's duty to see that the proper ribbons and trophies are laid out on the table and ready for the judge to present at the conclusion of the judging of each class. Following that, he also marks the winners' numbers on the large blackboard which stands in the corner of the ring.

Aiding the steward at the gate of the ring is a ring-runner. Runners are familiar with the arrangement of benching, and if all dogs entered in a class are not waiting at the gate when the class is called, they go to the benches, which also bear the catalog numbers, and find the missing dogs.

Our puppy dogs (let's say there are five between 9 and 12 months old) now enter the ring with their owners or handlers. The judge motions the handlers to circle the ring counter-clockwise with leashes held in the left hand. The judge stands in the center of the ring and observes the circling dogs.

He calls a halt and has the five dogs lined up in tandem along one side of the ring. The handlers quickly arrange the dogs in proper show stance so as to show each dog's conformation to best advantage. The judge makes a personal examination of each dog, starting with the dog which is first in the line-up. He examines its head, teeth, ears, neck, shoulders, and front feet. Stepping back he runs his hands over the dog's back, feels its girth, examines its coat, continues back and makes a careful examination of its rear quarters.

Then, to the next dog, and so on down the line. Finally, having examined each dog individually, he will ask each handler to gait his dog across the ring and back. He may send the dog over and back several times to make certain that its action is true.

Following this, the judge may choose to have the dogs lined up side by side while he examines them from the front, then from the rear. He may go over them all again with his hands. Finally, the various merits and demerits start taking rank in his mind and he decides that one dog most nearly approaches the standard of perfection for the breed; that another ranks second, and so on.

He then signals four of the handlers to positions which are marked along one side of the ring, 1st, 2nd, 3rd, and 4th. The fifth, unplaced, entrant is excused. The judge goes to the table and marks the judge's book with the ranking which he is to give to each dog. The steward gives him the proper ribbons, prize envelopes and, perhaps, a trophy, and the presentation is made to the four handlers.

Puppy dogs have been judged, and the steward announces that novice dogs are now to come into the ring. Class by class, this procedure is followed until the class winners in each of the male classes and the bitch classes are judged and the Winners dog and Reserve Winners dog as well as the Winners bitch and Reserve Winners bitch are selected.

Then, the Winners dog and the Winners bitch are brought together and the best of the two Winners is chosen. This selection is important for two reasons: First, the Best of Winners selection is entitled to compete for the distinction of Best of Breed. Even more important to some exhibitors is the fact that the Best of Winners dog (or bitch) is entitled to as much credit toward its championship as was earned by the Winner which it just defeated.

Credits toward championships are calculated on a "point" system. A dog is awarded a Championship Certificate by the American Kennel Club when it has won a total of 15 points. The greatest number of points which can be won at any show is five. Furthermore, two of the wins at which the necessary 15 points are won must be 3-point wins (or better) and these two wins must be made under different judges. In addition, some of the remaining wins must be made under a judge other than the two above referred to.

Thus, it is seen that the greatest of dogs must win the Winners dog or Winners bitch class at least three times under three different judges to earn its title.

Point ratings for each breed in five different territorial divisions of the country are established yearly by the American Kennel Club. These ratings are based upon the show records of each breed in the previous year. A breed which is extremely popular and extensively shown will have higher ratings than one of the rare breeds.

These ratings for all breeds are shown in the front of each catalogue for the geographic division in which the particular show is located. We remarked that the Best of Winners selection could be an important one from the standpoint of championship credit. The number of dogs of a sex which are shown deter-

mines the number of championship points which are to be awarded to the winner in that sex. Thus, 20 dogs entered and shown in the classes to which we have referred, may carry a point rating of three. Twenty-five dogs of the opposite sex might carry a point rating of four. The Winner in each sex is credited accordingly; but if the Winner which has won 3 points should be chosen over the 4-point winner for the *Best* of Winners, then it would be credited with a 4-point win—because it had defeated a 4-point winner of the opposite sex.

Except for the Best of Winners dog (or bitch) all dogs which are now to be judged for the honor of Best of Breed are champions. Only champions are permitted to be entered for this special prize, though the Best of Winners dog automatically competes.

Sometimes show-giving clubs include in their program some extra classes such as a class for dogs locally owned or for dogs which have won a prize in a field trial. These classes are judged before the Best of Breed is selected and the winners of these classes must compete for the special prize for Best of Breed. They seldom win it because they must meet the Best of Winners which has already proved its superiority over all the dogs entered in the regular classes. Furthermore, entries from these extra classes may be confronted with one to a dozen champions when they reach for the special Best of Breed prize.

While only champions may be specifically entered for the special prize for Best of Breed, it does not follow that the regular classes to which we have referred are for non-champions only. The Open dog class and the Open bitch class do not bar champions from entry.

Following the awarding of the Best of Breed prize, the judge selects the best dog of the opposite sex to his Best of Breed winner. It is designated "Best of Opposite Sex to Best of Breed."

With the completion of breed judging, we discover that a larger ring has been set up at our backs and that shortly we will see the judging of the Sporting Group. Best of Breed winners from all the recognized breeds in this group are brought together. It is frequently asked how a judge can decide that the Irish Setter entrant is better than, say, the Brittany Spaniel. The answer is that he is expected to have in his mind a picture of the perfect specimen of each breed in the group and rank the dogs according to their

The final judging phase in a Detroit dog show. Hank Babbitt phot

...uccess is encouraging. These winners in a county 4-H project will ...ably consider entering their dogs in other shows. Hank Babbitt ...to.

approximation to that perfect representative as defined in the standard of the breed. Four awards are made in the group and the first-prize winner then has the privilege of competing for the highest honor in the entire show—the special prize for Best Dog in Show.

The other five groups are judged in the same manner as the Sporting Group. The other groups are: the Hound Group, the Working Group, the Terrier Group, the Toy Group, and the Non-Sporting Group. Each of the more than one hundred recognized breeds falls into one of these six groups. Breed uses or characteristics have determined the group to which each breed is assigned.

The sixth group probably is a misnomer; surely it cannot be said that the Bulldog, for instance, which is a member of this group is less "sporting" than certain other breeds. It is thought that this designation traces to the fact that, in England, dogs were for many years divided into but two groups—sporting and non-sporting. As the sport has developed and grown in this country, many breeds have been removed from the Non-Sporting Group and assigned to more appropriate categories.

Organizing For Successful Shows. The staging of a major dog show calls for vast quantities of special equipment, organizing talent, and the ability to handle countless details. To meet this problem many show-giving clubs engage the service of a licensed superintendent. Other clubs appoint one of their members as their show secretary and this person obtains a license from the American Kennel Club to handle a particular show.

A complete service to clubs is offered by some superintendents—ring equipment, benching, seating. Huge tents for outdoor shows are obtainable from some superintending organizations along with their other services. These other services consist of assisting the club in the preparation of its premium list, printing, and distributing it to the superintendent's own mailing list of exhibitor-prospects.

Superintendents will also take over the job of printing the catalog, handling catalog advertising, the sale of tickets, and the sale of commercial exhibit space at the show.

Whether the show-giving club turns its superintending problem over to one of the 20-odd organizations which are licensed by the American Kennel Club or to one of their members who may undertake the work with volunteer work from his fellow club members, *somebody* must be designated for this work and approved by the American Kennel Club.

The rules of the American Kennel Club clearly define the duties of the superintendent of a show and he is held accountable for the carrying out of these responsibilities. He operates his business under a license which he obtains for a nominal fee but only after proof of his ability and dependability. The license is always subject to revocation and the Board of Directors of the American Kennel Club may fine superintendents for rules violation.

Sharing responsibility with the superintendent is the bench show committee of the show-giving club. This committee is in direct charge of the show, engages the judges, the superintendent, and attends to all arrangements which are not assigned to the superintendent.

In addition, the American Kennel Club grants to the bench show committee some very broad disciplinary powers over the affairs of its own show. This committee is called upon to rule on many questions which are certain to arise at its show. Furthermore, if major rule violations occur at the show, the committee is expected to sit as a court in a determination of such cases. The committee is granted the power to suspend persons from all privileges of the American Kennel Club for conduct at its show which is found to be prejudicial to the best interests of dog shows.

All in all, the hobby or sport of exhibiting dogs is a carefully supervised and regulated enterprise. The system represents a natural evolution of almost three-quarters of a century, a system which is unique to America but a system which the fanciers themselves have devised through trial and error and through their representation in the American Kennel Club.

The list of bench shows held annually in the United States is far too lengthy to include here. Also, the constant change in officers makes the inclusion of such a list impractical. However, information concerning bench show activities in any given area may be obtained by writing the American Kennel Club. 51 Madison Avenue, New York, N.Y. 10010.

GLOSSARY OF DOG SHOW TERMS

ANNUAL SPECIALS: Prizes which are offered by specialty clubs to their members for competition at all (or certain) American Kennel Club shows during the fiscal year of the specialty club.

BENCH: An elevated platform, divided into stalls, on which dogs are kept on exhibit when not being judged.

BENCH SHOW COMMITTEE: The Committee of a show-giving club which is given general responsibility for all arrangements in connection with the show; the Committee to which the

American Kennel Club looks for enforcement of all its rules at the show.

BEST OF WINNERS: The dog (or bitch) which is selected by the judge as the best of all entries in the regular official classes of a breed.

CATALOG: A book which all show-giving clubs are required to publish and which shows the particulars on every dog entered at the show, prizes offered, the scale of championship points awarded at that show, and other data pertinent to the event.

CLASSIFICATION: The list of breeds for which the show offers competition and the classes (regular and special) which are offered.

CHAMPION: The title which the American Kennel Club awards to a dog which has been awarded at least 15 points at licensed or member American Kennel Club shows. Of the 15 points, at least 6 or more points shall be won at two shows with a rating of 3 or more points each. These two 3-point (or better) wins must be made under different judges and

Judging Cocker Spaniels at a Westminster Kennel Club Show in Madison Square Garden, New York City.

the remainder must be awarded by at least one additional judge. Point ratings are determined annually by the American Kennel Club, based upon the extent of competition in each breed. Five points is the maximum which can be won at one show. No dog becomes a Champion until it is so officially recorded by the American Kennel Club.

CIRCUIT: A series of dog shows, the dates for which are arranged through the cooperation of a group of clubs, so as to permit exhibitors to travel from show to show in a direct route. There usually is an interval of a day or two between shows and a circuit may include a dozen or more cities.

CLASSES The "regular official classes of the American Kennel Club" are Puppy, Novice, American-bred, Open, Bred-by Exhibitor, Specials, and Winners. Most shows offer these classes in each sex.

In brief, these classes require the following conditions:

Puppy Class—For dogs between 6 and 12 months of age. At point-giving shows, no dogs under 6 months are exhibited. This class may be further divided into a class for puppies between 6 and 9 months and a class for puppies between 9 and 12 months.

Novice Class—For dogs that have never won a first place in a point-giving show, excepting competition in puppy classes.

American-Bred Class—For dogs, except champions, born in the United States from a mating which occurred in the United States.

Bred-by-Exhibitor—For dogs, except champions, owned and exhibited by the person recorded with the American Kennel Club as the breeder.

Open Class—For all dogs, including champions. (Champions are seldom exhibited here, but rather in the *Specials Class*.) The *Open Class* may be further divided into two or more classes on the basis of weight of the dogs, height, etc.

Specials Class—For champions of record.

Winners Class—No dog is initially entered in the *Winners Class*,

this placing is acquired by the ranking progress previously described.

ENTRY: The signed application of an exhibitor for the admission of his dog to competition at a show; the entry form is the contract between the exhibitor and show-giving club. Also, a term used for the dog so "entered."

GROUP: One of the six main subdivisions into which the American Kennel Club has classified each of the over one hundred breeds which it recognizes. The groups are: Sporting Group, Hound Group, Working Group, Terrier Group, Toy Group, and Non-Sporting Group.

HANDLER: One whose occupation is the exhibiting of dogs for others. Handlers are licensed by the American Kennel Club and are expected to meet certain minimum requirements as to ability and trustworthiness.

JUDGE: The person or persons chosen by the show-giving clubs to determine the relative merits of all dogs entered in their shows. They are licensed, after investigation, by the American Kennel Club, but each show must select its own judging panel. Some judges serve without compensation; others expect a full allowance for their expenses; still others serve professionally and receive a flat fee for their services.

LICENSED SHOW: A show given under American Kennel Club rules and awarding championship points by a club which is not a member of the American Kennel Club.

LISTED DOG: A dog entered at a dog show but which is not registered in the American Kennel Club Stud Book. Such an unregistered dog may be shown three times upon the payment of a "listing fee" for each show. Thereafter, it may not be shown unless the owner can prove that he is unable to register the dog due to technical difficulties (inability to procure a signature, etc.). In such case, the American Kennel Club may grant permanent listing privileges to the dog upon the payment of the above fee whenever shown. The fee is required to cover the added cost of maintaining a record of show wins on a dog which is not included in the registration files.

MEMBER SHOW: A show given by a club which is a member of the American Kennel Club and at which American Kennel Club championship points are awarded.

MISCELLANEOUS CLASS: A class which is offered by many clubs for a certain list of rare breeds which the American Kennel Club does not recognize or provide show classification but which are considered to be pure-bred dogs.

IRREGULAR CLASSES: Classes other than the regular official classes of the American Kennel Club which often are provided by show-giving clubs. Such classes are required to be judged after the judging of Best of Winners and the winners of these irregular classes must compete for the special prize for best of breed. Such irregular classes may be for dogs which have won a field trial, dogs which are locally owned, etc.

PREMIUM LIST: The printed offering of prizes by a show-giving club which is submitted to the prospective exhibitor when his entry is sought.

PROTEST: A written charge which may be filed at a show by an interested person with the superintendent or bench show committee alleging that a certain dog is being shown in violation of American Kennel Club rules. A cash deposit is required. Some protests must be adjudicated immediately by the bench show committee, others may be determined after the closing of the show. Certain protests may also be filed with the American Kennel Club after the show's closing.

RING: The roped-off enclosure (square or rectangular) in which dogs are judged.

RUNNER: One who acts as an assistant at the judging ring and aids the stewards in getting competing dogs into the ring when their classes are called.

RESERVE WINNER: The dog (or bitch) chosen by the judge to be second to the Winners dog or Winners bitch. In case the win of the latter is cancelled, the Reserve Winner is advanced to the position of the dog whose win was cancelled.

RECORDING FEE: A small fee which is collected by the show-giving club and which is remitted to the American Kennel Club to help defray the expense of maintaining the record of each dog.

SANCTIONED MATCH: A less formal show than a licensed or

member show. No championship points are awarded at sanctioned matches and Champions may not compete. Various classes may be provided excepting that nothing resembling the Winners class may be offered.

SHOW SECRETARY: One who acts in the capacity of superintendent for a show-giving club.

SPECIALTY SHOW: A show, offering championship points, for a single breed. These may be licensed or member specialty shows. They may be held only by a specialty club—a club devoted to the improvement of a single breed.

STEWARD: One who acts as ring-assistant to a judge. His duties do not include the judging of dogs.

SUPERINTENDENT: One who acts in a professional capacity in handling many or all the arrangements in connection with a show for a show-giving club.

SPECIAL FOR BEST OF BREED: The highest award which is made within a breed at a dog show. Contrary to the general opinion, it is not a class. It is a special prize for which the specifically entered and otherwise eligible dogs compete. Not being a class, no awards are made other than to the one dog declared Best of Breed.

WINNERS DOG: The dog which is declared to be the best in the Winners class, which class consists of the first prize winners from the other five regular official classes.

WINNERS BITCH: The bitch which is declared to be the best in the Winners class, which class consists of the first prize winners from the other five regular official classes.

—Obedience Trials—

PUBLIC ACCEPTANCE of the statement that "an obedient dog is a joy forever" is probably the reason for the fact that Obedience trials have become so popular a phase of the competitive dog sport.

Obedience has always been insisted upon by careful dog owners, and a certain amount of obedience is of course necessary in field trials and other forms of dog competition.

HISTORICAL NOTES

It is somewhat surprising, except perhaps to teacher-trainers, club guardians, long-time competitors and judges, that what was rated by veterans purely as a fad in 1934, when there existed only a single training class of eight and trials were unofficial, has resulted in more than 600 known training classes and/or organized clubs, scattered from coast to coast. Some of these trials attracted more than 300 entries. Yet it is easy to understand why dog owners are interested in better manners for their pets.

When going through dog records, one finds that from time to time some form of obedience training for competitive purpose has been attempted with the various groups and breeds, but none of the past efforts ever went beyond a small area or a single breed. Due to such restrictions, the public failed to be impressed, and little headway was made, for no form of competition can get far without public appeal.

Obedience trials had been a well-established sport in England for several years, but little was known of their operation in this country. It is understandable, then, that little impression was made in 1934 when a few dog magazines and fewer newspaper dog columnists announced that Mrs. Whitehouse Walker of Mt. Kisco, N.Y., owner of the Carillon Poodles, had returned after an extended study of England's "thrilling" sport, which was open to all breeds, but mainly participated in by Poodles and German Shepherds.

Mrs. Walker, known as the American "mother" of obedience work with dogs, was prompted to make her English study because she had been considerably annoyed around the show rings to hear that "bench show dogs were beautiful but dumb," and was seeking a means to prove the fallacy of this attitude. She felt that the new English obedience work might be the answer, and so sought out the English fancier, Mrs. Grace E. L. Boyd, whose Piperscroft Poodles were not only leading bench show winners in their native land and in the United States, but were also doing exceptionally well in the Obedience trials.

Mrs. Walker was convinced that obedience work would appeal to American fanciers and to the public. She brought back to this country the idea of starting with a single class and allowing the news of the new type of trials to spread by word of mouth. The first class started at Bedford Village, N.Y., with eight participating members. Week by week the group grew, and interested dog lovers came from as far away as New York City and Poughkeepsie, N.Y.

Possibly one of the greatest tests of whether this new form of dog work and the chance of competition could stand up was given Mrs. Walker when she noted the following breeds coming regularly to class: Cocker Spaniels, Poodles, German Shepherds, Irish Terriers, Bull Mastiffs, Doberman Pinschers, Skye Terriers, Dachshunds, Beagles, Great Danes, Collies, Miniature Schnauzers, Welsh Corgis, English and Irish Setters, Dandie Dinmont Terriers, and Boxers.

The number and variety of breeds that showed aptitude taught her that here was something that really had appeal, and that it now needed some form of competitive rules under which to operate, so that the general public might have a chance to see the work.

The American Kennel Club officials were cautious in giving the new activity official sanction but issued permission for Mrs. Walker's Obedience Test Club of New York to stage two trials in 1934. The first of these was held with the North Westchester Kennel Club show at Mt. Kisco, N.Y., and a second was held with the Somerset Hills Kennel Club show at Far Hills, N.J. Bayard Dominick judged the first trial and

Percy Stoddard the second.

These first trials called only for Open Classes, but the next year the Novice Class was added. This year, in addition to those held by the two original clubs, trials were staged by the Lenox, Mass., Kennel Club, the North Shore Kennel Club at Hamilton, Mass., the Westchester Kennel Club at Rye, N.Y., and the Kennel Club of Philadelphia. Over 15 different breeds were to be found in most of the competitive classes in 1935 which still were under the wing of Mrs. Walker's original club.

However, the key trial remained at North Westchester, and Dr. W. F. Vail, of Greenwich, Conn., noted bird dog field trial judge, was the arbiter the second year. Prior to this trial the original breeds in training had been expanded to include Irish Water

Dog in scent discrimination test. Photo by Evelyn M. Shafer.

Spaniels, Keeshonden, some of the retriever breeds, Bloodhounds, English Springer Spaniels, Shetland Sheepdogs, and Great Pyrenees.

It is interesting to note that at this time tracking tests, run only slightly differently than they are today, were introduced. They were first held on Henry J. Whitehouse's estate at Mt. Kisco, N.Y. The work, however, was not satisfactory and the judge was forced to mark all "not passed."

By this time the work had expanded from coast to coast with possibly 20 units in all, 15 of which were received as affiliates of Mrs. Walker's original club and remained so until the American Kennel Club had taken over more than an advisory capacity in the sport. Mrs. Walker and her group worked from 1936 to 1940 with the governing body for pure-bred dogs in the United States, and by the time the original club was dissolved in 1940 it had grown from eight members to something over 500.

The first branch units to affiliate with Mrs. Walker's club were the First Dog Training Club of Northern New Jersey, the Berkshire Training Club, the California Training Club, the Hawaiian Training Club, the Philadelphia Training Club, the Reading, Pa., Training Club, the Hartford, Conn., Obedience Training Club, the Port Chester, N.Y., Obedience Training Club, and the Morris and Essex Training Club.

The first trials found the ribbons and cash awards going to Poodles, German Shepherds, Doberman Pinschers, English Springer Spaniels, and Miniature Schnauzers, with the first two breeds more or less dominating the few Eastern events held prior to 1936.

It was in 1936, after many explanatory letters had passed between Mrs. Walker and the late Charles D. Inglee, Executive Vice-President of the American Kennel Club, and after enthusiastic reports had been received about the added attraction given to shows by the thrill of seeing dogs actually at work, that the American Kennel Club made the trials a formal part of the governing body's purebred program.

The first trial, under rules drawn up by Mrs. Whitehouse Walker and her aide, Miss Blanche M. Saunders, with the advice of the late Josef Weber, and approved by the American Kennel Club, was held with the North Westchester Kennel Club show at Mt. Kisco, N.Y. The judge was Mrs. Frederica Lewis Page, of Stamford, Conn. The same year saw the six trials of 1935 expand to 17, all over the country and in Hawaii.

The approved rules used for the first trial were so satisfactory that merely minor changes were made from 1936 until 1947, when, on October 8, the rules were heavily revised. It should be kept in mind that these rules are always under close scrutiny by officials and may be slightly changed from time to time so as to develop a more uniform standard of judging procedure.

The early growth of Obedience trials was made possible through the fact that interested persons working with the original Bedford Village class would return home and stir up interest among local dog owners. These were impressed not so much with the idea of competition for awards, but with the thought that this work would give their dogs better manners and thus make them more acceptable members of the community in which they lived.

Each of the early classes was able to get Mrs. Walker and Miss Saunders to attend and guide the first meetings, at which Miss Saunders would work one of Mrs. Walker's Poodles, while the owner explained each step and the reason for it. At times inexperienced dogs from the local group were handled and class teachers shown how to break in the dogs.

In 1937 Mrs. Walker received so many requests for help from distant clubs and classes that she purchased a house trailer, and with Miss Saunders and three Poodles, headed toward the South, traveling through Texas and on to California, giving talks on the subject of Obedience trials. More than 10,000 miles were covered from September to December.

The star of this trip, as well as at every other "missionary" appearance, was Carillon Epreuve, a fast and precise-working black standard Poodle who was better known as Glee. She was the first of all dogs in this country to win the three obedience degrees then awarded: C.D. for Champion Dog; C.D.X. for Champion Dog Excellent; and U.D. for Utility Dog, which at that time meant also passing the tracking test.

Glee was owned by Mrs. Walker, and on the day she became the first American dog to pass the tracking test and thus have all three degrees, Mr. Whitehouse's Poodle and a German Shepherd owned by Mr. and Mrs. Walter C. Pfeiffer also made their marks under the judging of the late Josef Weber.

The following year a few more dogs were entered in the tracking tests. Failure was, however, the order of the day, mainly because the handlers undertook to guide their dogs rather than rely on the dogs' noses.

school their dogs in the simple, practical exercises that will make them fit more securely into the life of the community. At the weekly sessions, which last from 90 minutes to two hours, even the rankest of cross-breds is admitted, but it is often found that the owner of such a pet winds up by having, as his second dog, a pure-bred of the type that appeals most to him.

As a matter of fact, these clubs and classes where the owner is taught to handle his own dog properly have provided a new market for the breeders of pure-bred dogs. When a certain breed has swept to the top of a succession of competitive trials there is a

The Long Sit test. Photo by Evelyn M. Shafer.

After lunch, when the trials were from 90 minutes to three hours old, Glee and Miss Saunders went out and found all five missing objects.

It is noteworthy that after the tracking tests had become well established many owners heeded the plea for using their dogs in public service. This was achieved by extending the length and difficulty of the training trials, and the dogs were registered with local police authorities as aides in finding lost persons. This custom was fairly prevalent prior to World War II. Since that time, however, many police agencies have acquired their own dogs for use in tracking and, in addition, for guard and patrol work.

TRAINING CLASSES AND CLUBS

The training classes and clubs are generally founded by amateurs, and all dog lovers of the community, as far as the capacity of the training site and the number of available teacher-trainers will allow, may

great urge to buy that breed.

Two important factors in the progress of Obedience trials as competitive events have contributed to drawing the main spectator interest in shows to this feature. First is the fact that the jumps to be made and the dumbbells to be retrieved are graduated in difficulty to the size and agility of the breeds in competition, thus putting all competitors on an even basis. The other is the fact that Obedience trials are rated in a manner which makes them comparable to a golf match, that is, both match and medal play at the same time. First, second, third, and fourth prizes are awarded in each of the five classes, and these awards go in the order of the highest scores attained on the day.

But however much an owner or handler may wish to win first prize, his actual goal is to acquire a sufficiently high score to earn a leg on the degree for which he is working. This means that, regardless of the class, he must be sure that his dog gets a score of at least 170 of the possible 200 points. In so doing, the dog has earned a minimum 50% of the total points allotted to each of the exercises. A dog that makes a perfect score in all but one exercise, even though in that one it may rate only one point under the half-credit mark, does not receive credit for a leg on the current degree.

In the Novice A and B Classes which lead to the Companion Dog degree, a dog must earn at least 170 points in the proper proportion, three times, with at least six dogs competing, to obtain the C.D. degree. In the Open A and B Classes the rating is the same, 170 points three times with at least six dogs competing. In the Utility Class the 170 or better standard must be maintained three times with at least two dogs competing. To add the tracking degree a dog must be marked "passed" by the two judges on the one day with at least three dogs competing. Thus the dog must be able to withstand the possible distraction of other dogs being present while he is working.

In the Novice and Open Classes all of the judging is done with only one dog in the ring at a time, save for the "long sit and down," when there must be at least six dogs in the ring, and no more than 15, although sometimes in the earlier days more than 30 dogs of 25 breeds were judged together on this "sit and down" with never a dog breaking. In the Utility work, until the new rules came into being, all the work was done individually, and even now the only part of this work that is done *en masse* is the stand for examination.

Although there are five classes in the trials that may be held either with all-breed shows or as separate entities (tracking must be held apart from a trial and on adequate grounds where non-conflicting trials of at least 440 yards can be laid out), there are really only three divisions of work: the Novice which leads to the Companion Dog degree, the Open which brings the Companion Dog Excellent honor, and the Utility by which a dog earns the Utility Dog degree.

The Novice A and the Open A Classes are for dogs of any breed and of either sex, and they must be handled by the owner or a member of the immediate family. No professional may handle a dog in this class, even though it be his own dog.

The Novice B and Open B Classes are for dogs of any breed and of either sex, and may be entered by any person, amateur or professional. A person may compete with his dog in the Novice A or B until he has acquired the Companion Dog degree, when he must shift to the Open A or B Classes, depending on his classification.

After a dog has acquired the Companion Dog Excellent degree, the owner may choose between going on into the Utility classes, where amateurs and professionals compete on even terms, or continuing to compete in the Open B for as long as he may wish. The same rule applies to Utility. Once a dog has been awarded that degree, he may compete forever in both Utility and Open B. Some of the country's seasoned performers with both the C.D.X. and U.D. or U.D.T. degrees have gone on competing at least 50 times more.

The tracking tests are open to dogs of any breed, and of either sex, that have acquired at least the Companion Dog degree. Here the amateur and professional compete again on even terms, and the dog may continue to participate in as many tracking tests as the owner may find convenient. Some dogs have passed this rather difficult work three or four times.

As has been stated previously, dogs may compete in Novice or Open A classes until they have won the degree, and many play safe against technical defaults by being sure to pass each class four times. There is no barrier, save that of sportsmanship, to prevent a person from competing in the two Novice Classes and the Open A as many times as there are shows before the owner is advised by the American Kennel Club that the certificate for the current degree has been awarded.

One of the interesting features of an Obedience trial is the wide variety of breeds that go through their paces in competing for degrees at the same trial. As many as 43 breeds have been observed in competition at one set of trials, and some training classes have reported as many as 60 breeds in school during one year.

The basic needs of the average owner, especially in the cities, are to train their dogs to come when called, to cease tugging at the end of the leash when out for a walk, to stop unnecessary barking, to refrain from jumping up on visitors, and to leave alien food alone.

More than half the trainees seeking help on these points remain on at classes to learn at least all of the Novice routine, and a possible half of these get the desire to see how well their dogs can make out in competition, at least in local shows where their neighbors can see them perform. Many persons whose hobby is hunting bring their dogs to class for a few lessons to instill obedience through the basic exercises.

A further attraction of obedience work is the fact that the age of the dog or its handler is of little consequence. Although many trainers advise that dogs should be at least a year old before taking training, it is generally acknowledged that the most important factor is how the temperament of the dog is suited to work.

As competition should be a point on which to judge age limitations, it is well to point out two extremes. The oldest dog to compete was Io, a Dalmatian owned by the Harland Meistrells of Long Island. Io was ten years old before she had a lesson, and, schooled by owners who never had had a dog in training before, made all three obedience degrees in the space of one year. At the other extreme is the Weimaraner, Grafmar's Ador, then owned by Grafmar Kennels of Hopkinton, Mass., which acquired the Companion Dog degree at the age of six months and two days. This early education did not spoil him for the field, for later on he made good in the hunting covers of five states.

Several clubs have on their training rolls three, in a few cases even four, generations of one family. Children of three years and great-grandmothers in their eighties have been seen in classes. One girl finished the C.D. degree on her mother's Cocker Spaniel when she was only six years old, and at least one grandmother put a German Shepherd through to all three degrees in a short space of time.

The appeal of Obedience trials to the spectator is indicated by the fact that more people will remain at the ringsides for longer periods watching obedience work than they will spend at all breed rings combined. One reason for this is that the average dog lover does not understand the fine points of conformation judging, why the judge puts dog A over dog B. However, the same person can appreciate the beauty of the dog's work at field trials or Obedience trials.

Scores at Obedience trials are gradually improving, so much so that perfect or near perfect work is now more often the rule than the exception. Most often found in the scoring brackets between 195 and 200 (perfect) in all classes are the following breeds: Cocker Spaniel, Doberman Pinscher, German Shepherd, Poodle, Dalmatian, Belgian Sheepdog, Golden Retriever, Pomeranian, Collie, English Springer Spaniel, Shetland Sheepdog, and Weimaraner.

A description of the exercises that make up the Tracking, Novice, Open, and Utility divisions of competition follows. The "on lead" work is done on a loose lead with the dog at the left side, a position he must retain when with the owner, even off lead.

Tracking. Dogs entered in this class are required to locate a missing object that shall be left at least 440 yards away from the starting point and on a trail that is at least 30 minutes old. Two judges officiate on trails that are plotted at least 24 hours previously, and redone 30 minutes or more before the dog is put down at the starting flag. A second marker is placed 30 paces from the start and after that the dog is on his own, with a special tracking harness from which trails a pliable rope or lead that is 30 or more feet long. The handler may not guide the dog.

The trail must not skirt fences, stone walls, or natural markers, and must have at least two turns in it. A dog may be kept down as long as he indicates he is working and, in order to be marked "passed", must find the object left at the end of the trail.

The majority of failures in this work are traced to the human element, for the handler often seriously handicaps the dog by trying to help him.

Novice Classes. In these classes a person may handle more than one dog in the individual exercises, but each dog must have a separate handler for the "long sit and down," where at least six dogs must be in the ring at the same time. In the event the class does not have six eligibles, it is permissible to "borrow" the remaining dogs from the Open Classes, as the time requirements are much less in Novice than in Open.

The first exercise is "heeling on leash," which has a valuation of 35 points. The handler may say "heel," and use the dog's name at the start of this and other

An obedience exhibition by a Baltimore Girl Scout Troop at Rockefeller Center, New York City.

The Long Down test. Photo by Hank Babbitt.

of these two exercises is 30 points, making a total of 200 points for a perfect score. At least 170 are needed to qualify, and the dog must have gained at least 50 per cent of the value of each of the six judging points.

In the Novice Class, as well as in the other classes, a judge must disqualify dogs that have a tendency to viciousness and females in season, and he may disqualify a handler who is unseemly in his handling of the dog.

The "sit and down" for the Novice A and B Classes may be judged together if there are not enough dogs in any one of the classes to make a qualifying score. The same is true in regard to the Open A and B Classes. An owner may have one dog in either A class, and one or more in the B classes, but he must have a separate handler for each dog if the A and B classes are combined for reasons sufficient to the judge.

Open Classes. In these classes dogs of all breeds and of either sex may compete, provided that they have earned Companion Dog degrees. A person may handle only one dog in Open A Class, but may have more than one in Open B Class or in a combination Open A and B Class. However, he must then provide individual handlers for each dog over and above the one handled by himself.

"Heeling on leash" is the first exercise in the Open Classes, and 20 points can be earned. The calls of the judge, not necessarily in this order, are: "Forward," "Halt," "Right turn," "Left turn," "About turn," "Slow," "Fast." The "About" may be called as a "Left about."

In the "heel free" exercise, for 30 points, the judge calls for the same commands as in "heel on leash," save that he adds the figure eight. Here, as in all exercises, the handler may give only the one command at the start and may, at the command, "Exercise finished," praise and pet his dog.

Third is the "drop on recall," worth 20 points. The dog is set at one end of the ring and the handler sent to the other end. The judge says, "Call your dog" and signals the handler when to drop, or cause to lie down, the oncoming dog by signal or voice. Then the dog is called in to a "sit" position before the handler. The judge orders, "Finish," and the dog goes smartly to heel position, after which the command is, "Exercise finished."

The "retrieve on the flat" comes next and requires the handler to throw a dumbbell graduated to the size of the dog. The dog must stay until asked by the judge to get it, via order to the handler. The dog returns with the dumbbell and sits before the handler until the judge commands, "Take it." He is then ordered to heel position. This is worth 25 points.

The "retrieve over the obstacle" requires the dog to stand steady as the handler throws the dumbbell over the high jump which is set to one and one-half the height of the dog at the shoulders. Exceptions are made in the case of the bulky breeds, such as St. Bernards and Great Pyrenees, where the obstacles are

exercises, but may give no other commands or signals, and must not operate with a tight leash. The judges' commands are: "Forward," "Halt," "Right turn," "Left turn," "About turn," "Slow," "Fast," "Figure eight." The last command is executed with two stewards as the turning posts. At the conclusion of this and other exercises, the judge says, "Exercise finished," at which time the handler may praise or pet his dog and make ready for starting the new exercise.

The second exercise is the "stand for examination" which carries a value of 30 points. The handler stands the dog for examination and moves in front of him to the end of the lead. The judge then goes over the dog but not as carefully as in breed examination, then commands the handler back to his dog, which he does by going around the dog and to its left side, and then commands, "Finish." The dog must show no shyness or movement during the exercise.

The "heel free," or off leash work is the same as that for heel on leash, except that there is no figure eight in this section in the Novice Class. As in the other heeling, the order of work is not necessarily as listed, but all the work must be done and the same pattern followed for all dogs to be judged.

The "recall" is the fourth exercise and counts for 30 points. The handler sits the dog at a spot designated by the judge, and moves as far away from the dog as the judge states. On command the handler calls his dog in by calling, "Come, Rover," or simply signaling him—never both. The dog sits directly in front of the handler and, at the judge's command, swings around to heel position, also sitting.

The "long sit" is for one minute and the "long down" for three minutes, with the handlers across the ring from the dogs. Steadiness in position counts here, and the dog may not shift until the judge declares, "exercise finished." In the case of the "long down," the judge commands, "Sit your dog," and then declares, "Exercise finished." The score for each

geared to their height. On command of the judge, the dog is sent for the dumbbell. He must go over the jump, pick up the dumbbell and return over the jump to the handler and sit before him, delivering only on the word of the judge, "Take it." The dog then finishes on the judge's command. The perfection mark here is 35 points.

The "broad jump" comes next and is worth 20 points. The boards are arranged in a series of four for larger breeds and sometimes reduced to two for the small breeds. The spread from first to last nested jump board is not to exceed six feet across, with the average being not more than three times the height of the dog at the shoulders.

The "long sit" calls for 25 points for a three-minute stay and the "long down" asks for a five-minute stay for another 25 points. In each case at least six dogs must "sit" or "down" while the handlers are out of sight of the dogs.

Utility Class. There are five exercises for the 200 points that count for perfection in the Utility Class. The first allows 60 points for scent discrimination. The dog must retrieve a metal, a leather, and a wooden object from a mass of four objects each of the same materials.

he cat does not distract this well-trained German Shepherd ping in a practice session, and he will jump as dependably in an dience Trial. Photo by Hank Babbitt.

The handler equips himself with fifteen objects. Five of these are made of leather, five of metal and five of wood. The judge selects one object of each type from this group and returns them to the handler. The judge than places the remaining twelve objects in a group on the floor or ground. The handler handles the three objects selected in such manner as to transmit his scent to them. He then blocks the vision of the dog and hands one of the objects to the judge.

Handling the object in a manner which will not interfere with the scent of the handler, the judge places the object among the group on the floor or ground. The dog is then ordered to find it and retrieve it to the handler. This is repeated with the other two types of objects. The dog is required to retrieve the object placed in the group by the judge.

Next comes the "seek back," worth 30 points. The handler is given a pattern to follow on a trail within the ring. He drops the object, usually a key case or a glove, without the dog seeing it, and concludes the pre-arranged pattern. On the judge's orders he places his hand on the dog's nose and commands him to find the lost object, either by scent or sight.

The "signal" exercise has only two commands from the judge, the "Forward" and the "Exercise finished." Between these commands the handler goes through the heeling routine, and must at some place in the work, which is all done on signals without vocal commands, go through Forward, Halt, Left turn, About turn, Right turn, Slow, Fast, Drop on recall (with the drop to be exactly in front of the handler), Sit, and Finish. The point value is 40.

The "hurdle and bar" exercise counts 35 points, and here the hurdle and bar are lifted to the same height as would be required for the "retrieve over obstacle." The dumbbell is placed in the dog's mouth and he is set before the high jump and commanded to stay as the handler takes a position to the side, nearer the bar jump. The handler then commands the dog, "Over," and the dog is required to clear both jumps, one at a time, still holding the dumbbell in his mouth, and turn back to face the handler until the judge commands, "Take it." Then follows "Finish" and "Exercise Finished."

The final exercise is the "stand for examination," worth 35 points, and the one part of the Utility Class work where all dogs of the class are in the ring together. The handlers leave their dogs on command and the judge goes over all of them as though in a cursory physical examination. On completion, the judge brings the dogs and handlers back together and commands, "Exercise finished."

The principal value of obedience training work is not that it promotes Obedience trials as a sport, but that it brings home to the general public the fact that it is a simple and easy matter to teach dogs of almost all breeds to obey commands readily and willingly. Anyone who wants to teach his dog the simple niceties of behavior, which make him a more pleasant companion and a more valuable animal, need only visit one of these obedience training classes. After having been a spectator for a session or two he will be convinced that anyone of even temper and reasonable patience can teach his own dog the exercises outlined in obedience training programs. If there are no obedience training classes available in the neighborhood, he can take advantage of the simple instructions contained in a number of good books on the subject. There is no reason now why every dog owned by an intelligent person should not possess at least a modicum of manners.

Outstanding Events. The American Kennel Club recognizes four classes of Obedience trials. These are: the trial held as an integral part of an all-breed bench show; the trial held as the official licensed or member trial of a separate obedience club but in connection with an all-breed bench show; the licensed or member club trial of an obedience unit held as a separate event; and the Obedience trial held in connection with the specialty bench show of a one-breed club.

The latter class are generally small trials, although on occasion there have been one-breed events which have registered larger entries than some of the trials held in conjunction with the smaller bench shows.

Entries in Obedience trials vary in number, with local interest the dominating factor in this respect. Interest in these events is growing throughout the country.

For a list of Obedience Trial Clubs, write Gaines Dog Research Center, 250 North Street, White Plains, New York, 10602. For a copy of the most up to date rules covering Obedience Trials, write to the American Kennel Club, 51 Madison Avenue, New York, New York, 10010.

GLOSSARY OF OBEDIENCE TRIAL TERMS

BROAD JUMP: Four separate hurdles painted white, built to telescope for convenience, largest measuring five feet wide and seven inches high. Spaced so as to cover a distance equal to not less than 2½ times the height of the dog at the withers, except that the maximum shall be no more than six feet. This applies to all breeds save those excepted in the High Jumps, which are limited to twice the withers' height. In removing hurdles, the highest is removed first.

C.D. Companion Dog: This signifies that the dog has completed three tests in the Novice A or B Classes, under at least two judges, and with at least six dogs in competition, and has made scores of 170 or better out of the possible 200; and in each instance has received at least 50 per cent of the allowable score for each individual exercise.

C.D.X. Companion Dog Excellent: This signifies that the dog, after first acquiring the C.D. degree, has completed three tests in the Open A or Open B Classes, under at least two judges, and with six dogs in competition; has made scores of 170 or better out of the possible 200, and in each case has received at least 50 per cent of the value of each individual exercise.

COLLAR: Either a leather or a chain slip collar must be used, with the latter preferred. Spike collars are forbidden even in training classes.

DOWN: All dogs, but not more than 15 at a time, must lay down for three minutes in the Novice class with the handlers across the ring; five minutes in the Open classes with handlers out of sight.

Mr. Chips Moler, a Miniature Schnauzer, goes through his pac He was the second dog in the world to win utility degrees in b the U.S. and Canada. Cleveland Press photo.

DROP ON RECALL: This is done in Open classes only. Dog sits at one end of ring and handler goes to the other end and calls the dog, dropping him on signal from the judge. He then calls him in as in the regular recall.

DUMBBELL: A wooden object shaped like the gymnasium work dumbbell, size and weight to vary with the size of the dog, with the bar wide enough to allow the dog to pick it up.

ELIGIBILITY: All the tests of obedience are progressive and may be entered by any pure-bred dog of either sex, registered with the American Kennel Club, or eligible for such registration, subject to the rule that dogs may not enter any form of competition regulated by the American Kennel Club under the age of six months. Bitches in season may not be entered in Obedience Test Classes or Tracking Tests, and a dog exhibiting viciousness must be disqualified from Obedience Trials or Tracking Tests.

HEEL: To have the dog walk at the left side with its head even with or in line with the left knee. This applies in "free heel" and "heel on leash."

HIGH JUMP: For Open Classes only, but used in Utility Class as part of one exercise. Side posts four feet high are provided with the jump bar five feet wide, so constructed as to provide adjustment for each two inches from 12 to 36 inches. Base board is eight inches wide, including space from ground or floor.

HURDLE AND BAR JUMP: Hurdle is as high as high jump and graduated the same. Uprights are four feet high and set five feet apart, with the bar placed so as to fall if hit. Bar is 2½ inches in diameter and painted alternate black and white sections of about 3 inches. Adjustable by two inches from 12 to 36 inches.

JUMP DEMAND: Applicable to "retrieving dumbbell over obstacle" in Open classes and for first half of "hurdle and bar jump" exercise in Utility Class. Never less than 1½ times height of dog at withers, but never more than three feet, except in cases of Bull-Mastiffs, Great Danes, Great Pyrenees, Mastiffs, Newfoundlands, and St. Bernards, which must jump once the height of the withers.

LEASH: Must be of leather with adequate snap and long enough that it can hang loosely, as tight leads call for penalties from judges. Most trainers prefer a leash that is as long as the handler is tall.

NOVICE A.: This class is for pure-bred dogs of either sex and of any breed which have not won the title "C.D." Each dog to have a separate handler and must be handled by owner or member of immediate family. No professional handler, trainer, or kennel employee may compete.

NOVICE B.: Same as above, except either amateur or professional handler may compete, and more than one dog may be shown by one person, but each must have separate handler for "Sit" and "Down."

OPEN A.: This class is for pure-bred dogs of either sex and of any breed which have won the C.D. degree but have not been awarded the C.D.X. degree. As in Novice A, no professional may compete and the dog must belong to the handler or member of immediate family.

RECALL: The dog sits at one end of the ring and the handler goes to the other, and calls the dog in at the judge's command. The dog sits directly in front of the handler and, on the judge's command, goes to heel, sitting.

RINGS: For indoor tests, exhibition rings must be 30x50 feet; and outdoors a minimum of 50x80 feet. Ground is required to be level and grass cut short.

SIGNALS: All signals of Obedience are done with the handler using a single command or signal, accompanied by the dog's name. Extra commands and signals are penalized, except in the "Stay," when command and signal may both be used.

SIGNAL EXERCISE: This is a section of Utility work wherein the handler controls dog entirely by signals through the complete heeling exercise—"Right Turn, Left Turn, About Turn, Slow, Normal, Fast, Halt"—with final work being "Recall," with dog dropped immediately in front of handler's feet and then signaled to "Finish" position, heeling at handler's left side.

SIT: All dogs, but not more than 15 at a time, sit stationary for one minute in the Novice Class with handlers across the ring; three minutes in the Open Class with the handlers out of sight.

TRACKING: This is a test of the dog's ability to follow a stranger's scent over a not obvious trail of from 440 to 500 yards, which has aged from 30 minutes to two hours. Tracklayer to wear leather-soled shoes and leave a leather object for dog to find. Dogs worked on lead of 30 to 60 feet.

T.D. Tracking Dog: This signifies that the dog, having acquired at least the C.D. degree under the rules, has been rated "Passed" by two judges officiating at the same time, in an outdoor tracking test under rules set forth by the American Kennel Club, charts of the trail to be signed and filed with the American Kennel Club.

UTILITY: In this Class the breed and sex eligibility is the same as in other classes, except that the dog must have acquired the C.D.X. degree. Amateur or professional may compete and the dog may be entered in these classes for an unlimited number of times.

U.D. Utility Dog: This signifies that the dog, having acquired the C.D. and C.D.X. degrees under the rules of the American Kennel Club, has completed three tests in the Utility Class, under at least two judges, and with two or more dogs in competition; has made scores of 170 or better of the possible 200, and has received each time at least 50 per cent of the valuation allowed in each individual exercise.

U.D.T. Utility Dog Tracker: This signifies that the dog has acquired the C.D., C.D.X. and U.D. degrees under the rules of the American Kennel Club, as well as having been marked "Passed" in at least one tracking test by two judges. Winning this degree does not bar the dog from further competition and the owner may carry the dog into as many Open and Utility Classes, or as many Tracking tests, as desired.

—Obedience Training—

TO MANY the term "obedience training" has come to mean the schooling of the dog in the various steps necessary to qualify him for competition in Obedience trials. In reality, the term means far more than that. It means bringing the dog completely under the control of his master, any time, any place, and under almost any conditions. It also means teaching the dog to accept this control quickly and cheerfully. In the final analysis, it is the development of good manners in the dog to the extent that his actions will be offensive to no one.

Perfect obedience is not accomplished overnight. It is the result of constant training and patient effort. While obedience training classes, to which any dog fancier can have access, are established throughout the country, obedience training does not stop in the class room. Practically every exercise taught in organized obedience training is useful in everyday life, and the dog may be rehearsed in these various exercises daily without his feeling that the rehearsal is a definite lesson. Soon he will accept the commands as a matter of course and obey them accordingly.

To successfully compete for the C.D. (Companion Dog) degree, the dog must show proficiency in the following exercises: heel on leash, heel free, stand for examination, recall, long sit, long down.

The C.D.X. (Companion Dog Excellent) degree requires successful qualifications in the following: heel on leash, heel free, drop on recall, retrieve on flat, retrieve over obstacle, broad jump, long sit, long down.

To secure the U.D. (Utility Dog) degree, the candidate must perform his exercises at *signals given by hand only*. Not even the judge speaks. The exercises are: scent discrimination, seek back, signal exercise, hurdle and bar jump, group examination.

The U.D.T. (Utility Dog Tracker) title is awarded U.D. titlists that have, in addition, won, through merit of performance, a Tracking Test Certificate.

Regardless of whether or not he ever competes in Obedience trials, the dog that becomes proficient in these exercises, or the majority of them, is a more valuable animal and a source of greater pleasure to his master.

Heeling on Leash. The dog should walk at your left side with his chest about on a line with your knee. There is a reason for having the dog walk always on the left: no matter in what direction you are traveling this places the dog between you and possible danger. The leash is held in the right hand, the left hand being free to control the dog's speed. Give the command "Heel" and start walking at regular pace. If he lags behind, a tug on the leash will bring him up in line. If he forges ahead, a light jerk will retard him. When you stop, make him "Sit" immediately, his fore quarters even with your left leg. To teach him to sit, use the command "Sit" and press down on his hips or hind quarters with your hand. Fifteen or 20 minutes of this is enough for one lesson. Stop sooner if the dog seems to grow tired. It should be practiced over and over again until the dog automatically walks at your left at the command "Heel" and assumes just as automatically "Sit" when you stop. Keep him on the alert by changing your pace occasionally from regular to fast and from fast to slow, having him keep his chest in line with your left knee as you go along. Stop short occasionally, making him come to "Heel" immediately and "Sit" if his pace causes him to go by you.

Learning to Turn. When the dog has learned to "Heel" properly at any pace you set, coming to "Sit" promptly when you stop, he should be schooled in the turns: right turn, left turn, right-about turn, and left-about turn. In making a right turn, a slight jerk on the leash to the right warns the dog that you are turning. In the left turn, a slight bump or shove with your left knee signals him that you intend to turn in that direction. If he goes too far, a slight jerk on the leash brings him back in line.

The first time the right-about turn is made, the dog will probably proceed a few paces before realizing that your are not with him. Always give the command "Heel" just before you turn about to the right. If he keeps straight ahead, let him go the full length of the leash, and just before he reaches the end give it a sharp jerk and call him by name, commanding "Heel." When he comes to "Heel" pet him and praise him. Allow him to think he made the error, praise him when he corrects it. In a few lessons he will learn to keep particularly alert when he hears the command "Heel."

The left-about turn is not so easy to negotiate. With the left hand grasp the leash a short distance from the collar. Use the leash to hold the dog under close control and your left leg to signal him for the turn. With a jerk of the leash and a shove with the leg, the dog will soon understand that he must turn completely around to the left. Another way is to walk around your dog, holding him tightly with the leash held in the left hand, giving sharp tugs on it to the left. It requires considerable practice to accomplish this with ease and grace.

The "Figure Eight" required in Obedience trials is a series of right and left turns around and between two judge's assistants standing a short distance apart.

Heeling Free. After the dog has become fully proficient in walking to heel on a slack leash, the leash should be removed from his collar. He should be watched carefully for a time; correct him promptly when he makes an error, and praise him lavishly for work well done. He should be just as much under

control without the leash as he is with it attached to his collar. In home lessons, alternately heel him with and without the leash. Make him feel almost a part of you.

Stand for Examination. Your dog has learned to automatically "Sit" when you stop while he is accompanying you. Now the task is to teach him to "Stand" at command and allow the judge to examine him, standing motionless the while. With the dog at heel, give the command "Stand" and stop. If he tries to sit down (as he certainly will if he learned his earlier lessons well), place your hands underneath his body and bring him to a standing position. It may be necessary to "pose" him by placing his legs squarely underneath him. Repeat the command "Stand" while handling him. When he is standing, walk in front of him and stand there a short while. Do not allow him to sit down. Boost him up each time he sits, repeating the command "Stand." Repeat this over and over until he will stand motionless until you return to him. After he will "Stand" while you are in front of him, walk around him, repeating the command. Next, have some friend approach him and walk around him while you repeat the command "Stand-stay". After he does this willingly, have your friend go over his body with his hands, as if testing him for soundness. Soon you will only need to give the one command "Stand." This exercise gives the dog show ring poise and eradicates any fear he might have of strangers.

The Recall. In this exercise the dog is taught to "Sit" and "Stay" while the owner walks away from him. He must then remain until called and respond quickly to the command "Come." Use a long leash in this training. "Sit" your dog. Command him to "Stay." Move a short distance away from him. If he attempts to follow, replace him in the original position, repeating the command "Stay." After repeated lessons in this, he will allow you to walk a considerable distance from him without moving. Then call his name and give the command "Come." If he is slow about responding, a sharp jerk on the leash will bring him along. Remember, he must respond quickly and come to you at fast pace. After he comes to you, he should be made to take his position "at heel" promptly.

Long Sit. Here the dog must remain in the sitting position while the trainer walks away from him and remains away from him for some time. In the "Sitting Three Minutes" test the trainer goes completely out of the dog's sight. The command is "Sit and Stay." In teaching this lesson, the trainer should have the dog sit as in the Recall, moving gradually farther away from him, but watching him in order to correct him and replace him quickly in the event the dog should move to follow. This is a matter of drill, drill, drill, but, once the dog realizes what you want him to do, little difficulty is experienced. He may be taught to remain sitting for long periods if desired.

Long Down. In the "Long Down" exercise the dog is

taught to lie down for three minutes while the handler moves a good distance away. At the end of that period the handler returns to the dog's right side and gives the command "Sit." An additional test called "Down for Five Minutes" is given, in which the handler leaves the ring and passes out of the dog's sight. The dog must remain "Down" until the handler returns and finishes the exercise at "Sit" position.

Teach the dog to lie down by giving the command "Down." This can be done in several ways. Press down on his shoulders; draw his front feet from under him; grasp the leash close under the dog's neck and pull him down; pass the leash under the foot and pull down. Use the command "Down" frequently in either method. Practice this until the dog goes down immediately at command. Praise him when he does it properly, but tolerate no delay. This should be done promptly. When he has learned to "Down" properly, add the command "Stay" and move away from him. Use the same tactics as in "Sit-stay," correcting him promptly until he will remain down for considerable periods. Then go out of his sight. Do not remain too long at first, and praise him highly when you return. Here again, as in all exercises, practice makes perfect. And here you can gradually substitute an upraised hand as a signal to "Down" instead of the command. This is important. The dog will learn it quickly if you patiently practice, rewarding him with praise or a tidbit when he responds properly. Soon you can drop him with a raised hand.

Drop on Recall. In this exercise the dog is caused to drop to the "Down" position at command or signal from the handler, while he is responding to the command "Come" in the Recall exercise. This is not likely to give much trouble if the dog has been taught to drop promptly on signal.

Retrieving. Many obedience trainers prefer to preface lessons in retrieving by teaching the dog to hold and carry objects in their mouths. This is, indeed, a valuable lead-in to retrieving, the teaching of which is often a difficult, and, to say the least, an irksome, chore. A rolled-up and taped magazine makes a good "dummy" in this work. The main task is to get the dog to open his mouth. Show him the "dummy." Hold it up against his mouth. Give the command "Take it." With the fingers of the left hand resting on the dog's upper lip, close behind his incisors, exert pressure. This will cause the dog to open his mouth. Place the magazine in his mouth and release the pressure, the right hand slipping under the jaw to prevent the dog's dropping or rejecting the magazine. With the left hand, stroke his head and ears. Praise him while you cause him to hold the object a short time, telling him to "Hold it."

Go easy with this for awhile. It is better to make progress slowly than to frighten your pupil unduly. Short lessons and frequent ones will accomplish much. After the dog learns to "Take it" and "Hold it" and to give the article up at the command "Give" or "Out," have him carry the article as you lead him along. In taking it from him, you should have him "Sit." Don't be in too big a hurry to take it from him If he should drop it, place it in his mouth again. Make him realize that he is to hold the article until you are ready to take it, and then release it only on command. You cannot be too lavish in your praise of good work during these lessons. The dog is most likely anxious to learn in order to please you, but he must also understand what he is supposed to do.

When the dog has learned to "Take it," "Hold it," "Carry," and "Give," retrieving comes comparatively easy with him. Before having him retrieve he may be taught to carry the object while at heel, with or without the leash, and while jumping the hurdle or bars.

With the dog in "Down" position, place the object a few inches in front of his nose and close to the ground. Give the command "Take it" and place it in his mouth. After a bit of this, place the article on the ground about a foot in front of the dog. Give the command "Take it" and jerk slightly on the leash, causing the dog to inch along toward the article. The right hand should be close to the object so that it can be quickly placed in the dog's mouth. When he will pick it up of his own accord, make a celebration of it. Praise him highly and show him he has done just what you wanted him to. With the right hand under the chin to prevent the dropping of the object, pull the dog up into sitting position with the left hand on the leash. Have him become proficient in this before proceeding to the next step.

Now, with the dog in "Sit" position, toss the article out a few feet in front of him and give the command "Take it" or "Fetch." With a tug on the leash, move along toward the object with the dog. It may be necessary for you to drop him close to the object. And it also may be necessary, for a time, for you to put the object in his mouth. But do not become discouraged. Retrieving proficiency is not obtained at once. Be satisfied with any little progress for the time being. Gradually increase the distance.

When definite progress is made, remove the leash, toss out the article as before and remain standing as the dog is ordered out. It may be necessary for you to go with him, at least part way, but encourage him to do the job by himself. When he has picked up the article, call "Come." Upon his return, which should be prompt, cause him to "Sit," wait a few seconds and command "Give" or "Out," and finish the exercise by commanding "Heel." The first time he does this all properly, spare no pains to show your pleasure. End the lesson there. It is tempting to keep on working a dog when he is performing well, but it is better to end a lesson on a sweet note than on a sour one. Take all of these lessons slowly. Haste can be disastrous. And don't forget to maintain a calm and even demeanor at all times, except when praising the dog. Show him what you want him to do, make him understand that he must do it, but also make him *know* you appreciate his obedience.

Other retrieving training methods are outlined in the article on Retriever Training.

In teaching the dog to retrieve over the hurdle or broad jump, throw the dumbbell far enough over the obstacle to allow the dog a clean, free jump on the return.

Over the Hurdle and Broad Jump. The dog should be worked on a long leash. Start out with a low hurdle about 12 inches high. Walk briskly toward it and step over it yourself. The dog will probably jump it. Praise him and repeat, giving the command "Over" or "Hop" each time you get to the obstacle. Increase the height of the hurdle gradually. Then send him over without stepping over it yourself, always giving the same command each time. He will find himself on the opposite side of the hurdle from you. A slight tug on the leash and the command will probably bring him back to you *over the hurdle*. Praise him lavishly when he does this well. He will soon begin to enjoy this. Be sure the leash is long, for you do not want to give him an unintentional jerk as he lands on the other side.

After a while you should work him without the leash, rewarding each time he performs well. Gradually raise the hurdle to the desired height.

An adjunct to this training is the use of a stick or broom handle, one end of which is placed against a post, a tree or building, and the other end held in your hand. Keep the stick horizontal. Such training will teach the dog he must jump *over* an obstacle he could more easily duck *under*.

In order to keep the dog under control at all times, some trainers cause the dog to "Down" immediately after each jump. Thus the dog is required to await the next command. This often serves to prevent his coming *around* rather than *over* the obstacle on his return trip.

Seek Back, Scent Discrimination, Tracking. All these are refinements of retrieving, and can be added to this accomplishment without much difficulty. After your dog is retrieving well, let him accompany you running free. Drop some object such as an old glove which you have worn a good deal or something you have handled a lot. Drop it as you walk along without the dog seeing it. Then stop, call him to you, point in the direction from which you came and give

the command "Take it. Go find it." or "Fetch. Go find." For the first few times go with him until he finds the object. When he realizes what you want him to do, he will soon search for it diligently. Gradually increase the distance from you to the object.

For scent discrimination, use a number of objects such as pieces of broom handle sawed to about five inches in length so that they all look alike. Handle one a great deal with your hands, carrying it in your pocket. Have it become thoroughly impregnated with your own scent. The others may be soaked in soapy water and carried with you in a pail or paper bag. Drop these as you go along, handling them with pliers or rubber gloves. Drop the scented stick close to one which does not hold your scent. Then send the dog back with the command "Fetch it. Go find." After he has shown his ability to determine the correct stick, place these, all of them, in a small circle, handling all but one with pliers or rubber gloves. Rub the other one thoroughly to impregnate it with your scent. Send him to fetch. When he has become proficient in identifying the proper stick, substitute other small articles, made of leather and metal, but all similar in size and appearance.

After he performs well in the "Seek Back" exercise, increase the distance gradually until he is finding and retrieving from as far as 1,000 yards. Drop the object in the trail at first. Later you may toss it to one side, causing him to seek harder. This exercise should be practiced over varying types of terrain, so that the task will not be too easy. Walk over short cover where the trail will be only the one you have made. Accompany the dog at first, seeing that he sticks fairly close to the trail. Later, let him go it alone.

These fundamentals of obedience training should give the beginner a good foundation on which to build. Attend a few Obedience trials and watch the procedures. Observe the actions of the handlers. Talk to them and ask questions. All will be glad to lend you a helping hand. Better still, join an obedience training class and grow in knowledge along with your own pupil. After you have started, you will learn much from your own dog. Remember that praise and rewards will accomplish far more than force. Be lavish in its bestowal when it is deserved.

—Training for the Show Ring—

IN TRAINING the dog for the show ring, a number of things must be considered. The dog must be constantly alert to his handler and practically oblivious to his surroundings. He must travel free and easily, with natural carriage, whether the leash be short or long. He must move willingly and freely with his handler in any direction. He must stand quietly in any position in which his handler cares to pose him, remaining motionless until allowed to relax. He must stand quietly and willingly for examination, allowing

a stranger, the judge, to examine him minutely, going over him thoroughly with his hands. And he must keep an even temper at all times.

The first lesson should be lead-breaking and should be continued throughout the dog's career. Not only can the dog be taught that he must remain under control at all times in this manner, but much good exercise can be secured by pacing him. With the lead held short, cause the dog to walk close to your side for several yards at a time. Then have him run close

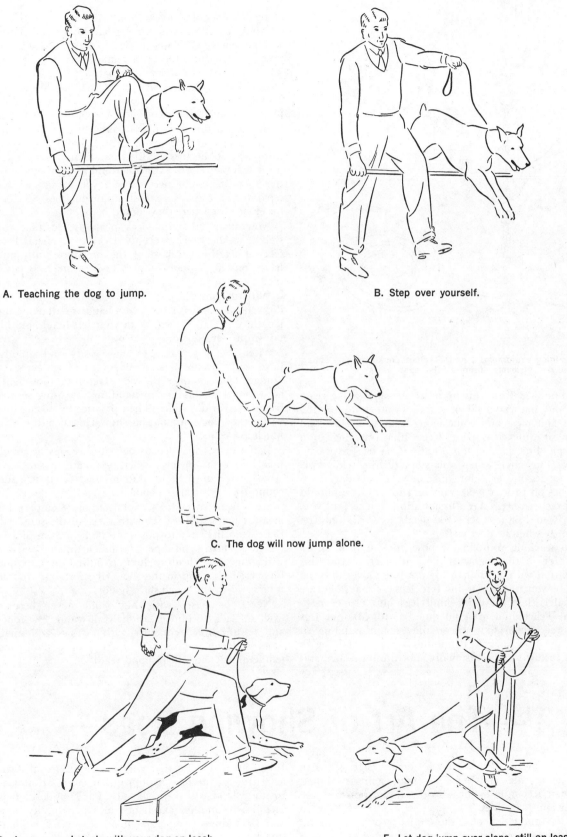

A. Teaching the dog to jump.

B. Step over yourself.

C. The dog will now jump alone.

D. Jump over obstacle with your dog on leash.

E. Let dog jump over alone, still on leash.

Obedience training.

Training equipment: 1 and 2—chain choke training collar; 3 and 4—retrieving dummies; 5—leash.

along his back and neck. This will require patience on your part, but with careful handling your efforts will be rewarded. Your task is to have him let you pose him as you desire and remain standing in that position until you allow him to change it. Keep his head up and alert, his ears where they should be, and his position such as to show his good points. The judge can only form his opinion on what he sees.

In posing the dog, place your left arm over the dog's back, and, with your right hand between his front legs at the brisket, lift him slightly and set his front legs parallel to each other and at right angles to the floor. It may be necessary for you to set each leg separately. See that he is well up on his toes. See that his elbows are where they should be.

Now place his hind legs properly, so that the weight of the body is evenly distributed on all four feet. Study the standard of the breed carefully and have your dog's pose conform to it as much as possible.

With the muzzle parallel with the floor, hold the dog's head out with the right hand, so that all the length of neck is shown. With your left hand hold his tail in proper position.

After the dog learns to pose easily and quietly, have some friend, a stranger to the dog, act as a "judge" and go over the dog. Get him thoroughly accustomed to this sort of handling, by using several friends at various times. Then practice by posing him with other dogs, simulating show ring conditions as much as possible.

If the dog is inclined to be self-conscious or timid, take him with you everywhere you can, in stores, in crowds, etc., until he has lost his fear of strange surroundings and strange people.

Study your own dog's conformation. Compare his measurements and weight with those of the standard. If he's too light try to put more flesh on him, if he's too heavy take it off. Spend as much time as possible with your dog, leading him, handling him, posing him. He'll pay you in the show ring for your trouble if he is worthy of bench show honors.

Never be hasty with him, and never become excited. Talk to him occasionally in calm, low tones and reward him frequently with caresses and small morsels. If he is possessed of the proper show ring temperament, he will respond readily.

to your side. Keep this up until he comes along readily and naturally. Then slacken your hold on the lead and have him come along with you, slow and then at quickened pace. Keep him traveling in a straight line, jerking him lightly if he tries to waver. Have him circle when you stop, turning clockwise. These lessons are not difficult, for the dog soon catches on to what you want him to do. They should be practiced every day. Do not allow him to pull you. He is to follow where you lead. Reward him frequently when he does well.

In teaching your dog to pose, step in front or to the side of the dog with the lead slack. Attract his attention with a tidbit or toy until he moves into the stance you desire. Set his fore legs so that they are parallel, then move his hind legs into proper position. Teach him to stand quietly with all four legs squarely under him. Have him remain standing in this position for several minutes at a time, talking to him in low tones occasionally and running your hand

—The Art of Showing Dogs—

WHAT IS art? The dictionary describes it as: "Any system of rules and principles that facilitates skilled human accomplishment, also the application of these rules and principles."

The production of a show quality puppy, coming as it does from registered and pedigreed stock, is a product of art—the breeder's art; the application of

rules and principles that govern inheritance of characteristics to produce a puppy that closely conforms to the standard of its breed. The standard that includes or implies excellence in type, quality, balance, soundness, temperament, intelligence, and hardiness.

Today in our world of specialization, to produce

such an animal is not enough, it must be conditioned mentally and physically to take its place among its peers.

To the artistic person in dogs, whether professional or amateur, this young animal represents a challenge not unlike the blank canvas to the painter, the lump of clay to the sculptor—the clean page to the writer. What can be done with the raw material—in this case the exciting challenge of a living, growing, understanding animal, one that is bred to conform with his forebears and ready to be molded into any outstanding patterns of behavior, showmanship, coat and condition that the artist wishes to attempt.

TO RAISE A CHAMPION

Many people are unaware of the fact that this molding begins very early in life. The puppy that is born into a home or kennel where it is handled constantly, almost from birth spoken to and played with, soon realizes there are other things in life than its mother's warmth and its sibling's rivalry. By three or four months of age it has had many new experiences, all of which are necessary for its future development. They are the framework of his being, and should follow a preplanned blueprint.

He has had his tail docked, dew claws removed, ears taped or trimmed—all of these things if he is of a breed where such practices are required. He has been properly inoculated, checked for worms and wormed if necessary. He has had his nails trimmed at regular intervals. His teeth throughout the upcoming teething period must have daily inspection to insure that no abnormalities will result from retained puppy teeth. He has learned to cope with his littermates; this an important psychological development for his mental well-being.

Now, according to the plan, he must learn many new things. His mental development at this point will depend on the artistry and perseverance of his teacher.

He learns his name and comes when called. Rewards throughout this phase of training will be in the form of praise or a pat, both of which he will learn to look forward to as being pleasurable, and which forges a bond between pupil and teacher. He learns to walk on lead, which can be accomplished so easily at this stage of training. To follow the teacher is a pleasure anyway, and to follow him with a connecting lead is no trouble at all.

He learns that going for a ride in the car is fun. It is a fact that a young puppy (three to four months) will adapt to riding in a car almost immediately with little or no distress. The same puppy a month or two older, with no previous experience in a car may become violently sick, and it can take many trips to cure him of this problem.

This also is the time he learns to sleep by himself, and in a crate. A puppy trained thusly at an early age will never think of the crate as punishment, but rather a special place of his own where he will be content and secure. If he is of a breed that requires

coat care and trimming, he learns to submit himself to these ministrations on a table, in a resigned fashion, perhaps, but not with a cowed or belligerent attitude. A mixture of reassurance and firmness of purpose on the part of the teacher is the order of the day, and between these two the puppy learns to be secure with, as well as to have respect for, his teacher.

And so day by day the puppy is taught as many things as possible that will allow him to be presented in the most favorable manner when it is time for him to enter the show ring. Additional lessons have to do with such things as learning not to chew his bedding. Also, not to remove his towel or coat if he is of a breed that requires these appointments when not actually in the ring. He learns simple commands such as "Stay" (on a table, in a car, etc.), "Go To Bed" (or kennel), "Keep Quiet" (or its alternatives) when he is making a fuss or barking unnecessarily.

He learns to play with a ball, a bone or a chew stick, to run after it, to carry it, or to chew it to amuse himself. Natural tendencies of showmanship are encouraged. Shyness, over-aggressiveness, unattractive traits of any sort—are discouraged and trained out insofar as the teacher is able.

In short, before he can become a show dog, this animal must be taken in hand by a person of talent who can make of him an interested and interesting member of society!

The unsocialized, unaware, strictly kennel-raised puppy who is used only to the regime of going out and coming in, food and sleep, etc., will never present to its handler or judge the kaleidoscope of character traits embodied in a puppy that has been properly prepared for his future. He will be, by comparison, colorless in competition, no matter how great his untapped intelligence.

POINTS TO WATCH

During his mental upbringing the young puppy must have conditioning as regards his muscle and body development. Free running, road walking, sharply-watched periods in his life when uncontrolled exercise might be detrimental, all of this must be figured into the blueprint. In the larger working breeds, too much weight before six months of age coupled with too much running may be disastrous to bone development. Too heavy a body on a Whippet puppy may leave its mark later in life, when, according to the standard of the breed, the body should have no tendency to barrel. The smaller varieties of Poodles which, if left to their own devices will stay on the thin side as puppies, may never mature with the correct body shape.

Young dogs crated to excess without the opportunity to run free or to be road walked may not only fail to develop in body properly, but may pick up "boredom vices" such as crate-chewing, box-walking, yapping without reason, and scratching without cause.

As the time approaches for his ring debut, the puppy's proper weight must be determined and achieved. His muscle tone must be that of the breed he is representing: the lithe, long, unbunched muscle of the sight hound; the hard firm flesh and muscle of the Boxer, Rottweiler and Bull Terrier; the firm feet, highly arched, found on so many breeds, all can be achieved and maintained only by proper exercise.

GROOMING AND TRIMMING

As the mental and physical development of our young hopeful has been likened to the artist working with living clay, the grooming and trimming of those breeds that require it must be likened to sculpture in hair. What a challenge to an artist to have before him a mature animal with coat ready to be trimmed not only according to the standard of the breed, but with enough allowance in that standard to fit it to the individual dog, to minimize its shortcomings, but so much more important, to bring out its good points to the fullest. To challenge the artistry further, the finished product must look its best, not only when standing on the grooming table, but able to continue that picture of close-to-breed-perfection while in motion!

The trimming of dogs is a worldwide profession, and a professionally-trimmed specimen will have that neat, finished look about it. However, an artistically trimmed or groomed dog will have a never-to-be-forgotten look about it of beautiful balance in line and symmetry. There have been praises sung of great Ter-

There is plenty of room for skill and talent in grooming a dog for bench or ring. Hank Babbitt photo.

rier men who knew where every hair was on their charges and why it was there. Poodles through the years have been presented by some in faultless manner, neither too much coat or too little, bracelets, packs, and pompons done to the last turn. The more subtly trimmed sporting dog may have his grace and line apparent, but without any mark of trimming knife, razor or clipper.

SHOWING AND HANDLING

And now, what of the person that will take hold of the lead to present our young hopeful to the dog show world? What of his (or her) artistic application to this art of showing dogs? This person may be professional, amateur, the person who has brought this youngster along the way to this point, or someone who merely puts on the finishing touches just before entering the ring. If this person is a great artist he will, like all great artists, have studied his art from the ground up. His background will have included the learning, by actual doing of everything that has to do with the production of a fine purebred animal.

It will be he who has whelped puppies, guided them through their ups and downs, the pitfalls and triumphs of their early life, so that he knows what has gone into the making of the dog he now stands with, ready and responsible. He has done this many times over and has become more knowledgable each time. He will have learned, and filed away in his subconcious the causes, effects and consequences of each stage in the animal's life, so that he may be able to call on his vast store when he enters the ring. He may be faced with a score of situations to which he must apply a good solution immediately, so that the job he does is smooth, effortless, and uninterrupted.

He must have a knowledge and understanding of the breed and its uses for this is the reason he is presenting the dog. He presents it as an individual embodying correct breed character and type, and unless he knows that is correct, he cannot do this job properly.

He must have a delicate sense of timing to have his dog just right at the right moment. He must have grace and a sense of rhythm when he moves his dog. He must not be clumsy in any of his hand motions, either when he poses his animal by hand, or gives it signals to pose on the end of the lead. He must have an awareness of what is going on in the ring about him, what the judge requires as regards ring procedure, which dog is the one to beat, what he can call on to make his dog shine just a little brighter. He must be a competitive person, but not an obnoxious one. He must not offend either fellow exhibitors or the judge, but he must be a team with his dog, and a team to be reckoned with. He must know rules inside and out, proper ring procedure and protocol for all occasions.

Above all, he must have a "pair of hands." He should be able to tell through his hands, what his dog is doing, how it is doing it, and why. It is through his hands that he gives confidence to the wary, encouragement to the confused, and correction to the over-zealous.

His instrument is his dog, and an artist at work will bring forth from this dog *harmony*—a harmonious blending of the art of breeding, the art of raising, the art of conditioning, the art of trimming, and the art of presentation in the show ring—the achievement of which, all in right combination forms altogether the art of showing dogs.

—The Art of Judging Dogs—

DOG JUDGING is an art. The statement is sometimes strongly debated by the losers. Yet there are judges who are almost universally acclaimed for their competence, while others are tabbed as having less competence, if indeed any at all. This grading by thousands of experienced exhibitors and breeders is the best proof that judging really is an art.

Dog judges themselves have been heard to say that judges are born, not made. This may be a bit of self-flattery indulged in by both good and poor judges alike. But it is true in the same sense that a great artist is superior to his training.

QUALITIES NEEDED IN JUDGES

A superior dog judge has integrity, thorough knowledge of the breed standards, experience, a thorough knowledge of ring procedures, and an emotional structure not easily upset. He also has the stamina to stand ten hours on concrete, or in broiling sun, while doing perhaps 200 full knee-bends within the same period.

In few other lines of work will a person have to make as many conscious decisions during a day as in dog judging, for the dog judge may be required to make a hundred to two hundred decisions, many of them close and over which he must struggle, during a single assignment.

But above all, the dog judge must "have an eye for a dog." The ability to recognize a good dog is the paramount requirement, of course, in the art of judging. While this ability improves with experience, it is instinctive, just as is the "natural" talent of the great artist.

A good dog is something more than the sum of his parts. He has some inner balance—some supreme quality which is greater than the sum of his parts, and indeed which may even minimize the sum of his flaws. One can make a comparison from the history of art. Sculptors coming after the Golden Age of Greece had the world's finest statues for models, yet they could not discover the Greek balance of parts.

Efforts were made to work out the proportions by a mathematical formula. They failed. Complicated geometric equations were developed. They contributed to the production of some geometric patterns in art, but they didn't produce art comparable to that of the great Greeks.

Efforts were made to make perfect statues by combining perfect parts. That is, a perfect skull shape, perfect nose, and perfect eye set—the marvelous chest from this model, the hips and thighs from that one.

The results were statues. But they weren't good ones. The bosom from one model belongs on that one, not on another. The legs of this one mold into the body of this man, not of another.

A human body, or a dog's, represents a kind of balance. "I wish," says the breeder, or the judge, "that I could put this dog's head on that dog's body." But, if it could be done, the result would be something less than either animal had before. For there would be no unity in the new organism.

Dog judges have, on occasion, been known to do an excellent job of judging in breeds which they had never seen before, and having standards which they had never read. What has carried them through has been this "having an eye for a dog." Yet the modern dog judge is required to have more than that. He must know the standards of the breeds he judges. He must know when a dog has a disqualifying fault peculiar to that breed, for example.

The judge may move from judging Great Danes to Beagles. His eye must be able to make a quick change from one size and type to the other. And it must tell the judge whether the Beagle is so close to height disqualification as to require an official measurement. He must keep within his mind, all the disqualifying height requirements of different breeds, and some 50 other points of disqualification in each of over 100 breeds of dogs.

Time was when judges seldom if ever required official measurements of dogs. Often they ignored disqualifying faults, unless these were entirely obvious to both exhibitors and spectators. Moreover, exhibitors seldom challenged other dogs when it was deemed they had disqualifying faults. They seldom do so even now. Apparently, they consider this to be poor sportsmanship. Or, they are afraid of making enemies. Exhibitors, too, seemed to feel that both the judge and other exhibitors were out of line if they challenged a dog on the question of disqualifying faults.

Yet the judge is, in a very real sense, the custodian of the breed standards. It is up to him to enforce the provisions of the standards, and to judge on the basis of those standards. Today, the American and Canadian Kennel Clubs, for instance, require their judges

Portrait of a Great Pyrenees family—four pups with their mother and father.

to do this. And so judges routinely call for measurements, veterinary examinations, or rulings on artificial coloring.

One great proof of a judge's competence is his ability to make choices between an even lot of average good dogs, or an even lot of poor ones. For it seldom happens that he will find a great dog in every class or breed.

The judge of any class considers breed type, soundness, balance of body parts, coat condition, movement, temperament, and handling. Having considered all these, and having struck a balance among all the dogs, he makes his decisions. His success in doing this is a test of his art.

A professional handler, in speaking of a certain judge remarked: "He can do a great job until he gets upset by something. Then he goes haywire!" The number of things which can upset a judge on a given day are legion. They include the knowledge that, in the last class, he made a mistake. The mark of his art is to remain undisturbed, to go on judging objectively, as though nothing had happened.

THE SEARCH FOR A PERFECT DOG

Sometimes ringsiders will say that they could "follow that judge all the way." Or, they'll say that they couldn't follow him. Or, that he reversed his type in dogs and bitches. In the first instance, they could follow the judge because in each class he could find dogs of the same general conformation. But, in the second case, he couldn't, because they weren't there to be found.

This brings up a major problem in judging. The judge has a preconceived picture in his mind of the perfect dog in this breed. If he can find dogs of this general quality, he is lucky. If he can't, then he must do the best he can.

His placings will not really satisfy him, and he knows that they won't satisfy exhibitors or spectators at ringside. For his choices may be no more defensible—and no less—than those of tomorrow's judge. And yet, if under these circumstances, his choices are generally accepted, then he has demonstrated a major ability in the art of judging—the ability to pick the best of a poor lot.

"Friendship ceases at the ring entrance" is a common expression at dog shows. Certainly among the best judges it is a simple statement of fact. The judge is there to judge dogs, not people. He cannot allow friendship, sentiment, or hatred to mar his judgment. He may detest some particular exhibitor or handler, but this must not affect his judgment of the dog before him.

THE SEARCH FOR THE BEST DOG

There are times when the winner's dog may get five points and the winner's bitch none. The hope then is that the bitch will defeat the dog for best of winners, and in doing so, pick up the same number of points. But the judge is not in the ring to award as many points as possible to this or that dog. He's there for one purpose only, to pick the *best* dog.

If the judge gives best of winners to the bitch in the example cited, though she doesn't merit it, he is being dishonest. And, moreover, he may be beating a male which is a best-in-show possibility.

JUDGES HAVE THEIR PROBLEMS

A handler, in speaking of a certain judge, said: "If you say anything out of line to that judge, or try in any way to promote your dog, he'll knock you down instantly." By that, he meant the judge would defeat his dog. The handler intended this as a compliment. But the judge probably would not have considered it as such. For he had to judge the dog, regardless of the actions of its handler.

In such a case, the judge knows that if he puts up this handler's dog, the handler will think that he was able to influence him. So he is in a dilemma. But there is an answer to it. The judge can always report the incident in his judge's book, or to the superintendent, or to the bench show committee. His action might cause the suspension of the handler or exhibitor. But it will have preserved his integrity as a judge.

Many a good judge ruins his own performance by talking too much. And thus, the art of judging includes also the ability to keep still.

A beaten exhibitor may accept a judge's placements with good grace, and may even agree with them. But his reasons may differ radically from those of the judge. And, in any case, he does not like to have his dog "picked apart" in public.

Some who have carried the art of judging to its highest point are "loners." They arrive at the show at the last possible moment, and they are the first to leave, or at least they leave as soon as the assignment is completed. In this way, they avoid those who would promote their dogs unfairly. They avoid the associations which cause scandal. And they avoid the "Why did you put my dog down?" episodes which so often cause hard feelings and misunderstandings.

In his *Encounter With The Future*, the world-famed astronomer Fred Hoyle points out that a mathematician who does not continue to do mathematical problems soon becomes a moss-covered has-been. The best dog judges never take their art for granted. They study the standards regularly. They keep familiar with the rules. And they always admit the possibility of their own errors, even as much as they try to avoid them.

Part VI

DOG AILMENTS AND FIRST AID

While a dog will diligently show in many ways that he is trying to carry out certain responsibilities to his master, as he sees them to be, a prime owner responsibility centers on looking after the dog's well-being. He must stay alert for health problems which the dog obviously cannot tell him about, but which, as they arise, usually manifest themselves through the dog's behavior. While most dogs normally lead robust healthy lives, some fall prey ultimately to illness, disorder, or accident. Fortunately, there has been much progress in veterinary medicine. In the bulk of cases it is possible for the owner to spare his dog pain and suffering and see him put back on the road to health through alertness and prompt consultation with a veterinarian whenever a health problem is suspected.

—Introduction—

IT WOULD be well to observe at the outset that author, publisher, and authorities agree that dog owners are best advised to consult a veterinarian whenever health problems arise with their dogs. As will be noted in this text, the veterinary practice of today has become a highly specialized profession and it would be extremely unwise for the average dog owner to attempt to diagnose and treat his dog only on the basis of consulting a book.

Most owners become accustomed to the pattern of their dog's normal behavior, it usually being abundantly clear when the dog is healthy and well. Departures from these customary patterns will, of course, raise questions in the owner's mind, one of the first of which should always be whether or not this may suggest a health problem. If so, the owner should not hesitate to consult a veterinarian.

Most professional kennel operators and dog breeders follow this same practice, regarding veterinarians as their foremost allies in the conduct of a successful business.

Nevertheless the information in this section was of educational value to many owners in the past and regarded as of considerable merit by readers of earlier editions. Considerable efforts have been made, therefore, to make it as up-to-date and useful as possible. There are times when an owner will wish to "read up" on specific dog health problems. Some of this information may prove helpful when an owner is uncertain whether a dog's behavior is merely a matter of eccentricity or indicates the need for a veterinarian's attention. When in doubt, check with your veterinarian.

—Progress in Veterinary Medicine—

THE VETERINARY profession has contributed to and profited by the rapid advancement of science during this century. For example, the modification of viruses to render them incapable of producing dis-

ease, but capable of producing immunity, was successfully accomplished during the early 1930's and the late 1940's in developing a modified vaccine against distemper. As has been true in other allied fields,

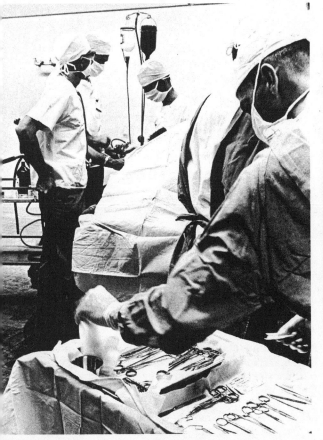

Administering fluids in preparation for animal surgery. Auburn University photo.

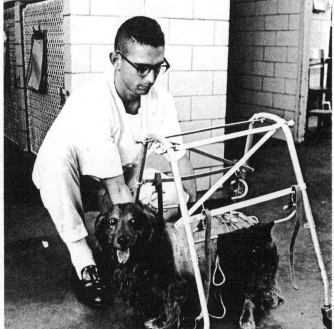

Providing postoperative support for a dog which has had spinal surgery. Auburn University photo.

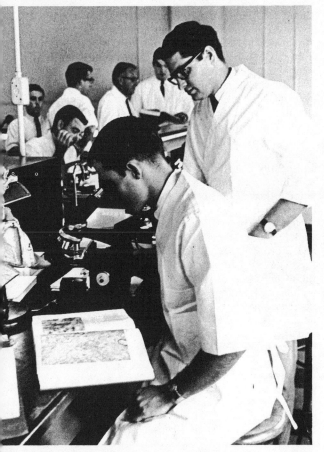

Many advances have been made in veterinary medicine in the last three decades. This is the Histology Laboratory at the Auburn U. School of Veterinary Medicine. Auburn University photo.

many diseases which were formerly grouped under a general heading have been accurately defined and identified. Infectious Canine Hepatitis is a good example of such a disease. The pioneer work accomplished in successfully immunizing animals with a modified live virus has resulted in the development of the Salk vaccine against infantile paralysis in humans as well as a modified live virus against rabies, the first significant change in immunization procedure since the original work of Pasteur.

This figurative "explosion of knowledge" has simultaneously influenced veterinary medical education which in the early part of the century began as a two-year university-level program and has subsequently increased to a minimum of a six-year program with the average number of years required at the present time of slightly less than seven years of training at the university level. This extended training has become necessary because of the many scientific developments which must be included in this traditional program. For example, prior to the 1930's there were few specific antibacterial agents. With the advent of the sulfonamides and antibiotics during the 1930's efficient tools became available to use for combating bacterial infections. The electronics industry has made significant contributions with the development of electrocardiographs, electroencephalographs and various other devices for detecting abnormalities in animals.

These developments created the need to establish the specialties which will become more numerous and more accurately defined in the future. The specialties will become a greater factor in practice and the development of allied groups of practitioners, rather than single general practitioners, appears to be the developmental pattern of the profession. Certainly no one can be proficient in all of the specialty requirements. The small animal practitioner is already experiencing divisions into canine, feline, exotic animals, pet birds, and other specialties. Specialties have developed in the various disciplines of surgery: for example, orthopedics, surgery of the eye, neurosurgery, etc.

Specialties are being developed within the field of canine medicine; namely, internal medicine, neuromedicine, or neurological diseases. Certainly this is a favorable situation for improved service to dog owners.

In summary, the empirical features of the science as it existed during the early part of this century are being replaced by a more nearly exact and predictable scientific approach.

──Some Common Dog Disorders──

IT IS virtually impossible to mention all of the diseases and disorders in dogs since volumes are written on the subject and veterinarians involve a lifetime of learning to stay abreast of all modern developments. It is felt that the dog owner must keep veterinary services prominent in his plans to maintain a healthy animal, not only as a *cure* for a disorder or disease but foremost as a *preventative* of trouble. The topics discussed will include the symptoms and possible causes of some common conditions, contagious diseases, external and internal parasites, poisons, breeding disorders, puppy diseases, old dog problems and eye and ear disorders.

SYMPTOMS . . . CAUSES

Abdominal Swelling. A frequent cause of abdominal distention in a puppy is a heavy internal parasite infection, such as roundworms, causing a so-called "pot belly" appearance. Occasionally a puppy will have acute abdominal distention from inability to defecate because of an obstruction or blockage at the anus, rectum, or intestinal tract. Accumulation of gas or fluids in the stomach can cause this disorder.

In older animals, one must consider ascites or "water belly" being caused by a liver or heart disorder; pregnancy; a pus infection of the womb called pyometritis; highly distended urinary bladder due to bladder stones, blockage, or paralysis; bloat; or tumors. It is obvious that the differential diagnosis of these disorders will usually require prompt veterinary services.

Appetite—Increase, Decrease, Depraved. An increase of appetite may occur during pregnancy and lactation, worm infection, sugar diabetes, pancreatic atrophy, or a psychic condition.

A decrease in appetite is an important clinical sign of certain diseases such as distemper, infectious hepatitis, leptospirosis, rabies, internal fungus and bacterial infections, kidney disease, stomach and intestinal disorders, heavy parasitism, pneumonia, and many others. Frequently inappetance is seen when foreign bodies such as sticks, fish bones, and chicken bones are lodged in the teeth, mouth, and esophagus. *Lack of appetite* is one of the most important signs of serious illness and should call for immediate veterinary consultation.

A depraved appetite is one in which material other than food is eaten, such as coal, manure, dirt and gravel. Causes of a depraved appetite are usually a mineral or vitamin deficiency, a chronic stomach condition, teething or gum inflammations, or an infectious disease like rabies. Occasionally this disorder is due to a psychic disturbance.

Bad Breath (Halitosis). The usual causes of bad breath are abnormalities of the teeth or gums, such as tartar, pyorrhea, dental caries or cavities, and inflammation of the gums. Other causes can be inflammations or ulcerations of the mouth from vitamin deficiencies, trench mouth, advanced kidney disease, stomach disorders, and lung abscesses. Oral health should be maintained by the owner if the animal is to live a long and happy existence.

Blood Deficiency or Bleeding. Anemia can be caused by severe hookworm infection, especially in a puppy. An owner must keep constant check of the lip and gum color (which should be a bright pink) and have a stool sample examined frequently to guard against an overwhelming hookworm infection. Nutritional deficiencies such as iron and vitamins can cause anemia. Anemia may also be caused by a general blood loss in disorders such as hemolytic puppy disease, wounds, warfarin poisoning, tumors, and external parasites such as ticks and lice. Other disorders and toxins which can suppress the formation of red cells and cause anemia are sugar diabetes, advanced kidney disease, and toxins from bacterial infections as in pyometritis (pus in the womb).

Nosebleed in hunting animals can be caused by foreign bodies in the nose such as lawn grasses, sticks, and thorns. Severe inflammation, allergies, and infections like distemper may also cause a nosebleed. Blood or vessel disorders can result in nosebleeds. In middle-aged and old dogs especially, tumors in the nasal and sinus passages frequently are the cause of nosebleeds. Most all of these causes involve sneezing and this act can initiate as well as perpetuate bleeding. Ice packs on the nose and head may be used to control profuse hemorrhage while the dog is on his way to the veterinarian.

Blood in the stool may make the feces bright red, dark brown, or black. The higher the bleeding occurs in the gastro-intestinal tract, the darker the blood.

Therefore, in a black stool, bleeding may be from the stomach or intestines while a bright red stool may be from bleeding in the colon, rectum, or anus. Black stools could result from hookworm infection, or a high content of iron or liver in the food. Bright blood in the stool may mean a sharp pointed foreign body in the rectum or ulcers in the colon or rectum.

Blood in the urine usually indicates the presence of stones in the kidneys, bladder, or outer urinary tract called the urethra. Stones generally cause frequent and incomplete urination and straining. However, severe inflammations or tumors of the urinary tract, especially the bladder or prostate gland, can cause bloody urine. It is obvious to an observant owner that the initial stage of estrus (heat period) in the bitch can cause blood tinged urine.

Breathing Difficulty. Breathing difficulty, air hunger or dyspenea can result from any partial or complete obstruction of the air passages, such as the nostrils, nose, throat, voice box, trachea, bronchi, and smaller bronchi called bronchioles. Any condition of the lungs that interferes with the transfer of gases as in congested lungs, pneumonia, abscesses, tumors, and foreign material in the lung tissue. Foreign material in the lungs can result from improper bottle feeding of very young puppies, or dosing a dog with liquid medication can cause air hunger. Any disorder that compresses the lungs such as chest fluids, pleuritis, infections, diaphragmatic hernia, and air in the chest cavity which is outside the lungs (as can be seen in broken ribs or wounds), can cause labored respiration.

Other conditions causing air hunger may be attributed to the heart and blood, severe anemia, congestive heart failures, pericarditis, and heartworms. High fever or severe poisonings can cause air hunger. Air hunger is seen in heat stroke. Severe air hunger demands prompt veterinary attention; it can be an emergency situation.

Convulsions. A convulsion or seizure is a disorder associated with violent muscular contractions with partial or total loss of consciousness. Usually convulsions are seen in infections, inflammations, or disorders of the brain or in diseases involving the body metabolism. Distemper can cause convulsions in the terminal state. Menigitis, brain hemorrhage, inflammations of the brain known as encephalitis, and brain tumors cause seizures. Epilepsy and so-called false epilepsy cause convulsions.

Metabolic conditions such as lack of blood calcium and sugar can cause symptoms like convulsions. Terminal kidney disease causes seizures and coma. Poisons like strychnine and some weed and insect poisons can cause seizures. Occasionally disorders like ear mites, severe skin inflammations, and internal parasites may stimulate convulsions, particularly in highly nervous individuals. Careful physical, x-ray, and laboratory examinations by a veterinarian may be needed to determine the cause. An electroence-phalogram may be needed to diagnose forms of epilepsy.

Cough. Coughing is common in dogs and is usually due to an irritation or inflammation somewhere in the breathing tract. Hacking or gagging coughs originate from the tonsils, pharynx, larynx, or trachea. Deep coughs originate from the bronchi or bronchioles. A cough is Nature's way of clearing the respiratory tract of mucus and other fluids. Most coughs are due to tonsillitis, pharyngitis, laryngitis, or bronchitis. Pneumonia produces a deep cough. Pleurisy, asthma, and roundworm larvae migrations in the lungs cause cough symptoms. An infection, tracheobronchitis, also known as kennel cough is frequently seen in kennels. This condition spreads from dog to dog.

A cough may be due to conditions involving the blood and heart. Congestive heart disease is a frequent cause and is characterized by a soft muffled type of cough. Heartworm infections can be a cause.

Persistent cough should receive veterinary attention since it may have public health significance. Conditions of human health importance could be tuberculosis, toxoplasmosis, histoplasmosis, and blastomycosis.

Dandruff. Dandruff or scurf is frequently seen in dogs having nutritional deficiencies and metabolic disturbances of internal organs as the liver, pancreas, or kidneys. Infestations of fleas, fungus infections, and mange can cause dandruff. One of the most common causes of dandruff is hypothyroidism or other endocrine disturbances of the gonads, adrenal, or pituitary glands. Irritating soaps, medications, and sunburn can cause a scaliness or dandruff. It is well to remember that the condition of the skin reflects the internal condition of the body and that dandruff may reflect an internal disturbance.

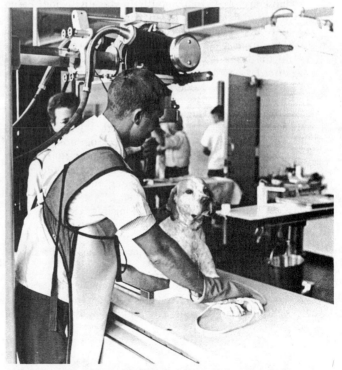

Positioning a Pointer for X-Ray. Auburn University photo.

Deafness. Occasionally an owner will notice that a puppy or several puppies in a litter seem deaf. Deafness in a puppy is usually a birth defect and may be inherited. Certain breeds seem to be predisposed and frequently this defect occurs concomitantly with other defects. It is important that such animals are examined carefully and if there is a chance of an inherited trait, these animals should not be used for breeding purposes.

Other causes for deafness can be outer ear infections (otorrhea), ear tumors, and extremely dirty or waxy ear canals. Brain injuries, tumors, or defects as well as abnormalities of the auditory nerve can cause deafness. Deafness seems to be prevalent among very aged animals.

Diarrhea. Diarrhea is one of the most common complaints and usually points to an abnormality of the digestive system. Diarrhea is characterized by a stool of thin consistency, even watery, is more frequently voided, and can be accompanied by much straining and abdominal distress. Inflammation of the intestinal tract usually manifests itself by a diarrhea. Such causes can be distemper; bacterial and fungus infections such as leptospirosis, salmonellosis, and histoplasmosis; parasitic infections such as hookworms, whipworms, coccidia, and strongyloides; other disorders such as advanced kidney disease, lung or womb infections, hepatitis, and pancreatitis. Poisons such as arsenic, lead, and phosphorus can cause a diarrhea. Diarrhea can be caused by a nervous colitis which may lead to ulcerations in the colon. This condition is seen occasionally in very high-strung hunting or field trial dogs.

Since persistent diarrhea might have public health significance in the case of pets, a veterinarian should be consulted for diagnosis and treatment.

Fainting. Fainting, passing out, falling out, and collapse are used synonymously in this discussion. Fainting is differentiated from coma because it involves only a transient loss of consciousness. Fainting can arise from a vessel spasm or transient vessel blockage in the brain. Fainting is more characteristic of heart disorder or a lack of blood sugar. Heartworms are the chief cause for a dog to "give out" in the field. Some hunting dogs "pass out" in severe exercise because of a lack of blood sugar. These animals have a disorder which does not allow fast enough release of stored sugar during extreme stress. Feeding honey, sugar, molasses, or other easily digestible sugar immediately before and during the hunt may alleviate the condition. This has been seen in young puppies or in cases of pancreatic or adrenal tumors.

If fainting persists into longer periods of time, coma develops. Brain disorders, sugar diabetes, advanced kidney disease or uremia, eclampsia, heat prostration, barbiturate or narcotic poisonings all can cause a coma.

Fever. Fever or increased body temperature can be due to some degree to fright or nervousness. A so-called dry, warm nose is not an accurate indication of fever. Extreme high fever can be seen in heat exhaustion or stroke, in hyperexcitability preceding convulsions as in eclampsia, or in virus infections as acute infectious hepatitis. Bacterial infections such as pneumonia, bronchitis, leptospirosis, bacterial stage of distemper, and metritis generally cause moderate fever. Internal fungus diseases can cause moderate or virtually no fever. In short, fever is a response to an infection except in heat stroke, eclampsia, or convulsions. Since fever is a symptom, the cause should be accurately diagnosed by a veterinarian early in the course of the disease.

Moderate subnormal temperature is usually seen before whelping. A marked subnormal temperature usually indicates a terminal disorder which may result in death.

Hair Loss. Localized loss of hair or baldness can be caused by mange, allergic dermatitis, fungus and ringworm disease, fleas, ticks, thermal or chemical burns, and endocrine disorders. Among the endocrine disorders, a deficient thyroid function is most frequent. Abnormal function of the pituitary, adrenal, and sex glands can cause baldness. Usually a malfunction of the ductless or endocrine glands is characterized by a bilaterally symmetrical loss of hair. Some breeds are characterized by a generalized thin hair coat and a complete absence on the undersurface of the body.

Itch. Itch or pruritis is an intense skin irritation and pain. In most cases of intense itching, the animal tries to alleviate the pain by scratching. Thus a vicious cycle of itch and scratching takes place and a severe lesion results from self mutilation. Fleas cause intense itching, while chiggers, ticks, lice, mange mites, and fungus infections are additional causes. Allergic reactions from pollens, blood transfusions, medications, and foods can all be causes. Liver, kidney, and diabetic disorders have also been known to cause itching. Chemical irritations, burns, excessive nervousness, and friction can cause itching. The services of a veterinarian are needed to help determine the cause so that relief can be afforded.

Jaundice. Jaundice or icterus is a yellow discoloration of tissue, seen best in the white of the eye or in nonpigmented skin. It is generally due to severe liver disease, a stoppage of the bile duct, or in severe blood destruction within the body. A common disease causing jaundice is leptospirosis especially when the particular spirochete called *Leptospira icterohemorrhagica* is involved. The blood disease in young puppies due to a factor similar to the rh factor in the human causes extensive blood destruction, icterus, and early death.

Lameness. Books have been written on the causes of lameness. Anything that causes man to limp can be compared to the dog. An inability to use a limb normally may require a careful and complete physical and possibly an x-ray examination by a veterinarian. An owner can examine the foot pads and between the toes of the affected limb for thorns, burrs, awns, and other foreign bodies which are causing pain. Frequently a cut or worn foot pad will cause lameness. More complex causes are sprains; ruptured tendons, ligaments, and muscles; fractures, infections, inflammations, or tumors of muscle or bone; various abnormalities of joints; foreign body wounds such as sticks; or injured nerves. Frequently a spinal condition such as a slipped disc, spinal inflammation or arthritis will start with pain and lameness in one leg and promptly affect both limbs.

In young dogs, a lameness, wobbly, or incoordination of the gait in the back legs may be due to congenital hip dysplasia. The basic feature of this disease is an improper anatomic relationship between the head of the femur and the socket joint. This improper fit results in a painful and progressive arthritis of the joint. Hip dysplasia occurs in all breeds, but the incidence is much greater in those breeds weighing 35 pounds or more at maturity. The exact mode of genetic transmission is not clearly understood.

For those interested in breeds with a high incidence of hip dysplasia, an evaluation program for breeding stock has been established by the Orthopedic Foundation for Animals, 817 Virginia Avenue, Columbia, Missouri 65201. For a small fee this panel of veterinary radiologists will certify as to the presence or absence of hip dysplasia. (*See also* discussion under *Congenital Diseases,* PUPPY DISEASES.)

Loss of Weight. Loss of weight and condition is a symptom that should be investigated when seen in dogs. Loss of weight can be observed when an animal has a normal appetite, especially if he is being worked hard when the animal has not been conditioned properly. However, a dog in proper training may only appear to be down in weight but usually weighs more. Loss of weight in the presence of a normal or abnormally large appetite is usually seen in metabolic disturbances such as a chronic pancreatic atrophy or in dietary deficiencies. Types of internal parasitism such as tapeworms can cause a weight loss and a normal or greater appetite.

Weight loss due to a decreased appetite generally indicates a serious viral, bacterial, fungus, parasitic, metabolic, or cancerous disease. A check for parasitism would be a good place to start. An evaluation of the diet should be standard procedure. It is quite likely that a veterinarian should be consulted early in the course of the condition for a more favorable outcome.

Nasal Discharge. Small amounts of clear moisture on the nostrils and muzzle are normal for the dog. Any discharge in excess of this is indicative of an abnormal situation in the nasal passages, sinus cavities, throat, or lungs. Inflammations due to viral infections as in distemper, and bacterial, yeast, and fungus infections may all cause a mucoid or purulent discharge. Allergies to pollens or irritants may cause a mucoid discharge. Foreign bodies such as ticks and awn grasses can cause a unilateral bloody discharge which may lead to a mucoid of purlent discharge if not

removed. Tumors or nasal mite infections can cause blood and other discharges. Infected upper teeth can cause nasal discharges. Sneezing is common with some types of nasal disorders. Many dogs will remove a discharge by constant licking, but depressing the nostrils will demonstrate the discharge.

Pain. The reaction to pain varies with types, breeds, and individuals within a breed. A miniature breed in a closely supervised environment will usually manifest pain more dramatically than a member of a large breed who is one among many in a kennel. Certain organs seem to be more sensitive to pain than others. For instance, pain in the abdomen produces less manifestation than a slipped disk in the neck. Abdominal and spinal pain usually produce an arched back and splinting of the abdominal muscles. Pain the the skin produces scratching. Spinal pain produces a reluctance to move the affected part, muscle spasms, and inability to move the legs. Affections of the brain produce a general irritability, pain, or lack of pain or depression. Acute pancreatitis and calculi passing in the ureters cause extreme colicky pain. Persistent pain should call for a physical examination to determine the cause so that humane relief can be secured.

Shivering. Shivering can be caused by being cold, feverish, frightened, or from a nervous disorder.

Vomiting. Dogs vomit easily and can feel very little discomfort in the process. Vomiting is an important symptom and usually is caused by an abnormality of the digestive tract. Tonsillitis, inflammations of the esophagus and stomach frequently are the cause. Obstructions in the passage of food in the esophagus and stomach such as choke, spasm of the inlet or outlet of the stomach, or obstructions or foreign bodies in the intestine can cause vomiting. The speed at which vomiting occurs after eating is an indication of the location of the trouble. Vomiting from esophagitis occurs within a few seconds after eating while an intestinal or stomach abnormality may cause vomiting to take place hours after eating. Strictures or enlargements of the esophagus may cause vomiting. Young puppies may vomit as soon as they start eating solid food because of a congenital vascular or esophageal defect. The esophageal worm and tumors can cause vomiting.

Other conditions can promote vomiting such as severe infections and absorption of bacterial toxins in pneumonia, pyometritis, hepatitis, peritonitis, and nephritis. Brain injuries, tumors, meningitis, and poisons may upon occasion produce vomiting.

Other Common Symptoms. Home diagnosis of ailments among dogs is seldom dependable and often dangerous, although it is well for the owner to have as much knowledge as possible concerning what common symptoms of disorder might indicate. It must be remembered that in a number of ailments or diseases the same symptoms are present, particularly in the preliminary stages.

For instance, loss of appetite may indicate any number of things. Among them are foreign bodies in

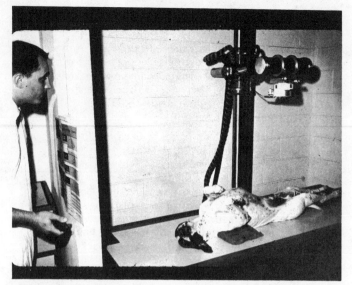

X-raying a dog to determine whether or not hip dysplasia is present. Photo by Purina.

the mouth or throat, insect stings, lead poisoning, mouth infection, loose teeth, tongue burned or cut, tonsillitis, ulcers, tumors or swelling in mouth, worms, and fever diseases.

If your dog needs treating for worms he will generally show one or more of the following symptoms: watery eyes, pus in inside corners of eyes (tape or whipworm indication), loose bowel movements, anemia (hookworm infestation), unthrifty coat, loss of appetite.

A number of troubles may be indicated by coughs of various types and degrees. Among them are asthma, upper respiratory infections, distemper (dry cough), Housedog Disease (gagging cough), eating grass (gagging cough), sore throat, tonsillitis, pneumonia, and heartworm. If the dog coughs only when pulling against the leash, and then frequently, heartworm is most likely indicated.

Frequent shaking of the head should make it obvious that something is wrong which needs correction. This may be ear canker, ear mites, a torn flap, "stick tight" parasites, lice, blood tumor or middle ear abscess.

If the dog runs at the nose he may be coming down with distemper, pneumonia, or Housedog Disease, have a nasal tumor or nasal infection, or be suffering from salmon poisoning. The latter trouble is not uncommon in certain areas on the West Coast.

Paralysis or partial paralysis may indicate a broken or injured back, infection of the spinal cord, brain lesion, Housedog Disease, or toxic poisoning.

Many dogs suffer from urinary troubles. Bloody urine indicates kidney or bladder stones or infection; cloudy urine, bladder infection; inability to urinate, stones in penis or uretha; dribbling urine or leaks, diabetes, kidney disease, or the aftermath of spaying.

Excessive nervousness may be inherited or caused by early puppy influences, training practices, tapeworms, whipworms, or brain inflammation.

If the dog frequently bites at himself it may be troubled with external parasites such as fleas, lice, red bugs or ticks, or may be suffering from skin diseases, mange (either form), or a vitamin deficiency (rare).

If the dog occasionally drags his rear along the ground this does not necessarily mean that he is infested with worms. Generally, it means that he is only squeezing out some of the accumulation in his anal glands.

Whenever at all practicable, it is always best to consult a competent veterinarian before administering any internal medicine.

COMMON CONTAGIOUS DISEASES OF DOGS

The most common contagious diseases in dogs are canine distemper, infectious canine hepatitis, leptospirosis, and rabies. All of these diseases are caused by a virus except leptospirosis which is caused by spirochete bacteria. Some of the other bacterial and mycotic diseases will be discussed under another section.

Canine Distemper. Canine distemper has been the leading disease threat to the dog for centuries. It is not contagious for man. Its incidence is world wide. It is characterized by a high mortality, causing some 50-80% of those affected to die. Those that live may have permanent impairment in the nervous system; senses of sight, smell, or hearing; or a chronic lung disease. The disease attacks all susceptible dogs, young or old. It is usually seen in young dogs only because older dogs have either been well immunized or recovered from the disease.

The cause of distemper is a filtrable virus. This virus can cause disease when contracted through direct exposure to a sick dog, through air, or by inanimate objects. Canine distemper can cause disease in foxes, wolves, and mink but not in cats. The so-called cat distemper is caused by an entirely different virus.

The clinical signs of canine distemper are variable, especially if a partial immunity may exist. The animal may run a moderate fever, be listless, and off feed. Respiratory symptoms of nose discharge, cough, and pneumonia develop commonly. Diarrhea is frequently seen. Nervous signs may include muscle twitching, fits, convulsions, and paralysis. Because of the widespread occurrence of the disease, any sick dog, especially a puppy, should receive prompt veterinary consultation for diagnosis and treatment.

Control. Since practically all dogs will eventually be exposed to virulent street virus of distemper, a competent vaccination program appropriate for the individual case should be outlined and administered by your veterinarian. Several programs are being used effectively, such as serum, globulin, killed virus vaccine, and modified live virus (MLV) of ferret, egg, or tissue culture origin. Most authorities agree that at least 2 doses of MLV vaccine should be given in puppies under 3-4 months of age, and annual boosters are strongly recommended. Regional variations in vaccination procedures are dictated by the virulence of the virus in the particular area.

Since even costly treatments for distemper are frequently ineffective, sound vaccination programs and health programs by your veterinarian cannot be emphasized too highly.

Infectious Canine Hepatitis. This disease has also been called Rubarth's disease, fox encephalitis, and canine adenovirus infection. It is an acute virus disease that can infect all members of the canine family but is not infectious to man. It can occur wherever dogs exist regardless of climatic conditions. Surveys have indicated that in dogs over a year of age, more than 50% have been infected. Therefore, its incidence is high, but it is characterized by a low mortality —about 10%.

The clinical signs of infectious hepatitis depend largely on its damage to the linings of blood vessels and to the liver cells. In very acute forms, especially in young puppies, the virus can cause death with few clinical symptoms. The incubation period is similar to that of distemper, that is about 5-9 days. Fever is high, usually a bit higher than in distemper. Other signs are listlessness, congested eye and mouth membranes, lack of appetite, large tonsils, small hemorrhages on mucous membranes, and abdominal pain behind the ribs. The course of the disease may be 4-9 days and a rapid return to health is common. In 15-25% of the dogs, a white or blue eye caused by an interstitial keratitis, occurs in 1-3 weeks after the initial signs.

The treatment and control measures depend on prompt veterinary assistance. Sick animals are treated symptomatically and should be isolated. The disease is spread in acute stages by saliva and feces, and in later stages in the urine. Recovered animals can shed the virus in the urine for several weeks. The virus is not airborne, as in distemper.

A preventative program is facilitated by vaccination at an early age. A program can be followed similar to that suggested for distemper, since many modified live virus products include both distemper and hepatitis vaccine. Annual boosters are recommended. The success of a vaccination program depends on a health program and examinations performed by your local veterinarian.

Leptospirosis. Canine leptospirosis in the United States is caused by spirochete bacteria, usually *Leptospira canicola,* and/or *icterohemorrhagica,* and rarely by *L. pomona.* The latter form is mild while the first two organisms cause severe illness. In man, the disease is called Weil's disease or rat fever. The disease is widespread throughout the world, is no respecter of age, and is infectious to man and other animals.

The clinical signs are attributed to blood destruction, liver, and kidney disease. A moderate fever occurs, the dog may be stiff, have abdominal pain, vomit, have black or tarry diarrhea, and congested oral and eye membranes. Oral membranes show spotty hemorrhages in acute forms. Yellow Jaundice or icterus can occur. Since degrees of kidney destruction are common, death may result from uremic convulsions or coma.

The treatment must be initiated early if any degree of success is to be attained. Antibiotics and special kidney care is imperative. Your veterinarian should be consulted immediately for treatment and control.

Control of the disease is of vital importance to the owner. The disease can spread by contact with excretions, especially urine. The disease can be spread by contact with infected rats or their excreta, therefore food and food containers must not be contaminated by infected urine and feces from dogs, rats, cattle, swine, and other animals. An infected animal must be isolated and handlers must, in addition to aforementioned facts, take particular care of their personal cleanliness.

Vaccination can help prevent the disease when combined with sanitation measures. Puppy vaccination programs should include the leptospirosis vaccines containing at least the two most pathogenic organisms, *L. canicola* and *L. icterohemorrhagica.* Annual boosters are essential since available vaccines confer a protection up to possibly a year. In outbreaks of leptospirosis, your veterinarian may need to give vaccines more frequently along with other control methods.

Rabies. Rabies is caused by a virus which attacks the nervous system and can affect all warm-blooded animals. It is a highly fatal disease and in man causes dreadful clinical signs. The disease is prevalent in certain areas in dogs, foxes, skunks, raccoons, cats, coyotes, bats, and cattle.

The virus can gain entrance in the body by a bite, scratch, or abrasion, usually through infective saliva. The virus can be airborne when huge numbers of infected bats are harbored in caves. The incubation period varies considerably from a few days to 6 months or longer, the average period being 3-8 weeks. Since the virus travels along nerves to the brain, the incubation period is shorter when the bite is close to the brain.

The clinical signs are due to changes in the nervous system. The furious form develops from an inflammatory encephalitis and the dumb or paralytic form may be from a terminal encephalitis. Therefore changes in temperament are important to note, such as extreme affection, seeking seclusion, viciousness, and hyperexcitability. A "dropped jaw", inability to eat, fear of water, (hydrophobia), dilated pupils, a "glassy" stare, fear of light, eating unusual objects such as sticks, straws, or soil can be clinical signs.

The disease demands effective control measures. Suspected animals must be examined and isolated by a veterinarian. All handling must be performed with utmost care. Isolation of unvaccinated exposed animals should be for not less than 4 months. Isolation of a vaccinated exposed animal can be reduced to 30 days. Prevention of the disease is being successfully performed by use of various types of vaccines. The most lasting immunity develops from use of modified live virus vaccine of low embryo passage. Vaccination programs will depend on local laws and circumstances prescribed by your local veterinarian or health department. Community control of the disease depends on vaccination of dogs, elimination of stray dogs, and elimination of infected wild animals.

If a person is bitten by a suspected animal, he should:

1. Apprehend the animal and have health officials or your veterinarian examine and confine him.

2. Cleanse the wound thoroughly and promptly with soap or detergent solution. See your physician immediately for treatment of the wound and possible specific preventative inoculations.

3. Diagnosis by a pathologist from the infected brain will prescribe further action.

BACTERIAL AND FUNGUS INFECTIONS

Bacteria cause most infections associated with a pus exudate. These could include all types of superficial abscesses which develop from skin abrasions, lacerations, wounds, and other injuries. Bacterial infections develop in the late stages or after virus infections such as distemper. Occasionally bacterial infections develop in the intestinal tract following the ingestion of spoiled or contaminated food, such as salmonellosis. Other bacterial infections include tetanus, septicemia, endocarditis, pyometritis, osteomyelitis, and pneumonia.

Other microorganisms which may cause pus-like infections are the fungi and occasionally yeasts. The fungi cause superficial infections and may be present with bacterial organisms. Frequently fungi are present but are not pathogenic until the bacteria have been destroyed, perhaps by use of antibiotics. Common fungus diseases are ringworm and other mycotic dermatitis, blastomycosis, toxoplasmosis, histoplasmosis, nocardiosis, coccidioidomycosis, and cryptococcosis. In this discussion we will discuss pneumonia and the internal fungus infections in more detail.

Pneumonia. This is an inflammation of the lungs which can be caused by a virus, bacteria, fungus or mycotic organisms, migrating parasites, or inhalation or aspiration of foreign material into the lungs. Frequently pneumonia results after a stress condition from another illness, exposure, surgery, and anesthesia. The body's resistance has been lowered and organisms already present cause disease. Penumonia is characterized by difficult breathing, exaggerated rib movements, extension of the head and neck, flaring of the nostrils, and dark mouth membranes. Cough is a prominent sign.

The successful treatment of pneumonia depends on prompt veterinary care not only to treat the condition but also to treat the cause. Owners must be careful in not allowing excessive climatic exposures to susceptible animals. Improper dosing or force feeding liquids to sick or newborn animals frequently causes the material to be accidentally aspirated into the lungs and a pneumonia results. A thoughtfully executed health and vaccination program will generally prevent such disorders as pneumonia.

Systemic Mycoses. Serious problems arise from this in certain areas of the country. These fungi are usually present in the soil and may cause a variety of conditions such as pneumonia, pleurisy, enteritis, abscesses, and osteomyelitis. Generally these organisms cause a progressive disease of long duration which may eventually cause death. In some instances, the body can react favorably and sustain or conquer the disease. Whenever, a disorder persists after usual therapy is given, a mycotic organism may be the cause. Special diagnostic tests and x-ray examinations by a competent veterinarian are necessary. State health laboratories can be of aid in diagnostic tests.

Treatment must be initiated early to be effective. Advanced cases are generally resistant to treatment. Many of these diseases are of public health importance since they affect other animals and man. One must be especially careful with infected animals around children, the aged, or persons who through other illness are in a state of lowered resistance. The advice of your veterinarian and health officials should be obtained.

POISONS

Diseases due to poisonous substances are encountered frequently in the dog as household products with potentially harmful effects continue to increase. There are numerous highly advertised products on the market which are dangerous when not used with the utmost caution and when directions are not carefully followed. Misuse of such products account for a large number of deaths to dogs each year. Another source of trouble is accidental access to toxic materials. Since most dogs will eat a variety of substances and cannot distinguish between the toxic and nontoxic, one should be especially careful when toxic substances are used around the house.

The following types of poisons are observed most commonly in the dog:

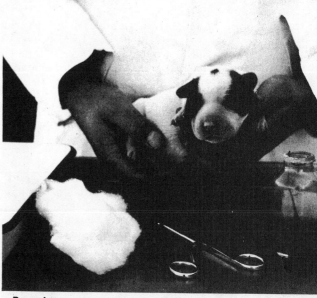

Preparing a very young puppy for dewclaw removal. Photo Purina.

1. Heavy metal poisoning which includes arsenic, lead, and thallium.

2. Insecticides, which include the chlorinated hydrocarbons and organic phosphates.

3. Rodenticides, which include strychnine and warfarin.

4. Insects, snakes, and common toads.

5. Miscellaneous, such as antifreeze.

Early recognition of the signs of the above poisons is important as dogs must be treated with specific drugs by your local veterinarian as quickly as possible.

Arsenic Poisoning. Arsenic is found in various ant, insect, and weed poisons. Arsenic trioxide is the most toxic form of arsenic on the market and is commonly found in cotton dust. The greatest damage from arsenic is to the stomach and intestinal tract.

If large amounts of arsenic are ingested, the dog may die in less than one hour. When lesser amounts are ingested, the first symptoms noted by the owner are usually vomiting, depression, and pain in the abdomen. The dog walks with an arched back as if in extreme pain and is very restless. The above symptoms are followed by weakness, straining, and diarrhea which is often bloody and has a very foul odor. Later there is loss of body fluids, dilation of the pupils and general collapse. The temperature is normal to subnormal. As death approaches the animal is in complete prostration.

In order for treatment to be effective, it must be started quickly. There is a specific antidote for arsenic and treatment for the severe damage to the gastrointestinal track is necessary. First aid treatment by the owner consists of inducing vomiting as quickly as possible with mustard or salt water; administer ¼-½ cup of strong tea and keep the animal warm and quiet. Raw eggs may be of value as a protein supplement and kaopectate may be administered to protect the stomach and intestine.

Lead Poisoning. Lead poison is not as common as other heavy metals, but may present a problem due to the fact that lead is found in some insect and rat poisons.

The symptoms observed in lead poison are a combination of central nervous system, stomach, and intestinal symptoms. The most common signs in dogs are vomiting, restlessness, extreme nervousness, and paralysis of muscles. Diarrhea is common and the temperature may be slightly elevated. The dog may show convulsions before death. Occasionally the dog will appear to be blind and will run into objects. Young dogs are most commonly affected.

Treatment must be started early and the administration of a specific antidote is necessary. The usual first aid treatment by the owner, as previously mentioned for arsenic, may be used.

Thallium Poisoning. Thallium sulfate is a heavy metal that is used extensively as a rat poison and is one of the most common types of poisoning seen in the dog. In most cases exposure is accidental, but one

should remember that dogs may be poisoned by eating rats that have ingested thallium.

In thallium poisoning, the symptoms vary depending upon the amount of thallium ingested. The usual symptoms observed include salivation, vomiting, loss of appetite, marked depression, and abdominal pain. The temperature is normal and there is usually an increase in the rate of breathing. The gums are extremely red in appearance. Skin lesions are commonly observed. The skin is red and there is a loss of hair. Later the skin will change to a black color and necrosis may occur. Since the hair follicles are not destroyed, new hair will grow on the affected areas after treatment. There is also considerable kidney damage from thallium poisoning.

The usual first aid treatment as mentioned for arsenic may be administered by the owner. Hospital treatment by your local veterinarian is extremely necessary, however, since specific antidotes and supportive treatment must be administered as quickly as possible.

Chlorinated Hydrocarbon Insecticides. This type of poison is still widely used, both in agriculture and as a household control of insects. Some of the more commonly used chlorinated hydrocarbons include DDT, Toxaphene, BHC, Chlordane, Lindane, and Methoxychlor. These substances will cause trouble either by ingestion or from application to the skin. When used in the recommended concentrations, however, and when not ingested, little trouble should result from their use. The presence of oil in the body or the use of these substances in combination with oily preparations greatly increases their toxicity. Toxaphene is perhaps the greatest source of trouble in the dog.

The chlorinated hydrocarbon insecticides act primarily on the central nervous system and are convulsive type poisons. The usual symptoms include an increase in respiration, restlessness, hyperexcitability, frequent urination, grinding of the teeth, muscular trembling, and convulsions. There may be salivation and the dog appears to be blind in some instances. Death generally occurs due to paralysis of the respiratory muscles.

First aid treatment consist of inducing vomiting with mustard or warm soapy water, bathing the animal to remove any toxic material from the skin and keeping the animal as quiet as possible until he can be treated by a veterinarian. Specific treatment is necessary to prevent death in most cases.

Organic Phosphate Insecticides. This group of insect poisons is the most widely used group of poisons on the market today. Their use in agriculture and around the house makes them a constant souce of trouble to our pets. If used in recommended concentrations, under proper circumstances, and where indicated they are relatively safe. However, many of them are quite toxic if ingested by an animal and many cases of organic phosphate poisoning are observed each year.

In cases of ingestion or absorption through the skin, the onset of symptoms is quite early. Affected

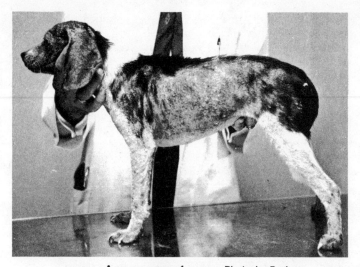

A severe case of mange. Photo by Purina.

animals show profuse salivation, vomiting, loss of control of urination and bowel movements, abdominal pain, breathing difficulty, incoordination, constriction of the pupils, and convulsions. The convulsions are usually more pronounced than those observed in chlorinated hydrocarbon poisoning.

First aid treatment is the same as for chlorinated hydrocarbons. Specific antidotes are available and must be administered as quickly as possible.

Strychnine. Strychnine poisoning is observed quite commonly in dogs. Generally the poison is accidently ingested by dogs when it has been placed in certain areas for the control of rats. It is used to some extent, however, for malicious killing of animals.

The onset of symptoms occurs early after ingestion and the severity of symptoms depends upon the amount ingested, and the amount of food in the stomach. The central nervous system is primarily affected. Dogs which have ingested strychnine show increased respirations, muscular twitching, severe hyperexcitability, and convulsions. The convulsions affect the limbs and face first and then extend to the rest of the body. Death is due to paralysis of the respiratory system.

First aid treatment consists of inducing vomiting with warm soapy water or mustard and the administration of strong tea. Prompt specific treatment by a veterinarian is indicated.

Warfarin. Poisons containing Warfarin are perhaps the most commonly used substances for the control of rats and mice. Poisoning in the dog may result from accidental ingestion of the material or from eating rats that have been fatally poisoned by the substance. Repeated exposure or one very large dose is necessary for toxic symptoms to develop.

Clinical signs include extreme depression, pale gums, normal or subnormal temperature, loss of appetite, and blood in the stool, urine, vomitus, and skin. The blood fails to clot normally after any type of trauma or needle puncture. If treatment is not

begun quickly the animal will die from loss of blood and shock.

First aid treatment by the owner consists of inducing vomiting with mustard or soapy water and the administration of Kaopectate. Specific treatment is indicated as quickly as possible.

Antifreeze (Ethylene Glycol). Antifreeze is a potential source of poisoning to all animals, however, the dog is most affected. This type of poisoning occurs most frequently in the early Spring and late Fall. Dogs seem to like the taste of antifreeze and quite often will drink from open containers or where it has been drained into gutters.

The material is quite toxic and causes extensive damage to the kidneys. The symptoms observed are primarily those of an acute kidney infection and include loss of appetite, vomiting, congestion of the gums, and severe depression. The animal is likely to develop kidney failure and die if the condition is not treated quickly. There is no first aid treatment other than inducing vomiting, and the animal should be taken to a veterinarian as quickly as possible.

Insects (Bee Stings, Ants, Wasps, and Spiders). Insect poisoning, especially bee stings, are quite common in the dog. The reaction is primarily that of an allergic response and in some cases, may be quite severe. The primary symptom noted by the owner is swelling in the area of the sting. This swelling is good, however, since the collection of fluid in the tissue dilutes the poison and makes it less serious. These stings are often confused with snakebites. Some dogs are unusually sensitive to a bee sting and death can occur very quickly. First aid treatment by the owner consists of the administration of any type of antihistamine or cortisone drug that may be in the house. Keep the animal quiet and obtain professional treatment as quickly as possible. This is especially important in the case of multiple stings.

The bite of a Black Widow Spider may be fatal to the dog. The poison is quite toxic and painful. The symptoms include swelling, redness, and pain around the site of the bite. Later the animal will show pain in the joints and paralysis may occur. There is no specific antidote, but supportive treatment is needed as soon as possible.

Toads. The skin and saliva of common toads contain a substance that is toxic to dogs on occasion. The condition occurs most commonly in the young, curious dog which delights in "nuzzling" these toads. Death is rare, but the symptoms can be severe. There is extreme salivation and vomiting, followed by depression and a slow, weak heart beat. The animal will salivate and remain depressed for about two hours. First aid treatment consists of keeping the animal warm and quiet. Specific drugs such as atropine should be administered to control salivation and vomiting.

In certain parts of Arizona there is a toad known as the Colorado River toad. These toads secrete a digitoxin-like substance which is located in wart-like lumps on the skin. The condition is observed primarily in hunting dogs and when the dog "mouths" these toads, he becomes hypersensitive and salivates profusely. Incoordination, rapid breathing, blindness, and convulsions may ensue. Symptoms generally last 45-60 minutes and many dogs recover spontaneously. However, small dogs will often die in strychnine-like convulsions. Specific treatment should be obtained as quickly as possible.

SNAKEBITES

In the United States we have primarily two types of poisonous snakes: the pit viper, which includes the rattlesnake, water moccasin or cottonmouth, and the copperhead or highland moccasin, and in the second type, the coral snake. A high incidence of snakebites is reported in the Southern states, although the distribution of pit vipers is general throughout the United States. The coral snake is found primarily along the coastal areas of the Southern United States. It is estimated that over 10,000 snakebites in dogs occur annually in this country. Rattlesnakes account for

about 80% of all deaths. The venom of the snake contains many toxic principles which are dangerous, however, the two basic types of substances are blood poisons and central nervous system poisons. Because of the limited exposure to the coral snake it will not be discussed and the symptoms presented will be those of the pit viper.

The most common early symptoms of pit viper poisoning are pain, swelling, discoloration of the skin, vomiting, and the presence of fang marks. In addition, weakness, a rapid pulse, and other signs of shock are usually present.

First aid treatment should be started quickly in order to be effective. A tourniquet should be placed proximal to the bite, tight enough to obstruct lymphatic and venous circulation, but not tight enough to obstruct blood flow through the arteries. The area of the bite should be packed with ice and the animal kept warm and quiet. Incision over the fang marks with suction is quite beneficial. Hospital treatment is extremely necessary and should be started as quickly as possible in order to save the life of the animal.

—Parasites—

DOGS ARE affected by many different parasites, both internal and external. Internal parasitism is the most common condition we see in young puppies. External parasites are a problem in all dogs, and contribute to many different types of skin problems. The following chart is given as a reference to the common drugs used in the treatment of parasitism in dogs. It will be referred to frequently in this discourse.

TREATMENT OF PARASITISM IN DOGS

Parasite	Treatment
Hookworms	Disophenol (DNP) N Butyl Chloride Tetrachloroethylene Dichlorvos
Roundworms	N Butyl Chloride Tetrachloroethylene Toluene Piperazine Dichlorvos
Whipworms	Phthalopyne (Whipside) Organic Phosphates Dichlorvos
Tapeworms	Nemural ArecolineR
Coccidia	Sulfa Drugs
Strongyloides	Dithiazanine Iodide Thibenzole
Esophageal worm	No specific treatment
Heartworms	Arsenical Compounds

One should be reminded, however, that drugs which will kill parasites are also toxic to the animal. It is advisable for a practicing veterinarian to examine the animal, determine the type parasite present, and prescribe the correct medication. If you are buying medication from a drug store, or from some mail order house, then follow the instructions carefully to avoid overdosing and possibly a state of poisoning resulting from the medication. It is emphasized that dogs may not need routine deworming every few months just for the sake of doing something. A stool sample should be submitted to your local veterinarian prior to any deworming procedure.

INTERNAL PARASITES

For purposes of discussion we will divide the section on internal parasites into *intestinal* and *cardiovascular*.

Intestinal Parasites

Hookworms. There are four species of hookworms which affect the dog. All are very similar in their life cycle, effect upon the host, and response to treatment. These are very small worms and are quite hard to see. The female parasite produces several thousand eggs per day which are passed in the feces. In a proper environment these eggs hatch into the infective larvae stage. The most favorable environment for the development of eggs is in a sandy loam soil in a moist shady place. Heat and cold are lethal to both the eggs and larvae.

After development of the larvae, infection of the dog may occur from: (1) ingestion with food; (2) penetration of the skin or (3) prenatal infection. In the case where the bitch is heavy with hookworms and prenatal infection occurs, puppies may die within the first 2 weeks of their life from hookworm disease. The worms attach themselves to the walls of the small intestine and suck blood. It has been shown that a single hookworm may withdraw as much as 0.8 cc. of blood in a 24 hour period (1,000 worms—27 ounces).

Canine hookworms may be picked up by man and in most cases produce a mild dermatitis or creeping eruption of the skin.

Treatment of hookworms is extremely important and since no drug kills the immature worms or migrating larvae, repeated treatment is necessary. For the drugs of choice *see chart* on treatment. Control or prevention of hookworm disease is an important consideration. The following suggestions are offered:

1. Worm the bitch prior to breeding and keep her in a clean place.

2. Let the bitch whelp in a clean dry place (on wire).

3. Raise the puppies on wire or on concrete.

4. Keep the pens clean at all times.

5. If dogs are kept on the ground, sodium borate may be used to kill the larvae.

6. Have puppies checked regularly after birth and deworm according to the advice of your local veterinarian.

Roundworms. There are three species of roundworms which affect the dog, all of which are similar in their life cycle and effect upon the dog. Roundworms are the most common intestinal parasites in dogs and the dog roundworm has been reported in man. They are relatively large, stout worms, generally white in color. The males and females measure several inches in length. The mature worms are normally found in the small intestine, but on occasion may occur elsewhere. The worms feed primarily on the food contained in the intestinal tract. In heavy infections there may be several hundred worms present in one animal.

The female passes eggs, which under proper conditions, embryonate and are ingested by a dog. These eggs may live on the ground for many months under optimal conditions. After the eggs are swallowed, the larvae are liberated, penetrate the wall of the intestine and migrate through the heart, pulmonary artery and lungs; are coughed up the windpipe and reswallowed. Here they grow to maturity. Changes may be produced in the lungs by the larvae, or in the intestine by the adult parasites. Prenatal infection is quite common and heavy infections may be present in young puppies. Diagnosis of infection is made by fecal examination. It is extremely difficult to diagnose the presence of parasites in the migratory phase. Although large numbers of parasites in the intestinal tract lead to unthriftiness, enlarged potbellied abdomen and in some cases blockage of the intestinal tract, the primary effect is the production of parasitic

pneumonia due to the migration of the infective larvae.

Control is based primarily on keeping dogs away from fecal contamination and regular fecal examination by your local veterinarian. Treatment— *see chart* (preceding).

Whipworms. Whipworm infection is a common and widespread parasitic disease of dogs and is observed quite often in the mature dog. This parasite is found in the cecum and colon of the dog and in a few cases the lower portion of the small intestine. The parasites are approximately one-half inch in length and are a pale pink in color. The female lays eggs which are eliminated in the feces of the infected dog. The nonparasitic phase of the life cycle is similar to the roundworm. When the infective eggs are ingested, the larvae escape into the small intestine and migrate to the cecum and colon where the adult worms attach themselves to the mucosa.

There is quite a variation in the symptoms produced by whipworms. Abdominal pain is frequently noted with diarrhea and/or constipation. Vomiting, depression, and loss of weight are frequently observed. Diagnosis of the infection is easily made by finding the eggs on fecal examination.

Control is based primarily on keeping dogs away from fecal contamination and regular fecal examination by your local veterinarian. Treatment— *see chart* (preceding).

Tapeworms. Tapeworms are frequently found in the dog and in many cases are more of a nuisance than actually causing harm to the animal. There are primarily two species of this parasite, one being found mostly in city dogs and the other in rural dogs. Both are very similar, however, in the effect upon the host. These parasites are found in the small intestine of dogs where they are attached to the inner lining of the intestine. The flea and louse serve as the intermediate hosts for this parasite and actually transmits the infection from one dog to another when ingested. Rural dogs are often infected from rodents and rabbits.

Tapeworms do not produce marked symptoms in the dog unless present in large numbers. Some discomfort and digestive upsets may occur. It is extremely difficult to find the eggs on fecal examination and diagnosis is most often based on finding the segments in the feces, and below the tail region of the dog. The control of tapeworms depends upon the control of the intermediate host, the flea, louse, and rabbit. Careful attention should be paid to the bedding of animals which should be cleaned and changed at regular intervals. The use of insecticides to kill the flea and louse is recommended. Treatment —*see chart*.

Coccidia. Coccidiosis is a protozoan parasitic disease of dogs which is common throughout the entire United States. The parasites are found in the small intestine where they produce a hemorrhagic enteritis, frequently with ulceration. The wall of the intestine becomes thickened and in severe cases necrosis of the tissue occurs. The mature parasites pass eggs which are known as oocysts which become infective to other dogs once they are outside the host's body. Infection is by ingestion of the sporulated oocyst.

The predominant symptoms are bloody diarrhea, progressive loss of weight, anemia, and general weakness. There may be a rise in temperature and muscular tremors of the rear limbs may be observed. Some animals which recover from the disease become carriers and although they show no clinical symptoms, they pass oocyst and infect other dogs. Diagnosis is made by finding oocyst on fecal examination.

The control of coccidiosis is very difficult. Removal of fecal material and clean kennels are necessary to reduce the intake of oocyst. Treatment—*see chart*.

Strongyloides. Strongyloides is an intestinal parasite of the dog which is quite common in the Southeastern United States. Many animals are infected with this parasite and show no clinical symptoms. This is due to the fact that the animal retains the parasite in its body for only a short period of time and no widespread damage to the intestinal tract is produced. When infection persists, however, the death rate is exceedingly high in puppies. The females pass eggs which hatch in the intestine and the first stage larvae are passed in the feces. The infective stage of these larvae is reached in about 48 hours. Infection of the dog is by skin penetration or ingestion.

The symptoms in young puppies usually begin with a soft cough, matted eyes, loss of appetite, and severe diarrhea. In the severe case it is hard to distinguish this condition from canine distemper. The intestinal disturbance becomes quite severe and the animal will pass pure blood, become dehydrated and anemic and death will result. Diagnosis is made by finding the larvae in fresh fecal samples.

Prevention of reinfection is necessary for treatment to be effective. This consists of protecting the animal by the most practical means from contaminated soil and the prompt isolation of infected animals. Treatment—*see chart*.

Esophageal Worm (Spirocerca Lupi). The esophageal worm is distributed throughout the entire world, especially in tropical areas. In the United States there seems to be certain areas where the degree of infection is greatest. Dogs infected are usually outdoor dogs and those found on the farm such as the hound.

The adult worms are found in the wall of the esophagus, stomach, and aorta of the dog. The female worms produce very small eggs which pass in the feces. The intermediate host appears to be the dung beetle. The larvae develop into the infective stage and when dogs ingest either the beetle or transport hosts such as chickens, mice, rats, and others infection occurs. Once inside the dog these larvae migrate through the walls of the stomach, through blood vessels, and finally into the largest one, the aorta. From here they usually migrate to the esophagus, but may remain in the wall of the aorta or wander to other tissues.

Symptoms are primarily those of an esophageal obstruction and pneumonia. These include vomiting, excessive salivation, cough, labored breathing, and finally dehydration and loss of weight. The adult worms occur in tumor-like masses in the wall of the esophagus, which are characteristic of a fibrosarcoma. There are characteristic bone changes present in prolonged cases.

Diagnosis is made by the symptoms, finding eggs in the feces, and examination of the esophagus with a gastroscope or by x-rays. Control is just about impossible due to the nature of the dog. Treatment—*see chart*.

Cardiovascular Parasites

Heartworms (Dirofilariae Immitis). Heartworm infection, once limited primarily to the Gulf Coast and Atlantic seaboard, is rapidly spreading throughout the entire United States. This spread can be attributed in part to the increased movement of dogs for breeding, hunting, and sporting purposes. The dogs most commonly infected with heartworms are the hunting breeds and outdoor dogs. House pets are seldomly infected except in certain coastal areas. This disease kills a large sumber of our dogs each year.

The most common location of the adult worm in the dog is in the main vessel to the lungs, the pulmonary artery. However, they may be found in the right side of the heart, the large veins leading to the heart, and the veins in the liver. The female worms shed larvae known as microfilariae which live in the blood stream for periods up to two years. These microfilariae are ingested by one of several species of mosquitoes which serve as the intermediate host. Once in the mosquito they develop into the infective stage in about two weeks, and are introduced into a dog's body when the mosquito feeds. The larvae live in the fat, muscles, and under the skin for 85-100 days before they reach the right side of the heart. Here they grow to maturity in about 4 months. For completion of the entire life cycle, approximately 8 months is required. Due to the length of time required for completion of the life cycle, heartworms are seldom seen in dogs under one year of age. The most common age for dogs to show symptoms of this parasitic infection is 3-6 years, depending upon the geographic location and the degree of exposure.

The symptoms exhibited by dogs infected with heartworms vary considerably, depending upon the location of the adult worms in the body, the severity and duration of the infection, and the type of dog. The first symptom usually noticed in hunting dogs is tiring upon exercise. A hacking cough may accompany the infection. Heavily infected dogs may collapse, show difficult breathing, and occasionally will have convulsions due to oxygen starvation. If the worms are located in the vena cavae, the symptoms are usually those of acute liver and kidney failure. Symptoms of congestive heart failure are attributed to interference of the blood flow through the heart and lung vessels. Other symptoms include anemia, rough hair coat, loss of weight, and dermatitis.

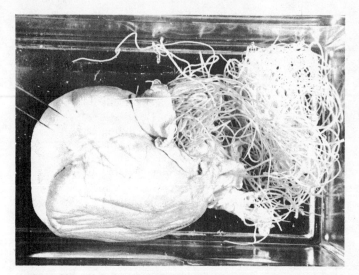

Dog's heart heavily infested with heartworms. Auburn University photo.

The diagnosis of this disease is based on finding the microfilariae on examination of a blood smear under a microscope. In most cases, however, it is impossible to tell the microfilariae of *D. immitis* from those of another canine filariid, *Dipetalonema reconditum* which causes little or no harm to the dog. For this reason practicing veterinarians collect a small amount of blood, and stain it with a dye before looking for the microfilariae. This way one can be sure of making a correct diagnosis. The precise determination of the severity of infection, which is important from a treatment standpoint, is often difficult to determine. The veterinarian must closely correlate the history, symptoms, findings on physical examination, and laboratory test before he can offer an opinion as to the outcome of the disease.

Treatment of heartworms is considerably different from treating an animal for intestinal parasites. When the adult heartworms are killed, they have but one place to go, down into the pulmonary vessels and lung tissue. For this reason if there are many adult parasites present, severe reactions may result from worms in the lungs. The small vessels of the lungs will be plugged with dead parasites and death can easily occur. It is for this reason that any treatment for heartworms should be done by a practicing veterinarian. The medication must be administered into the vein and in the correct dosage. The animal must be watched closely for any reactions, especially in the severe case. Lack of exercise and supportive therapy during the treatment period are necessary. It is the opinion of most people that dogs with light to moderate infections can survive the trestment with arsenicals with no apparent difficulty, while those animals with severe heartworm infection are best treated by surgery.

At present there is no specific control for heartworms. As long as we have no effective mosquito control program, we will be faced with this problem. There are ways in which we may attempt to limit the degree of infection. Animals, one year of age and older, that are in mosquito areas should be checked twice a year for the presence of microfilariae. In endemic areas annual or biannual treatment with arsenicals followed by a drug to kill the microfilariae has shown some value in keeping down a severe infection. Other measures which might be of value include spraying pens, screening outside runs, and avoiding the exercising of animals outside at twilight or on damp overcast days.

EXTERNAL PARASITES

The common external parasites affecting the dog include mange mites, ear mites, fleas, ticks, and lice. Detailed information on the appearance and life cycle will not be stressed, but considerable emphasis will be placed on the control of these parasites. Attention will also be given to the symptoms observed due to demodectic or red mange, sarcoptic mange, and ear mites.

There are numerous insecticides on the market, both internal and external, for the control of external parasites. These include the chlorinated hydrocarbons, organic phosphates, carbamates, rotenone, and pyrethrins. New and safer insecticides are being developed every day. These preparations are available as a dust, spray or dip. Some are extremely toxic and others are quite safe. In general, the dust is the safest form of insecticidal preparations. Dips are usually less toxic than sprays. The insecticides which are recommended for use on the dog are generally quite safe if instructions are carefully followed. It is only when excessive concentrations are used and products used that are not recommended for use on animals that trouble develops. A good example is Toxaphene, which is used primarily as a cotton dust. Many dogs are affected by this insecticide yearly due to its toxicity.

Some of the insectivides have a residual activity. That is, they will keep insects off the dog for a certain period of time. Others have only a quick killing power and no long lasting activity.

The most commonly used oral insecticide is Ronnell, an organic phsophate. This product has considerable value in the treatment of mange and in the control of fleas and ticks. It should be used, however, only on the advice of a veterinarian.

Treatment of the kennel and grounds, as well as treatment of the animal, is necessary for adequate control of external parasites, especially fleas and ticks. Careful attention should be given to the bedding and wooded areas around the household. It is only through continued effort by the dog owner to keep the animal clean, check him daily for the presence of external parasites, and the use of a proper, safe insecticide that control might be accomplished.

Demodectic Mange (Red Mange). This condition is caused by a tiny mite which lives deep in the hair follicles and the lymphatic system of most dogs and generally some stress condition precedes the development of symptoms. Transmission of the disease from one dog to another occurs with close physical contact such as dam and nursing pup. It rarely occurs in dogs over one year of age. Demodectic mange in the dog generally starts around the mouth and eyes and from there it will spread to other parts of the body. Loss of hair in small patches is usually the first symptom noted by the owner. The degree of infection depends upon the general condition of the dog, early treatment, and the presence of secondary bacterial infection. If left untreated progressively severe skin infection with pustule formations may develop. Diagnosis is made by observing the characteristic lesions and finding the mites on skin scrapings of the affected areas. Some dogs will spontaneously recover with no treatment; others require a long period to recover, and a low percent never recover. The recommended treatment consist of a good diet, topical application of an insecticide, medicated baths and dips, and the oral administration of an organic phosphate. Treatment in most instances is long and several months may be required for recovery. When topical application of insecticides are used around the face, care should be taken to protect the eyes and to prevent ingestion.

Sarcoptic Mange (Scabies). This disease is described as a contagious skin disease characterized by intense itching, loss of hair, thickening of the skin and crust formation. There is no apparent age, sex, or breed predilection, but the condition is observed most commonly in the young dog. Due to the contagious nature of the disease, many dogs in a kennel may become infected. The mites which produce this disease can be transmitted to man. The condition will vary in severity depending upon the condition of the dog, number of mites present, and host reaction to the parasite. Secondary bacterial infection is a common occurrence.

The diagnosis and treatment is essentially the same as for demodectic mange. Response to treatment is generally more rewarding, however.

Ear Mites. The common ear mite, *Otodectes cyanotis* inhabits the external ear canal of dogs and on occasion produces severe infection by damage to the lining of the ear canal. It is a lymph-sucker and because of the irritating properties of its excreta and its constant movement, additional self mutilation of the canal by scratching often results. The characteristic symptoms observed by the owner include scratching of the ear, head shaking, and a foul odor to the external ear. Secondary bacterial infection is common. Diagnosis is based on observing the mites in the external ear or by microscopic examination of exudate from the ear canal.

Treatment consist of proper cleaning of the ear and medication by bland oil and insecticidal preparations. Usually two to three weeks is required to clear up the problem. The condition is transmitted from one dog to another, so many dogs in a kennel may be affected.

Flea and Tick Infestation. This is a common occurrence and needs little further discussion. Some dogs are especially sensitive to fleas, however, and in some cases an acute allergic reaction may occur. This results in itching, loss of hair, and a reddening of the skin. Proper treatment is directed toward relief of symptoms and control of the parasite.

Ticks on occasion will produce a condition known as tick paralysis. The condition is characterized by a generalized weakness and generalized paralysis. Generally one or several ticks can be found along the back or neck region. Treatment consist of removal of the parasites and supportive therapy.

Lice. Infection with lice is not a common occurrence in the dog. When infested, considerable discomfort is afforded the animal. Intense irritation occurs and severe scratching is a constant symptom. The abrasion produced by scratching paves the way for secondary infections. The lice are often found in the vicinity of body openings where they gather to find moisture. Diagnosis is easy if careful examination of the animal is made. The lice are observed with the naked eye, however, they stay very close to the skin and in long-haired dogs may be overlooked. The eggs or nits may be readily found. Treatment is by bathing and dipping with insecticidal preparations. Remember that lice can be easily transmitted from dog to dog by combs, brush, or similar equipment.

—Breeding Problems—

MALE

LITTLE INFORMATION is available concerning infertility and impotency in the male dog. Infertility may result from neoplasia, disease of the spermatic cord, diseases of the epididymus, and hypoplasia or atrophy of the testes. Prostate infections and orchitis may also be causes of infertility. Impotency may result from some disease or congenital condition, and in most cases is physiological in nature. Some dogs have no desire to breed and others are so nervous and excitable that breeding becomes an impossibility.

A detailed physical examination of the male genital organs and careful examination of the semen is necessary. Depending on the findings on semen evaluation, several conditions may be suspected. In hypoplasia or atrophy of the testes and blockage of excretory ducts, very few sperm will be produced. Congenital defects in sperm formation such as testicular degeneration will give rise to a large percentage of abnormal sperm. Blood and exudate in semen have an adverse effect on the sperm and may cause infertility. Systemic disease, long periods of sexual abstinence will also cause abnormal sperm and perhaps infertility. Physical examination of the male genital organs may reveal some diseased condition which would interfere with fertility. In some cases treatment may be impossible and in other cases, correction of the diseased process by proper therapy may produce a fertile animal.

Lack of libido or impotency is not necessarily related to infertility. A dog without libido may be sterile, while a sterile dog may have excellent libido. If impotency is a problem, the administration of a hormone may correct the situation. In some cases it is necessary to breed certain animals in their natural surrounding, while in other cases breeding may be more successful away from home. Artificial breeding may be used when physiologic or psychological factors prevent natural breeding.

Tumors. Tumors of the urogenital system of the male dog occur to a moderate degree. Some of the most common tumors observed are of the penis, prostate gland, and testicles. The transmissible veneral tumor of the penis, adenocarcinoma of the prostate, and interstitial cell tumor, seminona, and sertoli cell tumor of the testicles may interfere with breeding or result in infertility. All have unique features and effects on the animals genital system. Proper examination by a veterinarian is extremely important in order that a diagnosis can be made and proper treatment initiated.

FEMALE

Agalactia is a condition characterized by inadequate milk secretion in the bitch. This condition may occur in any breed, however, it appears to be most common in the toy breeds. It may be permanent or temporary, and may or may not occur with subsequent litters. There is no specific treatment, but early recognition of the condition may enable one to prevent future recurrences.

Lack of normal mammary development prior to whelping is a common observation. This finding gives evidence that agalactia may occur. The condition can be definitely diagnosed by the absence of milk on examination of the mammary glands 12 to 24 hours after whelping. If the condition persists, puppies become restless and cry constantly. Examination of the puppies will reveal empty stomachs and a generally weakened condition. Supplemental feeding is necessary at this time.

Adequate milk secretion is a normal physiological response to specific hormones at the time of whelping in a normal healthy bitch. For adequate milk production to occur, proper exercise, good diet, freedom from infection, and whelping in a safe comfortable place are necessary. Specific treatment is recommended in some cases of true agalactia, however, response to such treatment is inadequate in many instances.

Estrus Abnormalities. Normal healthy dogs have estrus cycles at approximately 6 to 7 month intervals. In colder climates, however, one cycle per year may be considered normal. Females generally have their first estrus period at the age of 9 to 12 months. The period of estrus usually lasts for about 21 days. During this time the bitch goes through several stages of the cycle. Conception will vary, but generally is thought to be best if animals are bred on the 10th to the 14th day after first signs of estrus are noted. Variations in the normal estrus cycle may be considered abnormal and specific treatment is necessary.

Failure of estrus may be due to several factors. Malnutrition, overweight, after effects of infectious diseases, infection of the female genital system, endocrine disorders, and tumors are common causes for failure of estrus. Animals suffering from malnutrition must be treated in an effort to improve their physical condition before there is a reasonable chance of reproduction. Obese or fat animals are subject to partial or total repression of breeding activities. Infectious diseases may on occasion result in permanent sterility. Infection of the uterus, abdominal cavity, and cervix may result in scar tissue in the uterus and ovi ducts so that reproduction is impossible.

Short Estrus Periods. Such occurrences, where the dog is in estrus for only a few days is observed in some small breeds. The general cause of this abnormality is lack of stimulation from the pituitary gland and the symptoms of estrus regress without ovulation. Short cycles may also occur following heavy lactation and will result in small litters or infertile mating. Abnormally long estrus cycles may also result in infertile breeding due to the fact that sperm may not live long enough for ovulation to occur. This indicates that at least two matings are necessary.

Failure to Accept the Male. This usually does not occur in a normal female in full estrus. Occasionally very nervous bitches will not accept the male and this is due in most instances to psychological factors. If a bitch has a history of repeated nonacceptance, moderate stimulation with hormones might be indicated. Mild tranqualization is of help in highly nervous animals.

Hormonal Imbalance. Problems due to an imbalance of hormones are extremely difficult to diagnose. In most cases hormone imbalance is associated with abnormally short or long estrus periods. Care should be taken in the use of estrogenic substances for the induction of estrus, and the use of progesterone for the suppression of estrus. Excessive estrogen stimulation may produce cystic ovaries which in turn will continue to secrete estrogens and produce the condition known as nymphomania. Repeated administration of progesterone makes the uterus extremely susceptible to bacterial infection and resulting metritis.

Pseudopregnancy or False Pregnancy. This condition always occurs following ovulation when true pregnancy does not occur. Symptoms will vary from none to those of a complete pregnancy. The mammary glands will enlarge, milk production may be evident, and the dog becomes extremely nervous and makes her bed in the same manner as if whe were going to whelp. Pseudopregnancy is occasionally accompanied by bacterial infection resulting in mastitis or metritis. Normally no treatment is necessary and symptoms will subside near the end of the normal pregnancy period. In severe cases hormonal therapy may be indicated.

Mastitis. Mastitis is an inflammation of one or more mammary glands. The condition is usually bacterial in origin and may be acute or chronic. In most cases it is associated with the postpartum period, although trauma has, on occasion, produced the condition. Symptoms include hot, painful, swollen and sometimes discoloration of the mammary tissues. Depression, increased temperature, and loss of appetite are frequently noted. Puppies nursing an infected gland will cry, become listless, weaken, and die.

Treatment is directed toward overcoming the infection and is usually successful. If the condition is not detected early and proper treatment started, however, the disease may result in loss of puppies and functional gland tissue. The breasts should be milked frequently and sealed with tape to prevent the puppies from nursing. Milk samples should be taken for culture and the animal placed on proper antibiotic therapy. Local application of heat is helpful.

Chronic infection generally results from an acute infection and is evidenced by hard nodular swellings in the gland tissue. In the event of false or true pregnancy these glands may flare up with an acute infection. Careful evaluation of the lesion is important, for it is not uncommon for a mammary gland tumor to become activated. Examination of any abnormality of the mammary tissues by a veterinarian is advised.

Tumors. Tumors of the female genital system are quite common in occurrence, especially the transmissible venereal tumor and smooth muscle tumor of the vagina. Primary tumors of the uterus and ovaries are infrequent, but do occur. The transmissible venereal tumor in the female is manifested by a large pedunculated mass arising from the floor and walls of the vagina. Hemorrhage from the vagina is common and the tumor is more pronounced during the estrus cycle. Occasionally the tumor will obstruct the urethral orifice and stop urination. Spreading is not common, but occasionally the regional lymph glands may be involved. Surgical removal is the treatment of choice. Benign tumors such as the fibrous and smooth muscle tumor are the most commonly observed tumors in the vagina. They arise from the ventral or dorsal wall and protrude into the lumen. They are usually firm masses with a smooth surface. Occasionally the tumors are large enough to protrude from the vulva. Recurrence or malignancy is an uncommon finding. The treatment of choice is surgical removal.

Tumors of the uterus and ovaries produce very few outward signs. Occasionally a purulent or hemorrhagic vaginal discharge may be seen and treatment of such tumors is surgical removal.

—Eye Disorders—

Eye Discharge. This disorder is frequently seen in some diseases as distemper, or in an inflammation of the outer structure of the eye called the conjunctiva. Conjunctivitis can be caused by abnormalities of the lids; turned in eye lashes; the presence of foreign bodies such as dust, pollens, seeds, and sticks in the eye; by bacterial or fungus infections; or by contact with irritating chemicals. Exposure to cold air may be a contributing factor.

The clinical signs of conjunctivitis are photophobia (squinting, seeking darkness), a watery to heavy mucoid discharge, and a redness of eye membranes.

The treatment or control of conjunctivitis is frequently a matter of removing the cause. Eye washes such as boric acid will help remove foreign matter, cleanse the discharge, and sooth the membranes. If the symptoms persist, the dog should be taken to a veterinarian for careful examination and treatment.

Lid Disorders. Lid abnormalities are frequently the cause of conjunctivitis and corneal disease. The constant irritation of abnormal lids may cause serious problems. Usually these abnormalities require veterinary examination and surgery.

Corneal Disorders. Corneal disorders can be serious to the normal sight of the eye. These can be inflammations, infections, ulcerations, increased vascularity, pigmentation, or even rupture. Whenever the clear part of the eye is cloudy, ulcerated, or not clear, your veterinarian should be consulted immediately. Corneal ulcers can rupture in a matter of a few minutes, eye fluids will be lost, and sight may be lost or seriously impaired.

Cataract. A cataract is an opacity of the lens of the eye which is situated immediately behind the colored part of the eye called the iris. It appears as a white object which may be confused with a corneal opacity. However, close examination reveals a clear cornea, a functioning pupil, and the opaque object is behind the iris.

Cataracts can be present at a young age or in older animals. Cataracts can be inherited and if there is a high incidence in a blood line, it would be well to eliminate the offending parent from further breeding. Cataracts can be successfully removed by a veterinary surgeon in many cases.

Blindness. Blindness can be partial or complete from a variety of causes. The eye disorders described can affect sight or even cause a blindness. Severe corneal disorder, cataracts, glaucoma, retinal disease, degeneration of the optic nerve, brain disease, and distemper can cause blindness. If the pupil is dilated and will not close in the presence of bright light, the eye should be examined immediately by a veterinarian. This sign is frequently an early sign of severe disease and can be arrested by early diagnosis and treatment. Frequently neglected corneal disease or even conjunctivitis will result in a generalized infection and blindness.

Retinal Disorders. These conditions are disorders of the deep nervous layer of the eye. These disorders can be classified into those (1) present at birth and are probably hereditary, (2) due to injury, (3) secondary to severe illness and (4) those where the cause is unknown.

The dog lover should be especially cognizant about the congenital or hereditary anomalies. This group includes choroidal or optic nerve defects known as Collie eye. Retinal dysplasia and detachment is seen more in Bedlington Terrier puppies. Retinal atrophy is seen usually in Irish Setter puppies. Retinal atrophy can be seen more in older dogs, especially the Poodle. It is this group of hereditary disorders that diagnosis is mandatory by a competent veterinarian who has specialized in ophthalmology. A breeding program based on elimination of affected dogs is mandatory.

The other retinal problems mentioned are important to the dog but not necessarily to the future of the breed. A prompt examination is essential to the favorable outcome of the disorder.

——Ear Disorders——

External Ear. Disorders of the external ear are ones which the owner can see and smell and in many cases can be important to the life of the dog as well as his comfort and happiness. These conditions would include lacerations, abrasions, hematoma of the ear flap, parasites, skin diseases, and infection of the ear canal. Any irritations or abrasions of the ear flap should be cleaned up and treated with a mild medicant. If the dog persists in self-mutilation by shaking his head, scratching, or rubbing, these mild lesions rapidly become major ones. Every effort must be made to prevent this from happening.

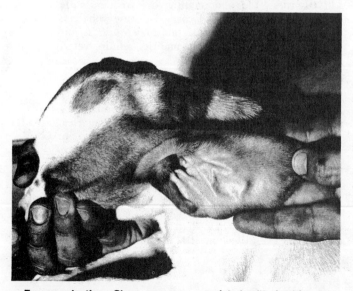

Ear examination. Clean ears are associated with healthy dogs. Photo by Purina.

Hematomas frequently occur from self-mutilation or from other direct blows. Frequently ear mites will initiate violent shaking of the head and cause a hematoma. If the veterinarian is not consulted, the condition may develop into a serious infection or mutilation, or if it heals, a so-called "cauliflower" ear will result.

Ear parasites usually are ear mites, but ticks, fleas, or skin mange mites may cause trouble. Ear mites can be seen under a microscope or a good magnifying glass. If these are not treated properly, a severe infection of not only the ear canal but the middle ear might develop.

Infection of the ear canal is sometimes called otorrhea, otitis externa, or in chronic cases, ear canker. The clinical sign of otitis externa are those of severe earache, pain, reddening, running or discharge, tilting the head to the affected side, and foul odor. The disorder is seen more frequently in "flop-eared" dogs. Predisposing causes are improper drainage of natural waxes or oils because of the anatomy of the ear canal, improper aeration causing a moist condition, and filth or dirt. Swimming or improper bathing may initiate trouble because of resulting moisture in the ear canal.

It behooves an owner who cares for his dog to keep checking the ears for dirt and signs of otitis. Removing outer dirt by means of a cotton swab is worthwhile. However, deep cleaning of the ear canal should be done by a veterinarian or his trained staff.

Much harm can be done to the ear by improper cleaning or washing. If it is a chronic problem, your veterinarian can advise you on how to help control the disorder. Occasionally surgical resection of part of the ear canal will alleviate the problem.

Middle and Inner Ear. Disorders of the middle and inner ear frequently develop from neglected otitis externa. Outer ear infections may rupture through the ear drum and cause deeper, more serious infection. Middle ear infections cause more serious symptoms of pain, head tilt, fever, and possibly circling. Many middle ear infections are also inner ear infections because of their continuity. Inner ear disorders are characterized by incoordination, severe head tilt or deviation, circling, falling, or even a fluctuating eyeball (nystagmus).

The successful outcome of middle and inner ear disorders depend on promptness in diagnosis and the initiation of proper therapy. If it is due to an extension of outer ear disease, treatment and/or surgery must be directed to this condition as well. A so-called mastoid operation can be performed in the dog for middle ear infection with satisfactory results. All surgical procedures will probably also require proper antibiotic therapy by your veterinarian.

——Puppy Diseases——

Congenital Diseases. Congenital deformities or those frequent at birth are becoming increasingly more common in the dog. This is due, perhaps, to the increased popularity of certain breeds and too much inbreeding and line breeding. Some of the most common congenital deformities will be briefly discussed. Young puppies should be examined at birth to check for any congenital deformities and those with congenital conditions should never be used for breeding purposes.

Congenital cleft of the lips or hair lip is a deformity which is only occasionally observed. In this condition the top lip of the puppy has an opening which usually extends up to the nasal area. The condition is rather unsightly and makes drinking and eating difficult. The condition is observed when the pup is first born. Surgical correction is possible in some cases, but has to be delayed until the puppy is old enough to undergo anesthesia.

Congenital cleft of the hard palate is a condition in which there is a communication between the oral cavity and nasal cavity. The hard palate failed to form properly in the development of the puppy. This opening may be very small, or in some cases may extend the entire length of the hard palate. Affected puppies have a difficult time eating as the food, either liquid or solid, will enter the nasal cavity from the mouth. Symptoms are a chronic nasal discharge consisting mostly of food. When the puppy eats, food will come back out of his nose. Foreign body pneumonia is a frequent complication. Surgical correction is possible in some cases.

Persistent right aortic arch is a condition characterized by abnormal development of the aorta and the result is a vascular ring surrounding the esophagus. This condition is seen most frequently in the German Shepherd and symptoms begin when the puppy is placed on solid food. The constriction of the esophagus is severe enough to restrict the passage of solid food. Liquids, however, can pass in most instances. Due to this constriction, the esophagus will become greatly enlarged anterior to the heart and will serve as a reservoir for the collection of food. Symptoms include vomiting and inhalation pneumonia. Surgical correction is possible, but must be attempted as soon as the dog is old enough to undergo anesthesia.

Cardiospasm or achalasia is a condition which is due to spasms, or a constriction of the muscles where the esophagus empties into the stomach. The result is a generalized enlargement of the esophagus leading to vomiting and inhalation pneumonia. This condition is observed most commonly in the toy breeds of dogs. Treatment may be conservative or surgical. Conservative treatment consist of feeding soft food and feeding the dog on an incline. This allows the food to enter the stomach with less difficulty. Surgical treatment is not satisfactory in most cases.

Pyloric stenosis is a condition involving the muscles of the pyloric spincter which is located where the stomach joins the small intestine. It is due to an apparent congenital hypertrophy of the circular muscles in this area and results in a stricture making the movement of food out of the stomach difficult.

Symptoms do not develop until the puppy is placed on solid food. Vomiting usually occurs 30-45 minutes after eating. Loss of weight and dehydration are noted after prolonged vomiting. Constipation is usually evident.

Diagnosis is made by correlating an accurate history with findings on x-ray examination. Surgical correction is possible.

Hip dysplasia is a condition characterized by subluxation or partial disclocation of the hip joint and occurs primarily in young dogs of large breeds. Hip dysplasia results in a malformation of the hip sockets and then of the head of the femurs. This condition is thought to be an inherited weakness associated with a lack of muscle mass in the hip area.

Clinical and radiographic signs of hip dysplasia are not present at birth, and changes do not become evident on radiographs until the animal is 4 to 6 months of age. In dogs that mature slowly, it may be difficult to diagnose the condition before an animal is 12-18 months of age. The occurrence of hip dysplasia is usually bilateral and is present about equally in both sexes.

Symptoms are variable and follow no particular pattern. Symptoms usually noticed by the owner include posterior weakness, difficulty in getting up, varying degrees of lameness, and a "clicking" of the hip joint when the animal walks. The dog will generally be "cow hocked" and there is an abnormal "slope" of the body from the wing of the ileum and the base of the tail. A definite diagnosis can only be made by radiographic examination.

Control or elimination of this condition is a difficult task. Breeding programs must be closely supervised and breeding of certified "dysplasia free" animals should be encouraged. There is hope that by careful selection, hip dysplasia abnormalities can be kept at a minimum. The task of selection calls for sympathy, patience, good judgment and perseverance. Owners should seek help from veterinarians in determining the presence of hip dysplasia in their breeding stock and in planning their breeding program.

Elbow dysplasia is an abnormality of the elbow joint which is manifested by an ununited anconeal process and arthritic changes of the joint. The condition is observed most frequently in the German Shepherd, although the St. Bernard, Irish Wolfhound, Basset Hound, Newfoundland, and Bloodhound have shown characteristic symptoms.

Symptoms will vary, depending on the degree of damage to the joint. Intermittent lameness is observed as early as 3 months of age. There may be some pain on manipulation of the joint.

The diagnosis of elbow dysplasia is based on radiographic findings. Treatment is both surgical and conservative. Owners of dogs with this condition are advised not to use them for breeding stock since it has been shown to be inherited.

Congenital patella luxation occurs primarily in the toy breeds and is classified as congenital or traumatic. The most common abnormality is an inward deviation of the knee cap, however, on occasion an outward luxation will occur. Congenital patella luxation in the young dog is considered to be hereditable and the dogs should not be used for breeding purposes.

Symptoms vary depending upon the degree of involvement and include occasional lameness, pain, outward rotation of the hocks, deformed knee joints, and complete disuse of the affected limb. Diagnosis is made by careful physical examination of the knee joint by a veterinarian. Surgical correction of the dislocation is the treatment of choice.

Blood Sugar Deficiency (Hypoglycemia). This is a condition observed in young puppies between the ages of 6 and 12 weeks. It is characterized by a low blood sugar with excessive storage of sugar in the internal organs of the dog's body. This condition seems to be preceded by some type of stress on the puppy.

Puppies can encounter all kinds of problems.

Symptoms begin suddenly and seem to follow a definite pattern. The puppy becomes weak, incoordinated, depressed, and there is recession of the eyes. Muscular trembling occurs and the puppy goes into a coma.

Treatment should be started as quickly as possible and is directed toward returning blood sugar levels to normal and relieving the stress condition of the puppy.

Rickets occurs in young fast growing puppies and is characterized by twisting and bowing of the bones. It is thought to be due to an improper balance of the minerals, calcium, and phosphorus. The disease usually affects the ends of the long bones of the body and most commonly the long bones in the front legs. There may be enlargement of the joints of the legs and along the ribs. In many cases lameness is quite evident in young, large dogs.

Diagnosis is based on the type dog, symptoms shown by the animal and radiographic findings. Treatment consists of determining the specific deficiency and then supplying the mineral needed. Vitamin D is also recommended to promote absorption and utiliation of the minerals.

The disease can be prevented by insuring that

there are adequate calcium and phosphorus levels in the diet. Supplementation of the diet with a vitamin mineral supplement may be advisable.

Sheath discharge is usually due to an inflammation of the prepuce or sheath in the male dog. This is a common condition both in young puppies and mature dogs and is characterized by a discharge from the preputial orifice. The skin area around the preputial orifice becomes inflamed and infected. Infected males lick the prepuce frequently, which causes more external irritation. The material is also ingested by the dog and may lead to internal infections.

Treatment is directed toward cleansing the preputial cavity daily and instilling an ointment containing antibiotics, sulfonamides, and a corticosteroid into the sheath. Treatment should be performed daily for 7-10 days. Recurrence is often noted and in some cases mild surgery may be necessary.

Puppy Septicemia. Bacterial infections in young puppies are a common cause of death. A variety of organisms may be involved, but the most common ones are streptococci, staphylococci, *Pseudomonas* and *Escherichia coli.* The puppies become weak, crawl off by themselves, cry, strain, and resist palpation of their abdomens. They usually die within 12 to 18 hours after onset of symptoms. The puppies should be taken to a veterinarian as soon as possible after symptoms are noted.

Parasites. See subsections on internal and external parasites (preceding).

Hand Rearing of Puppies. Hand rearing of puppies can be attained with moderate to good success if careful attention is paid to 3 very important considera-tions. These are: (1) an adequate substitute for the bitch's milk, (2) a suitable environment (proper temperature), and (3) a satisfactory feeding schedule. Perhaps the most important consideration in the first week of a puppy's life is proper temperature. This temperature should be constant and maintained at approximately 85°F. A gradual decrease in the temperature to 75° by the end of the 4th week is recommended.

The formula is an all important consideration. For best results Esbilac (Borden Company) in powdered form and SPF-lac in liquid form are recommended. These are simulated bitches milk products and are well formulated for the orphan puppy. If this product is not available, a suitable formula might be obtained from your local veterinarian.

The feeding schedule is based on the quality of the formula. It is a good policy to underfeed slightly, rather than overfeed. Puppies should be fed 3 to 4 times a day for the first 5 weeks of their life. After that two or three daily feedings will suffice. One should be careful not to feed too fast and produce a pneumonia by having food go down the trachea. If diarrhea develops overfeeding is probably the cause. Decrease the amount of food intake by one-half until the diarrhea stops.

In the preparation of the formula and in the handling of the equipment, proper sanitary conditions must prevail.

Regular gentle handling of the hand-reared puppy is recommended. This will stimulate circulation and serve as a form of passive exercise. If conventional methods of feeding present a problem, the owner may consult his veterinarian for instructions on how to feed the puppy by stomach tube.

—Vaccinations—

DISTEMPER, HEPATITIS, and leptospirosis causes death in a great number of puppies each year. Without vaccination the death rate would be much higher in certain areas of the United States. Every practicing veterinarian has a vaccination procedure that is best suited to his particular geographic location. The owners of young puppies should seek advice concerning vaccination prior to the breeding of the bitch and before the puppies are weaned. Improper use of across-the-counter vaccine is to be discouraged. Even though such vaccines may be cheaper, in most cases they are not the same quality as the veterinarian uses. In general, you pay for what you get. Don't blame anyone but yourself if an infectious disease occurs in your puppy when a proper vaccination program has not been followed.

As a general rule dogs are not at all bothered by modern vaccines and the dog vaccinated one day is usually ready for travel or whatever, the next.

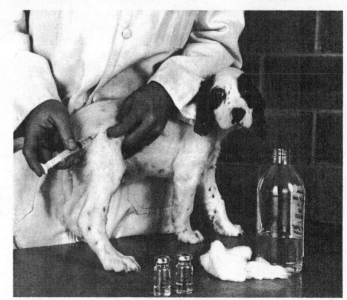

Vaccinating a young puppy. Photo by Purina.

-Geriatric Problems (Old-Dog Problems)-

PROBLEMS CONCERNING the aged dog confront every dog owner and practicing veterinarian. In too many cases one considers euthanasia in the aged dog once any type of trouble begins. Do we stop and think of all the pleasure we have received from the animal when he was young and healthy? We owe this animal the very best of care and due consideration should be given to some of the common problems which affect the older dog.

Diet Considerations. The diet of older dogs should not vary to a great extent from that of the young dog unless specific disease conditions are present. Older dogs require in general a low-level but high quality protein, low fat and carbohydrate, and in general a highly digestible diet. In some instances it is recommended that essential amino acids and vitamins be added to the basic diet. It is also considered better to feed the older dog two small meals a day rather than one large meal. Coarse foods should be avoided if dental problems are present. The prescription diets which can be purchased from a veterinarian meet the special needs of the older dog quite adequately and are convenient to use.

Heart Considerations. Cardiovascular disease is second in importance to kidney disease in the aged dog. A great majority of dogs over 8 years of age have some type of cardiac problem. Many of these go unnoticed until it is too late due to the fact that regularly physical examinations are not requested. It is realized that a dog with a cardiac problem can rarely be cured. With an early diagnosis and proper treatment, however, the life of the animal can be prolonged several years in some instances.

The most common cardiac problem observed in the aged dog is a chronic disease of the valves of the heart. This condition generally involves the valve in the left side of the heart and gives rise to signs of left heart failure. The most common signs observed are a productive or non-productive cough, restlessness, tiring on exercise, and fainting. The symptoms are much more pronounced on exercise. If not treated, the animal may go into congestive heart failure with the accumulation of fluid in the abdominal cavity and swelling of the extremities.

Diagnosis is made by hearing a pronounced murmur upon examination of the heart. Treatment should be started as soon as possible and consists of proper diet, restricted exercise, control of excitement, and specific drug therapy.

Other cardiac conditions which may be observed and give rise to similar symptoms include diseases of the heart muscle, heartworms, bacterial infection in the heart, and heart degeneration.

Kidney Disease. Chronic kidney disease is perhaps the most important condition affecting the aged dog and is observed most commonly in dogs 6 years of age and older. This condition accounts for more deaths in older dogs than any other condition. This disease consists of a chronic inflammation of the tissue until there is not enough renal function left to maintain life.

Dogs with this condition generally have a history of some previous attacks of acute kidney disease. The onset of the condition may be sudden or gradual. Symptoms most often observed are increased thirst, increased urination, loss of appetite, depression, weakness, mouth odor, and in some cases nervous disturbances. The diagnosis is based on history, symptoms, and specific laboratory tests. Early treatment is extremely necessary in order to maintain life. Proper care of the dog after treatment is equally important. Diet is of utmost importance. The prescription diet, KD, is recommended for dogs suffering from chronic kidney disease.

Dental Problems. Care of the teeth is extremely important in the older animal. There is a tendency to overlook these conditions because of the absence of symptoms. Dental problems are more prevalent in small housedogs than in larger outdoor dogs such as the hunting breeds. Regular dental check-ups should be a part of the general care of the dog. Frequent removal of tartar and examination of the teeth for looseness and infection are necessary. Loose or infected teeth should be extracted as soon as possible. Brushing the dog's teeth with salt and soda and giving it hard dog biscuits to chew helps keep the teeth clean. Enlargement of the gums with acute inflammation is a frequent occurrence when the teeth are not properly cared for and in severe cases a fetid odor and purulent exudate may be present. In the

Four generations of great Kinsman Beagles bred by Lee S. Wade, El Monte, California. Photo by Lee S. Wade.

case of dental hygiene, the old saying "an ounce of prevention is worth a pound of cure" is certainly a true one.

Other conditions which affect the aged dog include eye problems, hormonal deficiencies, ear problems, and skin problems. For proper diagnosis and treatment of these conditions, frequent examination by a veterinarian is advised.

—First Aid—

ALMOST EVERY dog owner at some time will be called upon to do something for his pet in the nature of first aid, possibly to stop a hemorrhage, pull porcupine quills, straighten and hold in place a broken leg. Every dog owner should be prepared should that possibility present itself.

The first thing to do is to restrain yourself from rushing to the injured dog's assistance. Approach him somewhat gingerly. He is probably in pain, Merely moving him adds to it, and in an instant you may be suffering more than he is. Therefore see that he can't bite you.

If he is a small dog, you may be able to procure a blanket which you can drop over him, folded, and thus pick him up. He won't be able to bite through its thicknesses. If he is large, muzzle him. Take a piece of cloth three to four feet long and four inches wide. Make a loop in the middle, take hold of both ends and let the loop swing around his nose. Pull the loop tight. Now tie a knot under his chin and carry the ends of the cloth back around his head and tie a bow knot behind the ears. He can't bite nor scratch the improvised muzzle off.

Shock. Nearly all dogs hurt in accidents suffer from shock. The heart beats faster but weakly, the dog shows prostration and often seems oblivious to pain which we think he must feel. Shock needs treatment before any minor cuts or breaks. It is best treated by covering the dog with a warm blanket and keeping him warm. His own body will furnish all the heat he needs, if well covered and in a temperature of 70 degrees. Otherwise he needs to be brought into a warm place. If he is not injured so badly that he cannot swallow, the simplest household stimulant to administer is coffee with sugar and cream so he won't fight it.

Gently lift his head, loosen the muzzle and if he won't bite, pour the coffee into a pocket made by pulling out his lip. A cupful is an excellent stimulant for a dog the size of a Setter. Do not give alcohol as is so often done; it is a depressant and produces the opposite from the desired effect.

Broken Bones. Keep the leg as straight as possible, if it is a broken leg. If the fracture is compound, that is, if the bone has broken through the skin, pull the leg so that the bone point no longer shows. If the pelvis, a rib, or shoulder blade is broken, let the dog alone until your veterinarian has been informed and tells you what to do. He may be able to set the last

two, but a broken pelvis generally knits without benefit of the veterinarian.

The principal thought should be to prevent the sharp point or edge of a bone from slashing about and cutting a blood vessel. To that end and for purposes of transporting him, it is best to attach a stick to the leg by tying it above and below the break.

Internal Hemorrhage. Look at your dog's gums after any severe accident. If they are blanched white he may be bleeding from a ruptured organ (liver or spleen) inside his abdominal cavity; of course you can see no external sign of blood. Get a long piece of cloth—an old bedsheet—and tear in into strips four of five inches wide. Roll them up. Now have an assistant or two hold the dog by the front and back legs, stretched out, while you wind his chest and abdomen firmly with your bandage. When he is bound, cover him and let him lie quietly. The firmness holds his organs in place and helps check hemorrhage. If a clot forms it is not likely to be shaken loose by body movement.

Poisoning. A poisoned dog needs instant treatment. Don't waste precious time taking him to the doctor but first empty his stomach. The easiest way is with hydrogen peroxide. Mix the regular drugstore strength (3%) with water 50-50 and pour it down the dog's throat. Use at least a tablespoonful to each 10 pounds of dog. It turns into oxygen and water and is harmless. He will vomit in about two minutes. After the stomach settles, give some Epsom salts, say a teaspoonful in a little water, to quickly empty the intestine. Hydrogen peroxide is an antidote for phosphorus, so often used in rat poisons. Epsom salts is an antidote for lead poisoning.

Slotted-floor boxes keep young pups off ground, clean and free from worms. Gunsmoke Kennels photo.

The following treatment can be tried for each specific poison. Naturally your first thought in knowing your dog was poisoned is to find out what it was. If you do not know and have used peroxide and Epsom salts, then obtain some "hypo" used by photographers and give a teaspoonful because it is an antidote for two other poisons.

HOUSEHOLD ANTIDOTES FOR COMMON POISONS

Poison	Antidote (for 40 lb. dog)
Mercuric compounds	Egg white, milk half a cup
Arsenic	Sodium thiasulphate (ordinary photographer's "hypo"), 1 teaspoonful in water
Acids	Bicarbonate of soda, eggshells, crushed plaster, 1 tablespoonful
Alkalis	Vinegar, lemon juice, several tablespoonsful
Lead	Epsom Salts, 1 teaspoonful in water
Phosphorus	Peroxide of hydrogen, as directed for emetic
Thallium	Table salt, 1 teaspoonful in water
Strychnine	Sedative drugs (nembutal, phenobarbital), 1 grain to each 7 lbs. of weight
Sedative drugs	Strong coffee, 1 cupful
Food poisoning	Peroxide of Hydrogen, empty bowels with enema of warm water, when stomach has settled give Epsom Salts, 1 teaspoonful in water

Porcupine Quills. Porcupines are spread over the country and more and more dogs are running afoul of them. Where you own a dog unacquainted with the animals, especially a courageous dog, keep a pair of pliers with tight-fitting jaws as part of owning the dog. Always go into the woods with these in your pocket.

If your dog attacks a porcupine, his mouth and lips will be filled with large body quills but the porcupine will generally have lashed his tail and swatted the dog on the chest, shoulders and legs, leaving the small, troublesome, fast-moving quills in dangerous places. The dog generally rolls and paws at himself, to make matters worse.

Get hold of him and put a chain around his neck and tie him to a tree so that he can't run away. Clip the quills in half with either scissors or pliers. This will make their removal less painful. Hold the dog and then pull the quills. Yank them out of his mouth and near his eyes first, and any behind the ribs. Those in his legs may be most troublesome, especially any in the wrist joints. Pull them out as cleanly as possible.

Some quills come out easiest by pushing them through tissue and pulling them out the other side. Quills in the tongue, lips, legs, and feet can be treated this way because it hurts the dog far less than pulling them backwards. This is because the quills on their business ends look like thistles with countless little scales protruding with points backward.

When it is available, vinegar will help considerably in removing porcupine quills. Sopped on liberally, the vinegar softens the quills, making them easier to pull. Many of the hound owners in the Rocky Mountain areas, where porcupines have become a constant problem, carry vinegar in their cars or trucks when they set out on a hunt. The quills have a somewhat hollow construction, however, which is why first cutting them in half allows them to contract and makes them easier to deal with.

Dog Bites. Even when a dog inflicts deep bites and jagged tears in another dog's skin, one need not be too much alarmed. It does no harm to allow your dog to lap and thus clean its open wounds before having them sutured. The worst that happens is where pus pockets develop and lockjaw germs grow. Where wounds are deep and inaccessible, it is best to ask a veterinarian to inject the dog with tetanus antitoxin, but be sure to tell him if it was ever used on the dog before.

If no veterinarian is available and you decide to suture the skin yourself, sew it with sterile thread that has been boiled, making sure the lower layers of the skin are touching each other, and healing usually will be prompt. Apply antiseptics to the stitches every day.

Cuts. Most troublesome of dogs' cuts are cut feet. They are so well supplied with blood that even a small cut bleeds profusely. If a cut on the leg or foot bleeds, apply a tourniquet above it, but relax it at least every ten minutes. Cut feet can best be managed temporarily by pressure bandages applied firmly. The idea is to let a clot form, even though it is a small clot. Nearly everyone applies the bandage too loosely. All a loose bandage does is to soak up the blood, not prevent its flow.

Such a bandage must not be kept in place too long or circulation may be impeded. When it is removed, it should be for a veterinarian to stitch the cut together and stop the blood flow.

Cut pads can incapacitate hunting dogs for weeks unless they are promptly treated because walking or running on the foot prevents healing of the pad. Suturing the cut closed and bandaging with changes of the bandages every other day can have a dog walking naturally in ten days or less.

Foreign Bodies in Mouth. If you see a dog having trouble closing his mouth, or pawing at his mouth, or strangling, try opening it and looking inside. He may be in such a frenzy that you will have to jump straddle him and hold his neck between your knees to restrain him.

You may find a bone or stick against the roof of his mouthed wedged between his teeth, or a needle in his throat, or a bone stuck on his teeth or a bone chip forced down beside his teeth. Any of these can usually be pulled out with a pair of pliers. It may be advisable to put a stick the size of a broom handle in his mouth to prevent the dog from closing his jaws while you are endeavoring to help him.

Drowning. If a dog can be rescued from drowning while his heart is still beating he can usually be saved. Artificial respiration is the answer. With your dog lying flat on his side, press down on the chest cavity and draw up. This pushes air out and his ribspring will cause inhalation. Keep this up at a rate of 20 a minute until he can breathe without your help.

Electric Shocks. If the dog is lying on a bare wire or the wire is lying on him, beware of moisture. If you try to get the wire off the dog use a dry stick. Dogs have been playing with electric cords and have bitten them while one foot was on a register and have been killed or made unconscious. They often urinate; the owner steps in the urine, picks up the dog which has the wire stuck to his foot, and becomes shocked himself.

If a dog's heart is beating after electric shock, apply artificial respiration and he may live.

——How to Give Medicine——

ADMINISTERING MEDICINES to dogs is not half the job most dog owners needlessly make of it. Liquids, powders, pills, tablets, and capsules are the forms of medicine commonly given. Here are the easy ways:

Liquids. To make a dog swallow a liquid you can place it on the back of his tongue, provided it is a small amount, say a teaspoonful. But if you expect him to swallow a larger amount, this method is not satisfactory, for he will almost certainly lose much of it if you simply pour it into his mouth. So you resort to the cheek method.

Try holding his head up with one hand and with the fingers of the other hand make a pocket in his cheek by pulling out his lips enough to enable you or an assistant to pour the medicine in through the opening. Continue to hold the head up until the liquid trickles between his teeth, and as it does so, he will swallow it. This eliminates the danger of having medicine inhaled which may cause pneumonia.

Powders. Open the dog's mouth just enough to insert the powder applicator which may be a flat stick or a teaspoon. Slip it between the front teeth and dump the powder in the back of the mouth. Snap the jaws closed as soon as the applicator is withdrawn. Hold the dog's head, allowing the mouth to open only

enough for the tongue to protrude a little. By working the tongue the dog mixes saliva with the powder and soon has a paste coating the inside of his throat and mouth. This is gradually swallowed with his saliva.

Pills, Tablets, Capsules. The method of administration is the same for all three. Place the medicine in a handy place near the dog where you can reach it easily. Assuming you are right-handed, place your left hand over the top of the dog's jaw with your thumb on one side and fingers on the other side of the lips just in front of the angle of the jaw, with his head pointed straight up. The pressure will cause the dog to open his mouth. With your right hand you can pull the lower jaw open. He won't close his mouth because he will bite his lips if he does. Now you drop your pill or capsule in the back of the mouth and, with your thumb out of the way, push the medicine down the throat over the bump you feel, which is the larynx (Adam's apple). Let the dog's mouth snap shut and he will usually stick out his tongue, showing he has swallowed. You don't need to massage his throat or pour water into his mouth. But watch him a few minutes to be sure the pill didn't slip off your fingers and lodge in the mouth.

——The Dog's Anatomy and Physiology——

THE DOG has been thoroughly studied because he has worked for mankind as a servant in a manner not ordinarily attributed to him: we owe to studies made with dogs many of the medicines and facts about physiology which are used daily to prolong human lives. Dogs gave us much of our knowledge about insulin, about reproductive hormones, about blood, even about cancer, to mention the barest fragments of their contribution.

The sciences of anatomy and physiology have often been considered independently, but we shall inquire

into the structure (anatomy) and function (physiology) both at once. The parts fall more or less into systems: skeleton and muscle; skin and hair; blood system; respiratory system; digestive system; genitourinary system, and nervous system. We shall consider each of these systems separately.

The Skeleton. There is little variation among dogs in the number and arrangement of the various bones in the different breeds of dogs. Variation is largely limited to differences in size or length. The chief excep-

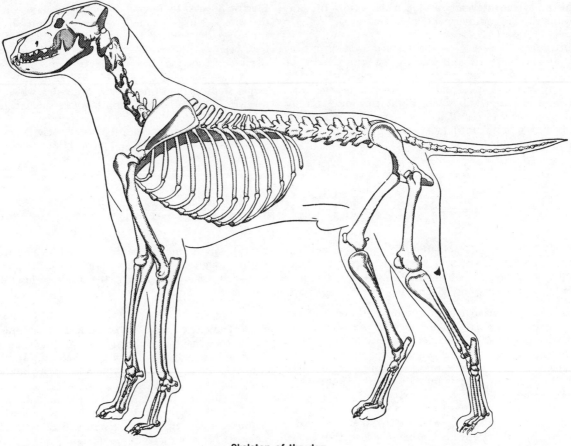

Skeleton of the dog.

tions are in the tail and the extra toe commonly called the dewclaw.

Behind the head we find the start of the spinal column consisting of 7 neck bones called *cervical vertebrae*, 13 bones above the chest cavity, called *thoracic vertebrae*, 7 bones above the loin, the *lumbar vertebrae*, 3 above the pelvis called *sacral vertebrae*, and from 20 to 23 in the tail of dogs with normal-length tails, called *coccygeal vertebrae*.

The bones of the head are variable in size according to breed. Dogs with broad heads and short faces contrast radically with dogs of breeds with narrow heads and long faces. But, for all the different exterior, their brain cases are approximately equal in capacity. Those with wide heads have better protected brains, and the jaws of such dogs are usually more powerful, due to the heavier jaw muscles.

It is not this book's intention to delve into the intricacies of details of impractical value to dog lovers. Whole books have been published on the subject of anatomy alone. The reader sufficiently interested in such details is referred to them. Here only some of the more interesting details of a dog's skull are considered. With a few exceptions the skull is composed of pairs of bones. The occipital bone—the one which makes the peak up between the ears—is single, and another, the vomer (which isn't visible) is also single. Even these are formed by the junction of

pairs of bones in the early development of the puppy. We call it the occipital bone, but technically anatomists call it the interparietal. Really it is a bone made by the fusing, before birth, of the occipital and interparietals.

Few animals have such a delicate development of the organs of olfaction (smelling) as have dogs. The air is inhaled and does not run from the nose down a tube to the lungs but first passes through a maze of the most frail network of bones covered with flesh and nerve endings. These bones are called the turbinates.

The lower jaw is composed of a pair of bones—the mandibles—which, at the rear, have right angle bends Very heavy muscles are attached to them and to the bones above. Mandibles are often broken. At the front they are joined together by cartilage so that when they break at this junction they heal rapidly, cartilage healing much more rapidly than bone.

The teeth of a puppy erupt starting at the third week of life, then fall out starting at the 14th week, on the average, and a new permanent set is grown in by the end of the seventh month. The last molar is in by the seventh month and most of the permanent set has erupted by the fifth. Dogs which have diseases causing fever and metabolic upsets during teething may develop deformed teeth or some with pits where enamel fails to deposit. At one time such teeth were called "distemper teeth," but we know now that any one of many maladies can be the cause.

Dogs' teeth are constructed for killing prey, for tearing it apart, for piercing, and the back teeth for cutting off the flesh. Dogs with short heads, like Boston Terriers, often have teeth so crowded that they erupt unevenly and some are turned sideways. Dogs with normal mouths have in the upper jaw, on each side, 3 incisors, 1 canine, 4 premolars, and 2 molars. On the lower jaw, on each side, they have 3 incisors, 1 canine, 4 premolars, and 3 molars. The dental formula is written thus:

$$2\left(I\ \frac{3}{3}\ C\ \frac{1}{1}\ P\ \frac{4}{4}\ M\ \frac{2}{3} \right) = 42$$

Hereditary abnormalities often produce dogs with no premolars, so their mouths resemble those of some horses, with a place for a bit to fit.

Dogs' teeth seldom develop cavities. Tartar often collect on them, pushing the gums back, and bacteria often grow deep along the teeth loosening them and allowing abscesses to develop. But even such teeth, when extracted, are usually free from cavities.

The skull has several sinuses which make trouble at times. They are called the frontal and maxillary. They vary in size with the shape of the head, and are connected.

Two large bones of the skeleton with which dog owners are especially concerned in these days of auto-mobile accidents are the shoulder blade (scapula) at one end, and the pelvis at the other. The shoulder blade covers a plexus of nerves. It is not uncommon for a blow on the shoulder to bruise or break the radial nerve, thus causing paralysis and a sagging of the whole leg so that the back of the paw drags the ground. The pelvis is a none-too-strong bone when subjected to blows and being run over. The dog's body was not evolved for any such extremes. Consequently we find the pelvis breaking, often into many pieces, with no adequate means at our disposal of setting it. Although it generally heals without much deformity to the dog, it may be deformed after breaking and mending so as to make the passage of large stools difficult and the normal birth of young impossible.

At each side is a socket into which the ball of the thigh bone fits. This joint is held together by a capsule and strong ligaments. A common accident in dogs is a dislocation of this joint, which dislocation can be reduced by a veterinarian while the dog is anaesthetized provided too many days are not allowed to elapse before the leg is set. The socket fills in, by growth, in a week's time and, after that, it is almost impossible to replace the thigh bone with any assurance that it will not dislocate with the first use of it by the dog.

Muscles not only cover the skeleton but help hold it together and perform many functions, from

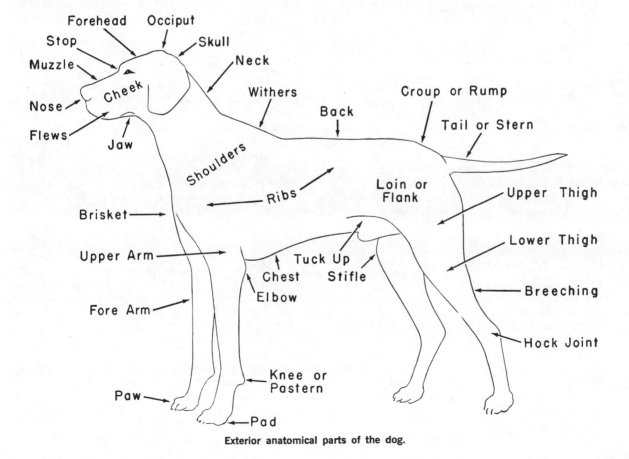

Exterior anatomical parts of the dog.

accounting for locomotion to breathing. There are two kinds of muscles, one called voluntary (under control of voluntary nerves); the other, involuntary. Those muscles which propel food through the intestines are involuntary and are usually spoken of as visceral muscles.

The dog's muscles are far more powerful than is usually realized. Feats of muscle prowess are boasted of for sled dogs which indicate that pound for pound they are far more powerful than horses. Feats of endurance in hounds, such as following a fox trail for 48 hours, border on the unbelievable. Dog muscles are uncommonly strong and almost tireless when properly trained.

Skin and Hair. The skin has considerable power to vary the density but not the length of its hairy protection. Southern dogs shipped north develop thicker coats and *vice versa,* but there is a limit apparently fixed by heredity as to this ultimate thickness or thinness, and to the coat's length. Some thin-coated dogs never do develop sufficiently heavy coats to stand cold northern winters, and some of the cold climate dogs grow coats much too heavy for comfort when moved south, and their puppies also fail to grow sufficiently sparse coats.

The mammary glands are actually skin glands, a fact not usually appreciated.

It was commonly held that dogs have no sweat glands in their skin, as do humans. Today we know they can and do sweat, especially from restricted areas, and these are not only the foot pads. Dogs do not raise welts on the skin as horses do when bruised, and their skin is affixed to the muscles beneath very loosely, so there is a definite sliding of the skin and greater protection from injury than many species possess.

Below the anus are two skin glands—the anal glands—which may discharge an evil-smelling thin liquid when the dog feels an extreme sense of terror. Most dogs are never frightened sufficiently to cause this discharge.

The skin of the ears especially is very well supplied with blood. Even the long, pendulous ears of hounds almost never freeze, a most remarkable fact especially when one considers the lack of protection to the ears which the body affords. But then, the skin is an organ with a good blood supply all over the body. It together with subcutaneous fat and hair outside, protects dogs against the bitterest cold.

Blood System. This consists, in brief, of a pump—the heart—with its ingenious and efficient construction. It is divided into four sections, two on each side, with valves fitted to close the proper sections to make the pump work. The muscular heart contracts and expands rhythmically. The contraction forces blood out through valves into arteries. From one side the blood flows to the lungs to be aerated and to discharge carbon dioxide and gaseous poisons, and from the other, out through the rest of the body and organs. The cavities of the heart fill as it relaxes, to be ready when the new contraction forces it along.

Between the beats the heart muscles rest.

The blood is borne about the body by arteries. As these divide they grow smaller and smaller with each division until at length the little arteries are called arterioles. The arterioles play out into still smaller units called capillaries, which are so small as to reach every cell in their vicinity. Capillaries become veinules, which unite to form veins which join to form large veins via which the blood returns to the heart.

Beside returning by way of the veins some of the blood plasma returns toward the heart via another system, called the lymph vessels. For that reason venous blood contains more cells than arterial blood. The lymph vessels conduct their contents through a system of purification plants known as lymph nodes. One very large lymph node is situated beside the stomach in the abdomen. Its functions are more than merely removing impurities, having beside this some part in the production of blood cells.

Having traversed the lymph vessels, the plasma or lymph is returned to the venous blood just before it reaches the heart thus making it normal blood, and this is then forced out to be purified in the lungs and liver.

Blood is composed of a clear fluid called plasma. This carries the blood-clotting chemical known as fibrinogen which, as everyone knows, is able to form a clot and, eventually, tough scar tissue. In the plasma are found the red cells; flattish, round cells containing hemoglobin, an interesting chemical with an affinity for oxygen which it also parts with under proper conditions. In the lungs it picks it up, and in the presence of oxygen-hungry cells of the body, gives it up and absorbs more on its next trip to the lungs. When it is loaded with oxygen the hemoglobin is bright red, which is the reason why arterial blood is bright red in contrast to the almost bluish venous blood.

We also find white cells in the plasma but in a much smaller percentage than red: 7,000,000 of red per milliliter to 5,000 of white. To give an idea of their size, a milliliter is about $1/_{30}$ of an inch cubed. White cells are disease destroyers and are of various shapes and sizes—not all uniform like red cells. There are many kinds—monocytes, leucocytes, etc., and counts of these cells are used sometimes in determining diseases.

Blood carries the properties called antibodies which are developed in the individual after a bout with every generalized disease. These chemical substances act as protection against the specific disease they were formed to combat, and usually last throughout the life of the dog.

Blood normally remains at a constant temperature, at a constant alkalinity, and with approximately the same amount of water per given quantity. Regulators in the body are at work controlling these factors. A dog's blood does not become "overheated" from what he eats, not over-acid unless he is sick, usually from kidney disease. When he has too much water, his kidneys take care of it and the bladder fills.

Respiratory System. The function of the respiratory system is to bring the oxygen in the air into close contact with the blood, and to provide one means of escape out of the body for waste gases.

We find the windpipe (trachea) leading from the back of the throat down to branches which in turn branch and branch into the various parts of the lungs. These organs are honeycomb tissues with innumerable air pockets with very thin walls, and in these walls the blood comes so close to the surface that there can be the desired transfer of gases. Here the red blood cells capture oxygen and give up carbon dioxide, and the blood loses other wastes. Air is inhaled, but that which is exhaled is of somewhat different composition—principally in that it has less oxygen and more carbon dioxide.

The movements of breathing—of the lungs filling and emptying—are accomplished by the great thin muscle called the diaphragm, which spreads across the dog's body forming the separator between the abdomen and the chest cavity, and the muscles of the ribs which synchronize with the diaphragm in making the chest cavity smaller and larger.

Digestive System. A dog's digestive system is a complex affair—far more than a tube through the body, as so many seem to think. It is a tube, yes, but one attended by nerves, glands, valves, and accessory organs—all of which help to move, digest, or absorb food. And even after food has been absorbed into the blood as end products of digestion, its utilization depends on regulators. All of these are most interesting.

The anatomy of the digestive system begins at the mouth. Dogs gulp food, made small enough by mastication to swallow if it is not furnished small enough by the dog's owners. Since no digestion takes place in the mouth, there is no point in chewing. It goes through the opening above the larynx over the flipper called the epiglottis. This keeps it from entering the windpipe which is a parallel tube having its opening just below the opening of the gullet (esophagus).

The gullet conducts it to the stomach through a valve. The stomach with its glandular wall might be considered an enlargement in the digestive tube. Highly acid digestive fluids with enzymes soak into the food there. Considerable digestion takes place in the stomach, all of it in breaking down protein from its original form into peptones and proteoses. Some influence is exerted on the fat, too, by an enzyme called lipase.

There is a valve—the pylorus—at the stomach's opening into the intestine. This valve is a regulator allowing properly prepared food to seep through and starting the material off in small sections. That part of the intestine just below the stomach is called the duodenum. It has heavier walls than the rest of the intestine and several openings from ducts—little tubes which conduct digestive fluids from (1) the pancreas, (2) the liver.

The pancreas has two tasks to perform: (1) secrete an enzyme which helps in starch digestion; (2) secrete insulin, not into the intestine, but into the blood. Insulin is a regulator which determines when the liver should store blood sugar and when it should cease storing it. In this way it is concerned with nutrition, for if the liver cannot store the sugar the dog must pass out a good deal of the surplus through his urine, and if he cannot accommodate all of it this way, he many have a convulsion.

The liver is a relatively large organ in a dog, being about ten per cent of the total weight (provided he is not excessively fat); it lies behind the diaphragm in front of the stomach. It stores blood sugar and has many functions such as purifying of blood, but our concern with it in digestion is in knowing that it secretes large quantities of bile which it stores in the gall bladder. As food comes into the duodenum, the bile is mixing with it constantly, producing an alkalizing effect, and the bile salts cause the fat to emulsify or split into innumerable tiny droplets so that digestive enzymes can break it down for absorption.

Without bile the dog cannot live. His stools become grey, pasty, and possess an odor of rancidity. Meals with fat cause a greater outpouring of bile than fat-free meals. Physiologists believe that a diet with 15 or 20 per cent fat produces optimum digestion because of its effect on the liver. At one time it was thought dogs should have no fat and dog owners are still being advised to feed only lean meat or low-fat diets—to the detriment of the dogs.

The duodenum blends into the intestine or may be considered a part of it, and the whole intestine which occupies most of the space from the stomach to the pelvis is only about five times as long as the dog, making it short in comparison with the intestines of other animals.

Its wall is filled with glands which secrete digestive fluids and it is here that the final digestive processes take place. What once was starch is broken down in steps until it becomes glucose; what once was crude protein is broken down into amino acids; what once was fat is broken down into glycerol and soap. In these forms the end products of digestion are absorbed, and with them soluble minerals, vitamins, and water.

Here it is important to understand the principle of osmosis. If a parchment bag is filled with a salt solution, and that bag is placed in a solution with no salt, there will be a passage of water into the bag as the salt solution attracts less concentrated solutions. In this way the bag will fill. If the stronger solution is outside, the bag will tend slowly to empty.

That principle accounts for the absorption of these end products of digestion. Fat won't penetrate the membrane represented by the intestines, but glycerol will. If a dog is given a physic of Epsom salts, the concentration of salt in the intestines is greater inside, so the water from the blood rushes out into the intestines, dilutes the salts, and flushes out the contents of the intestines.

But the blood contains salt. If the dog drinks

water, the concentration on the blood side of the intestinal membrane is greater and hence the water passes into the blood. As it does, it may carry with it glycogen and vitamins, or even poisons, but mineral salts are not utilized unless the concentration is less in the blood than outside. For instance, witness the huge amounts of calcium and phosphorus one finds in the stools of dogs after they have eaten bones. Such stools may be almost concretions of these minerals which were dissolved in the stomach by the hydrochloric acid, passed through the intestines unused except for the protein and fat which was removed, and the residue deposited in the lower bowel.

Absorption in the intestines is assisted by the structure of the intestinal lining which is like velvet with millions of microscopic fingers reaching out from its surface. These correspond to the fine threads standing on end which make up the surface of velvet. Because of these villi, as they are called, the total surface is tremendously increased and nutrients can pass into them and thus into the lymph from where they are conducted to the blood.

Once they pass this barrier the components of fat join together again into fatty acids. After a heavy meal of fat, if blood is drawn from a dog and allowed to stand, this fat (called chyle) will rise just as cream does on milk.

By the time the residue from what once was food reaches the lower end of the intestines, the colon, it passes through a valve called the ileo-cecal and thereafter there is little absorption except of surplus water if it is needed by the body.

The dog has an organ, the cecum, believed to be useful in the absorption of surplus liquid from the colon. It enters the upper side of the colon almost at the ileo-cecal valve. In some dogs it is a straight tube the size of the finger of a glove. In others, it may be six or more inches long with a corkscrew shape which winds about the intestine. This cecum is a favorite place for whipworms to live and is of little use to a dog, as has been amply demonstrated by all the dogs whose ceca were removed surgically before we had worm medicines which effectively removed the whipworms.

The rectum constitutes the lowest extremity of the intestine terminating at the anus, another valve of the sphincter type. The amount of residue from food consumed determines the quantity or volume of stool. The vegetable residue holds more water and is bulkier than residue from clear muscle meat. This latter, leaves so little residue that when dogs eat it alone, a whole day's food leaves such a small amount of stool that a dog might wait several days before defecating. On diets with vegetable content he may stool several times a day. The character of the stool depends on the food eaten; how much indigestible residue remains. Potatoes fed in lumps even though cooked may be found in the stool apparently undigested, whereas mashed potatoes have been well utilized, leaving only the cellulose behind.

The Genito-Urinary System. All of the dog's blood flows through large bean-shaped filter plants called kidneys, a pair of organs situated at the top of the abdominal cavity just under the last ribs in a well-protected location. Each kidney is about as large as a hen's egg. The structure of kidneys is one of the marvels of anatomy and physiology, for they effectively remove wastes and surpluses without changing the blood's general composition. Uric acid is the principal impurity removed, although surplus sugar can be found by appropriate examinations. Each kidney is composed of miles of tiny tubules which eventually discharge their products into a reservoir in the center called the pelvis. And from the pelvis runs a tube—the ureter—which joins the bladder at its neck. The ureters are equipped with valves which allow for downward passage of urine but no upward passage.

The bladder is an elastic organ, composed, of muscle, at whose neck is a sphincter muscle and, in male dogs, a gland, the prostate. This gland tends to swell from congestion by the mental stimulation to a dog of knowing that a bitch is in heat anywhere in the neighborhood. It also swells from other causes sometimes necessitating castration or hormone medication to reduce its size.

Being located in the pelvis, an enlarged prostate may cause not only pain but constipation by damming the feces sufficiently so that they cannot move over the swelling. Such dogs need special diets to be certain that constipation does not occur.

The urine is conducted from the bladder outside the body by the urethra. In the bitch it terminates in the floor of the vagina so that urine is discharged by her from that organ. In the male, the uretha runs the entire length of the penis to its very tip.

The male genital system consists of the penis which has toward its posterior portion a bulb which together with the anterior portion is composed of spongy tissue capable of becoming distended with blood. In copulation, when the penis enters the vagina of the bitch, the swelling of the bulb prevents the withdrawal of the penis, with the result that the pair remain tied until the blood leaves the penis and its reduction to nearer normal size make it small enough to slip out through the vaginal opening.

When the penis is first inserted the bulb is inside the pelvis, but with pulling apart by the dogs the bulb, now held firmly by the vaginal tissue, slips back through the pelvis and can be felt outside of it.

In addition to the penis, the male genital system also consists of a pair of testicles in which sperm are created from germinal cells which grow and divide to form them. The sperm are conducted into tubules and thence into a long coiled tube, the epididymus, where they are stored, which in turn becomes the vas deferens, and runs into the body through an opening in front of the pelvis—one on each side—along with an artery, vein, nerve, and muscle.

The vas deferens joins the urinary system at a point at the neck of the bladder above the prostate. It conducts sperm to the urethra through which they are ejaculated. When dogs first become tied, the first fluid ejaculated is clear and free from sperm and lightly alkaline, thus insuring an alkaline environment for the sperm. After the passage has thus been prepared, sperm fill the fluid making it a milky color.

Millions of sperm are discharged at each service by a dog not too frequently used as a stud. Only one is accepted by each egg and each sperm contains half the "architectural plans" for a pup. All the rest are wasted.

The female has no prostate but does have a rudimentary penis in the form of a clitoris which lies on the floor of the vagina, posterior to the opening of the urethra. Her uterus is long and Y shaped, the upper ends varying in length with her reproductive experience and her breed and size. Each ovary lies in a sac or capsule attached to one end of the uterus and to tissue near the kidney. The fallopian tube runs from the end of the uterus in a zigzag line across the surface of the capsule and ends in a spongy tissue —the fimbrae—which is situated above a slit in the side of the capsule.

The ovaries within this capsule are about as large as a yellow-eye bean, flattish in shape. At the time of "heat" or the mating cycle—twice a year, generally early winter and early summer—the ovaries ripen blister-like growth, each containing an ovum or egg. At anywhere from the tenth to the twentieth day of the mating cycle, usually about the sixteenth, the follicles burst liberating the eggs. The sperm are already in the sacs surrounding the ovaries and the eggs are at once besieged by sperm and each is fertilized by one.

The best time to mate dogs with assurance of success is close to the time of ovulation, as the rupturing of the follicles is called. Occasionally one finds a bitch which will ovulate at the first day of acceptance and others toward the very end of the period, but most bitches tend to ovulate at the middle of the acceptance period.

Several hormones are concerned in the mating cycle. The follicular hormone (estrin) generated in the follicles affects the bitch's behavior and makes her desire copulation. Another causes ovulation. This is called by various names but can be purchased as made from pregnant mare's serum.

As soon as the follicles have burst, the cavities fill with blood clots which organize and turn into tissue which secretes another hormone—the luteal—and it is this which puts a brake on the desire for copulation. Therefore, after ovulation, in a matter of a few days there is sufficient of this hormone in the blood to affect behavior. There is probably an odor about the bitch which this hormone causes that warns dogs to stay away because one sniff tells them the bitch is not in heat. The odor probably persists until the start of the next heat period.

Bringing bitches successfully in heat and ovulation can be engineered by injecting first the hormone, estrin, to be followed by pregnant mare serum in a week or ten days. Without the latter the bitch will come in heat but will fail to ovulate and will then come in heat again at her normal time. But if she ovulates, she will then be fertile and her next regular period will occur six months later unless some change in climate—such as being moved from North to South—or unusual light conditions produce it in a shorter time.

The Nervous System. The brain is the heart of the nervous system. In a dog it is small, weighing about 2½ ounces in a 40-pound dog. From it and to it go and come the nervous impulses over the nerves which run out from the brain and the spinal cord. The brain consists of a front part, the cerebrum, a rear section, the cerebellum, and at the extreme front we find the pair of olfactory bulbs most important to a dog. At the junction of the brain with the roundish spinal cord, the medula oblongata is located. Optic nerves attach underneath and ramify out in its substance. Each part, and there are many others, has some special function.

Nerves are white and fairly tough. The nervous system is not like the blood system in that liquid flows from small tubes into larger. The nerves close to the brain are large and seem to branch as they spread out, but this is due to the fact that every nerve fiber runs from some spot in the body all the way to the brain. As these minute nerve fibers spread out from trunks, they give the appearance of branching when actually they are losing a fiber here, another there.

Nerve impulses over these fibers travel with the speed of electricity. Too large an impulse of pain, such as an accident or severe burn, causes shock—a breakdown of the nervous system.

Part VII

DOG BREEDING

Dog breeding is a science, the successful pursuance of which requires great study and careful planning. The average breeder gives far too little thought to the choice of a sire, being content to breed to a winning or producing dog in the hope that outstanding progeny will result from the union with his bitch, and losing sight of the individual characteristics, good and bad, of the prospective parents.

—Breeding—

A SUCCESSFUL breeder not only studies the characteristics of the individual dogs he plans to use as breeding stock but also makes himself fully acquainted with the characteristics of the families from which these individuals come.

He sets a definite goal of accomplishment and strives, through selective breeding, to bring about an emphasis on desired characteristics, such as conformation, color, coat, and temperament, which meet the requirements of that goal.

He must also know a great deal about the physiology of reproduction. In brief, at a given time the ovary of the bitch develops follicles, each of which contains an ovum or egg. The follicles grow closer to the ovary's surface and, at about the fifteenth day of the mating period, rupture into the sac surrounding the ovary. If the bitch has mated with a dog, some of his semen is already in the sac, so that when the eggs appear they are set upon by large numbers of sperm, one of which manages to enter each egg.

The egg has within its nucleus a great many tiny packets of chemicals which we call genes. They are believed to be the bearers of heredity and their interaction determines the traits of the individual the cell forms. The egg has twice as many genes as the sperm, which has half the requisite number to develop a pup. But just at the time of fertilization the egg casts off half of its genes and the genes of both join together. Were it not for this unique provision—of each parent furnishing half the genes—the pups which developed would have double the prerequisite number of genes, and the number would double each generation.

At certain times the genes can be seen to gather into lines or bodies called chromosomes, so named because when stained they take up the stain and are clearly visible. Every dog, like all other normal creatures, has definite numbers of pairs of chromosomes. The exact figure for dogs has not been settled. Some flies have four pairs; humans, 24 pairs.

Each characteristic in the dog's body is determined by the interaction of all the genes, but the difference in a pair may make a great difference in any trait. This is more easily understood if we consider that a certain pair is responsible for each characteristic or trait. Let's say we are considering the inheritance of the character of pearl eye in Pointers.

This characteristic is determined in the pup by one gene given the pup from one parent and a mate given by the other parent. The principal thing to remember is that *each trait is thus determined by a pair of genes* and not by one.

Mendel's Law. If both of the pair are determiners (genes) for pearl eye, the pup will be pearl-eyed. If both are determiners for brown eye, the pup will be brown-eyed. But suppose one is a gene for pearl and the other for brown, what will the offspring be?

To understand that, we have to understand *Mendel's Law of Alternate Inheritance.* Ever since mankind began to speculate on how animals and humans inherit, it has been continually remarked that traits skipped a generation, but it was not known why. Such observations were the bases of many weird theories, some of which we shall consider later. Had our early scientists or animal breeders bothered to count as Mendel did, they might have learned Mendel's Law. Mendel bred garden peas and noted their differences in parallel columns. He crossed tall peas with dwarf peas, some wrinkled peas with peas which were smooth. In the first generation he got only one kind of character—not a type midway between.

If we crossed a pearl-eyed pointer with a pure-brown-eyed pointer we would have only brown-eyed pups. What would happen if we mated a pair of those brown-eyed pups? Just what happened to the peas of Mendel.

That scientist found his cross of tall with dwarf produced all tall peas and none in between. So he said the tall character dominated the dwarf. He called it dominant. The dwarf faded—receded from view—so he called it recessive. We call brown-eye dominant, pearl-eye recessive, because the first cross of these two pure types produces only brown-eyed pups.

Mendel counted the next generation and found he had 25 percent dwarf and 75 percent tall peas. The recessives had slipped a generation, but they did so with a nice mathematical precision. By continued breeding he found his recessives never gave rise to dominants, but that those which looked like the dominant often produced recessives. By more counting he learned that some of the talls were pure and produced only talls, but others produced both kinds always in the percentage of 4:1. So he figured he had (1) pure talls, (2) pure dwarfs, and (3) hybrids. The hybrids were mongrels for that trait. The ratio was 25 percent pure talls, 50 percent hybrids, 25 percent pure dwarfs.

If we had enough pups to count we should find we had a 25 percent pure-brown-eyed, 50 percent hybrid for the trait, and 25 percent pure-pearl-eyed.

Now right here we must understand what the word *hybrid* means. Many who have not studied genetics think a hybrid is a mule, that is, an offspring resulting from a cross of two species, such as a jackass and a mare or a canary bird with a finch. True they *are* hybrids but *species hybrids*. A *genetic hybrid* is a cross where a single pair of traits is involved.

Two genes for brown-eye do not make a hybrid; a dominant coupled with a recessive trait, such as a gene for brown coupled with a gene for pearl, do make a hybrid. And in the event, in your reading of genetic literature, you see the words homozygote and heterozygote, this is what they mean: the Greek word for yoke is *zygote*. *Homo* means same; *hetero* means different. Heterozygote means a yoke holding different things together, like an ox and a horse. In genetics heterozygote means two different genetic characters yoked and working together. Two genes for pearl-eye and two genes for brown-eye would be homozygotes. A pearl-eye gene yoked with a brown-eye gene would be heterozygotes. A heterozygote is the scientific name for a genetic hybrid.

Since Mendel's day all that we know about genes and chromosomes has been discovered. So we can say that the pearl-eyed pointers have a pair of genes (recessive) for pearl-eye; our hybrids have one of each kind of genes; our pure-brown-eyed (dominant) have a pair of genes for brown-eyes.

Consider all the characteristics of which dogs are composed and that every one is determined by genes in the germ plasm. Even some of the behavior patterns such as the propensity of puckering up the lips and smiling may be as simple a matter of inheritance as a pair of determiners. Many canine characteristics are doubtless determined by many pairs of genes working on the same end product. The principle holds nevertheless.

Some of us who study canine *genetics,* as the science of heredity is called, have been trying to factor dogs down into their lowest common hereditary denominators, as it were. We are trying to learn what all the inheritable characters are and how they are inherited. Quite a start has been made, but much remains to be accomplished. We find many characters are dominant or recessive. The list is appended on the end of this section. The mistake so many with too little knowledge make is to try to apply Mendel's Law to a single litter of, say, eight puppies, and assume it doesn't hold when the proportions do not come out according to expectations.

A breeder mates a gold-and-white (recessive) beagle to a tri-color (dominant). A friend has made the same type of mating. They each raise the pups. They decide to mate a pup from one litter with a pup from the other. All the pups are tri-colors because tri-color is dominant over gold-and-white.

The puppies from this cross of two hybrids should produce 25 percent gold-and-white. But there are four gold-and-whites and two tri-colors. This doesn't vitiate Mendel's Law. It simply shows there weren't enough pups for the mathematical expectancy to be realized. It is just as if we took a yellow and a mottled marble which one parent contributed and dropped them in a hat; then two more which the other parent contributed. You'd have two yellow and two mottled marbles. Reach into the hat now and take out two. Record the color. Put them back, mix them, and take out two more. Keep doing it and record what you had each time until you have drawn out 100 pairs. You will find you have very close to 25 times drawn a pair of yellow, 25 times drawn a pair of mottled, and 50 times a pair composed of one yellow and one mottled. Now you might draw a pair of yellows several times in a row, but the great average is 25-50-25.

Thus in any one litter the exact expectancy is not always realized, but there is an expectancy, nonetheless. It is governed by the Law of Alternate Inheritance. This question of skipping a generation is now, indeed, mathematically explainable.

Apply Mendel's Law to all the traits in dogs that can be resolved down to simple one-gene traits, and it helps greatly in understanding how dogs inherit.

A great many of the characteristics of dogs that we value most are not simple unit traits or one-gene traits. It is probably a fact that most of the traits are determined by a great many. Racing ability—speed—in greyhounds, bird-hunting ability in setters, "rabbit sense" in beagles, mantrailing in Bloodhounds, fighting ability in Staffordshires—such abilities are more often the sum total of a great many traits and one can't study them on a presence-or-absence basis as one can eye color. Rather we first understand the principle and then remember that improvement comes about by crossing the best families with the best.

Mutations. A mutation is a sudden change in heredity. Most mutations are downward, harmful to the bearer. An albino animal, while interesting to us, is a poorer bet to live in a wild state than a grey animal. A dog with very short legs is not so good a natural dog as a long-legged one. Suppose a breeder is interested in field trial pointers. His dogs are as fast as pointers come. In a litter he finds a puppy which grows with legs two inches longer than any of its litter mates, and more powerful muscles, but a body of the same length. When trained it can run much faster. That would probably be a mutation. It might breed true either as a dominant or recessive. By incorporating it into his stock, he breeds pointers able to run faster than another breeder's dogs.

By breed crossing and back crossing the breed improvements have come about. Many of our breeds have improved not a whit in 100 years. Few have regressed either. Some, through careless breeding and the notion of breeding bitches to champions irrespective of their mental qualities, have picked up many very undesirable characteristics. Poor selection on the part of breeders, perpetuating undesirable characteristics or incorporating undesirable mutations, and the failure to recognize and capitalize on desirable ones are all to blame for inferior strains of dogs today.

False Theories Once Accepted. Breeders in the past did not know of Mendel's Law and to explain how dogs and other animals inherit they concocted plausible theories which they often called "laws." Such "laws" were believed by nearly everybody:

The Inheritance of Acquired Characteristics. To explain how improvement came about, or deterioration progressed, we had the theory or law which, when applied to dogs, stated that if a dog hunted hard until he was old, the pups he sired in his old age would be better hunters because of his having hunted. If a sled dog worked hard at pulling, his pups would acquire his improved ability. It sounded reasonable. It was reasonable, if untrue, until we learned the more likely explanation—that changes come about by hereditary mutations.

Telegony. If a bitch were bred to a dog of another breed, and whelped a litter of mongrels, all the pups of subsequent litters the bitch might have would be marked by that sire of another breed. The bitch was believed ruined. The notion, without a vestige of truth, did much to insure purity of animal breeds. It had its basis in experiences which we know today have other explanations, but it was reasonable. We have no evidence that a stud dog affects any puppies other than those formed by the eggs which his sperm has fertilized. We can have puppies in a single litter sired by three studs and they will be as unmarked by the several half brothers or sisters as so many eggs in an incubator will be impressed by other eggs in the same tray.

Birth Marking. Another "law" which has long since been written off by scientists is that pertaining to a pregnant mother's ability to mark her child through mental impressions.

You can hunt a pregnant bitch or keep her in a pen, and there won't be the least difference in her puppies' ability as hunters. Frightening her by an automobile backfire won't impress her pups via her fright. They may, toward their latter weeks before birth, feel or sense explosions, but if there is any influence it has not been demonstrated. The bitch cannot mark them. Because she is frightened by a bear does not impress the puppies so they too will be more easily frightened.

Every dog breeder can forget prenatal influence so far as maternal impressions are concerned. Maternal nutrition, poisonings, parasites are a different matter. They can greatly affect pups, but they are not in the field of heredity.

The Blood Theory. How can a dog be pure-blooded? By having no chemical or parasite impurities in his blood. Years ago people thought heredity was a matter of dilution, not presence or absence, as modern genetics tells us it is. Heredity came via blood. But how absurd it is today to talk about pure-blooded, blooded, half-blooded, three-quarter-blooded, and all the other uses of blood. Many times fanciers, not understanding the simplest facts about heredity, have asked that in giving transfusions blood be used from dogs of the same breed and, if possible better representatives, so that their pups would be better than the parents—surely not contaminated with blood from another breed.

Red blood cells are larger than male sperm. How is blood going to influence heredity? We should talk about pure-bred, not pure-blooded. We should talk about genes and chromosomes, heredity, not blood.

Relationships. To be accurate each dog is only the custodian of the germ plasm he inherited. Inheritance is like a stream that goes on each generation, halving itself and joining with half of another line, producing individuals who carry the germ plasm as a trust and by mating pass it on where it produces other individuals who also are created by it and pass it on.

Inbreeding. Is inbreeding harmful? Is it beneficial? What is it? What is line-breeding? Is that harmful?

Inbreeding is the mating of a pair bearing fifty percent or more relationship to each other. Examples are parent to offspring, brother and sister, cousin to cousin, grandsire to grand-daughter.

Line-breeding is the mating of dogs having common distant relatives, such as grand- or great-grand-parents.

Outbreeding is the mating of dogs that are unrelated or only distantly related.

Outcrossing is the mating of dogs of two unrelated inbred lines.

Of these, line-breeding and outbreeding are the most common breeding methods used.

Since every dog is the product of his genes—that is, so far as his architectural plans are concerned—the kind of genes he has is all-important. If he has a number of inferior but recessive characters which are masked by dominants, he is safe. But let those recessive determiners of inferior traits double up and the pups show the inferior trait.

When dogs are inbred there is a greater chance of the genes for undesirable traits doubling up. That is why inbreeding is dangerous.

But it can also be desirable. Who wants a strain with lots of undesirable traits kept masked? An illustration is a strain of Boxers. Every now and then one or several white pups are born to solid-colored individuals of that strain. Whites are considered undesirable. Inbreeding determines which individuals produce white pups. The whites are eliminated and the breeder knows just which of his dogs carry white recessively.

Inbreeding doubles up the strain traits, good and bad. But continued inbreeding, without rigid selection, definitely decreases the size of the stock. It tends to decrease fertility to a certain extent, and it produces uniform stock. Uniform because the inbred offspring tend more and more to carry the same genes, and must develop similarly.

Mating of brother and sister, mother and son, father and daughter, down to first cousins, is considered inbreeding. Breeding father to daughter is genetically about equal to breeding half brother to half sister. Below first cousins is considered to be linebreeding which may be expressed as breeding not closely, within a strain.

Sex to Order. As this is written we have no practical means of producing sex to order, despite what you may have heard. The acid-alkaline theory, the North Wind theory, the sugar-salt theory, the left-right-side theory, or any of the thousands of theories which their proponents "proved" in the past yet remain to meet the acid test of science.

Sex is due to the sperm cells belonging to two classes. One half possesses an odd-shaped chromosome called the X chromosome; the other half possesses a full-sized one called the Y. All the female cells, have the corresponding chromosome of the Y. If an X-bearing sperm unites with an egg the pup will be a male. If a Y-bearing sperm unites, it will be a female pup. To look at sperm one can't tell which bear which chromosome. Drugs which kill one kind will kill both. Sex is almost a 50-50 proposition. Yet there are about 120 males born to every 100 females among our dog litters. The difference is believed due to those which die in embryo, not to the number conceived. There is considerable difference in the sex ratio according to the months of conception. In cold months there are many more males born, and in warm months the proportions tend to become nearer together.

The Computer and Selection of Breeding Stock. The idea of using the modern computer as a means of selecting potential dog breeding stock for various specific purposes sometimes arises as an attractive idea. So far, little seems to have been done in this area of any practical application.

Some of the studies referred to by Clarence Pfaffen-berger (*see* Part III) were aided by statistical data so assembled. And, according to one newspaper report in early 1970, at least one entrepreneur (having a dog grooming business in Philadelphia) was said to be exploring the use of the computer as an aid in making breeding selections so as to offer a dog owner or breeder wishing a candidate for mating his dog a choice of two "best selections," based upon qualities desired in the offspring.

As to the use of the computer respecting the maintenance of records on other animals such as livestock, race horses, etc., quite possibly the computer may have some applications in tabulating statistical data, but little, if anything, seems to have generated in its use so far of any great significance to identifying desirable breeding selections. For that matter, animal breeding—as a major field—offers enough complexities as it is, even to those well informed and experienced with such programs. Hence there seems no reason to believe the use of computers will revolutionize any animal breeding programs of the very near future.

Inherited Traits in Dogs. The known inherited genetic characters in dogs are as follows:

Color Inheritance

Dominant	Recessive
Black	All other colors
Solid Color	Ringneck pattern
Solid Color	Mostly white
Ringneck	Mostly white
Black-and-tan	Tri-color
Black-and-tan	Liver-and-tan
Black-and-tan	Red (type I)
Red (type II)	Black-and-tan
All colors	Albino-white
All colors	Dark-eyed white
Brindle	Tan
Black-and-brindle	Black-and-tan
Lemon-black nose and dark eyes	Lemon-pink nose and light eyes
Ticking	Non-ticking
Merling	Tri-color
Merling	Black-and-tan
Sable	Black-and-tan
Sable	Merling
Red	Cream

Leg Length

Short Legs (imperfectly)	Long Legs
Long legs	Short legs in Cockers

Eye Color

Brown eye	Yellow eye
Brown eye	Pearl eye

Coat Characteristics

Short hair	Long hair
Wire coat	Smooth coat
Coarse hair	Fine hair
Sparse coat	Dense coat
Straight	Curly

Miscellaneous

Dewclaws	No dewclaws
Stub tail (imperfectly)	Long tail
Straight tail	Curly tail
Glaucoma	Normal sight
Shorter ears	Longer ears

Mental Aptitudes

Open trailing	Still trailing
Chop voice	Drawling voice
High head carriage in hunt-ing	Low head carriage
Smiling	Nonsmiling
Bird interest	Lack of bird interest
Water-going	Non water-going
Quartering	Straight line hunting

MATING THE BITCH

It is best to wait until the bitch is in her second "season" or "heat" before breeding her. She will by that time very probably have reached her full maturity. The period of "heat" varies with individuals. It generally lasts about 18 days. This period has three divisions, each lasting a little less than a week. The first is the "coming in" time when the vulva starts swelling; the swelling grows more pronounced and a bloody vaginal discharge is noted. The second is the breeding period. Lastly is the "going out" period when the discharge stops and the swelling goes down. By the 18th day, or shortly thereafter, the bitch will no longer be willing to breed and will be safely "out of season."

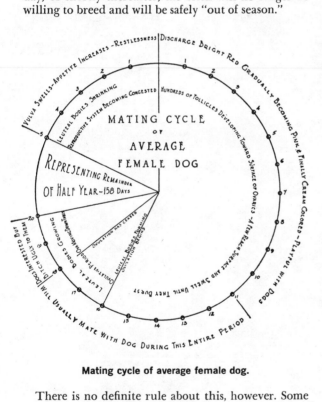

Mating cycle of average female dog.

There is no definite rule about this, however. Some bitches are "in season" only a short time while others remain receptive for three weeks.

Most breeders generally mate their bitches on about the tenth or eleventh day of "season." This is just after the vaginal discharge has stopped. Usually one mating is sufficient, but to provide against "mishaps" those who pay large stud fees try to insist upon two. Some bitches, particularly young bitches, are shy and nervous when approached by the prospective sire. In such cases, if assistance is required it should be given by someone with whom the bitch is acquainted, otherwise her fears may be aggravated.

If the bitch is to be shipped away for breeding, shipment should be made before she has been "in heat" a week. This will give her a chance to become accustomed to strange surroundings. It is better to be early than sorry you were late.

Before breeding her the bitch should be wormed thoroughly. Fecal slides should be made and the correct medicine administered by a veterinarian. No female should be bred while she is in run-down condition or overly fat.

CARE OF THE MATRON

The dog's period of gestation runs from 58 to 65 days, with the average 62 or 63 days, approximately nine weeks.

During this time, the diet of the matron is of much importance. It must be of sufficient quantity and quality to maintain the matron herself and bring about the development of her family in embryo. It should contain the vitamins, carbohydrates, fats, proteins, and minerals. Dry, commercial dog food may be kept available to her so she may meet the additional demands as required. This is especially important during the final weeks of gestation, when the puppies grow most rapidly.

Exercise is important. This should be mild but regular. As she grows heavy in whelp, she will be inclined to remain idle but should be taken for regular short walks on the leash.

A whelping box should be provided. This should consist of a wooden floor, with sides, but no top. A rail a few inches off the floor is advisable so that she cannot crowd the puppies against the sides and crush or suffocate them. Several layers of newspapers may serve as bedding. This will insulate against floor drafts and are easily removed when soiled. The bottom of the pen should be at least an inch off the floor. The bitch should be kept as quiet as possible during her period of travail.

The bitch should be disturbed as little as possible but watched carefully during whelping. After the first expulsive effort is seen, it is safe to allow one hour before the first delivery. However, if the straining is severe and the hour passes without results, the attention of a competent veterinarian should be sought immediately.

Bitches of the larger breeds may require all day for whelping. As long as the puppies arrive at fairly regular intervals there is no need to worry. Inexperienced breeders should not hesitate to call for veterinary assistance at the first indication that things are not going well with the whelping matron.

WEANING

Efforts to wean the puppies should start when they are about four weeks old. The mother will generally start this procedure herself.

```
─────────────────────────── WHELPING TABLE ───────────────────────────
                              (Based on 63 days from Mating Date)
Mating Date   January    1  2  3  4  5  6  7  8  9 10 11 12 13 14 15 16 17 18 19 20 21 22 23 24 25 26 27          28 29 30 31
Whelping Date March      5  6  7  8  9 10 11 12 13 14 15 16 17 18 19 20 21 22 23 24 25 26 27 28 29 30 31 April  1  2  3  4

Mating Date   February   1  2  3  4  5  6  7  8  9 10 11 12 13 14 15 16 17 18 19 20 21 22 23 24 25 26             27 28
Whelping Date April      5  6  7  8  9 10 11 12 13 14 15 16 17 18 19 20 21 22 23 24 25 26 27 28 29 30 May  1  2

Mating Date   March      1  2  3  4  5  6  7  8  9 10 11 12 13 14 15 16 17 18 19 20 21 22 23 24 25 26 27 28 28 29       30 31
Whelping Date May        3  4  5  6  7  8  9 10 11 12 13 14 15 16 17 18 19 20 21 22 23 34 25 26 27 28 29 30 30 31 Jun 1  2

Mating Date   April      1  2  3  4  5  6  7  8  9 10 11 12 13 14 15 16 17 18 19 20 21 22 23 24 25 26 27 28          29 30
Whelping Date June       3  4  5  6  7  8  9 10 11 12 13 14 15 16 17 18 19 20 21 22 23 24 25 26 27 28 29 30 July  1  2

Mating Date   May        1  2  3  4  5  6  7  8  9 10 11 12 13 14 15 16 17 18 19 20 21 22 23 24 25 26 27 28 29       30 31
Whelping Date July       3  4  5  6  7  8  9 10 11 12 13 14 15 16 17 18 19 20 21 22 23 24 25 26 27 28 29 30 31 Aug. 1  2

Mating Date   June       1  2  3  4  5  6  7  8  9 10 11 12 13 14 15 16 17 18 19 20 21 22 23 24 25 26 27 28 29       30
Whelping Date August     3  4  5  6  7  8  9 10 11 12 13 14 15 16 17 18 19 20 21 22 23 24 25 26 27 28 29 30 31 Sept. 1

Mating Date   July       1  2  3  4  5  6  7  8  9 10 11 12 13 14 15 16 17 18 19 20 21 22 23 24 25 26 27 28 29       30 31
Whelping Date September  2  3  4  5  6  7  8  9 10 11 12 13 14 15 16 17 18 19 20 21 22 23 24 25 26 27 28 29 30 Oct. 1  2

Mating Date   August     1  2  3  4  5  6  7  8  9 10 11 12 13 14 15 16 17 18 19 20 21 22 23 24 25 26 27 28 29       30 31
Whelping Date October    3  4  5  6  7  8  9 10 11 12 13 14 15 16 17 18 19 20 21 22 23 24 25 26 27 28 29 30 31 Nov. 1  2

Mating Date   September  1  2  3  4  5  6  7  8  9 10 11 12 13 14 15 16 17 18 19 20 21 22 23 24 25 26 27 28          29 30
Whelping Date November   3  4  5  6  7  8  9 10 11 12 13 14 15 16 17 18 19 20 21 22 23 24 25 26 27 28 29 30 Dec. 1  2

Mating Date   October    1  2  3  4  5  6  7  8  9 10 11 12 13 14 15 16 17 18 19 20 21 22 23 24 25 26 27 28 29       30 31
Whelping Date December   3  4  5  6  7  8  9 10 11 12 13 14 15 16 17 18 19 20 21 22 23 24 25 26 27 28 29 30 31 Jan. 1  2

Mating Date   November   1  2  3  4  5  6  7  8  9 10 11 12 13 14 15 16 17 18 19 20 21 22 23 24 25 26 27 28 29       30
Whelping Date January    3  4  5  6  7  8  9 10 11 12 13 14 15 16 17 18 19 20 21 22 23 24 25 26 27 28 29 30 31 Feb. 1

Mating Date   December   1  2  3  4  5  6  7  8  9 10 11 12 13 14 15 16 17 18 19 20 21 22 23 24 25 26 27          28 29 30 31
Whelping Date February   2  3  4  5  6  7  8  9 10 11 12 13 14 15 16 17 18 19 20 21 22 23 24 25 26 27 28 Mar. 1  2  3  4
```

For the first meal place the following mixture in a shallow dish:

One cup warm milk
One teaspoonful Karo syrup
One-fourth cup of warm water.

The puppies' heads should be repeatedly dipped into the dish until they begin to lap the mixture voluntarily. They learn quickly, and are generally quite gluttonous once they get the idea.

In a very short time they will be eagerly eating. The amount of milk should then be increased and dry, commercial dog food may be dissolved in the solution.

At about five weeks of age, the amount of commercial dog food should be steadily increased and the liquid content decreased until the result is a semi-moist, crumbly mixture composed of dog food and milk, or milky-water. Dry, kibbled food may be kept available at all times.

If the puppies seem reluctant to accept their prepared meals without the milk in them, the dry food may be removed. This way they will eagerly eat the prepared meals when presented. The transition to straight, commercial dog food is usually easy and without incident.

At this time, the mother is separated from her litter and is returned only for short nursing periods, if necessary to her comfort.

—Puppy Production—

(Purina Dog Care Center)

IN EVERY kennel the production of superior litters of healthy pups depends on the selection and mating of good brood stock that nicks, and following a good management program.

Over 10,000 pure-bred puppies have been produced in the Purina Dog Care Center since 1930. During the past fifteen years 90.2% of all puppies whelped alive were weaned. Good healthy brood stock maintained in an optimum nutritional and muscular condition can be expected to produce satisfactory offspring.

REPRODUCTION

After the eggs are fertilized they "float" in uterine fluids and become attached to the uterus wall where development of the young really gets off to a fast start. The young embryo starts developing a circulatory system very early. The heart circulates the body fluid of the young embryo up to a cotyledon band, in which a nutrient exchange takes place between the mother's blood and the blood of the developing embryo. It is by this method that nutrients are absorbed by the circulating blood of the embryo from the mother's blood. Many of the embryo waste products are returned to the mother's blood for elimination.

It is evident then that the nutrition supplied to the bitch is directly influencing the nutrition obtained by the developing embryo. If certain specific nutrients are not available in proper quantities, then the young embryo will not develop normally. For example, a deficiency of riboflavin in a bitch's diet may prevent the proper midline closure of the young puppy as it develops. This closure on the outside is most evident in the form of umbilical hernias. On the inside of the dog, this failure of the midline to close properly may be evident in heart defects or in cleft palate production. There are many other factors which can also influence both heart defects and cleft palates. It is known that specific strains of dogs have a genetic tendency toward the production of puppies with congenital heart defects. One strain of German Shepherds maintained by the Center in Missouri, for example, produced a high incidence of specific heart defect of a type commonly found in children.

The relationship between the nutrient balance of the bitch's diet and the development of the puppy pinpoints the necessity for optimum nutrition if the production of superior puppies is to be attained.

How do puppies grow? Many St. Bernard puppies will weigh 60-80 pounds at 6 months of age. St. Bernards have a mature weight equaling that of man. Most children during early growth, will only double their weight at six months of age, while the young St. Bernard puppy born with an average birth weight of 1½ lb. has increased his original weight by forty times.

A bitch should be in good muscular condition and have adequate exercise in order to produce good litters. Excessively fat bitches sometimes produce offspring which are malformed, perhaps attributable to the crowding condition in the uterus or have difficulty during parturition or whelping.

THE ESTRUS CYCLE AND MATING

Generally, a bitch at the Purina Center is mated on the day that she will accept a male and on alternate days until she has had three matings. This serves several purposes:

1. The bitch will be covered during the time of optimum egg liberation and fertilization.

2. It will give the male a chance to produce good sperm if he has not been used for a good period of time.

3. It will give the bitch the best opportunity to produce a maximum number of puppies.

When a stud is not used for a fairly long period of time, the semen that accumulates in the Cowper's gland may lose much of its potency. This is because the oxidation process that takes place in the body tends to let the sperm live its life at a fairly fast rate. Frequently, the first ejection after a rest of two or three weeks will be almost impotent. The second ejaculation following this is normally rich in live, active, normal sperm cells. It is recommended that a stud be used fairly regularly rather than trying to conserve his energy as is frequently the situation. A stud can be used for one mating each day without any decrease in his physical condition or in his potency.

Most bitches that have been fed good commercial rations without supplementation are large enough to mate by their first season or heat period. If she is still undersized, then it is best to wait for the second heat period.

Normally, the bitch will tend to come in season about twice a year, although some may operate on a shorter or longer cycle. When the vulva starts swelling the bitch is coming in season. As the swelling grows more pronounced discharge will follow. The correct date for mating can be determined by the use of a microscope and identification of the type of cells in the discharge. It is easier, however, to "try" the bitch at the end of seven days after swelling is first noted. If she accepts a male, then breed her that day, plus two additional matings, spaced two days apart. By mating on alternate days for three consecutive matings the chances of maximum fertilization of the eggs is optimized.

Parasite Control. Parasite control during the gestation period is extremely important. It is thought that some hormone in the bitch's body releases various parasites such as roundworms and possibly hookworms that can be transferred in the developing fetus. If a thorough program of parasite control can be maintained for the bitch the chances of transferring parasites into the fetus are reduced. Although there is no direct blood vessel connection between the developing fetus and its mother, the roundworm larvae is very efficient at crossing the placental membrane and is present when young puppies are whelped. Since the parasites are already in the young puppy's body at birth, they can develop into mature adults and be laying eggs by the time the puppy is three weeks of age. This provides a clue as to the treatment.

Bitches should be wormed about the 4th day after they are mated and again during the 4th week of gestation. Naturally it is most desirable to obtain fecal egg identification in order to be specific on the worming program.

After the puppies are whelped it is suggested that they be wormed by the 12th day. This will tend to eliminate almost all of the roundworms that were in their body at the time of birth and will help break the ascarid cycle.

Mange and other parasites can be transferred from the bitch to the puppy at the time of whelping. This

New pups—what a chore! Hank Babbitt photo.

sual odors from strange males are present. There is no indication whether this happens in a bitch or not, but it is generally recommended that after mating, a bitch not be moved into a new kennel alongside a strange male other than the one that serviced her for at least ten days.

ARTIFICIAL INSEMINATION

Artificial insemination has been used in dogs for more than 20 years. Although not difficult, the technique should be done under clean conditions by a veterinarian. Artificial insemination, although permitted by various registry associations, must be done under specific directions if the offspring are to be registered.

A litter can include pups sired by more than one male. Once a white bitch in the Purina Kennel was inseminated with mixed semen from three studs with dominance in color (one black, one red, and one white). All three studs were represented in the litter as indicated by markings on the puppies.

Artificial insemination holds a lot of promise for the future in the control of some diseases transmitted by contact during mating. These diseases include brucellosis, a bacteria that causes "fading disease" and other diseases.

CARE OF THE GESTATING BITCH

Gestation in the early stages does not produce a noticeable strain; in fact, the bitch can store a considerable quantity of nutrients in the developing embryos at no expense to herself since a hormone change takes place in her body after mating. Her metabolism efficiency increases to the point where very little extra demand is made during the first five or six weeks. After that the demand surges upward fairly rapidly, but the 20% increase in food intake will take care of this extra requirement by the developing litter.

Preparation of the Bitch for Whelping. When the bitch enters the whelping pen she should be prepared in such a way that she will have the easiest job during whelping and that the puppies will get off to a good start.

The bitch is placed in her whelping box approximately a week before she is due to whelp. This gives her an opportunity to become accustomed to the whelping box and she knows that this is a place where she can be free of excess excitment and intervention by distracting factors.

These preparations involve several steps:

1. *Washing.* Washing the bitch's udder to remove parasite eggs from the skin and from the orifices of the nipples. If you do not remove these with soap and water, the puppy will remove them. By washing the bitch thoroughly, the parasite contamination of exposure in the puppy is reduced.

2. *Sanitation.* The whelping pen should be sani-

increases the importance of maintaining the bitch parasite-free.

Post-Breeding. After the bitch has been mated, one must be careful not to overfeed in order that she does not gain too much weight. It is recommended that her feed intake be maintained at a normal level for the six weeks following mating. This will prevent her from becoming too fat. At six weeks of pregnancy she should have a 20% increase in food intake. This will supply ample nutrients for the development of the young embryos into good, healthy puppies, and at the same time prevent the bitch from becoming fat.

Environment After Mating. Work in other animals, notably mice, has indicated that a mated female placed in a new environment within thirty-six to forty-eight hours after mating may abort if a lot of unu-

tized so that any worm or other parasite eggs will be eliminated or minimized. This includes scrubbing the floor, the sidewalls, the litter box, and any other litter equipment. Clean, fresh litter, and clean food utensils are a must.

3. *Clipping.* Many bitches have excess hair around the udder and around the vagina. This hair should be clipped fairly short so that the puppies will not become entagled during whelping or/and so that they will have no trouble getting to the "dinner table." If the puppies cannot nurse on nipples unobstructed by hair they will have much more difficulty.

4. *Litter.* Satisfactory litter can include coarse soft-wood shavings, prairie hay, a blanket, sheet, or shredded paper. Shredded paper seems to be the litter choice since it is highly absorbent, easily obtained, inexpensive and provides a good footing for young puppies.

5. *Heating Pad.* Heating pads are extremely helpful in eliminating mortalities attributable to chilling. It is estimated that 50% of puppy losses are due to chilling.

WHELPING

Whelping may proceed over a period as short as a half-hour for an entire litter or it may extend up to six or even eight hours. Very seldom will it exceed eight hours, although it is not unusual for a puppy to be born as much as twenty-four hours after the other puppies in the litter have been born. Generally this indicates either an infection, a partial obstruction in the reproductive tract or something else of this type.

The care of the puppies immediately after whelping is important. Normally, the bitch will whelp and cut the umbilical cord without difficulty. If she does not, it is advisable to tie the cord, snip it off with sterile scissors, and paint the stump with an iodine solution or other good disinfectant.

The puppy after whelping loses several degrees of body temperature during the process of cooling and

Purina Sally I, English Setter, with litter of pups, one of the dogs owned by the Ralston Purina Pet Care Center, St. Louis, Missouri. Photo by Purina.

even when placed in a 90° environment the body temperature will still remain several degrees below that of a normal dog for at least a week. When puppies are born their rectal temperature may drop to as low as 94° during the first day and return slowly to the upper nineties by the end of the week. Those puppies whose temperatures dropped below 90° can generally be considered chilled and seldom will they live unless something is done to correct this lower body temperature.

Temperatures to Maintain the Whelping Box. A good schedule to follow is to maintain a temperature of 90°, 95° for the first week, 90° for the second week, 85° for the third week, and 80° for the fourth week. After the first week of a puppy's life he has gained almost his normal ability for controlling body temperature. During the first week he is almost a hypothermic animal and does not reach the normal temperature of an adult dog which generally ranges between 100° and 103° with an average of 102°F. These newborn puppies are much less resistant to cold than their parents.

How Many Puppies Can Be Expected? Beagles, pointers, and setters of the Purina Kennels average 7 pups in the first litter, then rise to an 8½ average for several litters, then start declining. Purina's strain of beagles will produce about 5-6 litters, the pointers about 7 or 8, and some of Purina's setters will produce up to 14-15 litters. These bitches are bred each heat period and there is nothing to indicate that this is detrimental to them in any way. There is some evidence that not breeding at least once each year may contribute to breast tumors.

Young puppies frequently have long toenails which may cut or irritate the udder of the bitch. These toenails should be clipped early if they are excessively long.

Dewclaws should be removed early since the puppy is almost insensitive to pain at this time. Dewclaws, when carefully removed during the third day will cause very little bleeding. Dewclaws, when left on some breeds, will bleed and become problems when dogs work hard in the field, through brush, and in other conditions.

SUPPLEMENTAL FEEDING

Sometimes it is necessary to supply milk to the young puppy from a source other than a bitch. When a bitch milk-replacer is needed, it is fairly easy to supply it by the use of some of the good commercial milk replacers on the market, such as Esbilac. If Esbilac or a similar product is not available then a good temporary formula can be made by using one cup of evaporated milk, one cup of water, one egg yolk, one tablespoon of corn oil, and a small quantity of salt, about as much as would be used to season an equal-size helping of potatoes. This ration can be used on a temporary basis if supplemented with a few drops of a good pediatric vitamin preparation. Those made available for human infants can usually take care of the needs of a puppy for several days without any serious nutritional deficiencies developing during this period. The only problem may be soft droppings or diarrhea production.

PARASITES AT BIRTH

Puppies are born with some parasites, including roundworms, if the bitch has an infection. It is suggested the puppies be wormed with a good anthelmintic such as piperazine during the twelfth or thirteenth day of life. This is 90% effective in controlling both kinds of roundworms that may be in the puppy at the time of birth. The puppy at 7 days of age is active and much less dependent on the mother for body warmth. At this point he will become almost independent in many respects and requires food only on an 8 hour basis.

By the third week, the eyes are open and the puppy is ready to accept food other than the bitch's milk. With very little help he will consume moistened solid food. Pups can be made to take food at two weeks or earlier if one will take the trouble to hand-feed the puppy. On his own at the third week the puppy is ready to eat solid foods. It is suggested that the bitch's food mixed with enough water to produce a crumbly-like consistency be made available to the puppies at all times. Then when the puppies are weaned, food intake of a puppy is at an adequate level to prevent any major setbacks at the time of weaning.

PSYCHOLOGY AND WEANING

Prior to weaning, if the puppies are to be sold, it is suggested that the puppies be separated for a couple of nights into separate boxes with one puppy in each box and left there overnight, and the next morning be placed back with the entire litter. This lets the puppies learn that they may be separated, but they will come back together. If this is done a couple of times when the puppies are sold to go to their new home there is much less problem with the puppies whining at night.

Pups should be weaned between the 5th and 7th week under normal circumstances. All puppies in the Purina Dog Care Center are weaned at 6 weeks of age since they go on growing tests starting at the 6th week.

When pups are weaned the bitch should not have been fed for the preceeding 24 hours, fed 1/4 normal food intake for the next 24 hours, 1/2 normal intake for the next 24 hours, then 3/4 for the next day, and then on to the normal maintenance level. The bitch's udder will have less tendency to become congested and cake when following this method of weaning.

Good healthy litters of puppies can be produced if you will follow the wise program of:

Good sanitation
Selective breeding
Planned management
Sound nutrition

Good commercial dog foods supply all of the nutrients needed by normal dogs. America's dogs fed these rations are better nourished than America's children.

ADDITIONAL BREEDING INFORMATION SOURCES

Two interesting treatises on the subject of breeding are Farmers Bulletin 1167 and Bulletin 905 (The Principles of Livestock Breeding), published by the U. S. Department of Agriculture. These (or newer versions) may be obtained from the Superintendent of Documents, Government Printing Office, Washington, D.C. A recommended book on the subject is *How to Breed Dogs* (Howell Books) by Dr. Leon F. Whitney.

Part VIII

THE DOG ON DUTY

The history of the development of the guide dog movement in the United States is one in which all America can take pride. Very seldom have people tried to make this a profitable enterprise for themselves and the few who have, have been discouraged effectively. There are eight notable philanthropic organizations that provide guide dogs and the education a blind person needs to gain not only mobility and independence, but self-assurance, self-esteem, and dignity. Dogs serve man in many other important ways, of course, for from time immemorial dogs have distinguished themselves by their versatility in guard and military service. In police and industrial security work today, specially trained dogs are being used on a wider basis than ever before. To this dog fraternity, before almost the exclusive province of the German Shepherd, have been added many other breeds. At finding marijuana, for example, beagles and many other breeds have proved adept.

—The Dog as an Aid To The Blind—

IN ANY town or city in the United States, a young business or professional man steps out to his carport and drives away a beautiful new shiny car. His means of locomotion has cost him $3,000 to $4,000, but it will be paid for in 18 to 36 months. Life is good.

Somewhere else in the same American town or city, another business or professional man emerges from his nice home. In his left hand he holds the handle of the harness of his guide dog. Both stride confidently down the street. This dog, a thing of beauty, is not a servant. He is a partner. The cost of teaching this man to use his dog, the board and room during the four weeks that they trained together, the equipment, the breeding and rearing of this dog, his education and all, have cost from $3,000 to $4,000. Life is good. (Many organizations publish a lower cost, but cold analysis shows that $3,000 is a minimum cost for an adequate product.)

Most of the blind people who own these wonderful dogs carry their own weight by making a living, often not only for themselves, but for a family. Many of the women with dogs care for their own home and family and do their own shopping and household work including cooking. Many blind women as well as men become professional people, even nurses.

But the dog that leads them will not have to be paid for at a rate of $3,000 or $4,000, although he costs that much. Most schools provide everything free.

The highest charge made for a dog is $150 and that includes the cost of transportation to and from the school.

Between 1925 and 1927 there were at least three different people in three different places working with different ideas and different techniques to supply guide dogs for American blind people, but at least one of them, Mrs. Dorothy Eustis, an American woman in Switzerland, did not know at that time her interest in dogs would lead to her establishment of The Seeing Eye, which has become somewhat of a model for similar schools throughout the world.

It is hard to believe that most states were still sending their blind people to asylums in 1925, and that the best they offered to the average blind person in the United States was a job in an industry established to use them in manual labor.

In a recent year there were an estimated 450,000 blind persons in the United States. At least ten percent of these could be liberated to move freely and take their place in society with the use of a guide dog. In a survey made by Columbia University, between only two and three percent of the 500 persons in the State of New York who received questionnaires said they would like to have a Seeing Eye dog. How many questionnaires were answered by someone else for the blind person is not reported. This has always made this type of study difficult. Parents and social workers answer letters and questionnaires for blind people. For some reason both parents and social workers are more likely to think a blind person *cannot* use a guide than are the persons who teach these people to use a dog, or the blind person himself.

To determine whether there are enough dogs for those who say they would like a dog and could use one according to the Columbia survey, take 2.5% of the 450,000 blind persons estimated to be in the United States and the result is 11,250 who want a dog now. The number of blind is increasing at about 10% each year. A guide dog's average life of usefulness is a little more than seven years. A blind person who has had a dog needs one even worse than before if he loses his dog, because his whole life has become adjusted to this companion's help. This means that at least one dog in every seven being trained for use must be reserved for the former student who will need a replacement. Or, at least 857 replacements are needed each year based upon an estimate just for replenishing the 6,000 guide dogs now in use. If the number grows, the needed replacements would be greater. It is useless therefore to try to evaluate the service that is being rendered by the existing schools or to speculate whether an expansion of some of them is justified without considering these facts.

THE MASTER EYE INSTITUTE

Mr. John L. Sinykin, a Minneapolis businessman, learned about the German blind veterans being trained with dogs to lead them in 1925. He had always been interested in dogs, and at his own expense went to Germany and other European countries to learn all he could about the use of guide dogs. When he returned, later that year, he set up The Master Eye Institute in Minneapolis. He had been well impressed with the German Shepherd dog and chose this breed for his project. During the next year he trained Lux. This dog he presented to Senator Thomas D. Schall, who had lost his sight. He trained Senator Schall and Lux to work together both in Minneapolis and at the Capitol. The team became the sensation of both Washington and Minneapolis.

Other people became interested in the project and helped Mr. Sinykin. Soon ministers, priests, and rabbis were all helping the cause, and a nonsectarian, non-racial organization was set up under the new name of The Master Eye Foundation, with training facilities in Minneapolis and offices in Chicago. A breeding program was started by Mr. Sinykin to produce dogs of the right size and inherited behavioral traits so as to be best suited for guide dogs. Most German Shepherds were too large and not enough selection was being made for good behavior and willingness by many of the breeders.

The second of the three who were to have an important part in the development of dogs to lead blind persons in the United States was Joseph Weber, a German dog trainer. Mr. Weber selected the dogs

The Master Eye dog is taught to disobey commands when occasion requires. Photo by Williams & Meyer Co.

he felt would be useful for breeding for police work and for leading blind people, and set up his breeding and training kennel near Princeton, New Jersey, at about the same time that Mr. Sinykin was starting his project in Minneapolis. When The Seeing Eye started in Nashville, Tennessee, Mr. Weber was asked to join them, both for his knowledge of the work and for the breeding stock he had developed.

THE SEEING EYE, INC.

The Seeing Eye had its origin in Switzerland also about this time. Mrs. Dorothy Harrison Eustis, an American, had become so impressed with the learning ability of her own dog, Hans (Jung), a German Shepherd, that she decided that a project to select the best strains of German Shepherds then available should be started. She had in mind the breeding and

Seeing Eye dogs must learn to judge height of overhanging obstructions and keep their masters from bumping their heads. Photo by Seeing Eye.

Most Seeing Eye dogs are German Shepherds, but other breeds are also used, principally Labrador Retrievers, Golden Retrievers, and Boxers. Photo by Seeing Eye.

training of these dogs especially for the Swiss Army, border guards and police. She called her project "Fortunate Fields" and selected Mr. Elliott Humphrey to use the new knowledge of genetics to further improve the German Shepherd dogs. The sort of study, on the scale she had in mind, had scarcely been done at all. Mr. Humphrey and his associates collected dogs from the six strains then believed to be the best in Europe; both conformation and ability to do superior work were used as criteria. Later, ability to work was found

Every Seeing Eye dog is thoroughly tested by blindfolded instructor. Photo by Seeing Eye.

to be the important quality, but good conformation was also sought. This was a serious project and excellent dogs resulted. The first Seeing Eye dogs in the United States were bred and trained at Fortunate Fields. (In 1967, the best line of brood bitches at Guide Dogs for the Blind, Inc. in San Rafael, California, was directly descended from guide dogs bred from Orkos of Longworth, a son of Fortunate Fields' Orkos, out of a bitch from the Fortunate Fields strain. So the project of breeding better German Shepherds dogs at Fortunate Fields has been beneficial to at least one other guide dog school's breeding program.)

A young man in Nashville, Tennessee, who had lost his sight, became interested in an *American Magazine* article by Mrs. Eustis about her project, and also in the fact that similar dogs were being trained for war veterans who had lost their sight in Germany.

Fortunate Fields had not trained dogs to lead blind people, but Mr. Morris Frank wrote Mrs. Eustis such an appealing letter asking how he could get such a dog that she invited him to come to Switzerland and be trained with a guide dog.

When Morris Frank returned to the United States with his dog, Buddy, they were not only the sensation of the entire country, but greatly surprised Mrs. Eustis and the trainers by their efficient ability to travel widely, more than 2,000 miles, over the country and cities using all sorts of transportation, and working safely even in such places as New York City.

The success of Morris Frank and Buddy caused Mrs. Eustis to set up The Seeing Eye, Inc., in Nashville. At first the dogs were all bred and trained at Fortunate Fields.

Mrs. Eustis now returned to the United States and interested many of her friends in her new project and after some time moved Seeing Eye to the estate which was her childhood home near Morristown, New Jersey. In 1965, a larger estate and new buildings especially planned for a guide dog school at Morristown, on the Washington Valley Road, became the modern home of The Seeing Eye.

Forward from 1928, when Mr. Frank and Buddy attracted so much favorable attention to the work of a guide dog, by 1958 The Seeing Eye, Inc., had not only become a model for other schools in many countries, but had amassed endowment funds so large it could operate all its activities on income from these alone and no longer needed to solicit any financial aid.

The new building provides living quarters for 200 students a year. They come in classes of eight and train for four weeks with their dogs under the direction of one of the ten trainers. These men are not only dog trainers—they are instructors qualified to teach blind people to become self-reliant and highly confident in their ability to use their dogs in any traffic and under all conditions. As many as three classes can operate in session at the same time, but each is the responsibility of the instructor who trained their dogs and selected them, one by one, to suit the personality of each student.

When new trainers and instructors are needed, young men are carefully screened for age, size and character, and especially for their attitude toward blind people and dogs. Such young men spend four years as apprentices under an experienced instructor before they have attained the experience and understanding to handle all the problems that will be encountered by them as regular instructors.

First steps in establishing The Seeing Eye were those taken by Morris Frank down the gangplank of the S.S. "Tuscania" as it arrived in New York in the spring of 1928. Photo by Seeing Eye.

Before a class comes to Seeing Eye to train, its members have already been screened. Age limits generally observed are from 16 to 55 years. Veterans of United States military service are all admitted free and given preference. Students who seem most likely to become self-supporting and reliant are also given preference. Other students than veterans pay $150 for their first dog and $50 for all replacements, but they receive their board and room, instruction, a dog fully-equipped, and their transportation is paid from any place in the United States or Canada. The Seeing Eye has found that their students like to pay something.

Ever since the establishment of The Seeing Eye, Inc., the school bred some of its own dogs. The breeding has been almost exclusively German Shepherd dogs. There is a special breeding farm with a manager and part-time geneticist who supervise the breeding and rearing of puppies. The breeding stock is all kept at the farm which is only a few miles from the school.

When the puppies are between 9 and 12 weeks of age, they are placed in 4-H Club Member homes, and there they are raised as family pets until they are 14 months of age. The Seeing Eye compensates the 4-H Member for the care and expense of raising these puppies. No dog aptitude tests are given until the dogs are returned at 14 months of age. The youngsters are not under supervision in an educational puppy-training way, but the dogs are inspected and tested at various times by a director in charge of the program, principally for health and physical and behavioral characteristics.

Since The Seeing Eye needs more dogs than it raises, it accepts dogs which it deems to be suitable for training, and buys suitable dogs when they are available. It uses besides German Shepherds, Labradors and Golden Retrievers, and some other breeds.

When the dogs are returned to The Seeing Eye from the 4-H homes or are accepted as donation or purchased, they are put into professional training by members of The Seeing Eye training staff for a period of four months or more, as each dog must learn how to lead a blind person. Each dog is thoroughly tested by his trainer, the latter blindfolded.

When students come to The Seeing Eye they are instructed by a staff member in the use of the harness, how they will control the dog, how they must learn to accept the dog's judgment if the dog indicates that it cannot do the thing that it is instructed to do. Once the student has learned these things from the instructor he is then assigned a dog especially selected to suit his personality, gait and attitudes. He must learn to walk at a 3-mile-an-hour pace on various routes about the city of Morristown, and learn to be enough independent so that he will reach his destination without getting lost. The Seeing Eye students are not trained in cities or towns other than Morristown.

While there is no financial or managerial relationship between The Seeing Eye and the other guide dog schools in the United States, they grow in tendency to be helpful to one another. Standard codes of ethics for this type of school have been drawn up and are discussed at meetings of the administrators of some of the guide dog schools. Several of the schools have accepted these as valid and useful guidelines.

The students, too, abide by a standard of ethics which is very high. They are independent and dignified citizens. Public indifference to the idea that anyone who lost his sight might fit into society once encouraged and even made it necessary for many blind people to beg.

Some of this indifference has carried over to affect some blind who have not been educated at any of the guide dog schools in the United States. In fact, since begging is often a very lucrative occupation, there are relatives and others who often exploit blind people by placing them on street corners in cities with a dog in harness and a tin cup. Some of these people pay as much as 50% of their take to racketeers. Actually, many are not even blind. None of the dogs used for begging come from recognized guide dog schools; this

Puppy is familiarized with strange objects. Ginny Kraft photo.

is one code which is strictly enforced. Every graduate must pledge to never use his or her dog for begging, and also that if the time ever comes when he or she no longer will use the dog as a guide, that the dog will be returned to the school where it was trained. The pledge also says that that the dog will never be loaned to any other blind or other person for any purpose whatsoever.

While it is generally thought by the public that a guide dog must be a German Shepherd female, all schools use both males and females. It is the practice to alter both before they are assigned to a blind person. Most states, in fact, require this.

The new building at Seeing Eye accommodates 200 students and is believed adequate for their needs for many years. The school is administered by a Board of Directors of 22 members.

With Seeing Eye as a model, it might appear that all that need be done to inform those interested in dogs as guides would be to list the other schools active in this work in the United States. But the fact is that while The Seeing Eye established a pattern largely followed by other schools, they each, like all

colleges, have developed so individually that it would not be fair to so assume.

GUIDE DOGS FOR THE BLIND, INC.

Early in 1942, five public-spirited women, working as volunteers in the United States Army Letterman Hospital in San Francisco, impressed by the large number of Servicemen being brought in from the Pacific combat area with eye injuries seemingly sure to result in blindness, asked the commanding officer if they would be supplied with guide dogs. They were told that The Seeing Eye, Inc., would take as many as it could.

It was the feeling of these women that Servicemen from the West should be able to get guide dogs nearer home, so they organized and financed Guide Dogs for the Blind, Inc., to supply dogs free to veterans who lived in the eleven western states. There was never to be any charge made for the dogs themselves, their training and equipment, or for the board, room, and instruction of Servicemen in the use of the dogs. As the movement gained popularity and the school grew, many others joined the original five, and operations were planned so that any blind person in those eleven western states could come to the school on the same conditions, except that the veterans were to always have preference, and those who needed to replace a dog would get second preference; after that the general public would always be welcome. Later, students were accepted from all states and the western Canadian provinces.

The original five women had two specialties which shaped the future of the school and made it different from any other guide dog school in the world. First, they were long accustomed to both working as volunteers and managing them. This talent they used to man much of the important work to be done. Secondly, three of them were dog owners and two were exhibitors, which meant an emphasis on good dogs from the very start. They were also from widely-separated but important parts of Northern California: Mrs. Doris Ryer Nixon, Santa Barbara; Mrs. Phyllis Tucker, Burlingame; Mrs. Mabel Deering, San Fran-

Because most users of guide dogs are employed and have to go and from their work regularly, the students train in all sorts weather. Ginny Kraft photo.

The three breeds trained at Guide Dogs for the Blind, Inc., San Rafael, California: (left to right) the Golden Retriever, German Shepherd, and Labrador Retriever. These 4-H members, who have raised the dogs from the age of 13 weeks, will soon return them to the school for their formal Guide Dog training. Photo by Guide Dogs for the Blind.

cisco; Mrs. Katheryn K. Breeden, Saratoga; and Mrs. Florence Kahn (Congresswoman from San Francisco).

Although the school grew so that a campus of 11½ acres was equipped to support a maximum of 144 students a year, by 1966 this San Rafael organization found that the new migration to the Coast and the new demands from the Vietnam war were beginning to overtax school facilities.

In the Spring of 1967, the Board of Directors decided that it would be necessary to appeal to the public for $6,000,000 so as to double the capacity of the breeding kennels, the training kennels, and the school. Plans were made to start with the kennels and the puppy-raising program.

Where all the dogs used as guides are bred and raised for this purpose as they are at Guide Dogs for the Blind, plans for breeding start three years in advance and the puppies must be whelped about 20 months before they will be graduated with their blind owners. Therefore, a five-year program for building was started, with the kennel, breeding, and raising facilities to take precedence.

Guide Dogs for the Blind started to breed its own dogs right at the start in 1942. The first ten years brought many discouragements. Only pure bred German Shepherds dogs were used and the puppies were raised from donated mothers from quality kennels. By 1946, the problems were so great that research to learn how to solve them was started and this research and its applications have continued.* When Golden and Labrador Retrievers were added to the program, the bitches were almost all young (one to four years of age) and their get proved more satisfactory. Their litters raised were larger than those from the older German Shepherd bitches. Thorough research has shown that over the 25-year breeding program, the best guide dogs and breeding stock both come from bitches who are from one to six years of age. Many good brood bitches produce few and

*(See *The New Knowledge of Dog Behavior.*—Part III.)

very poor puppies from age six on, regardless of breed. Many of the dogs donated in 1942 and 1943 were bitches who were proven good producers, but six years or older. All breeding stock now used is AKC-registered German Shepherds, Labradors, and Goldens. Each has been bred from successful working, hunting, field and obedience-trial stock and line-bred to supply the size and behavior traits which are required for guides. All the dogs used are home-bred.

From its beginning to January, 1967, the use of volunteers by this school has been extensive:

1. Volunteer committees enrolled members and raised funds.

2. Foster homes for all breeding stock are secured by volunteers.

3. Puppies are socialized at six weeks and seven weeks by volunteers and aptitude-tested by volunteers at 8, 9, 10, 11, and 12 weeks.

4. 4-H Club Members raise the puppies in their homes from 13 weeks of age until 12 months at their own expense, about $100.

5. Experienced obedience and field-trial people in each community where 4-H programs are active do liaison work for Guide Dogs, including approving of the homes and arranging for the proper care of the puppy before the home is approved. They, also, at their own expense, conduct weekly training classes and bring the youngsters to the graduations when their puppies graduate as Guide Dogs, so they may present the dogs to the graduates as their own property. Usually 400 to 500 people turn out every four weeks for the graduations.

Besides the volunteers, a large staff of paid professional people conduct the day-to-day activities of the school. California requires that all schools for guide dogs for the blind be licensed and that every instructor serve a four-year apprenticeship and pass a state board examination. This includes working a dog he

Prior to beginning training as a Guide, dogs are given basic obedience instruction. This German Shepherd is learning to retrieve a wooden dumbbell. When fully trained, the dog will assist his blind master in locating and retrieving any articles accidentally dropped. Photo by Guide Dogs for the Blind.

has trained under every condition which the board may require, with the trainer wearing a blindfold. The examination includes an oral and written test on the instructor's knowledge of problems of the blind and the proper care of the blind persons. In 1967 there were eleven licensed trainers, five in executive positions, and four apprentice trainers at San Rafael. A serious apprenticeship program with classes and regular study is conducted by the Director of Apprentices. Most apprentices have had two or more years of college and come to Guide Dogs seriously interested in social work, especially with blind people and the use of dogs to help them. Like the planning towards more suitable dogs to support the planned expansion, the apprenticeship program is also being expanded so as to have proper and qualified instructors ready to train the larger number of dogs and students.

Before the Board of Directors voted to expand the facilities at San Rafael, a capable organization researched the need carefully and made a detailed report.

This report brought out that even though the entire United States and the western provinces of Canada were eligible to send their blind people to this school, during its 25 years existence, 60% of the graduates came from California. Of these, 35% came from counties in Northern California, while Southern California, with a blind population almost double that of Northern California, had about 25%.

A few years previously, an officer of the Board of Directors visited ten of the counties in Northern California and talked to the welfare officers in each county. This visit was very revealing. None of the welfare officers had ever been to the campus of Guide Dogs for the Blind. Only one had ever thought of sending any of the blind people under her supervision to San Rafael to apply for a dog.

Correspondence with heads of various schools of ophthalmology brought a response that school emphasis was on teaching how to avoid blindness. The eye specialist, it was intimated, would always try to prevent blindness, not look for aids to the already blind.

The difference, then, between the surveys which

4-H Club members get their puppies and begin their own instruction through adult leaders. Photo by Guide Dogs for the Blind.

Golden Retriever puppy goes through "Sit Stay" exercise for 4-H Club trainer. Photo by Guide Dogs for the Blind.

With his Labrador Retriever Guide Dog this blind executive is able to keep business appointments with ease, both at home and out of town—an example of the mobility provided by trained Guide Dogs. Photo by Guide Dogs for the Blind.

This 11-week old Golden Retriever puppy has just learned to on hand signal. Photo by Guide Dogs for the Blind.

have indicated that between 35,000 and 45,000 people in the United States could live happier and more useful lives with a guide dog and the surveys which indicate that there are only 11,000 or 12,000 people who want dogs to lead them, can well be attributed to lack of knowledge about the availability and the usefulness of guides.

Guide dogs for the Blind, Inc., found this to be true. The school maintains a complete social service staff which not only screens all applications in the office, but sends instructors to visit homes and discuss applicant problems, explaining how they may or may not be overcome through the use of a guide. Just how the use of a dog is to affect the life of the applicant and his family is therefore threshed out before an application is approved. The applicant, for instance, is asked to walk along a familiar street unassisted; his medical record and his social service records are carefully checked, as the case may be. He is also asked to think of qualifying for employment, if he is not already employed. After the man or woman gets a guide and returns home, if he or she has a serious problem, an instructor is sent to the home to help solve the problem; if necessary, the student is returned to the school for further instruction.

At San Rafael, about twice as many men as women apply for dogs and the percentage of graduates runs in about the same proportion. Industrial blindness may influence this proportion.

The management of Guide Dogs for the Blind, Inc. is, under its constitution and articles of incorporation, in the hands of the president of the Board of Directors, the latter being limited to 20 members.

LEADER DOGS
FOR THE BLIND

Leader Dogs for the Blind, Rochester, Michigan, was established in 1939. It is mostly financed by Lions International, which specializes in work to aid blind people of the world. It was founded in Michigan, in the heart of industrial America, because many cases of blindness stem from industrial accidents. It has grown to be one of the world's largest guide dog schools. Lions have many sight-conservation programs and assist in the use of the white cane and instruction on how to use such a cane as well as providing guide dogs.

Lions International and Leader Dog School are convinced that the best defenses a blind person can build against the dead weight of pity are dignity, self-respect, and confidence. They believe that a happy heart and sound mind thrive better when a person can move with ease. The inefficiency that blindness causes often calls for special training to eliminate physical restrictions on mobility. It is a part of the Leader Dog Program to provide any help to bring about better mobility and greater freedom and happy hearts.

To a great degree The Leader Dog School depends

With a smile of confidence a Leader Dog graduate is able to travel at will. Photo by Leader Dogs for the Blind.

upon families of Lions, and others interested in their program, in raising many of its dogs. Lions from many parts of the United States contribute dogs. As in other guide dog schools, Leader Dogs are trained to protect their charges from traffic dangers by refusing to obey a command that would take them somewhere not safe. They are taught to respect both pedestrian and vehicular traffic and to avoid low-hanging awnings, limbs and wires, and any other dangerous footing.

Like The Seeing Eye and Guide Dogs for the Blind, the Leader Dog School provides a four-week instructional course for each student with board and room and 24-hour care for the students. The instructors train each dog for at least four months before it is isued to a student whereupon the training then proceeds for four additional weeks. Careful selections of dogs to fit the students' physical and emotional traits are made.

There is no charge for this service because Lions International and their friends not only maintain the school, but support its entire aid-for-the-blind program.

Lions have for many years carried on a program helping to educate the public in the care of the eyes, as well as the means by which a person can live virtually normally even if he does lose his sight.

Lions were among the most active of the organizations who brought to the attention of transportation companies, hotels and restaurants, and other public service organizations the need for admitting any blind person with a guide dog on the same basis they would a sighted person. Today states have laws which make it a serious offence for any such business to refuse to accept a blind person with a guide dog.

The more than 2,300 Leader Dogs presented to persons trained to use them at The Leader Dog School since 1939 have gone to every state in the Union, to Canada, Mexico and other countries.

If The Leader Dog School finds anyone qualified to

"Okay, let's git!" The minute this blind man picks up his Leader Dog's harness, he's in business and can step out with confidence. Photo by Leader Dogs for the Blind.

use one of their dogs, there is no restriction as to race, color or creed. This code is practiced in all guide dog schools.

During September, 1969, the Leader Dog School handled a relatively novel project, cooperating with Diadem, an organization devoted to the exchange of handicapped persons between Denmark and the United States—training a special class of 14 blind citizens of Denmark in the employment of Leader Dogs. Denmark does not have any Leader Dog schools, but the Diadem founders hope it someday will as there was much encouraging from this special and somewhat experimental project. Upon completing the course, the blind students and their guide dogs returned to Denmark, entirely new chapters in their lives opened to them with the help of their new intelligent and devoted canine companions.

GUIDING EYES FOR THE BLIND, INC.

In 1955, Guiding Eyes for the Blind, Inc., was founded by a voluntary group of directors and workers and incorporated under the laws of the State of New York. It is situated on a 10-acre campus in Yorktown Heights.

A breeding program has been started with special attention to Golden Retrievers of similar strains to those bred successfully at San Rafael. There is also a

German Shepherd breeding program. The school uses Labrador Retrievers, Boxers and Collies also. The training period of the dogs before being issued to students is approximately three months. The students and dogs are trained together for four weeks, in residence. There is a charge of $150 for the first dog and $50 for each dog after the first. Traffic training begins in Peekskill and progresses through White Plains to New York City.

PILOT DOGS

Church groups, service clubs, and others interested in helping blind people provide the principal support for Pilot Dogs, Inc. The dog training center is located on the outskirts of Columbus, Ohio, where the dogs are exposed to city traffic and living conditions during the entire time of their training. Since 1950 it has served all races, creeds and colors without any distinction with four-weeks in-residence instruction—the dog, equipment, and transportation to and from the school free. The Ohio State University Veterinarian School voluntarily cares for the dogs.

At least three months of training is given each dog before it is assigned to a student for a four-week in-residence training period. This school uses German Shepherds, Golden and Labrador Retrievers, Boxers, and Doberman Pinschers. In most of the breeds it prefers dogs that are smaller than the dogs which are usually shown in dog shows. It does not have a breeding program.

The downtown school for student training has a basement equipped with a training area where steps, planks over ditches, low-hanging objects stimulating low branches, awnings and wires, revolving doors, and other objects represent those which may later pose problems for the blind master and his dog. Downtown Columbus is used to acquaint the student and his dog with all types of city traffic and train them to meet any need adequately. The State Capital grounds, office buildings with elevators and revolving

Dog's-eye view of a Pilot Dogs, Inc. graduating class. Photo Columbus Dispatch.

With the aid of her new canine helper this blind woman can now expect to hold a job which, owing to transportation and traffic difficulties, might have been out of the question before. Second Sight photo.

doors, and all types of city hazards are used in training.

SECOND SIGHT GUIDE DOG FOUNDATION

Second Sight Guide Dog Foundation for the Blind, Inc., was incorporated under the laws of the State of New York to provide free guide dogs for the blind and the training of blind people to use them. It was established in 1946. The office of administration is located in Forest Hills, N.Y. The training center is in Smithtown, where the students receive their first training, progressing from there through Long Island, and then to New York City for advanced training including the use of subways.

This school does not have its own breeding program and uses only spayed females from 10 months to 3 years old. The breeds accepted are German Shepherds, Labrador, Golden, and Chesapeake Bay Retrievers, Smooth-coated Collies, and Boxers. They are given at least three months of professional training before they are issued to the students for a four-weeks in-residence course. Two trainers instruct a class of not more than ten students, dividing the students equally between them.

EYE DOG FOUNDATION

The parent corporation was founded in 1939 and devoted itself to the broad spectrum of aiding the blind. In 1952 Eye Dog Foundation was founded as a subsidiary for the purpose of devoting itself to the exclusive function of giving guide dogs to the blind. In 1954, Eye Dog Foundation became an independent entity, still retaining its exclusive function. Since April, 1956, it has operated a school for the blind students and guide dogs at Beaumont, California.

Supported entirely by public contributions, the Foundation receives its major financial aid from the endowments and bequests contained in wills as well as annual donations from public-spirited individuals.

The policy of Eye Dog Foundation is to supply (*absolutely free* of charge to the blind) eyes for the blind in the form of a guide dog along with harness and leash. Not only do they receive a guide dog free of charge, but while in attendence for the one month's training, the students live on Eye Dog Foundation premises in a dormitory provided by Eye Dog

Commuting by bus is no longer a problem for this blind man. Through the use of his guide dog he may come and go as he chooses. Second Sight photo.

Foundation where they are housed and boarded free of charge.

Prior to the commencement of the class wherein the blind person is trained with the dog, the dog is put through an intensive six-months training period by a trainer licensed by the State of California.

The Foundation has found that the German Shepherd is the most suitable for guide-dog work and insists that they be pure-bred with papers. In addition, since the female is more gentle in temperament, only the female is used. The dog must be between ten months and thirty months of age. The reason for this is that maturity is an essential element on the potential guide dog. With maturity comes the responsibility required to guide the blind person through all the obstacles of a sighted person; this then becomes a matter of life and death to the blind individual. However, another factor to be considered is the life span of the dog and therefore the length of service it will be able to render to the blind master, thus the rule that the Foundation limits the beginning training to dogs not over thirty months of age. Aside from the fact that the German Shepherd is one of the most intelligent, the short hair reduces the chore of the blind person in keeping her clean.

The first step in the training of the dog is that she learns to obey basic obedience commands such as: Come, Sit, Down, Fetch, Forward, Right and Left. Once that hurdle is attained, the dog must be trained under traffic conditions to:

(1) Stop at the curb at the end of each block as well as to stop at intersections where there are no curbs.

(2) To go forward on command only if it is safe to do so.

(3) To cross the street straight to the opposite curb and stop so the blind person will not stumble.

(4) The dog is taught to work at the left side of the blind person, but in addition is taught to clear her master safely of all obstacles on the right side as well as of any overhanging obstacles, low objects and manholes.

(5) To wait while approaching automobiles pass and not to guide the blind person within too close proximity to any automobile.

(6) To pass other animals (such as dogs, cats, birds, etc.) without being distracted from her work.

(7) Not to be distracted by noise or traffic.

(8) To guide her master to a bus, elevator, airplane, car or other vehicular transportation and ride with him.

(9) To find doors in and out of buildings.

(10) To stop at the top and bottom of stairways so that her master will not fall.

(11) To lie quietly under a table in a restaurant.

To insure complete safety to the blind recipient, at various stages during the training the trainer works under blindfold. This determines whether the dog is completely dependable in her work. The dog must learn to meet every situation expected to be encountered in her life's work because she must be the eyes of a blind person and upon that training depends the safety of her master.

Once this training is completed, the class is scheduled and the students are brought in to the Foundation. Since shepherds range in size from very large to small, it becomes a matter of matchmaking for the trainer to match the proper-sized dog with the individual student. Further, it is necessary that the temperament and character of the dog be compatible with that of the student. These are only minor phases of the ultimate goal though they will prove extremely important as the pair begin to live together.

While classes are in session, there is always a trainer in attendance, and a housekeeper who prepares the meals and serves the students.

The trainer supervises all training, kennels, and other Foundation facilities that include the housing and care of the guide dogs.

The Foundation recently acquired six and one-half acres in the Old Topanga Canyon area (1693 Jando Drive, Topanga, Calif.) where there is already a residence in existence. Grading of the new property commenced in the summer of 1969. A fifty-run kennel, kennelman's quarters, kitchen for preparing the dog food, whelping center, and a small kennel for the male German Shepherds, a twelve-bedroom dormitory containing recreation area, a kitchen and dining area are in the facility plan.

The property is in a rustic setting so that the blind students in residence will have a feeling of country atmosphere while they work and train with their dog.

Since the Foundation's birth, it has supplied hundreds of guide dogs to the blind. The administrative offices of Eye Dog Foundation are located at 257 South Spring Street, Los Angeles, California 90012.

—The Dog as a Guard—

SINCE THE prehistoric beginnings of man's relationship with *canis familiaris*, the dog has served not only as his pal but as his guardian, a trait which has proven of inestimable value. To this day, once a dog has accepted a person or family as his master, he immediately develops a well-defined sense of proprie-

torship and is ready to defend them, their home and possessions against all intruders. This sense of guardianship is present in almost all dogs, regardless of the breed, although it naturally asserts itself more in bolder or more aggressive animals.

This guardian trait, now recognized by science and

canine authorities as a definite instinct, may be traced back to the era before the dog became domesticated, to the times when it defended its lair in self-preservation and tolerated no encroachment upon its hunting areas.

Although the larger breeds have generally been used for protective purposes and after generations of breeding and training for this purpose might be termed "specialists" in this sort of work, many of the smaller types, such as the terriers, also possess the same highly developed instinct to guard and protect. The first dogs used exclusively for guarding were called "bandogs," i.e., dogs tied up with a band or chain. This name was used for a long time, but after the Norman conquest of England in 1066 the word "mastiff," said to be a corruption of "master of thief," came into common use. The custom of keeping "bandogs" chained up arose because it was believed that keeping them confined by chains during the day made them fiercer at night.

The "mastive or bandogge" was described by Abraham Fleming as "vast, huge, stubborn, eager, of a heavy and burdensome body, and therefore but of little swiftness," and it "took fast hold with its teeth and held on beyond all credit." The description suggests that the "bandog" was more likely to have been the Bulldog rather than the Mastiff, as we know the breeds today.

In 1641, Barnaby Goode, translating the work of Conrad Heresbach, described "The Bandog for the House" as follows:

Of first the Mastie that keepeth the house: for this purpose you must provide you such a one, as hath a large and mightie body, a great and shrill voyce, that both with his barking he mat discover and with his sight dismay the Theefe, yea, being not seene, with the horror of his voice put him to flight. His stature must neither be long nor fiery, either browne or grey, his lippes blackish, neither turning up, nor hanging too much downe, his mouth blacke and wide, his neather-jawe fat, and comming out of it on either side a fang, appearing more outward than his other teeth; his upper teeth even with his neather, not hanging too much over, sharpe, and hidden with his lippes; his countenance like a Lion, his brest great and shagayard, his shoulders broad, his legges big, his tayle short, his feet very great, his disposition must neither be too gentle, nor too curst, that he neither fawne upon a theefe, nor lavish of his mouth, barking without cause, neither maketh it any matter though he be not swift; for he is but to fight at home, and to give warning of the enemie.

Linnaeus described the Mastiff and his uses in *The Animal Kingdom* (1792):

MASTIFF—*Canis Anglicus.* Of very large size, having a robust body, and the lips are pendulous at the sides, or chops. Is very thick-set and strongly made, having a large head, and great lips, which hang down on each side. This dog is peculiar to England, and grows to a great size, being used principally as a watch dog, which duty he fulfills with great fidelity, and even judgement. Some will permit a stranger to come into the yard, or place which he is appointed to guard, and will go peaceably along with him through every part of it, so long as he touches nothing, but the moment he attempts to meddle with any of the goods, or endeavours to leave the place, he informs him, first by gentle growling, neither do mischief nor go away; and never uses violence unless resisted; will even, in this case, seize the person, throw him down, and hold him there for hours, or until relieved, without biting.

In the Middle Ages travel was exceedingly dangerous, and the man who ventured abroad was taking his life in his own hands unless accompanied by one or more faithful guard dogs. Carriages were invariably accompanied by dogs, some of which ran ahead to give warning. The use of "carriage dogs" continued even after travel became no longer dangerous, and developed into a fashion.

The value of the dog as a guard and protector has always been recognized and his services so utilized. The same applies to his capacity to track down highwaymen and criminals. Bloodhounds, as we know them today, were sometimes called "slough-dogs," for they were used to follow offenders through the sloughs, bogs, and mosses. The were also later called "Sleuth hounds," for obvious reasons. In Holinshed's *Chronicles* (1577) there is mention of a law to the effect that "whoso denieth entrance or sute to a Sleuth hound is persuit made after fellons and stollen goods, shall be holden as accessarie unto the theft."

Robberies and thefts became so prevalent in some sections of England that "Sleuth hounds" were ordered kept and cared for by the inhabitants. A warrant of 1616 reads:

. . . Whereas upon due consideration of the increase of stealths daily growing both in deed and report among you on the borders, we formerly conclude and agree, that for reformation therefore watches should be set, and slough dogs provided and kept, according to the contents of His Majesty's directions to us in that behalf prescribed.

Time has in no way diminished the value of the dog as a protector. With the rise of crime throughout the world in our day and age, the guard dog is playing an increasingly important role, and this protective trait of his is being more highly developed and utilized than ever before.

A canine baby sitter! Photo by Hank Babbitt.

This Boston Terrier is both guardian and playmate.

THE DOG AS HOME PROTECTOR

Families and individuals in cities and suburban areas are acquiring dogs of all kinds, not only as pets and companions, but for protection against intruders. Many a thief, rapist or would-be kidnaper has been foiled by the alert and courageous action of these faithful animals. Sensitive to impending danger, the dog gives quick warning by a faint growl or by raising the hackels or by breaking into an uproar of barking. In this respect the small "yappy" dog is often as effective as the large "attack-type" dog, for the prowler instinctively shuns the noisy, attention attracting situation.

And nearly every day newspapers somewhere report of a dog who has awakened a family in a burning house or in a dwelling threatened by escaping gas.

When this sense of protection is carefully trained and disciplined, the result is a highly-skilled guard dog that serves business and industry in many capacities.

THE DOG AND INDUSTRIAL SECURITY

Night watchmen around warehouses and factories are aided many times over by the service of a dog, especially in smaller operations which cannot afford elaborate protection services. Jewelry shops and liquor stores are similarly protected. Often delivery trucks carry a guard dog, as does an occasional taxi driver in large cities where holdups are constant. The dog sits in the front seat beside the driver and God help the hand, other than the master's, that reaches for the cash box.

Another interesting phase of guard dog work is that used by department stores. For example, Macy's in New York City, has had canine guards since October, 1952 when the store purchased four Doberman

Pinschers to patrol the store after hours in an effort to control the heavy losses inflicted by "sleep-ins." These are burglars who enter the store shortly before closing, remain overnight stealing merchandise and packing it, then leave early the next morning soon after the store opens.

Since their introduction at Macy's, the Dobermans have been directly responsible for the apprehension of numerous thieves who attempted to stay in the store overnight. The Dobermans have also prevented serious damage to the store by discovering machines that had been left on at store closing and also by discovering fire-smoldering and water-flows. On several occasions they have found runaway children who had secreted themselves in the store after closing.

The four original Dobermans were purchased fully trained. All subsequent Dobermans have been trained by Macy detectives assigned to the canine corps. Training classes are held on the roof where the kennels are located, and on the selling and reserve floors. The training is extensive and includes basic obedience exercises, searching, finding, flushing and attacking a

Five of the Dobermans which guard Macy's shown on the buildi‌ roof, up for an airing. Photo by Jerome Ducrot.

These two Dobermans and handler form part of the Macy security [syste]m. Photo by Jerome Ducrot.

assigned to a patrol car instead of the usual two men, thus spreading out the effectiveness of the police force. Whenever the patrolman investigates a suspicious situation, the dog goes with him. The animal can readily be sent up dark alleys, and when the officer captures and frisks a suspect, the dog sits at heel ready to defend upon command should the suspect suddenly attack the officer, as sometimes happens. The dogs are also trained to jump through an open car window and stop the driver if he attempts to escape in that manner.

German Shepherds are nearly always used for police work. They are fed, housed and trained by the patrolmen who handle them. The officers must have the approval of their wives for this, for they also must agree to keep the dogs kenneled at home. They must be fond of dogs and possess a level-headed temperament, and not be subject to hasty decisions or actions.

Describing the first contingent of police dogs used by the Winston-Salem Police Department, Philip Warner said in *The German Shepherd Dog Review*:

> The program of training started with the testing of all dogs for gun soundness and agitation; the willingness to attack, if necessary. The patrolmen were schooled in safety procedures, rules of the training area and care of their dogs' health. The men instructed their dogs in fifteen basic obedience commands by voice, signal and a combination of signal-voice commands. From the basic obedience work they advanced to attack work, on and off leash, with and without command. Tracking work was studied and carefully learned; patrol work and the very important building search was taught. During the course of training the men and dogs were developing a very close relationship and a deep affection for each other. Each dog learned that his first duty was to his master and to attack any aggressive move toward him, and that everything learned, other than this, was secondary. The key to all training was control, the handler's complete control over his dog.
>
> . . . The public relations value of the K-9 Unit (of the Winston-Salem Police Department) has been immeasurable and the public acceptance of these German Shepherds has been overwhelming. During the first year of operation the dogs and their handlers made appearances before a total audience of approximately 10,000 persons . . . the unit made 355 arrests, an-

prowler on instructions. The Dobermans are also trained to discover smoke, fire and waterflows.

THE DOG IN POLICE WORK

Still another increasingly important use of guard dogs is in police work. In the areas of searching, patrolling, tracking and deterrence of crime they have proven to be a definite asset. Particularly outstanding has been their night work, and as policing becomes more expensive as well as dangerous, they are playing an ever widening role. Among the cities which currently employ dogs are St. Louis, Boston, Baltimore, Winston-Salem, Providence, Cincinnati, Norfolk, and the Transit and Park Police of Philadelphia, to name but a few.

The dogs are particularly effective in flushing out a thief cornered in a store or building or alley, and in almost every instance a man running away from the scene of a crime will stop quicker for a dog than for a patrolman, regardless of the circumstances.

For this work one officer and his dogs are generally

A Chicago police dog-handler unit in training. Repeated goadings kindle dog's hostility, but the handler must control the dog's responses. Hank Babbitt photo.

A Michigan police dog-handler unit in training. Unleashed, the dog could very easily overtake a fleeing fugitive in the street and compel him to await arrival of a police officer. Hank Babbitt photo.

Police dog-handler teams, in which German Shepherds are preferred. Hank Babbitt photo.

As a family pet, the Shetland Sheepdog is affectionate, loyal and tolerant, and even in cold climates thrives as an "outdoor" dog for whom only simple shelters need be provided. Photo by Evelyn M. Shafer.

swered 577 calls, assisted other personnel 612 times, and apprehended a total of 32 suspects from building searches or while fleeing.

DON'T TRAIN PETS AS POLICE DOGS

Trained dogs under the charge of trained men have added to the efficiency of those police forces throughout the country which have seen fit to acquire them. But Arthur Frederick Jones, editor of the *American Kennel Gazette,* official magazine for the American Kennel Club, quickly points out that police dog

training is not for house pets. It is highly technical work involving an attack dog that must be kept under constant control by its master. "Most decidedly," he says, "they are not suited to private ownership in the capacity of pets." For if a child, in jest or by accident, gives the trained attack dog the wrong command, the consequences could be serious.

The protective instinct is present in almost all dogs. The fact that it can easily be encouraged and, in many cases, trained to a high degree of efficiency for special application, is making the guard dog more effective than ever before. Its role in our modern, high-powered society is assured. Relative to the use of dogs in investigative work, searching for drugs, see next topic (The Dog As A Soldier).

—The Dog as a Soldier—

AS LONG as there have been wars, the dog has fought loyally at the side of his master, or served in a multitude of other capacities allied with warfare. In earliest times he served as sentry and scout. Taught to fetch and carry over distances involving woods, hills, swamps, even jungles, he became a messenger. When his master was injured, the dog dashed off for aid, expanding his role into that of a casualty dog.

Later, learning to seek out wounded and fallen soldiers, he became a Red Cross helper. Working as a sled dog or a pack dog, he aided in the transportation of supplies under snowy Alpine conditions and over craggy mountainous terrain that other animals could not manage.

The dog most likely began his role when the offensive forays and defensive battles between warring tribes of cavemen began. The act of defense was a matter of course for the dog, and many a sleeping town and camp was saved by the alerting bark of guard dogs.

WAR DOGS OF THE OLD DAYS

War dogs appear in history as early as 700 BC. They accompanied the armies of the Assyrians, Persians, Greeks and Romans. Huge dogs of the mastiff type and the fierce Molassian hounds were launched in charges against the ranks of the enemy, and Homer mentions dogs which carried dispatches attached to their collars.

The Gauls and other nations developed a kind of armor for their war dogs. It was made with jointed plates of metal and light chain so as to permit freedom of movement while offering considerable protection. These war dogs also wore broad collars bristling with spikes and curved knives. As they dashed into the ranks of enemy cavalry, the blades and spikes cut horses' legs and often put whole squadrons to rout. Of necessity, these dogs were large and strong, and were often raised and trained especially for use in war.

"Let slip the dogs of war!" is an age-old order of army commanders. The huge rugged beasts were the first line of defense and, when sent charging into oncoming troops, they disrupted the enemy ranks and threw the attack off balance.

Alyattes, King of Lydia, maintained battalions of fierce war dogs which saw hard service in his campaigns. Annually, he issued instructions to his governors to requisition herds of oxen as food for these dogs. However, the Lydian dogs met their match at the battle of Thymbria in the greyhounds of Cyrus,

Armored dog.

and the victory was largely attributed to Cyrus' war dogs.

When Marius, the Roman Consul, won the battle of Versella, he had to overcome vast hordes of the enemy's war dogs led by women, and his victory was delayed for many hours by these gallant fighters.

After the Romans had come into contact with the war dogs of their enemies a few times, and had suffered many casualties from their vicious fangs, they

were not long in organizing companies of war dogs themselves. Attila, chieftain of the Huns, used large groups of dogs to guard his camps.

Aelian, writing in the early part of the third century A.D., said:

The Hyrani and Magnesii used to be accompanied into battle by their dogs, who were good allies and assistants; and there was an Athenian who took his dog with him to the Battle of Marathon, and the man and the dog were painted in a picture in the Painted Porch, and the dog was not held in dishonour but received the reward of heroism—the reward being to be seen in public along with the heroes.

Many dogs accompanied their masters on the Crusades and, according to some of their masters, were able to distinguish a Christian from an infidel by scent alone, and act accordingly!

During the Middle Ages, dogs were armored as completely as the knights and their charging horses.

Armored dog.

Suits of canine armor—plate, chain and canvas—were worn into battle and for the chase.

Attack dogs, brought to the New World by Cortez, helped the Spaniards conquer Mexico and Peru. Loosed by the Conquistadores, the swift and savage greyhounds dragged down and disemboweled the fleeing Aztecs.

When Charles V of Spain was at war with Francis I of France, his ally, King Henry VIII of England in 1518 sent to his aid a draft of soldiers accompanied by some 400 battle-mastiffs with iron collars. These war dogs were set on the French dogs at the seige of Valencia and drove them from the field, tails between their legs. The English war dogs performed with such splendid service in reconnaissance and trailing that they were commended by the Spanish Emperor and held up as examples of bravery and zeal to his troops.

Aldrovandus, a famous Italian naturalist born in 1522, wrote about war dogs and their training as follows:

Those dogs that defend mankind in the course of private, and also of public conflicts, are called, in Greek, *Symmachi*, or allies, and *Somatophylakes,* or bodyguards. Our authors consider that this kind of dog only differs from the dog which we have just described (the farm-and-sheep-dog) in the matters of training and teaching. The war dog, according to what is laid down by Blondus, should be a terrifying aspect and look as though he was just going to fight, and be an enemy to everybody except his master; so much so that he will not allow himself to be stroked even by those he knows best, but threatens every-body alike with the fulminations of his teeth, and always looks at everybody as though he was burning with anger, and glares around in every direction with a hostile glance. This dog ought to be trained up to fight from his earliest years. Accord-ingly some man or other is fitted out with a coat of thick skin, which the dog will not be able to bite through, as a sort of dummy; the dog is then spurred on against this man, upon which the man in the skin runs away and then allows himself to be caught and, falling down on the ground in front of the dog, to be bitten. The day following, he ought to be pitted

Armored dog.

against another man protected in the same manner, and at the finish he can be trained to follow any person upon whose tracks he has been placed. After the fight the dog should be tied up, and fed while tied up, until at the finish he turns out a first-class defender of human beings. Blondus is even of the opinion that from time to time it is a good thing to go for this dog with drawn swords; in this way, he thinks, the dog will develop his spirit and courage to the utmost; and then, of course, you can lead him against real enemies. And Blondus adds that such dogs are frequently to be met with in Spain of the present day.

Probably no better set of training rules has ever been set down on paper, for this is exactly how guard and sentry dogs are trained in this day and age by the U.S. Armed Forces. However, the employment of attack dogs in war has become a thing of the past though they have been increasingly employed in other capacities with outstanding success.

Sentry work remains one of their most important duties in war, as even Napoleon recognized. Just before the Battle of Aboukir in July, 1799, he wrote to General Marmont, saying, "You should have a large quantity of dogs which can be made use of by posting them in front of your fortifications."

DOGS IN EARLY AMERICAN MILITARY HISTORY

The history of war dogs in the United States is an interesting one, for our armies never officially recog-

nized nor employed them until our entrance in 1942 into World War II.

One of the earliest attempts to utilize them was in 1775 when Ben Franklin, organizing Pennsylvania's defense against Indian raids, suggested the use of scout dogs in a letter:

"Dogs should be used against the Indians. They should be large, strong and fierce; and every dog led in a slip string to prevent their tiring themselves by running out and in, and dis-covering the party by barking at squirrels, etc. Only when the party come near thick woods and suspicious places they should turn out a dog or two to search them. In case of meeting a party of the enemy, the dogs are then all to be turned loose and set on. They will be fresher and finer for having been pre-viously confined and will confound the enemy a good deal and be very serviceable. This was the Spanish method of guarding their marches."

But no action seems to have followed the proposal.

A few years later, John Penn, Lt. Governor of Pennsylvania from 1763 to 1771, urged the use of war dogs. In a letter to James Young, Pay Master and Commissioner of Masters, dated Philadelphia, June 28, 1764, he said:

" . . . You will acquaint the Captains that every Soldier will be allowed 3 Shillings per month who brings with him a strong Dog that shall be judged proper to be employed in discovering and pursuing the Savages. It is recommended to them to procure as many as they can, not exceeding 10 per company; Each Dog is to be kept tied and led by his owner . . ."

During the Revolution when the Indian allies of the British caused the Colonial troops considerable trouble, a third proposal for war dogs was made by William McClay in a letter dated Sunbury, April 27, 1779, to the State of Pennsylvania's Supreme Execu-tive Council:

" . . . I have sustained some Ridicule for a Scheme which I have long recommended, Viz., that of hunting the Scalping Parties with Horsemen and Dogs. The imminent Services which Dogs have rendered to our people in some late instances, seems to open People's Eyes to a Method of this kind . . . It may be objected That we have not proper Dogs. It is true that every new thing must be learned; But we have, even now, Dogs that will follow them, and the arrantest Cur will both follow and fight in Company. I cannot help being of opinion that a Single Troop of Light Horse, attended by Dogs under honest and active officers, would destroy more Indians than five thousand Men stationed in forts along the Frontiers; I am not altogether singular in this opinion, could not such a thing be tried?"

But it never was officially, although undoubtedly some dogs were used.

During the Civil War, a limited number of dogs was employed as messengers, and around the great encampments of both Northern and Southern armies sentry dogs often stood on the alert, though not in any officially-recognized capacity.

In the Spanish-American War a dog named Don became well-known among American troops. Not a single patrol which he led was ever ambushed. Don served with a U.S. Cavalry troop commanded by a Captain Steel who maintained: "Dogs are the only scouts that can secure a small detachment against ambuscade in these tropical jungles."

How prophetic these words were no one realized until American soldiers and marines began boring through the tropical jungles of the Pacific islands toward Japanese strongholds during World War II, later in Korea, and today in South Vietnam.

AMERICA OVERLOOKS ITS MILITARY DOG POTENTIAL

During World War I, the belligerents employed an estimated 75,000 dogs in a multitude of capacities. Germany alone trained and used some 30,000, while having 7,000 killed in action.

Lt. Colonel Edwin Hautenville Richardson, pioneer and authority in the art of training dogs for modern warfare, also famous for training and supplying the Russian Army with ambulance dogs in the Russo-Japanese War of 1904, took over the British War Dog School. Under his direction, hundreds of dogs were trained as messengers at the Front. Those which failed to qualify in this capacity were trained in guard duty. As manpower became a vital factor late in the war, many dogs replaced soldiers as guards of supply depots and ammunition dumps in the battle zones. Large numbers of dogs were also used in the British Isles to guard munitions factories and camps for prisoners of war.

Many soldiers on both sides kept dogs as companions, even during the fighting. Many of these dogs became exceedingly adept at detecting the approach of enemy planes long before the hum of their motors could be heard by the soldiers. This warning often allowed the soldiers time to take cover before bombing began.

At the request of the French, some 400 sled dogs were sent over from Alaska and were used to haul ammunition and supplies in snow-covered mountain sections, particularly in the Vosges Mountains.

The Italians used many St. Bernard dogs for draft purposes in the mountains, where a number of machinegun units used dogs of the working type to handle machinegun carriages, two dogs usually making up a team.

The American forces had no organized dog unit. However, they borrowed some from the British, French and Belgians. Most of these were employed in Red Cross, messenger and guard work. A bill providing for a war dog project failed to pass in the U.S. Congress. With the coming of peace in 1918, the project was shelved and forgotten.

The most famous war dog veteran was undoubtedly Rin-Tin-Tin who soon gained world wide renown as a film star. Born in a German trench at Metz, he was deserted by the Germans when they retreated. He was found in a dugout by Lieutenant Lee Duncan, an American officer who nursed him through puppyhood and brought him home. Mr. Duncan was a trainer of dogs for police work at Santa Monica, California, and after a training course, Rin-Tin-Tin was entered in the Police Dog Trials. These events were filmed and Rin-Tin-Tin performed spectacularly. Recognizing the screen possibilities of the dog, a representative of Warner Brothers was not long in contracting for his services, and a long and interesting movie career began. Rin-Tin-Tin undoubtedly did more to popularize the German Shepherd in this country than any other member of his breed.

During the intervening years from 1918 to 1941 the United States became the most populous dog country in the world—by 1942 there were an estimated 13-15 million dogs of which 500,000 were purebreds. Americans kept their dogs as pets and watchdogs and for hunting, never realizing the military potential they represented.

Meanwhile, Nazi Germany was training some 200,000 dogs, mostly German Shepherds, for war duty, mainly as messengers, scouts and sentries.

Russia, too, was keenly aware of the value of intelligent dogs in war, and both before and during the war, more than 50,000 war dogs were trained by the Russian forces.

At the outbreak of hostilities, the French immediately organized recruiting stations to augment the ranks of their military dogs. Great Britain did not start its war dog program until the war had been in progress for two years.

AMERICA'S DOGS IN WORLD WAR II

When Pearl Harbor occurred on December 7, 1941, America had no trained war dogs at all, but this situation was quick to change through the efforts of patriotic civilians who were canine-minded. Immediately after the debacle, Mrs. Milton S. Erlanger of New York, a well-known breeder and exhibitor of dogs, telephoned Roland Kilbon, a prominent writer on dog topics and member of the editorial staff of the *New York Sun*, to suggest the recruiting of war dogs. They contacted Mrs. William H. Long Jr., an obedience training authority, Leonard Brumby, President of the Professional Handlers' Association, and Feli-

. dog-handler teams relaxing after duty tour—European Theater,
d War II. U.S. Army photo.

This Marine Corps Doberman gave warning of enemy ambush troops on Bougainville during World War II and saved the lives of members of an American tank platoon. U.S. Marine Corps photo.

cien Philippe, artist and former chief of the Italian State Game Preserve, who had wide knowledge of European war dogs and their training. Soon the idea mushroomed into Dogs for Defense, Inc., with Harry I. Caesar, dog fancier, sportsman, banker and a director of the American Kennel Club, as its president.

Dogs For Defense, Inc. Throughout all the war years this organization supplied every one of America's war dogs in a whole-hearted volunteer effort so typically American, an effort in which dog fanciers—breeders, trainers, professional and amateur; kennel club members, show and field-trial judges, handlers, veterinarians, writers and just plain dog lovers—played a part with no recompense other than the knowledge that they were serving their country in her need. Men, women and children, in forming Dogs For Defense, Inc., gave time, effort, money and dogs. Without cost to the government, Dogs For Defense, Inc.* organized, recruited, at first trained and later shipped to military centers, the dogs which formed the K-9 Corps of the U.S. Armed Forces.

The American Theater Wing, guided by Miss Helen Menken, stage and radio star, and Sydney Wain, the Wing's public relations counsel, publicized the recruiting program and raised funds through benefits across the country.

Thus, almost two centuries after wise old Ben Franklin had urged the use of military dogs, his

* (See *The New Knowledge of Dog Behavior.*—Part III.)

countrymen followed his recommendation. Just as he had advised, dogs were employed when our troops approached "thick woods and suspicious places" and, as he had predicted, they did "confound the enemy a good deal" and proved "very serviceable."

The record they created is really an impressive one. The K-9 Corps saw action in North Africa, Sicily, Italy, France, and the Pacific Theater with the Army and Marine Corps. Ten thousand did sentry duty and beach patrol with the Coast Guard and helped protect military installations and war plants. Less heralded, but no less notable, was the rescue work done by Army sledge teams in the Arctic, retrieving and saving the lives of downed airmen.

But before any part of the program could begin, even before any dogs could be given, Dogs For Defense, Inc. had to convince a preoccupied and skeptical government to *use* war dogs. "One dog is worth six to eight sentries," it was argued, but war dogs had no place in American military tradition.

On March 13, 1942, the Army saw the light and requested 200 trained sentry dogs from Dog For Defense, Inc. Training began in kennels and clubs in New England, New York, New Jersey, Pennsylvania, Maryland and California, while 402 clubs throughout the Nation signified their willingness to cooperate by providing dogs.

The basis for war dog training is obedience work. By a quirk of fate, Mrs. Whitehouse Walker of Bedford Hills, N.Y. and Miss Blanche Saunders, pioneer obedience trainer, made a famous 10,000-mile trip from coast to coast in 1940, giving obedience demonstrations and exhibitions with three perfectly-trained dogs. Everywhere they stirred interest in this type of work, to the point that by 1941 there were 42 obedience clubs in operation throughout the country and providing training to dogs that would be of direct military value. The New England Dog Training Club under Bert D. Turnquist's guidance, schooled and

By straining at his leash and showing signs of excitement scout dog alerted a U.S. patrol of the proximity of the ene (Luzon, P.I., World War II.) U.S. Army photo.

A wounded American military dog receives prompt first aid in the [field]. International News Photo.

exhibited messenger dogs, as did the Long Island Dog Training Club under the supervision of Mr. and Mrs. Harland Meistrell and Mrs. William H. Long, Jr., an officer of Dogs For Defense, Inc. Sentry-dog work was organized by the Hartford Obedience Training club, while the Stockton English Springer Spaniel Training Club instructed casualty dogs.

When the war came in 1941, these pioneer efforts formed the basis upon which Dogs For Defense, Inc. could operate, and many of the dogs and members of obedience clubs and training schools were the first recruits for the K-9 Corps.

The first three trained sentry dogs went on duty at the plant of the Munitions Manufacturing Company, Poughkeepsie, N.Y., on April 13, 1942 and quickly proved their usefulness.

A month later, in May 1942, the first contingent of nine dogs trained under the supervision of Dogs For Defense, Inc., was assigned to Fort Hancock, N.J., for sentry duty. Their work won immediate approval. Two months later, Major General Edmund B. Gregory, the Quartermaster General, inaugurated a survey to determine the need for dogs in the Army. It revealed a far greater need than had been expected and convinced the general that the Army should take over the training of war dogs, with Dogs For Defense, Inc. remaining the procurement agency. An official order to this effect was issued by Under Secretary of War Robert P. Patterson, and thus the first step was taken in the establishment of the K-9 Corps.

The K-9 Corps and an Expanded Military Dog Program. The launching of the Army's ambitious program, which called for training large numbers of dogs for many duties other than guard and sentry, required quick expansion of Dogs For Defense, Inc. National headquarters were established in New York City, and regional directors and representatives were

appointed in every state of the Union and the Territory of Hawaii. Eventually the organization was procuring dogs for the Army, Coast Guard and Marine Corps at the rate of 1,500 dogs per month.

Dogs For Defense, Inc. supplied approximately 20,000 dogs for the Army in the first two years of operation. The enlistment cost of these dogs was less than $7 per dog. The owners donated the dogs, and the expenses for enlistment, physical examination and shipment to induction centers were assumed by Dogs For Defense, Inc. It is estimated that after two years dogs worth more than $2,000,000 were in the service of the country, but the value of their services in the Mediterranean Theater, the South Pacific, on Bougainville, Guadalcanal, New Guinea and New Britain cannot be computed in mere dollars and cents. The lives these dogs saved and the sacrifices they made provides another thrilling saga in the history of "Man's Best Friend."

The remarkable record of achievement established by dogs trained for a variety of duties during World War II removed any doubts which might have existed as to their value in time of war. Dogs saved the lives of a number of men in combat; they were instrumental in preventing ambush while operating with patrols and giving warning of enemy infiltration at night, and they performed valuable service in guarding various installations and in patrolling the coasts of the United States.

Five War-Dog Reception and Training Centers were established by the Quartermaster Corps. These were located at Front Royal, Virginia; Fort Robinson, Nebraska; Gulfport, Mississippi; Camp Rimini at Helena, Montana, and San Carlos, California.

Initially, the training program was limited to dogs for sentry work, but later it was expanded to include scout, messenger, sledge and pack dogs, and dogs to be used in connection with mine detection. Using dogs for mine detection did not, however, prove practical, and this phase of the program was subsequently abandoned.

Over 19,000 dogs, most of them donated, were processed through the training centers. About 45% of them were rejected as unsuited for training. Dogs actually trained and assigned to duty numbered for

After each mission scout dogs were given a thorough physical examination. (Burma-India Theater, World War II.) U.S. Army photo.

the various duties: messenger, 151; scout, 595; mine detection, 140; sentry, 9,298; sledge and pack, 268.

Many different breeds were tried out initially, and any one of 32 breeds and crosses thereof were at first acceptable and classified as War Dogs, but by the end of 1944 only five breeds were acceptable: German Shepherds, Belgian Sheepdogs, Doberman Pinschers, farm-type Collies, and Giant Schnauzers, plus crosses of these breeds. For sledge dogs, Malamutes, Eskimos and Siberian Huskies were favored. Under pack, Newfoundlands and St. Bernards were preferred. In 1946, the German Shepherd was named by the War Department as the official U.S. Army dog.

Terriers (Sealyhams and Wire-haired), Dachshunds, Bloodhounds, Cockers and Springers were tried in a secret project known as M-dogs for mine detection. In North Africa, the Germans introduced non-metallic, plastic mines which baffled electric mine-detectors. This slowed down Allied advances, so teams of trained mine-detection dogs and Americans were used to meet the situation. The dogs proved of excellent value in camp and rear areas, but at the Front they located at best 51%, and suffered many casualties. Dogs were distracted too much by the dead and debris of the battlefield to function well, it was decided, so the project was finally abandoned.

The Quartermaster General was charged with the responsibility of receiving, conditioning, training and issuance of dogs for all war purposes, as well as the military personnel assigned to such activities. Later, the Army, Marine Corps and Coast Guard procured and trained their dogs separately.

By 1943 thousands of sentry dogs had been assigned to duty at war plants, military installations, and with Coast Guard shore patrols. An experimental unit consisting of six scout and two messenger dogs with their handlers was dispatched to the Pacific Area for trials with combat units. Working successfully with both the Army and Marine Corps, taking part in both land campaigns and landing operations, this first dog platoon paved the way for many more to follow.

Reception and Training—U.S. Military Dogs. Extreme care was exercised in selecting military personnel to help in training dogs for duty. Emphasis was placed on a friendly attitude toward dogs, intelligence, patience and perseverance, mental and physi-cal endurance, resourcefulness and dependability. Qualified veterinarians were assigned to provide for the care of the canines.

Upon a dog's arrival at a reception center, a careful record was made of its background. A veterinarian then tattooed the dog's serial number inside the left ear, or on the flank or belly for identification purposes.

During basic training the dog was taught to carry out certain fundamental commands. On leash, they included Heel, Sit, Down, Cover, Stay, Come, Crawl, and Jump. Off-leash, the dog was trained to Drop and Jump. He was also accustomed to muzzles and gas masks, to riding in a variety of vehicles, and to gunfire. Some dogs were also transported by plane with little trouble.

Early in the program it was learned that a dog might be trained for scout, messenger or sentry work, but that he could not satisfactorily combine two or more duties.

Specialized training varied with the type of work for which the dog was being fitted.

The sentry dog worked on a short leash and was taught to give warning by growling, alerting or barking. He was especially valuable for working in the dark when attack from cover or the rear was most likely.

Scout or patrol dogs also worked on a leash, day and night, in all kinds of weather and over all types of terrain. Above all, this training taught the dog to work in silence in order to more easily detect snipers, ambushes and other enemy forces.

Messenger dogs were trained to work with two handlers, learning to make their way from one handler to another when unleashed. Taught to travel silently and by a circuitous route, if necessary, the messenger dog soon became adept at taking advantage of natural cover and at by-passing any group except the one which included his handler.

Battle conditioning was, of course, a necessary part of dog training. The dog was taught to be oblivious of all things which did not concern a given mission. The orientation course began with firing a rifle at a distance while the dog was engaged in regular activity. As the dog became more accustomed to this type of sound, he eventually came to pay little or no attention to the fire of small arms or even larger weapons.

Most dogs were trained in a period of 12 weeks. The sentry dog, however, usually completed his course in eight weeks. Expert instructors supervised the training, which was done by the handler who would actually be with the dog in the field.

Standard dog equipment included two collars, one leather, the other chain, a web harness, leash, kennel chain, muzzle, water-repellent blanket, brush and comb, individual feeding and watering pans, and gas mask.

Some Outstanding U.S. Military Dogs of World War II. A number of war dogs trained by the Quartermaster Corps established outstanding records overseas. At

Some Service dogs were used as shown here for carrying packets of small key supplies. These dogs were with the 89th Division during World War II. U.S. Army photo.

least one member of the K-9 Corps was awarded the Silver Star and the Purple Heart by an overseas command, but both were later revoked as contrary to an Army policy which prohibited the official commendation of animals. In January, 1944, the War Department relaxed restrictions on this regard and permitted publication of commendations in individual unit General Orders. Later, approval was granted for issuance by the Quartermaster General of Citation Certificates to donors of war dogs that had been unusually helpful during the war. The first to be issued were in recognition of the work of eight dogs which had comprised the first unit in the Pacific Area.

Among the first to be shipped overseas was Chips, a war dog donated by Edward J. Wren of Pleasantville, N.Y. Assigned to the 3rd Infantry Division, he served with that unit in the North African, Mediterranean, and European Theaters of Operation and did sentry duty at the Roosevelt-Churchill conference in January, 1943. Although trained as a sentry dog, Chips was reported on one occasion by members of Company I, 30th Infantry Regiment, to have broken away from his handler and attacked an enemy machinegun crew in Sicily. He seized one man and forced the entire crew to surrender. He was also credited by the units to which he was assigned with having been directly responsible for the capture of numerous enemy troops by alerting his handler to their presence.

Peefka, a German Shepherd donated by Kenneth W. Hayward of North Conway, N.H., was posthumously awarded a Certificate of Commendation for faithful and outstanding service. A scout dog with the Fifth Army, he was credited with the prevention of casualties to his patrol by giving unfailing alerts of enemy presence. Specifically mentioned was an instance when the dog had alerted his handler to a concealed wire across a mountain trail. Investigation revealed three mines which would have detonated had the wire been touched. Peefka was killed in action in March, 1945, by an enemy grenade, after leading his patrol through a mountainous region.

Silver, a scout dog donated by Anthony Schadd of Kenosha, Wisc., was commended for action in Italy. He alerted his handler to an enemy force which was preparing for a surprise bayonet attack that would have cost American lives. The dog was later killed by an enemy grenade thrown into his foxhole.

Dick, a scout dog donated by Edward Zan of New York City, was cited for working with a patrol in the Pacific Area for 48 out of 53 days. This dog not only discovered a camouflaged Japanese bivouac, but unerringly alerted his masters to the only occupied hut of five, permitting a surprise attack which resulted in the annihilation of the enemy without a single Marine casualty.

Lady, a messenger dog donated by John G. Macario of Minersville, Penna, was cited for extremely proficient work while attached to Australian troops during the drive through the Remu Valley and the attack on Medang.

Quite a different kind of military dog, this is Smokey, a pal and a Yorkshire Terrier, with Corporal William Wynne of Cleveland, Ohio during his service in Australia, New Guinea, the Dutch East Indies, the Philippines, and other parts of the Pacific Theater during World War II. Photo by Clayton Knipper.

Caesar, a German Shepherd, was one of the outstanding dogs attached to the Marine Corps. In writing to Max Glazer of Bronx, N.Y., who donated Caesar, General Thomas Holcomb, former Commandant of the Marine Corps, said:

"Caeser, a messenger dog, was the only means of communication between a Marine company and its battalion command post on the initial day, carrying messages back to the rear. On the second day, the telephone lines of his company were cut, and Caeser was again the only means of communication. Caeser was wounded on the third day and had to be carried back to the regimental command post on a stretcher, but he had already established himself as a hero. While with his company, Caeser made nine official runs between the company and the command post, and on at least two of these runs he was under fire."

Caesar's two handlers were Pfc. Rufus Mayo, Montgomery, Ala., and Pfc. John J. Kleeman, Philadelphia, Penna. On one occasion Caesar saved Mayo's life by attacking a Japanese soldier, causing him to drop the hand grenade he was about to throw. The Japanese fled, but not until he had wounded Caesar twice.

Andy, a two-year-old Doberman, was another Marine dog that did heroic work as a scout. On many occasions he led the advance of a Marine company and gave warning to scattered Japanese sniper opposition. He was donated by Theodore A. Wiedermann, Norristown, Penna., and his handlers were Pfc. John B. Mahoney, Clinton, Conn., and Pfc. Robert E. Lansley, Syracuse, N.Y.

Otto, a Doberman, alerted to a Japanese machinegun nest, and another Doberman, Rex, warned of a Jap surprise attack. As walkie-talkies went dead with jungle sweat, American war dogs further distinguished themselves. Duke flushed 50 Japs, was responsible for the capture of 22 others, and several times pointed out patrols pincering or ambushing his American buddies. Often the love between a war dog and his soldier master was fantastic, and so were the results. Many a doubting commanding officer came to this conclusion on Guadalcanal, the Solomon Islands, New Guinea, New Britain, Saipan, Guam, Peleliu, Iwo Jima, Okinawa, the Philippines, and other memorable fighting spots of World War II.

Fearlessly, they fought and fell as their masters did. Of the eight dogs in the first K-9 tactical unit sent to the South Pacific, none returned. Five died on duty; three had to be destroyed just before returning because of typhus.

As the war progressed, the K-9 Corps organized war dog platoons for combat work. A platoon consisted of a lieutenant, five sergeants and fifteen corporals with dogs. The Marine Corps has seven such platoons, one mine-detection team and two replacement drafts. The Army used fifteen platoons, seven against the Germans and eight against the Japanese.

But war dogs were not the only canines to serve their country. Scattered throughout the Aleutian Islands and Alaska were teams of sledge dogs working without fanfare to pick up downed flyers, haul emergency supplies and the like. These dogs were trained at Camp Rimini, high in the Rockies near Helena, Montana. In one instance a veteran driver, inducted into the Army, brought his own team of Siberian Huskies and enlisted them. Other drivers who were over-age, sold their entire teams to the Government.

On the mainland of the United States several thousand sentry dogs performed admirably along our sea coasts, around our harbors, factories and munitions plants. Many were the heroic instances that involved them.

One night at a West Coast embarkation port, a Dalmation caught a saboteur about to set fire to the dock area with a boatload of oily rags underneath a wharf. A Boxer at a Boston war plant spotted and trapped a prowler who had complete plans for destruction of the plant on his person.

A German Shepherd on beach patrol one foggy night warned of a fishing boat about to land. It turned out to be Japanese foreign agents trying to sneak ashore. At an airbase in Arkansas, K-9 sentries twice discovered fires before they became serious. In New Jersey, a Labrador retrieved the bodies of 34 drowned seamen.

Many were the known heroes, but many were unsung heroes also. The 28th Infantry Scout Dog Platoon received a unit citation because "not one of the more than 800 patrols led by its dogs was ambushed." The 26th Infantry Scout Dog Platoon's men earned on Silver Star, eight Bronze Stars, seven Purple Hearts, two with Oak Leaf Clusters, also unit citations from the 31st Division with which it worked. Six of its members died in line-of-duty.

Demobilization. When the end of the war came, demobilizing some 8,000 Service dogs became quite a chore. No dog, the Quartermaster Corps announced, would be considered ready for release by the Army until it had undergone a complete "demilitarizing" process. It was then thought that the dogs could be disposed of through public auction, but once again Dogs For Defense, Inc. stepped in and volunteered to find proper homes for those dogs which were not taken back by their owners. This it did merely for the price of shipment, which amounted to $14-24 each.

To be "demilitarized," each dog had its wartime lessons completely reversed. No longer were they encouraged to be one-man dogs, but their rehabilitation accustomed them to sights and sounds of cities and civilians, taught them to be friendly toward any and all people. Those which remained aggressive were humanely put to sleep, but the majority returned to happy home life.

Up to this point, Dogs For Defense, Inc. seemed to have fulfilled its mission, brilliantly but completely, nevertheless a strange thing happened. At an Army convalescent hospital in Pawling, N.Y., a mentally-depressed Air Corps officer, who could not be reached by all manner of modern therapy, acquired a puppy which became completely attached to him with the unstinting love and affection that characterizes the canine's relationship toward man. In only a short while, the officer began to improve; his depression faded and a new buoyancy of spirit marked his steady improvement.

Thus began The Healing Paw phase of Dogs For Defense, Inc. This was the acquisition of puppies for hospital patients and mental cases, to bring back that spark of life. The hospital at Pawling was the first test run. In a short time the place became a veritable dog show in itself as Dogs For Defense, Inc. sent out the order for spaniels, Boxers, terriers, Beagles, German Shepherds—all kinds. Sunken eyes and lost souls brightened as puppies romped among crutches and wheel chairs. Obedience training classes were held, and even K-9 Corps veteran dogs swaggering about brought back hope.

Soon the idea spread to Veterans Hospitals around the country and The Healing Paw branch of Dogs For Defense, Inc. had performed another miracle.

U.S. MILITARY DOGS AND THE KOREAN WAR

When the Korean War broke out in 1951, the Army had a few sentry dogs in Germany and some sledge dogs in Alaska, but it was not training specifically for war work in the front lines. However, to meet the situation it began acquiring dogs mainly for guard work, for it was thought that with the advances in military technology, modern warfare held little or no place for the age-old war dog in any other capacity.

But the very first group of dogs sent over proved highly effective not only for sentry duty, but for scout and patrol work at the Front. Thus did the K-9 Corps become important again, training dogs in basic obedience here in the United States and finishing the specialty work in South Korea among the people and in the environment where they had to operate. At the height of the conflict, the Army alone had two companies of K-9 Corps dogs and men in front-line fighting. These were broken down into individual dogs and men assigned to various combat units where they provided outstanding service.

S/Sgt. Melvin Powell of Yanceyville, N.C., who in the course of thirteen months of fighting with the 1st Cavalry Division, crossed the 38th Parallel four times, said of these dogs:

"They were really remarkable, particularly on patrols and during those bitter-cold, black nights when we couldn't see anything. The wind generally came from the north, so the scent of the enemy favored the dogs. Whenever they pricked their ears up and whined a little, we knew the enemy was within 150 yards of us and moving in, so we made ourselves ready. They were *never* wrong, to the extent that we got so we staked our lives on their ability."

By the end of the conflict, more than 500 war dogs had seen action in Korea. This time when the Armistice came they were not discharged, but remained as sentry and scout dogs around supply depots and along the demilitarized zone of the 38th Parallel, where they still serve today.

U.S. MILITARY DOGS IN VIETNAM

When the United States became involved in South Vietnam, war dogs were thought to be more obsolete than ever. First of all, it seemed unlikely that dogs raised in the U.S. could adjust satisfactorily to the extremely hot climate. Secondly, it was thought that

"Say 'Ah'!" Sentry dogs are given regular physical examinations. U.S. Army photo.

modern electronic devices, which could detect movement at considerable distances, would be more effective all-around. In both instances, this proved untrue.

The dogs that were sent over quickly adjusted to the tropical climate, and their first job was to guard important storage and staging areas as well as air bases against enemy attack by infiltration. So successfully did they work that just about all our air bases in Vietnam now have sentry dogs working around them, especially at night. It is the dog's extreme sensitivity to smell and sound that accounts for his effectiveness. In but a very short time they have learned to distinguish between the scent of an American and a Viet Cong. When a sentry dog indicates the presence of an unusual person in an unauthorized area, the handler sets off a flare which illuminates the surroundings, then calls for help. Immediately, Mobile Security Alert Teams, consisting of two more sentry-dog teams in a Jeep equipped with a machinegun, respond to the emergency.

In this manner infiltration and surprise attack by the Viet Cong has been held to a minimum under conditions where electronic detection devices proved not as reliable as first thought.

Viet Cong terrorists have used sprays, pepper, perfumes and other olfactory irritants in the hope of confusing the dogs enough so as to slip past them, but nothing has worked. Dogs can spot or scent an intruder well before he is able to lay a trap. As is always the case for military purposes, the dog's handler is the only person that the particular dog will obey.

Sentry Dog Training. At public demonstrations, sentry dogs are often put through their paces to show how easily the animals detect trespassers and how forcefully they will attack at the command of their handlers. During these demonstrations, the handlers work their dogs against policemen dressed in heavily-padded training uniforms.

These sentry dogs are trained at Lackland Air Force Base, San Antonio, Texas, which receives them from all parts of the country, sometimes after purchase, more often gratis. The dogs go through an

here is great mutual trust and confidence between this Air Force dler and his dog. U.S. Air Force photo.

In Vietnam and many other parts of the world—American military dog-handler teams take care of jobs that might otherwise require many more troops. U.S. Army photo.

eight-week course during which they are matched with their volunteer handlers. The training almost exactly parallels that recommended by Aldrovandus, the Italian, in 1522 and described earlier. Upon arrival at Lackland, the dog receives a physical examination, then is tested up to 21 days for temperament before being turned over to his permanent handler who, at the same time, has been learning how to care for the dog, groom, feed, and manage him. Basic obedience is then taught, after which comes the attack work. For this, a trainer agitates the dog with a stick or the like, then runs away while the handler encourages his dog to chase the fleeing man. This continues daily, the attacker always being chased away and the dog sent in pursuit upon command, then finally restrained upon command, until the animal learns the procedure.

Scout Dogs. Scout dogs for front-line patrol work are trained at Ft. Benning, Georgia. They are of high intelligence and ability, for they must learn to distinguish the enemy by scent and sound. In South Vietnam they have done such an outstanding job that our Armed Forces has sent out a nationwide call for more dogs which can be trained and used in the guerrilla and ambush-type combat being fought in the jungles and rice paddies there during the nights as well as the days. It is expected that from 2,000 to 5,000 war

dogs, mostly German Shepherds, will serve before the war ends.

About American Dogs In Vietnam. Associated Press correspondent Ronald Deutsch, reporting from South Vietnam, described the work of the U.S. war dogs there as follows:

Shortly before dusk 26 U. S. Infantrymen set out on a jungle patrol less than 30 miles from Saigon. Their mission: To ambush the Viet Cong. It was like hundreds of other patrols the 1st Infantry Division had made, except for one key difference: A hard, carefully-trained German Shepherd Dog led the way.

Nothing happened for three hours. Then the big dog became tense and stopped short. He pointed his body toward a clump of dense brush. The ambush was set.

Within ten minutes four Viet Cong walked into the trap and the Americans opened fire. One Viet Cong was killed; another wounded crawled into the jungle undergrowth. The Shepherd picked up his scent and tracked the wounded man, leading the Americans to him.

This incident typifies the increasing role played by scout dogs in the Vietnamese war.

"Our Shepherds will alert on any strange scent outside the patrol," said Sgt. 1/c Jesse Mendes, 38, of San Antonio, Texas. Sgt. Mendez is a military advisor on dogs. "They have been very instrumental in the discovery of mines, documents, food, weapons and ammunition."

Several hundred German Shepherds are presently in use. Most are sentry dogs on guard at key U. S. installations. Both the Army and Marine Corps are using more and more in the field. The scout dogs, or "four-footed radar", as the GI's call them, also come from basic training in the United States but they are further trained in Vietnam . . . Their handlers are experienced field soldiers. Often on patrols they are the first to take casualties because they walk ahead of the troops with the scout dogs.

Many a dramatic incident involving war dogs has come out of the Vietnam conflict, and many American lives have been saved by these canine heroes. Philip H. Warner described one such incident in *The German Shepherd Dog Review,* involving a dog named Tiger.

Assigned to the U.S. 1st Cavalry Division with his handler, T/5 S. Brown, Tiger set out on a search-and-destroy mission through the jungles, some 250 miles north of Saigon. Behind him were 200 American soldiers relying on his ability. After several hours of searching, Tiger stopped and alerted at some tall jungle grass about 75 yards away. It turned out to be 300 Viet Cong lying hidden and waiting in ambush. American planes were called in to attack the concentration which was broken up with a minimum of American losses, thanks to this war dog's ability. Tiger later died of wounds, a hero to the men who knew him.

One of the greatest enemies of the war dogs since they arrived in July 1965 has been snakes. Several of the Shepherds have taken fatal bites and also alerted their masters before the snakes could bite them. One of the smallest dogs on air-base patrol duty shoved aside Airman 2/C Clifford Davis of Knoxville, Tenn., to take a strike from a deadly snake. In a similar incident, a two-year-old German Shepherd on his first patrol saved the life of Airman 2/C Robert C. Horen of Detroit. The dog moved the airman out of a snake's range as the latter was about to strike. In

DOGS THAT FIND MARIJUANA

Increasing use of dogs is being made in investigative work such as in searching for hidden or concealed marijuana. The U.S. Army began training dogs for handling such problems within the military in 1969. Civilian police agencies experimented with such projects even earlier. It takes 12 weeks of schooling to teach "search" dogs to react to the smell of marijuana. In military use, these dogs are trained to be friendly, unlike the dogs trained for normal sentry duty.

Civil police agencies employ dogs also for such search purposes for it has been found that a properly trained "search" dog comes close to the 100% success mark in tests involving hidden caches of this drug. A dog, can be used to search a vehicle as well as a building, for example. If marijuana is hidden in a car's air filter under the hood, the dog will find it. He will find it even if it is behind the upholstered lining of a car door, hidden beneath objects or clothing in a car trunk, in a satchel, or elsewhere.

Dogs for detection of marijuana only within the military are trained at Fort Gordon, Georgia. Today, in many parts of the country, whether used by civilian police agencies or the military, dogs for detecting marijuana are making it increasingly difficult for drug purveyors or users to conceal or maintain illegal drug supplies. A number of these dogs are German Shepherds, but not always, for other breeds are successfully trained for this work, too.

Military dog-handler team on patrol outside an Air Force station, performing security duties protecting millions of dollars worth of property. U.S. Army photo.

other instances, dogs have killed snakes or given their handlers the opportunity to do so.

Thus it would seem that no matter how ingenious man becomes in perfecting and mechanizing warfare, the dog will always have a place beside his master in guarding and protecting what he feels is his, for his loyalty in time of peace is no less than in time of war.

Part IX

THE DOG IN COURSING AND RACING

England continues to lead the world in having the greatest number of active dog racing tracks, with Ireland standing in second place. Although track attendance in the U.S. is only about a third that in England, the money annually wagered runs nearly the same. As a sport, coursing events in the U.S. are centered mostly in the prairie states. Dog sled events, necessarily confined to areas having protracted winters, are important and especially well organized in Alaska. Otherwise they are prominent mainly in the New England region.

—Coursing and Racing—

MAN HAS long matched the speed of his dogs with that of wild game animals, both as a matter of pure sport and for the purpose of adding to his game bag. Held under natural conditions, with live animals as the incentive, the sport is called coursing.

HISTORICAL NOTES

Coursing with Greyhounds is undoubtedly the oldest competitive sport in which dogs were used. Centuries before Ovid, Grecian historian, 63 B.C.—A.D. 17— wrote the first known description of coursing, rival owners very probably matched their Greyhounds in informal contests and the sport, now organized into formal competitions, continues to this day.

Ovid's description, as translated by Dryden follows:
As when the impatient greyhound, slipped from far
Bounds o'er the glade to course the fearful hare,
She in her speed does all her safety lie,
And he with double speed pursues his prey,
O'erruns her at the sitting turns; but licks
His chops in vain; yet blows upon the flix.
She seeks the shelter which the neighboring covert gives,
And, gaining it, she doubts if yet she lives.

Necessity has caused some changes in the sport of coursing but its conduct remains essentially the same. In the early days in England, pointers or spaniels were used to find or start the hare. The Greyhounds (two, three, or four) were then uncoupled in pursuit. Later coursing was conducted in enclosed "paddocks," about a mile in length and about a quarter of a mile in breadth. As many as four, and even more, Greyhounds were set after one or more hares. The sport

was more of a slaughter of hares than a contest of dog speed. Later the use of the "paddock" was generally abandoned.

To give the hare a better chance, to make the sport a bit more humane, and to provide a better test of the speed of the dogs, the Duke of Norfolk drew up a set of coursing rules which were generally adopted, and coursing became a finer sport. This was during the reign of Queen Elizabeth, when coursing reached its greatest popularity in England.

The rules drawn up by the Duke of Norfolk follow:

1. No hare to be coursed with more than a brace of greyhounds.

2. The hare finder to give the hare three so-hos before he put her from her form, that the dogs might have notice to attend her being started.

3. The hare to have law of 12 score yards before the greyhounds were loosed unless the small distance between the hare and the covert would not admit it without danger of immediately losing her.

4. The dog that gave the first turn and during the course, if there was neither cote, slip, nor wrench, won.

5. A cote is when a greyhound goes endways by his fellow, and gives the hare a turn.

6. A cote served for two turns, and two trippings or jerkins for a cote; if the hare did not turn quite about she only wrenched, and two wrenches stand for a turn.

7. If there were no cotes given between a brace of greyhounds, but that one of them served the other at turning, then he gave the brace most turns won; and if one gave as many turns as the other, then he that bore the hare won.

8. If one dog gave the first turn, and the other lose the hare, he that bore the hare won.

9. A go-by, or hearing the hare, was equivalent to two turns.

10. If neither dog turned the hare, he that led last to the covet won.

11. If one dog turned the hare, served himself, and turned her again, it was as much as a cote—for a cote was esteemed two turns.

12. If all the course was equal, the dog that bore the hare won; if the hare was not borne, the course was adjudged dead, that is, undecided.

13. If a dog fell in a course, and yet performed his part, he might challenge a turn more than he gave.

14. If a dog turned the hare, served himself and gave divers cotes, and yet in the end stood still in the field, the other dog, if he ran home to the covert, although he gave no turn, was adjudged the winner.

15. If, by accident, a dog was run over in his course, the course was void, and he that did the mischief was to make reparation for the damage.

16. If a dog gave the first and last turn, and there was no other advantage between them, he that gave the odd turn won.

17. He that came in first at the death, took up the hare, saved her from being torn, cherished the dogs and cleansed their mouths from the fleck, was allowed to retain the hare for his trouble.

18. And those who were appointed judges of the course were to give their decision before they departed from the field.

The first organized meeting on record was that of the famous Swaffham Coursing Society in 1776. This club was organized by the Earl of Orford, in Norfolk, and its members were confined in number to the letters of the alphabet. There was no "I" and the membership consisted of twenty-five. The dogs of each member had to bear a name beginning with the letter assigned to the owner as a member of the club.

Lord Orford was the outstanding coursing enthusiast of his day and made endless experiments in Greyhound breeding and training. Gradually his mind became unbalanced and it was necessary that he be confined to his room. On the day that his favorite old bitch, "Czarina," was to race in a match of unusual importance, he escaped from his attendants and appeared upon the scene astride his well-known piebald pony. Entreated by his friends to return to the house, he refused and, galloping behind "Czarina," saw her win the trial. Suddenly he fell from his pony and died.

In 1780 coursing was established at Ashdown Park and the following year the Malton Coursing Club was organized. Interest in coursing as an organized sport grew rapidly in England, Scotland, and Ireland. Other early coursing societies were the Louth, Ilsley, Derbyshire, Newmarket, Beacon Hill, Morfe, Amesbury, Altcar, Deptford Union, and Burton-on-Trent in England; the famous Midlothian, the Larnarkshire and Renfrewshire Club, the Ardossan and the Biggar Club of Scotland and Bourbawn, Lurgan, Toombridge, Dunlavin, Black Brea, Dunsandle, and Kilwaunock of Ireland.

What the "Derby" is to the English horse-racing man, the "Waterloo Cup" is to the couring enthusiast. In 1836, a Mr. Lynn, proprietor of the Waterloo Hotel, organized an 8-dog stake which he called "The Waterloo Cup." The inaugural was run over Lord Sefton's estate at Altcar. In the second running, the race was enlarged to one for sixteen runners, and in 1838 this number was doubled. In 1857 it was made a 64-dog stake, and remains as such. The first year's race was won by Milanie, a red bitch by Milo ex Duchess, owned by Lord Malyneux, afterwards by Lord Sefton, and nominated, appropriately enough, by Mr. Lynn.

Throughout its long history The Waterloo Cup has remained the classic of the coursing world. To the "Cup" has been added the "Waterloo Purse" and the "Waterloo Plate."

In 1858 the National Coursing Club was organized and a new code of rules, based on those of the Duke of Norfolk, was adopted. This organization became the governing body of the sport and keeper of the Stud Book.

Snowball, a jet black Greyhound owned by Major Topham of Orford, was the first sire placed at public stud. From him, and other Greyhounds of that time, have come the racing dogs of today. King Cob, one-eighth Bulldog, is regarded as the keystone sire of all modern English Greyhounds. Practically every registered Greyhound, whether in England, Ireland, Australia, Africa, India or the United States, can trace its ancestry back to King Cob.

COURSING IN THE U.S.

Coursing in the United States is conducted under the supervision of the National Coursing Association (RFD #3, Abilene, Kansas), which acts as a register agency and maintains a stud book at Abilene, Kansas. Coursing meets are held at Abilene twice annually, in spring and fall, attracting from 300 to 3,000 enthusiasts, most of whom are breeders. Local coursing meets are held near breeding centers in Texas, Oklahoma, and California.

The nation's most important coursing feature is the National Waterloo Cup, staged annually since 1895, when Kilkirk, a fawn-colored bitch owned by Melrose and Dublin, was the winner. It takes its name from the "Waterloo Cup" of England.

The modern coursing field is a level, fenced area 450 yards in length and 150 yards in width. At one end of the sodded enclosure are caged or penned hares, which are driven out onto the coursing field when a brace of contestants are ready for the chase. At the opposite end of the park are escapes into

Predator animal hounds being unloaded and staked out. David M. Duffey photo.

which the hare may run if fortunate enough to avoid capture during a course. Near a point where the hares are released two Greyhounds are held on leash by a "slipper" who allows the hare to reach a point about 30 yards ahead of the dogs before releasing them.

In coursing the hare, the dogs are awarded points by a judge, or judges, stationed either in towers alongside the field or on horseback within the park.

Still playful and only a ten-months old pup, this dog is at the age where field experience would develop him so he could become (by age 18-24 months) a valuable coursing hound. An Irish Wolfhound.

Points are allowed for speed (1, 2, or 3), the go-bye (2), the turn (1), the wrench (½), the kill (2), and the trip (1). The dog gaining the greatest number of points is declared winner of the course. In stake events there are generally 36 or 64 entries (there can be any number), with winners meeting winners until the field is reduced to two finalists, who compete for the purse or prize. If the contestants earn an equal number of points, the purse is divided.

Close to the geographic center of the United States, in parts of Iowa, Missouri, Kansas, Nebraska, Colorado, north Texas and Oklahoma, the use of coursing hounds in hunting coyotes is not only well established as a sport, but reportedly is enjoying some

increase. Jackrabbits are also a proper coursing quarry in this region, for they as well as coyotes are a nuisance to both farmers and stockmen.

The hunts are made without guns, the dogs being transported in the backs of pickup trucks, confined in crates. The hunters seeing a coyote, the truck tries to overtake and pass it, the dogs being sprung as quickly as possible after they are able to spot the quarry out the back of the truck. If the coyote is to be caught, the dogs must do it very quickly after hitting the ground because they cannot long hold the sizzling speed required for overtaking it. In a good many cases, the coyote gets away.

Seeking to develop the best possible hounds for this work, coursing enthusiasts have tried crosses between just about all the major breeds of sight hounds against some basic Greyhound element—Irish Wolfhounds, Salukis, Scottish Deerhounds, etc., and in various combinations, the objectives sought being stamina, speed, tough feet, and other necessary characteristics.

Large dogs result; dogs very alert, deep of chest, strong-necked and powerful. And some predict that from it all there will eventually emerge a new breed, the American Coursing Hound.

DEFINITION OF POINTS

(From the Rules of the National Coursing Club)

a. In estimating the value of speed to the hare the Judge must take into account the several forms in which it may be displayed—*viz:*

1. Where in the runup a clear lead is gained by one of the dogs, in which case one, two or three points may be given, according to the length of lead, apart from the score for a turn or wrench. In awarding these points the Judge shall take into consideration the merit of a lead obtained by a dog which has lost ground at the start, either from being unsighted, or from a bad slip, or which has to run the outer circle.

2. Where one greyhound leads the other so long as the hare runs straight, but loses the lead from her bending round decidedly in favor of the slower dog on her own accord, in which case the one greyhound shall score one point for the speed shown, and the other dog score one point for the first turn.

3. Under no circumstances is speed without subsequent work to be allowed to decide a course, except where greater superiority is shown by one greyhound over another in a long lead to covert.

The Biscayne Track in Florida. Photo by Herb Davies.

The Flagler Greyhound Racing Track in Florida. Greyhound Racing
Record photo.

b. *The Go-bye* is where a greyhound starts a clear length
behind his opponent and yet passes him in a straight run and
gets a clear length before him.

c. *The Turn* is where the hare is brought round at not less
than a right angle from her previous line.

d. *The Wrench* is where the hare is bent from her line at less
than a right angle; but where she only leaves her line to suit
herself, and not from the greyhound pressing her, nothing to
be allowed.

e. *The Merit of a Kill* must be estimated according to whether
a greyhound, by his own superior dash and skill, bears the hare;
whether he picks her up through any little accidental circumstance favouring him, or whether she is turned into his mouth,
as it were, by the other greyhound.

f. *The Trip,* or unsuccessful effort to kill, is where the hare
is thrown off her legs, or where a greyhound flecks her, but
cannot hold her.

Allowances are made for bad starts, the hare's bearing decidedly in favor of one hound, and falls or acci-

dents. Penalties are charged for refusing to follow the
hare when slipped, standing still on a course, or
refusing to jump fences which the other dog takes.

COURSING TERMS

CUTE. Cleverness in coursing hare; heads it off, compels
running mate to do most of the work and collects points without great effort.

DROPPED MUSCLE. Rupture of inner loin or shoulder muscles.

FIGHTER. Dog that impedes or interferes with another; not
necessarily viciousness, but an attempt to hold back other contestants.

FOOT. Fleetness; speed.

GYP. Female Greyhound.

LOST BACK. Long back muscles torn loose from anchorage
due to over exertion.

RELIEF DOG. Courses are limited to three or four minutes.
When contestants continue beyond that time without making
a kill, a fresh dog, or dogs, are sent in to make the kill and end
the course.

RINGER. Where fraudulent substitution is made.

RUNUP. The dash from slips to the hare.

SAPLING. Untried pup of racing age, 10 to 18 months.

SPIKED. Cut by the claws of a contestant.

SPOOKY. Shy, easily frightened by crowds, or other dogs.

RACING ON TRACKS

The popularity of coursing declined in England to
some extent after the Queen Elizabeth era. It was
never a "popular" sport in the sense that it appealed
to or was participated in by all classes. Efforts to
popularize the sport were made by restricting the
dogs and hares to fenced enclosures. This led to the
employment of inanimate lures, the slaughter of
hares being offensive to many spectators. This marked
the beginning of the modern sport of Greyhound
racing as we know it today.

When the first lure was used to lead Greyhounds is

Aerial view of the racing plant of the Taunton Greyhound Racing Association, Inc., Taunton, Mass.

unknown. They were tried in connection with racing as early as 1740 and the Belgian express line attached lures to the carriages drawn by dogs in 1844. First record of a regular race meeting in which a lure was used is that at Hendon, England, in 1877. Here a stuffed rabbit attached to a cord was drawn over a 400-yard straight course by a reel. An English patent was issued in 1880 for a Greyhound lure installed within a circular track and in 1887 J. A. Pinard was granted a patent by the U.S. Patent Office on a similar hand-operated lure.

Three other Americans received patents on lures of varying types before Owen Patrick Smith made his first application for an electrically-propelled lure in 1912. Nevertheless, Smith is recognized as the father of Greyhound racing and his equipment, or improved variations, is now employed universally. Smith labored diligently, under the most discouraging handicaps, from 1905, when he conceived the idea of track racing while watching a coursing match at Chapman, Kansas, until 1919, when mechanical difficulties were overcome.

The first successful race meeting employing equipment comparable to that of today was held at Emeryville, Calif., in 1919 under the direction of O. P. Smith and George Sawyer. By 1926 more than 100 tracks had been constructed in the United States, Canada, and Mexico. That year a majority of the tracks then operating formed the International Greyhound Racing Association, with Smith as its high commissioner, and licensed race meetings here and in England. Charles Munn was granted a franchise that year covering the British Isles and a track was constructed at Wembley.

Although more than 150 dog tracks have been constructed in the United States and bordering cities of Mexico since 1921, only 33 tracks are now in operation. England supports more than 400 tracks; there are 125 in Ireland, 40 in Australia, and an unknown number in Germany, Italy, France, South Africa, India, China, and South American countries. In the United States, annual attendance at Greyhound race tracks totals 9,000,000 with wagering estimated at $400,000,000. Wagering at English tracks reaches $400,000,000 annually, with attendance of 26,000,000,

Before pups are placed in starting boxes they undergo training hand-schooling races to familiarize them with the lure. Note artifi "rabbit" lure in the foreground.

Greyhounds are transported to and from races in specially-b trailers. The truck body in the foreground will carry ten dogs; e of the trailers in the background will accommodate fifteen dogs.

crowds of 100,000 attending the larger London tracks.

Standard U.S. tracks are one-quarter mile oblongs, with a racing surface 18 to 22 feet wide illuminated by electric lights placed at 18-foot intervals. Lures, attached to light, electrically-propelled carriages, run on rails circling the racing strip either on the inside or outside. Racing distances are $3/16$ mile, $1/4$ mile, Futurity (495 yards), $5/16$ mile, $3/8$ mile, $7/16$ mile and $1/2$ mile. Most popular in the United States is the $5/16$ mile distance, in England 525 yards. Dogs of fair quality race over the $5/16$ mile distance in 32 seconds, traveling at the rate of 37 miles per hour. They cover about 18 feet in a running stride.

A race consists of eight dogs, equipped with leather racing muzzles and numbered blankets. They start from enclosed barriers or "boxes" with double doors that open simultaneously. Races are electrically timed and the finish photographed, most tracks having a camera that both times and photographs the contestants. The dogs follow an electrically-paced lure, the

A Greyhound racing stable—according to its owner, the building and runways completed, but landscaping and other finishing touches yet to be done. Greyhound Racing Record photo.

lure being a single or double synthetic replica of a rabbit skin stretched over a wire frame to give it a lifelike appearance. While the single lure is most commonly used, some tracks employ a double lure used either on the outside or inside rail.

A racing program, or nightly performance, consists of ten contests. The unit of wagering is $2.00. All U.S. tracks use the mutuel form of betting and wagers are made on first, second, and third (straight, place, and show) and daily double. Some tracks also

Greyhounds course by sight, so their eyes get special daily attention from their trainers.

have quiniela betting, a form requiring the bettor to select two dogs which must finish either first or second in a race. A recent innovation to pari-mutuel betting is the perfecta which requires the bettor to select two dogs which must finish first and second in the race in order for the bettor to win. In daily-double wagering a single bet couples a contestant in each of two races and both must finish first to complete a winning transaction.

Greyhounds bred for racing are well trained and well treated. Greyhound dams whelp an average of seven pups. Loss from sickness, injury and other causes averages 25% among racing dogs. Daily upkeep of a dog in training costs $1.25 to $2.00.

Racing Greyhounds are valued according to breeding and ability. Pups of 10 months and up sell for about $500. Pups ready for racing, but untried, have been sold for as much as $1,000 with the average price in the vicinity of $600. Experienced pups have sold as high as $3,500, but the usual price range is from $500 to $1,000. The price of fully experienced track dogs ranges upward from $1,000.

Equipment of the individual racing dog includes collar, lead, wire kennel muzzle, leather racing muzzle, and blanket. Kennel equipment for a small string of racing dogs costs from $600 to $1,000, not including the truck or trailer commonly used for transportation from breeding farm to race track. These special trucks or trailers range in cost from $500 to $5,000 (not including cost of a car or truck chassis) .

Comparatively few Greyhounds are bred for exhibition and as pets in the United States, but they enjoy considerable success in bench shows, and a number of racing dogs have won important show honors.

Owners of racing Greyhounds, however, are not greatly interested in blue ribbons. A racing kennel of good class, including 20 to 30 dogs, can gross up to $75,000 annually. Average purse earnings are $15,000. The more successful racing kennel owners maintain their own breeding farms (principally in Florida, Kansas, Texas, Oklahoma, and California) and keep in reserve as many as 100 dogs so that the kennel's strength may be maintained at a high level. Ten or more of the larger kennels value their holdings at over $150,000. Annual purse earnings of all racing Greyhounds in the United States reach $3,000,000. Purses paid winning dogs vary from $18 to $50,000, and at larger tracks average from $400 to $800 per race.

The most successful track in the United States is located at Wonderland Park, Revere, Mass., a suburb

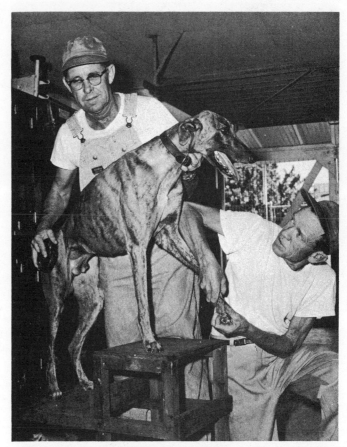

The racing Greyhound's feet must be kept in perfect condition for obvious reasons. Greyhound Racing Record photo.

Greyhounds are weighed before each race, the rules allowing only a slight variation from declared racing weights.

The racing Greyhound receives much care and attention from his trainer.

of Boston. Largest racing establishment is that maintained by the Multnomah Kennel Club at Portland, Oregon, a stadium seating 35,000. Florida has 13 dog tracks which operate during the winter with average nightly attendance of 5,000. Feature events attract 15,000 here, and a record crowd of 35,000 once filled the Multnomah Stadium.

A track's income is derived from commissions on wagers, the rate ranging from 12½% in Oregon to 17% in Massachusetts and Florida. The states share in these commissions, over $30,000,000 being paid into state treasuries. A modern racing establishment of normal size costs about $600,000 and track operators, after all costs are deducted, consider a race meeting successful if it produces a net profit of 1% on gross wagering. Nightly wagering ranges from $20,000 at the smaller tracks to more than $600,000 at the largest. Record handle for one night—$839,111 in 1964 at Wonderland Park, Revere, Mass.

A FEW FAMOUS COURSING AND RACING GREYHOUNDS

Master McGrath. In 1867 a shiftless tenant of an Irish nobleman was sleeping off the effects of a drunken spree on the banks of a stream running through the estate when he heard muffled cries coming from a sack caught on the root of a rotting stump. Staggering to the stream's edge the tenant drew from the water a half-drowned Greyhound puppy. When grown this puppy, having attracted the attention of the nobleman, was trained for coursing and became the most famous of all racing Greyhounds—Master McGrath. Today in County Waterford, Ireland, there stands a roadside shrine to Master McGrath, a splendid bit of bas-relief erected 75 years ago by admirers of the animal whose great courage and dazzling speed won the hearts of all true Irishmen. The Royal Dublin Society proudly displays an oil portrait of Master McGrath in its clubroom, from which was modeled the effigy that adorns the Irish sixpence. Master McGrath won the Waterloo Cup, in 1868, 1869, and 1871, and was defeated but once in his entire racing career, and then only because he fell through the ice of a frozen stream during a course. He died of heart failure in 1873.

King Cob. An English coursing champion of about 1835, notable because of his success as a dominant sire.

Mutton Cutlet. One of the most prolific and successful of modern sires, he produced more champions than any other sire in history. He was bred in Ireland by Brig. Gen. R. McCalmount, and later purchased and placed at public stud by T. A. Morris, Keeper of the Irish Stud Book. Perhaps 75% of modern racing Greyhounds trace their lineage to Mutton Cutlet.

Meadows. T. A. Morris selected this dog as the best available Irish sire and sent him to Charles Horne, Secretary of the National Coursing Association in

Before the race, the Greyhounds are paraded past the grandstand. Greyhound Racing Record photo.

1928, to strengthen the American stock. He is a key sire in a majority of American-bred Greyhounds.

Mission Boy. This Greyhound was the American track-racing counterpart of Master McGrath. Springing from a long line of coursing dogs bred by the Mission fathers of Southern California, Mission Boy was a cast-off that attached himself to J. J. Quill, a person of convivial nature who spent much of his time in neighborhood bars, with Mission Boy as his companion. When track racing was inaugurated at Emeryville, California, in 1919, Mission Boy became the first track champion, and many followers regard him as the greatest of all American racing Greyhounds. Under the training of Lawrence Freeman, Mission Boy won 23 of his 25 races at Tulsa, Oklahoma, in 1921, and set world records for the $\frac{1}{4}$, $\frac{5}{16}$, $\frac{3}{8}$ and $\frac{1}{2}$ mile distances. He once won two $\frac{1}{2}$-mile races the same afternoon—a feat never equaled by any other Greyhound. One of the smartest and handsomest of track dogs, Mission Boy, at the age of six, when most racing dogs have been retired, defeated Racing Ramp, an imported Irish champion then considered unbeatable, in a special match race arranged to honor the retiring veteran.

Racing Ramp. Imported by E. Loomis in 1922. Bred in Ireland by R. Ramp. Outshone all track stars of the 1922-1924 period. It became necessary to handicap this dog to give his competitors a fair chance. He was started 25 feet back of the regulation starting line.

Traffic Officer. Son of Meadows; a great coursing and track champion and famous sire. Bred by Art Wilson, Dow City and raced by Dan Oswald, Los Angeles, California, he won the first $5,000 match race at Agua Caliente, Mexico about 1930.

My Laddie. This famous son of Traffic Officer, won the $10,000 Gold Collar Sweepstakes match race in 1932 and set a $\frac{5}{16}$ mile world record. Owned by Frank Jones, Miami, Florida, he was very successful as a sire.

Just Andrew. Imported by John Pesek from Australia in 1933, at one time a most successful and prolific American sire.

Lucky Roll. Son of Just Andrew and Mustard Roll (an Irish dam sired by Mutton Cutlet). A track champion that stands as the greatest of the modern sires. His get—first and second generation—also won many important stake races. Bred by George Hackett, Anaconda, Montana.

Lucky Pilot. Grandson of Lucky Roll. Once held the leading United States records for most distances. Bred and owned by R. E. Holmes, Revere, Mass.

Flashy Sir. Another grandson of Lucky Roll, generally accepted as the greatest American racing Greyhound of all time. Flashy Sir won 62 of his 68 races, set many track records and defeated Lucky Pilot in two series of match races for purses of $10,000. He earned more than $50,000 in purses in two years of racing. Bred and owned by Ohlinger & Blair Kennel, Jewell, Kansas.

These are but a few of the outstanding racing Greyhounds. In 1948, Trev's Perfection, having distinguished himself by winning five of the most important stake events in England, Ireland, and Scotland, was brought to America to compete against Flashy Sir in a series of five two-dog match races for a total purse of $50,000. Flashy Sir having retired, Trev's Perfection was matched with less famous stars and met defeat in each of the five contests. This experience strengthened the claim of American breeders that United States Greyhounds are the finest in the world.

Following are the abbreviations used in registration of Greyhounds:

Bd. or Bdl.—Brindle.
Bl.—Blue.
Blk.—Black.
D. or Dr.—Dark, as in dark brindle.
D.F.—Dark Fawn.
F.—Fawn.
G.—Grey.
Imp.—Imported.
L.F.—Light Fawn.
L.R.—Light Red.
R.—Red.
W. or Wh.—White.

WHIPPET RACING

The Whippet is the fastest of all dogs at his weight or height. Snap-dog coursing, wherein rabbits were run down by Whippets in small or enclosed places, once enjoyed a vogue but was outlawed as unsportsmanlike.

The Whippet is known in some parts of England as the poor man's racehorse, but the sport of Whippet racing was long patronized by all classes, not only in England but in this country.

The conduct of the races required two men for each dog, one at the starting point and the other at the "over-mark," ten yards beyond the "finish line." The latter individual was called the "runner-up" and was someone known to the dog. He held a towel and stood at the "overmark" waving it and shouting encouragement to the competing dog.

Whippet tracks were generally straight stretches at least 220 yards in length and laid out over grass, race track or fair grounds. The winner was the first dog to cross the finish line.

Generally the dogs were matched for size and weight, but handicap races of 200 yards were popular, the lighter dogs being given the benefit of less yar-

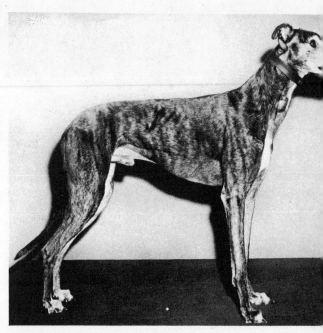

Flashy Sir, a National Champion and one of the greatest ra... Greyhounds. Taunton Greyhound Ass'n, Inc. photo.

dage. For instance, a dog weighing 22 pounds was given a 7-yard start when racing against dogs weighing 28 pounds. Twelve seconds for 200 yards was considered good time.

GLOSSARY OF GREYHOUND RACING TERMS

ALERT. Away quickly from the starting box.

BERTILLON. Record of identification. Age, breeding, owner, color, sex and all distinguishing marks such as scars, color of toenails, etc., are recorded on the Bertillon card.

BLANKET. Light satin blanket colored and numbered to correspond to post position in a race.

BLANKET FINISH. Closely bunched field at finish which, supposedly, might be covered by a normal sized blanket.

BLINKER. Leather shield attached to racing muzzle to obstruct view from either or both sides. Once commonly used, now obsolete.

BOOKING. Engagement or contract under which kennel terms of racing set up by track management.

BORE OUT. Interference by carrying another contestant wide.

BOX. Box-like barrier from which racing dog starts in a race.

BOX-BROKEN. A dog trained from a starting box.

BOX-BUSTER. (lid smasher)—Comes very fast out of the starting box, sometimes pushing through the doors before they are fully open. Earlier starting boxes were equipped with a hinged front, or lid, covering all eight starting stalls. Dogs often hit this lid before it could be raised.

BROKE DOWN. When a contestant pulls up suddenly, indicating internal or external injury.

BRUSH. Hurdles topped with broomstraw.

BUYING THE BOARD. Where a bettor purchases all combinations, in quiniela or daily double wagering.

CALCULATOR. One who calculates winning wagers in mutuel betting.

CANNONBALLING. Generally applied to dogs staging desperate rush near end of a race, where they drive through a field of contestants in a somewhat reckless manner.

CASHIER. Clerk who pays winning bets.

CERTIFICATE. A mutuel ticket, or receipt. In early days of

"They're off!" The start of a race at Wonderland, Revere, Mass. Wonderland photo.

Phototimer shows position of dogs during a race. Some races are timed photographically, a moving strip recording the time as the dogs pass the finish line.

Greyhound racing betting was illegal and tickets sold were claimed to represent stock certificates in the track's earnings, interests in earnings of the Greyhounds, rights to enter claims for dogs, seat reservations, and many other variations of mutuel wagering.

CHALK PLAYER. One who bets on favorites. In earlier days, before the advent of electric totes, odds were posted in chalk on blackboards; odds on favorites changed frequently and the board became smeared from erasures, thus "chalk" came to mean favorite.

CHART WRITER. Compiles information on running of races for past performance record.

CHECKED. Hesitation, during race. Similar to "propped."

COMBINATION. Mutuel ticket combining straight, place, and show; "a $6.00 combine."

COOLOUT SHELTER. Covered runway in which dogs may be walked after a race while "cooling out."

COURSER. Track racer that runs wide, or from side to side of the track like a coursing dog attempting to head off the hare.

CRATE. Stall or kennel in which a dog lives; crate used for shipping dogs or transporting them from kennel to track.

CURTAIN. Some lures are drawn into "escapes" at the end of a race; where there is no such hiding place a curtain is drawn across the track to conceal the lure after a race, and prevent dogs from continuing around the track. Sometimes an additional curtain behind the dogs trap them in a small space and make it easy for handlers to collect them.

DAILY DOUBLE. Form of wagering in which bettor selects entries from two races and combines them in a single wager; if both win their races he cashes in the ticket.

DUCAT. Mutuel ticket.

ENTRY. A dog nominated by its owner or trainer for a race; any starter, or any dog listed for starting in a race.

FAR TURN. The turn at the end of the backstretch; it is farthest from the finish line and from the grandstand.

FENCE-JUMPER. Bolts the course, running across infield in effort to head off lure.

FIGHTER. Dog that impedes or interferes with another contestant during a race. Not necessarily a vicious animal; one which tries to head off and impede a contestant. The English equivalent is "savager."

FIX. Where racing is not legal a "fix" or understanding with authorities must be arranged before operations are begun.

FLATBACK. Early English coursing Greyhounds had curved, rounded backs; modern racing dogs have developed broad, flat backs.

FORM. Variously applied to racing performance of a dog. Good form meaning consistency, bad form inconsistency; also the printed past performance record.

FOX-EARED. A Greyhound's ears should fold; those standing up stiffly are considered evidence of impure breeding.

GATE. Attendance at a race; number of spectators passing through the entrance gates.

GRADING. Method of classifying dogs for racing according to their past performance records.

GYP. Female Greyhound.

HAMBURGER HOUND. Low-grade racing dog.

HANDICAPPER. Classifies or grades dogs according to their racing ability; one who makes selections.

HANDLE. Total sum wagered during a night's racing program. Generally 85% of amount wagered is returned to winning bettors, 15% being retained by track management as commission and state taxes.

HEAD CHOPPED OFF. Colloquialism used when a dog is beaten to the first turn; headed off at the turn.

HIDE. Deprecatory term meaning generally, a dog of fair or ordinary class. "A pretty fair hide."

HOTBOX. Feature race; field of top grade performers.

HOTBOXER. Star performer.

HUGGED RAIL. Raced close to inner rail, or fence, to save distance.

HUSTLER. Tout; tipster. Seller of programs, newspapers, or tipsheets.

INFIELD. That part of the course enclosed by the racing strip, or track.

INSIDE RABBIT. Lure traveling on inside of racing strip.

INTERFERENCE. Same as fighting.

JINNEY PIT. Holdout, or lockout, kennels provided by race track in which to seclude dogs entered for racing. Dogs usually are held from 5:30 p.m. until post time of the race in which they are entered, which may be from 7:30 to 11:30 p.m.

JUDGE. Presiding judge at a race meeting.

JUMPER. Hurdler.

KENNEL. A complete establishment, including dogs, equipment, kennels, etc., individual stall or crate in which a dog is quartered.

KENNEL SICKNESS. Form of influenza accompanied by diarrhea and vomiting common to racing Greyhounds.

LEADOUT. Groom employed by track to lead contestants from paddock to starting barrier and return them after a race.

LEAKY ROOF. Derisive term indicating race track of low class, belonging to the "leaky-roof circuit."

LEFT (LEFT IN BOX). Where a starter is very late in emerging from starting box, or turns around and becomes wedged in the stall and must be extricated by attendants.

LOST BACK. Long back muscles torn loose from anchorage from over-exertion.

LURE. Electrically-propelled carriage carrying a stuffed rabbit attached to an arm which extends out over the track.

MEET. Scheduled race meeting.

MOUSY. Small, shy dog, usually a female.

MUTUEL PLANT. Department or enclosure reserved for acceptance, payment, and calculation of wages.

MUTUELS. Form of wagering in which odds are determined by amount of money wagered, with track management claiming a percentage of all wagers.

NUMBERS PLAYER. Race patron who bets position numbers rather than class or form.

ODDS MAN. Calculates approximate odds during progress of betting.

OFF. Start of a race; position of dogs at the start.

OPERATOR. Owner or manager of a race track.

OUTSIDE RABBIT. Lure constructed on outside of racing strip.

OVERLAND. Taking a wide swing around the track.

PADDOCK. Includes holdout kennels, scale room, inspection ring, grooms' quarters, etc.

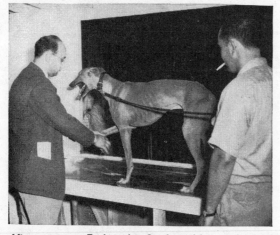

After-race care. Each racing Greyhound is examined carefully following a race. Here a veterinarian examines the dog while the trainer looks on.

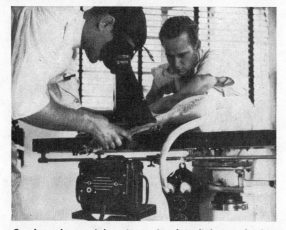

Greyhounds are taken to canine hospitals as check-ups are indicated. Here a veterinary surgeon examines a dog for possible bone injury.

PADDOCK JUDGE. Has charge of dogs before a race, makes identification inspection, supervises weighing, grooms, etc.

PARLAY. Where all the winnings from one wager are placed on the next selection in series.

PAYOFF. Sum returned or paid on winning wagers.

PHOTOFINISH. A close finish requiring use of photofinish camera to determine winner.

PHOTOGRAPHER. Operates photofinish camera.

PHOTOTIMER. Device that records time of each contestant on film as it crosses finish line.

PLACE. Second place in a race; contestant finished second.

PLANT. The whole of a racing establishment, including all structures and grounds.

POOL. Total sum of wagers bet on a race; total bets on

each of various forms, straight, place, show, daily double or quiniela.

POPPED THE BOX. Came away from starting barrier very fast.

POST. Starting position of a contestant; each position is numbered, from 1 to 8, No. 1 being stationed closest to inside of track.

POTLICKER. Racing Greyhound of poor class.

PRINT. Enlargement of picture taken by photofinish camera which is inspected by placing judges and then posted in a public place on the grounds.

PROGRAM. Schedule of races; printed list of night's races.

PROGRESSION. Form of wagering in which bettor doubles or adds to sum wagered each time he selects a loser on the theory that when a winner is selected a profit will be shown on series of bets.

PROPPED. Speed is retarded, during a race, by extending forelegs and "putting on the brakes." May be a momentary hesitation or complete stop. Interchangeable with "checked."

QUINIELA. Form of wagering originated in Mexico. Bettor selects two entries in a race, if both finish either first or second he wins.

QUITTER. Contestant that gives up the chase when outdistanced.

RACING SECRETARY. Handicapper who classifies dogs and assigns them to the various races.

RAIL RUNNER. Stays close to inner rail of track, thus saving distance.

RECKLESS. Rough, heedless. Mild form of interference.

REFUSED. Would not leave starting box, or would not run after emerging from box.

RAILBIRD. One who follows racing intensely; those who stand against rail, or fence, opposite finish line; one who comes to the track early, before racing starts.

ROUTER. Dog able to maintain fast pace for distance of $\frac{5}{16}$ mile or greater.

SCALE CLERK. Weighs dogs as they reach track from kennels and just before leaving paddock for a race.

SELLER. Dispenser of mutuel tickets.

SHAVED RAIL. Raced close to inner rail. Same as railrunner.

SHOTGUNNING. Where a racer swerves rather wide nearing a turn, then cuts sharply across bend to save ground.

SHOULDERING. Where a dog pushes or obstructs another with its body.

SHOW. Third position at finish.

SHUFFLED BACK. Contestant in race forced to withdraw from a bunched field due to crowding.

SPIKED. Injured by claws of a following contestant.

SPOOKY. Timid, shy, easily frightened by crowds or other dogs.

SPOT BETTOR. One who waits for what he considers exceptionally favorable prospects and odds.

SPRINTER. High early speed, weakening at distances of $\frac{5}{16}$ mile or greater.

STAYER. Dog with courage and stamina to race long distances.

STRAIGHT. First place; winning position at finish.

STRIP. The racing surface.

SWEATER. Dog that loses weight, through fretting, or "sweating" while in holdout kennels waiting its turn to race. Some dogs lose as much as four pounds. Also called weight-loser.

SYSTEM. Method of wagering. A system player is one who follows a routine method in wagering.

TAKE. Commission retained by track management from bets. Commissions, usually 15%, include state taxes, which range from 2½% to 7% of the take.

TAKEOFF. Recording sales of mutuel tickets on individual entries in a race so as to calculate winning wagers.

TIMBER. Hurdle.

TIMBER-TOPPER. A hurdle.

TIMER. Official in charge of timing races; timing mechanism, usually an electric clock which is automatically started when dogs leave strating box and stopped by winner's body breaking a light beam at finish line.

TIMID. Shy; a dog that refuses to race in closely bunched packs.

TOP DOG. Best dog at a track.

TOTE BOARD. Large structure in shape of a signboard on which results of races, time, odds, sums wagered, and sums returned are displayed.

TOUT. One who solicits wagers, for a commission or gratuity, generally by aid of a pretended exclusive knowledge of prospective winners.

TRAINING TRACK. Privately owned miniature or quarter-mile track equipped to train dogs for racing on standard tracks.

WHEELING. In quiniela and daily double wagering where a bettor selects a key entry and combines it with all other entries in a race.

—Sled Dog Racing—

NECESSARILY confined to sections where the winters' snows maintain over protracted periods, sled dog racing is, nevertheless, a definite part of the sporting life in the United States. In Alaska sled dog racing has long been a "national" pastime and has contributed much to the development of better dogs for work in that territory. Yet the fastest dogs, of course, are not always the most valuable for the "long haul." Sled dog racing is regarded as the Far North's greatest sport.

One of the most prominent and colorful of American organizations devoted to sled dog racing and the improvement of sled dog breeds is the New England Sled Dog Club. Organized in 1924 with Arthur T. Walden, famous Alaskan dog-driver, as its first president, the club annually stages a series of races which excite the interest of natives and winter vacationists alike. These events are held in various towns throughout New England.

Most of the teams now racing are composed of Siberian Huskies. The Alaskan Malamute is represented in a number of teams.

Sled dog racing has made important strides in the New England region, as well as parts of Canada and Alaska. Other breeds have been introduced into sled racing. R. G. Wehle of Scottsville, N.Y., several seasons ago had marked success with a team made up of pure-bred Pointers, some of them field-trial winners from his Elhew Kennels. These Pointers, when conditioned, possessed a turn of speed that enabled noteworthy success in a number of races.

There is no national organization as such that governs sled dog racing. However, the Alaskan circuit is extremely well organized and is considered the major league of sled dog racing on the North American continent. The New England Sled Dog Club, Inc., stages its World Championship Sled Dog Derby at Laconia, N.H., and the New England schedule of sled dog events is probably the most important circuit of races in this country.

Independent clubs, such as the Laurentian Sled Dog Club, have their own constitution, by-laws, and running rules. The race trial is mapped out—a race may be run in two heats—and specific race rules apply to the particular event.

The races are run over back roads as much as possible, the course distances ranging from 12 up to 30 miles, depending upon the snows and the amount of conditioning the teams have had. A good team can average 12 to 14 miles an hour when in proper condition.

The teams are driven in the "gang hitch" (a single leader), with the rest of the team in pairs. Teams usually consist of five, seven, or nine dogs. The pair

A New Hampshire racing team of Siberian Huskies.

A popular event, this being one for youngsters. Photo by Hank Babbitt.

behind the leader are called "point dogs," the next pair or pairs "swing dogs," and the last pair "wheel dogs." The entire control of the team is by voice. This makes a selection of a leader most important. Contrary to general opinion, the leader does not exercise control over the team by his physical prowess. The commands are "All right" or "Let's Go" to start, "Gee" for right and "Haw" for left. Colored flags are used to mark a course, a red flag on the right denoting a right turn, a red marker on the left meaning a

Another Siberian Husky team from New Hampshire where winters favor the sled dog sport.

left turn, and a blue marker signifying straight ahead.

Races are run on a handicap basis, with prizes for the handicap winner and the elapsed time winner. Handicap intervals are figured on past performances, the handicap committee regulating the individual starts so that each team should, theoretically, finish at the same time. The team crossing the finish line first is the handicap winner, the team making the fastest time is the elapsed time winner. Some condensed rules of sled dog racing follow:

The sled shall be capable of carrying the driver, big enough to carry a dog, and shall be equipped with a brake. For the first heat a team will consist of not less than five (5) dogs, and for each succeeding heat no team may start with less than four (4) dogs.

Starting times are drawn before the race for the first heat.

The order for the second heat shall be determined by the elapsed time for the first heat. The slowest team shall start first and the other teams will follow in order of elapsed time.

Drivers and teams are to be inspected by the veterinarian and judges before the start of the race.

Something unusual—a sled dog racing team made up of field trial Pointers! They have been raced regularly and successfully by R. G. Wehle of Scottsville, New York.

Notice that this is a sled dog team made up exclusively of Samoyeds—an Idaho team.

Dogs or teams coming to the starting line unfit or incapable of finishing the course can be disqualified.

Dogs must be carried on a sled if they become unfit after departure and drivers must return with the same dogs as registered at the start.

Whips are limited to a three-foot length. The use of a whip, other than snapping, except when dogs are unmanageable, is prohibited. Judges can disqualify drivers found guilty of using the whip otherwise. Any abuse of dogs is forbidden.

One team has the right of way over a preceding team when the rear team comes within 20 feet of the team ahead. When the right of way is asked for under these conditions, the forward team must make way for the following team or come to a full stop if requested, except when repassing or except within one-half mile of the start or finish line.

Use of internal medicament, injection or stimulant to the dogs before, after, or during a race is forbidden, except for medical purposes.

No dog shall be brought to any Club race from a kennel where there has been an indication of distemper within four weeks nor shall any person from such kennel attend a race. All dogs must be inoculated against distemper. No dog given live virus shall be brought to a race within four weeks.

Dog-drivers, owners, or any other person, are forbidden to assist a team by pacing. Outside assistance will be allowed only when teams are unmanageable.

Every driver shall wear a number visible in front and back *at all times.* This same number will be shown on the sled.

Part X

DOGS IN HARNESS AND HERDING WORK

The dog has proved himself of inestimable value as a worker for many centuries. Its abilities have been utilized in far more ways than those of any other animal, and a number of breeds have been developed especially to work in harness.

—The Dog as a Worker—

IN EVERY phase of harness-work, from pulling his small master's toy wagon to hauling heavy loads of freight over the frozen wastes of northern countries, the dog has been an apt and willing pupil. In Belgium, where the dog has been used as a draft animal in many rural districts, there is a saying that Sunday is the only day in the week when the draft dog is not happy. On this day he is not allowed to work. The leader of one of Arthur T. Walden's famous Yukon freight teams was Hootchinoo, three-quarters timber wolf. This dog never became completely domesticated, although born in an Alaskan village, and refused to associate with other dogs. Released from his harness after a freighting trip, he would disappear into the woods, to return only at feeding time, after which he disappeared again. However, the moment Walden showed him his harness, he became completely docile and immediately took his place at the head of the team.

Sheepdogs. After hunting and guarding, one of the first tasks for which the dog was trained was the herding of sheep or cattle. The sheepherder who has not one or more dogs is working under a tremendous handicap, for his dogs not only keep the herd intact, but also protect it against the raids of savage animals.

In many remote sections it was not uncommon for sheepherders to leave their dogs in sole charge of large flocks for weeks at a time, simply having left a cache of food for the dogs. On the long trips to market any one of the shepherd's dogs performed far more work, and with more efficiency, than could have been done by several men. With the dog as his only companion for long periods of time, it is only natural that the shepherd became exceedingly attached to the animal, and that the bond of understanding between

them became extremely close. The constant training which went on as a matter of course in the day's work developed the intelligence of these dogs to a high degree. The sheepherder's confidence in his own dog's ability often led to spirited contests on which large wagers were made. These resulted in annual sheepdog field trials, which are still held in some parts of Europe. The perfection with which the dogs perform is indeed extraordinary. The uncanniness with which they seem to anticipate every move of their charges cannot be appreciated without being seen. Their work has been made the subject for the programs of the Westminster Kennel Club at Madison Square Garden, New York, and for at least one motion picture, "Thunder in the Valley."

In ancient times any type of dog that could adapt itself to the work would be used as a sheepdog. Now, however, practically every country has its own breed of sheepdogs. In Germany there is the German Shepherd Dog (Alsatian in England); the Collie and the Old English Sheepdog; in Russia, the *Owtscharka,* a real giant of a dog that is a great defender against wolves and bears; in northern Italy, the *Picards,* the *Beauce* and the *Brie* in the midlands, and the Pyrenean Sheepdogs in the southwest.

In Poland there is the Polish Sheepdog, somewhat smaller than the Russian *Owtscharka.* Eight varieties of the Belgian Sheepdog are recognized: the Malinois; the short-coated; the wire-coated fawn; the wire-coated ash-grey; the wire-coated of other colors; the long-coated fawn; the long-coated of other colors; and the long-coated black (Groenendael).

The Dutch have two types of Sheepdogs, the Short-haired and the Wire-haired, but they have been largely replaced by German Shepherd Dogs.

In Egypt there is a sheepdog called the *Armant* by the natives. They are not very well known, but are used extensively in Egypt as watchdogs. The name *Armant* comes from a village in northern Egypt, the supposed place of origin for this breed. They are said to have been the result of the crossing of French dogs with native dogs of that section when Napoleon invaded Egypt.

On the Hungarian plains, the Komondor and the Kuvasz are found. The Istrian Sheepdog, from Istria, a peninsula on the Adriatic Sea, is considered of importance as it is a link between the ancient "molosses" and present-day sheepdogs.

The Shetland Sheepdog is a beautiful miniature of the Collie of Scotland. This versatile little fellow was the subject of much controversy when first attempts were made in Britain to have it officially recognized as a distinct breed. Some wanted to describe it as "a miniature show Collie" and call it the "Shetland Collie." For a time there were two types, one which resembled the original working Collie, and the other resembling the improved, or show-type, Collie. The breed had been originated in the Shetland Islands and was used for sheepherding.

Tibet is generally considered the country of the shepherd dog's origin. Perhaps nearest to the original sheepdog is the Mongolian Sheepdog.

A number of breeds in what is known as the "Working Group" were originally used as sheepdogs, although not now generally employed in that activity.

Dogs In Harness. In Belgium the dog has long been used as a draft-animal. In fact, a club existed in that country "for the improvement of the draft-dog." Professor Reul, one of the founders of the organization, said:

The dog in harness renders such precious services to the people, to small traders and to the small industrials (agriculturists included) in Belgium that never will any public authority dare to suppress its current use. A disatrous economic revolution would be the consequence. Penury and poverty would enter thousands of homes where a relative affluence is apparent now. The purpose of the Club for the improvement and the protection of the draught-dog in Belgium is to further the breeding of the dogs that are most suitable; to see that these dogs are better harnessed, better led, and that they are put to better-balanced and better-moving vehicles; to offer disinterested advise to drivers, relating to the doing away with the flaws of their vehicles; also to encourage the deserving ones by according them prizes in cash, in medals, in diplomas, and also in public congratulations.

Laws were passed and rigidly enforced protecting draft-dogs and insuring their proper treatment. Only dogs of the larger size were allowed to be used for the purpose; the type of harness, vehicle, and weight of loads were regulated. The load limit for a single dog was 300 lbs. and 400 lbs. for a pair. Draft-dogs were, and in some sections in Belgium still are, commonly used by milkmen, butchers, fruit and vegetable vendors, bakers, and coal dealers. The Belgian laws provided that no dog less than 24 inches high at the shoulder could be put to harness. Dogs could not be

harnessed with other animals, and it was unlawful to ride in a dog-drawn vehicle.

The draft-dog of Belgium resembles what is called in France a *Matin* (literally: a mastiff, cur). This dog is very strong, probably more powerful than a Great Dane, and is mostly black or fawn in color with large white patches. The Belgians contend that a good draft-dog can do as much work as a donkey and is easier to keep.

Dogs have been used for draft purposes also in Switzerland and Holland, and to some extent in other European countries. The dogs most generally used in Switzerland were the *Grosse Schweizer Sennenhunde* (large Swiss sheepdogs), formerly called "Metzgerhunde" (butcher's dogs).

The dog has been used for a wide variety of working purposes. It was often used as a beast of burden by the American Indians, and early settlers in Canada have been known to use them to pull the plow.

Sled Dogs. It is as the sledge-dog of the northern countries that the dog is best known as a worker. What the horse and the mule are to the people of the agricultural districts, the dog is to the inhabitants of the ice- and snowbound areas. For centuries the Eskimos of America and Greenland and the tribes living on the Siberian tundras have depended upon the dog as their sole means of transportation almost the whole year through. In the summer, when the snow is unfit for sleds, the dog is used as a pack animal, and most of them can carry one-third their weight for indefinite periods.

Of the use of sledge-dogs in the North, Marco Polo wrote:

You see the ice and mire are so prevalent, that over this tract, which lies for those 13 days' journey in a great valley between two mountains, no horses (as I told you) can travel, nor can any wheeled carriage either. Wherefore they make sledges, which are carriages without wheels, and made so that they can run over the ice, and also over mire and mud without sinking too deep in it. Of these sledges indeed there are many in our own country, for 'tis such that are used for carrying hay and straw when there have been heavy rains and the country is deep in mire. On such a sledge then they lay a bear-skin on

The Bouvier des Flandres is a draft dog, this one in harness in New Jersey rather than Europe. Deewal Kennels photo.

which the courier sits, and the sledge is drawn by six of those big dogs that I spoke of. The dogs have no driver, but go straight for the next post-house, drawing the sledge famously over ice and mire. The keeper of the post-house, however, also gets on a sledge drawn by dogs, and guides the party by the best and shortest way. And when they arrive at the next station, they find a new relay of dogs and sledges ready to take them on, whilst the old relay turns back; and thus they accomplish the journey across that region, always drawn by dogs.

The present development of Alaska could hardly have been accomplished without dogs, and they provide travel there today. Arthur Treadwell Walden, a native of New Hampshire, was one of the many adventurous souls who answered the call of Alaska's gold in 1896. Instead of becoming a miner, however, Walden realized the profits to be made in freighting and became one of Alaska's best-known "dog-punchers," as the freighters were called. At a later time, he handled the dogs of Admiral Byrd's expedition to the Antarctic. Walden in his book, *A Dog Puncher on the Yukon,* described freighting with dogs in Alaska as follows:

A dog-team with equipment for heavy freighting is totally different from that used for any other kind of dog driving. Six to seven large heavy dogs of the native breed made up a team. If it was possible, we liked to have two dogs that could act as leaders and thus relieve each other in breaking the trail.

We got most of our dogs from the Indians of the Malamute tribe, which lived at the mouth of the Yukon, and these dogs were called "Malamutes" for this tribe. The Eskimo dog, the Husky, and the Malamute are all the same breed. Variation in size is accounted for by the food they have, for generations, been reared upon in their various localities.

Another breed was called the "Porcupine River" or "Mackenzie" Husky. These were the best freight dogs I have ever seen, being far superior, much larger and stronger than the Eskimo. They came from a cross between the Eskimo and some large, domesticated breed. One team of these splendid dogs would weigh from 145 to 165 lbs. each in good working flesh.

The freight team was harnessed single file in the "tandem

hitch." Each dog wore a leather collar, fashioned somewhat on the order of a horse collar. Directly to this, the traces were hitched. There were no hames. The traces were held in place by a back-band and belly-band.

The traces of the lead dog ran back to those of the dog behind him and were hitched about four inches behind his hips. This method was continued until the dog immediately in front of the sled-dog was reached. His traces ran back past the sled dog and were hitched to a small whiffle-tree. The sleddog's traces were hitched to this whiffle-tree also, his traces working between the long ones. In this manner the sled-dog was free of the other dogs' traces and could jump out from between them and pull at right angles, thus helping the driver turn the sled.

A tug-rope about five feet in length came back from the whiffle-tree to the sled. The dog-driver walked straddle of this rope. The dogs were coupled up very closely when the sled was loaded and the dogs traveled at a walk. However, when the sleds were coming back unloaded and we could travel at a trot, the dogs were given about a foot and a half more freedom, which allowed fast traveling. With the sled fully loaded we made about three miles an hour. Coming back light we traveled at six or seven miles an hour.

Sleds of the so-called "Yukon-type" were used. These were about seven feet long, and sixteen inches wide on the runners. This allowed traveling on narrow trails. The clearance was about four inches. An overhang of about two inches on each side was allowed, making the loaded sled twenty inches wide. Lash-ropes extended about eighteen inches above the sides and two long lash ropes were attached to the front end.

A light canvas sheet was spread on the sled. This measured about eight by ten feet. The load was placed on this, the heaviest part about one third from the front end. The canvas was drawn up and the load wrapped as if it were a bundle. The long lash ropes from the front end were woven back and forth in the side ropes, securing the load. There were also V ropes at the front and back. The lash ropes were woven into these and the whole lashings tightened. A little water was splashed on these rope joints, which froze and held them solid.

A freight outfit generally consisted of three full-sized sleds, one behind the other. They were drawn up close and connected by cross-chains. This made each sled travel in the same track as the sled ahead. These sleds weighed from sixty to eighty pounds each, being heavily braced with iron. For the average

Alaskan Malamutes at work in the Far North. In their traditional travel in the Northlands, both dogs and masters brave ice made treacherous by repeated freezing and thawing conditions.

team they were loaded 600, 400, and 200 lbs., making a total of 1,200 lbs. for the team, or about 200 lbs. per dog.

A "gee-pole" corresponding to a wagon-pole, was lashed to the leading sled. The driver walked in front of the first sled with the tug-rope between his feet and the "gee-pole" was held in one hand. This allowed him to steer the sled, right it if it started to tip over, steady it on side hills and swing around corners in making a wide turn. It could be used to break loose a sled that was frozen in or act as a brake down small hills.

Braking a sled down steep hills was dangerous work. The dogs were unsnapped and the driver generally rode the "gee-pole,"

A typical dog cart for children, this one pulled by a St. Bernard. Such carts have all but disappeared from the American scene though they were once quite popular, especially among itinerant photographers who in many towns once went from house to house to sell photos of children posed in their carts.

using his legs as brakes. A number of fatal accidents have happened by the "gee-pole" breaking and the stub running through the driver's body. On very steep hills, the sleds were sometimes tipped over and dragged down on their sides. The use of three sleds instead of one long one made for much easier going. On long, hard hills, it allowed us to haul the sleds up separately.

I believe a dog-team can go farther on its own food than any other team in the world. It can travel with one man, loaded with 1,200 lbs. of food and equipment, over a long trip at the average rate of twenty miles a day. Barring accidents, it could travel

1,400 miles in 73 days. As the load grew lighter, the speed and mileage would increase.

We usually traveled about eight hours a day. On a long one-way trip, each sled was discarded when empty. With only one sled the going was easier and the pace faster. When we were coming back empty from freighting, we lashed one sled on top of the other.

The endurance of these dogs is a matter of wonder. On one actual trip over 900 miles, the first day's travel, loaded, probably did not exceed fifteen miles, but on the last day this team made a run of 55 miles, with both men riding an empty sled.

The price of these grand dogs depended upon circumstances. One of the best dogs I ever owned was Chinook, a large, half-bred Mackenzie River Husky. I got him in Dawson in 1898. The man who owned him had used him as a one-man's dog. He wouldn't sell him for money, but I traded him three sacks of flour, worth sixty dollars a sack, and two sacks of rolled oats, making two hundred dollars in all. He claimed that Chinook could start a heavier load than any other dog in the Yukon. He cried when he left, carrying his food.

Traveling light, the sled dogs of the North make remarkable time. What is said to be the record for dog travel was made by Albert Campbell, a Cree Indian. In answer to an appeal for medical aid and supplies, Campbell drove his dog team from Winnipeg to St. Paul, a distance of 522 miles, in 4 days and 22 hours!

Listed as the greatest load ever shifted by a dog was a 3,142-lb. sledge pulled by a husky named Charlie in a test at Anchor Point, Alaska, on Feb. 11, 1961. The dog was owned by Larry Clendenon.

The saga of Balto, leader of the team which brought the diphtheria serum into Nome, is universally known. A statue of Balto has been erected in Central Park, New York.

The duties performed by dogs on American farms are too numerous for detailed mention. They have ranged from herding cattle to hauling wood and drawing water by operating tread-mills.

In recognition of the dog's capacities for work, the American Kennel Club has a classification known as the "Working Group."

—Sheepdog Trials—

THE HIGH intelligence of the dog is nowhere better demonstrated than in the sheepdog trials of the British Empire. First introduced by Lloyd Price of Rhiwlas, Bala, North Wales, in 1873, the object of these competitions is the promotion of better training of sheepdogs. They are now held in England, Scotland, Canada, Australia, and New Zealand, and occasionally the work of these dogs is demonstrated as an added feature of one of the leading American bench shows. Sheepdog trials are held on an irregular basis elsewhere in this country.

In connection with leading livestock expositions, sheepdog exhibitions are given and the expert work of these fine dogs command the warm applause of spectators.

One has to see these exhibitions to fully appreciate

the high degree of intelligence possessed by these dogs and the many hours of patient training that have gone into their education. To the sheep-raising farmer of the hills or plains, these dogs mean as much as does improved machinery to the farmer of the lowlands.

The course for these trials is generally a large enclosure with a prominence from which the work can be viewed by the many spectators who gather for miles around to watch and to participate.

The number of sheep to be driven around the course is usually three, sometimes as many as five. Some of the stakes are for single dogs, while others are for two dogs working together. The competing handler or trainer takes his stand near the center with his dog or dogs. Each entry is alloted the same

A Working or Border Collie on an Ohio farm. Farm Journal photo.

time limit in which to complete the work. Excellence of performance coupled with the time necessary determine the awards.

The sheep are released from a cart which is some half mile distant and out of sight of the dogs. The dog must locate the sheep, the master remaining in the center of the course and directing his charge or charges by whistle or voice.

The first obstacle is termed a "false fence." This is made of two short lines of hurdles, so placed as to leave a wide gap through which the dog must drive the sheep. The animals must first be driven in a circle around a flag-post and then through a V-shaped gap made with two hurdles.

By this time the dog will have brought the sheep to within about 100 yards of his master. Here a different task confronts both master and dog. This is the "Maltese Cross," consisting of two lanes intersecting at right angles, each lane being only sufficiently wide enough to permit the sheep to pass through in single file. In this test the master may physically assist his dog. This is an exceedingly difficult task, as the sheep must go straight through in one direction. Having accomplished this, they must be driven straight through the other lane at right angles to the original course.

The final task is the "penning" of the sheep. Here again, the master may assist his dog. The pen is constructed of four hurdles with a space left open just sufficiently wide enough to admit one sheep at a time. With the time element playing such an important part, it is understandable that the anxiety of the master runs high at this point of the competition.

As in other field competitions, it is not always the best dog which wins these trials. The sheep drawn may be exceptionally wild or stubborn, and when this occurs, the ability of the dog and the patience of the master both undergo a rigid test.

Neither does it hold that the dogs which do the best work on their native heaths perform the best in these trials. Strangeness of surroundings, the presence of the crowds and the necessity of working against time all play their part. Some dogs, too, are not suited temperamentally to this work, while others seem to take to it naturally. But for competitive exhibitions of canine intelligence and training, these trials probably have no equal.

SHEEPDOG WORKING TERMS

A CUT: This refers to a number of sheep. When a shepherd selects a number from his herd to take to market this is called "a cut."

FLYING OFF: This refers to where the dog yields to the sheep instead of facing up to them.

HAULING: This term refers to the bringing in of the sheep by the dog.

RUN OUT: This term refers to the act of the dog in going after the sheep.

SET AND CRAWL: This describes the action of the dog in crouching and crawling toward the sheep to cause them to move slowly in the desired direction.

SHEDDING: This means the dividing of a lot of sheep, such as separating the lambs from their mothers.

SOFT-TEMPERED: When a dog shows little aggressiveness when pressed by wild or stubborn sheep, he is called "soft-tempered."

WEARING: This mean keeping the sheep from going in the wrong direction. Turning back is "wearing."

International Sheepdog Trials. Modern writings credit the 1873 Bals, Wales, Sheepdog Trial with being the first of its kind. From this beginning the popularity and value to the breed of competitive trials has grown steadily. The present stage of Sheepdog Trials is a series of eliminations leading to National Trials most years in England, Scotland, and Wales. Teams selected to represent these countries meet at the International Trial somewhere in the United Kingdom. Objectives of the "International" are "to stimulate public interest in the Shepherd and his calling; secure the better management of stock by improving the Shepherd's Dog. . ."

There are a number of classes of competition such as "singles" and "doubles." As "singles" suggests, the competitions are one man and one dog against the field, and "doubles" are one and two dogs working a single flock or two separated flocks merged into one on the course.

The course is an open area of at least 400 yards by 200 yards. The lay of the land affects the running of the course, but not so much its layout. The scale of points for each judge is commonly:

	Points
Gathering (outrun 5—lifting 5—bringing 10)	20
Driving (away from man to hurdles and back)	10
Shedding (separating marked sheep from the rest)	5
Penning	5
Single sheep (one marked sheep held off from rest)	5
Style	5

Time limit—15 minutes

NORTH AMERICAN
SHEEP DOG SOCIETY

The International Sheep Dog Society, founded in 1906, had from its beginning James A. Reid, Airdrie, Scotland, as secretary. His long service as secretary is largely responsible for pedigree record of many excellent bloodlines of Working Border Collies. A registered and pedigreed sheepdog has not only an abstract of his ancestry, but automatically high standing among sheepdog breeders the world over.

Imported or American-bred dogs of accepted breeding were regularly registered in the International Sheep Dog Society.

In 1940, partly as a war measure, to protect existing pedigrees, owners and breeders of the Working Border Collies formed the North American Sheep Dog Society which has maintained the closest possible relations with the older society. The secretary at its beginning was Don S. Bell, Wooster, Ohio. The North American Sheep Dog Society maintains its own breeding records. A young dog for purposes of pedigree record may be registered with the Society if its parents have "Certificates of Proven Working Ability." This dog's progeny are eligible for registration only when it in turn has on file its own Certificate of Proven Working Ability.

A sheepherding demonstration by two Border Collies.

The Society's present Secretary is Mr. Bernard L. Minton of McLeansboro, Illinois.

North American Sheep Dog Society Trials. From the time of the first trial in 1880 in Philadelphia until the formation of the North American Sheep Dog Society there were occasional sheepdog trials in the United States. There have been annual trials since, in conformity with Article V of the constitution of the Society.

Trials. Sec. 1. This Society shall encourage, plan, supervise and conduct competitive trials to promote the breeding and improve the training of Working Collie dogs of outstanding merit and ability.

There are not many sheepdog trials held in this country even now, but although the distances from trial course to trial course are great, the interest is increasing and the competition is keen.

The gather on present-day North American courses is at least 150 yards from the holding ring. The ring and gates make a triangle with each side 75 yards long. Scoring is as follows:

Gathering	20 points
Holding	5 points
Driving	15 points
Penning	15 points

HIRED SHEPHERDS' INTERNATIONAL CHAMPIONSHIP

(Supreme Championship Course)

The most difficult stake is known as the Hired Shepherds' International Championship. The rules follow:

(1) GATHERING: Distance about 800 yards for one lot of 10 sheep (unseen by dog) which must be brought through gate obstacle in the center of the field where dog will be redirected for another lot of 10 sheep (unseen by dog) which shall also be brought through gate and united with the first lot. Both the dog and the first lot of sheep must be past the gate before the dog is redirected for the second lot. First run to be on left side and second run on right side. Failure to negotiate the gate with either lot will involve a loss of points in the judges' discretion *according to circumstances*, and no re-try is permitted.

(2) DRIVING AWAY: Distance about 400 yards from where shepherd stands in triangular direction through two gate obstacles back to shepherd. Failure to negotiate the gates will in-

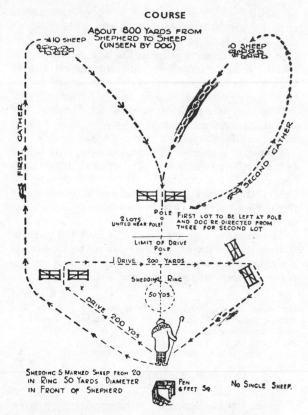

COURSE

ABOUT 800 YARDS FROM SHEPHERD TO SHEEP (UNSEEN BY DOG)

Supreme Championship Course, International Sheep Dog Society.

volve a loss of points in judges' discretion, *according to circumstances*, and no re-try is permitted at either gate. Drive, as such, ends when sheep are through or past second gate.

(3) SHEDDING: 20 sheep to be run off between shepherd and dog and dog brought in to stop *and turn back* five marked sheep. Ring 50 yards diameter. Maneuvering for "cuts" is forbidden. Until the five marked sheep are shed off, penning will not be permitted.

(4) PENNING: Five marked sheep shed off to be penned. Pen 6 feet square with gate. On completion of Shedding, competitors must proceed to pen leaving dog to bring sheep to pen. Competitors are forbidden to assist the dog to drive sheep to pen. Competitors to stand at gate end holding robe (6 feet) while dog works sheep into pen. A competitor who leaves the gate end before being ordered to do so by the judges, through the Course Director, will lose points in the judges' discretion.

SCALE OF POINTS: Gathering 30 (two runs, 15 each); Driving 10; Shedding 10; Penning 5; Style 5. Total 60. Aggregate 180.

TIME LIMIT: 30 minutes, which shall be extended in those cases in which the Competitor has completed the Shedding before the expiration of the 30 minutes. In these cases the Competitor shall be allowed such reasonable time as the judges think fit to pen, but the extra time taken in so doing beyond the 30 minutes shall be a factor in their discretion in placing the dogs.

BRACE CHAMPIONSHIP ("DOUBLES")

(1) GATHERING: (10 sheep). Sheep to be placed 500 yards from Shepherd. Both dogs to start at the same time, one going on the left hand and the other on the right hand. Crossing at head permitted. Straight fetch through gate 200 yards from shepherd. Failure to negotiate gate to be penalized by a loss of points in the judges' discretion. No re-try. Each dog to keep

Owned, trained and handled by Carl H. Bradford, Wooster, Ohio, these three Border Collies helped handle his sheep.

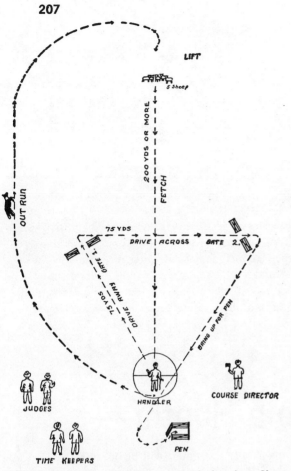

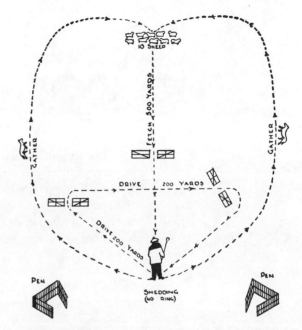

Brace Championship ("Doubles") Course, International Sheep Dog Society.

Official Sheep Dog Trial Course, North American Sheep Dog Society.

its own side till fetch finished. Crossing in fetch to be penalized in judges' discretion.

(2) DRIVING: 10 sheep with two dogs, 400 yds. in triangular direction through two gate obstacles back to shepherd. Failure

to negotiate the gates will be penalized by a loss of points in the judges' discretion. No re-try at either gate. Each dog to keep its own side till drive finished at second gate. Crossing to be penalized in judges' discretion.

(3) SHEDDING: Lot of 10 to be divided into two lots of 5 each.

(4) PENNING: One lot to be penned with either dog in V shaped pen with four feet entrance and no gate on the left. Dog to be left in charge while other lot penned by other dog in similar pen is 50 yards apart on the right.

SCALE OF POINTS: Gathering (running out, lifting and bringing) 20; Driving 10; Shedding 5; Penning (2 lots) 10; Style 5. Total 50. Aggregate 150.

TIME LIMIT: 25 minutes. No *extension*.

Part XI

THE DOG IN HUNTING

The first dogs, of course, were hunters. They were beasts of prey through necessity. And in practically all dogs of today the hunting instinct exists, to some small degree at least. To note this, one has only to watch a litter of puppies, or an individual, stalk butterflies or grasshoppers. While the bond between man and his hunting dog runs far back into history, the breeds emerging as best suited to hunting in the U.S. include not only those recognized by the various kennel clubs, but several hound strains such as the Redbone, the Bluetick, etc. For years these have bred true to type. For hunting in certain regions of America where terrain and trailing problems pose special requirements, they are unsurpassed.

——The Dog as a Hunter——

IN ALL probability, the first use made of the dog was as a hunting companion to his master. Year in and year out the dog has continued to remain as man's hunting aide, and even now a larger number are kept for that purpose than any other.

DOGS—HUNTERS OVER THE CENTURIES

Originally every dog was a hunter through necessity. Even now the hunting instinct is strong in almost every breed of dogs, although some of them have never been seriously used for hunting. In early civilizations, dogs were divided into two classes; those which hunted by scent, and those which hunted by sight. In the plains and desert sections of northern Africa and southwestern Asia, where the air was hot and dry, scenting conditions were found unfavorable but the visibility was good, and dogs which hunted by sight came to be favored. However, there were also areas in these sections where the vegetation was so thick that hunting by sight was hardly practical, and therefore it was only natural that the Assyrians and Egyptians developed breeds for both types of hunting.

The game, too, was quite varied in these areas, ranging from small animals, such as rabbits and birds, to the larger species, including lion. Large, strong, and heavy dogs were needed in lion hunting, and a very powerful dog of the mastiff type was produced for this purpose in both Assyria and Egypt. Lighter dogs of the hound type were probably used for the larger-hoofed game, while greyhound types were needed for

the gazelle and other swift plains animals. Typical of the latter type are the Afghan Hound and the Saluki, the latter being one of the oldest breeds in existence.

For a long period wild game was the principal source of food, and the use of dogs in hunting for sport was necessarily of secondary importance. Later, when sheep-herding and cattle-raising had become common in many sections, the practice of chasing wild game with dogs became more of a sport, yet one in which practically everyone engaged. In fact, not to engage in hunting was considered a mark of weakness.

In every era, hunting has been the favorite sport of mankind, and the dog has played an important part in every branch of that sport. Ancient rulers and kings of more modern times have almost all been devotees of the chase, some of them engaging in it almost to the point of fanaticism. Royal hunts were almost always accompanied by much show of pomp and pageantry, and many rulers maintained huge kennels of hunting dogs of various types.

The hunting expeditions of the Great Khan, referred to by Marco Polo, were perhaps those on the grandest scale. Yule's translation says:

The Emperor hath two Barons who are own brothers, one called Baian and the other Mingan; and these two are styled Chinuchi, which is as much to say "The Keepers of the Mastiff Dogs." Each of these brothers hath 10,000 men under his orders; each body of 10,000 being dressed alike, the one in red and the other in blue, and whenever they accompany the Lord to the chase, they wear this livery, in order to be recognized. Out of each body of 10,000 there are 2,000 men who are in charge of one or more mastiffs, so that the whole number of these is great. And when the Prince goes a-hunting, one of these Barons, with

Bas relief from the tombs at Thebe, about 1450 B.C.

his 10,000 men and something like 5,000 dogs, goes toward the right, whilst the other goes to the left of the party in like manner. They move along all abreast of one another, so that the whole line extends over a full day's journey, and no animal can escape them. Truly it is a glorious sight to see the working of the dogs and the huntsmen on such an occasion. And as the Lord rides a-fowling across the plains, you will see these big hounds come tearing up, one pack after a bear, another pack after a stag, or some other beast, as it may hap, and running the game now on this side and now on that, so it is really a most delightful sport and spectacle.

Xenophon, the Greek historian, led the life of a farmer in his later years. His *Hunting With Dogs* is one of the most unusual works in Greek literature, and his description of *The Perfect Dog* could as well have been written today, although its actual date is about 400 B.C.

Theodore Gaza, born at Thessalonica about A.D. 1400, was an eminent Greek scholar, who after the Turks had captured Thessalonica in 1429 migrated to Italy and taught Greek there. He presented a dog to Mohammed II and sent with it a lengthy and interesting letter explaining the dog's many virtues. The portion which pertains to the dog as a hunter follows:

And in the first place, the hunting of quadrupeds, which is generally agreed to be a pursuit of value and one which increases the amenities of life, retains the name which it originally derived from the dog, and is literally "dog-leading." And the gods followed this pursuit, and the men of the Heroic Age; and Greeks no less than barbarians both now, and in ancient times, and in all countries. And the patroness of the sport was Artemis, the sister of Apollo, the most honourable of the goddesses in heaven. Of heroes one might add Cheiron and Cephalus, and Asclepius, and Melanus, and indeed so many that it would be tedious to enumerate them. And does not Homer introduce the wisest of the Greeks hunting with Autolycus, and wounded in the thigh by a boar? His words are: "And him a boar wounded with his tusk when he had gone a-hunting to Parnassus with the sons of Autolycus."

Sparta, the most warlike city of antiquity, honoured this pursuit above all others; and they actually passed a law according to which a man who appeared at a banquet following the festival of Artemis without having hunted with the hounds was deemed to be guilty of an illegality and was punished. In the case of a young man the punishment was a pitcher of water poured over the head, and in the case of older men poured over the fingers of his hand: which so far as the pain endured goes, would seem to the reader slight enough; but was severe so far as the social disgrace it involved is concerned.

The attitude of the Macedonians towards the chase was similar, for the man who had wounded a boar without the use of nets was allowed as a concession to recline at dinner instead of being seated, which was considered a great honour amongst the

people. The same thing holds good of the Persians, amongst whom the king was as much devoted to the chase as he was to military pursuits, leading out the young men on hunting expeditions, and taking care that they actually performed their share of the task. And it was not without reason that they acted in this way, for hunting is the very best preparatory school for soldiers: this is so because it gets a man into the habit of rising early and going to bed late, and working during the night, and of enduring heat and cold and hunger and thirst. Yes, and more important still, it teaches him to run over smooth and level ground not more readily than through wild precipitous places, and to shoot and to wound, and not retreat if hit, and to put up with every kind of pain and danger and inconvenience; and the benefit one derives from such a life towards soldiering is incredible. And if you want to test by actual observation what good hunting is in war, just compare a hunting man and one who has had no experience of hunting and has never had anything to do with it, and you will at once see what an immense advantage the former has in the military field.

Or one might cite the authority of Plato. In his *Laws* he advises young men to go in for this pursuit, if they wish to become properly acquainted with their own country; but perhaps it would be more advisable to quote a passage from the text itself. He says: "I should imagine that one of the worthiest aims of public education would be to impart to every man an accurate knowledge of his own country. No doubt hunting either with dogs or in other ways is pleasant to any man and profitable to him also; but the scientific knowledge which he obtains is the real reason why a young man should pay attention to it." So much for the teaching of Plato. But by what voluntary assistance do we engage in hunting? Is it not clear that we do this by means of dogs? For, led out to the chase, they spot the animals and hunt them, or catching the trail they conduct us by means of this after the animals running themselves, while we run after as fast as we can; and they fight along with and in defence of us; and it often happens that before the huntsmen have followed up the track the hounds have torn the prey to pieces.

Enough for the help afforded us by dogs in hunting.

And without any great trouble it would be possible to prove point by point that if hunting had not been practised, the world

Babylonian hunting dogs.

Irish Setters staunch on point.

had been full of wild animals dealing destruction to mankind and besieging them in the cloistered safety of cities; from all such horrors, then, it is the help of dogs and hunting with dogs that has delivered us.

Dogs In English Hunting. The earlier English kings were especially keen on hunting with dogs, and were fully aware of the necessity for game conservation—for themselves. One of the first forest laws decreed that any dogs kept within ten miles of the King's forests must have their knees cut so that they would not be capable of chasing game. One law was to the effect that, "if a greedie, ravening dog doe bite a wild beast in the forest then the owner shall yeeld recompense for the same, according to the price of a free-man, which is twelve times a hundred shilling. But if the doe bite a royal beast, then he shall be guilty of the greatest offense."

Exceptions were made in the cases of small dogs, "little dogges (al which dogges are to sit in one's lap)," because in them "there is no daunger." To qualify for this exemption these "little dogges" had to be small enough to pass through a "dog gauge." Such a gauge, to which a swivel was attached by which it could be hung from a girdle, was in the form of an oval ring, seven by five inches in diameter.

A number of laws were passed providing for the maiming of dogs which might invade the King's property. One of these set forth the manner as follows: "Three claws of the forefoot shall be cut off by the skin, by setting one of his forefeet upon a piece of wood eight inches thick and one foot square, and with a mallet, setting a chisel two inches broad upon the three claws of his forefoot, and at one blow cutting them clean off."

Fines for the possession of unlawed dogs were levied and the keeping of dogs during certain seasons of the year by common people was prohibited. One of these laws, passed in 1603, during the reign of James I, reads as follows:

I. An Acte for the better execution of the intent and meaninge of former statutes "for the preservation of game" and "tracinge Hares in the Snowe", "by tracinge and coursinge them with Dogges in the Snowe" imprisonment for 3 months, or to pay 20/-per head.

II. And for the better preservation of Deare, Hare and other Games aforesaide, Bee it further enacted by the authority aforesaide, that all and everie person and psons which from and after the said first day of Auguste shall have or keep any Greyhound for coursing of Deare of Hare, or setting Dogges or Nette or Nettes, to take Pheasants or Partridges (except such per-

son or persons which shall be seized in their owne Right, or in the Right of their Wives, of Landes, Tenements or Hereditaments of the cleare yearlie value of Tenne pounds by the yeare or more above all charges and Reprises, of some Estate of Inheritance, or of Landes, Tenements or Hereditaments in his owne Right or in the Right of his wife, for tearme of life or lives; of the yearlie value of thirtie poundes, over and above all Charges and Reprises, or be posseste of Goods or Chattels to the full value of two hundred pounds to his owne use, or be son or sonnes of any knight, or of any Baron of Parliament, or of some pson of high Degree, or the Sonne or Heir Apparent of any Esquire) and beinge thereof convicted as aforesaid, shall be by the saide Justices of Peace committed and imprisoned in manner and forme, as in and by this p'sent Acte before is expressed specified and declared excepte such person or persons so offendinge, and thereof convicted as aforesaid, doe foorthwith pay or cause to be paide to the Churchwardens of the saide Parishe where the saide offence shal be committed, or the partie apprehended, to the use of the Poore of the saide Parishe the sume of fortie shillings of good and lawful money of England.

VI. And be it further enacted that ev'y Constable and Head borough in ev'y County, Citie, Towne, Corporation and other Place where they shall be sworne officers, shall and may by v'tue of this p'sent Acte, (bringing with them to that Purpose a lawfull warrant under the Hands of two Justices of Peace of the Counties Citie Libties or Towne Corporate) have full Power and Authoritie to enter into and search the House or Houses of any pson or psons (other than such as by this p'sent Act are allowed to take Pheasants and Partridges with Netts as aforesaid) being suspected to have any Setting Dogges or Netts for the taking of Pheasants and Partridges, and wheresoever they shall fvnd any such Setting Dogg or Netts, the same to take cary away and detaine, kill destroy and cut in Pieces as things phibited by this Act, and forefeit to such of the said Officers as shall finde out and take the same as aforesvd.

The British people have long been leaders in field sports. They were the first to develop "settinge dogges" and wing shooting. They were the first really to bring the retrievers to the forefront among gundogs. And it is to them that we are indebted for the development of practically every "specialist" dog in the sporting world.

However, sportsmen of all countries have since taken up hunting with dogs as a favorite pastime. Even during wars, solders have found the time to engage in this sport. In our own War Between the States, soldiers of the opposing armies occasionally declared "unofficial truces" to join each other in fox hunting between the lines.

Hunting Dogs Valuable In Present-Day Conservation. In World War I, several hound packs were maintained by British troops and "winked at" by commanding officers, despite regulations against such practices. American GI's used native dogs in frequent hunting forays behind the lines in foreign countries during World War II, and many of these fine sporting dogs were brought to this country by returning troops.

The erratic supply of upland game in the United States has not brought about a decrease in the numbers of gundogs. In fact, despite shortened hunting seasons and lower bag limits in some locales, the numbers of pure-bred hunting dogs have steadily increased in this country.

Wildlife conservationists have long urged the use of dogs in hunting. Many have gone so far as to declare the use of a retrieving dog the greatest individual contribution a hunter can make to the cause of game restoration. These dogs are particularly valuable in game salvage, as they will find and retrieve dead and crippled game which would otherwise have been lost to the gunner's game-bag and wasted. Millions of heads of game are annually saved by these dogs.

Not far from heavily populated areas where game is particularly scarce, shooting preserves more and **more** resort to artificial propagation of pheasants

and quail, releasing these birds in their favorite covers. In more instances than is generally realized, these birds are hunted not so much for the shooting pleasure, but for the thrill that comes to the hunter in watching the work of his pointing and retrieving dogs.

As long as wildlife populations will allow hunting, the sporting dog will be found in front or at the side of his master, helping him derive the fullest measure of enjoyment from his favorite sport.

——The Sport of Hunting——

FOR THE hunting of every species of North American game, except the larger hoofed animals of mountainous habitat where the use of dogs is neither practical nor to be desired, at least one breed of dogs is to be found which might well be termed "specialist." This fact is probably applicable to every country in the world where the sport of hunting is enjoyed.

This "specialization" is brought about by training, development of certain physical characteristics and the natural inclinations of the individual breeds or, more likely, through a combination of these factors.

For instance, trail hounds are more practical in the hunting of ground game such as furred animals; the pointing breeds and spaniels give far better results in hunting upland game birds; the retrievers are, by physical make-up and natural inclination, more efficient than any other breeds in waterfowl hunting.

THE DOG AS AN ASSET TO THE HUNTER

The dog is an asset to the hunter on practically every species of game, with the exception of a few of the larger types such as moose and elk in this country and some of the jungle and plain species of tropical climes. Naturally on species where the bag depends upon the skill of the hunter in stalking the use of the dog is not desired, nor would it be practical. The famous sportsman, Paul Rainey, once took a pack of American Foxhounds trained in bear hunting and fighting dogs of several breeds to Africa and used them with great success in hunting lion and other beasts of prey. The dogs were under the charge of the famous trainer, Er M. Shelley of Columbus, Mississippi, who originated unique training methods in teaching his dogs to leave hoofed game alone. His interesting book, *Hunting Big Game With Dogs In Africa* (1924), with the recording of his five years' experience in that country, along with the first motion pictures of that kind ever taken, was proof that dogs can be of great assistance in bringing the so-called "King of Beasts" to bay.

In Continental Europe hunting dogs of many types and for many purposes are to be found. There are roughhaired and smooth-coated pointers in Germany, as well as various hounds. The Griffons of France,

Holland, and Belgium are serviceable gundogs of great scenting powers.

The Wolfhounds of Russia derive their name from the sport in which they were first used. Generally they were employed as wolf-coursing dogs, the wolf having first been started by trail hounds or beaters. It was customary to slip three hounds after the wolf, once he was sighted.

Dogs of the Greyhound type were used centuries ago as coursing dogs in Arabia, Persia, and Egypt, and are still used for that purpose. The game is generally hare or antelope. In India, where feathered game is generally plentiful, the gundogs of the British Isles are very popular and in China and Japan, pointers, setters, and spaniels provide sport on pheasants.

In the South American countries there are several well-known breeds of native hounds, and crosses with the American and English Foxhounds have been made. Pointers and setters are also used. Australia and New Zealand offer some excellent upland game bird hunting and small furred game, on which hounds are used.

Beagles and Basset Hounds. In the United States, the most popular use of the dog in sport is, of course, in hunting. And in the various "divisions" of the gundog sports, rabbit-hunting ranks first in wide appeal. Probably the least publicized of American gunning

Labrador Retriever, Dhu, fetches downed pheasant to owner, Michael Duffy. Photo by David M. Duffey.

English Springer, Flirt, retrieves to owner, David Duffey, as Labrador Retriever looks on. Photo by David M. Duffey.

sports, the pursuit of the cottontail rabbit or the snowshoe rabbit (varying hare) attracts the greatest number of hunters in practically every state of the Union. The main reason for this is the wide distribution and great prevalence of the cottontail rabbit. Almost every American hunter who took up the sport of hunting at an early age received his introduction to gunning from the bobbing "powder-puff" of Br'er Rabbit.

Almost any sort of dog that will hunt through the coverts and rout game is used in rabbit hunting. Many pensioned-off foxhounds wind up their careers driving the so-called lowly rabbit to the guns of their masters' sons. On the farms throughout the country mongrel dogs are in general use and many pure-bred hounds of the largest strains are kept for this purpose. The "specialists" in this sport, however, are the Beagle and Basset hounds. Both breeds are small dogs and slow in speed when compared with larger hound breeds. Consequently, they are more proficient for this sport as they keep the rabbit on the move without driving him to earth or out of his regular range.

The Beagle is by far the more popular of the two breeds, in fact, this breed has earned a position as the second most popular breed in the U.S.A. He is faster and more energetic than his heavier-bodied cousin, although he does not possess a better "nose" nor is his voice as melodious. The Beagle, however, is well adapted to any type of American terrain and each year finds him increasing in popularity. More than 200 Beagle field trials are held annually in the United States. The Basset, unquestionably a good gundog on rabbits, has found comparatively small favor with the American gunner.

Dogs For Bird Hunting. The American game-bird hunter has a wide choice of canine "specialists" in his favorite shooting sport, whether his choice be pointing breed, retriever or spaniel. The pointing breeds far outnumber the others in this country.

The English Setter was the first gundog to be used in this country. The breed still holds high rank in popularity. Close on the English Setter's heels, and now perhaps outnumbering it, was the Pointer, which is not only in high favor as a shooting dog, but is garnering the major portion of bird dog field trial laurels. The Irish Setter was once a very popular gundog in this country and still makes an efficient gun asset on upland game birds. Though making it a beautiful dog to look at, the dark mahogany-colored coat of the Irish Setter renders it somewhat difficult to see in heavy color and many prefer the breeds of brighter markings. This applies also to the Gordon Setter. Once used extensively in the grouse and woodcock covers of the eastern United States, this breed is now seldom even afield, but is generally found somewhere competing for bench show honors.

The German Short-hair Pointer is a comparative newcomer to American game fields. Heavier-built, perhaps a little slower than the Pointer and English Setter, this dog makes an excellent hunting companion for the gunner who wants a close worker.

The Brittany Spaniel is another recent importation which has been accepted with considerable approval by American sportsmen. The only pointing spaniel, the Brittany possesses enough speed for the average gunner and has several characteristics distinctly in his favor. While their field competitions have been mainly confined to activities within the breed itself, a number of them have either won places or made excellent showings against the longer-legged pointers and setters.

The Weimaraner, a pointing dog of German origin, is highly touted by its exponents as a topnotch gundog on any species of upland game. It has also demonstrated exceptional intelligence by its performance in obedience and field trials.

Many upland gunners, particularly those who hunt the ring-necked pheasant, are swinging to the English Springer Spaniel. In fact, this versatile dog is considered by many authorities as the nearest approach to the "all-around" dog on American upland game and waterfowl. Large and strong enough to negotiate almost any cover to be found here, the Springer is also a strong swimmer and readily takes to the work of retrieving wildfowl from water. He is used extensively on grouse and woodcock, and he also makes a fine rabbit dog.

The Cocker Spaniel continues to be a popular

Springer Spaniel retrieves downed pheasant, still alive. Photo David M. Duffey.

Brace of Brittany Spaniels on point. Photo by David M. Duffey.

pure-bred dog, sporting or otherwise, although he could by no means be classed as America's leading hunting dog. Neither could he correctly be called America's "forgotten gundog," for many are gunned over each season. The fact remains, however, that this energetic little dog is overlooked by many who would take him into their kennels immediately if they only realized his capacities for field work. For many years the Cocker was used almost exclusively for the purpose for which he was developed . . . hunting. The lovable characteristics which equip him so ideally as a pet and companion attracted wide attention, and he became a favorite of the household and the show ring. Many breeders became more interested in bench shows than in the more active field sports, and the Cocker's field qualities suffered as a consequence. Nevertheless, his keen hunting instinct still remains, and a number of prominent proponents of the breed continue to promote the smaller Cocker in field trial competitions. While much of the cover to be encountered today is a bit too heavy for easy negotiation by the Cocker, this game little fellow can do a good job for the gunner in search of pheasants, grouse or woodcock. He also makes a good rabbit dog and is an excellent all-around retriever, performing well in water despite his small size.

The Clumber, Sussex, Welsh Springer, and Field Spaniels have never caught the fancy of American sportsmen to any appreciable degree, although each breed has its own champions in England.

Boykin Spaniel. Just what his ancestry is no one knows definitely, but the Boykin Spaniel has many admirers among the hunting gentry of the "low country" of the southeastern United States, and his fame is gradually spreading to other parts.

For a long time, gunners of South Carolina, Georgia, and north Florida have hunted wild turkey with dogs. No particular breed was used and generally a

pointer or setter was trained to flush the flock. Sometimes a small terrier was employed to scatter and "tree" these wary birds.

But seasoned turkey hunters have long been looking for a dog rugged and fast enough to flush the birds on the ground without scattering them too far. They also wanted a dog that was adept at finding and retrieving game. The story of the Boykin Spaniel goes to the effect that some 40 years ago a small brown puppy of undetermined breeding wandered into a church in Spartanburg, South Carolina. A. L. White, a member of the congregation, placed the puppy outside the church, and when the services were over, found the forlorn little fellow waiting there. The puppy was taken to the White home and grew into an active little dog that was an enthusiastic retriever. Mr. White sent the dog to his hunting partner, one Whit Boykin, once a noted sportsman of the Camden area. Undoubtedly part Cocker Spaniel, the little brown dog became a favorite of the Boykin family and developed into an exceptional retriever, with a flair for hunting wild turkeys. A brown spaniel bitch was found as a mate, and from that union sprang the foundation stock of what became locally known as the Boykin Spaniel.

In appearance these dogs are very much like small American Water Spaniels, weighing about 30 to 38 pounds and standing 15 to 17 inches high. Their tails are generally docked. Their coats are wavy or curly and deep mahogany or liver in color. The eyes are yellow to amber. It is said that a Chesapeake Bay Retriever was used as a cross to bolster the stock which was quite inbred during the first 20 years, but all trace of the Chesapeake seems to have disappeared and they are again breeding true to type now. Occasionally a white spot is seen on the chest.

The Boykin Spaniel is an enthusiastic water dog and is a strong swimmer. His small size makes him easy to transport in a duck boat, yet he is large and

There is nothing quite like a dog that retrieves with enthusiasm. Here such a dog—an English Springer Spaniel—hits the water on his way to retrieve. Photo by David M. Duffey.

strong enough to negotiate any type of southern waters.

They are especially quick in action and make excellent duck and dove retrievers. Very little training is necessary as most of them seem to be imbued with an intense desire to retrieve.

Retrievers. The shortages of waterfowl and the necessity for the conservation of these dwindling resources has had much to do with the increasing popularity of the retriever breeds in America. The slogan, "Get that cripple and save game!" is developing into a rallying-cry among sportsmen, and its importance is stressed by many sportsmen's organizations, thus emphasizing the value of the retrieving breeds.

The Chesapeake Bay Retriever is one of the few purely American-developed breeds, and for many years held first rank in numbers of retrievers in this country. However, the Labrador's popularity has been on the increase, and its spectacular performances in field trials has added materially to the interest in this breed.

The Golden Retriever is another breed that has made much progress in attracting the attention of American wildfowlers. The Irish Water Spaniel has long been used in this country to good effect, but the Curly-coated and Flat-coated Retrievers have enjoyed but small vogue. Both, however, are quite popular in England.

Another purely American product, long in the making, is the American Water Spaniel, the smallest of the retriever breeds. A strong, fearless swimmer, this little dog is capable of doing a good retrieving job even in rough water, and does not take up so much room in a duck boat or blind as his larger colleagues.

The Poodle originally was a sporting dog and an excellent retriever. Some few are still used for that purpose in this country, but the breed is now classified in the non-sporting group.

While the retriever breeds were primarily developed for work in water, many are used as non-slip

This Miniature Schnauzer owned by David Duffey became a good squirrel dog. Photo by David M. Duffey.

retrievers on upland game, and many crippled birds are saved each season through their employment. Many, too are used in actual field hunting in the manner of spaniels. Years ago, Charles Lawrence inaugurated a movement to hold field trials for retrievers, along the same lines as those under which spaniel trials are conducted. The original trial was fairly successful but the idea did not strike popular fancy.

Foxhounds and Fox Hunting. America's oldest sporting dog is the Foxhound. This hound, of which there are many strains in this country, is perhaps more versatile than any hunting dog because he can be used with great success on any type of ground game. His specialty, however, is the fox—the wide-ranging red or the circling grey, both of which have wide distribution in this country.

In color and tradition, fox hunting in the formal English manner is one of America's most glamorous sports. Despite the fact that much of the fine hunting country of the East and South has been taken over by intensive farming interests or utilized by industry, the sport maintains in many sections today, exemplifying the affinity between horse, hound, and hunter. Huge sums are spent annually in its furtherance, for enjoyment of this type of fox hunting is no inexpensive matter. Grounds maintenance is a considerable item

A yellow Labrador Retriever brings in a Canada goose. Sentinel photo.

with every hunt club. Fences must be gapped and paneled, and proper game habitat provided. Stables of hunting horses (hunters) represent large investments, and the hounds themselves are the least expensive of the accouterments of the chase.

The sport of "riding to hounds" has such a keen appeal to some sportsmen and sportswomen that in some sections where live foxes would have little chance for survival "drag hunts" are held regularly, where the scent is laid by artificial means. Hunt "breakfasts" and hunt balls are gala social events in the "season" of every organized hunt club.

Fox Hunting and Hunt Clubs. That the sport of fox hunting continues to flourish and grow is indicated in the 1969-1970 listing of hunt clubs of the United States and Canada recognized or registered by the Masters of Foxhounds Association of America. The listing follows:

AIKEN HOUNDS   Aiken Preparatory School, Aiken, South Carolina 29201

ARAPAHOE HUNT   Route 1, Box 62, Littleton, Colorado 80120

BATTLE CREEK HUNT   Route 1, 43rd Street, Augusta, Michigan 49012

BEAUFORT HUNT   c/o Dr. Rife Gingrich, R.D. 1, Middletown, Pennsylvania 17057

BEDFORD COUNTY HUNT   P.O. Box 123, Bedford, Virginia 24523

BELLE MEADE HUNT   P.O. Box 71, Thomson, Georgia 30824

BLUE RIDGE HUNT   Boyce, Clarke County, Virginia 22620

BRADBURY FOX HOUNDS   Route 3, Rehoboth, Massachusetts 02769

BRANCHWATER HUNT   3201 North Woodridge Road, Birmingham, Alabama 35223

BRANDYWINE HOUNDS   R.D. 5 West Chester, Pennsylvania 19380

BRIDLESPUR HUNT   Defiance, St. Charles County, Missouri 63341

BULL RUN HUNT   P.O. Box 390, Manassas, Virginia 22110

CAMARGO HUNT   7875 Buckingham Road, Indian Hill, Ohio 45243

CAMDEN HUNT   1822 Fair Street, Camden, South Carolina 29020

A well trained Springer Spaniel stops instantly at the flush of a game bird, waits for the shot, marks the fall, and retrieves to hand at command.

CASANOVA HUNT   Casanova, Virginia 22017

CHAGRIN VALLEY HUNT   Gates Mills, Ohio 44040

CHESTNUT RIDGE HUNT   New Geneva, Pennsylvania 15467

DEEP RUN HUNT   Manakin, Virginia 23103

EAGLE FARMS HUNT   127 North High Street, West Chester, Pennsylvania 19380

EGLINTON AND CALEDON HUNT   c/o Secretary, 41 Bathford Crescent, Willowdale, Ontario, Canada

ELKRIDGE-HARFORD HUNT   Monkton, Maryland 21111

ESSEX FOX HOUNDS   Peapack, New Jersey 07977

FAIRFAX HUNT   Sunset Hills, Virginia 22070

FAIRFIELD COUNTY HOUNDS   P.O. Box 32, Fairfield, Connecticut 06430

FARMINGTON HUNT   R.F.D. 5, Charlottesville, Virginia 22901

FORT LEAVENWORTH HUNT   P.O. Box 132, Fort Leavenworth, Kansas 66027

FOXCATCHER HOUNDS   Fair Hill (P.O. Elkton), Cecil County, Maryland 21921

FOX RIVER VALLEY HUNT   Donlea Rd., Barrington, Illinois 60010

FRONTENAC HUNT   Box 307, R.R. 1, Kingston, Ontario, Canada

GENESSEE VALLEY HUNT   "The Homestead," Geneseo, New York 14454

GLENMORE HUNT   Staunton, Virginia 24401

GOLDEN'S BRIDGE HOUNDS   North Salem, New York 10560

GOSHEN HUNT   P.O. Box 222, Olney, Maryland 20832

GREEN SPRING VALLEY HOUNDS   Glyndon, Maryland 21071

MR. HAIGHT, JR.'S LITCHFIELD COUNTY HOUNDS   Chestnut Hill, Litchfield, Connecticut 06753

HAMILTON HUNT   P.O. Box 331, Hamilton, Ontario, Canada

HARTS RUN HUNT   R.D. 3, Cedar Run Road, Allison Park, Pennsylvania 15101

Paul Merkle of Caroline, Wisconsin with a month's roster of wolves, cats and fox, taken with the aid of his predator hounds. Sentinel photo.

Rabbit takes to tree trying to elude the Beagles in pursuit. Tenn. Conservation Dept. Photo.

HILLTOWN HARRIERS   Spring House, Pennsylvania 19477

HILLSBORO HOUNDS   Brentwood, P.O. Box 50088, 4304 Harding Road, Nashville, Tennessee 37205

HOWARD COUNTY HUNT   Glenelg (P.O. Ellicott City) Maryland 21737

MR. HUBBARD'S KENT COUNTY HOUNDS   Chestertown, Maryland 21620

HUNTINGDON VALLEY HUNT   Doylestown, Pennsylvania 18901

IROQUOIS HUNT   Lexington, Kentucky 41001

MR. JEFFORDS' ANDREWS BRIDGE HOUNDS   Andrews Bridge, Christiana, Pennsylvania 17509

KESWICK HUNT   Keswick, Albermarle County, Virginia 22947

KINGWOOD FOX HOUNDS   Clover Hill, New Jersey

LAKE OF TWO MOUNTAINS HUNT   Como, Vaudreuil County, Quebec, Canada

LAURAY HUNT   Bath, Ohio 44210

LICKING RIVER HOUNDS   Far Cry Farm, Carlisle, Kentucky 40311

LIMEKILN HUNT   R.D. 4, Reading, Pennsylvania 19606

LIMESTONE CREEK HUNT   Troop "K" Road, Manlius, New York 13104

LONDON HUNT   P.O. Box 455, London, Ontario, Canada

LONG LAKE HOUNDS   850 North Star Center, Minneapolis, Minnesota 55402

LONGREEN FOX HOUNDS   Germantown, Tennessee 38038

LONG RUN HOUNDS   3804 Lexington Road, Louisville, Kentucky 40207

LOS ALTOS HUNT   3325 Woodside Road, Woodside, California 94062

LOUDOUN HUNT   P.O. Box 224, Leesburg, Virginia 22075

MARLBOROUGH HUNT   Upper Marlboro, Maryland 20870

MEADOW BROOK HOUNDS   Pound Hollow Road, Glen Head, Long Island, New York 11545

MECKLENBURG HOUNDS   Matthews, North Carolina 28105

MELLS FOX HOUNDS   The Mells, Route 1, Pulaski, Tennessee 38478

METAMORA HUNT   5614 Barber Road, Metamore, Lapeer County, Michigan 48455

MIAMI VALLEY HUNT   Locust Wood Farm, Springvalley, Bellbrook, Ohio 45305

MIDDLEBURG HUNT   Middleburg, Loudoun County, Virginia 22117

MIDDLEBURY HUNT   Middlebury, Connecticut 06762

MIDLAND FOX HOUNDS   P.O. Box 1360, Columbus, Georgia 30902

MILLBROOK HUNT   Millbrook, Dutchess County, New York 12545

MILL CREEK HUNT   Wadsworth, Illinois. (P.O. Address: Box 510, Lake Forest, Illinois) 60045

Scene at a Middleburg, Virginia hunt. Photo by Marshall Hawkins.

A fox hunting scene from Piedmont Hunt, Upperville, Virginia. Photo by Marshall Hawkins.

MISSION VALLEY HUNT   Bunting Farm, Stanley, Kansas 66084

MONMOUTH COUNTY HUNT   Cream Ridge and Allentown, New Jersey 08514

MONTPELIER HUNT   Montpelier Station, Virginia 22957

MONTREAL HUNT   St. Andrews East, P.Q., Canada

MOORE COUNTY HOUNDS   Southern Pines, Moore County, North Carolina 28387

MOORELAND HUNT   Post Office Drawer 526, Huntsville, Alabama 35804

MYOPIA HUNT   South Hamilton, Massachusetts 01982

NASHOBA VALLEY HUNT   Oak Hill Street, Pepperell, Massachusetts 01463

NEW BRITTON HUNT   Coventry Farm, Noblesville, Indiana 46060

NEW MARKET HOUNDS   P.O. Box 27, New Market, Maryland 21774

NORFOLK HUNT   P.O. c/o President, Farm Street, Dover, Massachusetts 02030

NORTH HILLS HUNT   4350 McKinley Street, Omaha, Nebraska 68112

OAK BROOK HOUNDS   P.O. Box 126, Oak Brook, Illinois, 60521

OAK GROVE HUNT   P.O. Box 39, Germantown, Tennessee 38038

OLD CHATHAM HUNT   Old Chatham, New York 12136

OLD DOMINION HOUNDS   Orlean, Virginia 22128

ORANGE COUNTY HUNT   The Plains, Faquier County, Virginia 22171

OTTAWA VALLEY HUNT   Donrobin, Ontario, Canada

PICKERING HUNT   R.D. 2, Phoenixville, Pennsylvania 19460

PIEDMONT FOX HOUNDS   Upperville, Fauquier County, Virginia 22176

POTOMAC HUNT   12200 Glen Road, Potomac, Maryland 20640

RADNOR HUNT   White Horse (P.O. Malvern), Chester County, Pennsylvania 19355

RAPIDAN HUNT   Retreat Farm, Rapidan, Virginia 22733

RAPPANANNOCK HUNT   Sperryville, Virginia 22740

REDLAND HUNT   Clover Hill, Brookeville, Maryland 20729

ROARING FORK HOUNDS   Box 1293 Aspen, Colorado 81611

ROCKBRIDGE HUNT   Box 1156, Lexington, Virginia 24450

ROCKY FORK-HEADLEY HUNT   Clarke State Road, Gahanna, Ohio 43020

ROLLING ROCK HUNT   Ligonier, Pennsylvania 15658

ROMBOUT HUNT   Salt Point, New York 12578

ROSE TREE FOX HUNTING CLUB   Red Lion, R.D. 1, Pennsylvania 17356

SEDGEFIELD HUNT   Box 21887, Greensboro, North Carolina 27420

SEWICKLEY HUNT   Sewickley, Pennsylvania 15143

SHAKERAG HOUNDS   3110 Maple Drive, N.E., Atlanta, Georgia 30305

SMITHTOWN HUNT   59 Mount Grey Road, Satauket, Long Island, N.Y. 11733

SOUTHERN ILLINOIS OPEN HUNT   P.O. Box "E", Herrin, Illinois 62948

SPRING VALLEY HOUNDS   Mendham, New Jersey 07945

MR. STEWART'S CHESHIRE FOXHOUNDS   Unionville, Chester County, Pennsylvania 19375

TORONTO and NORTH YORK HUNT   Beverley Farm, Aurora, Ontario, Canada

TRADERS POINT HUNT   R.D. 2, Zionsville, Indiana 46077

TRIANGLE HUNT   P.O. Box 686, Durham, North Carolina 27702

TRI-COUNTY HOUNDS   P.O. Box 453, Griffin, Georgia 30223

TRYON HOUNDS   Box 1360, Tryon, North Carolina 28806

VICMEAD HUNT   P.O. Box 3501, Wilmington, Delaware 19807

WARRENTON HUNT   P.O. Box 630, Warrenton, Virginia 22186

WATERLOO HUNT   Katz Road, Route 3, Grass Lake, Michigan 49240

WAYNE-DuPAGE HUNT   Wayne, Illinois 60184

WELLINGTON-WATERLOO HUNT   R.R. 1, Hespeler, Ontario, Canada

WEST HILLS HUNT   11050 Winnetka Blvd., Chatsworth, California 91311

WESTMORELAND HUNT   52 Northmont Street, Greensburg, Pennsylvania 15601

WHITELANDS-PERKIOMEN VALLEY HUNT   c/o Secretary, R.D. 1, Malvern, Pennsylvania 19355

WISSAHICKON HOUNDS   Gwynedd Valley, Pennsylvania 19437

WOODBROOK HUNT   6206 - 150th Street, S.W., Tacoma, Washington 98439

WOODSIDE HOUNDS   Woodside Plantation, R.R. 5, Box 396, Aiken, South Carolina 29801

The Labrador Retriever is both enthusiastic and businesslike about his retrieving work. Photo by Evelyn M. Shafer.

Popular Foxhound Strains. The most popular strain of American Foxhound is the Walker. Other strains enjoying wide acclaim are the Trigg, July, Hudspeth, and Wild Goose. Still other strains, which most likely formed the foundation of those mentioned, are the Buchanan-Henry-Birdsong, Goodman, Hampton-Watts-Bennett, Shaver, Sugar Loaf, Robertson, Whitlock Shaggies, Trumbo, Bywaters, Brooke, Byron, Cooke, Buckfield, and New England Native Hounds. Several of these are elaborated upon in another section of this book. The Plott Hound has been widely publicized in recent years. Originally developed for bear and boar hunting in the Great Smokies of Ten-

A typical hunt scene. These are English Foxhounds at the Oaks Hunt Club, Great Neck, Long Island.

nessee and North Carolina, these dogs are also used for fox, wolf, and coon hunting.

Dogs In Coon And Squirrel Hunting. Coon hunting has long been a thrilling and, in many cases, profitable, sport with the American hunter. While many Foxhound individuals develop into good "tree" dogs, a purely American-developed breed has come into being as a "specialist" on 'coons and 'possums. This is the Black and Tan Coonhound, recognized by both the American Kennel Club and the United Kennel Club. Other hound strains which are bred as "coon

specialists" are the Redbone, Bluetick, and English Treeing Walker.

Squirrel hunting is an "unsung" sport widely enjoyed throughout America. Many squirrel hunters prefer to still-hunt without dogs, and, truly, a boisterous or too-noisy dog can spoil the sport. Many of the terrier and small mixed breeds, however, develop into very efficient squirrel dogs and become practically priceless to their owners.

Dogs In Other Hunting. Mountain lion hunting is a sectional sport in this country in which hounds are used. These dogs are generally of "native" strains, mostly bred in the localities where they will be used. A good lion hound is another dog which is seldom offered for sale.

The smaller breeds, such as the Dachshund, used

Boykin Spaniel.

for small ground-game hunting in older countries, have never found much favor with American sportsmen, due largely to the difference in conditions and hunting customs.

Dogs play a major role in the hunting sports of every nation. The breeds most commonly used are listed by AKC as Sporting Dogs and Hounds, although, these do not include the terrier breeds, most of which, such as the Airedale, Fox and Scotch Terriers, were originally used for hunting purposes. The Airedale enjoyed quite a vogue with the American sportsman some years ago, and even today is found in many packs where fighting with the quarry is often to be expected.

There is an old saying that "the dog is the only hunting companion who pays his own way." Be that as it may, there is no denying the fact that the upland game hunter who goes afield without a dog is not getting the fullest measure of pleasure from his sport.

Under present conditions the time between shooting chances is sometimes irksomely lengthy, but those intervals can also be filled with thrills when the hunter enjoys watching his dog work. No hunter can cover the amount of ground his dog searches over, and no hunter possesses the "nose" of a dog. When the game is finally found and brought down, no hunter is as efficient in finding it and bringing it to bag as a good retrieving dog.

In the sport of hunting the dog is useful in so many various ways that his true worth is inestimable.

Some Distinctive American —Hunting Hounds—

THE AMERICAN sportsman has always been interested in improving his hunting dogs by crossbreeding with other strains or breeds. By careful selective breeding, various characteristics have become established and strains developed which breed true to type. This has been particularly true with the hound breeds. Until comparatively recent years, however, no serious thought was given to having these various "strains" recognized by the American Kennel Club, and in some instances the fanciers are still content to go without the sanction of that body, some preferring to register their dogs with the United Kennel Club and other Stud Books. Some, too, are content to breed their dogs without benefit of "official" pedigrees, yet nevertheless keeping careful account of the bloodlines.

Several of these strains have been breeding true to type for many years and have become generally accepted among the fancy which uses them. They are therefore worthy of a place in this book.

WALKER HOUND

The most popular strain of American Foxhound in the country today is the Walker. Wherever fox hunters gather the inevitable argument about strain supremacy provides the conversational sauce which allows the otherwise reticent sportsman to pop out of his shell and soar into forensic heights, often to his own surprise. But, also, wherever fox hunters gather there are sure to be found a number who champion the Walker Hound to the utmost of their ability. And, most likely, the exponents of that strain will be largely in the majority. For fullblooded Walker Hounds are now found in every section where the fox is chased for sport.

The history of the Walker Foxhound is an interesting one. The greatest portion of the credit for the development of the strain properly goes to two Kentucky sportsmen. Close friends and neighbors, George Washington Maupin, later more familiarly known as "Uncle Wash" Maupin, and John W. Walker had more than community interest in common. They were bound together by a mutual love of hounds and hunting, and this bond drew them closer as the years went by. There were others, of course, friends and neighbors, who contributed their share to the metamorphosis of the Walker Hounds. These were the Deatherages, Neil Gooch, Anse Martin, the Whites, the Williamses, the Gentrys, the Clays, the Goodmans, and others. But the roles they played were minor compared to that of Maupin and Walker.

Daniel Maupin, the father of George Washington Maupin, and William Williams came to Kentucky from Virginia. John W. Walker was a nephew of Mr. Williams and lived with his uncle until manhood. These gentlemen owned hounds of the native Virginia and Kentucky stock of that day, and bred them carefully and judiciously, selecting the best with which to carry on. Although the hounds of "Uncle Wash" Maupin and John W. Walker were of the same breeding, there existed between the two sportsmen that same spirit of friendly rivalry which still characterizes fox hunters the country over. For fifty years they bred from the same stock, taking care to weed out the unworthy and undesirables.

Then came the outcross, the influence of which was so profound as to result in the strain now called the Walker. Too much praise, however, cannot be given to the descendants and relatives of both gentlemen, particularly Mr. Walker, whose close adherence to the breeding principles laid down by their forebears was so basically essential to the development of the strain which now bears the Walker family name. Without a strict program of breeding and the keeping of careful records on the results, this strain would probably have passed into the limbo populated by other good strains which enjoyed, for a time, the limelight of popularity, but are not now well remembered.

This outcross was furnished, and at about the same time, by the almost legendary hound Tennessee Lead, and the two English importations, Rifler and Marth. It is interesting to note that one of the most, if not really the greatest, fountainheads of the Walker Foxhound was a "stolen" dog. Perhaps a kinder and more charitable word would be one made again popular in World War II—"Liberated." From what stock he stemmed, no one knows, and the circumstances of his acquisition probably precluded any serious attempt to find out. But, regardless of his origin, he made a great impression on the packs of "Uncle Wash" Maupin and John Walker, and the introduction of this new blood came at just the right time to effect the needed improvement in performance. This dog was known as Tennessee Lead.

Tom Harriss was one of "Uncle Wash" Maupin's friends and neighbors. He was a dealer in livestock and drove his stock overland to the Southern markets. Returning from one of his regular trips, he was passing through the mountains in Tennessee when he heard a pack of hounds running, headed directly toward him. Presently their quarry, a deer, crossed the road, closely followed by the pack. Harriss quickly dismounted and caught one of the hounds, bringing it back to Kentucky, where he presented it to Mr. Maupin.

The hound, later to be given the name Tennessee Lead, was not very prepossessing in appearance. He was a medium-sized black dog with a small tan spot over each eye, a thin coat, and no brush on his tail. He had an exceptional amount of fox-sense, plenty of drive and speed, a clear, short mouth, and, though not a standout in any department, was, over-all, a high-class, game-to-the-core Foxhound.

Mr. Maupin was not particularly impressed with the dog at first glance, but after a few races became enthusiastic about him—so much so, in fact, that he

sent two of his sons to the section of Tennessee in which Harriss had picked Lead up in an endeavor to purchase his duplicate or equals. His sons returned with two or three which resembled Lead in appearance—but in nothing else. Tennessee Lead became the idol of that section of Kentucky in which the Maupins and Walkers resided and was used extensively on Maupin-Walker bitches. His influence was immediately felt, and his blood became highly prized.

About this same time, Mr. Maupin and several of his fox-hunting friends arranged with Billy Fleming, a Philadelphia merchant with whom they transacted business, to purchase for them two foxhounds on his next trip to England. Mr. Fleming contacted the Buccleuch Kennels and secured a dog, Rifler, and a bitch, Marth. Upon arrival in New York, the dogs were sent by rail to Cincinnati and thence by stage to Richmond, Ky. Here they were met by nearly all the fox hunters in that section, who were anxious to see what the "foreigners" could do.

So high did that enthusiasm run that arrangements were made for a hunt that very night, and although he had been confined in a crate for more than two weeks, Rifler was tossed into the pack. This was, indeed, an entirely unfair test, prompted, of course, by impatient enthusiasm, and no doubt his new owners would have given this full consideration had

Walker Hound.

Rifler's efforts not proved up to proper standards. Regardless of his lack of condition, however, the "Englishman" proved himself a real fox dog that night and all those who had contributed toward his purchase felt themselves participants in a splendid investment. Their predictions were justified. This was perhaps the most severe test a foxhound had ever been subjected to. Although the group, of course, would have been charitable and reserved opinion until he could have been tested under more favorable conditions, it was, nevertheless, composed of seasoned hunters who were inclined to be particularly critical of individual hound work. The fact that Rifler was able to satisfy them makes his performance all the more outstanding. Marth, the bitch, had been bred in England before shipping and was showing in whelp. For this reason she was not subjected to the same extreme test which faced her kennel-mate.

There were other hounds in the Maupin and Walker packs which are said to have compared favorably with Lead and Rifler, but it was felt that new blood was needed and the three dogs mentioned above were the ones to provide it. This judgment proved to be sound.

Marth whelped a litter and from it four were raised, three males and one female. The three male puppies were called Fox, Bully, and Bragg. All were fine foxhounds and were used extensively at stud. The bitch puppy had the misfortune, when she was nearly grown, to be run over by a wagon which badly injured her foot. This prevented her from being hunted, and she was used for breeding purposes only. She was called Mash Foot. Due to the sketchiness of the early records, not a great deal is known about Mash Foot's progeny, although one of her sons figures quite prominently in the pedigrees of the older Walker Hounds. This was Rush, whose sire was Middleton's Eagle. Rush was a grand hound and his blood was prepotent. There have been some other outcrosses in the early days, but if so they were either discarded or not persisted in.

In 1892, however, another importation from England brought fresh blood to the Walker Hounds. Striver, Relish, and Clara were brought over from England by James Crawford of Chicago. Mr. Crawford presented these dogs to his friend, Colonel Jack Shinn. Colonel Shinn visited the Walkers for a hunt soon afterward and brought the trio of hounds with him, giving Striver to W. S. Walker, Relish to E. H. Walker, and Clara to Arch Walker. None of these hounds proved entirely satisfactory. Striver was an outstanding hound in every department except one: he was weak in mouth. His "open" was a mild squeal which could not be heard at any considerable distance. Otherwise, he was an excellent performer. A good hunter, tireless and game, he could generally be found near the front of the pack, but his voice was not one of the kind "heard throughout the country-side." Relish was what is known as an "in-and-outer." She could travel with the best—when she wanted to,

Eager Walker Foxhound pups. Photo by David M. Duffey.

which was seldom. The hound, Clara, is said to have been no good.

It has been said that the Walkers and Maupins were too jealous of their own stock to try to improve it by making outcrosses. This is denied. Hounds were brought in from New England, Maryland, and other points and the results of the crosses were carefully nurtured and watched, but none approached the high standard set by the Walkers and Maupins to such an extent that their continued use as breeding stock was warranted.

One of the hounds of the 1865-70 period which figures far back in the pedigrees of practically every present-day Walker Hound is Top, bred by Neil Gooch, later owned by "Uncle Wash" Maupin, who still later sold him to W. S. Walker for $100. According to Walker records, Top was the first dog to be sold for such a price, considered extremely high in those days. Top was by Maupin's Couchman and out of Gooch's Aggie II. His dam traced back to Tennessee Lead.

Red Mack II, whelped in 1883, was another outstanding hound which left his mark as a performer but unfortunately was not a great success as a sire. Red Scott, a brother, while an excellent fox dog, was not quite so good as Red Mack II but his blood carried on through generations.

Space limits will permit mention here of only a few of the outstanding hounds which, in later days, carried the Walker banner on to new heights and contributed to the well-deserved popularity which the strain enjoys today. Worthy of more than mere mention, however, are Cable, Big Stride, War Cry, White Rowdy, Cork, Mark, and String. Hub Dawson is another which should not be overlooked, as his name came much into evidence in many pedigrees.

Big Stride, whelped in 1916, and bred and owned by S. L. Woodridge, was the most famous Walker Hound of his day. An exceptionally fine fox dog, his greatest success came as a sire. It is unlikely that any other Walker Hound has been used more extensively for breeding purposes, and his progeny warranted his use. His name very probably appears in more pedigrees of recent Walker Hounds than that of any other dog, with the possible exception of Cable, his sire.

Cork, owned by Woods Walker, was an outstanding hound which left a lasting impression on the strain. He was in great demand as a stud and sired many exceptional foxhounds. An extremely game hound, Cork is known to have been in two hard races in close succession, in fact with hardly a let-up between, the combined time of which totaled about 19½ hours. During all that time Cork was either at the front of the pack or, indeed, leading it.

The Walker Foxhound is no longer a "family affair." Lovers of the chase all over the country have recognized the excellent qualities of the strain and it can be truly said that the mighty cry of the Walker Hound is a "voice heard throughout the land."

TRIGG HOUND

One of the most popular strains of foxhound in this country today is the Trigg Hound, which takes it name from its greatest exponent and originator, the late Colonel Haiden C. Trigg, of Glasgow, Ky., who wrote under the pseudonym "Full Cry." The strain may be properly described as the result of Colonel Trigg's carefully planned selective breeding program, using the Birdsong hound as foundation stock, with judicious crosses of July and Maupin or Walker blood. Years of patient experimentation and breeding, with a definite goal in mind, brought Colonel Trigg his reward in the establishment of a strain of foxhound noted for its speed, stamina, and gameness.

Dr. T. Y. Henry, a grandson of Patrick Henry, kept a pack of hounds in Virginia which had an enviable reputation as foxhounds of exceptionally high quality. Dr. Henry called these dogs "Irish" hounds, as they were descended from Mountain and Muse, imported from Ireland by Bolton Jackson of Maryland, and presented by him to Colonel Sterrett Ridgely. Colonel Ridgely gave them to Governor Samuel Ogle, of Maryland, who gave Mountain to Captain Charles Carroll, Jr., of Carrollton. Captain Carroll presented the dog to Dr. James Buchanan, who presented Captain, a direct descendent of Mountain and Muse, to Dr. Henry. Captain was by Traveler out of Sophy, both by Mountain out of Muse. Thus was laid the foundation of the Henry hounds, later known as the Birdsong hounds.

Early in the 1840's Dr. Henry presented a pair of puppies from his pack to George L. F. Birdsong, of Thomaston, Ga. Mr. Birdsong valued them so highly that he sent a wagon overland for them, there being no rail transportation at that time. These puppies and their progeny proved to be far superior to any hounds the famous Georgia sportsman had ever had before and he set about building a pack which soon was recognized as the best in that section.

Several years later Dr. Henry was threatened with tuberculosis, and his doctor ordered him to go South. Accompanied by several friends and his pack of hounds, Dr. Henry started overland for Florida, traveling by wagon and horseback. The trip was made in leisurely fashion, the party stopping occasionally to enjoy the hunting and fishing offered by the countryside. Knowing of the trip, Mr. Birdsong joined the party en route and spent several days hunting with Dr. Henry.

Although the move to Florida was beneficial to Dr. Henry's health, circumstances threatened to wipe out his famous pack. Deer abounded in the section in which the Virginia sportsman settled, and his dogs could not resist the temptation to chase them. Often the trail carried them across streams and lagoons infested with alligators. A number of the finest individuals in the Henry pack fell victim to alligators. Realizing that his pack would soon be wiped out if he continued to hunt them in his new location and desiring to preserve their good qualities for posterity, Dr. Henry wrote Mr. Birdsong and offered to give him the remnants of this famed kennel if he would come after them. Though saddened by his friend's plight, Mr. Birdsong was delighted to obtain these highly-prized hounds and left post-haste for Florida, bringing the dogs back to his Georgia home.

Miles G. Harris secured a very fine hound from a Nimrod Gosnell of Maryland and brought him to Georgia. The dog came to him on the first day of July and, for this reason, was named July. It is believed that July came from the same strain as old Captain, the foundation of Dr. Henry's "Irish" hounds.

In 1861, July was crossed on the Birdsong dogs. This cross was successful, although there existed some difference of opinion as to the comparative merits of the Birdsong dogs before and after the July cross. It brought fresh blood into the pack, however, and many considered that it strengthened the bloodlines.

Dr. Henry called his dogs "Irish" hounds. After the pack passed into the possession of Mr. Birdsong, he insisted that they be known as "Henry" hounds. However, as their fame spread through Georgia and the surrounding states, they became generally known as "Birdsong" hounds, and after the infusion of July blood, they were called by many "July" hounds. The straight-bred Birdsong hound is one whose breeding can be traced back to Captain without showing the July cross. Yet it is generally believed that July descended from Mountain and Muse, the progenitors of Captain.

In the meantime, Colonel Haiden C. Trigg, of Glasgow, Ky., was having good sport hunting gray foxes with his pack of long-eared, deep-toned, rat-tailed black-and-tan Virginia hounds. But in 1860 the red fox made its appearance in Colonel Trigg's territory and began to spoil his sport. His hounds were too slow to cope with the racing red raider. Not to be outdone, he was determined to secure, or develop, a pack of hounds game enough and fast enough to deal with the red fox.

Colonel Trigg bought five hounds from Mr. Birdsong in 1866 and 1867, paying $400 for them, at that time considered a high price. These were Chase and Bee (by Longstreet, a straight-bred Birdsong), George, Rip, and Fannie. Mr. Birdsong gave the colo-

Trigg Hound.

nel a dog named Lee, probably for "good measure."

In 1868, Colonel Trigg visited Mr. Birdsong, who was still ill with tuberculosis (he died the following year). He was, however, able to show his guest some excellent hunting. At that time Mr. Birdsong owned July and a number of his progeny. He also had Longstreet, a straight-bred Birdsong, and several promising puppies by this celebrated sire. After much pleading, Mr. Birdsong sold Colonel Trigg two young hounds for the sum of $500. These were Lightfoot, by July, and Delta, by Longstreet out of Echo, a daughter of July.

At about the same time, Colonel Trigg purchased from Colonel R. H. Ward, of Green County, Ga., Forest, by Boston, and Emma, paying $100 each. Rose, a full sister to Echo, and a splendid dog named Hampton were loaned to him. Colonel Trigg raised a litter of puppies from Rose and returned her; Hampton died shortly after he was received.

Shortly before his visit to Mr. Birdsong, Colonel Trigg spent a few days hunting with General George Washington Maupin, of Madison County, Ky., and purchased the young bitch Minnie, a close descendant of General Maupin's celebrated hound Tennessee Lead on one side and the imported English dogs Fox, Rifler, and Marth, on the other. At the same time

Colonel C. J. Walker presented Colonel Trigg with the young bitch Mattie, whose sire and dam both traced back to Tennessee Lead.

In 1869, after hunting with Colonel Trigg, W. L. Waddy and Thomas Ford of Shelby County, Kentucky, who had a pack of Maupin-bred hounds, insisted that the colonel try the qualities of some of their best dogs. Colonel Trigg selected Tip, Waxey, and One-Eyed King, and hunted them, breeding the latter to Delta, and getting the dog later known as Money, noted for his exceptional speed. Returning the courtesy, Colonel Trigg let Messrs. Waddy and Scott take his celebrated Forest for breeding purposes.

After General Maupin's death, W. S. Walker and brothers of Gerrard County, Ky., became the leading breeders of the Maupin or Walker Hounds, carefully preserving the bloodline of what is now known as the Walker Hound. In 1890 Col. Trigg secured the Walker Hound Trooper from Mr. Walker and used him to some extent as a stud dog.

In those days there were plenty of red foxes and plenty of good country in the South to run them in. Each line of breeding had its champions and match races were not unusual.

General Maupin, a pillar in the house of foxhound breeding, and his friends, among whom were the

Walkers, Sam Martin, the Gentrys, and the Whites, all famous fox hunters, were convinced beyond all change that the finest foxhounds of that day were Fox, Rifler, Marth, Queen, Tennessee Lead, Tickler, Doc, Kate, Top, Minnie, and others of their packs.

Equally high in the esteem of Mr. Birdsong and others of the Georgia contingent (the Wards, Robinsons, Ridgleys, and Jacksons), were Hodo, July, Longstreet, Flora, Forest, Echo, Hampton, Madcap, Lightfoot, Fannie, and others of their breeding.

Messrs. Waddy and Ford of Shelby County, Ky., also had their own ideas, and were confident that no hounds were better than their One-Eyed King, Tip, Josephine, and Venus.

After years of careful selection, judicious breeding, and crossing lines only for a definite purpose, Colonel Trigg developed the strain of hounds which now bears his name.

The Trigg Hound is a combination of blood from the Birdsong, Maupin, and Walker kennels. From 1867 to 1890 he mingled these strains with one end in view—the improvement of his pack. How well he succeeded is reflected in the deserved popularity the Trigg Hound enjoys today.

During that period Colonel Trigg had the following dogs in his kennels for breeding purposes, as well as for hunting:

Birdsongs: Chase, Bee, George, Lightfoot, Delta, Rip, Fannie, Lee, Forest, Emma, Hampton, Ward, Rose, and Emma Sampson; *Maupins:* Minnie, Mattie, Lead, Couchman, Bob, Dick, Rock, Venus, Mercy, Lee, and Brenda; *Walkers:* Buckner, Scott, and Trooper.

Colonel Trigg never bred his dogs for distinctive color or markings. His original dogs ranged from black and tan to fawn and included white, black and tan, tan with white points, red, red and white, black and white, red with white points, black with white points, light red with white points.

The Trigg Hound is a handsome, rugged individual in appearance, strong but without coarseness; rangy yet not gaunt. He has an abundance of bone but is not considered a heavy-boned dog. He has good length of muzzle, well-set ears and stern, strong shoulders and quarters, and is a workmanlike type of dog.

In height the Triggs run from 23 to 24½ inches, seldom 25 inches, in weight from 45 to 55 pounds. They are generally equipped with splendid noses and are noted for exceptional speed and splendid endurance.

REDBONE HOUND

The Redbone Hound is well known among coon hunters in all parts of the United States. In fact, not so many years ago practically every coon hunter who owned a solid red hound of unknown ancestry but proven proficiency in trailing and treeing raccoons called his dog a "Redbone." Some years ago, however, a few serious-minded devotees of the sport started a campaign of selective breeding to produce a hound which possessed the necessary nose, stamina and cour-

age to trail and tree furred game and breed true to type in color and conformation. The first dogs used were commonly called "Saddlebacks." The background color was red, and most of them possessed black saddle markings. By selective breeding the black saddle was bred out and the solid red dogs became known as Redbone Hounds. It is said that the foundation stock came from the hounds of George F. L. Birdsong, of Georgia, noted fox hunter and breeder, who obtained the remnants of the famous pack of Dr. Thomas Y. Henry. A Bloodhound

Redbone Hound.

cross is said to have been used on these dogs, and it is also said that blood of the Irish Hounds was also introduced. This latter cross is said to account for the white chest and feet markings which occasionally show up on the Redbone today.

These dogs are "specialists" in 'coon hunting, but are also proficient in trailing and treeing bear, cougar, and wildcat. "Treeing" (barking and remaining at tree) is instinctive with these dogs. Some of the "points" desired in the breed are as follows:

COLOR: Solid red preferred. Small amount of white on brisket and feet not objectionable.

HEAD: Ears set moderately low, fine in texture, not stiff and reaching near end of nose when stretched out. *Eyes:* Brown or hazel in color, set well apart and of pleading expression. *Skull:* Moderately broad, well proportioned with body. *Muzzle:* Well-balanced with other features of head, never dished or upturned.

TEETH: Even, neither over nor undershot.

NECK: Throat clean, medium in length, strong, slightly arched and held erect. Slight fold of skin below angle of jaw allowable.

SIZE: Slightly taller at shoulder than at hips. Never opposite. Males, 22 inches to 26 inches; females, 21 inches to 25 inches.

BODY: Deep broad chest, back strong and slightly arched, length well proportioned to height, thighs and shoulders up, clean and muscular. Well-sprung ribs, plenty of lung space.

LEGS: Legs straight, well boned, pasterns straight, well set, clean and muscular denoting combination of both strength and speed. Never cowhocked.

FEET: Cat paw type, compact, well padded, toes strong and well arched, stout, well-set nails. Feet should be set as directly under nails as possible.

TAIL: Medium in length, very slight brush, carried gaily but not hooked over back. Set moderately high.

COAT: Smooth and hard, medium to short in length, sufficient for protection.

MANNERS: A hound should always indicate a willingness to obey his master's command, denoting intelligence.

BLUETICK HOUND

The Bluetick or Bluetick-English, as some prefer to call him, is a hound descended from several strains of English Foxhounds, and bred with particular emphasis placed on the "bluetick" color phase. While these hounds are still excellent fox dogs, they have become especially popular with the coon-hunting fraternity,

Bluetick Hounds.

and the treeing instinct has been developed through generations of careful breeding to proven performers at the tree.

Rather large in size, the Bluetick has excellent speed, and many of them figure prominently in the coonhound field trials. They are generally easy to train and start trailing at an early age. With the blueticked body usually set off with tan points, these dogs make a very handsome appearance and are in great demand among coon hunters in all sections. They have been used to fine advantage in cougar hunting in the West.

TREEING WALKER

This is another "strain" of coonhound which is said to have been developed from certain individual Walker Hounds which showed especial proficiency in trailing and treeing raccoons. Through training and constant use in night hunting, the treeing "instinct" has been developed in a high degree and the "strain" has become a "specialist" in coon hunting, although they can be easily trained to trail any species of ground furred game. In appearance they have no characteristics which distinguish them from the Walker Foxhound.

PLOTT HOUND

Undoubtedly the breed of sporting dog which, as a breed, has received the widest publicity in recent years is the Plott Hound. Yet this dog is certainly not

a newcomer to the American sporting picture. He has, in fact, long been famous in the Great Smoky Mountains of Tennessee and North Carolina. It is only that his light has been hidden under the bushel of his somewhat restricted home venue. His great capabilities have been largely confined to hunting the bears and wild boars which range his native rugged terrain.

The Plott Hound has been successfully used on smaller game than bears and boars, and, properly trained, makes a splendid tree dog. But he has come into national prominence only since the annual wild boar hunts were inaugurated and conducted by the State of Tennessee in the great Smokies. The publicity given the breed through these annual affairs has won for him the recognition he has long deserved and the present demand for Plott Hound stock is far in excess of the supply.

Ancestors of this dog were used for boar hunting in Germany many years ago, but, of course, were not then called Plott Hounds. Jonathan Plott left his native Germany and came to this country in 1750, bringing a few wild-boar hounds with him. These dogs had been bred for generations for their stamina and gameness, for it took a great deal of both qualities to cope successfully with the big tuskers of that day. He settled in the mountains of western North Carolina and his dogs soon developed great proficiency in hunting the game of that area—the black bear which abounded in the wilderness.

It was not until many years afterward that a company of European sportsmen introduced the European wild boar into this section; in Plott's time the only "wild-boars" in the neighborhood were domesticated hogs which had gone feral through foraging for a living in the wilds. Plott was not interested in hunting these "razorbacks" and used his dogs almost exclusively for bear hunting. Their proficiency on

Bluetick Coonhound, a winner at a bench show. Photo by David M. Duffey.

Don Blodgett's Treeing Walker Hounds and their individual houses (Maine).

this species soon attracted attention among his neighbors, and it was not long before the hounds of Jonathan Plott had acquired a considerable reputation among the hunters of that section.

Mr. Plott kept his breeding and training secrets strictly to himself for 30 years, selecting his breeding stock carefully and jealously guarding the upbringing of their offspring. His were not the only bear dogs in those mountains, but his strain was kept entirely pure and free from any outcross during all those years. In this manner the breed became firmly established and his strict adherence to a careful program of breeding selectively not only kept the blood pure but improved the quality of his pack, for only the best performers were used for breeding purposes. A Plott Hound had to prove its worth in the hunting field before it was allowed to pass along its blood in succeeding generations.

The fame of the Plott pack spread, and word of the exceptional ability of these dogs reached the ears of a northern Georgia bear hunter, whose own pack had an enviable local reputation. In fact, the Georgia man was firmly convinced that nowhere in the land were there superior hounds to his own.

His dogs were known as "leopard dogs" originally

and later as the "leopard-spotted bear dogs." Authentic information concerning their origin is unavailable, but it is generally believed that they were brought over from Europe in the 1730's. It has been claimed by some that these dogs were from a strain used by English sportsmen in hunting leopards in foreign lands. They are also said to have been of the same strain from which the original Plott Hounds

Typical Plott Hound.

stemmed, some of the stud dogs having been shipped to Germany from England to bolster up the boar-hunting packs of that country.

The Plott pack passed into the management of Henry Plott in 1780. The fame of these dogs continued to spread and the curiosity of the Georgia hunter, whose name seems to have been lost, could no longer be denied. He simply had to find out if there were any better bear dogs anywhere than his own. So, with some of his best "leopard" dogs, he started the long trek through the mountains to North Carolina, finally locating the home of Henry Plott. The two hunters apparently had much in common and a staunch friendship developed. They hunted their packs separately and collectively, comparing notes and carefully checking performances.

The Plott Hounds evidently made quite an impression on the Georgia sportsman, for upon his return to his native state he took with him one of Henry's stud dogs to cross on some of his "leopard" bitches. The dog was only on loan from Plott; a year later he was returned by the Georgian, who presented Plott with a male puppy, sired by the Plott dog and out of one of the "leopard" bitches which had been selected by both men on the occasion of the Georgian's first visit.

The male puppy turned out to be an outstanding individual. So great were his good qualities that

Enthusiastic Treeing Walker coonhound at tree during a field trial.
Photo by David M. Duffey.

Henry Plott added him to his carefully selected pack and bred him to several of his bitches. This single cross is the only known instance of introduction of new blood into the Plott Hound since the original dogs were brought to this country in 1750. There have been rumors of numerous crossings with Bloodhound, Airedale, Black and Tan, and common mongrel, but this is strongly denied by members of the Plott clan and their friends. They maintain, in words which leave no doubt as to their sincerity, that, with this single exception, the strain of Jonathan Plott's hounds has been kept pure since 1750.

In 1946, the United Kennel Club recognized the Plott Hound as a distinct breed.

Despite the considerable publicity given the breed since its "rediscovery" by enthusiastic writers a number of years ago, there are probably but few *fullblooded* Plott Hounds in existence today. Certainly their numbers are few when compared with other hound strains. The Plott Hound has, for many generations, been a "family" strain. The members of the Plott family have not cared to publicize or commercialize the breed. Only in the past twenty-five years has the Plott Hound been given any considerable amount of publicity. These dogs had been famous among the bear and boar hunters of eastern Tennessee and western North Carolina mountain sections for many years, but no attempt had been made to exploit them and but few had passed out of the possession of the Plott family.

When the wild-boar hunting of that section took on a national flavor through "organized" hunts and prominent sportsmen from "outside" were invited to participate, knowledge of the real worth of this strain of hounds began to spread rapidly. A great demand for these dogs sprang up among hound lovers the country over and some were sold "outside." G. P. Ferguson, a neighbor of John and Von Plott, had been taken into their confidence, and these three men, with George Plott (who lost his life in the invasion of Normandy), are largely responsible for the program of careful breeding which has kept the strain intact. They bred their hounds with improved hunting performance as their prime objective, discarding those individuals which did not measure up to their rigid standards of field quality and keeping only the best. Their culls were not sold, but were done away with and, as a result, their packs always had their "best feet forward."

Of medium height, the Plott Hound has a rather large and somewhat beefy head, with the jaws of a fighter. His shoulders are muscular, his hind quarters strong, and his body is generally of the right proportions to give a well-balanced appearance.

In weight, the males average close to 60 pounds, and the bitches 8 to 10 pounds lighter.

The color is generally a deep brownish-brindle with a black saddle and often white points. Occasionally a white spot on the chest or a white "shirt-front" is seen. The Plott Hound is likely to breed true to type and color, although occasionally a lighter-colored individual is seen. This is attributed by most to the influence of the single cross with the "leopard dogs," as this strain was lighter than the original Plotts.

They are usually free-opening hounds with a bawling cry which often shortens to a chop when the trail is hot.

Although they are particularly good on the game of their native section, Plott Hounds have been used successfully on wolf, mountain lion, coyote, wildcat, deer, and various smaller game. They are said to be exceptionally good on game which runs and fights. Accustomed to the rugged terrain of the Great Smokies area, the Plott Hound is probably a bit too slow to fit in with a good pack of southern foxhounds, but as an all-purpose hound he merits serious consideration.

There are said to be three types or strains of the Plott Hound. Von and John Plott make their homes at Waynesville, N.C. Von Plott's hounds are of a long-eared variety, said to possess exceptionally good noses, enabling them to pick up and unravel colder trails than the other two.

John Plott's hounds have shorter ears and are a little "hot-nosed." They are faster and are particularly hard and courageous fighters. Mr. Ferguson's dogs seem to strike a happy medium between the other two. Mr. Ferguson lives at Cullowhee, N.C.

All three varieties were in the pack of George Plott. After his death, most of his hounds were perchased by H. T. Smithdeal, of Johnson City, Tenn. Mr. Smithdeal proceeded to bolster up his pack by buying selected hounds from the kennels of Von and John Plott and Mr. Ferguson. The Johnson City sportsman carried on the Plott tradition of selective breeding.

Proud owner displays his Plott Hound used on raccoon. As evident in this photo, the Plott Hound is not especially a small dog. Photo by David M. Duffey.

Part XII

TRAINING THE HUNTING DOG

There are those who, having had the experience both ways, say it would be a far better thing for a man to hunt without a dog than to hunt with an untrained one. Hardly anything is more frustrating, for instance, than to hunt with an untrained spaniel which, once released, proceeds immediately to tear down a cornfield, flushing wave after wave of ringnecks ahead—all out of range of the forgotten gunner behind. Or, to hunt behind a young pointer, one as equally concerned with pursuing a rabbit as in finding birds—or one that will only flash-point, then flush the bird before the gunner arrives. Or the beagle that won't come to a whistle or call when the hunter is ready to go home, but instead runs off on the trail of doves, pigeons, or some farmer's cat. Training a hunting dog can mean many years of enjoyable hunting seasons. Whether it is a hound, a bird dog, or a retriever, time spent in training will be well rewarded. Few things are as satisfying as the thrill of watching a hunting dog perform well in the field and realizing that he does so because you worked with him and helped bring him up to this fine performance. All it takes is a little know-how, patience and perseverance.

—Beagle Training—

TO SAY that Beagles are trained to hunt by giving them plenty of chances to "do what comes naturally" may be an over-simplification. But it's nearly true!

The Beagle, regardless of his popularity as a pet in recent years, is first and foremost a hound. No way has yet been devised to teach a hound to hunt. If a hound lacks a natural instinct to put his nose in a track and follow it, learning mostly through his own triumphs and mistakes, there is little the trainer can do about it.

Fortunately, most Beagles from hunting and field-trial stock have this strong hunting instinct and virtually any man or boy who likes to tramp about in the fields and woods can turn out a reasonably good hunting Beagle simply by letting the little hound know that a rabbit, his prime game, or other game you want him to drive, is what you are after.

First Lessons. Let's start with first things first. Two things which your Beagle must learn mechanically, something that he is taught—not something he figures out through experiencing it—is to come when

called and to understand that a command like "No!" means "Stop what you're doing, right now!" whether he starts running off-game or pestering the neighbor's chickens. You can do this at a tender age when you don't expect he'll be out hunting. So teach it first before you seriously hunt him.

To teach your Beagle to come, always use the same call and whistle. Start by calling him only when his attention is focused on you. Call and whistle and run away from him. Chances are almost certain he'll chase you. Let him catch you and praise him highly.

Always call him when you feed him, or you may want to reward him with a tidbit of food as well as a pat and verbal praise when he comes to you. When he reaches the point where he comes promptly or thinks there's play or praise in the offing, attach a long, light cord to his collar and wait until he gets interested in something else and ignores your command to come. Call him anyway, and when he refuses, reel him smartly and firmly to you. When he reaches you, pet and praise him. Usually just a few such lessons will suffice. Never scold or whip him when he comes to you, regardless of earlier misbehavior.

To teach him "No!" simply say that command whenever he's doing something he shouldn't be doing, reinforced with a sharp newspaper wave towards his flank if he's within reach, or a sharp yank on the check cord if he's away from you.

Some Beagle owners never teach these things to their hounds, but some Beagle owners as well spend a lot of time waiting for their dogs to get tired of hunting and find their own way out of the swamp hours after the hunter is ready to quit and go home. Response to the command "No!" may also save a lot of time chasing after a dog if he does start to run deer or some other off-game.

Take your pup, or the whole litter if you have one, out into the woods or to some strange vacant lot when eight to twelve weeks of age. If you stand still they'll get curious and start moving around. As they pick up confidence and start going out on their own, quickly and quietly hide somewhere. Soon the pup, or one or more of the litter, will start looking for you. Some may even try to track you. When it's evident they're looking for you, call and whistle them in until they find you. This helps teach them to keep track of you or to find their way back if they're some distance from you when a rabbit holes or the track peters out.

Beagles Are Precocious. Beagles are precocious and the age they are started on rabbits will depend on the individual dog. Some do a pretty good job at four or five months. Others don't seem to catch on until they're about a year. A good average time to start would be at about age six months. If you have a Beagle over two years of age who has never started a rabbit or run a line, forget him and try another.

Meanwhile, though, take that pup along to the woods every chance you get, from age 10 to 12 weeks on. Carry him, if you take too long a hike and he tires. He's only a little fellah! Let him find out all about the brush and fences and creeks he'll encounter when he's hunting and, above all, let him associate

Beagle checking out a "cold" trail. Hank Babbitt photo.

those pleasant trips with you. Keep him penned or otherwise confined except when you take him afield.

During this going-to-the-field period, if he happens to stumble on a rabbit or you can stomp one out of a brush pile that he'll chase, well and good. The sight chase will encourage him. But leave well enough alone. Let his own instincts be his guide. Don't shout or otherwise distract him from the rabbit. Let him run it as best he can. More than one Beagle has learned his hunting just this way and then become a really good gundog through plenty of experience.

A high-strung, excitable pup may come to his first check (a place and time when he temporarily loses the scent line) and, because he's eager and excited, turn around and go *back* on the track simply because it smells good. Discourage this and encourage the hound to cast around, not too wide, until he picks up the scent line once more. You don't want a back-tracking hound. If he can't pick up the line, call it a loss, and move on until you can start another bunny.

With a pup who is pretty calm and takes things slowly, you'll be likely to find him working his line over. He won't back-track, but he'll swing out until he strikes the old line and won't leave it.

Without snow, you'll have to make an educated guess as to what the young Beagle is doing, right or wrong. After a snowfall, it's simple because the story is there for you to read and you can definitely establish if the pup is following a good line in the proper direction. You may be able to help him pick up the line after a check, by calling him in and pointing to the track.

When the Pup is Ready for Serious Hunting. When you decide your pup's ready for the serious part of hunting you can introduce him to game by himself, with several pups of like age and development, or thrown in with an older Beagle or two or a pack.

Putting him down to run with the experienced hounds is a quick way to pick the most promising pups in a litter. But is has also spoiled many another pup who could have developed, except that he turned into a "follower" or quitter because he couldn't match the pace of older, experienced hounds.

Beagles—always quite ready to go, anxious to hunt! Hank Babbitt photo.

Instead, keep your pup with you until the older hounds start game and then take a station where the rabbit is likely to circle, holding your pup up where he can see. The baying of the hounds should interest him and when the rabbit comes around and the pup spots it, set him down quietly and let his instinct to chase take over. Repeated a few times, he'll connect the sight and sound of the chase with the scent and will start using his nose even when the bunny is out of sight. When he's really wild about this, put him down for short chases with the older hounds and

hunt him by himself as often as possible so he doesn't become dependent, but develops into a hard driver who figures things out for himself and will seek about so as to jump his own game.

If you don't have older Beagles available and start a single pup or brace of pups, try to kick out a rabbit in your hikes and encourage the pup to roust about in brush piles or cover edges where he's likely to jump a rabbit on his own. He should sight-chase and eventually get his nose down. If he doesn't see the rabbit start, call him to the hot track and encourage

As much fun as rabbit hunting is, it's many more times the sport with a good set of Beagles. Tennessee Conservation Dept. photo.

him to hunt. He'll take straight lines well and on his first check, when the rabbit abruptly switches direction, point out the line to him if he doesn't locate it himself. Be sure you know what direction the rabbit took so he'll trust your judgment and won't get discouraged by constant misleading "bum steers."

You can also start pups on liberated rabbits, ones that have been live-trapped. Rabbits often seem more abundant in the suburbs and towns than in the country. Take your live rabbit and your pups to your training place, which should include a large mowed field and some brush. Tease the pups with the rabbit, set the rabbit down and let it get well away before you let the pups go. A good bunny will lead them on quite a chase, even in strange country and may even escape a single pup. But if you work several at the same time, they'll eventually run it down and kill it. After they're keen about this you can allow a captive rabbit to run and hide and then put the pups on the hot scent until they work it out, using this as a supplement to actual hunting.

Introduction to Gun Noise. Shoot over your Beagle for the first time when he is driving hard and scenting conditions make it unlikely that he'll lose the line. Be sure you get the rabbit with that one shot, even if it means taking the bunny on the sit. Training your dog is of primary concern in this instance.

Don't shoot when your hound is too close, which means you may have to pass up some rabbits. After you've shot, if your hound keeps right on coming into the rabbit, fine. Let him pounce on it and "kill it," worry and chew it. You praise him, but that warm rabbit in his mouth will be all the reward he really needs.

If the sound of the shot stops him (which it shouldn't, if you've gotten him used to loud noises while he was a puppy—clapping hands, banging doors, dropping feed pans, etc.), get to him without frightening him, urge him on the track and offer encouragement. Get him to trail right up to the rabbit. You want him to connect the shot with the hot blood and meat which will excite him immensely. Should he hesitate about grabbing the rabbit, tease him with it and drag it in front of him until he does. Continue to use good judgment in firing in front of him until you are sure he's confident and that he knows that gunfire means a hot rabbit to chew.

Starting the Beagle Right. Don't overtire a young hound, no matter how willing or eager he is, or allow him to get discouraged. Run him an hour or two at a time, but every day you can. He won't learn anything in the kennel. Furthermore, if there are long lapses between training sessions he'll forget some of what he's learned. A Beagle gets smart through hunting. Take him often!

—Hound Training—

THE BEST way to train any hound is to hunt with him. Most hounds are imbued with a natural and intense desire to hunt, and the young hound that shows no inclination to do so after repeated opportunities is not worth keeping.

Trainers of sporting dogs have been able to teach their charges the niceties of manners and performance fairly easily, but no one has succeeded in *making* a dog actually *hunt*. Many have been taught to seek out hidden articles. Many have had their hunting instincts sharpened through encouragement. But no one has been able to instill keen hunting desire into a dog through force. Young hounds, whether they be Beagles, Foxhounds, Coonhounds or varmint hunters, should be started with dogs of their own kind. Often a few races with their elders are all that is necessary to teach them the species of game desired.

Occasionally, even frequently, young hounds are prone to run the first game trail they chance upon, such as young foxhounds chasing rabbits. If they persist in this, corrective measures must be taken. "Breaking scents," preparations so strong they sicken the dog of that specific odor, are readily available.

"Drag" races serve admirably in starting young hounds to trail and to tree, particularly during the

"off" seasons. This is done by laying a trail with a dragged hide or pelt, on which a few drops of anise oil has been sprinkled or a cloth drag laden with one of the excellent commercial training scents. These "drags" should be laid in fairly open country and over easy footing where the trainer can watch the progress of his pupils.

Trails may be laid by leading a pet coon through cover. The animal should be placed in a cage and hoisted into a tree at the end of the trail, where young hounds can view him and be encouraged to bark "treed."

One of the hardest things to teach a hound is to refrain from running any species of game other than that desired. Deer scent is particularly tempting and many a fox or coon chase has been interrupted by running hounds jumping deer. Here again the "breaking scents" are recommended.

The "blooding" of young hounds by allowing them to be in on the kill encourages them, but care should be taken to see that they are not badly mauled in the first battle.

There is no substitute for hunting experience in hound training. The more often young hounds are hunted without causing them to go stale, the more contacts they have with the desired game, the sooner they become proficient in the chase, and the quicker they learn the running habits of the quarry. The easiest and quickest way to cause a young hound to become "proof" against any other game than that desired is to hunt him in territory in which no other type of game, or few others, at best, range, and allow him to become so imbued with the desire to hunt that one particular species that he will pay no attention to any other.

Hounds need the same care given to other sporting breeds. Particular attention should be paid to the condition of their eyes and feet.

——Bird Dog Training——

THE FIRST step in field training is to take the dog while young to the field as often as possible and preferably where upland game birds may be encountered. Let the dog run and hunt to his heart's content. If he finds, flushes, and chases birds, so much the better. There is nothing gained by trying to restrain him until he has learned to hunt. If he has not enough natural hunting instinct, the chances are that he may never amount to much. Nevertheless, there are exceptions to all rules. It happens now and then that a dog showing little early heart for the hunt, may develop it later, with age and experience. It stands to reason, however, that it is better to work with a good prospect than a poor one. If one is not gifted with abundant patience—or has not yet formed a deep fondness for the dog—it is well to exchange a poor prospect for a good one as soon as possible. Beware of the prospect that does too much piddling around or puts his or her nose to the ground too incessantly. A high-class pointing dog should work for body scent only and seldom or never waste time on foot scent or attempts at trailing. All game birds will lie better to the bold, vigorous dog that dashes up to body scent and learns exactly how close he may approach with impunity.

Use A Whistle. It is a good idea every time you turn a dog loose to give a short, sharp double note on the whistle. If this is kept up, he associates this signal with the act of going away. The advantage is that if he ever later starts to potter, or you wish him to go wider to some destination, you can give him this signal and send him on. The come-in signal is prolonged whistling. The way to teach this is to practice it when attempting to take your dog up at the end of a workout. Some may respond naturally. Others may be both slower to catch on and to yield. You may have to call the dog by voice as an aid to the whistle. But if the whistle is used in connection with the calling, it will help the dog to get the idea of the signal. Most hunting-dog men prefer an Acme Thunderer-type whistle, and preferably one of bakelite. A metal whistle in zero weather may stick to the lips and take the skin off; a bakelite whistle is suitable for any weather.

Special Problems. It is assumed that in turning any dog loose in the field he will previously have been made proof against young pigs, poultry, sheep, or what not. If the average young dog is once exposed to an old hen with a brood of chicks, she will cure him in a hurry. To protect her chicks she will fly directly at the dog with a flapping, pecking, and stabbing that will cure him of poultry. If a dog has killed a chicken, the time-tested "country cure" is to get the dead chicken and wire it firmly up under the dog's neck. Wire it tight to his collar in a manner to make it secure. He may claw at it but he cannot reach it with his teeth. What he does to the chicken by clawing will but aid in sickening him of dead poultry. If the weather is warm for this cure, so much the better. The idea is to leave the chicken attached to the dog until he is thoroughly sick of it. Then remove the feet or whatever is left, and it is safe to bet that no repeat cure will be necessary.

For a dog that attacks young pigs no cure is known except to get to him and punish him. If the old sow gets to him first, there may be no dog left to cure. Many dogs have an almost insane desire to tackle sheep. If they ever taste blood, a high percentage may never be trusted again. Beward of the first sheep. Any extremity of punishment is in order and will be but

Training young Setter on liberated "planted" pheasant. Photo by Herb Levart.

flash-point. If he winds them first, however, he should stop, if but for an instant. Staunch pointing is simply prolonging that instantaneous pause until the dog will hold such a point for an indefinite time. There are dogs so full of the pointing instinct that they may practically be staunch themselves if they have opportunity to find enough game under good scenting conditions. Some of these dogs, having chased a lot of

Training young Setter on liberated or "planted" pen-raised quail. dog must become staunch on point. Photo by Herb Levart.

Teaching to "back." The young dog is brought up behind a pointing dog and caused to "honor" the point. Photo by Evelyn M. Shafer.

fair to the dog, whether he knows it or not. Otherwise he is sure to be killed some day by an irate farmer. The dog thoroughly trained in basic commands will never get into this situation, however.

Do not bother too much at first about a young bird dog chasing rabbits. You may talk to him in a tone of voice to indicate that you do not approve, but in the early stages do not take extreme measures. The idea above all else is that the dog should learn to hunt and learn to love it. Fur is naturally as attractive to a dog as feathers. Later, after a pointing dog is fully finished on game, and has had every reason in the world to know that you neither expect nor wish him to hunt rabbits—then will be time enough for a cure, if he still persists. Strong, severe commands, and a heavy hand on the check cord, will puzzle the dog, but usually teach the lesson.

Steadying. Any of the pointing breeds should at least "flash-point" on first contact with game. That is, they should flash-point if the scent is right. If flushing birds catch a young dog by surprise, there will be no

Teaching steadiness to shot. The handler is in position to grasp the check cord if the dog "breaks." Photo by Evelyn M. Shafer.

tice the check cord, a very valuable training aid, here being in training a Pointer. David M. Duffey photo.

game and found they cannot catch it, have sense enough to decide that pursuit is no use, and that tends toward a greater willingness to hold the point.

With more pupils than not, however, you will just have to be patient and wait for the day when you can get close enough to get your hands on them. For this

Teaching to point. The young dog is restrained from flushing the bird while the handler encourages it to point. Photo by Evelyn M. Shafer.

the breaks will have to favor you. The scent must be coming so strong as to help stop and hold the dog. You must be close enough so that he doesn't have to wait too long. When you get your hands on the dog,

Teaching to point. The handler continues to caution the dog as he slackens the check cord. Photo by Evelyn M. Shafer.

stroke him soothingly and let him know he is doing right. Stroke his tail up so that he will tend to hold it proudly. With your hands on him you can keep him steady for some little time. And here is a trick to be sure to use: Gently place a hand on his hind quarters and exert a little pressure to push him toward the birds. It is surprising how this tends toward steadiness. He might be wishing he could jump in and send the birds out. He does not, however, want to be shoved into them by you. Therefore, he resists the pressure. In the process of doing just that he is learning to be solid on point as nothing else can teach it. Naturally the dog should not be kept on point long enough to tire him out. Two or three minutes is plenty. Then step in, flush the birds, and let him go with them. Keep this up until he is so surely staunch on point that you can trust him under any and all circumstances to hold point for your arrival.

The next step is steadiness to wing and shot. For this you want a long, stout check cord. It must be really stout—one that will stand plenty of strain. For this lesson it is preferable to have someone with you to do the flushing. If that is impossible, you will just have to manage it yourself. Hold the check cord loose but wrapped firmly around your right hand at the end. When the birds are flushed, the dog will go with them as usual. Speak *"whoa"* to him very severely. He won't listen. Brace yourself. Just as he is about to hit the end of the check cord, speak *"whoa"* again. If he is going fast enough, and you are braced well enough, and if the check cord stands it, and you have a sufficiently good grip on the end of it, that dog will turn a somersault that will surprise him. Two or three times of this—if that many are necessary—and he will stay steady to wing when you say *"whoa."* He may even stay steady without the command. Being steady to wing, he will automatically be steady to shot. There is this exception: If a bird is killed, he may want to go in to retrieve without waiting for the command. A good many hunters do not object to this and some even prefer it. There is no question but that the dog will thus recover many a crippled bird that might otherwise be lost.

Accustoming the Dog to Gun Noise. It is presumed that the dog is already proof against gun shyness. Find out when you buy if he has ever heard gunfire —and to what extent. Even if he has, you should not at once try to test him. It is important first to make friends with him and win his confidence. Never shoot too close to any dog. Never shoot except in the field and when the dog is flushing, chasing, or pointing game. The point is that he should have his whole heart and soul centered on the game before him. Then if the gun is fired, and not too close—and you have previously won his confidence—he need never be gun shy. If a bird is killed, and he thus sees what the gun can accomplish, it will do much to assure that he will always love and never fear a firearm. Gun shyness is not natural. It is not hereditary. It is always some man's fault. It is never the fault of the dog.

—Training The Spaniel—

MORE IS asked of the English Springer Spaniel in the hunting field and in field-trial competition than is required of any other hunting dog breed. He must seek and find his game, flush it within range of the gun, mark its fall and recover it for the gunner, regardless of where it falls, both in water and in the uplands.

The requirements of a hunting Springer and the methods of channeling what are strong natural instincts in any good young dog, also apply to the other spaniels. What is outlined here may be equally well applied to Cocker Spanials, English Cocker Spaniels, American Water Spaniels or any of the retriever breeds which the hunter may ask to work in front of the gun in the manner of a spaniel. The only major exception here is the Brittany Spaniel, this last is really a pointer.

If a spaniel is to be brought to the high gloss and polish required of a field-trial performer, his training will be as arduous and time-consuming as that of a pointing dog. But, as a general rule, in the hunting field a spaniel can be expected to perform most satisfactorily at a much earlier age and with less field experience than a pointing dog.

Training Objectives. A hunting spaniel must learn two things. Everything beyond that is frosting on the cake. Assuming that he has the natural desire to hunt and a good nose, items which cannot be "trained" into a dog, he must be taught to restrict his eager questing to shotgun range, or approximately 40 yards from the gun. Obviously, since he is expected to chase the birds into the air, it will be frustrating if they are chased up at too great a distance to provide the gunner with good shooting.

The second requirement is retrieving. Hunters want crippled birds that run off, or game that falls dead in dense cover counted in their game bags and recovery of this game is vital as a conservation measure. So every hunting spaniel should "Fetch."

Start Them Early. Spaniels are precocious and should be allowed along on jaunts afield from the time they are three and four months old. While in the field let your spaniel be a puppy until about eight months of age when it's time to get serious with him. Because they are quick to learn, some spaniels are actually trained too early. Independence and love of game and gun must be encouraged and lapses in obedience treated tolerantly. Your pup should, however, come when called, sit on command and even be fetching dummies and bird wings reasonably well between the ages of three and eight months. He may also be taught to "Heel!" (walk at your side on command) and to "Stay!" (remain in one spot until sent on).

But take him into game cover and allow him to flush and chase to his heart's content anything that's available, including field sparrows, meadowlarks, rabbits or anything that leaves scent or attracts his attention when he gets out.

When you take your pup out, don't walk aimlessly. Set a zig-zag course and go to and into likely-looking spots that should hold game. This will help establish a quartering pattern in uniform cover, along with breaking the pattern to investigate particularly "birdy spots." When you change direction, blow a couple of beeps on your whistle to get his attention and, unless he's hot on the scent, he'll come to turn and head in the direction you are going. Accompany this change in direction with a wave of your arm and he'll start picking up the elements of responding to hand signals.

When he's come to enjoy these jaunts afield, get him used to responding to the commands he has learned in "yard training" when he's out in the field and allow him to work at will as long as he stays within gun range. With large numbers of spaniels this is all it will take. He'll develop a hunting pattern working about 25 to 30 yards to the front and sides as you move through the cover. But as soon as he kites off in a straight line and gets out of gun range, call him in to you and put him at heel for maybe a minute. Then send him out again. As long as he stays working within range, give him his head. When he takes the bit in his teeth, bring him back to heel. Keep repeating and the idea will come to him that he can hunt to his heart's content as long as he does it within the restrictions you lay out.

With a very headstrong dog, or later on, to train him to stop to allow you to catch up when he's hot on the trail of a hard running pheasant, for example, you have to resort to a check cord, in a manner similar to that used to steady a pointing dog.

If game is scarce, you can teach a spaniel to hunt and reward him at the same time by scattering the same dummies you use to teach retrieving about in the field, work him in the prescribed manner and let him home in on the scent (bird scent is available commercially to sprinkle on dummies) and "catch the bird." But planted pigeons or game farm birds are much better and should be used wherever possible, for the more experience your spaniel has with feathers and game the better he will be. Kill the birds he flushes. Shooting birds over a dog is what makes a hunter out of him. Basic retrieving and introduction to gunfire will be described later. But they can be done as part of yard-training procedure carried on at home during the same period you are introducing your pup to his field work, and then integrated into the field sessions.

These introductions to hunting should take place in the late summer and early fall, before the hunting seasons open, for spring-whelped spaniel pups. Then take the pup hunting. Don't worry about making him steady to shot and wing until he has had a full hunting season under his belt. Develop his desire first. Then when you crack down, forcing him to sit and mark a fall, or halt while hot on a moving bird, you won't confuse him as to his purpose in life or impair his desire to catch that bird. As a hunting dog, he may prove satisfactory to you without being steadied. That's your choice.

Retrieving. The only other basic requirement for a hunting spaniel is that he retrieve—from both land and water. At the same time, by getting him to connect the sound of gunfire with the fun of fetching, which is what retrieving should be to a spaniel, you should encounter no problem with gun shyness.

Spaniel pups can be "play-trained" into becoming satisfactory retrievers, starting at the age of eight weeks. Start with an old glove or a knotted wool sock. Play with the pup with it, then slide it out on the kitchen or garage floor or wherever you are conducting your training session; just a couple of feet away from the pup, at first. Chances are good he'll chase it, pounce on it, and return to you with it. Coax him to do so. After a short while you can toss it a little farther. Give the pup four or five tosses several times a day or whenever you have time. Don't keep at it too long. Quit when he's still interested and upon a successful retrieve. When you take the object from the pup, always say "Drop!" When you toss it, say the dog's name and tell him to "Fetch!" In these preliminary lessons always squat or kneel.

At three to four months of age, a small dummy (a kapok boat fender is excellent) that he can carry can be substituted for the glove or sock. Mix this up with tossing a game-bird wing saved from the hunting season. You are gradually lengthening your tosses. You can also tape the bird wing to the dummy. By the time the pup is about six months old he should be fetching a dummy from as far as you can throw it. Bring home intact small game birds like woodcock and ruffed grouse from your hunting trips, if your pup is still too young to be afield, and toss these for him to retrieve. Not only will this help his retrieving but it will get him used to feathers and the scent and taste of what he's to work with in the field.

Don't ever let him fail to bring you the bird. While you have here what could be termed a natural retriever, and this is fun, it's being done under your rules. When this becomes a habit, you will have just as reliable a retriever as any that has been "force trained", a tedious method which provides no enjoyment for either man or dog.

If your pup should want to run off with the dummy *do not chase him*. That's the game *he* wants to play. Run away from him and he'll chase you carrying the dummy. That's the game *you* want him to follow; then you praise him for his "delivery!"

If the pup is reluctant to pick up the dummy, tease him with it a little and play with him until he grabs it. When he's excited, toss it a little ways and he'll "attack" it. When he has it in his mouth, move away, calling and clapping to get him to chase you.

If he wants to lie on the dummy and chew it and your efforts to get him to chase you are ineffectual, walk up to him briskly and with no nonsense take it away, chastise him verbally, then squat and call him to you, make up with him and keep tossing the dummy and repeating this until he comes to you with it.

Accustoming the Dog to Gunfire. When the pup can be depended upon to retrieve the thrown dummy happily, it's time to introduce gunfire. You should have done a lot of hand-clapping, door and feed-pan slamming and general noise-making around your pup to pave the way and avoid any noise shyness.

Have a helper stand off some distance from you and toss the dummy. Have the pup make a couple of retrieves. Then have the helper—armed with a .22 blank pistol—get off about 50 yards from you, discharge the gun and toss the dummy towards the pup so it will land close enough to make for an easy retrieve. Practically every pup will be alerted by the sound of gunfire, see the dummy in the air, and go out to pounce on it when it lands. Praise him highly when he fetches. Three or four times of this and he'll be looking for the dummy in the air and something to fetch at the sound of gunfire. He'll associate gunfire with something that's pleasant and fun and which he is praised for doing—retrieving.

You can gradually move your helper in closer until finally you can shoot the gun yourself. Anytime the pup appears apprehensive, pretend not to notice, but retrogress until his confidence returns. In a short while you can move up to a small-gauge shotgun, following the same steps and also throw pigeons or game birds for him to fetch. Proper introduction to gunfire is a much more sane and effective program than attempting to "cure gun-shyness", once established.

Brittany Spaniel retrieves pigeon in training session. David M. Duffey photo.

a. In starting the spaniel's retrieving lessons, the handler "teases" the dog into taking the dummy.

b. The dog is allowed to play with it at first.

c. The spaniel is taught to hold the "dummy."

d. The dog must remain sitting while the "dummy" is thrown.

e. Promptness in retrieving is a "must."

f. The spaniel is taught to sit for the delivery.

Training a Spaniel. Photos by Evelyn M. Shafer.

The Finishing Stages. After you have introduced your pup to water, you can mix up this shooting and retrieving on both land and water. Acquaint your pup with water during the summer when it is warm. Go to a shallow pond or lake and wade out. You may have to coax, but you can usually get your pup to puddle around. Then toss your dummy just barely into the water so the pup can almost reach it from shore and tell him to "Fetch!" He'll reach for it, get his feet wet and come back with it. Very gradually lengthen the tosses until he is wading, and finally swimming a few strokes.

Keep at this, half a dozen or so retrieves a day, along with having your pup wade and swim alongside you and you'll develop the dog's confidence in water and a dog that can be depended upon to fetch a bird knocked down where it's wet.

From here on, developing a finished spaniel will be a matter of giving him experience on tougher tests, those you set up and those which occur as a natural thing when actually hunting the dog. It will also depend upon your diligence and practical application of common sense.

Having taught those two basics, you are well on your way with your spaniel to getting a full day's enjoyment out of those days in the uplands and marshes. To get complete enjoyment and to instill the many refinements that go into making a "brag dog", you'll be wise to obtain a good book on spaniel and retriever training, of which there are several on the market. They will go into detail not only in regard to the basics outlined, but the many other facets as well, steadying and handling among them, which will give the hunter a completely trained dog.

Meanwhile this outline should enable you to get your spaniel off on the right start and, if you give him plenty of attention and plenty of opportunity on birds, chances are he'll take it from there by himself and turn out to be a hunting dog you'll be both fond and proud of.

—Retriever Training—

THE RETRIEVERS are the following: Chesapeakes, Labradors, Goldens, Curly-coated Retrievers, Flat-coated Retrievers, Irish Water Spaniels, and American Water Spaniels. All of these are adapted by coat and nature to stand long, hard hours in a duck blind and retrieve wildfowl from icy water. Other breeds might retrieve ducks under moderate conditions, but have no business being subjected to the icy elements of a typical duck day. Individuals of many breeds will take naturally to retrieving. Some mere puppies like to play with a ball and retrieve it. Some dogs will naturally retrieve the first bird ever killed in front of them. Some excellent retrievers have been just naturally developed. The fact remains, however, that virtually all these dogs retrieve because they like to. If for any reason one such should ever get it into his head that he has changed his mind about liking it, then the master may well have quite a problem on his hands concerning how to correct the situation. Therefore, even the naturally inclined retrievers are usually given "force" training.

Starting the Training. The word "force," as here used, has nothing to do with cruelty in any respect whatever. It simply means that retrieving has been definitely taught and by a system which compels compliance. Since this same system applies equally to the retrievers, pointers, setters, spaniels, or any other breed asked to do the job, the following "force" system is recommended. (All hunting dogs should be taught to retrieve, because a good retriever is a true conservationist by saving game. Few hunters will dispute this; as a matter of fact, many hunters are as much interested in retrieving as in any other phase of hunting dog performance.)

Boykin Spaniel, rare breed, being trained in retrieving from wa
Chuck Morgan, trainer. David M. Duffey photo.

Golden Retriever delivers to Orin Benson, professional trainer, gle, Wisconsin. David M. Duffey photo.

Equipment for teaching "force" retrieving consists of several "dummies" or objects to retrieve, a leash so that the dog will be under constant control, a slip or choke collar, and, with some trainers, a spike collar. The latter is not recommended for amateurs, for one must be exceedingly careful in its use.

"Dummies" are made in varying forms. A piece of rubber hose about an inch in diameter and eight or ten inches long makes a good one. It is not too soft and is not injurious to the dog's teeth. A corn cob is a simple "dummy" as clean ones are easily available, but they are rather soft for dogs inclined to be a bit hard-mouthed. A small bundle of turkey feathers is often used. A small wooden dummy is easy to make and is quite serviceable.

Before beginning the lessons, the trainer must decide on the method to be used to cause the dog to open his mouth. There are many ways to accomplish this. One way will work with one dog while another way will be more satisfactory with another dog. Pinching an ear will work with some dogs nicely; squeezing a front paw gets results with another; others respond to a slight jerk on the choke collar. Find the most effective method for the individual and stick to it through his training.

Assuming your dog responds to the training collar, adjust it to his neck, with the running-free end on the upper side, and attach a short piece of stout cord. Grasp this up close to the ring with the right hand and hold the "dummy" with the left hand in front of the dog's nose where he can easily see it. Give the command "Fetch" in an ordinary tone of voice and accompany this command by a very slight jerk or

pressure on the collar. As the dog opens his mouth, instantly and gently place the "dummy" in it, slackening the pressure of the collar at the same moment. Hold your left hand under his mouth and thus keep it closed on the "dummy". Soothe his fears and induce him to hold the "dummy" steadily, caressing him if he holds it well. The first lesson should not be too prolonged. After one or two repetitions, call it a day.

Continue with this first lesson regularly, from day to day, until the dog will open his mouth promptly when you give the command "Fetch." Teach him to hold and carry the "dummy" reliably without mouthing it. These lessons should be given in a well-ventilated room, avoiding any distractions, diversions, or annoyances from spectators. A room has the further advantage of keeping the dog from cherishing ideas of escape, which may be his natural inclination during these early stages of training. In hot weather, the lessons should be given during the cool of early morning or late evening; under no circumstances should they be continued until the dog is manifestly discouraged under the restraint of discipline. Never end a lesson abruptly or with punishment. Lead the dog about for a few moments, praise and reassure him, then take off the training collar, thus concluding the lesson pleasantly.

Should the dog show strong tendencies toward an uncontrollably hard mouth, this fault must be corrected at once. Prepare a device as follows: Through a piece of wood about the size of a corncob drive some nails and clinch the end around the outside of it. Put in enough so that he cannot grasp the wood without somewhere touching the nails with his teeth. After grasping it once harshly he may afterward refuse to retrieve it. If so, force him to do it just as you began the first lesson with the dummy. All dogs have an intense dislike of closing their teeth on a hard substance. This device will enable you, after a bit of constant use, to achieve tenderness in retrieving.

Having taught the dog to open his mouth promptly to the order of "Fetch," the next stage is to teach him to step forward and grasp the object. In this lesson you need several feet of stout cord attached to the training collar so that the dog is free

Chesapeake Bay Retriever brings shackled duck to hand during training session. David M. Duffey photo.

to step forward when he hears the order. Hold the "dummy" a few inches in front of the dog's mouth and on a level with it, where he may both readily see and grasp it. Give the order "Fetch," exerting the necessary pressure on the collar at the same time and in a forward direction toward the dummy, thus assisting him to grasp it. The moment the "dummy" is in his mouth the collar pressure must be slackened. Be deliberate, and praise the dog when he has done well. Continue such lessons in this manner until he will, without the pressure of the collar, step forward promptly and grasp the "dummy" at the order of "Fetch."

At this juncture, the dog may continue holding the "dummy" when you wish him to release it, being apprehensive that, if it is not in his mouth, the pressure of the force collar may follow. Reassure him kindly every time he surrenders it to command. If he will not let go promptly upon order, grasp the end of the "dummy" in the left hand, but do not pull strongly on it. It is unwise to take it by *direct* force. When you have grasped the end of the "dummy" with your left hand, command him to "Give." Be prepared, if he refuses, to step on the toes of his forefoot. Use just enough pressure on his foot to force him to open his mouth—and this will require but very little. After a few repetitions, he should surrender the "dummy" instantly upon the order to "Give."

If you twirl the "dummy" temptingly and play-

fully before the dog's nose he may attempt to grasp it. It is a distinct gain if he will do so. Then he can be taught in a few lessons to *pick up* the "dummy". But too much playfulness should not be encouraged. The lessons must not lose the character of discipline. If too much playfulness is permitted, the force system will have no advantage over natural retrieving.

Having trained the dog so that he will step forward to grasp the "dummy" as ordered, the next stage is to teach him to lower his head to grasp it. This is accomplished simply by the process of gradually lowering the "dummy" at first only two or three inches at a time so that the change of position is not too suddenly radical. If you can tempt the dog with the "dummy", it should be easy to get him to follow it as it is lowered. If the dog takes kindly to this new lesson, he will sometimes even pick up the "dummy" from the floor after a very few attempts, particularly if you are tactful and do not proceed in too much of a hurry. A dog really anxious to please requires very little punishment and there may not be any perceptible stages in his progress; but in most instances the successive stages have to be formally and thoroughly observed. The dog requires time and schooling to comprehend his lessons. Hurrying him faster than he can comprehend or remember simply results in loss of time in the end.

At last the dog will pick up the "dummy" when he is ordered to "Fetch," provided it is held on the

His mind intent on only one thing, this enthusiastic English Springer Spaniel leaps for a fallen duck. Harvey's Photo Service.

floor; but if the hand is removed, he may at first make mistakes. He has previously been guided by following the hand. He may still follow the hand, which results in confusion if the hand is not near the "dummy." By keeping the hand close to the "dummy," after the latter has been placed on the floor, the dog is induced to pick it up. Finally, after many repetitions, he should gradually forget the hand and learn to concentrate on the "dummy" alone.

It must be admitted that it is sometimes difficult to persuade certain dogs to lower their heads. Some may be exceptionally obstinate in this respect. Force is the only answer in such cases. You must compel obedience. This means that you must be firm; it does not mean that you must be rough.

After the dog will pick up the "dummy," you may next throw it a foot or two in front of him and give him the order to "Fetch." In this lesson a longer check cord is required. If the dog does not move forward to the order, give him a pull to start him forward and at the same time repeat the order. If the previous stages of the training have been hurried over too rapidly, or imperfectly taught, the effect will be more manifest now than at any previous stage. It may even be necessary to return to some prior stage of development and begin all over again. If the dog has been properly prepared up to this point, it should be easy. This lesson should be thoroughly and regularly given, until the dog is reliably trained to fetch the object promptly without the use of the collar.

Then he should be given practice on a dead bird. If he shows any tendency to be hard-mouthed with this, you may tie some ten-penny nails to the bird, which may be removed after he begins to pick it up and carry it tenderly.

When he will retrieve the dead bird well (which may require a number of special lessons) he may next be taken to the yard or even an open field for practice. Be sure that you have him under perfect control; for if the pupil once learns that he may escape from discipline by using his heels, you will but give yourself a new problem before the training in retrieving can proceed.

No slovenly obedience should ever be accepted. Some men are satisfied if the dog brings the bird in and drops it close by. Do not accept such a performance. Insist that the dog complete his task. If you start slowly to walk away from him, this will often assist in inducing him to bring the bird in a direct line to you.

After your dog will fetch reliably, continue the lessons for many weeks so that the training will be indelibly imprinted upon his memory, and also to the end that perfect and prompt obedience may be established. He will then become so habituated to the work that disobedience or shirking never enters his mind.

In time, you may venture upon variations from the regular formula, with a view to developing the dog's intelligence. The "dummy" may be shown him and then thrown into bushes or tall grass, where he cannot see it, thereby forcing him to use his nose in finding it. The dog should learn to exercise a close watchfulness; this becomes an especially valuable trait later on in marking down game which falls to the gun.

He should be schooled to carry dead birds steadily to heel. You might drop a bird unobserved by the dog, but do it so that he will pass close and have a chance to smell it. Praise him highly if he picks it up. If he sniffs it but passes on, you should pretend to find it yourself and your manner should give evidence

The English Springer Spaniel, to whom retrieving comes almost naturally. Arthur M. Howath photo.

of pleasure at discovering such a prize, so that the dog's interest and desire to emulate may be aroused. Then require the dog to retrieve it.

As mentioned before, always insist on a perfect retrieve to hand. If you have adopted the method of giving him rewards, do not permit him to hurry through his work or half do it, in his eagerness to get the reward. Insist on having every detail properly observed. Nothing is more annoying in practical work than the dog's dropping a bird brought halfway in, or dropping the bird on the opposite side of a creek, necessitating a chase and retrieve on the part of the shooter, or another retrieve of the same bird by the dog.

Do not move when you send your dog in to retrieve game in the field. This is important. Tramping and stamping around in the vicinity of where you think the bird should be, you confuse your scent with that of the game you seek—and simply make it that much harder for the dog.

Introduction to Water Work. Most puppies of the spaniel and retriever breeds take naturally to water.

A. Teaching dog to stay at "heel" position.

B. Teaching dog to "sit."

C. Dog in "sit" position.

D. Teaching dog to sit at hand or whistle signal.

E. Teaching dog to hold the dummy.

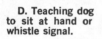

F. Teaching dog to mark the fall of the dummy.

Training a Retriever. Photos by Evelyn M. Shafer.

G. Use of check cord to teach dog to return with dummy to handler.

H. Forcing the dog to hold a live duck.

I. Dog must remain in blind until ordered to retrieve.

J. Teaching a dog to take hand directions.

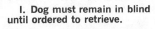

Training a Retriever (Continued). Photos by Evelyn M. Shafer.

Teaching the young dog to enter water is best accomplished in hot weather after he has had a good run and his body is heated. At this time a stream or body of water will look tempting to him. Several young dogs together often makes a "play-party" out of entering water and gives the timid youngster more confidence.

As soon as the young dog learns to swim, the hardest part is over. He will enjoy his new-found accomplishment. An older dog, fond of swimming, will be a great aid. If he is not encouraged by the example of other dogs, it will be necessary for you to take a hand. This should be done carefully. Encourage him to wade out with you, or even go in swimming with you. Do not force him or frighten him as this may cause his fear to become exaggerated and permanent.

Once your dog is at home in the water, it should be a fairly easy matter to have him become an efficient retriever from water, provided he is already a force-trained retriever. At first toss a bird or "dummy" for him close to the shore so that he will not have to swim for it. Repeat this several times, then increase the distance from shore until he has to swim for it. This may require some urging. Most young dogs are prone to stop and shake themselves immediately upon their return to shore, often dropping the retrieved object to do so. This should be dis-

couraged promptly. If he picks up the object and brings it on to you, the offense is not so serious but it will be a mark against him in field trials. Insist on a prompt retrieve to hand at all times.

Taking Directions. The ability to take directions, or hand signals, promptly and correctly is a valuable accomplishment in any dog hunted in front of the gun, in the blind or at heel as a non-slip retriever. Particularly valuable is it in a spaniel or retriever that has not seen the kill or properly marked the fall. These dogs should be taught to pause or look for directions immediately upon hearing several short blasts of the whistle.

When you have gained his attention in this manner, wave your hand in the direction you desire him to move and move yourself in that same direction. If you want him to "Go Back" wave your hand in a forward direction and move forward a little. If you want him to go to the right, wave your hand to the right and move to the right. The same applies to the left. If you want him to come closer to you, keep repeating the short blasts on the whistle and indicate your desire. By moving him in the direction desired, he will cross the line of scent and make the retrieve.

The dog should be allowed to use his own head as much as possible, and directions given only when necessary.

—Electronic Training Devices—

THE ADVENT of efficient miniaturized radio and electronic gear has made possible new equipment applications in the control of dogs employed in guard work as well as in dog training. A German Shepherd night watchdog at the Los Angeles County Museum of Natural History, for example, was found to respond to radio commands well enough to make it worthwhile equipping him with a special shoulder harness and small radio through which he could receive commands from building guards. The dog was worked on a 12-hour shift and helped keep the five-story museum under continuous night watch. Also, using miniaturized electronic equipment, the U.S. Army has experimented toward developing dogs to detect boobytraps and similar hazards. Electronic training aids are available today to dog trainers, most notable, perhaps, the shock collar.

Equipment Operation. Several firms produce electronic dog training equipment, this consisting usually of a special dog collar containing an electronic shock device which is activated only when the trainer pushes the button of a separate hand-held radio transmitter, and assuming, of course, that the dog is within receiving range of the tiny transmitter. Other equipment is available by which the shock may be

triggered—not by a radio signal, but an electrical impulse transmitted to the shock contact through a special leash.

Manufacturers usually offer a system by means of which the shock intensity can be varied. This is desirable, depending on the size and age of the dog, his temperament and faults, etc. As a general thing, devices of this kind are principally for use on dogs such as hounds, retrievers, bird dogs and other large dogs which occasionally prove exceptionally difficult to train and handle. Shock devices are not suitable for use on spaniels or any of the smaller groups which might be characterized as "softer" dogs. Nor should they be used on dogs which are less than a year old.

Applications. Shock collars are said by their exponents to be sure-fire cures for breaking a dog of bad faults such as chasing cars, poultry, fighting, making excessive noise, and other undesirable traits, but in each instance they should be used only when the owner or trainer can catch them right in the act. Also, these devices are intended to be used only when the dog can be seen by its owner or trainer, for training via the shock method is quite pointless unless administered with a very fine sense of timing. When

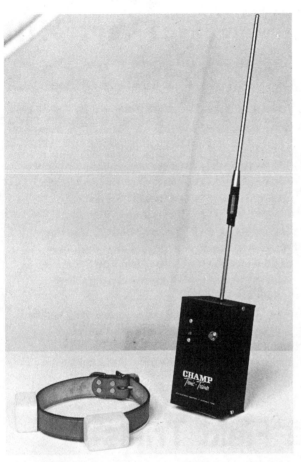

The Champ Tronic-Trainer, by JETCO. Photo by Jetco Electronic Industries, Inc.

used on dogs that point, care must also be exercised so as not to discourage the dog in any way from fol-

lowing his natural instincts to search out game and point.

In general, the electronic training devices are said to be highly effective. So much so that in obedience training, for example, it has been claimed that a dog may be taught yard work in a quarter of the time that would ordinarily be required. Once your dog has been taught what you want done, the electronic training device is useful in cases where the dog may refuse to conform to his training. Based on costs, however, electronic training equipment may not seem worthwhile to the owner of a single dog, whereas to one who trains many the equipment could prove valuable. The shock, itself, is harmless to the dog—is in no way disabling—and is felt for but a small fraction of a second.

Electronic dog training aids are usually advertised in outdoor or hunting magazines. Should he have the opportunity to talk with other owners and users of these devices, the dog owner contemplating their use might find such experience helpful as relating to the correction of some particular problem, for dogs are individuals and the faults which they exhibit as well as the problems to be corrected will vary.

The following are some of the firms which market electronic dog training equipment and from whom product information may be obtained by mail:

Jetco Electronics, P.O. Box 132, Huntsville, Texas 77340

Sensitronix, 2225 Lou Ellen, Houston, Texas 77018

Bill Boatman & Co., 244 Maple St., Bainbridge, Ohio 45612

Tri-Tronics, Inc., P.O. Box 5841, Tucson, Arizona 85703

(This firm also markets an "anti-bark" collar which automatically delivers a shock to the wearer each time he barks.)

—Some "Nevers" of Training—

NEVER NAG at a dog; when you speak to him, mean it. The dog constantly nagged at will never amount to much—and can't.

Never punish if in doubt. Always give the dog the benefit of any doubt. But if punishment is unconditionally called for, make it severe enough to count. Thus once should suffice for any given infraction. It is a question whether constant punishment is worse than constant nagging; both are bad.

Never tease a dog. Respect him and earn his respect. Don't accept partial or slovenly performance. Insist that the dog perform completely any task, as he has been taught he should.

Never vary commands. Make them always the same. Thus you preclude any confusion or uncertainty.

Never work or hunt your dog except with his equals or peers. If you go with men whose dogs will but spoil yours, leave them and hunt alone—or if you go with them, don't take your dog.

Never lend your dog to anyone, not even a best friend—any more than you would your wife. If you lend your dog to a friend the chances are you won't be friends for long.

Never ask anything unreasonable of a dog. Be jealous to guard his respect for you and his desire to perform as you would have him.

Never give him freedom to roam and find bad company. Dogs can become tramps and get into bad habits the same as people.

Never let companions who hunt with you spoil the dog by breaking shot or otherwise. If a man breaks shot you can't blame a dog for doing so.

Part XIII

THE DOG IN FIELD TRIALS

Nothing so quickly exposes the truth about a hunting dog's virtues and faults as his performance in the field. The field performance of several dogs of the same type may quickly be compared by any two or more hunting dog owners willing to team up on a hunt. This way, they will —in a sense and on a very small scale—be conducting their own field trials. But to learn what kind of performance they perhaps ought to expect of their dogs, they should attend a scheduled field trial for the breed they own. There they may observe the best in the competition and see what they can do. Often this proves a real eye-opener. But exciting as such events are to the spectators, the real importance of field trials lies in their influence on breeding, for such trials demonstrate the results of various breedings and thereby provide a sound basis for intelligent selective future breedings. Hence, it is correct, indeed, to say that field trials are "the weathervane" of hunting dog breeding programs.

—Beagle Hound Field Trials—

NO ORGANIZED sport which utilizes the talents of hunting dogs has known a faster or healthier growth in this country than that of Beagle Hound field trials. The National Beagle Club was formed in 1890 and held its first trial in November of that year. Conditions at Hyannis, Mass., the scheduled site of the trial, were so unfavorable that the venue was moved to Salem, N.H., where the event was successfully terminated.

In 1891 and 1892 the National Beagle Club was the only club holding formal or organized competitions for Beagles, but the following year the Northeastern Beagle Club and the New England Beagle Club came into being. For several years the sport knew a slow but nevertheless steady growth, but in recent years it has grown by leaps and bounds.

Beagle Trials—A Popular Sport. To the outdoor sportsman whose favorite pastime is hunting upland game, the growth of interest in Beagles and Beagle field trials is not surprising; in fact, it is only a natural sequel to the high popularity enjoyed by this great little gundog throughout this country.

The Beagle is universally recognized as a specialist in rabbit hunting. Although he possesses other qualities which endear him to the sporting public, rabbit hunting seems to be his mission in life. He was primarily bred for this purpose and it is in the chase of Molly Hare that he is at his best.

The cottontail rabbit is the most prolific of our upland game animals. He is found in practically all sections of the country and seems to withstand hunting pressure better than any other species. He provides great sport in the field, in hound music and gunning pleasure, and his succulent flesh can be whipped up into delicious dishes capable of tempting the jaded palate of the most blasé gourmet.

Pride of ownership is a human quality which glows in the breast of every beagler and the remark, "My hound is better than any around here," is a challenge which no true beagler can resist. If his own dogs are not "up to snuff", he is sure to have a friend whose pack or kennel can provide proper and instant competition.

The Beagle is an easy dog to keep. He requires but little room and his board bill is a minor matter. Unlike bird dogs and retrievers, it is not necessary to give him an extensive and expensive education in field work and manners before he can successfully compete in field trials. No great skill in handling is required of the owner and no specialized training is necessary. Some of the leading winners were taken directly from a farm where they had self-hunted all their lives to win highest honors at trials under the guidance of owners who had never before attended such an affair.

There is no dearth of good Beagle trial grounds in

this country. Suitable terrains well stocked with rabbits are to be found in almost every section and the application of simple yet sound game-management principles can provide favorable running conditions almost anywhere with a short time. The beagler is not confronted with the problems which beset the bird-dog fancier in this respect. And he has many more opportunities for training over a longer season each year.

The sport of Beagle field trials is comparatively inexpensive. The customary fee at licensed trials is $5; at sanctioned trials the fee is usually $2 or $3. If an unregistered Beagle wins at a licensed trial, it must be registered within thirty days. Entry fees in bird-dog trials range from $5 to $150. The greatest single item attached to Beagle trials is transportation. The sport is the least expensive of any in the gundog field.

These are only some of the reasons why Beagle Hound trials are growing in popularity. There is always a fine spirit of friendliness evident when beaglers get together, competitive yet cooperative. The Beagle is primarily a gundog, an ideal companion for the outdoorsman as well as a decorative friend at the fireside. He makes as much music as the foxhound and is far more tractable, for he keeps his master's gun in mind all the time. And his cocky manner and friendly disposition make him a favorite everywhere. It is no wonder that he is one of the best contenders for American popularity honors.

The avowed purpose of Beagle field trials is the improvement of the field qualities of the breed, as well as improvement in type. Proof that the sport has served well in this respect is the fact that field trial winners are frequently also winners of honors on the bench. Good type and conformation are necessary for the best field performance.

Fld. Ch. Hi Pine Wheeler, a Beagle owned by Dr. C. F. Partridge of Boaz, Alabama. Photo by Jimmy Wilson Studios.

How Trials Are Organized. All Beagle trial stakes, except a Championship stake, are divided by height into two divisions. These are stakes for Beagles not exceeding 13 inches in height and stakes for Beagles over 13 inches but not exceeding 15 inches in height.

Stakes may also be divided by sex if the field-trial giving club so desires and so states in its premium list of entry forms. The entries in Beagle trials have become so large in recent years that the division of stakes by sex has become a general practice.

Practically all Beagle trials in America are held under the jurisdiction, license, or sanction of the American Kennel Club. At each trial, all entries, except those mature beagles 18 months or older in age whose height has been officially determined by the American Kennel Club by its certificate of measurement, are measured by the standard of the National Beagle Club before starting, and if found to be incorrectly entered as to height, are transferred to the corresponding stake or stakes of their proper height.

At all field trials run on cottontail rabbits, Beagles are run in braces, but when the trial is run on hare all entries in a stake are run together as a pack. Small packs (four and six hounds) are also licensed.

When the dogs have been entered, the names are placed in a receptacle (such as a hat), stirred up, and drawn one at a time. The first dog drawn runs with the second dog drawn, constituting the first brace. The third and fourth dog drawn make up the second brace, and so on until all the dogs are drawn. Should there be an odd number or bye dog, such bye dog is run with a bracemate selected by the judges. This bracemate is under judgment when so running.

After the running of the first series has been completed, the judges may call for whatever dogs they wish to run in the second series, and brace them together in any manner they desire. In determining

Fld. Ch. Lucky Hunting Brownie, an Indiana Beagle, posed by ~~ce~~ **Tarrant.** Hounds and Hunting photo.

Handlers waiting to run Beagles in field trial. Sentinel Photo.

the final winners, the judges may run the hounds any number of times in any number of additional series they may desire. The idea is to give the competitors full opportunity to display their qualities under judgment. When hounds have been laid on a line together, or have been given the opportunity to hark in to one another, they are considered as in competition.

Procedures and Judging. Beagle trials are not elimination affairs, although the *modus operandi* may cause the novice to think otherwise. Judging is done under the "spotting" system and each brace does not constitute a race, with the loser being eliminated from further consideration. In fact, both dogs can be, and frequently are, called back into second and subsequent series.

However, one of the rules in Beagle trials reads as follows: "Before the judges announce the winners in a class, the placed hounds must have beaten the hound placed directly beneath them." This rule was once exclusive to Beagle trials and was not in effect in field trials for any of the other sporting breeds. Years ago, some important stakes in pointing dog trials had this requirement, but it has long since been discarded.

There are a number of rules of procedure and instruction to the judges in Beagle trials. While these rules are good guideposts for the judges, strict adherence to the letter of their wording sometimes brings about confusing situations which could be eliminated if the judges were allowed full leeway in conducting the competition to a successful conclusion. The less red tape in any gundog competition, the better. The selection of competent, unbiased, and impartial judges, who know what to look for in a good Beagle performance and how to find it, should insure correct decisions.

Beagle judges know that the Beagle is primarily a hunting hound. His primary object is to find game; then he must drive it in an energetic and decisive manner and show an animated desire to overtake it. Ability and desire to hunt are of first importance. It is not the quantity but the quality of the performance which should be given first consideration.

Interference by one hound with his bracemate is penalized. "Pottering" is remaining too long in one spot and not trying to advance. "Swinging" is making loops by reaching too far at checks or when the scent is lost. "Skirting" is running alongside those on the line and trying to get in front by catching the scent at a turn. "Babbling" is giving tongue when not trailing game. "Leaving checks" occurs when a hound refuses to come back to the place where he lost the scent. "Racing" occurs when a hound depends upon his heels rather than his nose to keep in front. He generally over-runs the track. "Running in hit-or-miss style" might be whipping the line by driving ahead, weaving back and forth trying to get ahead rather than sticking to the trail in an accurate manner. "Backtracking" is self-explanatory.

There is a considerable amount of luck in field trials, yet the worthy hound will generally make his mark eventually. Quality will not be continually denied. Beaglers all know that the vagaries of scent are many, that atmospheric conditions sometimes play havoc with a hound's ability to unravel a trail, that the "Luck of the Draw" is ever present. They also know "Old Lady Luck" will sometimes smile on them, and this, coupled with sheer love for the sport, keeps them knocking at the door of Beagle-trial fame.

Conscientious judges, and most of them are just that, know, too, that varying conditions may mean varying performances, and they try to equalize chances as nearly as possible.

The reduction of individual hound performance to a mathematical formula is extremely difficult, calling for an exceedingly analytical mind and probably much splitting of hairs. Each judge probably has his own method of arriving at percentages, if, indeed, he follows this rule strictly, and the figures may not always agree. But experienced men work a stake out to a logical conclusion, generally, particularly if they take the time necessary and do not resort to snap judgment, or jump to impulsive conclusions. The top-heavy sizes of some of the more important stakes make rather arduous undertakings of judging assignments and the conscientious fortitude of these officials under such circumstances is to be admired.

Championships and Championship Points. Championship points for Beagles are awarded only to winners of open All-Age Stakes. These points are

Merry Beagles from Gates Mills, Ohio, during a National Fi Trial. Hounds and Hunting photo.

awarded on the following basis: 1 point to the winner of first place for every hound started; ½ point to the winner of second place for each hound started; ⅓ point to winner of third place for each hound started; ¼ point to winner of fourth place for each hound started. At present a hound of either sex must win a total of at least 120 points, which must include three first places in licensed or member trials, to be declared to be a Field Trial Champion of Record by the American Kennel Club.

In the early days of Beagle trials, when annual events were few, only ten points were required to win a championship, but at least one win had to be made at a field trial that was rated 3 points or over and only one win of a hound was recognized at any trial. Beagle trials were rated as follows: 50 or more starters, 5 points; 40 starters and under 50, 4 points; 30 starters and under 40, 3 points; 20 starters and under 30, 2 points; under 20 starters, 1 point.

At Beagle trials, the gallery walks behind the judges, who are often mounted, and the handlers. Members of the gallery must remain far enough back not to interfere with the running and when game is raised they must stand fast. However, the gallery, as a general rule, can see a considerable portion of the running, and almost every Beagle trial is followed closely by a large and enthusiastic gallery of contestants and spectators. To insure ample opportunities on game for every competing dog, field trial clubs generally release captured or pen-raised rabbits prior to the start of the trials. In many instances these rabbits are released some days before the running in order to allow the animals to become oriented and accustomed to the area.

Not all good Beagles make good field trial contenders. Some dogs which do very fine work on their home grounds and when hunting with their kennelmates become too excited, nervous or timid to make a good showing when in competition. The change of environment, the presence of the gallery, the association with strange hounds and the general air of excitement attendant upon a field trial has an upsetting effect on some dogs and their performance in competition is far below the level of their known ability. Others catch the spirit of the occasion quickly and become what is known as "gallery dogs." They thrive on competition and seem to outdo themselves

Hot on the trail! Photo by Evelyn M. Shafer.

when braced with a strange dog in front of a gallery.

A good field trial Beagle must have more than a good nose, a properly used voice, and the desire to hunt. He must have great determination and independence; and while he must hark in to his bracemate's cry he must not depend upon his competitor to carry the trail. He must show intelligence in hunting the gamey spots, no matter how different the terrain may be to that with which he is accustomed. He must take advantage of every opportunity to display his good qualities and make the most of the limited time accorded him, and he must do it all with energy, enthusiasm, and style.

Beagle trials are of paramount importance to breeders of quality hounds. These competitions provide a sound basis for intelligent, selective breeding. Fans can keep abreast of Beagle developments and Beagle trials in *Hounds and Hunting*, the Bradford, Pa., publication devoted exclusively to the merry little hounds.

Under the point system and with the large number of trials being held annually, a Beagle has a better chance to gain the title of field trial champion than foxhounds and bird dogs which must win title events to annex such honors. But the acquiring of the necessary points, particularly when three first places must be won, is certainly no mean accomplishment, and many fine contenders have amassed far more than the necessary total of points only to miss the title because of failure to meet the first-place wins requirement.

As long as Br'er Rabbit and Molly Cottontail and their family continue to lay down scent-filled trails in America's fields and coverts, the Beagle will continue to be the favorite gundog of millions of American sportsmen.

—Bird Dog Field Trials—

ARE BIRD dog trials *really* of value in improving bird dog breeds? This question is frequently asked by novitiates witnessing their first field trial. Those who take an active interest in these events answer the question with an unqualified "Yes!"

Field trials are events wherein individual bird dogs

are given the opportunity to display their field qualities in direct competition.

They serve varied purposes. The primary object is the improvement of the bird-dog breeds through a more general dissemination of information concerning producing bloodlines and breeding procedure and a demonstration of the results of various breedings. This knowledge, so essential if future bird-dog generations are to measure up to the highest standards of field performance, can be best obtained through the avenue of public competition provided in field trials. Field trial standards approach the ideal, and the history of progress in American bird-dog breeding is found in the annals of the sport. Field trials provide the weathervane of bird-dog breeding programs.

The social side of a field trial is one of its most attractive features. The friendships formed are lasting. There is always a spirit of good fellowship and camaraderie and there is no class distinction among the devotees of the sport. Every field trial is a gathering of high-class sportsmen and sportswomen on common ground and in a common interest, and no higher degree of sportsmanship is prevalent in any sport. The sport provides a medium for the interchange of constructive ideas concerning everything pertaining to the gundog and, while the theories advanced may not always be in accord, the ensuing arguments are in the spirit of friendliness.

Field trials have always been and are now recognized as outstanding contributions to game restoration and conservation programs. Many game-management programs beneficial to the entire country-side have been launched on field trial grounds, the resulting research proving of great value to wildlife resources in general.

Historical Notes. The first public field trial in America was held at Memphis, Tenn., October 8, 1874. The winner was Knight, a black setter dog belonging to H. Clark Pritchett. The stake was sponsored by the Tennessee State Sportsmen's Association and the judges were J. W. Burton and J. H. Acklen. The contest was the result of some rather heated arguments among the members concerning the field merits of their respective dogs.

The Tennessee State Sportsmen's Association sponsored the sport exclusively until 1877, when the Hampton, Iowa, trials were held. Since that time the growth of interest has been steady. From 1880 to 1890, the sport recorded an average of six trials annually, with an average total of 120 dogs competing. After that period the sport rapidly spread to all sections of the country. In the decade from 1920 to 1930 an average of 144 trials, with 369 stakes, was held. During this period an average of 5535 bird dogs of various breeds competed annually in field trials. In more recent years the sport has grown by leaps and bounds until now there are a number of annual events in practically every section of the country. There are now almost 500 recognized field trial clubs in the country sponsoring over 750 recognized trials, embracing some 2,400 stakes (Open and Amateur) with about 40,000 starters.

In the early days the judges reached their decisions through the "point system." The scale of "points" used approximated the following: Nose, 30; pace and style, 20; backing, 10; breaking, 15; retrieving, 5; style and stanchness in pointing, 15; roading, 5; total, 100.

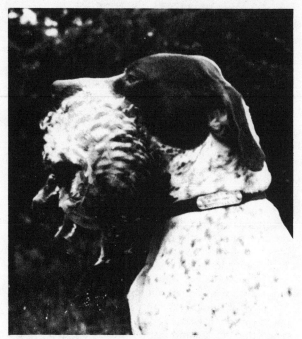

Three times National Pheasant Shooting Dog Champion Elhew Jungle retrieving grouse. (Owner: Robert G. Wehle, Scottsville, N.Y.)

("Breaking" here referred to handling or obeying the handler's commands.)

In 1879 the first "heat" system was adopted. Under this method, each dog that defeated his bracemate or competitor was carried into the next series until the final elimination was made and the winner declared. This system was found unsatisfactory as, in the drawing, it was possible for the two best dogs to be run together in the first heat, thereby penalizing one good dog to the advantage of an inferior one. Soon what is known as the "spotting system" came into being and it prevails today.

The "Spotting" Method. Under the "spotting" method, the judges are unhampered by red tape and unnecessary rules and are left free to pick the winners from the performances on that occasion. The contesting dogs are run in braces, the running time of the first-series heats being stipulated in the rules of the club. Unless the winners stand out decisively at the end of the first series, the dogs that have performed with the greatest brilliancy are picked as second-series contenders, braced in any manner the judges may desire, and put down again, running until the judges are satisfied as to the comparative merits of the contestants on that occasion.

The first-series heats in a field trial are all of the same duration, but the time allotted for second-series competition is at the discretion of the judges unless otherwise stipulated in the club rules.

Stakes, Circuits and Purses. With the increase in interest, it is only natural that there should be a number of changes in the *modus operandi* of field trials. Stakes according to age classification fall into

Puppy, Derby, and All-Age classifications. In many instances, like in the case of thoroughbred horses, January 1 serves as a universal birthday. Here it might be said that there are Puppy stakes for dogs up to certain age limits, as much as eighteen months, Derby events for candidates up to 30 months of age; and All-Age stakes open to all ages. There are amateur and professional stakes, winners' events, championship competitions, and shooting-dog stakes.

In the early days field trial dogs were handled on foot. Changes in conditions, the scarcity of game, and difference in standards have brought about almost an abandonment of this practice, and now practically everyone who attends a major field trial follows the running from horseback. Professional handlers train from horseback almost exclusively. This does not, of course, apply to shooting-dog stakes or the cover-dog trials in grouse country, where the handlers and, in some cases, the judges, walk.

The so-called "big circuit" of major trials is composed of a series of clubs holding annual events in the prairie chicken, pheasant and quail sections. These are inaugurated annually on the Canadian prairies, where prairie chicken, Hungarian partridge and, in recent years, the pheasant furnish the game. Prairie trials begin about September 1, leading pheasant competitions occur during the fall, and the circuit continues through the winter months in the South on quail, generally closing with the National Bird Dog Championship which has a traditional starting date of the third Monday in February.

These trials are all run under natural conditions, the courses being laid out across country. The entrance and starting fees are comparatively high and the cash purses correspondingly large. The heats range from 30 minutes to 3 hours.

When the curtain falls on the Winter competition, the Spring events are ushered in. These are generally held on one-course grounds in the East with liberated pheasants or quail providing the game.

The dogs that compete in the major stakes are considered the cream of the country, and it is upon their performance that the pendulums of breeding activity generally swing. Many of the dogs are developed for field trial and stud purposes only, although a large portion of them are annually used by their owners in the season's shooting.

Winners As Practical Hunting Dogs. There has been, and always will be, extensive discussion regarding the ability of the dog developed for field trials to adapt himself to the requirements of shooting. Years ago this question formed the basis of an interesting competition between the famous sportsmen, Herman B. Duryea and Pierre Lorillard. Duryea selected J. M. Avent, the veteran professional handler who had charge of the Duryea string of field trial dogs, as his shooting companion. Lorillard chose Charles Tucker, his handler, and pitted the bird-finding ability of his shooting dogs against the Duryea field trial winners. The contest was to be determined by the number of quail each party bagged on a given day.

Of course, marksmanship was an equation of the competition, but all were expert shots and no handicap was asked or given. The Duryea-Avent combination won by a wide margin, not only in the number of birds bagged but also in the number of coveys and singles found and handled. The great little setter bitch, Double National Champion Sioux (1901-02) was a member of the Duryea-Avent string. She was hunted in short heats several times during the day and found more birds than any other dog that competed.

There is no reason why the properly trained field trial winner cannot be used to the best advantage as a shooting dog in the type of country in which he has been developed. The winning setter, Phil Essig, was a shooting dog of the finest quality and the noted Eugene's Ghost, always difficult to handle in field trial competition, was shot over heavily after his field trial career was ended. National Champion Mary Blue was used extensively as a shooting dog by her owner, Walter C. Teagle.

Owner-Handler Stakes. Several of the major clubs hold "owner-handler" stakes, in which the competing dogs must be handled by the owners. To many judges these are most important events, for the owners are often strangers to their own dogs, as many of these dogs have been professionally trained and campaigned by their trainers in major trials.

Amateur Field Trials. The amateur handler is often handicapped in competition with professionals. Bird-dog training with him is a hobby, a source of pleasant and healthful recreation. Consequently he cannot devote as much time to his dogs as the professional, who makes bird-dog training a business. The professional is a valuable asset to the general bird-dog fraternity. He makes the sport of field trials or hunting with a bird dog possible for many enthusiasts who do not have the time, the facilities, or even the know-how to train their own dogs. He lives a hard life, his work returns comparatively little in a financial way, and he generally adopts his vocation as a life's work because of his love for bird dogs and the outdoors.

The amateur trials really constitute the backbone of the sport. In these events, the entries are generally

Elhew Jungle on point for his owner with two backers, each a holder of the Champion title.

Smokepole, the 1965 National Shooting Dog Champion. (Owner-handler, Herbert N. Holmes, Gunsmoke Kennels) Photo by Hendley's.

made up from the ranks of shooting dogs and are handled, in the main, by their fond owners. The trophies given as awards are highly prized, not so much for their intrinsic value; but as evidence of accomplishment. These trials are "feeders" for the major circuit, as many patrons of amateur events are ambitious to own and campaign a "big time" contender. The major amateur events each year are the Regional Amateur Championships, the National Amateur Quail Championships, and the National Amateur Pheasant Championship, sponsored by the Amateur Field Trial Clubs of America.

The American Field. The *American Field,* a weekly publication with headquarters in Chicago, devotes most of its editorial matter to field trial activities and subjects pertaining to the gundog. The publication maintains the Field Dog Stud Book and annually sponsors the American Field Futurity (run on quail) and the American Field Pheasant Futurity.

Other Stakes and Sponsors. Other breeders' stakes are the Grouse Futurity, sponsored by the Grand National Grouse Championship, and the New England Futurity, sponsored by the Association of New England Field Trial Clubs.

In the 1960s, Futurities were also established for shooting dog prospects—the National Shooting Dog Futurity run on pheasants in October, and the U.S. Quail Shooting Dog Futurity run on bob-white quail early in the year—January or February.

Getting Acquainted With Field Trial Activities. The novitiate in the field of bird dog activities should attend a few field trials. Ride the courses, see all the running, ask questions. They will provide an excellent medium for the comparison of the performance of your own dog with that of others. In attending these events you will meet genuine sportsmen always willing to extend a helping hand to a fellow fancier.

These contacts will prove of value in developing your own dog. Acquaintanceships formed at field trials often ripen into long and valued friendships.

National Bird Dog Championship. Most important of all bird dog field trials is, of course, the National Bird Dog Championship. With heats of 3 hours' duration, this is an endurance stake. Its standards are of the highest. Not only must the winner be able to go the long route at rapid pace but he must also handle to the gun. Whenever a dog wins this greatest of all bird-dog titles one can rest assured that here is a dog that is capable of providing a thrilling day of gunning. The National Championship is no place for an aimless runner. It is a stake for the highest type of shooting dog, the gundog at the very peak of his ability. The dog that will not handle kindly commands little consideration here. This is as it should be, for the bird dog's mission in life is to be an asset to his master's gun. The best field trial dog is nothing more than the shooting dog at his very best. The dog which cannot be gunned over is not deserving of the term "field trial dog."

National Free-For-All Championship. Next in field trial importance is the National Free-For-All Championship. In this stake the qualifying heats are one hour in length, the finals 3 hours. No dog is out of it until the decision is announced. This stake is quite a difficult one to win. The dog must qualify by turning in a sparkling performance in his one-hour appearance, and then he must go the long 3-hour route in impressive fashion. Some dogs may be quite capable of finishing the 3-hour grind at good pace, but an unlucky draw of courses or the lack of class in the first hour may prevent them from qualifying. On the other hand, a dog may turn in a wonderful performance in the first hour, but not be capable of finishing the long final heat in good form. Hence the winner generally is a dog which is keyed up to go the long heat, showing class and brilliance all the way. There are those who describe the National Championship as the quest for the ideal shooting dog, and the winner of the Free-for-All Championship the apotheosis of the highest class field trial dog.

Setters Vs. Pointers. "Which makes the best field trial dog, the setter or the pointer" is a frequently asked question, but few persons are qualified to give the answer. It all depends upon the individual, of course, for there are field trial winners and champions in both breeds. However, the pointers have held the major portion of the field trial spotlight in recent years, one reason being that more pointers are entered than setters.

This has not always been true—in fact, it is somewhat the reverse of what the situation was in the early days of field trials. Most field trial contenders then were setters; there were few pointers in the first trials. It was generally admitted that early-day pointer performance was not on a par with that of the setter, and the long-hairs held full sway. The first

Standing at the left in the rear row, the author with winners in the cond National Shooting Dog Futurity. Front (left to right): Dr. Thos. Flanagan with Grouse Ridge Buddy, 1st Place and the *Sports eld* plate; David Grubb with Pirate Dan Patch, 2nd Place; Carl Bark- with Tooth Acres Joe, 3rd Place. Rear (left to right): Henry P. Davis; Robert G. Wehle, Pres.; Judge rold A. Crane; Judge Rich Tuttle; and Richard Shear, Secretary. rdinali Studio photo.

winners were "native" setters, and then the progeny of imported English Setters of the Llewellin strain came into vogue, practically dominating the field for a number of years.

In order not to leave the pointer completely out in the cold, and also to promote more interest in the breed, field trial clubs began to hold separate stakes for two breeds, the winner of the setter stake being pitted against the winner of the pointer stake for the settlement of the "absolute." Seldom was the winner of the "absolute" not a setter.

The first pointer to win an important field trial was Don, owned by R. T. Vandevort. Don was first place ($250 cash) in the Free-For-All stake of the National American Kennel Club's trials, which were run on prairie chickens at Fairmont, Minn., begin- ning September 4, 1882, eight years after the first field trial was held. In addition to the cash purse, Vandevort's Don won the Pennsylvania State Field Trials Association cup for the best dog in the stake owned in Pennsylvania and a special prize of $20 for the best pointer in the stake.

Separate stakes for pointers continued to be held until around 1900, when the careful breeding pro- grams of the pointer fanciers began to show results.

The first pointer to win the National Champion- ship was Manitoba Rap. This was in 1909. Three pointers have won it three times each since. These were Mary Montrose, Becky Broomhill, and Ariel. Only one setter, Feagin's Mohawk Pal, has annexed this coveted crown three times. And only two setters, Sport's Peerless Pride (1939) and Mississippi Zev (1946), have been returned the winner since Feagin's Mohawk Pal won it for the third time in 1930.

During the past 25 years there has been much dis- cussion concerning the so-called "rise of the pointer and fall of the setter" in the realm of field trials. To speak of the "rise and fall" is to place an incorrect evaluation on the situation. The fact that the pointer is now more than holding his own with the setter in field trials does not indicate the deterioration of the setter as much as it does the improvement of the pointer. At the time the pointer fanciers were stick- ing strictly to their knitting and breeding to charac- teristics and proved ability rather than to pedigrees, the setter lovers had gone "purist" and frowned upon any dog which could not boast a 100% Llewellin pedigree, regardless of his field qualities. This fad is no longer in vogue and the setter breeders are again back on a sound foundation.

There was a time, too, not long ago, when "class," interpreted by too many as "heels," had its fling in field trials and a number of judges put too much emphasis on extreme range. This brought about the development of some whistle-running pointers and near-bolting setters to the detriment of both breeds. The pendulum has now swung back to proper bal- ance and the field trial contender of these days has to be endowed with a goodly portion of unusual ability in every department if he is to be successful. Not only must he have range which will take him to the limits of his country, but he must also hunt with intelli- gence and be amenable to his handler's commands. He must possess an excellent nose and use it well, show style and intensity in action and on point, and be perfectly mannered under the gun. When one consid- ers the high degree of excellence in so many phases of field performance that is expected of the field trial dog it is, indeed, surprising that so many make the grade. In the final analysis, the field trial dog is the shooting dog of the highest order.

Most judges insist that the English Setter has not deteriorated to any appreciable extent since the time when he was practically supreme in field trials. Rather, they explain, the pointer has improved. The setter wins the majority of places in grouse trials. Here again the main reason may be because he out- numbers the pointers in those events.

The Irish Setter, during the early days, played an important part in field trials. He was, however, a real field dog then and not the hothouse product that we see shuffling around in bench shows today. Many believe he would still be a contender had his fanciers been as much interested in the perpetuation of his field abilities as they were concerned about his beauty.

One reason for the enviable field trial position the pointer enjoys today is the fact that the short-hair, as a breed, develops a bit earlier than his long-haired rival. If care is used the pointer can be "pushed along" in his education without damage, but to bring him to the best the setter must be allowed to develop naturally. When all the arguments relative to which is the best breed for field trials are in and the shout- ing has died down the verdict is written in these

Start of a bird dog field trial in Piney Woods country.

words: "It all depends upon the individual." There are good ones and not-so-good ones in both breeds. There is one quality which is seldom mentioned but which is most important. That is the competitive spirit. Some dogs have it, some dogs do not. Without it the field trial contender is greatly handicapped. Any number of dogs seem to catch the spirit of competition and are at their best, often surpassing themselves, when hunting in front of a gallery. Others become too keyed-up, excited, or even a bit too frightened to be at their best in field trials. Dogs of the latter type generally do their best work at home and often their owners and trainers cannot understand why, when brought to field trials, they seem to have left their good races at home. It is simply because they do not have the competitive spirit.

Thrills A'Plenty. From a spectator standpoint a field trial is a thrilling thing to watch for anyone interested in bird dogs—or, for that matter, competitions between animals. Not all the races are brilliant, of course, but in every major field trial and in most smaller and amateur events some sparkling performances are registered. To see a high-class bird dog work out his country at good range, with dashing speed and lofty and merry carriage, showing rare judgment in his casts and swinging to the course with every evidence of having his master's gun in mind, is something not soon to be forgotten. And when such a ground-working performance is rewarded by a smashing find of game, stylishly and intensely pointed and perfectly handled, no sportsman, no matter how blasé, can fail to get a tingling sensation along his spine. It is not the quantity but the quality of the work that counts in field trials.

One of the most sensational races in the history of field trials was that of the diminutive setter bitch Sioux in 1902 when she won the National Champion-

ship for the second time. There is no one now alive who witnessed that race, but it has been discussed in detail by the late Hobart Ames, president and judge for many years of the National Bird Dog Championship Association, and the late Al F. Hochwalt, the great field trial authority, reporter, and author. Both of these gentlemen considered Sioux the greatest bird dog of all time.

On this occasion there were only two starters in the Championship, Sioux and the setter Clip Wind-'em. The dogs were cast off in the rain and before many minutes had passed it began to sleet and a cold north wind cut over the hills on the Ames preserve near Grand Junction, Tenn. Soon the vegetation was encrusted in ice, but Sioux seemed oblivious to this and raced over the rugged terrain as if it was a fair fall day. Her coat became covered with frozen mud and the under parts of her body matted with ice, but the game little setter found birds galore and finished the long 3-hour heat at a pace just as fast as it has been at the start. According to Mr. Ames, one of the judges, that race has never been equaled.

Manitoba Rap's race in 1909 when he became the first pointer to win the National Championship made real field trial history. No second series was necessary and the little underestimated pointer topped the field of 15, the largest to that date, by a wide margin.

Then there was the time when another small setter bitch made lasting history in this famous stake. She was La Besita, the last Llewellin to win the title. This was in 1915. Birds were unusually plentiful that year, but when La Besita was called to run with Brunswick Countess the weather took a drastic turn for the worse. The frozen ground had thawed during the middle of the morning but before the heat was long underway the weather turned colder and the mud on the dogs' bodies turned to dirty icicles. Yet the great heart of the little bitch carried her through and she ran up a bird score of nine coveys and three singles. Most of the gallery thought she had won it then, but the judges ordered her back to run the next day with the pointer Lewis C. Morris in a second series. During the early part of the night the alarming news came that La Besita had pneumonia! Serious consideration was given to withdrawing her, but it was decided to wait until morning. Careful nursing throughout the night seemed to check the ailment but La Besita was far from a well dog when she went to the mark the next afternoon. She crashed through to victory, however, in another demonstration, this time mercifully short, of great courage.

Few races in the National Championship ever caused more comment that that of the setter, Eugene's Ghost, in 1922. "Mike," as he was called found 17 coveys and 11 singles in his 3-hour heat, more than any other dog before or since—and still did not win the stake! The pointer bitch, Becky Broomhill, took the honors that year and again in 1923 and 1925. Her exhibition in 1922 was an example of perfect handling and she found birds in sufficient quantities. Many thought Eugene's Ghost lost the title when the high-strung young setter jumped and circled his birds, as a nervous young lady spectator slapped her slicker with her riding crop. Some thought the judges charged him with a blink, but such was not the case. The dashing setter was too headstrong on that occasion, as he usually was, and his canny handler, the veteran J. M. Avent, had scouts placed all along the sides of the course to turn him back on it when he got too wide. It is hard to realize that a dog could find and handle that many birds under judgment and still run too wide, but there was no limit to Eugene's Ghost's range.

Another outstanding race in National Championship history was that of the pointer, Doughboy, in 1924. Doughboy's performance not only sensationally surpassed the field but surprised the entire gallery, for the dog was not considered a serious contender. His previous performances that season were far below championship caliber but his trainer, John Willard Martin, had spent many hours in preparing him for this event and he came to the trial in top form. Old-timers still talk about the brilliance of his performance on that occasion.

One of the memorable heats between pointers at the National Championship was that between Doctor Blue Willing and Norias Annie. Between them, this brace found 20 coveys, with the bitch having something of an edge in bird-finding honors. She did not run with the dash and verve of her rival but her heat was the more consistent. A number of Doctor Blue Willing's finds were made off to one side or behind. In the last 40 minutes the dog was doing more running than hunting, while his less sensational bracemate continued to find coveys up to the last. The judges awarded the title to Norias Annie, but many in the gallery, who did not closely analyze the work, thought that Doctor Blue Willing had won it. That was in the 1934 National Championship.

One of the most thrilling second series was that between the pointer bitches, Homewood Flirtatious and Sulu, with the National Championship title of 1935 at stake. Flirtatious literally threw herself into point in less than a minute after being cast away. She had a covey nailed on barren ground, while her bracemate continued her first cast. Flirt scored again before Sulu could be turned, and then again within a few minutes. The judges saw range more than bird work, for each dog had found plenty during the first series. Flirtatious really gave evidence of amazing speed, with Sulu doing her share also. After 38 minutes of brilliant performance the judges were about to order them up when Flirt was seen pointing with exceptionally high head. Bevan, her handler, was unable to produce birds in front of her and the spirits of her backers sank, for they feared that she had marred this spectacular performance with an error. The keen eyes of Mr. Ames, however, spied Sulu on point up ahead. Flirtatious was backing! After a short heat between Sport's Peerless and Doctor Blue Willing, in which the setter flushed a covey and the pointer did nothing startling. Homewood Flirtatious was declared the champion.

Also to be remembered was the sensational performance of the pointer, Luminary, who won the National Championship in 1942. Here were 3 hours replete with thrills from start to finish, a phenomenal performance under the most trying weather conditions, yet the judges could not agree and called him back for a second series with that sterling pointer, Tarheelia's Lucky Strike. Fortunately, Luminary proved his superiority in the second series just as decisively, if not more so, than in his first try.

The nearest approach to Luminary's heat in the same decade was that of the little setter Mississippi Zev, winner in 1946. Zev scored on nine coveys and his finish was nothing short of sensational.

All brilliant heats, however, are not run in the National Championship. Most judges could name any number which have come under their judgment, such as the heats of Norias Roy and Evergreen Jersey Mack in the Continental; Eagle Farris' 45 minutes in the All-America; Ariel's one-hour qualifying heat in the 1944 National Free-For-All Championship, which he won, The Texas Ranger in the National Free-For-All; Titan in the National Pheasant Championship; Belle the Devil in the National Amateur Championship; Air Pilot's Sam in the Saskatchewan All-Age; Granite State Mischief in the New England Championship; Shore's Carolina Jack in the Southern New York All-Age; San Beau in the Continental Derby; Morpheus in the American Field Futurity; and others too numerous to mention.

The National Championship has grown in prestige and stature throughout its distinguished career. In more recent years, there have been large fields in competition—as many as 52 starters—and the eligibility requirements have been made more stringent. At this writing, two first-place wins in Open All-Age competition are necessary for qualification.

The stake has been run over the celebrated Ames Plantation near Grand Junction in west Tennessee for more than a century and some amazing records established. One does not have to harken back to the 1940s or before for thrilling exhibitions. In 1957, the scintillating Wayriel Allegheny Sport, a pointer stylist, set the bird-finding record for winners of the stake when he had 23 finds.

But, as though to prove that it is quality rather than quantity that counts, Sport had 26 game contacts in 1958, but did not win on that occasion!

Sometimes things happen fast in field trials. Did you ever hear of an unconscious dog winning a stake? The author has seen this happen. It was in the Cotton States derby of 1926. Twice National Champion Mary Blue was the dog. At the close of a brilliant ground-working second-series heat, Mary pointed a covey in fairly heavy sedge. Chesley Harris, her handler, picked up a rather heavy pine-knot as he walked toward her. His apparent intention was to throw the pine-knot into the sedge to flush the birds. Instead, fearful that Mary would break, he "dropped it rather heavily" on her head as he passed her. Mary dropped, knocked out cold. Harris flushed the birds, slowly returned to his dog, and before he could get her to her feet (he took his own time), the judges ordered her up and announced the decision, with Mary as the winner.

Some amusing things happen, too. Often a usually calm businessman will get tremendously excited when handling his own dog in an amateur stake. There is one instance in which an amateur handler was so excited when his dog pointed that he handed his gun to his scout and took his horse in to flush. Another man tried to blow his gun and shoot his whistle!

A Grand Sport. The sport of field trials is a grand one. Not only does it point the way to better bird dogs and promote the conservation and restoration of

wildlife resources, but it is also good, clean, healthful recreation where sportsmanship in the highest degree is manifest. It is the one sport in which the gambling element is conspicuous by its absence. For that reason alone the sport will continue to flourish. Gambling raised its head on one occasion, but the late Dr. T. W. Shore and the author were in position to take prompt action to halt it. The unthinking amateur, would-be "bookmaker" immediately saw the danger of such action and the error of his ways. He would be the first to frown on it now.

The best dog does not always win in field trials. If it did, many dogs would compete only one time. Bird dogs, like human beings, have their off-days when they are not feeling up to par physically or mentally. And the luck of the draw plays a considerable part in field trials. The very uncertainty of the sport makes it all the more fascinating. The field trial sport is no place for a poor loser. As a result, the highest type of sportsmanship will always maintain.

If you want to see how good—or how bad—your dog is, enter him in a field trial.

Important Organizations and Associations. The leading organizations that promulgate regulations for the holding of all the recognized bird dog field trials in America are *The American Field* and the Amateur Field Trial Clubs of America. There is a working agreement between *The American Field* which also published the *Field Dog Stud Book* and the A.F.T.C.A. The American Kennel Club also regulates field trials, principally Beagle, Retriever and Spaniel.

The large majority of trials are held by the member clubs of the Amateur Field Trial Clubs of America, and trials under the sanction of the American Kennel Club are generally those sponsored by the specialty club members of that organization.

The object of the Amateur Field Trial Clubs of America is: (a) to license trials, and to exercise regulatory power over trials run by member clubs; (b) to prevent conflicting dates of member trial clubs; (c) to provide uniform rules for running; (d) to approve a list of eligible Judges for member club's trials; (e) to record winners in amateur class trials, also winners in open stakes sponsored by member clubs, when handled by amateurs, and to issue certificates to owners of such winning dogs certifying that they have qualified and are eligible to compete in the Championship stakes sponsored by the organization; (f) to hold annual Championship stakes on quail and pheasants, and other Championships as the Board of Directors may determine; (g) to provide rules differentiating between a professional handler and an amateur handler, and (h) to provide a method procedure whereby the Board of Directors may conduct a hearing and render a decision whenever the charge of professionalism is made against any person who purports to be an amateur.

The association is supported by annual dues of member clubs.

There are approximately 750 recognized bird dog

Sam L's Skyhigh, a field trial winning Setter. (Owner: Sam Light, Punxsutawney, Pa.)

field trials held each year in this country with more than 40,000 dogs competing. This does not take into consideration the many "matinee" events, or "unofficial" or "non-registered" trials which are held informally in many sections.

From January to June, 1948, the *American Field,* the weekly publication recognized as the "official" chronicler of the sport, listed 196 separate trials, staging 648 stakes, in which 10,635 dogs started. The interest in such field trials has since increased tremendously when one notes that about 40,000 starters participate today.

HOW BIRD DOG FIELD TRIALS ARE JUDGED

There are no set rules for judging bird-dog field trials. Men who accept invitations to act in a judicial capacity in these events are generally men of considerable field hunting experience. They serve without pay. This fact makes the sport of bird-dog field trials the only field competition known in which the professionals must accept the decisions of amateurs as final.

Field trial judges are charged with the responsibility of interpreting individual bird-dog performances properly, evaluating them correctly, and selecting the winners on the basis of the performances of the occasion, impartially and without any regard for past records or performances.

While field trial standards, though unwritten "officially," are based on the highest concepts of excellence in gundog performance, the judges are not hampered by any red tape or bound by any set rules in their interpretation of individual action. This is as it should be, if their decisions are to be well balanced, for attending circumstances often play a considerable role in determining the manner in which a judge will interpret and evaluate a given situation or performance. Field trial judging may well be termed an inexact science. No magically mysterious qualities are required in the make-up of an able arbiter, yet he must possess certain capabilities if he is to be successful. He must know the ideal he seeks and be able to recognize the performances which most nearly approach it. He must be fearless in his opinions and absolutely fair and impartial in his decisions.

Each field trial is different in the situations which arise, and the necessary flexibility which attends their interpretation is sometimes confusing to the uninitiated who find difficulty in understanding a decision in which the reasoning of the judges would be perfectly obvious to the understandingly observant eye of the experienced spectator.

There are certain guideposts in judging field trials which are known to judges, handlers, and spectators alike. The all-age field trial dog must show "class," which embodies bird sense, speed, range, style, and stamina. He must hunt the course, responding to his handler's commands or directions. He must take advantage of the wind in his quest for game. He must locate and point his quarry accurately and posi-

tively. He must be staunch and steady; and he must back on sight. (See Glossary re terms.) These same requirements hold good for the derby dog, yet to some lesser degree, as allowances are made for his age and inexperience.

The best way the novice may learn what field trial judges are looking for and how they reach their decisions is by attending a number of these events. Follow each brace carefully, watching each contestant closely. Ask experienced spectators questions on the finer points of performance. Judge the trial for yourself and then compare your decision with that of the judges. If you can recognize quality in performance, your own decision is not likely to be far afield. For if the judges go about their work carefully, even painstakingly and unhurriedly, the dogs will generally judge themselves. Occasions will often arise, of course, when fine analysis is called for; herein lies the test of a good field trial judge.

Some Questions and Answers About Field Trials. For the benefit of the reader who is not entirely familiar with field trial procedure we here point out a number of situations which arise occasionally and illustrate how the experienced field trial judge will meet them. Let us put them in the form of questions and answers.

TRAILING—*Question:* If a dog is interfering with his bracemate's work by trailing in any form, what action should the judges take, if any?

Answer: After a warning from the judges, the handler of the offending dog should bring him in and cast him away in a different direction. If he persists in trailing, the judges should order him up, but only after he is given ample opportunity to hunt properly.

BACKING—*Question:* How much should a dog be penalized for refusal to back when it is obvious that he has seen the pointing dog?

Answer: An All-Age dog which refuses to back his pointing bracemate should be heavily penalized. Not long ago, some professional field trial handlers did not require their dogs to back, rather hoping that the refusal to back would be out of the sight of the judges and their dogs would be given credit for the find when they were finally discovered pointing closer to the birds. These handlers went on the theory that "A dog can't win a field trial backing." After seeing numerous demonstrations of the fact that "A dog can't win a field trial by refusing to back" these handlers, in the main, abandoned this practice and most All-Age dogs are now trained to back. In a championship stake each dog should be given an opportunity to back if possible, and refusal to back should disqualify. Derby dogs should not be required to back, but performance of this nicety reflects with credit on them.

GRABBING—*Question:* To what extent should a dog's standing in an All-Age stake be penalized when his handler grabs for his collar either before firing or so soon thereafter as to show lack of confidence in the dog's manners?

Answer: It is obvious that one cannot shoot birds while reaching for a dog. Such an action should be taken as evidence that the dog is unsteady until his staunchness is demonstrated on future finds in the same stake.

DELAYED SHOT—*Question:* Should a dog be penalized if his handler waits until the birds are out of gunshot before firing?

Answer: Such action on the part of the handler creates the impression that the dog is not a finished performer, and such an impression can be dispelled only by prompt shooting over future flushes. The handler is supposed to shoot before the birds have passed beyond killing range. If the birds have flushed wild, some delay is expected and permissible. A handler should never shoot when the dog is in error. Such action, however, should not penalize the dog.

INTIMIDATING—*Question:* Should a dog be penalized if his handler uses a quirt, leash, or riding crop, ostensibly to flush birds but in such manner as to intimidate the dog?

Answer: This practice is abused by some handlers and should be discouraged by the judges. If it is evident that the handler is deliberately intimidating the dog, the dog should be penalized. Judges should warn handlers against this practice.

STOPS TO FLUSH—*Question:* Should a dog be penalized for a stop to flush?

Answer: Circumstances determine this. If the conditions are such as to make it improbable that the flush was the fault of the dog he should not be penalized; in fact, his stopping should be treated as additional evidence of good manners. If a dog stops to flush on a number of occasions, faulty nose may be the cause.

BIRD WORK IN ALL-AGE STAKES—*Question:* Should bird work be required by judges before making placements in All-Age stakes?

Answer: Every effort should be made to secure bird work of acceptable quality before awards are made in an All-Age stake. This can usually be secured if the judges will take sufficient time and make the effort. In one-course trials there is little excuse for not providing every dog deserving of recognition an opportunity to show on game. On rare occasions in cross-country trials bird work of acceptable quality is at high premium and the judges are forced to make the best of a poor situation. No qualified judge is satisfied to make All-Age placements on "class" alone.

BIRD WORK IN JUNIOR STAKES—*Question:* What degree of bird work should be expected in different age classes?

Answer: Puppies, none; Fall derbies, flash points; Spring derbies, staunchness but steadiness to shot and wing not required.

STYLE—*Question:* To what extent should style be considered?

Answer: Joy in hunting is a most desirable characteristic and should always be looked for. It may be indicated by merriness, sometimes by dash and verve, sometimes by other physical attributes of a dog in motion; but it is unmistakable. Loftiness is a desirable characteristic of a dog on point but intensity is the most desirable characteristic of a pointing dog and is far more important than the position of the head or tail.

Illustrating how the gallery trails along at a typical Southern bird dog field trial.

Breaking away at a Border International Field Trial, Frobisher, Sask., Canada. Photo by Evelyn M. Shafer.

CHAMPIONSHIPS—*Question:* Should a championship be judged on a different basis than an ordinary All-Age stake?

Answer: While it is desirable that the winner of a championship be charged with no errors, it is better practice to award a title to a dog that displays all of the characteristics of style, pace, drive, bird sense, etc., even though such a dog be charged with some minor error or breach of manners, than to award a title to a dog lacking many of these characteristics even though with a high bird score and no errors. Champions should be named for brilliance of performance in spite of trivial errors rather than on the basis of errorless mediocrity.

RANGE—*Question:* How much should extreme range count, particularly if there are plenty of birdy objectives in sight?

Answer: Dogs should *hunt* their way out rather than cast in straight lines. A "straight-line" initial cast may be excused on the theory that field trial dogs are at high pitch and may be expected to work off some nervous energy on the first cast. A field trial dog should apply his range intelligently and with due regard to cover and objectives rather than with regard only to distance from the handler.

"OVERBIRDINESS" IN BIRD FIELD—*Question:* Should a dog be penalized if he shows "overbirdiness" or extreme caution in the bird field or approaching it, as a possible result of being worked often on planted birds?

Answer: Dogs should work the bird field naturally and at a fair pace. They are expected to locate birds by testing the air for body scent. Dogs that linger over ground scent, sneak from bush to bush at any unnaturally slow pace, or hunt the bird field in any unnatural manner, are to be regarded as "pottering" and should not be placed except as a last resort.

COMING FROM BEHIND—*Question:* To what extent should coming from behind penalize a dog?

Answer: Persistent back-casting should eliminate a dog. A dog that comes in from behind occasionally should not be faulted too much, particularly if the pace of the gallery is fast and the dog is hunting desirable objectives. It may be necessary for him to come up from behind occasionally to take advantage of the wind. It is deliberate or aimless back-casting which should be heavily penalized.

UNPRODUCTIVE POINTS—*Question:* How much emphasis should be placed on an unproductive point when the judges are unable to determine whether the game has recently flushed unobserved by dog, handler, or judges?

Answer: Dogs should be given the benefit of any doubt. No credit should be given and no penalty imposed unless the dog persists in making unproductive points.

DROPPING ON POINT—*Question:* How much should dropping on point count against the dog: (1) when found or dropping when point is made; (2) dropping at approach of handler?

Answer: There are only two good reasons for a dog dropping on point: (1) coming on birds too fast, especially downwind, and dropping to prevent a flush; (2) if cover is very thin and dog tries to make himself as inconspicuous as possible. Persistent dropping on point is poor style and should be considered. Dropping at the approach of handler should incur no penalty unless fear of punishment or gunshyness is evident.

DIVIDED FINDS—*Question:* When two dogs are found on point which should be given credit for the find?

Answer: This calls for keen analysis on the part of the judges. Generally the position of the dogs in relation to the birds, their postures and attitudes will give some clue. When it is impossible definitely to determine, each dog is given credit for a divided find.

The above situations are but a few which are

A group of famous field trial-winning Pointers owned by Robert G. Wehle's Elhew Kennels, Scottsville, New York.

common to field trials. They will serve, however, to give the reader some idea of the task which confronts the judges, who serve for love of the sport alone.

GLOSSARY OF BIRD DOG FIELD TRIAL TERMS

ACTION: Manner in which the dog moves.

BACK OR BACKING: When a dog comes to a point when he sights a pointing dog he is said to be "backing" the pointing dog. This is also called "honoring," for the backing dog does not scent the game himself.

BACK-CAST: Searching or casting to the rear.

BIRDS: The game birds hunted in field trials.

BIRD-WORK: The act of finding and handling game birds.

BIRDY: When a dog works his ground closely and carefully with intensity, he is called "birdy."

BRACE: In bird dog field trials, the dogs hunt in pairs and each pair is called a brace.

BRACE-MATE: Each dog in a brace is called the "brace-mate" of the other.

BYE: In a stake which contains an uneven number of dogs, the dog whose name is drawn last is called the "bye" and runs alone, unless the judges choose a brace-mate for him. Some clubs require that a brace-mate be paired with any bye.

CAST: The search a dog makes in any one general direction without an abrupt turn.

CHASING: Running after the flushed bird or birds.

CUTTING-BACK: Casting back toward the handler after a forward-cast has been made.

DELAYED SHOT: When a handler flushes the bird and waits an appreciable time before firing the shot in order to gain more control over his dog, he is charged with a "delayed shot."

DIVIDED FIND: When two dogs are found pointing and the judges are unable to determine which found the birds first, each is credited with a "divided find."

DIVIDED PLACEMENTS: When the performances of two dogs are considered equal the judges sometimes divide the purses. This is generally done only in third-place wins. Newest regulations preclude a division of places in any recognized trial.

DRAW: (A) To move upon game cautiously. (B) The manner of determining the sequence in which dogs will compete in field trials is called the "draw" or "drawing." The names of the dogs are written on individual slips of paper, folded and placed in a receptacle. They are then drawn out, one at a time. The first dog "drawn" competes with the second, etc. Should there be an uneven number, the last dog "drawn" is called the "bye." If two dogs drawn in the same brace are handled by the same person, the second dog so drawn is dropped to the first available position. Where it is permissible to draw bitches in season, they are paired with other females.

DROPPING ON POINT: Some dogs drop to the ground when scenting birds. Standing upright on point is preferred. Dropping on point is caused by over-cautiousness or fear of flushing the birds, although some handlers train their dogs to drop on point, as a precaution against breaking to shot.

FIND: When a dog makes an individual point on game, he is said to have made a "find."

FLUSH: The rise of a game bird. To cause a game bird or birds to fly.

INTIMIDATION: Using the flushing whip, riding crop, leash or other object in threatening manner when a dog is on point or the birds are being flushed.

MAKING GAME: When a dog shows, by his manner or attitude, that he is scenting game he is said to be "making game."

OVERBIRDINESS: Fussing about or dallying on old game scent. Searching the same ground over and over again.

RANGE: The distance at which the dog hunts from his handler.

RESTRAINT: Excessive cautioning or handling while the dog is hunting or on point.

SECOND SERIES: After the dogs have been run as regularly drawn, the judges may select some of the contestants to compete again. This is called a second series.

SCOUT: The handler's assistant. When a person other than the handler is hunting for the competing dog, he is said to be scouting.

SHOT-BREAKING: When the dog stands steady to the flush of a bird and breaks and chases when the shot is fired, he is charged with "shot-breaking."

STAUNCH OR STANCH: To remain still on point, standing or dropped, *until* the birds are flushed.

STEADY: To remain in original pointing position *after* the birds are flushed and the shot is fired.

Extracts of Running Rules*—Amateur Field Trial Clubs of America

MINIMUM REQUIREMENTS
FOR FIELD TRIALS
FOR ALL POINTING BREEDS

As adopted by Amateur Field Trial Clubs of America, The American Field Publishing Company and the Field Dog Stud Book.

Wins will not be recognized and recorded unless the trial and/or each stake in which such win is made conforms to the following conditions:

*(1966; updated to Fall, 1969.)

Section 1. The name of the club, place, and date of the trial, and the Secretary's name and address must be announced in an issue of the AMERICAN FIELD bearing publication date of at least seven days before the trials are to be run, and entry blanks, with complete description of each stake, be available to owners and handlers at least six days before the date of the drawing.

Section 2. RECOGNIZED STAKES ARE:

(a). Puppy Stakes. From January 1 to July 1 in each year for dogs whelped on or after January 1 of the year preceding.

From July 1 to December 31 of each year for dogs whelped on or after June 1 of the year preceding.

(b). Derby Stakes. From July 1 to December 31 in each year for dogs whelped on or after January 1 of the year preceding, and from January 1 to July 1 in each year for dogs whelped on or after January 1 of two years preceding.

(c). All Age Stakes. For dogs of any age. An "open stake" is one in which there are no limitations with respect to either dogs or handlers. An "amateur" stake is one in which all handlers are amateurs as defined by Article VIII, Section 1, herein.

Winners in Members and Gun Dog or Shooting Dog stakes shall be recorded, and win certificates issued, but winners of children's, ladies, brace, and other stakes not conforming to the definitions contained under this article will not be recognized.

(d). Championships, Winner's Stakes and Futurities: Wins will be recorded only in such amateur events of the above character as are recognized by the Amateur Field Trial Clubs of America, Inc., and in such open events as are recognized by the American Field Publishing Company and the Field Dog Stud Book.

Section 3. The minimum length or heats for all stakes other than Puppy Stakes shall be thirty minutes, on the basis of the time that an average brace takes to negotiate the course. In the case of one-course trials, no more than eight minutes of the thirty shall be spent in the bird field. Minimum length of heats for Puppy stakes shall be fifteen minutes.

Section 4. A stake must be drawn in a convenient and approved place open to the public not later than the night before the day the stake is due to run.

Section 5. Dogs shall not be substituted after the draw.

Section 6. All braces shall be run as drawn, except with the prior consent of the judges, which consent must not be given for the purpose of accommodating owners, handlers, or dogs that are not available when reached in the regular order of the draw.

Should there be a bye dog in the stake, the judges may, at their discretion, order it to be run alone or with a dog selected by them for the purpose. Provided, however, that if a dog from any regularly drawn full brace should be withdrawn, fail to appear or be disqualified, the bye dog shall be named by the judges to run with the dog remaining in that particular brace, the bye moved up to fill the vacancy caused by the absent dog. In the event there is no bye, then such dog losing its brace-mate, as previously contemplated, must be run in its regular order of drawing, either alone or with a dog as a running mate that is satisfactory to the judges. In the event that there be two withdrawals from different braces, the brace-mates of such withdrawn dogs may be run together where the first vacancy occurs, or in their regular order, at the discretion of the judges. This same rule applies if there be four or any even number of dogs withdrawn from the stake.

All stakes should be so arranged that if at all possible, no more than one bye dog is drawn or run. Except where there is an uneven number of starters in a stake no bye should ordinarily occur. For example, in the event the drawing by lot has two dogs handled by the same person remaining as the last in the stake, the bracing is rearranged with the last previous available dog drawn not so handled changing places with the first drawn of the final two dogs.

Section 7. No entry shall be accepted after the stake is drawn.

Section 8. No more than one brace of dogs shall run on a course, or any part of a course at the same time, irrespective of whether the dogs are in the same stake or in different stakes.

Section 9. Stakes shall be run only on recognized game birds whose flight has not been impaired by caging, hobbling, wing clipping, brailing, or in any other manner.

Section 10. Bitches in season shall not be permitted to run in one course trials. In multiple course trials they may start only if, in the opinion of the judges, it can be accomplished under conditions which will insure absolute fairness to other entries.

Section 11. Wins will not be recorded, or if recorded, will be cancelled if made at a trial or in a stake not conforming to the above requirements.

Section 12. It is recommended that courses contain sufficient bird cover and suitable objectives to induce intelligent searching by the dogs. Birdfields, if used, should be of adequate size to permit a dog to hunt without excessive hacking, and with cover sufficient to hold birds. A variety of cover and objectives is desirable. Five (5) acres is suggested as a minimum area for a birdfield.

RULES AND REGULATIONS
FOR FIELD TRIALS

ARTICLE I

Section 1. This corporation shall record the winners in stakes sponsored by active members of the corporation, when handled by amateurs and shall issue certificates, signed by the President and Secretary of this corporation, to owners of such winning dogs, provided, however,

1. The sponsoring member club shall have paid to this corporation membership dues for the year in which the trial is held in the sum of $35.00, and

2. The sponsoring member club shall have received a license from the corporation for such trial, and

3. The member club conforms to the "Minimum Requirements" as set out herein, in conducting said trial, and

4. The sponsoring member club certifies the winner, or winners, of its stake to the Secretary of this Corporation within thirty days after the close of the trials at which said win, or wins, was made, giving such information as may be required by the Secretary of this corporation, and

5. That in stakes with three or less dogs competing, one win certificate will be issued. In stakes with four or five dogs competing, two placements only will be recognized. In stakes with six or more dogs competing, three placements, with no division of any place, will be recognized.

6. After July 1, 1968, winner's certificates will not be issued for wins in amateur trials where a cash purse is given.

ARTICLE II
Championship Stakes

Section 1. Amateur Field Trial Clubs of America, Inc., shall hold each year.

A
A National Amateur Quail Championship.

B
A National Amateur Pheasant Championship.

C
A National Amateur Shooting Dog Championship.

D
A National Amateur Pheasant Shooting Dog Championship.

E
A National Amateur Chicken Championship.

F
Such other Championships as the Board of Trustees may determine for dogs of all pointing breeds registered or eligible for registration, regardless of previous wins, that have qualified as follows:

Section 2. For qualification in the National Amateur Quail Championship a dog shall have previously won a place, under an amateur handler, in a one hour multiple course all age stake, or a first place win in a one course or thirty minute all age stake duly held by an active member of this corporation in accordance with its regulations, or winner or runner-up in a Regional Championship sanctioned by this corporation.

Section 3. For qualification in a National Amateur Pheasant Championship or a National Amateur Chicken Championship, a dog shall have previously won a place, under an amateur handler, in a derby, all age, or Regional Championship Stake duly held by an active member of this corporation in accordance with its regulations.

Section 4. For qualifications in a National Amateur Shooting Dog Championship and in a National Amateur Pheasant Shooting Dog Championship or a National Amateur Chicken Championship, a dog shall have won a place, under an amateur handler, in a shooting dog stake held by an active member of this corporation, in accordance with its regulations. Gun Dog Stakes and Shooting Dog Stakes shall be considered one and the same.

Section 5. Within the meaning of this article an "All Age Stake" shall include Open Championships recognized by the American Field Publishing Company and Derby Stakes shall include all recognized Futurities.

Section 6. Championships. The National Amateur Quail Championship, The National Amateur Pheasant Championship, The National Amateur Shooting Dog Championship, the National Amateur Chicken Championship, and The National Amateur Pheasant Shooting Dog Championship shall be held annually at a place and date to be determined by the action of the President of this corporation. The winner of the first place in the National Amateur Quail Championship shall be declared the National Amateur Quail Champion of America for the year. The winner of first place in the National Amateur Pheasant Championship shall be declared the National Amateur Pheasant Champion of America for that year. The winner of first place in the National Amateur Shooting Dog Championship shall be declared the National Amateur Shooting Dog Champion of America for that year. The winner of first place in the National Amateur Pheasant Shooting Dog Championship shall be declared the National Amateur Pheasant Shooting Dog Champion of America for that year. The winner of first place in the National Amateur Chicken Championship shall be declared the National Amateur Chicken Champion of America for that year.

Section 7. A champion must be declared in all championships except the National Amateur Pheasant Shooting Dog Championship. The naming of the champion in this event and the naming of a runner-up in all championship events is optional with the judges.

Trophies

Section 8. A Championship trophy, to be won three times by the same owner, but not necessarily by the same dog, will be presented to the owner of the Champion in each stake, each year, to remain in his possession until the time of the running of the next such championship stake, when it must be returned in good condition to the Secretary of this corporation. The corporation will cause the name of the dog, the name of the owner and the year of the win to be engraved on each championship trophy each year. In addition to the regular championship trophies, the outright award to a suitable trophy of value shall go to the owner of the respective champions each year. If the judges declare a runner-up, his owner shall also be awarded a suitable trophy to commemorate the win. The Hawfield Trophy and the Championship Trophy in the National Amateur Quail Championship; the Mary M. Phillips Trophy in the National Amateur Shooting Dog Championship, and the W. H. McNaughton Trophy for Runner-Up in the National Amateur Shooting Dog Championship; the W. Lee White Trophy in the National Amateur Pheasant Shooting Dog Championship and the Gunsmoke Trophy in the National Amateur Pheasant Championship; being presently in competition shall each, upon being won three times by the same owner, become the property of said owner.

All trophies, other than the Brooke Week's Memorial Trophy and the Chimes Mississippi Jack Trophy, which are perpetual Trophies, that are now, or may be in the future, offered for competition shall, upon being won three times by the same owner, become the property of said owner.

ARTICLE III
The National Shooting Dog Championship

The National Shooting Dog Championship is an Amateur Free-for-All Championship run by the National Shooting Dog Championship Association at Union Springs, Alabama. Dogs are qualified for the championship finals in a preliminary qualifying series.

ARTICLE IV

Breed Championships. For recognition of a Breed Championship where a parent organization represents the breed and its regions, for approval to hold an Amateur Championship, the parent organization will accept conduct of the event as approved by an AFTCA Committee on Regulations. Fee for the recognition of such a championship event will be $150.00 annually.

ARTICLE V
REGULATIONS AND RUNNING RULES

Section 1. Judges. Each Championship Stake shall be judged by two or more judges selected by the Committee appointed by the President to plan the running of such Championship. The names of the judges shall, if possible, be announced at least thirty days prior to the running of the stake. If any judge so announced becomes unable to serve or fails to appear, a substitute judge may be named by said committee, or officers of the corporation, or the stake manager.

The judges shall be in general charge of the running of the dogs and how the same shall be handled, subject only to the regulations and running rules of this corporation.

Section 2. Entry Fees and Starting Fees. The nominating, starting and post entry fees in all championship stakes run by this corporation shall be fixed from time to time by the Board of Trustees, provided that post-entries may be made up to the time of drawing upon an additional payment to be fixed by the Board of Trustees, and provided further that dogs which qualify in trials held by active members of this corporation between the date of the closing of entries of the respective National Amateur Championships and the time of the drawing thereof may be entered and drawn without payment of post entry fees.

Section 3. Entry Blanks. The Secretary shall send entry blanks in advance to all owners who the Secretary anticipates may enter a dog in the respective Championships sponsored by this corporation. The owner of any and all dogs to be entered in any Championship Stake sponsored by this corporation must have his entries in the hands of the Secretary on or before the advertised closing date. All entries in Championship Stakes are required to show the serial number of the win certificate of the dog entered; the dog entered must be described by name, breed, age, color markings, sex, and stud book number; the name of the owner of the entry; and such other information as may be required by the Secretary of this corporation.

The Secretary of this corporation is authorized to refuse to accept the entry of any dog in any Championship Stake sponsored by this corporation unless and until the information herein set out is supplied to him.

Section 4. Objectionable Entries. Dogs afflicted with any disease which the Stake Manager may regard as contagious will not be permitted to start or to be handled in close proximity to other entries.

Bitches in season will not be permitted to start unless, in the opinion of the judges, it can be accomplished under conditions which insure absolute fairness to other entries, and in no circumstances will they be permitted to be kenneled or transported near other starters.

Objections to entries must be made in writing and addressed to the Secretary. Such objections will be given consideration of the Stake Manager prior to the running.

Section 5. Stake Manager. The entire conduct of the running of each Championship Stake, subject to the regulations and running rules of the corporation, and subject also to the jurisdiction of the judges, shall be vested in the Stake Manager. All questions arising, not determined by the regulations and running rules of the corporation and not within the jurisdiction of the judges, shall be determined by the Stake Manager, and his decision shall be final unless reviewed by the Board of Trustees. In such event, the decision of the Board of Trustees shall be final. In all Championships sponsored by this corporation, the President of the corporation shall be the Stake Manager, and in the absence of said President the ranking Vice President shall be Stake Manager, and if none of said officers are present, the Secretary of the corporation shall designate a Stake Manager. The Stake Manager is empowered to order any person in attendance at the trial removed from the field trial grounds and to prevent his return during the attendance of the stake if, in his judgment, such person has been guilty of conduct unbecoming a gentleman, and any such person may be permanently barred from attending future trials of this corporation by subsequent action of the Board of Trustees.

Section 6. Drawing and Running Rules. Starters shall be drawn by lot and numbered in the order drawn. Drawings will be for order of running only and not for any particular course. A dog that is absent from the place at which he is to start, may be disqualified at the discretion of the judges. The duty to have a dog at the time and place where he is to start rests solely upon the owner or handler. After the first series has been completed if the judges shall deem a second or additional series necessary, they may call the dogs wanted in whatever manner or order and for the length of time they may deem expedient.

(a). A stake may be drawn by lot in two separate groups, only if this is done to prevent the late starting of the trial being drawn when dogs entered in this trial have not completed running in a trial already in progress. The dogs available would be drawn in group one, and the dogs at the other trial in group two. This must be done only for the benefit of the Club running the stake and not for the convenience of any handlers or owners. This is done when one trial unexpectedly overlaps another trial.

Section 7. Handlers. A dog must be handled by his amateur owner, or a member of his family who is an amateur, or he may be handled by any other amateur handler, but that person must be a member in good standing of an active member of this corporation. An individual handler must be designated at the time of the drawing and such handler, if present and physically able to handle or scout, must handle the dog as drawn. If two dogs handled by the same handler should be drawn in the same brace, the second dog so drawn shall change place with the next dog to be handled by another handler.

(a). Any person under suspension by this corporation, or any person barred from competition in trials by this corporation, shall not be permitted to handle or scout a dog.

Section 8. Length of Heats.

1. In the National Amateur Quail Championship the first series heats shall be one and one half hours in length.

2. In the National Amateur Pheasant Championship, the National Amateur Chicken Championship, the National Amateur Shooting Dog Championship, and the National Amateur Pheasant Shooting Dog Championship the first series heats shall be one hour in length.

In each stake the judges may run as many additional series as they deem necessary and the time of running therein shall be determined solely by the judges.

Section 9. Shooting. No dog shall be placed in a Championship Stake until shot over when birds are flushed to his point. The shot shall be fired by the handler of the pointing dog only, with a gun not less than .32 calibre.

Section 10. Conduct of Handlers. All handlers must conform to any and all regulations and rules and directions of the judges which do not conflict with the regulations and running of this corporation, and should any such regulation be disregarded, the judges shall have authority to disqualify such handler and/or his dogs, or they may leave the matter to the Stake Manager for his action.

The judges are expected to prescribe and rigidly enforce a strict rule upon the interference of handlers with the opponents' dog.

Handlers shall be at liberty to inquire of the judges at any time as to any regulations within their province or of the Stake Manager concerning any rule beyond the jurisdiction of the judges.

Section 11. Scouting. No scouting other than by an amateur shall be permitted. It shall be illegal for anyone to scout for a handler unless permission of the judges has first been obtained. Lagging behind the field trial party for the purpose of locating dogs shall constitute scouting to the same extent as leaving the field trial party to go in any other direction.

(a). Scouting in Shooting Dog Championships. No scouting is permitted in a Shooting Dog Stake except that a person, with the permission of a judge, may be designated to go and see if a dog is on point at a specific location.

Section 12. Handling Dogs. During the running of a heat no dog in competition therein shall be removed from the ground for an appreciable length of time, placed on a leash or worked otherwise than in the accepted manner of handling by voice, whistle or signal.

(a). The use of any electronic device for the handling of a dog in competition in a field trial is forbidden.

Section 13. Backing. In an all-age or shooting dog stake, it is mandatory that a judge order a dog up if that dog, in the opinion of the judge, demonstrates conclusively that he refuses to back his brace-mate.

Section 14. Complaints. A handler may make a verbal complaint to either the judges or the Stake Manager concerning the conduct of his opponent, provided that such complaint be made promptly upon the alleged commission of the offense, this affording proper official opportunity of observing the immediate situation.

Section 15. Field Marshal. One or more Field Marshals shall be appointed by the Stake Manager, and the Field Marshal or Marshals shall give full authority to control the movement of the gallery or other spectators. The Field Marshal shall prevent interference with the judges, handlers and dogs.

Section 16. Instruction to Handlers. No one other than the handler of a dog may give a dog, while in competition, any command or direction, except with the permission of the judges.

Section 17. Impugning Judges. Any person who has, to the satisfaction of the Stake Manager, impugned the action of a judge officiating at any stake, or who has otherwise annoyed such official in connection with, or because of his official action with the trial, may be barred from further participation in or attendance at such trial by the Stake Manager, and such disbarment may be made permanent by subsequent action of the Board of Trustees.

Section 18. Blank Ammunition. The use of live ammunition is banned in all trials held by member clubs of the Amateur Field Trial Clubs of America, Inc, and in all Amateur Championships sanctioned by the Amateur Field Trial Clubs of America, Inc.

ARTICLE VI

Section 1. Definition of Professional and Amateur. Any person who receives or has received, either directly or indirectly, compensation for training or handling dogs, or who has accepted a cash prize or prizes, or other valuable consideration for handling dogs other than his own in field trial competition, or any person who works for or has worked for a professional handler in the training of dogs, or any member of the family of a professional handler who assists him in the training of dogs, is classified within the meaning of these regulations as a professional handler. All handlers not so classed as professional shall have amateur standing.

Section 2. Professionalism. Any active member of this corporation is empowered, upon consideration of evidence deemed sufficient, to declare any person who has actually handled a dog or dogs in stakes fostered by an active member, to be a professional and to disqualify his dog or dogs, or to bar him from handling in said stake as an amateur.

Section 3. Any active member of this corporation or any individual member thereof may file a written complaint with the Secretary of this corporation that a professional handler has handled, or attempted to handle, a dog or dogs in an amateur field trial event. The complaint shall state:

(a). The name and the address of the person alleged to be a professional.

(b). The time, place, name of the club and the event in which the person alleged to be a professional handled, or attempted to handle, in an amateur event.

(c). A concise statement of the events upon which the complaint relies as proof to establish such person is a professional handler.

If, in the opinion of the Secretary, such complaint has merit, he shall submit the same, and all evidence thereof, to the Board of Trustees, whose decision thereon shall be final. Before submitting such complaint to the Board of Trustees the Secretary shall notify the accused of the nature of the charge against him and the Secretary shall fix a time in which the accused may file a written answer to the charge and provide evidence thereon. The accuser shall be given the same opportunity to substantiate his complaint.

Upon expiration of the time so fixed by the Secretary, he shall submit copies of the complaint, the answer thereto, and all evidence submitted to him by either party, to each member of the Board of Trustees for their decision, and the Secretary shall also submit therewith any explanation or comment which he may desire. If majority of the Board of Trustees shall find in favor of the accused, his amateur standing shall remain unimpaired; but if the Board of Trustees shall find and decide that the accused is or was a professional handler, the person so accused shall be barred of and from handling any dog in competition in any amateur event in any stake sponsored by an active member of this corporation and no certificate of win made by a dog handled by such a person shall be issued by this corporation. The Secretary shall notify both the accused and the accusing party in writing the decision of the Board of Trustees.

Section 4. Reinstatement to Amateur Status. Any person who was admittedly a professional or who has been declared a professional by this corporation and any person who has been barred from competition in an amateur event because of the charge of professionalism or any person who has been embarrassed by unsupported charges of professionalism, even though he may not have been barred from competition in an amateur event, may, provided he has not, for a period of three years, violated either the letter or the spirit of the definition contained in Article VI, Section 1, hereof, qualify as an amateur handler in the following manner:

(a). Such individual may request, in writing a hearing by the Board of Trustees so that his status may be definitely established. Such individual must accompany the request with a statement and evidence supporting his claim that he is an amateur, as defined by these regulations, and shall prove his claim in the manner and procedure directed in Section 3 of this article.

If such a request is filed by an individual who has been barred from competition in an amateur event, the Secretary shall notify the President and Secretary of the active member which barred him and request that they provide, in proper form for presentation to the Board of Trustees, evidence on which their action was based.

(b). If a majority of the Board of Trustees find that the petitioner is entitled to amateur status, he shall be declared to be an amateur and the Secretary shall notify the petitioner and other interested parties of the Board's decision.

Section 5. Conduct Unbecoming a Gentleman. If a complaint is made by an active member of this corporation or by an individual associated with such active member that a person entering a dog or handling a dog in any field trial held by an active member of this corporation or by the corporation itself has acted in a manner contrary to good sportsmanship and detrimental to the best interest of field trials generally, such complaint shall be in writing and a hearing had in the same manner as is provided in Article VI, Section 3, hereof. If a majority of the Board of Trustees shall find and decide that the complaint is well founded and that the accused has acted in a manner contrary to good sportsmanship and detrimental to the best interests of field trials generally, the person so accused shall be barred of and from handling or entering any dog in competition in any amateur event sponsored by an active member of this corporation, and no certificate of win made by a dog entered or handled by such a person shall be issued by this corporation. The Secretary shall notify both the accused and the accusing party in writing of the decision of the Board of Trustees.

ARTICLE VII

Regions of the Amateur Field Trial Clubs of America. The Board of Trustees of the Amateur Field Trial Clubs of America may divide the country geographically into designated regions. The boundaries of these regions may be changed from time to time at the discretion of the Board. The present regions are as follows:

Region No. 1. New England—Maine, New Hampshire, Vermont, Massachusetts, Connecticut, Rhode Island and New Brunswick.

Region No. 2. Middle Atlantic States—New York, Pennsylvania, New Jersey and Delaware.

Region No. 3. Southeastern States—District of Columbia, Maryland, Virginia, North Carolina, South Carolina, Georgia and Florida.

Region No. 4. Central States—Michigan, Ohio, Indiana, West Virginia and Kentucky.

Region No. 5. Mid-Western States.—Illinois, Missouri, Iowa, Wisconsin and Minnesota.

Region No. 6. Southern States—Arkansas, Louisiana, Mississippi, Alabama, and Tennessee.

Region No. 7. Southwestern States—Texas and New Mexico.

Region No. 8. Plains States—Oklahoma, Kansas, Colorado, Nebraska, South Dakota, and North Dakota.

Region No. 9. Rocky Mountain States—Utah, Idaho, Montana, and Wyoming.

Region No. 10. Northwestern States—Washington, Oregon.

Region No. 11. Southern Pacific States—California, Nevada, and Arizona.

Region No. 12. Hawaiian Region—Hawaii.

Region No. 14. Western Canada-British Columbia, Alberta, Saskatchewan.

Region No. 15. Japan.

Section 1. The following procedures are set up:

(a). Wherever in a duly constituted region there are less than five member clubs, the member clubs of such a region may align themselves with the closest regional organization that they choose to join until such times as their region may qualify as an organization by having five member clubs.

(b). Any state or states may petition the Board of Trustees for realignment into a different region than they are now allocated to providing the majority of the clubs in said state or states express the desire for realignment.

(c). When any new region is duly constituted by action of the Trustees the President shall appoint a committee of three to be responsible for organizing the said new reigon. He shall do the same in the case of reactivating any region.

Section 2. Regional Organizations. The regions as constituted by the Board of Trustees shall be organized by the clubs within that region who are paid-up members of the Amateur Field Trial Clubs of America. The minimum of five member clubs shall be required in order that a region may be recognized as actively functioning. It is the intent of this corporation that after a region has been organized, the member clubs, should, so far as possible, and consistent with the following regulations, assume all direction and responsibility in the management and holding of stakes and other business affairs within said respective regions.

(a). The securing of sanction, supervision and general oversight of these regional events shall be under the direction of a president or chairman, to be selected annually in each region at a meeting called within said region for said purpose.

(b). At the annual meeting of the members of each region, or as soon thereafter as possible, the date and location for the regional all age and the regional shooting dog championships shall be chosen. All regional championships shall be sanctioned by this corporation when applied for by said regional organization and approved by five member clubs of said region.

(c). The respective regional president or chairman and the member, or members, of the Board of Trustees resident in any one of the respective regions shall be responsible to see that the annual meeting of the members of the region is properly called and held, and that the operation of the region is consistent with the By-Laws and Running Rules of the Amateur Field Trial Clubs of America.

(d). It shall be the duty of the president or chairman of the respective region to be personally present at each championship event within their region for the purpose of seeing that the rules of this corporation are complied with and the stakes run on a basis consistent with an event of this calibre. In the event said president or chairman is unable to attend the running of the regional championship, he shall have the power to appoint, in writing, a qualified person to act in his place.

(e). It shall be the duty of the president or secretary of the region to see that the list of officers, dates for trials, and other pertinent information about the region be sent to the office of the Secretary-Treasurer of the Amateur Field Trial Clubs of America.

(f). The president of each region shall be entitled to attend and have full voting power at the annual Trustees meeting of this corporation as provided in Article V. Section 4 (a) of the By-Laws of this corporation.

ARTICLE VIII
REGIONAL CHAMPIONSHIPS

Regional All Age and Regional Shooting Dog Championships may be sanctioned by the Board of Trustees of this corporation in such sections of the country as the Board may, in its discretion, deem advisable.

Section 1. Title Awards. The title awarded the dog winning these regional events shall be descriptive of the region in which the stake was held, thus the winner of an event in Region 1 would be designated Region 1 Amateur Champion or Region 1 Amateur Shooting Dog Champion, etc.

Section 2. Reward to Winners. The rewards to go with the title of Regional Champion and Runner-Up must be trophies. Money as a reward is prohibited and no sanction may be issued to any regional group which proposes a cash reward.

Section 3. Declaring Champion. It is not mandatory that a champion or runner-up be named, but is left to the discretion of the judges. This corporation will award the winner and the runner-up, if one is designated, in each regional event a certificate commemorative of the win.

Section 4. Courses and Game. All regional events must be held on a succession of courses under natural conditions, except

as otherwise specifically designated in these regulations under the heading "One Course Championships."

Except as provided under one course championships, at least three courses must be used in any regional event. There must be no birdfields on these courses, and the courses should be so arranged that no brace of dogs will have to cover the same ground the second time in the same heat.

Section 5. Length of Heats. The first series heats must be at least one hour in length, there may be as many additional series and for as long a time as the judges may deem necessary.

Section 6. Champions Must Be Shot Over. No dog shall be declared a winner or runner-up in a regional event until shot over when birds are flushed to his point. Shot to be fired by handler of pointing dog only with gun of not less than .32 calibre.

Section 7. Eligibility. Dogs to be eligible for the All-Age Championship shall have a winner's certificate from this corporation for a win in a derby or all-age event. Dogs to be eligible for the Regional Shooting Dog Championship must have a winner's certificate from this corporation for a win in a shooting dog event.

Section 8. Regulations Controlling. The regulations and rules of this corporation with specific attention to Article V, Sections 4, 6, 7, and 9 through 18, are to govern with respect to all matters not specifically covered by these Regional Regulations.

ARTICLE IX

Section 1. One Course Regional Championships. One course Championships may be sanctioned in Regions 1 and 2 and such other regions from time to time as may hereafter be determined by the Board of Trustees. The same regulations shall apply to one course championships as to other regional events except as follows.

(1). All dogs may be run over the same course.

(2). At least three birds (pheasant, quail, Hungarian or Chukar Partridges) must be liberated for each brace of dogs. No more than one-third of the birds liberated for each brace may be liberated in the so-called birdfields, and the remaining two-thirds to be liberated in at least two other well separated locations on the course.

(3). Not less than nine birds shall be liberated before the first brace is put down, not more than three of which shall be liberated in the birdfield, and the balance in at least two widely separated locations on the courses.

(4). No bird shall be dizzied or its physical powers otherwise impaired by any manipulations or device before being liberated; and so far as possible, birds should be liberated with a minimum of handling.

(5). Birds for the next brace shall be liberated within ten minutes after the field trial party has passed each point of liberation, so that all birds will be out a minimum of fifty minutes before being handled by dogs.

(6). The single course may be sufficiently large and the running so arranged that no one brace of dogs will have to cover the same ground a second time in the same heat.

(7). The course shall not end in a birdfield, but the last ten minutes of the running shall be in open country where birds are not liberated during the running of the stake, to enable the judges in the closing minutes of the heat to clearly estimate the stamina of the dogs.

(8). The winner of a one course event shall be designated as a One Course Champion.

(See also Part XVIII for the rules and regulations of other organizations relative Field Trials.)

NATIONAL SHOOTING DOG CHAMPIONSHIP ASSOCIATION
(Amateur Free-For-All Stake)

Year	Winner's Name	Breed and Sex*	Color*	Sire and Dam	Owner	Handler
1950	Braeside Prissy	PB	W & O	No Sale Buck–Miss Nancy	C. B. Williams	C. B. Williams
1951	Ginnie Sue	SB	W,B&Ti	Citation's Breeze–Fancy Lou	W. H. Wright	J. T. Ogletree
1952	Wyecott's Eufaula Celebration	PD	W & Li	Wyecott's Happy Harrigan–Wyecott's Debutante	C. P. Bentley	J. T. Ogletree
1953	Brandywine Dee	PB	W,Li&Ti	Sinetta Jake–Enigma	Mrs. D. P. Ross	J. T. Ogletree
1954	Wyecott's Eufaula Celebration	PD	W & Li	Wyecott's Happy Harrigan–Wyecott's Debutante	C. P. Bentley	Ernest Allen
1955	Perry's Field Marshal	SD	W,B,T&Ti	Dawson's Zev–Dean Lad Eugene	J. S. Dickinson	J. S. Dickinson
1956	Beau's Snow Man	SD	W,B,T&Ti	Snowstorm–Beau Don's Becky	Bullock Hunting Club	A. G. Simmons Jr.
1957	Just Rite Roz	PB	W & Li	Pin Up–Wahoo's Village Susie	R. R. Waugh	Bill Swift
1958	Satilla Nip Parades	PD	W,Li&Ti	Satilla Wahoo Pete–Village Lynn Firelight	Lee Smith	Lee Smith
1959	Paladin's Handy Man	PD	W,Li&Ti	Paladin–Nightcap's Hightide Pat	T. J. Smith	Bill Swift
1960	Storm Harrigan	PD	W,Li&Ti	Stormy Mike–Mary Helen Harrigan	Mrs. D. P. Ross	Leroy Upshaw
1961	Warhoop Jake II	PD	W & Li	Warhoop Jake–J. Pernelle	J. H. Bruce & J. S. O'Neall Jr.	J. S. O'Neall Jr.
1962	Blakemore's Candy Cake	PB	W,Le&Ti	Major Lexington Boy–Stanley's Candy	A. H. Hembree Jr.	A. H. Hembree Jr.
1963	War Eagle	PD	W,Li&Ti	Sunset Hill's Tuffy–Catalpa Ridge Melody	Dr. L. C. Cardinal	Dr. L. C. Cardinal
1964	Wahoo Chief	PD	W & B	Satilla Wahoo Pete–Sheila's Dot	Perry Gray	Perry Gray
1965	Smokepole	PD	W & O	Gunsmoke–Caney Valley Emma	H. N. Holmes	H. N. Holmes
1966	Blakemore's Ed Farrior	PD	W & B	Holly Lyn Joe–Bobette	A. H. Hembree Jr.	A. H. Hembree Jr.
1967	Cannonade	PD	W & Li	Gunsmoke–Caney Valley Emma	H. N. Holmes	H. N. Holmes
1968	Mr. Radar	PD	W & Li	Real Gone George–Marie's County Trixie	L. H. Cruse	L. H. Cruse
1969	Smokepole	PD	W & O	Gunsmoke–Caney Valley Emma	H. N. Holmes	H. N. Holmes
1970	Alabama Flying Cadet	PD	W & Li	Phantom Night Train–Storm's Melody	W. H. Chatfield	Rex Smith

NATIONAL AMATEUR QUAIL CHAMPIONSHIP

Year	Winner's Name	Breed and Sex*	Color*	Sire and Dam	Owner	Handler
1957	Home Again Mike	PD	W & Li	The Haberdasher–Ariel's Spunky Fireball	W. C. Jones	W. C. Jones
1958	Gunsmoke	PD	W & B	Satilla Sam–Luminary's Kate	H. N. Holmes	H. N. Holmes
1959	Northwester	PD	W & Li	Home Again Mike–Whispering Winds	G. H. Lewis, Jr.	G. H. Lewis Jr.
1960	Seairup	PD	W & Li	Titanup–Sierra June	Dr. G. E. Oehler	Dr. G. E. Oehler
1961	Pineland Johnny	PD	W & O	Satilla Wahoo Pete–Pineland Alice	M. C. Fleming	M. C. Fleming
1962	Mack's Chief Warhoop	PD	W & O	Warhoop Jake–Satilla Luminary Ruth	Mrs. E. M. Berol & Mr. & Mrs. J. G. Franks	Martin Best Jr.
1963	Kilsyth Sparky	PD	W & Li	Q's Delivery Doone–Resthaven Doone Gal	Mrs. G. M. Livingston	Bill Allen
1964	Vendetta	PD	W & Li	Cronus–Constant	H. S. Sharp	H. R. Ingram
1965	Primos Rowdy	PD	W, B & Ti	Holly Lyn Joe–Sutherland's Belle	Frank Stout	Frank Stout
1966	La Strega	PD	W & B	Rambling Rebel Jackson–Rambling Rebel Lady	Lloyd Reeves	J. W. Bales
1967	Haberdasher's Southerner	PD	W & Le	The Haberdasher–Huntland Paladin's Limoge	Dr. W. H. McCall	Dr. W. H. McCall
1968	Rinski Little Sam	PD	W & Li	Wayriel Allegheny Dan–Rinski Flying Girl	J. R. McClain	J. R. McClain
1969	A Rambling Rebel	PD	W & Li	Rambling Rebel Dan–Homerun Bess	W. S. Richardson	C. R. Scarborough
1970	Gunsmoke's Admiration	PB	W & Li	Gunsmoke–Colonial Rose M.	H. N. Holmes	H. N. Holmes

AMERICAN FIELD QUAIL FUTURITY

Year	Winner's Name	Breed and Sex*	Color*	Sire and Dam	Owner	Handler
1957	Dixie Melody	PD	W, Li & Ti	Satilla Wahoo Pete–Drug Package	H. E. Weil	John S. Gates
1958	Medallion II	PD	W, Li & Ti	Medallion–Stanton's June	Dr. W. B. Griffin	John S. Gates
1959	Gunsmoke's Jewel	PB	W, B & Ti	Gunsmoke–Santee Susan	Dr. T. J. Lattimore	John S. Gates
1960	Riggins White Knight	PD	W, O & Ti	Major Lexington Boy–Stanley's Candy	R. W. Riggins	D. Hoyle Eaton
1961	Gunsmoke's Yon Way	PB	W, Li & Ti	Gunsmoke–Titanup's Windy Way	J. D. Bayler	Howard Kirk
1962	War Exterminator	PD	W, Li & Ti	War Storm–Sugarplum	C. C. Coon	John S. Gates
1963	Fast Jake Delivery	PD	W, Li & Ti	Fast Drug Delivery–Renfro Delivery Girl	A. B. Bobbitt	Paul Walker
1964	Doctor's Stormy Mack	PD	W, Li & Ti	Storm's Romance–Doug's Pepper	Dr. D. E. Hawthorne	E. B. Epperson
1965	Stuart's Rambling Rebel	PD	W & Li	Rambling Rambling Dan–Deep Run Dot	G. H. Lewis Jr.	Fred Arant
1966	Homerun Jim	PD	W & Li	Homerun Johnny–Homerun Sis	W. H. Wimmer	Fred Arant
1967	Oklahoma Flush	PD	W & O	Paladin's Royal Flush–Baconrind's Sandy	Dr. I. J. Hammond	John R. Gates
1968	Jorwick's Papa J	PD	W & Li	Jorwick's Dixiecrat–Jorwick's Delilah	G. G. Jordan	Collier Smith
1969	Homerun Buddy	PD	W & Li	Homerun Johnny–Homerun's Sis's Dot	Claudia L. Phelps	Fred Arant, Jr.

* Key: PD—Pointer dog PB—Pointer bitch SD—English Setter Dog SB—English Setter Bitch W&Li—White and Liver W&Le—White and lemon W&B—White and black W&O—White and orange W&C—White and chestnut M, b, t & tk—White, black, tan and ticked

GRAND NATIONAL GROUSE CHAMPIONSHIP

Year	Winner's Name	Breed and Sex*	Color*	Sire and Dam	Owner	Handler
1957	TITLE WITHHELD					
1958	Vigorous	PD	W & Li	Frank's Boy Doc—Hunt's Lexington Judy	F. C. Ash	Luther Smith
1959	Doc's Girl Sis	PB	W & Li	Frank's Boy Doc—Hunt's Lexington Judy	F. C. Ash	Luther Smith
1960	Sam L's Rebel	ESD	W, B T & Ti	Eugene Crockett II—Tennessee Peerless Lou	Sam Light	Rich Tuttle
1961	Sam L's Rebel	ESD	W, B T & Ti	Eugene Crockett II—Tennessee Peerless Lou	Sam Light	Rich Tuttle
1962	Elhew Lucy Brown	PB	W & Li	Elhew Zeus—Elhew Abbygail	R. C. Shear	Rich Tuttle
1963	Orchard Valley Melody	ESB	W, B T & Ti	Orchard Valley Skylight—Fiesta Flo	R. P. Habgood Jr.	Luther Smith
1964	No Placements Awarded					
1965	Brenda Wahoo	PB	W & B	Anna Monroe's Pete—Tyson's Gay Tune	Alan Bartholomew	Alan Bartholomew
1966	Hussy	ESB	W & C	Skyhigh's Buckey—Marshall's Gold Dust	K. E. Undercoffer	A. I. Undercoffer
1967	Elhew Holly	PB	W & Li	Elhew Speculator—Elhew Grouse Queen	R. C. Shear and R. G. Wehle	R. C. Shear
1968	Elhew Holly	PB	W & Li	Elhew Speculator—Elhew Grouse Queen	R. C. Shear and R. G. Wehle	R. C. Shear
1969	Ghost Train	SD	W & O	Samson Montcalm—Fruchey's Ladybug	Wayne Fruchey	Wayne Fruchey

NATIONAL OPEN PHEASANT CHAMPIONSHIP

Year	Winner's Name	Breed and Sex*	Color*	Sire and Dam	Owner	Handler
1957	Rumson Farm Hayride	PD	W & Li	Louisiana Hayride—Nightcap's Aurora	W. H. McNaughton	Earl Crangle
1958	Rumson Farm Hayride	PD	W & Li	Louisiana Hayride—Nightcap's Aurora	Carmen Basilio & Earl Crangle	Earl Crangle
1959	Q's Delivery Doone	PD	W & Li	Newman's Delivery Dan—McCall's Mary Doone	H. A. Crane	Fred Arant
1960	Homerun Bess	PB	W & Li	Homerun—Homerun Spinet	Claudia L. Phelps	Fred Arant
1961	Little Frenchman	PD	W & O	Devious—Sporty King	Peter Lusardi	P. A. Brousseau
1962	Little Frenchman	PD	W & O	Devious—Sporty King	Peter Lusardi	P. A. Brousseau
1963	Rig A Jig	PD	W & O	Little Frenchman—Santee Tillie	A. L. Lippitt	P. A. Brousseau
1964	Rambling Rebel Dan	PD	W & Li	Newman's Delivery Dan—Alicia's Image	W. S. Richardson	Fred Arant
1965	Mike's Home Again	PD	W & Li	Mike's Delivery—Rico Paladin's Belle	Dr. A. W. Simpson Jr.	Fred E. Bevan
1966	Sugarshack	PB	W & O	War Storm—Sugarplum	Tom Peacock	Bob Lamb
1967	Tooth Acres Hawk	PD	W & Li	Latham's White King—John Oliver's Susie	Dr. F. B. Hines Jr.	Fred Arant
1968	Sugarshack	PB	W & O	War Storm—Sugarplum	Frank Stout	Bob Lamb
1969	Highway Lynn	PD	W & Li	Highway Man—Palamonium's Satilla Lynn	B. L. Ball	W. F. Rayl

NATIONAL AMATEUR PHEASANT CHAMPIONSHIP

Year	Winner's Name	Breed and Sex*	Color*	Sire and Dam	Owner	Handler
1957	Magnum	PD	W & O	Delivery Frank—Oak Hall Dottie	Dr. A. H. Nitchman	Dr. A. H. Nitchman
1958	Elhew Marksman	PD	W & O	Lexington's Lucky Trigger—Tick Thomee	R. G. Wehle	R. G. Wehle
1959	Magnum	PD	W & O	Delivery Frank—Oak Hall Dottie	Dr. A. H. Nitchman	Dr. A. H. Nitchman
1960	Seairup	PD	W & Li	Titanup—Sierra June	Dr. G. E. Oehler	P. E. Gray
1961	Orinda's Debutante	PB	W & Li	Buddy Tyson—Tysue	J. M. Thomas	J. M. Thomas
1962	Warhoop Jake II	PD	W & Li	Warhoop Jake—J Pernelle	Mr. & Mrs. J. S. O'Neal Jr.	J. S. O'Neal Jr.
1963	Chaney Farms Dan	PD	W & Li	Rambling Rebel Dan—Belle Doone	W. C. Chaney	W. C. Chaney
1964	Tybabe's Willing Doctor	PD	W & Li	Tybob—Kattie's Warhoop Babe	Ernest Mimms	Ernest Mimms
1965	Cannonade	PD	W & Li	Gunsmoke—Caney Valley Emma	H. N. Holmes	H. N. Holmes
1966	Cannonade	PD	W & Li	Gunsmoke—Caney Valley Emma	H. N. Holmes	H. N. Holmes
1967	Smokepole	PD	W & Le	Gunsmoke—Caney Valley Emma	H. N. Holmes	H. N. Holmes
1968	Gunsmoke's Admiration	PB	W & Li	Gunsmoke—Colonial Rose M	H. N. Holmes	H. N. Holmes
1969	Haberdasher's Royal Ace	PD	W & Li	Paladin's Royal Heir—Mike's Madonna	Dr. W. H. McCall	Dr. W. H. McCall

AMERICAN FIELD PHEASANT DOG FUTURITY

Year	Winner's Name	Breed and Sex*	Color*	Sire and Dam	Owner	Handler
1955	Tool Steel Man	PD	W & Li	Paladin—Sierra Doone	Mrs. Betty Hoover	John Thompson
1956	Northwester	PD	W & Li	Home Again Mike—Whispering Winds	G. H. Lewis Jr.	Paul Walker
1957	Rambling Rebel Dan	PD	W & Li	Newman's Delivery Dan—Alicia's Image	J. M. Culp	Fred Arant
1958	Resthaven Spunky Bill	PD	W & O	Tarengo Spunky Boy—Greenwood Anna	H. A. Crane	Fred Arant
1959	Elhew Zeus	PD	W & O	Elhew Marksman—Winsome Dinah	R. G. Wehle	R. G. Wehle
1960	Satilride	PD	W & O	Rumson Farm Hayride—Satilla Mary	H. H. Townshend	Earl Crangle
1961	Homerun Johnny	PD	W & Li	Rambling Rebel Dan—Homerun Bet	Claudia L. Phelps	Fred Arant
1962	Elhew Marmaduke	PD	W & O	Elhew Sharpshooter—Elhew Dior	R. G. Wehle	R. G. Wehle
1963	Blue Coast	PD	W & Li	Rambling Rebel Dan—Thorne	A. R. Smith	Pete Smith
1964	Mingo	PB	W & Li	Homerun Johnny—Homerun Sis	L. R. Tichenor & M. C. Best	Fred Arant
1965	Resthaven Bill Again	PD	W & Li	Resthaven Spunky Bill—Crossup	H. A. Crane	Fred Arant
1966	Roz's Image	PB	W & Li	Rambling Rebel Dan—Homerun Rozette	S. R. Cline	Fred Arant
1967	Storm Glider's Jess	PD	W & Li	Mr. Glider—Jennie Gal	Bill Coates	Fred Arant
1968	Toronado's Star	SB	W & O	Toronado—Sparkling Flame	E. A. DiMonte	Fred Arant
1969	Double Rebel	PD	W & Li	A Rambling Rebel—Hollybourne Cricket	C. R. Scarborough	Fred Arant, Jr.

* Key: PD—Pointer dog PB—Pointer bitch SD—English Setter Dog SB—English Setter Bitch W&Li—White and Liver W&Le—White and lemon
W&B—White and black W&O—White and orange W&C—White and chestnut W, b, t & tk—White, black, tan and ticked

WINNERS OF THE NATIONAL BIRD DOG CHAMPIONSHIP

Year	Name	F.D.S.B. Reg. No.	Breed and Sex	Color	Sire	Dam	Breeder	Owner	Handler
1896	Count Gladstone IV	......	Setter dog	Black, white and tan	Count Noble	Ruby's Girl	Charles Tucker	Avent and Hitchcock	J. M. Avent
1898	Tony's Gale	......	Setter dog	Black, white and tan	Antonio	Nellie G	Theodore Goodman	Eldred Kennels	D. E. Rose
1899	Joe Cumming	......	Setter dog	Black, white and tan	Antonio	Picciola	J. W. Renfroe	W. W. Titus	W. W. Titus
1900	Lady's Count Gladstone	1900	Setter dog	White blk. tan & ticked	Count Gladstone IV	Dan's Lady	G. G. Williams	G. G. Williamson	D. E. Rose
1901	Sioux	551	Setter bitch	White, black and tan	Count Gladstone IV	Hester Prynne	Avent, Thayer & Duryea	Avent and Duryea	J. M. Avent
1902	Sioux	551	Setter bitch	White, black and tan	Count Gladstone IV	Hester Prynne	Avent, Thayer & Duryea	Avent and Duryea	J. M. Avent
1903	Geneva	......	Setter bitch	White blk. tan & ticked	Tony Boy	Lena Belle	J. M. Avent	Pierre Lorillard	Charles Tucker
1904	Mohawk II	24504	Setter dog	White blk. tan & ticked	Tony Boy	Countess Meteor	J. M. Avent	Avent and Duryea	J. M. Avent
1905	Alambagh	18055	Setter dog	White blk. tan & ticked	Dash Antonio	Eldred Lark	Theo. Sturges	Hobart Ames	C. E. Buckle
1906	Pioneer	4647	Setter dog	White and orange	Dash Antonio	Bonnie Doone	R. H. Shannon	G. N. Clemson	E. Shelley
1907	Prince Whitestone	3289	Setter dog	White, black, tan and ticked	Count Whitestone	Queen Lilla	C. C. Burkhead	T. T. Pace	T. T. Pace
1908	Count Whitestone II	10620	Setter dog	White, black and tan	Count Whitestone	Mecca's Lady	W. W. Titus	Dr. H. B. McMaster	E. D. Garr
1909	Manitoba Rap	25709	Pointer dog	White, liver and tan	Ripple	Lady Cyrano Rush	W. T. F. Fielder	Thomas Johnson	C. H. Babcock
1910	Monora	......	Setter bitch	Black, white and tan	Mohawk II	Tankas	Avent and Duryea	J. M. Avent	J. M. Avent
1911	Eugene M	18277	Setter dog	White, black and ticked	Rosco Gladstone	Irene Cooper	M. E. Morehead	Frank Reily	W. H. Elliott
1912	Commissioner	18055	Setter dog	White and orange	Count Whitestone	Flossie May Fly	Calhoun and Avent	W. R. Craig	J. M. Avent
1913	Phillipides	18815	Setter dog	White, black and tan	Prince Rodney	Mary Tudor	F. S. Hall	Fred S. Hall	J. A. Gude
1914	Comanche Frank	19707	Pointer dog	White and liver	Fishel's Frank	Lady Johns	U. R. Fishel	U. R. Fishel	J. M. Avent
1915	La Besita	23014	Setter bitch	White, lemon & ticked	Count Whitestone	El Beso	J. L. Rynearson	F. M. Stephenson	W. H. Beazell
1916	John Proctor	25105	Pointer dog	White, lemon & ticked	Fishel's Frank	Miss Mariutch	A. L. Curtis	A. L. Curtis	C. H. Babcock
1917	Mary Montrose	38868	Pointer bitch	White and liver	Comanche Frank	Lorna Doone	F. M. Jones	William Ziegler Jr.	R. K. Armstrong
1918	Joe Muncie	33332	Setter dog	White and lemon	Jack Muncie	Miss Mathews	J. H. Mathews	Benjamin Weil	J. M. Avent
1919	Mary Montrose	38868	Pointer bitch	White and liver	Comanche Frank	Lorna Doone	F. M. Jones	William Ziegler Jr.	H. A. Tomlinson
1920	Mary Montrose	38868	Pointer bitch	White and liver	Comanche Frank	Lorna Doone	F. M. Jones	William Ziegler Jr.	H. A. Tomlinson
1921	Ferris' Jake	39833	Pointer dog	White and lemon	John Proctor	Lady Ferris	E. T. Cole	C. F. Griffith	Mack Pritchette
1922	Becky Broom Hill	43829	Pointer bitch	White and liver	Broom Hill Dan	Nell's Queen Cott	C. P. Hamel	L. L. Haggin	Chesley Harris
1923	Becky Broom Hill	43829	Pointer bitch	White and liver	Broom Hill Dan	Nell's Queen Cott	C. P. Hamel	L. L. Haggin	Chesley Harris
1924	Doughboy	46964	Pointer dog	White and liver	Nicholas Spettel	Kelona Lady	W. E. Hotchkiss	E. J. Rowe	J. W. Martin
1925	Becky Broom Hill	43829	Pointer bitch	White and liver	Broom Hill Dan	Nell's Queen Cott	C. P. Hamel	L. L. Haggin	Chesley Harris
1926	Feagin's Mohawk Pal	82979	Setter dog	White, black and ticked	Molemon	Mary Jepp	E. H. Hines	E. M. Tutwiler	Forrest Dean
1927	McTyre	69800	Setter dog	White and liver	Milligan's Dan	McPherson's Choice	Mrs. G. C. Moncrief	Jacob France	Chesley Harris
1928	Feagin's Mohawk Pal	82979	Setter dog	White, black and ticked	Molemon	Mary Jepp	E. H. Hines	E. M. Tutwiler Jr.	Forrest Dean
1929	Mary Blue	93971	Pointer bitch	White and liver	James Ben Hur	Lee's Grace	R. E. Lee	W. C. Teagle	Chesley Harris
1930	Feagin's Mohawk Pal	82979	Setter dog	White, black and ticked	Molemon	Mary Jepp	E. H. Hines	E. M. Tutwiler Jr.	Forrest Dean
1931	Mary Blue	93971	Pointer bitch	White and liver	James Ben Hur	Lee's Grace	R. E. Lee	W. C. Teagle	Chesley Harris
1932	Susquehanna Tom	169706	Pointer dog	White and liver	Highland Boy	Rap's Joy	Lebanon Kennels	Lebanon Kennels	Jake Bishop
1933	Rapid Transit	177658	Pointer dog	White and liver	The Hottentot	Milligan's Jane	A. G. C. Sage	A. G. C. Sage	Clyde Morton
1934	Nor'as Annie	163754	Pointer bitch	White, black and ticked	John Willing Jr.	Ben Hur's Countess	B. McCall	W. C. Teagle	C. H. Harris
1935	Homewood Flirtatious	174722	Pointer bitch	White, black and ticked	Seaview Rex	Wilder's Orange Lady	Dr. E. M. Wilder	Homewood Kennels	F. E. Bevan
1936	Sulu	207162	Pointer bitch	White, liver and ticked	The Hottentot	Lue's Sue	A. G. C. Sage	A. G. C. Sage	Clyde Morton
1937	Air Pilot's Sam	219719	Pointer dog	White, liver and ticked	Air Pilot	Nancy F	L. D. Johnson	Ed Farrior	Ed Farrior
1939	Sport's Peerless Pride	242136	Setter dog	White, black and ticked	Sport's Peerless	Gore's Blue Bonnie	L. M. Bobbitt	L. M. Bobbitt	W. D. English
1940	Lester's Enjoy's Wahoo	253324	Pointer dog	White, liver and ticked	Enjoy	Lester's Mary Lou	Dr. B. S. Lester	Dr. B. S. Lester	John S. Gates
1941	Ariel	289147	Pointer dog	White, liver and ticked	Air Pilot's Sam	Lullaby	A. G. C. Sage	A. G. C. Sage	Clyde Morton
1942	Luminary	275718	Pointer dog	White, black and ticked	Doctor Blue Willing	Lullaby	A. G. C. Sage	A. G. C. Sage	Clyde Morton
1943	Ariel	289147	Pointer dog	White, liver and ticked	Air Pilot's Sam	Lullaby	A. G. C. Sage	A. G. C. Sage	Clyde Morton
1945	Ariel	289147	Pointer dog	White, liver and ticked	Air Pilot's Sam	Lullaby	A. G. C. Sage	A. G. C. Sage	Clyde Morton
1946	Mississippi Zev	327886	Setter dog	White blk. tan & ticked	Peerless Eugene M	Red Flapper	J. E. Bufkin	Dr. W. R. Trapp	J. E. Bufkin
1947	Saturn	332801	Pointer dog	White and orange	Luminary	Hostess	A. G. C. Sage	A. G. C. Sage	Clyde Morton
1948	Peter Rinski	343012	Pointer dog	White and liver	Tennessee Dare Devil	Lady Willing Lady	Martin Watson	R. R. Waugh	Ray Smith
1949	Sierra Joan	347596	Pointer bitch	White and orange	Air Pilot Sammy	Titan's Girl	Frank Kirk	H. E. McGonigal	Howard Kirk

Year	Winner	Number	Breed	Color	Sire	Dam	Owner	Breeder	Handler
1950	Shore's Brownie Doone	375593	Pointer dog	White and liver	Claussen's Ran. Doone	Devotion's Kate	R. J. Reynolds Jr.	G. M. Livingston	G. A. Evans Jr.
1951	Paladin	390626	Pointer dog	White and liver	Ariel	Titan's Girl	Frank Kirk	A. G. C. Sage	Clyde Morton
1952	Paladin	390626	Pointer dog	White and liver	Ariel	Titan's Girl	Frank Kirk	Estate of A. G. C. Sage	Clyde Morton
1953	Shore's Brownie Doone	375596	Pointer dog.	White and liver	Claussen's Ranger Doone	Devotion's Kate	R. J. Reynolds Jr.	Mrs. G. M. Livingston	George A. Evans
1954	Warhoop Jake	426004	Pointer dog	White and liver	Lester's Enjoy's Wahoo	Spunky Willing Diane	C. D. Duke Jr.	Dr. H. E. Longsdorf	Ed Mack Farrior
1955	Lone Survivor	422955	Pointer dog	White and liver	Luminary	Titanette	Dr. E. R. Calame	Dr. E. R. Calame	Leon Covington
1956	Palamonium	487655	Pointer dog	White and liver	Paladin	Pandemonium's Dianah	Jimmy Hinton	Jimmy Hinton	Clyde Morton
1957	Wayriel Allegheny Sport	495832	Pointer dog	White and liver	Wayriel Jack	Allegheny Shendon Brownie	J. D. Barnhart	R. W. Riggins and Dr. J. A. Bays	Herman Smith
1958	The Arkansas Ranger	549564	Pointer dog	White and liver	Running W Wrangler	Ranger Bows	Mrs. G. B. Oliver	M. F. Mitchell	Jack Harper
1959	Palamonium	487655	Pointer dog	White and liver	Paladin	Pandemonium's Dianah	Jimmy Hinton	Jimmy Hinton	Clyde Morton
1960	Home Again Hattie	521919	Pointer dog	White and liver	The Haberdasher	Ariel's Spunky Fireball	C. H. Edwards	W. C. Jones	Paul Walker
1961	Spacemaster	526479	Pointer dog	White and liver	Fast Delivery	Knolwood Selene	A. Bracey Bobbitt and Mrs. P. E. Sherrill	Ralph E. Daniel	Paul Walker
1962	Home Again Hattie	587448	Pointer bitch	White and liver	Home Again Mike	Hattie of Arkansas	Mrs. G. B. Oliver	V. E. Johnson	Jack Harper
1963	Stormy Tempest	541103	Pointer dog	White and liver	Stormy Mike	Anytime	B. McCall	Dr. W. G. Arney and S. W. Hart	Gene Lunsford
1964	War Storm	594358	Pointer dog	White and liver	Warhoop Jake	Satilla Little Jane	Everett Reeves	B. McCall	John S. Gates
1966	Safari	578222	Pointer bitch	White and orange	Mercer Miller	Mercer Mill Judy	B. C. Goss	S. H. Vredenburgh	John Rex Gates
1967	Satilla Virginia Lady	647067	Pointer bitch	White and liver	Satilla Midnight Sun	Lady Bess	Dr. F. M. Phillippi	Dr. F. M. Phillippi	Herman Smith
1968	Riggins White Knight	613231	Pointer dog	White and orange	Major Lexington Boy	Stanley's Candy	W. R. Brown & D. H. Eaton	Dr. Nicholas Palumbo	D. Hoyle Eaton
1969	Red Water Rex	690437	Pointer dog	White and liver	Tiny Wahoo	Sea Island Gale	E. B. Alexander Jr.	E. B. Alexander Jr. & W. T. Pruitt	D. Hoyle Eaton
1970	Johnny Crockett	748513	Setter Dog	White and orange	Wonsover's Crockett Jed	Patterson's Flying Lady	Claud Patterson	H. P. Sheely	W. C. Kirk

WINNERS OF THE NATIONAL FREE-FOR-ALL CHAMPIONSHIP

Year	Name	F. D. S. B. Reg. No.	Breed and Sex	Color	Sire	Dam	Breeder	Owner	Handler
1916	John Proctor	25105	Pointer dog	White, lemon and ticked	Fishel's Frank	Miss Mariutch	A. L. Curtis	A. L. Curtis	C. H. Babcock
1917	De Soto Frank	29340	Pointer dog	White, black and ticked	Fishel's Frank	Alford's John's Fancy	John Jenkins	A. G. C. Sage	J. L. Holloway
1918	Candy Kid	31202	Setter dog	White, black, tan and ticked	Vallejo	Bond's Gypsy	Reford Bond	C. E. Duffield	Chesley H. Harris
1919	Jay R's Boy	31669	Setter dog	White, black, tan and ticked	Jay R Whitestone	Trixie Danstone	G. E. Stiller	Dr. T. H. Clark	Edw. Farrior
1920	Jay R's Boy	31669	Setter dog	White, black, tan and ticked	Jay R Whitestone	Trixie Danstone	G. E. Stiller	Dr. T. H. Clark	Edw. Farrior
1921	Shore's Ben	35028	Setter dog	White, black, tan and ticked	Ben's Sport	Mollie Cummings	T. W. Shore	Dr. A. F. Stone	John W. Martin
1922	Becky Broom Hill	43829	Pointer bitch	White and liver	Broom Hill Dan	Nell's Queen Cott	C. P. Hamel	L. L. Haggin	Chesley H. Harris
1923	Muscle Shoals' Jake	55621	Pointer dog	White and lemon	Ferris' Jake	Harris' Lady Pauper	J. J. Harris	James C. Foster Jr.	Edw. Farrior
1924	Muscle Shoals' Jake	55621	Pointer dog	White and lemon	Ferris' Jake	Harris' Lady Pauper	J. J. Harris	James C. Foster Jr.	Mack Pritchette
1925	McTyre	69800	Pointer dog	White and liver	Milligan's Dan	McPherson's Choice	Mrs. G. C. C. Moncrief	Jacob France	Pete Dixon
1926	Manrico	77183	Pointer dog	White, liver and ticked	Ferris' Jake	Griffith's Deenoya	Griffith's Kennels	C. E. Griffith	Chesley H. Harris
1927	McTyre	69800	Pointer dog	White and liver	Milligan's Dan	McPherson's Choice	Mrs. G. C. C. Moncrief	Jacob France	Chesley H. Harris
1928	Ireland's Greymist	114563	Pointer bitch	White, lemon and ticked	Griffith's Jack	Burger's Johanna	Griffith's Kennels	H. Glenn Ireland	Mack Pritchette
1929	Superlette	121950	Pointer bitch	White and liver	Milligan's Dan	Doughboy's Kelona Lady	S. G. McNeill	A. G. C. Sage	Clyde Morton
1930	Mary Blue	93971	Pointer bitch	White and liver	James Ben Hur	Lee' Grace	R. E. Lee	W. C. Teagle	Chesley H. Harris
1931	Superlette	121950	Pointer bitch	White and liver	Milligan's Dan	Doughboy's Kelona Lady	S. G. McNeill	A. G. C. Sage	Clyde Morton
1932	Superlette	121950	Pointer bitch	White and liver	Milligan's Dan	Doughboy's Kelona Lady	S. G. McNeill	A. G. C. Sage	Clyde Morton
1933	Norias Roy	166832	Pointer dog	White and liver	News Boy	Norias Lady	W. C. Teagle	W. C. Teagle	Prather Robinson
1934	Spunky Creek Joann	191432	Pointer bitch	White, orange and ticked	Muscle Shoals' Jake	Ireland's Greymist	Mrs. Glenn Ireland	Mrs. Nina Billingslea	Mack Pritchette
1935	Shanghai Express	191887	Pointer dog	White, liver and ticked	Richardson's Policeman	Touchstone Retrieving Roxy	P. C. Perry	G. M. Livingston	Henry Gilchrist
1936	Air Pilot's Sam	219719	Pointer dog	White, liver and ticked	Air Pilot	Nancy F	Edw. Farrior	L. D. Johnson	Ed. Mack Farrior
1937	Timbuctoo	211559	Pointer dog	White, liver and ticked	The Hotten:ot	Lue's Sue	A. G. C. Sage	A. G. C. Sage	Ed. Mack Farrior
1938	Norias Aeroflow	227615	Pointer bitch	White and lemon	Norias Jeff	Norias Kate	W. C. Teagle	W. C. Teagle	Chesley H. Harris
1939	Air Pilot's Sam	219719	Pointer dog	White, liver and ticked	Air Pilot	Nancy F	Edw. Farrior	L. D. Johnson	Edw. Farrior
1940	Rockabye Baby	265315	Pointer bitch	White and liver	Joe Willing	Lullaby	A. G. C. Sage	A. G. C. Sage	Clyde Morton
1941	The Texas Ranger	274144	Pointer dog	White and liver	Rex's Tarheel Jack	Miss Nellie Knolwood	P. E. Sherrill	D. B. McDaniel	Jack P. Harper
1942	Luminary	275718	Pointer dog	White, liver and ticked	Doctor Blue Willing	Lullaby	A. G. C. Sage	A. G. C. Sage	Clyde Morton
1943	The Texas Ranger	274144	Pointer dog	White and liver	Rex's Tarheel Jack	Miss Nellie Knolwood	P. E. Sherrill	D. B. McDaniel	Jack P. Harper
1944/1945	Ariel	289147	Pointer dog	White, liver and ticked	Air Pilot's Sam	Lullaby	A. G. C. Sage	A. G. C. Sage	Clyde Morton
1946	Saturn	322801	Pointer dog	White and orange	Luminary	Hostess	A. G. C. Sage	A. G. C. Sage	Jack P. Harper
1947	Texan Boy	325913	Pointer dog	White and liver	The Texas Ranger	Nola II	Gerald Jordan	D. B. McDaniel	F. W. Frazier
1948	Pandemonium	390628	Pointer dog	White and liver	Homerun Harrigan	Flying Girl	A. G. C. Sage	A. G. C. Sage	F. W. Frazier
1949	Pandemonium	390628	Pointer dog	White and liver	Homerun Harrigan	Flying Girl	A. G. C. Sage	A. G. C. Sage	Paul Walker
1950	Fast Delivery	375539	Pointer dog	White and liver	Delivery Boy	Ends Up	A. B. Bobbitt	A. B. Bobbitt	Ed. Mack Farrior
1951	Warhoop Jake	426004	Pointer dog	White, liver and ticked	Lester's Enjoy's Wahoo	Spunky Willing Diane	C. D. Duke Jr.	Dr. H. E. Longsdorf	Ed. Mack Farrior
1952	Warhoop Jake	426004	Pointer dog	White, liver and ticked	Lester's Enjoy's Wahoo	Spunky Willing Diane	C. D. Duke Jr.	Dr. H. E. Longsdorf	Howard Kirk
1953	Hall's Stonecroft Babe	467368	Pointer bitch	White, liver and ticked	Tyson	Gold Flame	Howard Kirk	Mrs. A. A. Hall	
1954	Lone Survivor	422955	Pointer dog	White, liver and ticked	Luminary	Titanette	Dr. E. R. Calame	Dr. E. R. Calame	
1955	Palamonium	487655	Pointer dog	White, liver and ticked	Paladin	Pandemonium's Dianah	Claude Hinton, Jr.	James Hinton	Leon Covington
1956	Volcano	438717	Pointer dog	White and lemon	Tyson	Ranger's Ariel Girl	Warren Clutter	Marc F. Mitchell	Clyde Morton
1957	Medallion	523361	Pointer dog	White and liver	Satilla Wahoo Pete	Sheila's Dot	John S. Gates	S. H. Vredenburgh	Jack Harper
1958	Medallion	523361	Pointer dog	White and liver	Satilla Wahoo Pete	Sheila's Dot	John S. Gates	S. H. Vredenburgh	John S. Gates
1959	Storm Trooper	509946	Pointer dog	White and liver	Stormy Mike	Bettie Shanks	Edward Farrior	B. McCall	John S. Gates
1960	Home Again Hattie	587448	Pointer bitch	White, liver and ticked	Home Again Mike	Hattie of Arkansas	Mrs. G. B. Oliver	V. E. Johnson	Jack Harper
1961	Farmer's Secret Weapon	531779	Pointer bitch	White, orange and ticked	Secret Weapon Boy	Farmer's Lady Tyson	J. S. Farmer	Peter Lusardi	P. A. Brousseau
1962	Stormy Tempest	541103	Pointer dog	White, liver and ticked	Stormy Mike	Anytime	B. McCall	Dr. W. G. Arney and S. W. Hart	Gene Lunsford
1963	Canon	654475	Pointer dog	White and orange	Tradition	Storm's Judy	Jimmie Hinton	Jimmie Hinton	Jimmie Hinton
1964	War Storm	594358	Pointer dog	White and orange	Warhoop Jake	Satilla Little Jane	Everett Reeves	M. McCall	John S. Gates
1965	Paladin's Royal Flush	689906	Pointer dog	White, lemon and ticked	Paladin's Royal Heir	Mike's Madonna	G. F. Wilson	Rogers H. Hays	John Rex Gates
1966	Jorwick's Dixiecrat	622864	Pointer dog	White and orange	Storm's Romance	Neill Bickerstaff's Mary	L. N. Bickerstaff	G. G. Jordon	Winfred Campbell
1967	Riggins White Knight	613231	Pointer dog	White and orange	Major Lexington Boy	Stanley's Candy	W. R. Brown & D. Hoyle Eaton	R. W. Riggins	D. Hoyle Eaton
1968	Air Control	709333	Pointer dog	White and lemon	Airflight	Sara Lee	Bob Cline	W. W. Till	David Grubb
1969	Oklahoma Flush	782916	Pointer dog	White and orange	Paladin's Royal Flush	Baconrind's Sandy	K. L. Keesee	Roger M. Kyes	John Rex Gates
1970	Wrapup	816192	Pointer dog	White and liver	Riggins White Knight	Bar Lane Dot	D. H. Eaton	J. Hinton/J. Payne	Billy Morton

—Foxhound Field Trials—

WHENEVER TWO or more fox hunters get together and combine their individual hounds into a single pack for a morning or evening of hunting, a foxhound field trial is in progress.

Not in any formal sense or stated event wherein decisions are handed down and prizes awarded, to be sure, but down deep within every owner of a good hound is the firm conviction that his hound is the *best,* and he is by no means bashful about declaring himself to that effect.

Historical Notes. Such vociferous arguments have been, and always will be, the natural order of the day whenever the fox is chased. Perhaps these arguments waxed particularly heated among the members of the Brunswick Fur Club and that organization set out to find some means of "officially" settling them. So the first foxhound field trial ever to be held in America was staged, under the club's sponsorship, at Albany Hills, Maine, November 11-15, 1889. E. L. Toothaker's Bugle won the Derby, with the Open Hound Class going to L. O. Dennison's Ben Butler.

Less than a month later—December 2, 1889—the Interstate Fox Hunters Club held its first recorded trials at Waverly, Miss. The Puppy Stake went to the Wild Goose Pack's Mounter, with the Avent Pack's Flora second, and the Wild Goose Pack's Boston third. Rock, of the Avent Pack, won the Speed class, with Callie Gates, of the Wild Goose Pack, second, and the Waverly Pack's Stonewall third. The Hunting and Trailing class was won by Callie Gates, with Stonewall Jackson, of the Wild Goose Pack, second, and Truman, carrying the Waverly Park's colors, third. Callie Gates was declared the best all-around foxhound. And the Wild Goose Pack won the honors for the best pack, with the Avent Pack second and the Willis Pack third.

The sport knew a slow, but steady, growth in the next few years and this interest brought out the need for a national organization. In 1893 a group of foxhunting enthusiasts gathered at the Waverly, Miss., home of Captain Billy and Val Young and organized the National Foxhunters Association.

The first trials of the new organization were not successful. Held at Olympia, Ky., the hunting continued for three days beginning November 20, 1894. A long spell of dry weather had, however, made scenting conditions very unfavorable and no decisive work was secured so the meet was called off.

The second trial was held at Owingsville, Ky., beginning December 2, 1895. The Derby went to Jay Bird, owned by Walker and Hagan, with second to Bourbon Kennels' Red Blaze, and third to A. Ware's Speed.

The All-Age stake was won by Kit, owned by Spencer Brothers. Lewis, owned by E. H. Walker, was second, while the Strode Valley Kennel Club's Bird annexed third.

The annual trials of the National Foxhunters Association present the climax of the sport each season in the National Championship. Just prior to this, the greatest event in foxhound field trials, the Chase Futurity, the classic for younger dogs, is held. The Futurity is sponsored by *The Chase* magazine, official organ of the National Foxhunters Association, and many state organizations. (*The Chase,* The Chase Publishing Co. Inc., 152 Walnut, Lexington, Ky. 40507.)

Long before the sport donned the official mantle of organization, many spirited contests were held throughout the southern states. The first prize ever given to the winner of one of these events which could be termed a foxhound field trial was a silver collar inscribed as follows:

A pack of American Foxhounds in action at the Warrenton, Virginia Hunt. Photo by Marshall Hawkins.

CHAMPION PRIZE COLLAR
State of Kentucky
Given by Madison County, April 25, 1866
TO THE FASTEST HOUND IN THE STATE

It was won by a hound named Rock, owned by W. C. Terrill. Rock won the collar twice, in 1866 and 1868. The events were held at Thorpe's Hollow on Drowned Creek, and the collar is still one of the prized possessions of the Terrill family.

Painted Dogs. Hounds competing in field trials are given numbers as they are entered. These numbers are painted on the dogs' sides to aid the judges as this is the only means by which the dogs may be identified satisfactorily and due fault or credit noted accurately for each dog. While few readers may have heard of painting dogs, this is one instance of such legitimate practice, quart cans of special dog paint being available in white, red, black, yellow, orange, and blue.

Judging and Titles. All-Age stakes usually last at least four days. Each morning at dawn the hounds are lined up for the roll call and then are cast away together. The task of keeping up with them, an extremely difficult one usually, is then the responsibility of the judges, who vary in number in accordance with the importance of the stake and the number of entries.

The dogs are judged on hunting and trailing, speed and driving, and endurance. They are faulted, or "scratched" (disqualified), for babbling (opening when not on scent), loafing, skirting or cutting (running wide of the line or leaving the line and trying

Posing hounds in the bench show at a Mississippi foxhound field trial.

to head off the fox), refusing to run with the pack, or, of course, quitting. Other faults are also taken into consideration.

Judging a foxhound field trial requires a great deal of physical stamina, as well as thorough knowledge of hound performance and the ability to interpret it. For the judges must be in the saddle from dawn until the hunt is called off for the day, usually about noon. Hard riding is a matter of course for them, for they must see the hounds before they can score their performances.

The standing of the hounds is generally posted after each day's running, along with a list of those

"scratched" or disqualified, so that each contestant knows how he stands.

The winner of the All-Age stake in a state trial is given the title of state champion and is entitled to the prefix "Ch." with the state abbreviation and the letter "f" for field, in parenthesis following.

The American Kennel Club recognizes as a champion the winner of an All-Age stake of any member or licensed club, provided the trial has lasted at least four days. The winner of the bench show in connection with these trials is entitled to the title "Champion" with the letter "b" for "Bench" following.

The roll call at daybreak, just before the cast, at a Tennessee State Foxhound Trial. Tennessee Conservation Dept. photo.

Perhaps the most important field trial, with the exception of the National Championship, is the United States Open, a hard-fought endurance race the requirements of which test the merits of the best hounds in the country.

That foxhound field trials make up a popular sport wherever Reynard, red or gray, roams is evidenced by the number of state organizations which have held or continue to hold annual championship events. Among them are those of Missouri, Kentucky, Alabama, Ohio, Texas, Georgia, West Virginia, Maryland, Virginia, Pennsylvania, New York, South Carolina, Connecticut, Arkansas, Florida, Minnesota, Mississippi, and North Carolina.

GLOSSARY OF FOXHUNTING TERMS

ACCOUNT FOR. When killed or run to earth, the fox is said to be accounted for.

BABBLER. A hound which opens or barks when not on the trail.

BILLET. The droppings of the fox.

BLANK. A cover or section of the country is blank or drawn blank when no fox is found in it. A day when hounds do not start a fox is called blank.

BLOODED. When hounds kill their quarry, they are said to have been blooded; the young or inexperienced hunter is "blooded" by anointing him with fox blood at his first "kill."

BLUE TICK. A white hound with small splashes of black mixed with the white giving the coat the effect of blue.

BRUSH. The tail of the fox.

BURROW. The underground home of small animals, such as rabbits.

Field trial foxhounds on the trail. Note the numbers, painted on each dog. Tennessee Conservation Dept. photo.

BURST. Any fast part of a run, generally the first part.

BURST HIM. When a fox is killed in a burst, the hounds have *burst him.*

CARRY A GOOD HEAD. When hounds keep abreast when running the line, they are carrying a good head.

CARRY A LINE. When hounds follow the scent well, they are carrying a line.

CAST. To spread out in search of scent.

CHALLENGE. The first hound to open on finding scent, *challenges.*

CHANGE. To leave the line of one quarry for that of another.

CHECK. A temporary loss of scent.

CHEER. Any hunting cry to encourage the hounds.

COLD (LINE). The faint scent of fox. May be minutes or hours old, according to scenting conditions.

COUPLES. A link with a swivel-snap at each end, so that hounds may be coupled together. A pack is said to consist of so many couples or couple. The expression got its origin from the practice of keeping hounds coupled until cast away on the hunt.

COURSE. To chase by sight and not by scent.

COVERT (COVER). A wood, thicket, or place where a fox is sheltered.

CRASH. When the pack gives tongue together on finding a fox.

CROPPER. A bad fall.

CRY (VOICE, TONGUE). The sound a hound makes when trailing or running a quarry. Different from the bark of common dogs, and varies materially at different phases of the chase.

CUB. The young of the fox.

CUB-HUNTING. Early season hunting.

DEN. The home of the fox.

DEN BARK. The peculiar cry of the hound when the fox is run to earth.

DETERMINATION. The will to try . . . and keep on trying.

DEWCLAW. The false toe and claw on the legs, generally removed. Dewclaws on the hind legs of hounds are said to indicate impure ancestry.

DEWLAP. The pendulous skin under the neck.

DOG FOX. The male fox.

DOG HOUND. The male hound.

DOUBLE. When the fox turns back on its course.

DRAFT. To remove hounds from a pack.

DRAG. An artificial line. Also the scent left by the fox on his return to his den.

DRAG HOUNDS. Hounds used to hunt an artificial line.

DRAW. To search for a fox in a given covert or cover.

DWELLING. The unnecessary lingering of hounds on scent.

EARTH. The hole of some burrowing animal which has been appropriated by a fox, or which the fox goes into for safety.

ENTER. When young hounds are first put in a pack they are said to be *entered.*

FAULT. See *Check.*

FEATHERING. Moving the stern from side to side with liveliness, indicating the hound has found interesting scent, but not in sufficient quantity to speak to it.

FIELD. Those, other than master and hunt staff, who follow the hounds.

FIND. When hounds first smell scent of the quarry, and open on it, they are said to have made a *find.*

FLIGHTY. Uncertain, changeable; applicable to both scent and hounds.

FOILED. When the ground has been much traversed by cattle, sheep, horses, hounds, etc., it is said to be foiled.

FORM. The seat, or kennel, of the rabbit, or hare.

FRESH. The opposite of cold, when applied to the line.

FULL CRY. The chorus of music from the pack. American hounds generally give their best cry at full speed.

GIVING TONGUE. See *Cry.*

GONE AWAY. When the fox has been found and the pack goes away at a fast rate.

GONE TO GROUND. When the fox has gone into an earth, a drain, den or other underground shelter.

HARK FORWARD. A huntsman's cheer to encourage his hounds to work forward.

HEAD. See *Carry a Head.*

HEADED. When the fox is made to turn back he is said to be headed.

HEADS UP. When hounds searching for scent raise their heads from the ground.

HIT OFF. To recover the line at a check.

HOICK (YOICK). A cheer to hounds.

Fox hunting clubs often put on hound shows. This is Orange County's Marker, a winner at one of the shows sponsored by the Rose Tree Fox Hunting Club of Media, Pa. Hank Babbitt photo.

HOLD HARD. A warning to riders to slow up and not press hounds closely.

HONEST. A hound that has no faults is said to be honest.

HONOR A LINE. When a hound gives tongue on the line of a known quarry.

JUMPED. When a pack has been working a line slowly and suddenly makes the fox go away at full speed, the fox is said to have been jumped.

KENNEL. The fox's lair. The housing place of the pack.

LAIR. The locality where the fox generally stays above ground in the daytime.

LIFT. To take the hounds from a lost scent, with the idea of trying to hit the line farther on.

LINE. The track of the quarry indicated by its scent.

LINE HUNTER. A hound which sticks close to the line.

LOSS. When hounds cannot longer follow the line they are said to have come to a loss.

MAIN EARTH. The fox's den and place of breeding.

MASK. The fox's head.

MEET. The gathering place of those taking part in the chase.

M.F.H. Master of Fox Hounds.

MOB. To surround and kill a fox without giving him a fair chance to run.

MOUTHY. A hound that is unnecessarily noisy is said to be mouthy.

MUTE. Descriptive of a hound which does not open on the line.

NOSE. Scenting ability.

OVERRUN. When hounds do not check when they no longer scent the line they are said to have overrun.

PACK. A group of hounds regularly hunted together.

PACK SENSE. When hounds run in mass formation well and honor each other's cry they are said to have pack sense.

PAD. The foot of the fox. The bottom of the hound's foot.

POINT. The distance in a straight line between two localities farthest apart in any particular hunt.

POINT-TO-POINT. A straight run.

POTTERER. A hound that dwells too long on scent.

PUT DOWN. To put to death.

QUARRY. The hunted animal.

RABBIT-EARTH. A burrow, in which the fox frequently goes for shelter.

RATE. To chastise a hound by whip or word.

RIOT. When hounds run anything but "legitimate" quarry.

ROACH-BACKED. An arch-backed hound.

RUN. The chase of the fox from find to kill.

SCORING. When the whole pack opens on a scent the hounds are said to be scoring.

SETTLE. When a find is made by one or more hounds and others, coming from different directions, join in on the line, the pack is said to settle.

SINKING. Descriptive of a nearly beaten fox.

SKIRTER. A hound which, in jealousy, runs wide of the pack.

SPEAK (OF A HOUND). To cry or open when on scent.

START. To find.

STERN. The tail of a hound.

STREAMING. Going across open country at full pace and cry.

STRIKE. To find, start.

STRIKE HOUNDS. Those possessing most keenness in finding traces of a line.

TAIL HOUNDS. Dogs at the rear of the pack.

TALLY-HO. The cheer announcing the viewing of a fox. Used in formal hunting.

THROWN OUT. When a hound or horseman loses his position in the chase.

TIMBER. A wooden fence, gate, stile or rail.

TONGUE. See Cry.

UP. Jumped.

VIEWED AWAY. When the quarry is seen to go away from cover.

VIXEN. The female fox.

VOICE. See Cry.

WHELP. A very young puppy.

WHIPPER-IN. The huntsman's assistant in controlling hounds.

WORKING A LINE. See Carry a Line.

WORRIED. Torn to bits by hounds.

YOICK. See Hoick. An old hunting cry.

—Retriever Field Trials—

IT HAS long been the conviction of experienced hunters that the most effective contribution any individual sportsman can make to the cause of wildlife conservation is the use of a retrieving dog while hunting. This statement is not limited to the specialists, the retrieving breeds, but includes *any* dog—which is not gunshy, has a nose, and will hunt!

The annual loss of game birds, both upland and waterfowl, which fall to the gun but are *not* retrieved, mainly through the lack of a retrieving dog, is enough to make the far-thinking sportsman who first used the term "game conservation" turn over in his grave. Yet almost all of this wasted game could be salvaged if a retrieving dog were made a "must" in the necessary equipment of every gunner. Although any sort of dog which will hunt and has a nose will be of value in game salvage, the retrieving breeds are specialists in this department of field performance and their importance in the overall picture of game conservation is inestimable. Their value cannot be overstated. For example, authorities freely estimate that at least one out of every five wild ducks which fall to the hunter's gun are cripples which get away to be taken by predators or to die lingering deaths, or are dead ducks which fall in such thick or heavy cover that they are extremely difficult to find, so that search for them is only cursory. The recovery of only a considerable portion of this annual waste, some of it needlessly wanton, would be a most effective contribution to the restoration of a priceless, natural, renewable resource which is in great danger today, and would materially assist in the preservation of wildfowling.

Hunting dogs have been taught to retrieve ever since they first became adjuncts to the gun, but until recent years the use of "specialists," retrievers developed solely and used exclusively for retrieving, has been comparatively limited in this country. The publicity given to retriever field trials in America, however, has given great impetus to interest in the various breeds to which this sport is devoted.

The performances of these dogs some of which have been nothing short of marvelous, have attracted the attention of many sportsmen who realize that the sport of field shooting loses its zest when the game downed is not retrieved. As a result, breeders of Chesapeakes, Labradors, Goldens, Flatcoated and Curlycoated retrievers in this country are hard pressed to supply the demand. The sport of retriever field trials is rapidly growing. First fairly well confined to the eastern seaboard, this sport has spread into all parts of the U.S. and Canada the Middle West, the Mississippi Valley, West Coast areas and some of the prairie states.

Historical Notes. Pioneers in the sport are the members of the Labrador Retriever Club, Inc., which held its first annual trial (licensed by the American Kennel Club) on Dec. 21, 1931. The competition was confined to Labrador Retrievers only, and two owners, Mrs. Marshall Field and Robert Goelet, won all places. Mrs. Field's Carl of Boghurst and Odds On accounted for first and second places respectively, while Mr. Goelet's Sab of Tulliallan won third-place honors. Fourth place was divided between Mrs. Field's May Millard and Mr. Goelet's Glenmere Joe. Sixteen Labrador competitors faced the judges, David Wagstaff and Dr. Samuel Milbank.

A Golden Retriever field trial winner in action. Photo by Evelyn M. Shafer.

The American Chesapeake Club held its inaugural trials in 1932, and these two clubs were the sole promoters of the sport until late in 1934 when the Brookhaven Game Protective Association held its first trial at Strong's Neck, East Setauket, N.Y.

The year 1935 saw the spread of the sport to the midwestern section of the country when 11 retrievers started in the first trials of the Midwest Field Trial Club at Barrington, Ill. Since that time the sport has known a healthy growth. Most of the events held in this country are now open to all members of the retriever breeds, although each breed organization, the Labrador Retriever Club, the American Chesapeake Club, the Golden Retriever Club, and occasionally the Irish Water Spaniel Club, hold trials in which the competition is confined to the individual breeds.

Retriever Trials—Their Regulation and Aims. The American Kennel Club of New York and the *American Field* of Chicago outlined, in considerable detail, rules and regulations for the holding of retriever trials. These formulas are quite similar; the *American Field* concept gives more latitude, perhaps, to the judges. The great majority of the trials are held under the licensing of the American Kennel Club.

Retriever trials in this country are not only public exhibitions of gundog proficiency. They are the best insurance retriever-breed fanciers can have against the relegation of their favorites to the somewhat cloistered confines of the bench-show ring. The Retriever is a workman and he reserves the opportunity to demonstrate his peculiarly outstanding capabilities in the wildfowl blind and game field. Retriever field trials are devoted to just that.

It might be well here to quote an extract from the Rules and Regulations governing retriever trials as formulated by the *American Field:*

> The object of retriever trails is the promotion and development of the high-class Retriever, to demonstrate by public performance the great intelligence, usefulness and

Action in land series, in a Retriever field trial. One Golden Retriever being sent, another honoring. David M. Duffey photo.

perfection of training attainable by dogs of the breeds named.

Retriever trails are designed to provide competition of the highest kind among the various retriever breeds, to stimulate enthusiasm among owners and to afford a practical guide to breeders by setting a high standard of performance. The tests in retriever trials should not vary from those encountered in an ordinary day's shooting, except that since the tests principally are artificially conducted they may be somewhat more exacting, but must be as uniform as possible for all contestants in a single stake.

Retriever trials educate the sportsman to a fuller appreciation of the work of his dogs and are a mighty influence in the significant work of conservation to promote perpetuation of wildlife.

Judging and Performance Expected. In these trials, as in other gundog trials, the competing dogs are judged on natural ability and training. Under natural ability come nose, pace, style, determination, drive, and marking. The refinements of training, which augment the dog's natural ability, include steadiness, obedience to handler, excellence of delivery, and tender mouth.

There are a number of factors which come under consideration by the judges in evaluating a retriever's performance in field trials. The most important quality of a good retriever is the possession of exceptional scenting ability. Without a good "nose" a retriever is practically hamstrung before his education begins. True, his ability to "mark" down his game will serve him in good stead, but his eyes alone are not sufficient to lead him to his quarry. An exceptional "nose" will lead him to the capture of a running cripple, no matter how elusive.

The successful retriever must not only work out the area of the fall quickly and thoroughly, but he must mark it down properly and go to it at command with dash and speed. If he fails to locate the fallen game immediately he will continue his search in determined and enthusiastic fashion, using initiative and independence, but responding promptly to the directions of his handler when they are given. He should quarter his ground thoroughly, taking every advantage of the wind to aid his nose, but conducting his search in accordance with his handler's directions as long as he can see or hear him.

Once the game is found it must be returned with promptness, without dallying, and delivered with tenderness. A slow delivery often mars an otherwise sparkling performance, although pace is not the prime requisite. A fast search, quick pick-up, and swift return make a well-rounded performance which always deserves high praise.

A good retriever must also be "water-wise." He must unhesitatingly enter the water when ordered to do so, no matter how cold or rough, and his ability to negotiate swiftly difficult water conditions is most essential to a successful and satisfactory performance. The "higher" a dog swims the better his chances are to end his quest with the greatest dispatch.

The retriever must be under perfect control at all times. Not only must he show obedience to his handler while actually at work, but he must be completely steady in the duckboat or blind or as a non-slip retriever (retriever working only at heel) in the field, particularly under the gun. Under actual waterfowl shooting conditions, many wildfowlers insist that their retrievers be on their way for the retrieve as soon as they have marked the fall, contending, and sometimes properly so, that the sooner he reaches the spot of the fall the better his chances are for a retrieve. Field trial procedures, however, will not permit such unsteadiness. The dog must remain "steady" until ordered to go. This is as it should be, for "steadiness" demonstrates the high degree of excellence which has been attained in the dog's training. And field trials are exhibitions of gundogs in performance approaching perfection as nearly as possible.

The argument concerning "shot-breaking" as an assistance to retrieving chances in "rough-and-tumble" shooting is as old as gundog training itself. There is an unnecessary element of danger present in "jump" shooting with a shot-breaking retriever in the boat, and numbers of capsizings have resulted. A shot-breaker can also upset things in a duck blind, although it is granted that the sooner he gets on the job the better. However, if a dog is allowed to break-shot he is more liable to become unsteady in other respects, and a successful and satisfactory retriever *must* be under control.

Proper retrieving performance includes tender retrieving. The "hard-mouthed" dog will be disqualified in field trials.

Much has been said about the speed and style of a retriever. The good retriever will go about his work with enthusiasm and dash, reaching his destination quickly and hunting his quarry at good pace. Pottering should not be tolerated. He should show animation and spirit in his work. Pleasure in his job and merry action are always pleasing to the eye.

Consistency of a high order is demanded in a retriever trial. Often in pointing-dog trials a single outstanding performance is sufficient to obtain a place in the stake, at least, and possibly means a first-

A Labrador Retriever in action at Weldon Springs, Missouri, during a National Championship Stake of the National Retriever Field Tr[ial] Club. Photo by Evelyn M. Shafer.

honors win. Such is not the case in retriever trials. One spectacular performance is not enough. Those dogs which win are called upon to repeat and repeat again as often as the judges deem necessary for the clear determination of the winner on that occasion.

While the dogs are drawn in braces, as in pointing-dog trials, and run in pairs, there is no definite time limit set on any single series. In this respect retriever trials differ from pointing-dog competitions. In the latter, too, it quite often occurs that a number of the contesting dogs run birdless heats and so have not demonstrated, in the first series, their ability to handle game. This is due to the considerable part the "luck of the draw" plays in bird dog trials. This "luck" is, in a large measure, eliminated in retriever trials, for in these events every competitor is assured of chances to prove his wares as a retriever of game. The shooting of pen-raised game assures this. The "luck" is not entirely eliminated, however, for it is simply impossible to give every dog identically the same retrieving problem to solve, although every effort is made to do so. One dog may draw a couple of kills which fall in fairly easy cover, while to the lot of his bracemate may fall a strong-running wing-tipped cripple which will give him quite a run for his money. The judges, however, have a way of balancing these performances one against the other so that the decisions are arrived at with equal fairness to all.

In the land tests the dogs compete in braces, although each dog performs his own task without aid or interference from his bracemate. The two dogs walk at the heels of their handlers, who are in line with the judges. Each must stand quietly or sit when the "line" comes to a halt. The game-bearers and the guns proceed at fair distance in front of the judges and handlers, and at a signal from the judges game birds are released and the guns go into action.

The dogs must remain, unleashed, quietly on the line and should mark the fall of the game. The judges then will order one handler to send his dog in for the retrieve, the bracemate remaining "steady" until its turn is called. It is indeed quite a temptation for a dog to watch his rival dash out and proudly make an enthusiastic return to be petted by his master when he knows that another bird is down. And it is doubly tempting when the same dog is again sent—to fetch the second bird. Yet control and "steadiness" play an extremely important part in retriever trials. Breaking to shot or retrieving without orders are errors which disqualify. The same applies to chasing rabbits in Open All-Age stakes.

In water tests, the dogs are worked singly, generally remaining in the blind with their handler until ordered to retrieve. Upon making the retrieve they must come around the blind and enter it from the rear or side to make the delivery.

Trials Offer Varying Challenges. There are no set programs which are required in all retriever trials. The judges and the field trial committee have com-

The Labrador Retriever is a consistently good performer in the field. Photo by Evelyn M. Shafer.

plete control over the requirements and mechanics of each stake. Difference in conditions which exist in various areas and over different field trial locales makes this latitude necessary. The general idea, however, that dogs are expected to retrieve any type of game bird under any and all conditions always prevails.

As an example of the diversified working procedure of a retriever trial we may cite some tests once given the winners of the Open All-Age stake of the Long Island Retriever Club. The first test was a long, widespread double mark in water. The second was a double mark in heavy cover on land, one bird 75 yards out and the other 10 to 15 yards farther on in the same line. The third was a combination marked retrieve and blind in water. The fourth was a long double mark in marsh grass. The fifth was a single mark across water and on land.

Another example was the tests one year given the winners of the Midwest Field Trial Club. First, a short triple-marked retrieve in water; second, a double-marked retrieve on land, both birds shot on the same line, one 40 yards out, the other 80 yards; third, a double land blind, one 40 yards out, the other 80, the dogs being required to return the near bird first; fourth, a short blind requiring water entry and handling in a narrow creek.

Simple problems, these? Most trainers do not think so. Their proper solution requires plenty of nose, brains, strength, and willingness.

Some retriever owners deride retriever trials as

Fld. Ch. King Buck, Labrador Retriever owned by Nilo Kennels, Brighton, Illinois, three times a winner of the National Champion Stake of the National Retriever Field Trial Club. Photo by Evelyn M. Shafer.

being "too artificial." "This is just a show. These are trick dogs," some have said. "You won't get these sort of conditions in actual wildfowling in a month of Sundays." The answer to such charges is: attend a modern retriever trial and see for yourself. True, some of the conditions do have an artificial flavor, for this is necessary to provide equal opportunities for all contestants and also to make the tests properly difficult. When one makes the statement that most the situations in retriever trials are not encountered in regular wildfowling he has merely admitted that he is not an experienced wildfowler.

"Trick dogs?" Some of the retrieving feats of the competing dogs in practically every retriever field trial are spectacular and sensational, and these dogs *do* know a lot of so-called "tricks" of the retrieving game, but they are "tricks" far different from the parlor variety. Do not forget that practically all the winning retrievers are top gunning companions in rough-and-tumble shooting and have had their share of open-season experience.

Noteworthy Performances. For evidence that these dogs get plenty of experience in field trials one should take a glance at the amazing record of Field Trial Champion Rip, a Golden Retriever which carved his niche in the Retriever Hall of Fame in the seasons of 1939, 1940, and 1941. Rip, according to his owner, Paul Bakewell, retrieved under judgment, from the fall of 1938 until his death in August, 1941, the remarkable total of 236 pheasants and ducks without a miss.

The champion Chesapeake Retriever, Dilwyne Montauk Pilot, declared the best retriever in 1936, was a marvelous gun dog and was heavily shot over by his owner, R. R. M. Carpenter of Montchanin, Del. A field trial performance of this grand retriever is considered one of the greatest exhibitions of canine sagacity. In the American Chesapeake Club's trials at Benton, Md., in 1937, Pilot was given a blind water retrieve of two ducks; one fell dead, the other was a strong swimming cripple. A sharp cross-wind was blowing and a fairly strong tide was running, making swimming difficult. Pilot picked up the dead duck and started for the blind, when he saw the cripple rapidly swimming away. He dropped the dead duck and started for the cripple. The bird was a strong swimmer, but the high-swimming Pilot was more than his equal. However, the bird was a clever diver and time after time eluded his pursuer. Pilot, too, was a diver and finally caught his quarry, returning the duck alive. He immediately started out after the dead duck, returning to the spot where he had left it. The duck, however, had floated far down the bay and was not in the dog's sight. The clever retriever started swimming in wide circles, caught his handler's direction, and finally made a bee-line for the fallen bird, retrieving it promptly. In all, the dog was in the water many minutes and he was busy every one of them. He won the stake.

Meadow Farm Night, Charles L. Lawrance's handsome black Labrador, is another who rendered an outstanding performance in the Long Island Retriever Club's trials. Night drew a wing-tipped

A Labrador completing a retrieve to his handler during a National Championship Stake of the National Retriever Field Trial Club, Smyrna, Delaware. Photo by Evelyn M. Shafer.

Springer returns with a pheasant to his owner-handler in an Eng-
Springer Spaniel National Championship Stake. Photo by Evelyn Shafer.

Ready for Water Retrieving Test in a typical Springer Spaniel field trial. David M. Duffey photo.

water retrieve. The duck was barely injured but was unable to fly. The big Labrador could not get his mouth on the bird because of its expert diving. Time after time he dived after the duck, only to see his quarry come up yards away. Finally, the dog drew on his instinctive intelligence and began to swim back and forth by the duck, crowding him just enough to cause the duck to swim toward shore but staying far enough away to keep from causing undue excitement. Once the duck was on land, the pick-up was easy for Night and a news photographer secured an excellent picture of the big fellow racing back to the blind with the live bird in his mouth. Night won that stake.

As demonstrations of gundog control, steadiness, willingness to tackle difficult situations, and plain canine intelligence, retriever field trials have no coun-

terpart in this country. They are here to stay. If they do nothing more than demonstrate to the shooting public the extreme value of the retriever breeds in game salvage and conservation, they have more than justified their existence!

The "Best Breed" Question. A frequent question is, "Which breed is the best retriever?" Discussion of this hotly debated matter has no place in this text. However, Labradors are most numerous among the winners, with Golden Retrievers and Chesapeake Bays next in order.

The sport of retriever field trials is growing every year, and more and more clubs are holding one or more retriever trials each year.

—Spaniel Field Trials—

THE FIRST field trials for spaniels were held in England in 1899, with all spaniel breeds competing. Fanciers of Cocker and English Springer Spaniels in this country, however, have kept their competitions separate, having events for Cockers, and events for Springers. The first championship spaniel field trials to be held in this country were those of 1924, when the Cocker Spaniel Field Trial Club of America held its inaugural event at Verbank, N.Y., and the English Springer Spaniel Field Trial Association held its first trial at Fisher's Island, N.Y.

Since that time the sport has spread to the Midwest and the Pacific coast. For a time these trials were held mainly in the East, but major spaniel field trial activities have spread to all sections of the country.

Spaniel trials differ in several ways from bird dog

Springer Spaniel flushes pheasants, then waits for shot and order to retrieve. David M. Duffey photo.

Shown here with four of her progeny, the dog at the left, Ch. Woodelf, was the dam of 8 champions, grand-dam of 26 champions, and ancestress of 114 champions. (Mrs. C. M. Buchanan, Orchard, Colorado, owner.)

trials. In only a few bird dog trials is game actually shot, while shooting is necessary in spaniel trials to test retrieving ability. In bird dog trials, the dogs are run as braces, two dogs working the same course at the same time. In spaniel trials the dogs are put down in braces but the bracemates work parallel courses each about 50 yards wide and must not interfere with each other. The field trial spaniel maintains the usual "shooting dog" range, while the field trial bird dog, particularly in the major trials, generally searches at considerably wider range than would be comfortable in hunting on foot. In spaniel trials, water retrieving tests are given.

The field trial spaniel is judged on game finding, retrieving, and steadiness. These qualities embrace nose, style, thoroughness, pace, facing cover, marking, watching handler for directions, speed, pick-up, carry mouth, control with commands, and control without command.

(See Part XVIII for field trial regulations.)

Completing his retrieve, one of the participants in a National Championship Stake of the National English Springer Spaniel Field Trial Association. Photo by Evelyn M. Shafer.

Part XIV

DOGS IN THE PRIMITIVE WORLD

Many people have contended that the dog is a direct descendant from the wolf; some have said that he was originally but a jackal domesticated, while others have written that the wild dogs of India came from a cross between the wolf and the tiger. Because of such far-fetched theories and beliefs, it is no small wonder that the dog has not been given as much credit for originality as other animals. Shrouded in mystery, the dog's origin has been the subject of many speculations, some purely of an amateur vein, and others seriously attempting to bridge the gap between scientific knowledge and findings and the dark unknown of eras referred to only in geological terms.

—The Origin of the Dog—

MAN, IN his never-ceasing search behind the veil of antiquity into the evolution and history of the human race, has not yet discovered the Adam and Eve of dogdom.

Perhaps the many and varied breeds of dogs, as our forebears knew them and as we know them today, have no common denominator. Perhaps they sprang from several species. Perhaps they came from one, the offspring of which spread to the four corners of the earth and adapted themselves to the climates and conditions of the respective lands which they chose to call "home."

There have been many, many theories concerning the origin of the dog, none of which has been entirely satisfactory. Some of them have been based on the impossible, others have been purely ridiculous. Some writers of the Eighteenth Century expounded rather fantastic notions regarding the origin of certain breeds, contending that all living dogs were the result of crosses between two other varieties. The eminent naturalists Pallas and Burchell stated that the mastiff came from a cross with the hyena, and Lowe in his more modern *Domestic Animals of Great Britain* stated this was possible. The Bengal tiger was even given credit for contributing to the origin of another breed.

It is probable that the earliest animals deserving to be called dogs were of the wolf type, but it has never been proved that all dogs descended from the true wolf. When one sees such wide divergences as the Dachshund and the St. Bernard, or the Irish Wolfhound and the Pomeranian, standing side by side, it is difficult to believe that these dogs trace back to common ancestors. Yet when we consider that man, sometimes within a half-century or so, has by selective breeding developed entirely new breeds among domestic animals, or changed the appearance and characteristics of existing breeds to almost full loss of recognition, does it not seem conceivable that, through the thousands of years that man has been closely associated with dogs, such amazing variations could have been developed from more or less common progenitors?

THE DOG IN VERY ANCIENT TIMES

History, in the written sense, did not begin until about 4,000 or 3,000 B.C., yet no one knows when the association or partnership between man and dog began. Geologists tell us that some close association existed during the Stone Age, probably about 50,000 years ago. Descriptions of the earliest "dogs" are made from attempts at the restoration of skeletons or partial skeletons, and are merely based on the conclusions of various authorities. According to Cecil G. Trew in *The Story of the Dog*, geology tells us nothing of the different breeds of dogs now existing.

Reproduction of the *Cynodictis*, the dog's ancestor.

Clues From Fossils. Close affinity to some of the present-day varieties is discernible in the remains of extinct species of dogs that have been found in many parts of the world. Information concerning them is very slight; the picture we can get depends mainly on skulls, fragments of teeth, jaws, and parts of bones. A complete skeleton of the Peat dog, *Canis palustris,* was found at Œningen, Switzerland. Unfortunately, it was somewhat crushed. A photo of this skeleton is used as an illustration in the *Transactions of the Geological Society,* London.

The remains of dog-like animals, which differ greatly from anything existing today, have been found as far back as the Oligocene period.

During the transition from the Eocene to the Oligocene period of geologic history, some 40 million years ago, the canid or dog family (to express the word "dog" in an inclusive sense) had its beginning. *Miacis,* a small carnivore with a long body and relatively short legs, lived in those times and from him, as direct lineal descendants, the first canids evolved in North America. These were of two types. One was a large, heavy, long-tailed dog known as *Daphaenus,* the first of the "bear dogs." The other was a much smaller, more slender animal called *Cynodictis.*

Daphaenus was an animal as large as a coyote, possessing a massive skull and an exceedingly long tail. These animals became much larger until in the late Miocene days they had reached gigantic proportions. Their methods of locomotion changed, their feet became shorter, and their skulls and teeth were modified. And thus the bears came into being.

Cynodictis retained the long body and short legs and most likely resembled the modern Old World civets. He became the "grandfather" of all the dog family. Two of his "grandchildren" in lower Miocene days were of distinct types. One was *Temnocyon,* the evolutionary line of which culminated in the hunting dogs of Africa and India. The African hunting dog, Lycaon, and the East Indian hunting dog, or dhole. are very doglike in appearance but are of quite an independent ancestry.

Cynodesmus, the other of these two lower Miocene canids, was the ancestor of a large and varied group of dogs, including modern American and Eurasiatic dogs, wolves, and foxes. The true dogs, as we know them, according to Dr. Edwin H. Colbert, American

Museum of Natural History, evolved between upper Miocene and recent times as an offshoot from the *Cynodesmus* stem and had their immediate origin in a genus known as *Tomarctus.* This animal must have been very doglike in appearance. With probably little general change, except a development of intelligence, it grew into the wild dogs and wolves through the north and east.

Fossil discoveries reveal that the dog-like animals of early times differed greatly from the Ungulates or "hoofed animals." The Ungulates lived then very much as they live now, in herds. Their numbers were far greater than those of the animals which preyed upon them. This probably explains why so many of their fossil remains have been found in various parts of the world. At Pikermi, Greece, great herds were discovered, apparently having been drowned in some devastating flood. No such quantity of the collective remains of carnivorous animals has been discovered.

Teeth have played a considerable part in aiding the tracing of the evolution of the dog. The foundation stock of modern carnivora most likely came from the order *Creodonta,* having incisors with closed roots. The number and form of the teeth of various species have indicated their relationships, and also pointed to the manner in which their food was obtained and broken up for consumption.

The first true carnivores were, for the most part, quite small animals resembling the civet-cat. In fact, the civet-cat of today has changed little since the Upper Eocene era. These creodonts varied in their feeding habits. Some were flesh-eaters, some insectivorous, and some omnivorous. In that era the whole assemblage apparently was in a state of plasticity, ready to specialize as necessity or occasion demanded.

The most important of these forms, according to Hutchinson in his *Dog Encyclopedia,* was the Family *Miacidae,* of the Eocene period, which he claims was undoubtedly the fountainhead of the true carnivora. They were the only members of the creodonts to develop "shearing teeth," characteristic in the dog and cat families. In the creodonts the shearing teeth were molars 1/2 or molars 2/3. In the *Miacidae* and the *Fissipeda* carnivores the shearing teeth are pre-molar 4/molar 1. This applies to all modern carnivores. However, most of them walked "flat-footed" like the bear, or only partially on the toes. The five toes on each foot spread out more widely than those of cats and dogs. By the Pleistocene period, however, wolves, jackals, foxes, and dogs all seem to have become established as such.

From the *Creodonta,* by evolution through the *Miacidae,* came three groups. The carnivores are:

> Fissipeda
>   Canoidea
>   Canidae
>   (Dogs, wolves, foxes, etc.)
>   Ursidae
>   (Bears)
>   Procyonidae
>   (Raccoons, pandas)
>   Murtelidae
>   (Weasel, otters, badgers,
>   mink, skunk, etc.)
>
> Creodonta, through
>   Miacidae
> Feloidae
>   Viverridae
>   (Civets)
>   Hyaenidae
>   (Hyenas)
>   Felidae
>   (Cats)
> Pinnipedia
>   Otariidae
>   (Sea-"lions")
>   Phocidae
>   (Seals)
>   Odobenidae
>   (Walruses)

These varied carnivores evolved through natural selection, utilizing mutation.

Stone Age and Peat Dogs. In writing of the Stone Age dog, Studer says "the skull has a length of 145 mm.; the bones of the extremities are larger and stronger than those of the dogs of the 'pile-dwellings' of the Neolithic period."

It may well be that the Peat dog, *Canis palustris,* was the first deserving of the name "dog." Jeitteles found evidence of its existence along the Rhine even down to the time of the Romans, its skull being found in an ancient urn. A skull showing the characteristics of the Peat dog was also found among the ruins of an old Roman military hospital in Baden.

Ancient dog, probably forerunner of the Saluki type.

This skull was perhaps of a later era and somewhat resembles the Spitz.

According to Jeitteles: "The skull cavity is nicely rounded, a weak parietal bone existing, the arc powerfully developed, the end of the face, which is rather stumpy, is strongly marked off from the brain cavity. As compared to the similarly constructed skulls of the Neolithic period, the Baden skull appears more contracted, the forehead is broader, the snout shorter and broader, the nose higher; as is the case with all modern races in contra-distinction with the prehistoric, with those of the Peat dog from the pile-dwellings in Luttrigen on Lake Buler, whereas the facial portion is much shorter."

He further writes: "I received from Dr. Scharff, Director of the National Museum in Dublin, the plaster-cast of a skull from the Caniological collection of Dunshauglin, County Meath, which, although in its dimensions is slightly larger, shows the characteristics of the dogs of the pile-dwellers. The length is 167 mm. In the somewhat narrow brain cavity in the development of the *crista parietalis,* the less marked facial portion is greater than the Ladoga dog of Anutschin, and may, therefore, represent the more primitive, influenced by less culture, of the form *C. f. palustris.* Although there is now in Europe no living example of the *C. f. palustris,* it appears to exist in its original form in Asia, namely in Siberia."

Excavations in the Danish kitchen middens revealed remains of prehistoric dogs of the modern type. Others have been found in the lake dwellings of Switzerland. A dog, almost the size of a Collie, was found buried with a woman in a burial mound of the Neolithic era. Strobel found remains of prehistoric dogs in the Terramare of Emilia, Italy. Naumann discovered skeletons and bones of dogs in the pile-dwelling ruins of Lake Starnberg, which date from the Bronze Age.

These and other findings of anthropologists and geologists are proof that the association between man and dog was well established thousands of years before the beginning of history.

Mittendorf found Spitz-like dogs among the Tungnes, Samoyedes, and Tschuktschese, the skulls of which showed much resemblance to those of the dogs of the pile-dwellers. Anutschin compared the dimensions with those of his Ladoga dog and found considerable similarity, although the snout of the Ladoga dog was shorter and stumpier and the top and side bones of the cranium were more pronounced.

In a paper discussing the findings and conclusions of earlier authorities, A. Brinkmann suggested that, because people of the Stone Age kept Samoyed or Spitz-type dogs, this group of dogs is of extreme antiquity.

Prior to Brinkmann's paper, however, Professor H. Kraemer, of Berne, advanced the thought that the skulls of prehistoric dogs are not of the Spitz type. He had particular reference to that of Vindonissa which he contended were more likely to be the skulls of the Tibet mastiff or St. Bernard type.

Perhaps the Peat dog, *Canis palustris,* was the first dog. Perhaps he himself was descended from the wolf of earlier eras. Be that as it may, we still face a perplexing problem when we consider the many varieties of domestic dogs which exist today—so vastly different in size, color, conformation and characteristics, and holding in common only a few primitive instincts, chief of which is the universal recognition of dog by dog.

Dog Varieties and Darwin's Views. From whence do all these varieties come? Is physical difference due in any great extent to such practices of forcible maltreatment as that resorted to in shortening the Bulldog's face? Has "mental impression" among dogs played much part in establishing physical characteristics? And how about environment and climatic conditions? All have undoubtedly had some influence, to greater or lesser extent, in establishing certain fixed characteristics in certain varieties, but who knows to what extent?

In addition to other variations, such as coat, color, etc., we have a number of different types of skeletons. There are the broad foreheads of the English Bull and the Mastiff; the long, narrow head of the Greyhound; the short skull of the Pekingese; the fox-like head of the Schipperke; the comparatively short, stocky body of the Boxer; the tall, lithesome build of the Irish Wolfhound. These are all dogs—types of dogs. Do they come from a common ancestor?

Regarding the principle of the establishment of varieties of the dog as we know him today, Darwin wrote in the first chapter of his *Origin of Species:*

"A breed, like a dialect of a language, can hardly be said to have a distinct origin. A man preserves and breeds from an individual with some slight deviation of structure, or takes more care than is usual in mating his best animals, and thus improves them, and the improved animals slowly spread in the immediate neighborhood. But they will as yet hardly have a distinct name, and from being slightly valued their history will have been disregarded. When further improved by the same slow and gradual process, they will spread more widely and will be recognised as something distinct and valuable, and will then probably first receive a provincial name. In semi-civilized countries, with little free communication, the spreading of a new subbreed would be a slow process. As soon as the points of value are once recognized, the principle, as I have called it, of unconscious selection will always tend—pehaps more at one period than at another, according to the state of civilization of the inhabitants—slowly to add to the characteristic features of the breed, whatever it may be. But the chances will be infinitely small of any record having been preserved of such slow, varying and insensible changes."

Darwin did not believe that the wolf was the original dog. Neither did he believe in mixtures of an impossible nature. He was not of the opinion that production under domestication accounted for the entire amount of difference in breeds of dogs, but granted some small part to their descent from distinct species. He also wrote: "Looking at the domestic dogs of the whole world, I have, after a laborious collection of all known facts, come to the conclusion that several wild species of *Canidae* have been tamed, and that their blood, in some cases, mingled together, flows in the veins of our domestic breeds." Darwin also doubted that varieties were developed by crossing aboriginal stock, and he apparently did not believe that such a dog as the later-developed Boston Terrier

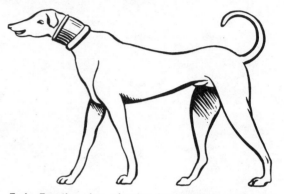

Early Egyptian dog, showing broad collar, probably for defense.

could be produced, for he said: "to obtain a race intermediate between two distinct races would be very difficult."

Views of Mivart and Boule. Professor St. George Mivart, in *Dogs, Jackals, Wolves and Foxes, Monograph of the Canidae,* said: "The problem of the origin of the domestic dog seems insoluble." Later in reference to dogs, jackals, wolves, and foxes, he says: "Close structural agreement yet remarkable divergence of its members."

M. Marcellin Boule in the *Bulletin de la Societé Geologique de France* expressed the opinion that *Amphicyin* were ancestors of both bears and dogs, while the *Cynodictus* was an ancestor of civets and foxes. The opinion was expressed in the broad sense.

Mivart did not agree with that. He said, in part: "Should it turn out to be a well-founded belief it would form another interesting example of that independent origin of similar structures for which we have long contended." And, further: "Mr. Boule very sensibly remarks that if dogs and foxes did have so diverse an origin, such a fact would constitute no reason why their descendants should not now be grouped in one single genus." Mivart also said: "The once supposed affinity of the Hyaena-Dog to the Hyaena and the Raccoon Dog to the Raccoon was due to mere superficial resemblances in external aspect."

If all the varieties of today had a common ancestor in a true dog living now, either in the wild form such as the dingo, or in an original type of domesticated dog such as the Saluki, for instance, then it would seem apparent that they all came from sports or from an occasional "monstrosity" such as Darwin calls a radical difference from racial type, or a malformed, or injured individual cultivated because of its peculiar characteristics.

Effects of Climate, Time, and Domestication. Climatic conditions no doubt played a considerable part in the development of varieties. And so did terrain. For instance, the hair between the pads of the Afghan Hound's feet is more pronounced than in many other breeds, enabling it to travel with more facility over the soft sands of its native land. The dogs of the colder climes have heavy coats, most of them with a close-knit covering of hair next to the skin. In rough and rugged country, where constant exposure to the elements is only natural, the dog is found to be remarkably well-equipped.

Time has never stood still. There has always been, and still is, a constant change, a shifting of conditions no matter how slight it may be. In some forms of life the change has been so gradual as to be hardly noticeable. But the dog has been readily adaptable to the control of man and its domestication is said by some to be man's greatest conquest. Certainly the dog has been, and is, exceedingly pliable, adapting itself to the controls and conditions imposed by man, and even bending to the vagaries of his whims.

Within a comparatively short time, man's breeding experiments with dogs reach fruition, physical characteristics and even habits become fixed and a new breed, breeding true to type, is on its way. Of course, the establishment of a new and distinct variety is not so simple as this might sound but man, through careful selective breeding, has brought about many changes and improvements in all his domesticated animals.

Area boundaries and difficulty of travel from one section to the other undoubtedly had much to do with the establishment and fixation of breeds. In isolated areas breeding material was concentrated. There was no opportunity for the introduction of new blood and no chance to pass on type to the outside world. So it was quite natural that selective breeding and rigorous culling was adopted. Unless litter mates were well up to the standard or showed signs of improvement, unless they could do the job for which they were intended, their chances of survival were small indeed. In practically all parts of the globe, dogs for certain purposes—hunting, work, herding—were developed from local blood, generally by some man in high position. These dogs were practically unknown, except within their own localities. The occasional introduction of a dog of a different type, producing undesirable individuals as often as not, was not particularly sought by dog breeders, and many of the progeny were passed on to lackeys or retainers, or were ordered destroyed.

Nevertheless, the produce of these matings played a part in the development of other breeds. Often a discarded dog was not destroyed, as ordered, but slipped away and traded into the "outside" by travelers. There were no systematic breeding practices, other than those of selectivity and convenience. Pedigrees and breeding records were not thought of, although many of the gentry could have probably traced their dogs through a number of generations by memory.

With the building of roads, and later the coming of the railroads, new areas were opened up and travel increased tremendously. Visitors to other sections found new, to them, and very much inbred breeds of dogs, and took them home to bolster their own breeds through outcrossings. Explorers exchanged dogs with inhabitants of new-found areas, dogs of different sizes, colors, and conformation. With the advent of new blood to heavily inbred varieties, a marked development of both constitution and brain was noted. And more new breeds began to take form.

The dog of today starts life on a higher plane. No longer is he forced to hunt for his livelihood, although he can do that, too, if necessity demands. He has adopted the customs and habits of his master and, in some instances, even his appearance reflects the human influence. Perhaps Nature used climatic conditions to mould and shape man and animal to some extent.

The saying, "like master, like dog," is certainly true in many instances. The dog of the jovial master is likely to have a happy disposition, while that belonging to the surly individual often reflects that attitude.

Greyhounds are said to possess exceptional eyesight. They, of course, hunt mainly by sight and it may be that the elongated muzzle is an aid to vision. It also

Dog from the Tombs of Beni-Hassan, about 2200-2000 B.C.

may have been that extra eyesight was necessary in the wide expanses of the area in which they were originally found.

Among the remains of dog-like animals, supposedly the ancestors of the wolves and bears, is the previously mentioned *Simocyon* of the Upper Miocene. This species had a broad and high skull unlike that of the Greyhound. It may be that the shortened face was a radical departure from type, a sport, so handicapped by this feature that it could not compete on even terms with other dog-like animals, and in time

Bahakaa, alias Mahut, one of four dogs on the lower portion of the Limestone Stele at Antef-aa. XII Dynasty, about 2000 B.C.

became cut off from them, establishing a separate evolutionary line. *Simocyon* represents a side branch of evolution and is not a direct ancestor of the dog.

The Dog-From-Wolf Theory. If one were to single out a number of his friends and ask them, "Where did the modern dog come from?" the almost invariable reply, given with glib assurance, would be, "Why, from the wolf, of course!" And then would probably follow a few of the usual reasons in substantiation of the claim: "The dog howls at the moon, so does the wolf. The dog frequently turns around several times before he lies down, so does the wolf."

The wolf-origin is, indeed, the most common, most generally accepted theory, particularly by those who have no great personal interest in the history of the dog. If we accept as fact that the varieties of the present-day dog descended from the existing types of wolves and evolved therefrom into varieties through man's manipulations, we are then confronted by the fact that there are more than three distinct types of dogs. There are wolf-like dogs, the fox-like, and jackal-like dogs, the Tibet Mastiff, the Bloodhound, and the short-faced dogs such as the Pekingese, the Japanese Spaniel, and the Pug.

The prominent naturalist, Dr. Thomas Bell, writing about a century ago, was a positive exponent of the wolf theory: "In order to come to any rational conclusion on this head, it will be necessary to ascertain to what type the animal approaches most closely, after having for many successive generations existed in a wild state, removed from the influences of domestication, and of association with mankind.

"Now we find that there are several instances of dogs in such state of wildness as to have lost that common character of domestication, variety of color and marking. Of these, two very remarkable ones are the dhole of India and the dingo of Australia; there is besides a half-reclaimed race among the Indians of North America, and another, also partially tamed, in South America, which deserve attention. It is found that these races, in different degrees, and in a greater degree as they are more wild, exhibit the lank and gaunt form, the lengthened limbs, the long, slender

muzzle, and the comparative strength which characterise the wolf; and that the tail of the Australian dog, which may be considered as the most remote from a state of domestication, assumes the slight bushy form of that animal. We have here, then, a considerable approximation to a well-known wild animal of the same genus, in races which, though doubtless descended from domestic ancestors, have gradually assumed the wild condition; and it is worthy of especial remark that the anatomy of the wolf, and its osteology in particular, does not differ from that of the dogs in general more than the different kinds of dogs from each other."

Dr. Edwin H. Colbert, American Museum of Natural History, says that Dr. Bell errs here in regard to the dhole, as this dog is a distinct genus, cyon, and was never domesticated.

Dr. Bell admits the difference in the eye—the forward direction of the eye in the dog against the oblique in the wolf. To this he attributes the dog's "constant habit of looking toward the master, and obeying his voice." He also points out that the dog and the wolf will interbreed and contends that their progeny are fertile.

It is well-known that the wolf and dog will cross or interbreed and that these crosses will produce when bred back to either dog or wolf. But the fertility of the wolf-dog cross, when bred back to each other, has never been established.

Stanley P. Young, Senior Biologist, Section of Biological Survey, Branch of Wildlife Research, U. S. Fish and Wildlife Service, and co-author of *The Wolves of North America*, in a letter to the editor says, "It is true that wolf-dog crosses can produce when bred back to either a wolf or dog. As far as my experience goes, I have never had any success when bred to each other. I cannot say the latter isn't possible, but I know of no instance to date where it has been done."

James Watson, in *The Dog Book*, takes issue with Bell regarding the latter's contention that the various wild dogs are feral dogs decending from domesticated stock and closely resembling the wolf. He maintains this claim will not stand investigation. Watson argues that the dingo was present when Australia was discovered by Europeans, and that there was no evidence of his being, or ever having been, a domesticated animal. He further points out that while wolves are gray in color, all wild dogs are reddish. Dr. Colbert says the dingo was brought to Australia by the aborigines.

Watson contends that if all dogs descended from the wolf, at least one of the wild, untamable and irreclaimable varieties would eventually breed back to their origin and become wolves. Not one single variety has done this; they remain dogs, Watson argues.

In *The Wolves of North America*, Edward A. Goldman writes: "The history of the Canidae, or dog family, as shown by fossil record, extends, with many ramifications, far back in geologic time. The phylogeny of the family has been clearly traced by Matthew to common ancestry with other carnivora in the Miacid family of Creodonts or primitive carnivora of the early Tertiary. The Canidae are principally a group of carnivora, with long slender limbs and non-retractile claws, that become adapted for speed on open ground and acquired long jaws for snapping and slashing at prey. Development of hunting methods led to association in groups, teamwork, and finally to the highly complex social instincts shown in modern dogs, wild and domestic. The dog family thus represents a wide contrast with the Felidae, or cat family, which represents another and even more exclusively carnivorous offshoot of Miacid ancestry. Unlike the dogs, the cats as a group developed shorter limbs with retractile claws and short jaws adapted to seizing and holding prey. Along with this physical equipment came the habits of concealment and lying in wait to pounce on a victim that could be quickly overpowered and killed. The cats evolved with similar success, but as a group more solitary in habits and lacking the social behavior exhibited by dogs. From the genus *Cynodictus,* a Miacid derivative of the Oligocene time in both the Old and New Worlds, slow evolution brought the typical line of the dog family through the Miocene period to the genus *Canis* in the upper Pliocene or lower Pleistocene period. Originating in the northern hemisphere, the family became nearly world-wide in dispersal, but was absent from Australasia until the introduction of the dingo, probably by man."

Both Count Buffon and Professor Mivart were very much interested in the crossing of wolves with dogs and dogs with foxes. Many others have experimented with such breeding, and the wolf-dog cross is not uncommon among the Eskimo people. Buffon tried to breed a bitch to a fox, but the experiment was unsuccessful. The fox would have nothing to do with her, neither did he quarrel with her while she was confined with him for ten days.

Mivart suggested that a probable reason for the difficulty in making dog-fox crosses was the peculiar

and penetrating odor of the fox, due to the secretion of its subcaudal gland. This is absent in the dog.

There has always been a seemingly deep and ingrained antagonism between the dog and the wolf, except when the dictates of sexual urge prompts association. Wolf hunting with dogs has long been a sport in many places, and in some sections the dog has been hunted by the wolf. Arctic explorers have many times recorded instances of wolves entering Eskimo villages and carrying away dogs. There also have been accounts of wolves enticing dogs away from the protection of their owners by manifestations of friendship and antics of play, only to turn on them and tear them to pieces when they had succeeded in luring them beyond the reach of their masters. Sled dogs have been known to succumb to the enticements of a female wolf in season, only to be devoured by members of the pack lying in wait.

Dogs—Wild and Domesticated. Domesticated dogs and wild dogs are quite similar in habit. Both are usually exceedingly jealous, yet seem to forget their differences and animosities when hunted in packs, concentrating on the trail or chase, and when the line is lost they readily and eagerly respond to the tonguing of the one that finds it again.

In practically every country where civilized man has explored he has found dogs, domesticated, semi-domesticated and/or wild, among the inhabitants. Some of these dogs had undoubtedly been tamed from wild stock, others were of different color and conformation. Packs of wild dogs, "dogs of the woods," "Chiens des Bois," as Buffon called them, were found in many sections.

Wild dogs, like domestic dogs, have been able to adapt themselves to the conditions of their habitat, feeding on whatever the country offered. Wild dogs, in one instance, at least, have been known to feed on the fruit of coconuts, scooping it out cleanly and neatly.

THE DOG'S WILD RELATIVES

The Dingo. The dingo of Australia is probably the nearest approach to the domesticated type among wild dogs. Around him much discussion has centered, many writers claiming that he is a feral dog which has reverted to the wild from domesticated dogs brought to Australia by explorers and early settlers. Dr. Edwin H. Colbert, American Museum of Natural History, says he was brought to Australia by the early blacks. The first mention of the dingo, according to Ash, is found in the writings (*A Collection of Voyages*) of Captain William Damphier who visited Australia in 1688: "My men saw two or three beasts like hungry Wolves, lean like so many skeletons, being nothing but skin and bones." The expression "like hungry wolves" indicates that Captain Damphier knew they were not wolves. Explorers of later days reported seeing more of these dog-like creatures. When man and his flocks came to Australia, the dingo seemed to flourish, preying on the settlers'

Abaker, or Abakaru, another of the four dogs on the lower portion of the Limestone Stele at Antef-aa.

stock to such extent that efforts to exterminate them were started, pushing them back into the bush. The dingo had no fear of the domesticated dog and seemed to treat it as its own kind.

The dingo, *Canis dingo,* is smaller than the wolf, has a slighter build, and is not nearly so strong. Its legs are somewhat long, and, as an average, the breed stands about 24 inches at the shoulder. It has a rather bushy tail, a somewhat long coat of yellowish or soiled white hair, except in the black variety, with a close, greyish under coat. In good flesh, the body is well formed and symmetrical. The fact that the dingo frequently has white feet and a white tip at the end of its tail suggests that it originated from domestic parentage. The muzzle is often black.

Dingoes are generally nocturnal in their habits, doing their hunting at night, a habit perhaps formed in the days when the early settlers made war against them. They usually travel in small groups, probably a family, although packs numbering as high as 100 have been seen. They often whelp in a hollow tree, the litter numbering about six or eight.

Regarding their adaptability to domestication, Dr. Carl Lumholz, in *Among Cannibals,* says that along the Herbert River each tribe had one or two dingoes, apparently of pure blood. "The natives find them in the hollow trunks of trees," he wrote, "and rear them with as great care as they do their own children. They sleep in the huts. They get plenty to eat, not only meat, but also fish."

The natives used them in hunting because they possessed a sense of smell. It is said that the masters never punished them, merely scolding them, probably because of their naturally timid disposition. Apparently these wild dogs, in that particular area, at least, were not so difficult to tame; but it is said that when the mating urge came, they often slipped away and never returned. The dingo carries his tail horizontally, uncurled, and drooping when in repose or watching something.

When the early settlers came, the dingo frequently interbred with domesticated dogs. And it is said that, when tamed he learned to bark something like the domesticated dog. The dingo, in his native haunts, made a distinct attempt at barking and had something like the cry of a young puppy.

Some writers maintained that the dingo is the last remnant of the wild ancestral dog. Dr. Nehring, who made an exceedingly careful study of the dingo's skeleton, contended that the dingo was not a feral dog, but one of a distinct wild race.

The dingo of New Holland did not take to domestication and was only partially reclaimed by the natives. When aroused or offended, it assumed a menacing attitude, the hair raising upright. When confined it was entirely mute, neither growling, barking nor howling.

Ash tells of an experience by a Mr. Oxley, Surveyor General of New South Wales, concerning the faithfulness of the dingo to its mate. Oxley's party killed a dingo and threw its body on a small bush. Passing the scene about a week later, he found the body had been dragged several yards from the bush and by it lay a female dingo, in dying condition, so weak that it could not move.

Professor McCoy advanced the opinion that the dingo is a wild dog of considerable antiquity. According to him it does not appear to be the ancestor of the European domestic dog, its dislike of human beings and difficulty of domestication being important reasons. Ash does not agree with this, claiming that it may have taken prehistoric man as many as thousands of generations of domesticated breeding of the dingo to fully eliminate the dingo's distrust and dislike of humanity, and to instill full confidence in mankind.

There have been many breeds or strains of wild dogs in many countries. Early naturalists were fairly well acquainted with several varieties in India.

The Buansu of Nepal. There was the Buansu of Nepal, to which Hodgson gave the name *Canis primaevus.* Its range was said to be between Suttledge and Brahmapootra, although Hodgson said its range, with immaterial differences, extended much farther.

Regarding this animal, the *Proceedings of the Zoological Society* for 1833 reported: "The Buansu preys at night as well as by day and hunts in packs of from six to ten individuals, maintaining the chase rather by powers of scent than by the eye, and generally overcoming its quarry by force and perseverance. In hunting, it barks like a hound, but its bark is peculiar and unlike that of the cultivated breeds of dogs and the strains of the jackal and the fox. Adults in captivity made no approach toward domestication, but a young one, which Mr. Hodgson obtained when it was not more than a month old, became sensible of caresses, distinguished the dogs of its own kennel from others, as well as its keepers from strangers, and in its whole conduct manifested to the full as much intelligence as any of the sporting dogs of its own age." There was also a letter by W. A. Wooler, addressed to the Secretary, which gave an account of a wild dog in the Presidency of Bombay, locally known as Dhale, and the habits described were similar to those of the Buansu. The word "Dhale" was probably a misspelling of the more usual word "dhole."

Wild Dog of Deccan. Writing in 1831, Colonel Sykes, sportsman and traveler, described what he called the wild dog of Dukhun, or Deccan, and which he designated as *Canis Duckhunensis.* "Its head is compressed and elongated; its nose not very sharp," he wrote. "The eyes are oblique, the pupils round, the irises light brown. The expression is that of a coarse, ill-natured Persian greyhound, without any resemblance to the jackal, the fox or the wolf; and is consequently essentially different from the *Canis Quao,* or *Sumatrensis* of General Hardwicke. Ears long, erect, and somewhat rounded at the top, without any replication of the tragus. Limbs remarkably large and strong in relation to the bulk of the animal, its size being intermediate between the wolf and the jackal." The *Canis Sumatrensis,* described by General Hardwicke, was a small, fox-like dog with reddish color and smaller ears.

The natives called the dog described by Sykes the *Kolsun,* and a report of a comparison with the Buansu appears in the *Transactions of the Asiatic Society* for 1834: " . . . and showed that the two dogs are perfectly similar in their general form and in the form of the cranium, and that in his (Sykes') specimen, as well as that of Mr. Hodgson, the hinder tubercular tooth of the lower jaw was wanting." The Buansu had a darker and denser coat. Ash says that these two and the dhole, a general term in India and

Pahates, alias Kami, another of the four dogs on the lower portion of the Limestone Stele at Antef-aa.

the East Indies for dog, are of the same variety, climatic conditions accounting for slight differences.

Congo Dog. Merolla describes the wild dogs he saw on his visit to the Congo in 1682 as follows: "In Sogno there are a sort of wild dogs, who going out to hunt in great numbers, whenever they meet with any lion, tiger or elephant in their way, set about him with that fury, that they commonly bring him to the ground."

The Dholes. One of the dholes was called the Quidoe, designated by naturalists as *Canis Scylax,* which was of much slighter build than the Kolsun, with a longer, less-bushy tail. In habits they were similar.

In central and southern India there was another dhole, called the Wah. This was a heavily-built dog, of ferocious appearance, with a large, broad, flat head. The muzzle was black. This dog was tan-colored with white underparts, had a short, dark-tipped tail. They hunted in packs and had a deep bay which was a sort of growl.

The Pariah Dogs. In many parts of the East—India,

Siam, Sumatra, Turkey, the whole of Southern Asia, and in Northern Africa—a variety of animals called Pariah Dogs were found. The name Pariah Dogs is a general term given to all dogs of the East that have no master. In its broader sense it is the term applied loosely to any of the lowest class of Hindustan who have no caste. Robert Leighton wrote that they were not wild dogs, but were the descendants of the sentinel and scavenger dogs of a nomad race. They were semi-wild but still remained in association with man. All being mongrels, they varied in type, color, and general appearance. Richard Strebel recognized three distinct varieties: one resembling the German Shepherd and found in Constantinople, often of a rougher coat than the German Shepherd; one being of smooth coat and part-colored; and the third, seen generally in Sumatra, being on the order of the Greyhound.

Professor Studer very likely took the latter type as his subject when, in *The Prehistoric Days in Their Relation to Present-Day Breeds,* he wrote: "The skull of these dogs is narrow, the brain part is elongated, but arched in its parietal region, tied up in the temporal bone; the forehead is narrow, low and falling off *processus supraorbitalis,* sunk in the median line, very contracted between the eyes; there is present a *crista parietalis,* and occiput is very much drawn backwards. The *bullae osseae* are fairly large with a blunt keel; the triangle of the back part of the head is not elevated. The facial part is narrow, gradually tapering toward the front, with little stop; the line of profile, on the root of the nose, is more or less concave; the bridge of the nose sinks gradually towards the tip of the muzzle. The jaw part is narrow at the set-on of the process of the cheek, so that the tie-up in front of the *por infraorbitale* is but slight. From the narrow bridge of the nose the side-walls of the upper-jaw fall very abruptly, perpendicularly in the fore-part. The cheekbones are strong, but are not much stretched; generally the brain part is longer or as long as the facial part; the orbitals are but little steep."

Many of the Pariah Dogs were mostly red, with a black mask, a black streak down the back, and black on the tail. Some, however, were colored like the wolf. Others were of greyish-yellow. They were scavengers, but in this respect were often of some value to the community.

The Turks never mistreated them, for in the teachings of the Mohammed religion animals, and especially dogs, will enjoy the pleasures of Paradise along with righteous human beings. They became so numerous in Turkey, however, that they were a nuisance and sometimes a menace. When, after World War I, the new regime forced sanitation practices upon Turkey, the problem of removing the nuisance of Pariah Dogs was tackled. Due to the reluctance of the Turk to kill dogs, this was no easy matter, but the government used tactics which, to say the least, were neither kind nor humane. Numbers of the dogs were herded into pits on the city walls and left to starve. Most were exiled to the rocky isle of Oxia, in the Sea of Marmora, and suffered the same fate or fell victims to the cannibalistic tendencies of their companions.

G. T. Jesse wrote of the Pariah Dogs: "The dogs of the towns associate in bands, and each dog has its district and its chief. No other dog is permitted to enter the territory without being at once assailed. If, however, a dog wishes to pass from one quarter to another, he is said to creep along in a humble manner, and immediately the dogs of that part come upon him, to throw himself on his back, and deprecate their attacks. After due examination, he is allowed to proceed, but repeats his submissive actions whenever he meets new foes, and so, after enduring repeated challenges, gains his destination." The aloofness of the Pariah from both wild and domesticated dogs keeps him fairly free from a number of dog diseases; but he is, naturally, quite subject to mange.

The Cape, or South African, Hunting-Dog. Known as the Hyena Dog, because of its close resemblance to that animal, the Cape, or South African, hunting dog is scientifically called *Lycaon pictus*. The early settlers named it *Vilde Honden,* which is Dutch for "wild dogs." The muzzle is short and rather pointed. The ears are dark-colored with little hair, comparatively broad, egg-shaped, and come to a point. These long-legged animals are about the size of a large Greyhound.

These dogs hunt in packs, usually at night, and are ruthless in their kill. If opportunity presents itself, they will do great damage to flocks or herds, slaughtering far more than they can eat, apparently destroying for the thrill of killing. They show very little fear of man, but rather a nonchalant curiosity which makes them a fairly easy target for the gunner. The Cape hunting dog has a sharp, angry-like bark, usually only given when aroused. They also have another cry, a sort of conversational chattering which is generally heard at night.

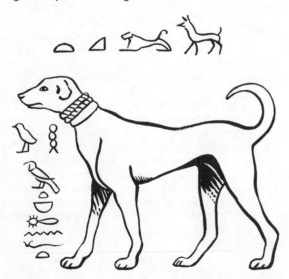

Tekal or Tekar, another of the four dogs on the lower portion of the Limestone Stele at Antef-aa.

Dog from the Tombs at Beni-Hassan, about 2200-2000 B.C.

H. A. Bryden described their method of hunting thus: "A pack of European hounds press their game steadily until it is run to a standstill, and overwhelm it in a body. But the 'wild honde' hunts quite differently. Each of the fleetest hounds in turn, or as it gets a chance, races up to the game and tears at some portion of the hinder parts; the flanks and under parts and hock tendons are favourite places. By this method the unfortunate antelope is finally overcome. As its paces grow shorter and more feeble, the attacks grow fiercer and more deadly and, finally, maimed, hamstrung and partly disemboweled, the quarry is pulled down and devoured."

The Cape hunting dog whelps its young in burrows, often connected. Should man approach during the breeding or rearing season, they do not seek safety underground, but take to the open; the young, if old enough, follow the parents.

These animals, whose long legs seem out of proportion to their bodies, are seldom marked alike. As a general rule the background color is yellowish-grey and the bodies are irregularly marked with splotches of white fringed with black.

They have been so destructive to domestic stock that repeated attempts have been made to exterminate them. Comparatively few specimens are left. Attempts have been made to tame them, without much success.

The "Indian" Wild Dog. There are a number of varieties of wild dogs in Indo-China. The one described by Walter Hutchinson in his *Dog Encyclopedia* is called "the Indian," or by the naturalists *Canis indicus or Canis pallepes.* The muzzle is pointed, the head large and flat. The eyes have an intelligent expression, the pupils slightly elongated. The forehead hollows out slightly in front of the eyes, and the neck is clean with no loose flesh. The average weight is around 60 pounds, making them rather high on the leg.

The color is a sort of reddish and gray, darker on the back and muzzle. The tail is quite bushy, the coat short and harsh. They do not bark, but howl in different tones, the voice sounding not at all like the domesticated dog. These dogs mate only once a year, the gestation period being ten weeks. The whelps are born during the dry season from November to March. The whelping usually takes place in some underground burrow and there the litter, from four to six, are nursed. These dogs have been tamed, when caught quite young, and interbred with the domestic dog.

The Golden Wolf. The Golden Wolf is an inaccurate name for another wild dog of Indo-China and the Malay Archipelago, known, by the naturalists, as *Canis latrans* or *Canis aureus*. It is also called the Dog of Java or the Dog of Sumatra, and it is more likely to be found on the Malay Islands. It is somewhat smaller than the "Indian." Its coat ranges in color from tan-red to brilliant brown. The tail is not so bushy but ends with black feather. In habits it is about the same as *Canis indicus*, but it is said that members of different packs never mingle. Its voice tends toward a bark only after being reared in captivity. When domesticated, these dogs seem to have a great liking for fruit.

Bush Dog of Brazil. Trew describes the Bush Dog of Brazil as having short legs and tail, short ears and a short face—in general, a rather insignificant specimen. It is said to have retained so many of its primitive characteristics that it is nicknamed "living fossil," showing very little change from the fossil remains found in the Pleistocene deposits in Brazilian caves.

Burmese Wild Dog. Found in Upper Burma, this dog resembles the wild dogs of Malay, with the exception that is is more strongly built. It is probably a member of the group of which the "Indian" and the Golden Wolf are members.

The Colpeo. The Colpeo, *Canis magellanicus*, found between Chile and Tierra del Fuego, is definitely more wolf-like than fox-like. Large and handsome in appearance, this breed apparently has great curiosity concerning man. It will often walk slowly up to men, staring at them, a habit which has often resulted in diasaster to the Colpeo. It is usually brownish gray, the back mottled with black, the long, bushy tail reddish. The cheeks, throat and under jaw are yellowish white, while the tail has a black patch on the underside near the root. It has exceptional speed.

Another dog from the Tombs at Beni-Hassan.

The Crab-Eating Dog. This dog, *Canis cancrivorus*, is found from Guano to La Plata. Seldom is it found on the Pampas. Generally called the Carasissi, this dog lives in the jungle and only occasionally preys on the natives' poultry or small stock. It feeds on small mammals, birds, crayfish, and plants. The natives highly value crosses between this and the domestic dog.

The Azara's Dog. If taken young, the Azara's Dog, *Canis azarae*, is easily tamed and shows its devotion to its master much in the same fashion as the domestic dog. They seem to be quite happy with domestic dogs of their own households, but show a distinct dislike for visiting canines. They vary considerably in color, with gray predominating, longer black and white hairs showing on the back. The underside of the body is whitish as is the innerside of the thighs. The legs are reddish, with some white on the upper parts. The tail is mottled black and white, like the back, but ends in a black tip. Its main food is small mammals, reptiles and birds, and it hunts with its nose to the ground. In general, its habits are foxlike. It does not make a burrow but seeks shelter above ground. It is smaller than the Crab-eating Dog.

The Hare Indian Dog. The Hare Indian Dog, *Canis lagopus*, found only with the Indian tribes which lived along the borders of Great Bear Lake and the Mackenzie, was much like the Collie in appearance. The natives were able to tame it fairly easily, but it could not be punished without resentment. It showed its appreciation of caresses by rubbing against the hand in the manner of cats. They did not bark, but howled like wolves. A short of attempt at barking was made, however, when they were particularly interested in something unusual or surprised. This was a half-growl, ending in a long howl. They possessed great endurance and were quite strong for their size.

The Hare Indian dog had a small head and slender muzzle, erect ears, rather oblique eyes and usually carried its bushy tail over its right hip. Its color was peculiar. Dark patches of blackish gray or lead color, mingled with fawn and white, covered its back and sides. These colors blended together without border lines. Its face, muzzle, belly, and legs were white and the head usually had a white blaze. A dark patch covered the eye. The hair was long, particularly about the shoulders, and gave the dog the appearance of having a ruffed neck when he was in full coat. He had an under coat of woolly fur. In describing it, Dr. Richardson wrote: "It, in fact, bears the same relation to the prairie wolf that the Esquimaux dog does to the great grey wolf. It is not, however, a breed that is cultivated in the districts frequented by the prairie wolf, being now confined to the northern tribes, who have been taught the use of firearms within a very few years. Before that weapon was introduced by the fur traders, a dog, so well calculated by the lightness of its body and the breadth of its paws for passing over the snow, must have been invaluable for running down game, and it is reasonable to conclude

Spotted dog from the Tombs at Beni-Hassan. As with the others illustrated from these Tombs, dating about 2200-2000 B.C.

that it was then generally spread amongst the Indian tribes north of the Great Lakes."

The Poe Dog. A dog used almost exclusively as an item of food by the natives of Tahiti and the Sandwich Islands was the Poe Dog, *Canis Pacificus*. Smooth haired of a tan or rust-yellow color, this dog had crooked limbs, long back, sharp muzzle and erect ears. It was an indolent animal and was fed or fattened on bread-fruit. Its flesh was considered a delicacy by the natives, who bred it strictly for food.

Wild Dogs of New Zealand. The dogs found in New Zealand were of the long-haired type resembling sheepdogs. They varied in color, some being spotted, while others were solid black or solid white. They were also killed and eaten by the natives, who trimmed their clothing with parts of the dogs' skins. They generally maintained themselves on the remains of fish left by the natives.

The Alco. The Alco figured in the works of some of the early writers. It was pictured as a small-headed dog with an abnormally fat body, a veritable lump of flesh. It was said to have originated from a variety of lapdog kept by ladies, specimens of which had escaped and reverted to the wild.

The Feral Dog of Natolia. These were of a feral race of shepherd or guard dogs, having bushy tails and resembling the yellowish-red wolf of that area. They differed from the local wolf in habits, however. They hunded in the open in packs of a dozen or so. They steered clear of man, but, if molested, would attack.

Wild dogs and domesticated dogs have similar traits. But wild dogs by no means have the wide variety of color combinations found in the many varieties of domesticated dogs. Rather somber in color on the whole, wild dogs do occasionally have varied markings, but these markings are generally found along the back and on portions of the limbs. They are seldom of a clearly defined nature, but are mostly variations in the depth of the background color. The winter coat is generally of a lighter shade than that of summer time, and in high altitudes the coat becomes thicker and, in some instances, changes to white, blending with the snow-covered terrain.

As to the relationship of the wild dogs to domestic varieties, we can only have our own thoughtful opinions. Wolf crosses and wild-dog crosses have been often obtained without difficulty. Both wolf and dingo can, and have, in a few generations become domestic dogs. There can be but little doubt that the wild dogs of widely separated areas played a not inconsiderable part in the establishment of a number of varieties of domesticated dogs. These wild species interbred freely with the domestic dogs that came with the early settlers, and in many instances these crosses brought inprovement. Many of these crossbred dogs were taken to other areas and countries, where again they were used in breeding.

The cloak of mystery still drapes the whole history of the dog's early development. Even the origin of the name "dog" remains in obscurity. "Hound" comes from the Teutonic *hund,* but there is no known derivative for the word "dog." Perhaps the *daw, daw, daw* sound of a distant dog's barking is its source. Who knows?

One thing seems fairly certain: environment and man's desire to make full use of the dog's potentialities, whether in sport, work, stock-tending, or pure companionship, played a major role in the development of varieties. In lands of wide expanses, where sight and speed were more important attributes than a keen sense of smell, the Greyhound, Saluki, and Afghan Hound fitted in with man's scheme of things. And in heavily-wooded cover where trailing the game was an absolute necessity, the hound-type dogs were found. When man needed a dog to help him dig out "earth game," the terriers were developed. When he needed brawn and strength to aid him in his work, he bred it.

And so it is in practically every phase of man's outdoor life . . . the dog has adapted himself to the climate, terrain and conditions imposed by man, forsaking his own kind to remain in contented association with one whose hand can be gentle and kind . . . and also, at times, cruel and ruthless.

Part XV

DOG'S EARLY ASSOCIATION WITH MAN

Man has ever been an opportunist. His early realization that it was possible to adapt the dog to his own service is a tribute to the progressiveness of his primitive intelligence. It has sometimes been said that the domestication of the dog is man's greatest conquest.

—Early Uses of the Dog—

JUST WHEN the association or partnership of man and dog began and how it was first brought about is unknown. Perhaps it happened that some kindly cavewoman took compassion on an orphaned puppy, or litter of puppies, and took them to her breast, nusing them through puppyhood as playthings for her children.

Perhaps some wandering hunter came upon a battle between a dog and some other animal for food, shared in the kill and partook of the spoils, having recognized the advantage of securing such a stout ally.

Link Between Man and Dog—The Search for Food. The story of civilization is unfolded in man's search for food. Lacking fangs or claws and endowed with only comparatively meager strength, man of necessity had to rely heavily upon his cunning. No doubt man and dog started as enemies, and it would be unreasonable to assume that the natural barriers of mutual fear and distrust were easily or quickly brushed away. It is very unlikely that primitive man possessed any great love for animals of any kind. His was a fight for existence of self, family and race. He had no allies, yet the spark of cunning was strong enough to prompt him to seek one. It is also possible that the dog, too, soon came to realize that a closer alliance with man might be to his own benefit, for he received in return for guarding the dwelling-place against common enemies and aiding in the search for food, the warmth and comfort of his ally's home and the assurance of plenty to eat. Regardless of how it came about, it was a fortunate alliance for both.

Dogs Became Helpers/Protectors. Early man could not hunt for food and guard his house at the same time. It is certain, therefore, that the first uses to which he put his new-found partner were the tasks of guarding the dwelling-place and of helping in the search and chase for food. That the guardian stewardship was well instilled is proved in the actions of every dog today. No matter what the breed, a modern dog gives notice of the approach of a stranger, and his actions quickly indicate his willingness to protect his master's person or property.

But perhaps the early association became even more closely cemented through mutual assistance in hunting. The dog could trail down a quarry and bring it to bay, so that it would fall victim to man's crude but effective weapons. Man might be unable to overtake a wounded animal himself, but it could easily be brought down by the dog. The two made a formidable combination for hunting, and life undoubtedly became easier for both.

Man and dog have come down through the ages side by side. Wherever man went he took the dog, or found a dog to domesticate. As civilization progressed and man began to seek greater security than that afforded by precarious day-by-day hunting, he started to annex certain properties. He gathered flocks of sheep and herds of cattle, and the dog became guardian of that property. At first he acted as a guard only, protecting the animals from marauding four-footed predators and bands of human robbers alike. Later he was taught to be a herder and a drover, performing his duties by virtue of his speed and agility, with more dispatch and efficiency than man himself.

Dogs Developed Further By Man for Different Purposes. Even before the days of herding, different types of dogs began to develop, and they were further developed by man for different hunting purposes, depending upon the kinds of game, the terrain, and the environment. And, as time went on, the dog came to play an increasingly important role in human life. The heavier and more ferocious dogs were trained as warriors to aid in conquests and invasions. (Discussion of this phase of the dog's service to man—see Part VIII.)

In many parts of the world the dog has been used as a beast of burden and a draft animal. This was particularly common among the Indian tribes. In isolated instances, some types of dogs have even been bred and raised to add to the food supply.

When the advance of civilization eliminated the necessity of hunting for a livelihood, the bonds between man and dog grew even closer. The dog became part of the family life, a companion and friend as well as a protector. In practically every phase of the development of civilization the dog has played a many-sided role of no little importance,

always to the benefit and pleasure of man, upon whom he is now dependent for his existence. The dog could, no doubt, shift for himself if need be, and many have done just that, but he prefers casting his lot with man, no matter how uncertain such a fate might be, than to reverting to the wild with his own kind. The bond between the two is now one of deep-rooted friendships, tempered and strengthened through many thousands of years of mutual affection and reciprocal aid.

The dog continues to perform his original services to man. But, in addition countless other uses have been made of his unusual abilities. As the only animal to willingly forsake its own kind to share man's uncertain fate, the dog has adapted itself to a multi-colored pattern of living, which often includes a complete change of feeding habits, and has proved its ability to fit into almost any sort of picture that man's desires may paint. Truly, the dog's capacity for usefulness seems boundless.

The Dog in
—Ancient Myth and Legend—

AS HE HAS BEEN so closely allied with man through the ages, it is not surprising that the dog plays an important part in ancient myth and legend. Many of these legends were wrapped in the nebulous garments of superstition; others have become interesting bits of everlasting literature.

Dog of Procris. Perhaps the most widely known myth is that concerning Diana, the virgin goddess of hunting, and the dog of Procris. This dog, according to

Roman sculpture reliefs on marble sarcophagus, Second Century, A.D. Courtesy Metropolitan Museum of Art.

Fifth Century tradition, was the progenitor of the Molossian hounds and those of Sparta.

Procris was Diana's dearest friend and the wife of Cephalus. The goddess gave Procris a dog always sure of its prey and a javelin which would never fail of its mark. These presents Procris gave to her husband. Cephalus was a great lover of hunting and was happy with his wife and treasures. According to the myth, some angry deity had sent a predatory fox to harass the countryside. Lelaps, the dog, was known to be able to outrun any rival, and so the hunters came to Cephalus and asked to borrow the dog in order to put an end to the fox's depredations. Set on the fox's trail, Lelaps started off with such great speed that the eye could not follow him. Had it not been for his footsteps in the sands, the hunters would have believed that he flew through the air. Try as it would, the fox could not elude him, even though it resorted to every ruse. Hard on the fox's heels came Lelaps, unsuccessfully snapping at the elusive fox. Just as Cephalus was about to hurl his javelin, both fox and dog stopped mid-stride. The gods, who had endowed both with speed and ability, were not willing that either should conquer, and turned dog and fox into stone, leaving them in the lifelike attitude of the chase.

A different version in mythology has it that Lelaps, the first Greyhound, was formed by Vulcan of Monesian brass. He liked his handiwork so well that he quickened it with a soul. Vulcan gave Lelaps to Jupiter, who gave him to Europa. Europa gave him to Minos, who made him a present to Procris, who gave him to Cephalus. It was written that this dog "had a nature so irresistible that he overtook all that he hunted, like the Teumesian fox, and Jupiter, to avoid 'confusion,' then turned both these 'incomprehensible' beasts into stone." It was also said that this dog was the ancestor of the great fighting dogs and shepherds' dogs, known as the Molossus dogs.

Cerberus. A number of dogs figure in the old Greek legends. To the dog Cerberus, Pluto entrusted the heavy responsibility of preventing the spirits of the dead from escaping from Hell. Evidently Cerberus performed his duties well, because when, with Christianity, Pluto was replaced by Satan, according to Dante the services of Cerberus were retained and he was given the task of guarding the third circle of the Inferno.

The Greeks and Dogs As Guardians of the Spirit. The ancient Greeks believed that the dog could protect them not only from earthly dangers but also from evil spirits. If a man suspected that he was going insane, he carried a dog along with him wherever he went, believing that it would keep the Evil One from disturbing his brain.

Legend of Dog and Adam and Eve. A legend, said to have originated in India, is to the effect that God made Adam and Eve and during the night a serpent came and devoured them. This made God extremely angry, but he made them again. And again, on the second night, the same thing happened. But God was not to be outdone. He remade Adam and Eve and this time made the dog to protect them. The serpent appeared that night, but was driven away by the dog's ferocious barking. That led to the belief in India that when a dog howls, a man is dying.

Argus. One of the most famous of ancient dog stories is that of Ulysses' dog, Argus. Argus spent the days of his youth in happy hunting with Ulysses, but when the latter set forth on his travels Argus was left behind. About ten years later Ulysses returned, disguised as a beggar. No one recognized him. However, as he approached the palace, he came upon Argus, weak and crippled with age, with only a dung-heap as his bed. The dog recognized his master's voice, and crawled to him. Argus tried to lick the hand of Ulysses, but was too weak to do so and sank dead at his master's feet. Ulysses was almost overcome by the loss of the only friend who had not forgotten him.

Two Legends of Dog's Loyalty. Titus Sabinus and all his slaves, according to Pliny, were condemned to death for conspiracy. One of the slaves owned a dog which stubbornly refused to leave him and followed him to prison. When the slave was executed, the dog sprang across the barrier and stood howling at the side of his fallen master. A spectator took pity on the faithful dog and tossed a piece of bread to it. The dog took the bread and held it to its dead master's lips. When the slave's body was thrown into the Tiber, the dog plunged in after it and swam at the side of the floating body until it sank from exhaustion.

Small bronze statuette—Greyhound—Hellenistic period. Courtesy Metropolitan Museum of Art.

Hyrcanus was the dog of King Lysimachus, who was killed in battle while fighting as one of Alexander the Great's generals. The dog sorrowfully followed the body as it was carried to the funeral pyre, and watched as the flames grew high. Then with a mournful howl, it sprang into the flames and perished.

Legend of Dog at the Beginning. Another, and very ancient, legend concerns the Beginning. It related that after God created the world and all its animals He made man as His masterpiece. But, through his own actions, man brought upon himself the wrath of God, who caused a great chasm to open between man and the other beasts. Among these beasts was the dog, which had become very much attached to man. As he watched the chasm slowly widen, the dog with a mighty leap cleared the widening gulf, landing at the side of man where he has remained ever since as faithful companion, protector and servant.

A Dog From King Pyrrhus' Day. Many stories have been told about the dog's faithfulness to the memory of his master. Among them is one dating back to about 250 B.C., during the reign of King Pyrrhus. One of the king's slaves was attacked and slain by two men, who also beat off the efforts of the slave's dog to protect him. The dog remained by the body which was left by the side of the road. King Pyrrhus, passing by, ordered the body to be buried and, taking compassion on the faithful dog, took it back to the palace, where the dog became his constant companion. One day, while the king was reviewing his troops, the dog suddenly rushed out and attacked two soldiers who confessed the crime to escape the violence of its fury.

Dogs In Indian Legend and Festival. The Dog-Rib Indians had a legend concerning their origin. Chapewee, according to the story, was the first man on earth. He, like Adam, met up with a forbidden fruit and had his troubles. A serious quarrel among his people caused the tribe to separate. One departing Indian founded his home on the banks of a lake, taking with him a female dog heavy in whelp. When the puppies were born the Indian cared for them and, after they had reached a playful age, tied them in his tepee to prevent their straying while he hunted and fished. Upon returning, he would often hear the sound of children's voices coming from the tent, but upon investigation would find nothing but the tethered puppies.

One day, determined to discover what was happening, he pretended to go fishing but concealed himself in a nearby spot from which he could watch. Shortly after his supposed departure he again heard children's voices in play, and rushing into the tepee, discovered beautiful children laughing and enjoying themselves heartily, the dog-skins lying by their sides. Snatching up these skins, he threw them into the fire. And so the children grew up in the form of humans and became the ancestors of the Dog-Rib tribe.

The sacrifice of the white dog played an important part in the annual festivals of the Six Nations of the Iroquois Indians. This took place during the New Year's Jubilee—the *Gi-ye-wa-no-us-qua-go-wa*—the last and most important of the six annual celebrations.

The Iroquois believed that, through a covenant made by their ancestors with the Great Spirit, they should sacrifice each year a spotless white dog, sending its spirit to the Great Spirit, who would receive it as an acknowledgment of their loyalty and open his ears to their prayers. A dog was selected because of its faithfulness to man and its assistance in the chase. It was thus considered as the most trustworthy animal to present their supplications to Ha-wen-yu.

During this celebration no weeping or mourning was allowed among the tribe. On the grand day of the white dog's sacrifice, the whole tribe gathered in the council-house, dressed in finest regalia. The Chief's talk was devoted to calling upon his people to offer full praise to the Great Spirit and give thanks for his love and goodness. After the speech the white dog was brought in and placed upon a bench.

The dog had previously been daubed with red paint and pure white feathers fastened to its body. The tribal members gathered around it and fastened colored ribbons to different parts of the body, decorating it so that finally very little of the dog's body could be seen. A string of wampum was also attached to the body, as a tribute to the Great Spirit. A basket containing a mixture of tobacco grown by the tribe and some purchased from others was placed at the head of the dog and set afire.

Another speech was then delivered, and the men left the council house. This was the signal for the arrival of another bedecked tribe member, in full feathers and paint, bearing paraphernalia representing the absent dead. Several solemn ceremonies were then performed and the messenger of the dead took his place near the bench occupied by the dog.

One of the tribe officials then took the dog and threw it over his shoulder, while another carried the basket containing the burning tobacco. After going twice around the bench, the twain filed out, followed, in single file, first by the men and then by the women. All marched to the place of sacrifice where a long address was delivered to the Great Spirit.

At the conclusion of this address, the dog was placed on the fire and another speech continued until the body and tobacco were reduced to ashes. Then

Greek vase in shape of dog. Courtesy Metropolitan Museum of Art.

the gathering dispersed, but the general rejoicing continued for two more days.

Dogs Of North Borneo, and Buddha. The natives of North Borneo have long believed that a fiery dog watches at the gates of Paradise, taking possession of the virgins.

In *Bouddhisme,* by L. Weiger, we find the following:

At Stravasti, Buddha entered into the house of one Tu-T'i, who was absent from home. Upon the divan a white dog was eating from a bowl. At sight of Buddha it leapt to the ground and barked at the Holy One. Buddha said, "Miser, how deep is thy degradation!" The dog betook itself to a corner in dejection. When Tu-T'i returned and saw his dog so sad, he asked the cause of its misery. The servants replied, "Buddha has done this." Tu-T'i was angered, and asked Buddha for an explanation. Buddha said, "I did but tell him the truth. This animal is thy dead father. Born a dog, as punishment for his avarice, he still guards his riches. Order him to reveal the treasure which he has hidden, even from thee, his son." Tu-T'i returned to his home and said to the dog, "As thou hast been my father in thy previous incarnation, all of that which was yours is now mine by right. Show me thy hidden treasure." The dog crept beneath the divan and began scratching the earth. There Tu-T'i dug, and discovered great treasures. Forthwith he was converted to Buddha.

The Dog In British Tales. One of the best known dog stories in British legend is that of the hound Gelert, presented by King John to Llewellyn, Prince of Wales. It is said that one morning on a hunt, Gelert, a favorite of the Prince, refused to start with the other hounds and returned home. The Prince had left his infant son at home, unattended. Upon his return he found Gelert at the castle door, covered with blood, "his lips and fangs ran blood." Horrified, the Prince killed his faithful hound, only to find his son alive and well, while at his side stretched the body of a huge wolf, showing the marks of Gelert's teeth.

There have been many tales of phantom and ghost dogs, some of mere local nature and others so oft-repeated that they have become a part of the folklore of many sections.

In England these include the Dartmoor Whisht Hounds, said to be the spirits of unbaptized children, doomed to hunt forever. Natives report that they are heard baying on the moors and running around in circles on the Abbot's Way on Dartmoor. During the day they are said to hide away at Hound's Tor and Hunt's Tor.

The Brixham Black Dog is another figure of fancy which is supposed sometimes to return to the home of his deceased master to guard a treasure buried before his death.

One Arscott, of Tetcott Park, once made the statement that he would follow the hounds until Doomsday. That section is now supposed to be haunted with his pack, which local folk often claim to hear running, urged on by their master's horn.

A gaunt bloodhound is supposed to run ahead of "my lady's" coach-and-four near Okehampton and Tavistock. Men are said to yield to her blandishments and enter the coach, never to be heard of again.

In Cornwall, the legend of Tregeagle is well known. Tregeagle, because he lived an evil life and sold his soul to the Devil, is hunted over the Dozemere Moors by Satan and his Hounds of Hell. Tregeagle's cries for mercy and the soundings of the hounds are said to be often heard in this vicinity.

The Black Dog of Salcombe Ridge is reported to accompany travelers abroad at night regardless of whether they desire it or not.

An interesting story of more recent origin is told of phantom hounds. After the World War I armistice, Field-Marshal Lord Allenby's headquarters in Palestine were located at Haifa. A number of his officers, keen on foxhunting, got together a pack of hounds, which they named the Vale of Acre Foxhounds. During the season they hunted twice a week in the Valley of the Kishon. When the military administration of Palestine was terminated, the hunt was discontinued and the pack disbanded.

An ex-officer and former member of the hunt returned to Haifa two years later and reported that he heard the hounds in full cry, the sounding of the horn and hunting cheers. Little credence was placed in his report and he was looked upon with sly amusement.

However, some years later, a noted English Master of Hounds and world-wide traveler reported that he had heard sounds of what he believed to be this same phantom pack running in some groves near Acre. Although he and his companion saw nothing, the sounds of hound cry, the notes of the horn and the hunters' cheers could be heard faintly in the distance.

Southern Legends. In the South many legends and tall stories of phantom and ghost dogs are heard among the negroes. These generally concern some huge Bloodhound or hunting dog which travels about only on dark and stormy nights, changing his form at will.

An Unfinished Egyptian Legend. One of the few stories of early Egyptian times in which dogs are mentioned was that of "The Prince of Doom." Unfortunately the papyrus on which it was written in about 1500 B.C. was torn and the ending is left to the conjecture of the reader. A king who desired a son prayed to the seven Hathors—cow-goddesses of fate—who granted his prayer but added that the son would be killed either by a dog, a serpent or a crocodile. The son spent his babyhood, childhood and early youth in a high tower, safe from all dangers. Grown to manhood he sought, and gained, permission to walk outside the tower. It was then he saw a dog for the first time, and begged his father to allow him to have a dog as a companion. Divided between fear and love, the King granted the request. One night, as the young prince was asleep, a serpent climbed the wall and entered the room, only to be killed by the dog. On another day, while his young master was bathing, the dog saved him from an attacking crocodile. Then . . . but here the papyrus is torn and the reader is left to imagine the ending for himself . . .!

—The Dog in Art—

DECORATIVE IN a high degree, the wide variety of breeds capable of lending almost any angle, curve, expression or color needed to illuminate or enhance any scene, it is not surprising that the dog has played no inconsiderable part in the art of all periods and times.

Many of our greatest painters have recognized the value of the dog as an adjunct to a portrait or the object of a sub-plot to the main subject, and have been quick to take advantage of it. The inclusion of dogs often added interest to the scene, and frequently gave an insight into the character of those portrayed.

The Dog Profusely Painted. Although Biblical references to the dog are seldom commendatory, it is not altogether surprising to find that many early painters of religious subjects included dogs in their works. This was particularly true among Italian masters. Paulo Veronese must have been a lover of dogs for they often appear in his paintings. In "Christ at the House of Simon the Pharisee," a group of dogs is seen apparently squabbling among the tables. Dogs also appear in his "The Adoration of the Magi," "Queen of Sheba Before Solomon," The Purification of the Virgin," "The Finding of Moses," "The Good

The dog plays an important part in stock herding throughout the world. Faithfulness to the task is dramatically pictured in the painting "Lost." Souvenir of Auvergne. By August Frederick Albrecht Schenck (1828-1901). French. Courtesy Metropolitan Museum of Art.

Samaritan," "Christ and the Centurion of Capernaum," "Jesus Disputing with the Doctors," and, unexpectedly, in "The Crucifixion." The dogs portrayed by Veronese ranged from Mastiffs to lapdogs.

Titian, too, used dogs in many of his religious paintings, among them being "Last Supper," (in which a small dog enjoys a bone under the table), "Archangel Gabriel with Tobias," "The Martyrdom of St. Lawrence," and "The Adoration of the Magi." In the latter a small dog relieves himself against one of the posts in the stable.

The paintings of Jacopo Bassano frequently contain dogs. These include "The Good Samaritan," "Adoration of the Magi," and "Christ and the Money-changers."

Bonifazio Veronese pictures a dog in his "Holy Family" group. His famous "Dives and Lazarus" shows a dog licking the sores of the beggar.

A hound appears in Raphael's "The Labours of Adam and Eve," but this master apparently had little regard for dogs, or else considered them unfit subjects for his brush. This might also be said of Michaelangelo. Botticelli, Orcagna, Pisanello, Crivelli, Morando, Piero di Cosimo, and Castiglione were among Italian painters in whose works dogs appear with more or less frequency.

Among the Spanish artists who employed dogs in their paintings were Luis da Vargas, Pedro Orrente, the great Velasquez (whose paintings tell us much of the dogs of his time), Francesco Collantes, Murillo, Mateo Carezo, and Goya.

The Dutch painters were especially given to the use of dogs in their works. This was particularly true of the portrait painters, some of whom seem to have preferred to pose their sitters with their favorite dogs. Dogs, too, frequently appeared in paintings depicting the country life of that nation. Rembrandt, however, passed the dog by in his paintings but frequently used dogs in his etchings. Among the Dutch painters who frequently added dogs to their scenes were: Willem Buytenwech, Frans Hals and his brother, Dirk, Van der Helst, Jan Victoors, Adriaen Ostade and his brother, Isaac, Terborch, Pieter van Slinge-landt, Lucas van Leyden, Geertgen van Sint Jans, and Anthony Mor. Others include Jan Steen, Adriaen van der Venne, Philips Wouverman, Nicolas Berchem, Albert Cuyp, Pieter de Hoogh and Abram Hondius, who spent much of his time in England. Perhaps, the greatest of all Dutch animal painters was Paul Potter.

The dog is a rather conspicuous figure in Flemish art. Jan van Eyck, Dirk Bouts, Memlinc, Bernard van Orley, Hans Bocksberger and Quentin Metsys frequently used dogs in their pictures, as did Hugo van der Goes and the Savery family, Jacob and Roelandt, brothers, and Jan, a nephew.

The great Rubens painted dogs many times, both in repose and in action. His associate, Jordeans, injected dogs into many of his pictures, no matter what the theme might be. Van Dyck was especially adept at picturing the bond of companionship and understanding between master and dog. In the painting of dogs, however, Jan Fyt was outstanding, some of his canvases being devoted entirely to dogs. Teniers was another whose work will long live.

German painters also included dogs in many of their finest works. Among them were Durer, Bernard Strigel, Lucas Cranach, Hans Holbein, and Johan Elias Ridinger.

The artists of France are by no means famous for their outstanding dog paintings, yet some of them did frequently include dogs in their canvases. The LeNain brothers were among the earliest to pay much attention to the dog. Some of France's most famous painters seem to have studiously avoided the use of dogs, but did paint other animals. Among those who occasionally found use for the dog in their works were: Jacques Stella, Gaspard Dughet, Francois Verchier, Alexander Francois Desportes, Watteau, Lancret, Fragonard, and Pater. Outstanding for his paintings of dogs was Jean Baptist Oudry, who painted the dogs of Louis XV, and was also famous for his hunting scenes.

The Dog In English Paintings. England heads the list of nations in producing artists who specialized in portraying the dog on canvas. By no means the first but certainly the best known to the layman was Sir Edwin Landseer (1802-1873), for whom was named a variety of the Newfoundland breed. The best known of his pictures, perhaps, is "Dignity and Impudence," depicting a Bloodhound and a Scotch Terrier. On a par in popularity is "The Shepherd's Chief Mourner," showing a Sheepdog guarding his master's coffin. "A Distinguished Member of the Royal Humane Society" is another famous picture, the "member" being a handsome Newfoundland. Other well-known pictures by Landseer are, "Highland Music," "The Hunted Stag," "The Sleeping Bloodhound," "The Dog, and His Shadow," "A Fireside Party," "The 'TWA' Dogs," "Suspense," "Collie Dog Rescuing A Sheep from a Snow-drift," "The Angler's Guard," "Impertinent Puppies Dismissed by a Monkey," and "Portrait of a Favourite Spaniel."

Hogarth frequently introduced dogs in his pictures, including his own dog Trump. Such famous portrait painters as Gainsborough and Reynolds included dogs in their portraits, the portrayal showing the same careful faithfulness to detail which characterized their human subjects.

George Stubbs, known principally for his excellence in horse portraiture, was also an excellent painter of dogs, often devoting entire canvases to them. Benjamin Marshall was another outstanding animal painter who frequently gave dogs the benefit of his talents. The Sartorius family (John, Francis, John N., and John F.) occasionally included dogs in their works. Sawrey Gilpin was another famous artist who frequently painted dog portraits.

The list of English artists who specialized in dog

painting, or quite frequently used them as incidental to the main subject of their works, is, indeed, a long one and space will not permit its full inclusion. Among them, however, are: Henry A. Alken, Samuel Alken, Samuel Howitt, James Pollard, Philip Reinagle, John Scott, James Seymour, Thomas Stothard, F. C. Turner, James Ward, Dean Wolstenholme, Sr., Dean Wolstenholme, Jr., John Wooton, Francis Wheatley, James Northcote, J. S. Copley, Thomas Rowlandson, George Morland, J. C. Ibbetson, Henry Singleton, Henry Bernard Chalon, Richard Barrett Davis, Tomas Bewick, Thomas Weaver, John E. Ferneley, Abraham Cooper, Edmund Bristow, J. Frederick Herring, W. P. Hodges, Frank Dicksee, Robert Motley, Cecil Aldin, Vernon Stokes, Lionel Edwards, Sir Alfred Munnings, Maud Earl, and T. Blinks.

The Dog In U.S. Art. In the United States there have been a number of very fine artists who specialized in dog paintings. J. M. Tracy, whose outstanding paintings of wildlife were all too few, was considered the foremost American dog painter of his time. Edmund Osthaus and G. Muss-Arnolt were brilliant in their portrayal of sporting dogs. Percival Rosseau's work, particularly with bird dogs and hounds, were great contributions to the American sporting scene. Among others are Edwin Megargee, Mildred J. Megargee, A. F. Tait, Fred McCaleb, Luis M. Henderson, William

Autumn. By Jan Joze Horemans, the younger. (1716-after 1790.) Flemish. Courtesy Metropolitan Museum of Art.

Harnden Foster, Wesley Dennis, Marguerite Kirmse, A. Lassell Ripley, and A. B. Frost.

"Butch," the winsome black and white Cocker Spaniel belonging to the artist Al Staehle, frequently adorned the cover of *The Saturday Evening Post*, much to the delight of that magazine's readers, while "Pluto," the canine character in Walt Disney's animated cartoons, is a source of delight to thousands of movie-going youngsters.

One of the world's most ousntading collections of dog paintings is that of the American Kennel Club, 221 Fourth Avenue, New York City. It contains some of the work of such outstanding painters as Richard Ansdell, R. A., Percival Rosseau, G. Muss-Arnolt, Martin T. Ward, B. Cooper, George Earl, Edwin Megargee, Abraham Cooper, John Sargeant Noble, Arthur Wardle, John Emms, Terri Bresnahan, Gilman Low, T. Blinks, J. M. Tracy, A. F. Tait, P. Jacoby, Maud Earl, F. T. Daws, C. Reichert, P. Reinagle, William Mangford, William Barraud, Ward Binks, James Walsham Baldock, Stephen Taylor, James Lambert, Louis Contoit, Dorothy Iola Keeler, Edmund Osthaus, H. Simon, N. DuBois, George Fenn and C. Cunaeus.

The Dog In Other Art. Centuries before dog painting became a specialized art, the animal figured prominently in carvings, murals, and sculpture of the ancients. In fact, ancient art has told us much about the evolution and development of the dog. He appears in many of the world's greatest tapestries. China, pottery, porcelain, bronze, gold, and silver are all mediums through which the dog has been portrayed.

The "spotted dog" seems to have been a favorite with artists of all periods. He was found on the walls of the tombs in Egypt, in the art of ancient Greece, sometimes with the build and body patches of the Harlequin Great Dane and at other times resembling in both shape and markings the Dalmatian. He was particularly intriguing to the makers of Staffordshire ware and practically every firm of potters in Battersea, Bow, Rockingham, and Delft produced the "spotted dog" in varying sizes, color combinations, conformations, and postures. Private collections of these interesting little ornaments, ranging from 30 inches to an inch, are not too uncommon.

In advertising and calendar art, the dog is known as a sure-fire "attention getter," ranking along with pretty girls and babies. And, adult and puppy, he is a favorite subject in the greeting card industry.

—The Dog in Religion—

THE DOG, so closely associated with man from earliest history, naturally entered into the religious beliefs of many peoples and many periods. Among primitive peoples, the dog was sometimes endowed with divine powers, and many of these early beliefs survived, in various forms, in later times.

The Dog In Biblical References. Although during the times of the Old Testament and early Christianity the dog was considered an "unclean" animal, almost every reference to him in the Bible being of a lowly and degrading nature, he took his place among the gods in other religions. Even in the contemporary period, he was a deified symbol among the Egyptians. The "graven images" which the Jews were forbidden to idolize might very well have included that of Anubis, the dog-headed deity of Egypt. It may very possibly be because of the reverence bestowed upon the dog in Egypt that the Hebrews were so emphatic in declaring him an object of abomination.

Dogs are mentioned in the Bible when the Jews were leaving Egypt: Exod., 2:7, "But against any of the children of Israel shall not a dog move his tongue." It has sometimes been interpreted that God rewarded the dog for his silence while the Jews were fleeing when in Exod. 22:31 we see, "Ye shall not eat any flesh that is torn of beasts in the field; Ye shall cast it to the dogs," thereby establishing that dogs should be fed. However, it is doubtful that anyone worried much about the feeding of dogs in general. The only ones so cared for were probably the useful watchdogs or shepherds' dogs. The Pariah Dog of the streets, a creature half wild and totally neglected, would excite our deepest pity today. He lived off the dead bodies of animals or whatever rubbish he could find. Therefore, it is not surprising that the most horrible fate that could befall one was the scourge of non-burial after death and to be eaten as offal by the dogs of the street.

Such was the fate of Jezebel: I Kings 21:19, "In the place where the dogs licked the blood of Naboth shall dogs lick thy blood, even thine"; 21:23, "The dogs shall eat Jezebel by the ramparts of Jezreel"; and, II Kings 9:35, "They found no more of her than the skull, and the feet, and the palms of her hands." The curse of the same horror is applied to the house of Jeroboam: I Kings 14:11 "Him that dieth of Jeroboam in the city shall the dogs eat." The same curse is applied in I Kings 16:4, to the house of Baasha, and to all rebellious Jews in Jer. 15:3: "And I will appoint over them four kinds, saith the Lord; the sword to slay, and the dogs to tear and the fowls and the beasts of the earth to devour and destroy."

It is, indeed, small wonder that the name "dog" was used in derogatory terms when we visualize the

Votive Plaque, Terracotta (Mastiff). Babylonian, ca. 2000 B.C. Courtesy Metropolitan Museum of Art.

poor animal of the streets and know, from the foregoing text, how base he appeared to the Hebrews. Under the Hebrew Laws in Lev. 2:27: "And whatsoever goeth upon his paws, among all manner of beasts that go on all fours, those are unclean to you," though basically governing the food laws, might well be construed the dog.

Allusions to the dog in the Bible are generally in the form of scorn. When in I Sam. 17:43, David goes forth to meet Goliath, the Philistine insultingly addresses the unarmed David: "Am I a dog that thou comest to me with staves?" And in I Sam. 24:14, David asks Saul: "After whom is the king of Israel come out? . . . after a dead dog, after a flea." In II Kings 8:13, Hazael, when told by Elisha that he should conquer Syria, said, "But what is thy servant which is but a dog that he should do this great thing?" using the term "dog" to show his great humility. Again, in II Sam. 3:8, Abner asks: "Am I a dog's head . . . that thou chargst me today . . . with a fault?"

Watchdogs are referred to in Isa. 56:10-11: "His watchmen are blind; they are all dumb dogs; they cannot bark; sleeping; lying down, loving to slumber. Yea, they are greedy dogs, they cannot have enough." In Biblical times the sheepdog was not trained in rounding up the sheep, but only guarded the flocks against marauding animals or strangers. It may be assumed that they were quite ferocious. Job, who had extensive flocks, refers to sheepdogs somewhat in scorn: Job, 30:1, "But now that they are younger than I have me in derision, whose fathers I would have disdained to set with the dogs of my flock."

From the time of the New Testament we have evidence that dogs were sometimes members of the household. Matt. 7:6, "Give not that which is holy unto the dogs, neither cast ye your pearls before swine," which, freely interpreted, might mean that dogs were cared for and fed around the house. Matt. 15 :26-27, "But he answered and said, It is not meet to take the children's bread and cast it to dogs. And she said, Truth, Lord, yet the dogs eat of the crumbs which fall from their masters' table," is further indication of the same fact. In Mark 7:28 we have the same parallel when the Syrophenician woman

answers, "Yes, Lord, yet the dogs under the table eat of the children's crumbs."

David prays in Pss. 22:20: "Deliver my soul from the sword. Deliver my darling from the power of the dog"—i.e., against the power of the infernal dogs in Hell.

The most charitable reference to the dog to be found in the Bible, one which in spite of the general feeling of revulsion toward the dog, is indicative of the animal's loyalty and friendship, is found in the incident of Lazarus and the rich man: Luke 16:20-21, "And there was a certain beggar named Lazarus, which was laid at his (the rich man's) gate, full of sores. And desiring to be fed with the crumbs which fell from the rich man's table: moreover the dogs came and licked his sores."

Cerberus. In Greek mythology, we have the guardian dog of the gates of Hell, Cerberus, the three-headed dog that only Hercules was ever able to subdue. Cerberus still retained his duties when Christianity's Satan replaced Pluto; Dante writes of him as the guardian of the third circle of the Inferno.

Sacrificial Dogs. The dog with his divine qualities figured conspicuously in the religious rites of primitive peoples. The Huron Indians sacrificed dogs as a dedication to their war god. Dogs were also believed capable of absorbing the ills and sins of human beings, and the savages used many different rites by which these afflictions were thought to be transferred

Babylonian bronze statuette—man with hunting dog, circa 1500 B.C. Courtesy Metropolitan Museum of Art.

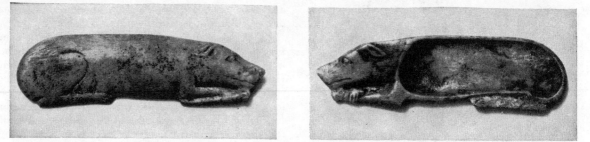

Toilet dish in shape of dog, XVIII Dynasty. Top view at left; underside shown at right. Ivory. Courtesy Metropolitan Museum of Art.

to dogs. Dogs were worthy, nevertheless, to substitute mythically for kings; as witness Ash's account of a dog that was killed instead of a king at Fazogli.

Sacred Dogs. In Turkey, until recently, the dog was considered sacred and as such allowed to roam unmolested. It naturally followed that great packs of miserable animals swarmed the towns and cities, and finally they had to be destroyed. Visitors to Constantinople in the early 1900's tell of the terrifying packs of barking dogs that would rush at them, barking as they walked along, all looking for a scrap of food.

Kitmer. The Mohammedans and Hindus, like the Hebrews, consider the dog "unclean." Mohammedans have for instance, used as abuse the phrase, "Christian dog." But, in contrast, Mohammedans also tell the legend of Kitmer, a dog that guarded the sleeping seven noble youths of Ephesus and watched over them for 309 years without food or water. This dog even gained a place in Paradise beside Balaam's ass and the camel which carried Mohammed in his flight from Mecca.

Dogs and the Egyptians. Evidence of dog worship in various forms has been found in many parts of the world. The esteem in which the dog was held in many of the eastern countries probably stemmed from Egypt where he was worshipped among the deities.

To the Egyptians, the dog was a symbol of fidelity, as well as a guardian god because of the dog-star Sirius, which never failed to herald the approach of the overflowing of the Nile. In lower Egypt, the prosperity of the people, and even their very lives, depended on the annual flooding of this river to keep their lands fertile. The coming of the great flood was foretold by the appearance of the very bright star, Sirius. As soon as this star appeared in the sky, the people would remove their flocks to pastures on higher levels and the lower ground would be fertilized by the waters of the river.

The earliest representations of dogs in Egypt were discovered in ceremonial objects unearthed at ancient Hierakonpolis near Thebes, and dating from the period 4400-4000 B.C. Casts of these objects exist in the British Museum, but their ritual purpose is unknown.

In the city of Cynopolis on the banks of the Nile, dogs were often sacrificed at special religious festivals and dedicated to Anubis. Archaeological discoveries have brought to light inscriptions on royal tombs (about 3000 B.C.) which indicate that dogs were buried with ceremonial pomp, even having individual tombs built for them that they might be honored before the great god Anubis.

Anubis, the god with the head of a dog or a jackal, was one of the oldest deities of the Egyptian pantheon. Anubis assisted Isis, the goddess, in her long search for the body of her husband, Osiris. In some accounts of the myth, Isis is instead aided by dogs. The myth of Isis' search is the very center of Egyptian mythology.

Since the dog played such an important part in the lives of their deities, it is not surprising that the Egyptians came to revere or even worship the dog. Every city had its cemetery for dog mummies—dog mummies may be seen in almost every large museum today—and when a dog died it was the custom for the entire family to go into mourning.

Pythagoras (6th century B.C.), the Greek philosopher who founded a powerful sect in southern Italy, was reported to have visited Egypt. At any rate, his religious cult was based on Egyptian philosophy, one of the doctrines of which was the transmigration of souls. The Pythagoreans believed that by holding a dog to the mouth of a dying friend one could make his soul enter into the animal form most worthy to receive the virtues of the departing spirit.

Dogs of Sicily and China. Aelian, an Italian by birth, living in the early part of the 3rd century A.C. relates that in a temple in the city of Adranus in Sicily sacred dogs served and waited upon the god of the temple. The dogs at Vulcan's temple on Mount Etna were also considered sacred. "And if people approach the temple and holy place decently, soberly and orderly, they fawn on these and receive them as friends and one would think they were familiar with and sympathized with them; but if any person approaches with unclean hands, him they bite and lacerate; and further they drive away anyone who comes there after forming one of a profligate company."

In China, the dog, along with the horse, the ox, the pig, sheep, and fowl, seems to have been domesticated since the earliest period.

The Chinese believed in the existence of dog demons, which could alternately take the form of a man or a dog, and which caused more consternation by wreaking mischief or frightening people than by any bloodthirsty tendencies.

The heavenly dog, T'ien Ken, was also a power in ancient times. In *The Religious System of China* by J. J. deGroot (1907) it is stated that the appearance of comets or the noise of thunder are said to be caused by the heavenly dog on his way from his celestial abode to the earth.

In olden times, the eclipse of the sun caused great alarm among the Chinese people. This account is given in J. H. Gray's *China* (1878):

> Five months prior to the eclipse, the head of the Li-Poo Board at Pekin, in obedience to the commands of the Emperor, forwards a dispatch to the chief rulers of each province and through them to the chief magistrate of each prefecture and each country, requesting them, at the approach of the eclipse, to save the sun. At the time, all the magistrates, dressed in black robes, assemble at the official residence of the chief magistrate. When they have arranged themselves before an altar erected in the courtyard, the chief magistrate burns incense and beats a drum three times. At this point, all the officials fall down before the altar and perform the kow tow. The officials, having concluded their part of the cermony, then retire but a number of underlings continue, until the eclipse is over, to beat drums and tom toms with the view of frightening and thereby preventing Tien-kow or the heavenly dogs from devouring the sun. During this din, priests of the respective sects of Buddha and Taou stand before the altar and chant appropriate prayers. Upon the tops of all the dwellings and shops of a Chinese city, men are also stationed who, by means of drums, tom toms and horns, add to the general din.

The dogs of the streets in ancient China (again the Pariah) were treated with no consideration whatsoever, but the dogs of the Imperial palace were held

very sacred. These dogs were the ancestors of the Pekingese. The Pekingese were to the Chinese symbols of the great protectors of their faith, Buddha's lions.

The marking on a dog also had symbolical value. Thus a white mark in the center of the forehead represented one of Buddha's thirty-two superior marks, and when such a mark appeared on a dog, it was considered to have close affiliation with Buddha. Likewise, a sash-like marking on the body of a dog indicated that the animal should command high regard, for it suggested the yellow belt worn only by certain members of the Imperial family.

The high regard in which dogs were held in ancient China is illustrated by the story of a certain Persian dog which was given the name of Ch'ih Hu

Plaque: Belt clasp or horse trapping (four dogs surrounding a goat). Caucasian, IX-VII Century, B.C. Courtesy Metropolitan Museum of Art.

or "Red Tiger" by the Emperor in A.D. 565. He also gave it the rank and privileges of Chun Chun (comparative to a duke), fed it with the choicest food, and granted it a revenue, and when the Emperor was mounted on his horse, the dog rode upon a mat placed in front of the saddle.

A Dog Ancestor Myth. In southern China dogs became objects of worship among the aboriginal tribes, and this worship was of a particular kind, being founded in a dog ancestor myth. (See the paper published by Chungsee Hsien Lin in *The Royal Anthropological Institute of Great Britain and Ireland Journal* [1932, Vol. 62, pp. 361-368]: "The Dog Ancestor Story of the Aboriginal Tribes of Southern China.")

According to the author, the dog ancestor myth can be found among the Kalangs of Java, the Nias of Sumatra, the Dog-Rib Indians of Alaska, the "black people" of Madagascar, and among some tribes of the South Sea Islands. The myth is also definitely traced

Jug—unglazed pottery showing Saluki. Mesopotamia, 13th Century, A.D. Courtesy Metropolitan Museum of Art.

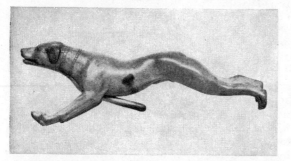

An Egyptian mechanical toy of the later XVIII Dynasty. This is in ivory; the lower jaw is activated by the rod. Courtesy Metropolitan Museum of Art.

among the aborigines of southern China, Burma and Indo-China.

According to the myth (the traditional date is 2435-2366 B.C.) the ancient Emperor Kaoshin was greatly disturbed by an invasion of the Chuan-jung, or dog tribe, a barbarous tribe whose chieftain was exceptionally formidable. The Emperor, therefore, proclaimed that anyone who could bring him the head of the chieftain, General Wu, would be rewarded with magnificent sums of gold, enough land for 10,000 households, and the hand of his youngest daughter.

The Emperor had a five-colored dog named Pan Hu, and soon after the announcement, the dog one day brought in and laid at the foot of the throne what proved to be the severed head of General Wu. The Emperor kept his promise; his daughter and the five-colored dog were married and went to live in a stone mountain. Here they had twelve children who married each other and became the ancestors of various tribes. Their descendants were known as Maui, or Barbarians, and became, in turn, the ancestors of the barbarous tribes in southern China.

There are various versions of the myth, but it has been definitely recorded among the Yao of the province of Kwangsi, the Taraho branch of the Taiyal tribe of Formosa, and the provinces of Chekiang and Fukian. It is told orally and the dog, Pan Hu, is personified as the ancestor god. On every seasonal festival, such as New Year's Day, faithful sacrifice is made to their honorable progenitor as a token of filial piety.

Frequent contact between the savage tribesmen and the civilized Chinese caused the story to be brought into Chinese communities where "it may not be believed but exists in folk tales, and there are instances of temples and place names bearing the name Pan Hu."

It is interesting to notice that in Ash's *History of the Dog*, a five-colored dog is referred to as having been given to the King in the Wei dynasty, A.D. 228, almost three thousand years later.

The same series of notes, collected by Ash from a Mr. Stenffen Hu, relates a story, supposedly from A.D. 502, of a sailor who was driven by wind to an island east of China. "This island was inhabited by a tribe.

Women had the same appearance as our Chinese, but spoke quite a different language which he could not understand. Man was in human body with dog head full of hair and spoke as the barking of the dog. . . . In their generation the girls they brought were human beings while the boys were dogs, and they married each other again." The sailor, imprisoned by the men, was set free by a woman and escaped. She gave him more than ten pieces of leg, telling him to drop each one of the legs after walking every ten miles. The dog men pursued him but in seeing the leg of his own in the way, would bring it back to his home and resume pursuit. In this way the sailor escaped to his ship and, presumably, thus carried home the story. (Ash interprets this as an interesting story suggesting the discovery of Japan.) But in certain aspects the similarity of the dog-ancestor myth is remarkable.

Japanese Dogs Respected. From Japan we have evidence from the 18th century that dogs were treated with exaggerated consideration. Kaempfer in his *History of Japan*, Vol. III, writes of a visit to Fusimi, a suburb of Miaco:

The temples which we had on our right, as we went up, being built in the ascent of the neighboring hills, were illuminated with many lamps, and the priests, beating some bells with iron hammers, made such a noise as could be heard at a considerable distance. I took notice of a large white dog, perhaps made of plaster, which stood upon an altar on our left, in a neatly adorned chapel, or small temple, which was consecrated to the Patron of the dogs.

[We] went by the place where publick orders and proclama-

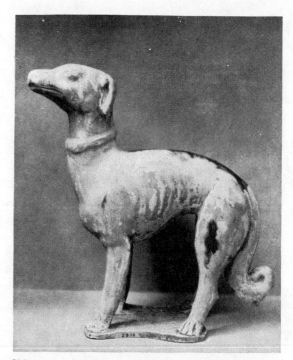

Chinese tomb pottery, the figure of a dog. Earthenware, buff, with cream-white glaze and green touches. T'ang Dynasty (618-906). Courtesy Metropolitan Museum of Art.

tions were put up, not far from the ditch of the castle, where we saw a new proclamation put up lately and twenty shuits of silver nailed to the post to be given as a reward to anybody that would discover the accomplices of a murder lately committed upon a dog. Many a poor man hath been severely punished in this country under the present Emperor's reign, purely for the sake of dogs. . . . Since the now-reigning Emperor came to the throne there are more dogs bred in Japan than perhaps, in any country whatsoever, and than there were before even in this empire. They have their masters, indeed, but lie about the streets and are very troublesome to passengers and travellers. Every street must, by special command of the Emperor, keep a certain number of these animals and provide them with victuals. There are huts built in every street, where they are taken care of when they fall sick. Those that die must be carried up to the tops of this hills as the usual burying places, and very decently interred. Nobody may, under servere penalties, insult or abuse them, and to kill them is a capital crime, whatever mischief they do . . .

All this because the Emperor was born in the sign of the Dog (one of the twelve celestial signs of the Japanese)! Kaempfer also relates an amusing story told by the natives:

A Japanese, as he was carrying up the dead carcass of a dog to the top of a mountain, in order to its burial, grew impatient, grumbled, and cursed the Emperor's birthday and whimsical commands. His companion, though sensible of the justice of his complaints, bid him hold his tongue and be quiet, and instead of swearing and cursing, return thanks to the gods that the Emperor was not born in the sign of the Horse, because in that case, the load would have been much heavier.

Fox Hunting and the Blessing of the Hounds. In our own civilization and in our own time, although not a necessary religious rite, the blessing of the hounds at the opening of the fox hunting season is a beautiful and impressive ceremony, performed sometimes in England and France and in some sections of this country where fox hunting takes on a formal flavor.

——The Dog in Superstition——

"EF YO' CUTS a piece of yo' dog's tail off and buries it under yo' front doorstep he'll nevuh run away and leave yo'."

This superstition and many others have been prevalent in the South for generations. But they are not the only ones to have supersitions about dogs. Such beliefs have existed ever since man adopted some form of worship in practically every area of the world where man and dog have been associated.

It is difficult to know just where to draw the lines between superstition, belief, and accepted legend. Because the dog instinctively drove away strange persons and animals from his masters, it was perhaps inevitable that many primitive peoples used the dog as an emblem or as a sacrificial device to drive away fears or evils, whether real, potential or imaginary.

In many of these superstitious legends the dog figures as a demon or devastating factor, but more frequently he is described as a protective power or omen of good.

Chinese literature occasionally depicts the dog as a monster of ill luck, but in Japanese legends the dog usually signifies the protector of mankind, while the cat personifies the enemy. It is the exception when the roles are reversed.

Legends of Dogs Transformed Into People. In Professor de Groot's *Religious System of China*, the chapter on Zoanthropy lists legends about dogs being transformed into human form. In one of these tales, such a transformed dog is found in a room and is beaten until he resumes his original shape and runs away. Immediately several men, harnessed and armed with spears and bows, attack the house. They are killed or wounded, however, and then change into dogs.

Another legend, written by T'ao Ts'ien, who lived about A.D. 365-427, tells of transformed dogs that played cards at night in a certain pavilion and caused death or disease to people who passed the night there. Many legends transfer the souls of dying humans into the bodies of dogs.

White Dogs. In the majority of the legends of supernatural dog prowess, white dogs are prevalent, mainly as instruments for good. The *Kojiki*, written A.D. 712, mentions the dog only once, and this dog was "white." The story concerns Emperor Yurkaku Tenno of Japan (A.D. 457-479) who was on his way to meet his bride when he saw a house built in exactly the same style as a palace. Very indignant at such impudence to the Imperial family, he ordered the house burned down at once. But the owner ran out and, with a thousand excuses, presented a white dog to the Emperor as a token of apology or remorse. Because a white dog was very rare, the Emperor was so delighted that he rescinded his order.

In the *Kojidan*, written A.D. 1210-1220, another

Wolfhound in bronze by Frederick George Richard Roth. 1872. American. Courtesy Metropolitan Museum of Art.

legend concerning a white dog is found. When Narit-sune was seriously ill, he awoke and saw near his pillow a large white dog. Whereupon he got up and tore out a handful of the dog's hair. He immediately felt better and soon recovered entirely. The hair is still preserved in the treasury of Hodo-In, a Buddhist temple in Kyoto.

In many ancient stories, varying versions of the same theme emphasize the dog's power to do good and his willingness to return good for evil. Most often the master, becoming outraged at his dog, cuts its head off. Whereupon, the severed head then performs some magical protective act. In several of these stories the severed head jumps to the bough of a tree under which the master is standing and attacks a poisonous snake which is about to strike the man.

While Chinese legend sometimes pictures the dog in an evil light, these people also had their superstitious beliefs concerning the dog's powers for good.

Egyptian faience—puppy. Courtesy Metropolitan Museum of Art.

Luig Chi-lung, writing during the Ming dynasty (A.D 1573-1619) reported: "Dogs were placed at the four gates of the capitol in order to keep thieves off, because according to popular opinion, they could distinguish strangers from the inhabitants and guard the houses." And, further, he wrote: ". . . for the same reason nowadays a *white* dog is killed and the gates are smeared with its blood in order to ward off calamity." According to Brinkley, the same custom was prevalent in Japan. But Dr. de Visser disagrees and writes: "but I have not found it mentioned in any Japanese work."

The Dog In Chinese and Other Supersitions. Unfortunately for the dog, the belief in his protective virtues caused him to be used as a sacrifice on numerous occasions, for we read: "Dogs were crucified at the four gates of the capitol in order to keep off evil spirits." Chang Shentsieh, in *On the Chingi,* explained this practice when he wrote: "In my opinion, crucification means driving away. A dog is an animal of Yang, the element of light. Thus when dogs are crucified at the four gates they drive away the spirits of fever. Ku is the evil spirit of fever. Dogs are crucified to keep the Ku off."

The protective power of the dog also had its place in Latin superstition. The mosaic or painted dog on the gates or entrances to ancient Italian houses probably was used to keep away evil as well as for decoration. Latins also believed, as did the Chinese, that the blood of a dog placed under the threshold kept away evil spirits, especially the spirits of the dead.

The primitives believed that the tooth of a dog possessed magical qualities—that its sharpness in real life was transferred to the realm of the unseen. They thought that the tooth of a puppy could banish fears; and that the longest tooth of a black dog could cure fever.

In many rites of primitive peoples the blood, teeth, urine, sexual organs and color—black—of the dog were used. In times of drought it was thought that rain could be brought on by the sacrifice of a black dog, according to J. G. Fraser in *The Golden Bough.*

Anubis, the dog-headed god.

Through superstition the dog was often made a scapegoat. Because of his supposed power over fever, so often mentioned in ancient literature, he became the recipient of disease. In certain rites he was made the victim and died, or was destroyed to cure the ailment. The practice of the rites of disease transference to dogs was prevalent among American Indians, and Plutarch wrote of Greeks who used puppies for this purpose.

Some Indians, particularly those of Kansas, believed that the courage and bravery of the dog would be transmitted to them if they ate dog-flesh before entering battle.

The Dakota Indians frequently feasted upon dog-flesh, but after the meal they carefully collected the bones, scraped, washed, and buried them as evidence that they meant no disrespect to the species itself in eating one of its members. They also believed that the buried bones would reproduce another dog.

In part of Wales the belief existed that if a white dog came near the house of a dying person, the soul would be saved; but that if the dog was black, the soul was destined for everlasting torment.

The Hindus believed in a dog-demon of epilepsy. When a person was stricken, friends or relatives wrapped him in a net and took him into the hall. The doorway could not be used, but there was a hole in the roof especially for that purpose. Some dirt was then taken from the place where people gambled, and the spot sprinkled with water. Dice were cast on it and the afflicted person placed on his back on the dice. The friends or relatives then prayed to the dog-demon of epilepsy, entreating: "Doggy, let him loose. Reverence be to thee, barker and bender!"

The black dog appears in many legends of European witchcraft, the dog-demon being of higher status than the cat-demon.

In China strips of yellow paper, upon which the head of a dog was stamped, were sold as charms—supposedly having the power to cause one to become

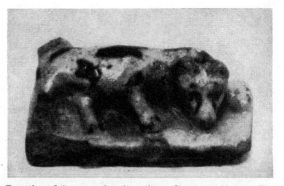

Egyptian faience—sleeping dog. Courtesy Metropolitan Museum of Art.

obedient to the will of another, to become sick, or even to die. These were secretly put in the unsuspecting victim's tea in the form of ashes, or rubbed on his person or clothing. "Ladies of the evening" were said to use these charms to insure the return of their most generous patrons.

In many countries there have been, and in some areas still are, superstitious beliefs that the howling of a dog is a herald of death. There are many versions of this belief, such as: dogs howl when the Angel of Death passes by; two howls by a dog mean a man's death; three howls mean a woman will die; dogs howl when they see coffins in the air; a corpse will be brought from the direction toward which a dog howls.

In some sections young engaged couples avoided dogs in the belief that should one walk between them their marriage would be unhappy. Another common superstition is that good luck will visit a person to whom a stray dog comes in friendly fashion and without having been called.

While the cat is the basis of many superstitions, many more have grown about the dog—undoubtedly because of the latter's longer and closer association with man.

Part XVI

DOG CLASSIFICATIONS

Kennel clubs in various parts of the world tend to classify breeds in groups, these usually centering on the chief class of service or utility expected of the breeds. Most clubs are confronted with practical considerations attending the registration services they offer and the show rules and standards which they must maintain. They are all quite well aware, of course, that many other breeds of dogs exist even though for various reasons they may not list nor carry such breeds as officially recognized. The various kennel clubs are, after all, service agencies for the dog owners and breeders in the country or region in which they are located. It follows that they therefore must be chiefly concerned with breeds numerically or geographically significant to their region's population if they are to render the services for which they are needed. Because various breeds fancied in one era may decline to insignificance in some other, the clubs find it necessary to recognize new breeds from time to time and similarly to drop or reclassify others.

—Classifications of Dogs—

SINCE MAN began to realize that certain types of dogs could serve certain purposes better than others, and this fact became generally recognized and capitalized upon, there has been some sort of classification of dogs. The earliest classification we know of dates back to Roman times when six classes were named as follows:

> House dogs (*Villatici*)
> Shepherd dogs (*Pastorales pecuarii*)
> Sporting dogs (*Venatici*)
> Pugnacious or war dogs (*Pugnaces* or *Bellicosi*)
> Dogs which ran by scent (*Nares sagaces*)
> Swift dogs which ran on sight (*Pedibus celeres*)

Before dog breeding became a matter of serious thought, there was no definite system of classification. Dogs of the same variety or breed might be known by different names in different countries or sections of countries. These names, however, indicated the type of use for which the dog was best fitted.

The *Boke of St. Albans*, attributed to Juliana Barnes or Berners, prioress of Sopwell nunnery, contained perhaps the earliest classification of dogs in the English language. This book was the first work on hunting to come from the English press and was published in 1486. It was said to have been largely copied from *The Master of Game*, written between 1406 and 1413 by Edward, the Second Duke of York, then Master of Game to his cousin, Henry IV, and, with interpolations, translated into Provencal by Gaston de Foix.

The *Boke of St. Albans* classified dogs as follows:

Greyhoun	Kenettys
Bastard	Teroures
Mengrell	Butchers Houndes
Mastif	Dunghill Dogges
Lemor	Tryndeltaylles
Raches	Prycheryd currys
	Small ladyes poppees that bere away the flees

As breeds became definitely established, more thought was given to their general classification, and when kennel clubs were formed in various countries, these classifications were revised and officially adopted. There have been subsequent revisions as new breeds have been developed and given official recognition, but only, however, after it has been practically established that they breed true to type.

——Early Classifications——

A NUMBER of writers and historians of the early days had their own ideas concerning the classifications of the various types and breeds of dogs. Most of these were dictated by the manner in which the dogs were used. Some were at considerable variance with others. Probably the most thorough of these chroniclers was Dr. Johannes Caius.

LETTER OF DR. JOHANNES CAIUS TO CONRAD GESNER

Dr. Johannes Caius, whose English name probably was John Key or Cay, but who also is known as Kaze or Kees, was a graduate of Cambridge University and founded the college that bears his name at Cambridge. After moving to London from his native town, Norwich, he was appointed Physician to Edward VI. He wrote, in Latin, the first book in England devoted to dogs. It was called, *Of English Dogges, the diversities, the names, natures and the properties. A Short Treatise written in Latin.*

Dr. Caius was a devoted student and a prolific writer. In 1570 he wrote a letter on English dogs to his friend Conrad Gesner, the eminent Swiss naturalist and scholar. The famous letter, often wandering but always intensely interesting, follows:

A few years ago, my dear Gesner, I sent you a discoursive treatise on the various forms of quadrupeds, birds and fishes; also on the kinds and shapes of plants and shrubs. I also sent specially for you some notes on dogs, and these you have promised to publish in the part of your book, on the forms of domestic animals of the second class, where you treat of Scotch Hounds: also at the end of a letter to William Turner about books published by you, the notes are among Unprinted Books. Still there are points in that treatise of mine which leave something to be desired, accordingly I stopped the publication and promised a revised edition. And so to be true to my promise, and to satisfy your expectations of me, I will try to explain to your comprehensive mind by a method of my own (1) the Genera and Species of Dogs, (2) the uses of this animal, (3) its character and disposition. I shall divide the subject under the 3 species of (1) Highbred, (2) Country, (3) Mongrel, and in that order I shall call them all British for two reasons: (1) The expression "British" really includes all English and the Scotch in one. (2) The Scotch being poor in livestock and much given to commerce do not indulge as much in the joys of hunting and the chase as do the English with greater pastoral wealth and larger leisure.

Well then: since the 1st class is exhausted by

    (a) those dogs that hunt wild beasts, or
    (b) that catch birds,

we name these first, as being 2 Genera, a Beast Class and a Bird Class. The Latin equivalent is *Canis Venaticus.*

Englishmen, however, regard the two pursuits as distinct: and would put hunting first; and just so give two different names to each class of dog:

    (1) the *Venatici*   (2)   the *Ancupatorii*

Further they subdivide (1) into 5 classes. Either they overcome the animals by (1) scent or (2) by sight or (3) by speed or (4) by scent and speed or (5) catch them by craft. The dog that wins by scent and is always swift is unusually keen in following up the trail: this dog we call *Sagax.* . . . Its hips protrude: its ears hang forward towards its mouth; it is of moderate size. This we call *Leverarius:* for the purpose of dividing a whole genus into separate species, for otherwise if one goes by duty or function one cannot class them into a unified species: one dog is keen to scent a hare only, another a fox, another a flat-horned animal, another a badger, or an otter, or a polecat, or rabbit only (this last, however, hunted only with a net and ferret), and each excels in his own class and in what he likes. There are hounds that will hunt fox and hare alternately, but not with the same luck as when following their natural bent, for they often go wrong. Some are Fox and Badger hounds only: called the *Terrarii* because they penetrate holes in the earth, as ferrets do when after rabbits, and so frighten and bite the fox and the badger that they either tear them on the ground with their teeth, or force them from their lairs into flight or into nets drawn over the burrows in the ground. These form the smallest class of *Sagaces.* The larger class remain to be mentioned: these, too, have drooping lips and ears, and it is well known that they follow their prey not only while alive but also after death when they have caught the scent of blood. For whether the beasts are wounded alive and slip out of the hunter's hands, or are taken dead out of the warren (but with a profusion of blood in either case), these hounds perceive it at once by smell and follow the trail. For that reason they are properly called *Sanguinarii.*

Frequently, however, an animal is stolen, and owing to the cleverness of the thieves there is no effusion of blood: but even so they are clever enough to follow dry human footsteps for a huge distance, and can pick a man out of a crowd however large, pressing on through the densest thickets, and they will still go on even though they have to swim across a river. When they arrive at the opposite bank, by a circular movement, they find out which way a man has gone, even if at first they do not hit on the track of the thief. Thus they supplement good luck by artifice and deserve what Ælian says of them in C59 of his *Historia Animalium,* where he argues that these dogs can think and reason and come to a decision; nor do they cease to follow until the thieves have been caught. During the day their masters keep them in darkness, and bring them out at night, the idea being that if they are used to the dark, they will be all the quicker in tracking robbers, who above all things are fond of the dark. When these dogs hunt thieves, they are not given the same liberty as when after beasts, unless they flee at great speed, but they are held back in the leash and so guide their master, on foot or horseback, at such speed as suits him.

On the Anglo-Scottish border, because of frequent cattle and horse raids, much use is made of these dogs, and they learn to follow animals first and to chase thieves later and as a secondary occupation.

In this class none is by nature aquatic unless it be the Otter Hound, for others frequent banks of earth and water in turn. But all of them will, if their prey takes to the water, take to it also, such being their desire to catch it. This, however, is more the working of desire than of instinct. And whereas some of these dogs are called Brachs in English (in Scotch, Rachs), this is because of sex, not race. For so we are used to name the females in *Genus Venaticum.*

Lastly, it is in the nature of the *Sagaces* that some, before the quarry is started, should quickly hunt about, and others start the animal by a noise at once at the first scent, though as yet it may be far off and in its lair: the younger they are, too, the less manageable and the more faulty they are.

For age and hunting practice breed experience and confidence in them as in all other animals, especially when they have learnt to obey a master's commands and prohibitions. As for what strikes his sense of sight, this he follows not with nose but with eye: with the eye he pursues fox or hare, selects from a herd the fattest and richest animal only, follows it up, finds it again if the view is lost, sees it return to the herd apart from all the rest, and finally when sighted hunts it to death. We call it *Agasaeus* because it aims at its prey with the eye. It is more frequently employed in Southern than in Northern England, and in level country districts than those that are thorny and woody. Also more by horsemen than by pedestrians; (for so they excite the horses to greater speed, the dogs taking more pleasure in them than in the prey itself, and accustom them lightly and fearlessly to leap over hedges and ditches and flee whither the riders may find refuge in flight through difficulty and danger, or pursue and kill an enemy at will). Should the hound ever deviate, it will run up on the instant at a signal and renewing the chase with sharp bark and at quick pace worry the hunted animal as before.

The *Leporarius* is so called from its speed: its value and its use are found in the hunting of hares. Although in catching fallow deer, stages, roebucks, foxes, etc., they excel in strength and traditional speed, their excellence varies with temperament and plumpness or slimness of body. For there is a thin sort comprising a larger and smaller variety: and some have smooth hair.

The larger the prey the larger the animal we select for it. I have found its value in hunting great; and in one respect it is a very odd animal.

Froissart relates in the 4th Book of his *Chronicles* that a *Leporarius* belonging to Richard II of England, which had before acknowledged only the King, did, when Henry IV (Duke of Lancaster) came to Flint Castle to arrest Richard, abandon Richard and receive Henry with the same loyal attentions as his rival, just as though he had perceived or got news of Richard's misfortunes. Richard was quick to see this and said in so many words that it was a presage of his doom.

There is a hound which has value for sagacity and speed, while in race and physical qualities it comes between the *Sagax* itself and *Leporarius*. This arrival is called *Levinarius* because of its light weight: *Lorarius* because it is led by Lora. Its speed enables it to press hard on its prey and catch it quickly.

The Greyhound obtained its name, *Vertagus*, originally from its craftiness. When in pursuit, it will turn itself (*vertat*) and with a revolution of the body it will with a sudden rush seize and catch its prey in the very opening of its lair. And it displays cunning in this way. When he comes to a rabbit-warren he does not worry the rabbit by running after them nor frighten them by barks, nor show any other marks of enmity, but casually and like a friend he passes by them in artful silence, carefully noting the rabbits' holes. On coming to the spot, he so arranges himself on the earth as to have the wind always against him and be out of view of the warren. In this way he easily perceived the smell of a rabbit coming in or going out, while the rabbit does not catch his scent at all and is baffled so as not to see him. So crouched, the hound lying in wait either cleverly seizes on the rabbit going out without thought of danger just at the burrow's entrance or catches them on his return and carries him to his master in his mouth, he being hidden near by. This dog is smaller than the *Sagax* we have mentioned, thinner, and with pricked-up ears. Were he larger you would call him from his shape *Bastard Leporarius*. But though much smaller he can catch in one day as many animals as are a fair cartload. Guile and bodily agility are to him what strength might be.

The Thief Dog is similar. At his master's commands he goes out at night and following up the rabbits without barking by the scent borne in his face he catches while coursing as many as his master allows and brings them back to where he stands. The inhabitants call him the Night Dog because he hunts at night But enough of those that hunt wild beasts.

Next of those that pursue birds already stated to be called *Aucupatorii*. These are bred dogs and of two kinds. Some pursue birds only on land, some by water. Those that confine themselves to land either track and start the bird, following it up openly and barking, or simply point it without noise. The first kind are used in hawking: the second in snaring. The first class have no special names but take their names from the birds

which they naturally pursue. So we get the names *Falconarii, Phasianarii, Perdiciarii* (Partridge).

The generic name in this country, however, is *Hispanioli*, as though the whole breed came from Spain. All are nearly all over white. If they have any spots, these are red, and scarce and big. There is a red and also a black variety: but such are very scarce.

Recently (so fond are we all now of novelties) a new variety has been imported from France, all white with black spots: this is always called the *Gallican*.

The dogs of the second kind follow the bird silently on foot and obey the directions of their master who helps them, and go forward, or back, or to the right or left as told. When I say the bird, I mean Partridges and Quails. When he has made a find carefully, noiselessly, stopping his course and on the secret watch he creeps forward low down; when he gets near he jumps and indicates the right spot by his paw: hence his is called *Canis Index*. The place once shewn, the birdcatcher spreads, and covers the bird with a net. This done, the dog at once rises to the familiar sign from his master or his voice, and startles the birds at closer quarters, so causing them to be *inextricably netted*. One need not wonder at the cleverness in the domestic dog when a hare, a wild animal, in the year of grace 1564 was actually seen in England to dance and to beat a drum with its forepaws like a drummer-boy and to go for a dog tooth and claw and retire with blood on its feet, this is not an idle story: and so I give it currency, for I think it well that nothing should be passed by that shows *design in nature*.

Those that hunt by water, by instinct, or perhaps after a little training, are larger in size, with a natural coat of rough, shaggy hair. I, however, my dear Gesner, have painted him for you shorn from shoulder to hindquarters and of tail, for it is our habit to shear them so, that they may be quicker when without hair and not checked in swimming.

In England he is also called *Aquatian*, taking his name from his watery haunts. With him we pursue birds on the water (and especially ducks whence he is called Duck-Dog: he is expert at that) or fish them out when killed with a dart, or recover darts and arrows that have fallen we don't know where, or find lost things; hence his name the Inquisitor Dog. And yet the duck can at times outwit a dog, and man too, either by making water or by natural cunning. If a man comes near where they lie, the ducks come forward and offer themselves voluntarily to the comers, and making believe to be lame of foot or wing, as though they could be caught at once, effect their exit slowly. By this trick they attract but elude those who come against them until having proceeded some way they are called off from the nests; and they are very careful on their return lest by being crowded together they should reveal where they are. Nor are the ducklings less careful to protect themselves. For as soon as they perceive that they are seen, they take refuge under a mound or under sedges, under the covering of which they are so cleverly protected that they would escape capture altogether if not scented out by the dog.

I have never personally known a *Canis Piscator* (of which Hector Boethius writes) which goes after fish on the rocks by scent, nor have I heard tell of such even after careful enquiries amongst anglers and sportsmen: unless you call the Otter a fish (which many believe it to be) just as the *Pupinus* bird is said and reputed to be a fish. Whether the dogs that go for fish—if any do—do it out of sport or out of hunger I will write and tell you when assured on the point: we know that there are dogs that will eat carrion if pressed by starvation.

In the meantime, we have the sanction of Ælian and Æbius for calling the Otter a River-Dog. And I know that the Otter, just like the dog, will if there is a dearth of fish, make raids on the land and rend lambs and then return fed up to the water. But we have none such amongst English dogs.

Again the Seal hunts fish over rocks and stones, but is not reckoned amongst our fish though we call him Sea-Dog.

There is another breed of high-bred dogs among us, apart from these, which Callimachus calls *Melitei*, from Melita, the island near Sicily (now popularly called Malta and famous from

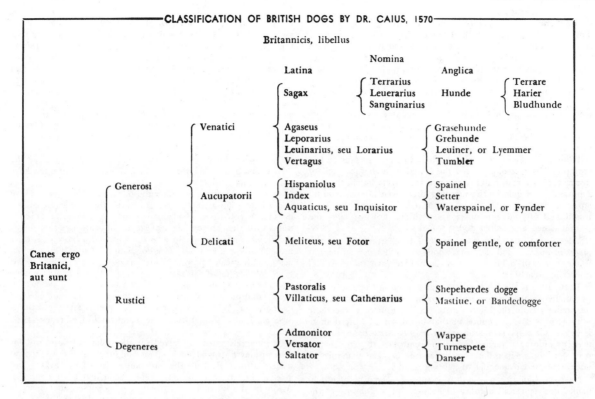

the Knights of St. John), from which the breed especially springs. And from Melta come the *Pachyni,* as Strabo says. This is a tiny breed of dog, and only sought after to be a luxurious plaything for women. The smaller it is the more welcome is it for that purpose and for being carried in the bosom in bed-chambers, or in their hands when driving out. It is no use at all except that it will relieve indigestion if pressed against the stomach, or moved up and down the breast of a sick person, because of the difference in temperature. Nay, it is even believed that diseases will pass, through the sickness and also the death of these: as though the evil passed into them because of the similarity of heat.

So much for the *Canis Generosus.* Now for the *Rusticus:*

In this class two only deserve mention, the *Pastoral* or *Pecurian* and the *Molossian* or *Villatic,* the one, useful to repel injury from beasts, the other against human strategy. In England the *Pastoral* is of smallish account since he has nothing to do with the wolf which is the natural enemy of sheep, for we have no wolves owing to the beneficial policy of Edgar, who imposed an annual tribute of 300 wolves on the Cambi as a tax (they were most frequent amongst them).

Writers say that King Lud of Cambria paid King Edgar an annual tax of 3,000 wolves, and so in four years all Cambria and all England were rid of them. Edgar reigned A. D. 959 about. Now since that date, we never read that a native wolf was seen in England; but by way of making money we have often seen one brought from abroad, simply to be seen as a rare and unfamiliar animal. But as to this dog. If his master utters a certain command, or a clear whistle through his closed fist, he will drive all stray sheep into one place, and this the one the master wants; so that with no real trouble and without even stirring the shepherd can govern the whole flock as he likes, making them advance or halt or retreat or move to and fro.

In England the shepherd follows his sheep: in France and Germany and Syria and in Tartary the practice is the contrary.

Sometimes, too, even without a dog running out or about, the wandering sheep will form into flock merely on hearing the whistle above described, because, I suppose, they are frightened of the dog and associate the sound with the probable reappear-

ance of the dog. And I have carefully made this observation when travelling, and noticed people curbing horses by the shepherd's whistle, so that one can visually test the truth of the fact. With this same dog the shepherd can get hold of a sheep to kill or to cure, without doing any injury to it.

The *Villaticus* is a big and robust breed. Its body has great weight but little speed. To look at it is, however, terrible and so is its voice and it has more strength and keenness than any Arcadian hound. Though it may be added that the Arcadian is reputed to be descended from the lion. The name *Villatic* comes from its function. If there is fear of thieves, it is used to protect the farm from them. He is useful also to cope with the fox and the badger who prey on the stock. He is also good at following wild boars, and driving swine from orchard and field, and for the purpose of capturing and keeping bulls when use or sport makes this desirable, one matched against one, or even one against two of the fiercest kind. For the breed is most bellicose and violent; and a danger even to men, for they do not fear men. Nor does war terrify them; and to make him even keener we help his propensity by science and by association. And they teach them to scare away bears, bulls, arctic bears, and other wild beasts, bear-leaders being appointed to conduct the contests; also often to fight with a man armed with a stake, a club or a sword, and so make them fiercer and keener and imperturbable. Their strength is miraculous; and their power of biting most keen, so much so, that three of them can hold a bear, four, a lion. There is a story that Henry VII, that wise monarch of England, ordered a number of them to be hanged, sore grieved that dogs of a lower and ignoble ancestry should do violence to the lion, the generous King of Beasts; a notable lesson to subjects not to rebel against a King. And another story relates that the Falconers commended a falcon of his for a daring attack on an eagle: with the same motive he ordered the falcon to be killed.

This kind of dog is also called *Catenarius* from "catena" "chain," for during the day it is chained to the door for fear of harm if it were loose, while at the same time it may frighten others by its bark. And though Cicero in the *Pro Roscio* thinks that dogs that bark in the day ought to have their legs broken, modern opinion guided by the need for securing life and property is widely different. For society is full of thieves, even in daylight; nor are they afraid of an infamous death by hanging. The reason is not merely lack of money, but the luxurious pride in clothes and fine living, and petulance, and love of ease such as characterises overweening profligates who care for nothing but horses prancing over the turf and gathering their proud footsteps and wheeling in a narrow circle, for nothing but lechery and idle begging and thieving, while they unjustly lay all to the score of bodily infirmity. The Emperor Valentinian had such men in his eye when he passed laws that men suffering from no bodily ill but lazily and worthlessly putting this forward as a pretext for begging should be the slaves in perpetuity for such cultivators of farms as should prosecute and expose their knavery, lest their idleness should be a burden to the state and a bad example. Alfred, too, governed the Kingdom with such vigilant justice that if a man walking through the streets lost in the dust a purse full of gold in the morning time, even after a month's lapse he would find it quite untouched. We know this from Ingulf of Croyland. But nowadays nothing hardly is safe even behind closed and bolted doors.

The *Canis Custos* is so called as defending farmsteads but also places of business and rich men's houses. For that reason dogs at Rome were fed publicly in the Capitol, to give the alarm of thieves approaching.

Then there is the *Laniarius*, so called because frequently used by butchers when driving and capturing beasts. Also the *Molossian* named from the Molossian district in Epirus, where there were good and keen hounds of that breed. Of this breed there is a class for a special reason called *Mandatorius*, because at its master's bidding it carries letters on from place to place tied to it or done up in its collar. And great care is taken that they be not intercepted if unequal to fighting or flight.

Next the *Lunarius*, whose duty is simply to be a night watchman, for sleepless all night it "bays"—to quote Nonius—at the moon. The larger and bigger will pump water out of deep wells for use in the country by pulling a long rope; hence called *Aquarii*.

The *Sarcinarii* are so called because with wonderful patience they relieve travelling merchants of the trouble of carrying their packs.

In addition to these qualities and uses the *Villatici* have the understanding merit of loving their masters and hating their enemies. And so they guard them on journeys, defending them from thieves and keeping them safe and sound, and so might also well be called Defenders. And if ever their master is called by a multitude of men and the strong arm, and falls, it has been found that they do not desert him even in death, but will lovingly and for many days endure hunger and cold, and if it should so turn out will kill the murderer or at any rate betray him by their bark or anger or hostile assault, as though a witness of their master's death.

A proof of this occurs to me: the case of a certain traveller who was travelling straight from London to Kingston, a town famous for the coronation of eight Kings, and who after he had travelled nearly all the way fell among thieves at Campareus, a broad and spacious valley covered with trees and infamous on account of robberies. And that dog of British breed mentioned by Blondus in his *History* when his master had been killed by a rival not far from Paris betrayed the murderer and would have killed him if the murderer had not protested against the vengeance of a dog. And when fires happen in the evening or at night, dogs a year old will bark even though prohibited until the servants wake and perceive the fire; and then stop of their own accord. This has been proved in England. And that dog was not less faithful who would not leave his master, who while hunting fell into a deep well, until by his own sagacity he had been drawn up by a rope on to which, when he was close to the top, the dog leapt to take him into his arms as it were, impatient of more delay. There are some who will not allow a fire to go out, but move coal on to it with their paws, having previously watched and wondered how it is done. If the coal is too hot, they cover it with ash and then shove it into the place with the nose.

There are others who do a Bailiff's work at night. For when the master goes to bed and a hundred brazen bolts close every-thing and the eternal strength of iron, and Janus Custos is not away from the door (as Vergil writes), then if the master tells the dog to go out, he goes all through the estate more carefully than any bailiff, and if he finds any stranger, be it man or animal, he drives them off, but leaves domestic animals and servants alone. But the variety of their cleverness is as great as their fidelity. For some without a muzzle will bark without biting: But these are less to be feared because they are more timid. For, as the proverb goes, the more timid the dog the greater the bark. Some bark and bite too. One should be careful of these because they mean to inflict injury at some time, but do not attack them, for they are provoked by anger to bite, being indeed bitter by nature. Some jump without noise and fly at a bound at the throat, and tear it terribly. Be in fear of these, for they have great courage and overcome careless men.

By such indications we distinguish a cowardly from a brave and a bold from a timid breed. But even from a bad breed one does not necessarily get bad progeny; no dog is more suitable for human use than the one named. For if one wished to sum up all their uses, what man could give the alarm of a beast or a thief more clearly and so loudly as a dog with his bark? Who subdues beasts with greater power? What servant is more loving to his lord? Who a more faithful companion? Who a more reliable defender? Or a more vigilant watchman? Who more staunch to avenge and punish? Who a better messenger? Who more effective in the water? What tailor carrying his wares is more patient?

So much of well-bred British dogs and rustic dogs, true to their breed.

Of mongrels and their mixed varieties I have little to say, for they display no signal mark of race or breed: I dismiss them as useless. Still in daytime they announce visitors by barking and give notice to their owners—hence their name *Admonitores*. Again in the kitchen when roasting is going on they help to turn the spits by a small wheel, walking round it, and making it turn evenly with their weight. No cook or servant could do it more cleverly. Hence the name *Versator*—or more commonly *Veru Versator:* these are also taught to dance to the drums and to the lyre and are the last of the classes at first mentioned. Our mongrels to perform in many other ways, standing or lying; they have learnt these tricks from their owners when they were in a state of vagrancy and want.

We have no native *Lyciscus* in England, just as we have no wolf: nor any other breed from dog and wolf except the *Lacaena* and the *Urcanus*, the former being a cross between dog and fox (there are several in England kept privately from motives of pride or morbid feeling); the latter between a bear and a house-dog (*Catenarius*), animals that are naturally enemies but here as elsewhere in the natural kingdom joined in union by a curious lust. For we read of union between *Hircani* and tigers, *Acadii* and lions, *Gallici* and wolves. In men, too, as Moria says, although they have reason, a senseless but instinctive lust will conciliate enmities. This *Urcanus* is a savage beast and of unappeasable anger (to use the word of the poet Gratius), which surpasses all our other dogs in ferocious cruelty: even its look is terrible and grim, in fight it is keen and vehement, and so tenacious that you could cut it in pieces sooner than shake it off; it fears neither wolf nor bull, bear nor lion; it can only be compared to that Indian dog of Alexander. But enough of British breeds.

Custom has long since admitted some foreign dogs and preferably the larger, I mean Icelandic and the Lithuanian: these being quite covered with hair, which is long and shaggy, have their faces and the shape of their bodies completely concealed. Many people are fond of them because they are foreign, and regard them as affectionately as they do a Maltese: so prone are we all to like novelties. We love the foreigner better than ourselves. And this happens in the case of workmen as well as in that of dogs. Our own men, though skilled and competent, we despise: but wonder at some animal from Barbary or a foreign country as the Cumans an ass or a Thales.

Hippocrates makes that observation at the beginning of his treatise *On Fractures* and we have enlarged on it in our treatise or argument *Emphemera Britannica addressed to the British people*. And one may add the more ignorant and impudent and frivolous a man is, the more we make of him, and the more he is made of by bejewelled princes and peers. But I will not talk of foreign dogs. All I want to do, my learned Conrad, is to tell you what you want to know of the English ones.

On another occasion I did separately treat of the *Gaetulian Dog*, on account of the rarity of the breed. Of the rest of them you yourself are writing at great length. But as I have written to you at greater length on this occasion than before, but too briefly for a proper exposition, remembering as I do the range of your interests, I will draw out a table to illustrate what I have said about British dogs. And as you are fond of modern names, as I know from your letter, I will add these to the Latin and add reasons for them, so as to make the whole thing plain and satisfactory to you.

Since being a foreigner our words are not intelligible to you without a translation, I shall now, following the same order as before, translate the English as I have already tranlated the Latin.

"Hound" then—the *Sagax* among the *Venatici*—comes from the word "hunt" with the change of one letter and "hunt" is translated "venari." And if taking from your language the word "Hund" ("dog" generally in German) you suppose it to be called that because of the similarity of the words, dear Gesner, I shall certainly be with you, for even now we retain many German words left over from the Saxon occupation of Britain, but I may also tell you the generic name for "canis" is "dog," and of "hunting dogs," "hound."

Similarly from English "gaze" (to look closely or attentively at anything) we derive *Gazehound*, or as we have called it *Agasaeus*. For it is not by scent but by careful and diligent sighting, that such a dog follows the prey, as we have observed, though of course I know *Agasaeus* is one of the Latin words for dog.

The English *Greyhound* comes from "grey," because it is of the first grade of dogs and of the best breed. "Grey" in English —"gradus". The Latin equivalent is *Leporarius*.

The dogs called *Levinarius* and *Lorarius* in Latin come from "Levitas" and "Leyner", "Lorum" and "Lyemmer." For in English "Lyemme"—"Lorum." That "Leyner" comes from "Levitas", the English from the Latin, and why generally so many of our words from Greek, Latin, Italian, German, French and Spanish, and how in course of time many have been altered by corruption, we have explained in our book on the symphony and consonance of English words.

The *Vertagus* is the last of the *Venatici*: and we call him *Tumbler*: "tumble" in English is "vertere" in Latin, and "tumbiere" among the Gauls, whence the name *Tumbler*, with a characteristic change of vowel into a liquid; just the opposite to what happens in French and Italian in which a liquid before a vowel is nearly always changed into another vowel: as Impiere, Piano, Implere, Plano, and many other instances.

After the *Venatici* the *Aucupatorii*, and 1st of these the *Hispaniolus*: a Spanish word as we have said. Leaving out the "h" and the "i" we say "spaniel" for the ease in pronunciation "spainel." The 2nd *Index* comes from English "set", to mark out a place: hence English *setter*. Next comes *Aquaticus* or *Water Spaniel* from "water" and "Spain"—"aqua" and Hispania". The "aqua" in which the dog plays is in English "water": and "Hispania" we call "Spain": and one assumes from the name that the breed comes from Spain. Still at the same time there is now an English breed of such dogs, but *Spaniel* is a common and general name for dogs believed to have come originally from Spain, and so they and other *Aucupatorii* are commonly referred there, though born in England and distinguished by a peculiar bark or a sign of breed: as is that sort by the addition of "water" or "aqua." The same dog is also called *Finder*, because he seeks for and finds lost things: "Find" in English—"invenire" in Latin. But because the principal part of finding lies in the Enquiring, we have given it this Latin name from Enquiring. From these two we pass to *Delicati Rustici*, and *Degeneres*. The *Delicatus, Melitaeus, Spanielgentle* or *Hispaniolus Generosus* is given us by the last name because of the generosity of its breed: for it is used to the society of titled men and women and is their companion at feasts and sports.

Compare Gorgo, the pet dog in a poem by Theocritus about a festival at Syracuse, which when she went out she gave to a slave to look after along with her baby, bidding her call the dog in and mind the crying child. This dog is useless for purposes except as I said to warm a stomach weakened by cold, or, also to show up an adultery: see hereon Ælian, Book 7, Cap. 25.

Rustici has for translation *Shepherd's Dog, Mastiff, Ban Dog: Pastor* in Latin—*Shepherd* in English, because he guards sheep, in Latin *oves*.

"Ban" is from "band" (in Latin "ligamenthum") and another word our Baliffs use, is "Masty"—"Sagina" (fat). For this breed called *Catenarii* is fat and well-fed.

I know at the same time that Augustinus Niphus considered the *Mastinus* or *Mastivus* to be properly a *Pecuarius*, and that Albertus Lyciscus says it is a half-breed from a dog and a wolf: but as a rule it passes for a *Molossian*. Lastly we have said certain mongrels are called *Wappe*, and *Turnspit*. The latter is from the English "turn"—Latin "verto". And "Spete" or "Spede" to represent the Italian equivalent for a "spit", namely "veru". "Wappe" comes from the natural sound "Wau" which a dog makes when barking to attract attention. Hence originally it was *Wauppe*. But for the sake of euphony, a vowel changing to a consonant, we say *Wappe;* then, too, Nonius derives *Baubari* from "Bau! Bau!" and so with the Greek.

As to the *Saltator*, it is sufficient to say that "dance" in English is "saltare" in Latin. And then I fancy you will not need to learn more on that head. And so you have, my dear Gesner, not only the kinds of our dogs, but also their names in English and Latin, their duties, functions, differentiae and peculiarities, natures and activities. What more could you possible desire? If you have not fully come up to your expectations (for perchance you are so eager that even speed seems slow) because I have suppressed the publication of that immature treatise which I sent you five years ago privately but not for publication, still I trust I have satisfied you in this respect, and that delay has made it appreciably better. Second thoughts, we are told, make a thing easier to read.

In his volume devoted to natural history, the versatile and learned Dr. Caius includes the following note on dogs:

There was a *Canis Gatulus* in England as early as 1554. Its body is compact, short and naturally curved, even when it walks. It has short or no neck: legs somewhat out of proportion in length to the body; a very short, or hardly any tail: a face sharp and black like that of a ground hedgehog: black eyes and canine teeth, there being a double row on one side of the head upper and lower, and on the other one row. It has a dog's bark, the walk of an ape, smooth hair on its face and fore parts, rough on the body otherwise. Its whole body on the inside is reddish, on the back and the outside, Lupine. Its length from head to tail is only one foot and a hand's breadth all but one finger.

In 1570 Dr. Caius made the classification of British dogs as outlined in the accompanying table.

FLEMING'S CLASSIFICATIONS

Dr. Caius' letter was used by Gesner and later published in London as a small book. In 1578, Abraham Fleming, a student, used the letter as the basis for his own published work, placing his personal and rather misleading interpretations on some of the text. Fleming classified British dogs as follows:

Harriers.—Some for the Hare, the Foxe, the Wolf, the Hart, the Bucke, the Badger, the Otter, the Polecat, the Lobster, the Weasel, the Conny.

Terrars.

Greyhounds.—Gradus in latine, in English degree, because among all dogs these are the most principall . . .

Tumblers.

Stealers.

Land Spaniels.—Are the most part white or spotted with red or black.

Setters.—. . . they will stand still . . . in silence by their face, eie and taile, they shew their game.

Water Spaniels.

Spaniel Gentle or Comforter.

Mastive or Bandogge.

Butcher's Dogge.

The Shepherd's Dogge.

Carrier.—. . . because at his master's voice and commaundment he carrieth letters from place to place, wrapped up cleverly in his lether collar.

Water Drawer.—. . . drawing water out of wells and deep pittes, but a wheele which they turne rounde about by the moving of their burthenous bodies.

Tynckers Cure.—Because with marveilous pacience they bear budgett fraught with Tinckers Tooles and metaill mette to mend kettels, porridge pottes, skellets and chafers and other such like trumpery requisite for their occupation.

The Mooner.—. . . because he doth nothing else but watch and ward at an inch, wasting the wearisome night season without slombering or sleeping, bawing and wawing at the moon—a quality in mine opinion strange to consider.

The Village Dogge or Housekeeper.—. . . being blacke coloured and great mouthed, or barking bigly so that he may the more terrifie the theefe, both by day and night, for in the night the beast may seize upon the robber before he discerne his blacke skin.

The Fencer.—. . . a certain wayefaring man travailing from the Cities of London to the Toune of Kingstone . . . was set upon . . . in Comeparck a perillous bottom compassed about wyth woddes. (The man was murdered and the dog tried to protect him and then to avenge him by attacking his assailants.)

Mongrel and Rascall Sort.

Daunser.—A performing dog.

Wappe or Warner. Turnespete.—(The Wappe warned of the approach of visitors by barking.)

CLASSIFICATIONS BY LINNAEUS

Carl Linnaeus, the famous Swedish naturalist, included an unusual division of the dog family in his *Systema Naturae* of 1756, giving the following classifications:

Dog with tail curved upwards to the left.

Domesticated Dog.

Wise Dog.

Greyhound.

A Great Dog. (Probably the mastiff.)

Water-dog.

Pet Dog. (Probably Maltese.)

Egyptian Dog.

Rubbing Dog or Cold Dog.

Weasel or weasel-coloured Dog.

These classifications were given Latin designations.

In 1792, *The Animal Kingdom . . . of Sir Charles Linnaeus . . . as lately published with great improvements by Prof. Gmelin of Gottingen . . . translated by Rober Kerr, F. R. and A. SS.E.* was published in London. It enlarged upon the Linnaeus classifications and included many additions from other and later authorities. Some of the text follows:

DOG. *Canis.*—This genus is naturally rapacious and greedy; bites very hard, and tears what it bites; it is very swift, and fitted for the chase, but does not climb trees: the head is in general flat on the crown, with a narrow lengthened visage and snout; the trunk of the body is thickest in its fore part, or at the chest; the fore feet have five toes, except the Hyaenas, which have only four, and the hind feet only four; while the genera of Cat, Seal, Bear, and Weasel have five toes on all the feet. The male has a large knob at its middle: the female brings forth a considerable number in each litter, and has generally ten paps, of which four are placed on the breast and six on the belly.

FAITHFUL DOG. *Canis Familiaris.*—The tail bends upwards, and towards the left side. Inhabits chiefly in society with man, though often found in a wild state; it is uncertain whether the species be native in the East Indies. This species is universally attached to mankind. It feeds on flesh, dead bodies, and farinaceous vegetables, refusing greens, and even digests bones. When sick, it eats some kind of grass which serves as an emetic, drinks by lapping with the tongue; is very delicate in the sense of smelling; runs obliquely, resting on the toes in walking; fiercely sweats when warm, but lolls out the tongue, and foams at the mouth; when about to lie down often goes round the place; and when asleep has a quick sense of hearing, and frequently seems to dream: the female, when in heat, receives the embraces of various males, who flock about her and are very quarrelsome among themselves, while she is equally ill-humored, biting and snarling at all around her. She goes sixty-three days with young, and litters from four to eight puppies; of which the males generally resemble the father, and the females the mother.

This is the most faithful of all animals, and perhaps the only one which is really attached to man, being hardly ever found wild, except in places where they have lost their masters and had no opportunity of finding others. It fawns at the approach of its master, and will not allow anyone to strike him; runs before on a journey, and coming to a division of the road, stops and looks back, as if asking which to choose: is very docile, and may be taught to seek for anything that is lost; is very watchful at night, and gives notice of the approach of strangers, and guards faithfully anything committed to its charge; drives cattle home from the field, and is employed to keep flocks and herds within due bounds, and to protect them from the attacks of wild beasts; points out game to the sportsman, by means of its acute sense of smelling, creeping with great caution to spring upon the game, and brings it when killed to its master, without destroying any; is employed in France and some other countries to turn spits, in Siberia is made to draw sledges; begs when his master is at table; and, when it has stolen anything, slinks away, slouching its tail between the hind legs, eat enviously with oblique eyes; and is always desirous of domineering over its fellows; is the enemy of all beggars, and often attacks strangers without any provocation; will lick wounds, and often by so doing relieves ulcers and the gout, howls at certain notes in music, and sometimes urines on hearing them, bites a stone when flung at it, grows sick at the approach of storms, is often afflicted with the *Taenia*, or tape-worm, in its bowels, sometimes becomes mad, which disorder it communicates to its kind, to other animals, and to man, by biting; makes a violent following when Empyreumatic oils are rubbed on the tail; is often infected with gonorrhea. Dogs are banished from their houses, as unclean, by Mahometans, who, notwithstanding, endow hospitals for their maintenance; is the victim of anatomists for demonstrating the circulation of the blood, the lacteal vessels, and for experiments on transfusion, cutting of nerves, and other cruel purposes; but has been made a useful martyr by some, for discovering the effects of remedies against poison.

The top of the head is flat, and has a projecting longitudinal ridge; the edges of the lower lips, at the sides, are divided into dentated or tooth-like projections, which are concealed by the upper lips, has five or six rows of whiskers on the snout; the upper margin of the external ear is reflected; the posterior one has two lobes, and the anterior three; the nostrils are in form of a semilunar furrow turned outwards at the lower end; the face usually has seven hairy warts; and the fur has eight ridges or whorls on the neck, the breast, the fore-legs, the belly, the eyes, the loins, the ears, and near the arms. The female has ten paps, of which four are on the breast. The feet have small membranes connecting the roots of the toes with each other, or are called sub-palmated.

This animal is subject to more varieties than any other. Each of these will reproduce, and, mixing with others, produce varieties almost without end: yet certain kinds are more numerous and more permanent than others, perhaps from their usefulness, having more attention paid to their breed. It is perhaps impossible to enumerate or describe all the varieties, but the following catalogue includes the most remarkable and best known. Various conjectures are formed concerning the original or parent stock; some deriving all dogs from the sheep-dog, and supposing that, by the influence of climate, and the crossing of breeds with the Shakal, Wolf, Fox and Hyaena, all the forms and sizes have been produced.

SHEPHERD'S DOG. *Canis domesticus.*—Has erect ears, the tail is wooly underneath.

POMERANIAN DOG. *Canis pomeranus.*—Has long hairs on the head, erect ears, and the tail is much curved upwards on the rump.

SIBERIAN DOG. *Canis sibiricus.*—Has erect ears, a curled-up tail, and the hair on the whole body is long.

ICELAND DOG. *Canis islandicus.*—The ears are erect, with pendulous points; and the hair is universally long, except on the snout, which is short.

GREAT WATER-DOG. *Canis aquaticus major.*—The hair is long and curled, like the fleece of a sheep.

LESSER WATER-DOG. *Canis aquaticus minor.*—Is of a small size, with long curly hair, which about the ears is longer and hangs downward.

PYRAME. *Canis brevipilis.*—Has a small rounded head, with short snout, and the tail is turned up on the back.

SPANIEL. *Canis extrarius.*—Has long, pendulous, wooly ears.

SHOCK-DOG. *Canis melitacus.*—Is about the size of a squirrel, having very long, soft, silky hair all over the body.

LION-DOG. *Canis Leoninus.*—Is exceedingly small, with long hair, like the foregoing, on the fore part of the body; that on the hind parts being shorter and smooth.

LITLE DANISH DOG. *Canis variegatus.*—Has small, half-pendulous ears, a small pointed nose, and thin legs.

BASTARD PUG-DOG. *Canis hybridus.*—Has small, half-pendulous ears, and a thick flattish nose.

PUG-DOG. *Canis fricator.*—The nose is crooked upwards, the ears are pendulous, and the body square built.

This variety has a resemblance to the bull-dog, but is much smaller and entirely wants his savage ferocity. Of this there are two sub-varieties, viz:

(a) The Artois dog, of Buffon, produced between the pug-dog and the bastard pug-dog.
(b) The Alicant dog, of Buffon, produced between the pug-dog and the spaniel.

BULL-DOG. *Canis Molossus.*—Is as large as a wolf having the sides of the lips very pendulous, and the body very strong and robust. The nose of this variety is short, and the under jaw is longer than the upper; this kind is exceedingly fierce and cruel, attacks without warning, but with little judgment, and never quits its hold. It is peculiar almost to England for baiting bulls, which practice, and consequently the kind of dog, is now much less frequent than formerly. There are several varieties of this in size and colour.

MASTIFF. *Canis anglicus.*—Of very large size, having a very robust body, and the lips pendulous at the sides, or chops.

Is very thick and strongly made, having a large head, and great lips, which hang down on each side. This dog is peculiar to England, and grows to a great size, being used principally as a watch-dog, which duty he fulfills with great fidelity and even judgment. Some will permit a stranger to come into the yard, or place which he has been appointed to guard, and will go peaceably along with him through every part of it, so long as he touches nothing; but the moment he attempts to meddle with any of the goods, or endeavours to leave the place, he informs him, first by gentle growling, or if that is ineffectual, by harsher means, that he must neither do mischief nor go away; and never uses violence unless resisted; and will even, in this case, seize the person, throw him down, and hold him there for hours, or until relieved, without biting.

GERMAN HOUND. *Canis sagax.*—Has pendulous ears, and a spurious toe, usually called a *dew-claw,* on each hind foot.

HOUND. *Canis gallicus.*—Is of a whitish ground-colour; has pendulous ears and a dew-claw on each hind foot.

BLOODHOUND. *Canis scoticus.*

POINTER. *Canis avicularius.*—The tail is short, and has the appearance of having been cut.

BARBET. *Canis aquatilis.*—The tail is truncated, or seems cut off in the middle, with long coarse hair.

GREYHOUND. *Canis cursorius.*—Has a long narrow head, with strong lengthened snout, and small half-pendulous ears; the legs are long and strongly made, and the body is long and thin.

IRISH GREYHOUND. *Canis cursorius hibernicus.*—Is nearly as large as a mastiff, having an arched body, and narrow projecting snout.

TURKISH GREYHOUND. *Canis cursorius turcicus.*—Is of the size of a mastiff, with an arched body and narrow snout; and having the fur somewhat curled.

COMMON GREYHOUND. *Canis grajus.*—About the size of a wolf; having a curved or arched body and narrow snout.

ROUGH GREYHOUND. *Canis grajus hirsutus.*—Same size body, and snout with the last, but having the hair somewhat longer and curled.

ITALIAN GREYHOUND. *Canis grajus italicus.*—Of a small size, but the same form of body and snout with the last.

ORIENTAL GREYHOUND. *Canis grajus orientalis.*—Tall, slender, with very pendulous ears, and very long hairs on the tail, hanging down a great length.

NAKED DOG. *Canis aegyptius.*—Has no hair on the body.

LURCHER. *Canis laniorius.*—The body is narrow, and covered with short, thick-set hair; the legs are long and the tail is thick and straight.

ROUGH LURCHER. *Canis laniarius aprirus.*—In body, legs and tail, resembles the last, but is covered with long harsh hair.

BOAR LURCHER. *Canis laniarius fuillus.*—The head and snout are strongly made; the hind part of the body is lank; the legs are long, and the hair is long and harsh.

TURNSPIT. *Canis vertegus.*—Has short legs and a long body, which is mostly spotted.

(a) With straight legs.
(b) With crooked legs.
(c) With long shaggy hair.

ALCO. *Canis americanus.*—About the size of a squirrel, having a small head, pendulous ears, a curved body and short tail.

Of this animal there are two kinds mentioned by authors.

FAT ALCO. *Canis americanus obesus.*—Is prodigiously fat; the head is very small, and the ears are pendulous; the fore part of the head is white, and the ears are yellowish; the neck is short; the back is arched, and covered with yellow hair; the tail is white, short and pendulous; the belly is large, and spotted with black, the legs and feet are white. The female has six conspicuous paps.

TECHNICHI. *Canis americanus plancus.*—Is like the small dogs of Europe, but has a wild and melancoly air.

NEW HOLLAND DOG. *Canis antarcticus.*—The tail is bushy, and hangs downwards; the ears are short and erect, and the muzzle is pointed.

Inhabits New Holland. This animal is rather less than 2 feet high, and about 2 feet and a half in length. His head resembles that of a fox, having a pointed muzzle, garnished with whiskers, and short erect ears; the whole body and tail is of a light brown colour, growing paler towards the belly, on the sides of the face, and on the throat; the hind parts of the fore legs, the fore parts of the hinds legs and all the feet are white. On the whole, it is a very elegant animal, but fierce and cruel; and from its figure, and the total want of the common voice of the dog, and from general resemblance in other respects, it seems more properly to belong to the wolf than dog kind.

BUFFON'S DIAGRAM

In 1798, Jean Louis Leclerc Buffon, the eminent French naturalist and writer, drafted a diagram giving his classifications of the dog. Buffon contended that all breeds of dogs came from the shepherd's dog, arguing that as all savage people who keep sheep

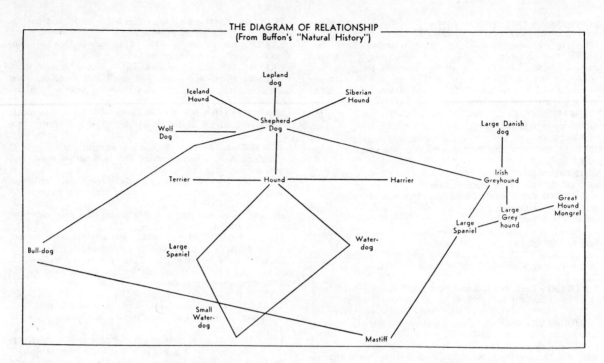

THE DIAGRAM OF RELATIONSHIP
(From Buffon's "Natural History")

have a sheepdog it must be that this sheepdog is the original dog! The eminent Frenchman overlooked or ignored the facts that dogs were the first domesticated animals, that they were used for other purposes, particularly hunting, long before they were used for herding, and that many types and breeds of dogs have been trained as sheepdogs.

A number of other writers of various periods made their own classifications of dogs. Among them were Thomas Pennant, John Whittaker, Thomas Beckley, W. C. L. Martin, and Professor Low. Dr. J. H. Walsh, writing under the *nom de plume* "Stonehenge," in 1859 published *The Dog,* which is considered the first dog book.

—American Classifications—

THE ENGLISH classifications set a standard which most of the other countries have followed to a considerable extent. The American Kennel Club classifications, however, are somewhat more extensive, embracing most of the breeds of other countries and those few that have been developed in this country. These classifications follow:

GROUP I—SPORTING DOGS

Griffon, Wirehaired Pointing	Spaniel, American Water
Pointer	Spaniel, Brittany
Pointer, German Shorthaired	Spaniel, Clumber
Pointer, German Wirehaired	Spaniel, Cocker
Retriever, Chesapeake Bay	Spaniel, English Cocker
Retriever, Curly-Coated	Spaniel, English Springer
Retriever, Flat-Coated	Spaniel, Field
Retriever, Golden	Spaniel, Irish Water
Retriever, Labrador	Spaniel, Sussex
Setter, English	Spaniel, Welsh Springer
Setter, Gordon	Vizsla
Setter, Irish	Weimaraner

GROUP II—HOUNDS

Afghan Hound	Foxhound, American
Basenji	Foxhound, English
Basset Hound	Greyhound
Beagle	Harrier
Bloodhound	Irish Wolfhound
Borzoi	Norwegian Elkhound
Coonhound, Black and Tan	Otter Hound
Dachshund	Rhodesian Ridgeback
Deerhound, Scottish	Saluki
	Whippet

GROUP III—WORKING DOGS

Alaskan Malamute	Great Pyrenees
Belgian Malinois	Komondor
Belgian Sheepdog	Kuvasz
Belgian Tervuren	Mastiff
Bernese Mountain Dog	Newfoundland
Bouvier des Flandres	Old English Sheepdog
Boxer	Puli
Briard	Rottweiler
Bullmastiff	St. Bernard
Collie	Samoyed
Doberman Pinscher	Schnauzer, Standard
German Shepherd Dog	Shetland Sheepdog
Giant Schnauzer	Siberian Husky
Great Dane	Welsh Corgi, Cardigan
	Welsh Corgi, Pembroke

GROUP IV—TERRIERS

Airedale Terrier	Lakeland Terrier
Australian Terrier	Manchester Terrier
Bedlington Terrier	Norwich Terrier
Border Terrier	Schnauzer, Miniature
Bull Terrier	Scottish Terrier
Cairn Terrier	Sealyham Terrier
Dandie Dinmont Terrier	Skye Terrier
Fox Terrier	Staffordshire Terrier
Irish Terrier	Welsh Terrier
Kerry Blue Terrier	West Highland White Terrier

GROUP V—TOYS

Affenpinscher	Papillon
Chihuahua	Pekingese
English Toy Spaniel	Pinscher, Miniature
Griffon, Brussels	Pomeranian
Italian Greyhound	Poodle (Toy)
Japanese Spaniel	Pug
Maltese	Shih Tzu
Manchester Terrier (Toy)	Silky Terrier
	Yorkshire Terrier

GROUP VI—NON-SPORTING DOGS

Boston Terrier	French Bulldog
Bulldog	Keeshond
Chow Chow	Lhasa Apso
Dalmatian	Poodle
	Schipperke

—Canadian Classifications—

THE CANADIAN Kennel Club classifications of the various breeds generally parallel those of AKC's. CKC's dog show rules of January, 1966* list the following as the recognized groups and breeds.

GROUP I—SPORTING DOGS

Griffons (Wire-haired Pointing) .	Setters (English) .
Pointers.	Setters (Gordon) .
Pointers (German Long-haired) .	Setters (Irish) .
Pointers (German Short-haired) .	Spaniels (American Cocker) .
Pointers (German Wire-haired) .	Spaniel (American Water) .
Pudelpointers	Spaniels (Brittany) .
Retrievers (Chesapeake Bay) .	Spaniels (Clumber) .
Retrievers (Curly-coated) .	Spaniels (English Springer) .
Retrievers (Flat-coated) .	Spaniels (Field) .
Retrievers (Golden) .	Spaniels (Irish Water) .
Retrievers (Labrador) .	Spaniels (Sussex) .
Retrievers (Nova Scotia Duck Tolling) .	Spaniels (Welsh Springer) .
	Tahl-Tan Bear Dogs.
	Vizslas
	Weimaraners.

GROUP II—SPORTING DOGS (HOUNDS)

Afghan Hounds.	Dachshunds (Miniature Wire-haired) .
Basenjis.	Dachshunds (Miniature Long-haired) .
Basset Hounds.	Deerhounds (Scottish) .
Beagles.	Drevers.
Bloodhounds.	Foxhounds (American) .
Borzois.	Foxhounds (English) .
Coonhounds (Black & Tan) .	Greyhounds.
Dachshunds (Standard Smooth) .	Harriers.
Dachshunds (Standard Long-haired) .	Norwegian Elkhounds.
Dachshunds (Standard Wire-haired) .	Otterhounds.
Dachshunds (Miniature Smooth) .	Rhodesian Ridgebacks.
	Salukis.
	Whippets.
	Wolfhounds (Irish) .

GROUP III—WORKING DOGS

Alaskan Malamutes.	Kuvasz.
Belgian Sheepdogs.	Newfoundlands.
Bouviers des Flandres.	Old English Mastiffs.
Boxers.	Old English Sheepdogs.
Briards.	Pulik.
Bullmastiffs.	Rottweilers.
Collies (Rough) .	Samoyeds.
Collies (Smooth) .	Schnauzers (Giant) .
Doberman Pinschers.	Schnauzers (Standard) .
Eskimos.	Shetland Sheepdogs.
German Shepherd Dogs.	Siberian Huskies.
Great Danes.	St. Bernards.
Great Pyrenees.	Welsh Corgis (Cardigan) .
Komondors.	Welsh Corgis (Pembroke) .

GROUP IV—TERRIERS

Airedale Terriers.	Lhasa Apsos.
Australian Terriers.	Manchester Terriers.
Bedlington Terriers.	Norwich Terriers.
Border Terriers.	Schnauzers (Miniature) .
Bull Terriers.	Scottish Terriers.
Cairn Terriers.	Sealyham Terriers.
Dandie Dinmont Terriers.	Skye Terriers.
Fox Terriers (Smooth) .	Staffordshire Bull Terriers.
Fox Terriers (Wire) .	Staffordshire Terriers.
Irish Terriers.	Welsh Terriers.
Kerry Blue Terriers.	West Highland White Terriers.
Lakeland Terriers.	

GROUP V—TOYS

Affenpinschers.	Mexican Hairless.
Cavalier King Charles Spaniels.	Papillons.
Chihuahuas (Long Coat) .	Pekingese.
Chihuahuas (Short Coat) .	Pinschers (Miniature) .
English Toy Spaniels.	Pomeranians.
Griffons (Brussels) .	Pugs.
Italian Greyhounds.	Silky Toy Terriers.
Japanese Spaniels.	Toy Manchester Terriers.
Maltese.	Toy Poodles.
	Yorkshire Terriers.

GROUP VI—NON-SPORTING

Boston Terriers.	Keeshonden.
Bulldogs.	Poodles (Miniature) .
Chow Chows.	Poodles (Standard) .
Dalmations.	Schipperkes.
French Bulldogs.	Shih Tzus.

* (Latest available at time of this edition.)

—English Classifications—

IN THE STUD book of the Kennel Club of Great Britain for the period 1859-1874 breeds were classified under the title "Pedigrees," as follows:

PEDIGREES
Sporting Dogs

Bloodhounds
Deerhounds
Greyhounds
Foxhounds
Otterhounds
Harriers
Beagles
Fox Terriers
Pointers
Setters (English)
Setters (Black and Tan)
Setters (Irish)
Retrievers
Clumber Spaniels
Irish Water Spaniels
Spaniels (Field, Cocker, and Sussex)
Water Spaniels Other than Irish
Dachshunds (or German Badger Hounds)

Non-Sporting Dogs

Mastiffs
St. Bernards (Rough and Smooth)
Newfoundlands
Dalmations (or Carriage Dogs)
Bulldogs
Bull Terriers (all sizes)
Sheep Dogs and Scotch Collies
Black and Tan Terriers (except Toys)
Dandie Dinmonts
Bedlington Terriers
Skye Terriers
Wire-Haired Terriers and Irish Terriers
English and Other Smooth-Haired Terriers
Broken-Haired Scotch and Yorkshire Terriers
Pomeranians
Italian Greyhounds
Pugs
Maltese
Blenheim Spaniels
King Charles's Spaniels
Toy Terriers (Smooth-Coated)
Toy Terriers (Rough and Broken-Haired)

The 1881 issue of the stud book shows very little change. The breeds are listed as follows:

PEDIGREES
Sporting

Bloodhounds
Deerhounds
Greyhounds
Foxhounds
Otterhounds
Harriers
Beagles
Fox Terriers
Wire-Haired Terriers
Pointers
Setters (English)
Setters (Black and Tan)
Setters (Irish)
Retrievers (Wavy-Coated)
Retrievers (Curly-Coated)
Spaniels (Irish)
Spaniels (Water, other than Irish.)
Spaniels (Clumber)
Spaniels (Sussex)
Spaniels (Field)
Dachshunds

Non-Sporting

Mastiffs
St. Bernards (Rough-Coated)
St. Bernards (Smooth-Coated)
Newfoundlands
Dalmatians
Colleys (Rough-Coated)
Colleys (Smooth-Coated)
Colleys (English Short-Tailed)
Bulldogs
Black and Tan or Manchester Terriers (except Toys)
Dandie Dinmont Terriers
Bedlington Terriers
Skye Terriers
English and Smooth-Coated Terriers (except Black and Tan)
Broken-Haired Scotch and Yorkshire Terriers
Pomeranians
Maltese
Italian Greyhounds
Pugs
Blenheim Spaniels
King Charles Spaniels
Poodles
Toy Terriers (Smooth-Coated)
Toy Terriers (Rough-Coated)
Irish Terriers

The Kennel Club (England), 1 Clarges Street, Piccadilly, London, W.I. has made available the following listing of breeds recognized (March, 1969) by that organization for the purpose of separate registration and stud book entries.

HOUND GROUP

Afghan Hounds.	Finnish Spitz.
Basenjis.	Foxhounds.
Basset Hounds.	Greyhounds.
Beagles.	Harriers.
Bloodhounds.	Irish Wolfhounds.
Borzois.	Otterhounds.
Dachshunds.	Rhodesian Ridgebacks.
Deerhounds.	Salukis.
Elkhounds.	Weimaraners.

GUNDOG GROUP

English Setters.	Pointers.
Gordon Setters.	German Shorthaired Pointers.
Irish Setters.	Retrievers.
Setters (Crossbred).	Weimaraners.

TERRIER GROUP

Airedale Terriers.	Lakeland Terriers.
Australian Terriers.	Manchester Terriers.
Bedlington Terriers.	Norfolk Terriers.
Border Terriers.	Norwich Terriers.
Bull Terriers.	Scottish Terriers.
Cairn Terriers.	Sealyham Terriers.
Dandie Dinmont Terriers.	Skye Terriers.
Fox Terriers.	Staffordshire Bull Terriers.
Irish Terriers.	Welsh Terriers.
Kerry Blue Terriers.	West Highland White Terriers.

UTILITY GROUP

Boston Terriers.
Bulldogs.
Chow Chows.
Dalmations.
French Bulldogs.
Keeshonds.
Poodles.

Schipperkes.
Schnauzers.
Miniature Schnauzers.
Shih Tzus.
Tibetan Apsos.
Tibetan Spaniels.
Tibetan Terriers.

TOY GROUP

Chihuahuas.
English Toy Terriers
    (Black and Tan).
Griffons Bruxellois.
Italian Greyhounds.
Japanese.
Toy Spaniels.

Maltese.
Miniature Pinschers.
Papillons.
Pekingese.
Pomeranians.
Pugs.
Yorkshire Terriers.

WORKING GROUP

Alsatians (German Shepherd
    Dogs).
Bearded Collies.
Boxers.
Bullmastiffs.
Collies.
Dobermanns.
Great Danes.
Mastiffs.

Newfoundlands.
Norwegian Buhunds.
Old English Sheepdogs.
Pyrenean Mountain Dogs.
Rottweilers.
St. Bernards.
Samoyeds.
Shetland Sheepdogs.
Welsh Corgis (Cardigan).
Welsh Corgis (Pembroke).

–Bermuda Kennel Club Classifications–

THE FOLLOWING listing of the regular official classes of the Bermuda Kennel Club appears through the courtesy of that organization.

GROUP I—SPORTING BREEDS

Griffons (Wire-haired
    Pointing).
Pointers.
Pointers (German
    Long-haired).
Pointers (German
    Short-haired).
Pointers (German
    Wired-haired).
Pudelpointers
Retrievers (Chesapeake
    Bay).
Retrievers (Curly-coated).
Retrievers (Flat coated).
Retrievers (Golden).
Retrievers (Labrador).
Retrievers (Nova Scotia
    Duck Tolling).

Setters (Gordon).
Setters (Irish).
Spaniels (American Cocker).
Setters (English).
Spaniels (American Water).
Spaniels (Brittany).
Spaniels (Clumber).
Spaniels (English Cocker).
Spaniels (English
    Springer).
Spaniels (Field).
Spaniels (Irish Water).
Spaniels (Sussex).
Spaniels (Welsh
    Springer).
Tahl-Tan Bear Dogs.
Vizslas
Weimaraners.

GROUP II—HOUND BREEDS

Afghan Hounds.
Basenjis.
Basset Hounds.
Beagles.
Bloodhounds.
Borzois.
Coonhounds (Black & Tan).
Dachshunds (Standard
    Smooth).
Dachshunds (Standard
    Long-haired).
Dachshunds (Standard
    Wire-haired).
Dachshunds (Miniature
    Smooth).

Dachshunds (Miniature
    Wire-haired).
Dachshunds (Miniature
    Long-haired).
Deerhounds (Scottish).
Drevers.
Foxhounds (American).
Foxhounds (English).
Greyhounds.
Harriers.
Norwegian Elkhounds.
Otterhounds.
Rhodesian Ridgebacks.
Salukis.
Whippets.
Wolfhounds (Irish).

GROUP III—WORKING BREEDS

Alaskan Malamutes.
Belgian Sheepdogs.
Bouviers des Flandres.
Boxers.
Briards.
Bullmastiffs.
Collies (Rough).
Collies (Smooth).
Doberman Pinschers.
Eskimos.
German Shepherd Dogs.
Great Danes.
Great Pyrenees.
Komondors.

Kuvasz.
Newfoundlands.
Old English Mastiffs.
Old English Sheepdogs.
Pulik.
Rottweilers.
Samoyeds.
Schnauzers (Giant).
Schnauzers (Standard).
Shetland Sheepdogs.
Siberian Huskies.
St. Bernards.
Welsh Corgis (Cardigan).
Welsh Corgis (Pembroke).

Best in Show award on the first day of the 1968 Bermuda International Dog Show went to this Miniature Poodle, Am. Ch. Harmo Gay Prospector, owned by Harmo Kennels and handled by William J. Trainor. Bermuda News Bureau photo.

GROUP IV—TERRIER BREEDS

Airedale Terriers.
Australian Terriers.
Bedlington Terriers.
Border Terriers.
Bull Terriers.
Cairn Terriers.
Dandie Dinmont Terriers.
Fox Terriers (Smooth).
Fox Terriers (Wire).
Irish Terriers.
Kerry Blue Terriers.
Lakeland Terriers.

Lhasa Apsos.
Manchester Terriers.
Norwich Terriers.
Schnauzers (Miniature).
Scottish Terriers.
Sealyham Terriers.
Skye Terriers.
Staffordshire Bull Terriers.
Staffordshire Terriers.
Welsh Terriers.
West Highland White
  Terriers.

GROUP V—TOY BREEDS

Affenpinschers.
Cavalier King Chas. Spaniels.
Chihuahuas (Long Coat).
Chihuahuas (Short Coat).
English Toy Spaniels.
Griffons (Brussels).
Italian Greyhounds.
Japanese Spaniels.
Maltese.

Mexican Hairless.
Papillons.
Pekingese.
Pinschers (Miniature).
Pomeranians.
Poodles (Toy).
Pugs.
Toy Manchester Terriers.
Yorkshire Terriers.

GROUP VI—NON-SPORTING BREEDS

Boston Terriers.
Bulldogs.
Chow Chows.
Dalmatianns.
French Bulldogs.

Keeshonden.
Poodles (Miniature).
Poodles (Standard).
Schipperkes.
Shih Tzus.

—F.C.I. Classifications—

FEDERATION CYNOLOGIQUE Internationale (F.C.I.) which with AKC and the British Kennel Clubs are the three leading canine authorities in the world, maintains offices at 12. Rue Leopold II, Thuin, Belgium. As the name implies, it is a federation, its members representing a number of countries, mostly European, all consenting to certain uniform practices, breed identifications, etc. Currently, F.C.I. lists its classifications as below; words asterisked merely indicate the name as related to a particular region or place.

Premiere Groupe (1st Group)

a) **Cheins de Berger** (Shepherd dogs, subject to work)

Beauce, noir et feu (Beauce*, black and red)
Beauce, fauves, gris (Beauce*, tawny, grey)
Brie, noir ardoisé (Brie*, slate-black)
Brie, fauves, gris (Brie*, tawny, grey)
Picards*
Pyrénées*
Allemands (Germans)
Bergers Belges (Belgium shepherds)
   noirs (Groenendaels) (black, long hair)
   fauve (Tervueren) (tawny) (long hair)
   autres que fauve et noirs (other than tawny and black)
      (long hair)
   fauves (Malinois) (tawny, from Malines) (short hair)
   noirs (black) (short hair)
   autres que noirs et fauves (other than black and tawny)
      (short hair)
Collies:
   Blue merle, poil long ("blackbird" blue, long hair)
   Toutes couleurs, poil long (all colors, long hair)
   A poil ras (short hair)
Shetland
Bobtails
Welsh Corgis (Pembroke)
Welsh Corgis (Cardigan)
Bouviers (Toilettage rigoureusement interdit) (cattle herding dogs—clippings strictly forbidden)
Bergers Hongrois (Hungarian cattle herding dogs)

b) **Garde-Utilité** (Watchdogs, not subject to work)

Rottweiler
Dobermann, noir et feu (black and rusty-red)
Dobermann, fauves (tawny)

Dogues Allemands (German Mastiffs)
   Fauves (tawny)
   Bringés (spotted, brindled)
   Noirs (black)
   Bleus (blue)
   Arlequins (Harlequins)
Dogues de Bordeaux (Bordeaux Mastiffs)
Mastiffs et Bull Mastiffs (Mastiffs and Bull Mastiffs)
Boxers jaunes (yellow Boxers)
   —bringé (brindled Boxers)
Bull Dogs
Rhodésian
Schnauzers géants (Giant)
   —moyens (Medium)
   —nains (Dwarf)
   Poivre et sel (black and white)
   Noirs (black)
Pinschers moyens (medium Pinschers)
Montagne Pyrénées (Pyrenees Mountain dog)
Saint Bernard poil long (with long hair)
   ——poil court (with short hair)
Terre-Neuve (Newfoundland)
Léonberg
Sennenhunde

Chiens de Trait (Draft dogs)

Esquimaux, blancs et couleurs (Huskies, Mémelutes) (Eskimo, white and other colors, Huskies, Malamutes)
Elkhounds (gris et poirs) (grey and white)
Samoyédes
   Blancs à poil long (white with long hair)
   couleurs à poil long (colored, with long hair)
   Blanc à poil ½ long (white, medium-length hair)
   Couleurs à poil ½ long (colored, medium-length hair)
Spitz Loup (ex-Keeshond) (Spitz Wolf) (ex-Keeshond)
   45 cm minimum (17½ inches, minimum)
Laihis

Deuxième Groupe (2nd Group)

Terriers
   Fox, poil lisse (smooth-haired)
   —, poil dur (wiry hair)
   Airedales
   Welsh
   Manchester
   Bull
   Sealyham
   Bedlington

Irish-Blue (Kerry blue)
Lakeland
Irish
Staffordshire
Jagd-Terriers
Scottish
Cairn
West Highland White
Dandie-Dinmonts
Skye
Border

Troisième Groupe (3rd Group)

Grands Chiens Courants Francais— (Chiens a Poil Ras)
Tall French runnings dogs—short hair)
Grands Bleus de Gascogne* (tail blue of Gascogne)
Grands Gascons Saintongeois* (tall Gascons Saintongeois)
Levesque*
Poitevins*
Billy*
Francais Tricolores (French, three colors)
Francais Blancs et Noirs (French, black and white)
Francais Blancs et Orange (French, white and orange)

Quatrième Groupe (4th Group)

Chiens Courants Francais de Moyenne Taille et Bassets
(French running dogs, medium-size and Dachshunds)
1 re Section—Chiens à Poil Ras (1st section—short hair)
Petits Bleus de Gascogne (small, blue, of Gascogne)
Petits Gascons Saintongeois (small Gascons Saintongeois)
Ariégeois*
Chiens d'Artois (dogs of Artois)
Porcelaines (China)
2 e Section—Chiens à Poil Long (2nd section—dogs with
long hair)
Griffons Nivernais* (setters Nivernais)
Briquets Griffons Vendéens (Brisquets setter Vendeens)
Griffons Bleus de Gascogne (blue setters of Gascogne)
Griffons Fauves de Bretagne (tawny setters of Bretagne)
3 e Section—Bassets Francais (3rd section—Dachshunds,
French; short-legged running dogs)
Bassets Artésians-Normands (Dachshunds of named re-
gions)
Bassets Bleus de Gascogne (blue Dachshunds of Gas-
cogne)
Bassets Griffons Vendéens (Dachshunds Setters of Vendee)
Bassets Fauves de Bretagne (tawny Dachshunds of
Brittany)

Cinquième Groupe (5th Group)

Chiens Courants de Races Anglaises (English running dogs,
hounds for big game—harts, wild boars)
1 re Section—Grands Chiens Anglais (1st section—tall
English running dogs)
Fox-Hounds
2 e Section—Petits Chiens Courants Anglais (2nd section
—Small English running dogs)
Harriers Modernes
Harriers du Somerset
Beagles-Harriers
Beagles

Sixième Groupe (6th Group)

Chiens Anglo-Francais (Anglo-French dogs, hounds for
small game—hares, rabbits)
1 re Section—Grand Anglo-Francais, o.m. 60 minimum
1st section—tall Anglo-French dogs, 23½ inches minimum)
Anglo Francais Tricolores (tricolor)
Anglo Francais Blancs et Noirs (black and white)
Anglo Francais Blancs et Orange (white and orange)
this includes crossbreeds between Fox-Hounds and Terriers)
2 e Section—Anglo-Francais de Moyenne Taille, 0, 51 à o,
60. (medium-sized Anglo-French dogs, 20" to 23½"
height)

Anglo-Francais Tricolores (tricolor)
Anglo-Francais Blancs et Noirs (white and black)
Anglo-Francais Blancs et Orange (white and orange)
(this includes crossbreeds from Harriers and French
running dogs, short-haired, Dachshund excepted, 16 to
19 inches height)
3 e Section—Anglo-Francais de petite taille (small-sized
dogs, height, 16 to 19½ inches)
Anglo-Francais
issus du croisement du Beagle ou Beagle Harrier avec
des races du quatrième Groupe à poil ras (bassets
exceptés). (Crossbreeds from beagle or beagle-harrier
or French running dogs, short-haired, Dachshunds
excepted.)

Septième Groupe (7th Group)

Arrêt-Continentaux (Continental setters, sporting dogs ex-
cept English breeds)
Braques (pointers)
De L'Ariège (from Ariège)
D'Auvergne*
Du Bourbonnais*
Du Puy*
Francais (French)
Saint-Germain*
Allemands (German)
Divers Étrangers (various foreigners)

Epagneuls (spaniels)

Bretons (bl. marron) (spaniels from Brittany-blue-brown)
— (bl. orange) (same, blue-orange)
— (bl. noirs) (same, blue-black)
Francais (French)
Picards*
Bleus Picards* (blue Picards)
Pont Audemer*
Allemands (German)
Griffons à poil dur (setters with wiry hair)
— à poil laineux (with woolly hair)
Barbets
Spinones
Drahthaar
Stichelharr
Pudel-Pointers
Wachtelhund

Huitième Groupe (8th Group)

Arrêt Anglais (English sporting dogs)
Pointers
Setters Anglais (English setters)
Setters Irlandais (Irish setters)
Setters Gordon (Gordon setters)
Retrievers (Flat coated)
— (Labrador)
— (Golden)
Chesapeake Bay
Cockers (Noirs) (black Cockers)
— Rouges et Golden) (red and golden)
— (Autres couleurs) (other colors)
Clumbers
Sussex
Welsh
Springers
Irish-Water

Neuvième Groupe (9th Group—breeds of fancy dogs)

Caniches a Poil Bouclé (poodles)
Blancs (white poodle, curled hair, 14 to 17½ inches
height)
Blancs (same, 17½ to 21½ inches height)
Marron (brown poodle, height 14 to 17½ inches)
Marron (same, 17½ to 21½ inches height)
Noirs (black poodle, height 14 to 17½ inches)
Noirs (same height, 17½ to 21½ inches)

Caniches a Poil Cordé (poodles with wiry hair)
   Mêmes tailles et couleurs que pour ceux à poil bouclé)
    (in same sizes and colors in preceding listing)
Caniches Nains (dwarf poodles)
   Blancs (white, less than 14 inches tall)
   Marrons (brown, same height specifications)
   Noirs (black, same height specifications)
Chow-Chows
   Bleus (blue)
   Crème (cream or light beige)
   Noirs (black)
   Roux-Fauve (rusty-tawny)
Dalmatiens (Dalmatians)
Bouledogues Francais (French bulldogs)
   Bringés, mâles (males, 17.6 to 24.2 lbs.)
   Mâles (brindled, 22.2 to 30.8 lbs.)
   Femelles (Females, 13.4 to 22 lbs.)
   Femelles (Females, 22 to 28.6 lbs.)
   Caille, mêmes poids
Bichons Polonais (Polish dog—Usually small)
   A Poil Frisé (with curled hair)
   Havanais (Cuban dog)
   Maltais (lap dog from Malta)
Espagneuls Nains Continentaux (dwarf Continental spaniels)
   — Poids minimum 1 kg 500 (minimum weight, 3.3 lb.)
   — Les phalènes (the Phalene)
   — Moins de 2 kg 500 (less than 5.5 lb.)
   — de 2 kg 5 à 4 kg (from 3.3 to 8.8 lbs.)
   — 4 kg 5 pour les femelles (females, 8.8 to 9.9 lb.)
Les Papillons
   Moins de 2 kg 5 (less than 3.3 lbs.)
   de 2 kg 5 à 4 kg (from 3.3 to 8.8 lbs.)
   4 kg 5 pour les femelles (females, 8.8 to 9.9 lbs.)
Epagneuls Japonais (Japanese spaniels) (There are two sub-divisions divided by specifications as to colors and weight.)
Epagneuls Pékinois (various Pekingese sub-divisions by color and weight specifications)
Epagneuls Nains Anglais (dwarf English spaniels)
   Blenheims
   King-Charles
   Prince Charles
   Ruby
Carlins
   Beige à masque noir (beige with black mask)
   Noirs (black)
Griffons Belges (Belgian setters) (subdivisions with specified weights)

Griffons Bruxellois (setters from Brussels; subdivisions as for Belgian setters)
Brabancons (dogs from Brabant)
Grands Spitz (ex-Grands-Loulous) (Tall Spitz; ex-tall Loulous) (Subdivisions for white, black, and brown, 16-inch minimum.)
Spitz Nains (ex-Loulons de Poméranie) (dwarf Spitz) (Color subdivisions for white, brown, orange, black, and wolf, 11-inch maximum.)
Affenpinschers
Pinschers Nains (dwarf Pinschers)
   A Poil Ras, unicolores (with short hair, one color)
   —, bicolors (same, two-color)
Schipperkes (There are several weight subdivisions)
Terriers du Yorkshire
Terriers de Boston
Terriers du Lhassa
Toy Terriers
Griffons Du Thibet (Thibetan setters)
Chiens Nus (naked or hairless dogs) (subdivisions for those with straight toupet and those without)
Chihuahuas

Dixième Groupe (10th Group)

Lévriers (Greyhounds—whippets)

   Greyhounds
   Whippets
   Sloughis
   Galgos
   Charnigues
   Barzois
   Deerhounds
   Irish Wolfhounds
   Persans (Salukis) (Persians—Salukis)
   Afghans
   Petits Lévriers Italiens (small Italian greyhounds)

Onzième Groupe (11th Group)

   Teckels (Dachshunds)
    Poil ras unicolore (short hair, monocolor)
    Poil ras bicolore (same, bicolor)
    Poil long unicolore (long hair, monocolor)
    Poil long bicolore (same, bicolor)
    Poil dur unicolore (wiry hair, monocolor)
    Poil dur bicolore (wiry hair, bicolor)

   (There are also subdivisions for dwarfs with specifications based on sex, hair texture, and a weight maximum of 8.8 lbs. for males, 7.7 lbs. for females.)

—German Classifications—

THE GERMAN classifications follow a simple line based on what the dog is supposed to do. The divisions follow:

I. Jagdhunde (shooting dog breeds—hounds)
II. Hetzhunde (Windhunde) (sporting dogs and stag hounds)
III. Gebrauchshunde (Diensthunde) (service or duty dogs)
IV. Schutz, Wach- und Haushunde (Gesellschaftshunde) (house dogs, watchdogs, miniature dogs)

GROUP I—SHOOTING DOG BREEDS

Bracken
Foxhounds
Hannoversche Schweisshunde (Hanoverian bloodhounds)

Bayerische Gebirgsschweisshunde (Bavarian mountain bloodhounds)
Deutsche Wachtelhunde (German spaniels)
Jagdspaniel (Hunting spaniels)
Kurzhaarige deutsche Vorstehhunde (German setters)
Weimaraner (dog bred in Weimer, a city in Germany)
Langhaarige deutsche Vorstehhunde (Long-haired German pointers)
Schwarzweisse grosse Munsterlander Vorstehhunde (Black and white large Munsterland pointers)
Kleine Munsterlander Vorstehhunde (Small Munsterland pointers)
Griffon
Pudelpointer (Poodle pointers)
Stichelhaarige deutsche Vorstehhunde

Deutsche drahthaarige Vorstehhunde (German wire-haired pointers)

Englische Vorstehhunde—Pointer und Setter (English pointers and setters)

Dachshunde Teckel, Dackel (Badger dogs)

Foxterrier

Deutsche Jagdterrier (German hunting terriers)

Schottische Terrier (Scottish terriers)

GROUP II—STAGHOUND AND SPORTING DOG BREEDS

Barsois (Borzois)

Salukis (Salukis or gazelle hounds)

Afghanische Windhunde (Afghan greyhounds)

Irische Windhunde (Irish greyhounds)

Irische Wolfshunde (Irish Wolfhounds)

Greyhounds

Whippets

Italienische Windspiele (Italian greyhounds)

GROUP III—SERVICE OR DUTY DOG BREEDS

Deutsche Schäferhunde (German sheepdogs)

Dobermannpinscher (Doberman pinschers)

Airedaleterrier (Airedale terriers)

Rottweiler (from Rottweil, a German city)

Boxer (Boxers)

Riesenschnauzer (Giant Schnauzers)

Hovawart-Hunde

GROUP IV—HOUSE, UTILITY AND WATCHDOG BREEDS

Bernhardiner (St. Bernard)

Neufundlander (Newfoundlands)

Leonberger (Leonberg dog—name of city where dog is raised)

Deutsche Doggen (German bulldogs or mastiffs)

Bordeaux-Doggen (Bordeaux bulldogs or mastiffs)

Ungarische Hitenhunde—Komondore, Kuvasz, Puli (Hungarian sheepdogs)

Schweizer Sennenhunde (Swiss sheepdogs)

Bodenständige Hütehunde (German watch dogs)

Bobtails

Englische Bulldoggen (English bulldogs)

Pudel (Poodles)

Spitze (Spitz dogs)

Chow-Chow

Nordische Spitze (Scandinavian Spitz dogs)

Samojeden (Samoyeds)

Schnauzer (Rough-haired terrier)

Pinscher

Kleine rauhhaarige Terrier—Schlage—Irische, Welsch, Sealyham, Weisse Hochland, Skye und Cairn-Terrier (Small, rough-haired terrier types—Irish, Welsh, Sealyham, White Highland, Skye, and Cairn Terriers)

Yorkshire-Terrier

Bedlington-Terrier

Bullterrier (Bull terriers)

Dalmatiner (Dalmatians)

Französische Bulldoggen (French bulldogs)

Black-and-Tan Terrier

Zwergschnauzer (Miniature schnauzers)

Zwergpinscher (Miniature pinschers)

Affenpinscher (Griffons—affe means ape, monkey)

Japan-Chin, Peking-Palasthunde und Zwergspaniel (Japanese-Chin, Peking Palace dogs and miniature spaniels)

Zwerggriffon (Miniature Griffons)

Malteser (Maltese dogs)

Mopse (Pugs)

—Spanish Classifications—

INQUIRIES RELATIVE the classifications of dogs in Spain should be addressed to the Real Sociedad Canina de Espana, Madrazo 20, Madrid, Spain. The following were listed in the previous edition of this text as officially-recognized Spanish breeds:

WATCH OR DEFENSE DOGS

Bardino

Perro de presa español (bull dog)

Perro de pressa mallorquin (from the Balearic Islands)

SPANISH GREYHOUND

Galgo español

SHEPHERD DOGS

Mastin español (large mastiff)

Mastin de los Pirineos (Border mastiff)

Perro de pastor catalin (shepherd dog)

TRACK HOUNDS

Alano

Podenco

Podenco ibicenco

Sabueso (beagle)

GUNDOGS

Barbas

Gorgas de Alciante

Pachon de Vitoria (pointer)

Pachon de Navarra (pointer)

Perdiguero (setter)

Perdiguero de Burgos

Perdiguero de Malorca

F.C.I. listings (Fall, 1969) indicate that specific standards have been approved by that organization for the following Spanish breeds:

Podenco ibicenco

Perdiguero de Burgos

Mastin español

Mastin de los Pirineos

Perro de presa malorquin

(For some details on the Perro de pastor catalin and the Ibizan Podenco, see Part XVII.)

—Swedish Classifications—

NATIVES OF Sweden have always been great dog lovers. The governing body of the fancy in that country is the Svenska Kennel Klubben. Norway, Finland, and Denmark are also represented as to standards and classifications by this organization. The breeds recognized by this organization follow.

GRUPP A. SPETSHUNDAR	GROUP A. SPITZDOGS
Akita inu	Akita dog
Alaskan malamute	Alaskan Malamute
Basenji	Basenji
Chow-chow	Chow-chow
Finsk spets	Finnish Spitz
Gråhund	Norwegian Elkhound, grey
Grönlandshund	Greenland dog
Jämthund	Swedish Elkhound
Karelsk björnhund	Karelian Beardog
Keeshond	Keeshond
Lapphund	Swedish Lapp Spitz
Lappsk vallhund	Finnish Lapp Spitz
Lundehund	Norwegian Puffin Dog or Norwegian Lundehund
Norrbottenspets	Norrbotten Spitz
Norsk buhund	Norwegian Buhund
Samojedhund	Samoyed
Siberian husky	Siberian Husky
Svart älghund	Norwegian Elkhound, black, or Black Elkhound
Welsh corgi cardigan	Welsh Corgi Cardigan
Welsh corgi pembroke	Welsh Corgi Pembroke
Västgötaspets	Vastgota Spitz
(21 raser)	(21 breeds)

GRUPP B. DRIVANDE HUNDAR	GROUP B. HOUNDS
Basset	Basset
Bayersk viltspårhund	Bayerischer Gebirgeschweisshund (German Hound)
Beagle	Beagle
Drever	Drever (Swedish Beagle)
Dunkerstövare	Dunker (Norwegian Fox Hound
Dvärgtax, korthårig	Smooth-haired Dachshund (miniature)
Dvärgtax, långhårig	Long-haired Dachshund (miniature)
Dvärgtax, strävhårig	Wire-haired Dachshund (miniature)
Finsk stövare	Finnish Foxhound
Foxhound	Foxhound
Haldenstövare	Haldenstovare (Norwegian Foxhound)
Hamiltonstövare	Hamiltonstovare (Swedish Foxhound)
Hanoveransk viltspårhund	Hannoverscher Sweisshund (German hound)
Hygenhund	Hygenhound (Norwegian Foxhound)
Kanintax, korthårig	Smooth-haired Dachshund (toy)
Kanintax, långhårig	Long-haired Dachshund (toy)
Kanintax, strävhårig	Wire-haired Dachshund (toy)
Luzernstövare	Luzerner Laufhund (Swiss Hound)
Schillerstövare	Schillerstovare (Swedish (Hound)
Schweizerstövare	Schweizer Laufhund (Swiss Hound)

Smålandsstövare	Smalandsstovare (Swedish Hound)
Tax, korthårig	Smooth-haired Dachshund
Tax, långhårig	Long-haired Dachshund
Tax, strävhårig	Wire-haired Dachshund
(24 raser)	(24 breeds)

GRUPP C. FÅGELHUDAR	GROUP C. GUNDOGS
Amerikansk cocker spaniel	American Cocker Spaniel
Bretagn spaniel	Brittany Spaniel
Chesapeake bay retriever	Chesapeake Bay Retriever
Clumber spaniel	Clumber Spaniel
Cocker spaniel	Cocker Spaniel
Curly-coated retriever	Curley-coated Retriever
Engelsk setter	English Setter
Flat-coated retriever	Flat-coated Retriever
Gammal dansk honshund	Old Danish Gundog
Golden retriever	Golden Retriever
Gordon setter	Gordon Setter
Irländsk setter	Irish Setter
Irländsk vattenspaniel	Irish Waterspaniel
Labrador retriever	Labrador Retriever
Liten munsterländer	Kleiner Münsterländer (German spaniel)
Pointer	Pointer
Springer spaniel	Springer Spaniel
Sussex spaniel	Sussex Spaniel
Wachtelhund	Wachtelhund (German spaniel)
Weimaraner	Weimaraner
Welsh springer spaniel	Welsh Springer Spaniel
Vorsteh, korthårig	German Pointer, short-haired
Vorsteh, strävhårig	German Pointer, wire-haired
(23 raser)	(23 breeds)

GRUPP D. BRUKSHUNDAR	GROUP D. WORKING DOGS
Bouvier des flandres	Bouvier des Flandres
Boxer	Boxer
Briard	Briard
Collie	Collie

Here on point is Cumberland Jake, a Swedish Pointer owned by Dr. R. G. Winkelbauer of Brunswick, Maine. Jake's parents were imported by Mr. H. O. Williams of Griffin, Georgia, from whom Jake was acquired. Photo courtesy R. G. Winkelbauer, M.D.

Doberman	Doberman
Groenendael	Groenendael
Hovawart	Hovawart (German working dog)
Riesenschnauzer	Giant Schnauzer (German working dog)
Rottweiler	Rottweiler
Schäfer	Alsation
Tervuerense	Belgian Tervuren (Belgian sheep dog)
(11 raser)	(11 breeds)

GRUPP E. TERRIER	**GROUP E. TERRIERS**
Airdale terrier	Airdale Terrier
Australisk terrier	Australian Terrier
Bedlington terrier	Bedlington Terrier
Border terrier	Border Terrier
Bull terrier	Bull Terrier
Cairn terrier	Cairn Terrier
Dandie dinmont terrier	Dandie Dinmont Terrier
Foxterrier, slåthårig	Fox Terrier, smooth-haired
Foxterrier, strävhårig	Fox Terrier, wire-haired
Irländsk terrier	Irish Terrier
Kerry blue terrier	Kerry Blue Terrier
Lakeland terrier	Lakeland Terrier
Manchester terrier	Manchester Terrier
Miniatyr bullterrier	Miniature Bullterrier
Norfolk terrier	Norfolk Terrier
Norwich terrier	Norwich Terrier
Sealyham terrier	Sealyham Terrier
Skotsk terrier	Scottish Terrier
Skye terrier	Skye Terrier
Staffordshire bull terrier	Staffordshire Bull Terrier
Tysk jaktterrier	German Hunting Terrier
Wheaten terrier	Wheaten Terrier
Welsh terrier	Welsh Terrier
West highland white terrier	West Highland White Terrier
(24 raser)	(24 breeds)

GRUPP F. VINTHUNDAR	**GROUP F. HOUNDS**
Afghanhund	Afghan hound
Greyhound	Greyhound
Irländsk varghund	Irish Wolfhound
Italiensk vinthund	Italian Greyhound
Podenco ibicenco	Podenco Ibicenco or Ibizan Hound or Pharaoh Hound (Spanish Hound)
Podenco portugues	Podenco Portuguese (Portoguise Hound)
Rysk vinthund	Borzoi
Saluki	Saluki
Skotsk hjorthund	Deerhound
Whippet	Whippet
(10 raser)	(10 breeds)

GRUPP G. SÄLLSKAPSHUNDAR	**GROUP G. NON-SPORTING DOGS**
Appenzeller sennenhund	Appenzeller Mountain Dog (Swiss breed)
Bearded collie	Bearded Collie

(English translations in corresponding right-hand columns.)

Berner sennenhund	Bernese Mountain Dog (Swiss breed)
Blodhund	Bloodhound
Bullmastiff	Bullmastiff
Dalmatiner	Dalmatian
Engelsk bulldog	English Bulldog
Entlebucher sennenhund	Entlebucher Mountain Dog (Swiss breed)
Grand danois	Great Dane
Grosser schweizer sennenhund	Great Swiss Mountain Dog
Kromfohrländer	Kromfohrländer (German breed)
Kuvasz	Kuvasz
Leonberger	Leonberger (German breed)
Mastiff	Mastiff
Mellanpinscher	German Pinscher, or Pinscher
Mellanschnauzer	Standard Schnauzer
Newfoundlandshund	Newfoundland
Old English Sheepdog	Old English Sheepdog
Polski owczarek	Polski Owczarek (Polish breed)
Pudle, dvärg	Poodle, toy
Pudel, mellan	Poodle, miniature
Pudel, stor	Poodle, large
Puli	Puli (Hungarian Sheepdog)
Pumi	Pumi (Hungarian Sheepdog)
Pyreneerhund	Pyrenean Mountain Dog
Rhodesian ridgeback	Rhodesian Ridgeback
S : t Berhardshund	St Bernard
Shetland Sheepdog	Shetland Sheepdog
Tibetansk terrier	Tibetan terrier
(29 raser)	(29 breeds)

GRUPP H. DVÄRGHUNDAR	**GROUP H. TOY DOGS**
Affenpinscher	Affenpinscher
Australisk silky terrier	Australian silky terrier
Bostonterrier	Boston Terrier
Cavalier king charles spaniel	Cavalier King Charles Spaniel
Chihuahua, långhårig	Long-haired Chihuahua
Chihuahua, korthårig	Smooth-haired Chihuahua
Dvärgpinscher	Miniature Pinscher
Dvärgschnauzer	Miniature Schnauzer
Dvärgspets	Toy Pomeranian
English toy terrier	English Toy Terrier
Fransk bulldog	French Bulldog
Griffon brabancon	Griffon Brabancon
Griffon bruxellois	Griffon Bruxellois
Japanese chin	Japanese
King charles spaniel	King Charles Spaniel
Lhasa apso	Lhasa Apso
Malteser	Maltese
Mops	Pug
Papillon	Papillon
Phalene	Phalène
Pekingese	Pekingese
Schipperke	Schipperke
Shih-tzu	Shih-tzu
Tibetansk spaniel	Tibetan Spaniel
Yorkshire terrier	Yorkshire Terrier
(25 raser)	(25 breeds)

—Other Classifications—

(See also UKC, Part XVIII—
KENNEL CLUBS)

Part XVII

DOGS AROUND THE WORLD

The average dog's life span of course, is much shorter than man's. While it is a difficult task indeed to try to comfort one disconsolate at the loss of the dog to which he had become strongly attached, it has frequently been suggested that dogs exist in such abundance and in so many different shapes, sizes and types that the individual dog may readily be replaced. Still, in every part of the world, the warm companionship and affection between dog and man tends to become of tender character, whether the dog happens to be pure-bred or mixed breed, whether he is of some little-known breed or is a dog of outstanding talents, as perhaps a dog movie star or an outstanding hunter. Within the families of American Presidents, dogs, too, have endeared themselves and by their antics kindled the lively interest of the public at large, for members of the press and news media have been ever sensitive of the human interest aspects surrounding the fables, capers and sometimes newsworthy exploits of White House dogs, whatever the era.

—Dogs of the World—

IT HAS been estimated that there are at least 400 reasonably distinct breeds of dogs in the world. Many of these breeds will not be pure-bred in the sense that the term is used in the United States. But they will conform sufficiently to type to be recognizable as a breed.

Of these, over one hundred breeds and varieties are recognized and registered by the American Kennel Club. In addition, half a dozen others are given a partial recognition by being placed in the "Miscellaneous Class."

Some of these breeds, such as the Akita, are quite close to complete recognition. That is, before long they may be given stud book status and may then compete for championships.

The Norwegian Elkhound is a representative of the Nordic dogs which is now known worldwide, but particularly popular in the United States and Canada. The sled dogs, too, may be considered Nordic dogs.

DOGS OF THE SPITZ TYPE

The Spitz group includes the Chow Chow, Pomeranian, Keeshond, and Schipperke. It also includes a breed which has been, so to speak, appropriated by a

number of countries. It is a medium-sized white dog which is often called just a Spitz.

In Germany, it is called the German White Spitz. But in Japan, where the breed is tremendously popular, it is called the Japanese Spitz. In the United States, the United Kennel Club registers the breed as the American Eskimo. The Hong Kong Kennel Club has been seeking recognition for the breed as the Miniature Samoyed.

The Japanese claim the dog is native to their islands. But White Russian refugees have said that they brought the dogs to Shanghai, Hong Kong, and other cities on China's Pacific Coast, from Russia. This from 1917 to 1920.

If the Peat Dogs spread originally from the Swiss Lakes, and from Finland, as is believed, then the White Russians would be making merely a later migration with Spitz dogs, for no later than 400 A.D., Spitz dogs (the Akita) had reached Japan and (the Chow Chow) China.

The Akita is the largest of three Spitz-type, but short-haired dogs of Japan. Following World War II, American military personnel became impressed by the dogs and began to bring them back to the United States.

The general qualifications for AKC recognition in this country are that there must be 600 dogs, pure-bred, and with certified pedigrees from their home-land, in the United States. Moreover, the 600 must be reasonably well scattered about the country. Today, the Akita is very close to U.S. recognition.

Largest of the ancient Nippon Inu or Japanese pure-bred, the Akita takes its name from the Province of Akita on the Japanese Island of Honshu where it was originally developed from the medium-size Kari, the Tosa Fighting Dog, and other breeds imported from Europe. (*Note:* In Japanese, the word "Inu" means "dog.") In addition to the Akita and Kari, there is a smaller-size of the Nippon Inu called the Shiba. The pointed, upright ears, tail curled over the back and rather full double-coat indicates a possible relationship to the ancestors of the sled-dog breeds. The Akita has been called a smooth-coated Chow Chow, but he lacks the blue tongue of the latter. He is slightly longer than tall.

The written history of the Akita is about 100 years old and tells of the care and training of these dogs to work with hawks in hunting both small and large game, as well as serving as an affectionate pet and protector of the home. A massive dog, the Akita stands about 20 to 27 inches at the shoulder and weighs from 95 to 125 pounds. Color varies from black through fawn and red through white with guard hairs being red, silver or black tipped. The eyes are dark brown. His coat is usually a solid color. Some even are a light cream, almost white.

The smaller edition of the Akita is sometimes called the Nippon Inu. But in Japan they are referred to only as the Japanese Middle-Sized Dog. They are almost identical to the Akita, but their size range is from 17 to 21 inches at the shoulder.

The smallest dog of this type is called the Shiba, or the Shiba Inu. It stands 14 to 16 inches at the shoulder. The Shiba differs from the Akita and the Nippon Inu in that it is born tail-less or with a short bob-tail. In this, it is like another minature Spitz, the Schipperke.

Japan also has a fighting dog which is as oversized for a dog as its wrestlers are among Japanese men. It is called the Tosa. In appearance, it is of Mastiff type, although larger. It probably contains both Mastiff and Great Dane blood.

As it is seen in Japan, the Japanese Spitz is a pure white dog, or white with light-biscuit ear markings. It weighs 20 to 25 pounds. It is double-coated with stand-off guard hairs. The tail plume is carried over the back.

Most of its close relatives are colored dogs. But the Volpino Italiano is also white, standing a maximum of 11 inches at the shoulder and weighing an average of nine pounds.

Most of the other very similar relatives to the Japanese Spitz are colored. They vary in size from the German Spitz, 10-11 inches at the shoulder, to the Lapland Spitz, 20 inches tall.

Other members of the group are the Norwegian Buhund, the Iceland Dog, the Great German Spitz, and the Pomeranian and Keeshond, the latter two known world-wide.

As said earlier, the so-called Nordic dogs may be almost indistinguishable from the Spitz family, except for such inherited aptitudes or instincts, such as hunting and guarding.

ELK AND BEAR HUNTING DOGS

The best known of the Nordic dogs is the Norwegian Elkhound. Others include the Finnish Spitz (so called in spite of the fact that he is a sporting dog); the Swedish Grahund, the Karelian Bear Dog, Tahl-Tan Bear Dog, and the Laikas.

The Grahund is quite similar to the better-known Norwegian Elkhound. The Karelian Bear Dog stands 20 to 23½ inches at the shoulder. It is of typical Northern type, with thick outer coat and plumed tail curled tightly over the back. The color is black with white markings. The black is sometimes tinged with brown.

The Karelian Bear Dog is one of the few sporting dogs to have a savage disposition. Because of their propensity for fighting, they are hunted alone. They make poor kennel dogs.

The Tahl-Tan Bear Dog is a Canadian breed developed by Indians of Northern Canada. An astonishing feature is the short tail, which is thick, and which gives the appearance of a round whiskbroom stuck upside down on the dog's rear end. (More about this breed, *see*—Little-Known Dogs, this Part.)

The Laikas are Russian hunting dogs. They stand 20 to 23 inches at the shoulder, and in general, conform to northern type. Little else is known about them. It appears unlikely that the Russians are keeping them pure-bred, or are breeding them to type.

TRAILING HOUNDS ABROAD

It can be said that, on the whole, the world's great sporting dogs have been sought out by British and American sportsmen. Thus, all major breeds are

Camille C. Wong and Karen Murskami of Reseda, California display an Akita at a Santa Barbara Kennel Club All-Breed event. Hank Babbitt photo.

known to some extent in the United States and Canada.

In the case of the hounds, this is not quite so true. In America and Canada, and in South America, only one type of Basset is generally known. This is the Artesien-Normand which has become standardized, and is now considered British.

Other Bassets are the Griffon Vendeen, Bleu de Gascogne, and the Fauve de Bretagne. They differ in some respects, and have never been brought to the perfection of the present Basset as it is known in Britain and North and South America.

The Drever, or Swedish Dachsbracke, is a somewhat taller dog of Basset type. Though taller, many of them have the crooked legs associated with Bassets. These dogs reach 16 inches in height; their ears are shorter than in the Basset. The breed has been recognized in Canada, and an occasional Drever is seen in shows, or in the hunting fields.

The Bavarian Schweisshund is an excellent trailing hound, about 20 inches tall, of foxhound-type in head and ears, but with a somewhat longer body. It is now quite rare outside Bavaria.

A hound which is catching on in South America is the Gran Bleu de Gascogne, called in Spanish the Azul de Gascon. This is a big, good looking hound, which might be mistaken for a long-eared American Bluetick coonhound.

Two hounds from Spain and Portugal seem anything but hound-like, since one has come to expect pendant ears in a hound.

One is the Ibizan Podenco, or Balearic Hound. It comes from the island of Ibiza, or generally from the Balearic Islands. It stands 22 to 24 inches at the shoulder, has erect ears, Greyhound-like flanks, and the Greyhound's ring-tail. A red color is preferred, but white, and red-and-white are seen.

Its counterpart, the Portuguese Podenco, comes in three sizes. The largest is slightly larger than the Spanish variety, and has a less pronounced ring, or sickle-tail. It comes in a variety of colors. Podencos are trained for deer or small game, according to size.

UTILITY DOGS

Before the coming of the railroad, pavements, and automobiles, each isolated farming area had its own breed of shepherd's dog. But fences, the disappearance of the wolf, and modern transportation for livestock from pasture to market ended this.

Today, dozens of fabled working breeds are only names written on the tablets of time. A few are seen often enough to indicate that they will survive. For them, the critical time is past, and fanciers have come forth to preserve them.

Bearded Collie. The Bearded Collie is slowly being returned to popularity in England. It looks a great deal like some of the European sheepdogs. It has dropped ears and a long, bushy tail. Bearded Collies are profusely covered with a long, harsh outer coat, which extends by feathers to the feet.

Gyokushu of Tojo Kensha, an Akita owned by Mr. and Mrs. Re E. Shaffer of Bonaire, Georgia. Photo by Olson's Studio.

These dogs stand 20 to 24 inches at the shoulder. Preferred colors are slate or reddish-fawn, but black and all shades of gray, brown, and sandy are allowed. Hair falls over the eyes, and there is a beard.

South American Dogs. The Beauceron is sometimes called the Berger de Beauce, and in South America, the Pastor de Beauce. It looks somewhat like a Doberman Pinscher with a long tail. The effect is heightened by cropped ears. The Beauceron is a short-coated shepherd dog. Besides the usual Doberman colors of black, black-and-tan, and red, gray dogs are often seen. Height is 24 to 27½ inches.

The Fila Brasileiro is a breed native to Brazil. It descends from huge dogs, probably erroneously called Mastiffs, which were brought in by the Portuguese conquerors.

The Fila Brasileiro looks very much like a Great Dane, but may be slightly smaller in size. Since the dogs have been used for guard work in the undeveloped back country of Brazil, many of them have extremely sharp dispositions.

Much of the credit for saving this breed from extinction must go to Luiz Hermanny Filho, a prominent Brazilian sportsman and dog breeder, who alerted others to the necessity of rescuing the last specimens of the breed.

Venezuela also has a dog which has descended from the great dogs brought in by the Spanish conquerors. This is the Mucuchies. It is a dog which resembles the Great Pyrenees in body structure, as well as in size. It appears probable, therefore, that it comes from the same basic stock. The modern Mucuchies is a rough-coated, good-natured dog, which comes in patched colors of black and white. It is found chiefly in the mountains where its hardihood is of great advantage to shepherds.

Owtchar. The Soviet Union possesses four shepherd dogs called Owtcharka, or Owtchar. The dogs are not necessarily related. But all four are said to be excellent sheepdogs, to have a high rate of intelligence and trainability, and to be excellent for police and military work.

Except for the largest of the four, the dogs are not well-known outside Russia. This one, called the Russian Owtchar, is a huge, shaggy dog, standing 32 inches at the shoulder, or more, and weighing 120 to 135 pounds.

The Owtchar looks something like a giant Old English Sheepdog. The thick shaggy coat tends to mat or cord. Colors are fawn, fawn-and-white, white-and-tan, slate, and other shades of gray. The tail is long, coming below the hocks, and it turns up at the tip.

Portuguese Water Dog. The Portuguese Water Dog is not, as its name might suggest, a retriever or duck dog. Instead, it is the friend and aid of fishermen. It is used as a guard dog, and for retrieving nets, or other objects from the water. This breed is known mainly to the fishermen of the southern Algrave province of Portugal. The dogs are also taught to act as messengers between boats, and even carry boat-to-shore messages.

Dogs stand 20 to 22½ inches at the shoulder and weight 42 to 55 pounds. They are black and white in color. There are two coat types. One has a glossy, long, but open coat. This is trimmed Poodle-fashion, so that the hind quarters are nearly bare.

The tail is trimmed except for a brush at the tip. The tail is carried curled slightly over the back. The second coat type calls for a short, flat, fairly dense coat. Both types have "wigs" or top-knots on the skull.

Tibetan Dogs. The Tibetan Mastiff is one of history's fabled dogs. It appears to be a descendant of dogs mentioned by Marco Polo. Many of the world's sheepdogs are believed to descend from it. Yet it is not known whether or not the breed has survived the conquest of Tibet by China. If it has not, then it can live only through careful nurturing of those specimens in other lands. (For more on this breed *see* head—Little-Known Dogs, this part.)

Tibet is the ancestral home of the Shih Tzu, the Tibetan Spaniel, and the Tibetan Terrier. The Shih Tzu was only recently given full recognition by the American Kennel Club. The dog resembles somewhat the larger Lhasa Apso.

The breed was created by crossing an unknown Tibetan dog with Pekingese. In quite recent times, additional Pekingese blood has been added, both in England and in the United States. This was a factor delaying AKC recognition. (For more on the Shih Tzu, *see* Group V breed coverage, Part XIX.)

The Tibetan Spaniel is a popular dog in India, where it is used as a house dog. It is quite a small dog and is discussed in more detail under the head—Little-Known Dogs, this part.

The Tibetan Terrier is not a terrier at all, but a small, active herding dog. A woman doctor, A. H. R. Greig, is credited with bringing these dogs from Tibet to India. The breed was recognized by the Indian Kennel Club in 1920, and by the Kennel Club, England, in 1937. The breed was brought to the United States in 1956.

The dog looks much like the Puli. It is 14 to 16 inches at the shoulder. Hair falls over the face, forms a beard under the chin, and is long and profuse on the body. The ears are pendant. The back is short and powerful. Weight varies from 15 to 30 pounds. Colors are white, cream, gray, smoke, black, and golden. Dogs may be whole-colored, parti-colored, or tri-colored.

Sinhala Hounds and Thai Dogs. Asia has other dogs which should be mentioned. One is the Sinhala Hound of Ceylon, and another the Thai Dog of Thailand. Both are roughly similar to the Basenji of Africa.

The Sinhala is of Basenji size, about 17 inches at the shoulder, and has a fine, short coat. The forehead is wrinkled, and the ears are erect. The tail curls over the back. Colors are brindle and dark brown.

Origin of the dog is not known. But it is able to live off the land—in a land which has deadly poisonous snakes and leopards. Unlike the Basenji, the Sinhala barks.

The Thai Dog appears to be a close relative of the Sinhala. And both belong to a very old type, that to which the Basenji also belongs. A chief difference between the Sinhala and the Thai Dogs is that the Thai breeders are attempting to breed out the curled tail in their dogs.

Phu Quoc. Since the legendary Phu Quoc is said to be an ancestor of the Rhodesian Ridgeback of South Africa and Rhodesia, it should be mentioned here. But whether the breed still exists is open to question. Recently, at least one animal dealer commissioned to do so, could not locate one in Thailand.

Shanah of Lamleh, Imp., Tibetan Terrier owned by Mrs. Henry S. Murphy, Kalai Kennels, Great Falls, Virginia.

The dog is sometimes called a terrier, sometimes a hound. If it still exists, its distinguishing feature is the ridge of hair along the backbone which grows *toward the head* instead of away from it.

DOGS WITHOUT HAIR

Hairless dogs are known the world over, although rare anywhere. The only ones which have gained recognition have been the Mexican Hairless, the Chinese Crested, and the Xoloitzcuintli.

An additional distinguishing feature of hairless dogs is the absence of many of the side teeth. The reason for this is not known. It has been suggested that the lack of some blood factor may inhibit the growth of both hair and teeth.

Another possibility is that hairlessness, and lack of complete tooth development are sex-linked characteristics. This seems the more likely since the Chinese Crested Dog (*see* Little-Known Dogs *and* Hairless Dogs, this part) has a prominent top-knot of hair on the skull.

For more on dogs without hair *see* head—Hairless Dogs, this Part.

Akita—an interesting head study.

FRANCE

There is a race of French toy dogs called Bichons. The Maltese is sometimes said to belong to this group. Except for the Maltese, most of the members are either extinct or very rare.

One, called the Bichon Frise is, however, beginning to attract attention. It is of Maltese size, pure-white in color, and has very fine, curly hair. It is one of those dogs which at one time may have been very common under the name of Toy Poodle, or Curly Poodle.

DOGS FOR CATTLE AND SHEEP

Australia has three types of cattle dogs, the Australian Cattle Dog, which has been given miscellaneous status in the United States as the Australian Heeler; the Australian Kelpie, and the Stumpy-Tail Cattle Dog.

Australian Cattle Dog. The Australian Cattle Dog is a distinctive blue or blue-mottled color, or he is a red-speckle. The origin of the dog is in doubt. He is a silent worker, and although his body is slightly longer than his height, he is capable of the quick turning motions needed of a herd dog. (More on this dog under head—Little-Known Dogs, this Part.)

Australian Kelpie. The Australian Kelpie is a sheepdog used to work sheep both in the yard and fold, and on the open range. His origin is in doubt, although the Border Collie is given as one ancestor. (More on this breed, *see* Little-Known Dogs, this Part.)

Stumpy-Tail Cattle Dog. The Stumpy-Tail Cattle Dog gets its name because it is born with a four-inch tail. He conforms in size and general type to the other two breeds, but is slightly shorter in back. He is a whole-color blue or blue-mottled. But there is also a red-speckled variety. In the latter, red body patches are permitted.

The Belgian Sheepdog. The Belgian Sheepdog is the oldest of three Belgian breeds which are recognized by the American Kennel Club. Until 1959, all three breeds were shown as Belgian Sheepdogs. But in that year, the Groenendael was given the title of Belgian Sheepdog.

A closely related dog was given separate classification as the Belgian Tervuren. A third variety, the Malinois, was taken from breed status and placed in the Miscellaneous class.

The Malinois was given full breed status in 1965.

A man named M. Rose, who lived in the village of Groenendael in Belgium, is given credit for founding the breed. In 1885, Rose noted a long-coated black bitch in one of his litters.

Rose was fascinated by this bitch. So he searched Belgium for a male of similar type. He found it in a dog called Picard D'Uccle. From the mating of these two came five puppies.

All were named "of Groenendael" after the village. That is, they were Duc de Groenendael, Margot de Groenendael, etc. And that is how the breed got its name.

Groenendaels were first brought to America in 1907. World War I interrupted their progress here. But American soldiers were impressed by their work as army and police dogs. And they brought back glowing stories of the "black police dogs."

About this time, the German Shepherds were coming to prominence through Strongheart and Rin Tin Tin. But the Belgian dogs were so famous that black German Shepherds were almost universally called Belgians. The Groenendaels continued to dominate the varieties so that while all three were shown as Belgian Sheepdogs, most people became accustomed to thinking of the black dog as the true Belgian.

It was for this reason that he was finally given full possession of the name.

Modern Belgians are quick, active, and remarkably alert. They have done well in obedience work, and have distinguished themselves as sensible home guards.

——Little-Known Dogs——

THERE ARE many rare foreign breeds virtually unknown outside of the countries of their origin. Some of these are listed below. None of these is a mongrel in any sense of the word, most of them having descended from pure-bred stock.

Australian Cattle Dog. Highly prized among the cattle ranchers of Victoria and New South Wales, the Australian Cattle Dog is a herder of high order, going about his work in businesslike manner without undue fuss. Known also as the Australian Heeler, he keeps the herds under control by nipping at the heels of lagging cattle.

His color is a distinctive blue, blue-mottled, or red-speckled. The coat is short, straight, somewhat harsh with a dense under coat. The tail reaches the hock, and has a brush. The ears are pricked and erect when at attention. Height ranges from 18 to 20 inches at the shoulder and weights range from 32 to 35 pounds. A rather handsome dog, the Australian Cattle Dog is supposed to have resulted from crossing the old blue-merle-type Collie with the Australian Kelpie or Sheepdog. Some contend that the Australian Wild Dog (dingo) and the Dalmatian have a part in his make-up. He is a workman of high intelligence.

Australian Kelpie. The origin of the Australian Kelpie, or Australian Collie, is subject to many theories. Serious students hold that the breed came from dogs imported from Scotland. Some stockmen advance the theory that the Kelpie comes from a cross between a black Smooth Collie, which a band of gypsies used in their poaching activities, and a fox! The Border Collie is sometimes given as one ancestor. The bushmen of Australia believe the Kelpie is the result of a cross between the dingo and the Smooth Collie. The name "Kelpie" came from a bitch named "Kelpie's Pup", which won the first sheepdog trials in Australia.

These dogs possess remarkable intelligence and virtually live for their work with sheep. Males are 18 to 20 inches at the shoulder and weigh about 30 pounds. Their coat is moderately short, with a dense under coat. The tail, which reaches the hock, has a brush. Ears are prick, and the body is slightly longer than tall.

Kelpies come in a variety of colors, black, black-and-tan, red, red-and-tan, fawn-chocolate, and smoke-blue. Red-colored puppies occur occasionally, which bolsters the bushmen's dingo theory. The breed has lost most of the Smooth Collie appearance.

Catalan Sheepdog. Found throughout Spain, the Catalan Sheepdog is known as the Perro de Pastor Catalan in Catalonia, the breed's point of origin. It is widely used as a sheepdog and is also a fine companion and guard dog. Two varieties, the long-haired and short-haired, are found, with the short-haired the more popular. The colors are black-and-grizzle, black-and-tan, brindle or tawny, with an occasional solid black or solid dark tan. Standing about 19 inches high, the dog weighs about 42 pounds.

Cavalier King Charles Spaniel. Based on the toy spaniel of King Charles II's reign, so often pictured in paintings of the Stuart period, a revival of interest

An Akita owned by Liz and Al Harrell of Stanton, California.

in this old type spaniel began about 1926, the Kennel Club of England recognizing the new breed in 1944. Although designated as a Toy breed, the Cavalier King Charles Spaniel is more the size of a Cocker than the English Toy Spaniels. The body is compact, rather square with deep chest, the head almost flat between the ears with no dome and a shallow stop. The coat is long and silky, free from curl but with generous feathering on ears and legs. Color may be any of the English Toy Spaniel patterns but is usually white with rich chestnut markings. Height about 12 inches, and average weight 15 pounds.

(The reader is reminded that the Cavalier King Charles Spaniel is *not* a member of the AKC varieties established under its English Toy Spaniel classification, AKC Group V—Toys.)

According to a *New York Times* article in the autumn of 1969, there were estimated to be about 800 Cavaliers now in the U.S.A. At one Cavalier King Charles Club gathering in Kentucky there were 104 entries in 1969 as compared to 77 in 1968. The Cavaliers are eligible to compete toward a championship under Canadian Kennel Club auspices. In England, the Cavalier King Charles Spaniel was stated to be the 15th most popular breed, circa 1969.

Chinese Crested Dog. A generally accepted theory is that the Mexican Hairless, called by the Mexicans themselves "the Chinese Dog," might have descended from this very ancient breed. Rare in any part of the world, legend has it that an emperor in an early dynasty had a pack of these dogs, but they were slain along with the rest of his court during a revolution, hence there were but few specimens to perpetuate the breed. Those with a long crest were raised as temple dogs, a short crest denoting a hunting strain. They have a cat-like way of stalking and other feline characteristics, such as cleaning themselves and flexing their toes in a way that enables them to cling or climb with their claws. In size, they may range from three to 25 pounds, their color speckled pink and brown or black, and the skin smooth and hairless. All are born pink, the final color and crest developing with maturity.

Chinook. Listed sometimes in reference books as the rarest breed in the world is the Chinook dog, only 125 of which were known to be alive as of March 31, 1965. A relatively unknown breed, the Chinook was a dog of the Far North, his association with man being, from whatever obscure beginnings, with certain Eskimo and Indian peoples.

Drentsche Partrijshond. A breed of considerable antiquity, the Drentsche Partrijshond (Partridge Dog) is a native of the Drentsche province of Holland. An excellent retriever, the dog is white with cinnamon head and orange ticking and about 24

Tolling Dog.

inches high. The coat is much similar to that of a Setter.

Finnish Spitz. Its origin the subject of much controversy, the Finnish Spitz is said to be the descendant of the Northern watchdog of the ancient Finns. Its ancestor was used for thousands of years as a hunting dog in Northern Finland, Lapland, and Karelia, and its counterpart of today is adept in hunting game birds in Finland, where it regularly figures in field trials for the breed. The dog finds feathered game by searching, drives it into a supposed sanctuary among the branches of a tree, and then calls the attention of its master to the game by barking and pointing it out. Through these unusual tactics, the dog has earned the name "Barking Bird Dog of Finland."

The colors are various shades of red, the darker being preferred. The coat is of medium length, with a ruff of greater length hair around the neck. Its plumed tail curls over its back in a complete single circle. In general appearance the dog is of typical Spitz type.

Istrian Pointer. The Istrian Pointer (Istriski Brak) is a great favorite among the sporting people of Yugoslavia. These dogs are in two varieties, smooth and rough-haired, with the smooth-haired much more popular. The height is about 20 inches and the weight about 45 pounds. The color is white with light tan, red or black markings on the head, ears and body. The rough-haired variety is the coarser and heavier-boned of the two.

Lurcher. A dog of great speed, intelligence, and hardiness, the Lurcher is called the outcast of dogdom and is not recognized as a breed by any official kennel club. Nevertheless the true Lurcher breeds true to type and is the subject of careful breeding by a number of gypsy tribes. Said to be the product of Greyhound and Bedlington Terrier blood, the Lurcher is about 24 inches high and weighs about 50 pounds. Its coat is short and harsh. The tail is long, thin, and tapering. Small prick ears are mounted on a head of the Greyhound type. Colors are grizzle, black or black-and-tan.

Maremma Sheepdog. A native of Italy, the Maremma Sheepdog is a handsome white herding dog somewhat similar to the Kuvasz. Occasionally specimens are found with a little lemon, biscuit or fawn about the head and ears. Weights range from 65 to 70 pounds, the height is about 25 inches. The coat is moderately long on the body but short on the head.

Portuguese Pointer. Standing about 25 inches at the shoulder, the Portuguese Pointer is, for a pointing dog, rather heavily boned and short backed. In color, the dog is fawn with red ears. His coat is smooth. An industrious, rugged dog, the Portuguese Pointer works with all game and is protected by the Club dos Cacadores Portugueses.

Rumanian Sheepdog. One of only three pure types of dogs remaining in Rumania, the Rumanian Sheepdog is both a shepherd and a guard. The guarding instinct has been highly developed and the dog is suspicious of all strangers, sometimes to the point of being a menace to travelers. It has a medium length coat of smooth, soft texture, is varied in color, the tri-colors being commonest. Sable with darker head points, black-and-tan and brindles are also known. Weights average about 110 pounds, heights about 25 inches.

Sealydale. A small South African Terrier, the Sealydale descends from the Sealyham and the Airedale,

Tahl-Tan Bear Dog.

the blood of the former predominating. About 13 inches high at the shoulder, this active little Terrier is used mainly for bolting game and vermin. In color it is white with tan or black markings.

Spinone. The Spinone is the best of the all-around Italian gundogs. Somewhat houndlike in appearance, the dog is white or white with red or blue markings and ticking. The coat is rough and the dog is able to withstand almost any weather. Its Piedmontese origin is said to date back several centuries. The dog has an excellent disposition.

Svensk Vallhund. Bearing a strong resemblance to the Pembroke Welsh Corgi, the Svensk Vallhund is one of the best stock dogs in Sweden. The two breeds are closely related in work, character, conformation and appearance, and this affinity probably originated during the raids the Norsemen made on the coast of Wales during the eighth and ninth centuries.

Tahl-Tan Bear Dog. Originally used by the Tahl-Tan Indians of Canada, the Tahl-Tan Bear Dog is the only breed believed to have originated in Canada. The Tahl-Tan Indians call him "their" dog, meaning the breeding stock has been passed down from generation to generation. Used for hunting black and grizzly bears, lynx and porcupine, the Tahl-Tan Bear Dog was customarily carried in a hide sack to conserve his energy and released only when the quarry was sighted. The little dog harried his game by circling, nipping and barking, holding it at bay and distracting its attention from the approaching hunter. Two dogs were usually used in hunting bear. Two

Drentsche Patrijshond.

Istrian Pointer.

Portuguese Pointer.

days before the planned hunt, the dogs were bled by stabbing them in the hind quarters, the Indians believing this practice gave them more agility and endurance. The instrument used in the bleeding was the fibula bone of the fox or wolf, no other instrument being considered proper. When training a puppy for lynx hunting, the Indians periodically scratched the puppy's nose with the claws and pad of the lynx in the belief that this would instill a greater desire to hunt this particular species of game.

The Tahl-Tan Bear Dog is an alert, gracefully-built dog of from 12 to 15 inches at the shoulder for males and proportionately smaller for females. The head is decidedly foxy in appearance with erect bat ears. The color scheme is usually black on the head, with irregular black and white patches covering the body. Many of the species, however, are blue-grey with irregular white patches, while some are wholly black.

The distinguishing characteristic of the breed is the tail. This is from 5 to 8 inches in length, carried erect. It is extremely thick from set-on to tip, usually black with white tip, depending upon the general coloring of the dog. This tail is quite dissimilar from that of all other breeds of dogs.

It is a general understanding that the Tahl-Tan Bear Dog will not live outside of Northern environment. A considerable number of these dogs have been taken "outside" in the past. Practically all have died, either from heat prostration or from unaccustomed diet. The dog is a fastidious eater, preferring small parcels of meat and fish. He is particularly fond of birds. The bark of the Tahl-Tan Bear Dog is a fox-like yap. His yapping and yodeling on moonlit nights is almost identical to that of the coyote. The mating season is usually fall or early winter.

The breed has been officially recognized by the Bermuda and Canadian Kennel Clubs and efforts are being made to preserve it, although drastic inroads have been made on the breed in recent years.

Tibetan Mastiff. Probably the ancestor of all the Mastiffs and the largest of this group, the Tibetan Mastiff runs in weight from 130 to 150 pounds and stands 24½ to 27½ inches at the shoulder. Used extensively as a guard, the dog is inclined to be quite fierce. The dog has a thick double coat, and an extraordinarily bushy tail, the latter carried over the back. Usual colors are black or golden, or black and tan. It is well-known in India and China and a few specimens have been imported into this country (U.S.). But while they have aroused considerable interest, the breed has gained no great degree of popularity here.

Tibetan Spaniel. Rarely found outside of Tibet or India, the Tibetan Spaniel is an alert little Toy somewhat similar in appearance to the Japanese Spaniel. He has a more pointed muzzle, a higher ear carriage and a less prominent eye than the dog of Japan, but the similarity in conformation, coat texture and tail carriage is striking.

The Tibetan Spaniel weighs from nine to 16 pounds and does not have the pushed-in muzzle of other toy spaniels. Instead, its muzzle is moderately-long, being joined to a very wide skull. The ears are set high, with the break coming above the skull line. They are well-feathered. The coat is dense and flat. The tail is set on high, is well-feathered, and is carried gaily, but not over the back. The body length is greater than the shoulder height. Colors are golden, sandy, white, black and tan, and parti-color.

Tolling Dog (Nova Scotia Duck Tolling Retriever). Few American sportsmen have ever heard of the Tolling Dog, and an even smaller number have ever hunted waterfowl with the aid of one of these animals. Although the Tolling Dog is occasionally used in parts of Europe, the only reports on their use on this continent come from Nova Scotia.

The Tolling Dog is officially recognized and classified under a Retriever heading by the Canadian Kennel Club, it being there listed as the Nova Scotia Duck Tolling Retriever. It is similarly recognized and classified by the Bermuda Kennel Club.

In France and England these dogs, of no special breed, were used to *toll* or lure waterfowl into large funnel-shaped nets, where they could be taken alive.

Usually the net was placed over a small stream which opened out into a larger body of water. The mouth of the funnel faced outward at the point where the stream entered the larger water, and the procedure employed in this method of taking waterfowl was quite simple.

The dog would run up and down the stream bank,

Portuguese Water Dog.   Sealydale.

Spinone.

from the mouth to a point 50 or 60 yards upstream. The sight of this dog running back and forth would be too much for the curiosity of the ducks, and they would swim toward the mouth of the funnel. As the ducks approached, the dog would shorten his runs, always keeping far enough from the ducks to allay their fears and leading them up the net-covered stream to the trap.

The modern method of employing the Tolling Dog is quite different. In Nova Scotia the dogs are used to lure waterfowl, but not to a net or trap. A hunter will locate a lake with a number of ducks on it. He will hide on the shore, preferably on a small point. The Tolling Dog then begins running up and down the shore, occasionally emitting a sharp bark. He normally runs back and forth between his master's hiding place and a point 60 to 70 feet distant. This attracts the attention of the ducks, who swim in to see what is causing the dog's excitement. Within a few minutes they come within range of the hunter's gun.

In Nova Scotia these dogs are bred to resemble a red fox in size, coat, and coloration, as local guides claim this method of luring ducks is one that is practiced by foxes, and that the waterfowl do not connect man with the fox. There are believed to be very few of these dogs even in Nova Scotia.

Wheaten Terrier. For many years found only in Ireland, the soft-coated Wheaten Terrier is an excellent farm dog as well as an asset to the sporting dog kennel of that country. Clear wheaten in color, the coat is soft and wavy. The dog is about 17 inches high. It is a descendant of the extinct Madadh, the ancestor of many soft-coated breeds in Ireland.

Working Border Collie. The working Border Collie is notably anxious and able to work livestock under the direction of its master.

The name was originally "Colley" which comes from the dog's close-working association with Colley sheep, an ancient Scotch breed. To do their work these dogs had to be fast and alert to the sheep and to the master.

Under his black and white coat his body is the perfect combination of the speed, the strength, and the spirit to control livestock, especially sheep. A full-

grown dog weighs from 30 to 50 pounds. Like any other group of skilled professional workers, the Working Border Collie has been selected for its intelligence and ability rather than for uniformity of size and appearance. Black and white are the dominant colors, but tan in the coat does not indicate impurity in the bloodlines, because some of the ancestors of these dogs carried tan markings. Some dogs are smooth and some are medium-coated; hair length of the dog is less important to the wise handler than energy and intelligence. The legs are strong and well adapted to body size for fast movement over smooth or rough ground that is level or steep. The body balance permits short bursts of high speed, sudden changes in direction and gait from a hard run to a creep, from a stalk to a steady lift, to a sudden disciplinary encounter with a stubborn animal.

Lighter dogs compensate with spirit and agility for their smaller size. Short-haired dogs can work more safely and comfortably in hot weather than long-haired, rough-coated dogs. Long-haired, shaggy dogs, of which the breed has some members, would seem best suited to cooler climates and slower work than the short-haired members of the breed.

The sturdiness of these dogs and their general stamina when combined with proper care, training, and handling on the part of the master, have more to do with their usefulness for any kind of work than the supposed physical advantages or limitations of size, coat, weight, or general build on any individual member of the breed.

The Working Border Collies of today are the descendants of a considerable variety of sheep-herding dogs chosen through the centuries to meet the changing needs of the shepherd and the sheep. The primal needs of shepherds for suitable dogs in sheeplands has been, and is, vigor, intelligence, courage, initiative, and obedience. There were dogs with these qualities in pastoral Britain and men to select the best qualified dogs for breeding. Dogs selected and bred for hundreds of generations to meet rigorous requirements for working ability will have high development and considerable uniformity in these traits, just as with other creatures selected and bred for specific physical characteristics.

In open country or in large fields a man and his

Svensk Vallhund.

Tibetan Spaniel.

Wheaten Terrier (Soft-coated).

flock of sheep are incomplete; the man is nearly helpless without his trained professional sheepdog. The dog gathers the flock which may be widely scattered on rough ground. By direction from the master he gathers the flock and drives it about the range or fields. He fetches it to the farmstead if so directed. In the paddock and in the barn, where sheep must be herded together rather than moved freely, the agility, speed, and perfect adaptation to the job of the skilfull working dog have no counterpart in man. In addition to this kind of close "inside" work, which consists of moving sheep in yards and feeding pens, the professional Working Border Collie can move sheep in loading into and unloading them from trucks or railroad cars when sheep are in transit.

In the western range country, where bands of sheep run to several thousands, you will find the Border Collie continuously on the job. One dog can handle about 1,000 sheep. He works nothing but sheep his entire lifetime. In the wide open spaces of the West with large numbers of sheep there will often be several dogs working at one time under one master to handle the bands properly. In eastern United States where flocks probably average 40 to 50 sheep, one dog will do everything with the sheep in field and barn.

Nearly all professionally-trained dogs are trained to work one kind of livestock. A dog trained on sheep can hardly be expected to work cattle or swine. Similarly, a dog trained for cattle or swine would probably be too rough for working sheep or poultry.

Another example of single-purpose dogs is their use with poultry, especially turkeys. People who raise turkeys by the thousands find Working Border Collies indispensable in the handling of their flocks. These are examples of the working specializations of which dogs of this breed are capable. But they can do even more.

Most farms have several kinds of livestock which spend considerable time in pastures. Working Border Collies on such farms frequently move the cattle or the hogs as well as sheep when the occasion demands. Many of the best-trained livestock dogs have learned to distinguish cattle from sheep and sheep from swine. They can bring to the master the kind he wants even if the Collie has to sort them in the field. One of the commonest duties of the general-purpose farm Working Collies is bringing in the cows. Horses respect the members of this breed in the same way that other livestock does for the same reasons.

Alert and Energetic. With his master until he receives working instructions, the Working Border Collie watches every move the master makes while he keeps an eye out for some creature to exercise his energies upon. If his attention wanders, the least signal from the master alerts his whole being for action. Whether the assignment is encircling a distant flock or driving them at a suitable pace along a lane, the trained Working Border Collie spares no energy in the performance of his assignment. Most members of this breed will exhaust themselves in their master's service if he demands it of them, whether from necessity or unwisely.

Spirited and Industrious. Difficulties of the terrain or of wild or unwilling animals do not discourage the well-trained Working Border Collie. He will take the hills on high and will stand his ground against the occasional unwilling animal that has not yet learned when the dog means business.

On the other hand, when the good dog errs or tends to develop bad practices, it will accept correction when wisely administered by the master without becoming sullen or timid. The evident feeling of oneness that the dog has for its master is the basis of the working relationship between the two.

The dog owns for a master only someone he finds worthy of respect. Owners of dogs of this breed should also be their masters or should completely delegate this privilege to someone else. It is wasteful and unkind to divide a dog's loyalty.

From these qualities come the dog's continued urge to work livestock under the direction of the master.

Obedience. The inherent alertness and willingness to cooperate with the master will develop obedience in the Working Border Collie, when the master knows what he wants and takes the trouble consistently to use the same signals for the same commands.

Intelligence. The undisciplined dog may have all the desirable qualities jumbled together in an attractive body. Until disciplined by contact with and working for a wise master, the best bred Working Border Collie is just another dog. What makes this breed valuable is the dog's capacity to accept training and to utilize ability to go beyond the detail of the master's instruction to accomplish the purpose of their working together. He learns quickly from the master and from experience. The dogs that have been able to obey and, within the limits of the master's will, to take the initiative in handling livestock properly, have become and are the bloodlines in this breed.

On the Range. The range being open country with its own natural water supply requires the movement of sheep to obtain feed and water. Range work consists as much in keeping the flock together as in moving it around. If the sheep are grazing far from water, the dog and shepherd will move them to and from their drinking places. The dog acts as warning of the approach of strange creatures, man or beast. He is the only companion that many shepherds have the season through.

In Enclosures. Upon occasion, when there is need, the trained Working Border Collie can keep the sheep back from the feed racks while they are being filled. When the flock is congested in an aisle or a lane and will not move, the trained Working Border Collie at the command of his master steps surely and lightly on the backs of the sheep to travel quickly to the front of the flock to start the leaders, then back over the top to the master. When the sheep require individual medication such as single dipping in a tank, or oral administration of capsules for worms, the dog will cut out a small number from the flock, bring them to the treatment point, and hold them.

Notable Individual Performances. The everyday duties of the Working Border Collie are commonplace to him and his master. People unfamiliar with the natural ability and working instinct of these dogs find some of their casual activities remarkable. Dogs know their flocks so well that they rarely come in with a flock until they have gathered them all.

For example, on one farm divided by a busy highway, sheep usually cross over through a water culvert instead of over the road. The dogs urge the sheep in the new flocks through the culvert until they are used to this passageway. The dog will press the flock until it will use the culvert even when water several inches deep is running through.

Dogs on this farm upon a single command from the master will gather the flocks from pasture and bring them through the culvert to the barn. Visitors one day watched a flock come through the culvert a few minutes after the dog had disappeared through it. Ordinarily the last through would be the dog, but this time no dog. One visitor spied a lamb across the road deserted by its young mother, but waited upon by the dog. The dog came back to the master on signal, then in obedience to other commands took the flock back through the culvert to bring young lamb and mother together. This trait of staying with the young lamb or any cast sheep seems to develop without special training.

Another time a dog fetched a flock from out of sight but did not follow the flock in. After a little while one sheep and one dog came up the path together. To people unused to such dogs these per-

formances are amazing, but when sheepdog men gather it would take more than this to raise an eyebrow. Some of the standard performances of the Working Border Collie in the line of regular duty are the more wonderful because dogs of this breed are simply doing what comes naturally.

Whenever a man and his dog work livestock, all three are on trial. It is natural for men with working dogs to tell of their dogs' accomplishments. Public performance of dogs working sheep under the critical eye of impartial judges in the presence of the competitors' partisans has become an accepted means of establishing standards of performances of animals of this breed.

The concentration of the Working Border Collie on the task makes it an ideal dog to perform before spectators.

Mr. Arthur N. Allen of McLeansboro, Illinois, is one of the more prominent owners and trainers of these dogs in recent years. His dogs—Rock and Nicky—were the canine stars of the movie *The Arizona Sheep Dogs* and Walt Disney's t.v. picture, *Border Collie.* His dogs give numerous performances in the many livestock shows and expositions held annually in the U.S., and many rodeos today feature exhibitions of the skill of this man and his dogs as a regular event or part of their programs.

The well-trained dog that is anxious to obey because of his respect and affection for the master is probably unaware of the different setting of his duties when he is moving sheep or other small stock short distances or through sharp turns in the oval on the fairgrounds, on the race track, in front of grandstand, or in an arena. Because the distances are small and possible distractions are many, the successful completion of a sequence of closely-timed parts of an act make this miniature field work more demanding on the dog and generally more difficult than the ordinary working requirements.

These staged performances are primarily to astonish and entertain by demonstration of the dog's ability rather than to prove to the spectators its real value as a working dog.

The real value of the Working Border Collie lies in its ability to move and hold livestock with greatest economy of the master's time and effort. (*See also* Part X—Sheepdog Trials.)

Working Border Collie.

—Hairless Dogs—

HAIRLESS DOGS have appeared from time to time in various parts of the world. Biologists and naturalists have given these dogs the technical name of Canis Africanus, because it is believed the origin of all hairless dogs is the African continent.

Local names for them have been African Sand Dog, Abyssinian Dog, Turkish Naked Dog, Chinese Crested Dog, and Mexican Hairless. In recent years, another Mexican dog, the Xoloitzcuintli has become prominent in that country.

QUESTIONS OF ORIGIN AND CAUSES

Many studies have been made of hairless dogs to determine the cause of their nakedness. But up to this time, no good explanation for it has ever been found. One supposition is that it is caused by a lack of some hair-promoting hormone. In these dogs, the body is more naked even than is that of a human being. But, as in man, there is more or less hair upon the head.

Since most hairless dogs have been kept in zoos where they have been regarded as freaks, little effort has been made to determine the inheritance factors. However, the factor for hairlessness appears to be linked with one governing the production of teeth. All hairless dogs are lacking in many of the side teeth, the molars and premolars.

The hairless dog, or African hound (Canis Africanus), according to Dr. A. E. Brehm, the noted German naturalist, has its origin in the African continent from where he migrated to Guinea, Manila, China, and then to America.

But the numbers and persistence of hairless dogs in Mexico has led some authorities to believe that the origin of all hairless dogs is Mexico and Central America.

Early References. The matter is confusing, and is made not the less so by repeated references to hairless dogs made by the Spanish Conquistadors.

The Conquistadors were mostly uneducated, and those who were, were not educated in the natural sciences. They saw thousands of life forms which were unlike any they had known in Europe. They had the problem of describing these forms in terms understandable for those back home.

They filled their reports with such names as "lions" and "tigers," "dogs" and "cats," even though some of these did not exist in the New World.

Jose de Acosta, a Jesuit priest, and the greatest naturalist of his time to come to the New World, was so astounded by the multitude of strange animals, that he was led to question the Biblical story of Noah and the Ark.

He reasoned that these animals could not have been on the Ark, since had this been so, they could not have come to the New World by swimming. And he speculated that the story was therefore either untrue, or that God made a Second Creation.

Father Bernardino de Sahagun is another author of a natural history, he having reached Mexico shortly after the Conquest. He speaks specifically of the Xoloitzcuintli in his Book XI.

"The little animals that they call down here 'xoloitzcuintli' have no hair on their bodies, and the natives cover them at night with their blankets. But these little dogs are not born like this, but the natives use a resin that they call 'oxtli,' and that they spread on the animals, and that way they pull all of its hair, leaving the body smooth."

Mexican Hairless Dog.

"Cuintli" appears to have been an Aztec root word, but its true meaning has been lost. Whatever it was, Sahagun's xoloitzcuintli was not a dog. It may have been a Guinea pig. The Guinea pig nevertheless is not really a pig either. And the use of the term by English-speaking people shows that early English writers were no better informed on New World species than were their Spanish contemporaries.

Many of the best authorities believe that the Aztecs had no true dogs. Acosta, in fact, made a careful study of the matter. He concluded that all the domestic animals—pigs, chickens, cattle, horses, dogs—were brought to the New World from Europe.

Whatever the hairless dog's origin, he appears to have been a favorite of Mexicans along the Texas, New Mexico, and Arizona borders as early as 1840. The dogs were particularly well-known about San Antonio, Austin, Nogales and Tucson.

The best—and yet most maddening—description of the dogs is this Texas account, written in 1848.

The Mexicans call him pelon. The Americans refer to him as the no-hair dog; while the stranger from the North, who sees him for the first time, calls him the cast-iron dog, for that is what he looks like at first glance. Although not particularly intelligent, the no-hair dog is susceptible of a high polish, for his hairless hide shines in the sun as if it had recently been touched up with stove polish.

His body is about the size, and somewhat the shape of a watermelon—that is, of one of those small watermelons that is about the size of a pelon dog. He differs, however, from the melon in that his tail is adorned with a tuft of blonde hair, which is never the case with the watermelon. He wears a tuft of hair—another tuft, of course, not the same one—on his head, which gives him a very striking appearance.

The pelon dog is found in Austin, San Antonio, and in tamales, the latter being a Mexican dish, the ingredients of which are as uncertain as those of hash.

The pelon is a descendent of the Barbary dog. He is of a purple-blue color, has bandy legs, and is always fat. His fatness is the result of an advantage he has over all other dogs, he being as bald (with the exception of the two tufts aforementioned) as the inside of a goose. He is not troubled, as other curs are, by detachments of fleas scouting over him, and *therefore does not keep himself thin with the exercise of scratching his left ear with his right hind leg. . . .*

The author was, no doubt, a very funny person. But he keeps us mystified as to the size of the dog. Another writer says the pelon was the size of a terrier. But, considering the wide variation in terrier size, how big is that?

And the first author throws more mystery on the dog by stating that the pelon is a descendant of the Barbary Dog. That dog does not exist today, and present researchers have not produced any evidence as to what it was.

Mexican Hairless Sometimes Confused with Chinese Crested Dog. Mexicans have often called the Mexican Hairless the Chinese Hairless. Two of five dogs regis-

tered by the Mexican Kennel Club in earlier years were direct imports from China. After many years of recognition, the American Kennel Club withdrew breed status in the mid-1960s.

The dogs can be any color, but slate seems to predominate. Dogs weigh about 14 to 15 pounds. Many have almost hairless skulls, but others have top-knots.

The Chinese Crested Dog is so similar to the Mexican Hairless that one has sometimes passed for the other. But the Chinese Crested is usually a somewhat larger dog, weighing up to 25 pounds. Colors are slate and slate-blue, with pink spots.

Chinese Crested Dog litters sometimes contain puppies with body hair. These dogs, if allowed to live, are called "powder puffs."

The Xoloitzcuintli. In Mexico today, a serious effort is being made to establish a breed with the ancient Aztec name of Xoloitzcuintli.

Compared with the Mexican Hairless and the Chinese Crested Dog, it is the largest of the three. The predominant color is slate-gray or blue. There is less mottling with pink than in the Chinese Crested, and less of a top-knot.

The skin feels hot to the touch, partly because of the absence of insulating fur. The skin is dark, elephant-like in color; it is somewhat thicker than in the ordinary dog, and there are sometimes a few short bristles distributed over the body. There may be a few hairs on the skull, and toward the end of the tail. The dog looks not unlike an oversized Standard Manchester Terrier. They are 16 to 20 inches tall and weigh 25 to 35 pounds. Molars and premolars are missing, and sometimes some of the incisors.

—Mixed Breeds—

COMMONLY CALLED mongrels or "mutts," mixed-breed dogs of almost every size, conformation, coat, and color are to be found in every city, town, hamlet, and rural section of this country. They are definitely a part of the American scene.

During the various phases of the development of America a breed usually known as the "cur" contributed much to the welfare of the pioneer. He acted as guard, hunter, shepherd, and companion, and in each capacity he was equally proficient. Originating, very probably, from crosses between hounds and herding dogs, the "cur" was a medium-sized dog of unlimited endurance, extreme hardiness, and remarkable intelligence. The length and texture of his coat varied with the climate of the section in which he was found and he came in any number of color combinations. He fought by the side of his master in the Indian Wars, he accompanied Dan'l Boone into the fastnesses of the New Country, he curled up by the

campfires of the Lewis and Clark Expedition, and he had a hand in the agricultural development of the South and Middle West. At one time the name "cur" indicated a dog of faithful devotion and great ability. The dignity which accompanied the name has long since been dropped and the "cur" is a forgotten dog. The term is now mainly used as an epithet.

Mongrels Unsatisfactory as Breeding Stock. There are reasons for the popularity of mixed breeds or mongrels. These blood mixtures produce some unusual progeny, unusual in both looks and sagacity. The novice who wants "just a dog for the children" is intrigued by the appealing expression and cunning looks of mixed-breed puppies and chooses one, but he little realizes that the alert, frisky, friendly little fellow may mature into a loose-jointed, shamble-gaited, heavy-boned adult far from the ideal sought or expected. Most mixed-breed matings are either accidental or the result of carelessness. Seldom are they deliberately planned. And even in the latter event, the type into which the progeny will eventuate is a matter of mere conjecture. The mixed-breed is generally incapable of reproducing his own kind, simply because he himself is generally the only individual of his own kind. While he may make a satisfactory worker, companion, guard or hunter, he will never do as breeding stock.

Most modern breeds, of course, can trace their origin to other breeds, but the establishment of any definite breed has seldom, if ever, been accidental. It has been the result of careful planning and selective breeding.

Are Mongrels Smarter? "Mongrels are smarter than pure-bred dogs" is a statement often made by the uninformed. Nothing is further from the truth! No mongrel is a specialist at any type of work or activity. True, many are exceedingly intelligent. One has only to watch vaudeville or circus troupes of performing dogs to have that fact verified. But the intelligence was handed down by pure-bred ancestors.

Many have the idea that mongrels are especially hardy and healthy. This idea, also, is not founded upon fact. Most of the mongrels we see today are living proof of the axiom "survival of the fittest." From puppyhood they have had to struggle hard for existence. Those who champion the hardiness of the mongrel fail to consider the large percentage of mongrel puppies that die in infancy.

Mixed Breed Dogs as Pets. Many people consider mongrels as ideal pets for children. Many individuals of mixed ancestry do make good companion dogs. Many are placid, tolerant, and willing to accept things as they come, simply because they do not have the benefit of ancestral instincts which give them a definite mission in life. Many of them, by temperament, however, are totally unfit for a child's pet, and some are outright untrustworthy. In selecting a pure-bred dog as a pet for children, the chooser has the advantage of knowing something of the dog's ancestry and of the temperament to be reasonably expected.

In summary, it costs no more to keep a pure-bred dog than to keep a mongrel. The pure-bred will match wits and hardiness with the mongrel, is capable of doing a better job in every way, and has the added advantage of being a valuable animal of distinctive appearance and able to reproduce similar animals of similar worth.

─Famous Dogs─

A few creatures fear us and endure our laws and our yoke but none of them loves us. Only the dog has made an alliance with us.
—Maurice Maeterlinck

OF ALL THE dog's qualities none is so characteristic and outstanding as his ability to be a true companion. The dog's natural instincts are to hunt and seek food for himself, or for his master, to protect from danger those whose affection and care he values, and to guard his master's household or livestock. All these basic characteristics of the dog do not compare with his chief attribute in all his alliance with man, in being just a companion.

Even the most "useless" dog, one that brings no perceptible benefit to his master, offers the answer to one of the greatest human needs—that for devoted and unquestioning comradeship. There are no whys and wherefores in a dog's absolute bond of love and friendship, come happiness or heartbreak. The master can feel assured that here is friendship in its highest form. The dog's extraordinary intuition sees man's very inner thoughts and feelings and responds in kind. It has been said that a real dog lover is one who has been hurt by life and needs a better opinion of himself; that there is something in the quality of a dog's admiration that gives this to him. The dog's faithful presence through the night and his approval in the morning does, indeed, have the power to obliterate a feeling of inadequacy and replace it with courage. A dog can even add humor, the saving grace of many of man's troubles. But there is more than all this. There is an understanding of mutual respect between a man and his dog companion.

To the dog it matters not at all whether his master is royal or rich, poor in the world's goods, or forsaken by his fellow man. The lean of "ol' houn' dawg" is as devoted a companion to a lonely mountaineer as a pampered toy dog is to his beautiful and elegant mistress. Many a sportsman would not go into the fields or woods with a gun unless he had the companionship of his hunting dog. The lone shepherd gains as much personal joy from the companionship of his dog as actual benefit from the dog's guarding of the flocks.

DOGS AND FAMOUS PEOPLE

Facts and fiction tell of the value of the dog's companionship through the ages. Many of the world's greatest men, writers, statesmen, philosophers, and scientists were never without the companionship of dogs.

It was the custom of Egyptian Pharaohs to have sculptures or pictures of their favorite dogs placed in their tombs. Cheops, who in 3773 B.C. began the construction of the great pyramid at Ghizeh, had as a constant companion a hound named Abakaru. The names and images of four of the favorite dogs of Rameses II were buried with him and when the tomb of Tutankhamen was opened, the effigies of two of

Polly Bergen, movie and t.v. star, with St. Bernard. Hank Babbitt oto.

attack, but thanks to the forced march the enemy was surprised and an important victory won.

One type of dog anecdote can be illustrated by a story from Kent, which reputedly took place during the 17th century. A country gentleman had noticed that every day a dog would swim from an island in the Thames to the main shore, disappear in the cover and swim back to the island about an hour later. Upon investigation he learned that the dog regularly visited a certain farmer, who fed him, and this, according to the farmer, had been going on for three months. The next time the dog had been ashore and started his return swim, he was accompanied by the curious man in a rowboat. The dog led him about 30 yards inland on the uninhabited island where a comparatively fresh mound of earth was found. Below was found the decomposing body of a man, whose skull had been shattered in apparent murder. The body was taken to the mainland and given decent burial. The gentleman adopted the dog, which soon showed evidence of great affection for him, but continued to spend several hours daily at his former master's grave. Several months later, the dog accompanied his new master to London. As the master was making arrangements with a boatman for his return home, another boatman pulled in to the wharf. The dog immediately hurled himself upon this man who was saved from death only by the interference of the dog's master. Threatened with the release of the dog, the boatman confessed to the crime and was subsequently tried, convicted and hanged. Upon returning home, the dog paid one last visit to his former master's grave, apparently satisfied that justice had been served.

An early Greek epitaph reads:

> Thou passest on the path, if haply thou dost mark this monument,
> Laugh not, I pray thee,
> Though it is a dog's grave; tears fell for me, and the dust was heaped above me by a master's hand, who likewise engraved these words upon my tomb.

Sir Walter Scott had a favorite Deerhound named Maida, another which he called Hamlet. Maida was his constant companion and appears in the novel *Woodstock* under the name of Bevis. The famous painter Landseer portrayed Maida with his master in a well-known painting. When Maida died, Scott had a stonemason erect a monument on his Abbotsford estate, which depicted the dog lying in his habitual attitude. The author himself dug Maida's grave and then went home to write a note cancelling a dinner engagement "on account of the death of a very dear friend."

Maida also inspired Scott to write, "I have sometimes thought of the final cause of dogs having such short lives, and I am quite satisfied it is in compassion to the human race; for if we suffer so much in losing a dog after an acquaintance of ten or twelve years, what would it be if they were to live double that time."

Scott's favorite must have endeared himself to most

his favored dogs were found. These are only a few instances of the esteem in which the Egyptian rulers held their dogs.

We have similar evidence from Assyria. The names of four of the best-loved dogs of Assurbanipal, who reigned about 625 B.C., have been identified as "He Who Must Bark," "Mischief-maker," "Holder of Enemies" and "Biter of Enemies." These names, descriptive of the dogs' characteristics, lead to the tentative identification of the latter two as Mastiffs, the first as an Assyrian Collie, and the second as a Terrier type.

The Prince of Condé (1621-1686), Louis XIV's general and one of Europe's greatest soldiers, was a dog lover, and many anecdotes are related about him. He had found a Great Dane mourning his dead master on the battlefield of Fleurus and adopted him, making him his inseparable companion. At the councils of war, after hearing the advice of his various generals, it is said that the general would often say: "Well, gentlemen, having heard all you have to say we will take the advice of a veteran." He would then explain the various arguments to the big dog and ask which plan he favored; often the dog would descend from his chair and solemnly offer his paw to one of the generals. As another anecdote has it, the dog on one occasion yawned and left the room, whereupon the great Condé decided to disregard all suggested plans and said: "I agree with the dog. We will march at dawn." The council had been trying to delay the

of his friends as well, for after his death Scott said, "My friends wrote as many elegies for him in different languages as ever were poured forth by Oxford or Cambridge on the death of a crowned head."

Recorded in verse by Scott and Wordsworth, and also in De Quincey's *Reminiscences* is the story of a young man, a Mr. Crouch, who on a tour of the Lake district climbed the mountain Helvellyn in April, 1805, accompanied by his dog. In the heavy mist he lost his way. In July, a shepherd in search of strays from his flock, heard a cry as of a young fox or dog, and followed the sound. Finally he came to a crevice where the body of the young man lay, and by his side was the meagre shadow of a dog, his companion.

In Shakespeare's time dogs were kept primarily for the purposes of utility or sport. His plays are full of references to dogs of the chase, and there is ample evidence of his intimate knowledge of the art of venery. However, it should be noted that in *Othello* there are also references to lap dogs. "He'll be as full of quarrel and offense as my young mistress' dog," says Iago of Cassio.

Mary, Queen of Scots, had a small Spaniel which hid beneath her voluminous robes when the Queen was taken to the execution chamber, keeping close to her feet under the long skirts, but history does not relate what became of him when he was discovered.

Another faithful Spaniel was Marie Antoinette's little dog Thisbe. He was prevented from riding with his mistress when she was taken to prison, but he trotted behind the carriage and was at the door of the prison to kiss the hand of his mistress. He was not allowed to enter, but watched faithfully at the door for several days.

The writings of Pope, Byron, and Lamb are strewn with interesting references to their domestic pets. But none compared with Charles Dickens in his fondness and understanding of dogs. Dickens loved dogs and had many in his household.

Dickens had a "small white shaggy terrier" named Timber Doodle, presented to him during his tour of America by the comedian Mitchell. His letters were full of references to this little dog. "Little doggy improves rapidly and now jumps over my stock at word of command. I have changed his name to Snittle Timbery as more sonorous and expressive."

From Italy Dickens wrote of his dog's troubles: "Timber has had every hair upon his body cut off because of the fleas and he looks like the ghost of a drowned dog come out of a pond after a week or so. He knows the change upon him and is always turning around and round to look for himself."

During Dickens' Gladshill Place days he had two Mastiffs, one of which was a favorite, Turk by name, "a noble animal, full of affection and intelligence," which died in a railway accident. Sultan, another pet, was a cross between a St. Bernard and a Bloodhound, "coloured like a lioness" and evidently with some lionlike characteristics, for it had to be destroyed for attacking a child of one of the servants. Dickens' interest in dogs was inexhaustible, and he was delighted with any new trait. There was a Newfoundland called Don, another named Linda and one known as Bumble because of the "peculiarly pompous and overbearing manner he had of appearing to mount guard over the yard when he was an absolute infant."

Charles Lamb had a large and handsome dog, Dash, of a "rather curious" breed. He was a "wild and wilful dog" that took advantage of Lamb's easy temper. He was devoted to his master but when walking would drag the good-natured Lamb on long, exhausting hikes. He was finally given to a friend, because, said Charles Lamb's sister, "he will be the death of Charles."

Dogs have a way of adjusting their lives to the lives of their masters. They will live the life demanded of them to answer man's need for companionship. One instance may be found in the celebrated Newfoundland, Boatswain, favorite of Lord Byron, which can be credited with the famous tribute in *Don Juan*, Canto 1:

> 'Tis sweet to hear the watch dogs' honest bark
> Bay deep-mouthed welcome as we draw near home;
> 'Tis sweet to know there is an eye will mark
> Our coming and look brighter when we come.

Here was a dog that, by nature, was a dog of the outdoors. But his master spent the nights at work or with his friends and slept through the morning and daylight hours when a dog should be abroad. Yet Boatswain happily lived the life of the poet, content to share his way of life.

No dog in literary history is more famous than Elizabeth Barrett Browning's Cocker Spaniel Flush. This was a lively little dog which, nevertheless, contentedly spent almost his entire life on a couch at the feet of his mistress. When Browning had married her and taken her out of the sickroom, her verses to Flush show what he had meant to her:

> Other dogs in thymy dew
> Tracked the hares and followed throngs,
> Sunny moor and meadow.
> This dog only, crept and crept
> Next a languished cheek that slept,
> Sharing in the shadow.
> But of thee it shall be said,
> This dog watched beside a bed
> Day and night unweary,
> Watched within a curtained room
> Where no sunbeam brake the gloom
> Round the sick and dreary.

Alexander Pope had a Great Dane at his home in Twickenham on the Thames. This dog was greatly admired by the then Prince of Wales, Prince Frederick. Pope would not part with his companion but later presented the Prince with a puppy sired by the Dane. This pup, in the royal kennels at Kew, wore a collar on which were the words written by Pope to accompany his gift:

> "I am His Highness' dog at Kew
> Pray tell me, sir, whose dog are you?"

Maurice Maeterlinck has been said to "worship dogs." Among his dogs was Pelleas, a little French

Bulldog, which had a "powerful head like Socrates and Verlaine." It was of Pelleas that Maeterlinck wrote his essay *On the Death of a Little Dog*. In Maeterlinck's words:

He knows to what to devote the best in him. He knows to whom above him to give himself. He has not to seek for a perfect superior and infinite power in the darkness and amid lies and dreams. He has a morality which surpasses all that he is able to discover within himself and which he can practice without scruples and without fear. He possesses truth in its fullness. He has a positive and certain ideal.

Although it would be impossible to find space to chronicle all the dogs that have been true friends to their masters and masters who have found the companionship of dogs of supreme importance in their lives, no list could exclude the famous little Terrier, Greyfriar's Bobby.

Bobby belonged to a Midlothian farmer named Gray, On every market day, the little dog accompanied his master to Edinburgh. They were to be seen together everywhere and at noon they went to a little restaurant near Greyfriar's cemetery, where the farmer would share his midday meal with his canine friend. In 1858, Gray died and was buried in Greyfriar's cemetery. The little dog hung about the gates and, when allowed by a compassionate attendant, would lie on his master's grave. At noon each day he went to the little inn and the innkeeper, remembering the two companions, gave him a bun. The dog would take the bun and disappear. One day Mr. Thraill, very curious, followed the dog and found that the bun was eaten at the side of Gray's grave, as if the two again shared their midday repast. The little dog never changed his habits. As dogs were not allowed to roam without licenses and collars, and beyond all, in the cemetery, a kindly Lord Provost presented Bobby with a collar and tag and he was unmolested when he sought his late master's side. When Bobby died, after years of faithfulness, a memorial statue was given by the Baroness Burdett-Couths, who loved dogs, and erected in Greyfriar's. It is simple inscribed, "A tribute to the affectionate fidelity of Greyfriar's Bobby."

The story of Greyfriar's Bobby was retold in a movie of the same name produced not long ago by Walt Disney.

One of the most famous tributes to the dog is Senator George G. Vest's eulogy delivered during a Missouri lawsuit involving the killing of a dog.

The best friend a man has in the world may turn against him and became his enemy. His son or daughter whom he has reared with loving care may prove ungrateful. Those who are nearest to us, those whom we trust with our happiness and our good name may become traitors to their faith. The money that a man has, he may lose . . . when he needs it most. A man's reputation may be sacrificed in a moment of ill-considered action. The people who are prone to fall on their knees to do us honor when success is with us may be the first to throw the stone of malice when failure settles its cloud upon our heels. The one absolutely unselfish friend that man can have in this selfish world, the one that never deserts him, the one that never proves ungrateful or treacherous, is his dog.

A man's dog stands by him in prosperity and in poverty, in health and in sickness. He will sleep on the cold ground where the wintry winds blow and the snow drives fiercely, if only he may be near his master's side. He will kiss the hand that has no food to offer, he will lick the wounds and the sores that come in encounter with the roughness of the world. He guards the sleep of his pauper master as if he were a prince. When all other friends desert, he remains. When riches take wings and reputation falls to pieces he is as constant in his love as the sun in its journey through the heavens. If fortune drives the master forth an outcast in the world, friendless and homeless, the faithful dog asks no higher privilege than that of accompanying him to guard him against danger, to fight against his enemies, and, when the last scene of all comes, and death takes the master in its embrace and his body is laid away in the cold ground, no matter if all other friends pursue their way, there, by the graveside will be found the noble dog, his head between his paws, his eyes sad but open in alert watchfulness, faithful and true even to death.

It can well be imagined how many lonely hours were lightened for Admiral Richard E. Byrd by his little dog companion, Igloo, during the great Antarctic exploration trip. Igloo was a Fox Terrier, a breed far remote from the Huskies of the polar regions, yet he adapted himself to the rugged, elemental living and travail of the expedition as easily as to life at home with the Byrd family, contented to be with his master. Igloo, moreover, well aware of his position as the pet of the leader, was quite cocky with the Eskimo dogs. After he got over the first surprise of seeing the huge sled dogs, he even became quite fierce with them! In his book *Little America*, Byrd writes that Igloo "feared not even the biggest dog among them; no doubt, he believed he was a great fighter because we saved his life so often."

Igloo accompanied the Admiral on his walks and as a little Fox Terrier's coat is not the kind to withstand the bitter cold of the Antarctic, one of the men made him a jacket of camel's hair which covered his body and his legs. This coat wasn't popular with Igloo and it was fascinating to the Eskimo puppies. They would steal up and nip at it at every opportunity, very curious about this odd covering. They so humiliated Igloo that he "could hardly contain himself." When his tormentors were off guard Igloo would try to reciprocate by attacking them in kind and it was a miracle to his master than he managed to escape his "amiable assassins."

The Eskimo dogs were great favorites of the expedition. Their proud and invincible spirit was much admired and most of them, contrary to the general belief, were gentle and playful. There were many instances of their drivers' love and attachment to these dogs. So these dogs, also, probably helped dispel loneliness and give courage as well as being a most necessary adjunct to the success of the expedition.

One of these dogs, Spy, became lame and sick as he had "pulled his heart out" during the unloading at Little America. His coat was not as heavy as the other dogs and Norman Vaughn, his master who "loved him as a brother," feared that he would have to be shot. However, Spy was taken into the house and slept in Byrd's room, much to the disgruntlement of Igloo! In time, the dog improved and Byrd writes of the beautiful sight it was to see Spy, out for exercise one day and still quite crippled, made a gallant dash to force his way to his place in the team which happened to go by. "The whole camp" stopped working to watch the tender greeting between the two dogs in the traces and the veteran. Spy gradually regained his health and was able to go back to his work in the harness.

Chinook, the famous lead dog of Arthur Walden's teams on the Byrd Expedition, is a name familiar to everyone. Byrd tells of an incident where Walden came within a hairsbreadth of falling into the ocean through a slush hole in the ice while trying to save the heavy sledge. Chinook showed the greatest anxiety and concern while watching his master's actions, almost as if he was determined to prevent him from taking what appeared to him to be a "foolish risk."

DOGS OF THE PRESIDENTS

From the very first President of the United States, there have been many since who had a fondness for dogs and many of the dogs of the White House are famous as companions to their masters.

George Washington was a great fox-hunting man. Naturally his interest lay with foxhounds. He enjoyed

During their residence in the White House, the dogs of President and Mrs. Calvin Coolidge were of much interest to news photographers. Courtesy Wide World Photos, Inc.

the chase so much so that during the Revolution when opportunity offered, he rode to the hounds. Hiltzheimer wrote in 1781, "My son, Robert, having been on a hunt at Frankfort, says that His Excel'y Gen. Washington was there."

The entries in Washington's diaries give many accounts of following the hounds. In one "Where and

How my time is spent," he wrote: "Jany. 1st. (1768) Fox huntg. in my own Neck with Mr. Robt Alexander and Mr. Colville—catched nothing." There were many such failures, but then in February there were two entries "catched two foxes" and again "catch two more foxes." On March 2, 1768, "Hunting again & catchd a fox with a bobd Tail & cut Ears, after 7 hours chase in which, most of the dogs were worsted."

Being so interested in fox hunting, Washington, with his usual painstaking care, started to build up a pack of hounds. They became his hobby and during the year 1768, his diaries are full of accounts of the breeding of hounds. Among his dogs in this period were: Mopsey, Taster, Tipler, Cloe, Lady, Forester, and Captain. Lady subsequently had four puppies which were named Vulcan, Searcher, Rover and Sweetlips.

Like all dog owners, Washington was beset by some troubles in his venture. He records how he anointed his hounds with "Hogs Lard & Brimstone" to cure an epidemic of mange. In spite of his efforts to breed his hounds according to scientific principles, the dogs often ignored the laws of eugenics and he was presented with puppies of quite different breeding from that of his planning.

From George Washington's time, the first dog we learn of in connection with the Presidents is the black and white spaniel which belonged to Maria Monroe, the first child to live in the Executive Mansion after it became known as the White House in 1817. She, also, was the first daughter of a President to be married in the White House.

Jefferson, Madison and Monroe all came from the

sporting sections of Virginia and all were lovers of hounds.

Andrew Jackson had a number of well-trained gundogs. Coonhounds, foxhounds, retrievers, and spaniels were the favorites of William Henry Harrison, John Tyler, James Polk, and Zachary Taylor.

Abraham Lincoln's love for dogs was immortalized in the famous statue of him as "The Hoosier Youth" executed by Paul Manship and erected in front of the Lincoln National Bank Building at Fort Wayne, Indiana. During his youth he befriended dogs on at least two occasions. One instance was when he rescued a dog which was marooned by a flooding mountain stream. At another time he nursed back to health an injured dog which he had found in the woods.

Ulysses S. Grant was another President who showed a fondness for dogs. During his service as General of the Union Army he was frequently accompanied by a hound which had attached itself to his troops.

Grover Cleveland was an ardent hunter and angler and owned a number of pointers, setters, spaniels, and beagles. Some of these almost always accompanied him on his hunting trips.

There were many kinds of small animals in Theodore Roosevelt's household, for he firmly believed in family pets. There were ponies, cats, lizards, guinea pigs, even kangaroos—and lots and lots of dogs. Scampt, a "rat terrier", was one of the President's companions. Mrs. Roosevelt had a dog named Gem. There was a Bull Terrier named Mike and a favorite dog, Black Jock.

For two consecutive administrations, Airedales reigned supreme in the White House. President Wilson had an Airedale called Davie. Then there was the well-known Laddie Boy, President Harding's Airedale, of which a bronze statue was made. Later there was another Airedale in the Harding household, a half-brother to Boy named Laddie Buck, but because of the confusion with Laddie Boy, his name was changed to Paul Pry.

The Coolidges' first White House dog was a Wire-

Charlie, at left, a Scotch Terrier, and Pushinka, pet dogs in the White House during President John F. Kennedy's tenure of office.

haired Terrier, Peter Pan, who took his guardian duties too seriously and proceeded to nip the heels of the workmen about the grounds, creating considerable havoc from time to time. Because of his excessive diligence, it was decided to give him to a friend who did not live where workmen and callers were so numerous.

One of President Coolidge's pets was a sheepdog from Wisconsin, Rob Roy. The latter was fond of coffee, and the President often poured a little in his saucer, much to the astonishment of guests, until they discovered that it was intended for Rob Roy. Prudence Prim, the beautiful white Collie, was so photogenic that cameramen besieged her and she was often pictured with her mistress. Prudence Prim's manners were as beautiful. She was a favorite with everyone and frequently mingled among the guests at tea parties, gracious and kindly, as if she understood the duties of a hostess.

President Hoover had a German Shepherd Dog named King Tut. After Tut's death there was one named Pat. The latter had a propensity for opening doors by himself and when another dog arrived from Norway for the President, a Norwegian Elkhound subsequently named Weejie, Pat opened doors for both of them to go through.

No President's dog has been so closely identified with the life of his master as Fala, the Scottish Terrier, the silent, affectionate, and devoted companion of Franklin Delano Roosevelt.

Fala was given to the President by Miss Katherine B. Davies of Westport, Conn., when he was a little puppy of four months. His sire, Peter the Reveller, and his dam, Kayfield Wendy, were very exceptional Scotties. Fala was registered as Murray of Fallahill, named after Roosevelt's relatives, the Murrays, whose estate in Scotland is Fallahill.

As Fala he was known to everyone in the nation. Fala's doings were news. And he was, moreover, a

Most American Presidents have been dog fanciers. No White House has ever been as close to his master as was Fala, President Franklin D. Roosevelt's Scottish Terrier. Courtesy United Press International.

These Beagles, shown here with President Johnson and the late Senator Dirksen, were all descendants of the original Johnson Beagle named Jefferson, but referred to always only as Beagle.

constant and vigilant attendant at the press conferences. He seemed to sense when they were to be held. When the doors opened and the newspaper men were admitted, Fala invariably took his place at the feet of the President.

He was not always an exemplary dog. The affairs of state sometimes bored him so that he had to have an occasional fling and run away. His truances never took him very far, and he was always discovered early, but as he liked to wander to the streets beyond the White House, it became eventually necessary to restrict him to the proper grounds in a wire-enclosed yard.

He disliked being separated from his master and undoubtedly his master missed the jovial little Scottie when he was not at his side. Fala was a constant source of amusement, comradeship, and consolation to President Roosevelt. When preparations were being made for the third inauguration exercises, Fala ran out and hopped into the car beside his master. He evidently felt he belonged at such an auspicious event, but he was gently removed by one of the bodyguards, and had to remain at home.

Fala made the last trip with his master, from Warm Springs to the White House; from the White House to Hyde Park, and to the rose garden on the banks of the Hudson.

President Truman and Eisenhower's years in the White House were relatively unmarked by publicity involving pets such as dogs. Fond of hunting in his earlier years, President Eisenhower admired the setters perhaps more than other breeds. But his health program following his illness while in office had to be directed to activities other than hunting.

In more recent years, President John F. Kennedy kept Charlie, a Scotch Terrier, and Pushinka, offspring of a Russian canine space traveler, at the White House. Charlie was a pet of the Kennedys prior to

JFK's election to the Presidency, remaining with the family throughout the time JFK was President. Charlie was the only dog traveling with them to Hyannis, Massachusetts and Palm Beach, Florida consistently. The others made these trips once in a while, too, but not as regularly.

Pushinka was a gift sent by Soviet Premier Nikita Krushchev to Caroline, President Kennedy's daughter. In 1963, Pushinka and Charlie had four puppies, surely a "first" of its kind to take place between world powers. President Kennedy gave these pups to various youngsters who had written the White House concerning their desire to own a dog.

Wolfie was a wolfhound given to the President as a gift during his trip to Ireland in 1963. A German Shepherd named Clipper was also given to Mrs. John F. Kennedy. She became very fond of Clipper.

Another dog, an Irish Setter named Shannon, was a gift to the President during his visit to Ireland. This dog and the President's son, John, became much attached and constant companions.

President Lyndon Johnson's beagles, Him and Her, attracted news attention by their "desire" to have their ears pulled. They descended from an original family beagle (named Jefferson, but always referred to only as "Beagle").

L.B.J. also had a white Collie named Blanco, a gift to the Presidential family received when they first moved into the White House. Another favorite target for news photographers was the President's dog Yuki, a white dog of mixed breed which had been found

While President Johnson conversed with a White House visit, Blanco, a white Collie given to the President when they first mov into the White House, relaxed nearby.

Dogs in President Nixon's household. From left to right, Pasha, a
rkshire Terrier, Vickie, a Miniature Poodle; and King Timahoe, an
sh Setter.

abandoned at a filling station and adopted by Luci
(Mrs. Patrick J. Nugent). Yuki, possessed of much
intelligence and a happy disposition, quickly became
popular within L. B. J's White House family.

President Richard Nixon moved into the White
House with Vickey, a Miniature Poodle, Pasha, a
Yorkshire Terrier, and King, an Irish Setter puppy,
thus carrying on a tradition as old as the office to
which he was elected.

From Washington's foxhounds to the Nixon trio,
Presidential dogs reflect the roles, whether hunting
companions or house pets, that dogs play in their
masters' lives. They also reflect an enthusiasm shared
by most Americans, whether or not their address is
1600 Pennsylvania Avenue.

DOGS OF THE MOVIES AND T.V.

Many dogs have been born "show-offs" and troupes of
performing dogs are almost as old as the stage itself.
But the highest degree of perfection to date in training dogs to run the gamut of human-like emotions
and perform deeds with sensationally uncanny understanding has been attained in the motion picture
industry.

In the days of silent films, it was not particularly
difficult to teach an intelligent and responsive dog to
act a part as if he lived it, for vocal and audible commands could be used. The advent of sound pictures,
however, made it necessary to develop an entirely different and much more difficult technique, and training dogs for work in the movies and T.V. became a
fine art, indeed.

These techniques embody the conventional employment of infinite patience coupled with a thorough

knowledge of the task at hand and complete understanding of the temperament of the dog. But the procedure is much more complex than that, for each dog
is an individual, sensitive to certain things in varying
degrees, and must be handled differently. There can
be no set rules, but an almost uncanny mutual understanding must be achieved.

In the words of Rudd Weatherwax, who, with his
brother, Frank, has been well-known in Hollywood
dog training, these methods highlight:

1. Kindness. A trainer must virtually live with his dog, learn
to know him, persuade the dog to like and trust him.
2. Patience. No one without it could possibly train a dog to
respond under movie-set conditions requiring silent cues in the
distracting presence of many persons.
3. Guidance. Weatherwax's principal tool—a leash or cord
about ten feet long.
4. Reward. A friendly word or a tidbit is the inevitable
consequence of a successful performance.

These simple principles make the task seem easy,
but they only form the foundation for the difficult
job ahead. The complexity of the work is reflected in
the fact that many, many patient dog lovers have
failed.

Other well-known Hollywood trainers, all of whom
have trained some exceptional performing dogs for
the screen, include Rennie Renfro, Henry East, Carl
Spitz (who served in the training program of the K-9
Corps), Frank Barnes, Earl Johnson, Bill Koehler,
Douglas Bundock, and Frank Inn; this listing is by
no means all-inclusive. Also, many of Hollywood's
dog trainers train other animals.

According to Carl Spitz, a good dog must go
through various training phases. These might be
termed: (a) Kindergarten, the ABCs of tractability
and response; (b) Grammer School, obedience to certain commands; (c) High School, advanced obedience training and instruction in response to silent

Lassie, star of a t.v. series of the same name.

DOGS AROUND THE WORLD

Here flanked by Stanley Livingston and Fred MacMurray is canine star Tramp, from the t.v. series, "My Three Sons." Hank Babbitt photo.

Trainer Bill Koehler explains to Emile Genest just what kind reaction is to be expected of Bodger during the shooting of the film "The Incredible Journey." Courtesy Walt Disney Productions.

At right, the late Walt Disney whose cartoon and animal movies delighted America for several decades, shown here with Gilles Payant (left) and the Irish Setter star of the movie, "Big Red." Courtesy Walt Disney Productions.

As night falls, Luath, the Labrador Retriever, followed by Bodger the Bull Terrier, and Tao, the Siamese cat, move on again in the long journey toward home through an unknown and forbidding wilderness in this scene from "The Incredible Journey." Courtesy Walt Disney Productions.

From left to right, Bodger, Tao and Luath are confronted by watery impasse, a problem which must be solved during their long wilderness journey toward home—a scene from "The Incredible Journey." Courtesy Walt Disney Productions.

cues; (d) College, development of personality as an actor.

The finishing phase gives the dog the background necessary to portray a villain, a comedian, a sentimentalist, or whatever. These abilities emerge after long and arduous practice, from repetitive reaction to the moods, gestures and will of the trainer. As Spitz has seen it:

Variety is the hardest part of the training. The dog must learn to take food avidly one minute; reject it the next. Practice is the key here. I have him do so many things that he gets used to variety. Nothing surprises him. Then, on a movie set, he doesn't mind strange objects, strange people or strange orders. He musn't become frightened. If he does, he'll miss the cue.

The peak point in training is instant reaction. It isn't enough that a dog responds to a word or gesture. He must respond *immediately;* otherwise he is no good for motion pictures. If he hesitates, he has failed just as completely as if he had refused to react at all. The slightest delay impedes the cues of the human actors or breaks the action. This ability to *act instantly* is far more valuable—and far more difficult to achieve—than any complicated trick.

Most of the well-known Hollywood training schools keep 40 to 50 dogs. Several full-time trainers are employed and separate classrooms are maintained for all the major stages of instruction.

A Russian Wolfhound named Czar was probably the first dog of prominence in motion pictures. He was in some of the old Universal productions, 50 or more years ago. Such dog names from past years as Rin-Tin-Tin, Strongheart, Teddy, Pete, Brownie, and Buck are still likely to be better remembered than the actors with whom they worked.

Rin-Tin-Tin, one of the highest paid dog actors of all time, was found in a World War I German trench as a puppy by Lt. Lee Duncan, who named him for the little woolen dolls fashioned by French girls as good luck charms for soldiers, and brought him home and trained him. Pictures in which he appeared were sensationally popular and are said to have saved the producing studio from bankruptcy. Rin-Tin-Tin's national popularity gave great impetus to the spread of the German Shepherd Dog in this country.

Hollywood today has many professionally-trained dogs working regularly in pictures. Half a dozen or so rate stardom more or less consistently. Heading the list has been Lassie, the Collie.

Pure breeding apparently offers no special advantage for dogs in motion pictures. Daisy, Loppy, Rags, Corky, and Shaggy were some of the outstanding mixed-breed players, but such names as Lassie, Flame, Asta, Buck, a St. Bernard, Prince, a Great Dane, and Ace, a German Shepherd, represent the bluebloods.

Some of these dogs might well be termed "finds." Lassie, then named Pal, was a cast-off because he chased motorcycles and barked constantly. He was given to Rudd Weatherwax in settlement of a $10 board bill.

The Cairn Terrier, Rommie, was an untrained house pet in the Weatherwax kennels. He caught the eye of Cecil B. DeMille, and Frank Weatherwax followed DeMille's instructions to "take him home and train him."

A scene from "Greyfriars Bobby," in which Old Jock, a Scottish shepherd, bids farewell to his faithful pet and companion, Bobby, before making his last trip into Edinburgh. Courtesy Walt Disney Productions.

Candy, a remorseful Welsh Corgi, howls in this scene from "Little Dog Lost" over the grave of a canine friend. Courtesy Walt Disney Productions.

Gilles Payant who with Walter Pidgeon starred in the film, "Big Red," here reassures Mollie, the starring Irish Setter, that he won't hurt the puppy. Courtesy Walt Disney Productions.

As "Old Yeller" in the movie of the same name, 115-pound Spike typifies a dog of "Mixmaster" background that hit it lucky on the "rags to riches" movie trail. In this film scene, he tolerantly ignores the rough play of children, but never for a moment neglects his self-assumed guard duties toward members of the wilderness family whose pioneer enterprise forms the story background. Courtesy Walt Disney Productions.

Actor Chuck Connors poses with his family and Spike, the canine star of "Old Yeller." Left to right: Michael, 6½; Jeffrey, 5; Stephan, 4; Mrs. Betty Connors. Courtesy Walt Disney Productions.

Rennie Renfro bought the mongrel Daisy (real name Spooks) for $2 in a pet show. The dog became a veteran actor.

Buck was a gun-shy hound which Renfro picked up at a dog pound and developed into a fine canine actor.

Corky, an appealing mongrel belonging to Henry East, was a $3 purchase. The little fellow became one of Hollywood's most consistent canine workers.

Earl Johnson secured the mongrel, Shaggy, for $2 at the city pound. The dog paid for himself, thousands of times.

The popular little dog in the "Petticoat Junction" television series also had humble beginnings, being a cross between a Cocker Spaniel and a Poodle. Owned by Mr. Frank Inn, the dog has no name, being known simply as "The Petticoat Junction dog." He was specially trained for about six months for his part on the show and was, circa 1969, about seven years old. This little dog, incidentally, has a girl friend named Hazel, who looks quite a bit like him and works on the film set frequently as his stand-in!

Spike, the canine hero of "Old Yeller," is another "rags-to-riches" celebrity whose history began as a month-old inmate of the Van Nuys, California Animal Shelter in 1953 where he was noticed by Frank Weatherwax.

"He was all head and feet, but he looked smart," recalled Weatherwax. "I thought he might make an actor, so I bailed him out for $3."

For Spike and Weatherwax, however, this was only a beginning, as a $20,000 investment in training (four years) followed before Spike outdid a dozen competitors for the role and got his "break" as "Old Yeller" from Walt Disney, who saw in the 115-pound rough-looking dog exactly what he was looking for. Another case of a dog making good despite a "Mixmaster" pedigree!

For sheer excitement, few animal scenes in Hollywood history rival the furious bear and dog fight in "Old Yeller." Unusual preparation was necessary to stage the outdoor battle without harming either animal.

With their welfare of first consideration, rehearsals for the skirmish began months ahead of actual shooting. Spike spent weeks on a leash getting acquainted with Doug, a nine-year-old movie bear owned by professional-handler Bryon Nelson.

Each animal learned the other's advantages. Spike was long on agility, Doug on strength.

With this knowledge the two enacted their screen scrap. And a mighty hubbub it was, full of sound, fury and primitive rage. Beyond all the seeming ferocity, however, it was a superb performance by a pair of experienced actors. This was testified to by Buster Matlock, a representative of the American Humane Association, present throughout the picture's filming.

"Both Spike and Doug knew exactly what to do," he affirmed. "Also, they were protected. They kicked up a lot of commotion and made it look good for the cameras, but when the dust cleared neither one had even a scratch."

The same care and consideration for the participants were taken in filming the wolf and hog fights. All animal sequences in "Old Yeller" were produced with the approval of the American Humane Association, whose "Animals Emancipation Proclamation" guaranteeing the welfare of movie animals has been part of the Screen Production Code since 1940.

Dogs in the Hollywood movie colony are outstanding examples of canine intelligence, the ability of dogs to learn. Many of them instantly recognize scores of cues and commands. Frank Barnes maintains that the German Shepherd, Grey Shadow, now retired, understood 200 words. It is sometimes hard to realize that back of these oft-times amazing performances there is a "man behind the scenes," but the fact remains that the Hollywood dog trainer has developed his work into a truly fine art.

To the late Walt Disney must go enormous credit for bringing alive some of the best and most famous dog stories of yesteryear, some produced for television as well as movie theaters.

To mention only a few of the prominent Disney productions featuring dogs, there was the movie "Big Red," the story of a backwoods orphan boy, a proud but lonely man in need of a son, and a happy-go-lucky Irish Setter whose courage brought man and boy together. The story, colorfully filmed in Quebec, Canada, employed as its canine lead, Champion Red Aye Scraps, an Irish Setter bred and trained originally by Larry and Eleanor Heist of Ontario, California, and further trained by Bill Koehler, who was allowed only four months for the task.

Ordinarily the bitterest of enemies, this Redbone Hound and a raccoon, star in the film "The Hound That Thought He Was a Raccoon," and showed that they could both tolerate each other and work together. Courtesy Walt Disney Productions.

Found as a pup and brought up by a family of raccoons, Nubbin, a Redbone Hound, learned later in his life that he was expected to hunt them! Another scene from "The Hound That Thought He Was a Raccoon." Courtesy Walt Disney Productions.

Canine star of the "Petticoat Junction" t.v. series. A dog of mixed breed which, since it had no name on the t.v. series, was referred to only as the "Petticoat Junction" dog. Courtesy Filmways.

Two other movies, each basically on the themes of dog's loyalty to man, were "Greyfriar's Bobby" and "The Incredible Journey."

"Greyfriar's Bobby" centered upon a cemetery in Edinburgh, Scotland, era—1859; the story of the little Skye Terrier that kept a fourteen-year vigil at his master's grave.

The canine hero of this film was a little stray Skye Terrier taken in off the streets of Churley, Scotland, by the 19-year-old daughter of a local police sergeant, the cost being only 12 shillings—roughly, $1.70. This is another "rags-to-riches" story, for eventually this dog, named Tam, made his paw print on a Hollywood contract and became insured with Lloyds of

London for 20,000 pounds—a far cry from his 12-shilling purchase price!

"The Incredible Journey" was a motion picture about an Ontario, Canada family who, departing for a several months' stay in England, entrusted their Bull Terrier, Bodger, a Labrador Retriever named

Buck, a one-time St. Bernard movie star.

Luath, and a Siamese cat named Tao, to the care of a family friend living some 200 miles away in the northwestern part of the Province. Left at their new location temporarily alone not long after their arrival, the three pets became lonesome and set out on the long, long journey through the wilderness back to their family home, encountering numerous perils and adventures along the way. Finally both family and pets were once more united.

The outstanding animal star of this film was "old" Bodger, the Bull Terrier, played by a 3-year-old dog actor named Muffey. Both Muffey and Rink, the latter the Labrador that played the part of Luath, were owned by William Koehler and Halleck H. Druscoll, who spent several months supervising the dogs' training before actual production began. The cat, Tao, incidentally, was actually named Syn Cat, a Siamese owned by Al Niemela, the trainer of a variety of animal species.

On an entirely different theme, "The Hound That Thought He Was a Raccoon" was a movie about a lost pup who, brought up fondly by raccoons and then returned to his owner, eventually found himself in the perplexingly adult role of pack leader on a raccoon hunt.

As described by the Disney Studios, this was a different kind of animal story in which the plot dealt with the conflicts, pressures and problems which an animal must face in its struggle for survival, the story being told from the animal's viewpoint.

So good, in general, has been the public acceptance of Disney animal films that whether it be in the television or the movie field, dog stories and dog actors are bound to continue as highly popular viewing fare, with new and even as remarkable canine stars appearing no doubt from time to time in the future to entertain both children and adults.

Part XVIII

KENNEL CLUBS

Quite probably there are today far more kennel clubs than ever before because such organizations now exist in many foreign countries including some in South America, Africa, and Asia, as well as Europe. Space permits covering only those kennel clubs whose programs or activities are widely known and thought to be of most interest to readers. There are also, however, similar organizations in such countries as Argentina, Australia, Brazil, Chile, Denmark, East Africa, Finland, West Germany, Ireland, Japan, Netherlands, New Zealand, Norway, Poland, and Spain. Also, in India, the kennel club is known as the Kennel Club of India; the Italian organization is known as the Italian Ente Nazionale Della Canofilia. In the Federated Malay States, the organization is the Malay Kennel Association; in Portugal, it is the Portuguese Club de Canicultura. In Sweden, it is the Svenska Kennel Klubben, and in South Africa, it is the South Africa Kennel Union.

—The American Kennel Club—

WHEN TEN sportsmen met in Philadelphia in September, 1884, talking of an association which might elevate the standards of the dog game, they probably didn't dream that the organization which was born that night could attain the size and influence of today's American Kennel Club. It was their idea that the organization should be established on a non-profit basis and that it should be representative of the nation's breeders and exhibitors.

While it has undergone several major reorganizations in its long and useful history, it has never deviated from its original purpose. Within a month after that first meeting, a constitution was prepared and it was adopted at an October meeting held in New York.

Major James M. Taylor of Lexington, Kentucky, was the first president and his friend, Elliott Smith of New York, another gundog man, was the first vice-president. These two were responsible for calling the first meeting. The other original officers were Samuel Coulson, second vice-president, E. S. Porter, secretary, and G. N. Appold, treasurer.

The organizers, of course, were the first members. Their new project had no more than made a start when it became clear to all that it should be revamped so as to eliminate individual memberships and, instead, invite already established kennel clubs and breed clubs to join. It has often been remarked that at this early date a new name, "The American Kennel Association," might have been adopted. Had that occurred, the public might have gained a better or easier understanding of the organization.

A Cooperative Association. It is true that many people among the scores of thousands who use the club's facilities do not know that it much more nearly resembles a cooperative association than a club. Each of the more than 300 clubs which now belong to the American Kennel Club is entitled to a delegate, a representative in the club's rule-making body.

Somewhat more than half of these member-clubs are known as all-breed show-giving clubs. The remainder are specialty clubs, devoted to the interests of a single breed. Through their membership, each of these clubs is entitled to conduct dog shows, field trials or obedience trails in the particular territory assigned to it. These events are conducted under an extensive set of rules and regulations. But the privilege of conducting such events under AKC rules is not limited to member clubs. Shows and trials of the same type are staged by an even greater number of non-member clubs simply by obtaining a license to conduct their program under these rules.

Early Problems and Growth. At the time of the Philadelphia meeting there was no recognized standard of perfection for each of the many breeds. Breeders and groups of breeders here and there went their own way in the development of strains which met their own fancies. True, there were breed clubs at that time, some of which had adopted standards for their breeds, but all had experienced difficulty in winning recognition on a national basis.

When AKC membership was opened to clubs rather than individuals, the first specialty club in each breed to be elected became designated as the parent club of the breed. The American Kennel Club looks to the parent clubs to define and revise their breed standards and generally to serve it in an advisory capacity in any problem relating to their particular breeds.

Just as specialty clubs were in need of an association which would give them national standing and aid in bringing together all interests within a breed, show-giving all-breed clubs were having their difficulties. Facilities did not exist for these clubs to standardize their operations. Irregularities of the worst sort occurred at many dog shows and fraud was rampant in certain quarters.

There was great need for an authentic stud book registry. There were registration organizations. Most of them were privately owned. Some were good, some were bad. Many breeders preferred to keep their own private records, and a pedigree issued over the signature of a man of good repute was considered by some to be more dependable than that issued by some of the registry organizations.

Of course, there was no way to deal with fraud excepting through the civil courts. The situation was made to order for a flourishing activity in pedigree mills, dishonest judging, and general skullduggery. These were the problems which confronted the new club in 1884. The acceptance which it has gained from the breeder-exhibitor public indicates the extent to which it has met the problem.

Present records would indicate that the doors of the new club were not stormed by early member-applicants. Among the club's present members, it is found that only perhaps 20 can date their membership prior to the turn of the century. Of those 20 clubs which were admitted during the first 16 years, only five gave shows open to the recognized breeds of the day. The other fifteen were specialty clubs.

The earliest all-breed members were the Westminster Kennel Club, Danbury Agricultural Society, Rhode Island Kennel Club, Texas Kennel Club, and the Ladies' Kennel Association. The breeds which were first to be represented were: Fox Terriers, Beagles, Spaniels, Bulldogs, Boston Terriers, Foxhounds, Dachshunds, Bull Terriers, French Bulldogs, Irish Setters, and the St. Bernards.

As the young organization grew, its services and facilities expanded. An official publication, *The American Kennel Gazette,* was launched. In addition to supplying reading matter of general interest to dog people, it undertook to report to the public on its own affairs. It also started publication of detailed reports on every show or field trial held under the club's rules.

The American Kennel Club Stud Book, a monthly publication listing the details on every dog registered in the club's offices, was brought out. Both publications are still considered an integral part of the club's service to the dog public though they do not operate at a profit.

The jurisdictional status of the club was frequently questioned in its early days. It had grown and proceeded on the theory that it was an organization whose members agreed to relinquish some personal rights in order to enjoy the benefits of association. Its representative delegates built up an extensive regulatory system for themselves. And, the club took the position that persons and clubs other than members might enjoy these facilities so long as they were willing to abide by the rules and conduct themselves in accordance with the club's aim and purposes.

Sometimes when the club denied the use of its facilities to a person, such as withholding the right to register one's dogs in its Stud Book, its right to do so was questioned. The exact status of the club in the affairs of pure-bred dogs, its purpose, and its rights were clearly set out when it underwent its second major organizational change.

Incorporation and Charter. The AKC was incorporated by special legislative act in 1909. The individual incorporators in behalf of the club were:

William G. Rockefeller, Dwight Moore, Howard Willets, B. S. Smith, Marcel A. Viti, Frederick H. Osgood, John E. De Mund, Clair Foster, Lawrence M. D. McGuire, Henry Jarrett, August Belmont, William B. Emery, Edward Brooks, Charles W. Cadwalader, Winthrop Rutherford, James Mortimer, George Lauder, Jr., William Rauch, Samuel R. Cutler, John G. Bates, J. H. Brookfield, Chetwood Smith, Hildreth K. Bloodgood, Singleton Van Schaick, Hollis H. Hunnewell, J. Sergeant Price, and William C. Codman.

The charter which they obtained says that:

The objects of the corporation shall be to adopt and enforce uniform rules regulating and governing dog shows and field trials, to regulate the conduct of persons interested in exhibiting, running, breeding, registering, purchasing and selling dogs, to detect, prevent and punish frauds in connection therewith, to protect the interests of its members, to maintain and publish an official stud book and an official kennel gazette, and generally to do everything to advance the study, breeding, exhibiting, running and maintenance of the purity of thoroughbred dogs.

It continues to say:

And for these purposes it shall have power to adopt a constitution, by-laws, rules and regulations, and enforce the same by fines and penalties, which it shall have the right to collect and enforce by suit, or by suspension or expulsion from membership, or by suspension or denial of any or all of the privileges of said corporation. It may, from time to time, alter, modify or change such constitution, by-laws, rules or regulations.

Delegates and Management. As has been stated, the delegates to the American Kennel Club serve as the congress for the club. They are the direct representatives of the member clubs. They meet quarterly in New York City and consider and adopt needed legislation. This body also votes upon all applications for membership which may come from other clubs. The delegates also pass upon all prospective delegates. A member club nominates its own delegate but he must be acceptable to his prospective colleagues.

Another important function of the delegates is to elect, from among their own number, three men each year to serve on the Board of Directors. The Board consists of twelve elected delegates, each elected for a four-year term so that there cannot be a turn-over of more than 25% in the Board's composition in any year.

The Board, under the club's constitution, is vested with broad powers in the general management of the club's affairs within the limits of its extensive by-laws. The Board meets each month. Following each annual meeting of the club, the Board holds an organization meeting and chooses one of its members as president. It also elects an executive vice-president, executive secretary, secretary, and treasurer.

All officers, except the president, devote their full time to the Club's affairs and they are responsible for its day-to-day management. A full-time staff (175 people some years ago) is required to handle the organization's affairs. Funds for the maintenance of this extensive operation come from fees for the registration of dogs. Additional income is derived from membership dues and the issuance of licenses for shows and trials which are held by non-member clubs.

Registrations. Registration is the club's biggest business, and probably its most important business because a majority of the nation's registered dogs are entered on the rolls of the A.K.C. Stud Book. Thus, the breeding of pure-bred dogs depends in no small measure on the accuracy and integrity of these records. While the A.K.C. does not have a monopoly, there being many other available registry organizations, the A.K.C. symbol on a pedigree has won wide acceptance as proved by the fact that thousands of breeders the country over feature this symbol in their advertising.

The club's Stud Book is at present open to over one hundred different breeds. These often are referred to as the "recognized" breeds; but club officials do not encourage the use of the term because it suggests that unrecognized breeds may not be sufficiently pure for admittance to this choice circle. The club is quick to point out that there are scores of other established breeds in various parts of the world which have not been admitted to the Stud Book mainly because of their rarity here.

Before a new breed is accepted and admitted to stud book records, it must be proved that it does breed true to type, it must have the sponsorship of a well-established club in this country, and there must be a sufficient number of the dogs in the hands of many owners to justify the setting up of a record-keeping system for it.

Registration is primarily restricted to dogs whose sires and dams were registered or were eligible for registration with the Club. Before an individual dog may be registered, the litter of which it is a part must be enrolled by the breeder. Reciprocal agreements with other stud books, particularly those of foreign lands, make possible the registration of some dogs which do not meet these general requirements.

Inquiries Handled and Services. The American Kennel Club receives well over one million applications for litter and individual registrations each year —and the rate increases about ten percent annually. In addition, there are over 160,000 applications for transfer of ownership, and this rate, too, increases at about the same pace.

It is said that a typical day's mail brings over 5,000 letters to the A.K.C. office. Most of them, of course, relate to registration; but many pertain to dog shows, field trials, and obedience trials. Then there are many which simply seek information on every imaginable phase of the dog and its welfare. There are thousands upon thousands of inquiries seeking special information. About half of these seek advice on buying a dog. The club maintains a special department for bringing buyers and sellers together. Any breeder whose dogs are registered with the A.K.C. may list his available stock with this department. The service is free and, of course, the club cannot vouch for the merits of any dog.

Much activity also centers in the license department. Show and trial-giving clubs first apply to this department for approval of a date. Club policy forbids the scheduling of two major events of the same type on the same day if they are less than 200 miles apart. After the approval of a date, the applying club submits its list of judges. Here, again, the club must avoid conflicts. It tries to avoid having any judge pass upon a given breed more than once in 30 days in an area of 200 miles radius. Finally, after approval of judges, premium lists are submitted to the department for approval. Since the premium list is considered as the contract between exhibitor and show- or trial-giving club, it is important that they comply in every particular with all A.K.C. regulations.

The licensing of several thousand judges also is a major responsibility of this department. The club maintains a list of judges who have been qualified to serve, but in the main they are licensed only for one event at a time.

Practically all dog shows and obedience trials in the United States are cleared through the American Kennel Club. The club does not fill the same important place in field trials, as many of the trials for pointing dogs are not run under the club's rules. The same applies to coonhounds, foxhounds, and certain other breeds. However, beagle trials, retriever trials, and spaniel trials are almost exclusively A.K.C. affairs.

Immediately after the conclusion of any A.K.C. show or trial, the superintendent or secretary is required to file a complete report with the show department of the American Kennel Club. Entry forms and judges' books, as well as marked catalogs, become a part of the club's permanent record. The reports are carefully audited to determine the eligibility of every participating dog and, finally, each placement of each dog is recorded on that dog's own card in the club files. On a minute's notice, the club can see the complete show record of any one of several hundred thousand dogs.

An important adjunct of the club's operation is its extensive library which is open to the public. All available American and foreign Stud Books are on file here as well as several thousand volumes devoted to the dog. An impressive art collection has been built through the generosity of the club's friends.

High Standards to be Maintained. The dog "game," whether viewed from the standpoint of breeder or exhibitor, is actually a participation-sport and, to maintain it on the highest possible plane, some regulatory facilities are required. Thus, the club's rules and by-laws provide that all may participate so long as they abide by these rules and do not prejudice pure-bred dogs by their activities. When they fail in that, the rules empower the Board of Directors to discipline such persons by suspension of all club privileges or by fine if there is no question of fact involved.

Handling of Certain Complaints or Disputes. If it becomes necessary to settle a question of fact, such cases are referred to a trial board. Nine such boards of three men each are appointed by the Board of Directors each year. They are strategically located throughout the United States. Their proceedings are not entirely unlike those of courts of law. Every accused person is given an opportunity to defend himself. Any person or any club is privileged to file charges with the American Kennel Club against either person or club.

AKC RULES, REGULATIONS, AND MEMBERSHIP

For a listing of breeds recognized by A.K.C., see Part XVI.

Up-to-date copies of A.K.C. rules and regulations may be secured by writing to The American Kennel Club, 51 Madison Avenue, New York, New York, 10010. Separate booklets are usually available for rules applying to registration and field trials, regulations and standards for obedience trials, and rules applying to registration and dog shows; the desired rules should therefore be specified.

For inquiries and correspondence, also available from A.K.C. are listings of member clubs together with the names and addresses of their respective delegates and secretaries. The A.K.C. also provides assistance to anyone wishing to contact breeders of specific kinds of dogs.

There follows a recent listing of member clubs and the rules and regulations of the organization as made available through the courtesy of A. K. C.

Afghan Hound Club of America   Sec'y, Mrs. Ralph L. Culver, 862 Schodack Landing Rd., Schodack Landing, N. Y. 12156.

Airedale Terrier Club of America   Sec'y, Mrs. Carl Macklin, R.D. 1, Box 190, Edinburg, Pa. 16116.

Alaskan Malamute Club of America, Inc.   Sec'y, Mrs. Dorothy S. Pearson, 8014 Shallowford Rd., Chattanooga, Tenn. 37421.

Albany Kennel Club   Sec'y, Mrs. Grace Pappas, R.D. 2, Castleton-on-Hudson, N. Y. 12033.

All Breed Training Club of Akron, Inc.   Sec'y, Mrs. Marilyn R. Hooper, 968 Stadelman Ave., Akron, Ohio 44320.

American Bloodhound Club   Sec'y, Mrs. Marion Pruitt, 41 Roxbury Dr., Commack, N. Y. 11725.

American Boxer Club, Inc.   Sec'y, Mrs. Lorraine C. Meyer, 807 Fairview Blvd., Rockford, Illinois 61107.

American Brittany Club   Sec'y, Nicky Bissell, Rt. 3, Box 14, Sherwood, Ore. 97140.

American Bullmastiff Association   Sec'y, Mrs. Russell E. Morris, Jr., Box 474, Rt. 1, Lutherville, Md. 21903.

American Chesapeake Club, Inc.   Sec'y, Edwin E. Gesner, Spring Cove Road, Pawson Park, Branford, Conn. 06405.

American Foxhound Club   Sec'y, William C. Elliott, Maple Hill Rd., Gladwyne, Pa. 19035.

American Fox Terrier Club   Sec'y, J. W. Smith, Box 190, Gowanda, N.Y. 14070.

American Maltese Association, Inc.   Corres. Sec'y, Mrs. Robert Stuber, 261 Primrose Pl., Lima, Ohio 45805.

American Manchester Terrier Club   Sec'y, Mrs. E. Floyd Deuel, 409 N. 2nd St., Hiawatha, Ka. 66434.

American Miniature Schnauzer Club   Sec'y, Mrs. R. L. Larson, 507 Redondo Dr., Ballwin, Mo. 63011.

American Pointer Club, Inc.   Sec'y, John G. Laytham, Laurel Hills, R.D. 2, Woodstown, N.J. 08098.

American Pomeranian Club   Sec'y, Miss Joy Brewster, R. R. 3, Rt. 6, Newtown, Conn. 06470.

American Sealyham Terrier Club   Sec'y, Mrs. Sharon Johnson, 5972 Columbia Rd., No. Olmstead, Ohio 44070.

American Shetland Sheepdog Association   Sec'y, Mrs. James Hausman, Farms Road, R. R. #1, Stamford, Conn. 06903.

American Spaniel Club   Sec'y, Mrs. Margaret W. Ciezkowski, 154 Maple Ave., Uniondale, N.Y. 11553.

American Whippet Club   Sec'y, Louis Pegram, c/o Ralston Purina Company, Checkerboard Square, St. Louis, Mo.

Anderson Kennel Club   Sec'y, Mrs. Dorothy Smullen, R.R. 4, Box 258, Anderson, Ind. 46011.

Arkansas Kennel Club, Inc.   Sec'y, Miss Margaret Wilbern, P.O. Box 126, Sweet Home Ark. 72164.

Asheville Kennel Club, Inc.   Corres. Sec'y, Mrs. Frank J. Chappell, 15 Dillingham Road, Asheville, N.C. 28805.

Atlanta Kennel Club   Corres. Sec'y, Miss Joyce A. Osburn, Karakel, Rt. 3, Lawrenceville, Ga. 30245.

Austin Kennel Club, Inc.   Sec'y, Mrs. Penny Bloomer, 2803 Vance Lane, Austin, Texas 78746.

Back Mountain Kennel Club, Inc.—Sec'y, Mrs. Robert Jewell, 52 W. Center Rd., Shavertown, Pa. 18708.

Badger Kennel Club   Sec'y, Miss Kay Stehr, 309 Grant St., Waunakee, Wisc. 53597.

Baltimore County Kennel Club, Inc.   Sec'y, Mrs. George Mueller, Sweet Air Rd., Phoenix, Md. 21131.

Basenji Club of America   Sec'y, Mrs. Donald Trottier, 174 Central St., Norwell, Mass 02061.

Basset Hound Club of America, Inc.   Sec'y, Mrs. Donald Bateman, Box 215, Warrenville, Ill. 60555.

Battle Creek Kennel Club   Corres. Sec'y, Mrs. Fred Myers, Rt. 8, Box 175, Battle Creek, Mich. 49017.

Beaver County Kennel Club, Inc.   Sec'y, Mrs. Nan Brasaemle, R.D. #1, Mars Rd., Evans City, Pa. 16003.

Bedlington Terrier Club of America   Sec'y, Mrs. L. H. Terpening, Bayberry Rd., R.D. 2, Princeton, N.J. 08450.

Belgian Sheepdog Club of America, Inc.   Sec'y, Mr. Myron E. Rowland, 1310 Hoyt Ave., Muncie, Ind. 47302.

Berks County Kennel Club   Sec'y, Mrs. David Diehl, 208 Columbia Ave., Hyde Park, Reading, Pa. 19605.

Birmingham Kennel Club, Inc.   Sec'y, Mrs. B. R. Boshell, Rt. 4, Box 980, Birmingham, Ala. 35210.

Borzoi Club of America   Sec'y, Mrs. Albert J. Groshans, Center Valley, Pa. 18034.

Boston Terrier Club of America, Inc.   Sec'y, Mrs. Caroline A. Morlock, 111 Birch St., Roslindale, Mass. 02131.

Briard Club of America   Sec'y, Mrs. Mary Lou Tingley, Yardley Road, Mendham, N.J. 07945.

Bronx County Kennel Club   Sec'y, Mrs. Debbie-Lynn Bowden, 2550 Independence Ave., Riverdale-on-Hudson, N.Y. 10471.

Bryn Mawr Kennel Club   Sec'y, Mrs. J. Sellers Walton, 639 Upper Gulph Rd., Wayne, Pa. 19087.

Buckeye Beagle Club   Sec'y, Mrs. Cathy Dowler, 622 Jordan Dr. N.W., New Philadelphia, Ohio 44663.

Bucks County Kennel Club   Sec'y, Mrs. Virginia S. Hampton, 500 E. Court St., Doylestown, Pa. 18901.

Bulldog Club of America   Sec'y, Kenneth R. Branion, 27905 W. 10 Mile Rd., Farmington, Mich. 48024.

Bulldog Club of New England, Inc.   Sec'y, Mrs. Arthur Lane, One North Ave., Weston, Mass. 02193.

Bulldog Club of Philadelphia   Sec'y, Mrs. Frances H. Williams, 198 Sherbrook Blvd., Upper Darby, Pa. 19082.

Bull Terrier Club of America   Sec'y, Mrs. Irene Mann, Lakeside Rd., R.D. 3, Newburgh, N.Y. 12550.

Burlington County Kennel Club   Corres. Sec'y, Mrs. Linda Willis, R.D. 1, Box 11, Medford, N.J. 08055.

Butler County Kennel Club, Inc.   Sec'y, Earl D. Poole, R.D. 1, Saxonburg, Pa. 16056.

Cairn Terrier Club of America   Sec'y, Mrs. L. O. Griffith Jr., 174 W. Ingomar Rd. Pittsburgh, Pa. 15237.

California Airedale Terrier Club   Sec'y, Mrs. Helen Piperis, 3903 Turnley Ave., Oakland, Calif. 94605.

California Collie Clan, Inc.   Corres. Sec'y, Jean Roche, 12311 Blodgett Ave., Downey, Calif. 90242.

Camden County Kennel Club, Inc.   Sec'y, Allen B. Mills, R.D. 2, Box 401, Medford, N.J. 08055.

Capital Dog Training Club of Washington, D.C., Inc.   Sec'y, Miss Barbara A. Ames, 3541 So. George Mason Dr., Alexandria, Va. 22302.

Cardigan Welsh Corgi Club of America, Inc.   Sec'y, Harold K. Nelson, 1072 Thomas Jefferson St. N.W., Washington, D.C. 20007.

Carolina Kennel Club   Sec'y, Miss G. C. Monroe, P.O. Box 11086, Guilford, N.C. 27409.

Catonsville Kennel Club   Corres. Sec'y, Mrs. John W. Barr, 2818 Roselawn Ave., Baltimore, Md. 21214.

Cedar Rapids Kennel Association, Inc.   Sec'y, Mrs. Ralph D. Willey, 215-217 3rd Ave. S.E., Cedar Rapids, Ia. 52406.

Central Beagle Club   Sec'y, Edmund Czwalga, Box 235, R.D. 1, Cheswick, Pa. 15024.

Central Florida Kennel Club, Inc.   Sec'y, Mrs. Viola H. Kastner, Rt. 1, Box 245, Sanford, Fla. 32771.

Central New York Kennel Club   Sec'y, Mrs. Paul M. Ferguson, R.D. #4, Cemetery Rd., Rome, N.Y. 13440.

Central Ohio Kennel Club   Sec'y, Miss Margaret Busch, 3803 Granden Road, Columbus, Ohio 43214.

Chain-O-Lakes Kennel Club   Corres. Sec'y, Mrs. Joan M. Ross, P.O. Box 274, Ingleside, Ill. 60041.

Charleston Kennel Club   Sec'y, Mrs. Candye Slay, 1046 Birchdale, Charleston, S.C. 29407.

Chattanooga Kennel Club   Sec'y, Mrs. Dorothy Pearson, 8014 Shallowford Rd., Chattanooga, Tenn. 37421.

Cheshire Kennel Club, Inc.   Sec'y, Mrs. Norris Robertson, Peg Shop Rd., Keene, N.H. 03431.

Chester Valley Kennel Club   Sec'y, Mrs. Alan R. Robson, R.D. 3, West Chester, Pa. 19380.

Chicago Bulldog Club, Inc.   Sec'y, Phillip E. Stonehouse, 515 Cumnor Road, Kenilworth, Ill. 60043.

Chicago Collie Club   Sec'y, Miss Jane Youngjohns, Rt. 25, Elgin, Ill. 60120.

Chihuahua Club of America   Sec'y, Simon M. Dickerson, Box 2025, Donelson, Tenn. 37214.

Chow Chow Club, Inc.   Sec'y, Mrs. Neva H. Gaspar, 22450 Santa Paula, Cupertino, Calif. 95014.

Cincinnati Kennel Club, Inc.   Sec'y, Charles Norris, 8100 Varner Rd., Cincinnati, Ohio 45243.

Cleveland All-Breed Training Club   Sec'y, Miss Irma Dixon, 16804 Fairfax Ave., Cleveland, Ohio 44128.

Cocker Spaniel Breeders Club of New England   Sec'y, Mrs. Kay Hardy, 8 West Dale Rd., Canton, Mass. 02021.

Collie Club of America, Inc.   Sec'y, John Honig, 72 Flagg St., Worcester, Mass 01602.

Colorado Kennel Club   Sec'y, Louis E. Surles, Star Rt., Box 85, Morrison, Colo. 80465.

Contra Costa County Kennel Club, Inc.   Sec'y, Dale J. Cook, 104 Lockwood Lane, Pleasant Hill, Calif. 94523.

Corn Belt Kennel Club   Sec'y, Miss Dorothy Banfill, 915 Hovey Ave., Normal, Ill. 61761.

Cornhusker Kennel Club, Inc.   Sec'y, Mrs. Fred C. Bookstrom, R.F.D. 7, Sheltered Acres, Lincoln, Neb. 68505.

Coulee Kennel Club, Inc.   Sec'y, Mrs. Shirley Kolhoren, 1021 Lasey Blvd., LaCrosse, Wisc. 54601.

Dachshund Club of America, Inc.   Sec'y, Mrs. William Burr Hill, 2031 Lake Shore Blvd., Jacksonville, Fla. 32210.

Dalmatian Club of America   Secretary, David G. Doane, M.D., 25 Franklin Rd., Walton, N.Y. 13856.

Dandie Dinmont Terrier Club of America   Sec'y, Dr. M. Josephine Deubler, 2811 Hopkinson House, Washington Square So., Philadelphia, Pa. 19106.

Dayton Kennel Club, Inc.   Sec'y, Mrs. Louis H. Kleinhans, 1404 E. Siebenthaler Ave., Dayton, Ohio 45414.

Delaware County Kennel Club   Sec'y, Miss Louise M. Scheirer, 135 Carre Ave., Essington, Pa. 19029.

Del Monte Kennel Club   Corres. Sec'y, Mrs. Charles A. Nelson, 725 Terry St., Monterey, Calif. 93940.

Des Moines Kennel Club   Sec'y, Mrs. Kathryn K. Foley, 213 42nd St., Des Moines, Ia. 50312.

Detroit Kennel Club   Sec'y, John P. Hackett, 1453 Pierce St., Birmingham, Mich. 48009.

Devon Dog Show Ass'n, Inc.   Sec'y, Mrs. William B. Lex, 418 Fishers Rd., Bryn Mawr, Pa. 19010.

Doberman Pinscher Club of America   Sec'y, Mrs. Milli Dold, P.O. Box 16031, Wichita, Ka. 67216.

Dog Fanciers Association of Oregon   Sec'y, Tom Masic, 14114 N.E. Siskiyou Ct., Portland, Oreg. 97220.

Dog Owners' Training Club of Maryland   Sec'y, Mrs. Thomas A. Knott, 2102 Meadowview Dr., Baltimore, Md. 21207.

Durham Kennel Club   Corres. Sec'y, Mrs. Lary K. Winberry, P.O. Box 1629, Durham, N.C. 28202.

Eastern Beagle Club, Inc.   Sec'y, Charles W. Dunham, 85 Ritter Lane, Newark, Del. 19711.

Eastern Dog Club   Sec'y, Chas. L. J. Noble, Lowell Rd., Concord, Mass. 01742.

Eastern German Shorthaired Pointer Club   Sec'y, Mrs. Judy Marden, Nedsland Ave., Titusville, N.J. 08560.

Elm City Kennel Club   Sec'y, Mrs. Milton Morris, 59 West Park Ave., New Haven, Conn. 06511.

El Paso Kennel Club   Sec'y, Mrs. Norman C. Gad, 2507 Nashville St., El Paso, Texas 79930.

Empire Beagle Club, Inc.   Sec'y, Mrs. James Fitzsimmons, Claverack, N.Y. 12513.

English Cocker Spaniel Club of America   Sec'y, Mrs. Collier Platt, Syosset, Long Island, N.Y. 11791.

English Setter Association of America, Inc.   Sec'y, Mrs. Ray Parsons, 12625 Farndon Ave., Chino, Calif. 91710.

English Springer Spaniel Club of the Central States   Sec'y, D. K. Langhans, 9124 Oak Park, Morton Grove, Ill. 60053.

English Springer Spaniel Club of Michigan   Sec'y, Mrs. Philip Shifferd, 33968 8 Mile Rd., Farmington, Mich., 48024.

English Springer Spaniel Field Trial Ass'n., Inc.   Sec'y, Mrs. Evelyn Monte, 250 Park Ave., New York, N.Y. 10017.

English Springer Spaniel Field Trial Club of Illinois   Sec'y, Mrs. Barry C. Phelps, 1699 Riverwoods Rd., Lake Forest, Ill. 60045.

Erie Kennel Club, Inc.   Sec'y, Mrs. Bonnie B. Reed, R.D. 6, Hartman Rd., Erie, Pa. 16510.

Evansville Kennel Club, Inc.   Sec'y, Donald Burks, 1111 W. Columbia St., Evansville, Ind. 47710.

Farmington Valley Kennel Club, Inc.   Sec'y, Mrs. Christine L. Swinkle, 20 Juniper Rd., Bristol, Ct. 06010.

Finger Lakes Kennel Club, Inc.   Sec'y, Miss Carolyn Pyle, Midline Rd., Freeville, N.Y. 13068.

First Company Governor's Foot Guard Athletic Ass'n. Sec'y, Lt. Charles E. Spencer, Jr., 159 High St., Hartford, Conn. 06103.

First Dog Training Club of Northern New Jersey, Inc. Sec'y, Clifford W. Webster, 7 Poplar St., Closter, N.J. 07624.

Forsyth Kennel Club, Inc. Sec'y, Mrs. Carl F. Newman, Hauser Rd., Rt. 1, Lewisville, N.C. 27023.

Fort Lauderdale Dog Club, Inc. Sec'y, Mrs. Jessie M. Rand, 234 Hibiscus Ave., Apt. 174, Lauderdale-By-The-Sea, Fla. 33308.

Fort Worth Kennel Club Sec'y, Mrs. C. D. Bourke, Jr., 1412 Bluebonnet Dr., Fort Worth, Texas 76111.

Framingham District Kennel Club, Inc. Sec'y, Mrs. Paul A. Wood, 478 Main St., Groveland, Mass. 01830.

French Bulldog Club of America Sec'y, Mrs. Richard M. Hover, 130 Troy Rd., Parsippany, N.J. 07054.

Genesee County Kennel Club Sec'y, Mrs. Russell Moffett, 1711 Overhill Drive, Flint, Mich. 48503.

Genesee Valley Kennel Club, Inc. Sec'y, Mrs. Henry D. Kingsley, 1627 Scottsville-Rush Rd., Rush, N.Y. 14543.

German Shepherd Dog Club of America, Inc. Sec'y, Miss Blanche L. Beisswenger, 17 W. Ivy Lane, Englewood, N.J. 07631.

German Shorthaired Pointer Club of America, Inc. Sec'y, Mrs. Geraldine Green, 125 Arlene Dr., Walnut Creek, Calif. 94596.

Golden Gate Kennel Club Sec'y, Stanley E. Hanson, 170 Ridge Rd., San Anselmo, Calif. 94960.

Golden Retriever Club of America Sec'y, Edward C. Syder, 3 Station Plaza, Ramsey, N.J. 07446.

Gordon Setter Club of America, Inc. Sec'y, Mrs. Louis C. Lustenberger, Jr., 14 Fargo Lane, Irvington-on-Hudson, N.Y. 10533.

Grand Rapids Kennel Club Sec'y, Mrs. Fred Engstrom, 1011 Allison, Grand Rapids, Mich. 49504.

Grand River Kennel Club Sec'y, Mrs. Raymond Bezdek, 6808 Melridge Dr., Painesville, Ohio 44077.

Great Barrington Kennel Club, Inc. Sec'y, Mrs. Marion G. Finke, Box 444, Great Barrington, Mass. 01230.

Great Dane Club of America, Inc. Sec'y, Mrs. Daniel Lasky, 73 Larchmont Ave., Waterbury, Conn. 06708.

Greater Miami Dog Club, Inc. Sec'y, Mrs. O. J. Smith, Rt. 1, Box 754, Ft. Lauderdale, Fla. 33314.

Greater St. Louis Training Club Sec'y, Mrs. Mildred Sypher, 59 Wilshire Terr., St. Louis, Mo. 63119.

Great Pyrenees Club of America Sec'y, Mrs. H. Carol Kilroy, 250 Governor's Hill Road, Oxford, Conn. 06483.

Greenville Kennel Club Sec'y, Mrs. Sharon Creasy, P.O. Box 923, Greenville, S.C. 29602.

Greenwich Kennel Club Sec'y, Mrs. William E. Larned, Burying Hill Rd., Greenwich, Conn 06830.

Greyhound Club of America Sec'y, Dr. Elsie S. Neustadt, P.O. Box 1185, Hanover, Mass. 02339.

Harrisburg Kennel Club, Inc. Sec'y, James J. Dilliplane, 2109 Kensington St., Harrisburg, Pa. 17104.

Hawaiian Kennel Club Sec'y, Paul D. Jones, 1501 First National Bank Bldg., Honolulu, Hawaii 96813.

Heart of America Kennel Club, Inc. Sec'y, Mrs. Carol McDermott, 8514 W. 56th Terr., Merriam, Ka. 66202.

Hollywood Dog Obedience Club, Inc. Sec'y, Miss Daphne R. Bell, P.O. Box 224, No. Hollywood, Calif. 91303.

Holyoke Kennel Club Sec'y, Mrs. Wilma G. Chamberlain, The Knolls, South Hadley, Mass. 01075.

Hoosier Kennel Club, Inc. Sec'y, Fred W. Meyer, Jr., 110 E. 11th St., Indianapolis, Ind. 46280.

Houston Kennel Club Sec'y, Richard R. Maze, P.O. Box 61122, Houston, Texas 77061.

Huntingdon Valley Kennel Club Sec'y, Mrs. Lenore F. Gomberg, 1032 Lindsay La., Rydal, Pa. 19046.

Huntington Kennel Club Sec'y, Miss Ann Harbulak, 6 Mohawk Trail, Garden Farms, Huntington, W. Va. 24705.

Hutchinson Kennel Club Sec'y, Mrs. Ruth Neill, 825 Lincoln, Hutchinson, Kans.

Illinois Capitol Kennel Club Sec'y, Mrs. Mary Jane Westbrook, 1408 W. Fayette, Springfield, Ill. 62704.

Illinois Valley Kennel Club of Peoria, Inc. Sec'y, Mrs. June Cross, 212 Craig Rd., Pekin, Ill. 61544.

Indianapolis Obedience Training Club, Inc. Sec'y, Mrs. Neva Scheffer, 807 Easy St., Indianapolis, Ind. 46227.

Ingham County Kennel Club, Inc. Sec'y, Mrs. Frank W. Mainville, 11940 Burke Hwy., Dimondale, Mich. 48821.

Inland Empire Kennel Ass'n. Sec'y, Mrs. Raymond M. Splawn, 220 So. Custer, Spokane, Wn. 99206.

Intermountain Kennel Club, Inc. Sec'y, Mrs. Frederick L. Glover, 1999 Siggard Dr., Salt Lake City, Utah 84106.

International Kennel Club of Chicago, Inc. President, Charles S. Potter, Union Stock Yards, 116 Exchange Bldg. Chicago, Ill. 60609.

Irish Setter Club of America Sec'y, Mrs. Edward F. Treutel, 204 Cumley Terr., Leonia, N.J. 07605.

Irish Terrier Club of America Sec'y, Miss Teresa M. Irving, 17 Agate Ave., Ossining, N.Y. 10562.

Irish Water Spaniel Club of America Sec'y, Mrs. John L. Hopkins, Center Rd., RFD, Bradford, N.H. 03221.

Irish Wolfhound Club of America Sec'y, Mrs. William W. Moir, 2531 No. Seventh St., Sheboygan, Wisc. 53081.

Italian Greyhound Club of America Sec'y, Mrs. Nancy Cochrane, 4407 Leedy Rd., Kingsport, Tenn. 37664.

Jacksonville Dog Fanciers Association, Inc. Sec'y, Mrs. Maggie Mills, 2739 Stanwood Ave., Jacksonville, Fla. 32207.

Japanese Spaniel Club of America Sec'y, Mrs. Herman H. Tietjen, 153 E. Market St., Rhinebeck, N.Y. 12572.

Jaxon Kennel Club Sec'y, Mr. Jerry B. Edwards, 8811 No. Territorial Rd., Plymouth, Mich. 48170.

Kalamazoo Kennel Club, Inc. Sec'y, John Stebbins, Rt. 2, Box 39A, Bangor, Mich. 49013.

Kanadasaga Kennel Club Sec'y, Mrs. Cecil Y. Smith, 213 W. Main St., Palmyra, N.Y. 14522.

K-9 Obedience Training Club of Essex Co., N.J., Inc. Sec'y, Mrs. Eleanor L. Rotman, 701 Valley Rd., Wayne, N.J. 07470.

Keeshond Club of America Sec'y, Mrs. Richard B. Hollaman, 9 Sunset Road, Darien, Conn. 06820.

Kennel Club of Beverly Hills Sec'y, Albert E. Van Court, 728 So. Windsor Blvd., Los Angeles, Calif. 90005.

Kennel Club of Buffalo, Inc. Sec'y, Mr. Thomas Cordy, 239 St. Lawrence Ave., Buffalo, N.Y. 14216.

Kennel Club of Northern New Jersey, Inc. Sec'y, Mrs. Dorothy P. Brown, 16 Westervelt Pl., Westwood, N.J. 07675.

Kennel Club of Pasadena Sec'y, Mrs. John Blanken Horn, 660 Westbridge Pl., Pasadena, Calif. 91105.

Kennel Club of Philadelphia, Inc. Sec'y, Alfred N. Snellenberg, Hague's Mill Rd., Ambler, Pa. 19002.

Kennel Club of Riverside Sec'y, Mrs. Mary B. Meyer, 10708 So. Morado Dr., Orange, Calif. 92667.

Kern County Kennel Club, Inc. Sec'y, Miss Judith Cappell, P.O. Box 817, Bakersfield, Calif. 93302.

Labrador Retriever Club, Inc. Sec'y, William K. Laughlin, P.O. Box 1392, Southampton, Long Island, N.Y. 11968.

Lackawanna Kennel Club Sec'y, Mrs. Elvera M. Wilson, 109 Seymour Ave., Scranton, Pa. 18505.

Ladies' Dog Club Sec'y, Mrs. Edward W. Anthony, 769 Harvard St., Whitman, Mass. 02382.

Ladies' Kennel Ass'n. of America Sec'y, Mrs. Arthur W. Higgins, Midland So., Syosset, L.I., N.Y. 11791.

Lake Shore Kennel Club, Inc. Sec'y, Mrs. Yvonne Shefcik, P.O. Box 2206, Hammond, Ind. 46323.

Lancaster Kennel Club, Inc. Sec'y, Mrs. D. Jean Marantz, 449 Hershey Ave., Lancaster, Pa. 17603.

Land o'Lakes Kennel Club, Inc. Sec'y, Mrs. Frances M. Wallace, 2353 Doswell Ave., St. Paul, Minn. 55108.

Langley Kennel Club Sec'y, Mrs. Bertil F. Swanson, 8 School La., Yorktown, Va. 23490.

Lehigh Valley Kennel Club Sec'y, Mrs. Emily J. Kinsley, R.D. 4, Box 179, Nazareth, Pa. 18064.

Lexington Kennel Club Sec'y, Mrs. Robert Woolcott, Rt. 2, Combs Ferry Rd., Winchester, Ky. 40391.

Long Island Kennel Club   Sec'y, Mrs. Collier Platt, R.F.D, 1, Syosset, L.I., N.Y. 11791.

Longshore Southport Kennel Club, Inc.   Sec'y, Mrs. Helen Boutell, 190 Westport Rd., Wilton, Conn. 06897.

Louisiana Kennel Club   Sec'y, Joseph C. Meyers, 500-C Lowerline St., New Orleans, LA. 70118.

Louisville Kennel Club, Inc.   Sec'y, Mrs. Dell Thomas, 5504 Morning Glory La., Pleasure Ridge Park, Ky. 40258.

Mad River Valley Kennel Club   Sec'y, Mrs. Ruth Ackley, Rt. 1, Plain City, Ohio 43064.

Magic Valley Kennel Club, Inc.   Sec'y, Mrs. James McMillion, 1235 Ridge Dr., Charleston, W. Va. 25309.

Mahoning-Shenango Kennel Club   Sec'y, Mrs. Oscar Turner, 4149 Lockwood Blvd., Youngstown, Ohio 44511.

Manitowoc County Kennel Club   Sec'y, Harold C. Klusmeyer, 1308 Cherry Rd., Manitowoc, Wisc. 54220.

Marion Kennel Club, Inc.   Sec'y, Mrs. Emily A. Lambert, R.R. 4, Marion, Ind. 46952.

Marion Ohio Kennel Club, Inc.   Sec'y, Mrs. Nancy T. Kesterson, 628 Penn Ave., Delaware, Ohio 43015.

Maryland Kennel Club   Sec'y, Helen C. Hottenbacher, 1508 Fidelity Bldg., Baltimore, Md. 21201.

Mastiff Club of America, Inc.   Sec'y, Dr. Samuel Schuster, 300 Longwood Ave., Boston, Mass. 02115.

McKinley Kennel Club   Sec'y, Miss Mildred I. Haag, 8565 Portage Rd., N.W. Massillon, Ohio 44646.

Memphis Kennel Club, Inc.   Sec'y, Mrs. C. L. Scanlon, 924 Beatrice, Memphis, Tenn. 38122.

Michiana Kennel Club   Sec'y, Rolland Jackson, P.O. Box 135, Osceola, Ind. 46561.

Mid-Contient Kennel Club of Tulsa, Inc.   Sec'y, Mrs. Marie DeShane, 1115 So. 129th E. Ave., Tulsa, Okla. 74108.

Middlesex County Kennel Club   Sec'y, Alonzo B. Reed, Westford Rd., Carlisle, Mass. 01741.

Mid-Hudson Kennel Club, Inc.   Sec'y, Mrs. John Coluccio, Primrose Hill, Rhinebeck, N.Y. 12572.

Mid-Jersey Companion Dog Training Club, Inc.   Sec'y, Mrs. Ruth Grigoza, 1015 Julia St., Elizabeth, N.J. 07201.

Midwest Field Trial Club, Inc.   Sec'y, T. J. Reames, Box 922, Burr Rd., St. Charles, Ill. 60174.

Miniature Pinscher Club of America, Inc.   Sec'y, Mrs. Joyce Helms, Rt. 4 Box 1550, Edmond, Okla. 73034.

Minneapolis Kennel Club   Sec'y, Mr. Frederick Brandt, 2055 Lilac Dr., Minneapolis, Minn. 55422.

Minnesota Field Trial Association, Inc.   Sec'y, R. N. Wolfe, 250 Hudson Rd., Bldg. 220, 6E, St. Paul, Minn. 55119.

Mississippi Valley Kennel Club   Sec'y, Mrs. Thomas C. Martin, 1808 No. Belt West, Belleville, Ill. 62223.

Mohawk Valley Kennel Club   Sec'y, Bernard G. Wandell, Jr., 15 Baldwin Rd., Scotia, N.Y. 12302.

Monmouth County Kennel Club, Inc.   Sec'y, Mrs. V. M. Wolontis, Windmill La., Rumson, N.J. 07760.

Montgomery County Kennel Club   Sec'y, Mrs. George V. Strong, 4 E. Sunset Ave., Philadelphia, Pa. 19118.

Mountain States Dog Training Club   Sec'y, Mrs. Beverly Roupp, 926 So. Cole Dr., Denver, Colo. 80228.

Mount Vernon Dog Training Club   Sec'y, Frank Reynolds, Jr., 5207 North Second St., Arlington, Va.

Muncie Kennel Club   Sec'y, William Warfel, 119 N. High St., Muncie, Ind. 47305.

Nassau Dog Training Club, Inc.   Sec'y, Mrs. Clement F. Plessner, 217 Dix Hills Road, Huntington Station, L.I., N.Y. 11747.

National Beagle Club   Sec'y, Morgan Wing, Jr., Millbrook, N.Y. 12545.

National Capital Kennel Club, Inc.   Sec'y, Mrs. Velma I. Agnew, 6611 Old Branch Ave. S.E., Washington, D.C. 20031.

Nebraska Dog & Hunt Club, Inc.   Sec'y, W. F. Somerhiser, 2810 No. Cotner Blvd., Lincoln, Neb. 68505.

Nebraska Kennel Club   Sec'y, Mrs. Thomas E. Harper, 10005 No. 72nd St., Omaha, Neb. 68112.

New England Beagle Club   Sec'y, Mrs. Ella Hewins, Blandford Road, Woronoco, Mass. 01097.

New England Dog Training Club   Sec'y, Mrs. Martin J. Meyer, 12 Pine Ridge Rd., Wellesley Farms, Mass. 02181.

New England Old English Sheepdog Club, Inc.   Sec'y, Mrs. Cathy Marino, 6 Franklin St., Dedham, Mass. 02026.

Newfoundland Club of America   Sec'y, The Reverend Robert L. Curry, Lenox School, Lenox, Mass. 01240.

New Jersey Beagle Club   Sec'y, Paul Paterson, 276 Riveredge Rd., New Shrewsbury, N.J. 07724.

New Mexico Kennel Club   Sec'y, Mrs. H. B. Davis, 2302 Calle Halcon, Sante Fe., N.M. 87501.

Newton Kennel Club   Sec'y, Mrs. Marilyn Terhune, E. Glen Rd., Rock Ridge Lake, Denville, N.J. 07834.

North Dakota Retriever Club, Inc.   Sec'y, Mr. James M. TeVogt, Rt. 1, Moorhead, Minn. 56560.

Northeastern Indiana Kennel Club   Sec'y, Mrs. George H. Bruning, Kress Rd., R.R. 1, Roanoke, Ind. 46783.

Northern Hare Beagle Club   Sec'y, Ralph DeWitt, R.F.D. Greenwich, N.Y. 12834.

Northern Ohio Beagle Club   Sec'y, Anna A. Billy, Rt. 1, Box 92-B, Medina, Ohio 44256.

North Shore Dog Training Club, Inc.   Sec'y, Mrs. Lucy A. Nowicki, 8219 N. Newland Ave., Niles, Ill. 60648.

North Shore Kennel Club   Sec'y, Mrs. George Marmer, 34 Prospect St., Peabody, Mass. 01960.

Northwestern Connecticut Dog Club, Inc.   Sec'y, John M. Menton, Wheaton Rd., Washington Depot, Conn. 06794.

Norwegian Elkhound Ass'n of America   Sec'y, Miss Doris H. Phillips, Elkins, New Hampshire 03233.

Norwich Terrier Club   Sec'y, Mrs. John L. Winston, Gladstone, N.J. 07934.

Oakland County Kennel Club   Sec'y, Mort Conrad, 1981 John R. Road, Rochester, Mich. 48063.

Oakland Dog Training Club, Inc.   Sec'y, Mrs. Winifred H. Handley, 2868 Alida St., Oakland, Calif. 94602.

Oakland Kennel Club   Sec'y, Miss April Ellwood, 1611 Paseo Del Campo, San Lorenzo, Calif. 94580.

Obedience Training Club of Hawaii   Sec'y, Mrs. Helen E. Markham, 2422 Ahaiki St., Pearl City, Hawaii 96782.

Obedience Training Club of Rhode Island   Sec'y, Mrs. John Drury, R.F.D. #1, Chepachet, R.I. 02814.

Ohio Valley Beagle Club   Sec'y, William F. Poe, 311 Glenroy Ave., Cincinnati, Ohio 45238.

Oklahoma City Kennel Club, Inc.   Sec'y, Mrs. Raymond L. Dickens, 4232 N.W. 39, Oklahoma City, Okla. 73112.

Old Dominion Kennel Club of No. Virginia   Sec'y, Mrs. Elizabeth C. Bell, 7904 Roswell Dr., Falls Church, Va. 22043.

Old English Sheepdog Club of America   Sec'y, Mrs. George Demko, 20 Donovan Dr., Cold Spring Harbor, N.Y. 11724.

Olympic Kennel Club, Inc.   Sec'y, Mrs. Charles Robins, 17808 2nd So., Seattle, Wash. 98178.

Onondaga Kennel Ass'n Inc.   Sec'y, Mrs. Joan Vaccaro, Johnny Cake Hill, Cato, N.Y. 13033.

Orange Empire Dog Clubs, Inc.   Sec'y, Miss Beth Gneck, 3130 No. Stoddard, San Bernardino, Calif. 92405.

Ox Ridge Kennel Club   Sec'y, Mrs. James Hausman, Farms Rd., R.D. #1, Stamford, Conn. 06903.

Pacific Coast Boston Terrier Club   Sec'y, Mrs. Lillian Huddleston, 17524 Lanark St., Northridge, Calif. 91324.

Pacific Coast Bulldog Club   Sec'y, Mr. Robert H. Armstrong, 6572 Oxford Dr., Huntington Bch., Calif. 92647.

Pacific Coast Pekingese Club   Sec'y, Mrs. Eugenie Kelly, 117 Linden Ct., Burbank, Ca. 91502.

Panhandle Kennel Club of Texas, Inc.   Sec'y, Mr. James Grubbs, 4223 Crouch St., Amarillo, Tex. 79106.

Papillon Club of America   Sec'y, Mrs. Lyle Robinette, Eleven O'Clock Rd., Weston, Conn. 06883.

Pasanita Obedience Club, Inc.   Sec'y, Bartje Miller 2200 Spaulding Pl., Altadena, Calif. 91001.

Pekingese Club of America   Sec'y, Miss Iris de la Torre Bueno, 400 Pelham Rd., New Rochelle, N.Y. 10805.

Pembroke Welsh Corgi Club of America   Sec'y, August Ramm, 95 Byram Lake Rd., Mt. Kisco, N.Y. 10549.

Penn Treaty Kennel Club, Inc.   Sec'y, Mrs. Betty Zimmerman, 578 Concord Rd., Chester, Pa. 19014.

Pensacola Dog Fanciers Association, Inc.   Sec'y, Miss Jane B. Hinesman, 40 E. Olive Rd., Pensacola, Fla. 32504.

Philadelphia Dog Training Club   Sec'y, Mrs. Nancy J. Stover, 2610 Quaint St., Secane, Pa. 19018.

Piedmont Kennel Club, Inc.   Sec'y, Mrs. Margaret Samples, 125 Old Bell Rd., Matthews, N.C. 28105.

Plainfield Kennel Club   Sec'y, Mrs. Henry H. Johnson, R.D., 14-C Rocky Run Rd., Glen Gardner, N.J. 08826.

Pocono Beagle Club   Sec'y, Russel Grove, R.D. #2 Elverson, Pa. 19520.

Poodle Club of America   Sec'y, Francis P. Fretwell, Rt. 1, Moore S.C. 29369.

Port Chester Obedience Training Club   Sec'y, Mrs. George McCrudden, 508 Benedict Ave., Tarrytown, N.Y. 10591.

Portland Kennel Club   Sec'y, Mrs. Geneive Cook, 6301 S.E. Hull, Milwaukie, Ore. 97222.

Providence County Kennel Club, Inc.   Sec'y, Warren D. Edman, 22 Hope Rd., R.F.D. 5, Cranston, R.I. 02920.

Pug Dog Club of America   Sec'y, Peter McLaughlin, Murphy Rd., R.R. 5, East Hampton, Conn. 06424.

Putnam Kennel Club   Sec'y, John A. Anderson, Sartorius Knls., Patterson, N.Y. 12563.

Queen City Dog Training Club   Sec'y, Miss Marjorie Hettrick, 961 W. Galbraith Rd., Cincinnati, Ohio 45231.

Queensboro Kennel Club   Sec'y, Mrs. David Knopf, 75-23 169th St., Flushing, N.Y. 11366.

Reno Kennel Club   Sec'y, Mrs. Helen V. Noyes, P.O. Box 1695, Reno, Nev. 89105.

Rhode Island Kennel Club   Sec'y, Mrs. Shirley Crossley, Tingley Rd., Cumberland, R.I. 02864.

Richland Kennel Club   Sec'y, Mrs. Barbara A. Hammons, 510 S. Keller St., Kenne-Wick, Wn. 99336.

Richmond Dog Fanciers Club, Inc.   Sec'y, Edith S. Cournow, 1817 San Benito St., Richmond, Calif. 94804.

Rio Grande Kennel Club   Sec'y, Miss Nancy Pollock, 908 Green Valley Rd., N.W., Albuquerque, N.M. 87107.

Rio Grande Obedience Dog Club   Sec'y, Mrs. Jeanne K. Weitz, 1413 Clausen Dr., El Paso, Texas 79925.

Roanoke Kennel Club   Sec'y, Mrs. Grady Spiegel, 2152 Bruce Ave., Salem, Va. 24153.

Rockland County Kennel Club, Inc.   Sec'y, Mrs. Henry A. Montandon, 31 North Greenbush Rd., West Nyack, N.Y. 10994.

Rock River Valley Kennel Club, Inc.   Sec'y, Mrs. R. T. Allen, 538 River Lane, Rockford, Ill. 61111.

Rubber City Kennel Club   Sec'y, Mrs. Esther Russell, 1440 E. Nimisila Rd., North Canton, Ohio 44720.

Sahuaro State Kennel Club   Sec'y, Mrs. Gladyse L. Armstrong, 122 W. Merrill, Phoenix, Ariz. 80513.

St. Bernard Club of America, Inc.   Sec'y, Mrs. Edward P. Wade, Jr., P.O. Box 151, West Chicago, Ill. 60185.

St. Joseph Kennel Club, Inc.   Sec'y, Mrs. Mary F. Pollock, 831 Trevillion Dr., St. Joseph, Mo. 64507.

St. Louis Beagle Club, Inc.   Sec'y., Mrs. Frances Coomes, Rt. 1, Box 181F, Foristell, Mo. 63348.

St. Louis Collie Club   Sec'y, Mrs. Virginia Smith, 5110 N. Hwy. 140 Florrisant, Mo. 63033.

St. Petersburg Dog Fanciers Ass'n., Inc.   Sec'y, Mrs. Alberta Gilholm, 5667 Hobson St., N.E., St. Petersburg, Fla. 33703.

Salinas Valley Kennel Club   Sec'y, Mrs. Dorothy Mattos, 19225 Locarno Way, Salinas, Calif. 93901.

Salisbury Maryland Kennel Club, Inc.   Sec'y, Miss Julia Crawford, 113 Lakeview Dr., Salisbury, Md. 21801.

Saluki Club of America   Sec'y, Mrs. Carol-Ann Lantz, 341 Providence St., W. Warwick, R.I. 02893.

Samoyed Club of America   Sec'y, Mrs. Nancy Alexander 1344 Via Del Carmel, Santa Maria, Calif. 93454.

San Antonio Kennel Club   Sec'y, Mrs. Nan S. Burke, 1000 Pennystone Ave., San Antonio, Texas 78223.

Sandemac Kennel Club   Sec'y, Mrs. Sally Jones, 1 Park Center, Pana, Ill. 62557.

Sandia Dog Obedience Club   Sec'y, Mrs. John Yarwood, 9008 La Barranca Ave., N.E. Albuquerque, N.M. 87711.

San Francisco Dog Training Club, Inc.   Sec'y, Mrs. Catherine Knight, 1851 Monterey Blvd., San Bruno, Calif. 94006.

San Gabriel Valley Kennel Club   Sec'y, Mrs. Fern Henrichsen, 120 E. Bay State St., Alhambra, Calif. 91801.

San Mateo Kennel Club   Sec'y, Mrs. M. W. Johnson, 9601 Broadmoor Dr., San Ramon, Calif. 94583.

Santa Ana Valley Kennel Club   Sec'y, Mrs. Vivian Brown, 2506 Larchmont St., Santa Ana, Calif. 92706.

Santa Barbara Kennel Club   Sec'y, Sidney F. Heckert, Jr., P.O. Box 3246, Hope Ranch, Santa Barbara, Calif. 95030.

Santa Clara Valley Kennel Club, Inc.   Sec'y, Mrs. Isabel S. Karkau, P.O. Box 871, Los Gatos, Calif. 95030.

Santa Cruz Kennel Club   Sec'y, Mrs. B. H. Markey, 3711 Soquel Dr., Santa Cruz, Calif. 95060.

Saw Mill River Kennel Club   Sec'y, Mrs. Wm. Bolton Cook, 20 Irenhyl Ave., Port Chester, N.Y. 10573.

Schipperke Club of America, Inc.   Sec'y, Mrs. Andrew H. Hundley, RR. 1, Box 28, Zionsville, Ind. 46077.

Scottish Terrier Club of America   Sec'y, Mrs. Ann W. Gilkey, Rt. 1, Box 11, Lovington, N.M. 88260.

Seattle Kennel Club, Inc.   Sec'y, W. A. Sperry, 9500 Rainier Ave. So., Apt. 309, Seattle, Wn. 98118.

Sewickley Valley Kennel Association   Sec'y, W. A. Hallett, 230 Hillendale Rd., Pittsburgh, Pa. 15237.

Shreveport Kennel Club   Sec'y, Mrs. J. W. Henderson, 3973 Huston St., Shreveport, La. 71109.

Siberian Husky Club of America   Sec'y, James A. Packard, 81 No. Mill St., Holliston, Mass. 01746.

Silky Terrier Club of America   Sec'y, Mrs. Merle E. Smith, P.O. Box 3521, San Francisco, Calif. 94119.

Silver Bay Kennel Club of San Diego   Sec'y, Mrs. Lois E. Lefebvre, P.O. Box 1362, El Cajon, Calif. 92022.

Sioux Empire Kennel Club, Inc.   Sec'y, Mrs. Audrey Lein, 5617 Circle Dr., Sioux Falls, S.D. 57106.

Sioux Valley Kennel Club, Inc.   Sec'y, Richard Ferguson, 5303 6th Ave., Sioux City, Ia. 51106.

Skokie Valley Kennel Club   Sec'y, Marie D. O'Brien, 1591 W. Dundee Rd., Palatine, Ill. 60067.

Skye Terrier Club of America   Sec'y, Mrs. John A. McDonald, RFD, Rt. 1, Bealeton, Va. 22712.

Somerset Hills Kennel Club   Sec'y, Mrs. Williams S. Ladd, Bernardsville Rd., Mendham, N.J. 07945.

Southeastern Iowa Kennel Club   Sec'y, Miss Carolyn D. Coughlin, R.R. 2, Ottumwa, Iowa 52501.

Southern Adirondack Dog Club, Inc.   Sec'y, Mrs. Merton Mason, 115 Evelyn Ave., Amsterdam, N.Y. 12010.

Southern Michigan Obedience Training Club   Sec'y, James Reynolds, 843 Pine Tree, Lake Orion, Mich. 48035.

Southern Tier Kennel Club, Inc.   Sec'y, Mrs. Rose Maher, 42 W. Van Scoter St., Hornell, N.Y. 14843.

South Jersey Kennel Club, Inc.   Sec'y, Miss Gertrude M. Tracey, 1026 Asbury Ave., Ocean City, N.J. 08226.

South Shore Kennel Club   Sec'y, Mrs. Doris E. Hurry, 1130 Main St., Randolph, Mass. 02368.

South Texas Obedience Club, Inc.   Sec'y, Miss Faye Spears, 4705 Pease, Houston, Texas 77023.

Spaniel Breeders Society   Sec'y, Mrs. William W. Brainard Jr., Glenara, Marshall, Va. 22115.

Spokane Kennel Club   Sec'y, Mrs. Louise Jackson, 511 W. Providence, Spokane, Wash. 99205.

Sportsman's Beagle Club   Sec'y, David Kilpatrick, 120 West King St., Malvern, Pa. 19355.

Springfield Kennel Club, Inc.   Sec'y, Mrs. J. M. Bordeaux, 60 Fort Pleasant Ave., Springfield, Mass. 01108.

Staffordshire Terrier Club of America   Sec'y, Mrs. Gladys C. Smith, 4676 Clairemont Dr., San Diego, Calif. 92117.

Standard Schnauzer Club of America   Sec'y, Mrs. Gloria Corey, 5241 Moonlight Dr., Indianapolis, Ind. 46226.

Staten Island Kennel Club, Inc.   Sec'y, Mrs. Edward L. Reardon, 279 Wardwell Ave., Staten Island, N.Y. 10314.

Steel City Kennel Club, Inc.   Sec'y, Mrs. Gary Gerber, 3601 West 105th Ave., Crown Point, Ind. 46307.

Suffolk County Kennel Club, Inc.   Sec'y, John C. Parry, 1476 14th St., W. Babylon, N.Y. 11704.

Sun Maid Kennel Club of Fresno   Sec'y, Mrs. Lucille Barton, 1035 E. Robinson Ave., Fresno, Calif. 93704.

Superstition Kennel Club   Sec'y, Mrs. Carol Cooper, P.O. Box 372, Mesa, Ariz. 85201.

Susque-Nango Kennel Club, Inc.   Sec'y, Miss Sarah O'Keefe, 85 Liberty St., Binghamton, N.Y. 13905.

Sussex Hills Kennel Club   Sec'y, Mrs. Alma Well, Dover-Chester Rd., R.D. 2, Dover, N.J. 07081.

Tampa Bay Kennel Club, Inc.   Sec'y, Mrs. Paul R. Bryant, 2507 Shell Point Rd., Tampa, Fla. 33611.

Tennessee Valley Kennel Club   Sec'y, Mrs. J. E. Fowler, 1101 Oaklett Dr., Knoxville, Tenn. 37912.

Terre Haute Chapter, Izaak Walton League of America   Sec'y, Mrs. Kathryn Williams, 2400 Idaho St., Terre Haute, Ind. 47802.

Texas Kennel Club   Sec'y, Mrs. Russell H. Lish, 2035 Willingham Dr., Richardson, Tex. 75080.

Tidewater Kennel Club of Virginia, Inc.   Sec'y, Mrs. Allan G. Decker, 1412 Centerville Tpke., Chesapeake, Va. 23322.

Toledo Kennel Club, Inc.   Sec'y, Mrs. Byron Hofman, Commodore Perry Hotel, 1601, 505 Jefferson Ave., Toledo, Ohio 43604.

Tonawanda Valley Kennel Club, Inc.   Sec'y, Mr. A. H. Beuler, P.O. Box 110, Batavia, N.Y. 14020.

Topeka Kennel Club   Sec'y, Mrs. Eileen McClintock, Rt. 6, Topeka Ka. 66608.

Town and Country Kennel Club, Inc.   Sec'y, Mrs. Roseann Cavanaugh, Rt. 3, Box 263C, Edmond, Okla. 73034.

Trenton Kennel Club   Sec'y, Mrs. Doris E. Moore, 105 Bonnie Ave., Trenton, N.J. 08629.

Tri-City Kennel Club, Inc.   Sec'y, Mrs. Eleanore A. Renihan, 828 Waverly Rd., Davenport, Ia. 52804.

Tri-State Kennel Association, Inc.   Sec'y, Miss Helen Gaither, 17 Walnut Ave., Wheeling, W. Va. 26003.

Troy Kennel Club, Inc.   Sec'y, Mrs. Robert L. Seekins, Jr., Scotchtown La., Scotchtown Estates, Middletown, N.Y. 19040.

Tucson Kennel Club   Sec'y, Mrs. John C. Haynes, Jr., 3100 N. Craycroft, Tucson, Ariz. 85716.

Union County Kennel Club   Sec'y, Mrs. Marie Grilla, 261 W. 1st Ave., Roselle, N.J. 07203.

United States Kerry Blue Terrier Club, Inc.   Sec'y, Mrs. Walter L. Fleisher, 443 Buena Vista Rd., New City, N.Y. 10956.

United States Lakeland Terrier Club   Sec'y, Mrs. John R. Loeffler, 1116 Elk St., Franklin, Pa. 16323.

Valley Forge Kennel Club   Sec'y, Miss Florence Hagan, 1335 Edge Hill Rd., Darby Pa. 19023.

Vancouver Kennel Club   Sec'y, Mrs. Bessie V. Pickens, 15300 S.E. Laurie Ave., Portland, Or. 97217.

Ventura County Dog Fanciers Ass'n.   Sec'y, Miss Diann Schiller, 440 So. Eva, Ventura, Calif. 93003.

Virginia Kennel Club, Inc.   Sec'y, Mrs. Charles L. Jordan, IV, Rt. 2, Box 142, Midlothian, Va. 23113.

Wachusett Kennel Club, Inc.   Sec'y, Mrs. Ruth Taft Hobbs, Bummet Brook Farm, Shrewsbury, Mass. 01545.

Walla Walla Kennel Club   Sec'y, Mrs. Jane T. Smith, Box 523, Pilot Rock, Ore. 97868.

Waterloo Kennel Club   Sec'y, Dean W. Tidrick, 2505 Timber Dr., Cedar Falls, Ia. 50613.

Waukesha Kennel Club, Inc.   Sec'y, Mrs. Joann Stanton, 2926 No. 80th St., Milwaukee, Wisc. 53129.

Weimaraner Club of America   Sec'y, Mrs. Jo Cox, Greenway Rd., Sun Prairle, Wisc. 53590.

Welsh Terrier Club of America   Sec'y, Mrs. Nell Benton Hudson, 8700 Wolftrap Rd., Vienna, Va. 22180.

Westbury Kennel Ass'n.   Sec'y, Bernard I. Nussinow, 24 Elm St., Woodbury, N.Y. 11797.

Westchester Kennel Club   Sec'y, Evan S. Ingels, Time Inc., Rockefeller Plaza, New York, N.Y. 10020.

Western Beagle Club   Sec'y, Jay Hinkle, RR 3, Logansport, Ind. 46947.

Western Fox Terrier Breeders Ass'n.   Sec'y, Mrs. Lettie M. Pilley, 3094 No. Lima St., Burbank, Calif. 91504.

Western Pennsylvania Kennel Ass'n., Inc.   Sec'y, Mrs. Joseph W. Babcock, 295 W. Prospect Ave., Pittsburgh, Pa. 15205.

Western Reserve Kennel Club   Sec'y, Mrs. Joan E. Bennett, 12978 Emerson Ave., Lakewood, Ohio 44107.

West Highland White Terrier Club of America   Sec'y, Eugene Clifford, 23 Alexine Ave., East Rockaway, N.Y. 11518.

Westminster Kennel Club   Sec'y, Robert E. Taylor, 41 East 57th St., Room 2704, N.Y., N.Y. 10022.

Westside Dog Training Club, Inc.   Sec'y, Miss Judy Schwarz, 2658 N. Marmora, Chicago, Ill. 60639.

Wilmington Kennel Club   Sec'y, Mrs. John R. Laurie, 728 Foulkstone Rd., Sharpley, Wilmington, Del. 19803.

Wisconsin Amateur Field Trial Club, Inc.   Sec'y, Roger Benjamin, 13275 W. Radisson Rd., New Berlin, Wisc. 53151.

Wisconsin Kennel Club   Sec'y, O. A. Keyes, 1232 N. Edison St., Milwaukee, Wisc. 53202.

Wolverine Beagle Club   Sec'y, Leslie Raber, Rt. 2, Hastings, Mich. 49058.

Worcester County Kennel Club   Sec'y, Bernard J. Kennedy, 80 Maple St., W. Boylston, Mass. 01583.

Yakima Valley Kennel Club   Sec'y, Mrs. Elsie Schmidt, 1019 So. 20th Ave., Yakima, Wn. 98902.

Yorkshire Terrier Club of America   Sec'y, Miss Valerie Kilkeary, 4105 Sheffield Ave., Hammond, Ind. 46327.

Never work or hunt your dog except with his equals or peers. Photo by Evelyn M. Shafer.

Rules Applying to Registration and Dog Shows

Amended to January 1, 1970

THE AMERICAN KENNEL CLUB
Incorporated
51 MADISON AVENUE
New York, N. Y. 10010

The American Kennel Club
Incorporated

Rules and Regulations
and
Extracts from By-Laws

CHAPTER 1

GENERAL EXPLANATIONS

SECTION 1. The word "dog" wherever used in these Rules and Regulations includes both sexes.

SECTION 2. The words "United States of America" wherever used in these Rules and Regulations shall be construed to include all territories and possessions of the United States of America and all vessels sailing under the American Flag.

CHAPTER 2

REGISTRABLE BREEDS BY GROUPS

The following breeds divided by groups shall be all the breeds now recognized by The American Kennel Club as being distinct breeds of pure-bred dogs eligible for registration in the Stud Book of The American Kennel Club.

GROUP 1

SPORTING DOGS

GRIFFONS (WIREHAIRED POINTING)
POINTERS
POINTERS (GERMAN SHORTHAIRED)
POINTERS (GERMAN WIREHAIRED)
RETRIEVERS (CHESAPEAKE BAY)
RETRIEVERS (CURLY-COATED)
RETRIEVERS (FLAT-COATED)
RETRIEVERS (GOLDEN)
RETRIEVERS (LABRADOR)
SETTERS (ENGLISH)
SETTERS (GORDON)
SETTERS (IRISH)
SPANIELS (AMERICAN WATER)
SPANIELS (BRITTANY)
SPANIELS (CLUMBER)
SPANIELS (COCKER)
SPANIELS (ENGLISH COCKER)
SPANIELS (ENGLISH SPRINGER)
SPANIELS (FIELD)
SPANIELS (IRISH WATER)
SPANIELS (SUSSEX)
SPANIELS (WELSH SPRINGER)
VIZSLAS
WEIMARANERS

FOREWORD

The American Kennel Club was formed principally for the protection and advancement of pure-bred dogs.

The State of New York by Special Act of its legislature incorporated The American Kennel Club and granted it a charter in Section 2 of which the objects of the corporation are described to be "to adopt and enforce uniform rules regulating and governing dog shows and field trials, to regulate the conduct of persons interested in exhibiting, running, breeding, registering, purchasing and selling dogs, to detect, prevent, and punish frauds in connection therewith, to protect the interests of its members, to maintain and publish an official stud book and an official kennel gazette, and generally to do everything to advance the study, breeding, exhibiting, running and maintenance of the purity of thoroughbred dogs."

Section 2 of this charter further states that "for these purposes it," The American Kennel Club, "shall have power to adopt a constitution, by-laws, rules and regulations, and enforce the same by fines and penalties, which it shall have the right to collect and enforce by suit, or by suspension or expulsion from membership, or by a suspension or denial of any or all of the privileges of said corporation."

Forms for the registration of pure-bred dogs may be obtained by writing to or calling in person at the offices of The American Kennel Club.

The holding of dog shows at which pure-bred dogs may be exhibited and be given an opportunity to compete for prizes and thereby enable their breeders and owners to demonstrate the progress made in breeding for type and quality, and the holding of obedience trials and field trials at which pure-bred dogs may be run in competition for prizes and thereby enable their breeders and owners to demonstrate the progress made in breeding for practical use, stamina and obedience have been found to be the best methods by which the progress which has been made in breeding can be shown.

The American Kennel Club has adopted certain By-Laws, Rules and Regulations designed to carry out these objects. This book contains such of these by-laws, rules and regulations as affect the registration of pure-bred dogs; or the club or association which wishes to hold a dog show or obedience trial; or the person who wishes to exhibit, compete or take part therein; or the person who by unsportsmanlike conduct or wrong-doing is believed to be injuring the welfare of the sport of breeding and showing pure-bred dogs.

for such length of time as to justify being designated as pure breeds. The Board of Directors also may remove any breed from the foregoing list or may transfer any breed from one group to another group whenever in its opinion sufficient evidence is presented to the Board to justify such removal or transfer.

CHAPTER 3

REGISTRATION

SECTION 1. The breeder of a dog is the person who owned the dam of that dog when the dam was bred; except that if the dam was leased at the time of breeding, the breeder is the lessee.

SECTION 2. An American-bred dog is a dog whelped in the United States of America by reason of a mating which took place in the United States of America.

SECTION 3. Any person in good standing with The American Kennel Club may apply for the registration of any pure-bred dog or litter of pure-bred dogs owned by him, by supplying The American Kennel Club with such information and complying with such conditions as it shall require.

SECTION 4. No individual dog from a litter whelped in the United States of America of which both parents are registered with The American Kennel Club shall be eligible for registration unless the litter has first been registered by the person who owned the dam at time of whelping; except that if the dam was leased at time of whelping, the litter may be registered only by the lessee.

SECTION 5. No dog or litter out of a dam under eight (8) months or over twelve (12) years of age at time of mating, or by a sire under seven (7) months or over twelve (12) years of age at time of mating, will be registered unless the application for registration shall be accompanied by an affidavit or evidence which shall prove the fact to the satisfaction of The American Kennel Club.

SECTION 6. No litter of pure-bred dogs and/or no single pure-bred dog which shall be determined by The American Kennel Club to be acceptable in all other respects for registration, shall be barred from registration because of the failure, by the legal owner of all or part of said litter, or said single dog to obtain some one or more of the signatures needed to complete the applicant's chain of title to the litter or dog sought to be registered, unless that person who, when requested, refuses so to sign the application form shall furnish a reason therefor satisfactory to The American Kennel Club, such as the fact that at the time of service an agreement in writing was made between the owner or lessee of the sire and the owner or lessee of the dam to the effect that no application for registration should be made and/or that the produce of such union should not be

GROUP 2—HOUNDS

AFGHAN HOUNDS
BASENJIS
BASSET HOUNDS
BEAGLES
BLOODHOUNDS
BORZOIS
COONHOUNDS (BLACK AND TAN)
DACHSHUNDS
DEERHOUNDS (SCOTTISH)
FOXHOUNDS (AMERICAN)
FOXHOUNDS (ENGLISH)
GREYHOUNDS
HARRIERS
IRISH WOLFHOUNDS
NORWEGIAN ELKHOUNDS
OTTER HOUNDS
RHODESIAN RIDGEBACKS
SALUKIS
WHIPPETS

GROUP 3—WORKING DOGS

ALASKAN MALAMUTES
BELGIAN MALINOIS
BELGIAN SHEEPDOGS
BELGIAN TERVUREN
BERNESE MOUNTAIN DOGS
BOUVIERS DES FLANDRES
BOXERS
BRIARDS
BULLMASTIFFS
COLLIES
DOBERMAN PINSCHERS
GERMAN SHEPHERD DOGS
GIANT SCHNAUZERS
GREAT DANES
GREAT PYRENEES
KOMONDOROK
KUVASZOK
MASTIFFS
NEWFOUNDLANDS
OLD ENGLISH SHEEPDOGS
PULIK
ROTTWEILERS
SAMOYEDS
SCHNAUZERS (STANDARD)
SHETLAND SHEEPDOGS
SIBERIAN HUSKIES
ST. BERNARDS
WELSH CORGIS (CARDIGAN)
WELSH CORGIS (PEMBROKE)

GROUP 4—TERRIERS

AIREDALE TERRIERS
AUSTRALIAN TERRIERS
BEDLINGTON TERRIERS
BORDER TERRIERS
BULL TERRIERS
CAIRN TERRIERS
DANDIE DINMONT TERRIERS
FOX TERRIERS
IRISH TERRIERS
KERRY BLUE TERRIERS
LAKELAND TERRIERS
MANCHESTER TERRIERS
NORWICH TERRIERS
SCHNAUZERS (MINIATURE)
SCOTTISH TERRIERS
SEALYHAM TERRIERS
SKYE TERRIERS
STAFFORDSHIRE TERRIERS
WELSH TERRIERS
WEST HIGHLAND WHITE TERRIERS

GROUP 5—TOYS

AFFENPINSCHERS
CHIHUAHUAS
ENGLISH TOY SPANIELS
GRIFFONS (BRUSSELS)
ITALIAN GREYHOUNDS
JAPANESE SPANIELS
MALTESE
PAPILLONS
PEKINGESE
PINSCHERS (MINIATURE)
POMERANIANS
PUGS
SHIH TZU
SILKY TERRIERS
YORKSHIRE TERRIERS

GROUP 6—NON-SPORTING DOGS

BOSTON TERRIERS
BULLDOGS
CHOW CHOWS
DALMATIANS
FRENCH BULLDOGS
KEESHONDEN
LHASA APSOS
POODLES
SCHIPPERKES

The Board of Directors of The American Kennel Club may add other breeds to the foregoing list whenever in its opinion sufficient evidence is presented to said Board to justify its belief that such other breeds have been in existence as distinct breeds registered. In all cases where such an agreement in writing has been made, any person disposing of any of the produce of such union must secure from the new owner a statement in writing that he receives such produce upon the understanding that it shall not be registered. For the purpose of registering or refusing to register pure-bred dogs The American Kennel Club will recognize only such conditional sale or conditional stud agreements affecting the registration of pure-bred dogs as are in writing and are shown to have been brought to the attention of the applicant for registration. The American Kennel Club cannot recognize alleged conditional sale, conditional stud or other agreements not in writing which affect the registration of pure-bred dogs, until after the existence, construction and/or effect of the same shall have been determined by an action at law.

The owner or owners of a stud dog pure-bred and eligible for registration who in print or otherwise asserts or assert it to be pure-bred and eligible for registration and on the strength of such assertion secures or permits its use at stud, must pay the cost of its registration. The owner or owners of a brood bitch pure-bred and eligible for registration who in print or otherwise asserts or assert it to be pure-bred and eligible for registration and on the strength of such assertion leases it or sells its produce or secures the use of a stud by promising a puppy or puppies as payment of the stud fee in lieu of cash, must pay the cost of its registration.

That person or those persons refusing without cause to sign the application form or forms necessary for the registration of a litter of pure-bred dogs or of a single pure-bred dog and that person or those persons refusing without cause to pay the necessary fees due from him, her or them to be paid in order to complete the chain of title to a pure-bred litter or a pure-bred single dog sought to be registered, when requested by The American Kennel Club, may be suspended from the privileges of The American Kennel Club, may be suspended from the privileges of The American Kennel Club or fined as the Board of Directors of The American Kennel Club may elect.

The registration of a single pure-bred dog out of a litter eligible for registration may be secured by its legal owner as a one-dog litter registration and the balance of the litter may be refused registration where the breeder or the owner or lessee of the dam at the date of whelping wrongfully has refused to register the litter and that person or those persons so wrongfully refusing shall be suspended from the privileges of The American Kennel Club or fined as the Board of Directors of The American Kennel Club may elect.

SECTION 7. No change in the name of a dog registered with The American Kennel Club will be allowed to be made.

SECTION 8. Any person in good standing with The American Kennel Club may apply for transfer of ownership to him of any registered dog acquired by him by supplying The American Kennel Club with such information and complying with such conditions as it shall require.

SECTION 9. The American Kennel Club will not protect any person against the use by any other person of a kennel name in the registration of dogs with The American Kennel Club or in the entry of registered dogs in shows held under The American Kennel Club rules, unless the kennel name has been registered with The American Kennel Club.

SECTION 10. On and after October 1, 1948, applications for the use of a kennel name as a prefix in the registering and showing of dogs shall be made to The American Kennel Club on a form which will be supplied by said Club upon request, and said application must be accompanied by a fee, the amount of which shall be determined by the Board of Directors of The American Kennel Club. The Board will then consider such application and if it approves of the name selected will grant the right to the use of such name only as a prefix for a period of five (5) years.

SECTION 11. The recorded owner shall have first consideration of the grant to use said kennel name for additional consecutive five (5) year terms upon receipt of the application for renewal accompanied by the renewal fee, the amount of which shall be determined by the Board of Directors, when received before the date of expiration of the original grant but the grant for any five (5) year renewal term will be made only at the expiration of the previous term.

In the event of the death of a recorded owner of a registered kennel name, his executors, administrators or legal heirs, upon submission of proper proof of their status may use the name as a prefix during the remainder of the five (5) year term of use and the legal heir of the deceased recorded owner, or the executors or administrators acting in his behalf, shall have first consideration of the grant to the use of said name for additional terms, as provided heretofore in this section.

SECTION 12. If the recorded owner of a registered kennel name granted after October 1, 1948, desires to transfer ownership of or an interest in said kennel name to a new owner, application to transfer such name for the unexpired term must be made to The American Kennel Club on a form which will be supplied by said Club upon request. The application must be submitted for the approval of the Board of Directors of The American Kennel Club and accompanied by a fee, the amount of which shall be determined by the Board of Directors of The American Kennel Club.

Any kennel name granted by The American Kennel Club prior to October 1, 1948 may be transferred by its present owner or owners to another only by consent and on certain conditions and payment of fee as determined by the Board of Directors of The American Kennel Club.

SECTION 13. In the case of any registered kennel name which is recorded as jointly owned by two or more persons, application to transfer the interest of one co-owner to another co-owner, may be made to The American Kennel Club on a form which will be supplied by said Club upon request. The application must be submitted for the approval of the Board of Directors of The American Kennel Club but no fee will be charged for such a transfer.

SECTION 14. The protection of all kennel names registered between March 1, 1934 and October 1, 1948 shall depend upon their continuous use by registered owners. Neglect by the recorded owner of a registered kennel name to use such name in the registration of dogs for a continuous period of six years or more shall be considered such an abandonment of the name as to justify The American Kennel Club in refusing to protect its use unless the owner or owners thereof prior to the expiration of such six-year period shall notify The American Kennel Club of his, her or their desire to retain the same.

CHAPTER 3-A

IDENTIFICATION AND RECORDS

SECTION 1. The word "person" as used in this chapter includes any individual, partnership, firm, corporation, association or organization of any kind.

The word "dog" as used in this chapter includes a dog or puppy of any age and either sex.

SECTION 2. Each person who breeds, keeps, transfers ownership or possession of, or deals in dogs which are registered or to be registered with The American Kennel Club, whether he acts as principal or agent or sells on consignment, must make in connection therewith and preserve for five years adequate and accurate records. The Board of Directors shall by regulation designate the specific information which must be included in such records.

SECTION 3. Each person who breeds, keeps, transfers ownership or possession of, or deals in dogs that are registered or to be registered with The American Kennel Club, whether he acts as principal or agent or sells on consignment, must follow such practices as, consistent with the number of dogs involved, will preclude any possibility of error in identification of any individual dog or doubt as to the parentage of any particular dog or litter.

SECTION 4. The American Kennel Club or its duly authorized representative shall have the right to inspect the records required to be kept and the practices required to be followed by these rules and by any regulations adopted under them, and to examine any dog registered or to be registered with The American Kennel Club.

SECTION 5. Each person who transfers ownership or possession of a dog that is registered or to be registered with The American Kennel Club must describe the dog in the records of The American Kennel Club in writing to the person acquiring the dog at the time of transfer, either on a bill of sale or otherwise. The Board of Directors shall by regulation designate the descriptive information required.

SECTION 6. The American Kennel Club may refuse to register any dog or litter or to record the transfer of any dog, for the sole reason that the application is not supported by the records required by these rules and the regulations adopted under them.

SECTION 7. Any person who is required to keep records and who fails to do so or who fails or refuses when requested to make such records available for inspection by The American Kennel Club or its duly authorized representatives, may be suspended from all privileges of The American Kennel Club by the Board of Directors.

Any person who fails to follow such practices as will preclude any possibility of error in identification of an individual dog or doubt as to the parentage of a particular dog or litter, or who fails or refuses to permit the American Kennel Club or its duly authorized representatives to examine such practices, or to examine a dog that is registered or to be registered with The American Kennel Club, may be suspended from all privileges of The American Kennel Club by the Board of Directors.

CHAPTER 4

DOG SHOWS DEFINED

SECTION 1. A member show is a show at which championship points may be awarded, given by a club or association which is a member of The American Kennel Club.

SECTION 2. A licensed show is a show at which championship points may be awarded, given by a club or association which is not a member of The American Kennel Club but which has been specially licensed by The American Kennel Club to give the specific show designated in the license.

SECTION 3. A member or licensed all-breed club may apply to The American Kennel Club for approval to hold a show at which championship points may be awarded with entries restricted to puppies that are eligible for entry in the regular puppy class and dogs that have been placed first, second or third in a regular class at a show at which championship points were awarded, provided the club submitting such an application has held at least one show annually for at least ten years immediately prior to the year in which application for a show so restricted is made, and further provided that there shall not have been less than 900 dogs entered in its show (or in one of its shows if the club holds more than one show a year) in the year preceding the year in which application is made for its first show with entries so restricted.

When an application for this type of restricted entry show has been approved by The American Kennel Club the only dogs eligible for entry shall be puppies that are eligible for entry in the regular puppy class and those dogs that have been placed first, second or third in a regular class at a show at which championship points were awarded held not less than sixty days prior to the first day of the show at which entries will be so restricted.

However, a club making application to hold a show restricted to entries of dogs as specified above may further restrict entries by excluding all puppies or all puppies 6 months and under 9 months and/or by excluding dogs that have placed third or dogs that have placed second and third, provided the extent of these further restrictions are specified on the application.

Any club whose application has been approved to hold a show with restricted entries as described in this section shall indicate the extent of the restrictions in its premium list.

SECTION 4. A member or licensed all-breed club may apply to The American Kennel Club for approval to hold a show at which championship points may be awarded with entries restricted to dogs that are champions on the records of The American Kennel Club and dogs that have been credited with one or more championship points, provided the club submitting such an application has held at least one show annually for at least 15 years immediately prior to the year in which application for a show so restricted is made, and further provided that there shall not have been less than 1200 dogs entered in its show (or in one of its shows if the club holds more than one show a year) in the year preceding the year in which application is made for its first show with entries so restricted.

When an application for this type of restricted entry show has been approved by the American Kennel Club, the only dogs eligible for entry shall be those dogs that have been recorded as champions and dogs that have been credited with one or more championship points as a result of competition at shows held not less than 60 days prior to the first day of the show at which entries will be so restricted.

However, a club making application to hold a show restricted to entries of dogs as specified above, may further restrict entries by excluding all puppies or all puppies six months and under nine months and/or by excluding dogs that have not been credited with at least one major championship point rating, provided the extent of these further restrictions are specified on the application.

Any club whose application has been approved to hold a show with restricted entries as described in this section shall indicate the extent of the restrictions in its premium list.

SECTION 5. A member or licensed show with a limited entry, at which championship points may be awarded may be given by a club or association in the event said club or association considers it necessary to LIMIT the TOTAL ENTRY at its show due to the limitations of space. The total number of entries to be accepted together with the reason therefor, must be indicated on the cover or title page of the PREMIUM LIST. A specified closing date, in accordance with Chapter 9, Section 9, must be indicated in the premium list together with a statement that entries will close on said date or when the limit has been reached, if prior thereto. No entries can be accepted, cancelled or substituted after the entry is closed. The specified closing date shall be used in determining whether a dog is eligible for the Novice Classes at the show.

SECTION 6. A specialty show is a show given by a club or association formed for the improvement of any one breed of pure-bred dogs, at which championship points may be awarded to said breed.

SECTION 7. An American-bred specialty show is a show for American-bred dogs only, given by a member club or association formed for the improvement of any one breed of pure-bred dogs at which championship points may be awarded to said breed.

SECTION 8. A sanctioned match is an informal meeting at which pure-bred dogs may compete but not for championship points, held by a club or association whether or not a member of The American Kennel Club by obtaining the sanction of The American Kennel Club.

CHAPTER 5

MAKING APPLICATION TO HOLD A DOG SHOW

SECTION 1. Each member club or association is entitled to hold one show and one field trial a year without payment of a fee to The American Kennel Club, but must pay a fee of fifteen ($15.00) dollars for each other show and/or field trial which it may hold during the same calendar year.

SECTION 2. Each member club or association which has held a show or shows in any one year shall have first right to claim the corresponding dates for its show or shows to be held in the next succeeding year.

SECTION 3. Each member club or association not a specialty club which shall hold a show at least once in every two consecutive calendar years shall have the sole show privilege in the city, town or district which has been assigned to it as its show territory.

SECTION 4. A member club or association must apply to The American Kennel Club on a regular official form, which will be supplied on request, over the signature of one of its officers, for permission to hold a show, stating in the application the day or days upon which, and the exact location where, it desires to hold such show, and sending a copy of any contract, or if verbal, a statement of the substance of the agreement made with the Superintendent or Show Secretary. This application will be referred to the Board of Directors of The American Kennel Club which will consider the same and notify the member club or association of its approval or disapproval of the dates and place selected.

SECTION 5. If a member club or association not a specialty club shall fail to hold a show at least once in every two consecutive calendar years, the Board of Directors of The American Kennel Club upon application may give a license to another club or association which need not be a member of The American Kennel Club to hold a show within the limits of the show territory of the member club or association which has so failed to hold its show.

SECTION 6. If a member club or association not a specialty club shall fail to hold a show within the next calendar year after a licensed show has been held within the show territory of said member club or association, The American Kennel Club will consider such failure sufficient reason to consider an application for membership in The American Kennel Club by any other club or association organized to hold shows within said territory which shall conform to the requirements and conditions of Article IV of the Constitution and By-Laws of The American Kennel Club although said member club or association so in default shall not consent thereto.

SECTION 7. Where there are two or more show-giving member clubs or associations not specialty clubs located in the same show territory, the jurisdiction of said clubs or associations shall be concurrent.

SECTION 8. The use of a club's name for show purposes cannot be transferred.

SECTION 9. If a non-member club or association wishes to hold a dog show, it must apply to The American Kennel Club on a regular official form, which will be supplied on request, over the signature of one of its officers, for permission to hold a show, stating in the application the day or days upon which, and the exact location where it desires to hold such show, and sending a copy of any contract, or if verbal, a statement of the substance of the agreement made with the Superintendent or Show Secretary. The American Kennel Club is to be supplied with such information with regard to Constitution, By-Laws, names of the officers and members, and the financial responsibility of the applying non-member club or association as The American Kennel Club may request. A non-member club shall pay a license fee for the privilege of holding such show, under American Kennel Club rules, the amount of which fee shall be fixed and determined by the Board of Directors of The American Kennel Club. The application will be referred to the Board of Directors of The American Kennel Club, which will consider the same and notify the non-member club or association of its approval or disapproval of the dates and place selected. If the Board of Directors shall disapprove the application, the license fee will be returned to said non-member club or association.

SECTION 10. A member specialty club may hold a show confined to the breed which it sponsors and such show shall carry a championship rating according to the schedule of points of the breed for which the show is given.

SECTION 11. A member specialty club may hold a show confined to American-bred dogs only in which show winners classes may be included and championship points awarded, provided that the necessary regular classes are included in the classification.

SECTION 12. A non-member specialty club may be licensed to hold a show, if the consent in writing that it may be given first shall be obtained from the member specialty club formed for the improvement of the breed sought to be shown which first was admitted to be a member of The American Kennel Club, which member club is commonly known as the Parent Club.

If a Parent Club unreasonably shall withhold its consent in writing to the holding of such show, the non-member specialty club may appeal to the Board of Directors of The American Kennel Club at any time after one month from the time when said consent was requested. A committee of said Board appointed by said Board or between sittings of said Board appointed by the President of The American Kennel Club, or, in his absence, by the Executive Vice-President of The American Kennel Club shall hear the parties who may present their respective contentions, either orally or in writing, and in its discretion may issue a license to the non-member specialty club to hold such show.

SECTION 13. Where a specialty club wishes to consider as its Specialty Show the breed classes at an all-breed show, written application must be made to The American Kennel Club and a fee of $15.00 sent with application. Consent of the parent member specialty club must be secured by the non-member specialty club and forwarded to The American Kennel Club.

SECTION 14. A specialty club that wishes to hold a futurity or sweepstake, either in conjunction with a show or as a separate event, must apply to The American Kennel Club on a form which will be supplied on request, for permission to hold the event, whether or not the futurity or sweepstake will be open to non-members.

SECTION 15. The Board of Directors of The American Kennel Club, may, in its discretion grant permission to clubs to hold sanctioned matches, which sanctioned matches shall be governed by such rules and regulations as from time to time shall be determined by the Board of Directors.

SECTION 16. American Kennel Club sanction must be obtained by any club that holds American Kennel Club events, for any type of match for which it solicits or accepts entries from non-members.

SECTION 17. The Board of Directors of The American Kennel Club will not approve applications for shows where dates conflict, unless it be shown that the granting of such applications will not work to the detriment of either show.

SECTION 18. A show-giving club must not advertise or publish the date of any show which it proposes to hold until that date has been approved by The American Kennel Club.

SECTION 19. All clubs holding shows under American Kennel Club rules must have available at each show through their bench show committees, a copy of the latest edition of *The Complete Dog Book* and at least one copy of the rules of The American Kennel Club.

SECTION 20. Any club holding a show for charity if requested must submit to The American Kennel Club within ninety days of date of show, a complete financial statement and receipt from the organization for which the show was held.

SECTION 21. The duration of a dog show will not exceed two days, unless permission be granted by The American Kennel Club for a longer period.

CHAPTER 6

DOG SHOW CLASSIFICATIONS

SECTION 1. The following breeds and/or varieties of breeds, divided by groups, shall be all the breeds and/or varieties of breeds for which regular classes of The American Kennel Club may be provided at any show held under American Kennel Club rules. The Board of Directors may either add to, transfer from one group to another, or delete from said list of breeds and/or varieties of breeds, whenever in its opinion registrations of such breed and/or variety of breed in the Stud Book justify such action.

GROUP 1—SPORTING DOGS

GRIFFONS (WIREHAIRED POINTING)
POINTERS

POINTERS (GERMAN SHORTHAIRED)
POINTERS (GERMAN WIREHAIRED)
RETRIEVERS (CHESAPEAKE BAY)
RETRIEVERS (CURLY-COATED)
RETRIEVERS (FLAT-COATED)
RETRIEVERS (GOLDEN)
RETRIEVERS (LABRADOR)
SETTERS (ENGLISH)
SETTERS (GORDON)
SETTERS (IRISH)
SPANIELS (AMERICAN WATER)
SPANIELS (BRITTANY)
SPANIELS (CLUMBER)
SPANIELS (COCKER)
    Three varieties: Solid Color, Black. Solid Color Other Than Black including Black and Tan. Parti-color.
SPANIELS (ENGLISH COCKER)
SPANIELS (ENGLISH SPRINGER)
SPANIELS (FIELD)
SPANIELS (IRISH WATER)
SPANIELS (SUSSEX)
SPANIELS (WELSH SPRINGER)
VIZSLAS
WEIMARANERS

GROUP 2—HOUNDS

AFGHAN HOUNDS
BASENJIS
BASSET HOUNDS
BEAGLES
    Two varieties: Not exceeding 13 inches in height. Over 13 inches but not exceeding 15 inches in height.
BLOODHOUNDS
BORZOIS
COONHOUNDS (BLACK AND TAN)
DACHSHUNDS
    Three varieties: Longhaired. Smooth. Wirehaired.
DEERHOUNDS (SCOTTISH)
FOXHOUNDS (AMERICAN)
FOXHOUNDS (ENGLISH)
GREYHOUNDS
HARRIERS
IRISH WOLFHOUNDS
NORWEGIAN ELKHOUNDS
OTTER HOUNDS
RHODESIAN RIDGEBACKS
SALUKIS
WHIPPETS

GROUP 3—WORKING DOGS

ALASKAN MALAMUTES
BELGIAN MALINOIS
BELGIAN SHEEPDOGS
BELGIAN TERVUREN
BERNESE MOUNTAIN DOGS
BOUVIERS DES FLANDRES
BOXERS
BRIARDS
BULLMASTIFFS
COLLIES
    Two varieties: Rough. Smooth.
DOBERMAN PINSCHERS
GERMAN SHEPHERD DOGS
GIANT SCHNAUZERS
GREAT DANES
GREAT PYRENEES
KOMONDOROK
KUVASZOK
MASTIFFS
NEWFOUNDLANDS
OLD ENGLISH SHEEPDOGS
PULIK
ROTTWEILERS
SAMOYEDS
SCHNAUZERS (STANDARD)
SHETLAND SHEEPDOGS
SIBERIAN HUSKIES
ST. BERNARDS
WELSH CORGIS (CARDIGAN)
WELSH CORGIS (PEMBROKE)

GROUP 4—TERRIERS

AIREDALE TERRIERS
AUSTRALIAN TERRIERS
BEDLINGTON TERRIERS
BORDER TERRIERS
BULL TERRIERS
    Two varieties: White. Colored.
CAIRN TERRIERS
DANDIE DINMONT TERRIERS
FOX TERRIERS
    Two varieties: Smooth. Wire.
IRISH TERRIERS
KERRY BLUE TERRIERS
LAKELAND TERRIERS
MANCHESTER TERRIERS
    Two varieties: Standard, over 12 pounds and not exceeding 22 pounds Toy (in Toy Group)
NORWICH TERRIERS
SCHNAUZERS (MINIATURE)
SCOTTISH TERRIERS
SEALYHAM TERRIERS
SKYE TERRIERS
STAFFORDSHIRE TERRIERS
WELSH TERRIERS
WEST HIGHLAND WHITE TERRIERS

GROUP 5—TOYS

AFFENPINSCHERS
CHIHUAHUAS
    Two varieties: Smooth Coat. Long Coat.
ENGLISH TOY SPANIELS
    Two varieties: King Charles and Ruby, Blenheim and Prince Charles.
GRIFFONS (BRUSSELS)
ITALIAN GREYHOUNDS
JAPANESE SPANIELS
MALTESE
MANCHESTER TERRIERS
    Two varieties: Toy, not exceeding 12 pounds Standard (in Terrier Group)
PAPILLONS
PEKINGESE
PINSCHERS (MINIATURE)
POMERANIANS
POODLES
    Three varieties: Toy, not exceeding 10 inches Miniature (in Non-Sporting Group) Standard (in Non-Sporting Group)
PUGS
SHIH TZU
SILKY TERRIERS
YORKSHIRE TERRIERS

GROUP 6—NON-SPORTING DOGS

BOSTON TERRIERS
BULLDOGS
CHOW CHOWS
DALMATIANS
FRENCH BULLDOGS
KEESHONDEN
LHASA APSOS
POODLES
    Three varieties: Miniature, over 10 inches and not exceeding 15 inches Standard, over 15 inches Toy (in Toy Group)
SCHIPPERKES

SECTION 2. No class shall be provided for any dog under six months of age except at sanctioned matches when approved by The American Kennel Club.

SECTION 3. The regular classes of The American Kennel Club shall be as follows:

Puppy
Novice
Bred-by-Exhibitor
American-bred
Open
Winners

been divided by sex, dogs of the same sex winning second or third prizes but not having been defeated by a dog of the same sex may compete in the Winners Class provided for their sex. At shows where the American-bred and Open Classes are not divided by sex there shall be but one Winners Class which shall be open only to undefeated dogs of either sex which have won first prizes in either the Puppy, Novice, Bred-by-Exhibitor, American-bred or Open Classes. There shall be no entry fee for competition in the Winners Class.

SECTION 4. The Puppy Class shall be for dogs that are six months of age and over, but under twelve months, that were whelped in the United States of America or Canada, and that are not champions. The age of a dog shall be calculated up to and inclusive of the first day of a show. For example, a dog whelped on January 1st is eligible to compete in a puppy class at a show the first day of which is July 1st of the same year and may continue to compete in puppy classes at shows up to and including a show the first day of which is the 31st day of December of the same year, but is not eligible to compete in a puppy class at a show the first day of which is January 1st of the following year.

SECTION 5. The Novice Class shall be for dogs six months of age and over, whelped in the United States of America or Canada, which have not, prior to the date of closing of entries, won three first prizes in the Novice Class, a first prize in Bred-by-Exhibitor, American-bred, or Open Classes, nor one or more points toward their championships.

SECTION 6. The Bred-by-Exhibitor Class shall be for dogs whelped in the United States of America, that are six months of age and over, that are not champions, and that are owned wholly or in part by the person or by the spouse of the person who was the breeder or one of the breeders of record.

Dogs entered in this class must be handled in the class by an owner, or by a member of the immediate family of an owner.

For purposes of this section, the members of an immediate family are: husband, wife, father, mother, son, daughter, brother, sister.

SECTION 7. The American-bred Class shall be for all dogs (except champions) six months of age and over, whelped in the United States of America, by reason of a mating which took place in the United States of America.

SECTION 8. The Open Class shall be for any dog six months of age or over except in a member specialty club show held only for American-bred dogs, in which case the Open Class shall be only for American-bred dogs.

SECTION 9. The Winners Class, at shows in which the American-bred and Open Classes are divided by sex, also shall be divided by sex and each division shall be open only to undefeated dogs of the same sex which have won first prizes in either the Puppy, Novice, Bred-by-Exhibitor, American-bred or Open Classes, excepting only in the event that where either the Puppy, Novice or Bred-by-Exhibitor Class shall not have

pionships are unconfirmed. The showing of dogs whose championships are unconfirmed is limited to a period of 90 days from the date of the show where a dog completed the requirements for a championship according to the owners' records.

After the Winners prize has been awarded in one of the sex divisions, where the Winners Class has been divided by sex, any second or third prize winning dog otherwise undefeated in its sex, which however, has been beaten in its class by the dog awarded Winners, shall compete with the other eligible dogs for Reserve Winners. After the Winners prize has been awarded, where the Winners Class is not divided by sex, any otherwise undefeated dog which has been placed second in any previous class to the dog awarded Winners shall compete with the remaining first prize-winners, for Reserve Winners. No eligible dog may be withheld from competition.

Winners' Classes shall be allowed only at shows where American-bred and Open Classes shall be given.

A member specialty club holding a show for American-bred dogs only may include Winners' Classes, provided the necessary regular classes are included in the classification.

A member club holding a show with restricted entries may include Winners' classes, provided the necessary regular classes are included in the classification.

SECTION 10. No Winners' Class, or any class resembling it, shall be given at sanctioned matches.

SECTION 11. Bench show committees may provide such other classes of recognized breeds or recognized varieties of breeds as they may choose, provided they do not conflict with the conditions of the above mentioned classes and are judged before Best of Breed competition.

Local classes, however, may not be divided by sex in shows at which local group classes are provided.

No class may be given in which more than one breed or recognized variety of breed may be entered, except as provided in these rules and regulations.

SECTION 12. A club that provides Winners classes shall also provide competition for Best of Breed or for Best of Variety in those breeds for which varieties are provided in this chapter. The awards in this competition shall be Best of Breed or Best of Variety of Breed.

The following categories of dogs may be entered and shown in this competition:

Dogs that are Champions of Record.

Dogs which according to their owners' records have completed the requirements for a championship but whose cham-

In addition, the Winners Dog and Winners Bitch (or the dog awarded Winners, if only one winners prize has been awarded), together with any undefeated dogs that have competed at the show only in additional non-regular classes shall compete for Best of Breed or Best of Variety of Breed.

If the Winners Dog or Winners Bitch is awarded Best of Breed or Best of Variety of Breed, it shall be automatically awarded Best of Winners; otherwise, the Winners Dog and Winners Bitch shall be judged together for Best of Winners following the judging of Best of Breed or Best of Variety of Breed. The dog designated Best of Winners shall be entitled to the number of points based on the number of dogs or bitches competing in the regular classes, whichever is greater. In the event that Winners is awarded in only one sex, there shall be no Best of Winners award.

After Best of Breed or Best of Variety of Breed and Best of Winners have been awarded, the judge shall select Best of Opposite Sex to Best of Breed or Best of Variety of Breed. Eligible for this award are:

Dogs of the opposite sex to Best of Breed or Best of Variety of Breed that have been entered for Best of Breed competition.

The dog awarded Winners of the -opposite sex to the Best of Breed or Best of Variety of Breed.

Any undefeated dogs of the opposite sex to Best of Breed or Best of Variety of Breed which have competed at the show only in additional non-regular classes.

SECTION 13. At specialty shows for breeds in which there are varieties as specified in Chapter 6, Section 1, and which are held apart from all-breed shows, Best of Breed shall be judged following the judging of Best of each variety and best of opposite sex to best of each variety. Best of Opposite Sex to Best of Breed shall also be judged. Dogs eligible for Best of Opposite Sex to Best-of-Breed competition will be found among the bests of variety or the bests of opposite sex to bests of variety, according to the sex of the dog placed Best of Breed.

At an all-breed show (even if a specialty club shall designate classes as its specialty show), the judge of a breed in which there are show varieties shall make no placings beyond Best of Variety and Best of Opposite Sex to Best of Variety.

SECTION 14. A club or association holding a show may give six group classes not divided by sex, such groups to be arranged in same order and to comprise the same breeds and recognized varieties of breeds as hereinbefore set forth in Chapter 2 and Section 1 of Chapter 6. All dogs designated by their respective breed judges Best of Breed at the show at which these group classes shall be eligible to compete in the group classes to which they belong according to this grouping, and all dogs designated Best of Variety in those breeds with more than one recognized variety, shall be eligible to compete in the group classes to which they belong according to this grouping. All entries for these group classes shall be made after judging of the regular classes of The American Kennel Club has been finished and no entry fee shall be charged. In the event that the owner of a dog designated Best of Breed or Best of Variety shall not exhibit the dog in the group class to which it is eligible, no other dog of the same breed or variety of breed shall be allowed to compete.

SECTION 15. A club giving group classes must also give a Best in Show, the winner to be entitled "Best Dog in Show". No entry fee shall be charged but the six group winners must compete.

SECTION 16. A club or association holding a show, if it gives brace classes in the several breeds and recognized varieties of breeds, may also give six brace group classes, not divided by sex; such groups to be arranged in the same order and to comprise the same breeds and recognized varieties of breeds as hereinbefore set forth in Chapter 2 and Section 1 of Chapter 6. All braces of dogs designated by their respective breed judges as Best of Breed or Best of Variety as the case may be at shows at which these brace group classes shall be given, shall be eligible to compete in the brace group classes to which they belong according to this grouping. All entries for these brace group classes shall be made after the judging of the regular classes of The American Kennel Club has been finished and no entry fee shall be charged. In the event that the owner of a brace of dogs designated Best of Breed or Best of Variety shall not exhibit the brace of dogs in the group class to which it is eligible, no other brace of dogs of the same breed or variety of breed shall be allowed to compete.

SECTION 17. If a club or association holding a show shall give these six group classes, it must also give a "Best Brace in Show", in which the six braces of dogs winning the first prizes in the six group classes must compete, but for which no entry fee shall be charged. The winner shall be entitled "The Best Brace in Show".

SECTION 18. A club or association holding a show, if it gives team classes in the several breeds and recognized varieties of breeds, may also give six team group classes not divided by sex, such groups to be arranged in the same order and to comprise the same breeds and recognized varieties of breeds as hereinbefore set forth in Chapter 2 and Section 1 of Chapter 6. All teams of dogs designated by their respective breed judges as Best of Breed or Best of Variety as the case may be at shows at which these team group classes shall be given, shall be eligible to compete in the team group classes to which they belong ac-cording to this grouping. All entries for these team group classes shall be made after the judging of the regular classes of The American Kennel Club has been finished and no entry fee shall be charged. In the event that the owner of a team of dogs designated Best of Breed or Best of Variety shall not exhibit the team of dogs in the group class to which it is eligible, no other team of dogs of the same breed or variety of breed shall be allowed to compete.

SECTION 19. If a club or association holding a show shall give these six group classes it must also give a "Best Team in Show," in which the six teams of dogs winning the first prizes in the six group classes must compete, but for which no entry fee shall be charged. The winner shall be entitled "The Best Team in Show".

SECTION 20. A club or association holding a show may give six group classes not divided by sex, open only to local dogs (as designated in its premium list), such groups to be arranged in the same order and to comprise the same breeds and recognized varieties of breeds as hereinbefore set forth in Chapter 2 and Section 1 of Chapter 6. All dogs designated by their respective breed judges "Best in Local Class of the Breed" or "Best in Local Class of the Variety of Breed" at the show at which these group classes shall be given shall be eligible to compete in the group classes to which they belong according to this grouping. No entry fee shall be charged. In the event that the owner of the dog designated "Best in Local Class" shall not exhibit the dog in the group class to which it is eligible, no other dog of the same breed or variety of breed shall be allowed to compete.

SECTION 21. A club giving local group classes may also give a "Best Local Dog in Show". No entry fee shall be charged but the local group winners must compete.

SECTION 22. The Miscellaneous Class shall be for pure-bred dogs of such breeds as may be designated by the Board of Directors of The American Kennel Club. No dog shall be eligible for entry in the Miscellaneous Class unless the owner has been granted an Indefinite Listing Privilege, and unless the ILP number is given on the entry form. Application for an Indefinite Listing Privilege shall be made on a form provided by the AKC and when submitted must be accompanied by a fee set by the Board of Directors.

All Miscellaneous Breeds shall be shown together in a single class except that the class may be divided by sex if so specified in the premium list. There shall be no further competition for dogs entered in this class.

The ribbons for First, Second, Third and Fourth prizes in this class shall be Rose, Brown, Light Green, and Gray, respectively.

At present the Miscellaneous Class is open to the following breeds:

Akitas
Australian Cattle Dogs
Australian Kelpies
Border Collies
Cavalier King Charles Spaniels
Ibizan Hounds
Miniature Bull Terriers
Soft-Coated Wheaten Terriers
Spinoni Italiani
Tibetan Terriers

SECTION 23. A registered dog that is six months of age or over and of a breed for which a classification is offered in the premium list may be entered in a show for Exhibition Only at the regular entry fee provided the dog has been awarded first prize in one of the regular classes at a licensed or member show held prior to the closing of entries of the show in which the Exhibition Only entry is made, and provided further that the premium list has not specified that entries for Exhibition Only will not be accepted. The name and date of the show at which the dog was awarded the first prize must be stated on the entry form.

A dog entered for Exhibition Only shall not be shown in any class or competition at that show.

CHAPTER 7

APPROVAL OF JUDGES LISTS AND PREMIUM LIST PROOFS

SECTION 1. After a club or association has been granted permission by The American Kennel Club to hold a show, it must send for approval by and in time to reach The American Kennel Club at least EIGHT WEEKS before the show date, a list of the names and addresses of the judges whom it has selected to judge its show, giving in each instance the particular breed or breeds of dogs and group classes, if any, which it is desired that each judge shall pass upon, and the name and address of the judge selected to pass upon Best in Show.

The show-giving club must not advertise or publish the name or names of any of the judges which it has selected until the complete list has been approved by The American Kennel Club.

SECTION 2. Each club or association which has been granted permission by The American Kennel Club to hold a dog show or obedience trial must submit in time to reach The American Kennel Club at least EIGHT WEEKS before its date, two printer's proof copies of its proposed premium list. The Show Plans Department of The American Kennel Club will return, not later than six weeks before the show or trial date, one copy of the proof indicating thereon all necessary corrections, deletions and revisions. Attached to the returned proof will be a conditional authorization of The American Kennel Club to print and distribute the premium list. This authorization will list the conditions to be observed or carried out by the show or trial-giving club and its superintendent or show or trial secretary, before printing the premium list.

SECTION 3. Premium lists and entry forms must be printed and sent to prospective exhibitors at least FOUR WEEKS prior to the first day of the show. Two copies of the premium list must be sent to The American Kennel Club at time of distribution.

SECTION 4. Premium lists and entry forms, in order to insure uniformity, must conform to The American Kennel Club official size of 6 x 9 inches and the entry form must conform in every respect with the official form, a sample of which may be had without charge by application to the Secretary of The American Kennel Club.

CHAPTER 8

RIBBONS, PRIZES AND TROPHIES

SECTION 1. All clubs or associations holding dog shows under the rules of The American Kennel Club, except sanctioned matches, shall use the following colors for their prize ribbons or rosettes, in the regular classes of The American Kennel Club and the regular group classes.

First prize—Blue.
Second prize—Red.
Third prize—Yellow.
Fourth prize—White.
Winners—Purple.
Reserve Winners—Purple and White.
Best of Winners—Blue and White.
Special prize—Dark Green.
Best of Breed and Best of Variety of Breed—Purple and Gold.
Best of Opposite Sex to Best of Breed and Best of Opposite Sex to Best of Variety of Breed—Red and White.

and shall use the following colors for their prize ribbons in all additional classes:

First prize—Rose.
Second prize—Brown.
Third prize—Light Green.
Fourth prize—Gray.

SECTION 2. The prize ribbon for Best Local Dog in Show shall be Blue and Gold, and the prize ribbons in local classes and local groups shall be:

First prize—Rose.
Second prize—Brown.
Third prize—Light Green.
Fourth prize—Gray.

SECTION 3. Each ribbon or rosette, except those used

at sanctioned matches, shall be at least 2 inches wide, and approximately 8 inches long; and bear on its face a facsimile of the seal of The American Kennel Club, the name of the prize, and the name of the show-giving club with numerals of year, date of show, and name of city or town where show is given.

SECTION 4. If ribbons are given at sanctioned matches, they shall be of the following colors, but may be of any design or size:

First prize—Rose.
Second prize—Brown.
Third prize—Light Green.
Fourth prize—Gray.
Special prize—Green with pink edges.
Best of Breed—Orange.
Best of Match—Pink and Green.
Best of Opposite Sex to Best in Match—Lavender.

SECTION 5. If money prizes are offered in a premium list of a show, a fixed amount for each prize must be stated. All other prizes offered in a premium list of a show must be accurately described or their monetary value must be stated. Alcoholic beverages will not be acceptable as prizes.

SECTION 6. A show-giving club shall not accept the donation of a prize for a competition not provided for at its show.

SECTION 7. All prizes offered in a premium list of a show must be offered to be awarded in the regular procedure of judging, with the exception of those prizes provided for in Sections 9 and 13 of this Chapter.

SECTION 8. Prizes may be offered for outright award at a show for the following placings:

First, Second, Third, Fourth in the Puppy, Novice, Bred-by-Exhibitor, American-bred or Open Classes, or in any division of these designated in the Classification.

First, Second, Third, Fourth in any additional class which the show-giving club may offer in accord with the provisions of Chapter 6, Section 11, and in the Miscellaneous Class (at all-breed shows only).

Winners, Reserve Winners, Best of Winners, Best of Breed or Variety, Best of Opposite Sex to Best of Breed or Variety. At all-breed shows only: First, Second, Third, Fourth in a Group Class and for Best in Show, Best Local in Show, Best Brace in Show and Best Team in Show.

SECTION 9. At specialty shows held apart from all-breed shows, prizes, for outright award, may also be offered for: Best in Puppy Classes, Best in Novice Classes, Best in Bred-by-Exhibitor Classes, Best in American-bred Classes, Best in Open Classes, Best in any additional classes which the show-giving club may offer in accord with the provisions of Chapter 6, Section 11, in which the sexes are divided.

(In breeds in which there are varieties, a prize may be offered for Best in any of the above classes within the variety.)

SECTION 10 At all-breed shows, prizes may be offered on a three-time win basis for the following awards, provided permanent possession goes to an exhibitor winning the award three times not necessarily with the same dog, and further provided such prizes are offered by the show-giving club itself or through it for competition at its shows only:

Best in Show, Best Local in Show, Best in any one group class.

SECTION 11. At specialty shows, prizes may be offered on a three-time win basis for the following awards, provided permanent possession goes to an exhibitor winning the award three times not necessarily with the same dog and further provided such prizes are offered by the specialty club itself or through it for competition at its specialty shows only:

Best of Breed or Best of Opposite Sex to Best of Breed (Where a specialty club considers the classes at an all-breed show as its specialty show, there can be no award for Best of Breed in those breeds in which there are varieties.) Best of Variety of Breed or Best of Opposite Sex to Best of Variety, Best of Winners, Winners Dog and Winners Bitch.

SECTION 12. Perpetual prizes and such three-time win prizes as have been in competition prior to September 9, 1952 and which would not be allowed under the terms of the sections in this Chapter will continue to be permitted to be offered under the terms of their original provisions until won outright or otherwise retired. Should premium list copy submitted to the AKC for approval contain such non-allowable prizes, a certification by the Club Secretary stating that the prizes have been in competition prior to September 9, 1952 must be included.

SECTION 13. Annual Specials are prizes offered by member or non-member specialty clubs for outright award at the end of a twelve-month period, the award to be based on the most number of wins at shows, in a designated competition, through-out the period.

Only those clubs which have held specialty shows can offer annual specials.

Specialty clubs must submit two lists of their proposed prizes to The American Kennel Club for its approval. When approval has been obtained, the specialty club shall send copies of the list to its members, with one such copy to The American Kennel Club.

No annual specials may be put into competition until these procedures have been followed and approval obtained.

The terms of such prizes are not to be printed in full in any premium list, but reference may be made to the prizes by listing the name of the specialty club under an appropriate heading. It shall be the obligation of the specialty club to contact superintendents, show secretaries and show-giving clubs, notifying them that their list of annual specials has been approved and that the offer may be published in premium lists by giving the name of the club under an appropriate heading. However, it shall be understood that competition for the various prizes is to count at all licensed or member club dog shows held in the designated period, whether the specialty club's name has been listed in a premium list or not.

If a specialty club wishes to confine competition for its annual specials to certain shows, it may do so, but such restriction must be specified in the terms of its proposed prizes submitted to the AKC and if approved, the copies of the list sent to members must include the restrictive provision.

SECTION 14. Regular Specials are prizes offered by show-giving member or non-member specialty clubs for outright and automatic award at any show where the terms have been published in full in the premium list and catalog of the show. No prize may be offered for an award higher than Best of Breed or Best of Variety of Breed. It shall be the obligation of specialty clubs offering such regular specials to notify superintendents, show secretaries and show-giving clubs that said prizes may be offered provided the terms are set forth in full in the premium list and catalog of the show. The specialty club will be solely responsible for the distribution of such prizes within 60 days after the completion of a show when it has been determined that all the terms of the awards have been met. No show-giving club is obligated to accept an offering of regular specials.

CHAPTER 9

PREMIUM LISTS AND CLOSING OF ENTRIES

SECTION 1. The awards at a dog show, or the scores made at an obedience trial, will be officially recorded by The American Kennel Club only if the certification of the Secretary of The American Kennel Club is published on the first, second or third page of the premium list stating that permission has been granted by The American Kennel Club for the dog show or obedience trial to be held under American Kennel Club rules and regulations.

If the show shall be given by a club or association not a member of The American Kennel Club the words "Licensed Show" must be plainly printed on the title page of the premium list.

SECTION 2. The premium list shall contain the following: A list of the officers of the show-giving club with the address of the secretary, a list of the members of the bench show committee (there must be at least five) together with the designation of "Chairman" and the Chairman's address (and "Obedience Trial Chairman'' if an obedience trial is being held by a club in connection with its dog show), the names of the Veterinarians (or name of local Veterinary Association), the names and addresses of the judges, together with their assignments, and the name and address of the superintendent or show secretary who has been approved by The American Kennel Club. The premium list shall also specify whether the show is Benched or Unbenched, and shall give the exact location of the show, the date or dates on which it is to be held, and the times of opening and closing of the show.

SECTION 2A. An all-breed show-giving club may, at its option, use a condensed form of premium list which shall be identical with the content and format of a regular premium list, and comply with all the pertinent rules except that the listing of breed prizes and trophies offered is omitted as well as the listing of all prizes and trophies offered for an obedience trial if held by the show-giving club with its show. Such prizes and trophies as are offered for best in show and group placements are to be included in a condensed premium list as well as any schedule of class cash prizes that a club proposes to offer.

Two copies of the proposed list of breed and obedience prizes and trophies are to be submitted to AKC for approval at the same time that printers proof copies of the condensed premium list are submitted. The conditions of all prizes and trophies offered must conform to the provisions of Chapter 8 of these rules and Chapter 1, Section 32 of the Obedience Regulations. A club using a condensed form of premium list is obligated to prepare lists of the breed and obedience prizes and trophies for distribution to prospective entrants and exhibitors on request. Such lists can be printed, multilithed, mimeographed or typed (and photostated) on paper of any suitable size with both sides of the paper being used if the club wishes. In each condensed form of premium list there must be the notation, "A list of breed and obedience prizes and trophies offered can be obtained by writing to (name and address of club secretary and/or superintendent and address)"

A club which chooses to use a condensed form of premium list may also prepare for printing a regular premium list for other than mail distribution. The regular premium list can then be used to fill requests for a listing of breed and obedience prizes and trophies offered and no separate list of breed and obedience prizes and trophies need be prepared.

However, if a regular premium list is used in addition to the condensed premium list, two copies of the printers proofs of the full premium list must be submitted to the AKC for approval with the notation that it is the club's intention to print a condensed premium list for mailing purposes.

An all-breed obedience trial-giving club may, at its option, use a condensed form of premium list which shall be identical with the content and format of a regular premium list, and comply with all the pertinent rules and regulations except that the listing of prizes and trophies offered is omitted. When a condensed form of premium list is used, the same procedure is to be followed with respect to the prize and trophy list as is required of show-giving clubs and as is set forth in this section.

SECTION 3. Except at specialty club shows, the general classification of recognized breeds divided into six groups and in the same order as set forth in Chapter 2, with the varieties of distinct breeds as described in Section 1 of Chapter 6 added thereto, in their proper groups and alphabetical position, shall be published in the premium list.

SECTION 4. If an all-breed club or association permits a specialty club to consider the classes at its show as their specialty show, the winner of Best of Breed or Best of Variety of Breed if no Best of Breed is awarded, may compete in the group classes of the all-breed show.

SECTION 5. If more than one judge has been approved to judge a specialty show held apart from an all-breed show, the premium list must designate the particular assignments of each judge as approved by The American Kennel Club, except when the specialty club has requested and received approval for the drawing of assignments at the show, in which case a statement to this effect shall appear in the premium list in place of designated assignments.

SECTION 6. A show-giving club shall assume the responsibility of collecting all recording fees for The American Kennel Club, which fact shall be stated in the premium list.

SECTION 7. Bench show committees may make such regulations or additional rules for the government of their shows as shall be considered necessary, provided such regulations or additional rules do not conflict with any rule of The American Kennel Club, and provided they do not discriminate between breeds or between dogs entered in show classes and those entered in obedience classes in the required hour of arrival and the hour of removal. If permission is granted to a club other than the show-giving club for the holding of an obedience trial in connection with a dog show, the obedience club so authorized, must comply with the show-giving club's rules adopted hereunder.

Such regulations or additional rules shall be printed in the premium list and violations thereof shall be considered the same as violations of the rules and regulations of The American Kennel Club.

SECTION 8. No prizes may be accepted or offered by a show-giving club unless they are published in the premium list of the show or in the separate list of prizes if the condensed form of premium list is used; nor may any be withdrawn or the conditions thereof changed after they have been published in the premium list or in the separate list of prizes.

If the donor of a prize that has been published in the premium list of a show or in the separate list of prizes shall fail to furnish the prize, the show-giving club shall promptly supply a prize of the same description and of no less value.

The show-giving club shall be responsible for all errors made in publishing offers of prizes and shall, in the event of error, award prizes of equal value; except that if an error has been made in the premium list or in the separate list of prizes in publishing the conditions of a specialty club's Regular Specials (as described in Chapter 8, Section 14) prizes shall be awarded according to the current terms of the specialty club's Regular Specials.

SECTION 9. Every premium list shall specify the date and time at which entries for a show shall close. The premium list shall also specify the name and address of the Superintendent or Show Secretary who is to receive the entries. For all shows other than specialty shows, the specified closing date and time must be no later than as outlined in the following schedule:

For a show which opens on Saturday, Sunday, or Monday, entries not accepted later than noon the Tuesday prior to the Tuesday immediately preceding the show.

For a show which opens on Tuesday, entries accepted not later than noon the Wednesday prior to the Wednesday of the week preceding the show.

For a show which opens on Wednesday, entries accepted not later than noon the Thursday prior to the Thursday of the week preceding the show.

For a show which opens on Thursday, entries accepted not later than noon the Friday prior to the Friday of the week preceding the show.

For a show which opens on Friday, entries accepted not later than noon the Saturday prior to the Saturday of the week preceding the show.

Whenever the closing day noted above falls on a postal holiday, entries received in the first mail only on the following day may be accepted.

CHAPTER 10

JUDGES

SECTION 1. Any reputable person who is in good standing with The American Kennel Club may apply for leave to judge any breed or breeds of pure-bred dogs which in his or her opinion he or she is qualified by training and experience to pass upon, with the exception of persons connected with any publication in the capacity of solicitor for kennel advertisements, persons connected with dog food, dog remedy or kennel supply companies in the capacity of solicitor or salesman, persons employed in and about kennels, persons who buy, sell and in any way trade or traffic in dogs as a means of livelihood in whole or in part,

whether or not they be known as dealers (excepting in this instance recognized private and professional handlers to a limited extent as will later appear) and professional show superintendents.

No Judge shall be granted a license to be an annual superintendent.

SECTION 2. The application for license to judge must be made on a form which will be supplied by The American Kennel Club upon request and when received by said club will be placed before the Board of Directors of The American Kennel Club who shall determine in each instance whether a license shall be issued.

SECTION 3. The American Kennel Club will not approve as judge for any given show the superintendent, show secretary, or show veterinarians, or club officials of said show acting in any one of these three capacities, and such person cannot officiate or judge at such show under any circumstances.

SECTION 4. Only those persons whose names are on The American Kennel Club's list of eligible judges may, in the discretion of The American Kennel Club, be approved to judge at any member or licensed show, except that if it becomes necessary to replace an advertised judge after the opening of the show and no person on the eligible judges list is available to take his place, the Bench Show Committee may select as a substitute for the advertised judge a person whose name is not on the eligible judges list provided such person is not currently suspended from the privileges of The American Kennel Club, is not currently suspended as a judge and is not ineligible to judge under the provisions of Sections 1 and 3 of this Chapter.

SECTION 5. The American Kennel Club may in its discretion approve as a judge of any sanctioned match, futurity or sweepstake a person who is not currently suspended from the privileges of The American Kennel Club or whose judging privileges are not currently suspended.

SECTION 6. Bench show committees or superintendents shall, in every instance, notify appointed judges of the breeds and group classes upon which they are to pass, and such notifications shall be given before the publication of the premium lists.

SECTION 7. Bench show committees or superintendents shall not add to or subtract from the number of breeds or variety groups which a selected judge has agreed to pass upon without first notifying said judge of and obtaining his consent to the contemplated change in his assigned breeds or variety groups, and the judge when so notified may refuse to judge any breeds or variety groups added to his original assignment.

SECTION 8. A bench show committee which shall be informed at any time prior to A WEEK before the opening day of its show that an advertised judge will not fulfill his or her engagement to judge shall substitute a judge in his or her place, which substitute judge must be approved by The American Kennel Club, and shall give notice of the name of the substitute judge to all those who have entered dogs in the classes allotted to be judged by the advertised judge. All those who have entered dogs to be shown under the advertised judge shall be permitted to withdraw their entries at any time prior to the opening day of the show and the entry fees paid for entering such dogs shall be refunded.

Since an entry can be made only under a breed judge, changes in Group or Best in Show assignments do not entitle an exhibitor to a refund.

SECTION 9. Should a Bench Show Committee be informed at any time within a week before the opening of its show, or after its show has opened, that an advertised judge will not fulfill his or her engagement to judge, it shall substitute a qualified judge in his or her place, and shall obtain approval of the change from The American Kennel Club if time allows.

No notice need be sent to those exhibitors who have entered dogs under the advertised judge.

The Bench Show Committee will be responsible for having a notice posted in a prominent place within the show precincts as soon after the show opens as is practical informing exhibitors of the change in judges. An exhibitor who has entered a dog under an advertised judge who is being replaced may withdraw such entry and shall have the entry fee refunded, provided notice of such withdrawal is given to the Superintendent or Show Secretary prior to the start of the judging of the breed which is to be passed upon by a substitute judge.

SECTION 10. In case an advertised judge shall have judged part of the classes of a breed and then finds it impossible to finish, a substitute judge shall be selected by the bench show committee, and in that event the awards made by the regular judge shall stand, and his or her substitute shall judge only the remaining entries in the breed. No dogs entered under the regularly selected judge shall be withheld from competition.

SECTION 11. A substitute judge shall finish the judging of the breed class or group he or she is adjudicating upon if he or she has begun to judge before the advertised judge arrives at the show.

SECTION 12. Any club or association that holds a dog show must prepare, after the entries have closed and not before, a judging program showing the time scheduled for the judging of each breed and each variety for which entries have been accepted. The judging program shall also state the time for the start of group judging, if any. The program shall be based on the judging of about 25 dogs per hour by each judge. Each judge's breed and variety assignments shall be divided into periods of about one hour, except in those cases where the entry in a breed or variety exceeds 30. A copy of the program shall be mailed to the owner of each entered dog and shall be printed in the catalog.

No judging shall occur at any show prior to the time specified in the judging program.

SECTION 13. The maximum number of dogs assigned in the breed judging to any judge, in one day, shall never exceed 175.

If a futurity or sweepstakes is offered in connection with a specialty show, which is held as part of an all-breed show, the above figure of 175 shall be reduced to 150 for the specialty show.

If a show-giving club so elects, it may place a limit of its own choosing lower than any of the limits provided for in the rule notifying The American Kennel Club of its intention and when the judging panel is submitted for approval. This limit will then govern the need for additional judges if, when the entries for the show have closed, any judge on the panel has drawn more dogs than the limit set by the club.

When the entries have closed, if the entry under any judge exceeds the above limits, the Bench Show Committee must select some other judge or judges to whom sufficient breeds or varieties can be assigned to bring the total assignment of every judge within the limits. In the case of a specialty show, if the limits are exceeded, at least one additional judge shall be assigned to bring each judge's assignment within the limits. Approval must be obtained from The American Kennel Club for each such reassignment.

Notice must be sent to the owner of each dog affected by such a change in judges at least five days before the opening of the show, and the owner has the right to withdraw his entry and have his entry fee refunded provided notification of his withdrawal is received before the opening of the show by the Superintendent or Show Secretary named in the premium list to receive entries.

SECTION 14. A judge shall not exhibit his dogs or take any dog belonging to another person into the ring at any show at which he is officiating, nor shall he pass judgment in his official capacity upon any dog which he or any member of his immediate household or immediate family (as defined in Chapter 6, Section 6) has handled in the ring more than twice during the preceding twelve months.

SECTION 15. A judge's decision shall be final in all cases affecting the merits of the dogs. Full discretionary power is given to the judge to withhold any, or all, prizes for want of merit. After a class has once been judged in accordance with these rules and regulations, it shall not be rejudged. A class is considered judged when the judge has marked his book which must be done before the following class is examined. If any errors have been made by the judge in marking the awards as made, he may correct the same but must initial any such corrections.

SECTION 16. A judge may order any person or dog from the ring. For the purpose of facilitating the judging, judges are required to exclude from the rings in which they are judging all persons except the steward or stewards and the show attendants assigned to the ring and those actually engaged in exhibiting.

SECTION 17. A judge shall be supplied with a book called the judge's book in which he shall mark all awards and all absent dogs. The original judges' books at shows shall be in the custody of the judge, steward, superintendent, or superintendent's assistant. None other shall be allowed access to them. At the conclusion of the judging, the book must be signed by the judge and any changes which may have been made therein initialed by him.

SECTION 18. A judge's decision, as marked in the judge's book, cannot be changed by him after filing, but an error appearing in the judge's book may be corrected by The American Kennel Club after consultation with the judge.

SECTION 19. Only one judge shall officiate in each Group Class and only one judge shall select the Best in Show.

The Board of Directors suggests that whenever possible the Best in Show be determined by one who has not already judged any breed or group class of said show.

SECTION 20. If a judge disqualifies a dog at any show, he shall make a note in the judge's book giving his reasons for such disqualification. In computing the championship points for a breed, said dog shall not be considered as having been present at the show.

CHAPTER 11

HANDLERS

SECTION 1. Any person handling dogs for pay or acting as agent for another for pay at any show held under the rules of The American Kennel Club must hold a license from The American Kennel Club.

Any reputable person who is in good standing with The American Kennel Club may apply to said Club for license to act as a handler or as an agent, which application must be made on a form which will be supplied by said Club upon request. When the application is received by The American Kennel Club the Board of Directors shall determine whether a license shall be issued to the applicant.

SECTION 2. The fee for being granted a license to be a handler or an agent, or an assistant to a handler or an agent, shall be determined by the Board of Directors of The American Kennel Club from time to time in its discretion. Any such license may be granted for any such period of time that the Board of Directors deems appropriate in its discretion. All granted licenses shall expire December 31 of the year in which they are granted.

Effective January 1, 1954, no fee is required with applications for Handlers or Assistant Handlers licenses.

No handler's license will be granted to a person residing in the same household with a licensed judge.

CHAPTER 12

SELECTION OF SUPERINTENDENT, SHOW SECRETARY AND VETERINARIANS

When a club or association, which has been granted permission to hold a show, sends to The American Kennel Club its list of Judges to be approved, it must enclose with that list the names and addresses of its proposed Superintendent or Show Secretary, and Veterinarian or Veterinarians, all of whom must be approved by the Board of Directors of The American Kennel Club before the premium list of the show can be printed.

CHAPTER 13

SUPERINTENDENTS AND SHOW SECRETARIES

SECTION 1. The Superintendent of a Dog Show held under the rules of The American Kennel Club must hold a license from The American Kennel Club.

SECTION 2. Any qualified person may make application to The American Kennel Club for approval to act as Show Secretary of a dog show.

SECTION 3. Superintendents and Show Secretaries will be responsible along with bench show committees for making complete arrangements for attendance at a show with each one of the veterinarians selected to service a show. In the event that a recognized Veterinary Association is to furnish the veterinarians, the complete arrangements shall be made with the secretary of the Association.

SECTION 4. Superintendents and Show Secretaries shall have on hand at every show the various official American Kennel Club forms for the use of veterinarians.

SECTION 5. Superintendents and Show Secretaries shall be prepared, at any show, to furnish the forms to be used by any exhibitor or handler who seeks a health examination of a dog. Upon the filing of the completed form by an exhibitor or handler, it shall be the superintendent's and show secretary's duty to see that the owner or agent of the dog takes his dog to the "Veterinarian Headquarters" for the examination.

SECTION 6. Superintendents and Show Secretaries will be responsible for providing at every show a suitable space which will serve as the headquarters of the show veterinarians. At an indoor show this space will be marked off in some adequate way and a sign "Veterinarian Headquarters" must be prominently displayed. At an outdoor show, where canvas is available, the veterinarians' office shall be set up under its own individual tent. Where no tenting is used the Headquarters must be arranged so that the veterinarians are afforded protection from the weather.

SECTION 7. Superintendents and Show Secretaries are required, with their report of a show, to list the names of all veterinarians who served at a show and give the hours that each veterinarian was present.

SECTION 8. Superintendents and Show Secretaries shall have the sole authority to enforce the rules having to do with the benching of dogs.

SECTION 9. Superintendents and Show Secretaries shall have the sole authority to excuse a dog from being shown on the recommendation of the veterinarian under Chapter 15, Section 4 (c) and to release dogs from a show prior to the published time for the releasing of dogs, except in the event that a dog has been dismissed from a show by a veterinarian under Chapter 15, Section 4 (b).

SECTION 10. Bench show committees and superintendents of dogs shows shall be held responsible for the enforcement of all rules and regulations relating to shows and must provide themselves with a copy of The American Kennel Club rules and regulations for reference.

SECTION 11. The Superintendent or Show Secretary will be held accountable for the maintenance of clean and orderly conditions throughout the precincts of the show during all hours when dogs are permitted to be present.

SECTION 12. Any reputable person who is in good standing with The American Kennel Club may apply to said Club for license to act as Superintendent of a Dog Show, which application must be made on a form which will be supplied by said Club upon request. When the application is received by The American Kennel Club its Board of Directors shall determine whether the applicant is reasonably qualified from training and experience to act as Superintendent of a Dog Show and whether a license shall be issued to said applicant.

The fee for being granted a yearly license to be a Superintendent and the fee for renewal of said license each year shall be determined by the Board of Directors of The American Kennel Club. The fee for being granted a license to superintend one show and/or one field trial only shall be determined in like manner.

No yearly license will be issued to any person until he or she has superintended at least three dogs shows or field trials.

No annual superintendent shall be granted a license to be a judge.

CHAPTER 14

ADMISSION AND EXAMINATION OF DOGS ENTERED IN A SHOW

SECTION 1. The bench show committee of an all-breed club or a specialty club holding a dog show must elect whether all dogs are to be inspected in respect to their apparent health before being admitted to the show or whether dogs will be allowed to enter a show's premises without inspection. If the bench show committee decides that all dogs are to be inspected, the designation "Examined Show" shall be printed on the title page of the premium list and catalog.

SECTION 2. An "Examined Show" is one at which each dog is subject to a health inspection by one of the show's veterinarians before being allowed to enter a show's premises.

SECTION 3. For an "Examined Show" a club must employ a sufficien number of qualified veterinarians to insure the inspection and admission of dogs without undue delay, and shall arrange to have its full complement of veterinarians present during the hours of the show when dogs will be admitted. If dogs are to be admitted to a show's premises before the published opening hour, then the bench show committee of a club must arrange to have one or more of its veterinarians on duty during such time.

SECTION 4. For an "Examined Show" a club or its superintendent shall provide a "Veterinarian Enclosure" into which and through which every dog must pass before it is admitted to a show's premises. The "Enclosure" is to be set up between an entrance to a show's building or grounds and the premises of a show and shall be of sufficient size to meet the needs of the veterinarians and allow for the orderly and prompt passage of exhibitors and dogs. Clubs and superintendents will be responsible for providing safeguards against the possibility of a dog getting into a show's premises without first having passed through the "Enclosure."

There shall also be provided within the "Enclosure" a quarantine area in which there will be benches for dogs that the show veterinarians may wish to hold for an examination.

SECTION 5. For an "Examined Show" a club or its superintendent shall provide in the enclosure for the use of its veterinarians the following items:

Examination tables (with non-slip footing surface and large enough to hold the largest dogs);
Tables for the use of the Veterinarians;
Rubber gloves;
Disinfectant (either zepheran chloride or roccal);
Wash bowls and paper towels;
Waste disposal cans;
"Passed" rubber stamps and stamp pads;
Forms to be completed by Veterinarians for all dogs not passed.

In addition a club or its superintendent shall appoint persons to serve in the Enclosure whose duty it will be to provide such help for the veterinarians as they may require and to direct the orderly passage of exhibitors and dogs through the Enclosure.

SECTION 6. If the bench show committee of a club chooses to hold an "Examined Show" the chairman shall complete a form that shall be supplied by The American Kennel Club which is to be attached to the club's application for a date. This form will include a representation that the club is prepared to provide an adequate number of veterinarians, that the layout of the club's proposed building or grounds is such that an adequate "Veterinarians Enclosure" (and benches) can be set up as described in these rules and that the club and its superintendent will properly administer the admission of dogs to the show premises in accordance with these rules.

SECTION 7. When a club is holding an "Examined Show" of more than one day's duration, all of the requirements set forth in this chapter shall be applicable to all dogs that have been temporarily removed from the show premises at the close of the first day and are required to be returned to the show premises on the second day.

CHAPTER 15

DUTIES AND RESPONSIBILITIES OF SHOW VETERINARIANS

SECTION 1. Any reputable person who is in good standing with The American Kennel Club and who has been duly qualified to practice his profession by law may act as veterinarian of a dog show.

SECTION 2. Every club that holds a licensed or member show shall employ one or more veterinarians who are qualified as described in Section 1, to serve in an official capacity. At least one of these veterinarians shall be in attendance during the entire progress of the show. The duties of the veterinarians shall be to give advisory opinions to Judges and to Bench Show Committees on the physical conditions of dogs, when requested by such officials as provided for in these rules; to examine the health of dogs at the request of exhibitors and handlers; and to render first aid to dogs in cases of sickness or injury occurring at the show. Show veterinarians are not required to be familiar with the Dog Show Rules or breed standards affecting the disqualification or eligibility of dogs, and should not attempt to interpret the effect of their advisory opinions on the status of dogs under the rules or standards. They should not discuss with exhibitors or handlers the advisory opinions given to Judges and Bench Show Committees. Show veterinarians are not to be called on to treat dogs for physical conditions that existed before they were brought to the show. In addition, at an Examined Show it will be the duty of the veterinarian to pass or reject all dogs coming into the Veterinarians Enclosure.

SECTION 3. At an "Examined Show," it will also be the duty of the show veterinarians to make a visual inspection of every dog that comes into the "Veterinarian Enclosure." Dogs with outward symptoms of illness or disease are to be held within the Enclosure for examination to determine whether they are to be admitted. The identification cards of admitted dogs shall be stamped "passed" by the examining veterinarian.

SECTION 4. Veterinarians serving a show will have complete authority to:

(a) Reject any dog at the entrance to a show's premises which he considers may endanger the health of any other dogs;

(b) Dismiss any dog that has been admitted to a show which he considers may endanger the health of other dogs;

(c) Recommend to the superintendent or show secretary the excusing of any dog from being shown or from the show premises provided he considers that the showing of the dog in the ring or its remaining within the show premises would impair the dog's health.

In all cases where a dog is rejected, dismissed or recommended for excusing from judging or the show premises, the veterinarian shall complete a form, which will be provided giving the basis for his decision, or opinion, and shall file the form with the superintendent or show secretary.

SECTION 5. Veterinarians may request exhibitors and handlers to open dogs' mouths, but when they consider it necessary may do so themselves, provided however that in the latter instance they wear rubber gloves and take proper sanitary precautions.

SECTION 6. Upon the presentation at the "Veterinarians Headquarters" of a dog whose health has been questioned by an exhibitor or handler, it shall be the duty of one of the show veterinarians, as soon as practical, to make an examination of the dog. If he considers that the dog should be dismissed from the show, he will ask the superintendent or show secretary to see that the dog is removed.

SECTION 7. Veterinarians serving a show will be expected to make full use of the area provided for them as a headquarters. Where practical, at least one veterinarian should be in attendance at the headquarters during the entire time that a show is in progress. At an "Examined Show" the "Veterinarians Enclosure" is to be used as a headquarters until such time as the entrance to the enclosure has been closed and no more dogs are to be admitted to it.

CHAPTER 16
DOG SHOW ENTRIES
CONDITIONS OF DOGS AFFECTING ELIGIBILITY

SECTION 1. No dog shall be eligible to be entered in a licensed or member dog show, except for dogs entered in the Miscellaneous Class, unless it is either individually registered in the AKC Stud Book or part of an AKC registered litter, or otherwise, if whelped outside the United States of America and owned by a resident of the U.S.A. or Canada, unless it has been registered in its country of birth with a foreign registry organization whose pedigrees are acceptable for AKC registration.

An unregistered dog that is part of an AKC registered litter or an unregistered dog with an acceptable foreign registration that was whelped outside the U.S.A. and that is owned by a resident of the U.S.A. or Canada may, without special AKC approval, be entered in licensed or member dog shows that are held not later than 30 days after the date of the first licensed or member dog show in which the dog was entered, but only provided that the AKC litter registration number or the individual foreign registration number and the name of the country of birth, are shown on the entry form, and provided further that the same name, which in the case of an imported or Canadian owned dog must be the name on the foreign registration, is used for the dog each time.

No dog that has not been individually registered with The American Kennel Club when first entered in a licensed or member dog show shall be eligible to be entered in any licensed or member dog show that is held more than 30 days after the date of the first licensed or member dog show in which it was entered, unless the dog's individual AKC registration number is shown on the entry form, or unless the owner has received from The American Kennel Club an extension notice in writing authorizing further entries of the dog for a specified time with its AKC litter number or individual foreign registration number. No such extension will be granted unless the owner can clearly demonstrate, in a letter addressed to the Show Records Department of The American Kennel Club requesting such extension, that the delay in registration is due to circumstances for which he is not responsible.

Such extension notice will be void upon registration of the dog or upon expiration of the period for which the extension has been granted if that occurs earlier, but upon application further extensions may be granted.

If a dog is later individually registered with a name that is not identical to the name under which it has been entered in dog shows prior to individual registration, each entry form entering the dog in a licensed or member dog show after the owner has received the individual registration certificate must show the registered name followed by "formerly shown as" and the name under which the dog was previously shown, until the dog has been awarded one of the four places in a regular class at a licensed or member show.

SECTION 2. At every show held under the rules of The American Kennel Club, a recording fee not to exceed 25 cents may be required for every dog entered. This recording fee is to help defray expenses involved in keeping show records, and applies to all dogs entered. If a dog is entered in more than one class at a show, the recording fee applies only to first entry. The Board of Directors shall determine, from time to time, whether a recording fee shall be required, and the amount of it.

Effective June 1, 1954 recording fees are not required.

SECTION 3. Every dog must be entered in the name of the person who actually owned the dog at the time entries closed. The right to exhibit a dog cannot be transferred. A registered dog which has been acquired by some person other than the owner as recorded with The American Kennel Club must be entered in the name of its new owner at any show for which entries close after the date upon which the dog was acquired, and application for transfer of ownership must be sent to The American Kennel Club by the new owner within seven days after the last day of the show. The new owner should state on the entry form that transfer application has been mailed to The American Kennel Club or will be mailed shortly. If there is any unavoidable delay in obtaining the completed application required to record the transfer, The American Kennel Club may grant a reasonable extension of time, provided the new owner notifies the show records department of The American Kennel Club by mail within seven days after the show, of the reason for the delay. If an entry is made by a duly authorized agent of the owner, the name of the actual owner must be shown on the entry form. If a dog is owned by an association, the name of the association and a list of its officers must be shown on the entry form.

SECTION 4. To be acceptable, an entry must be submitted with required entry fee, on an official American Kennel Club entry form, signed by the owner or his duly authorized agent, and must include all of the following information: Name of the club holding the show; date of the show; breed; variety, if any; sex; full description of the class or classes in which entered; full name of dog; individual registration number or AKC litter number or, for a dog entered in the Miscellaneous Class, ILP number; name and address of the actual owner or owners. For a dog whelped outside the U.S.A. that is not AKC registered, the entry form must show the individual foreign registration number and country of birth. In addition, an entry in the Puppy, Novice, Bred-by-Exhibitor, or American-bred class must include the place of birth; an entry in the Puppy Class must include the date of birth; and an entry in the Bred-by-Exhibitor class must include the name or names of the breeder or breeders.

No entry may be accepted unless it is received by the Superintendent or Show Secretary named in the premium list to receive entries prior to the closing date and hour as published in the premium list, and unless it meets all the requirements of the foregoing paragraph and all other specific requirements printed in the premium list.

SECTION 5. No entry shall be made and no entry shall be accepted by a Superintendent or Show Secretary which specifies any condition as to its acceptance.

SECTION 6. No change may be made in any otherwise acceptable entry form unless the change is received in writing or by telegraph, by the Superintendent or Show Secretary named in the premium list to receive entries, prior to the published closing date and hour for entries, except that a correction may be made in the sex of a dog at a show prior to the judging. No dog wrongly entered in a class may otherwise be transferred to another class. Owners are responsible for errors in entry forms, regardless of who may make such errors.

SECTION 7. No entry shall be received from any person who is not in good standing with The American Kennel Club on the day of the closing of the entries. Before accepting entries, a list of persons not in good standing must be obtained by the Show Superintendent or Show Secretary from The American Kennel Club.

SECTION 8. No entry shall be made under a kennel name unless that name has been registered with The American Kennel Club. All entries made under a kennel name must be signed with the kennel name followed by the word "registered." An "exhibitor" or "entrant" is the individual or, if a partnership, all the members of the partnership exhibiting or entering in a dog show. In the case of such an entry by a partnership every member of the partnership shall be in good standing with The American Kennel Club before the entry will be accepted; and in case of any infraction of these rules, all the partners shall be held equally responsible.

SECTION 9. A dog which is blind, deaf, castrated, spayed, or which has been changed in appearance by artificial means except as specified in the standard for its breed, or a male which does not have two normal testicles normally located in the scrotum, may not compete at any show and will be disqualified. A dog will not be considered to have been changed by artificial means because of removal of dew claws or docking of tail if it is of a breed in which such removal or docking is a regularly approved practice which is not contrary to the standard.

When a judge finds evidence of any of these conditions in any dog he is judging he must, before proceeding with the judging, notify the Superintendent or Show Secretary and must call an official show veterinarian to examine the dog in the ring and to give the judge an advisory opinion in writing on the condition of the dog. Only after he has seen the veterinarian's opinion in writing shall the judge render his own decision and record it in the judge's book, marking the dog "disqualified" and stating the reason if he determines that disqualification is required under this rule. The judge's decision is final and need not necessarily agree with the veterinarian's opinion. The written opinion of the veterinarian shall in all cases be forwarded to The American Kennel Club by the Superintendent or Show Secretary.

When a dog has been disqualified under this rule or under the standard for its breed, either by a judge or by decision of a Bench Show Committee, any awards at that show shall be cancelled by The American Kennel Club and the dog may not again be shown unless and until, following application by the owner to The American Kennel Club, the owner has received official notification from The American Kennel Club that the dog's show eligibility has been reinstated. The American Kennel Club will not entertain any application for reinstatement of a male which has been disqualified as not having two normal testicles normally located in the scrotum until the dog is twelve (12) months old.

SECTION 9-A. A dog that is lame at any show may not compete and shall not receive any award at that show. It shall be the judge's responsibility to determine whether a dog is lame. He shall not obtain the opinion of the show veterinarian. If in the judge's opinion a dog in the ring is lame, he shall withhold all awards from such dog and shall excuse it from the ring. A dog so excused shall not be counted as having competed. When a judge excuses a dog from the ring for lameness, he shall mark his book "Excused—lame."

SECTION 9-B. No dog shall be eligible to compete at any show and no dog shall receive any award at any show in the event the natural color or shade of natural color or the natural markings of the dog have been altered or changed by the use of any substance whether such substance may have been used for cleaning purposes or for any other reason. Such cleaning substances are to be removed before the dog enters the ring.

If in the judge's opinion any substance has been used to alter or change the natural color or shade of natural color or natural markings of a dog, then in such event the judge shall withhold any and all awards from such dog, and the judge shall make a note in the judge's book giving his reason for withholding such award. The handler or the owner, or both, of any dog or dogs from which any award has been withheld for violation of this section of the rules, or any judge who shall fail to perform his duties under this section shall be subject to disciplinary action.

SECTION 9-C. Any dog whose ears have been cropped or cut in any way shall be ineligible to compete at any show in any state where the laws prohibit the same except subject to the provisions of such laws.

SECTION 10. No dog shall be eligible to compete at any show, no dog shall be brought into the grounds or premises of any dog show, and any dog which may have been brought into the grounds or premises of a dog show shall immediately be removed, if it

(a) shows clinical symptoms of distemper, infectious hepatitis, leptospirosis or other communicable disease, or

(b) is known to have been in contact with distemper, infectious hepatitis, leptospirosis or other communicable disease within thirty days prior to the opening of the show, or

(c) has been kenneled within thirty days prior to the opening of the show on premises on which there existed distemper, infectious hepatitis, leptospirosis or other communicable disease.

SECTION 11. A club may engage dogs not entered in its show as a special attraction provided the written approval of The American Kennel Club is first obtained.

SECTION 12. No dog not regularly entered in a show, other than one engaged as a special attraction, shall be allowed within the show precincts, except when the club has stated in its premium list that space will be provided for dogs not entered in the show. The club must then provide an area, clearly identified by an appropriate sign. This area shall be exclusively for dogs which are either en route to or from other shows in which entered, or which are being delivered to new owners or custodians, or being returned to their owners. No dog may be placed in this area if it is entered in the show, nor unless it is registered or registrable and eligible to be shown under American Kennel Club rules and the standard for its breed.

An owner or agent who wishes to use this facility shall, upon entering the show, file with the Superintendent or Show Secretary a form giving the dog's registration data and the reason for its presence. The Superintendent or Show Secretary will then issue a tag identifying the dog. This tag is to be attached to the crate or container which the owner or agent must supply.

No one except owners or agents in charge of these dogs and show officials shall be admitted to the area, and there shall be no benching, nor any offering for sale, breeding, nor displaying of these dogs. Such dogs will not be permitted in any other part of the show precincts except for minimum periods when necessary for exercising, and then only when accompanied by the owners or their agents.

Dogs in this area shall be subject to all the rules relating to health and veterinarians. The Superintendent or Show Secretary shall be responsible for compliance with this rule.

SECTION 13. Any person acting in the capacity of Superintendent (or Show Secretary where there is no Superintendent), official veterinarian, or judge at a show, or any member of his immediate household or immediate family (as defined in Chapter 6, Section 6) shall not exhibit, act as agent or handler at the show, and dogs owned wholly or in part by him or by any member of his immediate household or immediate family shall be ineligible to be entered at that show.

SECTION 14. No entry shall be made at any show under a judge of any dog which said judge or any member of his immediate household or immediate family (as defined in Chapter 6, Section 6) has been known to have owned, handled in the ring more than twice, sold, held under lease or boarded within one year prior to the date of the show.

SECTION 15. Any show-giving club which accepts an entry fee other than that published in its premium list, or in any way discriminates between exhibitors or entrants, shall be disciplined. No show-giving club shall offer to any one owner or handler any special inducement, such as trophies, reduced entry fees, rebates, additional prize money, or any other concession, for entering more than one dog in the show.

SECTION 16. A Bench Show Committee may decline any entries or may remove any dog from its show for cause, but in each such instance shall file good and sufficient reasons for so doing with The American Kennel Club.

SECTION 2. Any club or association giving a dog show must provide arm cards and shall see that every person exhibiting a dog wears, when in the ring, an arm card containing thereon the catalog number of the dog being exhibited; but no badges, coats with kennel names thereon or ribbon prizes shall be worn or displayed, nor other visible means of identification used, by an individual when exhibiting a dog in the ring.

SECTION 3. The owner of a dog that is entered in a show, or the owner's agent, may request a determination of a dog's height or a dog's weight, if these factors are breed standard disqualifications, conditions of a class or conditions of a division of a class in which the dog is entered. Such requests may be made at any time after the opening of a show, but must be made before the scheduled time of the judging of the breed or variety. The determination, as made, shall be recorded on an American Kennel Club measuring and weighing form, and note of the height or weight of the dog, as the case may be, must promptly be made in the judge's book, by the superintendent or show secretary.

If the height or weight of the dog as determined under this Section is in accord with the breed standard or the conditions of the class or division thereof in which it is entered, the determination shall hold good for the duration of that show, and that show only and the dog cannot be in any way challenged or protested as to height or weight at that show, except that a judge may request a reweighing of the dog when it comes under judgment, and a determination made at that time shall supersede the previous determination.

If the height or weight of the dog as determined under this Section is not in accord with the breed standard or the conditions of the class or division thereof in which it is entered, the dog shall immediately be declared ineligible to compete by the Superintendent or Show Secretary and shall be marked absent in the Judge's Book. Such a dog shall not be brought into the judging ring and may be excused from the show immediately. The eligibility of such a dog to compete at subsequent shows shall not be affected.

SECTION 4. In those breeds where certain heights or weights are specified in the standard as disqualifications, or in any class or division of a class the conditions of which include a height or weight specification, it shall be the judge's responsibility to initiate a determination as to whether a dog is to be disqualified or declared to be ineligible for the class.

If, in the judge's opinion, the height or weight of a dog under judgment appears not to be in accord with the breed standard or the conditions of a class or division thereof, the judge, before proceeding with the judging, must notify the superintendent or show secretary and request that the dog's height or weight be determined by persons appointed by the bench show committee for that purpose, unless the dog's height has previously been determined at the show, or unless the dog's weight has previously been determined at the show other than under the provisions of

CHAPTER 17
THE CATALOG

SECTION 1. Every Bench Show Committee shall provide a printed catalog which shall contain all particulars required of exhibitors entering dogs as hereinafter provided. It shall also contain the exact location of the show, the date or dates on which it is to be held, the times of opening and closing of the show, a list of all officers and members of the Bench Show Committee, names and complete addresses of all judges and of the Superintendent or Show Secretary, the names of the veterinarians or local veterinary association providing veterinary service at the show, and an alphabetical list of the names and addresses of all exhibitors.

SECTION 2. Every catalog must bear on its cover or title page: "This show is held under American Kennel Club rules."

SECTION 3. If the show shall be given by a club or association not a member of The American Kennel Club the words "Licensed Show" must be plainly printed on the title page of the catalog.

SECTION 4. The catalog shall be in book form 6 x 9 inches in size. It shall contain the names and particulars of all dogs entered in the show, arranged as follows: catalog number; name of dog; AKC registration number, or litter number or "ILP" number for an unregistered dog, or foreign registration number and country for an unregistered imported dog; date of birth; name of breeder; names of sire and dam. The entries shall be catalogued by groups, breeds, varieties, and regular classes, in the order given in Chapter 6. The information on dogs entered in any additional classes shall appear following the space provided for recording Winners Bitch and Reserve Winners Bitch followed by the particulars of those dogs entered for Best of Breed except that the entries in those dogs entered for Best of Breed, Brood Bitch, or any other classes in which the judge's decision is based on the merits of more than one dog shall appear following the list of dogs entered for Best of Breed and the space provided for Best of Breed, Best of Winners and Best of Opposite Sex awards. The particulars of those dogs entered for Exhibition Only shall appear following all other entries in the breed or variety.

Additional requirements for format and contents of the catalog may be prescribed by the Board of Directors.

SECTION 5. The schedule of points toward championship governing each breed in the show shall be published in the catalog.

SECTION 6. All prizes offered in the premium list of a show or in the separate list of prizes if the condensed form of premium list is used, shall be printed in the catalog, and no change shall be made in the descriptions or conditions of these prizes, nor shall any prize or trophy be added that was not offered in the premium list or in the separate list of prizes.

CHAPTER 18
BENCHING OF DOGS

SECTION 1. At a Benched Show to which admission is charged, every dog twelve months old and over that is entered and present must be on its bench throughout the advertised hours of the show's duration, except for the necessary periods when it is actually being prepared for showing at its crate, or is being shown, or is in the exercise ring, or is being taken to or from these places. The advertised hours of the show's duration shall be the hours from the scheduled start of judging to the time shown in the premium list for the closing of the show. No such dog shall be in its crate during the advertised hours of the show's duration except by written permission of the Superintendent or Show Secretary, and except for a period of one hour before the time printed in the program for the judging of its breed or variety and, if it becomes eligible for its Group or for Best in Show, for a period of one hour before the time printed in the program for the judging of such competition.

SECTION 2. The provisions of Section 1 also apply to a dog under 12 months of age except that it need not be benched until after the judging of the breed classes for which it is entered or becomes eligible and it may be in its crate until the judging of those classes. At a two day show it is required to be present only on the day it is to be judged.

SECTION 3. Failure to comply with these rules may cause cancellation of the dog's winnings, and subject the owner, handler, and Superintendent or Show Secretary to a fine and suspension of license and privileges.

SECTION 4. No signs shall be displayed on a bench except the plaque or emblem of a show-giving specialty club to which the dog's owner belongs, and signs not over 11 x 14 inches offering dogs or puppies for sale, or giving the kennel name and address of the owner, or the dog's name and a list of awards won by it at that show, or the name of a show-giving specialty club of which the dog's owner is a member. No prizes or ribbons shall be displayed on the bench except those won by the dog at that show.

SECTION 5. At an Unbenched Show, a sign stating that the show is unbenched shall be prominently displayed wherever admission tickets are sold.

CHAPTER 19
MEASURING, WEIGHING AND COLOR DETERMINATIONS WHEN FACTORS OF DISQUALIFICATION IN BREED STANDARDS OR ELIGIBILITY UNDER THE CONDITIONS OF A CLASS OR DIVISION OF A CLASS.
CANCELLATION OF AWARDS

SECTION 1. Every dog entered and present at a show must compete in all competition in its breed or variety for which it is entered or becomes eligible, unless it has been excused, dismissed, disqualified or found to be ineligible, under the rules.

Chapter 19, Section 3. When a completed AKC measuring and weighing form has been submitted to the judge by such persons, giving the height or weight of the dog, the judge shall then disqualify the dog if its height or weight is such as to require disqualification under the standard of the breed, or shall declare the dog to be ineligible if its height or weight is such as to not conform with the conditions of the class or division in which it is competing, in either case making note of the fact in the judge's book.

If, in the opinion of any competing exhibitor or handler then in the ring, the height or weight of a dog under judgment (not previously determined at the show) appears not to be in accord with the breed standard or the conditions of a class or division thereof, such exhibitor or handler may, prior to the time the judge has marked his book, request the judge to proceed as above in obtaining a determination of the dog's height or weight. After the judge has obtained the completed AKC measuring and weighing form giving the height or weight of the dog, he shall then disqualify the dog if its height or weight is such as to require disqualification under the standard of the breed, or shall declare the dog to be ineligible if its height or weight is such as to not conform with the conditions of the class or division in which it is competing, in either case making note of the fact in the judge's book.

Any dog thus disqualified by the judge may not again be shown unless and until, following application by the owner to The American Kennel Club the owner has received official notification from The American Kennel Club that the dog's show eligibility has been reinstated.

Any dog thus declared ineligible by the judge for a class or division thereof shall be considered to have been wrongly entered in the class and cannot be transferred to any other class or division at the show.

Any dog that has been found to be ineligible as to height under the conditions of a class may not again be shown in that class unless and until, following application by the owner to The American Kennel Club, the owner has received official notification from The American Kennel Club that the dog's show eligibility has been reinstated. However, without making such application to The American Kennel Club, the owner of such a dog may enter the dog in a different class, provided the measurement made at the show is within the specified height limits of such class.

SECTION 5. Bench Show Committees shall be responsible for providing a suitable measuring stand and accurate scales at every show. Bench Show Committees must appoint three persons whose duty it will be, when called upon, to determine a dog's height or weight.

SECTION 6. In those breeds where certain colors or markings are specified in the standard as disqualifications, or in any

class or division of a class where a certain color, or colors or combinations of colors are required by the conditions of the class or division thereof, it shall be the judge's responsibility to determine whether a dog is to be disqualified or declared to be ineligible for the class.

If, in the opinion of the judge, the dog's color or markings are such as to require disqualification, the judge shall disqualify the dog, making note of the fact in the judge's book.

If, in the opinion of the judge, the dog's color or markings do not meet the requirements of the class or division of a class in which the dog is competing, the judge shall declare the dog ineligible to compete in that class or division of class, making note of the fact in the judge's book.

If, in the opinion of any competing exhibitor or handler then in the ring, the color or markings or combination of colors of a dog under judgment are such as to disqualify under the standard or are such as not to meet the requirements of the class or division thereof, such exhibitor or handler may, prior to the time the judge has marked his book, request the judge to render an opinion of the dog's color(s) and markings. Before proceeding with the judging, the judge must write his opinion on an AKC form that will be supplied by the superintendent or show secretary for that purpose, and shall disqualify the dog if its color or markings are such as to require disqualification under the breed standard or shall declare the dog ineligible if the color or markings do not meet the requirements of the class or division thereof in which the dog is competing, in either case making note of the fact in the judge's book.

Any dog thus disqualified by the judge under the standard may not again be shown unless and until, following application by the owner to The American Kennel Club, the owner has received official notification from The American Kennel Club that the dog's show eligibility has been reinstated.

Any dog thus declared by the judge to be ineligible for a class or division thereof shall be considered to have been wrongly entered in the class and cannot be transferred to any other class or division at that show.

SECTION 7. If an ineligible dog has been entered in any licensed or member dog show, or if the name of the owner given on the entry form is not that of the person or persons who actually owned the dog at the time entries closed, or if shown in a class for which it has not been entered, or if its entry form is deemed invalid or unacceptable by The American Kennel Club under these rules, all resulting awards shall be cancelled by The American Kennel Club. In computing the championship points such ineligible dogs, whether or not they have received awards, shall be counted as having competed.

SECTION 8. If the catalog and/or the judge's book of any show shall by error or mistake set forth any information contrary to the information which appears on the entry form of the dog for that show, the Bench Show Committee and/or the Superin-

tendent of the show, upon request of the owner or handler of said dog prior to the judging, shall correct the entry in the judge's book and in the marked catalog to be sent to The American Kennel Club and said dog properly may compete in all classes and for all prizes for which its entry form discloses it was properly entered.

SECTION 9. If an award in any of the regular classes is cancelled, the dog judged next in order of merit shall be moved up and the award to the dog moved up shall be counted the same as if it had been the original award. If there is no dog of record to move up, the award shall be void.

SECTION 10. If the win of a dog shall be cancelled by The American Kennel Club the owner of the dog shall return all ribbons and prizes to the show-giving club within ten days of receipt of the notice of the cancellation from The American Kennel Club. The show-giving club shall in each instance of failure to comply with this rule notify The American Kennel Club of such failure and The American Kennel Club upon receipt of such notice forthwith shall suspend the exhibitor so in default from all privileges of The American Kennel Club and notify the exhibitor so in default that it has done so, and said suspension shall continue until The American Kennel Club is notified that restitution has been made.

CHAPTER 20

PROTESTS AGAINST DOGS

SECTION 1. Every exhibitor and handler shall have the right to request through the superintendent or show secretary the examination, by one of a show's veterinarians, of any dog within a show's premises which is considered to endanger the health of other dogs in a show. The request is to be in writing and on a form obtainable from a superintendent or show secretary, whose duty it will be to see that the subject dog is promptly taken to the "Veterinarian Headquarters" by its owner or the owner's agent.

SECTION 2. A protest against a dog may be made by any exhibitor, entrant or any member of a member club of The American Kennel Club. It shall be in writing, and be lodged with the secretary of the show-giving club within seven (7) days of the last day of the show unless the same be made by The American Kennel Club, provided, however, that a protest calling for a decision as to the physical condition of a dog which can be determined only with the advice of a veterinarian or at the time of showing shall be made before the closing of the show.

No protest will be entertained unless accompanied by a deposit of five ($5.00) dollars, which will be returned if the protest is sustained. This does not apply to protests by The American Kennel Club, nor to a protest made in the ring previous to the rendering of his decision by the judge.

SECTION 3. If a protest shall be made during the holding of a show the bench show committee shall hold a meeting as soon as possible and give all parties concerned an opportunity to be heard and shall at once render its decision. If a protest shall be made subsequent to the show it shall be decided by the show-giving club within thirty (30) days of its receipt. Five days' notice of the date and place of hearing shall be given to all parties concerned. Written copies of all decisions on protests shall be forwarded immediately to The American Kennel Club.

SECTION 4. An appeal to The American Kennel Club from a decision of a bench show committee where a dog has been protested may be taken and shall be forwarded to The American Kennel Club within seven (7) days of the date on which the decision was rendered together with a deposit of ten ($10.00) dollars. If the decision be sustained the deposit shall be forfeited, but if reversed, the deposit shall be returned.

SECTION 5. Any person who is handling a competing dog in the ring in any breed competition may then verbally protest to the judge before the judge has marked any award in his book, alleging that a dog being shown in the competition has a condition which makes it ineligible to compete under Chapter 16, Section 9, or Chapter 16, Section 9-B, of these rules, or a condition requiring disqualification under the standard for the breed; except that a verbal protest alleging that the height or weight or natural color and markings of a dog requiring its disqualification under the breed standard or a determination of its ineligibility under the conditions of its class must be made under Chapter 19, Sections 4 or 6.

When such a protest is made, the judge, before proceeding with the judging, must notify the superintendent or show secretary and must call an official show veterinarian to examine the dog in the ring and give the judge an advisory opinion, in writing, on the condition of the dog. Only after he has seen the veterinarian's opinion in writing shall the judge render his own decision and record it in the judge's book, marking the dog "Disqualified" and stating the reason if he determines that disqualification is required under Chapter 16, Section 9, or under the breed standard.

If the judge, after seeing the veterinarian's written opinion, determines that the dog is ineligible to compete because of violation of Chapter 16, Section 9-B, he shall withhold any award to the dog and mark the judge's book "Ineligible to compete award withheld," stating the reason for his decision.

A dog determined by a judge to be ineligible to compete under Chapter 16, Section 9-B, unless such determination is based on the use of a substance only for cleaning purposes, may not again be shown until an official record has been made by The American Kennel Club of its true color or markings. If the color and markings of the dog as recorded are such as not to be a disqualification under the standard of its breed, the dog's show eligibility will be reinstated.

The written opinion of the veterinarian shall in all cases be forwarded to The American Kennel Club by the Superintendent or Show Secretary.

CHAPTER 21

CHAMPIONSHIPS

SECTION 1. Championship points will be recorded for Winners Dog and Winners Bitch, when Winners Classes are divided by sex, for each breed or variety listed in Chapter 6, Section 1, at licensed or member dog shows approved by The American Kennel Club, provided the certification of the Secretary as described in Chapter 9, Section 1, has been printed in the premium list for the show.

Championship points will be recorded according to the number of eligible dogs competing in the regular classes of each sex in each breed or variety, and according to the Schedule of Points established by the Board of Directors. In counting the number of eligible dogs in competition, a dog that is disqualified, or that is dismissed, excused or ordered from the ring by the Judge, or from which all awards are withheld, shall not be included.

If the Winners Class is not divided by sex, championship points will be recorded for the dog or bitch awarded Winners, based on the schedule of points for the sex of the breed or variety for which the greater number in competition is required.

SECTION 2. A dog which in its breed competition at a show shall have been placed Winners and which also shall have won its group class at the same show shall be awarded championship points figured at the highest point rating of any breed or recognized variety or height of any breed entered in the show and entitled to winners points in its group, or if it also shall have been designated Best in Show, shall be awarded championship points figured at the highest point rating of any breed or recognized variety or height of any breed entered and entitled to winners points in the show. The final points to be awarded under this section shall not be inclusive of any points previously awarded the dog in its breed competition or under the provisions of this section.

SECTION 3. At shows in which the winners' classes of certain breeds are divided into recognized varieties of those breeds as specified in Section 1 of Chapter 6 of these Rules and Regulations, the procedure for computing championship points shall be the same as if each recognized variety were a separate breed.

SECTION 4. Any dog which shall have won fifteen points shall become a Champion of Record, if six or more of said points shall have been won at two shows with a rating of three or more championship points each and under two different judges, and some one or more of the balance of said points shall have been won under some other judge or judges than the two judges referred to above. A dog becomes a champion when it is so officially recorded by The American Kennel Club and when registered in the Stud Book shall be entitled to a championship certificate.

SECTION 5. Any dog which has been awarded the title of Champion of Record may be designated as a "Dual Champion" after it also has been awarded the title of Field Champion, but no certificate will be awarded for a Dual Championship.

CHAPTER 22

SUBMISSION OF A SHOW'S RECORDS TO AKC

SECTION 1. A show-giving club shall pay or distribute all prizes offered at its show within thirty (30) days after The American Kennel Club has checked the awards of said show.

SECTION 2. After each licensed or member club dog show a catalog marked with all awards and absent dogs, certified to by the superintendent or show secretary of the show, together with all judges' books, all original entry forms and a report of the show must be sent to The American Kennel Club so as to reach its office within seven (7) days after the close of the show. Penalty for noncompliance, one ($1.00) dollar for each day's delay and such other penalties as may be imposed by the Board of Directors of The American Kennel Club. All recording fees shall be paid to The American Kennel Club within seven (7) days after the close of the show.

CHAPTER 23

STEWARDS

The following policy has been adopted by the Board of Directors regarding stewarding at dog shows:

Clubs should appoint a chief steward well in advance of the date of their show whose duty it will be to invite a sufficient number of experienced persons to act as stewards in the judging rings on the day of the show. No person should be asked to serve as a steward whose judging or handling privileges are suspended or whose superintending privileges have been revoked. The chief steward should, as soon as practicable, confirm in writing, to each person who accepts an invitation to steward, the date and location of the show, the time at which they are to report for duty, and their particular ring assignment.

In preparing the schedule of ring assignments, the chief steward and other club officials should keep in mind that no person should serve as a steward with a judge under whom be has an entry, or under whom, in the course of the day's judging, such entry may become eligible to compete. If it becomes necessary during the show to reshuffle stewarding assignments, care should be taken to see that a person is not assigned to serve as steward with a judge if there is any possibility that the judge, later in the show, will be passing upon an entry of the steward.

Persons should be selected who are familiar with judging procedure, breed classifications and rules. It should be borne in mind that a good steward makes the work of judging easier by relieving the judge of necessary detail; by assembling classes promptly, he will be able to keep the judging program on schedule and eliminate to a large extent delays between classes.

The chief steward should use his discretion in the assigning of more than one steward to a ring, but it is advisable that two stewards be asked to serve in those rings where judges have heavy assignments.

Stewards will notify the judge when all the dogs are in the ring for each class and call his attention to known absentees. Under no circumstances should a steward make any notation in the judge's book or erase or strike out any notation made by the judge.

Stewards will be responsible for returning to the chief steward or superintendent upon the completion of the judging all prize money, trophies and ribbons not awarded.

Stewards should have in mind that they have been selected to help the judge and not to advise him. They should carefully refrain from discussing or seeming to discuss the dogs or the exhibitors with the judge and should not, under any circumstances, show or give the appearance of showing the catalog to a judge. Stewards should not take or seem to take any part in judging. When they are not actively engaged in their duties, they should place themselves in such part of the rings as will not interfere with the view of those watching the judging, and should not permit persons to crowd about the ring entrance and interfere with access to the ring.

The foregoing policy should be observed by clubs holding member and licensed obedience trials, in addition to the applicable obedience regulations and the practices established for persons stewarding in obedience rings.

EXTRACTS FROM BY-LAWS

CHAPTER 24

DISCIPLINE

Article XII of the Constitution and By-Laws of The American Kennel Club provides:

SECTION 1. Any club or association or person or persons interested in pure-bred dogs may prefer charges against any other club or association, or person or persons, for conduct alleged to have been prejudicial to the best interests of pure-bred dogs, dog shows, obedience trials or field trials, or prejudicial to the best interests of The American Kennel Club, which charges shall be made in writing in duplicate setting forth in detail the nature thereof, shall be signed and sworn to by an officer of the club or association or by the person or persons making the same before some person qualified to administer oaths and shall be sent to The American Kennel Club together with a deposit of ten ($10.00) dollars, which sum shall become the property of The American Kennel Club if said charges shall not be sustained, or shall be returned if said charges are sustained, or if The American Kennel Club shall refuse to entertain jurisdiction thereof.

SECTION 2. The bench show, obedience trial or field trial committee of a club or association shall have the right to suspend any person from the privileges of The American Kennel Club for conduct prejudicial to the best interests of pure-bred dogs, dog shows, obedience trials, field trials or The American Kennel Club, alleged to have occurred in connection with or during the progress of its show, obedience trial or field trial, after the alleged offender has been given an opportunity to be heard.

Notice in writing must be sent promptly by registered mail by the bench show, obedience trial or field trial committee to the person suspended and a duplicate notice giving the name and address of the person suspended and full details as to the reasons for the suspension must be forwarded to The American Kennel Club within seven days.

An appeal may be taken from a decision of a bench show, obedience trial or field trial committee. Notice in writing claiming such appeal together with a deposit of five ($5.00) dollars must be sent to The American Kennel Club within thirty days after the date of suspension. The Board of Directors may itself hear said appeal or may refer it to a committee of the Board, or to a Trial Board to be heard. The deposit shall become the property of The American Kennel Club if the decision is confirmed, or shall be returned to the appellant if the decision is not confirmed.

SECTION 3. Upon receipt of duly preferred charges the Board of Directors of The American Kennel Club at its election either may itself consider the same or send the same to a Trial Board for hearing.

In either case a notice which shall state that said charges have been filed and shall set forth a copy of the same shall be sent to the club or association, or person or persons against which or whom said charges have been preferred, which club or association, or person or persons herein shall be known as and called the defendant. The club or association or person or persons which or who shall have preferred said charges herein shall be known as and called the complainant.

Said notice also shall set forth a time and place at which the defendant may attend and present any defense or answer which the defendant may wish to make.

If the complainant shall fail or refuse to appear and prosecute said charges or if the defendant shall fail or refuse to appear and present a defense at the time and place designated for the hearing of said charges, without giving a reasonable excuse for such failure or refusal, the Board of Directors or the Trial Board to which said charges have been referred may suspend whichever party shall be so in default from the privileges of The American Kennel Club for a period of six months or until such time as the party so in default shall be prepared to appear ready and willing to prosecute or defend said charge, as the case may be.

SECTION 4. The Board of Directors shall have the power to investigate any matters which may be brought to its attention in connection with the objects for which this Club was founded, or it may appoint a committee or Trial Board to investigate, in which event the same procedure shall be followed and the same rules shall apply as in a trial before a Trial Board.

If after such investigation the Board of Directors believes that sufficient evidence exists to warrant the filing of charges, it may file or direct the filing of such charges. The Board of Directors acting in accordance with the provisions of this Article may prefer charges for conduct prejudicial to the best interests of The American Kennel Club against persons who shall bring to its attention any matter which upon investigation shall be found to have been reported to it from malicious or untruthful motives or to have been based upon suspicion without foundation of fact or knowledge.

SECTION 5. The Board of Directors of The American Kennel Club shall have power to prefer charges against any association or other club, or person or persons, for conduct alleged to be prejudicial to pure-bred dogs, dog shows, obedience trials or field trials or to the best interests of The American Kennel Club, and pending the final determination of any such charges, may withhold the privileges of The American Kennel Club from any such other person or body against whom charges are pending.

SECTION 6. The Board of Directors shall have the power to suspend from the privileges of The American Kennel Club any member or delegate pending final action by the delegates in accordance with the provisions of this section, for conduct alleged to have been prejudicial to the best interest of The American Kennel Club or for violation of its constitution, by-laws or rules.

The Board of Directors shall then file charges and promptly set a date for a hearing and send to such suspended member or delegate by registered mail at least ten days prior to the date so fixed, notice of the time when and the place where the suspended member or delegate may be heard in its or his defense. Said notice shall also set forth a copy of the charges. The Board of Directors may itself hear the evidence of the suspended member or delegate and any witnesses or may refer the charges to a committee of the Board or to a Trial Board to take the testimony and to report its findings or recommendations to the Board of Directors.

The Board of Directors, after hearing or reviewing the evidence, shall report its findings to The American Kennel Club at the next regular meeting of the Club, whereupon the dele-

fixed and determined by the Board of Directors of The American Kennel Club. Until said fee has been paid the application shall not be acted upon.

SECTION 19. As much of Article XII of these By-Laws as the Board of Directors of The American Kennel Club shall indicate shall be printed in any book or pamphlet which The American Kennel Club shall cause to be published containing the Rules of said Club.

CHAPTER 25

TRIAL BOARDS

Article XIII of the Constitution and By-Laws of The American Kennel Club provides:

SECTION 1. Trial Boards shall be appointed from time to time by the Board of Directors of The American Kennel Club and shall consist of three members for each Board, one of whom, if practicable, should be an attorney-at-law, and no one of whom shall be a director of The American Kennel Club. In case one or more members of a Trial Board shall be unable to sit in any given case, the President, or in his absence, the Executive Vice-President of The American Kennel Club, may appoint a substitute or substitutes for such case. In case of the absence of one or more members of said Board, the remaining member or members may hear and determine a case if the parties being heard shall consent thereto.

SECTION 2. Trial Boards shall hear and decide by a majority vote matters submitted to them by the Board of Directors and shall have power to impose a fine not to exceed twenty-five ($25.00) dollars and/or withhold the privileges of the Club for a period of not more than six months, or may recommend to said Board of Directors the withholding of privileges for a longer period or may recommend disqualification or the imposition of fines exceeding twenty-five ($25.00) dollars.

If a Trial Board recommends the withholding of privileges or disqualification to the Board of Directors, the privileges of the Club shall be automatically withheld until the Board of Directors has adopted or refused to adopt such recommendation.

SECTION 3. Trial Boards shall have power to disqualify any person or withhold from any person all the privileges of The American Kennel Club for a period of not more than six months or to recommend to said Board of Directors the penalty of disqualification or the withholding of privileges for a longer period for improper or disorderly conduct during a hearing or a trial.

SECTION 4. Trial Boards shall keep minutes of their sittings.

SECTION 5. The decisions of Trial Boards shall be in writing signed by all members attending, and have annexed

---

gates shall take action upon said findings and by a majority vote of the delegates present may reinstate, continue the suspension for a stated time or expel such member or delegate from The American Kennel Club.

SECTION 7. The American Kennel Club shall have the power by a two-thirds vote of the Delegates present and voting at any regular meeting to suspend from the privileges of The American Kennel Club any member or delegate for conduct alleged to have been prejudicial to the best interests of The American Kennel Club or for violation of its constitution, by-laws or rules.

The order of suspension thus made shall then be referred to the Board of Directors for hearing and report under the procedure as set forth in Paragraphs 2, 3 and 4 of Section 6 of this article.

SECTION 8. The Board of Directors of The American Kennel Club shall have power to hear as an original matter any charges preferred and to review and finally determine any appeal which may be made to the Board of Directors from the decision of a Trial Board or Bench Show, Obedience Trial or Field Trial Committee, and in each instance in which it shall find the charges to have been sustained, it shall impose such penalty as said Board of Directors may decide to be just and proper.

SECTION 9. The Board of Directors of The American Kennel Club and any Trial Board of The American Kennel Club with the permission of the Board of Directors of The American Kennel Club first obtained in writing, may in the discretion of said Board of Directors, and if necessary at the Club's expense, summon witnesses or a member of any Trial Board, Bench Show Committee, Obedience Trial Committee or Field Trial Committee to attend any and all hearings held under the provisions of Articles XII and XIII of the Constitution and By-Laws of The American Kennel Club. Said Board of Directors may suspend from the privileges of The American Kennel Club for a period of six months or until such time as he or she shall appear and be prepared and willing to testify any person so summoned who without reasonable excuse shall fail to appear and testify.

SECTION 10. The Board of Directors of The American Kennel Club shall, at the next meeting of the Board after an appeal is made from the decision of a Trial Board or Bench Show, Obedience Trial or Field Trial Committee, name a date for the hearing of such appeal and shall cause notice of the time when and place where said hearing is to be held to be sent to all parties in interest by registered mail at least fourteen (14) days prior to the date named.

SECTION 11. Penalties may range from a reprimand or fine to suspension for life from all privileges of The American Kennel Club.

SECTION 12. The Treasurer of The American Kennel Club shall enforce all monetary penalties.

SECTION 13. The suspension or disqualification of a person shall date from the day of the perpetration of the act or from any date subsequent thereto which shall be fixed after hearing by a Trial Board or by the Board of Directors of The American Kennel Club and shall apply to all dogs owned or subsequently acquired by the person so suspended or disqualified.

SECTION 14. All privileges of The American Kennel Club shall be withheld from any person suspended or disqualified.

SECTION 15. Any club, association or organization which shall hold a dog show, obedience trial, field trial or dog exhibition of any kind not in accordance with the rules of The American Kennel Club which apply to such show, obedience trial, field trial or exhibition may be disciplined even to the extent of being deprived of all privileges of The American Kennel Club for a stated period of time or indefinitely, and if such club, association or organizaion shall be a member of The American Kennel Club, it may be expelled from membership therein.

SECTION 16. No Club or association licensed by The American Kennel Club to give a show, obedience trial, hold a field trial or give a dog exhibition of any kind shall employ in any capacity, accept the donation of a prize or money from, or permit to be within the walls or boundaries of its building or grounds, if a dog show or obedience trial, or its grounds, if a field trial, save only as a spectator, any person known to be under suspension or disqualification from the privileges of The American Kennel Club or any employee or member of a corporation which shall be under suspension or disqualification from the privileges of The American Kennel Club. And any contract for floor space at a show, or contract for advertising space in a catalog, premium list or other printed matter, in connection with the giving of said show, shall bear upon it the following condition: "This space is sold with the understanding that should the privileges of The American Kennel Club be withdrawn from the purchaser of this space prior to the carrying out of this contract, this contract is thereby automatically cancelled, and any money paid by the purchaser for such space shall be refunded."

SECTION 17. No member club or association under suspension shall be represented by its delegate and no delegate under suspension shall act for a member or in any official capacity for The American Kennel Club during the period of suspension.

SECTION 18. Any association, club, person or persons suspended or disqualified by The American Kennel Club or from whom the privileges of The American Kennel Club have been withheld, may apply for reinstatement or restoration of privileges upon paying a fee, the amount of which may be

OBEDIENCE REGULATIONS

Purpose

Obedience trials are a sport and all participants should be guided by the principles of good sportsmanship both in and outside of the ring. The purpose of obedience trials is to demonstrate the usefulness of the pure-bred dog as a companion of man, not merely the dog's ability to follow specified routines in the obedience ring. While all contestants in a class are required to perform the same exercises in substantially the same way so that the relative quality of the various performances may be compared and scored, the basic objective of obedience trials is to produce dogs that have been trained and conditioned always to behave in the home, in public places, and in the presence of other dogs, in a manner that will reflect credit on the sport of obedience. The performances of dog and handler in the ring must be accurate and correct and must conform to the requirements of these regulations. However, it is also essential that the dog demonstrate willingness and enjoyment of its work, and smoothness and naturalness on the part of the handler are to be preferred to a performance based on military precision and peremptory commands.

OBEDIENCE REGULATIONS

January 1, 1969
Revised
June 2, 1969
and
December 1, 1969

The American Kennel Club

51 Madison Avenue

New York, N. Y. 10010

thereto all exhibits and papers offered before them. Each decision, together with complete copies of the minutes and testimony taken, shall be filed with the Secretary of The American Kennel Club within ten days of the date of the rendering of the decision. It shall be the duty of the Secretary of The American Kennel Club, when received, at once to notify in writing all parties in interest of the decision of a Trial Board.

SECTION 6. An appeal may be taken to the Board of Directors from any decision of a Trial Board, whether it be a decision in which the Trial Board itself imposes a certain penalty and/or fine, or one in which the Trial Board recommends that the Board of Directors shall impose a certain penalty and/or fine. Notice in writing claiming such appeal together with a deposit of twenty-five ($25.00) dollars must be sent to The American Kennel Club within thirty days after the receipt of the notice of the decision or recommendation of the Trial Board. The Board of Directors may itself hear said appeal or may refer it to a committee of the Board to be heard. The deposit of twenty-five ($25.00) dollars shall become the property of The American Kennel Club if the decision or recommendation of the Trial Board shall be confirmed, or shall be returned to the appellant if it shall not be confirmed. If the aggrieved party shall fail to take such appeal to the Board of Directors, there shall be no further right of appeal of any kind.

SECTION 7. Article XIII of these By-Laws shall be printed in any book or pamphlet which The American Kennel Club shall cause to be published containing the Rules of said club.

CHAPTER 1
General Regulations

Section 1. Obedience Clubs. An obedience club that meets all the requirements of The American Kennel Club and wishes to hold an Obedience Trial at which qualifying scores toward an obedience title may be awarded, must make application to The American Kennel Club on the form provided for permission to hold such trial. Such a trial, if approved, may be held either in conjunction with a dog show or as a separate event. If the club is not a member of The American Kennel Club it shall pay a license fee for the privilege of holding such trial, the amount of which shall be determined by the Board of Directors of The American Kennel Club. If the club fails to hold its trial at the time and place which have been approved, the amount of the license fee paid will be returned.

Section 2. Dog Show and Specialty Clubs. A dog show club may be granted permission to hold a licensed or member obedience trial at its dog show, and a specialty club may also be granted permission to hold a licensed or member obedience trial if, in the opinion of the Board of Directors of The American Kennel Club, such clubs are qualified to do so.

Section 3. Obedience Classes. A licensed or member obedience trial need not include all of the regular obedience classes defined in this chapter, but a club will be approved to hold Open classes only if it also holds Novice classes, and a club will be approved to hold a Utility class only if it also holds Novice and Open classes. A specialty club which has been approved to hold a licensed or member obedience trial, if qualified in the opinion of the Board of Directors of The American Kennel Club, or an obedience club which has been approved to hold a licensed or member obedience trial may, subject to the approval of The American Kennel Club, offer additional non-regular classes for dogs not less than six months of age, provided a clear and complete description of the eligibility requirements and performance requirements for each such class appears in the premium list. Pre-Novice classes will not be approved at licensed or member obedience trials.

Section 4. Tracking Tests. A club that has been approved to hold licensed or member obedience trials and that meets the requirements of The American Kennel Club, may also make application to hold a Tracking Test. A club may not hold a tracking test on the same day as its show or obedience trial, but the tracking test may be announced in the premium list for the show or trial, and the tracking test entries may be included in the show or obedience trial catalog. If the entries are not listed in the catalog for the show or obedience trial, the club must provide, at the tracking test, several copies of a sheet, which may be typewritten, giving all the information that would be contained in the catalog for each entered dog. If the tracking test is to be held within 7 days of the obedience trial the entries must be sent to the same person designated to receive the obedience trial entries, and the same closing date should apply. If the tracking test is not to be held within 7 days of the obedience trial the club may name someone else in the premium list to receive the tracking test entries, and may specify a different closing date for entries at least 7 days before the tracking test.

The presence of a veterinarian shall not be required at a tracking test.

Section 5. Obedience Trial Committee. If an obedience trial is held by an obedience club, an Obedience Trial Committee must be appointed by the club, and this committee shall exercise all the authority vested in a dog show's Bench Show Committee. If an obedience club holds its obedience trial in conjunction with a dog show, then the Obedience Trial Committee shall have sole jurisdiction only over those dogs entered in the obedience trial and their handlers and owners; provided, however, that if any dog is entered in both obedience and breed classes, then the Obedience Trial Committee shall have jurisdiction over such dog, its owner, and its handler, only in matters pertaining to the Obedience Regulations, and the Bench Show Committee shall have jurisdiction over such dog, its owner and handler, in all other matters.

When an obedience trial is to be held in conjunction with a dog show by the club which has been granted permission to hold the show, the club's Bench Show Committee shall include one person designated as "Obedience Chairman". At such event the Bench Show Committee of the show-giving club shall have sole jurisdiction over all matters which may properly come before it, regardless of whether the matter has to do with the dog show or with the obedience trial.

Section 6. Sanctioned Matches. A club may hold an Obedience Match by obtaining the sanction of The American Kennel Club. Sanctioned obedience matches shall be governed by such regulations as may be adopted by the Board of Directors of The American Kennel Club. Scores awarded at such matches will not be entered in the records of The American Kennel Club nor count towards an obedience title.

All of these Obedience Regulations shall also apply to sanctioned matches except for those sections in which it is specified that the provisions apply to licensed or member trials, and except where specifically stated otherwise in the Regulations for Sanctioned Matches.

Section 7. American Kennel Club Sanction. American Kennel Club sanction must be obtained by any club that holds American Kennel Club obedience trials, for any type of match for which it solicits or accepts entries from non-members.

Section 8. Dog Show Rules. All the Dog Show Rules, where applicable, shall govern the conducting of obedience trials and tracking tests, and shall apply to all persons and dogs participating in them except as these Obedience Regulations may provide otherwise.

Section 9. Immediate Family. As used in this chapter, "immediate family" means husband, wife, father, mother, son, daughter, brother, or sister.

Section 10. Pure-Bred Dogs Only. As used in these regulations the word "dog" refers to either sex but only to dogs that are pure-bred of a breed eligible for registration in the American Kennel Club stud book or for entry in the Miscellaneous Class at American Kennel Club dog shows, as only such dogs may compete in obedience trials, tracking tests, or sanctioned matches. A judge must report to The American Kennel Club after the trial or tracking test any dog shown under him which in his opinion appears not to be pure-bred.

Section 11. Unregistered Dogs. Chapter 16, Section 1 of the Dog Show Rules shall apply to entries in licensed or member obedience trials and tracking tests, except that an eligible unregistered dog for which an ILP number has been issued by The American Kennel Club may be entered indefinitely in such events provided the ILP number is shown on each entry form.

Section 12. Dogs That May Not Compete. No dog belonging wholly or in part to a judge or to a Show or Obedience Trial Secretary, Superintendent, or veterinarian, or to any member of such person's immediate family or household, shall be entered in any dog show, obedience trial, or tracking test at which such person officiates or is scheduled to officiate. This applies to both obedience and dog show judges when an obedience trial is held in conjunction with a dog show. However, a tracking test shall be considered a separate event for the purpose of this section.

No dog shall be entered or shown under a judge at an obedience trial or tracking test if the dog has been owned, sold, held under lease, handled in the ring, boarded, or has been regularly trained or instructed, within one year prior to the date of the obedience trial or tracking test, by the judge or by any member of his immediate family or household, and no such dog shall be eligible to compete. "Trained or instructed" applies equally to judges who train professionally or as amateurs, and to judges who train individual dogs or who train or instruct dogs in classes with or through their handlers.

Section 13. When Titles Are Won. Where any of the following sections of the regulations excludes from a particular obedience class dogs that have won a particular obedience class title, eligibility to enter that class shall be determined as follows: a dog may continue to be shown in such a class after its handler has been notified by three different judges that it has received three qualifying scores for such title, but may not be entered or shown in such a class in any obedience trial of which the closing date for entries occurs after the owner has received official notification from The American Kennel Club that the dog has won the particular obedience title.

Where any of the following sections of the regulations requires that a dog shall have won a particular obedience title before competing in a particular obedience class, a dog may not be shown in such class at any obedience trial before the owner has received official notification from The American Kennel Club that the dog has won the required title.

Section 14. Disqualification and Ineligibility. A dog that is blind or deaf or that has been changed in appearance by artificial means (except for such changes as are customarily approved for its breed) may not compete in any obedience trial or tracking test and must be disqualified. Blind means having useful vision in neither eye. Deaf means without useful hearing.

If a judge has evidence of any of these conditions in any dog he is judging at an obedience trial he must, before proceeding with the judging, notify the Superintendent or Show or Trial Secretary and must call an official veterinarian to examine the dog in the ring and give to the judge an advisory opinion in writing on the condition of the dog. Only after he has seen the opinion of the veterinarian in writing shall the judge render his own decision and record it in the judge's book, marking the dog disqualified and stating the reason if he determines that disqualification is required under this section. The judge's decision is final and need not necessarily agree with the veterinarian's opinion. The written opinion of the veterinarian shall in all cases be forwarded to The American Kennel Club by the Superintendent or Show or Trial Secretary.

Section 15. Disturbances. Bitches in season are not permitted to compete. The judge of an obedience trial or tracking test must remove from competition any bitch in season, any dog which its handler cannot control, any handler who interferes willfully with another competitor or his dog, and any handler who abuses his dog in the ring, and may excuse from competition any dog which he considers unfit to compete, or any bitch which appears so attractive to males as to be a disturbing element. In case of doubt an official veterinarian shall be called to give his opinion. If a dog or handler is expelled or excused by a judge, the reason shall be stated in the judge's book or in a separate report.

The judge must disqualify any dog that attempts to attack any person in the ring. He may excuse a dog that attacks another dog or that appears dangerous to other dogs in the ring. He shall mark the dog disqualified or excused and state the reason in his judge's book, and shall give the Superintendent or Show or Trial Secretary a brief report of the dog's actions which shall be submitted to AKC with the report of the show or trial.

When a dog has been disqualified under this section as being blind or deaf or having been changed in appearance by artificial means or for having attempted to attack a person in the ring, all awards made to the dog at the trial shall be cancelled by The American Kennel Club and the dog may not again compete unless and until, following application by the owner to The American Kennel Club, the owner has received official notification from The American Kennel Club that the dog's eligibility has been reinstated.

Spayed bitches, castrated dogs, monorchid or cryptorchid males, and dogs that have faults which would disqualify them under the standards for their breeds, may compete in obedience trials if otherwise eligible under these regulations.

A dog that is lame in the ring at any obedience trial or at a tracking test may not compete and shall not receive any score at the trial. It shall be the judge's responsibility to determine whether a dog is lame. He shall not obtain the opinion of the show veterinarian. If in the judge's opinion a dog in the ring is lame, he shall not score such dog, and shall promptly excuse it from the ring and mark his book "Excused—lame".

No dog shall be eligible to compete if it appears to have been dyed or colored in any way or if the coat shows evidence of chalk or powder, or if the dog has anything attached to it whether for medical or corrective purposes, for protection, for adornment or for any other reason, except for Maltese, Poodles, Shih Tzu, and Yorkshire Terriers which may be shown with the hair over the eyes tied back as they are normally shown in the breed ring. The judge, at his sole discretion, may agree to judge such a dog at a later time if the offending condition has been corrected.

An obedience judge is not required to be familiar with the breed standards nor to scrutinize each dog as in dog show judging, but shall be alert for conditions which may require disqualification or exclusion under this section.

Section 16. Novice A Class. The Novice A class shall be for dogs not less than six months of age that have not won the title C.D. No person who has previously handled a dog that has won a C.D. title in the obedience ring at a licensed or member trial, and no person who has regularly trained such a dog, may enter or handle a dog in this class. Each dog in the class must have a separate handler, who must be its owner or a member of the owner's immediate family. The same person must handle each dog in all exercises.

Section 17. Novice B Class. The Novice B class shall be for dogs not less than six months of age that have not won the title C.D. Dogs in this class may be handled by the owner or any other person. A person may handle more than one dog in this class, but each dog must have a separate handler for the Long Sit and Long Down exercises when judged in the same group. No dog may be entered in both Novice A and Novice B classes at any one trial.

Section 18. Novice Exercises and Scores. The exercises and maximum scores in the Novice classes are:

1. Heel on Leash .... 35 points
2. Stand for Examination .... 30 points
3. Heel Free .... 45 points
4. Recall .... 30 points
5. Long Sit .... 30 points
6. Long Down .... 30 points
   Maximum Total Score ...... 200 points

Section 19. C.D. Title. The American Kennel Club will issue a Companion Dog certificate for each registered dog, and will permit the use of the letters "C.D." after the name of each dog that has been certified by three different judges to have received scores of more than 50% of the available points in each of the six exercises and final scores of 170 or more points in Novice classes at three licensed or member obedience trials, provided the sum total of dogs that actually competed in the regular Novice classes at each trial is not less than six.

Section 20. Open A Class. The Open A class shall be for dogs that have won the C.D. title but have not won the title C.D.X. Obedience judges and licensed handlers may not enter or handle dogs in this class. Each dog must be handled by its owner or by a member of his immediate family. Owners may enter more than one dog in this class but the same person who handled each dog in the first five exercises must handle the same dog in the Long Sit and Long Down exercises, except that if a person has handled more than one dog in the first five exercises he must have an additional handler, who must be the owner or a member of his immediate family, for each additional dog, when more than one dog he has handled in the first five exercises is judged in the same group for the Long Sit and Long Down.

Section 21. Open B Class. The Open B class will be for dogs that have won the title C.D. or C.D.X. A dog may continue to compete in this class after it has won the title U.D. Dogs in this class may be handled by the owner or any other person. Owners may enter more than one dog in this class but the same person who handled each dog in the first five exercises must handle each dog in the Long Sit and Long Down exercises, except that if a person has handled more than one dog in the first five exercises he must have an additional handler for each additional dog, when more than one dog that he has handled in the first five exercises is judged in the same group for the Long Sit and Long Down. No dog may be entered in both Open A and Open B classes at any one trial.

Section 22. Open Exercises and Scores. The exercises and maximum scores in the Open classes are:

1. Heel Free — 40 points
2. Drop on Recall — 30 points
3. Retrieve on Flat — 25 points
4. Retrieve over High Jump — 35 points
5. Broad Jump — 20 points
6. Long Sit — 25 points
7. Long Down — 25 points
Maximum Total Score — 200 points

Section 23. C.D.X. Title. The American Kennel Club will issue a Companion Dog Excellent certificate for each registered dog, and will permit the use of the letters "C.D.X." after the name of each dog that has been certified by three different judges of obedience trials to have received scores of more than 50% of the available points in each of the seven exercises and final scores of 170 or more points in Open classes at three licensed or member obedience trials, provided the sum total of dogs that actually competed in the regular Open classes at each trial is not less than six.

Section 24. Utility Class. The Utility class shall be for dogs that have won the title C.D.X. Dogs that have won the title U.D. may continue to compete in this class. Dogs in this class may be handled by the owner or any other person. Owners may enter more than one dog in this class, but each dog must have a separate handler for the Group Examination when judged in the same group.

Section 25. Division of Utility Class. A club may choose to divide the Utility class into Utility A and Utility B classes, provided such division is approved by The American Kennel Club and is announced in the premium list. When this is done the Utility A class shall be for dogs which have won the title C.D.X. and have not won the title U.D. Obedience judges and licensed handlers may not enter or handle dogs in this class. A dog may be handled in the Group Examination by a person other than the person who handled it in the individual exercises, but each dog must be handled in all exercises by the owner or by a member of his immediate family. All other dogs that are eligible for the Utility class but not eligible for the Utility A class may be entered only in the Utility B class to which the conditions listed in Section 24 shall apply. No dog may be entered in both Utility A and Utility B classes at any one trial.

Section 26. Utility Exercises and Scores. The exercises and maximum scores in the Utility classes are:

1. Scent Discrimination—
   Article No. 1 — 30 points
2. Scent Discrimination—
   Article No. 2 — 30 points
3. Directed Retrieve — 30 points
4. Signal Exercise — 35 points
5. Directed Jumping — 40 points
6. Group Examination — 35 points
Maximum Total Score — 200 points

Section 27. U.D. Title. The American Kennel Club will issue a Utility Dog certificate for each registered dog, and will permit the use of the letters "U.D." after the name of each dog that has been certified by three different judges of obedience trials to have received scores of more than 50% of the available points in each of the six exercises and final scores of 170 or more points in Utility classes at three licensed or member obedience trials in each of which three or more dogs actually competed in the Utility class or classes.

Section 28. Tracking Test. This test shall be for dogs not less than six months of age, and must be judged by two judges. With each entry form for a licensed or member tracking test for a dog that has not passed an AKC tracking test there must be filed an original written statement, dated within six months of the date the entry is received, signed by a person who has been approved by The American Kennel Club to judge tracking tests, certifying that the dog is considered by him to be ready for such a test. These original statements cannot be used again and must be submitted to The American Kennel Club with the entry forms. Written permission to waive or modify this requirement may be granted by The American Kennel Club in unusual circumstances. Tracking tests are open to all dogs that are otherwise eligible under these Regulations.

This test cannot be given at a dog show or obedience trial. The duration of this test may be one day or more within a 15 day period after the original date in the event of an unusually large entry or other unforeseen emergency, provided that the change of date is satisfactory to the exhibitors affected.

Section 29. T.D. Title. The American Kennel Club will issue a Tracking Dog certificate to a registered dog, and will permit the use of the letters "T.D." after the name of each dog which has been certified by the two judges to have passed a licensed or member tracking test in which at least three dogs actually competed.

The owner of a dog holding both the U.D. and T.D. titles may use the letters "U.D.T." after the name of the dog, signifying "Utility Dog Tracker".

Section 30. Obedience Ribbons. At licensed or member obedience trials the following colors shall be used for prize ribbons or rosettes in all regular classes:

First Prize — Blue
Second Prize — Red
Third Prize — Yellow
Fourth Prize — White
Special Prize — Dark Green

and the following colors shall be used for non-regular classes:

First Prize — Rose
Second Prize — Brown
Third Prize — Light Green
Fourth Prize — Gray

Each ribbon or rosette shall be at least two inches wide and approximately eight inches long, and shall bear on its face a facsimile of the seal of The American Kennel Club, the words "Obedience Trial", the name of the trial-giving club, the date of the trial, and the name of the city or town where the trial is given.

Section 31. **Match Ribbons.** If ribbons are given at sanctioned obedience matches they shall be of the following colors and shall have the words "Obedience Match" printed on them, but may be of any design or size:

First Prize .... Rose
Second Prize .... Brown
Third Prize .... Light Green
Fourth Prize .... Gray
Special Prize ...... Green with pink edges

Section 32. **Prizes.** Ribbons and all other prizes offered for competition placings and all other prizes offered for competition within a single regular class at a licensed or member trial, shall be awarded only to dogs that earn scores of more than 50% of the available points in each exercise and final scores of 170 or more points.

Prizes for which dogs in one class compete against dogs in one or more other classes at a licensed or member trial may, at the option of the club holding the trial, specify that scores of more than 50% of the available points in each exercise and final scores of 170 or more points, are required.

Ribbons and all prizes offered at sanctioned obedience matches, and in non-regular classes at licensed and member trials, shall be awarded on the basis of final scores without regard to more than 50% of the points in each exercise.

Prizes at a licensed or member obedience trial must be offered to be won outright, with the exception that a prize which requires three wins by the same owner, not necessarily with the same dog, for permanent possession, may be offered for the dog with the highest qualifying score in one of the regular classes, for the highest scoring dog in the regular classes, or for the highest combined score in the Open B and Utility classes.

Subject to the provisions of paragraphs 1 and 2 of this section, prizes may be offered for the highest scoring dogs of the Groups as defined in Chapter 2 of the Dog Show Rules, or for the highest scoring dogs of any breeds, but not for a breed variety. Show varieties are not recognized for obedience. In accordance with Chapter 2, all Poodles are in the Non-Sporting Group and all Manchester Terriers in the Terrier Group.

Prizes offered only to members of certain clubs or organizations will not be approved for publication in premium lists.

Section 33. **Risk.** The owner or agent entering a dog in an obedience trial does so at his own risk and agrees to abide by the rules of The American Kennel Club, and the Obedience Regulations.

Section 34. **Decisions.** At the trial the decisions of the judge shall be final in all matters affecting the scoring and the working of the dogs and their handlers. The Obedience Trial Committee, or the Bench Show Committee if the trial is held by a show-giving club, shall decide all other matters arising at the trial, including protests against dogs made under Chapter 20 of the Dog Show Rules, subject, however, to the rules and regulations of The American Kennel Club.

Section 35. **Dogs Must Compete.** Any dog entered and received at a licensed or member obedience trial must compete in all exercises of all classes in which it is entered unless disqualified, expelled, or excused by the judge or by the Bench Show or Obedience Trial Committee, or unless excused by the official veterinarian to protect the health of the dog or of other dogs at the trial. The excuse of the official veterinarian must be in writing and must be approved by the Superintendent or Show or Trial Secretary, and must be submitted to The American Kennel Club with the report of the trial. The judge must report to The American Kennel Club any dog that is not brought back for the group exercises.

Section 36. **Judging Program.** Any club holding a licensed or member obedience trial must prepare, after the entries have closed, a program showing the time scheduled for the judging of each of the classes. A copy of this program shall be mailed to the owner of each entered dog and to each judge, and the program shall be printed in the catalog. This program shall be based on the judging of no more than 8 Novice entries, 7 Open entries, or 5 Utility entries, per hour during the time the show or trial will be open as published in the premium list, taking into consideration the starting hour for judging if published in the premium list, and the availability of rings. No judge shall be scheduled to exceed this rate of judging. In addition, one hour for rest or meals must be allowed if, under this formula, it will take more than five hours of actual judging to judge the dogs entered under him. No judge shall be assigned to judge for more than eight hours in one day under this formula, including any breed judging assignment if the obedience trial is held in conjunction with a dog show.

If any non-regular class is to be judged in the same ring as any regular class, or by the judge of any regular class, the non-regular class must be judged after the regular class.

Section 37. **Limitation of Entries.** If a club anticipates an entry in excess of its facilities for a licensed or member trial, it may limit entries in any or all regular classes, but non-regular classes will not be approved if the facilities are limited; or a club may limit entries in any or all regular classes to 64 in a Novice class, 56 in an Open class, or 40 in a Utility class.

Prominent announcement of such limits must appear on the title or cover page of the premium list for an obedience trial or immediately under the obedience heading in the premium list for a dog show, with a statement that entries in one or more specified classes or in the obedience trial will automatically close when a certain limit or limits have been reached, even though the official closing date for entries has not arrived.

Section 38. **Additional Judges, Reassignment, Split Classes.** If when the entries have closed, it is found that the entry under one or more judges exceeds the limit established in Section 36, the club shall immediately secure the approval of The American Kennel Club for the appointment of one or more additional judges, or for reassignment of its advertised judges, so that no judge will be required to exceed the limit.

If a judge with an excessive entry was advertised to judge more than one class, one or more of his classes shall be assigned to another judge. The class or classes selected for reassignment shall first be any non-regular classes for which he was advertised, and shall then be either the regular class or classes with the minimum number of entries, or those with the minimum scheduled time, which will bring the advertised judge's schedule within, and as close as possible to, the maximum limit. If a judge with an excessive entry was advertised to judge only one class, the Superintendent, Show Secretary, or Obedience Trial Secretary, shall divide the entry as evenly as possible between the advertised judge and the other judge by drawing lots.

The club shall promptly mail to the owner of each entry affected, a notification of any change of judge. The owner shall be permitted to withdraw such entry at any time prior to the day of the show, and the entry fee shall then be refunded. If the entry in any one class is split in this manner, the advertised judge shall judge the run-off of any tie scores that may develop between the two groups of dogs, after each judge has first run-off any ties resulting from his own judging.

Section 39. **Split Classes in Premium List.** A club may choose to announce two or more judges for any class in its premium list. In such case the entries shall be divided by lots as provided above. The identification slips and judging program shall be made up so that the owner of each dog will know the division, and the judge of the division, in which his dog is entered, but no owner shall be entitled to a refund of entry fee. In such case the premium list shall also specify the judge for the run-off of any tie scores which may develop between the dogs in the different groups, after each judge has first run-off any ties resulting from his own judging.

Section 40. **Split Classes, Official Ribbons.** A club which gives a split class, whether the split is announced in the premium list or made after entries have closed, shall not award American Kennel Club official ribbons in either section, but may offer prizes on the basis of qualifying scores made within each section if the split class is announced in the premium list. The four dogs with the highest qualifying scores in the class regardless of the section in which they were made, shall be called back into the ring and awarded the four American Kennel Club official ribbons by one of the judges of the class who shall be responsible for recording the entry numbers of the four placed dogs in one of the judges' books.

Section 41. **Training of Dogs.** There shall be no drilling nor intensive or corrective training of dogs on the grounds or premises at a licensed or member obedience trial. No practice rings or areas shall be permitted at such events. All dogs shall be kept on leash except when in the obedience ring or exercise ring. Spiked or other special training collars shall not be used on the grounds or premises at an obedience trial or match. These requirements shall not be interpreted as preventing a handler from moving normally about the grounds or premises with his dog at heel on leash, nor from giving such signals or such commands in a normal tone, as are necessary and usual in everyday life in heeling a dog or making it stay, but physical or verbal disciplining of dogs shall not be permitted except to a reasonable extent in the case of an attack on a person or another dog. The Superintendent, or Show or Trial Secretary, and the members of the Bench Show or Obedience Trial Committee, shall be responsible for compliance with this section, and shall investigate any reports of infractions.

Section 42. **Abuse of Dogs.** The Bench Show or Obedience Trial Committee shall also investigate any reports of abuse of dogs or severe disciplining of dogs on the grounds or premises of a show, trial, or match. Any person who, at a licensed or member obedience trial, conducts himself in such manner or in any other manner prejudicial to the best interests of the sport, or who fails to comply with the require-

ments of Section 41 above after receiving a warning, shall be dealt with promptly, during the trial if possible, after the offender has been notified of the specific charges against him, and has been given an opportunity to be heard in his own defense in accordance with Section 43 below.

Article XII Section 2 of the Constitution and By-Laws of The American Kennel Club provides:

Section 43. **Discipline.** The Bench Show, Obedience Trial or Field Trial Committee of a club or association shall have the right to suspend any person from the privileges of The American Kennel Club for conduct prejudicial to the best interests of pure-bred dogs, dog shows, obedience trials, field trials or The American Kennel Club, alleged to have occurred in connection with or during the progress of its show, obedience trial or field trial, after the alleged offender has been given an opportunity to be heard.

Notice in writing must be sent promptly by registered mail by the Bench Show, Obedience Trial or Field Trial Committee to the person suspended and a duplicate notice giving the name and address of the person suspended and full details as to the reasons for the suspension must be forwarded to The American Kennel Club within seven days.

An appeal may be taken from a decision of a Bench Show, Obedience Trial or Field Trial Committee. Notice in writing claiming such appeal together with a deposit of five ($5.00) dollars must be sent to The American Kennel Club within thirty days after the date of suspension. The Board of Directors may itself hear said appeal or may refer it to a committee of the Board, or to a Trial Board to be heard. The deposit shall become the property of The American Kennel Club if the decision is confirmed, or shall be returned to the appellant if the decision is not confirmed.

(See Guide for Bench Show and Obedience Trial Committees in Dealing with Misconduct at Dog Shows and Obedience Trials for proper procedure at licensed or member obedience trials.)

(The Committee at a Sanctioned event does not have this power of suspension, but must investigate any allegation of such conduct and forward a complete and detailed report of any such incident to The American Kennel Club.)

CHAPTER 2

Regulations for Performance

Section 1. **Ring Conditions.** If the judging takes place indoors the ring should be rectangular and should be about 35' wide and 50' long for all obedi-

ence classes. In no case shall the ring for a Utility class be less than 35' by 50', and in no case shall the ring for a Novice or Open class be less than 30' by 40'. The floor shall have a surface or covering that provides firm footing for the largest dogs, and rubber or similar non-slip material must be laid for the take off and landing at all jumps unless the surface, in the judge's opinion, is such as not to require it. At an outdoor show or trial the rings shall be about 40' wide and 50' long. The ground shall be clean and level, and the grass, if any, shall be cut short. The Club and Superintendent are responsible for providing, for the Open classes, an appropriate place approved by the judge, for the handlers to go completely out of sight of their dogs. If inclement weather at an outdoor trial necessitates 'he judging of obedience under shelter, the requirements as to ring size may be waived.

Section 2. **Obedience Rings at Dog Shows.** At an outdoor dog show a separate ring or, rings shall be provided for obedience, and a sign forbidding anyone to permit any dog to use the ring, except when being judged, shall be set up in each such ring by the Superintendent or Show Secretary. It shall be his duty as well as that of the Show Committee to enforce this regulation. At an indoor show where limited space does not permit the exclusive use of any ring for obedience, the same regulation will apply after the obedience rings have been set up. At a dog show the material used for enclosing the obedience rings for the regular classes shall be at least equal to the material used for enclosing the breed rings. The ring must be thoroughly cleaned before the obedience judging starts if it has previously been used for breed judging.

Section 3. **Compliance with Regulations and Standards.** In accordance with the certification on the entry form, the handler of each dog and the person signing each entry form must be familiar with the Obedience Regulations applicable to the class in which the dog is entered. A handler with a physical handicap may compete, provided he can move himself about the ring as required, without physical assistance or guidance from another person, except for guidance to the proper location in the ring which may be given by the judge or, in the group exercises, by a person who is handling a competing dog in the ring.

Section 4. **Praise and Handling between Exercises.** Praise and patting are allowed between exercises, but points must be deducted from the total score for a dog that is not under reasonable control while being praised. A handler must not carry or offer food in the ring.

Imperfections in heeling between exercises will not be judged. In the Novice classes the dog may be guided gently by the collar between exercises and to get it into proper position for the next exercise. There shall be a substantial penalty for any dog that is picked up or carried at any time in the obedience ring, and for a dog in the Open or Utility classes that is not readily controllable or that is physically controlled at any time, except for permitted patting between exercises, and posing, or if the judge requests the handler to hold his dog for measuring. Minor penalties shall be imposed for a dog that does not respond promptly to its handler's commands or signals between exercises in the Open and Utility classes.

Section 5. Use of Leash. All dogs shall be kept on leash except when in the obedience ring or exercise ring. Dogs should be brought into the ring and taken out of the ring on leash. Dogs may be kept on leash in the ring when brought in to receive awards, and when waiting in the ring before and after the group exercises. The leash shall be left on the judge's table between the individual exercises, and during all exercises except the Heel on Leash and group exercises. The leash may be of fabric or leather and, in the Novice classes, shall be of sufficient length to provide adequate slack in the Heel on Leash exercise.

Section 6. Collars. Dogs in the obedience ring must wear well-fitting plain buckle or slip collars of leather, fabric, or chain. Fancy collars, spiked collars or other special training collars, or collars that are either too tight or so large that they hang down unreasonably in front of the dogs, are not permitted, nor may there be anything hanging from the collars.

Section 7. Misbehavior. Any disciplining by the handler in the ring, any display of fear or nervousness by the dog, or any uncontrolled behavior of the dog such as snapping, barking, relieving itself in the ring, or running away from its handler, whether it occurs during an exercise, between exercises, or before or after judging, must be penalized according to the seriousness of the misbehavior, and the judge may expel or excuse the dog from further competition in the class. If such behavior occurs during an exercise, the penalty must first be applied to the score for that exercise. Should the penalty be greater than the value of the exercise during which it is incurred, the additional points shall be deducted from the total score under Misbehavior. If such behavior occurs before or after the judging or between exercises, the entire penalty shall be deducted from the total score.

Section 8. Commands and Signals. Whenever a command or signal is mentioned in these regulations, a single command or signal only may be given by the handler, and any extra commands or signals must be penalized; except that whenever the regulations specify "command and/or signal" the handler may give either one or the other or both command and signal simultaneously. When a signal is permitted and given, it must be a single gesture with one arm and hand only, and the arm must immediately be returned to a natural position. Delay in following a judge's order to give a command or signal must be penalized, unless the delay is directed by the judge because of some distraction or interference.

The signal for downing a dog may be given either with the arm raised or with a down swing of the arm, but any pause in holding the arm upright followed by a down swing of the arm will be considered an additional signal.

Signaling correction to a dog is forbidden and must be penalized. Signals must be inaudible and the handler must not touch the dog. Any unusual noise or motion may be considered to be a signal. Movements of the body shall be considered additional signals except that a handler may bend as far as necessary to bring his hand on a level with the dog's eyes in giving a signal to a dog in the heel position, and that in the Directed Retrieve exercise the body and knees may be bent to the extent necessary to give the direction to the dog. Whistling or the use of a whistle is prohibited.

The dog's name may be used once immediately before any verbal command or before a verbal command and signal when these regulations permit command and/or signal. The name shall not be used with any signal not given simultaneously with a verbal command. The dog's name, when given immediately before a verbal command, shall not be considered as an additional command, but a dog that responds to its name without waiting for the verbal command shall be scored as having anticipated the command. The dog should never anticipate the handler's directions, but must wait for the appropriate commands and/or signals. Moving forward at heel without any command or signal other than the natural movement of the handler's left leg, shall not be considered as anticipation.

Loud commands by handlers to their dogs create a poor impression of obedience and should be avoided. Shouting is not necessary even in a noisy place if the dog is properly trained to respond to a normal tone of voice. Commands which in the judge's opinion are excessively loud will be penalized.

Section 9. Heel Position. The heel position as used in these regulations, whether the dog is sitting, standing, or moving at heel, means that the dog shall be straight in line with the direction in which the handler is facing, at the handler's left side, and as close as practicable to the handler's left leg without crowding, permitting the handler freedom of motion at all times. The area from the dog's head to shoulder shall be in line with the handler's left hip.

Section 10. Heel on Leash. The handler shall enter the ring with his dog on a loose leash and shall stand still with the dog sitting in the heel position until the judge asks if the handler is ready and then gives the order "Forward". The handler may give the command or signal to Heel, and shall start walking briskly and in a natural manner with the dog on loose leash. The dog shall walk close to the left side of the handler without crowding, permitting the handler freedom of motion at all times. At each order to "Halt", the handler will stop and his dog shall sit straight and smartly in the Heel position without command or signal and shall not move until the handler again moves forward on order from the judge. It is permissible after each Halt before moving again, for the handler to give the command or signal to Heel.

The leash may be held in either hand or in both hands, at the handler's option, provided the hands are in a natural position. However, the handler and dog will be penalized if, in the judge's opinion, the leash is used to signal or give assistance to the dog.

Any tightening or jerking of the leash or any act, signal or command which in the opinion of the judge gives the dog assistance shall be penalized. The judge will give the orders "Forward", "Halt", "Right turn", "Left turn", "About turn", "Slow", "Normal", and "Fast", which order signifies that both the handler and dog must run, changing pace and moving forward at noticeably accelerated speed. These orders may be given in any sequence and may be repeated if necessary. In executing the About Turn, the handler will do a Right About Turn in all cases. The judge will say "Exercise finished" after the heeling and then "Are you ready?" before starting the Figure Eight.

The judge will order the handler to execute the "Figure Eight" which signifies that the handler may give the command or signal to Heel and, with his dog in the heel position, shall walk around and between the two stewards who shall stand about 8 feet apart, or if there is only one steward, shall walk around and between the judge and the steward. The Figure Eight in the Novice classes shall be done on leash only. The handler may choose to go in either direction. There shall be no About Turn in the

Figure Eight, but the handler and dog shall go twice completely around the Figure Eight with at least one Halt during and another Halt at the end of the exercise.

Section 11. **Stand for Examination.** The judge will give the order for examination and the handler, without further order from the judge, will stand or pose his dog off leash, give the command and/or signal to Stay, walk forward about six feet in front of his dog, turn around, and stand facing his dog. The method by which the dog is made to stand or pose is optional with the handler who may take any reasonable time in posing the dog, as in the show ring, before deciding to give the command and/or signal to Stay. The judge will approach the dog from the front and will touch its head, body and hindquarters only, and will then give the order "Back to your dog", whereupon the handler will walk around behind his dog to the heel position. The dog must remain in a standing position until the judge says "Exercise finished". The dog must show no shyness nor resentment at any time during the exercise.

Section 12. **Heel Free.** This shall be executed in the same manner as Heel on Leash except that the dog is off the leash. Heeling in both Novice and Open classes is done in the same manner except that in the Open classes all work is done off leash, including the Figure Eight.

Section 13. **Recall and Drop on Recall.** To execute the Recall to handler, upon order or signal from the judge "Leave your dog", the dog is given the command and/or signal to stay in the sitting position while the handler walks forward about 35 feet towards the other end of the ring, turns around, and faces his dog. Upon order or signal from the judge "Call your dog", the handler calls or signals the dog, which in the Novice class must come straight in at a brisk pace and sit straight, centered immediately in front of the handler's feet and close enough so that the handler could readily touch its head without moving either foot or having to stretch forward. The dog shall not touch the handler nor sit between his feet. Upon order or signal from the judge to "Finish", the dog on command or signal must go smartly to the heel position and sit. The method by which the dog goes to the heel position shall be optional with the handler provided it is done smartly and the dog sits straight at heel.

In the Open class, at a point designated by the judge, the dog must drop completely to a down position immediately on command or signal from the handler, and must remain in the down position until,

on order or signal from the judge, the handler calls or signals the dog which must rise and complete the exercise as in the Novice class.

Section 14. **Long Sit.** In the Long Sit in the Novice classes all the competing dogs in the class take the exercise together, except that if there are 12 or more dogs they shall, at the judge's option, be judged in groups of not less than 6 nor more than 15 dogs. Where the same judge does both classes the separate classes may be combined provided there are not more than 15 dogs competing in the two classes combined. The dogs that are in the ring shall be lined up in catalog order along one of the four sides of the ring. Handlers' armbands, weighted with leashes or other articles if necessary, shall be placed behind the dogs. On order from the judge the handlers shall sit their dogs, if they are not already sitting, and on further order from the judge to "Leave your dogs" the handlers shall give the command and/or signal to Stay and immediately leave their dogs, go to the opposite side of the ring, and line up facing their respective dogs. After one minute from the time he has ordered the handlers to leave their dogs, the judge will order the handlers "Back to your dogs" whereupon the handlers must return promptly to their dogs, each walking around and in back of his own dog to the heel position. The dogs must not move from the sitting position until after the judge says "Exercise finished".

Section 15. **Long Down.** The Long Down in the Novice classes is done in the same manner as the Long Sit except that instead of sitting the dogs the handlers, on order from the judge, will down their dogs without touching the dogs or their collars, and except further that the judge will order the handlers back after three minutes. The dogs must stay in the down position until after the judge says "Exercise finished".

Section 16. **Open Classes, Long Sit and Long Down.** These exercises in the Open classes are performed in the same manner as in the Novice classes except that after leaving their dogs the handlers must cross to the opposite side of the ring, and then leave the ring in single file as directed by the judge and go to a place designated by the judge, completely out of sight of their dogs, where they must remain until called by the judge after the expiration of the time limit of three minutes in the Long Sit and five minutes in the Long Down, from the time the judge gave the order to "Leave your dogs". On order from the judge the handlers shall return to the ring in single file in reverse order, lining up facing their dogs at the op-

posite side of the ring, and returning to their dogs on order from the judge.

Section 17. **Retrieve on the Flat.** In retrieving the dumbbell on the flat, the handler stands with his dog sitting in the heel position in a place designated by the judge, and the judge gives the orders "Throw it", whereupon the handler may give the command and/or signal to Stay, which may not be given with the hand that is holding the dumbbell, and throws the dumbbell; "Send your dog", whereupon the handler gives the command or signal to his dog to retrieve; "Take it", whereupon the handler may give a command or signal and takes the dumbbell from the dog; "Finish", whereupon the handler gives the command or signal to heel as in the Recall. The dog shall not move forward to retrieve nor deliver to hand on return until given the command or signal by the handler following order by the judge. The retrieve shall be executed at a fast trot or gallop, without unnecessary mouthing or playing with the dumbbell. The dog shall sit straight, centered immediately in front of its handler's feet and close enough so that the handler can readily take the dumbbell without moving either foot or having to stretch forward. The dog shall not touch the handler nor sit between his feet.

The dumbbell, which must be approved by the judge, shall be made of one or more solid pieces of one of the heavy hardwoods, which shall not be hollowed out. It may be unfinished, or coated with a clear finish, or painted white. It shall have no decorations or attachments but may bear an inconspicuous mark for identification. The size of the dumbbell shall be proportionate to the size of the dog. The judge shall require the dumbbell to be thrown again before the dog is sent if, in his opinion, it is thrown too short a distance, or too far to one side, or against the ringside.

Section 18. **Retrieve over High Jump.** In retrieving the dumbbell over the High Jump, the exercise is executed in the same manner as the Retrieve on the Flat, except that the dog must jump the High Jump both going and coming. The High Jump shall be jumped clear and the jump shall be as nearly as possible one and one-half times the height of the dog at the withers, as determined by the judge, with a minimum height of 8 inches and a maximum height of 36 inches. This applies to all breeds with the following exceptions:

The jump shall be once the height of the dog at the withers or 36 inches, whichever is less, for the following breeds—

Bloodhounds
Bullmastiffs

Great Danes
Great Pyrenees
Mastiffs
Newfoundlands
St. Bernards

The jump shall be once the height of the dog at the withers or 8 inches, whichever is greater, for the following breeds—

Spaniels (Clumber)
Spaniels (Sussex)
Basset Hounds
Dachshunds
Welsh Corgis (Cardigan)
Welsh Corgis (Pembroke)
Australian Terriers
Cairn Terriers
Dandie Dinmont Terriers
Norwich Terriers
Scottish Terriers
Sealyham Terriers
Skye Terriers
West Highland White Terriers
Maltese
Pekingese
Bulldogs
French Bulldogs

The handler has the option of standing any reasonable distance from the High Jump, but must stay in the same spot throughout the exercise.

The side posts of the High Jump shall be 4 feet high and the jump shall be 5 feet wide and shall be so constructed as to provide adjustment for each 2 inches from 8 inches to 36 inches. It is suggested that the jump have a bottom board 8 inches wide including the space from the bottom of the board to the ground or floor, together with three other 8 inch boards, one 4 inch board, and one 2 inch board. A 6 inch board may also be provided. The jump shall be painted a flat white. The width in inches, and nothing else, shall be painted on each side of each board in black 2 inch figures, the figure on the bottom board representing the distance from the ground or floor to the top of the board.

Section 19. Broad Jump. In the Broad Jump the handler will stand with his dog sitting in the heel position in front of and anywhere within 10 feet of the jump. On order from the judge to "Leave your dog", the handler will give his dog the command and/or signal to stay, and go to a position facing the right side of the jump, with his toes about 2 feet from the jump, and anywhere between the first and last hurdles. On order from the judge the handler shall give the command or signal to jump and the dog shall clear the entire distance of the Broad Jump without touching and, without further command or signal, return to a sitting position immediately in front of the handler as in the Recall. The handler shall change his position by executing a right angle turn while the dog is in mid-air, but shall remain in the same spot. On order from the judge, the handler will give the command or signal to Heel and the dog shall finish as in the Recall.

The Broad Jump shall consist of four hurdles, built to telescope for convenience, made of boards about 8 inches wide, the largest measuring about 5 feet in length and 6 inches high at the highest point, all painted a flat white. When set up they shall be arranged in order of size and shall be evenly spaced so as to cover a distance equal to twice the height of the High Jump as set for the particular dog, with the low side of each hurdle and the lowest hurdle nearest the dog. The four hurdles shall be used for a jump of 52" to 72", three for a jump of 32" to 48", and two for a jump of 16" to 28". The highest hurdles shall be removed first.

Section 20. Scent Discrimination. In each of these two exercises the dog must select by scent alone and retrieve an article which has been handled by its handler. The articles shall be provided by the handler and these shall consist of two sets, each comprised of five identical articles not more than six inches in length, which may be items of everyday use. One set shall be made entirely of rigid metal, and one of leather of such design that nothing but leather is visible except for the minimum amount of thread or metal necessary to hold the article together. The articles in each set must be legibly numbered each with a different number, and must be approved by the judge.

The handler shall present all 10 articles to the judge and the judge shall designate one article from each of the two sets, and shall make a written note of the numbers of the two articles he selects. These two handler's articles shall be placed on a table or chair in the ring until picked up by the handler who shall hold in his hand only one article at a time. The handler's scent may be imparted to the article only from his hands which must remain in plain sight. The handler has the option as to which article he picks up first. Before the start of the Scent Discrimination exercises the judge or the steward will handle each of the remaining 8 articles as he places them at random in the ring about 6 inches apart. The handler will stand about 15 feet from the articles with the dog sitting in the heel position. The handler and dog will face away from the articles that are on the ground or floor from the time the judge takes the handler's article until he orders "Send your dog". On order from the judge, the handler immediately will place his article on the judge's book or work sheet and the judge, without touching the article with his hands, will place it among the other articles.

On order from the judge to "Send your dog", the handler and dog will execute a Right About Turn to face the articles and the handler will simultaneously give the command or signal to retrieve. The dog shall not again sit after turning, but shall go directly to the articles. The handler may give his scent to the dog by gently touching the dog's nose with the palm of one open hand, but this may only be done while the dog is sitting at heel and the arm and hand must be returned to a natural position before handler and dog turn to face the articles. The dog shall go at a brisk pace to the articles. It may take any reasonable time to select the right article, but only provided it works continuously and does not pick up any article other than the one with its handler's scent. After picking up the right article the dog shall return at a brisk pace and complete the exercise as in the Retrieve on the Flat.

The same procedure is followed in each of the two Scent Discrimination exercises. Should a dog retrieve a wrong article in the first exercise, it shall be placed on the table or chair, and the handler's article must also be taken up from the remaining articles. The second exercise shall then be completed with one less article in the ring.

Section 21. Directed Retrieve. In this exercise the handler will provide three regular full-size, predominantly white, work gloves, which must be open and must be approved by the judge. The handler will stand with his dog sitting in the heel position, midway between and in line with the two jumps. The judge or steward will drop the three gloves across the end of the ring in view of the handler and dog, one glove in each corner and one in the center, about 3 feet from the end of the ring and, for the corner gloves, about 3 feet from the side of the ring, where all three gloves will be clearly visible to the dog and handler. There shall be no table or chair at this end of the ring.

The judge will give the order "Left" or "Right" or "Center". If the judge orders "Left" or "Right", the handler must give the command to Heel and shall pivot in place with his dog in the direction ordered, to face the designated glove. The handler shall not touch the dog to get it in position. The handler will then give his dog the direction to the designated glove with a single motion of his left hand and arm along the right side of the dog, and will give the command to retrieve either simultaneously with or immediately following the giving of the direction. The dog shall then go directly to the glove at a brisk pace and retrieve it without unnecessary mouthing or playing with it, completing the exercise as in Retrieve on the Flat.

The handler may bend his knees and body in giving the direction to the dog, after which the handler will stand erect with his arms in a natural position. The exercise shall consist of a single retrieve, but the judge shall designate different glove positions for successive dogs.

Section 22. **Signal Exercise.** In the Signal Exercise the heeling is done in the same manner as in the Heel Free exercise except that throughout the entire exercise the handler uses signals only and must not speak to his dog at any time. On order from the judge "Forward", the handler may signal his dog to walk at heel and then, on specific order from the judge in each case, the handler and the dog execute a "Left turn", "Right turn", "About turn", "Halt", "Slow", "Normal", "Fast." These orders may be given in any sequence and may be repeated if necessary. Then on order from the judge, and while the dog is walking at heel, the handler signals his dog to Stand in the heel position near the end of the ring, and on further order from the judge "Leave your dog", the handler signals his dog to Stay, goes to the far end of the ring, and turns to face his dog. Then on separate and specific signals from the judge in each case, the handler will give the signals to Drop, to Sit, to Come and to Finish as in the Recall. During the heeling part of this exercise the handler may not give any signal except where a command or signal is permitted in the Heeling exercises.

Section 23. **Directed Jumping.** In the Directed Jumping exercise the jumps shall be placed midway in the ring at right angles to the sides of the ring and 18 to 20 feet apart, the Bar Jump on one side, the High Jump on the other. The handler from a position on the center line of the ring and about 20 feet from the line of the jumps, stands with his dog sitting in the heel position. On order from the judge "Send your dog", he commands and/or signals his dog to go forward at a brisk pace toward the other end of the ring to an equal distance beyond the jumps and in the approximate center where the handler gives the command to Sit, whereupon the dog must stop and sit with its attention on the handler, but need not sit squarely. The judge will then designate which jump is to be taken first by the dog, whereupon the handler commands and/or signals his dog to re-

turn to him over the designated jump, the dog sitting in front of the handler and finishing as in the Recall. While the dog is in mid-air the handler may turn so as to be facing the dog as it returns. The judge will say "Exercise finished" after the dog has returned to the heel position. When the dog is again sitting in the heel position for the second part of the exercise, the judge will ask "Are you ready?" before giving the order "Send your dog" for the second jump. The same procedure is to be followed for the dog taking the opposite jump. It is optional with the judge which jump is taken first but both jumps must be taken to complete the exercise and the judge must not designate the jump until the dog is at the far end of the ring.

The height of the jumps shall be the same as required in the Open classes. The High Jump shall be the same as that used in the Open classes, and the Bar Jump shall consist of a bar between 2 and 2½ inches square with the four edges rounded sufficiently to remove any sharpness. The bar shall be painted a flat black and white in alternate sections of about 3 inches each. The bar shall be supported by two unconnected 4 foot upright posts about 5 feet apart. The bar shall be adjustable for each 2 inches of height from 8 inches to 36 inches, and the jump shall be so constructed and positioned that the bar can be knocked off without disturbing the uprights. The dog shall clear the jumps without touching them.

Section 24. **Group Examination.** All the competing dogs take this exercise together, except that if there are 12 or more dogs, they shall be judged in groups of not less than 6 nor more than 15 dogs, at the judge's option. The handlers and dogs that are in the ring shall line up in catalog order, side by side down the center of the ring with the dogs in the heel position. Each handler shall place his armband, weighted with leash or other article, if necessary, behind his dog. On order from the judge to "Stand your dogs", all the handlers will stand or pose their dogs, and on order from the judge "Leave your dogs", all the handlers will give the command and/or signal to Stay, walk forward to the side of the ring, then about turn and face their dogs. The judge will approach each dog in turn from the front and examine it, going over the dog with his hands as in dog show judging. When all dogs have been examined, and after the handlers have been away from their dogs for at least three minutes, the judge will promptly order the handlers "Back to your dogs", and the handlers will walk around behind their dogs to the heel position, after which the judge will say "Exercise finished". Each dog must remain standing at its position in the

line from the time its handler leaves it until the end of the exercise, and must show no shyness nor resentment.

Section 25. **Tracking.** The tracking test must be performed with the dog on leash, the length of the track to be not less than 440 yards nor more than 500 yards, the scent to be not less than one half hour nor more than two hours old and that of a stranger who will leave an inconspicuous glove or wallet, dark in color, at the end of the track where it must be found by the dog and picked up by the dog or handler. The article must be approved in advance by the judges. The tracklayer will follow the track which has been staked out with flags a day or more earlier, collecting all the flags on the way with the exception of one flag at the start of the track and one flag about 30 yards from the start of the track to indicate the direction of the track; then deposit the article at the end of the track and leave the course, proceeding straight ahead at least 50 feet. The tracklayer must wear his own shoes which, if not having leather soles, must have uppers of fabric or leather. The dog shall wear a harness to which is attached a leash between 20 and 40 feet in length. The handler shall follow the dog at a distance of not less than 20 feet, and the dog shall not be guided by the handler. The dog may be restrained by the handler, but any leading or guiding of the dog constitutes grounds for calling the handler off and marking the dog "Failed". A dog may, at the handler's option, be given one, and only one, second chance to take the scent between the two flags, provided it has not passed the second flag.

The Club or Tracking Test Secretary, after a licensed or member tracking test, shall forward two copies of the judges' marked charts, the entry forms with certifications attached, and a marked and certified copy of the catalog pages or sheets listing the dogs entered in the tracking test, to The American Kennel Club so as to reach its office within seven days after the close of the test.

CHAPTER 3

Regulations for Judging

Section 1. **Standardized Judging.** Standardized judging is of paramount importance. Judges are not permitted to inject their own variations into the exercises, but must see that each handler and dog executes the various exercises exactly as described in these regulations. A handler who is familiar with these regulations should be able to enter the ring under any judge without having to inquire how the particular judge wishes to have any exercise performed, and without being confronted with some unexpected requirement.

Section 2. **Handicapped Handlers.** Judges may modify the specific requirements of these regulations for handlers to the extent necessary to permit physically handicapped handlers to compete, provided such handlers can move about the ring without physical assistance or guidance from another person, except for guidance from the judge or from the handler of a competing dog in the ring for the group exercises. Dogs handled by such handlers shall be required to perform all parts of all exercises as described in these regulations, and shall be penalized for failure to perform any part of an exercise.

Section 3. **Judge's Report on Ring and Equipment.** The Superintendent and the officials of the club holding the obedience trial are responsible for providing rings and equipment which meet the requirements of these regulations. However, the judge must check the ring and equipment provided for his use before starting to judge, and must report to The American Kennel Club after the trial any undesirable ring conditions or deficiencies that have not been promptly corrected at his request.

Section 4. **Stewards.** The judge is in sole charge of his ring until his assignment is completed. Stewards are provided to assist him, but they may act only on the judge's instructions. Stewards shall not give information or instructions to owners and handlers except as specifically instructed by the judge, and then only in such a manner that it is clear that the instructions are those of the judge.

Section 5. **Training and Disciplining in the Ring.** The judge shall not permit any handler to train his dog nor to practice any exercise in the ring either before or after he is judged, and shall deduct points from the total score of any dog whose handler does this. A handler who disciplines his dog in the ring must be severely penalized. The penalty shall be deducted from the points available for the exercise during which the disciplining may occur, and additional points may be deducted from the total score if necessary. If the disciplining does not occur during an exercise the penalty shall be deducted from the total score. Any abuse of a dog in the ring must be immediately reported by the judge to the Bench Show or Obedience Trial Committee for action under Chapter 1, Section 43.

Section 6. **Catalog Order.** Dogs should be judged in catalog order to the extent that it is practicable to do so without holding up the judging in any ring for a dog that is entered in more than one class at the show or trial.

Judges are not required to wait for dogs for either the individual exercises or the group exercises. It is the responsibility of each contestant to be ready with his dog at ringside when required, without waiting to be called. The judge's first consideration should be the convenience of those exhibitors who are at ringside with their dogs when scheduled, and who ask no favors.

A judge may agree, on request in advance, to judge a dog earlier or later than the time scheduled by catalog order if the same dog is entered in another class which may conflict. However, a judge should not hesitate to mark absent and to refuse to judge any dog and handler that are not at ringside ready to be judged in catalog order if no such arrangement has been made in advance, nor if the dog is available while its handler is occupied with some other dog or dogs at the show or trial.

Section 7. **Judge's Book and Score Sheets.** The judge must enter the scores and sub-total score of each dog in the official judge's book immediately after each dog has been judged on the individual exercises and before judging the next dog. Scores for the group exercises and total scores must be entered in the official judge's book immediately after each group of dogs has been judged. No score may be changed except to correct an arithmetical error or if a score has been entered in the wrong column. All final scores must be entered in the judge's book before prizes are awarded. No person other than the judge may make any entry in the judge's book. Judges may use separate score sheets for their own purposes, but shall not give out nor allow exhibitors to see such sheets, nor give out any other written scores, nor permit anyone else to distribute score sheets or cards prepared by the judge. Carbon copies of the sheets in the official judge's book shall be made available through the Superintendent or Show or Trial Secretary for examination by owners and handlers immediately after the prizes have been awarded in each class. If score cards are distributed by a club after the prizes are awarded they must contain no more information than is shown in the judge's book and must be marked "unofficial score".

Section 8. **Announcement of Scores.** The judge shall not disclose any score or partial score to contestants or spectators until he has completed the

judging of the entire class or, in case of a split class, until he has completed the judging of his division; nor shall he permit anyone else to do so. After all the scores are recorded for the class, or for the division in case of a split class, the judge shall call for all available dogs that have won qualifying scores to be brought into the ring. Before awarding the prizes, the judge shall inform the spectators as to the maximum number of points for a perfect score, and shall then announce the score of each prize winner, and announce to the handler the score of each dog that has won a qualifying score.

Section 9. **Explanations and Errors.** The judge is not required to explain his scoring, and should not enter into any discussion with any contestant who appears to be dissatisfied. Any interested person who thinks that there may have been an arithmetical error or an error in identifying a dog may report the facts to one of the stewards or to the Superintendent or Show or Trial Secretary so that the matter may be checked.

Section 10. **Rejudging.** If a dog has failed in a particular part of an exercise, it shall not ordinarily be rejudged nor given a second chance; but if in the judge's opinion the dog's performance was prejudiced by peculiar and unusual conditions, the judge may at his own discretion rejudge the dog on the entire exercise.

Section 11. **Ties.** In case of a tie for any prize in a class, the dogs shall be tested again by having them perform at the same time all or some part of one or more of the regular exercises in that class. In the Utility class the dogs shall perform at the same time all or some part of the Signal exercise. The original scores shall not be changed.

Section 12. **Judge's Directions.** The judge's orders and signals should be given to the handlers in a clear and understandable manner, but in such a way that the work of the dog is not disturbed. Before starting each exercise, the judge shall ask "Are you ready?" At the end of each exercise the judge shall say "Exercise finished". Each contestant must be worked and judged separately except for the Long Sit, Long Down, and Group Examination exercises, and in running off a tie.

Section 13. **A and B Classes and Different Breeds.** The same methods and standards must be used for judging and scoring the A and B Classes, and in judging and scoring the work of dogs of different breeds.

Section 14. No Added Requirements. No judge shall require any dog or handler to do anything, nor penalize a dog or handler for failing to do anything, that is not required by these regulations.

Section 15. Additional Commands or Signals, and Interference. If a handler gives an additional command or signal not permitted by these regulations, either when no command or signal is permitted, or simultaneously with or following a permitted command or signal, or if he uses the dog's name with a permitted signal but without a permitted command, the dog shall be scored as though it had failed completely to perform that particular part of the exercise. A judge who is aware of any assistance, interference, or attempts to control a dog from outside the ring, must act promptly to stop any such double handling or interference, and should penalize the dog or give it less than a qualifying score if in his opinion it received such aid.

Section 16. Standard of Perfection. The judge must carry a mental picture of the theoretically perfect performance in each exercise and score each dog and handler against this visualized standard which shall combine the utmost in willingness, enjoyment and precision on the part of the dog, and naturalness, gentleness, and smoothness in handling. Lack of willingness or enjoyment on the part of the dog must be penalized, as must lack of precision in the dog's performance, and roughness in handling. There shall be no penalty of less than ½ point or multiple of ½ point.

Section 17. Qualifying Performance. A judge's certification in his judge's book of a qualifying score for any particular class constitutes his certification to The American Kennel Club that the dog on this particular occasion has performed all of the required exercises at least in accordance with the minimum standards and that its performance on this occasion would justify the awarding of the obedience title associated with the particular class. A qualifying score must never be awarded to a dog whose performance has not met the minimum requirements, nor to a dog that shows fear or resentment, or that relieves itself at any time in an indoor ring, or that relieves itself while performing any exercise in an outdoor ring, nor to a dog whose handler disciplines or abuses it in the ring, or carries or offers food in the ring.

In deciding whether the faulty performance of a particular exercise by a particular dog warrants a qualifying score or a score that is something less than 50% of the available points, the judge shall consider whether the awarding of an obedience title would be justified if all dogs competing in the class performed the exercise in a similar manner; and must give a score of less than 50% of the available points if he decides that it would be contrary to the best interests of the sport if all dogs competing in the class performed in a similar manner on all occasions.

Section 18. Orders and Minimum Penalties. The orders for the exercises and the standards for judging are set forth in the following sections. The lists of faults are not intended to be complete but minimum penalties are specified for most of the more common and serious faults. There is no maximum limit on penalties. A dog which makes none of the errors listed may still fail to qualify or may be scored zero for other reasons.

Section 19. Heel on Leash. The orders for this exercise are "Forward", "Halt", "Right turn", "Left turn", "About turn", "Slow", "Normal", "Fast", "Figure eight". These orders may be given in any order and may be repeated, if necessary, but the judge shall attempt to standardize the heeling pattern for all dogs in any class. The principal feature of this exercise is the ability of the dog to work as a team with its handler. A dog that is unmanageable must be scored zero. Where a handler continually tugs on the leash or adapts his pace to that of the dog, the judge must score such a dog less than 50% of the available points. Substantial deductions shall be made for additional commands or signals to Heel and for failure of dog or handler to change pace noticeably for Slow and Fast. Minor deductions shall be made for such things as poor sits, occasionally guiding the dog with the leash, heeling wide, and other imperfections in heeling. In judging this exercise the judge shall follow the handler at a discreet distance so that he may observe any signals or commands given by the handler to the dog, but without interfering with either dog or handler.

Section 20. Stand for Examination. The orders for this exercise are "Stand your dog and leave when ready", "Back to your dog". The principal features of this exercise are to stand in position before and during examination and to show no shyness nor resentment. A dog that sits before or during the examination or growls or snaps must be marked zero. A dog that moves away from the place where it was left before or during the examination, or a dog that shows any shyness or resentment, must receive less than 50% of the available points. Depending on the circumstances in each case, minor or substantial deductions must be made for any dog that moves its feet at any time, or that sits, or moves away after the examination is completed. The examination shall consist of touching only the dog's head, body and hindquarters with the fingers and palm of one hand. The scoring of this exercise will not start until the handler has given the command and/or signal to Stay, except for such things as rough treatment of the dog by its handler or active resistance by the dog to its handler's attempts to make it stand, which shall be penalized substantially.

Section 21. Heel Free. The orders and scoring for this exercise shall be the same as for Heel on Leash except that the Figure Eight is omitted in the Heel Free exercise in the Novice classes.

Section 22. Recall. The orders for this exercise are "Leave your dog", "Call your dog", "Finish". The principal features of this exercise are the prompt response to the handler's command or signal to Come, and the Stay from the time the handler leaves the dog until he calls it. A dog that does not come on the first command or signal must be scored zero. A dog that does not stay without extra command or signal, or that moves from the place where it was left, from the time the handler leaves until it is called, or that does not come close enough so that the handler could readily touch its head without moving either foot or having to stretch forward, must receive less than 50% of the points. Substantial deductions shall be made for a slow response to the Come, depending on the specific circumstances in each case; for extra commands or signals to Stay if given before the handler leaves the dog; for a dog that stands or lies down; for extra commands or signals to Finish; and for failure to Sit or Finish. Minor deductions shall be made for poor or slow Sits or Finishes, and for a dog that touches the handler on coming in or sits between his feet.

Section 23. Long Sit and Long Down. The orders for these exercises are "Sit your dogs" or "Down your dogs", "Leave your dogs", "Back to your dogs". The principal features of these exercises are to stay, and to remain in the sitting or down position, whichever is required by the particular exercise. A dog that at any time during the exercise moves a substantial distance away from the place where it was left, or that goes over to any other dog, must be marked zero. A dog that stays on the spot where it was left but that fails to remain in the sitting or down position, whichever is required by the particular exercise, until the handler has returned to the heel position, and a dog that repeatedly barks or whines, must receive less than 50% of the available points. A substantial deduction shall be made for any dog that moves even a minor distance away from the place where it was left or that barks or whines only once or twice. Depending on the circumstances in each case, a substantial or minor deduction shall be made for touching the dog or for forcing it into the Down position. There shall be a minor deduction for sitting after the handler is in the heel position but before the judge has said "Exercise finished" in the Down exercises. The dogs shall not be required to sit at the end of the Down exercises.

If a dog gets up and starts to roam or follows its handler, the judge shall promptly instruct the handler or one of the stewards to take the dog out of the ring or to keep it away from the other dogs. The judge should not attempt to judge the dogs or handlers on the manner in which they are made to Sit. The scoring of the Long Sit exercise will not start until after the judge has given the order "Leave your dogs", except for such general things as rough treatment of a dog by its handler or active resistance by a dog to its handler's attempts to make it Sit.

During these exercises the judge shall stand in such a position that all of the dogs are in his line of vision, and where he can see all the handlers in the ring, or leaving and returning to the ring, without having to turn around.

Section 24. **Drop on Recall.** The orders for this exercise are the same as for the Recall, except that the dog is required to drop when coming in on command or signal from its handler when ordered by the judge, and except that an additional order or signal to "Call your dog" is given by the judge after the Drop. The dog's prompt response to the handler's command or signal to Drop is a principal feature of this exercise, in addition to the prompt responses and the Stays as described under Recall above. A dog that does not stop and drop completely on a single command or signal must be scored zero. Minor or substantial deductions shall be made for a slow drop, depending on whether the dog is just short of perfection in this respect, or very slow in dropping or somewhere between the two extremes. All other deductions as listed under Recall above shall also apply.

The judge may designate the point at which the handler is to give the command or signal to drop by some marker placed in advance which will be clear to the handler but not obvious to the dog, or he may give the handler a signal for the Drop, but such signal must be given in such a way as not to attract the dog's attention.

If a point is designated, the dog is still to be judged on its prompt response to the handler's command or signal rather than on its proximity to the designated point.

Section 25. **Retrieve on the Flat.** The orders for this exercise are "Throw it", "Send your dog", "Take it", "Finish". The principal feature of this exercise is to retrieve promptly. Any dog that fails to go out on the first command or a dog that fails to retrieve, shall be marked zero. A dog that goes to retrieve before the command or signal is given, or that does not return with the dumbbell sufficiently close so that the handler can readily take it without moving either foot or stretching forward, must receive less than 50% of the points. Depending on the specific circumstances in each case, minor or substantial deductions shall be made for slowness in going out or returning or in picking up the dumbbell, mouthing or playing with the dumbbell, dropping the dumbbell, slowness in releasing the dumbbell to the handler, touching the handler on coming in, sitting between his feet, failure to sit in front or to Finish. Minor deductions shall be made for poor or slow Sits or Finishes.

Section 26. **Retrieve over High Jump.** The orders for this exercise are "Throw it", "Send your dog", "Take it", and "Finish". The principal features of this exercise are that the dog must go out over the jump, pick up the dumbbell and promptly return with it over the jump. The minimum penalties shall be the same as for the Retrieve on the Flat, and in addition a dog that fails both going and returning to go over the High Jump, must be marked zero. A dog that retrieves properly but goes over the High Jump in only one direction, must receive less than 50% of the available points. Substantial deductions must be made for a dog that climbs the jump or uses the top of the jump for aid in going over, in contrast to a dog that merely touches the jump. Minor deductions shall be made for touching the jump in going over.

The jumps may be preset by the stewards based on the handler's advice as to the dog's height. The judge must make certain that the jump is set at the required height for each dog. He shall verify in the ring with an ordinary folding rule or steel tape to the nearest one-half inch, the height at the withers of each dog that jumps less than 36 inches. He shall not base his decision as to the height of the jump on the handler's advice.

Section 27. **Broad Jump.** The orders for this exercise are "Leave your dog", "Send your dog", and "Finish". Any dog that refuses the jump on the first command or signal or walks over any part of the jump must be marked zero. A dog that fails to stay until the handler gives the command or signal to jump, or that fails to clear the full distance with its forelegs, shall receive less than 50% of the available points. All other penalties as listed under Recall shall also apply. It is the judge's responsibility to see that the distance jumped is that required by these Regulations for the particular dog.

Section 28. **Scent Discrimination.** The orders for each of these two exercises are "Send your dog", "Take it", and "Finish". The principal features of these exercises are the selection of the handler's article from among the other articles by scent alone, and the prompt carrying of the right article to the handler after its selection. The minimum penalties shall be the same as for the Retrieve on the Flat and in addition a dog that fails to go out to the group of articles, or that retrieves a wrong article, or that fails to bring the right article to the handler, must be marked zero for the particular exercise. Substantial deductions shall be made for a dog that picks up a wrong article, even though it puts it down again immediately, and for any roughness by the handler in imparting his scent to the dog. Minor or substantial deductions, depending on the circumstances in each case, shall be made for a dog that is slow or inattentive, or that does not work continuously. There shall be no penalty for a dog that takes a reasonably long time examining the articles, provided it is working smartly and continuously.

The judge shall select one article from each of the two sets and shall make written notes of the numbers of the two articles selected. The handler has the option as to which article he picks up first, but must give up each article immediately when ordered by the judge. The judge must see to it that the handler imparts his scent to the article only with his hands and that, between the time the handler picks up each article and the time he gives it to the judge, the article is held continuously in the handler's hands which must remain in plain sight. The judge or his steward must handle each of the eight other articles as he places them in the ring. The judge must make sure that they are properly separated before the dog is sent so that there may be no confusion of scent between articles.

Section 29. **Directed Retrieve.** The orders for this exercise are "Right", or "Center", or "Left", "Take it" and "Finish". The principal features of this exercise are that the dog stay until directed to retrieve, that it go directly to the designated glove, and that it retrieve promptly. A dog that fails to go out on command or that fails to go directly in a straight line to the glove designated, or that fails to retrieve the glove, shall be marked zero. A dog that goes to retrieve before the command is given or that does not return promptly with the glove sufficiently close so that the handler can readily take it without moving either foot or stretching forward, must receive less than 50% of the available points. Depending on the specific circumstances in each case, minor or substantial deductions shall be made for touching the dog or for excessive movements in getting it to pivot at heel facing the designated glove. All of the other penalties as listed under Retrieve on the Flat shall also apply.

Section 30. **Signal Exercise.** The orders for this exercise are "Forward", "Left turn", "Right turn", "About turn", "Halt", "Slow", "Normal", "Fast", "Stand", and "Leave your dog", and in addition the judge must give the handler signals to signal his dog to Drop, to Sit, to Come, to Finish. The orders for those parts of the exercise which are done with the dog at heel may be given in any order and may be repeated if necessary, except that the order to "Stand" shall be given when the dog and handler are walking at a normal pace. The signals given the handler after he has left his dog in the Stand position shall be given in the order specified above. The principal features of this exercise are the heeling of the dog and the Come on signal as described for the Heel and Recall exercises, and the prompt response to the signals to Drop, to Sit, and to Come. A dog that fails, on a single signal from the handler, to stand or remain standing where left, or to drop, or to sit and stay, or to come, or that receives a command or audible signal from the handler to do any of these parts of the exercise, shall receive less than 50% of the available points. All of the deductions listed under the Heel and Recall exercises shall also apply to this exercise.

Section 31. **Directed Jumping.** The judge's first order is "Send your dog", then, after the dog has stopped at the far end of the ring, the judge shall designate which jump is to be taken by the dog, whereupon the handler commands and/or signals his dog to return to him over the designated jump, the dog sitting in front of the handler and finishing as in the Recall. After the dog returns to the handler the order "Finish" is given followed by "Exercise Finished". The same sequence is then followed for the other jump. The principal features of this exercise are that the dog goes away from the handler in the direction indicated, stops when commanded, jumps as directed, and returns as in the Recall.

A dog that, in either half of the exercise, anticipates the handler's command and/or signal to go out, that does not leave its handler, that does not go out between the jumps and a substantial distance beyond, that does not stop on command, that anticipates the handler's command and/or signal to jump, that does not jump as directed, or a dog that knocks the bar off the uprights or climbs over the High Jump or uses the top of the High Jump for aid in going over, must receive less than 50% of the available points. Substantial deductions shall be made for a dog that does not stop in the approximate center of the ring, that turns, stops, or sits, before the command to Sit, or that fails to sit. Substantial or minor deductions shall be made for slowness in going out, and all of the minimum penalties as listed under Recall shall also apply.

The judge must make certain that the jumps are set at the required height for each dog by following the same procedure described for the Retrieve over High Jump.

Section 32. **Group Examination.** The orders for this exercise are "Stand your dogs", "Leave your dogs", and "Back to your dogs". The principal features of this exercise are that the dog must stand and stay, and must show no shyness nor resentment. A dog that moves a substantial distance away from the place where it was left, or that goes over to any other dog, or that sits or lies down before the handler returns to the heel position, must be marked zero. A dog that moves a minor distance away from the place where it was left, or a dog that shows any shyness or resentment or that repeatedly barks or whines, must receive less than 50% of the available points. Depending on the specific circumstances in each case, minor or substantial deductions must be made for any dog that moves its feet at any time during the exercise, or sits or lies down after the handler has returned to the heel position. The judge should not attempt to judge the dogs or handlers on the manner in which the dogs are made to stand. The scoring will not start until after the judge has given the order "Leave your dogs", except for such general things as rough treatment of a dog by its handler, or active resistance by a dog to its handler's attempts to make it stand. The dogs are not required to sit at the end of this exercise. The examination shall be conducted as in dog show judging, the judge going over each dog carefully with his hands. The judge must make a written record of any deductions immediately after examining each dog, subject to further deduction of points for subsequent faults. The judge must instruct one or more stewards to watch the other dogs while he conducts the individual examinations, and to call any faults to his attention.

Section 33. **Tracking Tests.** For obvious reasons these tests cannot be held at a dog show, and a person, though he may be qualified to judge Obedience Trials, is not necessarily capable of judging a tracking test. He must be familiar with the various conditions that may exist when a dog is required to work a scent trail. Scent conditions, weather, lay of the land, ground cover, and wind, must be taken into consideration, and a thorough knowledge of this work is necessary.

One or both of the judges must personally lay out or walk over each track after it has been laid out, a day or so before the test, so as to be completely familiar with the location of the track, landmarks and ground conditions. At least two of the right angle turns shall be well out in the open where there are no fences or other boundaries to guide the dog. No part of any track shall follow along any fence or boundary within 15 yards of such boundary. The track shall include at least two right angle turns and should include more than two such turns so that the dog may be observed working in different wind directions. Acute angle turns should be avoided whenever possible. No conflicting tracks shall be laid. No track shall cross any body of water. No part of any track shall be laid within 75 yards of any other track. In the case of two tracks going in opposite directions, however, the first flags of these tracks may be as close as 50 yards from each other. The judges shall make sure that the track is no less than 440 yards and that the tracklayer is a stranger to the dog in each case. It is the judges' responsibility to instruct the tracklayer to insure that each track is properly laid and that each tracklayer carries a copy of the chart with him in laying the track. The judges must approve the article to be left at the end of each track, must make sure that it is thoroughly impregnated with the tracklayer's scent, and must see that the tracklayer's shoes meet the requirements of these regulations.

There is no time limit provided the dog is working, but a dog that is off the track and is clearly not working should not be given any minimum time, but should be marked Failed. The handler may not be given any assistance by the judges or anyone else. If a dog is not trailing it shall not be marked Passed even though it may have found the article. In case of unforseen circumstances, the judges may in rare cases, at their own discretion. give a handler and his dog a second chance on a new track. A track for each dog entered shall be plotted on the ground not less

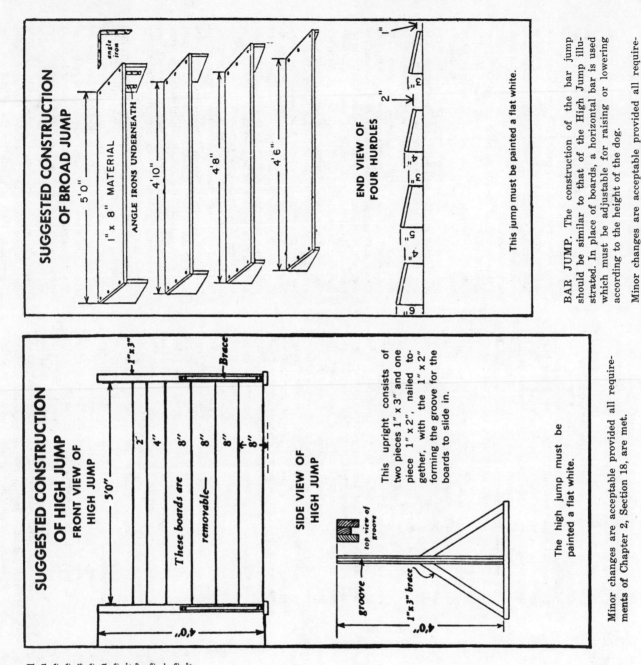

SUGGESTED CONSTRUCTION OF BROAD JUMP

5'0"

1" x 8" MATERIAL

ANGLE IRONS UNDERNEATH

angle iron

4'10"

4'8"

4'6"

END VIEW OF FOUR HURDLES

1"

2"

3"

4"

3"

5"

4"

5"

6"

This jump must be painted a flat white.

BAR JUMP. The construction of the bar jump should be similar to that of the High Jump illustrated. In place of boards, a horizontal bar is used which must be adjustable for raising or lowering according to the height of the dog.

Minor changes are acceptable provided all requirements of Chapter 2, Sections 19 and 23 are met.

SUGGESTED CONSTRUCTION OF HIGH JUMP

FRONT VIEW OF HIGH JUMP

5'0"

1" x 3"

Brace

2"

4"

8"

These boards are

8"

removable—

8"

8"

4'0"

SIDE VIEW OF HIGH JUMP

groove

top view of groove

1" x 3" brace

4'0"

This upright consists of two pieces 1" x 3" and one piece 1" x 2", nailed together, with the 1" x 2" forming the groove for the boards to slide in.

The high jump must be painted a flat white.

Minor changes are acceptable provided all requirements of Chapter 2, Section 18, are met.

than one day before the test, the track being marked by flags which the tracklayer can follow readily on the day of the test. A chart of each track shall be made up in duplicate, showing the approximate length in yards of each leg, and major landmarks and boundaries, if any. Both of these charts shall be marked at the time the dog is tracking, one by each of the judges, so as to show the approximate course followed by the dog. The judges shall sign their charts and show on each whether the dog "Passed" or "Failed", the time the tracklayer started, the time the dog started and finished tracking, a brief description of ground, wind and weather conditions, the wind direction, and a note of any steep hills or valleys.

Registration and FIELD TRIAL RULES and Standard Procedures for

POINTING BREEDS
DACHSHUNDS
RETRIEVERS
SPANIELS

Amended to June 13, 1967

The American Kennel Club
Incorporated

New York, N. Y.

THE AMERICAN KENNEL CLUB
Incorporated

Registration and Field Trial Rules

CHAPTER 1

GENERAL EXPLANATIONS

SECTION 1. The word "dog" wherever used in these Field Trial Rules and Regulations includes both sexes.

SECTION 2. The words "United States of America" wherever used in these Field Trial Rules and Regulations shall be construed to include all territories and possessions of the United States of America and all vessels sailing under the American flag.

CHAPTER 2

REGISTRATION

SECTION 1. The breeder of a dog is the person who owned the dam of that dog when the dam was bred; except that if the dam was leased at the time of breeding, the breeder is the lessee.

SECTION 2. An American-bred dog is a dog whelped in the United States of America by reason of a mating which took place in the United States of America.

SECTION 3. Any person in good standing with The American Kennel Club may apply for the registration of any pure-bred dog or litter of pure-bred dogs owned by him, by supplying The American Kennel Club with such information and complying with such conditions as it shall require.

SECTION 4. No individual dog from a litter whelped in the United States of America of which both parents are registered with The American Kennel Club shall be eligible for registration unless the litter has first been registered by the person who owned the dam at time of whelping; except that if the dam was leased at time of whelping the litter may be registered only by the lessee.

SECTION 5. No dog or litter out of a dam under eight (8) months or over twelve (12) years of age at time of mating, or by a sire under seven (7) months or over twelve (12) years of age at time of mating, will be registered unless the application for registration shall be accompanied by an affidavit or evidence which shall prove the fact to the satisfaction of The American Kennel Club.

SECTION 6. No litter of pure-bred dogs and/or no single pure-bred dog which shall be determined by The American Kennel Club to be acceptable in all other respects for registra-

tion, shall be barred from registration because of the failure, by the legal owner of all or part of said litter, or said single dog to obtain some one or more of the signatures needed to complete the applicant's chain of title to the litter or dog sought to be registered, unless that person, who, when requested, refuses so to sign the application form, shall furnish a reason therefor satisfactory to The American Kennel Club, such as the fact that at the time of service an agreement in writing was made between the owner or lessee of the site and the owner or lessee of the dam to the effect that no application for registration should be made and/or that the produce of such union should not be registered. In all cases where such an agreement in writing has been made, any person disposing of any of the produce of such union must secure from the new owner a statement in writing that he receives such produce upon the understanding that it shall not be registered. For the purpose of registering or refusing to register pure-bred dogs The American Kennel Club will recognize only such conditional sale or conditional stud agreements affecting the registration of pure-bred dogs as are in writing and are shown to have been brought to the attention of the applicant fo. registration. The American Kennel Club cannot recognize alleged conditional sale, conditional stud or other agreements not in writing which affect the registration of pure-bred dogs, until after the existence, construction and/or effect of the same shall have been determined by an action at law.

The owner or owners of a stud dog pure-bred and eligible for registration who in print or otherwise asserts or assert it to be pure-bred and eligible for registration and on the strength of such assertion secures or permits its use at stud, must pay the cost of its registration. The owner or owners of a brood bitch pure-bred and eligible for registration who in print or otherwise asserts or assert it to be pure-bred and eligible for registration and on the strength of such assertion leases it or sells its produce or secures the use of a stud by promising a puppy or puppies as payment of the stud fee in lieu of cash, must pay the cost of its registration.

That person or those persons refusing without cause to sign the application form or forms necessary for the registration of a litter of pure-bred dogs or of a single pure-bred dog and that person or those persons refusing without cause to pay the necessary fees due from him, her or them to be paid in order to complete the chain of title to a pure-bred litter or a pure-bred single dog sought to be registered when requested by The American Kennel Club may be suspended from the privileges of The American Kennel Club or fined as the Board of Directors of The American Kennel Club may elect.

The registration of a single pure-bred dog out of a litter eligible for registration may be secured by its legal owner as a one-dog litter registration and the balance of the litter may be refused registration where the breeder or the owner or lessee of the dam at the date of whelping wrongfully has refused to register the litter and that person or those persons so wrongfully refusing shall be suspended from the privileges of The American Kennel Club or fined as the Board of Directors of The American Kennel Club may elect.

SECTION 7. No change in the name of a dog registered with The American Kennel Club will be allowed to be made.

SECTION 8. Any person in good standing with The American Kennel Club may apply for transfer of ownership to him of any registered dog acquired by him by supplying The American Kennel Club with such information and complying with such conditions as it shall require.

SECTION 9. The American Kennel Club will not protect any person against the use by any other person of a kennel name in the registration of dogs with The American Kennel Club or in the entry of registered dogs in field trials held under The American Kennel Club rules, unless the kennel name has been registered with The American Kennel Club.

SECTION 10. On and after October 1, 1948, applications for the use of a kennel name as a prefix in the registering and running of dogs shall be made to The American Kennel Club on a form which will be supplied by said Club upon request, and said application must be accompanied by a fee, the amount of which shall be determined by the Board of Directors of The American Kennel Club. The Board will then consider such application and if it approves of the name selected will grant the right to the use of such name only as a prefix for a period of five (5) years.

The recorded owner shall have first consideration of the grant to use said kennel name for additional consecutive five (5) year terms upon receipt of the application for renewal accompanied by the renewal fee, the amount of which shall be determined by the Board of Directors, when received before the date of expiration of the original grant but the grant for any five (5) year renewal term will be made only at the expiration of the previous term.

In the event of the death of a recorded owner of a registered kennel name, his executors, administrators or legal heirs, upon submission of proper proof of their status may use the name as a prefix during the remainder of the five (5) year term of use and the legal heir of the deceased recorded owner, or the executors or administrators acting in his behalf, shall have first consideration of the grant to the use of said name for additional terms, as provided heretofore in this section.

SECTION 11. If the recorded owner of a registered kennel name granted after October 1, 1948, desires to transfer ownership of or an interest in said kennel name to a new owner, application to transfer such name for the unexpired term must be made to The American Kennel Club on a form which will be supplied by said Club upon request. The application must be submitted for the approval of the Board of Directors of The American Kennel Club and accompanied by a fee, the amount of which shall be determined by the Board of Directors of The American Kennel Club.

Any kennel name granted by The American Kennel Club prior to October 1, 1948 may be transferred by its present owner or owners to another only by consent and on certain conditions and payment of fee as determined by the Board of Directors of The American Kennel Club.

SECTION 12. In the case of any registered kennel name which is recorded as jointly owned by two or more persons, application to transfer the interest of one co-owner to another co-owner, may be made to The American Kennel Club on a form which will be supplied by said Club upon request. The application must be submitted for the approval of the Board of Directors of The American Kennel Club but no fee will be charged for such a transfer.

SECTION 13. The protection of all kennel names registered between March 1, 1934 and October 1, 1948 shall depend upon their continuous use by registered owners. Neglect by the recorded owner of a registered kennel name to use such name in the registration of dogs for a continuous period of six (6) years or more shall be considered such an abandonment of the name as to justify The American Kennel Club in refusing to protect its use unless the owner or owners thereof prior to the expiration of such six (6) year period shall notify The American Kennel Club of his, her or their desire to retain the same.

CHAPTER 2A

SECTION 1. The word "person" as used in this chapter includes any individual, partnership, firm, corporation, association or organization of any kind.

The word "dog" as used in this chapter includes a dog or puppy of any age and either sex.

SECTION 2. Each person who breeds, keeps, transfers ownership or possession of, or deals in dogs which are registered or to be registered with The American Kennel Club, whether he acts as principal or agent or sells on consignment, must make in connection therewith and preserve for five years adequate and accurate records. The Board of Directors shall by regulation designate the specific information which must be included in such records.

SECTION 3. Each person who breeds, keeps, transfers ownership or possession of or deals in dogs that are registered or to be registered with The American Kennel Club, whether he acts as principal or agent or sells on consignment, must follow such practices as, consistent with the number of dogs involved, will preclude any possibility of error in identification of any individual dog or doubt as to the parentage of any particular dog or litter.

SECTION 4. The American Kennel Club or its duly authorized representatives shall have the right to inspect the records required to be kept and the practices required to be followed by these rules and by any regulations adopted under them, and to examine any dog registered or to be registered with The American Kennel Club.

SECTION 5. Each person who transfers ownership or possession of a dog that is registered or to be registered with The American Kennel Club must describe the dog in the records of The American Kennel Club in writing to the person acquiring the dog at the time of transfer, either on a bill of sale or otherwise. The Board of Directors shall by regulation designate the descriptive information required.

SECTION 6. The American Kennel Club may refuse to register any dog or litter or to record the transfer of any dog, for the sole reason that the application is not supported by the records required by these rules and the regulations adopted under them.

SECTION 7. Any person who is required to keep records and who fails to do so or who fails or refuses when requested to make such records available for inspection by The American Kennel Club or its duly authorized representatives, may be suspended from all privileges of The American Kennel Club by the Board of Directors.

Any person who fails to follow such practices as will preclude any possibility of error in identification of an individual dog or doubt as to the parentage of a particular dog or litter or who fails or refuses to permit The American Kennel Club or its duly authorized representatives to examine such practices, or to examine a dog that is registered or to be registered with The American Kennel Club, may be suspended from all privileges of The American Kennel Club by the Board of Directors.

CHAPTER 3

FIELD TRIALS DEFINED

A MEMBER FIELD TRIAL is a field trial at which championship points may be awarded, given by a club or association which is a member of The American Kennel Club.

A LICENSED FIELD TRIAL is a field trial at which championship points may be awarded, given by a club or association which is not a member of The American Kennel Club, but which has been specially licensed by The American Kennel Club to give the specific field trial designated in the license.

A SANCTIONED FIELD TRIAL is an informal field trial at which dogs may compete but not for championship points, held by a club or association, whether or not a member of The American Kennel Club, by obtaining the sanction of The American Kennel Club.

CHAPTER 4

MAKING APPLICATION TO HOLD A FIELD TRIAL

SECTION 1. Each member club or association is entitled to hold one show and/or one field trial a year without payment of a fee to The American Kennel Club, but must pay a fee of fifteen ($15.00) dollars for each other show and/or field trial which it may hold during the same calendar year.

SECTION 2. Each member club or association which has held a field trial or field trials in any one year shall have first right to claim the corresponding dates for its trial or trials to be held in the next succeeding year.

SECTION 3. A member club or association must apply to The American Kennel Club for leave to hold a field trial, stating in the application the day or days upon which and the place where it desires to hold such field trial. This application will be referred to the Board of Directors of The American Kennel Club which will consider the same and notify the member club or association of its approval or disapproval of the dates and place selected.

SECTION 4. The use of a club's name for field trial purposes cannot be transferred.

SECTION 5. If a non-member club or association wishes to hold a field trial it must apply to The American Kennel Club, on a form which will be supplied by The American Kennel Club upon request, for leave to hold such field trial stating in the application the day or days upon which and the place where it desires to hold such field trial and giving to The American Kennel Club such information which regard to the Constitution and By-Laws, and the names of the officers and members and the financial responsibility of the applying non-member club or association as The American Kennel Club may demand and shall pay a license fee for the privilege of holding such field trial, the amount of which fee shall be fixed and determined by the Board of Directors of The American Kennel Club. This application will be referred to the Board of Directors of The American Kennel Club which will consider the same and notify the non-member club or association of its approval or disapproval of the dates and place selected.

If the Board of Directors shall disapprove the application, the license fee will be returned to said non-member club or association.

SECTION 6. A non-member specialty club may be licensed to hold a field trial, if the consent in writing that it may be given first shall be obtained from the member specialty club formed for the improvement of the breed sought to be run which first was admitted to be a member of The American Kennel Club, which member club is commonly known as the Parent Club.

If a Parent Club unreasonably shall withhold its consent in writing to the holding of such field trial the non-member specialty club may appeal to the Board of Directors of The American Kennel Club at any time after one month from the time when said consent was requested and a committee of said Board appointed by said Board or between sittings of said Board appointed by the President of The American Kennel Club or in his absence by the Executive Vice-President of The American Kennel Club shall hear the parties who may present their respective contentions either orally or in writing and in its discretion may issue a license to the non-member specialty club to hold such field trial.

SECTION 7. If a member or non-member club or association wishes to hold a sanctioned field trial, it must apply to The American Kennel Club for leave to hold such field trial, stating in the application the date or dates upon which and the place where it desires to hold such field trial, the names and addresses of the officers of the club or association, and the names and addresses of the Judges, provided, however, that a Beagle Association's Secretary may file a blanket application for the regular Spring Derby Sanctioned Trials of the member clubs of that Association. The application will be referred to the Board of Directors of The American Kennel Club, which will consider the same and notify the club or association of its approval or disapproval of the dates, place and Judges selected. No fee is charged by The American Kennel Club for holding a sanctioned field trial.

Sanctioned field trials shall be governed by such simple rules and regulations as from time to time shall be determined by the Board of Directors.

SECTION 8. The Board of Directors of The American Kennel Club will not approve applications for field trials where dates conflict unless it be shown that the granting of such application will not work to the detriment of either field trial club which has applied.

A club holding field trials must not advertise or publish the date of any field trial which it proposes to hold until that date has been approved by The American Kennel Club.

CHAPTER 5
RIBBONS AND PRIZES

SECTION 1. All clubs or associations holding field trials under the rules of The American Kennel Club, except sanctioned field trials, shall use the following colors for their prize ribbons or rosettes:

First prize—Blue.
Second prize—Red.
Third prize—Yellow.
Fourth prize—White.
Special prize—Dark Green.

SECTION 2. Each ribbon or rosette, except those used at sanctioned field trials, shall be at least 2 inches wide, and approximately 8 inches long; and bear on its face a facsimile of the seal of The American Kennel Club, the name of the prize, and the name of the field trial-giving club with numerals of year and date of trial.

SECTION 3. If ribbons are given at sanctioned field trials, they shall be of the following colors, but may be of any design or size:

First prize—Rose.
Second prize—Brown.
Third prize—Light Green.
Fourth prize—Gray.
Special prize—A combination of any of these colors.

SECTION 4. If money prizes are offered, a fixed amount for each prize shall be stated.

SECTION 5. All prizes not money which may be offered shall be accurately described or the value stated. Stud services shall not be accepted as prizes.

CHAPTER 6
JUDGES

SECTION 1. Persons judging field trials are not required to obtain licenses and a field trial club may submit the name of any reputable person who is in good standing with The American Kennel Club for approval to judge at its field trial. Such approved Judges may run dogs in any stakes in which they are not judging, excepting as the rules applying to trials for particular breeds may provide otherwise.

SECTION 2. Substitute or additional Judges may be appointed by a field trial club at its field trial, if occasion demands it, provided however that said substitute or additional Judges are persons in good standing with The American Kennel Club. When additional Judges are used, they shall always act in conjunction with one or more of the regularly approved Judges if present. The American Kennel Club shall be promptly notified of additional or substitute Judges officiating.

CHAPTER 7
APPOINTMENT OF FIELD TRIAL SECRETARY
APPOINTMENT, RESPONSIBILITIES AND AUTHORITIES OF FIELD TRIAL COMMITTEE

SECTION 1. A club or association that has been granted permission by The American Kennel Club to hold a field trial must appoint a Field Trial Secretary and submit his or her name to The American Kennel Club for its records on a form that will be supplied by the AKC. Any qualified person who is in good standing with The American Kennel Club may act as Field Trial Secretary.

SECTION 2. A club or association that has been granted permission by The American Kennel Club to hold a field trial must appoint a Field Trial Committee which will have complete responsibility for the planning and conducting of the trial. This committee shall be comprised of at least five members of the club and may include the Field Trial Secretary.

SECTION 3. The field trial committee of a club holding a licensed or member trial shall have the authority to decide upon any matter arising during the running of the trial, except a matter coming within the jurisdiction of the judges, but such committee decisions must be made in accord with the general field trial rules and with the rules that apply to the particular type of trial being held.

CHAPTER 8

PREMIUMS LISTS, ENTRY FORMS, CLOSING OF ENTRIES, DRAWING OF ENTRIES

SECTION 1. After a club or association has been granted permission by The American Kennel Club to hold a field trial and before its premium list is printed, it must send to The American Kennel Club, for approval, two copies of a Questionnaire Form (supplied by the AKC) which will give the exact location of the trial, the dates on which it will be held, and set forth in detail the stakes to be run and their conditions; a complete list of the money, ribbon prizes and other prizes which it wishes to offer; a list of the names and addresses of the judges and the stakes they are to judge; the names and addresses of the officers of the club, including the field trial secretary; the name and address of the chairman and the names of the other members of the field trial committee; the date, hour and place of the closing of entries; and the date, hour and place of the drawing of entries.

The place where entries are to be drawn need not be identical with the place where entries are received. Each premium list shall specify that the Field Trial Secretary is to receive entries.

Premiums lists, when printed, shall contain all the information set forth on the Questionnaire Form as approved by The American Kennel Club and shall be the official size, 6 by 9 inches.

SECTION 2. Every premium list shall contain one or more copies of the official American Kennel Club entry form as approved by the Board of Directors of the AKC. Any club may obtain a sample of the official entry form applicable to the particular type of trial to be held. Requests should be in writing, addressed to the Secretary of The American Kennel Club.

SECTION 3. Two copies of the premium list and entry form when printed must be sent to The American Kennel Club at time of distribution to prospective entrants.

SECTION 4. Such extracts from the rules as shall be designated by the Board of Directors of The American Kennel Club shall be furnished with every premium list and entry form.

SECTION 5. Field Trial Committees may make such regulations or additional rules for the government of their field trials as shall be considered necessary, provided such regulations or additional rules do not conflict with any rule of The American Kennel Club. Such regulations or additional rules shall be printed in the premium list and violations thereof shall be considered the same as violations of the Rules and Regulations of The American Kennel Club.

SECTION 6. If the rules of a particular type of trial provide for the acceptance of entries after the published closing date and hour, the conditions under which such entries will be accepted must be stated in the premium list.

CHAPTER 9

ELIGIBILITY OF DOGS FOR ENTRY
FULL COMPLETION OF ENTRY FORMS

SECTION 1. Every dog entered in a licensed or member trial must be at least six months of age on the first day of the trial and must either be registered in The American Kennel Club stud book, or be part of a previously registered litter or, if imported into the United States, must be registered with a foreign registry organization whose pedigrees are acceptable for AKC registration; except that the foregoing shall not apply until January 1, 1967 to dogs that have won points or credits toward a Field Championship on or before March 13, 1962.

SECTION 2. An unregistered dog that is part of a registered litter or an imported dog with an acceptable foreign pedigree may, without special AKC approval, be entered in three trials before it is registered, but only if the litter registration number or the foreign registration number and the name of the country are shown on the entry form and if the same name, which in the case of an imported dog must be the name on the foreign pedigree, is used for the dog each time. No unregistered dog may be entered more than three times unless the owner has received from The American Kennel Club an extension notice authorizing further entries for a specified time. The owner may apply by letter to the Field Trial Records Department of The American Kennel Club for such an extension, explaining the reasons for the delay in registration and demonstrating that it is due to circumstances for which he is not responsible.

All extension notices issued will be void upon the registration of the dog or at the expiration of the period for which the extension has been granted, if that occurs earlier, but upon written application further extension may be issued.

SECTION 3. If a dog should become registered under a name that is different from that under which it was entered prior to registration, the registered name followed by "formerly shown as" and the former name shall be given on the entry form for subsequent trials until the dog has placed in one of the regular stakes at a licensed or member trial.

SECTION 4. Every dog must be entered in the name of the person who actually owned the dog at the time entries closed. The right to enter and run a dog cannot be transferred. A registered dog which has been acquired by some person other than the owner as recorded with The American Kennel Club must be entered in the name of its new owner at any field trial for which entries close after the date on which the dog was acquired, and application for transfer of ownership must be sent to The American Kennel Club by the new owner within seven days after the last day of the trial. The new owner should state on the entry form that transfer application has been mailed to The American Kennel Club or will be mailed shortly. If there is any unavoidable delay in obtaining the completed application required to record the transfer, The American Kennel Club may grant a reasonable extension of time provided the new owner notifies the field trial records department of The American Kennel Club by mail within seven days after the trial, of the reason for the delay. If an entry is made by a duly authorized agent of the owner, the name of the actual owner must be shown on the entry form. If a dog is owned by an association, the name of the association and a list of its officers must be shown on the entry form.

SECTION 5. Each entry form must be completed in full and the information given on the entry form must be that which applies to the entered dog. Each entry form must be signed by the owner or his agent duly authorized to make the entry.

SECTION 6. No entry shall be accepted from any person who is not in good standing with The American Kennel Club on the day of the closing of the entries. Before accepting any entries, a list of persons not in good standing must be obtained by the Field Trial Secretary from The American Kennel Club.

SECTION 7. No entry shall be made under a kennel name unless that name has been registered with The American Kennel Club. All entries made under a kennel name must be signed with the kennel name followed by the word "registered." An "entrant" is the individual, or, if a partnership, all the members of the partnership entering in a field trial. In the case of such entry by a partnership every member of the partnership shall be in good standing with The American Kennel Club before the entry will be accepted; and in case of any infraction of these rules, all the partners shall be held equally responsible.

SECTION 8. Owners are responsible for errors made in entry forms, regardless of who may have made such errors.

SECTION 9. No dog shall be eligible to compete at any field trial, no dog shall be brought into the grounds or premises of any field trial, and any dog which may have been brought into the grounds or premises of a field trial shall immediately be removed, if it

(a) shows clinical symptoms of distemper, infectious hepatitis, leptospirosis or other communicable disease, or

(b) is known to have been in contact with distemper, infectious hepatitis, leptospirosis or other communicable disease within thirty days prior to the opening of the trial, or

(c) has been kenneled within thirty days prior to the opening of the trial on premises on which there existed distemper, infectious hepatitis, leptospirosis or other communicable disease.

SECTION 10. A dog is not eligible to be entered in any field trial in any stake in which championship points are given, if the Judge of that stake or any member of his family has owned, sold, held under lease, boarded, trained or handled the dog within one year prior to the date of the field trial.

SECTION 11. Any field trial-giving club which accepts an entry fee other than that published in its premium list or entry form, or in any way discriminates between entrants shall be disciplined. No club or member of any club shall give or offer to give any owner or handler any special inducements, such as reduced entry fees, allowances for board or transportation or other incentive of value for a certain number of entries or shall give or offer to give in consideration of entering a certain number of dogs, any prizes or prize money, except the officially advertised prizes or prize money, which prize money shall be for a stated sum or a portion of the entry fees. Any club found guilty of violating this rule shall be barred from holding licensed or sanctioned trials, and if a member of The American Kennel Club, may be expelled from membership therein. All persons found guilty of paying or receiving any monies, special inducements or allowances in violation of the foregoing shall be disciplined, even to the extent of being deprived of all privileges of The American Kennel Club for a stated time or indefinitely.

SECTION 12. A Field Trial Committee may decline any entries or may remove any dog from its trial for cause, but in each such instance shall file good and sufficient reasons for so doing with The American Kennel Club.

SECTION 13. Any dog entered and present at a field trial must compete in all stakes in which it is entered, unless excused by the Field Trial Committee at that trial after consultation with the Judges.

CHAPTER 10
CANCELLATIONS OF AWARDS

SECTION 1. If a dog has been entered in any stake for which it is ineligible, or in the name of an owner other than the actual owner at the time entries closed, or if run in a stake for which it has not been entered or if its entry is deemed invalid by The American Kennel Club under the provisions of Section 9, Chapter 5, of these rules, any resulting award shall be cancelled by The American Kennel Club, and such dog shall not be counted as having been in competition in determining championship ratings.

SECTION 2. If the win of a dog shall be cancelled, the dog next in order of merit shall be moved up, and the win of the dog moved up shall be counted the same as if it had been the original award.

SECTION 3. If the win of a dog shall be cancelled by The American Kennel Club, the entrant of the dog shall return all prizes for such win to the Secretary of the field trial-giving club within ten (10) days of receipt of notice from The American Kennel Club of said cancellation.

CHAPTER 11
PROTESTS AGAINST DOGS

SECTION 1. A protest against a dog may be made by any entrant or any member club of The American Kennel Club. It shall be in writing, and be lodged with the Secretary of the field trial-giving club within seven (7) days of the last day of the field trial unless the same be made by The American Kennel Club, provided, however, that a protest calling for a decision as to the physical condition of a dog which can be determined only by a veterinarian or at the time of running shall be made before the closing of the field trial. No protest will be entertained unless accompanied by a deposit of five ($5.00) dollars, which will be returned if the protest is sustained. This does not apply to protests by The American Kennel Club.

SECTION 2. If a protest shall be made against a dog during the holding of a field trial, the Field Trial Committee shall hold a meeting as soon as possible and give all parties concerned an opportunity to be heard and shall at once render its decision. If a protest shall be made subsequent to the field trial, it shall be decided by the field trial-giving club within thirty (30) days of its receipt. Five days' notice of the date and place of hearing shall be given to all parties concerned. Written copies of all decisions on protests shall be forwarded immediately to The American Kennel Club.

SECTION 3. An appeal to The American Kennel Club from a decision of a Field Trial Committee where a dog has been protested may be taken, and shall be forwarded to The American Kennel Club within seven (7) days of the date on which the decision was rendered together with a deposit of ten ($10.00) dollars. If the decision be sustained the deposit shall be forfeited, but if reversed, the deposit shall be returned.

CHAPTER 12
RECORDING OF A FIELD CHAMPION

SECTION 1. Dogs that complete the requirements for a field championship as described in the various chapters of these rules and if registered in The American Kennel Club Stud Book will be recorded Field Champions by The American Kennel Club and Championship Certificates issued to owners of record.

Such Field Champions may be designated as "Dual Champions" when and if they become Show Champions. No certificate will be issued for a Dual Championship.

CHAPTER 13
JUDGES' AWARD OF MERIT

At any licensed or member field trial, other than Basset Hound Trials, the judges may make a "Judges' Award of Merit" in any stake to any unplaced dog for particularly excellent work. The name and registration number of each dog to which such an award is made shall be noted on the back of the page in the judges' book for the stake in which the award was made.

CHAPTER 14
WHAT HAS TO BE SENT TO THE AMERICAN KENNEL CLUB AFTER A FIELD TRIAL

SECTION 1. At the conclusion of the judging of each stake, a club holding a field trial shall provide, for the Judges' signatures, a judging sheet of the stake judged, showing full particulars of all dogs placed. At the conclusion of the trial, the Field Trial Secretary shall certify to the Judges' signatures on each judging sheet and shall certify to the number of entries and starters in each stake.

The judging sheets, inserted in the covers of the judging book, together with all entry forms and a full report of the trial, shall be sent to The American Kennel Club so as to reach The American Kennel Club no later than seven days after the closing date of the trial. Clubs which do not get the records of their trials in to The American Kennel Club within the seven day period will be fined at the rate of one dollar per day for each day's lateness and will be subject to such other penalties as may be imposed by the Board of Directors.

The trial report shall contain a list of the names of all members of the Field Trial Committee who were present at the trial, the names and complete addresses of all of the Judges, and the name and address of the Field Trial Secretary.

SECTION 2. A Judge's decision shall be final in all cases affecting the merits of the dogs. Full discretionary power is given to the Judge to withhold any, or all, awards for want of merit.

CHAPTER 15
ENFORCEMENT OF RULES

Field Trial Committees and Field Trial Secretaries shall be held responsible for the enforcement of all rules and procedures relating to field trials, and must provide themselves with a copy of this book for reference.

CHAPTER 16
EXTRACTS FROM BY-LAWS
DISCIPLINE

Article XII of the Constitution and By-Laws of The American Kennel Club provides:

SECTION 1. Any club or association, or person or persons interested in pure-bred dogs may prefer charges against any other club or association, or person or persons for conduct alleged to have been prejudicial to the best interests of pure-bred dogs, dog shows, obedience trials or field trials, or prejudicial to the best interests of The American Kennel Club, which charges shall be made in writing in duplicate setting forth in detail the nature thereof, shall be signed and sworn to by an officer of the club or association or by the person or persons making the same before some person qualified to administer oaths and shall be sent to The American Kennel Club together with a deposit of ten ($10.00) dollars, which sum shall become the property of The American Kennel Club if said charges shall not be sustained, or shall be returned if said charges are sustained, or if The American Kennel Club shall refuse to entertain jurisdiction thereof.

SECTION 2. The Bench Show, Obedience Trial or Field Trial Committee of a club or association shall have the right to suspend any person from the privileges of The American Kennel Club for conduct prejudicial to the best interests of pure-bred dogs, dog shows, obedience trials, field trials or The American Kennel Club, alleged to have occurred in connection with or during the progress of its show, obedience trial or field trial, after the alleged offender has been given an opportunity to be heard.

Notice in writing must be sent promptly by registered mail by the Bench Show, Obedience Trial or Field Trial Committee to the person suspended and a duplicate notice giving the name and address of the person suspended and full details as to the reasons for the suspension must be forwarded to The American Kennel Club within seven (7) days.

An appeal may be taken from a decision of a Bench Show, Obedience Trial or Field Trial Committee. Notice in writing claiming such appeal together with a deposit of five ($5.00) dollars must be sent to The American Kennel Club within thirty (30) days after the date of suspension. The Board of Directors may itself hear said appeal or may refer it to a Committee of the Board, or to a Trial Board to be heard. The deposit shall become the property of The American Kennel Club if the decision is confirmed, or shall be returned to the appellant if the decision is not confirmed.

SECTION 3. Upon receipt of duly preferred charges the Board of Directors of The American Kennel Club at its election either may itself consider the same or send the same to a Trial Board for hearing.

In either case a notice which shall state that said charges have been filed and shall set forth a copy of the same shall be sent to the club or association, or person or persons against which or whom said charges have been preferred which club or association, or person or persons herein shall be known as and called the defendant. The club or association, or person or persons which or who shall have preferred said charges herein shall be known as and called the complainant.

Said notice also shall set forth a time and place at which the defendant may attend and present any defense or answer which the defendant may wish to make.

If the complainant shall fail or refuse to appear and prosecute said charges or if the defendant shall fail or refuse to appear and present a defense at the time and place designated for the hearing of said charges, without giving a reasonable excuse for such failure or refusal, the Board of Directors or the Trial Board to which said charges have been referred may suspend whichever party shall be so in default from the privileges of The American Kennel Club for a period of six (6) months or until such time as the party so in default shall be prepared to appear ready and willing to prosecute or defend said charge, as the case may be.

SECTION 4. The Board of Directors shall have the power to investigate any matters which may be brought to its attention in connection with the objects for which this Club was founded, or it may appoint a Committee or Trial Board to investigate, in which event the same procedure shall be followed and the same rules shall apply as in a trial before a Trial Board.

If after such investigation the Board of Directors believes that sufficient evidence exists to warrant the filing of charges, it may file or direct the filing of such charges. The Board of Directors acting in accordance with the provisions of this Article may prefer charges for conduct prejudicial to the best interests of The American Kennel Club against persons who shall bring to its attention any matter which upon investigation shall be found to have been reported to it from malicious or untruthful motives or to have been based upon suspicion without foundation of fact or knowledge.

SECTION 5. The Board of Directors of The American Kennel Club shall have power to prefer charges against any association, or other club, or person or persons, for conduct alleged to be prejudicial to pure-bred dogs, dog shows, obedience trials or field trials or to the best interests of The American Kennel Club, and pending the final determination of any such charges, may withhold the privileges of The American Kennel Club from any such other person or body against whom charges are pending.

SECTION 6. The Board of Directors shall have the power to suspend from the privileges of The American Kennel Club any member or Delegate pending final action by the Delegates in accordance with the provisions of this section, for conduct alleged to have been prejudicial to the best interests of The American Kennel Club or for violation of its Constitution, By-Laws or Rules.

The Board of Directors shall then file charges and promptly set a date for a hearing and send to such suspended member or Delegate by registered mail at least ten days prior to the date so fixed, notice of the time when and the place where the suspended member or Delegate may be heard in its or his defense. Said notice shall also set forth a copy of the charges.

The Board of Directors may itself hear the evidence of the suspended member or Delegate and any witnesses or may refer the charges to a Committee of the Board or to a Trial Board to take the testimony and to report its findings and recommendations to the Board of Directors.

The Board of Directors, after hearing or reviewing the evidence, shall report its findings to The American Kennel Club at the next regular meeting of the Club, whereupon the Delegates shall take action upon said findings and by a majority vote of the Delegates present may reinstate, continue the suspension for a stated time or expel such member or Delegate from The American Kennel Club.

SECTION 7. The American Kennel Club shall have the power by a two-thirds vote of the Delegates present and voting at any regular meeting to suspend from the privileges of The American Kennel Club any member or Delegate for conduct alleged to have been prejudicial to the best interests of The American Kennel Club or for violation of its Constitution, By-Laws or Rules.

The order of suspension thus made shall then be referred to the Board of Directors for hearing and report under the procedure as set forth in Paragraphs 2, 3, and 4 of Section 6 of this Article.

SECTION 8. The Board of Directors of The American Kennel Club shall have power to hear as an original matter any charges preferred and to review and finally determine any appeal which may be made to the Board of Directors from the decision of a Trial Board, Bench Show, Obedience Trial or Field Trial Committee, and in each instance in which it shall find the charges to have been sustained, it shall impose such penalty as said Board of Directors may decide to be just and proper.

SECTION 9. The Board of Directors of The American Kennel Club and any Trial Board of The American Kennel Club with the permission of the Board of Directors of The American Kennel Club first obtained in writing may, in the discretion of said Board of Directors, and if necessary at the Club's expense, summon witnesses or a member of any Trial Board, Bench Show Committee, Obedience Trial or Field Trial Committee to attend any and all hearings held under the provisions of Articles XII and XIII of the Constitution and By-Laws of The American Kennel Club. Said Board of Directors may suspend from the privileges of The American Kennel Club for a period of six months or until such time as he or she shall appear and be prepared and willing to testify any person so summoned who without reasonable excuse shall fail to appear and testify.

SECTION 10. The Board of Directors of The American Kennel Club shall, at the next meeting of the Board, after an appeal is made from the decision of a Trial Board, Bench Show, Obedience Trial or Field Trial Committee, name a date for the hearing of such appeal and shall cause notice of the time when and the place where said hearing is to be held to be sent to all parties in interest by registered mail at least fourteen (14) days prior to the date named.

SECTION 11. Penalties may range from a reprimand or fine to suspension for life from all privileges of The American Kennel Club.

SECTION 12. The Treasurer of The American Kennel Club shall enforce all monetary penalties.

SECTION 13. The suspension or disqualification of a person shall date from the day of the perpetration of the act or from any date subsequent thereto which shall be fixed after a hearing by a Trial Board or by the Board of Directors of The American Kennel Club and shall apply to all dogs owned or subsequently acquired by the person so suspended or disqualified.

SECTION 14. All privileges of The American Kennel Club shall be withheld from any person suspended or disqualified.

SECTION 15. Any club, association or organization which shall hold a dog show, obedience trial, field trial or dog exhibition of any kind not in accordance with the rules of The American Kennel Club which apply to such show, obedience trial, field trial or exhibition may be disciplined even to the extent of being deprived of all privileges of The American Kennel Club for a stated period of time or indefinitely, and if such club, association or organization shall be a member of The American Kennel Club, it may be expelled from membership therein.

SECTION 16. No club or association licensed by The American Kennel Club to give a show, obedience trial, hold a field trial or give a dog exhibition of any kind shall employ in any capacity, accept the donation of a prize or money from, or permit to be within the walls or boundaries of its building or grounds, if a dog show, obedience trial, or its grounds, if a field trial, save only as a spectator, any person known to be under suspension or disqualification from the privileges of The American Kennel Club or any employee or member of a corporation which shall be under suspension or disqualification from the privileges of The American Kennel Club. And any contract for floor space at a show, or contract for advertising space in a catalogue, premium list or other printed matter, in connection with the giving of said show, shall bear upon it the following condition: "This space is sold with the understanding that should the privileges of The American Kennel Club be withdrawn from the purchaser of this space prior to the carrying out of this contract, this contract is thereby automatically cancelled, and any money paid by the purchaser for such space shall be refunded."

SECTION 17. No member club or association under suspension shall be represented by its Delegate and no Delegate under suspension shall act for a member or in any official capacity for The American Kennel Club during the period of suspension.

SECTION 18. Any association, club, person or persons suspended or disqualified by The American Kennel Club or from whom the privileges of The American Kennel Club have been withheld, may apply for reinstatement or restoration of privileges upon paying a fee the amount of which may be fixed and determined by the Board of Directors of The American Kennel Club. Until said fee has been paid the application shall not be acted upon.

SECTION 19. As much of Article XII of these By-Laws as the Board of Directors of The American Kennel Club shall indicate shall be printed in any book or pamphlet which The American Kennel Club shall cause to be published containing the Rules of said Club.

CHAPTER 17

EXTRACTS FROM BY-LAWS

TRIAL BOARDS

Article XIII of the Constitution and By-Laws of The American Kennel Club provides:

SECTION 1. Trial Boards shall be appointed from time to time by the Board of Directors of The American Kennel Club and shall consist of three members for each Board, one of whom, if practicable, should be an attorney-at-law, and no one of whom shall be a Director of The American Kennel Club. In case one or more members of a Trial Board shall be unable to sit in any given case, the President, or in his absence, the Executive Vice-President of The American Kennel Club may appoint a substitute or substitutes for such case. In case of the absence of one or more members of said Board the remaining member or members may hear and determine a case if the parties being heard shall consent thereto.

SECTION 2. Trial Boards shall hear and decide by a majority vote matters submitted to them by the Board of Directors and shall have power to impose a fine not to exceed twenty-five ($25.00) dollars and/or withhold the privileges of the Club for a period of not more than six months, or may recommend to said Board of Directors the withholding of privileges for a longer period or may recommend disqualification or the imposition of fines exceeding twenty-five ($25.00) dollars.

If a Trial Board recommends the withholding of privileges or disqualification to the Board of Directors, the privileges of the Club shall be automatically withheld until the Board of Directors has adopted or refused to adopt such recommendation.

SECTION 3. Trial Boards shall have power to disqualify any person or withhold from any person all the privileges of The American Kennel Club for a period of not more than six months or to recommend to said Board of Directors the penalty of disqualification or the withholding of privileges for a longer period for improper or disorderly conduct during a hearing or a trial.

SECTION 4. Trial Boards shall keep minutes of their sittings.

SECTION 5. The decisions of Trial Boards shall be in writing signed by all members attending, and have annexed thereto all exhibits and papers offered before them. Each decision, together with complete copies of the minutes and testimony taken, shall be filed with the Secretary of The American Kennel Club within ten days of the date of the rendering of the decision. It shall be the duty of the Secretary of The American Kennel Club, when received, at once to notify in writing all parties in interest of the decision of a Trial Board.

SECTION 6. An appeal may be taken to the Board of Directors from any decision of a Trial Board, whether it be a decision in which the Trial Board itself imposes a certain penalty and/or fine or one in which the Trial Board recommends that the Board of Directors shall impose a certain penalty and/or fine. Notice in writing claiming such appeal together with a deposit of twenty-five ($25.00) dollars must be sent to The American Kennel Club within thirty days after the receipt of the notice of the decision or recommendation of the Trial Board. The Board of Directors may itself hear said appeal or may refer it to a Committee of the Board to be heard. The deposit of twenty-five ($25.00) dollars shall become the property of The American Kennel Club if the decision or recommendation of the Trial Board shall be confirmed, or shall be returned to the appellant if it shall not be confirmed. If the aggrieved party shall fail to take such appeal to the Board of Directors, there shall be no further right of appeal of any kind.

SECTION 7. Article XIII of these By-Laws shall be printed in any book or pamphlet which The American Kennel Club shall cause to be published containing the Rules of said Club.

CHAPTER 18

RULES FOR POINTING BREED TRIALS

Held By Specialty Clubs For the Following Breeds:

BRITTANY SPANIELS
POINTERS
GERMAN SHORTHAIRED POINTERS
GERMAN WIREHAIRED POINTERS
ENGLISH SETTERS
GORDON SETTERS
IRISH SETTERS
VIZSLAS
WEIMARANERS
WIREHAIRED POINTING GRIFFONS
(Chapters 1 through 17 also apply)

SECTION 1. A Specialty Club formed for the improvement of Brittany Spaniels, Pointers, German Shorthaired Pointers, German Wirehaired Pointers, English Setters, Gordon Setters, Irish Setters, Vizslas, Weimaraners or Wirehaired Pointing Griffons, may be approved to hold field trials for its breed or its breed plus any or all of the above named breeds. The premium list for a licensed or member trial shall name the breeds which may be entered. Unless all the breeds so specified may be entered in any of the stakes offered, then, in the conditions of each stake the breeds eligible for entry in it shall be named.

SECTION 2. Any of the following regular stakes may be offered at such trials:

Open Puppy Stake for dogs six months of age and under fifteen months of age on the first advertised day of the trial.

Open Derby Stake for dogs six months of age and under two years of age on the first advertised day of the trial.

Gun Dog Stake (Open or Amateur) for dogs six months of age and over on the first advertised day of the trial.

All-Age (Open or Amateur) for dogs six months of age and over on the first advertised day of the trial.

Limited All-Age (Open or Amateur) for dogs six months of age and over on the first advertised day of the trial which have won first place in an Open Derby Stake or which have placed first, second, third or fourth in any All-Age or Gun Dog Stake. A field trial-giving club may give an Amateur Limited All-Age Stake in which places that qualify a dog have been acquired in Amateur Stakes only.

In an Amateur Stake at a licensed or member field trial all dogs must be owned and handled by persons who, in the judgment of the Field Trial Committee, are qualified as Amateurs.

Definition of an Amateur Owner or Handler for Pointing Breed Trials

An Amateur Owner or Amateur Handler is a person who, during the period of two years preceding the trial, has not accepted remuneration in any form for training or handling dogs in any form of dog activity, and who at no time in the past has for any period of two years or more operated as a professional trainer or handler of field trial dogs.

SECTION 3. The premium list for a licensed or member trial shall specify date, time and place for the closing of entries, and time and place for the drawing of all stakes. The specified closing hour may be no later than the published hour for the drawing which must be held not later than the night preceding the running of the first stake. However, at a trial at which a Limited All-Age Stake is offered, additional entries of particular dogs which first qualify at that trial for such a stake may be accepted and the drawing of that stake may occur immediately before the running of the stake.

SECTION 4. Bitches in season may not compete and cannot be on the field trial grounds even though entered in the trial. No dog not entered in a field trial shall be allowed on the grounds.

SECTION 5. The requirements for a dog of one of the pointing breeds competing in field trials under these rules to be recorded a Field Champion shall be established by the Board of Directors of The American Kennel Club.

At present a dog will be recorded a Field Champion after having won 10 points under the point rating schedule below in regular stakes in at least three licensed or member field trials, provided that 3 points have been won in one 3 point or better Open All-Age, Open Gun Dog, or Open Limited All-Age Stake, that no more than 2 points each have been won in Open Puppy and Open Derby Stakes, and that no more than 4 points have been won in Amateur Stakes;

EXCEPT THAT a German Wirehaired Pointer or Weimaraner shall not be recorded a Field Champion after June 30, 1968 unless it has also been certified by two Judges to have passed a Water Test at a licensed or member field trial held by a specialty club for one of these two breeds.

Championship points shall be credited only to dogs placed first in regular stakes. The number of points shall be based on the actual number of starters in each stake according to the following schedule:

4 to 7	starters	1 point
8 to 12	starters	2 points
13 to 17	starters	3 points
18 to 24	starters	4 points
25 or more	starters	5 points

SECTION 6. A National Championship Stake at German Shorthaired Pointer Field Trials shall be for dogs over six months of age, which by reason of wins previously made qualify under special rules approved by the Board of Directors. This stake shall be run..not more than once in any calendar year by the Parent Association of the Breed or by a Club or Association formed for this purpose and duly licensed by The American Kennel Club. The winner of such stake shall become a Field Champion of Record if registered in The American Kennel Club Stud Book, and shall be entitled to be designated "National German Shorthaired Pointer Field Champion of 19—".

SECTION 7. The National Amateur Championship Stake for German Shorthaired Pointers shall be held no more than once in any calendar year, and shall be for dogs which by reason of wins previously made qualify under regulations submitted by the Parent Club and approved by the Board of Directors of The American Kennel Club. The stake shall be held by the Parent Club which shall file an application for permission to run it under procedures approved in advance by The American Kennel Club. The winner of this stake, if registered in the American Kennel Club stud book, shall be recorded an Amateur Field Champion by The American Kennel Club and may be

designated "National Amateur German Shorthaired Pointer Field Champion of 19—".

SECTION 8. A National Championship Stake for Brittany Spaniels may be run not more than once in any calendar year, by the parent club for the breed, or by an association formed for the purpose of running a national championship stake, which association shall be comprised of one representative of the parent club and one representative of each of the various regional Brittany Spaniel clubs. The stake shall be for dogs six months of age or over, which by reason of wins previously made qualify under regulations made by the parent club or the national association, all of which regulations shall be subject to the approval of the Board of Directors of The American Kennel Club. The winner of such stake shall be credited with championship points in accord with the schedule in Section 5 of this chapter, and the stake shall have the same value as an Open All-Age Stake. The winner of such stake shall be entitled to be designated "National Brittany Spaniel Field Champion of 19—".

SECTION 9. The National Amateur Championship Stake for Brittany Spaniels shall be held no more than once in any calendar year, and shall be for dogs which by reason of wins previously made qualify under regulations submitted by the Parent Club and approved by the Board of Directors of The American Kennel Club. The stake shall be held by the Parent Club which shall file an application for permission to run it under procedures approved in advance by The American Kennel Club. The winner of this stake, if registered in the American Kennel Club stud book, shall be recorded an Amateur Field Champion by The American Kennel Club and may be designated "National Amateur Brittany Spaniel Field Champion of 19—".

STANDARD PROCEDURE FOR POINTING BREED FIELD TRIALS

Held By Specialty Clubs For The Following Breeds:

BRITTANY SPANIELS
POINTERS
GERMAN SHORTHAIRED POINTERS
GERMAN WIREHAIRED POINTERS
ENGLISH SETTERS
GORDON SETTERS
IRISH SETTERS
VIZSLAS
WEIMARANERS
WIREHAIRED POINTING GRIFFONS

PROCEDURE 1. STANDARD OF PERFORMANCE

1-A PUPPY STAKES. Puppies must show desire to hunt, boldness, and initiative in covering ground and in searching likely cover. They are not expected to point but should flash point or otherwise indicate the presence of game if the opportunity is presented. Puppies should show reasonable obedience to their handlers' commands. They are to be judged on their future promise as high class Derby dogs. Game will not be killed in a Puppy Stake. Blanks shall not be fired in a Puppy Stake unless so specified in the premium list, in which case every dog that makes game contact shall be fired over if the handler is within reasonable gun range. At least 15 minutes and not more than 30 minutes shall be allowed for each heat.

1-B DERBY STAKES. Derbies must show a keen desire to hunt, be bold and independent, have a fast, yet attractive, style of running, and demonstrate not only intelligence in seeking objectives but also the ability to find game. Derbies must point, but steadiness to wing and shot are not required. Should birds be flushed after a point by handler or dog within reasonable gun range from the handler a shot must be fired. Lack of opportunity for firing over a Derby dog on point shall not constitute reason for non-placement when it has had game contact in acceptable Derby manner. However, Judges must arrange to have all placed dogs fired over if a natural opportunity does not occur. Derbies must show reasonable obedience to their handlers' commands. Derbies are to be judged on their promise as either future Gun Dogs or future All-Age Dogs. At least 20 minutes and not more than 30 minutes shall be allowed for each heat.

1-C GUN DOG STAKES. A Gun Dog must show a keen desire to hunt, have a bold and attractive style of running, and demonstrate not only intelligence in quartering and in seeking objectives but also the ability to find game. The dog must hunt for its handler at all times at a range suitable for a handler on foot, and should show or check in front of its handler frequently. It must cover adequate ground but never range out of sight for a length of time that would detract from its usefulness as a practical gun dog. The dog must locate game, must point staunchly, and must be steady to wing and shot. When the brace mate has established point it should back, preferably on sight, but if not, then on command. Intelligent use of the wind and terrain in locating game, accurate nose, style and intensity on point, are highly desirable. Intentional flushing and lack of steadiness to wing and shot are serious faults. The dog should automatically relocate game that moves out, but may be encouraged to relocate by its handler. The dog should give a finished performance and should be under its handler's control at all times. A Gun Dog should handle well with a minimum of noise or backing by the handler. At least 30 minutes shall be allowed for each heat.

1-D ALL-AGE AND LIMITED ALL-AGE STAKES. An All-Age dog shall demonstrate all of the same qualities as a Gun Dog as defined in the foregoing, except that it must hunt with greater speed and at a much greater range if the terrain permits, with a greater degree of independence, and covering the course in a forward-moving, pattern so as to locate any game on the course. It should respond to handling but should show an indication of using its own judgment in negotiating the course to find birds, and should not wait for the handler to direct it as to where to go. Style and intensity on point are essential. At least 30 minutes shall be allowed for each heat.

1-E In a Gun Dog, All-Age, or Limited All-Age Stake held by a German Shorthaired Pointer, German Wirehaired Pointer, Vizsla or Weimaraner Club, the dog placed first must have demonstrated backing in addition to the basic requirements for hunting and pointing as described above. A dog should not be placed on the basis of its backing performance alone, but failure of a dog to back or honor when its brace mate has established point must be heavily penalized. Backing should be done naturally but may be done on command, but greater credit shall be given for a natural back. Judges should try to have each dog that is being considered for placement back in a natural situation. However, if the opportunity to back does not occur naturally in these stakes the Judges may set up a brace for this purpose. The backing dog may not be touched before the blank is fired, nor before the retrieve if game is shot, unless directed by a Judge in case of an unproductive find.

1-F No Gun Dog, All-Age, or Limited All-Age Stake shall be run in heats of more than 30 minutes at a licensed or member trial unless the running time is given in the premium list.

1-G In any stake in which birds are not shot, except in Puppy or Derby Stakes as specified in Sections 1-A and 1-B, a blank cartridge must be fired by the handler over any dog on point, after the game has been flushed. The handler must shoot within the time that would be required to kill a bird at natural shotgun range. Any deliberate delay in shooting must be severely penalized.

1-H A reasonable move of a dog to mark a bird flushed after a point is acceptable, but this shall not excuse a partial break or a delayed chase.

1-I Any club that anticipates an entry in a licensed or member field trial that might exceed the number of dogs that could be judged on the available running grounds during the available judging hours, should specify in its premium list that entries in any or all stakes will be limited and that entries will close when the limit or limits have been reached if this occurs before the specified closing time for entries.

PROCEDURE 2. JUDGES

2-A Each stake must be judged by two Judges.

2-B The decisions of the Judges shall be final with respect to the running and placement of the dogs, and in all questions concerning the merits of the dogs. They shall have full power to turn out of any stake any dog that does not reasonably obey its handler or that interferes with the work of its brace mate, and any handler who, in their opinion, willfully interferes with another handler or his dog.

2-C Any person who, during the running of a stake, strikes or otherwise abuses or mistreats a dog, or conducts himself in a manner prejudicial to the best interests of the sport, must be expelled from that stake by the Judges who shall also report the matter to the Field Trial Committee for possible action under Chapter 16, Section 2. A report of the incident and the action taken shall be sent promptly to The American Kennel Club by the Field Trial Secretary.

2-D Any additional running of the dogs after the first series of heats has been completed shall be entirely at the discretion of the Judges unless further series are specified in the premium list, and the Judges shall determine the length and scope of any subsequent series and the bracing of the dogs.

2-E If the two handlers with their dogs become separated while both are on course and under judgment, one Judge shall accompany each handler; except that a Judge should not follow a dog that cuts the specified course in order to reach the bird field.

2-F The Judges may appoint an official observer at the bird field to report to them whether or not a dog had game contact before a Judge reached the bird field.

PROCEDURE 3. FIELD TRIAL MARSHALS

3-A The Field Trial Committee shall appoint one or more field trial Marshals. It shall be the duty of one Marshal to assist the Judges and to carry out their instructions, including regulating and controlling the gallery, and seeing to it that the gallery is kept separate from and behind the Judges, and that no one in the gallery talks to the Judges while the dogs are down. Other Marshals shall see to it that braces are ready when called, and assist the Field Trial Committee in all other matters necessary for the smooth and expeditious running of the trial.

3-B No person shall serve as Marshal assisting the Judges in any stake in which he has entered or will handle a dog.

PROCEDURE 4. DRAWING AND BRACING

4-A The dogs shall generally be run in braces, and each dog in a brace must have a separate handler.

4-B If every dog entered in a stake at a licensed or member field trial has a different handler, the bracing of the dogs in that stake shall be established by a straight drawing and the braces shall then be run in the order drawn.

4-C If two or more dogs with the same handler are entered in a stake at a licensed or member field trial, such entries shall be segregated for the drawing for bracing so that no two dogs handled by the same person can be drawn for the same brace. The running order for all complete braces shall then be determined by a separate drawing after the bracing has been established. If, during the drawing for running order, any handler is drawn to handle in more than two consecutive braces in the same stake, and if there is a later brace to be drawn in which he has no entry, the next brace drawn in which that handler has no dog may be moved up to run following the second consecutive brace, so that the handler would not be required to run in more than two consecutive braces. However, this shall not apply if an alternate handler has been named.

4-D The bracing and running order established by either method shall not be changed under any circumstances; except that

(1) in case of a scratch or absentee the brace mate of the absent dog shall be run with the dog from the next incomplete brace or, if there is no other incomplete brace with the bye dog; and except further that

(2) if the foregoing procedure would result in the bracing together of two dogs handled by the same person, the two odd dogs shall be rebraced consecutively with the two dogs in the last brace in the stake in which that handler has no dog.

4-E Any new brace or braces so created must be run in the running order drawn for one of the two dogs in the brace, as the Field Trial Committee may decide. If there is no bye dog and no other incomplete brace, the brace mate of a scratched or absent dog shall run last as the bye dog.

4-F If a bye dog remains after all the braces have been run, its brace mate shall be selected by the Judges at their sole discretion from among the dogs that have run in that stake; or the Judges may, if the Field Trial Committee agrees, run such a bye dog without a brace mate. The Judges alone shall decide whether or not any brace mate they select for such a bye dog shall be under judgment, and if under judgment, for what portion or portions of the heat, and their decision shall be publicly announced before the brace is started.

PROCEDURE 5. COURSES AND BIRDS

5-A Stakes at licensed or member field trials may be run on any of the following types of courses, all of which must include sufficient acreage, adequate cover for birds, and suitable objectives:

(1) *Single Course With Bird Field* consisting of a back course and a bird field which has sufficient cover to hold birds and which is of adequate size to permit a dog to hunt naturally and without excessive hacking. A bird field must not be less than 5 acres, and 10 acres is recommended. At a licensed or member trial no less than two birds must be released in the bird field for each brace in first series in all stakes except the Puppy Stake. Additional birds may be released either in the bird field or on the back course.

(2) *Single Course Without Bird Field* consisting entirely of a course without any specific bird field, on which birds are released in suitable places around the course. At a licensed or member trial no less than two birds must be released for each brace at a suitable place on the course in all stakes except the Puppy Stake.

(3) *Multiple Courses* consisting of a series of courses on which each brace starts where the last brace was picked up. On such a course it is assumed that there is adequate natural or released game.

5-B The same requirements for released birds that apply to other stakes at a licensed or member trial shall also apply to the Puppy Stake unless the premium list specifies that no birds will be released in the Puppy Stake.

5-C No released bird shall be picked up on the course or in the bird field unless dead or crippled.

5-D Regular stakes at a licensed or member trial shall be run only on recognized game birds, and the birds should be strong, healthy, full-feathered and clean; except that in Puppy Stakes non-game birds may be used if specified in the premium list.

5-E Birds should, if possible, be released in natural cover rather than in artificially created cover. They should not be placed in holes nor in such cover as will impede their ability to fly or run. Hobbles are highly undesirable, and must never be used if there is adequate cover. If hobbles are used they must be of soft yarn which the birds themselves can remove, and must allow a minimum of three inches space between the birds' feet. Other artificial restraints may never be used. Birds may be rocked or dizzied but not to such an extent as to affect their ability to fly. Game stewards should wear gloves. Successive birds should not be released in or near the same spot.

5-F The premium list for a licensed or member trial shall specify the type of course and species of game to be released in each stake.

PROCEDURE 6. RUNNING AND HANDLING

6-A The duty of having a dog ready in place when required for judging rests solely with its handler or owner. All dogs should be ready on the grounds well in advance of the scheduled times for their braces so that the Judges will not be held up in case of an absent brace. If a dog is not present at the place where it is to start within 5 minutes after it is called for by the Judges to run in any series it must be disqualified. The Judges are responsible for keeping the time.

6-B No more than one brace shall be run on a course or on any part of a course at the same time, irrespective of whether the dogs are in the same stake or in different stakes.

6-C In a stake on a single course with bird field the time of each heat shall include no more than 8 minutes in the bird field, except that in Puppy Stakes the time in the bird field shall not exceed 6 minutes. The time shall start when the first dog enters the bird field, except that a dog may be disqualified if it has cut the specified course in order to reach the bird field, in which case time starts when the second dog enters. Otherwise the Judges, or the Marshal if instructed by the Judges, shall see to it that both dogs in each brace are directed to the bird field at as nearly the same time as possible. If one dog has strayed or is otherwise held up on the course, the brace mate and its handler may ordinarily proceed on the course and enter the bird field unless otherwise directed by a Judge.

6-D Time shall not be called when a dog is on point in the bird field unless so specified in the premium list.

6-E In a Derby Stake, if the second dog is not on point or backing, its handler may, without penalty, hold or otherwise control the dog if there is any likelihood that it would interfere with the dog on point.

6-F A dog that is on point, roading, or obviously on game, when time is up, shall be allowed a reasonable time to complete its work.

6-G Judges must discourage continuous or excessive noise or loud vocalizing by handlers in any stake, and particularly in Gun Dog Stakes. Failure to heed the Judges' instructions may result in disqualification.

6-H Intimidation, blocking, or the use of any training aid or other means to restrain the dog from breaking wing or shot, shall be severely penalized.

6-I A dog that remains steady to wing and shot with a minimum of handling or commands must be given credit in a Gun Dog, All-Age or Limited All-Age Stake.

6-J A dog that is out of judgment for a continuous period of more than 5 minutes, or for more than 1/6 of the time specified for the heat if over 30 minutes, shall not be placed unless seen on point by a Judge or unless, in the opinion of the Judges, the dog's absence was due to unusual conditions.

6-K No person shall in any manner assist a handler in controlling his dog or in finding a dog that is lost, unless specific permission is first obtained from a Judge. A dog may be disqualified if it receives direction of any kind from anyone except its handler.

6-L No dog shall be picked up during a heat except on direction or permission from a Judge.

6-M All dogs started in a stake must remain on the grounds

until the stake is completed unless excused by the Judges or by the Field Trial Committee.

6-N No one shall be permitted in the bird field at any time during the running of a stake; except for the Judges, the official guns, the Marshal, and the handlers of the competing dogs while the dogs are in the bird field; and except for the game stewards to the extent necessary to release game.

6-O No person shall serve as an official gun or game steward in a stake in which he handles a dog or in which a dog owned by him is entered.

6-P Promiscuous firing of guns or blank pistols on the field trial grounds is prohibited. The handler of a dog shall fire one blank and no more for each flush of one or more birds.

6-Q There shall be no training of dogs anywhere on the course during the trial.

6-R The Field Trial Committee shall not permit severe training, correcting, or disciplining of dogs on any part of the field trial grounds. The Committee shall investigate any reports of such conduct or of any other conduct prejudicial to the best interests of pure-bred dogs, field trials, or The American Kennel Club. Any person who conducts himself in a manner prejudicial to the best interests of the sport shall be dealt with promptly during the trial if possible, after the offender has been notified of the specific charges against him, and has been given an opportunity to be heard in his own defense, in accordance with Chapter 16, Section 2.

6-S The premium list for any licensed or member field trial must specify whether or not handling from horseback will be permitted in any or all stakes. If handling from horseback is permitted in any stake the club must have suitable horses available. Mounted and foot handlers are not to be segregated in the draw.

The Judges shall see to it that any mounted handler uses his horse only as a means of conveyance on the course and never as an active aid in handling. The handlers shall remain on the specified course with the Judges. If one handler is mounted and the other is on foot, the Judges shall set a reasonable pace to accommodate the foot handler. Mounted handlers must keep their horses at a walk at all times unless otherwise authorized by a Judge.

A handler must always dismount before handling his dog on game and before firing. No handler's horse may be brought into the bird field.

PROCEDURE 7. SHOOT-TO-KILL STAKES

7-A The premium list must identify any Shoot-to-Kill Stake, and must specify, for each stake in which birds are to be shot, whether the shooting will be done by official guns or whether handlers will be required to shoot their own birds, and the

shooting for all braces in the stake shall be done in the manner specified.

7-B The Judges shall have complete authority over all shooting. They may require a change of official guns at any time during the running of a stake, except for the Judges, the official guns, and may bar from further shooting in that trial any official gun or gunning handler who does not abide strictly by safe gunning rules.

7-C If the shooting is done by official guns, two qualified guns are required for each brace, one to accompany each handler. Provision must also be made for alternate or stand-by guns in case they should be required.

7-D One official gun must join each handler as he enters the bird field, or if a bird field is not used, at a designated place on the course. The official gun must always keep himself in the correct position for safety of dogs and persons.

7-E Game should be shot cleanly, in a sportsmanlike manner, in full flight, and at a distance that will give the dog a reasonable retrieve. An official gun represents the handler up to the time that game is shot, but must not interfere in any manner with his work nor direct the work of the dog.

7-F Game flushed by a free running dog or birds that flush wild shall not be shot except on instructions from a Judge. If a bird does not fly after an attempt to flush by a handler, it shall not be shot on the ground except on instructions from a Judge.

7-G Retrieving is required in all Shoot-to-Kill Stakes, except Derby Stakes as specified below, and counts as an important part of a dog's performance. After the shot the dog shall not be sent to retrieve by the handler until the dog's steadiness to wing and shot has been positively demonstrated. The handler commands and/or signals the dog to retrieve but may not touch the dog. The dog must retrieve promptly and tenderly to hand. In Shoot-to-Kill Derby Stakes retrieving will also be required unless otherwise specified in the premium list, but the dog is not required to be steady to wing and shot.

CHAPTER 19

RULES FOR DACHSHUND TRIALS

(Chapters 1 through 17 also apply)

SECTION 1. In Single Stakes for Dachshunds, the order of running in pairs in the first series shall be decided by lot at the draw, dogs worked by the same person or belonging to the same owner being separated when possible. In event of a bye dog, the Judge or Judges shall choose its bracemate. At the end of the first series, the Judges will call up the two dogs with the highest score, and any other dogs they require further to be run in additional series.

SECTION 2. In Couple or Pack Stakes the order of running in the first series shall be decided by draw, and the dogs composing a couple or pack must belong to the same owner. No dog shall form part of more than one couple and one pack at the same Meeting, and each couple or pack shall have but one handler. A couple consists of two dogs. A pack consists of two or more couples (the number to be specified in the premium list). Dogs will be expected to work their ground harmoniously together, performing as in a Single Stake.

SECTION 3. In Pack Stakes each entry in the stake shall be run separately as a pack.

SECTION 4. A Derby Stake at a Dachshund field trial shall be for dogs whelped on or after the first day of January of the year preceding that year in which the field trial is run.

SECTION 5. A Non-Winners Stake at a Dachshund field trial shall be for dogs which never have won first place in any field trial stake at a licensed or member Dachshund field trial.

SECTION 6. The field trial-giving club may run such other stakes as are printed on the premium list and/or entry form and which have been approved by The American Kennel Club.

Note: In all Stakes the principal qualifications to be considered by the Judges are good noses, courage in facing punishing coverts, keenness, perseverance, obedience and willingness to go to earth. Should a rabbit lodge in any earth, or run through any drain large enough for the Dachshund to enter, the dog should, of course, be expected to enter without hesitation; and failure to do so should automatically render them ineligible for first award, even though their performance was in all other respects outstanding.

SECTION 7. Only trials that are run on live cottontails, or hare, or both, shall be permitted to carry championship points.

SECTION 8. Stakes may be divided by sex if the field trial-giving club so desires and so states in its premium list and/or entry form. If, however, the premium list and/or entry form states that the stakes are divided by sex, and thereafter when the entries are received it is found there are less than six entries of each sex in any stake, that stake shall be combined and run with both sexes in a single stake, but no stakes which the premium list and/or entry form states are to be divided by sex shall be combined into a Single Stake under any other circumstances.

SECTION 9. Judges shall have the power to turn out of the stake any dog which does not obey its handler, and any handler who wilfully interferes with another competitor, or his dog; and the power to exclude from competition bitches in heat, or any dog which the Judges may consider unfit to compete. The entry fees of all such dogs shall be forfeited.

SECTION 10. The owner or agent entering a dog in a trial does so at his own risk, and agrees to abide by the rules of The American Kennel Club.

SECTION 11. In the event of the weather proving unsuitable for holding the trials, it shall be in the power of the Field Trial Committee to postpone the meeting from day to day for a maximum of three days following the last advertised day, provided said postponement does not conflict with any other Dachshund field trial. After postponements for three days the provisions of Section 12 of this Chapter shall come into operation.

SECTION 12. In the event of the weather still proving unsuitable after postponements for three days, the Field Trial Committee may then abandon the meeting at any time, on returning the entry fees to the competitors. If, from unforeseen circumstances, the Field Trial Committee deem it advisable to alter the date of the meeting after the closing of the entries, this may be done with the consent of The American Kennel Club and by sending formal notices to all competitors, who may exercise the option of cancelling their entries within four days from the date of such notice, in which event their entry fees will be returned to them. All entries, however, in regard to which no such option is exercised, will stand good for the meeting at its altered date.

SECTION 13. Splitting of prizes and/or places at Dachshund field trials is prohibited.

SECTION 14. Championship points for Dachshunds shall be awarded only to the first and second place winners of Open All-Age Stakes. A Dachshund winning first place in an Open All-Age Stake will be awarded a number of championship points equal to the number of actual starters in the stake in which it competed. A Dachshund winning second place in an Open All-Age Stake will be awarded one-third as many points as the first place winner of the stake, provided there are nine or more actual starters in the stake.

SECTION 15. No Dachshund shall be recorded a Field Champion unless it is registered in The American Kennel Club Stud Book and unless some of its required championship points have been won as a first place winner of an Open All-Age Stake.

SECTION 16. The total number of championship points necessary for a Dachshund to win in order to be declared a Field Champion of Record shall be fixed and determined by the Board of Directors of The American Kennel Club.

At present the total number of points required is 25.

CHAPTER 20

RULES FOR RETRIEVER TRIALS

(Chapters 1 through 17 also apply)

SECTION 1. Wherever used in this chapter and in the Standard Procedure for Non-Slip Retriever Trials, the word Retriever shall be deemed to include the several breeds of Retrievers and/or Irish Water Spaniels.

DACHSHUNDS

Field trial clubs or specialty clubs formed for the improvement of any one of the several breeds of Retrievers may give field trial stakes in which one of said breeds only may compete, or in which more than one of said breeds may compete together.

Championship points may be awarded where two or more of said breeds compete together in a mixed stake as well as where a separate stake has been provided for each breed.

SECTION 2. Only pure-bred Retrievers over six months of age may be entered in field trials.

The owner or agent entering a dog in a trial does so at his own risk, and agrees to abide by the rules of The American Kennel Club.

A dog is not eligible to be entered in any licensed or member trial in any stake, if the judge of that stake or any member of his family has owned, sold, held under lease, boarded, trained or handled the dog within one year prior to the starting date of the field trial, or if the judge or any member of his family holds a direct financial interest contingent upon the dog's performance.

No post entries will be accepted and entries shall close not later than the time of the drawing which drawing shall take place at least three days before the first day of the trial.

Judges shall have the power to disqualify any dog which shall not appear within fifteen minutes of the time designated for its turn to be tried.

Bitches in season shall not be eligible for competition in any stake and shall not be allowed on the field trial grounds. The entry fees of bitches withdrawn because of coming in season shall be refunded.

Judges shall have the power to exclude from competition any dog which the judge may consider unfit to compete. The entry fee of all such dogs will be forfeited.

SECTION 3. Only Amateurs shall be asked to judge licensed or member Retriever Trials. In Stakes carrying championship points there shall be only two Judges, and their combined experience shall conform to the provisions set forth in Section 24 of the Standard Procedure.

SECTION 4. In stakes for Retrievers the order of running shall be decided by lot at the draw, dogs worked by the same person or belonging to the same owner being separated when possible. At the option of the trial giving club, the drawing may be arranged so that all bitches are drawn after all dogs.

Dogs may be run in an order different from the order in which they were drawn, when in the opinion of the judges or Field Trial Committee, such procedure would result in a reasonable and desirable saving of time in the conduct of the trial.

SECTION 5. Only stakes which are run on game birds and on both land and water shall be permitted to carry championship points. Premium lists should specify the kind of game to be used in each stake, and, unless otherwise specified in the premium list, only pheasants and ducks may be used in stakes carrying championship points, and pheasants or pigeons and ducks in other stakes.

SECTION 6. After a Field Trial Committee has selected field trial grounds, no competing dog shall be trained on that part of the grounds to be used for the trial.

SECTION 7. In the event of the weather proving unsuitable for holding the trials, the Field Trial Committee may suspend or postpone any or all stakes up to three days. Notice of such postponement shall be forwarded immediately to The American Kennel Club.

Postponement beyond three days must have the approval of The American Kennel Club.

In the event of postponement of 24 hours or more in the starting time of any stake, any competitor shall have the right to withdraw his entries and his entry fees shall be returned to him.

SECTION 8. Splitting of prizes and/or places at a Retriever Trial is prohibited. No cash or merchandise shall be given as prizes for placing dogs. There shall be no prizes or trophies of any kind offered to handlers in any stake, except (a) trophies to Amateur Handlers and (b) a trophy to the handler of the winning dog in the National Championship Stake.

SECTION 9. The regular official stakes at a Retriever Trial shall be Derby, Qualifying, Open All-Age, Limited All-Age and Amateur All-Age.

SECTION 10. A Derby Stake at a Retriever Trial shall be for dogs which have not reached their second birthday on the first day of the trial at which they are being run. For example, a dog whelped May 1, 1965, would not be eligible for Derby Stakes at a trial starting May 1, 1967, but would be eligible at a trial the first day of which was April 30, 1967.

A Qualifying Stake at a Retriever Trial shall be for dogs which have never won first, second, third, or fourth place or a Judges' Award of Merit in an Open All-Age or Limited All-

Age or won first, second, third or fourth place in an Amateur All-Age Stake, or won two first places in Qualifying Stakes at licensed or member club trials. In determining whether a dog is eligible for the Qualifying Stake, no award received on or after the date of closing of entries shall be counted

An Open All-Age Stake at a Retriever Trial shall be for all dogs.

A Limited All-Age Stake at a Retriever Trial shall be for dogs that have previously been placed or awarded a Judge's Award of Merit in an Open All-Age Stake, or that have been placed first or second in a Qualifying or placed or awarded a Judges' Award of Merit in an Amateur All-Age Stake carrying championship points.

An Amateur All-Age Stake at a Retriever Trial shall be for any dogs, if handled in that stake by persons who are Amateurs (as determined by the Field Trial Committee of the trial-giving club).

SECTION 11. At any field trial, there shall not be more than one of the following stakes:—Open All-Age or Limited All-Age, and no club shall hold more than two of such stakes in one calendar year.

In a two-day trial, when one of the above stakes is held, not more than two other stakes shall be held unless more than one stake is run at the same time under different Judges.

SECTION 12. A National Championship Stake at a Retriever Trial shall be for dogs which by reason of wins previously made qualify under special rules subject to approval by the Board of Directors of The American Kennel Club. This stake shall be run not more than once in any calendar year by a club or association formed for this purpose and duly licensed by The American Kennel Club. The winner of such stake shall become a Field Champion of Record if registered in the American Kennel Club stud book and shall be entitled to be designated "National Retriever Field Champion of 19—".

SECTION 13. A National Amateur Championship Stake at a Retriever Trial shall be for dogs which by reason of wins previously made, qualify under special rules subject to approval by the Board of Directors of The American Kennel Club. This stake shall be run not more than once in any calendar year by a club or association formed for this purpose, or by the club formed to conduct the National Championship Stake, and the stake shall be duly licensed by The American Kennel Club. The Winner of such stake shall become an Amateur Field Champion of Record if registered in the American Kennel Club stud book, and shall be entitled to be designated "National Amateur Retriever Field Champion of 19—".

SECTION 14. Non-regular stakes may be held at Retriever Trials subject to the approval of The American Kennel Club, and provided the premium list sets forth any special conditions regarding eligibility for entry, and any special conditions regarding the method of conducting or judging the stake. Such stakes will not carry championship points or be considered as qualifying a dog for any other stake.

SECTION 15. A Retriever shall become a Field Champion of Record, if registered in the American Kennel Club stud book, after having won points in Open All-Age or Limited All-Age Stakes at field trials of member clubs of The American Kennel Club or at field trials of non-member clubs licensed by The American Kennel Club to hold field trials.

SECTION 16. A Retriever shall become an Amateur Field Champion of Record, if registered in the American Kennel Club stud book, after having won points in Open All-Age or Limited All-Age Stakes when handled by an Amateur (as determined by the Field Trial Committee of the trial-giving club) and in Amateur All-Age Stakes at field trials of member clubs of The American Kennel Club or at trials of non-member clubs licensed by The American Kennel Club to hold trials.

SECTION 17. The total number of points required for a championship, the number of places in a stake for which points may be required, and the number of points to be acquired for each place, and the number of starters required and their qualifications for eligibility to acquire points in each stake shall be fixed and determined by the Board of Directors of The American Kennel Club.

At each trial having an Open All-Age Stake, or an Amateur All-Age Stake, the Field Trial Secretary in his report must certify whether at least twelve (12) of the starters in each of those stakes were eligible to compete in a Limited All-Age Stake.

At each trial having an Open All-Age or Limited All-Age Stake, the Field Trial Secretary in his report must specify which handlers of placing dogs, if any, in either such stake are determined to be Amateurs by their Field Trial Committee.

At present, to acquire a Field Championship, a Retriever must win:

(1) a National Championship Stake or (2) a total of 10 points, which may be acquired as follows.—In each Open All-Age or Limited All-Age Stake there must be at least 12 starters, each of which is eligible for entry in a Limited All-Age Stake, and the winner of first place shall be credited with 5 points, second place 3 points, third place 1 point, and fourth place ½ point, but, before acquiring a championship, a dog must win first place and acquire 5 points in at least one Open All-Age or Limited All-Age Stake open to all breeds of Retriever, and not more than 5 points of the required 10 shall be acquired in trials not open to all breeds of Retriever.

At present, to acquire an Amateur Field Championship, a Retriever must win: (1) a National Championship Stake, handled by an Amateur, or a National Amateur Championship Stake or (2) a total of 10 points in Open All-Age or Limited All-Age Stakes or a total of 15 points in Open All-Age, Limited All-Age or Amateur All-Age Stakes, which may be acquired as follows:

In each Open All-Age, Limited All-Age or Amateur All-Age Stake, there must be at least 12 starters, each of which is eligible for entry in a Limited All-Age Stake, and the handler must be an Amateur (as determined by the Field Trial Committee of the trial-giving club), and the winner of first place shall be credited with 5 points, second place 3 points, third place 1 point, and fourth place ½ point, but before acquiring a championship, a dog must win a first place and acquire 5 points in at least one Open All-Age, Limited All-Age or Amateur All-Age Stake open to all breeds of Retriever, and not more than 5 points shall be acquired in trials not open to all breeds of Retriever.

STANDARD PROCEDURE FOR NON-SLIP RETRIEVER TRIALS

In order that trials may be conducted as uniformly as practicable, standardization of objectives is essential and, therefore, all Judges, guns, contestants and officials who have a part in conducting trials should be familiar with and be governed so far as possible by the following standard:—

BASIC PRINCIPLES

1. The purpose of a Non-Slip Retriever trial is to determine the relative merits of retrievers in the field. Retriever field trials should, therefore, simulate as nearly as possible the conditions met in an ordinary day's shoot.

Dogs are expected to retrieve any type of game bird under all conditions, and the Judges and the Field Trial Committee have complete control over the mechanics and requirements of each trial. This latitude is permitted in order to allow for the difference in conditions which may arise in trials given in widely separated parts of the United States, which difference well may necessitate different methods of conducting tests.

2. The function of a Non-Slip Retriever is to seek and retrieve "fallen" game when ordered to do so. He should sit quietly on line or in the blind, walk at heel, or assume any station designated by his handler until sent to retrieve. When ordered, a dog should retrieve quickly and briskly without unduly disturbing too much ground, and should deliver tenderly to hand. He should then await further orders.

Accurate marking is of primary importance. A dog which marks the fall of a bird, uses the wind, follows a strong cripple, and will take direction from his handler is of great value.

TRIAL PROCEDURE

3. The Judges, with due regard to the recommendations of the Field Trial Committee, shall determine the tests to be given in each series—and shall try to give all dogs approximately similar tests in the same series.

4. At the end of the first series, and every series thereafter, the Judges will call back all dogs which they wish to try further, and will cause them to be run in additional series until the stake is decided.

5. Judges shall in their discretion determine the number of dogs that shall be worked or kept on line simultaneously. In at least one series in all stakes, except Derby, every dog should be kept on line off leash while another dog works.

6. When coming to line to be tested, the dog and handler should assume any position directed by the Judges.

Dogs should be considered under judgment from the time they are called to come to the line until they have left the line and are back of all the Judges and on leash.

In stakes carrying championship points, dogs should be brought to the line and taken from the line off leash and without collar and remain without collar while under judgment. In these stakes collars and leashes may be put on the dogs after they leave the line and are back of all of the Judges.

In Qualifying stakes, unless otherwise instructed by the Judges, dogs should be brought to the line and taken from the line off leash; leashes may be put on the dogs after they leave the line and are back of all the Judges. In Derby stakes, solely at the handler's option, dogs may be brought to the line on leash or off leash—the leash being removed from the line on leash or off leash until the dog has completed his work and honoring, if any. However in Qualifying and Derby stakes, when the handler is instructed to pick up his dog because of a missed bird or other condition of which he is expected to return to the line, the collars or leashes may be put on the dogs at once on line.

No dog should run with bandages or tape of any kind without the approval of the Field Trial Committee. The Committee should inspect the injury for which the bandage or tape is being used unless, of their own knowledge, they already possess such information, or unless they are furnished with a veterinary's certificate setting forth this information to their satisfaction.

7. The dogs should be shot over by guns appointed by the Field Trial Committee, or, at the option of the Judges, by the handler. In the event of the handler shooting, he should be backed up by official guns.

8. On marked retrieves, a dog should be able to see each bird in the air and as it falls, and the guns should be so stationed as to be conspicuous to and easily identified by the dog. Guns may be requested to shoot twice at every bird. After birds have been shot, all guns shall remain quietly and only move their positions in accordance with specific instructions by Judges. Judges may request guns to disappear from sight after their bird is down, but they should not have them move to another position to deliberately mislead the dogs in their marking. On marked retrieves the order in which birds are to be retrieved should not be specified by the Judges, unless it is to be considered a test of control (i.e. a handling test).

9. When possible in land series, game should be dropped on fresh territory for each dog and not on ground already fouled.

10. When on line, a handler should not place his dog or himself so that the dog's full vision of any birds or falls is blocked. This applies to the working dog and the honoring dog. Violation of this provision, if determined by the Judges to be deliberate, is sufficient cause to justify elimination from the stake.

11. Unless otherwise instructed by the Judges, no dog should be sent to retrieve until his number has been called by one of the Judges.

12. Judges should call the number of the dog ordered to retrieve rather than the name of the handler or dog.

13. If, when a dog is ordered by the Judge to retrieve a fall, another dog breaks for the same fall and interferes with the working dog to the extent of causing him in any way to make a faulty performance, the dog interfered with should be considered as not having been tried¹ and given a chance for another performance.

14. If the Judges decide to re-run a dog by reason of the occurrence of any situation that makes for a relatively unfair test for such dog, the dog should be picked up immediately and tested on a new set of birds, if practicable after waiting behind the line until several other dogs have been tested.

If the dog has completed a portion of the test when the unfair situation develops, that dog should be judged on the portion of the test completed in his original try and on the uncompleted portion in the re-run; provided however, that if in the re-run of the previously completed portion of the test, the dog (1) does not complete that portion in accordance with the Judges' instructions for the test or (2) commits any of the faults set forth herein as usually justifying elimination from a stake, he should be penalized for such errors in the same manner as the Judges would deal with him regardless of the re-run. Faults not set forth herein as usually justifying elimination, committed on the re-run, on the previously completed portion, should be ignored and the dog judged on his original work.

However, the performance should be sharply penalized if, in the opinion of the Judges, the handler deliberately attempts to divert the dog's attention from previously completed portion or portions first.

15. When ordered to retrieve, the handler shall direct his dog from any position designated by the Judges.

16. Retrievers should perform equally well on the land and in the water, and should be thoroughly tested on both.

17. During at least one water test in all stakes, dogs should be worked over artificial decoys, anchored separately.

18. Except in compliance with Judges' instructions in tests in which dogs are required to honor before themselves being run, all competing dogs should be kept where they can neither see the falls for another dog nor see any particular dog work in any water series they have not completed. Violation of this provision, unless in the opinion of the Judges there exist adequate contrary mitigating circumstances, is sufficient cause to justify elimination from the stake.

19. Nothing should be thrown to encourage a dog to enter the water or direct a dog to the fall. Violation of this provision is to be considered sufficient cause for elimination from the stake.

20. In stakes carrying championship points, there should be at least one handling test or blind retrieve—and preferably two, one on land and one in water.

21. All competing dogs must be kept where they cannot see blind retrieves planted and where they cannot see another dog working on a blind retrieve in any series which they have not completed. Members of the Field Trial Committee should report violations of this section to the Judges. Violations of this section should be penalized by elimination of the dog and the handler from the stake.

22. Tests or retrieves which are not to be considered by the Judges at the final summing up should not be held.

JUDGING

Because of its concise statement of purpose, Section 2 of this Standard Procedure is repeated here:

2. The function of a Non-Slip Retriever is to seek and retrieve "fallen" game when ordered to do so. He should sit quietly on line or in the blind, walk at heel, or assume any station designated by his handler until sent to retrieve. When ordered, a dog should retrieve quickly and briskly without unduly disturbing too much ground, and should deliver tenderly to hand. He should then await further orders.

Accurate marking is of primary importance. A dog which marks the fall of a bird, uses the wind, follows a strong cripple, and will take direction from his handler is of great value.

23. The Judges must judge the dogs for (a) their natural abilities including their memory, intelligence, attention, nose, courage, perseverance and style, and (b) their abilities acquired through training, including steadiness, control, response to direction, and delivery. Decisions to eliminate a dog from a stake as a result of faulty performance must be the consensus of the Judges.

24. In Stakes carrying championship points, the experience of the two Judges shall be such that their combined experience includes the judging of 8 Stakes carrying championship points.

LINE MANNERS

25. When called to be tested, a dog should come tractably at heel and sit promptly at the point designated by his handler and remain quietly where placed until given further orders. Retrievers which bark or whine on line, in a blind or while retrieving should be penalized. Loud and prolonged barking or whining is sufficient cause to justify elimination from the stake.

26. No handler shall (1) carry exposed any training equipment (except whistle) or use any other equipment or threatening

gestures in such a manner that they may be an aid or threat in steadying or controlling a dog; (2) hold or touch a dog to keep him steady; or (3) noisily or frequently restrain a dog on line, except in extraordinary circumstances, from the time the first bird is being thrown until the dog's number is called. Violation of any of the provisions of this paragraph is sufficient cause to justify elimination from the stake.

A handler may, without penalty, give a command to sit as the first bird is being thrown in a "walk up." In other tests, during the period from the moment when, in accordance with the Judge's signal, the bird thrower commences his motion to throw the first bird until the dog's number is called, the handler of the working or honoring dog should remain silent. Also, in all marking tests, during such period, the handler's hands should remain quietly in close proximity to his body. A handler who projects his hand during such period, whether for the purpose of assisting his dog to locate a fall or otherwise, should be considered to have used a threatening gesture, and his dog penalized accordingly.

27. In an All-Age Stake, if a dog makes a movement which in the opinion of the Judges indicates a deliberate intent to retrieve without having been ordered to do so, that dog shall be deemed to have broken and shall be eliminated. In any stake other than an All-Age stake, if a dog makes a slight break and is brought immediately under control, the dog need not be eliminated, but shall be penalized for unsteadiness.

If a dog on line creeps or jumps forward short of breaking as birds are shot and no effort is made by the handler to stop and restrain him, the Judges should not interpret such as a deliberate intent to retrieve, since nothing was done to stop the dog. On the other hand, if the handler does make an effort to stop the dog, the Judges should assume that the handler believed the dog intended to break and should deal with such infraction accordingly.

The Judges may require that dogs which have so jumped or crept forward be brought back to heel before being sent for their birds. A handler so ordered should bring his dog to a position satisfactory to the Judges and remain with him in such position until his number is called. In tests including honoring, care should be exercised to treat creeping, on the part of either dog, in a manner not grossly unfair to the other.

In all stakes, after the Judges have directed that a dog be ordered to retrieve, that dog is entitled to run in and retrieve and shall not be accused of, or penalized for breaking, even though the Judges did not see or hear the handler send the dog.

When a dog that is still in a stake, but not on line under judgment, breaks for a fall for a dog under judgment, in such a manner that the dog or his handler interferes, in the opinion of the Judges, with the normal conduct of the stake, that dog shall be eliminated from the stake.

When the handler of a dog under judgment is ordered by the Judges for any reason to pick up his dog, he is under judgment until he is back of all the Judges with his dog on leash, and all provisions of this section shall apply until that time.

28. After delivering a bird to his handler, a dog should stand or sit close to handler until given further orders.

THE RETRIEVE

29. When ordered to retrieve, a dog should proceed quickly and eagerly on land or into the water to marked falls or on the line given him by his handler on falls he has not seen. He should not disturb too much ground or area and should respond quickly and obediently to any further directions his handler might give him. Failure to enter either rough cover, water, ice, mud or any other situation involving unpleasant or difficult going for the dog, after having been ordered to do so several times, is sufficient cause to justify elimination from the stake.

A dog who pays no attention to many whistles and directions by his handler can't be said to be "out-of-control," and unless in the opinion of the Judges there exist valid mitigating circumstances, should be eliminated from the stake.

30. In marking tests, a dog whose handler gives him a line in the direction of the fall, provided that such lining is accomplished briskly and precisely, should not by reason of such lining be outscored by a dog not so lined. However, conspicuously intensive lining is undesirable and should be penalized.

31. In marked retrieves, if a dog, after having been sent to retrieve, (1) returns to his handler before finding the bird, with or without having been called in, except in those cases of confusion of the dog as to whether he was really ordered to retrieve; (2) stops his hunt; or (3) fails to pick the bird up, actually leaving it after finding it, it shall be sufficient cause, unless there exist in the opinion of the Judges valid mitigating circumstances, to justify elimination from the Stake.

32. A dog that goes to the area of a fall, hunts, fails to find and then leaves the area to hunt for another fall, or that drops a bird he is retrieving and goes for another, shall be considered to have "switched." Unless in the opinion of the Judges there exist valid mitigating circumstances, this fault constitutes sufficient justification for elimination from the stake.

33. A dog which fails to find a bird which, in the opinion of the Judges, he should have found, shall be eliminated from the stake.

34. Repeated evidence of poor nose is in itself sufficient justification for elimination from the stake. Because scenting conditions are affected by so many factors, Judges should exercise extreme caution in invoking this penalty.

35. A dog retrieving a decoy should be eliminated.

36. Upon finding the game, he should quickly pick it up and return briskly to his handler.

A dog should not drop his game on the ground, but distinction should be made between deliberately dropping a bird, and readjusting a bad hold or losing his grip because of a struggling bird or running over uneven terrain.

37. Upon returning, he should deliver the bird promptly and tenderly to his handler. A dog sitting to deliver should not outscore a dog making a clear delivery without sitting to do so. A dog that is unwilling to release a bird on delivery should be penalized, and if compelled to do so by severe methods should, unless in the opinion of the Judges there exist valid mitigating circumstances, be eliminated.

38. A dog should be eliminated for hard mouth or badly damaging game. but, before doing so, all Judges should inspect the bird and be satisfied that the dog alone was responsible for the damage.

GENERAL

39. Any handler who displays unsportsmanlike conduct or who is seen to kick, strike or otherwise roughly manhandle a dog while on the grounds of a field trial at any time during the holding of a trial, may be expelled from competition in a stake, or from competition at the trial, by the Field Trial Committee.

It shall be the duty of the Committee to investigate, at once, any report that is made to it of alleged unsportsmanlike conduct on the part of a handler, or a report that a handler has been observed kicking, striking, or otherwise roughly manhandling a dog. If a Field Trial Committee, after investigation, determines that a handler is in violation of this section, it shall promptly notify the handler of its decision, specifying whether the handler is expelled from a particular stake or from further competition at the trials.

The judges of a particular stake shall have the authority to expel a handler from any further competition in the stake, if they observe unsportsmanlike conduct on the part of the handler or see the handler kicking, striking, or otherwise roughly manhandling a dog while the judging of the stake is in progress. It will be the duty of the judges to promptly report to the Field Trial Committee the expulsion of a handler from a stake and the Field Trial Committee may then expel the handler from all remaining competition at the trial, if in the Committee's opinion such further action is warranted.

Whenever a handler is expelled from a stake or from competition at a trial under this section, the dog or dogs that he is handling may continue in competition with one or more other handlers.

The Field Trial Secretary of a trial shall submit to The American Kennel Club, with the records of the trial, a report of any action taken under this section by either the Field Trial Committee or the Judges.

40. Judges shall have the power to turn out of the stake

any dog which does not obey its handler and any handler who interferes wilfully with another handler or his dog.

42. No dog shall be given a place in a stake unless the dog has competed in all tests held for any dog in such stake.

42. The awarding of a Judges' Award of Merit to dogs which have passed every required test in a stake and have shown themselves to be well trained and qualified retrievers, should be encouraged.

GENERAL PROVISIONS

43. All field trial-giving clubs should clearly recognize that Open or Limited Stakes are of the first importance and that all other stakes are of relatively lesser importance, and are requested to adjust the timing of stakes so that time shall be available for a fair test in those stakes.

44. It is essential that all spectators attending a trial should be kept far enough from the line to enable the dog working to clearly discern his handler, and nothing shall be done to distract the dog's attention from his work. A handler has the right to appeal to the Judges if the gallery is interfering with his work in any way, and the Judges in their discretion may, if they believe the dog has been interfered with, give him another test.

45. There should be no practicing or training on any part of the field trial grounds from the start of the trial until its conclusion.

46. In sanctioned trials or non-regular stakes, any sections of this Standard Procedure may be relaxed or eliminated, but all contestants should be advised in what respects this is true.

RETRIEVER ADVISORY COMMITTEE RECOMMENDATIONS

The Retriever Advisory Committee has adopted Standing Recommendations to all Retriever trial-giving clubs, including a Supplement to the Standard Procedure that deals in more detail with the conduct and judging of these trials.

Judges and officials of trial-giving clubs should make themselves familiar with these recommendations and the supplement, copies of which can be obtained from The American Kennel Club (Field Trial Plans Department), 51 Madison Avenue, New York, N. Y. 10010.

CHAPTER 21

RULES FOR SPANIEL TRIALS

(EXCEPT BRITTANY SPANIELS AND IRISH WATER SPANIELS)

(Chapters 1 through 17 also apply)

SECTION 1. Field trial clubs or specialty clubs formed for the improvement of any one of the several breeds of hunting Spaniels recognized by The American Kennel Club may give field trial stakes in which one of the said breeds only may compete or in which more than one of said breeds may compete together. No championships points, however, shall be awarded where two or more breeds of hunting Spaniels (excepting English Cocker Spaniels and Cocker Spaniels) compete together in a mixed stake.

SECTION 2. In single stakes for Spaniels the order of running in pairs shall be decided by lot at the draw, dogs worked by the same person or belonging to the same owner being separated when possible. The Judges will carry on the trial of two dogs simultaneously, working parallel beats as far as possible and not requiring any co-operation in quartering. At the end of the first series the Judges will call up any dogs they require further to be run in additional series. In Championship Stakes dogs should be run in pairs for at least the first two series, but it is required that each dog competing must be paired with another dog in at least one of these series, in both if possible. In no event may a dog not under judgment be used to create a pair. After the second series the Judges, at their discretion, may elect to run additional series with the dogs running singly under both judges. At National Championship trials, and at the National Amateur Championship trial for English Springer Spaniels, the dogs should run in pairs for at least four land series, but it is required that each dog competing must be paired with another dog in at least two of these series, in all four if possible. In no event may a dog not under judgment be used to create a pair. They may thereafter be run singly under both Judges, at their discretion, in additional land series. All dogs that are awarded places or a Judges' Award of Merit shall have been down for one performance under each of the two officiating Judges. A dog to receive any award must compete in all land series, and all water tests if any be held.

SECTION 3. No Judge of an Open All-Age, a Qualified Open All-Age or an Amateur All-Age Stake at a Spaniel Trial shall enter or run a dog or allow any dog that he owns to be entered or run, in any stake at that trial.

A Judge of any stake, other than an Open All-Age, a Qualified Open All-Age or an Amateur All-Age Stake at a Spaniel Trial may enter or run a dog or allow any dog that he owns to be entered or run in any stake at that trial that he is not judging.

SECTION 4. In Brace or Team Stakes the order of running in the first series shall be decided by draw, and the dogs composing a brace or team must belong to the same owner. No dogs shall form part of more than one brace or team at the same meeting and each brace or team shall have but one handler. A brace consists of two dogs and a team consists of three or more dogs. Dogs will be expected to work their ground harmoniously together, performing as in a single stake.

When a retrieve is to be made, the Judge shall designate the dog.

SECTION 5. In all stakes the Spaniels shall be regularly shot over in the customary sporting manner, and may be worked up and down wind, as well as in water when possible. No handler shall carry any training or other handling equipment (except whistle) exposed or in such manner that it may be used as a steadying aid or threat.

SECTION 6. Only stakes which in their land series are run on live full-winged game birds shall be permitted to carry championship points.

SECTION 7. The use of any trap or contrivance from which game can be released is prohibited in any Open All-Age Stake carrying championship points.

SECTION 8. The Judges are empowered to turn out of the stake any dog that does not obey its handler, or any handler who wilfully interferes with another competitor, or his dog, or any dog they may consider unfit to compete. Bitches in season shall not be allowed for competition in any stake and shall not be allowed on the field trial grounds. The entry fee of all such dogs will be forfeited except in cases of bitches in season.

SECTION 9. The owner or agent entering a dog in a trial does so at his own risk, and agrees to abide by the rules of The American Kennel Club.

SECTION 10. In the event of the weather proving unsuitable for holding the trials, it shall be in the power of the Field Trial Committee to postpone the meeting from day to day for a maximum of three days following the last advertised day, provided said postponement does not conflict with any other Spaniel field trial. After postponements for three days the provisions of Section 11 of this Chapter shall come into operation.

SECTION 11. In the event of the weather still proving unsuitable after postponements for three days, the Field Trial Committee may then abandon the meeting at any time, on returning the entry fees to the competitors. If, through unforeseen circumstances, the Field Trial Committee shall deem it advisable to alter the date of the meeting after the closing of the entries, this may be done with the consent of The American Kennel Club and by sending formal notices to all competitors, who may exercise the option of cancelling their entries within four (4) days from the date of such notice, in which event their entry fees will be returned to them. All entries, however, in regard to which no such option is exercised, will stand good for the meeting at its altered date.

SECTION 12. The regular official stakes at a Spaniel field trial shall be Puppy, Novice, Limit, Open All-Age, Qualified Open All-Age, and Amateur All-Age.

SECTION 13. Only one open all-age stake may be run at any trial. When an open all-age stake is referred to, it shall be understood to mean either an Open All-Age or a Qualified Open All-Age stake.

An Amateur All-Age stake, when offered for English Springer Spaniels, will be a championship stake.

SECTION 14. A Puppy Stake at a Spaniel field trial shall be for dogs that have not reached their second birthday on the first day of the trial in which Puppy Stake is included.

SECTION 15. A Novice Stake at a Spaniel field trial shall be for dogs that have never won first, second, third or fourth in an Open All-Age Stake, a Qualified Open All-Age Stake or an Amateur All-Age Stake or first in any other regular stake (Puppy stake excepted) in a licensed or member Spaniel trial.

SECTION 16. A Novice Handler Stake at a Spaniel field trial shall be for novice handlers only and only for dogs that qualify for a Novice Stake as set forth in Section 15. A Novice handler is one who has never handled a dog placed first, second, third or fourth in an Open All-Age Stake, a Qualified Open All-Age Stake or an Amateur All-Age Stake or a dog placed first in any other regular stake (Puppy stake excepted) in a licensed or member Spaniel trial.

SECTION 17. A Limit Stake at a Spaniel field trial shall be for dogs that have never won first place in an Open All-Age Stake, or two firsts in any regular official stake (Puppy Stake excepted), at a licensed or member club Spaniel trial in the United States or at any Spaniel trial in any other country.

SECTION 18. An Open All-Age or Qualified Open All-Age Stake at a Spaniel field trial shall be for all dogs over six months of age.

SECTION 19. A Qualified Open All-Age Stake at a Spaniel field trial shall be for dogs over six months of age that have placed first, second, third or fourth in any stake (Puppy Stake excepted), at a licensed or member club Spaniel field trial. A dog imported from Canada or the United Kingdom may be admitted to such stake on presentation of evidence of such dog having placed in an equivalent stake in either of those countries.

SECTION 20. A Shooting Dog Stake at a Spaniel field trial shall be open to all dogs over six months of age.

SECTION 21. An Amateur All-Age Stake shall be for dogs over six months of age that are handled by amateurs. The status of the handler is to be determined by the field trial committee of the club holding the trial.

SECTION 22. A National Championship Stake at English Springer Spaniel field trials shall be for dogs over six months of age, which by reason of wins previously made qualify under special rules approved by the Board of Directors. This stake shall be run not more than once in any calendar year by the Parent Association of the breed or by a Club or Association formed for this purpose and duly licensed by The American Kennel Club. The winner of such stake shall become a Field Champion of Record and shall be entitled to be designated "National Springer Spaniel Field Champion of 19—."

SECTION 23. A National Amateur Championship Stake for English Springer Spaniels shall be for dogs over six months of age, which by reason of wins previously made qualify under special regulations adopted by the Board of Directors of The American Kennel Club. This stake shall be run not more than once in any calendar year by the Parent Association of the breed under procedures approved by The American Kennel Club. The winner of such stake shall become an Amateur Field Champion of Record and shall be entitled to be designated "National Amateur Springer Spaniel Field Champion of 19—."

SECTION 24. A National Championship Stake for Cocker Spaniels including English Cocker Spaniels shall be for dogs over six months of age, which by reason of wins previously made qualify under special rules approved by the Board of Directors of The American Kennel Club. This stake shall be run not more than once in any calendar year by the Parent Club or Association of the breed or by a Club or Association formed for this purpose and duly licensed by The American Kennel Club. The winner of such stake shall become a Field Champion of Record and shall be entitled to be designated "National Cocker Spaniel or English Cocker Spaniel Field Champion of 19—."

SECTION 25. Before a dog shall receive its field championship, it must have shown its ability to retrieve game from water, after a swim. The holding of Water Tests during a field trial will be left to the discretion of the Field Trial Committee of the club conducting the trial. Dogs competing must, if required by the Judges to do so, take such a test. Refusal by an owner or handler to let his dog take such tests will disqualify the dog in the stake in which it is competing and for the remainder of the trial. It is the responsibility of the Field Trial Secretary or Committee to submit the results properly signed by the Judges so that they will carry championship credit.

SECTION 26. Two Judges only shall officiate at one time. Both Judges of a stake are required to examine game before a decision is made as to hard mouth.

SECTION 27. Splitting of prizes and/or places at Spaniel field trials is prohibited.

SECTION 28. In the event of a disagreement between the Judges on any question, the Field Trial Committee of the club giving the trial shall appoint a referee to cast the deciding vote.

SECTION 29. The gun to be used in a Spaniel field trial shall be a double barrel hammerless 12 gauge. No load less than 3¼ drams of powder and 1⅛ ozs. of No. 5, No. 6, No. 7 or No. 7½ shot may be used. All shooting in other than Shooting Dog Stakes will be done by Guns appointed by the Committee. In Shooting Dog Stakes only, it is permissible to use any type 12, 16 or 20 gauge gun, provided not more than two shells are in the gun at any time.

SECTION 30. A spaniel shall become a Field Champion of Record, if registered in the American Kennel Club stud book, after having won Open All-Age or Qualified Open All-Age Stakes (limited to its own breed of Spaniel excepting in the case of Cocker Spaniels and English Cocker Spaniels, both of which may compete in the same stake) at field trials of member clubs of The American Kennel Club or at field trials of non-member clubs licensed by The American Kennel Club to hold field trials.

SECTION 31. The number of Open All-Age or Qualified Open All-Age Stakes to be won in order to become a Field Champion, and the number of starters necessary in each Open All-Age or Qualified Open All-Age Stake, shall be fixed and determined by the Board of Directors of The American Kennel Club.

At present to acquire a Field Championship an English Springer Spaniel must win (1) a National Championship Stake or (2) two Open All-Age Stakes or two Qualified Open All-Age Stakes or one Open All-Age Stake and one Qualified Open All-Age Stake at different trials with at least ten starters in either stake.

At present to acquire a Field Championship a Cocker Spaniel or English Cocker Spaniel must win (1) a National Championship Stake or (2) two Open All-Age Stakes or two Qualified Open All-Age Stake or one Open All-Age Stake and one Qualified Open All-Age Stake at different trials with at least six starters in either stake.

SECTION 32. The number of Amateur All-Age Stakes to be won by English Springer Spaniels in order to become an Amateur Field Champion and the number of starters necessary in such stakes shall be fixed and determined by the Board of Directors of The American Kennel Club. No English Springer Spaniel shall be recorded an Amateur Field Champion unless it has been registered in the American Kennel Club stud book.

At present to acquire an Amateur Field Championship an English Springer Spaniel must win (1) a National Amateur Championship Stake or (2) two Amateur All-Age Stakes at different trials with at least ten starters in each stake.

STANDARD PROCEDURE FOR SPANIEL FIELD TRIALS

1. The purpose of a Spaniel field trial is to demonstrate the performance of a properly trained Spaniel in the field. The performance should not differ from that in any ordinary day's shooting, except that in the trials a dog should do his work in a more nearly perfect way.

2. The function of a hunting Spaniel is to seek, find and flush game in an eager, brisk, quiet manner and when game is shot, to mark the fall or direction thereof and retrieve to hand. The dog should walk at heel or on a leash until ordered to seek game and should then thoroughly hunt the designated cover, within gun shot, in line of quest, without unnecessarily covering the ground twice, and should flush game boldly and without urging. When game is flushed, a dog should be steady to flush or command, and, if game is shot should retrieve at command only, but not until the Judge has instructed the handler. Dogs should retrieve quickly and briskly when ordered to do so and deliver tenderly to hand. They should then sit or "hup" until given further orders. Spaniels which bark and give tongue while questing are objectionable and should be severely penalized.

3. If a dog, following the line of a bird, is getting too far out he should be called off the line and later he should again be cast back on it. A dog which causes his handler and gun to run after him while line running, is out of control. Handlers may control their dogs by hand, voice, or whistle, but only in the quiet manner that would be used in the field. Any loud shouting or whistling is evidence that the dog is hard to handle, and, in addition, is disturbing to the game.

4. A dog should work to his handler and gun at all times. A dog which marks the fall of a bird, uses the wind, follows a strong runner which has been wounded, and will take direction from his handler is of great value.

5. When the Judge gives a line to a handler and dog to follow, this must be followed and the dog not allowed to interfere with the other contestant running parallel to him.

6. The Judges must judge their dogs for game-finding ability, steadiness, and retrieving. In game finding the dog should cover all his ground on the beat, leaving no game in his territory and showing courage in facing cover. Dogs must be steady to wing and shot and obey all commands. When ordered to retrieve they should do this tenderly and with speed. No trials for Spaniels can possibly be run without retrieving, as that is one of the main purposes for which a Spaniel is used.

7. In judging a Spaniel's work Judges should give attention to the following points, taking them as a whole throughout the entire performance rather than giving too much credit to a flashy bit of work.

Control at all times, and under all conditions.
Scenting ability and use of wind.
Manner of covering ground and briskness of questing.
Perseverance and courage in facing cover.
Steadiness to flush, shot and command.
Aptitude in marking fall of game and ability to find it.
Ability and willingness to take hand signals.
Promptness and style of retrieve and delivery.
Proof of tender mouth.

Where facilities exist and Water Tests are held in conjunction with a stake the manner and quality of the performance therein shall be given consideration by the Judges in making their awards. Such tests should not exceed in their requirements the conditions met in an ordinary day's rough shoot adjoining water. Land work is the primary function of a Spaniel but where a Water Test is given, any dog that does not complete the Water Test shall not be entitled to any award.

8. The Guns should shoot their game in a sportsmanlike manner, as they would in a day's shoot. The proper functioning of the Official Guns is of the utmost importance. The Guns are supposed to represent the handler up to the time the game is shot, although not interfering in any manner with his work or that of the down dogs. They are supposed, if possible, unless otherwise directed, to kill cleanly and consistently the game flushed by the Spaniels, at a point most advantageous to a fair trial of the dogs' abilities, with due regard to the dogs, handlers, Judges, gallery and other contingencies.

9. Care should be taken not to shoot so that the game falls too close to the dog. If this is done it does not afford a chance for the dog to show any good retrieving ability and often results in a bird being destroyed. The Guns should stand perfectly quiet after the shot, for otherwise they may interfere with the dog and handler. When a dog makes a retrieve no other birds or game should be shot unless ordered by the Judge for special reasons. The Gun must also keep himself in the correct position to the handler and others.

10. It has been repeatedly proven that the most efficient gun and load for this work, in all fairness to the dogs, handlers and those responsible for the trial, is a well-choked twelve gauge double gun, and a load of not less than three and one-fourth drams of smokeless powder or equivalent, and one and one-eighth ounces of No. 5, No. 6, No. 7 or No. 7½ shot.

11. All field trial-giving clubs should clearly recognize that Open All-Age Stakes are of the first importance and that all other stakes are of relatively lesser importance and that an entire day should be reserved for the running of an Open All-Age Stake unless there is a very small entry.

12. The Shooting Dog Stake.

(a) The stake should be judged on dog work and on gun handling and shooting, emphasizing the manner in which the Gun and the dog work together.

(b) Any type 12, 16 or 20 gauge gun may be used with the following restrictions:

(1) When a pump or automatic gun is used contestant shall load no more than two (2) shells including the one in the gun chamber.

(2) Immediately upon sending dog to retrieve contestant shall break his gun. In the case of a pump or automatic gun any remaining shell shall be ejected so that gun chamber is empty.

(3) The Gunner shall retain his gun at all times.

(4) No gun shall be loaded until contestant is instructed to do so by the Judge.

(5) The gun shall be carried in a safe manner and position at all times.

(6) A Gunner must never shoot toward or over the gallery.

(7) Carelessness in handling his gun shall be grounds for the immediate elimination of the contestant by the Judges.

(c) Dogs shall be run singly in the stake and their work and that of the Gunner be observed by both Judges.

(d) Particular attention is called to the provisions of the standard procedure that provides that Guns should shoot their game in a sportsmanlike manner as they would in an ordinary day's shoot.

THE AMERICAN KENNEL CLUB

Incorporated

BEAGLE FIELD TRIAL
AND REGISTRATION RULES

Amended to September 1, 1968

(Copyright 1968 by The American Kennel Club)

This issue of the Registration and Beagle Field Trial Rules and Procedures contains all revisions up to September 1, 1968, and will apply to all trials starting on and after that date.

REGISTRATION AND BEAGLE FIELD TRIAL RULES

CHAPTER 1
GENERAL EXPLANATIONS

SECTION 1. The word "dog" wherever used in these Field Trial Rules and Regulations includes both sexes.

SECTION 2. The words "United States of America" wherever used in these Rules and Regulations shall be construed to include all territories and possessions of the United States of America and all vessels sailing under the American Flag.

CHAPTER 2
REGISTRATION

SECTION 1. The breeder of a dog is the person who owned the dam of that dog when the dam was bred; except that if the dam was leased at the time of breeding, the breeder is the lessee.

SECTION 2. An American-bred dog is a dog whelped in the United States of America by reason of a mating which took place in the United States of America.

SECTION 3. Any person in good standing with The American Kennel Club may apply for the registration of any pure-bred dog or litter of pure-bred dogs owned by him, by supplying The American Kennel Club with such information and complying with such conditions as it shall require.

SECTION 4. No individual dog from a litter whelped in the United States of America of which both parents are registered with The American Kennel Club shall be eligible for registration unless the litter has first been registered by the person who owned the dam at time of whelping; except that if the dam was leased at time of whelping the litter may be registered only by the lessee.

SECTION 5. No dog or litter out of a dam under eight (8) months or over twelve (12) years of age at time of mating, or by a sire under seven (7) months or over twelve (12) years of age at time of mating, will be registered unless the application for registration shall be accompanied by an affidavit or evidence which shall prove the fact to the satisfaction of The American Kennel Club.

SECTION 6. No litter of pure-bred dogs and/or no single pure-bred dog which shall be determined by The American Kennel Club to be acceptable in all other respects for registration, shall be barred from registration because of the failure, by the legal owner of all or part of said litter or said single dog to obtain some one or more of the signatures needed to complete the applicant's chain of title to the litter or dog sought to be registered, unless that person, who, when requested, refuses so to sign the application form, shall furnish a reason therefor satisfactory to The American Kennel Club, such as the fact that at the time of service an agreement in writing was made between the owner or lessee of the sire and the owner or lessee of the dam to the effect that no application for registration should be made and/or that the produce of such union should not be registered. In all cases where such an agreement in writing has been made, any person disposing of any of the produce of such union must secure from the new owner a statement in writing that it shall not be registered. For the purpose of registering or refusing to register pure-bred dogs, The American Kennel Club will recognize only such conditional sale or conditional stud agreements affecting the registration of pure-bred dogs as are in writing and are shown to have been brought to the attention of the applicant for registration. The American Kennel Club cannot recognize alleged conditional sale, conditional stud or other agreements not in writing which affect the registration of pure-bred dogs, until after the existence, construction and/or effect of the same shall have been determined by an action at law.

The owner or owners of a stud dog pure-bred and eligible for registration who in print or otherwise asserts or assert it to be pure-bred and eligible for registration and on the strength of such assertion secures or permits its use at stud, must pay the cost of its registration. The owner or owners of a brood bitch pure-bred and eligible for registration who in print or otherwise asserts or assert it to be pure-bred and eligible for registration and on the strength of such assertion leases it or sells its produce or secures the use of a stud by promising a puppy or puppies as payment of the stud fee in lieu of cash, must pay the cost of its registration.

That person or those persons refusing without cause to sign the application form or forms necessary for the registration of a litter of pure-bred dogs or of a single pure-bred dog and that person or those persons refusing without cause to pay the necessary fees due from him, her or them to be paid in order to complete the chain of title to a pure-bred litter or a pure-bred single dog sought to be registered, when requested by The American Kennel Club, may be suspended from the privileges of The American Kennel Club or fined as the Board of Directors of The American Kennel Club may elect.

The registration of a single pure-bred dog out of a litter eligible for registration may be secured by its legal owner as a one-dog litter registration and the balance of the litter may be refused registration where the breeder or the owner or lessee of the dam at the date of whelping wrongfully has refused to register the litter and that person or those persons so wrongfully refusing shall be suspended from the privileges of The American Kennel Club or fined as the Board of Directors of The American Kennel Club may elect.

SECTION 7. No change in the name of a dog registered with The American Kennel Club will be allowed to be made.

SECTION 8. Any person in good standing with The American Kennel Club may apply for transfer of ownership to him of any registered dog acquired by him by supplying The American Kennel Club with such information and complying with such conditions as it shall require.

CHAPTER 3

IDENTIFICATION AND RECORDS

SECTION 1. The word "person" as used in this chapter includes any individual, partnership, firm, corporation, association or organization of any kind.

The word "dog" as used in this chapter includes a dog or puppy of any age and either sex.

SECTION 2. Each person who breeds, keeps, transfers ownership or possession of, or deals in dogs which are registered or to be registered with The American Kennel Club, whether he acts as principal or agent or sells on consignment, must make in connection therewith and preserve for five years adequate and accurate records. The Board of Directors shall by regulation designate the specific information which must be included in such records.

SECTION 3. Each person who breeds, keeps, transfers ownership or possession of, or deals in dogs that are registered or to be registered with The American Kennel Club, whether he acts as principal or agent or sells on consignment, must follow such practices as, consistent with the number of dogs involved, will preclude any possibility of error in identification of any individual dog or doubt as to the parentage of any particular dog or litter.

SECTION 4. The American Kennel Club or its duly authorized representative shall have the right to inspect the records required to be kept and the practices required to be followed by these rules and by any regulations adopted under them, and to examine any dog registered or to be registered with The American Kennel Club.

SECTION 5. Each person who transfers ownership or possession of a dog that is registered or to be registered with The American Kennel Club must describe the dog in the records of The American Kennel Club in writing to the person acquiring the dog at the time of transfer, either on a bill of sale or otherwise. The Board of Directors shall by regulation designate the descriptive information required.

SECTION 6. The American Kennel Club may refuse to register any dog or litter or to record the transfer of any dog, for the sole reason that the application is not supported by the records required by these rules and the regulations adopted under them.

SECTION 7. Any person who is required to keep records and who fails to do so or who fails or refuses when requested to make such records available for inspection by The American Kennel Club or its duly authorized representatives, may be suspended from all privileges of The American Kennel Club by the Board of Directors.

Any person who fails to follow such practices as will preclude any possibility of error in identification of an individual dog or doubt as to the parentage of a particular dog or litter, or who fails or refuses to permit The American Kennel Club or its duly authorized representatives to examine such practices, or to examine a dog that is registered or to be registered with The American Kennel Club, may be suspended from all privileges of The American Kennel Club by the Board of Directors.

CHAPTER 4

KENNEL NAMES

SECTION 1. The American Kennel Club will not protect any person against the use by any other person of a kennel name in the registration of dogs with The American Kennel Club or in the entry of registered dogs in field trials held under The American Kennel Club rules, unless the kennel name has been registered with The American Kennel Club.

SECTION 2. On and after October 1, 1948, applications for the use of a kennel name as a prefix in the registering and running of dogs shall be made to The American Kennel Club on a form which will be supplied by said Club upon request, and said application must be accompanied by a fee, the amount of which shall be determined by the Board of Directors of The American Kennel Club. The Board will then consider such application and if it approves of the name selected will grant the right to the use of such name only as a prefix for a period of five (5) years.

The recorded owner shall have first consideration of the grant to use said kennel name for additional consecutive five (5) year terms upon receipt of the application for renewal accompanied by the renewal fee, the amount of which shall be determined by the Board of Directors, when received before the date of expiration of the original grant but the grant for any five (5) year renewal term will be made only at the expiration of the previous term.

In the event of the death of a recorded owner of a registered kennel name, his executors, administrators, or legal heirs, upon submission of proper proof of their status may use the name as a prefix during the remainder of the five (5) year term of use and the legal heir of the deceased recorded owner, or the executors or administrators acting in his behalf, shall have first consideration of the grant to the use of said name for additional terms, as provided heretofore in this section.

SECTION 3. If the recorded owner of a registered kennel name granted after October 1, 1948, desires to transfer ownership of or an interest in said kennel name to a new owner, application to transfer such name for the unexpired term must be made to The American Kennel Club on a form which will be supplied by said Club upon request. The application must be submitted for the approval of the Board of Directors of The American Kennel Club and accompanied by a fee, the amount of which shall be determined by the Board of Directors of The American Kennel Club.

Any kennel name granted by The American Kennel Club prior to October 1, 1948 may be transferred by its present owner or owners to another only by consent and on certain conditions and payment of fee as determined by the Board of Directors of The American Kennel Club.

SECTION 4. In the case of any registered kennel name which is recorded as jointly owned by two or more persons, application to transfer the interest of one co-owner to another co-owner, may be made to The American Kennel Club on a form which will be supplied by said Club upon request. The application must be submitted for the approval of the Board of Directors of The American Kennel Club but no fee will be charged for such a transfer.

SECTION 5. The protection of all kennel names registered between March 1, 1934 and October 1, 1948 shall depend upon their continuous use by registered owners. Neglect by the recorded owner of a registered kennel name to use such name in the registration of dogs for a continuous period of six (6) years or more shall be considered such an abandonment of the name as to justify The American Kennel Club in refusing to protect its use unless the owner or owners thereof prior to the expiration of such six (6) year period shall notify The American Kennel Club of his, her or their desire to retain the same.

CHAPTER 5

DEFINITIONS

SECTION 1. A MEMBER FIELD TRIAL is a field trial at which championship points may be awarded, held by a club which is a member of The American Kennel Club.

SECTION 2. A LICENSED FIELD TRIAL is a field trial at which championship points may be awarded, held by a club which is not a member of The American Kennel Club but which has been licensed by The American Kennel Club to hold the specific field trial designated in the license.

SECTION 3. A SANCTIONED FIELD TRIAL is a field trial at which dogs may compete but not for championship points, held by a club, whether or not a member of The American Kennel Club, or by a Beagle Association, by obtaining the sanction of The American Kennel Club.

SECTION 4. A BEAGLE FIELD TRIAL SEASON is a period of twelve months starting July 1.

CHAPTER 6

APPLICATIONS FOR LICENSED AND SANCTIONED TRIALS

SECTION 1. No more than one licensed or member field trial will be approved for any one club in any one Season.

SECTION 2. All applications to hold licensed or member Beagle field trials during a season should be filed with The American Kennel Club not later than March 1 before the start of that season. Any club filing such an application which is received by The American Kennel Club after March 1 shall, before its application is approved, pay a penalty fee of $25.00 plus an additional $5.00 for each full week of delinquency, and any application received after April 1 shall be rejected.

SECTION 3. A club which wishes to hold a licensed or member field trial must apply to The American Kennel Club on a form which will be supplied on request to clubs which meet the requirements of The American Kennel Club. This application will be referred to the Board of Directors of The American Kennel Club which will consider it and notify the club of its approval or disapproval.

SECTION 4. A non-member club shall submit with its application a check or money order in payment of the license fee, the amount of which shall be fixed and determined by the Board of Directors of The American Kennel Club. If the Board of Directors shall disapprove the application, the license fee will be returned to the club.

At present the license fee for a Beagle field trial is $25.00.

The following Section 5 does not apply to Beagle field trials as the parent club has granted blanket consent to the holding of field trials and specialty shows for Beagles.

SECTION 5. A non-member specialty club may be licensed to hold a field trial, if the consent in writing that it may be given first shall be obtained from the member specialty club formed for the improvement of the breed sought to be run which first was admitted to be a member of The American Kennel Club, which member club is commonly known as the Parent Club.

If a Parent Club unreasonably shall withhold its consent in writing to the holding of such field trial the non-member specialty club may appeal to the Board of Directors of The American Kennel Club at any time after one month from the time when said consent was requested and a committee of said Board appointed by said Board or between sittings of said Board appointed by the President of The American Kennel Club or in his absence by the Executive Vice-President of The American Kennel Club shall hear the parties who may present their respective contentions either orally or in writing and in its discretion may issue a license to the non-member specialty club to hold such field trial.

SECTION 6. A club holding a licensed or member field trial must not advertise or publish the dates of the field trial which it proposes to hold until they have been approved by The American Kennel Club.

SECTION 7. A member or non-member club or **Beagle Association** which wishes to hold a sanctioned field trial must apply to The American Kennel Club on a form which will be supplied upon request; provided, however, that the secretary of a Beagle association may file a blanket application for the regular Spring Derby sanctioned field trials of all of the clubs belonging to that association. American Kennel Club sanction must be obtained by any club that holds American Kennel Club events, for any type of event for which it solicits or accepts entries from non-members. An application for a sanctioned Beagle field trial will be referred to the Board of Directors of The American Kennel Club which will consider it and notify the club or association of its approval or disapproval. No fee is required to be paid for approval of an application for a sanctioned field trial.

SECTION 8. All of these rules and procedures shall apply to sanctioned field trials as well as to licensed or member field trials, except for those rules and procedures that state specifically that they apply to licensed or member trials only. Such rules will not apply to Plan B sanctioned trials unless the club specifies in the announcement for the event that a particular rule or procedure will apply.

SECTION 9. The use of a club's name for field trial purposes cannot be transferred.

CHAPTER 7
RIBBONS, MONEY PRIZES, AND SPECIAL PRIZES

SECTION 1. A club holding a licensed or member field trial shall offer prize ribbons or rosettes of the following colors in the four regular classes:

First prize—Blue.
Second prize—Red.
Third prize—Yellow.
Fourth prize—White.
N.B.Q.—Dark Green.

SECTION 2. Each ribbon or rosette at a licensed or member field trial shall be at least 2 inches wide and approximately 8 inches long and shall bear on its face a facsimile of the seal of The American Kennel Club, the words Field Trial, the name of the prize, the name of the field trial-giving club, and the date of the trial.

SECTION 3. If ribbons or rosettes are given at sanctioned field trials they shall be of the following colors, and shall bear the words Field Trial, but may be of any design or size:

First prize—Rose.
Second prize—Brown.
Third prize—Light Green.
Fourth prize—Gray.
N.B.Q.—Orange.

SECTION 4. If money prizes are offered, a fixed amount or percentage of the entry fee for each prize shall be stated.

SECTION 5. All special prizes not money which may be offered shall be accurately described or the value stated. Stud services shall not be accepted as special prizes.

CHAPTER 8
JUDGES AND THEIR DECISIONS

SECTION 1. Persons judging field trials are not required to obtain licenses and a field trial club may submit the name of any reputable person who is in good standing with The American Kennel Club for approval to judge at its field trial. Such approved Judges may run dogs in any classes which they are not judging.

SECTION 2. Substitute or additional Judges may be appointed by a field trial club at its field trial, if occasion demands, provided however that said substitute or additional Judges are persons in good standing with The American Kennel Club. When additional Judges are used they shall act in conjunction with one or more of the advertised Judges if practicable. The American Kennel Club shall be promptly notified of additional or substitute Judges officiating.

SECTION 3. Before any advertised Judge shall be eligible to judge a licensed or member field trial, he shall first sign an agreement certifying that he has a thorough knowledge of the rules, regulations and procedures, and will judge in strict accord with them.

SECTION 4. The decisions of the Judges shall be final in all matters relating to the merits of the hounds.

CHAPTER 9
FIELD TRIAL COMMITTEE, FIELD TRIAL SECRETARY, PREMIUM LISTS

SECTION 1. A club or Beagle association that has been granted permission by The American Kennel Club to hold a field trial must appoint a Field Trial Committee which shall have charge of the organization and management of the trial. The committee shall have at least five members and may include the Field Trial Secretary.

SECTION 2. A club that has been granted permission by The American Kennel Club to hold a licensed or member field trial must appoint a Field Trial Secretary acceptable to The American Kennel Club whose name and address must be submitted to The American Kennel Club before the premium list for the trial can be printed. Any reputable person who is in good standing with The American Kennel Club may act as Field Trial Secretary.

SECTION 3. The Field Trial Committee and Field Trial Secretary shall be held responsible for compliance with the Beagle Field Trial Rules and Procedures, and must provide themselves with copies of the latest edition of this book.

SECTION 4. A club that has been granted permission by The American Kennel Club to hold a licensed or member field trial, before its premium list and entry forms shall be printed, must send to The American Kennel Club for approval two copies of a questionnaire form supplied by The American Kennel Club which will specify the exact location of the grounds where the trial is to be run; whether the trial will be run in braces, small packs, or large packs; the classes to be run and their conditions; the place where the drawing or numbering will be done and, for a Large Pack trial, the hours during which hounds will be measured for each class; the time entries close for each class; the date each class is to start; the names and addresses of the Judges and the classes which each is to judge; a complete list of money, ribbon prizes and special prizes which the club wishes to offer; the entry fee; the names and addresses of the officers of the club and of the Field Trial Secretary; the name and address of the chairman and the names of the other members of the Field Trial Committee. The premium list for each licensed or member field trial shall contain all of the information set forth on the questionnaire form as approved by The American Kennel Club and shall be the official size, 6 x 9 inches.

SECTION 5. Every premium list for a licensed or member field trial shall contain one or more copies of the official American Kennel Club entry form, samples of which will be supplied on request.

SECTION 6. Such extracts of the rules as shall be designated by the Board of Directors of The American Kennel Club shall be furnished with every premium list or entry form for a licensed or member field trial.

SECTION 7. Field Trial Committees may make such regulations or additional rules for the government of their field trials as shall be considered necessary, provided such regulations or additional rules do not conflict with any rule or procedure of The American Kennel Club. Such regulations or additional rules shall be printed in the premium list of a licensed or member field trial and violations thereof shall be considered the same as violations of the Rules and Regulations of The American Kennel Club.

CHAPTER 10

ENTRY REQUIREMENTS AND ELIGIBILITY

SECTION 1. Every hound entered in a field trial must either be individually registered in The American Kennel Club Stud Book, or be part of an AKC registered litter, or otherwise, if whelped outside the United States of America and imported by a resident of the U.S.A. or owned by a resident of Canada, must have been registered in its country of birth with a foreign registry organization whose pedigrees are acceptable for American Kennel Club registration.

SECTION 2. An unregistered hound that is part of an AKC registered litter or a hound with an acceptable foreign registration that has been imported by a resident of the U.S.A. or that is Canadian owned may, without special AKC approval, be entered in licensed or member field trial classes which are started not more than 30 days after the first entry in a licensed or member field trial, but only provided that the AKC litter registration number, or the individual foreign registration number and the name of the country of birth, are shown on each entry form, and provided further that the same name, which in the case of an imported or Canadian owned hound must be the name on the foreign registration, is used for the hound each time.

SECTION 3. No hound that has not been individually registered with The American Kennel Club when first entered in a licensed or member field trial shall be eligible to be entered in any licensed or member field trial class that is started more than 30 days after the first entry in a licensed or member field

trial, unless the hound's individual AKC registration number is shown on the entry form, or unless the owner has received from The American Kennel Club an extension notice authorizing further entries of the hound for a specified time with its litter number or foreign registration number. No such extension will be granted unless the owner can clearly demonstrate, in a letter addressed to the Field Trial Records Department of The American Kennel Club requesting such extension, that the delay in registration is due to circumstances for which he is not responsible. Any such extension notice will be void upon registration of the hound or upon expiration of the period for which extension has been granted, but upon application further extensions may be granted.

SECTION 4. If a hound is later individually registered with a name that is not identical to the name under which it has been entered in field trials prior to individual registration, each entry form entering the hound in a licensed or member field trial after the owner has received the individual registration certificate must show the registered name followed by "formerly run as" and the name under which the hound was previously run, until the hound has been awarded one of the four official places at a licensed or member trial.

SECTION 5. Each entry in a licensed or member field trial form must be made on an official American Kennel Club entry form. Each entry form must be completed in full and must be signed by the owner or his agent duly authorized to make the entry, and the information given on the form must be that which applies to the entered hound.

SECTION 6. Every hound must be entered in the name of the person who actually owned the hound at the time entries closed. The right to enter and run a hound cannot be transferred. A registered hound which has been acquired by some person other than the owner as recorded with The American Kennel Club must be entered in the name of its new owner at any field trial for which entries close after the date on which the hound was acquired, and application for transfer of ownership must be sent to The American Kennel Club by the new owner within seven days after the last day of the trial. The new owner should state on the entry form that transfer application has been mailed to The American Kennel Club or will be mailed shortly. If there is any unavoidable delay in obtaining the completed application required to record the transfer, The American Kennel Club may grant a reasonable extension of time provided the new owner notifies the Field Trial Records Department of The American Kennel Club by mail within seven days after the trial, of the reason for the delay. If an entry is made by a duly authorized agent of the owner, the name of the actual owner must be shown on the entry form. If a hound is owned by an association, the name of the association and a list of its officers must be shown on the entry form.

SECTION 7. Owners are responsible for errors made on entry forms regardless of who may have made such errors.

SECTION 8. No entry shall be accepted from any person who stands suspended from the privileges of The American Kennel Club.

SECTION 9. No entry shall be made under a kennel name unless that name has been registered with The American Kennel Club. All entries made under a kennel name must be signed with the kennel name followed by the word "registered." An "entrant" is the individual, or, if a partnership, all the members of the partnership, entering in a field trial. In the case of such entry by a partnership every member of the partnership shall be in good standing with The American Kennel Club before the entry will be accepted; and in case of any infraction of these rules, all the partners shall be held equally responsible.

SECTION 10. No hound shall be eligible to compete at any field trial, no hound shall be brought into the grounds or premises of any field trial, and any hound which may have been brought into the grounds or premises of a field trial shall immediately be removed, if it

(a) shows clinical symptoms of distemper, infectious hepatitis, leptospirosis or other communicable disease, or

(b) is known to have been in contact with distemper, infectious hepatitis, leptospirosis or other communicable disease within thirty days prior to the opening of the trial, or

(c) has been kenneled within thirty days prior to the opening of the trial on premises on which there existed distemper, infectious hepatitis, leptospirosis or other communicable disease.

SECTION 11. A hound is not eligible to be entered or to compete in any field trial in any class if an advertised or actual judge of that class or any member of his immediate family or household has owned, sold, held under lease, boarded, trained, or handled, the hound within one year prior to the date of the field trial. Immediate family means husband, wife, father, mother, son, daughter, brother, or sister.

SECTION 12. Any field trial-giving club which accepts an entry fee other than that published in its premium list, or in any way discriminates between entrants, shall be disciplined. No club or member of any club shall give or offer to give any owner or handler any special inducements, such as reduced entry fees, allowances for board or transportation or other incentive of value for a certain number of entries or shall give or offer to give in consideration of entering a certain number of hounds, any prizes or prize money, except the officially advertised prizes or prize money, which prize money shall be for a stated sum or a portion of the entry fees. Any club found guilty of violating this rule shall be barred from holding licensed or sanctioned trials, and if a member of The American Kennel Club, may be expelled from membership therein. All persons found guilty of paying or receiving any monies, special inducements or allowances in violation of the foregoing shall be disciplined, even to the extent of being deprived of all privileges of The American Kennel Club for a stated time or indefinitely.

SECTION 13. A Field Trial Committee may decline any entries or may remove any hound from its trial for cause, but in each such instance shall file good and sufficient reasons for so doing with The American Kennel Club.

SECTION 14. Any hound entered and present at a field trial must compete in any class in which it is entered unless it is disqualified or marked absent by the Judges, or is found to be ineligible or is excused by the Field Trial Committee after consultation with the Judges.

CHAPTER 11
CANCELLATIONS AND PROTESTS AGAINST HOUNDS

SECTION 1. If at a licensed or member trial, an ineligible hound has been entered in any class, or if a hound has been entered in the name of an owner other than the actual owner at the time entries closed, or if a hound has been run in a class for which it was not entered, or if its entry form is deemed invalid by The American Kennel Club under these rules, any resulting awards shall be cancelled by The American Kennel Club and such hound shall not be counted as a starter in determining championship ratings.

SECTION 2. If the win of a hound at a licensed or member trial is cancelled, the hound next in order of merit shall be moved up, if eligible, and the win of the hound moved up shall be counted the same as if it had been the original award.

SECTION 3. If the win of a hound is cancelled by The American Kennel Club, the owner of the hound shall return all prizes for such win to the Secretary of the field-giving club within ten (10) days of receipt of notice from The American Kennel Club of said cancellation.

SECTION 4. A protest against a hound may be made by the owner of any hound entered in a field trial or by the duly authorized agent of any such owner, or by any member of a member club of The American Kennel Club. It shall be in writing, and be lodged with the Secretary of the field trial-giving club within seven (7) days of the last day of the field trial unless the same be made by The American Kennel Club, provided, however, that a protest calling for a decision as to the physical condition of a hound which can be made only by a Veterinarian or at the time of running shall be made before the closing of the field trial. No protest will be entertained unless accompanied by a deposit of five ($5.00) dollars, which will be returned if the protest is sustained. This does not apply to protests by The American Kennel Club.

SECTION 5. If a protest against a hound is made during the holding of a field trial, the Field Trial Committee shall hold a meeting as soon as possible and shall give all parties concerned an opportunity to be heard and shall at once render its decision. If a protest is made after the field trial, it shall be decided by the field trial-giving club within thirty (30) days of its receipt. Five days notice of the date and place of hearing shall be given to all parties concerned. Written copies of all decisions on protests shall be forwarded immediately to The American Kennel Club.

SECTION 6. An appeal may be taken to The American Kennel Club from a decision of a Field Trial Committee where

a hound has been protested. Any such appeal shall be forwarded to The American Kennel Club within seven (7) days of the date on which the decision was rendered, together with a deposit of ten ($10.00) dollars. If the decision be sustained the deposit shall be forfeited but if reversed the deposit shall be returned.

CHAPTER 12
DESCRIPTION OF CLASSES AND CHAMPIONSHIP REQUIREMENTS

SECTION 1. All licensed and member Beagle field trials shall be run under one of the three following procedures:

    A. Braces on Rabbit or Hare.
    B. Small Packs on Rabbit or Hare.
    C. Large Packs on Hare.

At a licensed or member Beagle field trial there shall be separate classes for:

Open Dogs not exceeding 13 inches in height.

Open Bitches not exceeding 13 inches in height.

Open Dogs over 13 inches but not exceeding 15 inches in height.

Open Bitches over 13 inches but not exceeding 15 inches in height.

However, if when the entries are closed, it is found that there are less than six hounds of a sex eligible to compete in any class, that class shall be combined and run with both sexes in a single class if possible, but no classes shall be combined under any other circumstances.

No hound shall be eligible to run in more than one of these classes at any field trial.

SECTION 2. Splitting of prizes or places is prohibited.

SECTION 3. Field Championship points for Beagles shall be awarded only to hounds placing in licensed or member trials in Open Classes in which there were six or more starters. The championship points shall be awarded on the following basis:

    1 point to the winner of first place for each starter;
    ½ point to the winner of second place for each starter;
    ⅓ point to the winner of third place for each starter;
    ¼ point to the winner of fourth place for each starter.

A starter is an entered eligible hound that has not been disqualified and that has been cast or laid on a line with its brace mate at the start of its first series heat at a brace trial; or that has been cast at the start of its first series pack at a small pack trial; or that has been cast at the start with the rest of the pack at a large pack trial.

SECTION 4. The total number of wins and championship points necessary for a Beagle to be recorded a Field Champion by The American Kennel Club shall be established by the Board of Directors of The American Kennel Club. The wins and points may be acquired in both the 13 inch and 15 inch divisions.

To be recorded a Field Champion, a hound of either sex must have won three first places and 120 points in classes with not less than six starters at licensed or member field trials.

SECTION 5. A Beagle that has won the required number of classes and championship points will, when registered in the Stud Book, be recorded a Field Champion, and a championship certificate will be issued to the owner. A hound becomes a Field Champion when it is so officially recorded by The American Kennel Club.

SECTION 6. A Field Champion may be designated as "Dual Champion" if it has also been awarded the title of Champion. No certificate will be awarded for a Dual Champion.

CHAPTER 13
JUDGES' BOOKS AND REPORTS

SECTION 1. At the conclusion of the judging of each class at a licensed or member field trial the club shall provide for the Judges' signatures a book showing the class judged and the full particulars of each hound placed at a brace trial, or the number of each hound placed at a pack trial. The Judges shall certify to the number of actual starters, which shall not include any hound that has been disqualified or measured out for second series or for the winners pack or that has been otherwise found to be ineligible. At the conclusion of the field trial the Field Trial Secretary shall certify to the Judges' signatures for the respective classes and shall also certify to the number of hounds drawn for a Brace or Small Pack trial or entered for a Large Pack trial, and to the number of starters. At a trial run in small or large packs he shall also certify as to the identity of each hound according to its number.

The Judges' book, together with all the entry forms, and a full report of the trial, shall be sent to The American Kennel Club in time to be received by them no later than seven days after the closing date of the trial. A penalty fee of $1.00 per day must be paid if these records are not received by The American Kennel Club within seven days, and the Board of Directors may impose additional penalties.

The report shall contain a list of the names of all members of the Field Trial Committee who were present at the trial, the names and complete addresses of all of the Judges, and the name and address of the Field Trial Secretary.

Extracts from By-Laws

CHAPTER 14
DISCIPLINE

Article XII of the Constitution and By-Laws of The American Kennel Club provides:

SECTION 1. Any club or association or person or persons interested in pure-bred dogs may prefer charges against any other club or association or person or persons for conduct alleged to have been prejudicial to the best interests of pure-bred dogs, dog shows, obedience trials or field trials, or prejudicial to the best interests of The American Kennel Club, which charges shall be made in writing in duplicate setting forth in detail the nature thereof, shall be signed and sworn to by an officer of the club or association or by the person or persons making the same before some person qualified to administer oaths and shall be sent to The American Kennel Club together with a deposit of ten ($10.00) dollars, which sum shall become the property of The American Kennel Club if said charges shall not be sustained, or shall be returned if said charges are sustained, or if The American Kennel Club shall refuse to entertain jurisdiction thereof.

The power conferred by Section 2 below to suspend a person from all privileges of The American Kennel Club applies only to Field Trial Committees at licensed or member field trials. At a sanctioned trial, the Field Trial Committee should collect evidence, hold a hearing, and report its findings and conclusions to The American Kennel Club.

SECTION 2. The Bench Show, Obedience Trial or Field Trial Committee of a club or association shall have the right to suspend any person from the privileges of The American Kennel Club for conduct prejudicial to the best interests of pure-bred dogs, dog shows, obedience trials, field trials or The American Kennel Club, alleged to have occurred in connection with or during the progress of its show, obedience trial or field trial, after the alleged offender has been given an opportunity to be heard.

Notice in writing must be sent promptly by registered mail by the Bench Show, Obedience Trial or Field Trial Committee to the person suspended and a duplicate notice giving the name and address of the person suspended and full details as to the reasons for the suspension must be forwarded to The American Kennel Club within seven (7) days.

An appeal may be taken from a decision of a Bench Show, Obedience Trial or Field Trial Committee. Notice in writing claiming such appeal together with a deposit of five ($5.00) dollars must be sent to The American Kennel Club within thirty (30) days after the date of suspension. The Board of Directors may itself hear said appeal or may refer it to a committee of the Board, or to a Trial Board to be heard. The deposit shall become the property of The American Kennel Club if the decision is confirmed, or shall be returned to The appellant if the decision is not confirmed.

SECTION 3. Upon receipt of duly preferred charges the Board of Directors of The American Kennel Club at its election either may itself consider the same or send the same to a Trial Board for hearing.

In either case a notice which shall state that said charges have been filed and shall set forth a copy of the same shall be sent to the club or association or person or persons against which or whom said charges have been preferred which club or association, or person or persons herein shall be known as and called the defendant. The club or association or person or persons which or who shall have preferred said charges herein shall be known as and called the complainant.

Said notice also shall set forth a time and place at which the defendant may attend and present any defense or answer which the defendant may wish to make.

If the complainant shall fail or refuse to appear and prosecute said charges or if the defendant shall fail or refuse to appear and present a defense at the time and place designated for the hearing of said charges, without giving a reasonable excuse for such failure or refusal, the Board of Directors or the Trial Board to which said charges have been referred may suspend whichever party shall be so in default from the privileges of The American Kennel Club for a period of six (6) months or until such time as the party so in default shall be prepared to appear ready and willing to prosecute or defend said charge as the case may be.

SECTION 4. The Board of Directors shall have the power to investigate any matters which may be brought to its attention in connection with the objects for which this Club was founded, or it may appoint a committee or Trial Board to investigate, in which event the same procedure shall be followed and the same rules shall apply as in a trial before a Trial Board.

If after such investigation the Board of Directors believes that sufficient evidence exists to warrant the filing of charges, it may file or direct the filing of such charges. The Board of Directors acting in accordance with the provisions of this Article may prefer charges for conduct prejudicial to the best interests of The American Kennel Club against persons who shall bring to its attention any matter which upon investigation shall be found to have been reported to it from malicious or untruthful motives or to have been based upon suspicion without foundation of fact or knowledge.

SECTION 5. The Board of Directors of The American Kennel Club shall have power to prefer charges against any association, or other club, or person or persons, for conduct alleged to be prejudicial to pure-bred dogs, dog shows, obedience trials or field trials or to the best interests of The American Kennel Club, and pending the final determination of any such charges, may withhold the privileges of The American Kennel Club from any such other person or body against whom charges are pending.

SECTION 6. The Board of Directors shall have the power to suspend from the privileges of The American Kennel Club any member or Delegate pending final action by the Delegates in accordance with the provisions of this section, for conduct alleged to have been prejudicial to the best interests of The American Kennel Club or for violation of its Constitution, By-Laws or Rules.

The Board of Directors shall then file charges and promptly set a date for a hearing and send to such suspended member or Delegate by registered mail at least ten days prior to the date so fixed, notice of the time when and the place where the suspended member or Delegate may be heard in its or his defense. Said notice shall also set forth a copy of the charges.

The Board of Directors may itself hear the evidence of the suspended member or Delegate and any witnesses or may refer the charges to a committee of the Board or to a Trial Board to take the testimony and to report its findings or recommendations to the Board of Directors.

The Board of Directors, after hearing or reviewing the evidence, shall report its findings to The American Kennel Club at the next regular meeting of the Club, whereupon the Delegates shall take action upon said findings and by a majority vote of the Delegates present may reinstate, continue the suspension for a stated time or expel such member or Delegate from The American Kennel Club.

SECTION 7. The American Kennel Club shall have the power by a two-thirds vote of the Delegates present and voting at any regular meeting to suspend from the privileges of The American Kennel Club any member or Delegate for conduct alleged to have been prejudicial to the best interests of The American Kennel Club or for violation of its Constitution, By-Laws or Rules.

The order of suspension thus made shall then be referred to the Board of Directors for hearing and report under the procedure as set forth in Paragraphs 2, 3, and 4 of Section 6 of this Article.

SECTION 8. The Board of Directors of The American Kennel Club shall have power to hear as an original matter any charges preferred and to review and finally determine any appeal which may be made to the Board of Directors from the decision of a Trial Board, Bench Show, Obedience Trial or Field Trial Committee, and in each instance in which it shall impose such penalty as said Board of Directors may decide to be just and proper.

SECTION 9. The Board of Directors of The American Kennel Club and any Trial Board of The American Kennel Club with the permission of the Board of Directors of The American Kennel Club first obtained in writing may, in the discretion of said Board of Directors, and if necessary at the Club's expense, summon witnesses or a member of any Trial Board, Bench Show Committee, Obedience Trial Committee or Field Trial Committee to attend any and all hearings held under the provisions of Articles XII and XIII of the Constitution and By-Laws of The American Kennel Club. Said Board of Directors may suspend from the privileges of The American Kennel Club for a period of six months or until such time as he or she shall appear and be prepared and willing to testify any person so summoned who without reasonable excuse shall fail to appear and testify.

SECTION 10. The Board of Directors of The American Kennel Club shall, at the next meeting of the Board after an appeal is made from the decision of a Trial Board, Bench Show, Obedience Trial or Field Trial Committee, name a date for the hearing of such appeal and shall cause notice of the time when and the place where said hearing is to be held to be sent to all parties in interest by registered mail at least fourteen (14) days prior to the date named.

SECTION 11. Penalties may range from a reprimand or fine to suspension for life from all privileges of The American Kennel Club.

SECTION 12. The Treasurer of The American Kennel Club shall enforce all monetary penalties.

SECTION 13. The suspension or disqualification of a person shall date from the day of the perpetration of the act or from any date subsequent thereto which shall be fixed after hearing by a Trial Board or by the Board of Directors of The American Kennel Club and shall apply to all dogs owned or subsequently acquired by the person so suspended or disqualified.

SECTION 14. All privileges of The American Kennel Club shall be withheld from any person suspended or disqualified.

SECTION 15. Any club, association or organization which shall hold a dog show, obedience trial, field trial or dog exhibition of any kind not in accordance with the rules of The American Kennel Club which apply to such show, obedience trial, field trial or exhibition may be disciplined even to the extent of being deprived of all privileges of The American Kennel Club for a stated period of time or indefinitely, and if such club, association or organization shall be a member of The American Kennel Club, it may be expelled from membership therein.

SECTION 16. No club or association licensed by The American Kennel Club to give a show, obedience trial, hold a field trial or give a dog exhibition of any kind shall employ in any capacity, accept the donation of a prize or money from, or permit to be within the walls or boundaries of its building or grounds, if a dog show or obedience trial, or its grounds, if a field trial, save only as a spectator, any person known to be under suspension or disqualification from the privileges of The American Kennel Club or any employee or member of a corporation which shall be under suspension or disqualification from the privileges of The American Kennel Club.

SECTION 17. No member club or association under suspension shall be represented by its Delegate and no Delegate under suspension shall act for a member or in any official capacity for The American Kennel Club during the period of suspension.

SECTION 18. Any association, club, person or persons suspended or disqualified by The American Kennel Club or from whom the privileges of The American Kennel Club have been withheld, may apply for reinstatement or restoration of privileges upon paying a fee the amount of which may be fixed and determined by the Board of Directors of The American Kennel Club. Until said fee has been paid the application shall not be acted upon.

SECTION 19. As much of Article XII of these By-Laws as the Board of Directors of The American Kennel Club shall indicate shall be printed in any book or pamphlet which The American Kennel Club shall cause to be published containing the Rules of said Club.

CHAPTER 15

TRIAL BOARDS

Article XIII of the Constitution and By-Laws of The American Kennel Club provides:

SECTION 1. Trial Boards shall be appointed from time to time by the Board of Directors of The American Kennel Club and shall consist of three members for each Board, one of whom, if practicable, should be an attorney-at-law, and no one of whom shall be a Director of The American Kennel Club. In case one or more members of a Trial Board shall be unable to sit in any given case, the President, or in his absence, the Executive Vice-President of The American Kennel Club may appoint a substitute or substitutes for such case. In case of the absence of one or more members of said Board the remaining member or members may hear and determine a case if the parties being heard shall consent thereto.

SECTION 2. Trial Boards shall hear and decide by a majority vote matters submitted to them by the Board of Directors and shall have power to impose a fine not to exceed twenty-five ($25.00) dollars and/or withhold the privileges of the Club for a period of not more than six months, or may recommend to said Board of Directors the withholding of privileges for a longer period or may recommend disqualification or the imposition of fines exceeding twenty-five ($25.00) dollars.

If a Trial Board recommends the withholding of privileges or disqualification to the Board of Directors, the privileges of the Club shall be automatically withheld until the Board of Directors has adopted or refused to adopt such recommendation.

SECTION 3. Trial Boards shall have power to disqualify any person or withhold from any person all the privileges of The American Kennel Club for a period of not more than six months or to recommend to said Board of Directors the penalty of disqualification or the withholding of privileges for a longer period for improper or disorderly conduct during a hearing or a trial.

SECTION 4. Trial Boards shall keep minutes of their sittings.

SECTION 5. The decisions of Trial Boards shall be in writing signed by all members attending, and have annexed thereto all exhibits and papers offered before them. Each decision, together with complete copies of the minutes and testimony taken, shall be filed with the Secretary of The American Kennel Club within ten days of the date of the rendering of the decision. It shall be the duty of the Secretary of The American Kennel Club when received at once to notify in writing all parties in interest of the decision of a Trial Board.

SECTION 6. An appeal may be taken to the Board of Directors from any decision of a Trial Board, whether it be a decision in which the Trial Board itself imposes a certain penalty and/or fine, or one in which the Trial Board recommends that the Board of Directors shall impose a certain penalty and/or fine. Notice in writing claiming such appeal together with a deposit of twenty-five ($25.00) dollars must be sent to The American Kennel Club within thirty days after the receipt of the notice of the decision or recommendation of the Trial Board. The Board of Directors may itself hear said appeal or may refer it to a committee of the Board to be heard. The deposit of twenty-five ($25.00) dollars shall become the property of The American Kennel Club if the decision or recommendation of the Trial Board shall be confirmed, or shall be returned to the appellant if it shall not be confirmed. If the aggrieved party shall fail to take such appeal to the Board of Directors, there shall be no further right of appeal of any kind.

SECTION 7. Article XIII of these By-Laws shall be printed in any book or pamphlet which The American Kennel Club shall cause to be published containing the Rules of said Club.

THE AMERICAN KENNEL CLUB
Incorporated

STANDARD PROCEDURES

GENERAL PROCEDURES GOVERNING BEAGLE FIELD TRIALS RUN IN BRACES, SMALL PACKS OR LARGE PACKS.

Effective September 1, 1968

Approved by the Board of Directors of The American Kennel Club

GENERAL PROCEDURES GOVERNING BEAGLE FIELD TRIALS RUN IN BRACES, SMALL PACKS, OR LARGE PACKS

All of these procedures apply to sanctioned field trials as well as to licensed or member field trials except for those procedures that state specifically that they apply to licensed or member trials.

PROCEDURE 1. MANAGEMENT

1-A The Field Trial Committee shall have full charge of the organization and management of the trial, and shall have the power subject to the by-laws, rules and procedures of The American Kennel Club, to interpret any special rules published by the club holding the field trial, and to decide any matter, whether arising from an unforeseen emergency or not, which is not specifically provided for in these rules and procedures. Whenever such matters arise, the Field Trial Committee shall exercise the specific powers and carry out the duties described in these rules and procedures and submit a complete report of the incident to The American Kennel Club.

1-B Each club holding a licensed or member field trial must have at least three members of the Field Trial Committee present on the grounds at all times during the running of the trial. If a split class or two classes are run at the same time on different running grounds there must be at least three members of the Field Trial Committee on each grounds throughout the running, unless the separate running grounds are immediately adjacent to each other. A club which fails to comply with this requirement will not be approved for a licensed or member field trial during the next field trial season.

1-C The Field Trial Committee shall appoint a Marshal or Marshals to carry out the orders of the Judges. Marshals may advise Judges but must carry out the instructions of the Judges whose decision is final. At a trial run in Large Packs no person shall act as Marshal for a class in which he has a hound entered; and at a trial run in Small Packs no person shall act as Roving Marshal for a class in which he has a hound entered. Marshals shall be identified by badges or arm bands carrying the designation "Marshal."

1-D At a field trial run in Small Packs there shall be two Marshals. One Marshal shall guide and supervise the gallery. The other Marshal, known as the Roving Marshal, shall assist the Judges and supervise the handlers.

1-E At a trial run in Large Packs there shall be three or more Marshals. One of the Marshals shall assist Judges in becoming acquainted with the running grounds and act as guide and liaison man between the Judges, the other Marshals, the Field Trial Committee and the gallery. The other Marshals shall keep owners, handlers and spectators out of the running grounds, and report to the Judges immediately in writing any hound that has pulled out of the running pack, together with the number, time, and length of time out of the pack. After the class is completed, one Marshal shall account for all hounds and guide the handlers from the running grounds.

1-F At a field trial run in Braces or Small Packs each class or division of a class shall be judged by two Judges. At a field trial run in Large Packs there shall be two Judges for each class or division of a class up to 30 hounds, three Judges for 31 to 40 hounds, four Judges for 41 to 50 hounds, and so forth. If substitute Judges are required, or if additional Judges are required for a split class or for a Large Pack class of more than 30 hounds, they may be appointed by the Field Trial Committee at the trial provided they are persons in good standing with The American Kennel Club. When such Judges are used they should, if possible, act in conjunction with one or more of the advertised Judges provided this does not prevent any advertised Judge from completing the judging of a class which he has already started. If two such Judges have to judge together without one of the advertised Judges, at least one should be an experienced Judge of American Kennel Club licensed Beagle field trials. The American Kennel Club shall be promptly notified of additional or substitute Judges officiating.

1-G No licensed or member Beagle field trial may be run on released game unless the game has been released prior to the first day of the trial.

1-H Any advertising a club decides to use for a licensed or member trial shall include the following information which must be identical with the information approved by The American Kennel Club for the premium list copy: Names of approved Judges and the classes they are to judge; type of trial whether run in Braces, Small Packs, or Large Packs; location of trial; date on which each class is to start; entry fee; the place where the drawing or numbering will be done and, for a Large Pack trial, the hours during which hounds shall be measured for each class; and time entries close for each class.

1-I One person only may handle or hunt each hound, whether it be the owner, his agent or the agent's deputy. All others must remain in the gallery at a licensed or member trial. When game is raised or the hounds are away on the trail, the gallery shall stand fast or change position only as instructed by the Judges or the Marshal.

At trials run in Large Packs everyone except Judges and Marshals must go to an advantageous point designated by the Judges or Marshal, and may change positions only at the discretion of the Judges or Marshal.

1-J If unforeseen circumstances make it impossible to complete the judging of a licensed or member field trial on the last date applied for and approved by The American Kennel Club, the Field Trial Committee may continue the judging on one or two days immediately following the last date approved. The Field Trial Secretary's report to The American Kennel Club shall include a report of the circumstances requiring the extension and a list of the classes or series judged on each additional day.

PROCEDURE 2. ENTRIES

2-A If any question should arise as to a different hound having been substituted in place of the hound described on the entry form, the question shall immediately be investigated by the Field Trial Committee, who shall decide whether or not the entered hound has been run, after giving all parties an opportunity to be heard, and submit a complete report of its findings and decision to The American Kennel Club. If the Field Trial Committee decides that a hound other than the hound entered and drawn has been run, the entered hound that did not run shall be disqualified and its entry fee and any awards shall be forfeited. At a trial run in braces or small packs the hound that was substituted and run in the brace or pack, if entered and drawn in an earlier or later brace or pack, shall also be disqualified if owned or entered in the same class, shall also be disqualified if owned or entered in that trial by the same person who owned or entered the hound for which the substitution was made or by a member of that person's immediate family or household; but otherwise shall not be disqualified and shall be permitted to run again if drawn for a later brace or pack. At a brace trial the brace mate of a hound disqualified under this section before the completion of judging of first series, shall run in the last brace as or with the odd hound, and any previous scoring it received shall be cancelled. The Field Trial Committee at a licensed or member trial shall exercise its authority under Chapter 14, Section 2, if there is any indication that the substitution was intentional.

2-B Castrated dogs and spayed bitches are ineligible for entry and shall not be permitted to compete in Beagle field trials.

2-C In a class for combined sexes, any bitch which in the opinion of the Field Trial Committee is in season, shall be excluded from the running grounds and regular kennels. A separate kennel shall be provided for such bitches.

2-D All entered hounds must be present on the field trial grounds at the time entries close at a licensed or member trial when entries close on the day the class is to be run.

2-E No hound which is entered and present may be withheld from competition at any trial and no hound may be withdrawn during the running of a class, unless it is disqualified by the Judges, or is found to be ineligible, or is excused by the Field Trial Committee after consultation with the Judges. No hound will be excused by a Field Trial Committee except in the most unusual and deserving circumstances, and never to meet the convenience or caprice of its owner or his agent. If any hound should be withheld or withdrawn with or without the consent of the Field Trial Committee, that committee shall make a full report of the incident in writing and the report shall be forwarded to The American Kennel Club by the Field Trial Secretary. At a licensed or member trial the committee shall also use its authority under Chapter 14, Section 2, if the evidence justifies such action.

2-F A hound is not eligible to be entered or to compete in any class of any field trial if an advertised or actual Judge of that class, or any member of his immediate family or household has owned, sold, held under lease, boarded, trained, or handled, the hound within one year prior to the date of the field trial. Immediate family means husband, wife, father, mother, son, daughter, brother, or sister.

PROCEDURE 3. MEASURING

3-A At all Beagle Field Trials hounds shall be measured in accordance with the following procedures; except that measurement shall not be required for any hound with whose entry form the owner or agent has submitted an official American Kennel Club measurement card; and except further that such measurement will not be required at certain sanctioned trials the announcements for which specify that all hounds shall be measured in advance or that a hound may be entered without measurement in the class into which it was measured on some specified earlier occasion.

(1) *Brace and Small Pack Trials.* At all field trials run in Braces or Small Packs, only the hounds called back by the Judges for second series or for the winners pack shall be required to be measured; except that if there are eight or less entries in a class, all hounds in that class shall be measured before the drawing. The actual measuring shall be done by the Judges, who may select a third person to assist them, and shall be done in the presence of the owners or handlers of all hounds called back, before starting second series or the winners pack. Such measuring at a Brace trial shall be done immediately following the conclusion of judging of first series and prior to announcement of second series bracings.

The owner or handler of any hound whose eligibility for the height requirements of the class may be considered doubtful may notify the Field Trial Secretary when he presents the completed entry form entering the hound in a specific class, that he wants the hound measured before closing of entries.

All hounds on which such advance measurement has been requested shall be measured at the place where the drawing will be held within one-half hour prior to the closing time for entries for the class in which the hounds are entered, and the start of such advance measuring shall be publicly announced by the Field Trial Secretary. The actual measuring shall be done by the Judges of the class who may select a third person to assist them. As each hound is measured the owner or handler shall give its name to the Judges and the name and measurement shall be announced to the spectators by the Field Trial Secretary or Field Trial Committee Chairman.

A hound measured in advance on request shall not be subject to further measurement at that trial. The owner or handler of a hound that is, prior to the drawing, measured out of the class in which it has been entered, shall have the option of having his entry fee returned or of transferring the entry to a class at that trial for which the hound is eligible as measured, if entries for such other class have not yet closed, and the hound shall not be counted as an entry in the class from which it was measured out. Hounds measured out after being called for second series or winners pack shall not be eligible to run in another class at that trial.

The actual measurement of each hound measured by the Judges at a licensed or member trial, whether measured in advance on request or measured for second series or winners pack, shall be entered in ink on an AKC measurement report form, and the form shall be signed by the Judges and forwarded by the Field Trial Secretary to The American Kennel Club with the results of the trial.

(2) *Large Pack Trials.* At a Large Pack trial all hounds entered in each class shall, before they are numbered, be measured by the Field Trial Committee or by one or more measuring committees, each consisting of at least three persons appointed by the Field Trial Committee. The measuring shall be done only during the hours specified in the premium list and in any advertising the club may decide to use, except that measuring immediately before the numbering may continue after the published time if it is impossible to measure all hounds within the time advertised.

3-B The actual and recorded owner of a Beagle 18 months of age or older registered with The American Kennel Club, which has not completed its Field Championship, may apply to The American Kennel Club for an official determination of his hound's height. The American Kennel Club will assign the measurement to a qualified measurer who shall select two assistants or witnesses to measure the hound with him. The measuring shall be done in public at a licensed or member field trial, or at a recognized Federation Winners Stake or Futurity. At a Large Pack Trial such measuring shall be done only during the hours specified and at the place designated for measuring in the premium list and in any advertising the Club may use. When the measurer has determined the height of the hound, he and his two assistants shall sign the certification form supplied by The American Kennel Club. Upon receipt of this properly executed form, The American Kennel Club will issue a card giving the height of the hound provided it does not exceed 15 inches. The card shall be recognized at all field trials held under American Kennel Club rules and procedures as the hound's official measurement, in lieu of the requirements of Procedure 3-A above, and the hound shall be ineligible to compete in a class for hounds of any other height. A fee of two dollars shall accompany the original application for measurement.

3-C Official measurement cards issued by The American Kennel Club shall be subject to revocation at any time. The measurer under Procedure 3-B shall refuse to make an official measurement, and shall notify The American Kennel Club of his refusal, if the hound at the time it is presented for the measurement is in such physical condition that in his opinion it might be measured into a different division or over 15 inches if presented in good physical condition. The owner or handler of a hound on which an official measurement card has been issued who has reason to doubt the accuracy of the official measurement, must report his opinion and the reasons for it to The American Kennel Club.

3-D A measuring stand made entirely of metal and meeting the requirements of The American Kennel Club must be used for all measuring at field trials including official measurement. The contact bar shall have a smooth edge, and there shall be no markings or calibrations on the measuring stand or stick. Any calibrations shall be on a separate part or sleeve, so that the stick is set and locked before the measurers know the hound's height in inches. The calibrations must be checked with a gauge or rule for each class. The contact bar shall be loosely placed across the shoulder blades at the highest point, the hound standing in a naturally alert position with the head up but not stretched upward and with its feet well under it and forelegs vertical, on a smooth non-polished board placed at floor or ground level. The contact bar must never be set in advance at a specified height, but may only be set at the height of the particular hound being measured. The hound shall be posed for measurement by the measurers.

PROCEDURE 4. JUDGING

4-A All Judges prior to assuming their duties shall familiarize themselves with these rules and procedures and make their findings in accordance therewith. If any Judge shall fail to judge in accordance with these procedures, **the Field Trial Committee shall report the irregularity in detail to The American Kennel Club.**

4-B In all classes the Judges shall award places as follows: 1st, 2nd, 3rd, and 4th. After these places have been awarded the Judges shall designate the next best qualified hound as "N.B.Q." N.B.Q. is not a place and in case of disqualification of a placed hound at a licensed or member trial, the N.B.Q. hound shall not be moved up.

4-C No person shall make any remarks nor give any information which might affect the actions of the persons handling the hounds or the running of the hounds. Any person so offending may be expelled from the running grounds on orders from the Judges, and points of merit shall not be allowed any hound whose handler acts upon such information. The Judges must be informed of any such misconduct before the close of the race in which it occurs, and their decision shall be final.

4-D The Judges shall not permit any person who is handling a hound to make any unnecessary noise, nor to conduct himself in a disorderly manner, nor to interfere in any way with an opponent's hound. Judges shall report promptly to the Field Trial Committee for appropriate action, any person handling a hound who, during the running of a class, fails or refuses to comply with the Judges' orders, or who uses abusive language to a Judge or otherwise conducts himself in a manner prejudicial to the best interests of Beagle field trials.

PROCEDURE 5. STANDARD FOR JUDGING

5-A Foreword

(1) The Beagle is a trailing hound whose purpose is to find game, to pursue it in an energetic and decisive manner, and to show a determination to account for it.

(2) All phases of its work should be approached **eagerly**, with a display of determination that indicates **willingness** to stay with any problem encountered until successful. Actions should appear deliberate and efficient, rather than haphazard or impulsive.

(3) To perform as desired, the Beagle must be endowed with a keen nose, a sound body, and an intelligent mind, and must have an intense enthusiasm for hunting.

(4) Beagle Field Trials are designed and conducted for the purpose of selecting those hounds that display sound quality and ability to the best advantage.

(5) This Standard of Performance contains descriptions of both desirable and faulty actions. Judges will use it as a guide in evaluating performances, and will credit or demerit performance to whatever degree their actions indicate quality or fault, and to the extent that these actions contribute to accomplishment, fail to contribute to accomplishment, or interfere with accomplishment.

(6) Judges should approach their work with the attitude that the future welfare of the breed is in their hands, and should make their findings and selections on a basis calculated toward keeping the Beagle useful for both field trials and hunting purposes.

5-B Definitions — Desirable Qualities

Searching ability is evidenced by an aptitude to recognize promising cover and eagerness to explore it, regardless of hazards or discomfort. Hounds should search independently of each other, in an industrious manner, with sufficient range, yet within control distance of the handler, and should be obedient to his commands.

Pursuing ability is shown by a proficiency for keeping control of the trail while making the best possible progress. Game should be pursued rather than merely followed, and actions should indicate a determined effort to make forward progress in the surest most sensible manner by adjusting speed to correspond to conditions and circumstances. Actions should be positive and controlled, portraying sound judgment and skill. Progress should be proclaimed by tonguing. No hound can be too fast provided the trail is clearly and accurately followed. At a check, hounds should work industriously, first close to where the loss occurred, then gradually and **thoroughly** extending the search further afield to regain the line.

Accuracy in trailing is the ability to keep consistent control of the trail while making the best possible progress. An accurate trailing hound will show a marked tendency to follow the trail with a minimum of weaving on and off, and will display an aptness to turn with the trail and to determine direction of game travel in a positive manner.

Proper use of voice is proclaiming all finds and denoting all forward progress by giving tongue, yet keeping silent when not in contact with scent that can be progressed. True tongue is insistent claiming that running mates can depend on.

Endurance is the ability to compete throughout the duration of the hunt and to go on as long as may be necessary.

Adaptability means being able to adjust quickly to changes in scenting conditions and being able to work harmoniously with a variety of running mates. An adaptable hound will pursue its quarry as fast as conditions permit or as slowly as conditions demand. At a loss, it will first work close, and then, if necessary, move out gradually to recover the line.

Patience is a willingness to stay with any problem encountered as long as there is a possibility of achieving success in a workmanlike manner, rather than taking a chance of making the recovery more quickly through guesswork or gambling. Patience keeps a hound from bounding off and leaving work undone, and causes it to apply itself to the surest and safest methods in difficult situations.

Determination is that quality which causes a hound to succeed against severe odds. A determined hound has a purpose in mind and will overcome, through sheer perseverance, many obstacles that often frustrate less determined running mates. Determination and patience are closely related qualities and are generally found in the same hound. Determination keeps a hound at its work as long as there is a possibility of achievement and quite often long after its body has passed the peak of its endurance. Determination is desire in its most intense form.

Independence is the ability to be self-reliant and to refrain from becoming upset or influenced by the actions of faulty hounds. The proper degree of independence is displayed by the hound that concentrates on running its game with no undue concern for its running mates except to hark to them when they proclaim a find or indicate progress by tonguing. Tailing, or watching other hounds, is indication of lack of sufficient independence. Ignoring other hounds completely and refusing to hark to or move up with running mates is indication of too much independence.

Cooperation is the ability to work harmoniously with other hounds by doing as much of the work as possible in an honest, efficient manner, yet being aware of and honoring the accomplishments of running mates without jealousy or disruption of the chase.

Competitive spirit is the desire to outdo running mates. It is a borderline quality that is an asset only to the hound that is able to keep it under control and to concentrate on running the game rather than on beating other hounds. The overly competitive hound lacks such qualities as adaptability, patience, independence, and cooperation, and in its desire to excel is seldom accurate.

Intelligence is that quality which influences a hound to apply its talents efficiently, in the manner of a skilled craftsman. The intelligent hound learns from experience and seldom wastes time repeating mistakes. Intelligence is indicated by ability to adapt to changes in scenting conditions, to adapt and to control its work with various types of running mates, and to apply sound working principles toward accomplishing the most under a variety of circumstances.

The hound that displays the aforementioned qualities would be considered the Ideal Beagle for all purposes afield, capable of serving as a field trial hound, a gun dog, or a member of a pack, on either rabbit or hare.

5-C Definitions — Faulty Actions

Quitting is a serious fault deserving severe penalty and, in its extreme form, elimination. Quitting indicates lack of desire to hunt and succeed. It ranges from refusing to run, to such lesser forms as lack of perseverance, occasional let up of eagerness, and loafing or watching other hounds in difficult situations. Quitting is sometimes due to fatigue. Judges may temper their distaste when a hound becomes fatigued and eases off, if such a hound has been required to perform substantially longer than those with which it is running. During the running of a class a hound may have to face several fresh competitors in succession. In such instances a short rest period would be in order. Otherwise, Judges should expect hounds to be in condition to compete as long as necessary to prove their worthiness, and no hound that becomes unable to go on should place over any immediate running mate that is still able and willing to run.

Backtracking is the fault of following the trail in the wrong direction. If persisted in for any substantial time or distance it deserves elimination. However, hounds in competition sometimes take a backline momentarily, or are led into it by faulty running mates. Under these circumstances Judges should show leniency toward the hound that becomes aware of its mistake and makes a creditable correction. Judges should be very certain before penalizing a hound for backtracking and, if there is any doubt, take sufficient time to prove it to be either right or wrong. Backtracking indicates lack of ability to determine direction of game travel.

Ghost trailing is pretending to have contact with a trail and making progress where no trail exists, by going through all the actions that indicate true trailing. Some hounds are able to do this in a very convincing manner and Judges, if suspicious, should make the hound prove its claim.

Pottering is lack of effort or desire to make forward progress on the trail. Hesitating, listlessness, dawdling, or lack of intent to make progress, are marks of the potterer.

Babbling is excessive or unnecessary tonguing. The babbler often tongues the same trail over and over, or tongues from excitement when casting in attempting to regain the trail at losses.

Swinging is casting out too far and too soon from the last point of contact, without first making an attempt to regain scent near the loss. It is a gambling action, quite often indicating over-competitiveness or an attempt to gain unearned advantage over running mates.

Skirting is purposely leaving the trail in an attempt to gain a lead or avoid hazardous cover or hard work. It is cutting out and around true trailing mates in an attempt to intercept the trail ahead.

Leaving checks is failure to stay in the vicinity of a loss and attempt to work it out, bounding off in hopes of encountering the trail or new game. Leaving checks denotes lack of patience and perseverance.

Running mute is failure to give tongue when making progress on the line.

Tightness of mouth is a failure to give sufficient tongue when making progress. This will often be evidenced by the hound tightening up when pressed or when going away from a check.

Racing is attempting to outfoot running mates without regard for the trail. Racing hounds overshoot the turns and generally spend more time off the trail than on it.

Running hit or miss is attempting to make progress without maintaining continuous contact with the trail, or gambling to hit the trail ahead.

Lack of independence is a common fault that is shown by watching other hounds and allowing them to determine the course of action. Any action which indicates undue concern for other hounds, except when harking in, is cause for demerit.

Bounding off is rushing ahead when contact with scent is made, without properly determining direction of game travel.

5-D Credits

(1) Hounds shall be credited principally for their positive accomplishments. The extent of any credit should be governed by the magnitude of the accomplishment and the manner in which it is achieved. Credit is earned for searching ability, pursuing ability, accuracy in trailing, proper use of voice, endurance, adaptability, patience, determination, proper degree of independence, cooperation, controlled competitive spirit, intelligence displayed when searching or in solving problems encountered along the trail, and success in accounting for game.

(2) When crediting hounds for working style or methods used to gain accomplishments, Judges should keep the purpose of the breed constantly in mind and be alert for hounds, deficient in ability, that make simple problems appear difficult. They also should guard against becoming impressed by fascinating actions that do not produce results. Credit for working style should be used chiefly to differentiate between successful performers, and should never be applied to a degree which might indicate that style or method has been preferred to accomplishment, except in instances where excessive faultiness is involved. Credit for any accomplishment should be in proportion to its contribution to the performance. Mere lack of fault is not grounds for credit. While faultiness is not to be considered lightly, the slightly faulty hound that succeeds should be preferred to the stylist that fails.

5-E Demerits

(1) Faults, mistakes, lack of accomplishment, and apparent lack of intelligence, shall be considered demerits and shall be penalized to whatever extent they interfere with or fail to contribute to a performance.

(2) Faults are undesirable traits indicating lack of sound quality, and shall be penalized in proportion to the degree of commitment, the frequency of repetition, and the distractions they afford running mates, as well as for the interruptions or lack of progress they cause during the performance. Quitting, backtracking, ghost trailing, and running mute, are the more serious faults. Pottering, swinging, skirting, babbling, leaving checks, racing, running in hit-or-miss fashion, tightness of mouth, and lack of desire or ability to find and move game, shall be considered demerits.

(3) Mistakes are erratic judgments, sometimes committed under pressure of competition and prompted by a desire to excel, and sometimes due to influence of faulty running mates. Where mistakes are not committed with a frequency that would indicate lack of sound quality, consideration should be shown according to the hound's aptitude for realizing its errors, and its efforts to overcome them.

(4) Lack of accomplishment is failure to get enough done to compare favorably with the competition, and is often due to lack of such qualities as determination, patience, intelligence, or endurance. In instances where this is apparent the

penalty should be severe. Judgment on hounds that fail to accomplish as desired should be based on the circumstances under which the failure occurred and the determination and intelligence displayed in the effort to overcome it. Where failure is no fault of the hound, such as interference with the game or trail, or where a worthy hound encounters an especially hazardous or abnormal circumstance unlike anything the majority of contestants are expected to overcome, new game should be provided without penalty. Lack of intelligence is apparent in the hound that does not portray sound judgment and skill during its performance.

THE AMERICAN KENNEL CLUB

Incorporated

ADDITIONAL STANDARD PROCEDURES FOR BEAGLE FIELD TRIALS RUN IN BRACES ON RABBIT OR HARE

Effective September 1, 1968

Approved by the Board of Directors of The American Kennel Club

ADDITIONAL STANDARD PROCEDURES FOR BEAGLE FIELD TRIALS RUN IN BRACES ON RABBIT OR HARE

PROCEDURE 6. CLOSING, DRAWING, BRACING ABSENTEES

6-A Immediately prior to the closing of entries for each class at a licensed or member trial the Field Trial Secretary shall call out the names of all hounds entered in that class and shall then announce that entries have closed and that the drawing will begin. Any necessary change in Judges for the class shall also be announced at this time.

6-B The running order of the hounds entered in each class shall be determined by drawing, and the hounds shall be braced for the first series according to the drawing. Should two hounds owned by the same person be drawn in the same brace, the last hound so drawn will change places with the next hound drawn which is not so owned. This change will be made with a hound drawn later if possible, but may be made with a hound drawn earlier if necessary. The running order of two such hounds may be permitted in the first series when a separation is impossible, but in no other case.

6-C The Field Trial Committee shall have the option of splitting a class in which there are 50 or more entries into two divisions, A and B, except that at a licensed or member field trial no class may be split on any day on which the club has scheduled the start of more than one class. If a class is to be split, the Judges and running grounds for each division shall be assigned by the Field Trial Committee and announced before the drawing is started. The entire class shall be drawn as one, the first half of the class as drawn constituting Division A, and the second half as drawn constituting Division B. There shall be the same number of hounds in each Division, except that any odd brace shall be added to Division A and any odd hound shall be added to Division B. At least one advertised Judge must officiate in each Division if possible. After the first series, an equal number of hounds shall be brought back from each Division. The high hounds from both Divisions shall be the first brace in the second series, the other braces being similarly made up of one hound from each Division in the order in which each was scored in first series. The two hounds in each second series brace shall start equal. The second and subsequent series shall be judged by the advertised Judges if possible.

6-D The brace mate for an odd hound in first series shall be selected by the Judges.

6-E Owners and handlers must keep themselves informed as to the running order and progress of the judging, and must be ready within hailing distance when their hounds are called by the Marshal on instructions from the Judges. The running order cannot be changed under any circumstances once the hounds have been drawn, except as specifically provided in

Procedures 2-A and 6-F.

6-F Any hound, except the brace mate for the odd hound in first series, that does not appear within 15 minutes after the Judges have called for its brace, shall be marked absent in any series and shall not be permitted to run, and its absence shall be reported by the Judges to the Field Trial Committee who shall investigate the absence and submit a complete report to The American Kennel Club. The brace mate of an absent hound in first series shall run in the last brace as or with the odd hound. If a hound is absent after the bracings have been announced in second or subsequent series, the remaining hounds shall be moved up and each hound below the absent hound shall be braced with the next highest scored hound with which it has not previously been braced. The Judges shall establish a reasonable time limit before disqualifying for absence a hound they have selected as the brace mate for an odd hound in first series.

PROCEDURE 7. INSTRUCTIONS TO JUDGES

7-A Whenever practicable the hounds shall be cast to search for game, but the decision as to whether the hounds are to be cast or whether they are to be kept on leash until they are laid on a line where game has been sighted, shall be made by the Judges alone.

7-B Each heat shall be conducted in a manner best calculated to give the competitors equal opportunity to display the qualities under judgment. No hound shall be started without a brace mate at the start of a brace. The Judges shall establish a reasonable time before dropping a hound that is missing after the start of a brace. The brace mate of an odd hound in any series shall be under judgment.

7-C When a hound gives signs of being on game, the Judges shall allow it opportunity to prove whether or not it is on true trail. Judges shall not penalize or fault a hound without ample proof. If reasonable doubt exists, the hound shall be given the benefit of the doubt.

7-D When hounds have been laid on a line together or have been given an opportunity to hark in to one another in any series, this shall be considered as competition, except that when neither hound opens the brace shall be given a second rabbit or hare unless the first rabbit or hare was seen by one of the Judges.

7-E Trailing game other than announced, such as pheasants or game animals, shall not be considered a demerit.

7-F Should a brace become split, the hounds going away on different rabbits or hare, the Judges shall order both hounds up and the brace shall be put on game different from that previously run by either hound.

7-G Judges shall not eliminate a hound in any series for the sole reason of losing game.

7-H When additional game is required the search shall start at the point where the last game was found.

ADDITIONAL STANDARD PROCEDURES FOR BEAGLE FIELD TRIALS RUN IN SMALL PACKS ON RABBIT OR HARE

PROCEDURE 8. DRAWING, MARKING AND RUNNING

8-A All of the procedures governing Beagle field trials run in Braces and Beagle field trials run in Large Packs shall, to the extent that they are applicable and not in conflict with the following procedures, also govern Beagle field trials run in Small Packs on Rabbit or Hare.

8-B The hounds shall be numbered consecutively as entered, starting with the number "1". Each hound shall have its number painted on both its sides with a durable paint, the figures to be at least 3½ inches high and clearly visible. The Field Trial Secretary and his assistant, if any, shall be the only persons, to record each number against the name of the corresponding hound. These numbers shall be used in the drawing and running of the packs and the names of the hounds must not be used.

8-C The Field Trial Committee shall decide how the class will be divided in first and subsequent series, the number of packs, and the number of hounds in each pack. The packs in first and subsequent series shall consist of four or five hounds except when the class is composed of six, seven, or eleven hounds. When there are eleven hounds, they shall be divided into two packs of five and six. When there are six or seven hounds they shall be run as one pack. The packs shall be drawn for in first and second series. The hounds shall be run in packs as drawn regardless of ownership, and the packs must be run in the order drawn. In third and subsequent series the hounds shall be arranged in packs in numerical order.

8-D The hounds shall be cast to search for game in first and subsequent series. Handlers will control the hounds in the search for game and will get the hounds in the pack when game is started. After game is started handlers will have five minutes in which to get hounds in the pack unless one or more hounds are running another rabbit. In such case, or in case of a split pack, the Roving Marshall will instruct, advise, and assist, the handlers in getting the hounds running together as a pack.

8-E In each pack the hounds that are to be considered for running in the next series must run at least 20 minutes on game. The Judges may run any pack for as long a time as they deem necessary in order to select the best hounds.

8-F This procedure shall apply to all packs and to all series except the winners pack. Judges may select all, any, or none, of the hounds from each pack for further running. At any time during the running of a pack the Judges shall

THE AMERICAN KENNEL CLUB
Incorporated

ADDITIONAL STANDARD PROCEDURES FOR BEAGLE FIELD TRIALS RUN IN SMALL PACKS ON RABBIT OR HARE

Effective September 1, 1968

Approved by the Board of Directors of The American Kennel Club

7-I After the running of first series has been completed the Judges shall announce which hounds they wish to see in second series and no other hounds shall be called to run in second series following this announcement except in the case of an error by the Judges in identification of a hound, and except further that the Judges may call for an additional hound to replace any hound that has been measured out at second series or is absent for second series measuring. In bracing the hounds in second series, the hound having the highest score from first series must be announced as the first hound in the first brace, and its brace mate shall be the next highest scored hound which has not been braced with it in first series. The remaining braces in second series shall be braced in the same manner. No two hounds shall be braced together in more than one series.

7-J All hounds called for second series shall be considered as having an opportunity to win or place regardless of their relative positions when called back, except that no hound shall be placed higher than another placed hound by which it has previously been defeated in direct competition during the running of the class. In deciding whether one hound has defeated another in direct competition in second or subsequent series, the scoring of the two hounds in earlier series shall not be considered. After first series the Judges shall run each brace until one hound in their opinion has clearly defeated the other, unless both hounds are so faulty as not to merit further consideration for placement. If required, additional rabbits may be given at the Judges' discretion.

7-K The Judges may announce the four placed hounds at any time after completion of second series, provided each placed hound has been placed in direct competition by the hound placed immediately above it. All placed hounds must have run in second series. No series nor any part of any series shall be re-run, except for any part of a series which may have been affected by an error made by the Judges in bracing or in identification of a hound, and except further that the Judges may continue the running of a brace at a later time or on the following day if darkness or severe weather conditions make it necessary to pick up the hounds before the judging of that brace is completed.

7-L The Judges should agree on the scoring of each hound before starting the next brace.

7-M Should there arise at any time during the running of a heat a question concerning the actual running of the hounds that is not provided for in these Procedures, the Judges shall handle the situation in a manner not contrary to these Procedures, and shall so decide the matter as to give each hound an equal opportunity.

7-N No owner or handler shall have any right to question or refuse to follow the Judges' orders.

7-O Handlers, while their hounds are down, shall go together and keep within sight of the Judges and each other when possible. When hounds are cast, a handler may speak or whistle to his hound or work it in any way he may deem proper, if not contrary to these Procedures, but he shall not make any unnecessary noise, nor interfere with an opponent's hound in any way. When hounds have been laid on a line together or have harked in to one another, the duties of the handlers shall cease until further instructed by the Judges. The handlers shall at all times keep back of the Judges and hounds unless otherwise instructed by the Judges. Judges shall enforce these requirements at all times.

order up any faulty hound that is interfering with the smooth running of the pack and shall also order up any hound whose performance does not merit further consideration. Hounds to be eliminated shall be ordered up one or two at a time until only those to be considered for subsequent series remain in the pack. If there appear to be no worthy hounds in a pack, they shall be gradually eliminated by ordering up the most faulty hounds as such are determined one or two at a time down to the last hound, if necessary, to make sure no worthy hound is overlooked before the entire pack is eliminated.

8-G When the Judges have seen enough and a pack is ordered up, they shall announce which hounds, if any, may be considered for next series. After the running of all packs in each series, the Judges shall submit to the Roving Marshal or Field Trial Secretary a list of the numbers of the hounds to be called back for the next series.

8-H Hounds selected for succeeding series shall not be rated but shall enter each series equally rated.

8-I When the class has been reduced to from five to seven hounds by running sufficient series to accomplish this end, the remaining hounds shall be run as a pack and will be known as the Winners Pack. Hounds in the Winners Pack that are to be placed must be run at least 30 minutes on game, and as long thereafter as the Judges deem necessary in order to place the hounds. The four place hounds must be run as a pack with fourth and third place hounds being picked up as their respective places are determined. The second and first place hounds must be run as a brace until the Judges are able to determine their respective places.

THE AMERICAN KENNEL CLUB

Incorporated

ADDITIONAL STANDARD PROCEDURES FOR BEAGLE FIELD TRIALS RUN IN LARGE PACKS ON HARE

Effective September 1, 1968

Approved by the Board of Directors of The American Kennel Club

ADDITIONAL STANDARD PROCEDURES FOR BEAGLE FIELD TRIALS RUN IN LARGE PACKS ON HARE

PROCEDURE 9. MARKING AND DRAWING

9-A The hounds shall be numbered as entered and measured, starting with the number "1". Each hound shall have its number painted on both its sides with a durable paint, the figures to be at least 3½ inches high and clearly visible. The Field Trial Secretary and his assistant, if any, shall be the only persons to record each number against the name of the corresponding hound. These numbers shall be used in any drawing and in the running of the packs and the names of the hounds must not be used.

9-B All entries in a class shall run as a pack; except that when there are more than 25 starters the pack may, at the option of the Field Trial Committee, be split and the two Divisions run simultaneously for not less than two hours, with at least one advertised Judge with each pack if possible. If the Field Trial Committee decides to split the pack, the hounds shall be drawn so that their handlers will not have a choice of Judges or running grounds. The first half as drawn shall constitute Division "A", and the remainder of the class including any odd hound shall constitute Division "B". An equal number of hounds from each pack will then run together for not less than one hour under all officiating Judges.

PROCEDURE 10. INSTRUCTIONS TO JUDGES

10-A In Open Classes the pack shall run for not less than 3 hours, and Derbies shall run for not less than one and one half hours, subject to the exceptions contained in Procedures 9-B, 10-O, 10-P and 10-Q.

10-B Before each class the Judges shall agree upon a uniform point system of crediting and demeriting hounds, and shall inform the Chairman of the Field Trial Committee of the system they are going to use, and he in turn shall inform the handlers of this system.

10-C All Judges must confer and agree on those hounds eligible for first place, and further must agree on all hounds to be picked up under Procedure 10-R.

10-D Should there arise at any time during the running of a class, questions bearing upon the actual running of the hounds and not provided for in these procedures, the Judges are instructed to seek advice from the Field Trial Committee and so decide the matter as to give each hound an equal opportunity.

10-E Each class shall be conducted in the manner best calculated to give every competitor an opportunity to display the qualities under judgment. The Judges shall allow each owner or handler the right and privilege to see his entry has a fair start and is fairly started on the line of scent with the balance of the pack at the beginning of each race.

10-F Should the pack split, hounds going away on different hares, the Judges shall order the Marshals to order and assist the handlers to get their hounds into the largest running pack, or to pick up all hounds and get a new start on fresh game. If too many splits occur in one locality, all hounds shall be ordered up and moved to a different location for a new start.

10-G After a class has been ordered up, all handlers shall have thirty minutes in which to group their hounds. All hounds in the handlers' possession after this thirty minutes may then be cast. Handlers of missing hounds shall then be allowed thirty minutes after fresh game has been started to get their hounds back into the pack.

10-H Judges are to consider that the Beagle is primarily a hunting hound and that its object is first to find game and second to drive it in an energetic and decisive manner and show an animated desire to overtake it.

10-I Trailing game other than announced shall not be considered a demerit, nor shall any hound be demerited for failing to pack if the pack shall be proven to be on game other than announced. In the event such hound shall be ordered up under Procedure 10-R it shall be reinstated in the pack.

10-J The number of times a hound finds game shall not necessarily give it the preference, but the quality of the performance shall be given first consideration. Ability and desire to hunt are of first importance. These points are evidenced by intelligence, the method of working ground, and the ambition and industry displayed whether game is found or not.

10-K When a hound gives signs of being on game, the Judges shall allow it opportunity to prove whether or not it is on true trail. Judges shall not penalize or fault a hound without ample proof. If reasonable doubt exists, the hound shall be given the benefit of the doubt.

10-L The Judges shall give credit to the hound that is a better searcher and sticks to its work. A hound will be expected to maintain an efficient range throughout a race and to show hunting sense in its work. Hunting sense is shown by the desire to hunt for game, the selection of likely places to hunt in, the method of hunting the places, the industry in staying out at work, and the skill in handling and trailing the game after it is found.

10-M At a check all hounds should work industriously, close to where the loss occurred, before going further afield to look for the line.

10-N Undue credit shall not be given a hound with an outstanding voice, when not seen by the Judges, nor for speed nor flashy drive if the trail is not clearly followed. Accuracy in trailing, proper use of mouth, endurance, good pack qualities, should be the principal points of merit.

10-O When a hare pursued by the pack runs into the gallery, cars or trains, or any such unforeseen obstacle, and the hounds come to a complete loss, the Judges shall then have all hounds picked up and get a new start. The time the pack was down in the first race prior to the move, shall be added to the time after the second start is made, to determine when the scheduled time has elapsed. If it is necessary to order up the hounds on the first day due to unavoidable circumstances such as darkness, a severe storm, or lack of game, when the pack has run less than two and a half hours in an Open class or less than one hour in a Derby, the same hounds must be put down again to run the balance of the required time under the same Judges, either on the same day or on the following day; otherwise there shall be no championship points awarded.

10-P If no scoring is obtained on the first day, or if different Judges shall be used on the second day, then the class shall be considered as a continuation and shall be run for the full time, but the points shall be awarded on the basis of the number of starters the first day. Any hound being withdrawn from the second day run must be reported to the Judges by the handler of the hound, but in no case shall an entry fee be refunded as the opportunity to compete is still present. In the event that less than five hounds are on hand for the second day's class, the class shall be declared no contest.

10-Q If the Judges require more time in order to make a satisfactory decision in the class, the hounds must remain down until the Judges order them up, but in no case, unless all the hounds "quit cold" can the scheduled time be curtailed. Time not to count if pack gets on game other than hare.

10-R The Judges must order out of the race any hound which in their opinion is found to disorganize the smooth running of the pack, such as cutting in front of a pack, backtracking, overrunning and giving tongue, stealing a line, ghost trailing, running mute, rioting, failing to pack, pulling out of the race and failing to get back in while the pack is in hearing. This procedure must be strictly adhered to. Pottering, swinging wide, skirting, babbling, leaving checks, racing, running in hit or miss style, shall be considered faults and demerited, or if sufficiently serious the hound may be ordered up.

10-S The Judges at the conclusion of approximately two hours of running time may, at their discretion, order up any or all hounds on which they have little or no score and continue for the final period of time judging only those hounds on which they have scored, and in no case shall a running pack be broken up to eliminate these hounds.

10-T The placings of the hounds shall be posted in a conspicuous place at the Field Trial Headquarters within one hour after the close of the race.

10-U Owners and handlers shall not talk to the Judges from the time the pack is started until the judging of the pack is completed.

10-V When hounds have been laid on a line, or have harked in to one another, the duties of the handlers shall cease until further instructions are received from the Judges or the Marshals.

10-W Immediately after the Judges have ordered the hounds up they shall consult with the Marshals after which they shall meet and decide among themselves which hounds are the winners. The results are to be given to the Field Marshal in writing who in turn will hand them over to the Field Trial Secretary who will check the numbers against the names and announce the winners.

10-X The Judges shall appoint a spokesman from their number and all orders or information concerning the running of the class shall be given by him in a clear and impartial manner, so that each person handling a hound may be fully informed.

Sanctioned Beagle Field Trials

Any club that holds American Kennel Club events must obtain sanction for any type of field trial that is advertised to, or open to entries from, non-members of the club.

Sanctioned Beagle Field Trials are trials sanctioned by and run under the rules and procedures of The American Kennel Club at which NO CHAMPIONSHIP POINTS ARE AWARDED. (see Chapter 6, Section 7).

A PLAN A SANCTIONED BEAGLE FIELD TRIAL is a qualifying trial held by a club that wishes to qualify for the holding of its first licensed trial. Such a club will receive approval to hold a Plan A trial only if AKC is satisfied that the club will shortly be fully equipped and ready to hold a licensed trial which will be a credit to the sport. A Plan A trial is a two day event, and shall be conducted in accordance with all of the rules and procedures that apply to licensed or member trials, except those rules relating to championship points, and except further that both sexes may be combined in a single class. The club is required to prepare regular premium lists and entry forms for the trial and to submit to The American Kennel Club after the trial all of the records described in Chapter 13, Section 1.

A PLAN B SANCTIONED BEAGLE FIELD TRIAL is any other type of sanctioned field trial held by a club or Beagle association. It may be a one day event or may continue for two or more days. No premium list is required and the club does not have to submit records of the trial to The American Kennel Club.

Applications for sanctioned Beagle field trials should be filed with The American Kennel Club at least FOUR WEEKS before the first day of the event applied for.

Definition of a Beagle Derby

A Beagle is a Derby throughout the calendar year, January 1 through December 31, if it was whelped not later than June 30 of the previous year and not earlier than July 1 of the year before that.

Information for New Beagle Clubs

The following information is given to assist and guide new clubs, or persons who are considering forming new clubs, with the ultimate purpose of holding Beagle Field Trials under American Kennel Club rules and procedures.

Trials shall be run under one of the three following procedures:

(a) Braces on Rabbit.

(b) Small Packs on Rabbit or Hare.

(c) Large Packs on Hare.

SECTION 3. At a licensed or member Basset Hound Field Trial the regular classes shall be Open All-Age Dogs and Open All-Age Bitches. If, however, when entries are closed there are less than six entries in one of the classes, the classes shall be combined, if possible, and run with both sexes in a single class.

SECTION 4. Additional non-regular classes may be run if specified, and if the conditions of each such class are described in the premium list.

A Derby Class is a non-regular class. A Basset Hound remains a derby through the calendar year in which it is whelped and through the succeeding calendar year.

SECTION 5. Splitting of prizes or places is prohibited.

SECTION 6. Judges may place hounds first, second, third, and fourth, in each class, but full discretionary power is given to the Judges to withhold any or all awards for want of merit. After these places have been awarded the Judges may designate the next best qualified hound as "N.B.Q.". N.B.Q. is not a place, and in case of disqualification of a placed hound at a licensed or member trial, the N.B.Q. hound shall not be moved up.

SECTION 7. Field championship points for Basset Hounds shall be awarded only to hounds placing first at licensed or member field trials in Open All-Age Classes in which there are six or more starters; and to hounds placing second, third and fourth at licensed or member field trials in Open All-Age Classes in which there are fifteen or more starters; and shall be awarded on the following basis:

1 point to the winner of first place for each starter;

$\frac{1}{2}$ point to the winner of second place for each starter;

$\frac{1}{4}$ point to the winner of third place for each starter;

$\frac{1}{8}$ point to the winner of fourth place for each starter.

A starter is an entered eligible hound that has not been disqualified and that has been cast or laid on a line with its brace mate at the start of its first series heat at a brace trial; or that has been cast at the start of its first series pack at a small pack trial; or that has been cast at the start with the rest of the pack at a large pack trial.

SECTION 8. In order to be recorded a Field Champion a Basset Hound must be registered in The American Kennel Club Stud Book and must have won championship points in Open All-Age Classes at four or more licensed or member Basset Hound Field Trials, and must have placed first in at least one such class.

SECTION 9. The total number of championship points required for a Basset Hound to be recorded a Field Champion by The American Kennel Club shall be fixed and determined by the Board of Directors of The American Kennel Club.

At present the total number of points required is 40.

THE AMERICAN KENNEL CLUB

Incorporated

BASSET HOUND

FIELD TRIAL RULES

Amended to September 1, 1968

(Copyright 1968 by The American Kennel Club)

CHAPTER 12

RULES FOR BASSET HOUND TRIALS

SECTION 1. Basset Hound Field Trials shall be run under the rules and procedures for Beagle Field Trials, except that the following Beagle Field Trial rules and procedures shall not apply to Basset Hound Field Trials:

Chapter 5, Section 4,

Chapter 6, Sections 1 and 2,

Chapter 12, all Sections,

Procedure 3 and all other references to measuring,

Procedure 4-B.

SECTION 2. All licensed and member Basset Hound Field

Change of Running Grounds

Any club holding Beagle field trials under the rules and procedures of The American Kennel Club, which is contemplating arrangements for new running grounds, whether for the regular activities of the club or for its licensed field trial, should consult The American Kennel Club before making any commitment on such new grounds. American Kennel Club approval is based in part on the location of the grounds and it should not be assumed that The American Kennel Club will continue to grant approvals to the club at the new location. In notifying The American Kennel Club of a contemplated change, the club should give a detailed report of the old and new grounds and their locations, and of the reasons for the proposed change.

A new club should not initiate its contact with The American Kennel Club by submitting an application for a sanctioned field trial to be held in the immediate future. Before the initial application of any new club can be considered, that club must first have been placed formally on American Kennel Club records as being eligible for approval to hold certain types of events.

The first step for any such new club to take is to write to The American Kennel Club giving a full report on the club, its history and its plans for the future, and describing tentative or definite arrangements for grounds and facilities. With this report the club should submit a copy of its by-laws and an alphabetical list of names and addresses of its members, with a brief account of each member's activity and interest in Beagles.

The American Kennel Club does not expect that a new club will come into being fully equipped with the finest running grounds and club house. The American Kennel Club is willing to work along with a club starting in the simplest fashion, if it has sound and adequate plans for steady improvements which show promise of a well equipped club within a few years, with year-round facilities for its members to meet and to train their hounds.

Such a club is expected to have a good number of members who reside within a reasonable distance of its grounds, and a democratic set of by-laws which place control of the club in the hands of a majority of its members. Membership should be open to any person of good character residing in the area who is really interested in the sport, and the location of the club's grounds and the area in which its members reside should not conflict with those of another Beagle Field Trial Club.

Before any new club can be approved for a licensed field trial at which championship points are awarded it must have held, with American Kennel Club approval, at least two successful Plan A sanctioned trials with an interval of not less than six months between trials, in each of which at least 40 hounds were entered and run. The American Kennel Club strongly advises that before applying for the first Plan A trial, a club should have held several Plan B trials.

The fact that a club has held two such Plan A trials will not automatically qualify it for approval of a licensed trial. The American Kennel Club will not grant a license, and no club should apply for one, unless the club is fully equipped and ready to hold a first-class trial which will be a credit to the club and to the sport.

A club which is equipped and ready but which has not yet held its second Plan A trial, may file before March 1 an application for dates for a licensed trial to be held in the season starting the following July 1, provided its second Plan A trial will be finished before April 15.

——The United Kennel Club, Inc.——

ELSEWHERE MENTIONED is the fact that in the last quarter of Nineteenth-Century America there was no widely-recognized standard of perfection for the various dog breeds. Breeders—both as individuals and groups—went much their own way in developing dog strains, suiting less the ideas of others, even customers, than their own. There were very few breed clubs then in existence, anyway, and the ones that held forth found it difficult to attract wide recognition.

He who sought to purchase a good dog of proven lineage, one likely to be a good performer—a good hunting dog, for example—in those days often became the victim of fraud. In all too many instances he was, after all, forced to rely upon the private records of the individual breeder or compelled to try to appraise a good strain from only "word of mouth" vantage.

If the particular breeder was a man of good repute, his pedigree records might have been diligently and honestly kept. If not, the most applicable doctrine was "buyer beware!" A few dog registration organizations came into being, some as forms of private enterprise, but many of them falling quickly by the way, unable to attract a thriving following. From this, it may be seen that there then was plenty of room and demand for the services of a dependable dog registrate, one which could be relied upon to maintain authentic and systematic records.

UKC Founded In 1898. At least one registration service formed in those days by private enterprise, nevertheless did survive, emerging to become the second oldest and largest registration office of pure-bred dogs in the United States. This was the United Kennel Club, Inc., founded by Mr. Chauncey Zachariah Bennett in 1898. Its offices and mailing address are at 321 West Cedar Street, Kalamazoo, Michigan 49007.

Mr. Chauncey Z. Bennett, an outstanding authority in his day on pure-bred dogs, thought that a great deal more should be done to promote breed standards and assist dog breeders. He had never been satisfied with the practices of other organizations undertaking to register dogs at that time, and thought it both timely and possible to form a new organization with a more complete registration system, one that would become respected and unite both breeders and owners yet at the same time promote the different breeds, especially those breeds for which there was at that time no registration service available at all.

Unlike a number of other private breed registrars of that day, Mr. Bennett saw clearly the need for an efficient, flexible, and durable registration system, one that would carry forward pedigrees from generation to generation with records of integrity, regardless of how many generations might be handled eventually. It took a great deal of his time to evolve it, but he finally developed a registration system that proved so complete in detail and workable that it is used by UKC substantially unchanged even at the present time.

Registrations and Organizational Growth. The breed first registered by UKC was the American (Pit) Bull Terrier—the brindle and white. Many men were interested in this great sporting dog in those days, and Mr. Bennett, himself, one of its great fanciers, was well versed in the breed.

The first dog placed on UKC record was Bennett's Ring. Other breeders and fanciers were contacted, and soon registrations of the breed mounted.

With the registration system proving fully satisfactory, Mr. Bennett next undertook to register other breeds, selecting the Old Glory strain of Black & Tan Coonhound as the second breed acceptable for registration. Associated with this choice, no doubt, was the fact that as much as Mr. Bennett loved hunting, a serious health problem compelled him to give up the trail and the chase, yet his special fondness continued for hunting dogs. Recognition of the Redbone Coonhound came next, followed by the English Coonhound; registrations now were accruing at a fast pace. The next undertaking was the inauguration of UKC's official journal, a magazine named *Bloodlines Journal*. This periodical was mailed to all breeders and fanciers doing business with UKC. It was soon

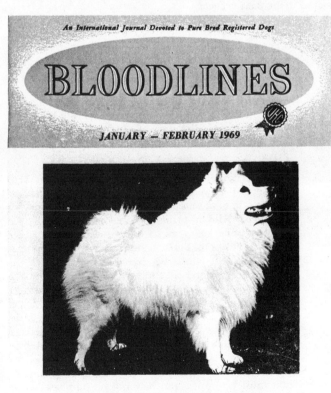

Our Good Omen For 1969

Sample cover of *Bloodlines* magazine, the official UKC journal. Courtesy—UKC.

Scene from a coon dog trial; note how hound's ears are protected by a cloth tie, possibly to help cure some recent injury and prevent another. Hank Babbitt photo.

soundly established and its circulation began to grow. It is now published every two months.

Now having its own official publication, the growth of UKC began to snowball.

One rather little-known fact, perhaps, is that at a very early point in its history, UKC undertook for a short period to register also goats, rabbits and cats. This, however, was a part of the enterprise given up with little regret as the registration of pure-bred dogs increased.

Purple Ribbon. As registrations mounted, Mr. Bennett sought to work out some special advanced registration system, developing in the process provision for the Purple Ribbon pedigree. This was and is still the highest caliber of pedigree record achievable under UKC registration. To earn such rating, an unbroken pedigree chain must be recorded with UKC for enough generations to entitle the offsprings to the Purple Ribbon rating of six or seven generations of breeding. This system and seal was early trademarked and registered with the U.S. Department of Commerce.

Purple Ribbon pedigree status is much coveted by all breeders and owners of UKC-registered dogs. As UKC's President says, since this rating is something that must be earned and may not be purchased, it is a rating commanding wide respect.

Promotion of Field Trials and Other Activities. UKC's founder helped promote English Beagle Field Trials in America. These are trials in which it is necessary for spectators to follow on horses.

The founder's last great interest was the (all hounds) UKC-licensed field trials for Coonhounds. Many of these trials were held in the East, with a few held in Midwestern states as early as 1924 and continuing on through the early 1930's. But, as time passed, it became more of a test each year for Mr. Bennett to keep up the demanding active pace commensurate with the expanding UKC program. His daughter, Frances Ruth, joined the staff of UKC and *Bloodlines Journal* even before she was through high school, taking on ever-growing responsibilities with the UKC program.

Upon Mr. Bennett's death, December 20, 1936, Frances left college and assumed full-time responsibility for the UKC program. In the early 1940's, she married Dr. E. G. Fuhrman of Lawton, Michigan, who gave up his practice and joined the UKC staff in Kalamazoo during 1942. (Dr. Fuhrman is a graduate of Missouri's Kirksville College of Osteopathy and Surgery.)

Under Dr. Fuhrman's efforts, program emphasis shifted more and more to UKC-sponsored field activities and events with corresponding benefit to the organization's growth. In time, Dr. Fuhrman became President of UKC and continues in this position today.

As its program developed, UKC licensed (All Breed) bench shows and inaugurated its own system of benching and awards, with provisions for ribbons and silver cups.

Shows and Hunts In An Expanding Program. The organization has established licensed shows for six breeds of Coonhounds, and UKC-licensed Night Hunts. The latter have proved so popular that UKC now lists officially approximately 1,200 recognized hunting clubs in the United States and Canada holding these events. UKC Water Races have been inaugurated and field trials licensed by UKC continue to be held.

Cross-bred coon dogs at tree in a field trial. David M. Duffey pho

Coonhound tree in Coon Dog Field Trials, Kenton, Ohio.

Under UKC license, the dogs winning at these events receive, according to a scale of points, UKC Night Hunt points-earned toward a Night Champion and a Grand Night Champion, UKC points-earned and show licenses toward a Show Champion and a Grand Show Champion. Under its licensed water races, there are awards for Water Race Champion, Grand Water Race Champion, and Field Champion. UKC-licensed Night Hunts have probably been the fastest growing such events in the United States, attracting the greatest following and interest. Competition is really keen in these events, and the sport is enjoyed not only by men and women, but by young people, too.

In such typical event, the six breeds of Coonhounds are tried out in the woods under actual hunting conditions with a judge who scores the dogs according to their hunting ability, all overseen by a Master of Hounds from a local hunting club sponsoring the event under the club name. Regular UKC-licensed shows have the second-largest following. In popularity, these are followed next by the UKC Water Races, then by UKC Field Trials. (See Night Hunt Honor and licensed Water Race rules accompanying text.)

On the accompanying list are the breeds recognized and now registered by UKC. Those with an asterisk

are the breeds originally recognized by UKC, for which the organization served as original registrar.

UKC is also a registered trademark with the United States Department of Commerce.

BREEDS RECOGNIZED AND REGISTERED BY UKC

(Consult *Bloodlines Journal* and UKC for detailed Standards.)

American (Pit) Bull Terrier*	Toy Fox Terrier*
American Eskimo*	German Shepherd
American Toy Terrier*	Great Dane
Airdale Terrier	Greyhound
American Water Spaniel*	Pekingese
Alaskan Malamute	Pomeranian
Arctic Huskie*	Poodle
Basset Hound	St. Bernard
Beagle	Scottish Terrier
Bloodhound	Spaniel, Cocker
Boston Terrier	Whippet
Boxer	
Miniature Boxer*	
Chihuahua	COONHOUND BREEDS
Chow Chow	American Black & Tan
Collie	Coonhound*
Collie, Columbian*	Bluetick Coonhound*
Collie, Smooth	English Coonhound*
Dachshund, Smooth	Plott Hound*
Dashshund, Longhaired	Redbone Coonhound*
Dalmatian	Walker (Treeing)
English Shepherd*	Coonhound*
Fox Terrier, Smooth	American Black & Tan Fox
Fox Terrier, Wire	& Coonhound*

* (UKC—Original; see Text)

UKC continues to thrive and grow today, and has become the second-largest (all-breed) office for the registration of pure-bred dogs in the United States. It also does business with breeders and owners in Canada, Mexico, as far away as Japan, South Africa, and, in fact, all the way around the world.

The latest UKC program concerns the UKC-recognized American Eskimo breed. A national UKC program will soon be put into effect and an organization formed expressly for the purpose of promoting this breed and holding licensed shows and other activities involving the breed.

Today there is a national Toy Fox Terrier Association, also various state Toy Fox Terrier Associations —all chartered through UKC. The Toy Fox Terrier is probably one of the numerically largest Toy breeds as far as breed activities, registration, and involvement in UKC programs, or as far as individual Toy breed activities are concerned anywhere.

Chartered also by UKC are The American Black & Tan Coonhound Association, The National Redbone Coonhound Association, The Bluetick Breeders of America, The National English Coonhound Association, The Walker (Treeing) Breeders and Fanciers Organization, and the National Plott Hound Association. These are all national UKC-chartered breed associations that are responsible for many of the programs, events and activities conducted under UKC license for the general promotion and betterment of these breeds.

As a matter of policy, UKC's Dr. Fuhrman believes in encouraging breeders and owners to take an active part in UKC affairs by their suggestions and proposals so that the various UKC activities and programs will advance and better the breeds and best serve the interest of UKC's many program associates and registrants.

UKC does not encourage in-breeding,* believing that where family breeding is carried on over a period of time subdominant weaknesses may become dominant, thus causing various types of deformity. This policy has been advocated from the very beginning of UKC registrations, with the philosophy followed that in evaluating a dog in the hunting and working breeds, especially, his performance should as much be stressed as his conformation and appearance.

Today, in the *Bloodlines Journal* and UKC offices, there is another young lady following her mother's footsteps—Susan Frances Fuhrman—who, since her college days, has served as editor and secretary.

UKC's slogan: "We lead where others follow."

1969 OFFICIAL NITE HUNT HONOR RULES**

1. One night only. All casts to hunt three hours. Three or four dogs in cast, but not more than four, this is up to the management. Dogs must prove to be open trailers. One handler to each dog. Any handler unable to complete hunt must pick up his dog. Scorekeeper may give permission for another handler to complete hunt. All dogs, including Champions, to hunt entire hunt unless emergency arises or scratched.

2. POINT SYSTEM:

   (a) 100 points for dog that opens first; 75 points second; 50 points third; 25 points fourth.
   (b) 100 points for dog declared treed first; 75 points second; 50 points third; 25 points fourth.

3. POINTS WILL BE PLUS:

   (a) When dogs strike and tree, and coon is seen by a majority of the cast members present and the scorekeeper. Only one tree is counted even if more than one coon is up the tree.
   (b) When dog is declared struck and treed and coon is seen other than in tree, dog declared treed to receive strike and tree points. Dogs not declared treed, strike points only. Coon caught on ground, strike points only.

Hot in pursuit, a good coonhound will not become discouraged simply because his quarry's trail leads to the edge of water. Here a caged coon is pulled across a stretch of water and the dogs race after him. Hank Babbitt photo.

   (c) One set of strike points in case of split tree, and each will be counted as separate trees for tree points.
   (d) Dog cannot receive trail points if he is not on trail when first dog is declared treed unless he trees on separate tree. However, he may receive tree points if he trees within 5 minutes.

4. POINTS WILL BE MINUS:

   (a) For treeing game other than coon. Both strike and tree will be minus.
   (b) When dogs open and do not tree.
   (c) When dogs tree and scorekeeper can plainly see that no coon is there.
   (d) When dog has been declared treed and dog leaves tree. (If he goes on on the trail just his tree points will be minus.)
   (e) If dog declared treed after five minutes has elapsed no additional dog can be declared treed at that particular tree but if they come in to tree will get minus on track and nothing on tree if coon is seen. He has had plenty of time to have treed.
   (f) When a dog quits a trail that is being worked and comes in he should be minused; scorekeepers decision, or if none of the dogs open within ten minutes the strike will be considered finished and minused. However, if the dog goes back on the trail he will get 25 points for going back but these points will be minused every time he comes out. He is not to be tied or encouraged to go back.

5. POINTS WILL BE CIRCLED: Will count neither for or against the dog.

   (a) When dog strikes and trees up a tree or a hole in the ground where there could be a coon yet scorekeeper does not see coon and no off game is seen.
   (b) If dogs are trailing when time is out.
   (c) If scorekeeper has to call time out. (When dogs tree where no game is seen, yet a coon could be there, such as den hole, tile or leafy tree.) (No tree climbing.) When dogs are trailing when time is up, make circle (O). Note: In case of running coon in hole or tile, track may be considered finished if dogs, by actions either tree barking or otherwise, show to the satisfaction of the scorekeeper coon to be there. When scorekeeper orders dogs to be called off because of livestock or nearness to highway, buildings, etc.
   (d) Points will be circled when dogs return to tree that they had previously been scored on.
   (e) No dog to receive minus points for coming into tree after the five minutes are up unless a coon is seen and the dogs treeing are awarded plus points. If points are circled, all points are to be circled.

6. DOGS WILL BE SCRATCHED:

   (a) If a dog has a total of 400 minus points, regardless of how many plus points the dog has.
   (b) Fighting or attempting to fight.
   (c) Failing to make any attempt to hunt within first hour.
   (d) If handler refuses to claim his dog. (This rule is to be rigidly enforced.)
   (e) For running stock. (Only one offense.)
   (f) If a handler is drinking or if he seems to want to stir up trouble.
   (g) Bitches smelling strong enough to attract dogs or a dog that is just bad to bother bitches while other dogs pay them no attention.
   (h) If dog is continuously silent on trail.
   (i) Unnecessarily delaying completion of a cast.

---

* Inbreeding—the mating of a pair bearing fifty percent or more relationship to each other. Examples are parent to offspring, brother and sister, cousin to cousin, grandsire to grand-daughter. In respect to the breeding of race horses, some authorities also much oppose inbreeding for while this sometimes produces horses with good speed, too many other undesirable characteristics also are found, hence tending to defeat the purpose.

Having followed the coon across the water, the dogs keep up suit. Hank Babbitt photo.

(j) In Championship and Grand Championship casts, dog is automatically scratched for treeing and running game other than coon.

(k) Club may set an overall time limit and cast will be scratched for violation.

7. TIME OUTS: (Scorekeeper may call time out.)

(a) When dogs are getting on highway, trail onto posted land or trail into a place where there is danger to dogs or men.

(b) When other hunters get too close. If dogs get with another group of dogs.

(c) If new ground must be found to finish cast.

(d) In case of accident or sickness.

(e) If group becomes lost.

(f) 15 minutes of hunting time may be demanded to search tree which is not additional time out.

NOTE: If scorekeeper calls time out then time is out and if dog should tree in the next minute it would not count. NO TIME IS TO BE CALLED OUT TO SEARCH A TREE OR WHEN DOGS ARE TIED TO BE LED AWAY FROM A TREE. (THIS IS A PART OF THE HUNT.)

8. HANDLERS:

The handler's duties are to know his dog's voice and nature. He is to tell scorekeeper when dog opens and when dog trees.

9. SCOREKEEPERS:

The scorekeepers are men picked by the sponsors because they believe them to be honest and capable of keeping score just as it is given them by handlers. They will show no favors to any dog or hunter. Scorekeepers may be handlers if agreeable by all four members of the cast and Master of Hounds.

10. HANDLERS AND SCOREKEEPERS:

You must not call another handler's dog. Scorekeeper only may scratch dogs in woods. Dogs must be claimed if scorekeeper demands. If scorekeeper finds dog treeing off game, he will give minus points even if not claimed. No trees to be climbed or coon to be killed. Where dogs split up, scorekeeper will go with handler to the dog that trees first. Permission may be given for other handlers to go with their dogs; however, they must stay at tree until checked. After 5 minutes, first dog's tree may be checked and that dog kept on leash until he can be turned loose with other dogs on their trail and will receive 25 points credit or discredit as deserved; handler to decide if he wishes to turn his dog in with the others on their trail. However, if their coon is already treed, no credit allowed for dog brought to the tree. All handlers must stay with the scorekeeper at all times unless given permission by scorekeeper to leave. Scorecards to be carried by an agreeable party or scorekeeper and must be scored by scorekeeper in plain view of all. If there is a question in the woods, score with a question mark (?) and check with Master of Hounds later. Master of Hounds will hear each viewpoint and have last say. Remember, handler may state his case plainly, but if unreasonable, his dog may be scratched by Master of Hounds or Scorekeeper. The management has the right to refuse entry to any dog or handler. Scorecards must be finished in the woods and no changes later except where a question arises in the woods. Master of Hounds shall be at the club house at all times. All scores must be posted.

11. COMPLAINTS:

In case of a complaint, that man is to go with the scorekeeper and other members of that cast to the Master of Hounds as soon as cast is over. He will state his case and Master of Hounds will make final decision. After scorecards have been turned in, no complaints will be considered after a period of thirty minutes has elapsed.

12. SCORECARDS:

Scorecards must be finished in the woods and signed by each handler. (Any changes must be made by Master of Hounds with members of entire cast present.) This rule must be strictly adhered to. Club Secretary must keep scorecards and make them available to contestants or U.K.C. for one year.

13. WINNERS:

(a) A dog must have a total score of plus points before he can receive Championship Points.

(b) The ten high point winners from different casts will be judged the first ten winners. If there are not ten cast winners with plus points, the placing will follow in order of total plus points.

14. TIES:

All ties to be broken for U.K.C. points. Dog will win out

Coondog enthusiasts assembling for a field event. Hank Babbitt photo.

Scene at a night hunting event. Lamps, flashlights and maps help, but it's not always just a coon dog who sometimes gets lost in such events. Hank Babbitt photo.

over other dog; dog that has least number of minus points; if still a tie, dog that has most plus tree points; if still a tie, dog that has the most plus strike points; if still a tie. dog that has the most circled .tree points. If still a tie, two dogs involved will hunt one hour or until tie is broken.

15. GENERAL INFORMATION:

When dogs are turned loose from the car, you have 3 minutes to call your dog. After that handler must call on or before third bark or dog is subject to be scratched. However, if a handler wants to claim his dog struck he may do so and score started on him. (Dogs have been hauled long distances and are in strange woods with strange dogs.) After the 3 minutes are up handler must claim his dog when he opens on or before third bark or be scratched for refusing to call his dog. When a dog is declared treed scorekeeper is not to let anyone go to the tree and start shining in less than 5 minutes, unless all dogs have been declared treed. This is a courtesy to other handlers and also to see that a dog will hold his tree. If men are so far from tree that it will take more than 5 minutes to get to tree he is to start walking toward tree but stopping all along to let other handlers see if their dog is treeing. Scorekeeper is not to let any handler keep holding him away from tree just to let a dog get to tree after 5 minutes are up. Dog must hold the tree for 5 minutes. Scorekeepers are not to let hunters call dogs off a trail without counting those points minus. No shouting encouragement to dogs. Dog should not be minused tree points if he comes back a short distance to meet handler if dog goes back in and trees satisfactorily. Judge should be informed of such peculiarities before hunt. Club has authority to set an overall time limit.

All hunters have opportunity of drawing for their cast.

16. Dogs not U.K.C. Registered must enter grade part of hunt.

17. DISPUTES:

All disputes must be settled at Club Level according to the above rules before sending in official U.K.C. final report of this hunt.

18. NITE CHAMPIONS:

Each nite hunt must have a Champions cast. At least one coon must be treed and seen in order for Champion to receive credit and a total plus score. This is to apply even if only one Champion is present to be entered in this cast. A Champion cannot hunt in open competition. This cast should be reserved for spectators, if any. All classes of Nite U.K.C. Champions are eligible to compete.

19. U.K.C. Nite Hunts must be advertised to the public and in at least one Coonhound Publication.

Final report form must be sent to United Kennel Club, Inc. 321 West Cedar Street, Kalamazoo, Michigan 49006 within ten days if credit is to be given to top ten winners. Fee of 25 cents for each U.K.C. dog in Hunt must accompany report.

(Qualifications for Nite Champion degree: Dog must have a minimum of 100 recorded U.K.C. points and must win at least one U.K.C. Licensed Hunt.)

1969 LICENSED WATER RACE RULES*

1. Under U.K.C. Rules dogs are run for Trophies and Points only. (No money may be involved for prize money.)
2. Only U.K.C. Registered coonhounds accepted in the Licensed Water Race.
3. U.K.C. registered coonhounds and grade dogs are run separately. (Never compete.)
   A. Where possible, 6 or 5 dogs to a heat.
4. Each Water Race must have a Champion heat even if only one Water Race Champion present.
5. Heat winners receive no points.
6. All dogs must start from starting line. Line must be established 15 to 25 feet from water's edge, depending on circumstances and conditions present. Stakes are to set at water's edge and are thirty feet apart.
   A. All dogs must pass between these stakes or be disqualified.
7. Dog started by starting signal.
   A. Any dog released before starting signal will be disqualified.
   B. Dogs not to be encouraged by handlers after being released.
8. Float is to be placed a uniform distance from shore for entire race.
   A. A live coon must be used on float and in tree.
9. Line Flags: Placed in swimming water 75 feet apart.
10. Judge Requirement: Two Line Judges, Three Tree Judges, One Starting Judge.
    A. Chairman of Judges must be appointed by organization. He has to be a Tree Judge.
    B. The Clerk's word is final on entries and when heats are drawn or to be run.
11. Dogs must tree within a 15 feet radius of tree inside or circle to qualify for Tree Winner.
12. Dogs must Tree to the satisfaction of Tree Judges in order to be declared a winner.
13. Tree Dog: Tree dog declared tree winner within 5 minutes after first dog arrives at tree. If no dog has qualified for a Tree decision, the Judge blows his whistle and declares the heat over.
14. To win a Line Decision, a dog must pass free and clear in swimming water, between line flags going in direction of home tree.
15. First Tree and First Line Winners advance to semi-finals.
16. All semi-finals will be run under same set of rules.
17. Line Winners and Tree Winners will run separately in "Semi-Finals and Finals."

---

* Reproduced by written permission of UKC; address all inquiries to UKC.)

18. In case of Ties: All Ties will advance into semi-finals and finals.
19. In case of Dead Heat: Heat will not be run over.
20. No owner or attendant will be permitted within 30 feet of the Judge's tree until after the Judges have rendered their decision. No owner or attendant shall make any noise or movement to encourage his entry under penalty of being disqualified. If the dogs start fighting, the Judge will call the owners to part them.
21. The management shall assume the responsibility of calling the names and number of each heat, but they assume no responsibility if the owner or attendant, through negligence, fails to get to the starting post in time for the heat.
22. The management assumes no responsibility for the safety of the dogs or the individuals.
23. All dogs, owners and attendants at the starting post are in charge of the Starting Judge and will remain so until he explains to them his systems of starting so each owner and attendant will be familiar with his system.
24. RULES TO BE USED FOR SMALL ENTRY: When entry is 36 dogs or less, it is not large enough for semi-finals. Use six dogs or less to the heat. Heat winners will advance to finals.
   A. Regular rules to be followed.

POINT SYSTEM FOR SMALL ENTRY:

HEAT WINNERS:

A dog winning First Tree receives .... 5 points
A dog winning First Line receives .... 5 points

GRAND FINAL WINNERS:

A dog winning First Tree receives .... 15 points
A dog winning First Line receives .... 10 points
If dog should win "First Tree" and "First Line"
in the Grand Finals he will receive .... 25 points

No dog may receive over 35 points in any Water Race.

NOTICE: When there are enough dogs for "Semi-Finals" follow regular Point System.

DISQUALIFICATIONS:

1. For false entry of dog.
2. For encouraging dog in ane manner while starting or swimming or at tree.
3. For fighting while swimming or at tree.
4. For any un-sportly act by owner of dog while on the grounds or in the water.
5. If handler is drinking.
6. If a dog gets away before the Judge gives the signal, the dog shall be disqualified, and the owner forfeits the entry fee.

Preparations for a night hunt—unloading the hounds. Hank Babbitt photo.

U.K.C. LICENSED WATER RACE RULES
REGULAR POINT SYSTEM*

No Heat points are given.

SEMI-FINALS:

A dog winning First Tree receives .... 10 points
A dog winning First Line receives .... 5 points

GRAND FINAL:

A dog winning First Tree receives .... 15 points
A dog winning First Line receives .... 10 points

If dog should win "First Tree' and "First Line"
in the GRAND FINALS, he will receive .... 25 points

No dog may receive over 35 Points in any Water Race.

Requirements for U.K.C. Water Race Champion is 100 Champion Points and must include one First Tree and First Line win in Grand Finals at least one time; as of March 1, 1969.

Requirements for U.K.C. Grand Water Race Champion: Must win three Grand Finals, including at least one Grand Tree Final.

Judges decision is final.

* (Reproduced by written permission of UKC.—Address all inquires to the latter.)

—The Canadian Kennel Club—

IN ORDER to write a comprehensive story of the history of the Canadian Kennel Club, let us go back to the year 1876, when dogdom on the North American continent was controlled by one organization—the National American Kennel Club. In that year, a Canadian-owned dog won at the Chicago show. He was an English Setter named Leicester, owned by L. H. Smith of Strathroy, Ontario. His registered American Kennel Club Stud Book number was 148.

When the representatives of ten show-giving clubs met at Philadelphia on September 17th, 1884, three of the men who voted the American Kennel Club into being were from clubs outside the borders of the United States. The clubs represented were the Montreal Kennel Club, the New Brunswick Kennel Club, and the London Kennel Club. Later a fourth club, the Manitoba Kennel Club, became a member of the American Kennel Club.

CKC—Formed In 1888. In 1887, the Canadian breeders decided that some measure of canine government for Canada was indicated, and on September 27, 1888, the Canadian Kennel Club was formed in the

Tecumseh House at London, Ontario. On February 21, 1889, a delegation of these members attended the American Kennel Club in New York City, where they were most cordially received and a request that the American Kennel Club recognize the Canadian Kennel Club as being the governing body in the Dominion of Canada was unanimously granted.

A reciprocity agreement was drawn up, part of which made provision for Canadian dogs to compete at shows held under American Kennel Club rules without such dogs first being compelled to register in the American Kennel Club Stud Book if such dogs had already been registered in the Canadian Kennel Club Stud Book. It was further agreed that each club would uphold all disqualifications made by the other.

Early Years. As many of the Canadian fanciers were only familiar with the substantial contact of sponsoring their shows under the banner of the American Kennel Club, they were hesitant about supporting a new organization—so much so, that the only shows which were held in the first year under the C.K.C. rules were in Ottawa and London. Toronto, Kingston, and Hamilton came later.

The honor of having registered the first dog in the first stud book fell to the late Charles A. Stone, who registered a Blue Belton English Setter bitch born in 1884, named Forest Fern, sired by Prince Royal ex Forest Ruby. The Forest Setters, both English and Irish, became famous throughout Canada and the United States.

It was when the first Constitution of the C.K.C. of Canada was drawn up that it was decided to have the club governed by the members, and so it has come down through the years. Today the C.K.C. is composed of members who by paying a fee become active participants in the affairs of the Kennel Club. Every two years they elect the officers by ballot; the president, first vice-president, second vice-president, and the directors for each province. In two important meetings during the year, the directors from across the country meet and discuss the affairs of the club for ensuing periods. Amending the Constitution and rules is done by means of a referendum ballot mailed to all members. This is the only kennel club in the world which is governed by individual membership. The president, officers, and directors serve without remuneration.

The end of the first year of the C.K.C. history found that the club had been instrumental in procuring an order-in-council whereby all dogs of breeding certified to by the club could be brought into Canada duty free. Individual dog registrations were 402 for 1889; 455 for 1890, and 847 for 1891. These figures represent the groundwork of the C.K.C.

The distinction for registering the first kennel name fell to Harry A. Carter, Simcoe, Ontario, who registered the name "Canadian." The second kennel name to be granted was "Mount Royal," for Dr. T. Wesley Mills of Montreal, Quebec. The third name to be registered was "Corktown," on behalf of C. E. Living of Westville, Ontario.

The first president was Richard Gibson of Delaware, Ontario; the secretary was Charles A. Stone of London, Ontario, the same gentleman who registered the first dog in the C.K.C. Stud Book.

There was but $17.51 left in the treasury for the officers to start the year 1894. The first reciprocity agreement with the American Kennel Club had been cancelled. The young club was holding literally only by the faith placed in it by the officers who had formed the club in the beginning. A proposition was then put forth that the C.K.C. share the advantages of the American Kennel Club as a member club and so have delegate representation.

At that time, the English Kennel Club, although the strongest Kennel Club in the world, was not recognized on the same footing by the A.K.C. While their pedigrees were accepted, their registrations were not, and while the dog might measure up to the American standards, it could only compete in an open class at any show held under A.K.C. rules.

In view of the fact that the American Club had done so much to help in the formation of the C.K.C., it was decided that it carry on under its own banner.

It was an uphill struggle, for after seven years only one Stud Book had been published and an accumulation of registrations marked the years 1893 to 1900. Money was not available to finance the obligations of printing a Stud Book. It was not until 40 years later that Stud Book No. 2 was compiled. It is a leather-bound copy of typewritten pages, probably the only Stud Book of its kind in the world. It took almost three years of labor by the late J. D. Strachan, aided and abetted by the directors of the Canadian National Live Stock Records. This was done without any thought of remuneration.

Confusion In The Ranks. Going back to the year 1907, the scarcity of dog shows and registrations worked hardships on the financial structure. It was, therefore, particularly aggravating when the Montreal Canine Association became a member club of the A.K.C. and held shows under their rules. Victoria, B. C., and St. John, New Brunswick, also changed their

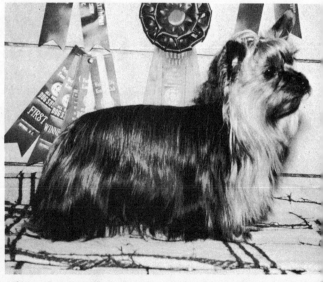

Champion Amber of Abon Hassan, Yorkshire Terrier. (Owner, R. D. Thompson of Vancouver, B.C., Canada)

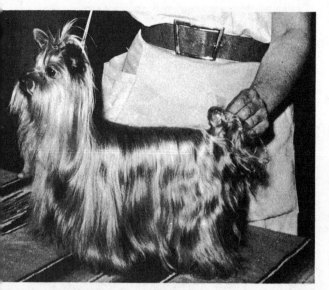

American and Canadian Champion Kathleen Pride (Imp), another [Yor]kshire Terrier from the Abon Hassan Kennels in Vancouver, B.C., [Can]ada.

status, with the result that the Canadians became confused by working under the various rulings.

In 1910, another difficulty arose when rabies became prevalent on both sides of the border and all dogs were compelled to be muzzled. By 1912, the none too substantial structure of the C.K.C. had its very existence challenged—the Vancouver Kennel Club decided to sever connections and become an affiliated member club of the A.K.C. One must remember that of 22 dog shows held in Canada there were 13 of them staged between Winnipeg, Manitoba, and Victoria, British Columbia. Western Canada formed a club of its own known as the Dominion Kennel Club. Registrations were arranged and a club register started. To the Alberta Kennel Club goes the distinction of giving allegiance to the parent club when almost every other club in Western Canada had deserted her. For their summer show in 1913, Alberta brought America's greatest judge of that time, the late James Mortimer of New York City, to judge its show under C.K.C. rules.

The *Canadian Kennel Gazette*, which had been the official organ, was sold to Winnipeg interests, and on July 3rd, 1914, A. P. Muchmore, on behalf of the Dominion Dog Fanciers Association, made formal application for incorporation under the Live Stock Pedigree Act. There is no doubt this association was the Dominion Kennel Club. However, matters were kept in abeyance until on February 20, 1915, application for incorporation under the Live Stock Pedigree Act by the C.K.C was filed with the Department of Agriculture. Behind this application was the background of 27 years built up by the C.K.C. which organization had published 19 Stud Books containing approximately 16,000 registrations, and had successfully sponsored shows featuring pure-bred dogs since 1888.

Crisis Survived—Growth Begins. In the life story of any organization are a few dates around which the entire history for that period must revolve. On the happenings of those dates depend to a great extent the entire success or failure of the efforts and may dictate the upward or downward trend of the result. Just such a date was 1915 for the C.K.C., Inc. In that year, in the old offices at 777½ Yonge Street, Toronto, final papers were signed incorporating the C.K.C. with the National Live Stock Records. With the registration certificates bearing the seal of the Department of Agriculture for the Dominion of Canada, the entire course of the club's history changed. In two years, membership was doubled; in four years it was tripled, and the C.K.C. began to feel the security which follows in the train of substantial, all-round business improvement. The stability of the rally was speedily sensed, the only worry was the fact that the club no longer had an official organ.

However, on May 2, 1917, the interests in the magazine were purchased by the C.K.C. and with the June, 1917, issue of *Kennel and Bench* the club, for the first time since it was organized in 1888, owned its own official organ.

One of the most remarkable paragraphs in that issue was the following: "Since the C.K.C. became incorporated under the National Live Stock Pedigree Act of the Federal Department of Agriculture, it has risen from a practically obscure organization to an honoured place among the most prominent live stock associations of Canada." Further distinction came when His Grace, the Duke of Devonshire, Governor General of Canada, consented to become the C.K.C.'s patron.

1918 marked a banner year, for Humphrey Eliott, of Ottawa, had taken his beautiful Bull Terrier, Champion Haymarket Faultless, to the Westminster Kennel Club Show. In an entry of 1636 dogs benched, this Canadian dog won Best Dog in Show, All Breeds, at the Westminster Kennel Club, the only Canadian dog to bring that honor to Canada since the club's inception. In 1922, a Canadian-bred Cocker Spaniel, Lucknow Lottery, won Best Sporting Dog,

Int. Ch. Winna Lady Jenifer, bred and owned by Winifred Stuggall of Montreal, Canada.

Canadian-bred Russian Wolfhound. (Owner, Mrs. Janet Patterson of Brantford, Ontario, Canada)

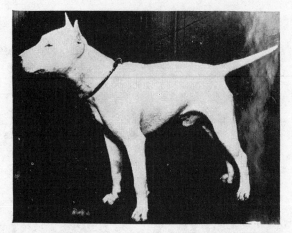

Ch. Haymarket Faultless, one of the greatest Bull Terriers of all time. (Owner, Humphrey Elliott, Ottawa, Canada)

All Breeds, at Westminster. He repeated this again in 1923, and in his year's campaigning in the United States won at the most prominent specialty shows and large all-breed bench shows. He was bred by Jack Sutton of Winnipeg, Manitoba.

The next big event in the club's history was September 30, 1926, when Dr. J. De Mund, the president of the A.K.C., Inc., and Newton H. Day, secretary, met Colonel G. F. MacFarland, president, and J. D. Strachan, the secretary-treasurer of the C.K.C., and a reciprocity agreement was drawn up which solidified the two clubs on a definitely satisfactory basis. One cannot stress too emphatically, the courtesy and spirit of cooperation which has been manifest at all times between the officers and directors of the A.K.C. and the C.K.C. Without this assistance the story might have been a different one.

The name of the official organ was changed from *Kennel and Bench* to *Dogs in Canada*, in March, 1940.

Most, but not all of the Canadian breed standards correspond with those adopted by A.K.C. There is some variation between the rules under which dog shows, field trials, Obedience trials, etc. are held but the line of demarcation is scarcely discernible. In the main, whatever has been accepted in one country has soon been duplicated in the other.

Field Trials and Shows. The first field trials in Canada on record were held in the vicinity of Winnipeg, Manitoba, in the year 1885, by the Northwest Field Trial Club. Thomas Johnson of Winnipeg, Manitoba, was the dean of all field trialers at that time. He owned and campaigned Manitoba Rap, a consistent winner. He also owned the noted and famous Manitoba Frank and Manitoba May, great field trial dogs of the day, which left their stamp on many of the more prominent dogs of that time. W. B. Wells, of Chatham, Ontario, was an early owner and importer. In 1888, Mr. Smith of London, Ontario,

imported the Llewellyn Setter Champion Paris which turned out to be a big field trial winner. It was said that $5,000 was refused for Champion Paris at that time.

The German Shepherd Dog Club of Canada sponsored field trials for Working dogs similar to the trials held in Germany in 1932 and the first dog to win a field trial championship under these rules was Int. Ch. Hettal Von Bodman, German Shepherd Dog imported from Germany by Mrs. Hartley Dodge of Giralda Farms, Madison, New Jersey, and owned by Alex Gooderham of Toronto, Ontario.

When the Obedience trial rules similar to those of the A.K.C. were adopted in 1940, the German Shepherd Dog Club dropped their trials to join under the one banner.

The first Obedience trial of an official nature was held in Vancouver, B.C., at the Canada Pacific Exhibition Show on August 30, 1940. These trials have become as popular in Canada as in the United States. To Canada fell the honor of breeding and owning the first dog of any breed to win all Obedience trial degrees on both sides of the border. The dog was the Welsh Corgi (Pembroke) Champion Windrush Redwing, International C.D., C.D.X., U.D. He was owned by Mrs. M. H. Page, of York Mills, Ontario.

The first field trials for Spaniels ever held in North America were those organized by E. Chevrier, North America's greatest English Springer Spaniel breeder, and held at Lorette, near Winnipeg, in September, 1922. The winner of the Open stake was imported Champion Don Juan of Gerwyn.

Many professional bird dog trainers from the United States are allotted training grounds on the Canadian prairies each summer and the "major circuit" of prairie chicken field trials are generally made up of dogs owned in the States. Many of the finest gun and field trial dogs in America receive their early educations on the Canadian training grounds, and some American trainers have been maintaining establishments in Canada for 30 years or more.

As many of the fairs and exhibitions across Canada have an agricultural background or section, it is only natural that dog shows should be included. Most prominent of the exhibitions holding all-breed dog shows are the Canadian National Exhibition at Toronto, and the Pacific National Exhibition at Vancouver.

Representatives are appointed from the membership of the Canadian Kennel Club to the exhibitions which sponsor dog shows.

The allocation of dog shows in Canada differs from that of any other country in the world. The number of shows a club may hold in one year is left to the discretion of the board of directors. The clubs once often combined to make what was known as a "circuit," but today many clubs will hold instead, say two championship shows on a weekend rather than one, and this cuts down on the time and travel expenses to exhibitors.

On the statistical side, CKC has some 7,000 members, registers approximately 50,000 dogs a year, and in 1969 there were 249 championship shows, 165 licensed obedience trials, 109 licensed field trials, and six tracking tests held under CKC rules.

Rules. Inquiries for copies of CKC rules, etc. may be addressed to The Canadian Kennel Club, Inc., 1173 Bay St., Toronto, Ontario, Canada.

——The Kennel Club of England——

THE KENNEL CLUB of England, known in that country simply as the Kennel Club, was born of the necessity to bring order out of chaos to the sport of public competitive dog exhibitions. The first dog show in England was held in 1859, and for 14 years these competitions, growing in popularity, were held in a rather haphazard manner.

Abuses of many kinds were practiced for, while individual clubs had rules of sorts, these organizations had no power to punish transgressors. Faking became a frequent violation; dog were borrowed for certain shows and returned to the owners after the awards were announced; the same dog was shown under different names in various novice classes, and other flagrant violations of decent ethics were not uncommon.

Recognizing the necessity for the establishment of a governing body with punitive powers, S. E. Shirley, M.P., called a group of well-known fanciers together in 1873 and the Kennel Club was formed. The Prince of Wales, who was later to become King Edward, became the Patron of the club.

One of the first important actions of the club was to publish a Stud Book, which contained the pedigrees of 4027 dogs which had won prizes at shows in the previous 14 years. Rules were formed and classifications established. Some of the most important rules met with considerable opposition and attempts were even made to establish a rival body, but the leadership of the Kennel Club maintained until that body was firmly entrenched in the commanding position it holds today.

All dog shows in England now come under the supervision of the Kennel Club. Before a dog may be exhibited, it must be registered with the Kennel Club, for which service a small fee is charged. Should it be sold, official transfer must be filed with the club before it can be exhibited again. The practice of cropping dogs' ears was prohibited by the club in 1895.

To become a champion in England a dog must win three challenge certificates under three different judges. These wins are comparable to that of Winners, Dog and Winners, Bitch under the rules of the American Kennel Club.

Before any gundog can become a champion of record it must have won a working certificate in a recognized field trial.

Between 2,000 and 3,000 dog shows are held annually in England.

KENNEL CLUB REGULATIONS

Regulations of The Kennel Club, 1 Clarges Street, Piccadilly, London, W.I.—formed in 1873 and known simply as Kennel Club—as relate to classification and registration appear through the courtesy of that organization. The first paragraph of these regulations lists the breeds of dogs recognized by The Kennel Club which, since the complete listing appears in Part XVI of this volume, has been here omitted.

* * *

2. Breed Registers and Varieties of Breeds—A separate Register, called the Breed Register, is kept by the Kennel Club for each breed, except in the cases of the following breeds, for which a separate Register is kept for each of the varieties of the breed specified.

SPANIELS

Clumber.
Cocker.
Cocker, American.
Field.
Irish Water.
Springer, English.
Springer, Welsh.
Sussex.
Interbred.
Crossbred.

DACHSHUNDS

Long-Haired.
Smooth-Haired.
Wire-Haired.
Miniature (Long-Haired).
　(Not exceeding 11 lbs. for exhibition.)
Miniature (Smooth-Haired).
　(Not exceeding 11 lbs. for exhibition.)
Miniature (Wire-Haired).
　(Not exceeding 11 lbs. for exhibition.)

BULL TERRIERS

Bull Terriers.
Bull Terriers (Miniature).
　(Not exceeding 14 inches for exhibition.)

FOX TERRIERS

Smooth.
Wire.

English Bulldog. Photo by Evelyn M. Shafer.

IRISH SETTERS

Red.
White and Red. (A.O.V.).

RETRIEVERS

Curly-Coated.
Flat-Coated.
Golden.
Labrador.
Interbred.
Crossbred.

COLLIES

Rough.
Smooth.

POODLES

Standard, 15 inches and over
   for exhibition.
Miniature, under 15 inches for
   exhibition.
Toy, under 11 inches for exhibition.

CHIHUAHUAS

Long Coat.
Smooth Coat.

TOY SPANIELS

Cavalier King Charles
   Spaniels.
King Charles Spaniels.

3. Breeds Eligible for Challenge Certificates—Challenge Certificates are issued by the Kennel Club for each breed or variety of breed of which a separate Register is kept.

4. Other Registers—A dog which is not eligible for entry in any of the above Registers may be entered in one of the following Registers kept by the Kennel Club.

    Any other Breed.
    Interbred Dogs.
    Crossbred Dogs.

Obedience and Working Trials Record.—Any dog will be accepted for registration in the Obedience and Working Trials Record, irrespective of its ancestry, on condition that it competes only in Obedience Tests and/or Working Trials.

5. Grouping of Breeds—For the purpose of competition between dogs of differing breeds, the grouping of breeds as shown in Regulation 1 shall be held to define Sporting (Hounds, Gundogs and Terriers) and Non-Sporting (Utility, Working and Toys).

6. A Dog's Breed—A dog is of the breed or variety of breed named in the Breed Register in which it is held to be eligible for entry.

7. Breed Registration—A dog bred from parents of the same breed or variety of breed can be entered only in the Register of that breed or variety except that such a dog bred from Chihuahuas, Dachshunds, Collies, Fox Terriers and Poodles must be entered in the Register of the variety it most closely resembles. If either parent or both parents are not registered in the Breed Register, the Kennel Club may permit registration on production of such evidence as it requires.

8. Crossbreed Registration—A dog bred from parents of different breeds must be registered as Crossbred, and the names of the breeds making the cross must be stated.

9. Interbred Dogs—A dog bred from parents of the same breed, but different varieties, must be registered as an Interbred, except that such a dog bred from Chihuahuas, Dachshunds, Collies, Fox Terriers and Poodles, must be entered in the Register of the variety it most closely resembles. In all cases the names of the varieties making the interbreeding must be stated.

10. Crossbred Retrievers or Spaniels—Any Retriever or Spaniel ineligible for registration as Pure Bred or Interbred may be registered under the heading of Retriever (Crossbred) or Spaniel (Crossbred).

11. Interbred Dogs in Breed Register—A dog bred from a parent registered as Interbred must be registered as Interbred, but, provided the Interbred ancestors are registered at the Kennel Club, a dog can be registered in a Breed Register if in each of the first three generations of its pedigree one of the parents making the Interbreeding is eligible for entry in that Register.

12. Crossbred Dogs in Breed Register—A dog bred from a parent registered as Crossbred must be registered as Crossbred, but, provided the Crossbred ancestors are registered at the Kennel Club, a dog can be registered in a Breed Register if in each of the first four generations of its pedigree one of the parents making the Crossbreeding is eligible for entry in that Register.

13. Dogs of Pedigree Unknown in the Whole or in Part—A

Ch. Pugville's Imperial Imp. II, Pug, owned by the Duke a Duchess of Windsor.

dog a part or the whole of whose pedigree is unknown may be entered in a Breed Register by permission of the Committee.

14. Breeder—The Breeder of any dog is the owner of the dam at the time of whelping, unless a Registration varying this definition has been effected under the Regulations for Loan or Use of Bitch for breeding purposes.

15. Name—Three names besides the one desired should be given in case the one entered in the body of the form is not available for registration. The names of notable persons, places, kennels, countries, cities, common names, colours or of a general character should not be selected. Numbers in figures or words cannot be accepted.

A name once entered in the Stud Book cannot be again registered in the same breed.

A name once registered cannot again be registered in the same breed for ten years after the 1st of January following the last registration.

When a dog is registered the name, including prefix or affix, shall not exceed 24 letters.

16. Prefixes and Affixes constitute part of a name and cannot be used for registration by any other than the person who for the time being is entitled under a subsisting grant of the Committee. The Committee will not grant the use of a prefix or affix of the names of counties, large towns, or titles, a letter or number, or an adjective or noun appropriate to the name of a dog, and any grant will be at the discretion of the Committee, who may cancel any grant at any time. In no circumstances may the grantee dispose or attempt to dispose of a prefix or affix.

17. Change of Name—The registered name of a dog may be changed once only in its lifetime and the only change permitted is the addition of the owner's registered prefix or affix to the original name. A Kennel Club change of name form must be used for the purpose and the dog must be transferred to the applicant. The new name must not be used until the change of name Certificate has been issued.

The name of a dog cannot be changed after 30 days have elapsed from the date of the win which qualifies it for entry in the Kennel Club Stud Book.

18. Imported Dogs—The name of a dog imported from, and already entered in, any country with which the Kennel Club has a reciprocal agreement, cannot be changed except by the addition of a registered prefix or affix. Before the name of an imported dog can be accepted for registration, applicants must give the date of importation, the address of the quarantine station at which it was detained, and the name and address of the importer.

19. Cancellation—If a registered dog dies before it has been exhibited or bred from, or before it has been entered in the Stud Book, the owner may cancel the name and the same shall be deemed never to have been registered.,

20. Non-acceptance of Registration—The Committee may decline an application for any registration or cancel any registration already made. The Committee will refuse for registration any cropped dog bred in Great Britain and the progeny of any such dog. If it should be proved that a dog has been cropped after registration, then the registration will be cancelled.

21. Hereditary Disease—Should the Kennel Club decide that a disease which in their opinion is hereditary is prevalent in a breed, it may require at the time of application for registration or transfer signed declarations regarding the disease on forms issued by the Kennel Club, and any registration or transfer may be cancelled should it be proved to the satisfaction of the Kennel Club that any of the statements made in the declarations are no longer correct.

22. Registration of Dogs with Unregistered Parentage—The Kennel Club accepts registration of dogs whose parents are not registered, but in such cases the name of an unregistered parent is printed in italics in the official list of registrations published monthly in *The Kennel Gazette*.

23. Service of a Bitch by more than one Dog—If, intentionally or unintentionally, a bitch is served by two dogs in the same heat, the names of both dogs must be given when the puppies are registered.

24. The Acceptance of a Registration is not a guarantee of its accuracy.

* * *

—The Bermuda Kennel Club*—

THE BERMUDA Kennel Club, Inc. was founded in 1955 and held its first show the following year. With dog shows under its auspices ever increasing in popularity, the club conducted its Seventeenth International Show in November, 1969. Rules of the Canadian Kennel Club governed the show until 1967, however, the club then adopted its own rules, these having governed the shows from that year forward. In 1968, the club also set up its own registration system.

This club conducts its International Shows during the autumn, usually November, they all being held within a one-week period. Four all-breed shows and obedience trials are conducted, with a fifth obedience trial held the morning after the last show.

It is difficult to conjecture a more attractive place for dog shows, the shows being held in Botanical Gardens, a beautiful and well-know Bermuda attraction. During 1968 there were 350 show entries, with nearly

four hundred for the 1969 program. Entries list from all parts of the U.S.A., from many points in Canada, and even from such relatively distant points as British Columbia and England, reflecting their increasing popularity where participation may be combined with a delightful Bermuda holiday.

By permission of The Bermuda Kennel Club., the following information is reproduced as of interest to possible show participants.

* * *

BERMUDA CHAMPIONSHIP — SCHEDULE OF POINTS

To be awarded a Bermuda Championship, it is necessary to obtain 10 points under at least three different judges. The points may be accumulated from one show to another and must include one 3-point win, either in breed or group. Any dog placing 1st, 2nd, 3rd or 4th in the group shall be awarded the highest number of points for any dog of any breed it defeats in that group, or its own points, whichever is higher. These points shall not be in addition to, but inclusive of, the points previously won in the breed. The Best Dog in Show shall be awarded the highest point rating of the show. Maximum number of points awarded in any one show shall be five.

---

* (The authors are indebted to Bermuda Kennel Club's President of 1968, Mrs. Edward Flieger, who served also as Show Secretary in 1969, for informaton relative this club and its autumn shows.)

Rating Applies to Each Sex

Scale of Points   1   2   3   4   5
All Breeds and Varieties   1   2   3   4   5

The Rules of the Bermuda Kennel Club, effective May 17, 1967, require the payment of a "listing fee" of 7/—or $.85 on the entry of a dog not registered individually in the records of the Bermuda Kennel Club. A "listed dog" may not be entered in shows or trials more than six times unless application for registration with the Bermuda Kennel Club has been made. In order to receive a Bermuda Kennel Club championship certificate or obedience title certificate, a dog must be registered with the Bermuda Kennel Club.

From Bermuda Kennel Club "Registration Rules," Chapter 4, Eligibility, Section (1):

"The following dogs are eligible for registration provided that in each instance the application for registration is acceptable to the Club's Registration Officer and is in accordance with the terms of these rules and is accompanied by the required fees and documents:

(a) A dog born in Bermuda of a litter registered with the Club.

(b) A dog registered in any of the following stud books or records:

The Canadian Kennel Club
The Kennel Club, England
The American Kennel Club
The Association of Masters of Harriers and Beagles
The Association of Masters of Foxhounds
The National Coursing Club, England
The Irish Kennel Club
The Irish Coursing Club
Newfoundland Live Stock Register"

Dogs entered in both breed and obedience pay only one listing fee.

CLASSIFICATION

Dogs may be entered in any of the following classes for which they are eligible.

(EXTRACTS FROM BERMUDA KENNEL CLUB DOG SHOW RULES)

Chapter 4. Breeds, Classes and Awards

Section 2.

(b) Every dog entered at a show must be entered in one of the regular official classes as set forth in Chapter 4, Section 2 (c) to (h) inclusive, or entered for "Specials Only" or "Exhibition Only," except in the case of Veterans' Classes for dogs and bitches 7 years of age and over if such special classes are provided for in the Premium List.

(c) The JUNIOR PUPPY CLASS shall be for dogs at least six months of age on the first day of the show and under nine months of age on the first day of the show.

(d) The SENIOR PUPPY CLASS shall be for dogs at least nine months of age on the first day of the show and under 12 months of age on the first day of the show.

(e) The NOVICE CLASS shall be for dogs never having won a first prize at a show in any regular official class. In determining whether a dog is eligible for this class, no award received on or after the official date of the closing of entries for a show at which the dog is to be shown shall be counted.

(f) The BERMUDA BRED CLASS shall be for dogs born in Bermuda, champions in any country excluded.

(g) The BRED BY EXHIBITOR CLASS shall be for dogs owned and handled in the ring by the breeder or a member of his immediate family.

(h) The OPEN CLASS shall be for all dogs that have not gained a Bermuda Championship.

Section 3.

(g) BEST OF VARIETY (applicable to American Cocker Spaniels only). Best of Variety in each colour shall compete for Best of Breed. This one Best of Breed will represent all varieties of American Cocker Spaniels in the group.

(h) SPECIALS ONLY. Only Bermuda Champions of Record may be entered in this class. In the case of American Cocker Spaniels, such dogs shall compete with the dog awarded Best of Winners for the Best of Variety award.

(a) No dog eligible to compete for any official awards may, except if excused by the Show Superintendent, be withheld from competition, and any exhibitor withholding a dog in contravention of this rule shall be subject to disciplinary action by the Board of Governors.

The "Brace Class" is an unofficial class. To be eligible for entry in an unofficial class, it is required that the dog first be entered in one of the official classes.

Only visitors coming to Bermuda expressly for the purposes of entering their dogs in the shows are eligible to compete for the award of Best Visitor's Dog.

A puppy entered in any official class may be eligible to compete for Best Puppy in Breed.

All dogs entered must compete in all classes and groups for which they are eligible except such dogs as may be excused by the Show Superintendent. Penalty for non-compliance cancels all wins and championship points earned by the dog withheld from competition. (Chapter 7, Section 7, B.K.C. Rules.)

1. JUNIOR PUPPY CLASS (6-9 months)
2. SENIOR PUPPY CLASS (9-12 months).
3. NOVICE CLASS.
4. BERMUDA BRED CLASS. The Bermuda Bred Class shall be for dogs born in Bermuda, champions in any country excluded. All Bermuda-bred dogs (progeny of a Bermudian-owned dam at the time of service) will be eligible to compete for the Best Bermuda Bred trophy.
5. BRED BY EXHIBITOR CLASS. The Bred by Exhibitor Class shall be for dogs owned and handled in the ring by the breeder or a member of his immediate family.
6. OPEN CLASS. The Open Class shall be for all dogs that have not gained a Bermuda Championship.
7. SPECIALS ONLY. ONLY Bermuda Champions of Record may be entered in this class.
8. LOCALLY OWNED. Unofficial Class. Not Bermuda Bred, but must be owned by a permanent resident of Bermuda. A dog entered in any official class may be eligible to compete in the locally owned class.
9. BRACE CLASS. Unofficial class.
10. EXHIBITION ONLY. Dogs to be shown by Junior Showmen in Junior Showmanship Competition must be entered in this class if not entered in a breed or obedience class.

Classes for the following breeds will be divided as indicated hereunder:

COCKER SPANIELS (AMERICAN): (1) Black; (2) Ascob (any solid colour other than black); (3) Parti-Colour; (4) Black and Tan.

COCKER SPANIELS (ENGLISH): (1) Solid Colour; (2) Parti-Colour.

BEAGLES: (1) 13″ and under; (2) Over 13″ and not exceeding 15″.

GREAT DANES: Open Classes only: (1) Harlequin; (2) Any other colour.

* * *

REQUIREMENTS FOR BRINGING DOGS INTO BERMUDA

Providing the basic requirements are met, there are no quarantine restrictions either bringing your dogs into Bermuda or returning them to the United States or Canada. Bermuda has NO RABIES. Following are the requirements necessary to bring a dog into Bermuda:

1. IMPORT PERMIT: For normal travel of dogs back and forth, or for dogs being brought in for re-

sale, an import permit, which can be obtained by writing to the Department of Agriculture and Fisheries, Paget, Bermuda, is necessary. For the purposes of the Bermuda Kennel Club's shows and trials, however, individual import permits for each dog entered will be obtained by the Show Committee from the Department of Agriculture and Fisheries and mailed to each exhibitor with the identification card, so that individual exhibitors need not apply to the Department of Agriculture for permits for dogs entered in the shows and trials. This permit must accompany the dog. Please indicate to whom identification card should be sent IF OTHER THAN THE OWNER.

2. HEALTH CERTIFICATE: Each dog entering Bermuda must have a certificate from a licensed veterinarian identifying the animal by reference to its breed, sex, age and colour, and certifying that:

1. It is not infected with any communicable disease or carrying any external parasite;

2. It has not, as far as is ascertained by reasonable inquiry, been infected by or exposed to rabies and has not been present within the last six months within an area officially quarantined or designated as a rabies area, and

3. It has been vaccinated since attaining the age of three months, with anti-rabies vaccine of a type specified in the certificate not less than one month nor more than twelve months prior to the date of its arrival in Bermuda.

The requirements for re-entry of dogs into the United States are as follows:

1. Certificate regarding vaccination against rabies, as described above, for entry into Bermuda.

2. Certificate of Health signed by a veterinarian not more than seven days prior to entry into the United States. These health certificates can be issued by the veterinarian in charge of the show.

The requirements for re-entry of dogs into Canada are as follows:

1. A certificate from the Bermuda Government veterinarian certifying that Bermuda is free from rabies and that your dog has been inspected and found free of any symptoms of contagious disease. This certificate can be issued by the veterinarian in charge of the show.

* * *

DOG SHOWS AND BERMUDA HOLIDAYS

The firm of Penboss Associates, Ltd., 66 Front Street, Hamilton, Bermuda, offers special services to visitors wishing to combine a Bermuda holiday with Show participation; this includes reservation service for both entries and visiting owner/handlers. A helpful brochure will be furnished by that firm upon request.

For show schedules and other data, full particulars may usually be obtained through travel agencies or Penboss. The official mailing address of The Bermuda Kennel Club is P.O. Box 1455, Hamilton, Bermuda.

BREEDS RECOGNIZED

The Bermuda Kennel Club Registration rules recognize, in general, the same breeds as A.K.C., however, there are a few exceptions as follows:

Bermuda Kennel Club adds the following breeds to Group I—Sporting Dogs:

German Long-haired Pointers
Pudelpointers
Retrievers (Nova Scotia Duck Tolling)
Tahl-Tan Bear Dogs

In Group II listings, Sporting Dogs (Hounds), the Bermuda Kennel Club lists separately six classes of Dachshunds, depending on size, and type of coat. It also lists the Drever dog as a separate breed.

Under Group III—Working Dogs, the Bernese Mountain Dog does not appear, neither are Belgian Sheepdogs listed by separate classes as to whether Malinois or Tervurens, as is the A.K.C. practice.

Collies are listed in two divisions by kind of coat, whether rough or smooth. The Eskimo dog is listed and Mastiffs are listed as Old English Mastiffs.

Under its Group IV—Terriers, the Bermuda Kennel Club has separate divisions for Smooth and Wire Fox Terriers. Whereas A.K.C. lists the Lhasa Apsos in Group VI classifications, this breed appears instead in Group IV (Terriers) in the Bermuda listings. Bermuda also lists the Staffordshire Bull Terrier in Group IV as a separate breed.

Bermuda Kennel Club listings in Group V include the Cavalier King Charles Spaniels, Chihuahuas (by two classes, long and short coat), the Mexican Hairless dog, Toy Poodles and Toy Manchester Terriers.

Bermuda Kennel Club's Group VI—Non-Sporting Dogs, includes the Shih Tzu. Poodles appear under two classes, miniature and standard. As before mentioned, the Lhasa Apsos appears under the Terrier grouping rather than here.

(For a complete listing, see Part XVI of text.)

Irish Setter, Flann's Sir Boss, owned and handled by George F. Pool of Hallsville, Texas, named Best in Show in one of the annual Bermuda Dog Shows. Judge Theodore Gunderson (left) of Ontario, Canada, and, making the presentation, Bermuda's Governor, His Excellency, Lord Martonmere.

Part XIX

BREEDS RECOGNIZED BY THE AMERICAN KENNEL CLUB

The American Kennel Club recognizes over one hundred different breeds of dogs. To secure this "recognition" a breed club must be formed, its constitution, by-laws and membership list submitted to AKC, together with the proposed standard for the breed and supporting evidence that the breed in question is a pure breed which reproduces a true type. When one hundred individual registrations have been made in the AKC Stud Book, the breed is entitled to show classification. To maintain this status at least fifteen individual registrations must be made annually.

—Introduction—

IT HAS been estimated that there are perhaps 40 million to 50 million dogs in America. Only a small portion of these animals are registered in the various stud books, and many of them are unlicensed. Nevertheless this total, which approximates one dog to every four or five persons, attests to the popularity of the dog in this country.

The American Kennel Club, composed of a large number of kennel clubs and field trial associations, has long been looked upon as the largest "official" body of American dogdom. Its Stud Book contains the registration of members of the pure breeds recognized by that organization, whose owners have seen fit to give their individual dogs the benefit of "certified" pedigrees. Other stud books, however, also have a considerable following. For instance, the Field Dog Stud Book, maintained by the *American Field* Publishing Company, registers by far the largest number of pointers and setters and many other sporting dogs. Most of the registrations of foxhounds and coonhounds in this country are to be found in the stud books of those breed organizations, and a good many are registered also with UKC.

The American Kennel Club classifies its recognized breeds into six groups. These are: Sporting Dogs, Hounds, Working Dogs, Terriers, Toys, and Non-Sporting Dogs. In the sequence of this grouping, the following text has been prepared by well-known breed authorities. They trace the origin and development of the various breeds, outline their characteristics and uses, and present the most up to date official breed standards available at the present time. These standards are occasionally changed by official action of the specialty clubs concerned, subject to the approval of the American Kennel Club.

The illustrations have not been selected with outstanding bench show and field trial records as the paramount consideration. They merely represent typical specimens of the individual breeds. Space limitations preclude the possibility of using the photos of many noted and even famous winners deserving of a place in this book.

—Group 1—Sporting Dogs—

WIREHAIRED POINTING GRIFFON

REGARDED AS a French breed but originating in Holland, the Wirehaired Pointing Griffon was the first pointing breed with a harsh coat to be recognized by the American Kennel Club. First brought to this country in 1901, the dog has enjoyed several spasmodic spurts of popularity. None of these periods, however, has been very long, for the dog's unique appearance and lack of speed kept it from becoming popular with the American sportsman, and its coat and color also failed to appeal. There are still a number of these dogs on this side of the ocean, and serious attempts at breeding them are made, but in terms of wide popularity, the Pointing Griffon has never gained a real solid foothold in American game fields.

This dog owes its existence to one man, E. K. Korthals, son of a wealthy banker who lived at Schooten, near Haarlem, Holland. Young Korthals desired to develop a new breed of hunting dog which would possess such great utility that it could be used on any type of game. Its characteristics had to include keenness of nose, ability to trail, possession of the pointing instinct and a rugged constitution which would enable it to cope with the toughest of cover and also to retrieve from icy and rough waters.

Korthals bought a gray and brown Griffon bitch named Mouche from M. G. Armand of Amsterdam in 1874 as the keystone of his proposed new breed. Five other dogs were purchased during the next three years. These were Janus, a wooly-haired dog, Junon, a short-hair, and Hector, Satan, and Banco, all three rough-coated. Mouche was mated to Janus and this union between rough-coat and woolly-coat produced one puppy, Huzaar. Mouche was mated to Hector, and a bitch puppy from that mating named Madame Augot was bred to the dog Satan, producing Zampa.

The first really productive cross, however, was effected when Huzaar was bred to the short-haired bitch Junon. Here was a combining of the wooly-haired, rough coated and short-haired types, and from this mating came a bitch named Trouvée, whose coat was harder than any other of the Korthals dogs. When bred to Banco, another rough-coat, Trouvée produced Moustache I, Querida, and Lina. These three dogs proved the fountainheads of the breed.

Korthals' father did not share his son's enthusiasm for dog breeding and, apparently, they quarreled over the matter, for the young man left Holland, going to Germany where he resumed his breeding operations. It was in France, however, that most of the development work on the breed was done, and in that country the Wirehaired Pointing Griffon is today known as the Korthals Griffon.

Just what breeds made up the background of the dogs which formed the foundation of this pointing

Wirehaired Pointing Griffon. Photo by Evelyn M. Shafer.

breed is not known, but authorities claim that in their veins ran Spaniel, Setter, and Otterhound blood. It has also been fairly well established that an infusion of German Shorthaired Pointer blood was used.

The Wirehaired Pointing Griffon is a rather slow, close-working dog who does his best work in the heavy growth of marshy country where his harsh coat provides him much protection. He is intelligent and takes to training readily, but, even though versatile, he is unable to compete on even terms with several other breeds among American pointing dogs. Most of them, in fact, can give him "cards and spades" and still take almost every trick.

Description and Standards. The description and standards follow:

GENERAL APPEARANCE: The Wirehaired Pointing Griffon is a dog of medium size, fairly short-backed, rather low on his legs. He is strong-limbed, everything about him indicating strength and vigor.

His coat is harsh like the bristles of a wild boar, and his appearance, notwithstanding his short coat, is as unkempt as that of the long-haired Griffon, but, on the other hand, he has a very intelligent air.

HEAD: Long, furnished with a harsh coat, forming a mustache and eyebrows, skull long and narrow, muzzle square.

EYES: Large, open, full of expression, iris yellow or light brown.

EARS: Of medium size, flat or sometimes slightly curled, set rather high, very lightly furnished with hair.

NOSE: Always brown.

NECK: Rather long, no dewlap.

SHOULDERS: Long, sloping.

RIBS: Slightly rounded.

FORE LEGS: Very straight, muscular, furnished with rather short wire hairs.

HIND LEGS: Furnished with rather short stiff hair, the thighs long and well developed.

FEET: Round, firm and well formed.

TAIL: Carried straight or gaily, furnished with a hard coat without plume, generally cut to a third of its length.

COAT: Hard, dry, stiff, never curly, the undercoat downy.

COLOR: Steel gray with chestnut splashes, gray-white with chestnut splashes, chestnut, dirty white mixed with chestnut, never black.

HEIGHT: 21½ to 23½ inches for males, and 19½ to 21½ inches for females.

POINTER

BROCKTON'S BOUNCE, Statter's Major, Whitehouse's Hamlet, Garth's Drake! What names to conjure up visions of great glory in the game fields of England! Mention this quartet and you have named the four cornerstones in the foundation of the Pointer breed. Add the name of Price's Champion Bang, and you have heralded the principal fountainhead of the breed as we know it in this country today.

These were not the first Pointers of exceptional quality, for behind each lay many generations of careful breeding, as early-day Pointer breeders kept meticulous records of their breeding operations long before bench shows and field trials came into being and before the Kennel Club was organized. But these five dogs, more than any others, exerted a lasting influence on many future generations and many of their individual characteristics and good qualities are seen in the everyday performances of "short-hair" gundogs and field trial contenders in every state.

The Pointer is a favorite gundog in Italy. Although many fanciers of the breed are under the impression that the Pointer originated in Spain, it is a matter of history that dogs of similar conformation and characteristics were to be found in France, Belgium, and other countries at about the same period when the breed was seen in Spain. The "braques" of France "that stop at scent and hunt with the nose high" may have come from Spain but that is a question which has never been settled. There are seventeenth and early eighteenth-century paintings by French artists which show the Pointer. It may have been that the Pointer was brought into England from both France and Spain. Be that as it may, it is the English sportsman to whom we are indebted for the *development* of the Pointer.

Among the pioneering English breeders of Pointers were: Thomas Webb Edge, George John Legh, J. C. Antrobus, Lord Combermere, Sir Vincent Corbet, the Earl of Sefton, Thomas Statter, Lord Derby, Sir Richard Garth, J. W. Whitehouse, R. J. Lloyd Price, J. Lang, and George Moore. These were not all, of course, and many others who contributed much came later.

It is fortunate for the Pointer that these men were thoughtful breeders, attaching great importance to field performance and the intermingling of the blood of Bounce, Major, Hamlet, and Drake, the "four aces" of pointerdom, carried on for improvement.

Although Brockton's Bounce was considered a medium-sized dog, he would be called a very large specimen today. He was dark liver and white in color, with the white heavily ticked. Most of his progeny were much like him in appearance and many inherited his good field qualities. In the first field trials ever held in England, in April, 1865, Brockton's Bounce, along with Whitehouse's Hamlet and J. A. Hanley's Moll, scored 90 out of a possible 100 per cent, while Sir Richard Garth's Jill and Mr. Fleming's Dandy made perfect scores. The judging was done on a point system, an untried method, of course, and the rather crude way in which the conclusions were arrived at did not prove a great deal. Bounce produced many good sons and daughters, one of which was Price's Vesta, the dam of Price's Champion Bang, the most famous pointer of his day.

Statter's Major was an even larger dog than Brockton's Bounce but, despite his size, was of good conformation. He was said to be the greatest stud pointer which had been seen in England in 30 years and his ancestry traced directly back to Spanish origin. He was considered a fast dog of great determination with excellent range. Major sired a number of dogs which figure far back in present-day pedigrees. Among them was Lord Sefton's Sam, which was the sire of the well-known Faust, imported in the eighties

Pointer—National Shooting Dog Champion (1966) Blakemore's Ed rrior. (Owner: A. H. Hembree, Union Springs, Ala.)

by the St. Louis Kennel Club. Sefton's Sam was the sire of Jane, the dam of Croxteth, a dog which did so much for the Pointer on this side of the waters.

Whitehouse's Hamlet was a somewhat different type of dog, both in color and conformation. At the same time the Antrobus, Edge, Sefton, and Moore strains, from which Bounce and Major descended, held sway in England, there was a strain of lemon and white Pointers, which, while not generally popular, were in high favor with an enthusiastic few. Leading these fanciers was H. Gilbert, and with the advent of public competitions his dogs created much favorable comment. Hamlet, a white and lemon son of Gilbert's Bob and Whitehouse's Juno, made a score of 90 per cent in the first English field trial. He soon became exceedingly popular as a sire. Hamlet was a powerfully-built dog, a bit short in muzzle, yet representing a clean-limbed, lithe type somewhat in contrast to the bulky conformation of Bounce and Major.

Garth's Drake was, according to authorities, the greatest bird dog—Pointer or Setter—of his day, particularly when it came to the matters of speed and handling of game. His speed was something to marvel at, and he approached his game at such a reckless pace that it became necessary for him to put on all brakes and slide into a dropping point in order to keep from running over his game. It was not until his seventh season that he began to slow down to such an extent that he could really assume a standing position on point. He was a large, rangy dog, clean in the shoulders and particularly good in loin. In action he was a frictionless-moving machine which seemed fairly to glide over the terrain, rough and smooth alike. There are probably many Pointers today which are just as fast as Drake was, but in those days excessive speed was unusual and Drake's gait attracted much attention. He was not a beautiful dog in conformation, but his splendid style and extreme intensity

were qualities much to be desired and he became the most famous Pointer stud of his time. He possessed remarkable prepotency and his fame, both as a producer and performer, was justified. Sir Richard Garth, his breeder and owner, disposed of his dogs in 1874 just before going to India. Drake, then seven years old, was purchased by Mr. R. J. Lloyd Price for 150 guineas, considered a very high figure at that time. The dog left his mark on the Pointer breed, and even today when a dog of particularly smooth action comes before the field-trial public oldtimers are prone to remark, "He has the Drake gait."

Price's Champion Bang was a powerful white and liver Pointer considered, in his prime, the handsomest Pointer in England. His sire was Coham's Bang, a son of Whitehouse's Hamlet, and his dam was Vesta, the daughter of Brockton's Bounce. In him we see the combining of the blood of two of the "cornerstones," a most happy combination.

Bang was quite different from Drake, not only in conformation but in action. His was not the smooth, gliding stride, but rather a reckless, powerful fling marked with fire and dash. His breeder was Sam Price, of Bow, Devonshire, England, one of the most successful breeders of his day. Bang nicked well with the daughters of Drake, Brockton's Bounce, Whitehouse's Hamlet, Statter's Major, Sefton's Sam, and others and it is most fortunate for the Pointer fancy that he did, for he was bred to extensively. In addition to his grand manner of going, he was extremely bold and stylish on point. He was not, however, so fast as Drake.

The two sons of Bang which are held in highest regard by American breeders were Croxteth and Priam. The latter never came to the States but he sired King of Kent and Beppo III, both of which were imported to this country in the eighties.

Croxteth was the head of the first important field trial family here, for his sons and daughters were quite successful and their progeny were also frequent winners, carrying on through generations.

King of Kent, the son of Priam, established a family which was not only exceedingly successful in field trials but also in bench shows. Among the field winners he produced were the famous Rip Rap, Maid of Kent, Zig Zag, Tapster, Hal Pointer, Kent Elgin, and Tick Boy. His many sons and daughters were the sires and dams of a long succession of winners and producers.

Beppo III, a son of Priam out of a full sister to the dam of King of Kent, was not so successful but his sons and daughters produced many winners in the field and on the bench.

Probably the best producing son of Price's Champion Bang was Mike, which, like Priam, never left England's shores. Through his son, Mainspring, he established a very important field trial family. Mainspring, brought over to this country, became the sire of Jingo, whose name and deeds are familiar to students of Pointer breeding. Jingo's progeny are among the Pointer greats.

The so-called "native" Pointers of the early days also played their part in the development of the Pointer of this country. One of the most famous was Champion Rush, bred and owned by Mr. Edmund Orgill, a very careful and thoughtful breeder who preferred the white and lemons. Rush was a successful bench show winner.

The Westminster Kennel Club and the St. Louis Kennel Club, two organizations interested in Pointers, imported a number of good ones and some which did not exactly please the American fancy. The St. Louis group imported Sleaford in 1877, but had indifferent success. Undaunted, they continued their importations. In 1877 they secured, through E. C. Stirling, the heavyweight, white and liver Bow, imported by T. H. Scott. He proved a bench show winner and also placed in field trials. In 1879, S. A. Kaye a member of the club, imported Faust, paying $1,350, the largest price to be paid for a Pointer in America up to that time. Faust enjoyed a series of bench show victories in this country and was a successful sire. A number of very fine bitches were also imported during this period, among them Jessamine, Lassie, Zeal, Trinket, and Lena.

The families of Rip Rap and Jingo have long been the subject of comparison, both having supporters contending superiority of one over the other. Both were wonderful field dogs and both established families which made Pointer history. Both were top-flight field trial winners and both were great producers. As a sire, Jingo perhaps had some advantage as he came before the field trial public some three seasons later than did Rip Rap and consequently had the opportunity of mating with many of Rip Rap's best daughters.

Rip Rap was one of the first white and black Pointers to make a big mark in the field trial world. For many years prior to his appearance, black in a Pointer was frowned upon with suspicion, but it was not long before this prejudice was dispelled. So prominently did his name become associated with the white and blacks that to this day many of those not so well informed as they consider themselves refer to every white and black Pointer as a "Rip Rap." Rip Rap sired 19 field trial winners, many of them fine producers. His best son was Young Rip Rap, a brilliant performer and a successful sire.

His most neglected son, from a breeding standpoint, was probably Fishel's Rip Rap, owned by the well-known breeder, U. R. Fishel, of Hope, Ind. Fishel's Rip Rap had no field trial record and was used at stud but little because of the availability of more brilliant sires. He sired, however, the famous Fishel's Frank, and that one accomplishment is enough to clinch for him a place in Pointer history. Unfortunately he died just about the time Fishel's Frank began his brilliant career, and when Pointer breeders wanted to use him it was too late.

Jingo sired 22 field trial winners, eight of them being the result of his matings with Dot's Pearl, a daughter of Rip Rap. Lad of Jingo was Jingo's best

Pointer—Triple Champion Gunsmoke. (Owner: H. N. Holm Springfield, Ill.)

producing son, which was the sire of the sensational Hard Cash, one of the few really great prairie-chicken dogs.

What the "four aces" were to the Pointers of the early days, what Croxteth and King of Kent were to a later period, and what Rip Rap and Jingo were still later, Alford's John and Fishel's Frank were in the period following the turn of this century. Their advent marked the real rise of the Pointer in field trial competitions. The blood of these two great bird dogs, more than that of any others, brought the Pointer up to a basis of even competition with his long-haired rival, the English Setter.

Alford's John was a "country town dog" about which much has been written. It was by accident that he attracted the attention of W. J. Baughn of Ridgeville, Ind., who recommended his purchase to C. H. Foust of Warren, Ind. Mr Foust had invited Mr. Baughn to look over a couple of Setter puppies he had purchased from Mr. Baughn as field trial prospects. The puppies were a disappointment to the latter, but the younger Pointer which accompanied them uninvited set such a pace that the Ridgeville sportsman suggested that he be acquired immediately if he wanted a winner. Mr. Foust, primarily a Setter fancier, did not take too kindly to the suggestion but did acquire an interest in the Pointer from his owner, Thomas Alford, a druggist of Warren. Later, while he was already successful, he became the property of R. R. Dickey, Jr., of Dayton, Ohio.

Winner of the Manitoba Chicken Championship, along with other victories, Alford's John set a hot pace for the Setters of that period and his puppies were in great demand. He did not come from a long line of winners and but few dogs of any prominence appear in his pedigree, but he was a peerless performer and his daughters were the best producers of any family of Pointers before or during his time.

Three years after Alford's John made his first appearance, U. R. Fishel, Hope, Indiana, brought out a youngster named Fishel's Frank, and won second with him in the Nebraska Derby. Frank, a son of Fishel's Rip Rap (Rip Rap ex Ghay Estill) and Boy's Queen (Jingo's Boy ex Nellie Rush), soon attracted much attention by his spectacular performances and it was not long before breeders were flocking to his banner. He won on many occasions, but the race which brought him more fame than any was a race he lost. This was the National Championship of 1908. Frank was drawn in the last brace with the Setter Danfield. He had the misfortune to contact a bevy of quail early in his three-hour heat. The birds were on barren ground and the sight of them proved too great a temptation for Frank, for he dashed forward as they went up but stopped promptly at command. After that his exhibition was flawless and many in the gallery thought he had won the stake even with the slight error. The judges felt otherwise, however, and called the Setters Count Whitstone II and Danfield back to run for the title.

Count Whitstone II won, but for months afterwards the field trial gallery buzed with the argument that Fishel's Frank should have been the new champion. And the dog's fame continued to spread. After this race he was retired to stud.

Fishel's Frank sired 58 field trial winners, many of them champions and top-flight performers. The list and their deeds are far too long to enumerate here, but two of his sons made Pointer history. They were Comanche Frank and John Proctor, both out of daughters of Alford's John. Close behind them were two more sons, Lewis C. Morris and Desota Frank.

The first Pointer to win the National Championship was Manitoba Rap, whose bloodlines combined those of Rip Rap, Jingo, and Rush of Lad. He was retired from competition immediately after winning the championship in 1909, when he was still less than three years of age.

The two sons of Fishel's Frank which brought the Pointer to the pinnacle of success and proved beyond a doubt his worthiness to compete on even terms with the Setter were Comanche Frank and John Proctor. Both won the National Championship (Comanche Frank in 1914 and John Proctor in 1916) in addition to other field trial title events. Both established winning and producing families which have made Pointer history.

Comanche Frank was a dog of unusual stamina and courage, no matter under what conditions he was called upon to hunt. He was one of the greatest, most consistent, and most intelligent ground-working bird dogs ever known. His nose, particularly in his younger years, was not always at its best and his location was sometimes none too good. But in his more mature seasons he proved that he was an excellent bird finder and handler on both quail and prairie chickens, winning titles on both.

Comanche Frank was the sire of the sensational Mary Montrose, winner of the National Championship when still a derby and the first dog to win this title three times. When she was right, "Peerless Mary," as she was called, was practically unbeatable.

John Proctor, whose dam was Miss Mariutch, another daughter of Alford's John, won four championships, including the National Championship of 1916. In all he had 23 wins, 14 of them being first places, and left a long list of winning progeny, 47 in all. Like Comanche Frank, John Proctor had a magnificent way of going and showed remarkable intelligence in working his ground. But, unlike his illustrious half-brother, he was inclined to loaf occasionally, for he would not hunt on barren ground.

Later on two more families of Pointers added to the further glory of the breed. These were the families of Triple Champion Muscle Shoals Jake, a son of Ferris Jake and a grandson of John Proctor, and Amateur Champion Seaview Rex, a son of Tarheel John.

Muscle Shoals Jake was not only a most successful sire but also an outstanding field trial performer. He was an extremely bold dog, sometimes bold to a fault, and for several seasons had a bad fault which kept him out of the money on occasions. This was the lust to kill which would occasionally assert itself in the dog; when it did he would tackle almost anything which came in his path: goats, sheep, pigs, turkeys, and even colts or calves were not immune from his attacks. In his later years he was broken of this habit, although the trait occasionally cropped up in some of his many sons. The dog was exceedingly prepotent and was bred to extensively. His winning progeny, also, are too numerous to list here. One of his best sons, however, was Champion Air Pilot, which produced, among other good ones, National Champion Air Pilot's Sam. Sam also proved a splendid producer.

Seaview Rex was not a frequent winner in major field trials but he produced a family of great renown. An extreme stylist himself, he possesed the ability to transmit this exceedingly attractive quality to the majority of his get and to such a degree that they were generally easily recognized. He stamped his progeny with other qualities, too, among them being a rather heavily-shouldered gait. Perhaps his most prominent son was the sensational National Pheasant Champion Village Boy, whose son, Champion Spunky Creek Boy, became a leading Pointer sire.

No treatise on the Pointer would be complete without prominent mention of the famous Pointers of the late A. G. C. Sage. This New York sportsman maintained an extensive hunting preserve near Alberta, Alabama, called "Sedgefields," and more Pointer breeding history was made at this establishment than in any other single area.

Mr. Sage was a great patron of field trials; in fact, his connection with the sport had extended over a longer period than any other man's at the time of his death. He never campaigned his dogs extensively,

Pointer—National Amateur Pheasant Champion Elhew Marksman, here retrieving grouse. (Owner: R. G. Wehle, Scottsville, N.Y.)

but he was outstandingly successful wherever his dogs started. His derbies won more *American Field* Futurities than those of any other breeder and he won more National Championships, National Free-for-All, and National Derby Championships than any other individual.

Space will not permit the mention of all of his winners here but a few of his Futurity winners have been: Superlette, Morpheus, Rockaby Baby, Ariel, Astra, Bye Bye, Oration, and Bolero. Some of his National Free-for-All winners have been: Superlette, a repeater, Timbuctoo, Ariel, and Saturn. His National Champions have been: Rapid Transit, Sulu, Luminary, Ariel (three times), Saturn, and Paladin.

Three Pointers won the National Championship three times. These were Mary Montrose, Becky Broomhill, and Ariel. Only one Setter, Feagin's Mohawk Pal, has ever held that distinction.

Time was when a professional brought a Pointer to a field trial with half an apology. In fact, in the early days of public competition the Pointer was not considered the equal of the Setter and, consequently, separate stakes were run for Pointers only.

At the present time there are more Pointers being entered in field trials than Setters, and more places are won by Pointers. Perhaps the numerical force has something to do with it, but it is a fact that, as a breed, the Pointer develops faster than the Setter and can be brought to the peak of his ability at an earlier age.

More force can be used with the average Pointer than with the average Setter, but too much force, of course, will either ruin the dog entirely or make him into a mechanical performer who does not have his heart in his work. This type of dog is entirely unsuitable for field trials and is not to be desired as a gunning companion.

The Pointer, while not unresponsive to kind treatment, does not have the affectionate disposition of the Setter and is much less apt to become a one-man dog. In fact, the desire to hunt is so firmly imbedded in many of them that they will usually hunt for anyone who has a shotgun. Yet there are Pointers who are loyal in the extreme.

The Pointer, because of the shortness of his coat, can generally stand hot weather and arid terrain better than a Setter. By the same token, the Setter can generally stand cold weather and heavy, briary cover better than the Pointer. In both cases, though, much depends on the individual.

As a rule, the Pointer is a dog of rugged constitution, in which the desire to hunt and a well-defined pointing instinct are deeply ingrained. As in any breed, some are rather phlegmatic, others are brilliant. But if one will choose carefully from well-known bloodlines of proved merit and give his prospect the proper training, he will have a gundog second to none on any type of upland game birds. The Pointer was developed for a hunting dog—a gundog—and a gundog he will be as long as present breeding practices continue.

Description and Standards. The description and standards follow:

GENERAL APPEARANCE: The Pointer is bred primarily for sport afield; he should unmistakably look and act the part. The ideal specimen gives the immediate impression of compact power and agile grace; the head noble, proudly carried; the expression intelligent and alert; the muscular body bespeaking both staying power and dash. Here is an animal whose every movement shows him to be a wide-awake, hard-driving hunting dog possessing stamina, courage, and the desire to go. And in his expression are the loyalty and devotion of a true friend of man.

TEMPERAMENT: The Pointer's even temperament and alert good sense make him a congenial companion both in the field and in the home. He should be dignified, yet showing at all times a responsive attitude.

HEAD: Skull long and proportionately wide, but indicating length rather than width. Slight furrow between the eyes, cheeks cleanly chiseled. A pronounced stop midway between nostrils and occiput. Muzzle long, in the same plane as the skull. Jaws ending level and square, with scissors or even bite. The flews clean. Nostrils large, spongy, widely open.

EARS: Set on at eye level. When hanging naturally, they should reach just below the lower jaw, close to the head, with little or no folding. They should be somewhat pointed at the tip—never round—and soft and thin in leather.

EYES: Of medium size, rounded, pleasant in expression and the darker the better.

NECK: Long, dry, muscular and slightly arched, springing cleanly from the shoulders.

SHOULDERS: Long, thin, and sloping. The top of blades close together.

FRONT: Elbows well down, directly under the withers and truly parallel, so as to work just clear of the body. Forelegs straight and with oval bone. Knee joint never to knuckle over. Pasterns of moderate length, perceptibly finer in bone than the leg, and slightly slanting. Chest, deep rather than wide, must not hinder free action of forelegs. The breastbone bold, without being unduly prominent. The ribs well sprung, descending as low as the elbow-point.

BACK: Strong and solid, with only a slight rise from croup to top of shoulders. Loin of moderate length, powerful and slightly arched. Croup falling only slightly to base of tail. Tuck-up should be apparent, but not exaggerated.

TAIL: Heavier at the root, gradually tapering to a fine point. Length no greater than to reach to the hock joint. Carried straight, ideally on a level with the back.

HINDQUARTERS: Muscular and powerful, with great propelling leverage. Thighs long and well-developed. Stifles well bent. The hocks clean and parallel. Decided angulation is the mark of power and endurance.

FEET: Oval, with long, closely-set, arched toes, well padded, and deep.

COAT: Short, dense, smooth with a sheen.

COLOR: Liver, lemon, black, orange; either in combination with white or solid-colored. A good Pointer cannot be a bad color. In the darker colors, the nose should be black or brown; in the lighter shades it may be lighter or flesh-colored.

GAIT: Smooth, frictionless, with a powerful hindquarters' drive. The head should be carried high, the nostrils wide, the tail moving from side to side rhythmically with the pace, giving the impression of a well-balanced, strongly-built hunting dog capable of top speed combined with great stamina.

BALANCE AND SIZE: Balance, overall symmetry, is much more important in the Pointer than size. It is just as vital in a dog bred for field work as it is in an athlete or a race horse, and for the same reasons: it indicates muscular coordination, endurance, and an equilibrium of power. Whether large or small, a well put-together Pointer, "smooth all over," is to be preferred to an uneven one with contrasting good and bad points. Provided there is balance, considerable variation in size and weight is permissible.

FAULTS:

GENERAL APPEARANCE: Lack of true Pointer type. Hound or terrier characteristics.

TEMPERAMENT: Timidity, unruliness.

HEAD: Blocky or apple head. Short or snipy muzzle or frog face. Bulging cheeks or pendulous flews. Lack of stop, down-face, Roman nose. Undershot or overshot. Small or dry nostrils.

EARS: Low set, round, heavy, folded, leathery or hound ears.

EYES: Light, hard, almond, or staring eyes.

NECK: Ewe neck. Throatiness. Short, thick neck.

SHOULDERS: Loaded or bossy shoulders. Set wide apart at top. Straight shoulders, no slope.

FRONT: Elbows turned either in or out. Forelegs knuckled over. Straight pasterns, terrier front. Bone of forelegs coarse, fine, or round. Narrow chested, shallow, shelly, pigeon-breasted. Chest too wide, resulting in elbows out. Ribs too flat or too barrelled.

BACK: Roach or sway back. Unbalanced length of body. Cobbiness. Steep rise, or none at all, in topline. Sagging or long, thin loin. Croup falling away too sharply.

TAIL: Rat tail. Set on too high or too low. Carried between the legs, or carried high, flagpole tail.

HINDQUARTERS: Straight stifles. Cow hocks. Lack of angulation or straight in stifle. Any suggestion of weakness in hindquarters.

FEET: Cat-foot. Thin or soft pads. Splayed feet. Flat toes.

COAT: Long hair or curl. Soft or silky coat.

COLOR: Weak or washed-out colors. Light or flesh-colored nose in a dark-colored dog. Butterfly nose.

GAIT: Crossing-over, sprawling or side-tracking. Stepping too high in front—the hackney gait.

SCALE OF POINTS:	Points
Head	10
Ears	3
Eyes	4
Neck	5
Shoulders	8
Front	6
Back	4
Tail	5
Hindquarters	15
Feet	9
Coat and color	5
Gait	6
Balance and true Pointer type	20
TOTAL	100

(March 10, 1959)

GERMAN SHORT-HAIRED POINTER

IN THE American gundog kennel there is a dog to fit the individual tastes and requirements of every upland game bird gunner. Whether his desires run to a wide-ranging, high-stepping, swashbuckling ground-coverer or to a close-working, careful plodder that is amenable to his owner's every command, there is a dog to fill the bill if the gunner will only take the time to look for it.

No longer so much a comparative newcomer to America, the German Shorthaired Pointer is fairly made to order for the sportsman who prefers to take his hunting in a somewhat leisurely manner and needs a pointing dog with a choke-bore nose, medium range, and moderate speed. If the gunner wants to combine a bit of waterfowling along with his upland game shooting, he will do well to give the German serious consideration. For a combined job of pointing game and retrieving from land and water, the German Shorthaired Pointer takes a back seat for no dog. But if he wants great speed and high style on point along with the rest he must choose lines carefully, for this dog generally goes about his job in the fashion of the true workman he is—all business, with no fancy frills. Because of this thorough-going trait, German Shorthairs have been walking away with many important field trials in recent years.

As his name implies, the German Shorthaired Pointer originated in Germany. The basic stock of the breed was the old Spanish Pointer. A cross with the Bloodhound brought more nose, greater intelligence, and better trailing ability. The cross also brought bigger bone, greater size, and less speed. This dog was not entirely satisfactory, and so a cross on the Foxhound was used, which added the speed but probably diminished the pointing instinct. So again new blood was brought in, this time the English Pointer providing it. After several generations of careful selective breeding, the patient and thorough

German breeders had the dog they were seeking—a dog of great versatility, able and willing to track down ground game with the gameness and keen nose of the hound, to point instinctively his feathered game with the sure location and staunchness of the Pointer and Setter and, in addition, with the strength and fortitude to brave rough and icy water in retrieving wildfowl. The German Shorthaired Pointer possesses all three traits.

The versatility of this dog is attracting considerable attention among American sportsmen and he is growing in popularity. In Minnesota, Michigan, and near-by states where a varied game supply allows full use of his capabilities, he is in great demand. The average German Shorthaired Pointer owner is generally unwilling to admit that the big fellow has any superior as an all-around gundog. Generally the jack-of-all-trades is a master of none, and so it might be with this dog—but you should be sure of your own dog before you challenge the owner of a German Shorthair to a rough-and-tumble, catch-as-catch-can game-getting contest on feather and fur, with retrieving ability to count.

The Shorthair is not a fast dog. His rugged, somewhat bulky make-up prevents him from being as speedy as his smaller, more wiry rivals. And, too, he is not intended for speed, for it is the nature of this dog to work his ground carefully and pick up, with his keen nose, the faintest scent, working it out to a contact with game. His excellent nose causes him to carry a rather low head generally, although when scenting conditions are good he travels with it held high. On point he is intense enough, though many are inclined to crouch to some extent, apparently in an endeavor to make their bulk as inconspicuous to game as possible.

The German Shorthair is a dog of an exceedingly kind and mild disposition, seldom quarrelsome but more than capable of holding his own with a more pugnacious opponent.

The German Shorthaired Pointer is the favorite gundog in Germany.

There are many breed trials in the country and exponents of the breed are growing more interested in this form of breed display and promotion. Several German Shorthaired Pointer field trials have been held here sponsored by the mother club, the German Shorthaired Pointer Club of America, with headquarters in Minneapolis, and those sponsored by the German Shorthaired Pointer Club of Michigan, at Detroit. All trials are conducted under the rules of the American Kennel Club and field trial championship points are awarded the winners.

The man who hunts on foot and wants a tractable dog of medium range for combination shooting will do well to consider the Shorthair. He might need to look no further.

Description and Standards. The description and standards, adopted by the German Shorthaired Pointer Club of America, Inc., and approved by the American Kennel Club, May 7, 1946, follow:

GENERAL APPEARANCE: The overall picture which is created in the observer's eye should be that of an aristocratic, well-balanced, symmetrical animal with conformation indicating power, endurance, and agility, and a look of intelligence and animation.

The dog should be neither unduly small nor conspicuously large. It should rather give the impression of medium size, but be like the proper hunter, "with a short back, but standing over plenty of ground." Tall, leggy individuals seldom possess endurance or sound movement.

Dogs which are ponderous or unbalanced because of excess substance should be definitely rejected. The first impression should be that of keenness which denotes full enthusiasm for work without indication of nervous or flighty character. Movement should be alertly coordinated without waste motion.

Grace of outline, clean-cut head, sloping shoulders, deep breast, powerful back, strong quarters, good bone composition, adequate muscle, well-carried tail and taut coat, all of which should combine to produce a look of nobility and an indication of anatomical structure essential to correct gait which must indicate a heritage of purposefully conducted breeding.

HEAD: Clean-cut, neither too light nor too heavy, in proper proportion to the body. Skull should be reasonably broad, arched on side and slightly round on top. Scissura (median line between the eyes at the forehead) not too deep, occipital bone not as conspicuous as in the case of the Pointer.

The foreface should rise gradually from nose to forehead—not resembling the Roman nose. This is more strongly pronounced in the dog than in the bitch, as befitting his sex. The chops should fall away from the somewhat projecting nose. Lips should be full and deep, never flewy. The chops should not fall over too much, but form a proper fold in the angle. The jaw should be powerful and the muscles well developed.

The line to the forehead should rise gradually and should never possess a definite stop as in the case of the Pointer, but rather a stop-effect when viewed from the side, due to the position of the eyebrows.

The muzzle should be sufficiently long to enable the dog to seize properly and to facilitate his carrying game a long time. A pointed muzzle is not desirable. The entire head should never give the impression of tapering to a point. The depth should be in the right proportion to the length, both in the muzzle and in the skull proper.

EARS: Ears should be broad and set fairly high, lie flat and never hang away from the head. Placement should be above eye level.

The ears, when laid in front without being pulled, should about meet the lip angle. In the case of heavier dogs, they should be correspondingly larger.

German Shorthaired Pointer—Dual Champion Kamiak Desert Sand. (Owner: Lowell and Gay Dorius, Kamiak Kennels, Oakdale, Calif.)

German Shorthaired Pointer—These dogs not only point, but are excellent retrievers. David M. Duffey photo.

EYES: The eyes should be of medium size, full of intelligence and expressive, good-humored, and yet radiating energy, neither protruding nor sunk. The eyelids should close well.

The best color is a dark shade of brown. Light yellow, china or wall (bird of prey) eyes are not desirable.

NOSE: Brown, the larger the better; nostrils well opened and broad. Flesh-colored and spotted noses are not desirable.

TEETH: The teeth should be strong and healthy. The molars should intermesh properly. Incisors should fit close in a true scissor bite. Jaws should be neither overshot nor undershot.

NECK: Of adequate length to permit the jaws reaching game to be retrieved, sloping downwards on beautifully curving lines. The nape should be rather muscular, becoming gradually larger towards the shoulders. Moderate hound-like throatiness permitted.

BREAST AND THORAX: The breast in general should give the impression of depth rather than breadth; for all that, it should be in correct proportion to the other parts of the body with fair depth of chest.

The ribs forming the thorax should be well-curved and not flat; they should not be absolutely round or barrel-shaped. Ribs that are entirely round prevent the necessary expansion of the chest when taking breath. The back ribs should reach well down.

The circumference of the breast immediately behind the elbows should be smaller than that of the breast about a handsbreadth behind elbows, so that the upper arm has room for movement.

BACK AND LOINS: Back should be short, strong and straight with slight rise from root of tail to withers. Excessively long or hogbacked should be penalized. Loins strong, of moderate length and slightly arched. Tuck up should be apparent.

ASSEMBLY OF BACK MEMBERS: The hips should be broad with hip sockets wide apart and fall slightly toward the tail in a graceful curve. Thighs strong and well muscled. Stifles well bent. Hock joints should be well angulated with strong, straight bone structure from hock to pad. Angulation of both stifle and hock joints should be such as to combine maximum combination of both drive and traction. Hocks should turn neither in nor out.

ASSEMBLY OF FRONT MEMBERS: The shoulders should be sloping, movable, well covered with muscle. The shoulder blades should lie flat. The upper arm (also called the cross bar, i.e., the bones between the shoulder and elbow joints) should be as long as possible, standing away somewhat from the trunk so that the straight and closely muscled legs, when viewed from in front, should appear to be parallel. Elbows which stand away from the body or are pressed right into same indicate toes turning inwards or outwards, which should be regarded as faults. Pasterns should be strong, short, and nearly vertical.

FEET: Should be compact, close-knit, and round to spoon-shaped. The toes sufficiently arched and heavily nailed. The pad should be strong and hard.

COAT AND SKIN: The skin should look close and tight. The hair should be short and thick and feel tough and hard to the hand; it is somewhat longer on the underside of the tail and the back edge of the haunches. It is softer, thinner and shorter on the ears and the head.

TAIL: Is set high and firm, and must be docked, leaving approximately two-fifths of length.

The tail hangs down when the dog is quiet, is held horizontally when he is walking, never turned over the back or considerably bent but violently wagged when he is on the search.

BONES: Thin and fine bones are by no means desirable in a dog which should be able to work over any and every country and should possess strength. The main importance accordingly is laid not so much on the size as being in proper proportion to the body. Dogs with coarse bones are handicapped in agility of movement and speed.

WEIGHT AND HEIGHT: Dogs, 55 to 70 pounds; bitches, 45 to 60 pounds. Heights: dogs, 23 to 25 inches; bitches, 21 to 23 inches at the shoulders.

COLOR: Solid liver, liver and white spotted, liver and white spotted and ticked, liver and white ticked, liver roan. Any colors other than liver and white (gray white) are not permitted.

Symmetry and field quality are most essential. A dog well balanced in all points is preferable to one with outstanding good qualities and defects. A smooth, lithe gait is most desirable.

German Shorthaired Pointer—A head study.

Faults: Bone structure too clumsy or too light. Head too large. Too many wrinkles in forehead. Dish-faced. Snipey muzzle. Ears too long, pointy, or fleshy. Flesh-colored nose. Eyes too light, too round, or too closely set together. Excessive throatiness. Cowhocks. Feet or elbows turned inward or outward. Down on pasterns. Loose shoulders, swayback. Black coat or tri-colored. Any colors except liver or some combination of liver and white.

GERMAN WIREHAIRED POINTER

RECENTLY ADDED to the recognized list of general purpose hunting dogs who point their game and retrieve it after it is shot is the German Wirehaired Pointer. The breed became a part of the American Kennel Club's official family in 1959 but had been recognized for some years before by the Field Dog Stud Book.

The FDSB still registers the breed as Deutsche Drahthaar, its German sobriquet, but the AKC has translated literally and tacked on the descriptive term "pointer" and registers the breed as German Wirehaired Pointer.

But whether he's called a Drahthaar or a Wirehaired Pointer, he's in the process of establishing himself as a useful and interesting breed of dog. In appearance it would be an oversimplification to describe the Drahthaar as "a German Shorthaired Pointer who needs a shave," but for starters that might be as apt a description as any.

In temperament, while inclined to be aloof with strangers, the German Wirehair is affectionate almost to a fault with those he knows, has a strong trace of clownishness in his make-up, and a strong desire to be with people. They are not good kennel dogs, are easily bored by lack of attention and the more they are asked to learn the happier they are. They are eager to learn, quick to try to please and have retentive memories.

While firmness is the only way to earn this dog's respect in training sessions, it should be counterbalanced by not only praise, but some light-hearted horsing around and affection. Tough and resilient, both physically and mentally, the Wirehaired Pointer in many ways is a "soft" dog and a regimen of all work and no play can result in either a fawning, overly eager-to-please attitude, or one of stubborn sulkiness.

German Wirehaireds are at their best with persons who enjoy being with and training their one-at-a-time dogs so they have a home companion as well as a proficient hunter.

As a hunter, the Drahthaar is expected to be a close to medium-ranging seeker of upland game birds, pointing them upon location and retrieving them after they are shot. Most members of the breed possess strongly the right instincts, both to hunt out, point and fetch. They are very trainable for this reason. German Wirehaireds may also be expected to work well in marsh and water, within reason. They take to retrieving from water quite readily and their harsh coats have amazingly quick-drying properties.

Like other pointing breeds from the European region, in his home country the Drahthaar is asked to do any of a number of other tasks as a companion to the gamekeeper and hunter. But his supporters in the U.S. have wisely refrained from selling him to the public as an amazing jack-of-all-trades with an unbelievable list of accomplishments, all acquired with a minimum of training.

Although first brought to the U.S. around 1920 and known to exist in some numbers in the 1930s, the breed began to "catch on" in the 1950s. The breed is most popular in the Midwest, and was first popularized in Illinois and Wisconsin, but is still classed as a rare breed. Hunting conditions in the North-Central part of the U.S. make this kind of pointing dog practical and have led to the popularity of other Continental pointing breeds like the Brittany Spaniel, German Shorthaired Pointer, Weimaraner, and so on.

Haar Baron's Mike was the first Wirehaired to win an AKC-recognized field championship, competing in October, 1959. His dam, Dual Ch. Haar Baron Gremlin, won both her show and field titles in 1960, as well as the German Pointing Dog National Trial, which Haar Baron's Mike captured in 1959. Both were owned and handled by Cliff Faestel, Brookfield, Wisconsin.

Informed speculation is that the early Wirehaired Pointers (development began in Germany in 1870) are a combination of Griffon, Stichelhaar, Pudelpointer and German-Shorthaired. A recognized breed in Germany, the Pudelpointer is the result of a cross between a Poodle and an English Pointer and the Griffon and Stichelhaar were developed with the use of Pointers, Foxhounds, Pudelpointers and a Polish water dog.

Reportedly the Wirehairs are more popular in Germany than the Shorthairs, which are now among the

German Wirehaired Pointer—Ch. Haar Baron's Mike, first of breed to win an AKC Field Trial Championship. (Owner: Cliff Faest Brookfield, Wisc.) David M. Duffey photo.

German Wirehaired Pointer—Many hunting dogs are tolerant of children and make themselves popular as family dogs. David M. Duffey photo.

most popular multi-purpose pointing breeds in the U.S., leading in registrations in the German Hunting dog studbook since 1923.

They are alert, agile dogs, with good stamina and gait, possessing fine nose and the proper instincts that lead to easy training and refinement in developing top notch and practical performers in the field. Because of their bewhiskered faces, they are different enough in looks to catch the fancy of some dog exhibitors. There is a set standard with which the breed's coarse, wiry coat must conform if the dog is to be shown, but German Wirehaireds used in the field vary greatly in the composition and texture of their coats.

This "new" breed won't get popular because it fills some gap in the U.S. hunting scene. But it will be around for a long time because it can compete honestly with a number of breeds already established, filling the bill well for the sportsman who enjoys a variety of upland bird hunting on foot and wants a dog that will locate his game, point and retrieve it and, within reason, occasionally serve as a waterfowl retriever.

Description and Standards. In detail, the standard for the German Wirehaired Pointer follows:

GENERAL: The German Wirehaired Pointer is a dog that is essentially Pointer in type, of sturdy build, lively manner, and an intelligent, determined expression. In disposition the dog has been described as energetic, rather aloof but not unfriendly.

HEAD: The head is moderately long, the skull broad, the occipital bone not too prominent. The stop is medium, the muzzle fairly long with nasal bone straight and broad, the lips a trifle pendulous but close and bearded. The nose is dark brown with nostrils wide open, and the teeth are strong with scissors bite. The ears, rounded but not too broad, hang close to the sides of the head. Eyes are brown, medium in size, oval in contour, bright and clear and overhung with bushy eyebrows. Yellow eyes are not desirable. The neck is of medium length, slightly arched and devoid of dewlap, in fact, the skin throughout is notably tight to the body.

BODY AND TAIL: The body is a little longer than it is high, as ten is to nine, with the back short, straight and strong, the entire back line showing a perceptible slope down from withers to croup. The chest is deep and capacious, the ribs well sprung, loins taut and slender, the tuck-up apparent. Hips are broad, with croup nicely rounded and the tail docked, approximately two-fifths of original length.

LEGS AND FEET: Forelegs are straight, with shoulders obliquely set and elbows close. The thighs are strong and muscular. The hind legs are moderately angulated at stifle and hock and as viewed from behind, parallel to each other. Round in outline, the feet are webbed, high arched with toes close, their pads thick and hard, and their nails strong and quite heavy. Leg bones are flat rather than round, and strong, but not so heavy or coarse as to militate against the dog's natural agility.

COAT: The coat is weather resisting and to some extent water repellent. The undercoat is dense enough in winter to insulate against the cold but so thin in summer as to be almost invisible. The distinctive outer coat is straight, harsh, wiry and rather flat-lying, from one and one-half to two inches in length, it is long enough to protect against the punishment of rough cover but not so long as to hide the outline. On the lower legs it is shorter and between the toes of softer texture. On the skull it is naturally short and close fitting, while over the shoulders and around the tail it is very dense and heavy. The tail is nicely coated particularly on the underside, but devoid of feather. These dogs have bushy eyebrows of strong, straight hair and beards and whiskers of medium length.

A short smooth coat, a soft woolly coat, or an excessively long coat is to be severely penalized.

COLOR: The coat is liver and white, usually either liver and white spotted, liver roan, liver and white spotted with ticking and roaning or sometimes solid liver. The nose is dark brown. The head is brown, sometimes with a white blaze, the ears brown. Any black in the coat is to be severely penalized. Spotted and flesh-colored noses are undesirable and are to be penalized.

SIZE: Height of males should be from 24 to 26 inches at the withers, bitches smaller but not under 22 inches.

(February 7, 1959)

CHESAPEAKE BAY RETRIEVER

WHEN CONDITIONS are so tough a hunter is reluctant to ask his dog to perform, the Chesapeake Bay Retriever gives every indication that he's really enjoying his work.

The work that this rugged dog was developed for and has remained best suited to, is retrieving downed waterfowl. Once the top retriever breed in the U.S., he still remains mighty popular with the waterfowl gunner who wants a dog that thrives on the difficult and won't be daunted by anything the elements or man can dish out.

The Chesapeake, now trailing the Labrador and Golden Retriever in popularity, is one of the few breeds developed in the U.S.—specifically in the Chesapeake Bay region of Maryland from which it derives its name, spreading along the East Coast waterfowl-

Chesapeake Bay Retrievers—In this photo, four generations. (Owner: Dr. Daniel Horn, Fairfax, Virginia) Photo by Evelyn M. Shafer.

ing areas, then to the upper Mississippi flyway marshes, and finally to the West Coast.

There are a number of conjectural versions about how the Chesapeake came about. The favored tale, approved by the American Chesapeake Club, is that two dogs were rescued along with the crew of a ship that was wrecked off the Maryland coast in 1807. The black bitch and the dingy red dog named Canton and Sailor, respectively, were good waterfowl retrievers and subsequently mated with other dogs in the region used for water work. In the course of this development, until about 1885 when a definite type emerged, it's possible that not only the nondescript dogs but Setters, Irish Water Spaniels, Bloodhounds, Coonhounds, Otterhounds and other retrievers may have made their contribution.

Both the salty "Baymen" of the Chesapeake waterfront and cultured sportsmen had a hand in establishing the Chesapeake. The breed's innate toughness, both physical and mental, probably stems from its adaptability to conditions along the waterfront and acceptance by its residents. But credit for establishing a breed that bred true to type, one that gained official recognition and public acceptance, must rest with the gun clubs and interested sporting gentry who long ago invested in breeding programs and kept careful records.

The American Chesapeake Club was formed in 1918, but it wasn't until 1933 that the American Kennel Club approved a breed standard. A rough and ready character, the Chesapeake's lack of physical beauty has mitigated against popularity with the show fancy, and his independent bent of mind has made him too much of a handful for most field trial trainers. So he remains the favorite of the man who hunts ducks and geese almost exclusively, and who wants a no-quit dog willing to do the job of collecting dead and crippled waterfowl with complete disregard for his own comfort.

The Chesapeake's unique coat gives him an advantage over the other breeds when the weather is roughest. The breed's love of water is proverbial. Some modern Chesapeakes still retain the long, swayback that was once almost a trade-mark of a dog used almost exclusively in water. But in recent years, apparently in an effort to get a better mover on land in order to compete with the other retriever breeds, a more compact dog is seen. The coat features the most impervious-to-water-and-weather hair ever attached to a tough hide. Utilitarian rather than beautiful, the rather harsh outercoat is rough, dull, has no shine, and blends with the marshes. Underneath is a wool-like undercoat. The coat contains plenty of oil and the skin is loose, both factors in the breed's ability to withstand wet and cold.

Even if a dog has the physical equipment, he won't accomplish difficult tasks without the right determined mental attitude. The Chesapeake's stubbornness and individualism are proverbial. This temperament, while unacceptable to some, is what makes him the great dog he is. There are a few notable exceptions, for there are "soft" Chesapeakes just as there are a few "tough" Goldens. But the average big Chessie is about as sensitive as a Sherman tank. The man who desires the most from this breed must adhere to the axiom of "Spare the rod and spoil the child."

Devoted to his master, although seldom subservient, the Chesapeake looks askance at strangers and will drive off both human and canine interlopers. He makes an excellent guard or watchdog and has a strong sense of possessiveness whether it's about the ducks he's retrieved or the family that belongs to him. He can also be utilized as a flushing and fetching dog on upland game although his performance there won't match that of the spaniels or the other retriever breeds, as a rule. Possessing a long memory, once the trainer gets through to a Chesapeake and the dog learns what the hunting game is all about, he'll stay sharp from season to season without constant work and brushing up.

Despite their toughness, one woman handler, Mrs. Eloise Heller, a Californian, achieved outstanding success with Chesapeakes in field trials and contends that a firm but kindly approach to training is more effective than the thump-'em-good-when-they-defy-you procedures most successful Chesapeake trainers advocate.

Individual Chesapeakes have given good accounts of themselves in field trials including FT Ch.-AF Ch. Atom Bob owned by Dr. John C. Lundy, Boise, Idaho; FT Ch-AF Ch. Meg's Pattie O'Rourke, owned by Dr. and Mrs. F. A. Dashnaw, Cupertino, Calif.; and Slow Gin, owned by Dr. Lawrence Reppert, San Antonio, Tex.

A dog found in many of the pedigrees of top Chesapeakes is Dual Champion Sodak's Gypsy Prince, a great competitor in bench and field and one of the top sires from 1932 to 1938. He was owned by Anthony Bliss, who was credited with revitalizing the

American Chesapeake Club after he became its president in 1935.

When this tough, unsophisticated dog, with a no nonsense attitude toward his work is understood and trained in a manner compatible with his ruggedly individual temperament, it may not result in a lovable dog. But it is firm testimony to the ability of this great waterfowler that even his most severe critics are unanimous in their admiration and respect for his capabilities.

Description and Standards. The description and standards, adopted by the American Chesapeake Club and approved by the American Kennel Club follow:

HEAD: Skull broad and round with medium stop, nose medium short—muzzle pointed but not sharp. Lips thin, not pendulous. Ears small, set well up on head, hanging loosely and of medium leather. Eyes medium large, very clear, of yellowish color and wide apart.

NECK: Of medium length with a strong muscular appearance, tapering to shoulders.

SHOULDERS, CHEST, AND BODY: Shoulders, sloping and should have full liberty of action with plenty of power without any restrictions of movement. Chest strong, deep, and wide. Barrel round and deep. Body of medium length, neither cobby nor roached, but rather approaching hollowness, flanks well tucked up.

BACK QUARTERS AND STIFLES: Back quarters should be as high as or a trifle higher than the shoulders. They should show fully as much power as the fore quarters. There should be no tendency to weakness in either fore or hind quarters. Hind quarters should be especially powerful to supply the driving power for swimming. Back should be short, well-coupled, and powerful. Good hind quarters are essential.

LEGS, ELBOWS, HOCKS, AND FEET: Legs should be medium length and straight, showing good bone and muscle, with well-webbed hare feet of good size. The toes well rounded and close pasterns slightly bent and both pasterns and hocks medium length—the straighter the legs the better.

STERN: Tail should be medium length—varying from: males 12 to 15 inches, and females, 11 to 14 inches; medium heavy at base, moderate feathering on stern and tail permissible.

COAT AND TEXTURE: Coat should be thick and short, nowhere over 1½ inches long, with a dense, fine, woolly under coat. Hair on face and legs should be very short and straight with tendency to wave on the shoulders, neck, back, and loins only. Curly coat or coat with a tendency to curl not permissible.

COLOR: Any color varying from a dark brown to a faded tan or dead grass. Dead grass takes in any shade of dead grass, varying from a tan to a dull straw color. White spot on breast

Chesapeake Bay Retriever—Noted for dependable retrieving under even the roughest conditions. Photo by Evelyn M. Shafer.

and toes permissible, but the smaller the spot the better, solid color being preferred.

WEIGHT: Males, 65 to 75 lbs.; females 55 to 65 lbs.

HEIGHT: Males, 23 inches to 26 inches; females, 21 inches to 24 inches.

SYMMETRY AND QUALITY: The Chesapeake dog should show a bright and happy disposition and an intelligent expression, with general outlines impressive denoting a good worker. The dog should be well proportioned, a dog with a good coat and well balanced in other points being preferable to the dog excelling in some but weak in others.

The texture of the dog's coat is very important as the dog is used for hunting under all sorts of adverse weather conditions, often working in ice and snow. The oil in the harsh outer coat and woolly under coat is of extreme value in preventing the cold water from reaching the dog's skin and aids in quick drying. A Chesapeake's coat should resist the water in the same way that a duck's feathers do. When he leaves the water and shakes himself, his coat should not hold the water at all, being merely moist.

Color and coat are extremely important as the dog is used for duck hunting. The color must be as nearly that of his surroundings as possible, and together with the fact that dogs are exposed to all kinds of adverse weather conditions, often working in ice and snow, the color of coat and its texture must be given every consideration when judging on the bench or in the ring.

Courage, willingness to work, alertness, nose, intelligence, love of water, general quality, and, most of all, disposition should be given primary consideration in the selection and breeding of the Chesapeake Bay dog.

SCALE OF POINTS:	Points
Head, including lips, ears and eyes	16
Neck	4
Shoulders and body	12
Back quarters and stifles	12
Elbows, legs, and feet	12
Color	4
Stern and tail	10
Coat and texture	18
General conformation	12
TOTAL	100

Note: The question of coat and general type of balances takes precedence over any scoring table which could be drawn up.

A Chesapeake Bay Retriever and her litter of pups. Sentinel Photo.

APPROXIMATE MEASUREMENTS: *Inches*

Length head, nose to occiput	9½ to 10
Girth at ears	20 to 21
Muzzle below eyes	10 to 10½
Length of ears	4½ to 5
Width between eyes	2½ to 2¾
Girth neck close to shoulder	20 to 22
Girth of chest to elbows	35 to 36
Girth at flank	24 to 25
Length from occiput to tail base	34 to 35
Girth forearms at shoulders	10 to 10½
Girth upper thigh	19 to 20
From root to root of ear, over skull	5 to 6
Occiput to top shoulder blades ...	9 to 9½
From elbow to elbow over the shoulders	25 to 26

Disqualifications. Black or liver colored. Dewclaws on hind legs, white on any part of body, except breast, belly or spots on feet. Feathering on tail or legs over 1¾ inches long. Undershot, overshot, or any deformity. Coat curly or tendency to curl all over body. Specimens unworthy or lacking in breed characteristics.

(July 9, 1963)

CURLY-COATED RETRIEVER

THE CURLY-COATED Retriever is living proof that quality of performance and good looks do not always bring popularity. This is a dog of great beauty, and there never has been any question as to his water ability. Yet the breed has never reached great prominence, either on the bench or in the duck marshes. Perhaps the only exception to this is the great popularity of the breed in New Zealand. There he is used both for wildfowling and quail shooting. Apparently the New Zealanders greatly prefer him.

Perhaps the first allusion to them occurs in the *Sportsmen's Cabinet* (1803): "These dogs are exceedingly singular in their appearance, and most probably derive their origin from the Greenland dog, blended with some particular race of our own."

Stonehenge, in 1859, guessed that this cross was the Irish Water Spaniel. ". . . This variety of retriever is always a cross between the St. John's Newfoundland and the water spaniel, which is generally Irish." Stonehenge may have been right, but other writers disputed this, pointing out that in crosses with the Irish Water Spaniel, the peculiar top-knot of the Irish usually showed up, but it is absent in the Curly-Coated Retriever.

Other suggested crosses were the English Water Spaniel, the Poodle, and perhaps the Gordon Setter. These crosses undoubtedly were tried, but their final influence on the Curly-Coat is not known.

The Curly-Coated Retriever was first shown on the bench in 1859. At the Islington International show in 1864, he was given a separate classification from other retrievers. Mr. Corse's Jet was the victor. Jet and Jet II dominated the show for several years. Later William Arkwright's Sweep and Mr. Salter's King Koffie gained fame.

The Curly-Coated Retriever Club was formed in England in 1896. In February 1933, the Curly Retriever Club was formed. Since that day, it has sponsored the breed, and has given trials for Curly-Coats.

Perhaps the best known English field dogs of later

Curly-Coated Retriever. Photo by Evelyn M. Shafer.

vintage have been Calgary Grizzly and Pycombe Sable. Both dogs, and others later, have shown up well enough in competition with other breeds.

Writing in 1905 and 1906, the great American dog authority James Watson predicted that retrievers would never gain a foothold in the United States. He could not foresee modern hunting conditions, with duck flights dangerously reduced. Yet Watson felt that if any retriever breed was destined for popularity here, it was the Curly-Coat. He thought the breed a beautiful one, compared its coat favorably with that of the Chesapeake, and thought the dog's coat was superior to that of the Irish Water Spaniel.

Still, the Curly-Coat has not gained popularity here, even though he was perhaps the first in the field so far as English retriever breeds are concerned. There were a scattered few of the Curly-Coats in America from pre-Civil War days on. Two are mentioned in 1907 as having created a very favorable opinion by their working ability.

J. Gould Remick tried to popularize the breed just before World War II. During this period there were at least three Curly-Coats who proved themselves in field trial competition with Chesapeakes, Labradors, Goldens, and Irish Water Spaniels. These were Sarona Sam of Marvadel, Sarona Jacob of Marvadel, both owned by Mr. Remick, and Carbon of Marvadel, owned by F. Royal Gammon.

This dog is a square-built dog standing about 24 inches tall at the shoulder. He is a mass of tight curls from the occipital crest of the head to the end of his tail.

The Curly-Coated Retriever is either black or dark liver. There are occasional white hairs on the chest, but a patch of white is severely penalized. Actual size and weight are not important, and the standard for the breed gives neither maximum nor minimum height or weight qualifications.

The outstanding characteristics of the breed are water-going eagerness and stamina in cold water. The dogs will dive continuously after crippled ducks. They are good markers and have excellent memories. Most of them are good land workers, and are said to stand out in locating "runners."

An early criticism of them, which is not generally true today, was that they were hard-mouthed. Most authorities, however, consider them easy to train, and all are agreed as to the sweetness of their temper. Most Americans criticize them as being too slow in field trial work, while admitting their competence. In England, they are considered very fast, particularly in the water.

Description and Standards. The description and standards follow:

HEAD: Long and well proportioned, skull not too flat, jaws long and strong but not inclined to snipiness, nose black, in the black coated variety, with wide nostrils. Teeth strong and level.

EYES: Black or brown, but not yellow, rather large but not too prominent.

EARS: Rather small, set on low, lying close to the head, and covered with short curls.

COAT: Should be one mass of crisp curls all over. A slightly more open coat not to be severely penalized, but a saddle back or patch of uncurled hair behind the shoulder should be penalized, and a prominent white patch on breast is undesirable, but a few white hairs allowed in an otherwise good dog. Color, black or liver.

SHOULDERS, CHEST, BODY, AND LOINS: Shoulders should be very deep, muscular, and obliquely placed. Chest not too wide, but decidedly deep. Body, rather short, muscular, and well ribbed up. Loins, powerful, deep and firm to the grasp.

LEGS AND FEET: Legs should be of moderate length, fore legs straight and set well under the body. Quarters strong and muscular, hocks low to the ground with moderate bend to stifle and hock. Feet round and compact with well-arched toes.

TAIL: Should be moderately short, carried fairly straight and covered with curls, slightly tapering toward the point.

GENERAL APPEARANCE: Strong, smart, upstanding, showing activity, endurance, and intelligence.

FLAT-COATED RETRIEVER

KNOWN AS the game-keeper's dog for its extensive use on estate and moors all over Great Britain, the Flat-Coated Retriever, has never become very popular in this country, although it is found in some sections.

The breed was originally called the Wavy-Coated Retriever, and for years the various strains produced types which differed from each other considerably. The dog which, in the early days, more nearly approximated the present standard of the Flat-Coated Retriever was Wyndham, owned and exhibited by R. Braisford. Wyndham made his first appearance at the Birmingham (England) show in 1860. He was very much on the type of the Labrador Retriever in conformation. His coat was almost wholly black, but was considerably heavier than that of the Labrador. It is supposed, from his coat, that this was inherited from the St. John's type Newfoundland. The blood of the Labrador very probably also flowed in his veins. It is generally believed that crosses of the Gordon Setter and Irish Setter were also used to establish the Flat-Coated Retriever as a dog which bred true to type.

When he made his first appearance, Wyndham excited considerable comment and much was written about him. Dogs of this type were to be found on many of the hunting preserves in Great Britain, where they were generally used by the game-keepers. Whenever these men were given assignments to kill some game for the larder of the estate owner, they usually hunted on the edges of the preserves so that they would not disturb the main hunting covers. The Flat-Coated Retrievers were close-working dogs, of a rather phlegmatic disposition and easily controlled. They went about their work in a quiet, business-like manner and took direction readily.

The "Riverside" strain, developed by Reginald Cook, of Shropshire, England, were especially popular for many years, being bred for great utility and a number were champions both in the field and on the bench. Ellis Ashton, of Derbyshire, was another prominent British breeder.

Probably the best known Flat-Coated Retriever in this country was Blackdale Ben of Wingan, imported by Jay F. Carlisle. Ben was a great sire and an exceptional performer in field trials. His name appears in practically all the Flat-Coated Retrievers in this country. His son, Black Royal, owned by Dr. H. I. Hoen, had an enviable record in the field. Another well-known descendant was Black Trumpeter, owned by Mr. and Mrs. Peter C. Englehart, who have owned quite a number of good breed specimens. Star Lea Solitaire, owned and trained by the well-known

Flat-Coated Retriever.

trainer, Bill Gladwin, and later sold to Charles E. Dinky, Jr., was a daughter of Blackdale Ben. A well-known grandson of this famous dog was Black Ben Benjamin. John McL. Simpson, of Chicago, and J. Gould Remick, of New York, have owned several excellent performers in the field.

In England these dogs have worked very well on upland game and waterfowl, but in this country their efforts have been almost wholly confined to retrieving.

Description and Standards. The description and standards follow:

GENERAL APPEARANCE: A bright, active dog of medium size (weighing from 60 lbs. to 70 lbs.) with an intelligent expression, showing power without lumber and raciness without weediness.

HEAD: This should be long and nicely molded. The skull flat and moderately broad. There should be a depression or stop between the eyes, slight and in no way accentuated so as to avoid giving either a down or a dish-faced appearance. The nose of good size with open nostrils. The eyes, of medium size, should be dark brown or hazel, with a very intelligent expression (a round, prominent eye is a disfigurement), and they should not be obliquely placed. The jaws should be long and strong, with a capacity of carrying a hare or pheasant. The ears small and well set on close to the side of the head.

NECK, SHOULDERS, AND CHEST: The head should be well set in the neck, which latter should be long and free from throatiness, symmetrically set and obliquely placed in shoulders running well into the back to allow of easily seeking for the trail. The chest should be deep and fairly broad, with a well-defined brisket, on which the elbows should work cleanly and evenly. The fore ribs should be fairly flat showing a gradual spring and well arched in the center of the body but rather lighter towards the quarters. Open couplings are to be ruthlessly condemned.

BACK AND QUARTERS: The back should be short, square and well ribbed up, with muscular quarters. The stern short, straight, and well set on, carried gaily, but never much above the level of the back.

LEGS AND FEET: These are of the greatest importance. The fore legs should be perfectly straight, with bone of good quality carried right down to the feet which should be round and strong. The stifle should not be too straight or too bent and the dog must neither be cowhocked nor move too wide behind, in fact he must stand and move true all round on legs and feet, with toes close and well arched, the soles being thick and strong and when the dog is in full coat the limbs should be well feathered.

COAT: Should be dense, of fine quality and texture, flat as possible.

COLOR: Black or liver.

GOLDEN RETRIEVER

A BEAUTIFUL dog, intelligent, biddable and very affectionate, the Golden Retriever, would be a popular companion and pet, regardless of hunting ability. But when one adds to these attributes outstanding nose and retrieving instinct, which make him a much enjoyed adjunct to the hunter during a day in the marsh or upland, it is easy to understand the breed's popularity with the U.S. public.

The Golden Retriever's history in the U.S. is relatively recent. Recognized by the American Kennel Club in 1932, for 15 years or more the Golden remained a relative rarity. Officially recognized as a breed in England in 1910 and in Canada in 1927, largely through the efforts of Bart Armstrong, Winnepeg, Manitoba, it was field trial wins that started the Golden on its rise in popularity.

In 1939, Rip, owned by Paul Bakewell III, St. Louis, Mo. became the first Golden accorded the title of field trial champion. That year and in 1940 Rip was named the year's outstanding retriever. Goldens were on their way.

The fact that the dog is particularly good looking has resulted in great popularity for the Golden Retriever on the bench. But from the start, the concept of a dual dog, one that would work and also be a presentable representative of the breed, has been the goal of the breed's parent organization, the Golden Retriever Club of America.

Three now-legendary Goldens, all dual champions, did yeoman service in popularizing the breed with the U.S. public following World War II. Winning both field trial and show championships were Stilrovin Rip's Pride and Tonkahof Esther Belle, both owned by Kingswere Kennels, Winona, Minn. and Stilrovin Nitro Express, owned by Ben Boalt, Milwaukee, Wisconsin. Add to the ability of this breed to remain both a field and show dog its successes in

Golden Retriever. Photo by Evelyn M. Shafer.

the obedience ring and you have a very versatile performer.

Golden Retriever fanciers can always boast that "one of theirs" won the first National Championship stake for retrievers. He was F. T. Ch. King Midas of Woodend, owned by E. N. Dodge, Wayzata, Minn. and handled by F. M. Hogan. The year was 1941 in a field of 15 dogs.

A fanciful tale, containing a germ of truth, was once used as the official explanation of how the Golden came into being, ignoring a logical supposition that all the retriever breeds probably shared common ancestors which eventually evolved into strains and finally breeds on the basis of coat color and texture.

The tale of Lord Tweedmouth and his troupe of circus dogs, referred to as Russian Trackers, and how he "made" a breed using these sheepdogs, especially one named Nous, as the foundation of the Golden Retriever breed, is now generally discredited.

The story now accepted is that in 1864, according to records and accounts made public by a grand-nephew of Lord Tweedmouth in 1952, his lordship (also known as Sir Dudley Marjoribanks) bought not a troupe of eight, but a single dog, which he named Nous, reportedly the only yellow pup in a litter of blacks. Breeding this dog to a bitch of a now extinct spaniel strain—the Tweed Water Spaniel—he kept three of the resulting four puppies. This foundation stock was crossed out to another spaniel and to a

black retriever and the progeny closely line-bred until the early 1880s. Allegedly some Irish Setter and Bloodhound blood was introduced between 1875 and 1885.

Physically like the other retrievers, the Golden is a good-sized, well put together dog with a dense, long coat that ideally should have a rich gold sheen. Almost spaniel-like in temperament, most have soft dispositions and they respond best to coaxing and affectionate discipline in training. But while there should be no short-cuts, patient repetition paying off, Goldens possess an almost overwhelming desire to please, and this coupled with intelligence and the right instincts makes them a very trainable breed.

In competitive dog activities among the retrievers, Goldens rank second to the Labradors in field trial and practical hunting use and in total registration figures, but doubtlessly head all other retriever breeds in participating in conformation shows and in the obedience ring.

As a hunting dog he can be expected to perform creditably on land as well as in water, not only marking and recovering downed game, but with a bit of training can be adapted as a flushing dog working in front of the gun.

The honest, completely trusting Golden facial expression tells a dog fancier just about all he has to know about this breed. It's as a versatile dog, devoted family friend and companion, proficient hunter and striking competitor, that the Golden has made his mark in the U.S., one which will likely carry him on a fairly level keel of popularity regardless of fads and fancies among the dog-buying public.

Description and Standards. The description and standards follow:

GENERAL: A symmetrical, powerful, active dog, sound and well put together, not clumsy or long in the leg, displaying a kindly expression and possessing a personality that is eager, alert and self-confident. Primarily a hunting dog, he should be shown in hard working condition. Over-all appearance, balance, gait and purpose to be given more emphasis than any of his component parts.

SIZE: Males 23-24 inches in height at withers; females 21½-22½. Length from breastbone to buttocks slightly greater than height at withers in ratio of 12-11. Weight for dogs 65-75 pounds; bitches 60-70 pounds.

HEAD: Broad in skull, slightly arched laterally and longitudinally without prominence of frontal or occipital bones. Good stop. Foreface deep and wide, nearly as long as skull. Muzzle, when viewed in profile, slightly deeper at stop than at tip; when viewed from above, slightly wider at stop than at tip. No heaviness in flews. Removal of whiskers for show purposes optional.

EYES: Friendly and intelligent, medium large with dark rims, set well apart and reasonably deep in sockets. Color preferably dark brown, never lighter than color of coat. No white or haw visible when looking straight ahead.

TEETH: Scissors bite with lower incisors touching inside of upper incisors.

NOSE: Black or dark brown, though lighter shade in cold weather not serious. Dudley nose (pink without pigmentation) to be faulted.

EARS: Rather short, hanging flat against head with rounded tips slightly below jaw. Forward edge attached well behind and just above eye with rear edge slightly below eye. Low, hound-like ear-set to be faulted.

NECK: Medium long, sloping well back into shoulders, giving sturdy muscular appearance with untrimmed natural ruff. No throatiness.

BODY: Well balanced, short-coupled, deep through the heart. Chest at least as wide as a man's hand, including thumb. Brisket extends to elbows. Ribs long and well sprung but not barrel shaped, extending well to rear of body. Loin short, muscular, wide and deep, with very little tuck-up. Top line level from withers to croup, whether standing or moving. Croup slopes gently. Slabsidedness, narrow chest, lack of depth in brisket, excessive tuck-up, roach or sway back to be faulted.

FOREQUARTERS: Forequarters well coordinated with hindquarters and capable of free movement. Shoulder blades wide, long and muscular, showing angulation with upper arm of approximately 90 degrees. Legs straight with good bone. Pastern short and strong, sloping slightly forward with no suggestion of weakness.

HINDQUARTERS: Well-bent stifles (angulation between femur and pelvis approximately 90 degrees) with hocks well let down. Legs straight when viewed from rear. Cowhocks and sickle hocks to be faulted.

FEET: Medium size, round and compact with thick pads. Excess hair may be trimmed to show natural size and contour. Open or splayed feet to be faulted.

TAIL: Well set on, neither too high nor too low, following natural line of croup. Length extends to hock. Carried with merry action with some upward curve but never curled over back nor between legs.

COAT AND COLOR: Dense and water repellent with good undercoat. Texture not as hard as that of a shorthaired dog nor silky as that of a Setter. Lies flat against body and may be straight or wavy. Moderate feathering on back of forelegs and heavier feathering on front of neck, back of thighs and underside of tail. Feathering may be lighter than rest of coat. Color lustrous golden of various shades. A few white hairs on chest permissible but not desirable. Further white markings to be faulted.

A Golden Retriever in action.

GAIT: When trotting, gait is free, smooth, powerful and well coordinated. Viewed from front of rear, legs turn neither in nor out, nor do feet cross or interfere with each other. Increased speed causes tendency of feet to converge toward center line of gravity.

Disqualifications. Deviation in height of more than one inch from standard either way. Undershot or overshot bite. This condition not to be confused with misalignment of teeth. Trichiasis (abnormal position or direction of the eyelashes).

(September 10, 1963)

LABRADOR RETRIEVER

SLEEK AND powerful, with an amiable, no-nonsense disposition and a record unsurpassed by any other retriever breed, the Labrador Retriever is in an enviable position. No apologies need be made for the breed's appearance, performance or demeanor. Strictly on the basis of being able to *produce,* the Lab has become one of the most popular gundogs in the U.S. and undisputed king in the retrieving field.

But the Labrador had an uphill fight to accomplish this, competing against a rugged native American performer, the Chesapeake, the beauty of another British import, the Golden, and, at the time of his introduction on the American scene, even the now rare Irish Water Spaniel.

But the record now speaks for itself—No. 1 among the retrievers in American Kennel Club registrations, a favorite as a practical hunter and retriever of both waterfowl and upland birds, an honest record in conformation shows, competent in the obedience ring and boasting a field trial record that can only be described as phenomenal.

Most dog breeds have produced a few outstanding individuals. But when individual dogs among the Labrador Retriever breed are mentioned, it is a sure bet that a number of other equally outstanding performers will be slighted.

From the time field trials for retrievers have been

held, Labradors have dominated them and continue to do so.

The first U.S. trial, open to all retriever breeds took place at East Setauket, N.Y. in December 1934. Labradors finished first, second and third. No other retriever breed has won the National Retriever Championship since 1951 to the present printing, and in the years from 1941, when the competition began and until 1964, only three times has a breed (Golden) other than the black Labrador won the cup. Nor has the National Amateur Field Trial Championship been won by other than a black Labrador to date.

While some of this can be ascribed to the sheer numbers of Labs that now compete in trials, the ability of this breed to produce earned them this recognition among serious competitors. While establishing themselves from 1931 to 1948, 66 percent of the field trial champions named were Labradors and in 1948, Labradors making up only 47 percent of the entries in trials, won 94 percent of the first places and 79 percent of all placements! While the numbers of participants has understandably increased off that record, the performance hasn't fallen off the pace.

But the Labrador, coming in three basic colors, black, yellow and chocolate, has made his mark not only as a flashy performer in competition, but as a workaday retriever of ducks and geese and a practical flusher and retriever of upland and shore birds. Hardy, good looking, easy to care for and to train, this breed has demonstrated its versatile potential by working as a guard, stock and police dog, children's playmate, and an unobtrusive companion in the U.S., Canada and the British Isles.

The ancestors of our modern day Lab, may have been taken to England on the boats of Newfoundland fishermen. Or it may be that these dogs evolved because English fishermen took dogs with them when they went to Newfoundland in the 1500s. Anything said about these early origins is chiefly speculative.

However, they were *developed* in England. Between 1835 when the Earl of Malmesbury got his

dogs and 1878, the date of the first British pedigrees, there was doubtless much crossing between various strains and individual dogs used for retrieving in England. No records exist that can establish that Pointers may have been used in the development, but the fact that a few of today's Labs show a strong pointing instinct when used on upland game lends some credence to the theory. It is likely, that the base stock brought to England by Malmesbury stemmed from the long-coated, large Newfoundland, and the short coats, agility and smaller size of these offshoots were advantageous in the hunting field. Labs were first recognized as a distinct breed by the English Kennel Club in 1903.

The oldest recorded dog age, by the way, is attributed to a black Labrador gundog once owned by James Hawkes, a game-keeper at Revesby Estate near Boston, Lincolnshire, England. "Adjutant," the dog's name, was whelped on August 14, 1936 and died on November 20, 1963 at the age of 27 years and 3 months. He had only the one owner during his lifetime.

The distinction of being the first field trial champion of record in the U.S. goes to Blind of Arden in 1935, and the first dual champion was Michael of Glenmere, owned by Jerry Angle, Lincoln, Nebraska, in 1941. From there on, the winner's list is too long to record. But the history of the Labrador's development would not be complete without mention of the names of two importers and breeders.

Dozens of kennels and even more professional handlers have established names and reputations on the basis of their work with Labradors in the past 35 years. But most of our best American dogs can trace their bloodlines back to Wingan Kennels, owned by J. F. Carlisle, Long Island and Arden Kennels, owned by Averill Harriman, New York.

Good balance, physically and mentally, can be used to explain the success and popularity of the Labrador Retriever. They adjust and are suitable to all temperatures and climes, their short coats water-and-weather-resistant, but unattractive to burrs, mud and odor.

The fire and drive of a good Labrador is balanced by serenity, courage—by common sense, eagerness—by patience, and independence by docility. In performing the chores laid out for him he exudes an aura of willingness, enjoyment and pride. A working dog throughout his history and to the present day, with generation after generation operating in close association with man, the Lab is capable of learning by rote or by happenstance and he can satisfy the most rank amateur trainer or the most demanding professional.

The breed's popularity is now established and has leveled off. But as long as there are men and women seeking a practical hunting dog, a polished competitor, a biddable companion or just a plain understanding dog to talk to, the Labrador's place on the U.S. scene is assured.

The Labrador Retriever is a favorite gundog in several countries—Australia, Great Britain, New Zealand, and South Africa.

Labrador Retriever. Hank Babbitt photo.

The Labrador is a fairly consistent winner in Retriever field trials. Photo by Evelyn M. Shafer.

Description and Standards. The description and standards follow.

GENERAL APPEARANCE: The general appearance of the Labrador should be that of a strongly-built, short-coupled, very active dog. He should be fairly wide over the loins and strong and muscular in the hind quarters. The coat should be close, short, dense, and free from feather.

HEAD: The skull should be wide, giving brain room; there should be a slight "stop," i.e., the brow should be slightly pronounced, so that the skull is not absolutely in a straight line with the nose. The head should be clean-cut and free from fleshy cheeks. The jaws should be long and powerful, and quite free from snipiness; the nose should be wide and the nostrils well developed. Teeth should be strong and regular, with a level mouth.

The ears should hang moderately close to the head, rather far back; should be set somewhat low and not be large and heavy. The eyes should be of a medium size, expressing great intelligence and good temper, and can be brown, yellow or black, but brown or black is preferred.

NECK AND CHEST: The neck should be medium length and powerful and not throaty. The shoulders should be long and sloping. The chest must be of a good width and depth, the ribs well sprung and the loins wide and strong, stifles well turned, and the hind quarters well developed and of great power.

LEGS AND FEET: The legs must be straight from the shoulder to ground, and the feet compact with toes well arched and pads well developed; the hocks should be well bent, and the dog must neither be cowhocked nor move too wide behind; in fact, he must stand and move true all round on legs and feet. Legs should be of medium length, showing good bone and muscle, but not so short as to be out of balance with rest of body. In fact, a dog well balanced in all points is preferable to one with outstanding good qualities and defects.

TAIL: The tail is a distinctive feature of the breed; it should be very thick toward the base, gradually tapering toward the tip, of medium length; should be free from any feathering, and should be clothed thickly all round with the Labrador's short, thick, dense coat, thus giving that peculiar "rounded" appearance which has been described as the "otter" tail. The tail may be carried gaily, but should not curl over the back.

COAT: The coat is another distinctive feature; it should be short, very dense and without wave, and should give a fairly hard feeling to the hand.

COLOR: The colors are black, yellow, or chocolate and are evaluated as follows:

(a) Blacks: All black, with a small white spot on chest permissible. Eyes to be of medium size, expressing intelligence and good temper, preferably brown or hazel, although black or yellow is permissible.

(b) Yellows: Yellows may vary in color from fox-red to light

Labrador Retrievers are usually all black, but some are all yellow or yellowish-tan.

cream with variations in the shading of the coat on ears, the underparts of the dog, or beneath the tail. A small white spot on chest is permissible. Eye coloring and expression should be the same as that of the blacks, with black or dark brown eye rims. The nose should also be black or dark brown, although "fading" to pink in winter weather is not serious. A "Dudley" nose, (pink without pigmentation) should be penalized.

(c) Chocolates: Shades ranging from light sedge to chocolate. A small white spot on chest is permissible. Eyes to be light brown to clear yellow. Nose and eye-rim pigmentation dark brown or liver colored. "Fading" to pink in winter weather not serious. "Dudley" nose should be penalized.

MOVEMENT: Movement should be free and effortless. The forelegs should be strong, straight and true, and correctly placed. Watching a dog move towards one, there should be no signs of elbows being out in front, but neatly held to the body with legs not too close together, but moving straight forward without pacing or weaving. Upon viewing the dog from the rear, one should get the impression that the hind legs, which should be well muscled and not cowhocked, move as nearly parallel as possible, with hocks doing their full share of work and flexing well, thus giving the appearance of power and strength.

APPROXIMATE WEIGHTS: Dogs—60 to 75 pounds; bitches—55 to 70 pounds.

HEIGHT AT SHOULDERS: Dogs—22½ inches to 24½ inches; bitches—21½ inches to 23½ inches.

(April 9, 1957)

ENGLISH SETTER

THE ENGLISH SETTER is America's oldest gundog. Long before his short-haired rival, the Pointer, came into popularity, the English Setter was proving a prime asset to the gun wherever American upland game birds were found. His firm entrenchment in the affections of the American gunner made it doubly hard for the Pointer to gain a foothold.

Concerning the origin of the Setter, the old-time writers agreed upon one thing. He was called "A spaniel improved," and most of the early writers maintained that the Setting Spaniel is an older breed than the Pointer. Some others, including Stonehenge, intimate that there might have been an introduction of Pointer blood in the early Setting Spaniels, but no proof of this has ever been offered.

England has long had a number of varieties or strains of Setters. Among them were the Featherstone, Southesk, Lovat, Naworth Castle, Seafield, and Ossulton. Later came the Laveracks, established by Edward Laverack. Wales also had Setters, the strain of that section being known as Llandidloes, chalk white in color. Ireland had the Irish Setters of solid red or red and white in color. Scotland had the black and tans, later known as the Gordons.

Specimens of most of these breeds came to America in the early days. Occasionally a Russian Setter came over. These strains were frequently intermingled and the offspring became known as "natives." This designation was, of course, erroneous but the name "native" served as well as any.

One of the earliest and most popular strains of "natives" was the Gildersleeve, held in high esteem particularly by the gunners of Maryland, Delaware, and eastern Pennsylvania. Most of these medium-sized dogs were orange and white and were said to possess excellent noses and spendid action.

Another orange and white strain was the Morford, established by Theodore Morford of Newton, N.J. The Morfords enjoyed considerable popularity and bred true to type.

The Ethan Allens, founded by a sportsman of that name who lived at Pomfret, Conn., came in a variety of colors and were not level in conformation. These dogs were especially good on grouse, woodcock, and snipe.

Another breed of so-called "natives" which bred true to type and characteristics was that established by Asa Sherwood of Skaneateles, N.Y., and William Vie of St. Louis, Mo. These dogs probably bred as true to type as any strain established before or since.

The Campbell Setter, a strain established by M. C. and George M. Campbell of Springhill. Tenn., was the most popular and noted of the "natives." The Messrs. Campbell entered their dogs fearlessly in Southern field trials where they acquired an enviable reputation. The strain was, like many others, a mixture of many lines, with the Gordon probably, and the Irish Setter certainly, contributing most. The original fountainheads of the strain were Mason's Jeff, a black dog, and Fan or Old Fannie, a white and lemon bitch. It has been said that every puppy from this mating developed into an exceptional bird dog.

One of the first of these offspring was Old Buck, which produced Buck, Jr., when bred to Old Joe, a son of Otto and Fannie. Buck, Jr., when bred to Elcho, probably the best, and certainly the most famous, Irish Setter of all time, produced Joe, Jr., the greatest of all the Campbells. The first dog to win a field trial in America was a black Setter named Night, the property of H. C. Pritchett of Nashville, Tenn. Night was a native-bred dog but his dam was a Campbell Setter, being by Otto and out of Fan. He won the free-for-all stake of the first American field trial, sponsored by the Tennessee Sportsman's Association and held near Memphis, Tenn., October 8, 1874.

Edward Laverack, whose Laverack strain was attracting much attention on both sides of the water, began to experiment with the Duke-Rhoebe-Laverack cross and these dogs quickly came to the forefront. They attracted the attention of R. Purcell-Llewellin, at that time an extensive breeder, and it was from this stock that the strain now known as the Llewellin Setter was established.

One of Mr. Llewellin's early exportations to North American was Petrel, who was bred to Dan and then sold to L. H. Smith of Strathroy, Ontario. Petrel whelped after her arrival and one of her puppies was Gladstone, later to become one of the greatest of the early-American Llewellins. Mr. Smith gave Gladstone, as a very young puppy, to P. H. Bryson of Memphis, Tenn. The dog developed rapidly and soon became famous, both as a field performer and as a sire. He had much to do with the great popularity of the so-called Llewellin strain in this country.

English Setter—Ch. Aspetuck's Shadow. (Owner: Mrs. Joyce Rosen, Commack, N.Y.) Photo by Evelyn M. Shafer.

Interest in the Setters increased rapidly and it was only natural that there was much difference of opinion concerning the merits of the Campbell "natives" and the vaunted "blue-blooded" Llewellins. These discussions reached a climax in the great match race between Joe, Jr., the greatest of the Campbells, and Gladstone, the chief of the American Llewellin tribe, and the greatest exponent of the Duke-Rhoebe-Laveracks.

The race was scheduled as a three-day endurance test, but shortly before the date set Gladstone had the misfortune to fracture the tip of his tail and came to the mark with the tip wrapped in bandages of canvas glued together. At the request of his owner the race was limited to two days, $500 a side, with the number of actual points on quail to be the only determining factor. Style, speed, range, and other field trial qualifications were to be disregarded.

At the end of the first day Joe, Jr. was four points up on the "blueblood," having 34 to Gladstone's 30. Early the next day Gladstone passed his rival, and the Campbell, which had gone lame, looked like a sure loser. Joe, J., recovered, however, and at noontime was one point in the lead. He worked out of his lameness in the afternoon and began scoring rapidly, winning at sundown with the decisive score of 61 points to Gladstone's 52.

The Llewellins, however, continued to gain popularity, due to general excellence in field performance coupled with a well-planned advertising campaign. So great did the Llewellin vogue become that, with some American breeders, it amounted to almost a fetish. For more years than were good for the strain, the owner who could not boast that his dog's pedigree traced back in an unbroken line to the Duke-Rhoebe-Laveracks was looked upon as one who could not recognize the best. Too many Llewellin breeders began to pay more attention to pedigrees than to proved field qualities and the popularity of the strain began to decline. The Field Dog Stud Book recognizes the "Llewellin" as a separate and distinct strain,

but no dog is designated as a "Llewellin" whose pedigree does not trace back to the original fountainheads without an outcross.

At the present time there are comparatively few 100 per cent Llewellins in the country, although the majority of our English Setters have a preponderance of that blood. Color had nothing to do with the strain, but many novices today erroneously classify any lightly-marked blue-ticked English Setter as a "Llewellin."

Mr. Laverack's breed of dogs stemmed from Ponto and Old Moll, a brace of dogs he obtained from the Reverend Mr. Harrison of Carlisle in 1825. Mr. Laverack stated that the Rev. Mr. Harrison had kept the strain pure for 35 years before he acquired Ponto and Old Moll.

Duke, the property of Barclay Field, was a black and white dog which came to be known as Field's Duke. His dam was descended from the North of England Border breed which was favored by Sir Vincent Corbett. His sire was Sir F. Graham's Duke. According to early writers, he had quite a reputation but was never able to display his good qualities in public, appearing, on these occasions, to be deficient in nose.

Rhoebe was a heavily-marked black, white, and tan with little quality of conformation. Neither was she considered a field performer, but this cross produced excellent dogs which continued to produce exceptional performers when bred to Laverack bitches. Rhoebe was owned by Mr. Statter.

In 1871, while attending the field trials at Shrewsbury, Mr. Llewellin purchased Dan and Dick, sons of Field's Duke and Statter's Rhoebe, for breeding to his Laverack bitches. Thus was the foundation of the "Llewellin" strain laid. Much has been written about the origin of this strain, and some authorities claim that the Duke-Rhoebe-Laveracks were bred by Mr. Laverack some time before Mr. Llewellin became interested in the cross. It was the latter, and his kennel manager, G. Teasdale Buckell, who popularized the "Llewellin breed" and gave it its accepted name.

Llewellin's Dan was a dog of great prepotency and when he was crossed with the flighty Laverack bitches he seemed to add just what was needed and his offspring were dogs of sterling qualities. Foremost of these, of course, was the great Gladstone. This handsome white, black, and tan dog possessed unusual stamina, great hunting intelligence, an unusual nose, and the right amount of highstrung nervous energy. In addition he was a great sire.

Count Noble, imported by David Sanborn of Baltimore, was another early Llewellin who had a great influence on the Setters of America. He came over at just the right time, for there were many daughters of Gladstone to come to his court and this cross was very successful. He was also a fine field performer and won several times in trials. He was especially good on prairie chickens. He sired 30 winners, five more than Gladstone. Another successful cross with Count Noble were the daughters of Dashing Rover. Count Noble made a great impression and his name is found in the pedigrees of many present-day Setters.

Leicester, also imported by L. H. Smith, enjoyed considerable patronage and is generally considered one of the pillars of American field trial Setters, but he produced to Dart alone. His daughters, however, were good producers.

Druid, imported by Arnold Burgess of Hillsdale, Mich., in 1877 is another which exerted considerable influence on the setter in this country.

Space will not permit a tabulation of anything like all the Setters which helped make the field-type English Setter as we know him today. Among them, however, were Dan Gladstone, Ruby's Dan, Sportsman, Gath, Roderigo, Count Gladstone IV, and Eugene T. Also not to be overlooked were Antonio, Rodfield, Tony Boy, Mohawk II, Prince Rodney, and Connell's Gleam. Later came Candy Kid, Eugene M, Fairy Beau, Marse Ben, Eugene's Ghost, Phil Essig, and still later Sport's Peerless and Florendale Lou's Beau.

Lamberton's Mack was a great grouse dog which produced a good number of grand gundogs in the East. But the Setter which is more responsible than any other single Setter sire for the excellence of the grouse and woodcock dogs in this country is Nugym, the son of Eugym Mohawk and Bridge's Bonnie Lassie. Nugym produced 93 winners which ran up a total of 400 wins. Sam L's Skyrocket was another noted producer of excellent grouse dogs.

Time was when the English Setter had things pretty much his own way in American field trials. In fact, so superior was his performance to that of the Pointer that competition between the two breeds was considered not very sporting, and the Pointer had separate stakes in which to display his wares. This is certainly no longer true today, for, in annexing field trial laurels, the Pointer has surpassed his long-haired rival, who finds himself hard put to hold his own.

The argument concerning the merits of Setters of the early days and Setters of the present is always in evidence where "old-timers" gather. It will, of course, never be settled, for hunting conditions have changed, game supplies have had their ups and downs, and modern requirements are a bit different. There are those who contend, and with sound argument, too, that the Setter has not gone backward but, rather the Pointer has improved. Be that as it may, it is a fact that the period when preference for the "Llewellin" strain bordered on the fanatic and many Setter breeders paid far more attention to pedigrees than to the field performance and qualities of prospective sires and this was concurrent with the Pointer's rise in field trials. Breeders of the short-hair have always flocked to the sire that could and did prove his ability in the hunting field.

The first National Bird Dog Championship was won by the Setter, Count Gladstone IV, in 1896. Each succeeding year found a Setter at the top of the class, the diminutive Setter bitch, Sioux, proclaimed by many as the greatest bird dog of all times, having

won the title twice, 1901 and 1902, until 1909, when the Pointer Manitoba Rap gained the crown.

Setters held forth for the next four years, with Monora, Eugene M, Commissioner, and Phillipides winning the title, until the Pointer Comanche Frank was crowned in 1914. From 1918, when Joe Muncie won it, until 1926, when Feagin's Mohawk Pal won it, the Pointers held the stage. Feagin's Mohawk Pal is the only Setter to have won the title three times (1926, 1928, and 1930). It was not until 1939 that another Setter, Sport's Peerless Pride, could gain the honors; and then began another period of Pointer supremacy until 1946, when the sensational little Setter, Mississippi Zev, won the stake outstandingly. In addition, Zev won the National Amateur Championship, the Texas Open Championship, and the Regional Amateur title.

The English Setter thrives on attention and affection. He loves to be in the company of a kind master, to hunt for him and to worship him. His performance is at its best when his training has not been hurried or forced. Once the Setter learns a lesson he learns it well and is not so apt to forget or disregard it as the Pointer. He is also much more prone to become a "one-man" dog than his short-haired rival.

The first American Field Quail Futurity was won by the Setter Tonopaugh, in 1905. For many years Setters dominated this stake—until 1947—but no Setter had won it since 1929 when Outacite topped the field, and only four Setters have even placed in this classic since 1935. In 1947, however, the sensational Tennessee Zev, son of the illustrious four-times champion, Mississippi Zev, won the stake with a brilliant performance, defeating 93 other entrants. It is a rather significant fact that no Setter has ever won a place in the American Field Pheasant Futurity established in 1934. No Setter has ever won the National Derby Championship, and only five have gained runner-up honors since the inaugural stake in 1920. This is interpreted by some authorities as proof that the Setter does not mature as early or reach the peak of his capabilities as soon as the Pointer.

Field trials, while serving as an indicator of breed performance and popularity, do not tell the whole

English Setter—Ch. Regent. (Owner: Harry Townshend, New Haven, Conn.)

story. The many splendid qualities of the English Setter will always endear him to the sportsman who prefers gunning success to field trial wins. And for the sportsman who fully appreciates the pleasures of a day afield with a willing, industrious, loyal, and affectionate gundog companion that is also a thing of beauty in action and repose, the English Setter knows no peer.

In choosing a young Setter gundog prospect, one should look for boldness, grace of carriage, and sturdy, yet not bulky, conformation. Setters come in a variety of colors: white and black; white, black, and tan; white and orange; blue belton, orange belton, and, occasionally white and chestnut. Color makes no difference in field performance or a dog's general abilities, yet, all other factors being equal, it is best to choose one on which white predominates. A heavily-marked dog or one of the belton types is sometimes rather difficult to see in the field, particularly on a cloudy, hazy, or rainy day.

Be sure that he comes from ancestors that have proved their worth as hunting dogs. If his parents are good field performers the chances are high that he will also, under proper training, develop into a good gundog.

Do not try to rush his education or crowd him in his training. Allow his natural instincts to develop and direct them in the proper channels. Be extremely careful in the use of force. Many good young Setters have been ruined by too much correction or punishment when they did not know why it was being administered. Be sure that your dog knows *why* before you punish him. A sharp scolding or a bit of shaming can often accomplish much more than painful force. Never take a chance on cowing the young dog. The Setter, while sensitive, is not generally a timid fellow, but his reaction to kind treatment and his aversion to punishment that he does not understand are parts of his nature. He can be led into doing great deeds, but he hates to be forced, and once he begins to sulk you have a problem on your hands.

Above all, make a companion of your Setter. Spend as much time with him as possible. You will grow to understand each other better and more quickly. It is safe to prophesy that your Setter will meet you more than halfway.

"Once a Setter-man, always a Setter-man," is an old saying which is by no means a half-truth. The man who owns one English Setter shouts the praises of the breed to the housetops. The one who owns two English Setters does the same thing—only louder!

A complete roster of the breeders of English Setters in this country would fill a sizable volume itself and, of course, is impracticable here. There is no section of the country where this grand bird dog cannot be found and there is no type of upland game bird which he cannot or will not handle successfully. His versatility and his ability to adapt himself to almost any type of hunting make him popular wherever the shotgun is used in hunting.

For strong, healthy puppies like these English Setters, choose well-qualified brood matron.

Description and Standards. The description and standards follow.

HEAD: Long and lean, with a well-defined stop. The skull oval from ear to ear, of medium width, giving brain room but with no suggestion of coarseness, with but little difference between the width at base of skull and at brows and with a moderately defined occipital protuberance. Brows should be at a sharp angle from the muzzle. Muzzle should be long and square, of width in harmony with the skull, without any fullness under the eyes and straight from eyes to tip of the nose. A dish face or Roman nose objectionable. The lips square and fairly pendant. Nose should be black or dark liver in color, except in white, lemon and white, orange and white, or liver and white dogs, when it may be of lighter color. Nostrils should be wide apart and large in the openings. Jaws should be of equal length. Overshot or undershot jaw objectionable. Ears should be carried close to the head, well back and set low, of moderate length, slightly rounded at the ends, and covered with silky hair. Eye should be bright, mild, intelligent and dark brown in color.

NECK: The neck should be long and lean, arched at the crest, and not too throaty.

SHOULDERS: Shoulders should be formed to permit perfect freedom of action to the forelegs. Shoulder blades should be long, wide, sloping moderately well back and standing fairly close together at the top.

CHEST: Chest between shoulder blades should be of good depth but not of excessive width.

RIBS: Ribs, back of the shoulders, should spring gradually to the middle of the body and then taper to the back ribs, which should be of good depth.

BACK: Back should be strong at its junction with the loin and should be straight or sloping upward very slightly to the top of the shoulder, the whole forming a graceful outline of medium length, without sway or drop. Loins should be strong, moderate in length, slightly arched, but not to the extent of being roached or wheel-backed. Hipbones should be wide apart without too sudden drop to the root of the tail.

FORELEGS: The arms should be flat and muscular, with bone fully developed and muscles hard and devoid of flabbiness; of good length from the point of the shoulder to the elbow, and set at such an angle as will bring the legs fairly under the dog. Elbows should have no tendency to turn either in or out. The pastern should be short, strong and nearly round with the slope from the pastern joint to the foot deviating very slightly forward from the perpendicular.

HIND LEGS: The hind legs should have wide, muscular thighs

with well developed lower thighs. Stifles should be well bent and strong. Hocks should be wide and flat. The hind pastern or metatarsus should be short, strong and nearly round.

FEET: Feet should be closely set and strong, pads well developed and tough, toes well arched and protected with short, thick hair.

TAIL: Tail should be straight and taper to a fine point, with only sufficient length to reach the hocks, or less. The feather must be straight and silky, falling loosely in a fringe and tapering to the point when the tail is raised. There must be no bushiness. The tail should not curl sideways or above the level of the back.

COAT: Coat should be flat and of good length, without curl; not soft or woolly. The feather on the legs should be moderately thin and regular.

HEIGHT: Dogs about 25 inches; bitches about 24 inches.

COLORS: Black, white and tan; black and white; blue belton; lemon and white; lemon belton; orange and white; orange belton; liver and white; liver belton; and solid white.

MARKINGS: Dogs without heavy patches of color on the body, but flecked all over preferred.

SYMMETRY: The harmony of all parts to be considered. Symmetrical dogs will have level backs or be very slightly higher at the shoulders than at the hips. Balance, harmony of proportion, and an appearance of breeding and quality to be looked for, and coarseness avoided.

MOVEMENT AND CARRIAGE: An easy, free and graceful movement, suggesting rapidity and endurance. A lively tail and a high carriage of head. Stiltiness, clumsiness or a lumbering gait are objectionable.

SCALE OF POINTS:		Points
HEAD		
Skull	5	
Ears	5	
Eyes	5	
Muzzle	5	20
BODY		
Neck	5	
Chest and shoulders	12	
Back, loin and ribs	10	27
RUNNING GEAR		
Forelegs	5	
Hips, thighs and hind legs	12	
Feet	6	23
COAT		
Length and texture	5	
Color and marking	3	8
TAIL		
Length and carriage	5	5
GENERAL APPEARANCE AND ACTION		
Symmetry, style and movement	12	
Size	5	17
TOTAL	100	100

(Approved May 8, 1951)

GORDON SETTER

"WHAT HAS become of the Gordon Setter?" That is a question frequently asked of every writer on canine topics, and a rather difficult one to answer to the inquirer's satisfaction. Yet there is a definite reason for the comparative scarcity of the Gordon and his somewhat dubious standing as a field dog.

The wearer of the tan-trimmed ebony-hued coat, once the darling of the ruffed grouse and woodcock covers and a fair favorite in the quail fields, has lost little of his imposing appearance, but many, probably the majority, of the breed members in this country today go through life without ever having enjoyed the intoxicating thrill of upland game bird scent or heard the cracking report of a fowlingpiece. Yet there was a time when the Gordon Setter knew no peer as a cover-working gundog.

"Frank Forester" wrote thrillingly about the outstanding field abilities of a brace of Gordons which hunted to his gun in his favorite New York-New Jersey covers and on the marshy snipe flats of the Eastern Shore. He fairly sang their praises to the housetops, and many other sportsmen of his day preferred the Black and Tans to all other pointing dogs.

It is indeed a rare day now when one comes across a fellow gunner depending upon a Gordon Setter to find his game. True, the dog will hunt, has a good nose, and will point. But his English cousin and his Irish neighbor so far surpass him in dash, ambition, determination, and all-around "class" that the field merits of his breed are hardly to be compared with those of the other long-haired clans.

The Gordon today might be called a "collection piece" in the dog world. Like collectors of antique furniture, unusual objects of art, ancient armor, etc., there are always certain people who like to own "something different." Dog fanciers are no exception to this rule, and some people have "taken on" the Gordon Setter simply because he is now a rather rare animal of great beauty—forgetting, overlooking, or caring little about his utilitarian capabilities. Those owners seldom take him afield except for casual walks or to give him the exercise necessary to round him into what is called "show condition." Such breeders are largely responsible for the Gordon Setter's decline in popularity as a gundog, for they have bred for a type which could hardly do an acceptable day's work in the field under present conditions. While the present accepted standard calls for a rather racily built, medium-sized dog of clean Setter type, comparatively few of the specimens of today could approach that ideal.

There are, however, serious-minded breeders among the Gordon Setter fanciers who are earnestly trying to promote more interest in the dog as he was originally intended, an asset to the hunt and an adjunct to the sportsman's gun. In these days of short game supplies they are having added difficulties, for the Gordon is not a fast dog but a rather slow one, as a rule, and his range is generally restricted. With game as scarce as it is in some places, the modern topflight gundog must be a hustler from the word "go"; not only must he work his ground thoroughly, but he must cover a lot of it at a fast clip if he is to give his owner a fair number of shooting chances.

There are other reasons why the Gordon Setter does not enjoy high favor among the gunning public. As stated above, he is a rather slow dog and somewhat methodical, even to the point of being phlegmatic, in his work. He is, however, thorough and goes about his work in a businesslike manner.

His black and tan color, strikingly handsome as it

is in the show ring, works against him to some extent in the field. It makes him rather hard to see in heavy cover—and it is in heavy cover that the Gordon does his best work.

Even his splendidly loyal disposition may handicap him at times. The Gordon is generally very much a one-man dog. He is exceedingly loyal to his owner or trainer and when professionally trained often finds it difficult to adjust himself to a new "boss" when returned to his owner. His loyalty is indeed an admirable trait, but his desire for his master's companionship should not interfere with his ambition to hunt.

These characteristics, however, should not weigh too heavily against the dog, for he has many other good qualities. His handsome and shiny coat of black, set off with its trimmings of mahogany tan, makes a pretty picture in the field or before the fireside. While the dog is not particularly lofty in action he is attractive enough to catch the eye. He possesses a splendid nose, and, given the opportunity to use it, can prove his worth in this respect. He is quite a tractable dog and takes to training quickly and kindly. He makes a good retriever from land or water.

There are some specimens which show dash and verve comparable to the English Setter. It is to these individuals that Gordon Setter fanciers should turn if they are to improve the breed's hunting qualities and restore him to gunning favor. Unfortunately for the breed, however, too many fanciers are more interested in the Gordon's ornamental features and prefer to keep him as a pet and show dog. It has been a good many years since the Gordon played any considerable part in field trials. The Gordons of today just do not, as a rule, have that snap and dash so necessary in the makeup of a successful field trial contender.

The Gordon Setter gets his name from the Duke of Gordon, at whose castle kennels the breed is supposed, by some, to have originated. This is a disputed question, for it is known that quite a few wealthy Scottish sportsmen were breeding black-and-tan Setters at about the same time, and even before, the Duke of Gordon showed his preference for Setters of that color.

The Duke of Gordon is said to have used a Collie bitch named Maddy in his breeding operations. Maddy is reported to have been an exceptionally intelligent dog of extreme "birdness." She did not actually "point" her game but stopped upon some game scent and "watched," as writers of that day described her actions. Whatever influence Maddy might have exercised upon the breed has long since been dissipated, and the Gordon can now claim as much "legitimacy" as any other of the sporting breeds.

The Gordon Setter is an old established member of bird-dogdom's aristocracy. In the eyes of many of us who admire and value bird dogs for their field qualities above all else, the Gordon is not getting a fair deal from present exponents of the breed in this country. He deserves a much better break and, given it, will take his rightful place among American gundogs.

Description and Standards. The description and standards, adopted by the Gordon Setter Club of America and approved by the American Kennel Club, follow.

GENERAL IMPRESSION: The Gordon Setter is a good-sized, sturdily built, black and tan dog, well muscled, with plenty of bone and substance, but active, upstanding, and stylish, appearing capable of doing a full day's work in the field. He has a strong, rather short back, with well-sprung ribs and a short tail. The head is fairly heavy and finely chiseled. His bearing is intelligent, noble, and dignified, showing no signs of shyness or viciousness. Clear colors and straight or slightly waved coat are correct. He suggests strength and stamina rather than extreme speed. Symmetry and quality are most essential. A dog well-balanced in all points is preferable to one with outstanding good qualities and defects. A smooth, free movement, with high head carriage, is typical.

SIZE: Shoulder height for males, 24 to 27 inches. For females, 23 to 26 inches.

WEIGHT: Males, 55 to 80 pounds; females, 45 to 70 pounds. Animals that appear to be over or under the prescribed weight limits are to be judged on the basis of conformation and condition. Extremely thin or fat dogs should be discouraged on the basis that under- or overweight hampers the true working ability of the Gordon Setter. The weight-to-height ratio makes him heavier than other setters.

HEAD: The head is deep, rather than broad, with plenty of brain room; a nicely rounded, good-sized skull, broadest between the ears. The head should have a clearly indicated stop. Below and above the eyes should be lean, and the cheek as narrow as the leanness of the head allows. The muzzle is fairly long and not pointed, either as seen from above or from the side. The flews should not be pendulous. The nose should be broad, with open nostrils and black in color. The muzzle is the same length as the skull from occiput to stop, and the top of the muzzle is parallel to the line of the skull extended. The lip line from the nose to the flews shows a sharp, well-defined, square contour.

EYES: Of fair size, neither too deep-set, nor too bulging, dark brown, bright, and wise. The shape is oval rather than round. The lids should be tight.

EARS: Set low on the head approximately on line with the eye, fairly large and thin, well folded and carried close to the head.

TEETH: The teeth should be strong and white, and preferably should meet in front in a scissors bite, with the upper incisors slightly forward of the lower incisors. A level bite is not to be considered a fault. Pitted teeth from distemper or allied infections should not be penalized.

NECK: Long, lean, arched to the head, and without throatiness.

SHOULDERS: Should be fine at the points, and lying well back, giving a moderately sloping topline. The tops of the shoulder blades should be close together. When viewed from behind, the neck appears to fit into the shoulders in smooth, flat, lines that gradually widen from neck to shoulder.

CHEST: Deep and not too broad in front; the ribs well sprung, leaving plenty of lung room. The chest should reach to the elbows. A pronounced forechest should be in evidence.

BODY: The body should be short from shoulder to hips, and the distance from the forechest to the back of the thigh should approximately equal the height from the ground to the withers. The loins should be short and broad and not arched. The croup is nearly flat, with only a slight slope to the tailhead.

FOREQUARTERS: The legs should be big-boned, straight, and not bowed, with elbows free and not turned in or out. The angle formed by the shoulder blade and upper arm bone should be approximately 90° when the dog is standing so that the foreleg is perpendicular to the ground. The pasterns should be straight.

Gordon Setter. The color and flecking in his coat—difficult to ~ow except via a color photo—is what usually identifies the Gordon ~tter. Chiefly black, with brown or tan flecking. Photo by Evelyn M. ~afer.

HINDQUARTERS: The hind legs from hip to hock should be long, flat, and muscular; from hock to heel, short and strong. The stifle and hock joints are well bent and not turned either in or out. When the dog is standing with the hock perpendicular to the ground the thigh bone should hang downward parallel to an imaginary line drawn upward from the hock.

FEET: The feet should be formed by close-knit, well-arched toes with plenty of hair between; with full toe pads and deep heel cushions. Feet should not be turned in or out. Feet should be cat-like in shape.

TAIL: Short and should not reach below the hocks, carried horizontal or nearly so; thick at the root and finishing in a fine point. The feather which starts near the root of the tail should be slightly waved or straight, having triangular appearance, growing shorter uniformly toward the end. The placement of the tail is important for correct carriage. If the croup is nearly flat, the tail must emerge nearly on the same plane as the croup to allow for horizontal carriage. When the angle of the tail bends too sharply at the first coccygeal bone, the tail will be carried too gaily or will droop. The tail placement should be judged in its relationship to the structure of the croup.

TEMPERAMENT: The Gordon Setter should be alert, gay, interested, and aggressive. He should be fearless and willing, intelligent and capable. He should be loyal and affectionate, and strong-minded enough to stand the rigors of training.

GAIT: The action of the Gordon Setter is a bold, strong, driving, free-swinging gait. The head is carried up and the tail "flags" constantly while the dog is in motion. When viewed from the front the forefeet move up and down in straight lines so that the shoulder, elbow, and pastern joints are approximately in line with each other. When viewed from the rear, the hock, stifle, and hip joints are approximately in line. Thus the dog moves in a straight pattern forward without throwing the feet in or out. When viewed from the side the forefeet are seen to lift up and reach forward to compensate for the driving hindquarters. The hindquarters reach well forward and stretch far back, enabling the stride to be long and the drive powerful. The over-all appearance of the moving dog is one of smooth-flowing, well-balanced rhythm, in which the action is pleasing to the eye, effortless, economical and harmonious.

COAT: Should be soft and shining, straight or slightly waved, but not curly, with long hair on ears, under stomach and on chest, on back of the fore- and hind legs, and on the tail.

COLOR AND MARKINGS: Black with tan markings, either of rich chestnut or mahogany color. Black penciling is allowed on the toes. The borderline between black and tan colors should be clearly defined. There should not be any tan hairs mixed in the black. The tan markings should be located as follows: (1) Two clear spots over the eyes and not over three quarters of an inch in diameter; (2) On the sides of the muzzle. The tan should not reach to the top of the muzzle, but resembles a stripe around the end of the muzzle from one side to the other; (3) On the throat; (4) Two large clear spots on the chest; (5) On the inside of the hind legs showing down the front of the stifle and broadening out to the outside of the hind legs from the hock to the toes. It must not completely eliminate the black on the back of the hind legs; (6) On the forelegs from the carpus, or a little above, downward to the toes; (7) Around the vent; (8) A white spot on the chest is allowed, but the smaller the better. Predominantly tan, red, or buff dogs which do not have the typical pattern of markings of a Gordon Setter are ineligible for showing and undesirable for breeding.

While not a part of the official breed standard, the following may be helpful in placing proper emphasis upon qualities desired in the physical make-up of the breed.

SCALE OF POINTS: | | Points
---|---
Head and neck (incl. ears and eyes) .... | 10
Body .... | 15
Shoulders, forelegs, forefeet .... | 10
Hind legs and feet .... | 10
Tail .... | 5
Coat .... | 8
Color and markings .... | 5
Temperament .... | 10
Size, general appearance .... | 15
Gait .... | 12
TOTAL .... | 100

Disqualification. Predominantly tan, red, or buff dogs which do not have the typical pattern of markings of a Gordon Setter.

(November 13, 1962)

IRISH SETTER

IF ONE TOOK the time to canvass almost any group of bird dog fanciers, he would find that a goodly percentage would say, "The first gundog I ever owned was an Irish Setter." This will be hardly true of the sportsmen of the next generation, but that is not the Irish Setter's fault. It is, rather because the beauty of this breed has caused it to become the darling of the bench show sporting-dog world—so much so that its sterling field qualities have been sadly neglected by too many people, who have grown to love the red dog for his beauty alone.

His great popularity on the bench has caused many newcomers to the sport of upland game shooting to labor under the misconception that the Irish Setter is a thing of beauty only and a second-rate gundog at best. Fortunately for the breed, there are a few breeders who know that this is not true and through their own breeding programs are proving that this dog can still take his place alongside the English Setter and the Pointer in the niches set aside for pleasant and efficient gunning companions.

Recent showings of some of these dogs in field trial competitions, running on even terms with their English cousins and the short-hairs, offer fairly potent evidence that the standing of the Irish Setter is definitely improving in the eyes of sportsmen. It is true that the number of Irish Setters competing in present-day field trials is comparatively small, but if present breeding tendencies continue his position in this sport is likely to become much improved.

Although this dog does not shine with consistent brilliancy in field trials he takes his place in the winner's circle often enough to prove that, despite his bench show popularity, he is definitely *in* the gundog picture and is certainly not *out* of the field trial scene. In thousands of towns and communities will be found a red dog or two which, perhaps without benefit of extended pedigree, uphold the traditions of field excellence left him by his ancestors.

Now hailed as the most beautiful sporting dog, the Irish Setter was not always the solid-red-coated animal we know today. Most of the original Irish Setters were red and white, with red predominating, and even today a bit of white on the breast or toes is not exactly uncommon.

In earlier days he was a great favorite because he was a general-purpose dog. Rough and rugged, he did a good job for the gunner, whether pointing quail, grouse or woodcock, or retrieving ducks from icy waters. The flashy Llewellin Setters came into vogue along in the Eighties and became quite the fashion. With this, and the rise of the Pointer, the Irish Setter was placed somewhat in the gundog background and most of the breeding stock fell into the hands of men who cared for their dogs more for their private shooting or bench shows rather than for engaging in field competitions.

In the early days of field trials, however, Irish Setters played an important part. In 1876 an imported dog, Erin, won the Greenwood Stake of the Tennessee State Sportsmen's Association trials, which were held near Memphis. These were the third trials in the history of the sport.

A year later, Berkely, the son of Elcho and Lou II, won second in the puppy stake and Carrie, a bitch owned by the late Jesse Sherwood, was third. In the next trials of the Tennessee State Sportsmen's Association, Champ was second and Ida, Jr., a daughter of Erin and Ida, was third. First in the Championship Stake went to Joe, Jr., the son of Elcho and the Campbell bitch, Buck, Jr. In a match endurance race between Joe, Jr., and Gladstone, most prominent

English Setter of his day and one of the fountainheads of the field trial strain, Joe, Jr., emerged the winner. The race was for $1000 and lasted from sunrise to sunset for two days. It was judged on the number of actual points scored on game birds. Joe, Jr., had 61 points to Gladstone's 52.

Space will not permit a recounting of Irish Setter achievements in early field trials; suffice it to say that the breed garnered a surprising number of places, considering the limited number of representatives competing.

Elcho might properly be considered the fountainhead of the breed in this country. He probably had more influence than any of the earlier importations and there are few pedigrees of the present day which do not contain the name of this great individual. Elcho, a second-place winner in the Irish Setter class at the Dublin show, was brought to this country by Charles H. Turner of St. Louis. His bench show career in this country was a succession of victories.

No account of the Irish Setter would be complete without mention of the late Otto Pohl of Fremont, Nebr. During his career in the early part of the century, Mr. Pohl gathered together a remarkable kennel of red dogs which, for a combination of bench and field quality, were not to be equaled. Some of his well-known dogs were Drug Law, Pat-A-Belle, Rheola Clanderrick, and Morty Oge. His famous field trial winning bitch, Donegal's Alizon, won the cup offered to the best Setter with a field trial record awarded by Bob Weil, owner of National Champion Joe Muncie, an English Setter. This was at the Dayton show in 1918. Her victory at Dayton the following year was even greater than that, for she won the "Master Benson" trophy, offered by the noted sportsman, Harry D. Kirkover, to the best Pointer, English, Irish, or Gordon Setter with a field trial record.

Another sportsman who did much for the Irish Setter was Elias C. Vail, of Ridgefield, Conn. Mr. Vail's Modoc Bedelia won a number of places in field trials, the most important of which was a place in the trials of the English Setter Club of America, at Medford, N.J., in 1924. Competition at this club is usually exceedingly keen, many famous field trial dogs having started their careers on these grounds, and not until 22 years later did another Irish Setter place in these events. This, appropriately enough, was Rufus McTybe O'Cloisters, a great grandson of Bedelia, owned by the late Edwin M. Berolzheimer.

Mr. Vail also had good success with Elcova's Kinkie, Elcova's Admiration and Elcova's Terence McSwimey, running them against Pointers and English Setters.

An outstanding breeder of field-working Irish Setters in the country not so many years ago was the late Edwin M. Berolzheimer, Tarrytown, N.Y., and Ridgeland, S.C. Mr. Berolzheimer maintained a considerable breeding establishment at his New York home, The Cloisters, and his "O'Cloisters" suffix is familiar to every Irish Setter fancier. In the South, he hunted over his dogs on his plantation each season

Irish Setter.

and campaigned them fearlessly on the Eastern field trial circuit. His famous performer, Rufus McTybe O'Cloisters, considered by authorities as one of the best field trial Irish Setters ever raised in this country, won in the hot competition of the South.

Mr. Berolhzheimer had his share of bench show wins, but was more concerned with the development of the field qualities of the breed. If the breed had a few more champions of the same caliber as was Mr. Berolzheimer, who would strive as earnestly for breed improvement, the Irish Setter would soon become a more serious contender for field trial and field honors.

Among Mr. Berolzheimer's more prominent field trial winners were: Elcova McTybe, the only dog to win first place in the All-Age stake of the trials of the Irish Setter Club of America three times, Shaun McTybe O'Cloisters, a 14-times winner, Clodagh McTybe O'Cloisters, Tyron McTybe O'Cloisters, Brian McTybe O'Cloisters, Wheeler's Kildare Rusty, Wheeler's Red Boy, and the well-known Rufus, mentioned above.

The reputation given the Irish Setter—headstrong, hard to handle, etc.—is not well deserved. This bad name was given him by several of the Irish Setters brought over in the early Eighties from Ireland and England; to those who really know him, he has long since lived this down. The average Irish Setter of today is as easily broken as his English cousin.

True, as in any other breed, some individuals develop more slowly than others and consequently more time and patience are required to bring them to the fulfillment of their capabilities. This dog is not one to be forced or abused. He responds to kindness with apparent gratefulness and once he realizes what his master expects of him, his desire to please is quickly apparent.

It is true that the Irish Setter is somewhat lacking in "style," as the term is interpreted today. Few possess the rather exaggerated loftiness on point which characterizes some of our English Setters and Pointers, but most of them show a decided intensity on point. Many Irish Setters—in fact, most of them—point with a rather low tail which detracts somewhat from the beauty of the pointing posture. Efforts are being made by seriously interested breeders to correct this fault through selective breeding and progress is being made, although at present a low-stationed point seems characteristic of the breed.

The Irish Setter may not possess the excessive dash on the breakaway which field trialers fancy, but he goes about his work in a businesslike manner which generally produces results. He seldom shows the extreme range of the English Setter or the Pointer, but generally is more restricted in his course, although he covers his territory thoroughly. Above all, he works to the gun, and whether for horseback hunting in the South or searching the close coverts of the ruffed-grouse country he has his master's gun constantly in mind. His dark coat, although beautiful, works against him to some extent by making him

Irish Setter—Here on point.

rather hard to see in heavy cover. This is one reason why some gunners lost interest in him and chose lighter-colored gundogs.

There is no particular age at which to start field education of the Irish Setter. A year or a year and a half is early enough, for the youngster should be allowed to develop naturally. He should never be crowded and if correction becomes necessary it should be administered in mild doses at first and only when he knows why he is being punished. The young dog should never be punished severely. He is generally quite sensitive and needs careful handling. If treated harshly he will probably not understand why, and there is great danger of thus breaking his spirit and diminishing his desire to hunt. This should be avoided by all means.

The Irish Setter is decidedly an individual. The accepted training methods work well with this breed, but they must be modified or intensified to fit each individual case. He is no more timid than any other breed, but he definitely does not take kindly to harsh treatment.

Of all the pointing breeds, the Irish Setter is most likely to become a "one-man" dog. He forms a great attachment for his master and no matter how keen he is to hunt he is not prone to follow the first man who comes along with a shotgun over his shoulder.

By nature he is a very affectionate dog, and though he has a good sense of property rights, he seldom becomes vicious. The best advice to any prospective Irish Setter owner is to make a companion of the dog. Treat him like one of the family. Lavish affection on him, but not to the extent of coddling him. He will meet you more than halfway and be anxious to please. By making a close friend of him, your job of bringing him under control is almost finished.

His nose is equal to that of any pointing dog. He is strong, sturdy, can stand any kind of weather, and makes an ideal companion afield or in the home. As an ornament he knows no equal in the realm of dogdom.

Edwin M. Berolzheimer, Tarrytown, N.Y., once an outstanding breeder of field-working Irish Setters, with five of his famous "O'Cloisters," the suffix familiar to many an Irish Setter fancier, even today. Photo by August J. Bucker.

BODY: Sufficiently long to permit a straight and free stride. Shoulder blades long, wide, sloping well back, fairly close together at the top, and joined in front to long upper arms angled to bring the elbows slightly rearward along the brisket. Chest deep, reaching approximately to the elbows; rather narrow in front. Ribs well sprung. Loins of moderate length, muscular and slightly arched. Top line of body from withers to tail slopes slightly downward without sharp drop at the croup. Hindquarters should be wide and powerful with broad, well-developed thighs.

LEGS AND FEET: All legs sturdy, with plenty of bone, and strong, nearly straight pastern. Feet rather small, very firm, toes arched and close. Forelegs straight and sinewy, the elbows moving freely. Hind legs long and muscular from hip to hock, short and nearly perpendicular from hock to ground; well angulated at stifle and hock joints, which, like the elbows, incline neither in nor out.

TAIL: Strong at root, tapering to fine point, about long enough to reach the hock. Carriage straight or curving slightly upward, nearly level with the back.

COAT: Short and fine on head, forelegs, and tips of ears; on all other parts, of moderate length and flat. Feathering long and silky on ears; on back of forelegs and thighs long and fine, with a pleasing fringe of hair on belly and brisket extending onto the chest. Feet well feathered between the toes. Fringe on tail moderately long and tapering. All coat and feathering as straight and free from curl or wave.

COLOR: Mahogany or rich chestnut red, with no trace of black. A small amount of white on chest, throat, or toes, or a narrow centered streak on skull, is not to be penalized.

SIZE: There is no disqualification as to size. The make and fit of all parts and their over-all balance in the animal are rated more important. Twenty-seven inches at the withers and a show weight of about 70 pounds is considered ideal for a dog; the bitch 25 inches, 60 pounds. Variance beyond an inch up or down to be discouraged.

GAIT: At the trot the gait is big, very lively, graceful, and efficient. The head is held high. The hindquarters drive smoothly and with great power. The forelegs reach well ahead as if to pull in the ground, without giving the appearance of a hackney gait. The dog runs as he stands: straight. Seen from the front or rear, the forelegs, as well as the hind legs below the hock joint, move perpendicularly to the ground, with some tendency toward a single track as speed increases. But a crossing or weaving of the legs, front or back, is objectionable.

BALANCE: At his best the lines of the Irish Setter so satisfy in overall balance that artists have termed him the most beautiful of all dogs. The correct specimen always exhibits balance whether standing or in motion. Each part of the dog flows and fits smoothly into its neighboring parts without calling attention to itself.

(June 14, 1960)

AMERICAN WATER SPANIEL

DESPITE HIS nearly unique "made in America" origins, the American Water Spaniel, a compact, curly-coated dog, with the intelligence and ability to do almost anything today's small game hunter asks of a dog, remains relatively unknown throughout most of the U.S.

Nevertheless this breed, once called the American Brown Water Spaniel, or just plain "water spaniel," has been known to Midwestern and New England sportsmen for more than three-quarters of a century,

Description and Standards. The description and standards follow.

GENERAL APPEARANCE: The Irish Setter is an active, aristocratic bird-dog, rich red in color, substantial yet elegant in build. Standing over two feet tall at the shoulder, the dog has a straight, fine, glossy coat, longer on ears, chest, tail, and back of legs. Afield he is a swift-moving hunter; at home, a sweet-natured, trainable companion. His is a rollicking personality.

HEAD: Long and lean, its length at least double the width between the ears. The brow is raised, showing a distinct stop midway between the tip of nose and the well-defined occiput (rear point of skull). Thus the nearly level line from occiput to brow is set a little above, and parallel to, the straight and equal line from eye to nose. The skull is oval when viewed from above or front; very slightly domed when viewed in profile. Beauty of head is emphasized by delicate chiseling along the muzzle, around and below the eyes, and along the cheeks. Muzzle moderately deep, nostrils wide, jaws of nearly equal length. Upper lips fairly square but not pendulous, the underline of the jaws being almost parallel with the top line of the muzzle. The teeth meet in a scissors bite in which the upper incisors fit closely over the lower, or they may meet evenly.

NOSE: Black or chocolate.

EYES: Somewhat almond-shaped, of medium size, placed rather well apart; neither deep-set nor bulging. Color, dark to medium brown. Expression soft yet alert.

EARS: Set well back and low, not above level of eye. Leather thin, hanging in a neat fold close to the head, and nearly long enough to reach the nose.

NECK: Moderately long, strong but not thick, and slightly arched; free from throatiness, and fitting smoothly into the shoulders.

although his official recognition by the American Kennel Club didn't come until 1940.

The American Water Spaniel is often confused with the Irish Water Spaniel and understandably so. Many waterfowl and upland hunters are less concerned with purity of breeding than performance. In years past many Irish-American Water Spaniel crosses were made and many a Midwest riverman still owns a dog that is obviously a cross between these two separate breeds. However, when pure-bred, there are distinct differences.

The American Water Spaniel usually stands about 15 to 18 inches high and weighs 25 to 40 pounds. There are some outsize strains which run larger. The Irish standard calls for a 21 to 24 inch dog, weighing 45 to 65 pounds, but one will see many much larger individuals, particularly those shown on the bench. Where the American is compact and spaniel-like, the Irish is up on legs and has a springy, rolling gait. After comparing size, look at the dog's head. The American's dome is broad and smooth, the Irish head is narrower and has a poodle-like topknot. The American's coat has a more marcelled appearance, the Irish's is ropy and longer. Finally, the American's tail should be hair-covered or plumed. That of the Irish is bare, resulting in the nickname "rat-tail."

Just as Maryland's Chesapeake Bay region has been credited with the development of the Chesapeake Bay Retriever, so must the Wolf and Fox River Valley region of East-Central Wisconsin be noted as the place from whence came the American Water Spaniel. The rivers and the large lakes they feed, Poygan, Butte des Morts and Winnebago, provided a waterfowl gunner's paradise in the late 1800s. Then duck hunters reached their favorite spots via waterway. They required a dog that could shake off cold and wet, work marsh cover, yet fit handily into a small skiff or canoe. It was for this purpose, a skiff dog—small but hardy—that the American was developed.

The sturdy little dog has also adapted to work as a flushing dog in the uplands, being particularly adept at working out ruffed grouse, woodcock and pheasant. Some also jump rabbits and tree squirrels and are favorites of the mink and muskrat trapper as a trapline dog having a good nose and fondness for water. In the uplands, the American lacks the dash of a good Springer, but he is a busy sure worker, eager to please and easily trained, and he will please the hunter whose pace is leisurely.

Prominent in the development of American Water Spaniels were Driscoll Scanlan, Nashville, Ill., Karl Hinz, Milwaukee, Wis., John Sherlock, Kenmore, N.Y., Louis Smith, Holliston, Mass. and Thomas Brogden, Rush Lake, Wis. who with John Scofield in the late 1930s formed the American Water Spaniel Club which led to recognition by the Field Dog Stud Book in 1938 and the AKC in 1940.

But if one man can be rated as the sponsoring originator of any breed of dog, this honor must be vested in one Dr. F. J. Pfeifer, a practicing physician and surgeon since 1909 in New London, Wisconsin, at the confluence of the Embarrass and Wolf rivers. Dr. Pfeifer was the first man in the U.S. to register an American Water Spaniel with an official registry.

On Feb. 8, 1920, the United Kennel Club registered "Curly Pfeifer" as an American Water Spaniel after the doctor—convinced that since the dogs he had known since boyhood were producing pups that looked just like themselves, there must be a strong strain present making it genotypically feasible to establish a breed—had attempted to convince the FDSB and AKC that the American was eligible for recognition.

Recognition by the UKC started Dr. Pfeifer on an extensive breeding program and at one time in the 1920s his Wolf River Kennels on the Trambauer brothers' farm near New London contained 132 Americans. By 1924, when his kennel was awarded Purple Ribbon status by the UKC, indicating that quite a few successive generations of the strain had been registered and found to maintain the required standards, Dr. Pfeifer was selling over 100 puppies annually, some going to Canada, Missouri, Illinois, Texas, and Louisiana as well as other areas in Wisconsin.

Each pup sold (price was $20 for bitches, $25 for dogs) was accompanied by a small training pamphlet Dr. Pfeifer wrote, and the dogs were unconditionally guaranteed. In a year, if the purchaser wasn't satisfied with the American as a hunter and companion, he could get his money back or a new puppy. The doctor couldn't recall ever having to make good this offer.

During the 1920s when the demand for these dogs was high, other kennels sprang up, other breeding programs were undertaken, and it is most probable that there was a considerable degree of crossing with Irish Water Spaniels which also enjoyed some popularity with Midwestern waterfowlers at that time.

The generally accepted theory regarding the far back origins of the American Water Spaniel has it that numbers of old English Water Spaniels, now extinct, were imported by sportsmen seeking a retriever smaller than the popular Irish Water Spaniel. But the Wisconsin rivers and lakes during both annual seasonal waterfowl migrations proved too cold

American Water Spaniel. Photo by Carhart's.

for the English dog, who reputedly had great scenting powers. So the Irish Water Spaniel and Curly-coated retriever were introduced—so this version goes—a strain was stabilized, and line breeding produced the skiff dog we now know as the American Water Spaniel.

Dr. Pfeifer, who had his first "American Brown" in 1894, always disagreed with parts of this theory. He contended that it wasn't until after he had registered and was breeding Americans successfully that other breeders made some introductions of Irish Water Spaniel, and that he culled many pups from breedings between dogs purchased away from his own kennel which showed indications of being mixed with the Irish spaniels. When Irish Water Spaniels are crossed into any strain their progeny almost invariably display a prominent top-knot. The doctor contended every American he had from 1894 on had a broad, smooth head, very short curls, and a bushy tail. In his opinion, the chief progenitors of the American Water Spaniel were the Curly-coated Retriever and the Field Spaniel.

Today, the American is a bit sharper in temperament than most spaniels, not as large and powerful as the retrievers and lacking the speed and dash of the English Springer Spaniel. But as a plain, ordinary, all-around huntin' dog, he stacks up very well.

He should be more popular, but he isn't, for two reasons. Because he is not a pretty dog, and because most of his breeders and users have been practical hunting men, the American has never caught on for show fancy. Secondly, despite his strong natural inclination to hunt and retrieve which makes training easy, there is no niche in the field trial world, with its attendant publicity, for the American. Capable of a dual role as waterfowl retriever and upland game flusher to an extent that would satisfy most hunters, he isn't large enough to compete with the Labradors, Chesapeakes and Goldens in the retriever trials, or dashing enough to shine when pitted against a Springer in the spaniel trials.

But talk to virtually any hunter carrying 50 years or more on his shoulders and he will recall some old "Brownie" or "Curly" he owned or knew as a boy or young man; a dog that learned almost by "doing what comes naturally," which was hunted hard, bragged about, followed the kids to school and did tricks for saloon patrons. That's the kind of dog the American Water Spaniel still is.

Description and Standards. The description and standards follow:

GENERAL APPEARANCE: Medium in size, of sturdy typical spaniel character, curly coat, an active, muscular dog, with emphasis placed on proper size and conformation, correct head properties, texture of coat and color. Of amicable disposition; demeanor indicates intelligence, strength and endurance.

HEAD: Moderate in length, skull rather broad and full, stop moderately defined, but not too pronounced. Forehead covered with smooth, short hair and without tuft or top-knot. Muzzle of medium length, square, and with no inclination to snipiness; jaws strong, and of good length, and neither undershot nor overshot; teeth straight and well shaped. Nose sufficiently wide,

American Water Spaniel—An expert in retrieving. Photo by D. M. Duffey.

and well developed nostrils to insure good scenting power.

FAULTS: Very flat skull, narrow across the top, long slender or snipey muzzle.

EYES: Hazel, brown, or of dark tone to harmonize with coat; set well apart. Expression alert, attractive, intelligent.

FAULT: Yellow eyes to disqualify.

EARS: Lobular, long and wide, not set too high on head, but slightly above the eyeline. Leather extending to end of nose and well covered with close curls.

NECK: Round and of medium length, strong and muscular, free of throatiness, set to carry head with dignity, but arch not accentuated.

BODY STRUCTURE: Well developed, sturdily constructed, but not too compactly coupled. General outline is a symmetrical relationship of parts. Shoulders sloping, clean and muscular. Strong loins, lightly arched and well furnished, deep brisket but not excessively broad. Well sprung ribs. Legs of medium length and well boned, but not so short as to handicap for field work.

LEGS AND FEET: Fore legs powerful and reasonably straight. Hind legs firm with suitable bent stifles and strong hocks well let down. Feet to harmonize with size of dog. Toes closely grouped and well padded.

FAULT: Cow hocks.

TAIL: Moderate in length, curved in a slightly rocker shape, carried slightly below level of back; tapered and covered with hair to tip, action lively.

FAULTS: Rat or shaved tail.

COAT: The coat should be closely curled or have marcel effect and should be of sufficient density to be of protection against weather, water, or punishing cover, yet not coarse. Legs should have medium short, curly feather.

FAULTS: Coat too straight, soft, fine, or tightly kinked.

COLOR: Solid liver or dark chocolate, a little white on toes or chest is permissible.

HEIGHT: 15 to 18 inches at the shoulder.

WEIGHT: Males 28 to 45 pounds; females 25 to 40 pounds.

Disqualification. Yellow eyes.

BRITTANY SPANIEL

A POINTING spaniel has proved to be the answer to what an upland gunner, who walks through restricted coverts, wants in a shooting dog and at the same time has won hundreds of admirers who have never fired a shotgun in their lives. This unique dog, the only spaniel that points its game, is the Brittany Spaniel.

Generally known in this country for less than three decades, the breed has made great strides in popularity with Eastern and Midwestern gunners who want to shoot their grouse, woodcock and pheasant over a point, but need a dog who works close. Particular improvement has been noted in the Brittany's work under the gun during the past ten years and at the same time its admirers have diligently attempted to meet the approved physical standard for the breed as well as maintain and improve upon the mental qualities that permit quickly absorbing field training.

Sizing up the Brittany among the gundogs, he would be classed as a small to medium dog, not exceeding 20½ inches in height and weighing about 40 pounds. He gives the impression of having legs proportionately long in comparison to a rather cobby body. He is either born with a short tail or it is docked. His general appearance is about what you might expect to get if you crossed an English Setter with an English Springer Spaniel. His hunting pattern also is about halfway between these two breeds, for while the bigger running Brittanys are more desirable, a large number of this breed range no farther out than a flushing dog like a Springer Spaniel, even though they point their birds.

But despite appearances and action, the Brittany is no cross-breed. Old French woodcuts show the *Bretagne* being used in the uplands on rabbits, in the wetlands on snipe, and even in the water on ducks. Some romantic researchers have tried to establish some connection between the Brittany, the Welsh Springer Spaniel and the old red and white dogs from which the Irish Setter is supposed to have descended, on the basis of color similarity. This theory holds that the ancient Celts driven from France to Wales and Ireland brought Brittany-like dogs with them to establish the two other breeds.

More prosaically, it seems that if there is a connection, it probably came in more recent times as the normal result of commerce, war and piracy between peoples of the British Isles and the main European Continent.

Credit for much of the Brittany's early development goes to a French sportsman, Arthur Enaud, using two pointing breeds, the Italian *Bracco* and the French *Braque de Bourbonnais* to increase scenting ability and intensify the orange and white coloring he favored. This French pointer may also be the factor establishing the hereditary transmission of short tails in some Britts, since it was a breed characteristic.

Louis Thebaud first called U.S. attention to the Brittany with his importations in the mid-'30s, although the breed named after the French province has been known on the Continent for centuries. They began to catch on rapidly after World War II as more persons took up hunting only to find game populations declining and hunting areas reduced both in size and scope. Their acceptance by the U.S. gunning public has paralleled that of the other Continental pointing breeds, chiefly those stemming from Germany. Not only did the hard-running, far-reaching, superbly stylish pointers and setters become less practical, but many a hunter, just getting acquainted with dogs and hunting, felt more comfortable with a dog he could keep track of while on foot.

So while the changing complexion of things to the American hunter and the type of hunting he does has been responsible for creating a spot on the U.S. scene for close-working dogs that will point and, more often than not, fetch game birds, the Brittany itself is responsible for its current popularity, sharing credit with an active breed organization for development of its good hunting potential.

The American Brittany Club is a live-wire organization equally devoted to field, show and obedience tests to prove out its favorite. A regular publication, *The American Brittany*, is the official organ of the Club.

It must be borne in mind that essentially the Brittany is not a bold dog. He responds best to coaxing and to kid glove rather than by whip and rough command. This makes him easily trainable for some, but a problem for the short-tempered. Because his range is restricted at best, every effort should be made to encourage the Brittany to reach out and seek game, rather than encourage his remaining so close to the handler that he's stumbled over. Too many of the breed still show a distressing tendency to hang tight to the handler, so he leads the dog into birds rather than the dog going out and finding his own as he should. But on the other hand, the bustling, busy Brittanys developed through proper breeding and handling are highly appreciated dogs and excellent

Brittany Spaniel—Unlike most other spaniels, the Brittany will point as well as retrieve. Photo by Evelyn M. Shafer.

bird finders. While they may lack the reach and style of the wide-going, high-tailed Pointers and Setters, once on game they lack nothing in hunting intensity and their more developed inclination to retrieve makes up for any of their real or imagined short-comings when compared with the long-tailed dogs.

More aloof in temperament than the other spaniels, the Brittany is a fine family pet, and his size makes it possible for apartment-house dwellers to consider him as a combination house dog and hunting companion.

Most Brittanys can be expected to work on any species of upland birds and some individuals will even do a reasonably good job of duck fetching if conditions aren't too arduous. The Britt is a best bet on ruffed grouse, woodcock and, in most cases, pheasant hunting, and a secondary preference as far as quail, prairie grouse or Hungarian partridge go, where other breeds have more to offer.

The Brittany Spaniel is considered the favorite gundog in Belgium and is highly popular in France and Italy as well as in America.

Description and Standards. The description and standards, adopted by the American Brittany Club and approved by the American Kennel Club follow.

GENERAL DESCRIPTION: A compact, closely knit dog of medium size, a leggy spaniel having the appearance as well as the agility of a great ground coverer. Strong, vigorous, energetic and quick of movement. Not too light in bone, yet never heavy-boned and cumbersome. Ruggedness, without clumsiness, is a characteristic of the breed. So leggy is he that his height at the withers is the same as the length of his body. He has no tail, or at most, not more than 4 inches.

WEIGHT: Should weight between 30 and 40 pounds.

HEIGHT: 17½ to 20½ inches—measured from the ground to the highest point of the back—the withers.

COAT: Hair dense, flat or wavy, never curly. Not as fine as in other spaniel breeds, and never silky. Furnishings not profuse. The ears should carry little fringe. Neither the front nor hind legs should carry heavy featherings. Note: Long, curly, or silky hair is a fault. Any tendency toward excessive feathering should be severely penalized, as undesirable in a sporting dog which must face burrs and heavy cover.

SKIN: Fine and fairly loose. (A loose skin rolls with briars and sticks, thus diminishing punctures or tearing. But a skin so loose as to form pouches is undesirable.)

COLOR: Dark orange and white, or liver and white. Some ticking is desirable, but not so much as to produce belton patterns. Roan patterns or factors or orange or liver shade are permissible. The orange and liver are found in standard particolor, or piebald patterns. Washed out or faded colors are not desirable. Black is a disqualification.

SKULL: Medium length (approximately 4¾ inches). Rounded, very slightly wedge-shaped, but evenly made. Width, not quite as wide as the length (about 4⅜ inches) and never so broad as to appear coarse, or so narrow as to appear racy. Well defined, but gently sloping stop effect. Median line rather indistinct. The occipital crest only apparent to the touch. Lateral walls well rounded. The Brittany should never be "apple-headed" and he should never have an indented stop. (All measurements of skull are for a 19½-inch dog.)

MUZZLE: Medium length, about two thirds the length of the skull, measuring the muzzle from the tip to the stop, and the skull from the occipital crest to the stop between the eyes. Muzzle should taper gradually in both horizontal and vertical dimensions as it approaches the nostrils. Neither a Roman nose nor a concave curve (dish-face) is desirable. Never broad, heavy, or snipy.

NOSE: Nostrils well open to permit deep breathing of air and adequate scenting while at top speed. Tight nostrils should be penalized. Never shiny. Color, fawn, tan, light shades of brown or deep pink. A black nose is a disqualification. A two-tone or butterfly nose should be severely penalized.

EYES: Well set in head. Well protected from briars by a heavy, expressive eyebrow. A prominent, full or pop eye should be heavily penalized. It is a serious fault in a hunting dog that must face briars. Skull well chiseled under the eyes, so that the lower lid is not pulled back to form a pocket or haw for catching seeds, dirt and weed dust. Judges should check by forcing head down to see if lid falls away from the eye. Preference should be for darker-colored eyes, though lighter shades of amber should not be penalized. Light and mean-looking eyes to be heavily penalized.

EARS: Set high, above the level of the eyes. Short and leafy, rather than pendulous, reaching about half the length of the muzzle. Should lie flat and close to the head, with the tip rounded very slightly. Ears well covered with dense, but relatively short hair, and with little fringe.

LIPS: Tight to the muzzle, with the upper lip overlapping the lower jaw only sufficiently to cover under lip. Lips dry so that feathers do not stick. Drolling to receive a heavy penalty. Flews to be penalized.

Brittany Spaniels, pointing and backing. These are all National Field Champions. Photo by Evelyn M. Shafer.

TEETH: Well joined incisors. Posterior edge of upper incisors in contact with anterior edge of lower incisors, thus giving a true scissors bite. Overshot or undershot jaw to be penalized heavily.

NECK: Medium length. Not quite permitting the dog to place his nose on the ground without bending his legs. Free from throatiness, though not a serious fault unless accompanied by dewlaps. Strong, without giving the impression of being over-muscled. Well set into sloping shoulders. Never concave or ewe-necked.

BODY LENGTH: Approximately the same as the height when measured at the withers. Body length is measured from the point of the forechest to the rear of the haunches. A long body should be heavily penalized.

WITHERS: Shoulder blades should not protrude much. Not too widely set apart with perhaps two thumbs' width or less between the blades. At the withers, the Brittany is slightly higher than at the rump.

SHOULDERS: Sloping and muscular. Blade and upper arm should form nearly a 90-degree angle when measured from the posterior point of the blade at the withers to the junction of the blade and upper arm, and thence to the point of the elbow nearest the ribs. Straight shoulders do not permit sufficient reach.

BACK: Short and straight. Slight slope from highest point of withers to the root of the tail. Never hollow, saddle, sway or roach-backed. Slight drop from hips to root of tail. Distance from last rib to upper thigh short, about three to four finger widths.

CHEST: Deep, reaching the level of the elbow. Neither so wide nor so rounded as to disturb the placement of the shoulder bones and elbows, which causes a paddling movement, and often causes soreness from elbow striking ribs. Ribs well sprung, but adequate heart room provided by depth as well as width. Narrow or slab-sided chests are a fault.

FLANKS: Rounded. Fairly full. Not extremely tucked up, nor yet flabby and falling. Loins short and strong. Narrow and weak loins are a fault. In motion the loin should not sway sideways, giving a zigzag motion in the back, wasting energy.

HINDQUARTERS: Broad, strong and muscular, with powerful thighs and well-bent stifles, giving a hip set well into the loin and the marked angulation necessary for a powerful drive when in motion. Fat and falling hindquarters are a fault.

TAIL: Naturally tailless, or not over four inches long. Natural or docked. Set on high, actually an extension of the spine at about the same level.

FRONT LEGS: Viewed from the front, perpendicular, but not set too wide as in the case of a dog loaded in shoulder. Elbows and feet turning neither in nor out. Viewed from the side, practically perpendicular to the pastern. Pastern slightly bent to give cushion to stride. Not so straight as in terriers. Falling pasterns, however, are a serious fault. Leg bones clean, graceful, but not too fine. An extremely heavy bone is as much a fault as spindly legs. One must look for substance and suppleness. Height to the elbows should approximately equal distance from elbow to withers.

HIND LEGS: Stifles well bent. The stifle generally is the term used for knee joint. If the angle made by the upper and lower leg bones is too straight, the dog quite generally lacks drive, since his hind legs cannot drive as far forward at each stride as is desirable. However, the stifle should not be bent as to throw the hock joint far out behind the dog. Since factors not easily seen by the eye may give the dog his proper drive, a Brittany should not be condemned for straight stifle until the judge has checked the dog in motion from the side. When at a trot, the Brittany's hind foot should step into or beyond the print left by the front foot. The stifle joint should not turn out making a cowhock. (The cowhock moves the foot out to the side, thus driving out of line, and losing reach at each stride.) Thighs well feathered, but not profusely, halfway to the hock. Hocks, that is, the back pasterns, should be moderately short, pointing neither in nor out; perpendicular when viewed from the side. They should be firm when shaken by the judge.

FEET: Should be strong, proportionately smaller than other spaniels, with close-fitting, well-arched toes and thick pads. The Brittany is not "up on his toes." Toes not heavily feathered. Flat feet, splayed feet, paper feet, etc., are to be heavily penalized. An ideal foot is half way between the hare- and cat-foot.

The points below indicate only relative values. To be also taken into consideration are type, gait, soundness, spirit, optimum height, body length and general proportions.

SCALE OF POINTS: Points
  Head 25
  Body 35
  Running gear 40
  TOTAL 100

Disqualifications. Any Brittany Spaniel measuring under 17½ inches or over 20½ inches. Any black in the coat or a nose so dark in color as to appear black. A tail substantially more than 4 inches in length.

(November 18, 1952)

CLUMBER SPANIEL

THE CLUMBER Spaniel was once described as the "retired gentleman's shooting dog." This was because retired British military men and civil servants found the Clumber ideal for shooting in the turnip patches and other truck garden areas close to the city. The fields were small, the pace leisurely, and the dogs were easily handled.

The story of the origin of the Clumber is based entirely on an article which appeared in *Sporting Magazine* in 1807. A British writer misquoted from this article, and most authors have continued the error ever since. The original article showed part of a dog painting. Part of this article is given here:

. . . The annexed engraving is the portrait of William Mansell, game keeper to His Grace, Henry Clinton, Duke of Newcastle, and painted by F. Wheatly, Esq., R. A., now in the Duke's possession at Clumber House, Nottinghamshire.

The group of springers, or cock-flushers, by which the game keeper is so tastefully surrounded in the picture, was a gift to Duke Henry when in France, from the Duke of Noailles; and William Mansell, during a uniform attention to the duties of his office (near 30 years) has, above other things, studied to increase, unmixed, this peculiar race of flushers.

Since this Duke of Noailles died about 1766, it is supposed that the dogs may have been given to the Duke of Newcastle about 1760. However, no other kennel of dogs of similar type was ever found in France, though many British sporting authorities tried to trace dogs of that type there.

The dogs pictured were obviously Clumbers, about as we know them today. Early writers ascribed the long, low body to Basset crosses, and the heavy head to St. Bernard or "Alpine" Spaniel crosses. Probably neither is correct, since most spaniels tend to short legs and heavy heads.

A good description of the Clumber of 100 years ago was given by Colonel Hamilton in his Recollections, published in 1860.

This spaniel is red and white, is larger than the usual spaniel, strong made, an intelligent countenance, dark eyes, and the ears not very long.

These dogs have excellent noses and display great spirit in beating strong covert, and after having been shot over two or three seasons, become very valuable for pheasant and cock shooting. They are naturally ill tempered, and rarely form any attachment but to their master or game keeper.

A dog of that period, Mr. Holford's Jock, is described by Stonehenge (1859) as being 2 feet 10 inches long from the tip of the nose to the root of the tail. He had an 11-inch tail, and he was 17 inches tall.

James Watson, the American dog authority, was something of a Clumber enthusiast, having taken part in drawing the American standard for the breed. But his opinion of the dogs in the field was not too high. In 1906, he wrote:

One dog was of little use, so slow are they in their movements, and it called for a team of several braces, as many as could be obtained, in fact, to be of use for a shooting party. This entailed special training, and looking after by a man who could handle them, for they would not work for every person, or any person.

Despite Watson's uncomplimentary opinion, Clumbers almost monopolized the early spaniel trials, and at the very time Watson was writing. The first spaniel trials were held in 1899, and all spaniel breeds competed together in them. J. Sharpe's Stylish Price, a Cocker, won both the puppy and open stakes. But Clumbers took all other placings. In the open stake, Mr. Watt's Hoar Cross Shortly was second, and Mr. Cockburn's Carry One was third. Second in the puppy stake went to F. Winton Smith's Beachgrove Toy, and Mr. Warwick's Compton Roger was third.

At the second trial, held the same year, Mr. Smith's Clumber, Beachgrove Bee, won both puppy and open stakes. This dog dominated the trials for years, and became the first field trial champion spaniel of record. Here is a description given of him at this trial: ". . . A dog with a narrow face, but good body, and well ahead of anything in competition. Way he worked coverts and hedgerows was a treat, and he retrieved capitally; sensible but did not show great excellence of nose."

In those days it was said: "In almost any litter of spaniel puppies, there will be three kinds, Cockers, Springers or Field Spaniels, and Sussex." Clumbers were not included because it was felt they were of a radical type, with little relationship to the others. Yet the pedigrees of all these breeds were mixed up. Thus, Beachgrove Teal, a Clumber, was the dam of Longbranch Teal, one of the first Springers ever to be shown in Canada.

Primarily, it was the field trials which changed this. With Clumbers taking the honors, breeds began to be separated, and trials were held for the separate

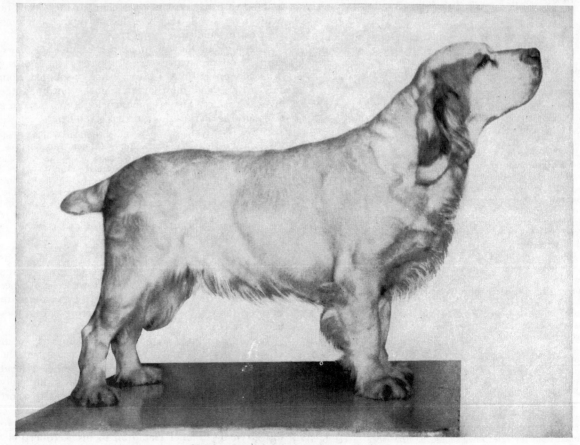

Clumber Spaniel. Photo by Evelyn M. Shafer.

breeds. The Clumbers then gradually lost out because the Cockers and Springers became faster, and gained in favor as all-around dogs.

Among the great English Clumbers were Beachgrove Minette, Beachgrove Maud, Rivington Honey, Ch. Hempstead Toby, and Ch. Tramp of St. Mary's. All these dogs won in the field and on the bench.

In America, our hunting conditions have not been such as would show the dogs to advantage. This does not necessarily doom the Clumber forever in America, for our population is building up rapidly, and game supply has its ups and downs. Gamefarm shooting is apt to become more common, and conditions may come around to the point where the Clumber will fit well into the American shooting scene.

The Clumber is perhaps the most easily trained of any of the spaniel family. He is not headstrong. Once he has learned his lessons, he remembers them, even if only hunted once or twice a year. Perhaps because of his white coat and his "sedate" pace, he is said to be the finest of all hot-weather hunting dogs.

The Clumber is to the spaniel family what the Basset is to the hounds—a slow-moving, short-legged, large-bodied dog. He does not, however, give tongue when on a hot scent as the Basset does, and as does also the Sussex Spaniel.

The modern Clumber Spaniel is 17 to 18 inches tall at the shoulder, and males will weigh 55 to 65 pounds. This may be compared to the Springer which, at 18.5 inches at the shoulder, will average 45 pounds in weight.

The Clumber is orange and white, or lemon and white, with almost no orange or lemon on the body. The head somewhat resembles that of a St. Bernard, both in type and in markings. Considering the size of the dog, the head is very heavy, the lips are pendulous, and the eyes often show haw (the lid droops to show the red membrane).

Description and Standards. The description and standards follow.

GENERAL APPEARANCE AND SIZE: General appearance, a long, low, heavy-looking dog, of a very thoughtful expression, betokening great intelligence. Should have the appearance of great power. Sedate in all movements, but not clumsy. Weight of dogs averaging between 55 and 65 pounds; bitches from 35 to 50 pounds.

HEAD: Head large and massive in all its dimensions; round above eyes, flat on top, with a furrow running from between the eyes upon the center. A marked stop and large occipital protuberance. Jaw long, broad and deep. Lips of upper jaw overhung. Muzzle not square, but at the same time powerful-looking. Nostrils large, open and flesh-colored, sometimes cherry colored.

EYES: Eyes large, soft, deep-set and showing haw. Hazel in color, not too pale, with dignified and intelligent expression.

EARS: Ears long and broad at the top, turned over on the front edge, and there but slightly. Hair short and silky, without the slightest approach to wave or curl.

NECK AND SHOULDERS: Neck long, thick and powerful, free from dewlap, with a large ruff. Shoulders immensely strong and muscular, giving a heavy appearance in front.

BODY: Long, low and well ribbed up. The chest is wide and deep, the back long, broad, and level, with very slight arch over the loin.

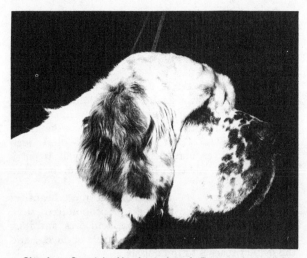

Clumber Spaniel—Head study of Eng. and Am. Ch. Thornville Silver. (Owner: R. W. Meyer, Santa Ana, Calif.)

LEGS AND FEET: Forelegs short, straight, and very heavy in bone; elbows close. Hind legs only slightly less heavily boned than the forelegs. They are moderately angulated, with hocks well let down. Quarters well developed and muscular. No feather above the hocks, but thick hair on the back of the legs just above the feet. Feet large, compact, and well filled with hair between the toes.

COAT AND FEATHERS: Coat silky and straight, not too long, extremely dense; feather long and abundant.

COLOR AND MARKINGS: Color, lemon and white, and orange and white. Fewer markings on body the better. Perfection of markings, solid lemon or orange ears, evenly marked head and eyes, muzzle and legs ticked.

STERN: Stern set on a level and carried low.

SCALE OF POINTS:	Points
General appearance and size	10
Head	15
Eyes	5
Ears	10
Neck and shoulders	15
Body and quarters	20
Legs and feet	10
Coat and feather	10
Color and marking	5
TOTAL	100

(February 6, 1960)

COCKER SPANIEL

THE COCKER Spaniel is one of the world's most popular dogs. It leads or has led other breeds in almost every country where dogs are registered. Yet the Cocker's popularity does not carry over into the field, where only the bitterest kind of struggle has kept intact any of the Cocker's former reputation as a great sporting companion. This has been due not so much to the Cocker's lack of ability in the field as to his extraordinary beauty and quality as a pet and show dog.

The modern Cocker Spaniel is divided into two

main types, the English Cocker and the American. Until some years ago, the two were very much the same. Many had common ancestors, and differed chiefly in size. At present, the two are divided both as to size and type.

The English Cocker is the larger of the two, and somewhat resembles a small Springer. Males run from 28 to 34 pounds. The muzzle is slightly longer than that of the American dog, and there is not the excess of hair of the American black type. Self-colors, such as all black, liver, and red are seen, as well as parti-colors, and roan colors of blue, red, orange, liver, and lemon.

The American type is perhaps the most beautiful of all the spaniels. He has a pronounced stop, rounded skull, large, rather prominent eyes, and long ears. The ears are set on at eye level, or lower, and the leather reaches to the muzzle.

The body is short, with a much broader chest than is true in other spaniels. The top line slopes from the withers to the croup. The stifle angulation is pronounced, sometimes excessively so in blacks. A serious fault in many is a weak, spreading foot, with thin pads.

The American Cocker is divided into three varieties, based primarily on color. These are black; any other solid color, but including black and tan; and parti-colors. The blacks, generally, have a much more profuse coat and feathering than the others. Weight limits for all American types are 22 to 28 pounds.

Good Cockers have a merry, effervescent disposition which is a distinct mark of the breed. But, in some, shyness and hysteria were once manifest to a serious degree. Responsible Cocker breeders, however, have been waging an apparently successful battle to eliminate these character faults.

The history of the Cocker as a breed starts with the birth of Mr. Farrow's Obo, June 14, 1879. Obo is generally considered to have been the first modern Cocker. He was by Fred, out of Betty, weighed 22 pounds, and was 10 inches tall.

Four years after Obo's birth, Cockers were granted a separate classification at British dog shows, and in 1893, separate Cocker registrations were made in the English stud book. The first field trial was given in 1899, and these have continued to grow in popularity in England ever since.

On the whole, the great English Cocker families of the early days played an equal role in the United States and Canada. For instance, many of Obo's descendants were sent to America. Braeside Bob, one of these, is sometimes called the father of the American Cocker.

Both the Ware and Rivington kennels in England bred both Springers and Cockers. Both sent great dogs to America. Among the famous Rivington Cockers were Rivington Signal, Rivington Red Coat, Rivington Blue Gown, and Rivington Sam. The latter, though a Cocker, founded one of the strongest Springer lines.

From 1850 to 1900 in America, hunting with span-

Cocker Spaniel. Photo by Paul Toppelstein.

iels went out of favor. After the organization of the American Spaniel Club in 1881, some efforts were made to bring hunting Cockers into favor again. But these efforts failed, and for many years Cockers remained merely pets and bench dogs.

Among the early bench Champions can be mentioned: Hornell Dandy, 1881; Hornell Silk (by Obo), (1882); Black Pete (by Obo, Jr.), 1885; and Bambo (by Bob Obo), 1890.

The first championship field trial given in the United States was sponsored by the Cocker Spaniel Field Trial Club of America at Verbank, N.Y., in 1924. The judges were William Hutchinson and A. Clinton Wilmerding, the latter one of the founders of the American Spaniel Club.

Because of the backing of such people as Colonel H. S. Nielson, Elias Vail, Ralph Craig, Herman Mellenthin, Leonard Buck, and Ella B. Moffitt, Cocker trials began to prosper. These people selected top stock for training, with the result that many dual champions were made. The first dual, or bench and field, champion was My Own High Time. Others include such noted performers as Live Oak Spring Storm, Miller's Esquire, Don Pablo from Jourdains, and Rowcliffe Hill Billy.

At first, the trials were mainly in the East. This section produced such great field dogs as Latch Up George, Rowcliffe Blue Streak, Rowcliffe Bangaway, High Time Elcova, Horsford Delight Em, and the famous Blue Waters Magnificent. All were field champions.

The Midwest produced Jimmie, a field champion of extraordinary class but of unknown pedigree, and field champions Ravine Top Freckles, Stipe's Cricket, and Miller's Esquire.

On the Pacific Coast a great many top performers have been produced. Two of these, field champions Nugget and Bunny, could not be registered. Nugget, however, ran for seven years and won five open all-age stakes. Other noted field champions from this section include Roanfeather Argonaut, Isleton Boy, Rex of Windsor, Camino Boy, Aubrey Squib, and Chequamegan Laddie. The last three are English champions.

Just before World War II, a number of English Cockers were imported. Many of them made field championships here or produced them. In this group are Rivington Bean, Cinar's Chuck, Cinar's Dash, Cinar's Ring, and Cinar's Spot of Earlsmoor.

The war almost mortally injured Cocker trials. Only a couple of trials were held. The old dogs died off, and the dilemma of the cockerites was that they no longer could buy field trial strains. However, Ralph Craig, as head of the American Spaniel Club led that organization in an aggressive policy of rebuilding.

Arguments as to the value of field trials are never ending. But there can be no doubt that, so far as Cockers are concerned, they are of tremendous value. They prove performance, set standards for performance, help to identify blood lines which will produce top field dogs, and generally stimulate the breeding for character.

An argument against field trials is that, because of the competitive angle, performance standards are set far above the reach of the amateur trainer-owner, and even above the requirements for top hunters. There is considerable truth to these points as far as field trials in general are concerned. But, probably because of the overshadowing of field Cockers by their bench brothers, this has never been true in Cocker trials. There simply have not been enough performers to make it true. Even if true, however, the great advantages conferred by the trials would outweigh the disadvantages.

All the spaniels—including the Springer, Cocker, Clumber, Sussex, Welsh Springer, and Brittany—are called bird dogs. This assumes that they search the air currents for the body scents of birds, in contrast to the hounds which search out and follow trail scents. The majority do hunt by locating body scents in the air. But because hounds, or dogs with hound-trailing proclivities, were sometimes bred with the spaniels, many do have a trailing, rather than a body

scent, nose. This explains why a good flusher is not always a good finder.

The dog who hunts by body scent is at an advantage when working into the wind, or when game is "setting." If the wind is right, he may have equal chances of locating and flushing moving game. The dog with the trailing nose is, however, at a heavy disadvantage except when game is moving and he can pick up a trail. He has a distinct advantage when he is after the "runner," as, for instance, the pheasant which has been knocked down but can still run.

The best performers are those dogs which learn by experience to use their noses both ways. Many of the better Cockers and Springers have this ability. But the truly observing spaniel owner will note which dogs have the desired body-scenting nose, and will breed for this quality.

It is the tendency among sportsmen to buy from a pedigree. This is excellent as far as it goes, since, if the parents were field winners, most of the offspring may be expected to have some field ability. But the puppy buyer does not want to be the one to get the non-performer in the litter.

In general, spaniels inherit certain aptitudes which are necessary for high class workmanship in the field. By aptitude is meant an innate or inherited proficiency in doing a certain thing. These appear in varying numbers in Cockers and Springers. Here are some of them: Water going, briar hitting, retrieving, proper carry of the retrieve, soft mouth, capacity for training, bird hunting, and fence crashing.

It is easily observable that some spaniels will dive into water no matter how rough or cold. Others enter grudgingly, and some refuse entirely. Puppies of six to eight weeks of age can be tested for this as easily as older dogs. The tester merely walks out into the water and calls the pups to follow. Some walk out and swim without hesitation. Others will not enter.

Spaniels, or at any rate the good ones, are supreme workers in briars. Many of them will smash through cockleburrs or a patch of briars at top speed, come out bleeding, and hit the next patch just as hard. While few want their dogs so badly matted or torn up this way, the briar-shy dog is nearly useless, particularly in the Midwest.

Many dogs seem to retrieve naturally. The only training they require is to be taught "must." Others resent retrieving and are taught only with difficulty. Most spaniels belong to the former class. Some of the better ones also appear to have a very definite aptitude for carrying. They never seem to be able to pick up a bird incorrectly, while others always have to lay the bird down several times in order to get a better grip.

Capacity for training is an important feature in the spaniel. Most of them are highly alert, give you their complete attention, and take correction in stride. Most spaniels are primarily interested in flying things. If spaniel pups and Beagle pups are placed in the same run, the spaniels will show interest in every

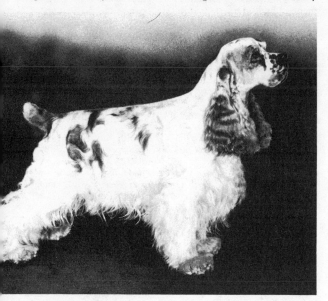

Cocker Spaniel—Parti-color. Photo by Evelyn M. Shafer.

Cocker Spaniel Pups. Photo by Evelyn M. Shafer.

flying thing, whereas the Beagles will pay little attention. Their interests are on the ground.

Many spaniel pups are hard to contain behind a fence. They crawl through, or over, or under. In the field, you need never worry about them. They will always find a way to get through the fence, or up the creek bank, even when very young and inexperienced.

The prospective purchaser of a Cocker field dog, having little to go on in pedigree research, can make simple tests to prove almost all of these aptitudes before he buys. He can test the pups for water, briars, fences, curiosity, and courage in going out and away into cover, simply by taking them for a walk.

Description and Standards. The description and standards, adopted by the American Spaniel Club and approved by the American Kennel Club, follow:

SKULL: Well developed and rounded with no tendency toward flatness, or pronounced roundness, of the crown (dome). The forehead smooth, the eyebrows and stop clearly defined, the median line distinctly marked and gradually disappearing until lost rather more than halfway up to the crown. The bony structure surrounding the socket of the eye should be well chiseled; there should be no suggestion of fullness under the eyes or prominence in the cheeks which, like the sides of the muzzle, should present a smooth, cleancut appearance.

MUZZLE AND TEETH: To attain a well-proportioned head, which above all should be in balance with the rest of the dog, the distance from the tip of the nose to the stop, at a line drawn across the top of the muzzle between the front corners of the eyes, should approximate one-half the distance from the stop at this point up over the crown to the base of the skull. The muzzle should be broad and deep, with square, even jaws. The upper lip should be of sufficient depth to cover the lower jaw, presenting a square appearance. The teeth should be sound and regular and set at right angles to their respective jaws. The relation of the upper teeth to the lower should be that of scissors, with the inner surface of the upper in contact with the outer surface of the lower when the jaws are closed. The nose of sufficient size to balance the muzzle and foreface, with well-developed nostrils, and black in color in the blacks and black and tans; in the reds, buffs, livers, and parti-colors, and in the roans it may be black or brown, the darker coloring being preferable.

EYES: The eyeballs should be round and full and set in the surrounding tissue to look directly forward and give the eye a slightly almond-shaped appearance. The eye should be neither weak nor goggled. The expression should be intelligent, alert, soft and appealing. The color of the iris should be dark brown to black in the blacks, black and tans, buffs and creams, and in the darker shades of the parti-colors and roans. In the reds, dark hazel; in the livers, parti-colors, and roans of the lighter shades, not lighter than hazel, the darker the better.

EARS: Lobular, set on a line no higher than the lower part of the eye, the leather fine and extending to the nostrils, well clothed with long, silky, straight or wavy hair.

NECK AND SHOULDERS: The neck sufficiently long to allow the nose to reach the ground easily, muscular and free from pendulous "throatiness." It should rise strongly from the shoulders and arch slightly as it tapers to join the head. The shoulders deep, clean-cut and sloping without protrusion and so set that the upper points of the withers are at an angle which permits a wide spring of rib.

BODY: Its height at the withers should approximate the length from the withers to the set-on of tail. The chest deep, its lowest point no higher than the elbows, its front sufficiently wide for adequate heart and lung space, yet not so wide as to interfere with straightforward movement of the forelegs. Ribs deep and well-sprung throughout. Body short in the couplings and flank, with its depth at the flank somewhat less than at the last rib. Back strong and sloping evenly and slightly downward from the withers to the set-on of tail. Hips wide with quarters well-rounded and muscular. The body should appear short compact and firmly knit together, giving the impression of strength.

LEGS AND FEET: Forelegs, straight, strongly boned and muscular, and set close to the body well under the scapulae. The elbows well let down and turning neither in nor out. The pasterns short and strong. The hind legs strongly boned and muscled with well-turned stifles and powerful, clearly defined thighs. The hocks strong, well let down and paralleled when in motion and at rest. Feet compact, not spreading, round and firm, with deep, strong, horny pads and hair between the toes; they should turn neither in nor out.

TAIL: Set on and carried on a line with the topline of the back and when the dog is at work, its action should be incessant.

COAT: On head, short and fine. On body, flat or slightly wavy (never curly), silky in texture, of medium length, with enough undercoating to give protection. The ears, chest, abdomen, and posterior sides of the legs should be well feathered, but not so excessively as to hide the Cocker Spaniel's true lines and movement or affect his appearance and function as a sporting dog. Excessive coat or feathering shall be penalized.

COLOR AND MARKINGS: Blacks should be jet black; shadings of

brown or liver in the sheen of the coat shall not disqualify; but shall be penalized. A small amount of white on the chest and throat shall not disqualify, but shall be penalized; however, white in any other location shall disqualify.

Solid Colors Other Than Black should be of sound shade. Lighter coloring of the feathering, while not favored, shall not disqualify. A small amount of white on the chest and throat shall not disqualify, but shall be penalized; however, white in any other location shall disqualify.

In Parti-Colors, at least two definite colors appearing in clearly defined markings, distinctively distributed over the body, are essential. Primary color which is ninety (90%) per cent or more of the specimen, shall disqualify; secondary color or colors which are limited solely to one location shall disqualify. Roans are classified as Parti-Colors and may be of the accepted roaning patterns of mottled appearance or alternating colors of the hairs throughout the whole coat.

Black and Tan, shown under the Variety of Any Solid Color Other Than Black, should have definite tan markings on a jet black body, with clearly defined lines between the two colors. The tan markings should be distinct and plainly visible, and the shade of the tan markings may be from the lightest cream to the darkest red color. The quantity and location of the tan markings are the essence of this description. The amount of tan markings is restricted to ten (10%) per cent or less of the color of the specimen; tan markings in excess of ten (10%) per cent shall disqualify. A mere semblance of tan markings at the specified locations shall not disqualify, but shall be severely penalized; the total absence of tan markings at any of the specified locations, shall disqualify. The marking should be located as follows:

(1) A clear spot over each eye. (2) On the sides of the muzzle, and on the cheeks. (3) On the undersides of the ears. (4) On all feet and legs. (5) Under the tail.

Tan on the muzzle which extends up and over and joins, or tan on the cheeks which is solid, or tan on the feet which does not extend upward towards the knees and hock joints, shall not disqualify, but shall be penalized. Black hairs and penciling on the tan markings shall not be penalized, but tan markings which are "brindled" shall be penalized. A small amount of white on the chest and throat shall not disqualify, but shall be penalized. However, white in any other location shall disqualify.

HEIGHT: The ideal height at the withers for an adult dog should be 15 inches. The ideal height at the withers for an adult bitch should be 14 inches. The maximum height at the withers for a dog shall be 15½ inches and the maximum height at the withers for a bitch shall be 14½ inches. A dog or bitch whose height exceeds the maximum heights specified herein shall be disqualified. Note: Height is determined by a line perpendicular to the ground from the top of the shoulder blades, the dog standing naturally with its forelegs and the lower hind legs parallel to the line of measurement.

GENERAL DESCRIPTION: Embodying the foregoing we have a serviceable-looking dog with a refinedly chiseled head; standing on straight legs and well up at the shoulders; of compact body and wide, muscular quarters. The Cocker Spaniel's sturdy body, powerful quarters and strong, well-boned legs show him to be a dog capable of considerable speed combined with great endurance. Above all he must be free and merry, sound, well-balanced throughout, and in action show a keen inclination to work; equable in temperament with no suggestion of timidity.

SCALE OF POINTS: Points

Skull	8
Muzzle	10
Teeth	4
Eyes	6
Ears	3
Neck and Shoulders	15
Body	15
Legs	9
Feet	6
Stern	3
Coat	6
Color and Markings	3
Action	12
TOTAL	100

Disqualifications. Color and Markings: Blacks—White markings except on chest and throat. Solid Colors Other Than Black —White markings except on chest and throat. Parti-Colors— Ninety (90%) per cent or more of primary color; secondary color or colors limited solely to one location. Black and Tans— Tan markings in excess of ten (10%) per cent; total absence of tan markings at any of the specified locations; white markings except on chest and throat. Height: males over 15½ inches; females over 14½ inches.

(December 10, 1957)

ENGLISH COCKER SPANIEL

IN 1892 the Kennel Club (England) officially distinguished between the Springer Spaniel and the Cocker; this Cocker Spaniel was the English Cocker Spaniel. Even so, both Springers and Cockers appeared in those days often in the same litters, size of the individual dog alone being the dividing line between them. The English Cocker Spaniel Club of America was formed in 1935 to discourage the interbreeding of English and American Cocker varieties, there being too much confusion as to which Cocker was which. Many a large American Cocker, for instance, had entered the show ring as an English Cocker, for without genetic distinction no one really could say which were the legitimate contenders.

Under direction of Mrs. Geraldine R. Dodge, then president of the club, an extensive pedigree search was inaugurated to trace authentic English lines. Nevertheless, it was not until 1941 that the club found itself in a position to handle problems of selection and breeding authoritatively.

Despite this, the English Cocker was recognized as a separate breed by the Canadian Kennel Club in

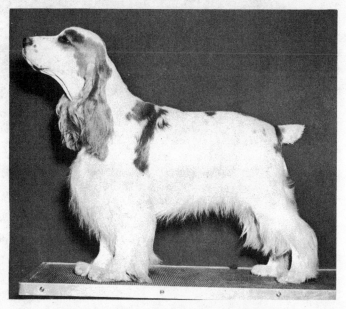

English Cocker Spaniel. Photo by Ken Smith.

1940 and by AKC in 1946. Not until 1947, however, did English Cocker registrations appear in the *Stud Book* under their own heading.

Certainly usually always the merriest of companions in either case, it is somewhat amusing to think that the chief distinction to be seen between these breeds is their height, this measurable at times as merely a fraction of an inch.

The Cocker Spaniel, presumably tending toward the larger English size, is considered the favorite breed in Denmark, and the favorite gundog in Holland, New Zealand, and Sweden. He is, of course, a highly popular dog in Great Britain.

Description and Standards. The description and standards, as adopted and approved by the American Kennel Club, follow.

GENERAL APPEARANCE: The English Cocker Spaniel is an attractive, active, merry sporting dog; with short body and strong limbs, standing well up at the withers. His movements are alive with energy; his gait powerful and frictionless. He is alert at all times, and the carriage of head and incessant action of his tail while at work give the impression that here is a dog that is not only bred for hunting but really enjoys it. He is well balanced, strongly built, full of quality and is capable of top speed combined with great stamina. His head imparts an individual stamp peculiar to him alone and has that brainy appearance expressive of the highest intelligence; and is in per-

fect proportion to his body. His muzzle is a most distinctive feature, being of correct conformation and in proportion to his skull.

CHARACTER: The character of the English Cocker is of extreme importance. His love and faithfulness to his master and household, his alertness and courage are characteristic. He is noted for his intelligence and merry disposition; not quarrelsome; and is a responsive and willing worker both in the field and as a companion.

HEAD: The skull and forehead should be well developed with no suggestion of coarseness, arched and slightly flattened on top when viewed both from the stop to the end of the skull as well as from ear to ear, and cleanly chiseled under the eyes. The proportion of the head desirable is approximately one-half for the muzzle and one-half for the skull. The muzzle should be square with a definite stop where it blends into the skull and in proportion with the width of the skull. As the English Cocker is primarily a sporting dog, the muzzle and jaws must be of sufficient strength and size to carry game; and the length of the muzzle should provide room for the development of the olfactory nerve to insure good scenting qualities, which require that the nose be wide and well developed. Nostrils black in color except in reds, livers, parti-colors and roans of the lighter shades, where brown is permissible, but black preferred. Lips should be square, full and free from flews. Teeth should be even and set squarely.

FAULTS: Muzzle too short or snipy. Jaw overshot or undershot. Lips snipy or pendulous. Skull too flat or too rounded, cheeky or coarse. Stop insufficient or exaggerated.

EYES: The eyes should be of medium size, full and slightly oval shaped; set squarely in skull and wide apart. Eyes must be dark brown except in livers and light parti-colors where hazel

English Cocker Spaniel. As well as the American Cocker Spaniels, some of the English Cockers also have solid black coats (not shown).

is permissible, but the darker the better. The general expression should be intelligent, alert, bright and merry.

FAULTS: Light, round or protruding eyes. Conspicuous haw.

EARS: Lobular; set low and close to the head; leather fine and extending at least to the nose, well covered with long, silky, straight or slightly wavy hair.

FAULTS: Set or carried too high; too wide at the top; insufficient feathering; positive curls or ringlets.

NECK: Long, clean and muscular; arched towards the head; set cleanly into sloping shoulders.

FAULTS: Short; thick, with dewlap or excessive throatiness.

BODY: Close coupled, compact and firmly knit, giving the impression of great strength without heaviness. Depth of brisket should reach to the elbow, sloping gradually upward to the loin. Ribs should spring gradually to middle of body, tapering to back ribs which should be of good depth and extend well back.

FAULTS: Too long and lacking depth; insufficient spring of rib; barrel rib.

SHOULDERS AND CHEST: Shoulders sloping and fine; chest deep and well developed but not too wide and round to interfere with the free action of the forelegs.

FAULTS: Straight or loaded shoulders.

BACK AND LOIN: Back short and strong. Length of back from withers to tail-set should approximate height from ground to withers. Height of the dog at the withers should be greater than the height at the hip joint, providing a gradual slope between these points. Loin short and powerful, slightly arched.

FAULTS: Too low at withers; long, sway-back or roach back; flat or narrow loin; exaggerated tuck-up.

FORELEGS: Straight and strong with bone nearly equal in size from elbow to heel; elbows set close to the body with free action from shoulders; pasterns short, straight and strong.

FAULTS: Shoulders loose; elbows turned in or out; legs bowed or set too close or too wide apart; knees knuckled over; light bone.

FEET: Size in proportion to the legs; firm, round and catlike with thick pads and strong toes.

FAULTS: Too large, too small; spreading or splayed.

HINDQUARTERS: The hips should be rounded; thighs broad; well developed and muscular, giving abundance of propelling power. Stifles strong and well bent. Hock to pad moderately short, strong and well let down.

FAULTS: Excessive angulation; lightness of bone; stifle too short; hocks too long or turned in or out.

TAIL: Set on to conform with the topline of the back. Merry in action.

FAULTS: Set too low; habitually carried too high; too short or too long.

COLOR: Various. In self colors a white shirt frill is undesirable. In parti-colors, the coloring must be broken on the body and be evenly distributed. No large portion of any one color should exist. White should be shown on the saddle. A dog of any solid color with white feet and chest is not a parti-color. In roans it is desirable that the white hair should be distributed over the body, the more evenly the better. Roans come in various colors: blue, liver, red, orange and lemon. In black and tans the coat should be black; tan spots over the eyes, tan on the sides of the muzzle, on the throat and chest, on forelegs from the knees to the toes and on the hind legs on the inside of the legs, also on the stifle and extending from the hock to the toes.

FAULTS: White feet are undesirable in any specimen of self color.

COAT: On head short and fine; on body flat or slightly wavy and silky in texture. Should be of medium length with enough undercoating to give protection. The English Cocker should be well feathered but not so profusely as to hide the true lines or interfere with his field work.

FAULTS: Lack of coat; too soft, curly or wiry. Excessive trimming to change the natural appearance and coat should be discouraged.

HEIGHT: Ideal heights at withers: Males, 16 to 17 inches; females, 15 to 16 inches. Deviations to be severely penalized but not disqualified.

WEIGHT: The most desirable weights: Males, 28 pounds to 34 pounds; Females, 26 pounds to 32 pounds. Proper physical conformation and balance should be considered more important than weight alone.

(September 13, 1955)

ENGLISH SPRINGER SPANIEL

THE ENGLISH Springer Spaniel is a medium-sized hunting dog, weighing from 45 to 55 pounds, and standing 18 to 22 inches tall at the shoulder. He has a dense but not curly coat, long ears set on at eye level, and a docked tail. His colors are black and white, liver and white, often with tickings of either color, and blue or liver roan.

The dog is relatively heavy-boned. His feet are webbed for swimming and work in swamps, with well-arched toes and deep, horny pads. Viewed from the side, the dog should be square, from the withers to the ground, and from the withers to the set of the tail.

The term "spaniel" comes from the Roman term for Spain-Hispania. Dr. Caius, an English dog authority who wrote about 1570, says the English took the name of "Hispaniolus." But it could have come to us from the French "Chiens du Espagnol," meaning "dogs of Spain." Early English writers used Spagnell, Spainell, and Spanyell.

Dr. Caius, and others, divided the spaniels into Land Spaniels and Water Spaniels. Gradually the former became known as Springers, those who flushed game for the Greyhounds or the falcon, and Setting Spaniels, those which pointed out setting game, or kept it setting for the net. Of the Springers, Dr. Caius said, "they have no special names but take their names from the birds which they naturally pursue." Hence, the origin of Cockers, "cocking spaniels," which were used for woodcock hunting. The Setting Spaniels became our Setters.

Though the early writers said the spaniels came from Spain, this is by no means certain. Indeed, the long-eared spaniel may have been an established type the world over. The Cyriote Collection in the Metropolitan Museum has a figure of a dog which must have been a spaniel, so that the type may be as old as 3000 B.C. And one of the first white men to visit North America remarked that the Indians had spaniel dogs. There is a single reference to spaniels in the Irish laws, about A.D. 17, and later in Welsh law. But we have no means of knowing whether or not these were spaniels as we know them.

Gaston de Foix is the first to tell us of the work of spaniels. Gaston was a French nobleman who kept as many as a thousand hunting dogs in his kennels.

About 1387, he wrote one of the most famous hunting books of all time, the *Livre de Chasse*.

In it he tells us of "hounds for the hawk and [or] spaniels." He says the dogs quarter about in front of their masters, sometimes becoming so active as to lead the hounds astray. He praised the dogs for their ability in water, and their efficiency at retrieving ducks which had dived under water.

Two hundred years later, Dr. Caius wrote: "Some pursue birds only on land, and start the bird, following it up openly and barking, or simply point it out without noise. . . . All are nearly all over white. If they have spots, these are red and scarce and big. There is a red and also a black variety."

In 1637, another English sporting authority, Aldrovandus, gives a description of a "spaniel dog with floppy ears, the chest, belly, and feet white, picked out with black, the rest of the body black."

From about 1800 on, spaniels were divided about as follows: Those under 14 pounds were called comforter spaniels, or lap spaniels, Spaniels from 14 to 28 pounds were called Cockers. Those over 28 pounds, with 35 about average, were called Springers, English Spaniels, or Field Spaniels.

At least among the Cockers and larger spaniels, bloodlines were not kept separate. Moreover, a dog might be called a Cocker until he outgrew the Cocker weight limits, after which he would be called a Springer, Clumber, or Field Spaniel, depending on his looks. But about 1812, the Boughey family of Aqualate, Shropshire, began to keep a pure line of Springer Spaniels. Many modern Springers trace back to Mop and Frisk, who lived in that early period. In the Norfolk hunting country, a fairly typical Springer was developing as the Norfolk Spaniel.

The modern history of the Springer Spaniel begins on January 3, 1899, when the Sporting Spaniel Club gave its first field trial on the estate of William Arkwright of Sutton Scarsdale. Arkwright and Elias Bishop judged. A second trial was held on December 12, 1899, on the estate of B. J. Warwick. At neither trial did a Springer place among the first three. But at succeeding trials, the larger and faster dogs began to whip the Clumbers and the Cockers, and those loosely called Field Spaniels. Agitation therefore grew for a separate classification. This came in 1903 when Springers were first exhibited at English bench shows. F. Winton Smith's famous field dog, Beechgrove Will, became the first male champion, and Harry Jones' Fansome, the first bitch to win a championship.

Sportsmen now combed the British Isles for dogs which looked like Springers. These were registered as Springers, though previously they might have run in trials under other breed names. Sometimes, as in the case of Beechgrove Will, they had descendants which were registered as still other breeds. Despite this variable background, it is an extraordinary fact that all modern American and Canadian champions, both

English Springer Spaniel. Photo by Evelyn M. Shafer.

bench and field, trace back to six patriarchs. These were Sam, Bruce, Rivington Sam, Horsford Honour, Dash of Hagley, and Velox Powder.

Three great British dogs which set up powerful families in North America were the the bench and field (dual) champions, Flint of Avendale and Horsford Hetman, and the field trial champion, Rivington Sam. Other field champions who have had the greatest influence on American field dogs were Dalshangan Dandy Boy, Rex of Avendale, Cally Podge, Spy O'Vara, half a dozen of the famous Banchory dogs, and Bryngarw Firearm.

The old liver and white or black and white "English Spaniels" had been popular in America up to the period of the Civil War. After that, the breed disappeared. It seems probable that the reason was the opening up of the great quail hunting territories of the Midwest. On the Great Plains, long-legged, wide-ranging dogs were required to locate the coveys, and staunch points were necessary to hold the birds until the hunters could come up. Thus the Spaniel gave way to the Pointer and Setter.

The upsurge of the Springer Spaniel in America, however, was due to the rise of the pheasant as the chief game bird in the North. In the Southern quail territories, Springers are still few in number. Only the best of the Pointers and Setters can pin and hold a pheasant, since this bird loves to scurry off. This continued running away from point corrupts many an otherwise satisfactory bird dog, who suddenly begins to break his points and chase.

But the Springer is a flushing dog. He quarters his ground, stays within gun range, and flushes the pheasant to his master's gun. Thus the running tactics of the pheasant fit into his natural hunting procedure.

It is as hard to teach a Springer to drop to flush and shot as it is to teach a Pointer to hold a point. But a Springer can be very useful gundog even though he does not drop to flush, whereas a ranging Pointer who will not hold a point is useless.

It is probable, too, that restricted hunting areas, by reason of the increasing population of the country, have played a part in the advance of the Springer. Short hunting fields are an advantage to a dog whose natural hunting range is only the reach of his master's shotgun, whereas they are a disadvantage to a Pointer or Setter, who is a wide-ranging dog by long usage and nature.

On the whole, the Springer is easily trained. He quarters naturally, and is taught to work to a gun without difficulty. The majority inherit an aptitude for retrieving, and learn to mark the fallen bird with great rapidity. They are readily adaptable to other hunting besides pheasant, and are superb workers in briar patches and swamps.

Certainly many Springers are kept because of their all-around ability. This is particularly true of those hunters who desire a combination duck and pheasant dog. Springers cannot stand icy waters as some of the other retrievers do, but they will take all the duck work the average hunter cares to, or can, give them.

English Springer Spaniel—Nat'l. Fld. Trial Ch. Micklewood Scud. (Owner: Mrs. Julia Armour, Chicago, Ill.) Photo by Evelyn M. Shafer.

Many of these dogs inherit great water-going aptitude.

Pure-bred Springers came to America as early as 1907. But they did not catch on here until Eudore Chevrier of Winnipeg, Manitoba, began to import and train them in huge numbers about 1921. Chevrier is credited with importing more dogs, particularly Springers, than any other kennel. He sold these dogs trained, or partly trained, all over North America.

In the United States, Freeman Lloyd interested a group of New York sportsmen in the breed. The English Springer Spaniel Field Trial Association was formed in 1924, and held its first trial at Fisher's Island that year. Aughrim Flash won that year, and the next. The annual Fisher's Island trials are still the "blue riband" of Springerdom.

First American field trial champions were Tedwys's Trex and Aughrim Flashing in 1929. Trex was an English field trial champion, and became an American dual champion. Those early years in the East produced three more dual champions. Fast, Bozo's Bar Mate, and Green Valley Punch.

Other noted field champions which were produced on the Eastern circuit were Fleet and Flight of Falcon Hill, Trex and Squire of Chancefield, and Indian, English, and American Field Trial Champion Wake's Wager of Greenfair.

The Midwest developed its own field trial circuit which, at first, was not recognized by the Eastern clubs in national championship competition. However, in the period from 1935 to 1946 they swept everything before them. Perhaps the greatest of these dogs, and perhaps the greatest ever to run in this country, was Solo Event. She was owned by James Simpson, Jr., who imported her; Clifford Wallace trained her.

Field trials on the Pacific Coast have grown steadily in importance. Famous early field dogs in the Far West include Dual Champion King Lion, and Field

Champions Elysian Eric and Elysian Echo. Others include Field Champions Russet of Middlefield, Pendleton Static, and Pendleton Rocket.

In spaniel trials, dogs are put down in braces. Brace mates work parallel courses each about 50 yards wide. They must not interfere with each other. Live, full-winged pheasants are "planted" ahead of the dogs, and in this manner each dog is given an equal chance to find, flush, and retrieve game.

Dogs are expected to drop to flush and shot, or to the shot of the other dog's flush. Each dog is followed by a handler, gunner, and judge. The gunner gives the bird a long lead and then brings it down. The dog must drop to flush and must stay there until the judge orders the retrieve. The dog is scored on his ability to mark the fall, to follow the bird if it is a runner, and to bring it quickly to hand.

When all dogs have worked, those dogs which have shown merit are called back to work under the other judge on the other course. A third and fourth series may be called when needed. Dogs are thrown out for breaking to flush or shot, for hard mouth and other errors. Water tests are given, though by no means as difficult as conducted for the Midwest dogs.

A dog becomes a field champion when he has won two stakes at which there were sufficient starters to qualify as a championship trial. At first, six starters were sufficient. The number jumped to ten, but then fell back to eight during the war years.

The majority of Springer Spaniels are registered in the American Kennel Club Stud Book. A few however, are registered in the Field Dog Stud Book.

Description and Standards. The description and standards follow.

GENERAL APPEARANCE AND TYPE: The English Springer Spaniel is a medium-size sporting dog with a neat, compact body, and a docked tail. His coat is moderately long, glossy, usually liver and white or black and white, with feathering on his legs, ears, chest and brisket. His pendulous ears, soft gentle expression, sturdy build and friendly wagging tail proclaim him unmistakably a member of the ancient family of spaniels. He is above all a well proportioned dog, free from exaggeration, nicely balanced in every part. His carriage is proud and upstanding, body deep, legs strong and muscular with enough length to carry him with ease. His short level back, well developed thighs, good shoulders, excellent feet, suggest power, endurance, agility. Taken as a whole he looks the part of a dog that can go and keep going under difficult hunting conditions, and moreover he enjoys what he is doing. At his best he is endowed with style, symmetry, balance, enthusiasm and is every inch a sporting dog of distinct spaniel character, combining beauty and utility. To be penalized: Those lacking true English Springer type in conformation, expression, or behavior.

TEMPERAMENT: The typical Springer is friendly, eager to please, quick to learn, willing to obey. In the show ring he should exhibit poise, attentiveness, tractability, and should permit himself to be examined by the judge without resentment or cringing. To be penalized: Excessive timidity, with due allowance for puppies and novice exhibits. But no dog to receive a ribbon if he behaves in vicious manner toward handler or judge. Aggressiveness toward other dogs in the ring *not* to be construed as viciousness.

SIZE AND PROPORTION: The Springer is built to cover rough ground with agility and reasonable speed. He should be kept to medium size—neither too small nor too large and heavy to do the work for which he is intended. The ideal shoulder height for dogs is 20 inches; for bitches, 19 inches. Length of topline (the distance from top of the shoulders to the root of the tail) should be approximately equal to the dog's shoulder height—never longer than his height—and not appreciably less. The dog too long in body, especially when long in loin, tires easily and lacks the compact outline characteristic of the breed. Equally undesirable is the dog too short in body for the length of his legs, a condition that destroys his balance and restricts the gait.

Weight is dependent on the dog's other dimensions: a 20-inch dog, well proportioned, in good condition should weigh about 49-55 pounds. The resulting appearance is a well-knit, sturdy dog with good but not too heavy bone, in no way coarse or ponderous. To be penalized: Over-heavy specimens, cloddy in build. Leggy individuals, too tall for their length and substance. Over-size or under-size specimens (those more than one inch under or over the breed ideal).

COLOR AND COAT: Color may be liver or black with white markings; liver and white (or black and white) with tan markings; blue or liver roan; or predominantly white with tan, black or liver markings. On ears, chest, legs and belly the Springer is nicely furnished with a fringe of feathering (of moderate heaviness). On his head, front or forelegs, and below hocks on front of hindlegs the hair is short and fine. The body coat is flat or wavy, of medium length, sufficiently dense to be water-proof, weather-proof and thorn-proof. The texture fine and the hair should have the clean, glossy, live appearance indicative of good health. It is legitimate to trim about head, feet, ears; to remove dead hair; to thin and shorten excess feathering particularly from the hocks to the feet and elsewhere as required to give a smart, clean appearance. To be penalized: Rough, curly coat. Over-trimming especially of the body coat. Any chopped, barbered or artificial effect. Excessive feathering that destroys the clean outline desirable in a sporting dog. Off colors such as lemon, red or orange not to place.

HEAD: The head is impressive without being heavy. Its beauty lies in a combination of strength and refinement. It is important that the size and proportion be in balance with the rest of the dog. Viewed in profile the head should appear approximately the same length as the neck and should blend with the body in substance. The skull (upper head) to be of medium length, fairly broad, flat on top, slightly rounded at the sides and back. The occiput bone inconspicuous, rounded rather than peaked or angular. The foreface (head in front of the eyes) approximately the same length as the skull, and in harmony as to width and general character. Looking down on the head the muzzle to appear to be about one-half the width of the skull. As the skull rises from the foreface it makes a brow or "stop," divided by a groove or fluting between the eyes. This groove continues upward and gradually disappears as it reaches the middle of the forehead. The amount of "stop" can best be described as moderate. It must not be a pronounced feature as in the Clumber Spaniel. Rather it is a subtle rise where the muzzle blends into the upper head, further emphasized by the groove and by the position and shape of the eyebrows which should be well-developed. The stop, eyebrow and the chiseling of the bony structure around the eye sockets contribute to the Springer's beautiful and characteristic expression.

Viewed in profile the topline of the skull and the muzzle lie in two approximately parallel planes. The nasal bone should be straight, with no inclination downward toward the tip of the nose which gives a down-faced look so undesirable in this breed. Neither should the nasal bone be concave resulting in a "dish-faced" profile; nor convex giving the dog a Roman nose. The jaws to be of sufficient length to allow the dog to carry game easily; fairly square, lean, strong, and even, (neither undershot nor overshot). The upper lip to come down full and rather square to cover the line of the lower jaw, but lips not to be pendulous nor exaggerated. The nostrils, well opened and broad, liver color or black depending on the color of the coat. Flesh-colored ("Dudley noses") or spotted ("butterfly noses") are undesirable. The cheeks to be flat, (not rounded, full or thick) with nice chiseling under the eyes. To be penalized: Oval, pointed or heavy skull. Cheeks prominently rounded, thick and protruding. Too much or too little stop. Over heavy muzzle. Muzzle too short, too thin, too narrow. Pendulous slobbery lips. Under- or over-shot jaws—a very serious fault, to be heavily penalized.

TEETH: The teeth should be strong, clean, not too small; and when the mouth is closed the teeth should meet in an even bite or a close scissors bite (the lower incisors touching the inside of the upper incisors). To be penalized: Any deviation from above description. One or two teeth slightly out of line not to be considered a serious fault, but irregularities due to faulty jaw formation to be severely penalized.

EYES: More than any other feature the eyes contribute to the Springer's appeal. Color, placement, size influence expression and attractiveness. The eyes to be of medium size, neither small, round, full and prominent, nor bold and hard in expression. Set rather well apart and fairly deep in their sockets. The color of the iris to harmonize with the color of the coat, pre-

ferably a good dark hazel in the liver dogs and black or deep brown in the black and white specimens. The expression to be alert, kindly, trusting. The lids, tight with little or no haw showing. To be penalized: Eyes yellow or brassy in color or noticeably lighter than the coat. Sharp expression indicating unfriendly or suspicious nature. Loose droopy lids. Prominent haw (the third eyelid or membrane in the inside corner of the eye).

EARS: The correct ear set is on a level with the line of the eye; on the side of the skull and not too far back. The flaps to be long and fairly wide, hanging close to the cheeks, with no tendency to stand up or out. The leather, thin, approximately long enough to reach the tip of the nose. To be penalized: Short round ears. Ears set too high or too low or too far back on the head.

NECK: The neck to be moderately long, muscular, slightly arched at the crest gradually blending into sloping shoulders.

Nothing hesitant about the retrieving spirit in these lively Springers! (Owner: Maxwell Riddle, Ravenna, Ohio)

Not noticeably upright nor coming into the body at an abrupt angle. To be penalized: Short neck, often the sequence to steep shoulders. Concave neck, sometimes called ewe neck or upside down neck (the opposite of arched). Excessive throatiness.

BODY: The body to be well coupled, strong, compact; the chest deep but not so wide or round as to interfere with the action of the front legs; the brisket sufficiently developed to reach to the level of the elbows. The ribs fairly long, springing gradually to the middle of the body then tapering as they approach the end of the ribbed section. The back (section) between the withers and loin) to be straight and strong, with no tendency to dip or roach. The loins to be strong, short; a slight arch over loins and hip bones. Hips nicely rounded, blending smoothly into hind legs. The resulting topline slopes *very gently* from withers to tail—the loins from withers to back descending without a sharp drop; the back practically level; arch over hips somewhat lower than the withers; croup sloping gently to base of tail; tail carried to follow the natural line of the body. The bottom line, starting on a level with the elbows, to continue backward with almost no up-curve until reaching the end of the ribbed section, then a more noticeable up-curve to the flank, but not enough to make the dog appear small waisted or "tucked up." To be penalized: Body too shallow, indicating lack of brisket. Ribs too flat sometimes due to immaturity. Ribs too round (barrel-shaped), hampering the gait. Sway-back (dip in back), indicating weakness or lack of muscular develpment, particularly to be seen when dog is in action and viewed from the side. Roach back (too much arch over loin and extending forward into middle section). Croup falling away too sharply; or croup too high—unsightly faults, detrimental to outline and good movement. Topline sloping sharply, indicating steep withers (straight shoulder placement) and a too low tail-set.

TAIL: The Springer's tail is an index both to his temperament and his conformation. Merry tail action is characteristic. The proper set is somewhat low following the natural line of the croup. The carriage should be nearly horizontal, slightly elevated when dog is excited. Carried straight up is untypical of the breed. The tail should not be docked too short and should be well fringed with wavy feather. It is legitimate to shape and shorten the feathering but enough should be left to blend with the dog's other furnishings. To be penalized: Tail habitually upright. Tail set too high or too low. Clamped down tail (indicating timidity or undependable temperament, even less to be desired than the tail carried too gaily).

FOREQUARTERS: Efficient movement in front calls for proper shoulders. The blades sloping back to form an angle with the forearm of approximately 90 degrees which permits the dog to swing his forelegs forward in an easy manner. Shoulders (fairly close together at the tips) to lie flat and mold smoothly into the contour of the body. The forelegs to be straight with the same degree of size to the foot. The bone, strong, slightly flattened, not too heavy or round. The knee, straight, almost flat; the pasterns short, strong; elbows close to the body with free action from the shoulders. To be penalized: Shoulders set at a steep angle limiting the stride. Loaded shoulders (the blades standing out from the body by overdevelopment of the muscles). Loose elbows, crooked legs. Bone too light or too coarse and heavy. Weak pasterns that let down the feet at a pronounced angle.

HINDQUARTERS: The Springer should be shown in hard muscular condition, well developed in hips and thighs and the whole rear assembly should suggest strength and driving power. The hip joints to be set rather wide apart and the hips nicely rounded. The thighs broad and muscular; the stifle joint strong and moderately bent. The hock joint somewhat rounded, not small and sharp in contour, and moderately angulated. Leg from hock joint to foot pad, short and strong with good bone structure. When viewed from the rear the hocks to be parallel whether the dog is standing or in motion. To be penalized: Too little or too much angulation. Narrow, undeveloped thighs. Hocks too short or too long (a proportion of ⅓ the distance from hip joint to foot is ideal). Flabby muscles. Weakness of joints.

FEET: The feet to be round, or slightly oval, compact, well arched, medium size with thick pads, well feathered between the toes. Excess hair to be removed to show the natural shape and size of the foot. To be penalized: Thin, open or splayed feet (flat with spreading toes). Hare foot (long, rather narrow foot).

MOVEMENT: In judging the Springer there should be emphasis on proper movement which is the final test of a dog's conformation and soundness. Prerequisite to good movement is balance of the front and rear assemblies. The two must match in angulation and muscular development if the gait is to be smooth and effortless. Good shoulders laid back at an angle that permits a long stride are just as essential as the excellent rear quarters that provide the driving power. When viewed from the front the dog's legs should appear to swing forward in a free and easy manner, with no tendency for the feet to cross over or interfere with each other. Viewed from the rear the hocks should drive well under the body following on a line with the forelegs, the rear legs parallel, neither too widely nor too closely spaced. Seen from the side the Springer should exhibit a good, long forward stride, without high-stepping or wasted motion. To be penalized: Short choppy stride, mincing steps with up and down movement, hopping. Moving with forefeet wide, giving roll or swing to body. Weaving or crossing of fore or hind feet. Cow-hocks—hocks turning in toward each other.

In judging the English Springer Spaniel the overall picture is a primary consideration. It is urged that the judge look for type which includes general appearance, outline and temperament and also for soundness especially as seen when the dog is in motion. Inasmuch as the dog with a smooth easy gait must be reasonably sound and well balanced he is to be highly regarded in the show ring, however, not to the extent of forgiving him for not looking like an English Springer Spaniel. A quite untypical dog, leggy, foreign in head and expression, may move well. But he should not be placed over a good all-round specimen that has a minor fault in movement. It should be remembered that the English Springer Spaniel is first and foremost a sporting dog of the spaniel family and he must look and behave and move in character.

(June 12, 1956)

FIELD SPANIEL

ONCE BRED with such heavy bone and length of body as to become almost a grotesque caricature of a spaniel, the Field Spaniel has, in more recent years, settled into a type which makes this breed a workmanlike dog of great beauty.

Phineas Bullock of England was a great fancier of the Field Spaniel and dogs of his breeding possessed tremendous length and exaggerated lowness to the ground. The efforts of Mortimer Smith, however, have been largely responsible for developing this breed, which was originally established by repeated crosses of the "Welsh Cocker" with the Sussex Spaniel, into a well-balanced, practical, and handsome dog. With his present conformation he is a dog of agility, speed, and endurance. The Field Spaniel is level-headed, intelligent, easily trained, and possesses great perseverance. The breed has never been very popular in America.

According to one newspaper account, no Field Spaniels were entered at all in the Madison Square Garden dog shows during the years 1930 to 1967, inclusive. Field Spaniels were also referred to as extinct in the U.S. from 1940 until very recently, their number dwindling to only six in 1958, these latter all being in Great Britain. Through British breeding efforts, the half dozen have increased to some 20 to 30, or thereabouts, only two or three of which were shipped to U.S. buyers.

In the U.S., Mr. Richard H. Squier of Randolph, Ohio, has succeeded in efforts to continue the breed through raising puppies from Field Spaniels imported from England, and three of his dogs have won AKC championships. (See accompanying photo.)

Description and Standards. The description and standards, by courtesy of AKC follow.

HEAD: Should be quite characteristic of this grand sporting dog, as that of the Bulldog, or the Bloodhound; its very stamp and countenance should at once convey the conviction of high breeding, character and nobility; skull well developed, with a distinctly elevated occipital tuberosity, which, above all, gives the character alluded to; not too wide across the muzzle, long and lean, never snipy or squarely cut, and in profile curving gradually from nose to throat; lean beneath the eyes—a thickness here gives coarseness to the whole head. The great length of muzzle gives surface for the free development of the olfactory nerve, and thus secures the highest possible scenting powers.

EYES: Not too full, but not small, receding or overhung, color dark hazel or brown, or nearly black, according to the color of the dog. Grave in expression and showing no haw.

EARS: Moderately long and wide, sufficiently clad with nice Setterlike feather and set low. They should fall in graceful folds, the lower parts curling inwards and backwards.

NECK: Long, strong and muscular, so as to enable the dog to retrieve his game without undue fatigue.

BODY: Should be of moderate length, well ribbed up to a good strong loin, straight or slightly arched, never slack.

NOSE: Well developed, with good open nostrils.

SHOULDERS AND CHEST: Former long, sloping and well set back, thus giving great activity and speed; latter deep and well developed, but not too round and wide.

BACK AND LOIN: Very strong and muscular.

HINDQUARTERS: Strong and muscular. The stifles should be moderately bent, and not twisted either in or out.

STERN: Well set on and carried low, if possible below the level of the back, in a straight line or with a slight downward inclination, never elevated above the back, and in action always kept low, nicely fringed with wavy feather of silky texture.

FORELEGS: Should be of fairly good length, with straight, clean, flat bone, and nicely feathered. Immense bone is no longer desirable.

FEET: Not too small; round, with short soft hair between the toes; good, strong pads.

COAT: Flat or slightly waved, and never curled. Sufficiently dense to resist the weather, and not too short. Silky in texture, glossy and refined in nature, with neither duffleness on the one hand, nor curl or wiriness on the other. On the chest, under belly and behind the legs, there should be abundant feather, but never too much, especially below the hocks, and that of the right sort, *viz.* setterlike. The hindquarters should be similarly adorned.

COLOR: Black, liver, golden liver, mahogany red, or roan; or any one of these colors with tan over the eyes and on the cheeks, feet, and pasterns. Other colors, such as black and white, liver and white, red or orange and white, while not disqualifying, will be considered less desirable since the Field Spaniel should be clearly distinguished from the Springer Spaniel.

HEIGHT: About 18 inches to shoulder.

WEIGHT: From about 35 pounds to 50 pounds.

GENERAL APPEARANCE: That of a well-balanced, noble, upstanding sporting dog; built for activity and endurance. A grand combination of beauty and utility, and bespeaking of unusual docility and instinct.

SCALE OF POINTS:	Points
Head and jaw	15
Eyes	5
Ears	5
Neck	5
Body	10
Forelegs	10
Hind legs	10
Feet	10
Stern	10
Coat and feather	10
General appearance	10
TOTAL	100

(July 14, 1959)

IRISH WATER SPANIEL

THE IRISH WATER SPANIEL was one of the first retrievers to be imported into this country. Many old books mention this breed as used in the 1860's, but the first accurate record we have is in the first volume of the American Kennel Club published in 1878. Richard Tuttle of Chicago registered a male Irish Water Spaniel named Bob as number 1352 in the Stud Book of the National American Kennel Club, whcih later became the American Kennel Club. This dog was bred by J. H. Whitman, another Midwesterner, and was out of Queen by Sinbad.

There were 12 dogs and 11 bitches of this Irish breed registered in 1878. The only other retrievers registered on this date were two Chesapeakes. There were no Labradors or Golden Retrievers. The majority of Irish Water Spaniels registered in the next 20

Field Spaniel—Ch. Jeannie of Mittina. (Owner: Mr. Richard H. [Squ]ier, Randolph, Ohio.) According to this dog's owner, there were [only] eleven Field Spaniels in America in early 1970, he having eight [of t]hem. Mr. Squier's dogs finished three champions in 1969 and [the]se were, according to AKC records, the first Field Spaniel Cham[pion]s in the U.S. since 1916. Photo by Ritter.

Irish Water Spaniel.

years were owned by sportsmen living around Milwaukee, St. Louis, Chicago, and Cleveland. At the time there were no restrictions on shooting waterfowl, which were plentiful; thousands were killed for market and sport from early fall to spring. The Irish Water Spaniel was imported from Ireland to provide a rugged water dog that could work in heavy cover and icy water day after day when the flight was on. Ducks and geese that had been shot formed a large part of the nation's food supply at the time and the market shooter could not afford to waste powder and shot on crippled birds if he were going to compete successfully in the market, but every cripple brought in was a quarter-dollar saved.

Gradually the breed's popularity spread to the East and sportsmen on Long Island and Cape Cod began to use and register Irish Water Spaniels. There is no way of determining the number of Irish Water Spaniels in the country in this period when American waterfowl shooting was at its peak, as many of the owners did not register their dogs in the stud books, but between 1880 and 1920 it was one of the popular retrievers because it could really do a day's work when large bags were common. In the Field Dog Stud Book of 1922 the Irish Water Spaniel outregistered the other popular retriever breeds.

In Ireland, where this breed originated, it is easy to trace their history back to Justin McCarthy who lived

there and was actively breeding Irish Water Spaniels in 1850 as we know them today. His most famous dog was Boatswain, who lived to an old age and was found in the pedigree of one of the early dogs registered in our American Stud Book. Before McCarthy started his breeding experiments there were two distinct breeds of Water Spaniels in Ireland. The one in the north was small, parti-colored with a wavy coat, and very similar to the English Water Spaniel. A larger Water Spaniel with a curly coat was found in the South of Ireland around the bogs of the River Shannon, and this Water Spaniel is believed to be an ancestor of the modern dog. Many theories have been advanced on the ancient origin of the Irish Water Spaniel. One authority claims that they are a cross between an Irish Setter and a Poodle. This is unlikely, because both breeds have long hair on the tail and the Irish Water Spaniel, except for a few inches at its base, has a tail like a Pointer. The Poodle has long hair on his face and comes in a variety of colors, whereas the Irish Water Spaniel has a smooth face covered with short hair and shows only one color, solid liver.

There is no doubt about the Irish Water Spaniel being the largest member of the spaniel family. His face, ears, and disposition are typical of the spaniel family which originated in Spain. So, somewhere in the background is an ancestor from the Iberian Peninsula where so many of our good sporting dogs originated. The Irish Water Spaniel has bred true to type for the last 90 years in this country and except for size, looks no different from the dogs of McCarthy's breeding. Whether this Irishman developed our modern Irish Water Spaniel by selective breeding of the South of Ireland Water Spaniel or cross-breeding with a liver-colored Spanish Pointer, no one will ever know because McCarthy left no records of his breeding experiments. Regardless of lack of records, however, we know that his breeding theories were sound, as we have a dog today that looks entirely different from any other breed. The Irish Water Spaniel is always solid liver in color, curly-coated, with short straight hairs on face and tail. It is never seen in a parti-color or the range in coat shades found in other retriever breeds.

About the same time the eastern American gunners began to find the Irish Water Spaniel useful, West Coast duck hunters started to use them. Although American gunners originally imported these dogs from Ireland because the conditions and cover in the Irish rough shoots were similar to those found in this country, they soon began to breed larger dogs that were heavier and longer legged and even better suited to working in western sloughs and tidal rivers.

Although Flat-Coated Retrievers were imported from England where the cover was more open and the shooting of driven game was more in vogue, the Irish Water Spaniel maintained his popularity for years because of his background of experience in the heavy Irish covers where he was used on upland game as well as waterfowl.

Today the Irish Water Spaniel is still popular among a small group of sportsmen and guides who are confirmed duck shooters and consider their Irishman as essential a piece of equipment as their gun or decoys. These dogs originated in the Irish marshes and the love of working in water is bred into them to the point where a real duck hunter, who really kills a lot of birds under natural conditions, realizes their value as a meat dog. In the 1930's, registrations of Irish Water Spaniels dropped as the popularity of the newer imports of other retrieving breeds increased. Unfortunately registration in a recognized stud book is the only real record of a breed's popularity as compared with other breeds, but there are many good Irish Water Spaniels of pure breeding scattered all over this country, a number of which are never registered because their owners are typical of the old-time gunners who appreciate the dog for the honest day's work he will give, but cannot be bothered to fill out a form.

It is doubtful if the Irish Water Spaniel will ever reach the popularity of other retrievers unless some moneyed group makes an effort to popularize the breed with the modern sales tactics that have been used to help other breeds. The small group of gunners who really love and share their hunting with this grand Irish dog are not over-anxious to see him become popular anyway because too much popularity

would be beyond the pocketbook of the average hunter.

The Irish Water Spaniel is a large sporting dog classified as a retriever and used mainly for retrieving upland game and waterfowl; many owners use him to spring game. The majority of these Irish dogs have excellent noses which they must inherit from their spaniel ancestors. They have sufficient length of legs that they move fast on the land and can go through broken-down sedge and rice in marshland that slows shorter-legged breeds almost to a standstill. A 65-pounder is large enough for rough going.

The Irish Water Spaniel will work from a short blind, a duckboat in open water or one that is surrounded by sedge grass, or will work off of rocks. He is not afraid of mud and will wade into the mud that keeps sucking the hunter's boots off if he attempts to wade through it. He soon learns how to pick up fallen birds in a tidal river where the current is strong, and will always cut below the fall of the bird and wait for it to drift down to him. He is a strong swimmer, usually swimming with a level back and the rat tail moving all the time and occasionally coming out of the water. He learns quickly from experience, and it is not long before he knows enough to distinguish the fall of a dead black duck from one that is down crippled, and head for the creek below the fall instead of wasting time going directly to the fall as he would on a stone-dead bird. He soon learns all the tricks of a skulking black duck, and before he is many years old he can out-

Irish Water Spaniel—This breed was highly popular among duck hunters during the 1920s and early 1930s.

smart a crippled duck of any species found in the marsh.

The Irish Water Spaniel will retrieve all kinds of upland game as well as he does waterfowl. There is even a record of one retrieving a large red dog fox. These big spaniels are used in may parts of the country to spring pheasants and many of them learn to circle a running bird. They are particularly adapted for country where the going is rough and a shorter legged dog is slowed down to the point of being handicapped. He will trail rabbits and provide many a shot at a cottontail if the country is not too open.

The Irish Water Spaniel Club of America was founded in 1937 to help this dog, and eight Irish Water Spaniels ran the first trial at that time. Since then a scattering of Irish Spaniels have run against other retrievers in trials all over the country. A number have placed in large trials, but most of their owners have not brought their field trial training to the high perfection found in the other breeds that are winning most of the trials. Probably one out of 20 in any breed of retrievers is suited for successful field trial competition. The majority of the Irish Water Spaniels that have run in trials, however, have just been good field dogs; although they usually did everything asked of them in a trial, they lacked that extra something that is found only in a retriever which has been selected as outstanding in temperament from a large group of dogs. The Irish Water Spaniel has a nose, is fast on land and water, marks well, and handles easily yet can think for himself. Some of them would certainly be capable of winning field trials if the same time and money were spent on them as on other breeds who nowadays win field trials. Most Irish Water Spaniel owners are mainly interested in a dog who will give them a good day's shoot. However, there are people who remember Irish Singer, Bog's Jiggs, Blackwater Bog, Step and Mike—all Irish Water Spaniels who did well in competitive retriever trials.

The first sporting dog in this country to win his obedience title was an Irish Water Spaniel; these are willing, happy workers in an obedience test, giving pleasure to anyone watching them. The Irish puppy can start training at four months and, if the water is warm, start swimming at the same time. Although many Irish Spaniels are natural retrievers, they all should be force broken, as this type of training makes a more useful dog. Extreme patience must be used at all times, as an Irish Water Spaniel will not stand abuse. They develop physically only slowly, and do not reach their full growth until they are two years old and in many cases retain many of their playful traits until they are full grown.

Description and Standards. The description and standards follow.

HEAD: Skull is rather large and high in dome with prominent occiput; muzzle square and rather long with deep mouth opening and lips fine in texture. Teeth strong and level. The nose should be large with open nostrils and liver in color. The head should be cleanly chiseled, not "cheeky," and should not present a short, wedge-shaped appearance. Hair on face should be short and smooth.

TOP-KNOT: Top-knot, a characteristic of the true breed, should consist of long loose curls growing down into a well-defined peak between the eyes and should not be in the form of a wig, i.e., growing straight across.

EYES: Medium in size and set almost flush, without eyebrows. Color of eyes hazel, preferably of dark shade. Expression of the eyes should be keenly alert, intelligent, direct, and quizzical.

EARS: Long, lobular, set low, with leathers reaching to about the end of the nose when extended forward. The ears should be abundantly covered with curls, becoming longer toward the tips and extending 2 or more inches below the ends of the leathers.

NECK: The neck should be long, arching, strong, and muscular, smoothly set into sloping shoulders.

SHOULDERS AND CHEST: Shoulders should be sloping and clean; chest deep but not too wide between the legs. The entire front should give the impression of strength without heaviness.

BODY, RIBS, AND LOINS: Body should be of medium length, with ribs well sprung, pear shaped at the brisket, and rounder toward the hind quarters. Ribs should be carried well back. Loins should be short, wide, and muscular. The body should not present a tucked-up appearance.

HIND QUARTERS: The hind quarters should be as high as the shoulders, or a trifle higher, and should be very powerful and muscular with well-developed upper and second thighs. Hips should be wide, stifles should not be too straight, the hocks low set and moderately bent. Tail should be set on low enough to give a rather rounded appearance to the hind quarters and should be carried nearly level with the back. Sound hind quarters are of great importance to provide swimming power and drive.

FORE LEGS AND FEET: Fore legs medium in length, well boned, straight and muscular with elbows close set. Both fore and hind feet should be large, thick, and somewhat spreading, well clothed with hair both over and between the toes, but free from superfluous feather.

TAIL: The so-called "rat-tail" is a striking characteristic of the breed. At the root it is thick and covered for 2 or 3 inches with short curls. It tapers to a fine point at the end, and from the root-curls is covered with short, smooth hair so as to look as if the tail has been clipped. The tail should not be long enough the reach the hock joint.

COAT: Proper coat is of vital importance. The neck, back, and sides should be densely covered with tight, crisp ringlets entirely free from wooliness. Underneath the ribs the hair should be longer. The hair on lower throat should be short. The fore legs should be covered all around with abundant hair falling in curls or waves, but shorter in front than behind. The hind legs should also be abundantly covered by hair falling in curls or waves, but the hair should be short on the front of the legs below the hocks.

COLOR: Solid liver; white on chest objectionable.

HEIGHT AND WEIGHT: Dogs 22 to 24 inches; bitches 21 to 23 inches. Dogs 55 to 65 pounds; bitches 45 to 58 pounds.

GENERAL APPEARANCE: A smart, upstanding, strongly built but not leggy dog, combining great intelligence and rugged endurance with a bold, dashing eagerness of temperament.

GAIT: Should be square, true, precise and not slurring.

SCALE OF POINTS: Points

Head

Skull and top-knot 6
Ears 4
Eyes 4
Muzzle and Nose 6   20

Body

Neck 5
Chest, Shoulders, Back, Loin, and Ribs . 12   17

Driving Gear

Feet, Hips, Thighs, Stifles, and Continuity of Hind Quarters Muscles	14	
Feet, Legs, Elbows, and Muscles of Fore Quarters	9	23

Coat

Tightness, denseness of curl, and general texture	16	
Color	4	20

Tail

General appearance and "set on," length, and carriage	5	5

General Conformation and Action

Symmetry, Style, Gait, Weight, and Size ..	15	15
TOTAL	100	100

SUSSEX SPANIEL

PARTICULARLY distinctive in appearance from its rich, golden, liver-colored coat, the Sussex Spaniel is inclined to give tongue on scent, a characteristic not generally found in other spaniels. The Sussex is a rather slow dog, somewhat massive in appearance, and his lack of speed has been the main factor in keeping him from being popular with American sportsmen.

The first and most important kennel of Sussex Spaniels in England belonged to Mr. Fuller of Brightling. Phineas Bullock, who had much to do with the development of the Field Spaniel, was also a well-known fancier of the Sussex.

They have long been used in rough shooting in England and, when properly trained, make good retrievers. Their conformation mitigates against speed, although the dog is a lively worker. He possesses an excellent disposition.

Description and Standards. The description and standards, by courtesy of AKC follow.

HEAD: The skull should be moderately long and also wide with an indention in the middle and a full stop, brows fairly heavy; occiput full, but not pointed, the whole giving an appearance of heaviness without dullness.

EYES: Hazel color, fairly large, soft and languishing, not showing the haw overmuch.

NOSE: The muzzle should be about three inches long, square, and the lips somewhat pendulous. The nostrils well developed and liver color.

EARS: Thick, fairly large and lobe shaped; set moderately

Sussex Spaniel.

low, but relatively not so low as in the black Field Spaniel; carried close to the head and furnished with soft, wavy hair.

NECK: Is rather short, strong and slightly arched, but not carrying the head much above the level of the back. There should not be much throatiness about the skin, but well-marked frill in the coat.

CHEST AND SHOULDERS: The chest is round, especially behind the shoulders, deep and wide giving a good girth. The shoulders should be oblique.

BACK AND BACK RIB: The back and loin is long and should be very muscular, both in width and depth; for this development the back ribs must be deep. The wholy body is characterized as low, long and level.

LEGS AND FEET: The arms and thighs must be bony as well as muscular, knees and hocks large and strong; pasterns very short and bony, feet large and round, and with short hair between the toes. The legs should be very short and strong, with great bone, and may show a slight bend in the forearm, and be moderately well feathered. The hind legs should not appear to be shorter than the forelegs, nor be too much bent at the hocks. They should be well feathered above the hocks but should not have much hair below that point. The hind legs are short from the hock to the ground, and wide apart.

TAIL: Should be docked from 5 to 7 inches, set low, and not carried above the level of the back, thickly covered with moderately long feather.

COAT: Body coat abundant, flat or slightly waved, with no tendency to curl, moderately well feathered on legs and stern, but clean below the hocks.

COLOR: Rich golden liver; this is a certain sign of the purity of the breed, dark liver or puce denoting unmistakably a recent cross with the black or other variety of Field Spaniel.

GENERAL APPEARANCE: Rather massive and muscular, but with free movements and nice tail action, denoting a cheerful and tractable disposition. Weight from 35 pounds to 45 pounds.

POSITIVE POINTS:	Points
Head	10
Eyes	5
Nose	5
Ears	10
Neck	5
Chest and shoulders	5
Back and back ribs	10
Legs and feet	10
Tail	5
Coat	5
Color	15
General appearance	15
TOTAL	100

NEGATIVE POINTS:	Points
Light eyes	5
Narrow head	10
Weak muzzle	10
Curled ears or set on high	5
Curled coat	15
Carriage of stern	5
Top-knot	10
White on chest	5
Color, too light or too dark	15
Legginess or light of bone	5
Shortness of body or flat sided	5
General appearance—sour or crouching	10
TOTAL	100

(July 14, 1959)

WELSH SPRINGER SPANIEL

IT MAY well have been that the Welsh Springer Spaniel is the oldest, or was the first, of the spaniel breeds to be used in front of the sportsman's gun. Old pictures, prints, and writings depict early-day gunners hunting over a medium sized spaniel, red and white in color. This is the only color of the Welsh Springer. In this he differs from the English Springer, Cocker, and Field Spaniels.

The Welshman is a larger dog than the Cocker but a bit smaller than the English Springer. He originated in Wales and is principally found there today, although the dog has been exported to many countries.

The dog is a rough-and-tumble worker, no cover being too difficult, no weather too rough. His flat, even coat has a soft under coat which enables him to withstand the rigors of cold climates, and, when properly trained, he makes a first-rate retriever from both land and water. In this country his cousin, the English Springer, has been far more popular, perhaps because the Welshman is more independent and not so easily trained. If started young, however, this dog learns his lessons well and retains what he learns.

The late Theodore Sturgis used these dogs for years in New England gunning, while the late Hobart Ames had a number which performed well in retrieving quail on his plantation-preserve in Tennessee. The dog is particularly hardy, easy to keep, adapts himself well to all conditions and possesses an even disposition.

Description and Standards. The description and standards, by courtesy of The Welsh Springer Spaniel Club, England, follow.

The "Welsh Spaniel" or "Springer" is also known and referred to in Wales as a "Starter." He is of very ancient and pure origin and is a distinct variety which has been bred and preserved purely for working purposes.

HEAD—SKULL: Proportionate, of moderate length, slightly domed, clearly defined stop, well chiselled below the eyes.

MUZZLE: Medium length, straight, fairly square, the nostrils well developed and flesh colored or dark.

JAWS: Strong, neither under nor over shot.

EYES: Hazel or dark, medium size, not prominent, nor sunken, nor showing haw.

EARS: Set moderately low and hanging close to the cheeks, comparatively small and gradually narrowing towards the tip, covered with nice setter-like feathering.

A short chubby head is objectionable.

NECK AND SHOULDER—NECK: Long and muscular, clean in throat, neatly set into long and sloping shoulders.

FORE LEGS: Medium length, straight, well boned, moderately feathered.

BODY: Not long; strong and muscular with deep brisket, well-sprung ribs; length of body should be proportionate to length of leg, and very well balanced; with muscular loin slightly arched and well coupled up.

QUARTERS: Strong and muscular, wide and fully developed with deep second thighs.

Welsh Springer Spaniel. Photo by Evelyn M. Shafer.

HIND LEGS: Hocks well let down; stifle moderately bent (neither twisted in nor out), moderately feathered.

FEET: Round with thick pads.

STERN: Well set on and low, never carried above the level of the back; lightly feathered and with lively action.

COAT: Straight or flat and thick, of a nice silky texture, never wiry nor wavy. A curly coat is most objectionable.

COLOR: Dark rich red and white.

GENERAL APPEARANCE: A symmetrical, compact, strong, merry, very active dog, not stilty, obviously built for endurance and activity.

VIZSLA

EVERY COUNTRY in Europe has its pointing breed. In fact, bracques or pointers may be of a certain region and known by that name or, perhaps, the name of an estate or a royal house where a certain type of pointer was developed, but most often it is that of the country itself. And so it was with the Vizsla, known in its homeland as the Hungarian Pointer.

The antiquity of this pointing breed is established by primitive stone etchings of the tenth century showing a Magyar huntsman with his falcon and his dog, a dog that closely resembles the Viszla of today. And in a chapter on falconry in a 14th Century manuscript of early Hungarian codes, a similar dog appears in one of the illustrations.

Although its origin is obscured by the centuries, historical reference bring the Vizsla into focus about 1,000 years ago, when the Magyars with their falcons and their hunting dogs swept Central Europe, finally settling in Hungary. These dogs were highly valued by early barons and war lords and since only such eminent personages could keep hunting dogs, these dogs were zealously guarded. It was probably as much by their segregation as by actual intention that the purity of the breed was preserved.

The plains of Hungary were ideal for the hunting of game. Almost entirely agricultural, the country's climate brought a long, hot growing season and winter temperatures moderated with the nearness of water, a combination that made it possible to raise grains in great abundance. Partridge, hare and other small game naturally flourished amid such plenty and the huntsman took advantage of it. However, he needed a keen but cautious-working hunting dog, one that combined the ability to find and point game and serve as a retriever as well.

The Vizsla filled this role and is still doing so, not only in its native land but in the United States where it first became admitted to the Field Dog Stud Book and, in 1960, joined the breeds registered in the American Kennel Club Stud Book.

Still relatively rare compared to the long-established pointing breeds, the Vizsla is being seen more and more frequently in the shooting field, in field trials, and in dogs shows. The Vizsla Club of America is today an enthusiastic and active group with members who represent a wide geographical area.

Texas, Washington, Missouri and California also boast their Vizsla fanciers. At the Harbor Cities Kennel Club Show in California in 1963, with a record entry of 3,300 dogs, Vizslas also had their record entry in America with 23. The best-of-breed award went to Ch. Warhorse O-Jay, owned by the t.v. and cinema star, Zsa Zsa Gabor, and bred by

Dr. Walter and Marie Campbell, whose bitch, Ch. Duchess of Shirbob, C.D., produced in one litter, the five other champions shown in Specials.

The very existence of the Vizsla is a tribute to the tenacity and fortitude of its admirers in its native land for otherwise the continued development of the breed might have ended during the great war years. After World War I, the breed almost became extinct.

Yet, as in many cases where a breed has been in jeopardy, there were those staunch supporters who refused to let it die out. Hungarians who fled to Austria in 1945 took their Vizslas with them. One of these dogs, Pannu IV, has progeny in the United States. Other Vizslas were taken into Germany and Italy by their owners. Some went to Czechoslovakia and Turkey and others to southern Russia. Thus, a substantial nucleus of breeding stock was preserved, to bring eventually to America an efficient sporting dog. Pointer in type, averaging 23 inches at the shoulder and weighing 50-60 pounds, the Vizsla has a distinctive solid color-coat of rusty gold. Its name, in the Hungarian vernacular, is said to mean "alert", "responsive."

Description and Standards.

GENERAL APPEARANCE: That of a medium-sized hunting dog of quite distinguished appearance. Robust but rather lightly built, his short coat is an attractive rust-gold, and his tail is docked. He is a dog of power and drive in the field, and a tractable and affectionate companion in the home.

HEAD: Lean but muscular. The skull is moderately wide between the ears, with a median line down the forehead. Stop moderate. The muzzle is a trifle longer than the skull and, although tapering is well squared at its end. Jaws strong, with well-developed white teeth meeting in a scissors bite. The lips cover the jaws completely but they are neither loose nor pendulous. Nostrils slightly open, the nose brown. A black or slate-gray is objectionable.

EARS: Thin, silky, and proportionally long, with rounded-leather ends; set fairly low and hanging close to the cheeks.

EYES: Medium in size and depth of setting, their surrounding tissue covering the whites, and the iris or color portion harmonizing with the shade of the coat. A yellow eye is objectionable.

NECK: Strong, smooth, and muscular; moderately long, arched and devoid of dewlap. It broadens nicely into shoulders which are well laid back.

BODY: Strong and well proportioned. The back is short, the withers high, and the topline slightly rounded over the loin to the set-on of the tail. Chest moderately broad and deep, and reaching down to the elbows. Ribs well sprung, and underline exhibiting a slight tuck-up beneath the loin.

LEGS AND FEET: Forelegs straight, and muscular, with elbows close. The hind legs have well-developed thighs, with moderate angulation at stifles and hocks. Too much angulation at the hocks is as faulty as too little. The hocks, which are well let down, are equidistant from each other from the hock joint to the ground. Cowhocks, are faulty. Feet are cat-like, round and compact, with toes close. Nails are brown and short; pads thick and tough. Dewclaws, if any, to be removed. Hare feet are objectionable.

TAIL: Set just below the level of the back, thicker at the root, and docked one third off.

COAT: Short, smooth, dense, and close-lying, without woolly undercoat.

COLOR: Solid. Rusty gold or rather dark sandy yellow in different shades, with darker shades preferred. Dark brown and pale yellow are undesirable. Small white spots on chest or feet are not faulted.

TEMPERAMENT: That of the natural hunter endowed with a

Vizsla. Photo by Evelyn M. Shafer

good nose and above-average ability to take training. Lively, gentle-mannered, and demonstratively affectionate. Fearless, and with well-developed protective instinct.

GAIT: Far-reaching, light-footed, graceful, smooth.

SIZE: Males 22 to 24 inches, females 21 to 23 inches at the highest point of the shoulders. Any dog measuring over or under these limits shall be considered faulty, the seriousness of the fault depending on the extent of the deviation. Any dog that measures more than 2 inches over or under these limits shall be disqualified.

WEIMARANER

IF YOU DO not like to hear the virtues of another's dog extolled hour after hour, do not engage the owner of a Weimaraner in conversation. The enthusiasm of all the Weimaraner owners is contagious. No breed ever brought to this country has been accorded such an ardent welcome, nor has the possession of any breed been so carefully guarded, for the promoters of the Weimaraner in this country are following the precedent of the Weimaraner Club of Germany, which was extremely careful concerning ownership of surplus stock, breeding practices, and prohibition of the infusion of new blood.

The Weimaraner originated at the German court of Weimar a little more than 125 years ago. The nobles of Weimar wanted an all-around hunting dog which would do everything; point, retrieve, trail, work in all sorts of cover and all kinds of weather—and with it all be a loyal, loving companion and house dog. Probably the heaviest contributor to the Weimaraner's hunting ability was the old red Schweisshunde, a sort of super-Bloodhound which provided the background for most of Germany's hunting breeds.

Just how long it took and what crosses were needed to establish the Weimaraner as a distinct breed is not a matter of exact record. But once established, the breed was carefully guarded and no exploitation was allowed. It is said that there have never been more than 1500 of these dogs in all of Germany at one time and none were allowed outside. It was the desire of the club that the Weimaraner remain Germany's own dog exclusively, and club members were subjected to rigid breeding regulations. This same careful supervision prevails today and is practiced, to a large extent, by members of the Weimaraner Club of America.

Howard Knight of Providence, R.I., succeeded in obtaining and bringing to this country a pair of these dogs in 1929. Several others were imported shortly afterwards, and so a foundation stock for the breed in this country was obtained. The Weimaraner is thus one of the more recent additions to America's sporting-dog group.

Naturally, the breed is not numerically strong in this country and, under the careful supervision of the Weimaraner Club of America, it is possible that it will never be. This is as the Club would have it, as the members are determined to keep the quality high, regardless of the excellent opportunity for commercial exploitation. For the "Gray Ghost," as the dog has been dubbed in this country, has had fine publicity and the club's avowed intention to confine ownership to those who meet certain qualifications has whetted the desire of many to own these dogs. "Make it hard to get" is always good promotion, but backers of the Weimaraner are quick to deny any such purpose and equally ready to declare the breed equal to the extraordinary claims made for it.

So far the Weimaraner has not attracted much attention by his prowess in the hunting field. It is, of course, still early for that. But the high intelligence and tractability of the breed has definitely been demonstrated in many obedience trials. Grafmar's Ador, C.D. (Companion Dog), won his obedience degree at the age of six months, the youngest dog ever to

Weimaraner on point. Photo by Shep Shepherd.

acquire it. He also proved proficient on game and an excellent producer of quality puppies.

The Weimaraner is a large dog, but free from coarseness. Males weigh from 65 to 85 pounds, females 55 to 75. Despite their size, 24 to 26 inches for males and 22 to 25 inches for females, they are remarkably smooth in gait and their stealthy movements in the field, together with their solid coat, has won for them the nickname "gray ghost."

As a family dog, the Weimaraner has also achieved noticeable popularity and he is not uncommon any longer in suburban areas. To strangers he exhibits a cold and closely-watchful attitude, and he seems well endowed with the qualities desired in an efficient guard or watchdog. He may, in fact, be today acquired by many as much or more for that purpose than for use in hunting.

The solid color ranges from silver-gray to a dark gray called silver taupe. The outer coat is slick and velvety, with a dense woolly under coat which gives the dog comfort in rigorous weather.

The eyes are blue-gray or amber, changing with light conditions, and adding to the unusualness of the dog's appearance. The tail is always docked to one-half or two-thirds its length.

The Weimaraner learns his lessons early and well. He is exceedingly tractable and willing to obey whenever he understands. He is a striking dog in appearance and never fails to attract attention.

Description and Standards.

GENERAL APPEARANCE: A medium-sized gray dog, with fine aristocratic features. He should present a picture of grace, speed, stamina, alertness and balance. Above all, the dog's conformation must indicate the ability to work with great speed and endurance in the field.

HEIGHT: At the withers: dogs, 25 to 27 inches; bitches 23 to 25 inches. One inch over or under the specified height of each sex is allowable but should be penalized. Dogs measuring less than 24 inches or more than 28 inches and bitches measuring less than 22 inches or more than 26 inches shall be disqualified.

HEAD: Moderately long and aristocratic, with moderate stop and slight median-line extending back over the forehead. Rather prominent occipital bone and trumpets well set back, beginning at the back of the eye sockets. Measurement from tip of nose to stop equal that from stop to occipital bone. The

Weimaraner. Photo by Wm. Brown.

flews should be straight, delicate at the nostrils. Skin drawn tightly. Neck clean-cut and moderately long. Expression kind, keen and intelligent.

EARS: Long and lobular, slightly folded and set high. The ear when drawn snugly alongside the jaw should end approximately 2 inches from the point of the nose.

EYES: In shades of light amber, gray or blue-gray, set well enough apart to indicate good disposition and intelligence. When dilated under excitement the eyes may appear almost black.

TEETH: Wellset, strong and even; well developed and proportionate to jaw with correct scissors bite, the upper teeth protruding slightly over the lower teeth but not more than $\frac{1}{16}$ of an inch. Complete dentition is greatly to be desired. Nose-gray.

LIPS AND GUMS: Pinkish flesh shades.

BODY: The back should be moderate in length, set in a straight line, strong, and should slope slightly from the withers. The chest should be well developed and deep, with shoulders well laid back. Ribs well sprung and long. Abdomen firmly held; moderately tucked-up flank. The brisket should extend to the elbow.

COAT AND COLOR: Short, smooth and sleek, solid color, in shades of mouse-gray to silver gray, usually blending to lighter shades on the head and ears. A small white marking on the chest is permitted, but should be penalized on any other portion of the body. White spots resulting from an injury should not be penalized. A distinctly long coat is a disqualification.

FORELEGS: Straight and strong, with the measurement from the elbow to the ground approximately equaling the distance from the elbow to the top of the withers.

HINDQUARTERS: Well-angulated stifles and straight hocks. Musculation well developed.

FEET: Firm and compact, webbed, toes well arched, pads close and thick, nails short and gray or amber in color. Dewclaws should be removed.

TAIL: Docked. At maturity it should measure approximately 6 inches with a tendency to be light rather than heavy and should be carried in a manner expressing confidence and sound temperament. A non-docked tail shall be penalized.

GAIT: The gait should be effortless and should indicate smooth coordination. When seen from the rear, the hind feet should be parallel to the front feet. When viewed from the side, the topline should remain strong and level.

TEMPERAMENT: The temperament should be friendly, fearless, alert and obedient.

MINOR FAULTS: Tail too short or too long. Pink nose.

MAJOR FAULTS: Doggy bitches. Bitchy dogs. Improper muscular condition. Badly affected teeth. More than four teeth missing. Back too long or too short. Faulty coat. Neck too short, thick or throaty. Low-set tail. Elbows in or out. Feet east and west. Poor gait. Poor feet. Cowhocks. Faulty backs, either roached or sway. Badly overshot or undershot bite. Snipy muzzle. Short ears.

VERY SERIOUS FAULTS: White, other than a spot on the chest. Eyes other than gray, blue-gray or light amber. Black mottled mouth. Non-docked tail. Dogs exhibiting strong fear, shyness and extreme nervousness. A color darker than mouse-gray.

DISQUALIFICATIONS: Oversize or undersize. A distinctly long coat.

(June, 1965)

—Group II—Hounds—

AFGHAN HOUND

THE AFGHAN Shikaris call him "the dog of Noah's Ark." This is, of course, "drawing a long bow," but there is no doubt that the Afghan hound is one of the oldest breeds in the world. And it is a fact that the type has not changed with the centuries.

Sinai, the small peninsula between the Gulf of Suez and the Gulf of Akaba where Jebel Musa, or the Mountain of Moses, is located is said to be the spot where the breed originated. This area was a part of ancient Egypt in the period 3,000 to 4,000 B.C. A papyrus of that section and era mentions the dog many times. It was, according to Major H. Blackstone, an English authority on antiquities, referred to as "cynocephalus," which, freely translated means "monkey-faced hound."

The breed derives its name from Afghanistan, but its origin is not confined to that country as it is found in large numbers all along the Borderland and Northern India, where it is known as the Barakzai, Kurram Valley Hound. Barukhzy is the name of the royal family of Afghanistan.

The breed has many uses in its native lands. It is valuable as a guard of flocks and herds and is a good hunter of deer and other small animals. Usually hunted in couples, the Afghan has been known to give a good account of himself in fights with leopards and animals of like ferociousness.

Hutchinson's *Dog Encyclopedia* (London) contains an interesting account of the service of dogs of this breed at a military outpost on the Northwest Frontier of India. Using the nom-de-plume of "Mali," the author wrote as follows:

Chaman, you must know, is one of our principal posts of the North-West Frontier. A former Commander-in-Chief decreed that a post should be established at Chaman to be fed by a light railway from Quetta. Two mud forts guard the railway station, one on each side; each fort is manned by one company of Indian infantry, and one squadron of native mounted levies and *by dogs*.

What strikes the newcomer entering either of the forts at any hour of the day is the large, extraordinary-looking creatures sprawling all over the place, fast asleep. In size and shape they somewhat resemble a large greyhound, but such slight resemblance is dispelled by the tufts with which all are adorned: some having tufted ears, others tufted feet, and others, again, possessing tufted tails.

They are known as Baluchi Hounds, and they get their daily food ration from the commissariat babu; he is the only permanent resident of the fort. They will have no truck with any stranger, white or black.

When Retreat sounds, the pack awakes, yawns, pulls itself together, and solemnly marches out to take up position close to the newly arrived night guard. *They appear to be under no leadership*, yet as the patrols are told off a couple of dogs attach themselves to each patrol, and they remain with their respective patrols till Reveille next morning. Between a deep ditch and wall of the fort is a narrow path. Throughout the night, this path is patrolled by successive couples of dogs. Immediately one couple has completed the circuit of the walls and arrives back at the main gate, another couple starts out.

When it is remembered that these extraordinary hounds have never had any training whatsoever, that their duties are absolutely self-imposed—for no human being has the slightest control over them—the perfection of their organization and the smoothness with which they carry out their tasks make mere man gasp!

The Afghan Hound is, indeed, a product of the wide expanses. He would probably never have prospered in urban surroundings. He is peculiarly equipped to negotiate rough and waste country with comparative ease, the shape of his feet allowing him to travel over desert sands at good speed. The Afghan's hip bones are set higher and much wider apart than in the ordinary dog. These allow him to move over hill country and uneven ground easily, and to turn at great speed. They also give him a peculiar gait.

In disposition, the Afghan is naturally bold and courageous. But he is very much a one-man dog, and his reluctance to take up with strangers make him seem somewhat shy when, in reality, his apparent timidity is merely an expression of his desire to be left alone by those with whom he is not acquainted.

The Afghan is a striking dog in appearance, and his silky coat and dignified demeanor never fail to attract attention. The heavy feathering on his legs, resembling "chaps" to some extent, often cause him to be referred to as "the cowboy dog."

It was at the Kennel Club Championship Show of 1907 that the breed first came before the British public. Mrs. Barff took first prize in the Foreign Dog class with her Zardin, which later became the accepted model of the Afghan Hound, and the standard of points was fixed from him. His embalmed body is now in the British Museum.

The breed soon became popular in England. Champion Sirdar of Ghazni was brought to that country by Mrs. Amps, from her kennels in Cabul and his progeny became the foundation stock of most of the principal English kennels. Another imported hound which did much to establish the breed in that country was Champion Buckmal. Other early English breeders were: Major Bell Murray, Major Mackenzie, F. Carter, Mrs. J. Chesterfield-Cooke, Mrs. T. S. Couper, the Hon. Florence Amherst, Mrs. M. Wood, and Mrs. M. E. Till.

The Afghan Hound made its first appearance in America in the late 1930's and, while it attracted immediate attention, it did not attain any great promise of popularity at that time. Since that time interest in the breed has moved forward substantially.

Description and Standards. The description and standards, adopted by the Afghan Hound Club of America and approved by the American Kennel Club, follow.

Afghan Hound—Ch. Nigro's Zarak. (Owner: Alice E. Nigro and F. Karasec; handler, Robert Forsyth.) Photo by Evelyn M. Shafer.

GENERAL APPEARANCE: The Afghan Hound is an aristocrat, his whole appearance one of dignity and aloofness with no trace of plainness or coarseness. He has a straight front, proudly carried head, eyes gazing into the distance as if in memory of ages past. The striking characteristics of the breed—exotic or "Eastern" expression, long silky top-knot, peculiar coat pattern, very prominent hip bones, large feet, and the impression of a somewhat exaggerated bend in the stifle due to profuse trouserings—stand out clearly, giving the Afghan Hound the appearance of what he is, a King of Dogs, that has held true to tradition throughout the ages.

HEAD: The head is of good length showing much refinement, the skull evenly balanced with the foreface. There is a slight prominence of the nasal bone structure causing a slightly Roman appearance, the center line running up over the foreface with little or no stop, falling away in front of the eyes so there is an absolutely clear outlook with no interference; the underjaw showing great strength, the jaws long and punishing; the mouth level, meaning that the teeth from the upper jaw and lower jaw match evenly, neither overshot nor undershot. This is a difficult mouth to breed. A scissors bite is even more punishing and can be more easily bred into a dog than a level mouth, and a dog having a scissors bite, where the lower teeth slip inside and rest against the teeth of the upper jaw, should not be penalized. The occipital bone is very prominent. The head is surmounted by a top-knot of long silky hair.

EARS: The ears are long, set approximately on level with outer corners of the eyes, the leather of the ear reaching nearly to the end of the dog's nose, and covered with long, silky hair.

EYES: The almond shaped (almost triangular), never full or bulgy, and dark in color.

NOSE: Nose is of good size, black in color.

FAULTS: Coarseness; snipiness; overshot or undershot; eyes round or bulgy or light in color; exaggerated Roman nose; head not surmounted with top-knot.

NECK: The neck is of good length, strong and arched, running in a curve to the shoulders which are long and sloping and well laid back.

FAULTS: Neck too short or too thick; a ewe neck; a goose neck; a neck lacking in substance.

BODY: The back line appearing practically level from the

Afghan Hound and puppy. Photo by Evelyn M. Shafer.

shoulders to the loin. Strong and powerful loin and slightly arched, falling away toward the stern, with the hip bones very pronounced; well ribbed and tucked up in flanks. The height at the shoulders equals the distance from the chest to the buttocks; the brisket well let down, and of medium width.

FAULTS: Roach back, sway back, goose rump, slack loin; lack of prominence of hip bones; too much width of brisket causing interference with elbows.

TAIL: Tail set not too high on the body, having a ring, or a curve on the end; should never be curled over, or rest on the back, or be carried sideways; and should never be bushy.

LEGS: Fore legs are straight and strong with great length between elbow and pastern; elbows well held in; forefeet large in both length and width; toes well arched; feet covered with long thick hair; fine in texture; pasterns long and straight; pads of feet unusually large and well down on the ground. Shoulders have plenty of angulation so that the legs are well set underneath the dog. Too much straightness of shoulder causes the dog to break down in the pasterns, and this is a serious fault.

All four feet of the Afghan Hound are in line with the body, turning neither in nor out. The hind feet are broad and of good length; the toes arched, and covered with long thick hair; hind quarters powerful and well muscled with great length between hip and hock; hocks are well let down; good angulation of both stifle and hock; slightly bowed from hock to crotch.

FAULTS: Front or back feet thrown outward or inward; pads of feet not thick enough; or feet too small; or any other evidence of weakness in feet; weak or broken down pasterns; too straight in stifle; too long in hock.

COAT: Hind quarters, flanks, ribs, fore quarters, and legs well covered with thick, silky hair, very fine in texture; ears and all four feet well feathered; from in front of the shoulders, and also backwards from the shoulders along the saddle from the flanks and ribs upwards, the hair is short and close forming a smooth back in mature dogs—this a traditional characteristic of the Afghan Hound.

The Afghan Hound should be shown in its natural state; the coat is not clipped or trimmed; the head is surmounted (in the full sense of the word) with a topknot of long, silky hair—this

also an outstanding characteristic of the Afghan Hound. Showing of short hair on cuffs on either front or back legs is permissible.

FAULTS: Lack of short haired saddle in mature dogs.

HEIGHT: Dogs, 27 inches, plus or minus one inch; bitches, 25 inches, plus or minus one inch.

WEIGHT: Dogs, about 60 pounds; bitches, about 50 pounds.

COLOR: All colors are permissible, but color or color combinations are pleasing; white markings, especially on the head, are undesirable.

GAIT: When running free, the Afghan Hound moves at a gallop, showing great elasticity and spring in his smooth, powerful stride.

When on a loose lead, the Afghan can trot at a fast pace; stepping along, he has the appearance of placing the hind feet directly in the foot prints of the front feet, both thrown straight ahead. Moving with head and tail high, the whole appearance of the Afghan Hound is one of great style and beauty.

TEMPERAMENT: Aloof and dignified, yet gay.

FAULTS: Sharpness or shyness.

BASENJI

COMPARATIVELY new to America, but rapidly growing in popularity and destined for still further prominence is the Basenji, an ancient breed. Companions of the Pharaohs, the Basenji faded into obscurity when the civilization of Ancient Egypt declined. Originating in Central Africa, the breed is still valued in its native land and its bloodlines kept pure. It is understandable that the breed should survive through the centuries, for it is highly intelligent and possesses a great hunting instinct.

The Basenji is known as "the barkless dog," but is

not entirely noiseless as it gives a peculiar and appealing sound when happy or extremely pleased, and growls and snarls on occasion. The "happy" sound has been described as somewhere between a chortle and a yodel and is pleasant to hear.

A dog of extremely proud bearing, the Basenji is highly intelligent, anxious to please, and easily trained. In his native country, he is used in pointing game, retrieving, and is of particular value in hunting small game where silence is especially desired.

In addition to the quality of silence, the unusual characteristics of the breed are a broad forehead deeply furrowed with wrinkles, prick ears standing straight up from the head; dark, intelligent and apparently far-seeing eyes. Their habits are somewhat unusual, as the Basenji is extremely fastidious, cleans himself all over in the manner of a cat, and his lack of doggy odors make him ideal as a house pet.

This unusual dog has a splendid disposition and makes an ideal companion for children. Extremely playful, his happiness seems contagious, and when more dog lovers become acquainted with his characteristics he will most likely be in greater demand as a companion for the house and the field.

The coat of the Basenji is quite distinctive both in texture and color. The texture, in keeping with the tropical climate of its native land, is fine and somewhat silky, with an extremely attractive sheen. The coat becomes coarser in colder climates, but never

loses its brilliance. The most desired color is red, although shadings of red and fawn are seen, and occasionally a chestnut as well as black and tan. The dog's coat always has white points with a white tip to the tightly curled tail which is carried over one side of the back.

It was in 1895 that the first pair of Basenjis were brought to England. They fell victim to the dread disease, distemper, and died shortly after. It was not until 1937 that the breed was successfully introduced into the British Isles.

Mrs. Byron Rogers of New York City brought a pair to the United States about that time. A litter of puppies was whelped but again distemper took its toll and only one of the entire group survived. This was Bois, the older male dog.

A young female Basenji was brought to Boston from Africa in 1941. Alexander Phemister of Kingston, Mass., obtained her as well as the dog, Bois, from Mrs. Rogers. The mating between Bois and the female, Congo, produced the first litter of Basenjis to be raised to maturity in the United States. Dr. A. R. B. Richmond established a kennel of Basenjis in Canada and some of his stock was sent to this country and later others came from England.

The Basenji Club of America was formed in 1942, with Mr. Phemister as president; Miss Ethelwyn Harrison of Euclid, Ohio, and Dr. Eloise Gerry of Madison, Wisc., vice presidents; George Gilkey of Merrill, Wisc., treasurer; and George E. Richards of Lynn, Mass., secretary. In 1943, the American Kennel Club accepted the standard of the Club as official and accepted the breed for registration in the A.K.C. Stud Book Register. In 1945 the breed was classified in the Hound Group. A few months later Phemister's Melengo became the first American Basenji Champion.

As a sprightly, graceful, intelligent companion of happy disposition, the Basenji is ideal, particularly for fanciers who are city dwellers.

In England the Basenji has been used successfully in bird hunting. They reputedly have a soft mouth with retrieved birds.

Description and Standards. The description and standards, adopted by the Basenji Club of America and approved by the American Kennel Club, follow.

CHARACTERISTICS: The Basenji should not bark, but is not mute. The wrinkled forehead and the swift, tireless running gait (resembling a race-horse trotting full out) are typical of the breed.

GENERAL APPEARANCE: The Basenji is a small, lightly built, short backed dog, giving the impression of being high on the leg compared to its length. The wrinkled head must be proudly carried, and the whole demeanor should be one of poise and alertness.

HEAD AND SKULL: The skull is flat, well chiseled and of medium width, tapering towards the eyes. The foreface should taper from eye to muzzle and should be shorter than the skull. Muzzle, neither coarse, nor snipy but with rounded cushions. Wrinkles should appear upon the forehead, and be fine and profuse. Side wrinkles are desirable, but should never be exagerated into dewlap.

NOSE: Black greatly desired. A pinkish tinge should not pen-

Basenji—Ch. Khajah's Gay Enchantress. (Owner: Khajah Basenjis, hirley A. Chambers, Altoona, Pa.) Hank Babbitt photo.

Basenji—Head studies of a red and white and a tri-color Basenji from Khajah Basenjis.

alize an otherwise first class specimen, but it should be discouraged in breeding.

EYES: Dark hazel, almond shaped, obliquely set and far seeing.

EARS: Small, pointed and erect, of fine texture, set well forward on top of head.

MOUTH: Teeth must be level with scissors bite.

NECK: Of good length, well crested and slightly full at base of throat. It should be well set into flat, laid back shoulders.

FOREQUARTERS: The chest should be deep and of medium width. The legs straight with clean fine bone, long forearm and well defined sinews. Pasterns should be of good length, straight and flexible.

BODY: The body should be short and the back level. The ribs well sprung, with plenty of heart room, deep brisket, short coupled, and ending in a definite waist.

HINDQUARTERS: Should be strong and muscular, with hocks well let down, turned neither in nor out, with long second thighs.

FEET: Small, narrow and compact, with well arched toes.

TAIL: Should be set on top and curled tightly over to either side.

COAT: Short and silky. Skin very pliant.

COLOR: Chestnut red (the deeper the better) or pure black, or black and tan, all with white feet, chest and tail tip. White legs, white blaze and white collar optional.

WEIGHT: Bitches 22 pounds approximately. Dogs 24 pounds approximately.

SIZE: Bitches 16 inches and dogs 17 inches from the ground to the top of the shoulder. Bitches 16 inches and dogs 17 inches from the front of the chest to the farthest point of the hindquarters.

FAULTS: Coarse skull or muzzle. Domed or peaked skull. Dewlap. Round eyes. Low set ears. Overshot or undershot mouths. Wide chest. Wide behind. Heavy bone. Creams, shaded or off colors, other than those defined above, should be heavily penalized.

(June 8, 1954)

BASSET HOUND

THE MOST distinguished looking member of the hound family is, undoubtedly, the Basset. In appearance, he is somewhat of a conglomerate, having the coloring of a Foxhound, the head of a Bloodhound, the running gear of an extra-boned Dachshund, and a long, heavy body. In action he belies his looks to some extent, being considerably more agile than his appearance would indicate.

The breed, an ancient one, flourished chiefly in Belgium and France, and also in some sections of Russia. The Basset originated in France and was developed through crossing the old French Bloodhound on the white hounds of the Abbots of St. Hubert. The hounds of St. Hubert were used for hunting in very heavy cover, and a dog which held its nose close to the ground, because of its short legs, was to be preferred to one which could not easily put its nose close to the ground. Through selective breeding the shorter leg was intensified and the crooked forelegs of the Basset developed.

The first Bassets came to England in 1866, when the Comte de Tournow sent Lord Galway a pair of hounds, which were named Basset and Belle. Some of their offspring were sold to Lord Onslow, who supplemented his pack from the kennels of Comte Canteleu le Contealx. Some of the descendants of these hounds were imported into America and were crossed upon earlier importations from Russia.

From this breeding has come the American Basset, a bit sounder in limb than the lighter French type and more compact and not so bulky as the English type, which was considered too large.

In height the Basset runs from 10 to 15 inches; 13 inches is about right. Weight runs from 25 to 50 pounds, although some dogs weigh as much as 60 pounds in show condition. This dog is exceedingly heavy in bone and weighs more than he appears to.

The Basset Hound is the favorite hound in Italy, but he has never been very popular in this country. Perhaps his rather grotesque appearance militates against him to some degree, but he makes a good gunning companion for one who likes a slow, painstaking hunter. He is used on rabbits and hares and has found some favor as a pheasant dog. In some sections of the country he is used on grouse also and is taught to retrieve. He can be easily taught to tree and makes a good dog for coon, opossum, and squirrel hunting. Of excellent disposition, the Basset readily takes to training, and if worked by a single person, soon becomes a one-man dog.

Basset Hound—Ch. Lime Tree Micawber. (Owner: Mrs. Robert V Lindsay, Syosett, N.Y.) Photo by Evelyn M. Shafer.

Basset Hound—Ch. Questa of Blue Hill. (Owner: Mr. and Mrs. ▪uglas Kolvenbach, North Reading, Mass.) Photo by Evelyn M. afer.

One of his outstanding characteristics is the Basset's voice. Deep and resonant, his bell-like note makes fine "music" and carries well. The "cry" is fairly heavy in quality and the tonguing of a pack of Bassets will set the welkin a-ring.

Another outstanding characteristic is the keenness of his nose. The Basset possesses what is generally conceded to be the best nose in the hound group with the exception of the Bloodhound's.

For rabbit hunting, or even fox hunting where the fox is shot, many prefer the Basset to all other hounds. They maintain that his slowness will keep the game on the move without frightening it too much, will cause it to make smaller circles, and hence will give the gunner a better chance for a shot.

In recent years, breeders of Bassets have emphasized the dog's value as a pheasant hunter. It is best to hunt the Basset by himself or with one or more of his own breed. His main value is lost when he is hunted with dogs of greater speed.

In all-around appearance the Basset Hound is a docile, somewhat awkward dog of great dignity. In action he is every inch the workman.

Description and Standards. The AKC description and standards follow.

GENERAL APPEARANCE: The Basset Hound possesses in marked degree those characteristics which equip it admirably to follow a trail over and through difficult terrain. It is a short-legged dog, heavier in bone, size considered, than any other breed of dog, and while its movement is deliberate, it is in no sense clumsy. In temperament it is mild, never sharp or timid. It is capable of great endurance in the field and is extreme in its devotion.

HEAD: The head is large and well proportioned. Its length from occiput to muzzle is greater than the width at the brow. In overall appearance the head is of medium width. *The skull* is well domed, showing a pronounced occipital protuberance. A broad flat skull is a fault. The length from nose to stop is approximately the length from stop to occiput. The sides are flat and free from cheek bumps. Viewed in profile the top lines of the muzzle and skull are straight and lie in parallel planes, with a moderately defined stop. The skin over the whole of the head is loose, falling in distinct wrinkles over the brow when the head is lowered. A dry head and tight skin are faults. *The muzzle* is deep, heavy, and free from snipiness. *The nose* is darkly pigmented, preferably black, with large wide-open nostrils. A deep liver-colored nose conforming to the coloring of the head is permissible but not desirable. *The teeth* are large, sound, and regular, meeting in either a scissors or an even bite. A bite either overshot or undershot is a serious fault. *The lips* are darkly pigmented and are pendulous, falling squarely in front and, toward the back, in loose hanging flews. *The dewlap* is very pronounced. *The neck* is powerful, of good length, and well arched. *The eyes* are soft, sad, and slightly sunken, showing a prominent haw, and in color are brown, dark brown preferred. A somewhat lighter-colored eye conforming to the general coloring of the dog is acceptable but not desirable. Very light or protruding eyes are faults. *The ears* are extremely long, low set, and when drawn forward, fold well over the end of the nose. They are velvety in texture, hanging in loose folds with the ends curling slightly inward. They are set far back on the head at the base of the skull and, in repose, appear to be set on the neck. A high set or flat ear is a serious fault.

FOREQUARTERS: *The chest* is deep and full with prominent sternum showing clearly in front of the legs. *The shoulders* and elbows are set close against the sides of the chest. The distance from the deepest point of the chest to the ground, while it must be adequate to allow free movement when working in the field, is not to be more than one-third the total height at the withers of an adult Basset. The shoulders are well laid back and powerful. Steepness in shoulder, fiddle fronts, and elbows that are out, are serious faults. *The forelegs* are short, powerful, heavy in bone, with wrinkled skin. Knuckling over of the front legs is a disqualification. *The paw* is massive, very heavy with tough heavy pads, well rounded and with both feet inclined equally a trifle outward, balancing the width of the shoulders. Feet down at the pastern are a serious fault. *The*

Basset Hound—Their temperament often belies their melancholic expression. Photo by Evelyn M. Shafer.

toes are neither pinched together nor splayed, with the weight of the forepart of the body borne evenly on each. The dewclaws may be removed.

BODY: The rib structure is long, smooth, and extends well back. The ribs are well sprung, allowing adequate room for heart and lungs. Flat-sidedness and flanged ribs are faults. The topline is straight, level, and free from any tendency to sag or roach, which are faults.

HINDQUARTERS: The hindquarters are very full and well rounded, and are approximately equal to the shoulders in width. They must not appear slack or light in relation to the over-all depth of the body. The dog stands firmly on its hind legs showing a well-let-down stifle with no tendency toward a crouching stance. Viewed from behind, the hind legs are parallel, with the hocks turning neither in nor out. Cowhocks or bowed legs are serious faults. The hind feet point straight ahead. Steep, poorly angulated hindquarters are a serious fault. The dewclaws, if any, may be removed.

TAIL: The tail is not to be docked, and is set in continuation of the spine with but slight curvature, and carried gaily in hound fashion. The hair on the underside of the tail is coarse.

SIZE: The height should not exceed 14 inches. Height over 15 inches at the highest point of the shoulder blades is a disqualification.

GAIT: The Basset Hound moves in a smooth, powerful, and effortless manner. Being a scenting dog with short legs, it holds its nose low to the ground. Its gait is absolutely true with perfect coordination between the front and hind legs, and it moves in a straight line with hind feet following in line with the front feet, the hocks well bent with no stiffness of action. The front legs do not paddle, weave, or overlap, and the elbows must lie close to the body. Going away, the hind legs are parallel.

COAT: The coat is hard, smooth, and short, with sufficient density to be of use in all weather. The skin is loose and elastic. A distinctly long coat is a disqualification.

COLOR: Any recognized hound color is acceptable and the distribution of color and markings is of no importance.

DISQUALIFICATIONS. Height of more than 15 inches at the highest point of the shoulder blades. Knuckled over front legs. Distinctly long coat.

(January 14, 1964)

BEAGLE

RATED AS the most popular of the hound breeds is the Beagle. There are several reasons for this. First, the Beagle is essentially a gundog. Second, he is a specialist on the cottontail rabbit, the most prolific of all species of American upland game animals and the most widely hunted. Third, his merry and affectionate disposition make him a favorite as a pet and companion for children, a loyal and ornamental house dog. And fourth, his great versatility allows his use on almost any type of upland game. He is particularly effective on squirrels and pheasants.

As with practically all hound breeds, the exact origin of the Beagle is not definitely known. It is established, however, that the little fellow was in favor in the days of King Henry VIII and came into even greater vogue during the reign of that monarch's daughter, Elizabeth. It was the custom in those days for the hunting gentry to take their Beagles to the fields in the panniers of the saddles. From this we may judge that the Beagles of those days were very small—from 8 to 12 inches high.

It has been said that the Beagle resulted from experiments in crossing the Harrier with the old South of England or Southern Hound. In some instances they were called "little Harriers." The claim is that selective breeding, using only the smallest specimens, brought the Beagle down to the diminutive size known in the days of good Queen Bess. This miniature hound, however, did not enjoy sustained popularity; they were too small for use.

Early Beagles were classified as "shallow-flewed" or "deep-flewed" in proportion to the deepness of the upper lip. The shallow-flewed were said to be the fastest and the deep-flewed the surest and more musical. The wire-haired Beagle was considered the stronger and better dog.

Though most of our information concerning the early Beagles came from England, it is known that the name originated from the corrupted French word *beigle,* meaning small.

The present-day Beagle gets his keen nose probably from the Kerry Beagle, in color and general appearance a miniature Bloodhound. Except for that, however, it is doubtful that the Kerry Beagle exerted any influence over the Beagle of today, and his contribution was more likely made to the Foxhound and Coonhound breeds.

General Richard Rowett, of Carlinville, Ohio, is generally credited with bringing the first Beagles to America, in the early 1870's; among them were Rosey and Dolly. At about the same time, C. H. Turner brought over Sam and Warrior, and Norman Elmore of Granby, Conn., imported Ringwood, a dog of exceptional ability, and others.

From the matings of Warrior and Rosey a number of excellent dogs were produced. Among them was Dodge's Rattler, a dog which had a profound influence in developing what was known as the Rowett strain. This blood has carried on through many generations and the Rowetts are recognized as the fountainheads of the present-day Beagles. These early importations found immediate favor among American sportsmen who wanted a small hound of excellent type, large enough to cope with the cover in this country and small enough to be "handy."

Along in the Eighties there was much discussion as to what constituted the ideal Beagle. These controversies resulted in the formation of the American-English Beagle Club in 1884. General Rowett, Mr. Elmore, and Dr. L. H. Twadell, of Philadelphia, were appointed as a committee to draft the standard for the breed. That they were men of foresight and wrote well is demonstrated in a comparison of the standard adopted by the American-English Beagle Club and the present standard of the National Beagle Club of America, for few changes have been necessary.

General Rowett was not a commercial breeder and the dogs from his kennel were not distributed indiscriminately. However, he did let some of the more enthusiastic fanciers, who were seriously interested in breeding better Beagles, have some of his stock. The progeny of these dogs added to the prestige of the

Beagle puppies

Rowett strain and these bloodlines became justly famous.

Upon the noted Carlinville sportsman's death most of his stock was acquired by Pottinger Dorsey of New Market, Md., and C. Staley Doub of Frederick, Md. These gentlemen carried on in the Rowett manner, without thought of profit to themselves, and Beagle fanciers of today owe much to their breeding operations. Their efforts produced Lee, Triumph, Wanderer, Welcome, Harker, Hooker, and many other of the outstanding performers of their day. Dogs from the Dorsey and Doub kennels were field performers, backed by generations of practical dogs, and while neither cared to commercialize his dogs they did dispose of some top-flight individuals to thoughtful breeders who carried on to the further fame of the Rowetts.

Another famour strain is the Blue Cap, developed largely by Hiram Card, a Canadian breeder. The foundation stock of this strain were the imported blueticks, Blue Cap and Blue Bell, brought over by Captain William Assheton of Virginia from the kennels of Sir Arthur Ashburnham of England. A mating of these two produced Card's Blue Cap, a dog which when crossed on the Rowetts and bitches of Champion Bannerman blood exerted a startling influence on the dogs of his time.

Champion Bannerman was imported by Dr. L. H. Twadell for Lewis Sloan, of Philadelphia, about 1884 and proved a great sire. One of his sons, Jack Bannerman, was used extensively by Mr. Card in the development of the Blue Cap strain. Mr. Card always preferred the blue-ticked or mottled color with black markings and tan trimmed, and bred for that color, producing some very handsome Beagles which were excellent workers in the field.

Another imported dog of the early days which proved a prepotent sire was Chimer, imported by Mr. Diffendoeffer of Pennsylvania.

The outstanding dog of the early Nineties was Frank Forest, a line-bred Rowett on his sire's side, and out of Skip, which stemmed from the blood of the kennels of Sir Arthur Ashburnham. Mated with Sue Forest, Frank Forest, owned by H. L. Kreuder of Nanuet, N.Y., produced Champion Clyde, Sunday, and Gypsy Forest and through them established a well-nigh unbeatable family. Clyde was the sire of many excellent hunters and his son, Champion Trick, also produced many rabbiters of exceptional ability.

Soon after the turn of the century Beagles and beagling in America began gaining rapidly in popularity. Quite a number of organized or privately-owned packs were established and in some sections the sport took on a more formal flavor. Among some of the well-known packs of yesteryear are the Hempstead Beagles, the Round Hill, the Thornfield, the Rockridge, the Dungannon, the Somerset, the Wolver, the Piedmont, the Sir Sister, the Belray, the Old Westbury, the Ragdale, the Fairfield, the Mt. Brilliant, and the Windholme.

The first Beagle field trials in this country were those held at Hyannis, Mass., November 4, and Salem, N.H., November 7, 1890. The change of venue was necessitated by conditions. These trials were held under the auspices of the newly-formed National Beagle Club. The noted Frank Forest was the winner of the all-age stake for dogs 15 inches and under. Second was Don and third was Sunday, a son of Frank Forest out of Sue Forest. Tone, owned by the Glenrose Kennels, won the stake for bitches 15 inches and under, while Gypsy Forest, another member of the Frank Forest-Sue Forest litter, was second. Belle Ross, owned by B. S. Turpin, was the winner of the stake for bitches 13 inches and under.

A larger entry was noted in the trials of 1891, and the sport of Beagle field trials has enjoyed a steady growth ever since. Hundreds of these contests are held every season and there is hardly a section of the

Beagle—Eng. Ch. Rozavel Elsy's Diamond Jerry, a 15-inch Beagle. (Owner: Thelma Gray, Surrey, England)

country where the bugle mouth of the merry little Beagle is not heard in competition with members of his breed.

Training Beagles for work in the field is now a recognized profession and many professional trainers take their charges over a regular circuit of field trials, beginning in early fall and running into late spring. Field trial clubs set their dates so they will not conflict and will allow time enough for the competitors to travel from one event to the other and also give their charges the needed rest or tune-up workouts in between events.

Professional trainers map out their campaigns months in advance, planning to enter their charges in trials that are easily accessible, that are of greatest importance, or where they consider they have the best chances of winning.

At bench shows and field trials, Beagles are divided into two classes, those of 15 inches in height or under, and those of 13 inches or under. Beagles over 15 inches in height are automatically disqualified for competition.

At Beagle trials, the dogs are run in braces or pairs. The names of individual hounds are placed on single slips of paper and drawn from a receptacle, the first dog drawn running with the second dog drawn, and so on. After all braces have been run, the judges may call back any competing hounds they may desire to see again and brace them in any manner they desire, running them a second time, a third, or even more until they have found the best performers on that particular occasion. The cottontail rabbit is the game used although occasionally in some sections hares are employed.

Not all Beagles have field trial qualifications. Some do not perform so well in strange country or with a gallery of enthusiastic beaglers following as they do when they are hunting in familiar territory with their masters. Others seem to have a highly developed competitive spirit and do their best work when urged on by the incentive of competition.

The ideal Beagle is a dog of great determination. He should possess the desire to hunt in a marked degree, a keen nose which will allow him to work out a comparatively cold trail and rout out his quarry, and stick to the line until that quarry has gone to earth or has been caught. He should be able and willing to work in rough, heavy, briar-infested cover as well as in the easy going of the open, and in any kind of weather. A major requisite is a good mouth, not too freely used, but freely and happily given when the rabbit is up and going. Beagles are truly the music-makers of the meadows and the rippling cry of a well-balanced pack will thrill the most sophisticated.

The Beagle is a hardy dog, easy to keep in condition. He does not need much kennel room and adapts himself quickly to all climates. Like all hounds, he thrives on work and the more he is hunted the better he likes it.

While not a particularly sensitive dog, the Beagle likes attention and readily responds to kindness and affection. He is quick to learn and about all the training he needs is work. The more hunting his owner can give him the closer the bond between them will become, and the more finished performer he will be.

Bred and developed primarily for rabbit hunting, the Beagle is a very useful dog on practically every species of upland game. He makes a master squirrel dog, is extremely valuable on the trap line, and as a pheasant dog doffs his hat only to the pointing breeds and spaniels. Though he is not fast enough to be used to best advantage on fox, there have been instances when the Beagle proved himself proficient on this species, even running an occasional fox to the death.

Carrying himself with the cocky air of the sportsman he is, the Beagle attracts attention wherever he goes. He has the quality of combining ruggedness with daintiness which is possessed by no other dog in such degree and as an ideal dog around farm or home he is hard to excel. His dignity is not akin to aloofness and he is willing to meet any friendly advances more than halfway.

Beagles come in all hound colors, and any hound color is good. However, the most popular color is white, black, and tan. The Beagle is a favorite hound in both America and Canada.

Description and Standards. The description and standards, adopted by the National Beagle Club of America and approved by AKC follow.

HEAD: The skull should be fairly long, slightly domed at occiput, with cranium broad and full.

EARS: Ears set on moderately low, long, reaching when drawn out nearly, if not quite, to the end of the nose; fine in texture, fairly broad—with almost entire absence of erectile power—setting close to the head, with the forward edge slightly inturning to the cheek—rounded at tip.

EYES: Eyes large, set well apart—soft and houndlike—expression gentle and pleading; of a brown or hazel color.

MUZZLE: Muzzle of medium length—straight and square-cut—the stop moderately defined.

JAWS: Level. Lips free from flews; nostrils large and open.

DEFECTS: A very flat skull, narrow across the top; excess of dome, eyes small, sharp and terrierlike, or prominent and protruding; muzzle long, snipy or cut away decidedly below the eyes, or very short. Roman-nosed, or upturned, giving a dish-face expression. Ears short, set on high or with a tendency to rise above the point of origin.

BODY, NECK AND THROAT: Neck rising free and light from the shoulders strong in substance yet not loaded, of medium length. The throat clean and free from folds of skin; a slight wrinkle below the angle of the jaw, however, may be allowable.

DEFECTS: A thick, short, cloddy neck carried on a line with the top of the shoulders. Throat showing dewlap and folds of skin to a degree termed "throatiness."

SHOULDERS AND CHEST: Shoulders sloping—clean, muscular, not heavy or loaded—conveying the idea of freedom of action with activity and strength. Chest deep and broad, but not broad enough to interfere with the free play of the shoulders.

DEFECTS: Straight, upright shoulders. Chest disproportionately wide or with lack of depth.

BACK, LOIN AND RIBS: Back short, muscular and strong. Loin broad and slightly arched, and the ribs well sprung, giving abundance of lung room.

DEFECTS: Very long or swayed or roached back. Flat, narrow loin. Flat ribs.

FORELEGS: Straight, with plenty of bone in proportion to size of the hound. Pasterns short and straight.

FEET: Close, round and firm. Pad full and hard.

DEFECTS: Out at elbows. Knees knuckled over forward, or bent backward. Forelegs crooked or Dachshundlike. Feet long, open or spreading.

HIPS, THIGHS, HIND LEGS AND FEET: Hips and thighs strong and well muscled, giving abundance of propelling power. Stifles strong and well let down. Hocks firm, symmetrical and moderately bent. Feet close and firm.

DEFECTS: Cowhocks, or straight hocks. Lack of muscle and propelling power. Open feet.

TAIL: Set moderately high; carried gaily, but not turned forward over the back; with slight curve; short as compared with size of the hound; with brush.

DEFECTS: A long tail. Teapot curve or inclined forward from the root. Rat tail with absence of brush.

COAT: A close, hard, hound coat of medium length.

DEFECTS: A short, thin coat, or of a soft quality.

A brace of Beagles running a rabbit.

COLOR: Any true hound color.

GENERAL APPEARANCE: A miniature Foxhound, solid and big for his inches, with the wear-and-tear look of the hound that can last in the chase and follow his quarry to the death.

SCALE OF POINTS:		Points
Head		
Skull	5	
Ears	10	
Eyes	5	
Muzzle	5	25
Body		
Neck	5	
Chest and shoulders	15	
Back, loin and ribs	15	35
Running Gear		
Forelegs	10	
Hips, thighs and hind legs	10	
Feet	10	30
Coat	5	
Stern	5	10
TOTAL		100

VARIETIES: There shall be two varieties. Thirteen Inch—which shall be for hounds not exceeding 13 inches in height. Fifteen Inch—which shall be for hounds over 13 but not exceeding 15 inches in height.

Disqualification. Any hound measuring more than 15 inches shall be disqualified.

BLOODHOUND

SUBJECT OF fantastic tales and legends, credited with almost supernatural powers by the uninformed, and possessor of a name which automatically brings fear to the ears of the criminally bent, the Bloodhound is one of the most misunderstood of all breeds.

Many of the tales were really not as fantastic as they sounded and have been born of more truth than fiction, but some have been pure fabrications. Bloodhounds have been known to follow a trail more than 100 hours old, so to some they might well seem to be endowed with supernatural sense in addition to powerful scenting ability. It is easy to understand why their sensational contributions to crime detection, coupled with the word "blood," would cause the criminal to cringe with apprehension whenever the name "Bloodhound" is mentioned. Yet in reality the Bloodhound is one of the most gentle of all dogs. His formidable appearance and deep, roaring bay cause miscreants to shy away from his neighborhood, but

**Beagle—Ch. Elsy's Rumboat, a 13-inch Beagle. (Owner: W. S. and **
J. D. Elsy, Portland, Ore.)

by nature this stately hound is placid and even affectionate.

Many early writers have assumed that the Bloodhound descended from the hounds of St. Hubert, who died A.D. 727. Descendants of St. Hubert's hounds came into England at the time of the Norman Conquest. The tri-colors or white hounds were later known as Talbots and the blacks and black-and-tans were given the name Bloodhound. However, Gratius, writing before the Christian era, and Strabo, at a later date, recorded the importation of sleuth-hounds into Gaul from Britain. St. Hubert is supposed to have obtained his hounds from Gaul.

Early English laws recognized the ability of sleuthhounds and made search of homes to which such hounds trailed a legal action.

In Barbour's *The Bruce* (1316-95) is found the following passage:

"A sleuth hund had he thar alsua.
Sa gud that wald chang for nathing."

The famous letter of Dr. Johannes Caius, written in 1570 to Conrad Gesner, contains an interesting description of the dog we now call the Bloodhound.

From this letter one could easily assume that the name "Bloodhound" may have been given these dogs because they were adept at following the line of wounded animals. Several authorities do not accept this concept of the origin of the term, suggesting that the word "Bloodhound" was used in the same sense as blood horse, meaning thoroughbred. Bloodhound may imply the desire for blood or ferocity, but if so the term is indeed a misnomer, for this is a well-mannered breed, most individuals apparently welcoming friendly overtures and taking correction in training without resentment.

A description of the breed is found in Bellenden's translation of Boece's Latin *History Of Scotland* (1527). It follows:

The third kind is mair than ony rache; reid hewitt, or ellis blak, with small sprainges (tints or markings) or spottis; and ar callit be the peple, Sleuthoundis. This doggis hes sae mervellus wit, that serche tevir and followis on thaim allanerlie be sent of the guddis (goods) that are tane away; and nocht allanerlie findis the thief, bot invadis him with gret cruelte; and, thoucht the thevis oftimes cors the watter, quhair they pass, to caus the hound to tine the sent of thaim and the guddis, yet he serchis heir and thair with sic diligence that, be his fut, he findis baith the trace of the theif and the guddis. The mervellous nature of thir hounds will have no faith with uncouth people; howbeit, the samin ar richt frequent and rife on the bordouris of Ingland and Scotland: atteur it in statue, be the lawis of the Bordouris, he that denyis entres to the sleuthound, in time of chace and serching of guddis, sal be haldin participant with the crime and thift committis.

The sport of tracking has long been sponsored by the Association of Bloodhound Breeders in England, which held its first meet in 1898 on the moors a few miles north of Scarsborough. The tests were made more difficult as time went on.

The Birmingham (England) Show has the distinction of holding the first classes for Bloodhounds.

This was in 1860. Leading hounds of that day were: C. E. Holford's Regent, Trimbush and Matchless; G. Rushton's Juno and Duchess; Dr. E. Reynolds' Rosewell and Ray's Peeress; J. Leigh Becker's Brenda, and two great hounds named Druid, one owned by T. A. Jennings and the other by Col. A. J. Cowen.

Probably the man who did most to establish the Bloodhound on its modern lines and keep its working qualities foremost in mind was Edwin Brough, who was for many years England's leading breeder. Mr. Brough kept two strains from which he could interbreed successfully. One was headed by Champion Beckford and Champion Bianco, and the other by Champion Bono. From a union of those two lines came Champion Panther, the greatest Bloodhound of his day and a most successful sire. When Mr. Brough retired, his bloodlines were taken over by Mrs. Edmunds of Ledburn Manor, Leighton Buzzard, and Henry Hylden of Brighton, who were successful in their breeding operations.

The First American to take an active interest in the breed was L. L. Winchell of Fair Haven, Vermont. Dr. Lougest of Boston, Mass., was next to take up the breed, and then Dr. Knox of Danbury, Conn., entered the field. Dr. Knox for a long time maintained an extensive kennel which enjoyed a greater success at bench shows than perhaps any other establishment in the country. Roger Williams, of Lexington, Ky., is another noted authority on the breed.

Dr. Leon F. Whitney, Orange, Conn., long bred and trained Bloodhounds, and his authoritative writings on the breed have done much to bring its true worth to public attention. In his book *Bloodhounds and How to Train Them* (1947), Dr. Whitney describes three types of Bloodhounds. These are: (a) the show type, (b) the man-trailers used on a leash, and (c) the penitentiary type. Dr. Whitney holds little brief for the show type, which he calls the English type, maintaining these are fragile dogs of low

Bloodhound—Ch. The Ring's Imp. (Owner: Mrs. Robert V. Lindsay, Syosset, N.Y.) Photo by Evelyn M. Shafer.

vitality. He holds their chief value to the breed to be in crossing with other types to keep them looking like Bloodhounds.

Dogs of the man-trailer type may be somewhat of a departure from the show type but they are workmen all the way. These might be termed the medium type and are not the heavy, ponderous loose-skin dogs usually found at bench shows.

The penitentiary type are of even racier build. They need to be faster and are capable of being taught to attack. They are used to track criminals at large, usually escaped convicts, and most of them are good tree dogs. It is not necessary that they possess exceptional noses as the trails they are called upon to follow are seldom old ones. These dogs have done exceptional trailing work, especially in the South where many of the penal institutions are in the form of state farms and attempted escapes are not uncommon.

Dr. Whitney contends that, regardless of the personal preferences of the exponents of each of these types, there are needs for all three types, each of which is called upon to do a different job.

Bloodhounds have long been used in many sections of this country as trailers of lost persons and criminals. Innumerable lives have been saved through the sagacity of these dogs and a recounting of the crimes solved through their trailing would fill many volumes.

Possibly the greatest "Bloodhound detective" ever to live was Captain Volney G. Mullikin, of Kentucky. Through his Bloodhound activities more than 2,500 cases of criminology and missing persons were solved. His best hound was Nick Carter, said to be the greatest man-trailer in history. Over 600 convictions were secured through this dog's work and he held the world's record for following a trail 105 hours old that resulted in a confession. This trail started at a burned chicken-house and ended at a house a mile away.

Captain Mullikin held the distinction of having his dogs work out the shortest trail ever to result in a confession. It was only 10 feet long! His longest trail was 55 miles, during which one of his dogs whelped puppies. The bitch and her young were sent home and the officer went on with the male dog of the pair to catch his man. Perhaps the longest trail on record was that of a burglar, which started in Oneida, Kansas, and ended with the burglar in custody at Elwood, 135 miles away.

Corporal "Cy" Horton of Troop K, New York State Police, had outstanding success with his Bloodhounds, some of which were trained by Dr. Whitney. Trooper Brown of the Rhode Island State Police is another officer who did excellent work with Bloodhounds.

One of the greatest penitentiary dogs was Boston, owned by the state penitentiary at McAlester, Okla. One of his sensational exploits was to aid in rounding up 23 escaped convicts. He worked for a day and a half, with feet torn and nose and lips bleeding.

Bloodhound puppies. Photo by Evelyn M. Shafer.

Another famous dog was Red Eagle, whose master resided at Crystal Springs, Miss. Eagle was in constant demand throughout the state of Mississippi, but officers in his home county (Copiah) maintained that the dog's fabulous reputation kept crime at low tide in that area.

Living conditions have changed greatly since the Bloodhound was first introduced into this country, and the breed appears occasionally in both movies and t.v. Present conditions would seem to render the great dog practically worthless as a crime detector or finder of missing persons. Yet Bloodhound breeders contend that the very opposite holds true and back their statements that practically every trained Bloodhound in the country finds little time for loafing. If one lost child is found by a Bloodhound that dog has saved the community much expense and inconvenience to say nothing of possibly averting a painful death to an innocent youngster.

Description and Standards. The description and standards, by courtesy of the Association of Bloodhound Breeders, England, and followed also by AKC are as follows below.

GENERAL CHARACTER: The Bloodhound possesses, in a most marked degree, every point and characteristic of those dogs which hunt together by scent (Sagaces). He is very powerful, and stands over more ground than is usual with hounds of other breeds. The skin is thin to the touch and extremely loose, this being more especially noticeable about the head and neck, where it hangs in deep folds.

HEIGHT: The mean average height of adult dogs is 26 inches, and of adult bitches 24 inches. Dogs usually vary from 25 inches to 27 inches and bitches from 23 inches to 25 inches; but, in either case, the greater height is to be preferred, provided that character and quality are also combined.

WEIGHT: The mean average weight of adult dogs, in fair condition, is 90 pounds, and of adult bitches 80 pounds. Dogs attain the weight of 110 pounds, bitches 100 pounds. The greater weights are to be preferred, provided (as in the case of height) that quality and proportion are also combined.

EXPRESSION: The expression is noble and dignified, and characterized by solemnity, wisdom, and power.

TEMPERAMENT: In temperament he is extremely affectionate, neither quarrelsome with companions nor with other dogs. His nature is somewhat shy, and equally sensitive to kindness or correction by his master.

HEAD: The head is narrow in proportion to its length, and

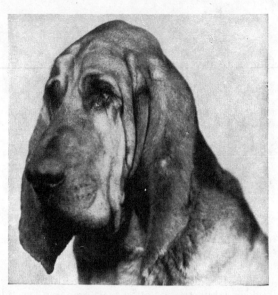

Bloodhound—Head study.

long in proportion to the body, tapering but slightly from the temples to the end of the muzzle, thus (when viewed from above and in front) having the appearance of being flattened at the sides and of being nearly equal in width throughout its entire length. In profile the upper outline of the skull is nearly in the same plane as that of the foreface. The length from end of nose to stop (midway between the eyes) should be not less than that from stop to back of occipital protuberance (peak). The entire length of head from posterior part of the occipital protuberance to the end of the muzzle should be 12 inches, or more, in dogs, and 11 inches, or more, in bitches.

SKULL: The skull is long and narrow, with the occipital peak very pronounced. The brows are not prominent, although, owing to the deep-set eyes, they may have that appearance.

FOREFACE: The foreface is long, deep, and of even width throughout, with square outline when seen in profile.

EYES: The eyes are deeply sunk in the orbits, the lids assuming a lozenge or diamond shape, in consequence of the lower lids being dragged down and everted by the heavy flews. The eyes correspond with the general tone of color of the animal, varying from deep hazel to yellow. The hazel color is, however, to be preferred, although very seldom seen in red-and-tan hounds.

EARS: The ears are thin and soft to the touch, extremely long, set very low, and fall in graceful folds, the lower parts curling inwards and backwards.

WRINKLE: The head is furnished with an amount of loose skin, which in nearly every position appears superabundant, but more particularly so when the head is carried low; the skin then falls into loose, pendulous ridges and folds, especially over the forehead and sides of the face.

NOSTRILS: The nostrils are large and open.

LIPS, FLEWS, AND DEWLAP: In front the lips fall squarely, making a right angle with the upper line of the foreface; whilst behind they form deep, hanging flews, and, being continued into the pendant folds of loose skin about the neck, constitute the dewlap, which is very pronounced. These characters are found, though in a less degree in the bitch.

NECK, SHOULDERS, AND CHEST: The neck is long, the shoulders muscular and well sloped backwards; the ribs are well sprung; and the chest well let down between the fore legs, forming a deep keel.

LEGS AND FEET: The fore legs are straight and large in bone, with elbows squarely set; the feet strong and well knuckled up; the thighs and second thighs (gaskins) are very muscular; the hocks well bent and let down and squarely set.

BACK AND LOIN: The back and loins are strong, the latter deep and slightly arched.

STERN: The stern is long and tapering, and set on rather high, with a moderate amount of hair underneath.

GAIT: The gait is elastic, swinging and free, the stern being carried high, but not too much curled over the back.

COLOR: The colors are black-and-tan, red-and-tan, and tawny; the darker colors being sometimes interspersed with lighter or badger-colored hair, and sometimes flecked with white. A small amount of white is permissible on chest, feet, and tip of stern.

BORZOI

THE NOVICE at a dog show, seeing the exotic beauty of a Borzoi for the first time, might well be surprised to learn that this seeming aristocrat actually is a hound bred in its native land for a highly specialized purpose: to hunt wolves, hence its common name, Russian Wolfhound.

The exact origin of the breed is unknown, although it has been recorded in Russia for more than three centuries. It was first listed in England in 1875 and later in this country. Many believe that the Borzoi may be a descendant of the earliest dogs known to modern man, the Greyhound type pictured in early Persian and Egyptian art. Where the rough coat came from is open to argument. Some believe it may have evolved through centuries of adaptation to the rigors of the Russian winter; others think it may be the result of cross-breeding with a wolf. With either theory, many centuries must have elapsed between the time man and his dog left the warmth of the Middle East until he described his dog in written language in a country far to the north.

Men always have guarded jealously the secrets of their hunting dogs and this, together with great distances, slow means of travel with incidental great expense, also quarantine laws, all undoubtedly tended to prevent earlier distribution of the breed throughout Europe and this country. Probably the first dogs to be exported from Russia were gifts to very important people.

It is believed that the first Borzoi to be imported into this country was a bitch named "Elsie," purchased in England by William Wade of Hulton, Pennsylvania, in 1889. In the last decade of the nineteenth century, C. Stedman Hanks imported several which critics described as good specimens.

Borzoi breeders are indebted to the late Joseph M. Thomas of Valley Farm Kennels for research which led to the standards fixed by the Russian Wolfhound Club in 1905 and continued by the Borzoi Club of America. Mr. Thomas had owned various Borzois and had been puzzled because they did not breed true to any particular type. Much study of the subject convinced him that there was a fixed standard at one time which he referred to as the "ancient type of hounds."

In July, 1903, he made a trip to England to see some dogs which had been imported at great expense by their owners. He visited a number of kennels but was dissatisfied with what he saw. Hardly any two dogs looked alike and practically all had what he had come to believe were faults. He was convinced the key to his problem was in Russia, so he made his first trip there later that same year. He visited many places, including the Imperial Kennels, but still was confronted with the same lack of uniformity, the same evidence of cross-breeding with other types of hounds. It appears that for a considerable period of time in the eighteenth century, there had been a craze in Russia to cross-breed the Borzoi with other hound types, such as various Greyhounds, so that the true ancient type had practically disappeared.

Almost discouraged, he finally was discussing the matter with the editor of a small sports paper, from whom he learned of the kennels of Artem Balderoff at Woronzova and those of His Royal Highness, the Grand Duke Nicholas at Tula. Upon request, he was given permission to visit both kennels and to his great delight found that these men had become interested a quarter of a century earlier in exactly his own problem. Here he found Borzois as close to his idea of perfection as possible. He learned that his mental picture of the "ancient type of hound" was true. It had taken these Russians many generations of careful selection and great care in breeding with full knowl-

An identical brace of Borzois.

edge of lineage to weed out the alien strains and to revert to the true type of Borzoi. He explained to Mr. Walzoff, in charge of the kennels of Grand Duke Nicholas, the difficulties Borzoi breeders were having in England and in America to obtain really good dogs. His knowledge and enthusiasm made such an impression that he was permitted to buy a dog that year, in 1904, and again in 1911.

The first dog Mr. Thomas imported was Bistri of Perchina, an excellent specimen of the "true ancient type"; the second was Sorva of Woronzova, an outstanding bitch of superb form. From the few pictures available of these two Borzois, one is impressed with their symmetry, poise, alert expression, and fluid lines indicative of power and speed.

In the eastern part of the United States the breed is known principally as a show dog and pet. In the West he has been used successfully by ranchers and sheepmen to hunt coyotes and the breed has been advocated by the Department of Agriculture for that purpose.

Borzois have been trained successfully for both theatre and movie appearances. Their lithe grace of movement blends well with the showing of glamorous gowns by fashion mannequins.

A prominent publisher, Alfred A. Knopf, took a stylized design of a Borzoi as his colophon and the word "Borzoi" as his trade-mark in tribute and admiration for the breed.

To Joseph M. Thomas, in his book, *Observations on Borzois,* we are indebted for the following list of names commonly used by Russian owners for their dogs:

Charadei	magician
Blistai	brilliant
Sverkai	flashing
Nadmen	proud
Lubim	beloved
Atmen	"One among many"
Almaz	diamond
Lebid	swan
Aspor	the winner of a dispute
Atamen	chief of Cossacks
Rasboi	brigand
Tiran	tyrant
Naian	troublesome for beasts
Cornnitza	Clever one
Malodietz	brickbat
Oudaloi	brickbat
Oudar	a blow, or to give a blow
Kopchick	a small falcon
Karatai	rapid
Ardagan	favorite falcon of John The Terrible—a Tartar name
Bistri	rapid
Krilatka	white falcon
Zorka	dawn
Lada	bride

The first club organized in this country to further the interest of the breed was The Russian Wolfhound Club of America. It had its constitution adopted on February 19, 1904, with the following officers elected: Edward L. Kraus, president; John G. Kent, vice president; Joseph B. Thomas, Jr., secretary-treasurer. Its objective was defined as follows:

Borzois—A matron and her puppies.

The Russian Wolfhound Club of America is established with a view to promote the breeding of Russian Wolfhounds; to define precisely and publish a definition of the true type; and to urge the adoption of such type by breeders, judges, dog-show committees, etc., as the only recognized and unvarying standards by which Russian Wolfhounds shall be judged, which may in the future be uniformly accepted as the sole standard of excellence in breeding and in awarding prizes of merit to Russian Wolfhounds; and (by giving prizes, supporting shows, and taking other steps) to do all in its power to protect and advance the interests of the breed.

After some years had passed, members felt that the term "Russian Wolfhound" was a misnomer and that the exact Russian word for the breed "Borzoi" would be a more appropriate description. In 1935 the name was changed to the Borzoi Club of America, the Club retaining the same standards and aims.

Description and Standards. The revised description and standards, by courtesy of the Borzoi Club of America, follow:

HEAD: Skull slightly domed, long and narrow, with scarcely any perceptible stop, rather inclined to be Roman-nosed; jaws long, powerful and deep; teeth strong, clean and even, neither pig-jawed nor undershot; nose large and black.

EARS: Small and fine in quality, lying back on the neck when in repose with the tips when thrown back almost touching behind occiput; raised when at attention.

EYES: Set somewhat obliquely, dark in color, intelligent, but rather soft in expression, never full nor staring, nor light in color, eyelids dark.

NECK: Clean, free from throatiness, somewhat shorter than in the Greyhound, slightly arched, very powerful and well set on.

SHOULDERS: Sloping, should be fine at the withers and free from coarseness or lumber.

CHEST: Rather narrow, with great depth of brisket.

RIBS: Only slightly sprung, but very deep, giving room for heart and lung play.

BACK: Rising a little at the loins in a graceful curve.

LOINS: Extremely muscular, but rather tucked up, owing to the great depth of chest and comparative shortness of back and ribs.

FORE LEGS: Bone, flat, straight, giving free play for the elbows, which should be neither turned in nor out; pasterns strong.

FEET: Hare-shaped, with well-arched knuckles, toes close and well padded.

HIND QUARTERS: Long, very muscular and powerful, with well bent stifles and strong second thighs, hocks broad, clean and well let down.

TAIL: Long, set on and carried low in a graceful curve.

COAT: Long, silky (not woolly), either flat, wavy, or rather curly. On the head, ears and front of legs, it should be short and smooth; on the neck the frill should be profuse and rather curly. Feather on hind quarters and tail, long and profuse, less so on the chest and back of fore legs.

COLORS: Any color, white usually predominating, more or less marked with lemon, tan, brindle, grey or black. Whole colored specimens of these tints occasionally appear.

GENERAL APPEARANCE: Should be that of an elegant, graceful aristocrat among dogs, possessing courage and combining muscular power with extreme speed.

SIZE: Dogs, average height at shoulder from 28 to 31 inches; average weight from 75 to 105 pounds. Larger dogs are often seen, extra size being no disadvantage when it is not acquired at the expense of symmetry, speed and staying quality. Bitches are invariably smaller than dogs, and two inches less in height, and from 15 to 20 pounds less in weight is a fair average.

SCALE OF POINTS:	Points
Head	12
Eyes	5
Ears	3
Neck	5
Shoulders and brisket	10
Ribs, back and loins	15
Hind Quarters, stifles and hocks	12
Legs and feet	10
Coat and feather	10
Tail	3
Conformation and gait	15
TOTAL	100

BLACK AND TAN COONHOUND

ALTHOUGH A relative newcomer to official lime-light, there is nothing really *new* about the old-fashioned, long-eared "cooner." The very word "old-fashioned," in his description, stamps him as an old-timer. For many years, night hunters in almost every section of the country where the raccoon is the object of the chase have used Black-and-Tans and preferred them to all other breeds. Generations of intensive use in coon and possum country have developed the Black-and-Tan into a specialist on these two species of furred game. His super-bored nose, keeness on trail, and great determination to force his quarry to take to a tree or log for safety have made him the choice of many coon hunters and his popularity is growing.

There are other breeds of hounds which are known as "coonhounds" and are used almost exclusively on small furred game. Notable among these are the Redbone and Bluetick. There are many packs of these dogs which have been bred from the same foundation stock for many generations and whose blood might well be considered pure.

It remained, however, for a group of far-sighted fanciers of the Black-and-Tan strain to practice careful, selective breeding, to keep detailed breeding records and pedigrees, and to adopt programs pointed to the improvement of their favorite breed. Through such progressive activities and aggressive promotion work, the Black-and-Tan became the first breed to be officially recognized as worthy of the name Coonhound.

Of course, there are many who contend that any hound which will run and tree a coon is entitled to the appellation "coonhound," and this argument has merit. But that brings up the question as to whether the ancestors of that particular hound were proved Coonhounds and whether his progeny will instinctively take to the trail of a coon. Breeders of the old-fashioned Black-and-Tan will not dispute the point and are willing to admit that many types of hounds coming from Foxhound breeding can be trained and developed into proficient cooners—and many are. But, through generations of careful breeding, using only dogs of undisputed ability as trailers and honest treers, the Black-and-Tan exponents have developed a dog which, as a breed, has a natural instinct for night hunting on coons and possums.

Comparatively little has been written about the origin of the old-fashioned Black-and-Tan. The first ancestor is said to have been the now extinct Talbot hound, which came to England with William the Conqueror. It is generally conceded that the foundation stock came from the old Virginia Foxhound known locally as the "black-and-tan," many of which were used in coon hunting. Most of the old Virginia Foxhounds were black and tan in color, although among them were also reds, white-spotted, and fawns. Some of these Black-and-Tans were selected for breeding purposes, not only for their proficiency as coon hunters, but the color factor also played a part. This was not a common practice among foxhound breeders, as color has counted but little with them. These hounds, however, were developed particularly

Black and Tan Coonhound—The ones that perform well are highly prized by their owners. Hank Babbitt photo.

for coon-hunting and trained in this sport for years.

The general appearance of the Black and Tan Coonhound is proof positive that considerable Bloodhound blood was introduced years ago, exactly how many seems unknown. Nevertheless, the blood of the Bloodhound is most obvious, and though the characteristic wrinkles are not present, the flews are not so heavy, and the expression is more alert, the low-hung, somewhat ponderous ears and the general make-up of the dog are indicative of that cross. In fact, the Black-and-Tan is frequently mistaken for a Bloodhound by those unfamiliar with both breeds. Closer inspection, however, or a side-by-side comparison, will quickly reveal the differences.

The Bloodhound influence is also seen in the manner in which the Black-and-Tan works his trail. The Black-and-Tan works entirely by scent and keeps his nose close to the trail. The "breast-high" scent frequently so important to a good fox race is apparently not so interesting to the Black-and-Tan, who sticks to foot-scent. The Bloodhound has undoubtedly contributed the Coonhound's nose. At the same time he has caused him to work his trail at a somewhat slower pace than that of the Foxhound, although he is fast enough for the type of game in which he specializes.

Although a specialist on raccoons, the Black-and-Tan does excellent work in hunting bear, deer, bobcat, mountain lion, and other big game, and many of the "lion" hunters of the West find him of particular value in helping control these cats and other predators in the stock country.

The big hound is a hardy animal and is capable of standing the rigors of winter and the heat of summer and is able to negotiate the rough and difficult terrain over which he is called upon to work.

The Black and Tan Coonhound is easily trained. He is a dog of great determination, his keen nose allows him to pick up and stick to the trail, his deep, musical voice is thrilling, and when he points his handsome nose skyward and lets go with his roaring "tree bark" it generally means the end for Mr. Coon.

The UKC is the largest registrar and focal point of programs involving this much-admired hunting breed.

Description and Standards. The AKC description and standards follow.

The Black and Tan Coonhound is first and fundamentally a working dog, capable of withstanding the rigors of winter, the heat of summer, and the difficult terrain over which he is called upon to work. Judges are asked by the club sponsoring the breed to place great emphasis upon these facts when evalu-

Black and Tan Coonhound. Photo by Evelyn M. Shafer.

the rear. The stride of the Black and Tan Coonhound should be easy and graceful with plenty of reach in front and drive behind.

COAT AND COLOR: The coat should be short but dense to withstand rough going. As the name implies, the color should be coal black, with rich tan markings above eyes, on sides of muzzle, chest, legs and breeching with black pencil markings on **toes.**

SIZE: Measured at the shoulder: males, 25 to 27 inches; females, 23 to 25 inches. Height should be in proportion to general conformation so that dog appears neither leggy nor close to the ground. Dogs oversized should not be penalized when general soundness and proportion are in favor.

Judges should penalize the following defects: Undersize, elbows out at shoulder, lack of angulation in hindquarters, splay feet, sway- or roach back, flatsidedness, lack of depth in chest, yellow or light eyes, shyness and nervousness.

FAULT: Dewclaws; white on chest or other parts of body is highly undesirable and if it exceeds 1½ inches in diameter should be disqualified.

Disqualification. White on chest or other parts of the body if it exceeds 1½ inches in diameter.

(July 10, 1945)

DACHSHUND

OFTEN THE subject of facetious ridicule at the hands of the uninformed, the Dachshund is one of the most interesting of all breeds of dogs. He is frequently referred to as "the sausage dog," described as "half-a-dog high and a dog-and-a-half long," and mentioned as an ideal family dog "because the entire family can pet him at the same time!" He has also been called "the dog that is sold by the yard."

His name implies the early purpose for which he was used, badger hunting; "dachs" meaning badger and "hund" meaning dog in Germany. Although generally associated with a German origin, the Dachshund is very probably of ancient lineage. A long-bodied, low-hung dog is revealed on the statue of an early Egyptian king. This dog's name was "Tekal" and this may be the origin of the name "Teckel," by which the Dachshund is usually known in Germany. The *Teckelklub*, managing Dachshund bench shows, was founded in that country in 1888. The *Gebrauchsteckel-Klubs* conducted the hunting activities of the breed.

A comparatively little-known fact is that there are no less than six varieties of the Dachshund; the original smoothhaired variety from which the others stemmed, the longhaired and the wirehaired, and miniatures of each type. Although the Dachshund is considered the national dog of Germany, other countries have adopted him with even greater enthusiasm and England had a specialty club for the breed before one was established in Germany. The *Gebrauchsteckel-Klubs* of Germany maintained separate stud books on the breed. In this registry only dogs of known hunting ability were recorded, with but little attention to conformation or coat. Pedigrees have extended as far back as 1859 and 1860. In 1915, however, the *Teckelklub* adopted the coat-identifying initials "K" for *Kurzhaar* or smooth, "L" for *Langhaar* or long-hair, and "R" for *Rauhhaar* or wire-

Black and Tan Coonhound—Black predominates in the coat of is one. Hank Babbitt photo.

ating the merits of the dog. The general impression should be that of power, agility, and alertness. His expression should be alert, friendly, eager, and aggressive. He should immediately impress one with his ability to cover the ground with powerful rhythmic strides.

HEAD: The head should be cleanly modeled, with medium stop occurring midway between occiput bone and nose. The head should measure from 9 to 10 inches in males and from 8 to 9 inches in females. Viewed from the profile the line of the skull is on a practically parallel plane to the foreface or muzzle. The skin should be devoid of folds or excess dewlap. The flews should be well developed with typical hound appearance. Nostrils well open and always black. Skull should tend toward oval outline. Eyes should be from hazel to dark brown in color, almost round and not deeply set. The ears should be low set and well back. They should hang in graceful folds giving the dog a majestic appearance. In length they should extend well beyond the tip of the nose. Teeth should fit evenly with slightly scissors bite.

NECK, SHOULDERS, AND CHEST: The neck should be muscular, sloping, medium length, extending into powerfully constructed shoulders and deep chest. The dog should possess full, round, well-sprung ribs, avoiding flatsidedness.

BACK AND TAIL: The back should be level, powerful and strong, with a visible slope from withers to rump. Tail should be strong, with base slightly below level of back line, carried free, and when in action at approximately right angle to back.

LEGS AND FEET: The forelegs should be straight, with elbows well let down, turning neither in nor out; pasterns strong and erect. Feet should be catlike with compact, well-arched toes and thick strong pads.

HINDQUARTERS: Quarters should be well boned and muscled. From hip to hock long and sinewy, hock to pad short and strong. Stifles and hock well bent and not inclining either in or out. When standing on a level surface the hind feet should set back from under the body, and leg from pad to hock be at right angles to the ground when viewed both from profile and

hair. Later the letter "Z" was added to denote *Zwergh* and *Kaninchenteckel* for miniatures.

Field trials are conducted for the breed, both in the European countries and America, the game generally being rabbits. For a while the artificial-burrow "dig" test (Schliefen) was a part of field trial procedure but this was abolished in 1933. The artificially-laid-scent "drag" (Schweiss-Suchen) was also frowned upon as dogs trained for this test began to show little natural hunting desire. The Dachshund's very make-up, with his long-backed body and short, crooked legs, prevents him from hunting with material speed. His main value in the hunting field lies in his ability to rout and kill ground game, but the game resources of this country offer him limited opportunities to display his capabilities in this regard.

Generally, however, in this country he is found as a house pet and companion. Extremely clean in his habits, he is ideal as a house dog, and his cheerful and loyal disposition makes him a fine companion. The smoothhaired variety, with a finely-textured coat which glistens attractively when the dog is properly conditioned and groomed, is a particular favorite. The Dachshund is an especially good dog for children. He generally attaches himself to one master, although his loyalty to the entire family is well known.

The characteristics of the breed and the evenness of type have been maintained in this country by constant importation of new blood and careful adherence to a program of breeding selectivity.

It has been no easy matter to maintain the popularity of the breed in this country, or in England. During World War I there were only about six breeders in England who continued their breeding programs. In this country antipathy to anything German during that period reflected against the chipper little dog that had won many friends here, and owners who appeared in public with their pets were often subjected to contemptuous remarks and accusations of being "pro-German." During the years between the two great wars, however, the Dachshund had regained his place in the hearts of many American dog fanciers and the general public took a saner view of him during World War II.

The Dachshund got his name from his early use in badger hunting but since the breed was established the type has changed to some extent. The successful badger dog was heavier, coarser, larger, and more houndy in appearance. The ability to dig was a requisite and the Dachshund is so equipped. Generally on the lower slopes of the mountainous sections of Germany where the badger did much damage to growing crops of maize, the dogs were used to drive these animals to the guns which were posted between the game and their earths. The badger makes a formidable opponent when brought to bay and although the Dachshund is a fearless fellow, he would have a rough time of dispatching this prey in a fair fight.

The Dachshund has been used successfully in hunting deer, due to the fact that he can penetrate almost any cover and his physical make-up forces him to travel at slow pace, consequently he does not so frighten the deer as to make it "run out of the country." His bay is much deeper than one would expect of so small a dog.

In this country the Dachshund is now seldom used as a sporting dog, although promoters of the breed have held field trials in an endeavor to definitely establish him as a sporting dog in this country. The American Kennel Club classifies the Dachshund as a sporting dog in the hound class, but it has been argued that he is not a hound and he is certainly not generally considered a gundog. Nevertheless, he possesses hunting instinct in a high degree and if given the chance can give his owner much pleasure on small ground game.

The origin of the breed is a matter of conjecture. Now recognized as distinctly German, they were to be found throughout Western Europe at an early date. Some early writers maintained that they evolved from the old Turnspits, the dogs that did such fine yoeman work in kitchen service. Certainly the dogs used for this purpose were long of body and low of leg.

Other writers held that the breed descended from the Basset Hounds of France, with much of the hound type being eliminated by the infusion of terrier blood. In the small person of the Dachshund we do, indeed, find the characteristics of both the hound and terrier. In many respects he resembles the Basset, while his small stature, courage, and willingness to go to earth bespeak terrier blood.

Two dogs which did much to establish accepted Dachshund type in the early days in England were Jackdaw, owned by Harry Jones of Ipswich, and Pterodactyl, whelped in 1888, bred by a Mr. Willink and eventually purchased by Sidney Woodiwiss, who had the largest kennel of Dachshunds in England. Both left a lasting stamp upon the breed and were used in the stud extensively.

In this country, the dogs of Dr. C. Motschenbacher of New York City, and Mr. and Mrs. Karl A. Keller of Wellesley, Mass., were the most prominent winners around the turn of the century. Dr. Motschenbacher's Champion Young Phoenomen, Jr. was in great demand, as was the Keller's Champion Parsifal.

Dachshund—Smooth-coated. Photo by Evelyn M. Shafer.

Dachshund—Long-haired. Photo by Evelyn M. Shafer.

The high popularity of the breed in all its variations is definitely well established in this country. Large entries are to be seen in practically every important bench show. With these conditions prevailing it is only natural that there are many champion Dachshunds throughout the country and competition is exceedingly keen among breeders and exhibitors.

The Dachshund is a favorite breed in Australia and is considered a favorite hound in Great Britain, Denmark, Holland, and India. The smooth Dachshund is a favorite hound in Great Britain.

The Dachshund is a lively friendly fellow, affectionate with his family but somewhat a one-man dog. He is unusually clean, having practically no "doggy" odor about him, and requires little grooming. One of the most amusingly fascinating sights is to watch a litter of young Dachshund puppies at play. And they are generally playing when not sleeping.

Description and Standards. The description and standards follow.

SUMMARY

GENERAL APPEARANCE: Short-legged, long-bodied, low-to-ground; sturdy, well muscled, neither clumsy nor slim, with audacious carriage and intelligent expression; conformation preeminently fitted for following game into burrows.

HEAD: Long, uniformly tapered, clean-cut; teeth well fitted, with scissors bite; eyes medium oval; ears broad, long, rounded, set on high and well back; neck long, muscular. Forequarters—Muscular, compact. Chest deep, long, full and oval; breastbone prominent. Broad, long shoulder, and oblique humerus forming right angle; heavy, set close; forearm short, inclined slightly in. Foreleg straight and vertical in profile, covering deepest point of chest. Feet broad, firm, compact, turned slightly out. Hindquarters—Well-muscled and rounded. Pelvis, femur and tibia oblique, forming right angles; tarsus inclined forward. Hip should be level with shoulder, back strong, neither sagged nor more than very slightly arched. Tail strong, tapered, well-covered with hair, not carried gaily.

VARIETIES: Three coat types: Smooth or Shorthaired, short and dense, shining, glossy. Wirehaired, like German Wirehaired Pointer, hard, with good undercoat. Longhaired, like Irish Setter.

NOTE: In each coat variety there are divisions of open classes restricted to Miniatures, under 9 pounds, minimum age 12 months.

COLOR: Solid red (tan) of various shades, and black with tan points, should have black noses and nails, and narrow black line edging lips and eyelids; chocolate with tan points permits brown nose. Eyes of all, lustrous, the darker the better.

FAULTS: Overshot or undershot, knuckling over, loose shoulders; high on legs, clumsy gait, long, splayed or twisted feet, sagged or roached back, high croup, small, narrow or short chest, faulty angulation of fore or hindquarters, weak loins, narrow hindquarters, bowed legs, cowhocks; weak or dish-faced muzzle, dewlaps, uneven or scanty coat.

GENERAL FEATURES

GENERAL APPEARANCE: Low to ground, short-legged, long-bodied, but with compact figure and robust muscular development; with bold and confident carriage of the head and intelligent facial expression. In spite of his shortness of leg, in comparison with his length of trunk, he should appear neither crippled, awkward, cramped in his capacity for movement, nor slim and weasel-like.

QUALITIES: He should be clever, lively, and courageous to the point of rashness, persevering in his work both above and below ground; with all the senses well developed. His build and disposition qualify him especially for hunting game below ground. Added to this, his hunting spirit, good nose, loud tongue, and small size, render him especially suited for beating the bush. His figure and his fine nose give him an especial advantage over most other breeds of sporting dogs for trailing.

CONFORMATION OF BODY

HEAD: Viewed from above or from the side, it should taper uniformly to the tip of the nose, and should be clean-cut. The skull is only slightly arched, and should slope gradually without stop (the less stop the more typical) into the finely-firmed slightly-arched muzzle (ram's nose). The bridge bones over the eyes should be strongly prominent. The nasal cartilage and tip of the nose are long and narrow; lips tightly stretched, well covering the lower jaw, but neither deep nor pointed; corner of the mouth not very marked. Nostrils well open. Jaws opening wide and hinged well back of the eyes, with strongly developed bones and teeth.

(a) Teeth: Powerful canine teeth should fit closely together, and the outer side of the lower incisors should tightly touch the inner side of the upper. (Scissors bite.) (b) Eyes: Medium size, oval, situated at the sides, with a clean, energetic, though pleasant expression; not piercing. Color, lustrous dark reddish-brown to brownish-black for all coats and colors. Wall (fish or pearl) eyes in the case of gray or dapple-colored dogs are not a very bad fault, but are also not desirable. (c) Ears: Should be set near the top of the head, and not too far forward, long but not too long, beautifully rounded, not narrow, pointed, or folded. Their carriage should be animated, and the forward edge should just touch the cheek. (d) Neck: Fairly long, muscular, clean-cut, not showing any dewlap on the throat, slightly arched in the nape, extending in a graceful line into the shoulders, carried proudly but not stiffly.

FRONT: To endure the arduous exertion underground, the front must be correspondingly muscular, compact, deep, long and broad. Forequarters in detail: (a) Shoulder Blade: Long, broad, obliquely and firmly placed upon the fully developed thorax, furnished with hard and plastic muscles. (b) Upper Arm: Of the same length as the shoulder blade, and at right angles to the latter, strong of bone and hard of muscle, lying close to the ribs, capable of free movement. (c) Forearm: This is short in comparison to other breeds, slightly turned inwards; supplied with hard but plastic muscles on the front and outside, with tightly stretched tendons on the inside and at the back. (d) Joint between forearm and foot (wrists): These are closer together than the shoulder joints, so that the front does not appear absolutely straight. (e) Paws: Full, broad in front, and a trifle inclined outwards; compact, with well-arched toes and tough pads. (f) Toes: There are five of these, though only four are in use. They should be close together, with a pronounced arch; provided on top with strong nails, and underneath with tough toe-pads.

Trunk: The whole trunk should in general be long and fully muscled. The back, with sloping shoulders, and short, rigid pelvis, should lie in the straightest possible line between the withers and the very slightly arched loins, these latter being short, rigid, and broad. (a) Chest: The breastbone should be strong, and so prominent in front that on either side a depression (dimple) appears. When viewed from the front, the thorax should appear oval, and should extend downward to the mid-point of the forearm. The enclosing structure of ribs should appear full and oval, and when viewed from above or from the side, full-volumed, so as to allow by its ample capacity, complete development of heart and lungs. Well ribbed up, and gradually merging into the line of the abdomen. If the length is correct, and also the anatomy of the shoulder and upper arm, the front leg when viewed in profile should cover the lowest point of the breast line. (b) Abdomen: Slightly drawn up.

Hindquarters: The hindquarters viewed from behind should be of completely equal width. (a) Croup: Long, round, full, robustly muscled, but plastic, only slightly sinking toward the tail. (b) Pelvic Bones: Not too short, rather strongly developed, and moderately sloping. (c) Thigh Bone: Robust and of good length, set at right angles to the pelvic bones. (d) Hind Legs: Robust and well-muscled, with well-rounded buttocks. (e) Knee Joint: Broad and strong. (f) Calf Bone: In comparison with other breeds, short; it should be perpendicular to the thigh bone, and firmly muscled. (g) The bones at the base of the foot (tarsus) should present a flat appearance, with a strongly prominent hock and a broad tendon of Achilles. (h) The central foot bones (metatarsus) should be long, movable towards the calf bone, slightly bent toward the front, but perpendicular (as viewed from behind). (i) Hind Paws: Four compactly closed and beautifully arched toes, as in the case of the front paws. The whole foot should be posed equally on the ball and not merely on the toes; nails short.

Tail: Set in continuation of the spine, extending without very pronounced curvature, and should not be carried too gaily.

Note: Inasmuch as the Dachshund is a hunting dog, scars from honorable wounds shall not be considered a fault.

SPECIAL CHARACTERISTICS OF THE THREE COAT-VARIETIES

The Dachshund is bred with three varieties of coat: (1) Shorthaired (or *Smooth*); (2) Wirehaired; (3) Longhaired. All three varieties should conform to the characteristics already specified. The longhaired and shorthaired are old, well-fixed varieties, but into the wirehaired Dachshund, the blood of other breeds has been purposely introduced; nevertheless, in breeding him, the greatest stress must be placed upon conformity to the general Dachshund type. The following specifications are applicable separately to the three coat-varieties, respectively:

SHORTHAIRED (OR SMOOTH) DACHSHUND

(1) Hair: Short, thick, smooth and shining; no bald patches. Special faults are: Too fine or thin hair, leathery ears, bald patches, too coarse or too thick hair in general. Tail: Gradually tapered to a point, well but not too richly haired; long, sleek bristles on the underside are considered a patch of strong-growing hair, not a fault. A brush tail is a fault, as is also a partly or wholly hairless tail.

Color of hair, nose and nails: (a) One-colored Dachshund: This group includes red (often called tan), red-yellow, and yellow, with or without a shading of interspersed black hairs. Nevertheless a clean color is preferable, and red is to be considered more desirable than red-yellow or yellow. Dogs strongly shaded with interspersed black hairs belong to this class, and not to the other color groups. No white is desirable, but a solitary small spot is not exactly disqualifying. Nose and Nails—Black; red is admissible, but not desirable.

(b) Two-Colored Dachshund: These comprise deep black, chocolate, gray, and white; each with rust-brown or yellow marks over the eyes, on the sides of the jaw and underlip, on the inner edge of the ear, front, breast, inside and behind the front leg, on the paws and around the anus, and from there to about one-third to one-half of the length of the tail on the under side. (The most common two-colored Dachshund is usually called black-and-tan.) Except on white dogs, no white is desirable, but a solitary small spot is not exactly disqualifying. Absence, or undue prominence of tan markings is undesirable. Nose and Nails—In the case of black dogs, black; for chocolate, brown or black; for gray, gray or even flesh color, but the last named color is not desirable; in the case of white dogs, black nose and nails are to be preferred.

(c) Dappled and Striped Dachshund: The color of the dappled (or tiger) Dachshund is a clear brownish or grayish color, or even a white ground, with dark irregular patches of dark-gray, brown, red-yellow or black (large areas of one color not desirable). It is desirable that neither the light nor the dark color should predominate. The color of the striped (brindle) Dachshund is red or yellow with a darker streaking. Nose and Nails—As for One- and Two-Colored Dachshund.

WIREHAIRED DACHSHUND

(2) The general appearance is the same as that of the shorthaired, but without being long in the legs, it is permissible for the body to be somewhat higher off the ground.

Hair: With the exception of jaw, eyebrows and ears, the whole body is covered with a perfectly uniform tight, short, thick, rough, hard coat, but with finer, shorter hairs (undercoat) everywhere distributed between the coarser hairs, resembling the coat of the German Wirehaired Pointer. There should be a beard on the chin. The eyebrows are bushy. On the ears the hair is shorter than on the body; almost smooth, but in any case conforming to the rest of the coat. The general arrangement of the hair should be such that the wirehaired Dachshund, when seen from a distance should resemble the smoothhaired. Any sort of soft hair in the coat is faulty, whether short or long, or wherever found on the body; the same is true of long, curly, or wavy hair, or hair that sticks out irregularly in all directions; a flag tail is also objectionable. Tail: Robust, as thickly haired as possible, gradually coming to a point, and without a tuft. Color of Hair, Nose and Nails: All colors are admissible. White patches on the chest, though allowable, are not desirable.

LONGHAIRED DACHSHUND

(3) The distinctive characteristic differentiating this coat from the shorthaired, or smoothhaired Dachshund is alone the rather long silky hair. Hair: The soft, sleek, glistening, often slightly wavy hair should be longer under the neck, on the underside of the body, and especially on the ears and behind the legs, becoming there a pronounced feather; the hair should attain its greatest length on the underside of the tail. The hair should fall beyond the lower edge of the ear. Short hair on the ear, so-called "leather" ears, is not desirable. Too luxurious a coat causes the longhaired Dachshund to seem coarse, and masks the type. The coat should remind one of the Irish Setter, and should give the dog an elegant appearance. Too thick hair on the paws, so-called "mops," is inelegant, and renders the animal unfit for use. It is faulty for the dog to have equally long hair over all the body, if the coat is too curly, or too scrubby, or if a flag tail or overhanging hair on the ears are lacking, or if there is a very pronounced parting on the back, or a vigorous growth between the toes. Tail: Carried gracefully in prolongation of the spine; the hair attains here its greatest length and forms a veritable flag. Color of Hair, Nose and Nails: Exactly as for the Smoothhaired Dachshund.

Note: Miniature Dachshunds are bred in all three coats. They are not undersized or underdeveloped specimens of full-size Dachshunds, but have been purposely produced to work in burrows smaller than standard Dachshunds can enter. The limits set upon their size have inevitably resulted in a more

Dachshund—The three varieties shown here are (left) a wirehaired Dachshund; (center) a long-haired Miniature Dachshund; (right) a smooth Dachshund. Photo by Paul Toppelstein.

slender body structure. Depth of chest and shortness of leg proportionate to the regular conformation would, in these diminutive animals, prove impractical for their active hunting purposes.

The German specifications limit Zwergteckel (dwarf Dachshund) to a chest circumference of 13.8 inches and limit Kaninchenteckel (rabbit Dachshunds) to a chest circumference of 11.8 inches, certified at a minimum age of 12 months. Rather than the ideal, these sizes represent instead the upper limit for miniature re-registration; and thus in pedigrees provide an index to purity of miniature breeding.

In the United States Miniature Dachshunds have not been given separate classification. At American shows, a division of the open class for "under 9 pounds and 12 months old or over" permits class competition as miniatures, and opportunity in winners classes to compete for championship points in each coat variety. Within the limits imposed, symmetrical adherence to the general Dachshund conformation, combined with smallness, and mental and physical vitality should be outstanding characteristics of the Miniature Dachshund.

GENERAL FAULTS

Serious Faults (which may prevent a dog from receiving any show rating): Overshot or undershot jaws, knuckling over, very loose shoulders.

Secondary Faults (which may prevent a dog from receiving a high show rating): A weak, long-legged, or dragging figure; body hanging between the shoulders; sluggish, clumsy, or waddling gait; toes turned inwards or too obliquely outwards; splayed paws; sunken back, roach (or carp) back; croup higher than withers; short-ribbed or too weak chest; excessively drawn-up flanks like those of a Greyhound; narrow, poorly muscled hindquarters; weak loins; bad angulation in front or hindquarters; cowhocks; bowed legs; "glass" eyes, except for gray or dappled dogs; a bad coat.

Minor Faults (which may prevent a dog from receiving the highest rating in championship competition): Ears wrongly set, sticking out, narrow or folded; too marked a stop; too pointed or weak a jaw; pincer teeth, distemper teeth; too wide or too short a head; goggle eyes, "glass" eyes in the case of gray and dappled dogs, insufficiently dark eyes in the case of all other coat-colors; dewlaps; short neck; swan neck; too fine or too thin hair.

(July 9, 1935)

SCOTTISH DEERHOUND

SHADES OF plumed knights in armour, laden banquet tables in tapestried halls, the splendor of the Age of Chivalry! And woven into the pattern as a symbol is the Scottish Deerhound.

Truly a dog of the nobility, for years possessed by no one of lesser rank than an earl, the calm demeanor and characteristic faraway expression of the Deerhound seems to recall those olden, golden days. Extremely rugged in appearance, yet remarkably graceful, the dog's stately carriage denotes aristocracy in every line.

Early writings on the breed are somewhat confusing, as the reader is often unable to determine whether the passage refers to the Deerhound or to the Irish Wolfhound. Many names were used to describe the breed, principal of which are Rough Highland Greyhound, Highland Greyhound, Wolfdog, and Staghound. The breed is known to have existed in Scotland and elsewhere before A.D. 1526. Both Rough and Smooth Greyhounds are mentioned in Arrian's writings and Dr. Johannes Caius, writing in 1576, described Greyhounds as: "Some are of greater sorte and some of a lesser. Some are smoothe skynned and some are curled, the bigger therefor are appointed to hunt the bigger beastes . . ." and he defines these "beastes" as "the buck, the harte, and the doe." Holinshed in 1577 used practically the same description, but used the term "Shaggy haired" instead of "curled."

Dalziel stated that the text of Pitscottie's *History of Scotland,* published about 1600, contained the term "deer hounds," but later writers argued that this was in error. The passage referred to follows: "The King (A.D. 1528) desired all gentlemen that had dogges that war guid to bring thame to hunt in the saidis boundis, quhilk the most pairt of the noblemen of the Highlandis did, sick as the Earles of Huntlie, Argyle, and Athol, who brought their deir hounds with thame and hunted with his majestie."

Chronicles of Scotland, written in 1728 by Robert Linsay, contains a similar passage but eliminating the word "deir." It follows: "And also warned all Gentlemen that had good Dogs to bring them, that he might hunt in the said country, as he pleased, the whilk, the Earl of Argyle, the Earl of Huntley, the Earl of Athole, and so all the rest of the Gentlemen of the Highland did, and brought their Hounds with them in like manner, to hunt with the King, as he pleased." But in the 1814 edition of Robert Linsay's work, the quotation as given by Dalziel is used.

Scrope's work, published in 1838, contains a chapter on the Deerhound written by a Archbold Macneile which is the first detailed description of the breed in British literature. He stated that the finest Deerhounds at that time were Buskar and Brass and the bitches, Runa and Cavack, belonging to his brother. Buskar, a pale, yellow dog with wiry hair, stood 28 inches at the shoulder, with a chest girth of 32 inches and weighed about 85 pounds.

Youatt, in 1845, stated that the Scotch Deerhound was a typical Greyhound, only with a rough coat and stronger in build. He described the Highland Greyhound or Deerhound as being larger than the Scottish Greyhound.

Stonehenge, writing in 1859, stated that the rough Greyhound was identical in conformation with the pure Deerhound and "can only be distinguished by their style of running when at work or play."

Stonehenge contended that Maida, the famous hound whose noted master, Sir Walter Scott, described as "the most perfect creature of Heaven," was not a Deerhound but a cross between a Greyhound and a Bloodhound. Captain Graham stated that the sire of Maida was a Pyrenean wolf-dog.

Along in the 1860's the most famous Deerhounds were Old Torunn and Young Torunn, owned by Mr. Chaworth of Kirk Langton. Both became noted sires. Queen Victoria was interested in the breed. Her Kieldar was the sire of Hylda, the dam of the famous Morni. Morni stood 30¼ inches at the shoulder and had a chest girth of 34 inches.

Early breeders of the Deerhound jealously guarded them, and as a result of inbreeding, the struggle for breed survival was, in several periods, a hard one. However, Deerhound fanciers managed to hold the breed together and Deerhounds were by no means rare in the Highland districts in the middle '80's. The sport of deer coursing declined and gradually faded from the picture, first, because hunters contended the hounds drove the deer out of the forests into areas where no hunting was allowed; secondly, because stalking and shooting became more popular. But the breed became fairly popular with the bench show fancy.

The Birmingham show of 1860 was the first show at which there were classes for Deerhounds. One class was for dogs, the other for bitches. Lieut. Col. Inge, of Thorpe, won both classes with Valiant and Brimstone.

Among the early breeders were: Lord Henry Bentinck, the Duke of Sutherland, W. Gordon, Lord Breadalbane, Dr. Hadden, Spencer Lucy, Sir St. George Gore, Captain Graham of Durnock, and H. C. Musters.

Near the turn of the century the best known dogs were Sir Gavin, Fingal II, Ensign, Shepherd, Swift, Earl II, Enterprise, Royal Lufra, and Rossie Bluebell. Several left their stamp on the breed.

The Deerhound has always been held in high value. His worth in the chase of the large Scottish deer was long established. In addition he was a splendid guard and companion for the Highland Chieftains, and while he is essentially a hunting dog, he has a well-grounded love of human companionship. At one time he was held in such high esteem that a nobleman condemned to die could buy his freedom with a leash of these hounds. He has fine powers of scent and is a good tracker. In disposition, he is friendly, tractable and easily trained, possessing devotion and loyalty to his master.

Description and Standards. The description and standards, adopted by the Scottish Deerhound Club of America and approved by the American Kennel Club follow.

HEAD: Should be broadest at the ears, narrowing slightly to the eyes, with the muzzle tapering more decidedly to the nose. The muzzle should be pointed, but the teeth and lips level. The head should be long, the skull flat rather than round with a very slight rise over the eyes but nothing approaching a stop. The hair on the skull should be moderately long and softer than the rest of the coat. The nose should be black (in some blue fawns—blue) and slightly aquiline. In lighter colored dogs the black muzzle is preferable. There should be a good mustache of rather silky hair and a fair beard.

EARS: Should be set on high; in repose, folded back like a Greyhound's, though raised above the head in excitement without losing the fold, and even in some cases semi-erect. A prick ear is bad. Big thick ears hanging flat to the head or heavily coated with long hair are bad faults. The ears should be soft, glossy, like a mouse's coat to the touch, and the smaller the better. There should be no long coat or long fringe, but there is sometimes a silky, silvery coat on the body of the ear and the tip. On all Deerhounds irrespective of color of coat, the ears should be black or dark colored.

NECK AND SHOULDERS: The neck should be long—of a length befitting the Greyhound character of the dog. Extreme length is neither necessary nor desirable. Deerhounds do not stoop to their work like the Greyhounds. The mane, which every good specimen should have, sometimes detracts from the apparent length of the neck. The neck, however, must be strong as is necessary to hold a stag. The nape of the neck should be very prominent where the head is set on, and the throat clean cut at the angle and prominent. Shoulders should be well sloped; blades well back and not too much width between them. Loaded and straight shoulders are very bad faults.

TAIL: Should be tolerably long, tapering and reaching to within 1½ inches off the ground and about 1½ inches below the hocks. Dropped perfectly down or curved when the Deerhound is still, when in motion or excited—curved, but in no instance lifted out of line of the back. It should be well covered with hair, on the inside, thick and wiry, underside longer and towards the end, a slight fringe is not objectionable. A curl or ring tail is undesirable.

EYES: Should be dark—generally dark brown, brown or hazel. A very light eye is not liked. The eye should be moderately full, with a soft look in repose, but keen, far-away look when the Deerhound is roused. Rims of eyelids should be black.

BODY: General formation is that of a Greyhound of larger size and bone. Chest deep rather than broad, but not too narrow or slab-sided. Good girth of chest is indicative of great lung power. The loin well arched and drooping to the tail. A straight back is not desirable, this formation being unsuited for uphill work, and very unsightly.

LEGS AND FEET: Legs should be broad and flat, and good broad forearms and elbows are desirable. Forelegs must, of course, be as straight as possible. Feet close and compact, with well-arranged toes. The hind quarters drooping, and as broad and powerful as possible, the hips being set wide apart. A narrow rear denotes lack of power. The stifles should be well bent, with great length from hip to hock, which should be broad and flat. Cowhocks, weak pasterns, straight stifles and splay feet are very bad faults.

COAT: The hair on the body, neck and quarters should be harsh and wiry, about 3 or 4 inches long; that on the head, breast and belly much softer. There should be a slight fringe on the inside of the fore and hind legs but nothing approaching the "feather" of a Collie. A woolly coat is bad. Some good strains have a mixture of silky coat with the hard which is preferable to a woolly coat. The climate of United States tends to produce the mixed coat. The ideal coat is a thick, closelying ragged coat, harsh or crisp to the touch.

Color is a matter of fancy but the dark blue-grey is most preferred. Next comes the darker and lighter greys or brindles, the darkest being generally preferred. Yellow and sandy red or red fawn, especially with black ears and muzzles, are equally high in estimation. This was the color of the oldest known strains—the McNeil and Chesthill Menzies. White is condemned by all authorities, but a white chest and white toes, occurring as they do in many of the darkest colored dogs are not objected to, although the less the better, for the Deerhound is a self-colored dog. A white blaze on the head, or a white collar, should entirely disqualify. The less white the better but a slight white tip to the stern occurs in some of the best strains.

HEIGHT OF DOGS: From 30 to 32 inches, or even more if there be symmetry without coarseness, which is rare.

HEIGHT OF BITCHES: From 28 inches upwards. There is no objection to a bitch being large, unless too coarse, as even at her greatest height she does not approach that of the dog, and therefore could not be too big for work as overbig dogs are.

WEIGHT: From 85 to 110 pounds in dogs and from 75 to 95 pounds in bitches.

SCALE OF POINTS:

Arranged in Order of Importance

1. *Typical*—A Deerhound should resemble a rough-coated Greyhound of larger size and bone.

Scottish Deerhound.

2. *Movements*—Easy, active and true.
3. *Height*—As tall as possible consistent with quality.
4. *Head*—Long, level, well balanced, carried high.
5. *Body*—Long, very deep in brisket, well sprung ribs and great breadth across hips.
6. *Fore legs*—Strong and quite straight, with elbows neither in nor out.
7. *Thighs*—Long and muscular, second thighs well muscled, stifles well bent.
8. *Loins*—Well arched, and belly well drawn up.
9. *Coat*—Rough and hard with softer beard and brows.
10. *Feet*—Close, compact, with well knuckled toes.
11. *Ears*—Small (dark) with Greyhound-like carriage.
12. *Eyes*—Dark, moderately full.
13. *Neck*—Long, well arched, very strong with prominent nape.
14. *Shoulders*—Clean, set sloping.
15. *Chest*—Very deep but not too narrow.
16. *Tail*—Long and curved slightly, carried low.
17. *Teeth*—Strong and level.
18. *Nails*—Strong and curved.
   Disqualification. White blaze on the head, or a white collar.

AMERICAN FOXHOUND

American Foxhound—A head study. Hank Babbitt photo.

THE FOXHOUND is America's oldest sporting dog. Just when he first came to this country is a matter of uncertainty, but Hernando DeSoto, the Spanish explorer, had "hounds" with him when the discovered the Mississippi River in 1541. These hounds were not used for hunting fox, however, but for hunting Indians!

Robert Brooke, a friend of Lord Baltimore, brought the first pack of hounds to America on June 30, 1650, after Baltimore had appointed him a member of the "Privy Council of State within our said Province of Maryland." Mr. Brooke lived for only five years after coming to America, but he is recognized as the first Master of Foxhounds in this country. The sport which he established, fox hunting, spread rapidly and widely and now is enjoyed in practically every state of the Union. As the dates of the establishment of the first pack of hounds in England to be used exclusively for fox hunting have been variously reported as 1666, 1690, and 1698, it has been authoritatively maintained that packs of foxhounds have existed in this country almost as long as they have in England.

Many of the founders of this nation were fox hunters. Foremost among them was, of course, George Washington, who learned much of the sport, while still in his teens, from Thomas, Lord Fairfax. Thomas Jefferson, Alexander Hamilton and Thomas Marshall were all ardent fox hunters, and the Marquis de Lafayette, in August, 1785, sent seven "stag hounds" to Washington in the thought that they would augment the first President's pack. These large French hounds did not take well to fox and Washington was disappointed in them.

There have been, and still are, many strains of American Foxhounds, practically all of which had their fountain-heads in the Brooke hounds, later importations from England, France, and Ireland or some combinations of these blood lines. Most prominent of these strains are the Walker and the Trigg, which are discussed at greater length elsewhere in this text.

Other strains were the Travis, Goodman, Hampton-Watts-Bennett, Shaver, July, Sugar Loaf, Roberston, Whitlock Shaggies, Trumbo, Bywaters, Arkansas Traveler, Spalding-Norris, Byron, Cook, Buckfield, and New England Natives. All of these strains flourished in their various localities for a time, and some of them still exist, but the Walker, Trigg, and July are by far the best known and in highest favor today.

The versatility of the foxhound is something at which to marvel. He can be trained to trail any species of ground game and even Man himself. A truly good foxhound possesses more qualities than any other domestic animal used for sport. He must have an amazing amount of endurance, more than the quarry he seeks. He must have a better nose than any other sporting dog, exceptional speed, good, free cry, strength to carry him through heavy covers and over rugged country, the agility to negotiate any sort of terrain quickly, and remarkable intelligence. In addition he must possess determination in a high degree, a high desire to reach his quarry, and the gameness and stamina to match his determination. He must be willing to "packup" or run with the pack, "harking in" immediately when another casting member of the pack "speaks" the trail. And he must possess that mysterious quality which has brought so many wandering hounds home, a homing instinct.

This is, indeed, a large package, yet it is wrapped up in countless blocks of hound hide wherever hounds are bred and hunted.

For versatility, stamina, nose, natural hunting intelligence, and gameness the foxhound knows no superior in the American sporting scene. Running the trail hour after hour, with seldom or never a glimpse of his quarry, the foxhound gives his best in the sheer joy of the chase.

The largest recorded litter of pups was born to a foxhound bitch, by the way, there being 23 pups born February 11, 1945 to Lena, owned by Commander W. N. Ely of Ambler, Pennsylvania.

It is not possible to list many of the breeders of foxhounds in this country, for their number has been legion. A few who once were, and some who may still be well-known fanciers, breeders, and authorities are listed as follows:

Walker strain: Woods Walker, Paint Lick, Kentucky; Ed Power, Frankfort, Kentucky; Roger Stone, Lexington, Kentucky; S. L. Wooldridge, Jr., Versailles, Kentucky; Robert J. Goode, Gastonburg, Alabama; J. Wade Walker, Paint Lick, Kentucky; Jack Malone, Portersville, Alabama, and Alex Parish, Richmond, Kentucky.

Trigg strain: Robert Rodes, Bowling Green, Kentucky; J. S. Kirby, Bowling Green, Kentucky; L. S. McMillan, Laurens, South Carolina, and Paul Greer, Glasgow, Kentucky.

Spalding-Norris strain: Ralph Wingo, Monroe, Missouri.

Goodman strain: John H. Allen, Iuka, Mississippi; Tom Davis, Hazelwood, North Carolina; and Hughes Atkinson, Owingsville, Kentucky.

July strain: E. Burton Cooke, Asheville, North Carolina.

Trumbo strain: Glenn Sutton, Hurley, New Mexico, and John W. Scott, Shelbyville, Indiana.

Description and Standards. The description and standards, by courtesy of the American Foxhound Club, follow.

HEAD: *Skull*—Should be fairly long, slightly domed at occiput, with cranium broad and full. *Ears:* Ears set on moderately low, long, reaching when drawn out nearly, if not quite, to the tip of the nose; fine in texture, fairly broad, with almost entire absence of erectile power—setting close to the head with the forward edge slightly inturning to the cheek—round at tip. *Eyes:* Eyes large, set well apart—soft and houndlike—expression gentle and pleading; of a brown or hazel color. *Muzzle:* Muzzle of fair length—straight and square cut—the top moderately defined. *Defects:* A very flat skull, narrow across the top; excess of dome; eyes small, sharp and terrier-like, or prominent and protruding; muzzle long and snipey; cut away decidedly below the eyes, or very short. Roman nosed, or upturned, giving a

Foxhounds at a bench show in Florida. David M. Duffey photo.

American Foxhounds on the trail. David Duffey photo.

Young Walker Foxhounds trying to solve a loss in the trail. David Duffey photo.

dish-face expression. Ears short, set on high, with a tendency to rise above the point of origin.

BODY: *Neck and Throat:* Neck rising free and light from the shoulders, strong in substance yet not loaded, of medium length. The throat clean and free from folds of skin, a slight wrinkle below the angle of the jaw, however, is allowable. *Defects:* A thick, short, cloddy neck carried on a line with the top of the shoulders. Throat showing dewlap and folds of skin to a degree termed "throatiness."

SHOULDERS, CHEST AND RIBS: Shoulders sloping—clean, muscular, not heavy or loaded—conveying the idea of freedom of action with activity and strength. Chest should be deep for lung space, narrower in proportion to depth than the English hound—28 inches (girth) in a 23-inch hound being good. Well sprung ribs, back ribs should extend well back—a three inch flank allowing springiness. *Defects:* Straight, upright shoulders, chest disproportionately wide or with lack of depth. Flat ribs.

BACK AND LOINS: Back moderately long, muscular and strong. Loins broad and slightly arched. *Defects:* Very long or swayed or roached back. Flat, narrow loins.

FORE LEGS AND FEET: *Fore Legs:* Straight, with fair amount of bone. Pasterns short and straight. *Feet:* Fox-like. Pad full and hard. Well arched toes. Strong nails. *Defects:* Out at elbow. Knees buckled over forward, or bent backward. Fore legs crooked. Feet open, long or spreading.

HIPS, THIGHS, HIND LEGS AND FEET: *Hips and Thighs:* Strong and muscled, giving abundance of propelling power. Stifles strong and well let down. Hocks, firm, symmetrical and moderately bent. Feet close and firm. *Defects:* Cowhocks, or straight hocks. Lack of muscle and propelling power. Open feet.

TAIL: Set moderately high; carried gaily, but not turned forward over the back; with slight curve; with very slight brush. *Defects:* A long tail. Teapot curve or included forward from the root. Rat tail, entire absence of brush.

COAT: A close, hard, hound coat of medium length. *Defects:* A short thin coat, or of a soft quality.

HEIGHT: Dogs should not be under 22 or over 25 inches. Bitches should not be under 21 or over 24 inches measured across the back at the point of the withers, the hound standing in a natural position with his feet well under him.

COLOR: Any color.

SCALE OF POINTS:

	Head	Points
Skull	5	
Ears	5	
Eyes	5	
Muzzle	5	
	—	20
	Body	
Neck	5	
Chest and shoulders	15	
Back, loins and ribs	15	
	—	35
	Running Gear	
Fore legs	10	
Hips, thighs and hind legs	10	
Feet	15	
	—	35
	Coat and Tail	
Coat	5	
Tail	5	
	—	10
TOTAL		100

ENGLISH FOXHOUND

ORIGINALLY FOX hunting did not come under the category of sport, rather it was practiced for the purpose of ridding sections of the country of what was supposed to be a species of destructive vermin.

The sole idea was to kill the fox, and the methods employed were in wide variance with the sometimes formal, but always sportsmanlike, field ethics with which the fox is hunted in England and America today. Coverts or sections of woods were once surrounded by nets and the fox driven into them without any thought of giving him a fair chance for his life.

Fox hunting in England followed stag hunting. Gradually it became recognized as a sport and followers began to pay more attention to the type of hounds used. The larger hounds were not needed, but a faster, smaller dog was desired. A number of crosses were undoubtedly used before the English Foxhound became an established type. It is more than likely that all of the English hounds were derived from French hounds. Four types of French hounds were described in George Tirberville's *Art of Venerie,* written during the reign of Queen Elizabeth. These were known as *The White,* used principally for stag hunting; *The Fallow,* used on all sorts of game, mainly the stag; *The Dun,* to be found more frequently than any other hound breed and good on any game; and *The Black* or *St. Hubert's,* of many

English Foxhound.

colors and no doubt the forbears of the **Bloodhound** and the Southern Hound.

Some of the early packs of hounds were those of the Earl of Yarborough (Brocklesby), the Earl of Fitzwilliam (Milton), Lord Fitsharding (Berkeley), the Duke of Beaufort (Badminton), the Duke of Ruland (Belvoir). These packs are said to have laid the foundation of the English Foxhound of today. In fact, it has been frequently advanced that the blood of the Brocklesby hounds is contained in every foxhound in England.

Belvoir Gambler, whelped in 1885, was said to have been one of the greatest English Foxhounds ever bred. In his *Reminiscences of Frank Gillard,* Cuthbert Bradley described him as follows:

Although Belvoir Gambler cannot be bred from rule of thumb, the proportions of this remarkable foxhound are worth preserving as an example of what symmetry should be. Standing 23 inches at the shoulder, from the extreme point of his shapely shoulders to the outer curve of his well-turned quarters, he measured 27½ inches in length whilst from elbow to ground his heights was only 12 inches. Possessing great depth of rib and room around the heart, he girthed 31 inches, and his arm below was 8¼ inches round. Below the knee he measured 8¼ inches of solid bone, while round the thigh he spanned full 9¼ inches. The extended neck was 10 inches from cranium to shoulder and the head 10½ inches long. His color was of the richest, displaying all of the beautiful "Belvoir Tan," and his head had that brainy appearance expressive of the highest intelligence. Gambler might have inspired that earnest poet, Cannon Kingsley, when he described the modern foxhound. "The result of Nature not limited, but developed by high civilization. Next to an old Greek statue there are few such combinations of grace and strength as in a fine foxhound.

Since the days when fox netting was abandoned and fox hunting became the sport of the English aristocracy, the English hound has played an important part in the country life of England's gentry. Many organized foxhound packs throughout England have made English hunting tradition. Among them were the Warwickshire, Cotswold, Pytchley, Cottesmore, Quorn, Belvoir, Fitzwilliam, Croome, Heythrop, Blankney, the Duke of Beaufort's, and the **Cricklade.**

The Foxhound Stud Book in England dates back to 1880.

There have been many great English Foxhounds, in fact too many to enumerate here. But a few of the outstanding performers and sires were: Rector (Milton); Dexter and Weaver (Belvoir); Potentate (Pytchley); Whynot (Meynell); Sergeant (Lord Lonsdale's); Woodman (Crafton) and Rallywood Brocklesby).

For additional discussion of foxhounds, see Parts XI and XIII, this text.

Description and Standards. The description and standards, by courtesy of the Masters of Foxhounds Association of America follows.

HEAD: The head should be of full size, but by no means heavy. Brow pronounced, but not high or sharp. There should be a good length and breadth, sufficient to give in a dog hound a girth in front of the ears of fully 16 inches. The nose should be long (4½ inches) and wide, with open nostrils. Ears set on low and lying close to the cheeks. Most English hounds are "rounded" which means that about 1½ inches is taken off the end of the ear. The teeth must meet squarely, either a *pig-mouth* (overshot) or undershot being a disqualification.

NECK: The neck must be long and clean, without the slightest throatiness, not less than ten inches from cranium to shoulder. It should taper nicely from shoulders to head, and the upper outline should be slightly convex.

SHOULDERS: The shoulders should be long and well clothed with muscle, without being heavy, especially at the points. They must be well sloped, and the true arm between the front and the elbow must be long and muscular, but free from fat or lumber.

CHEST AND BACK RIBS: The chest should girth over 31 inches in a 24-inch hound, and the back ribs must be very deep.

BACK AND LOIN: The back and loin must both be very muscular, running into each other without any contraction between them. The couples must be wide, even to raggedness, and the top line of the back should be absolutely level, the *stern* well set on and carried gaily but not in any case curved *over* the back like a squirrel's tail. The end should taper to a point and there should be a fringe of hair below.

HIND QUARTERS: The hind quarters or propellers are required to be very strong, and as endurance is of even greater consequence than speed, straight stifles are preferred to those much bent as in a Greyhound. Elbows set quite straight, and neither turned in or out are a *sine qua non*. They must be well let down by means of the long true arm above mentioned.

LEGS AND FEET: Every Master of Foxhounds insists on legs as straight as a post, and as strong; size of bone at the ankle being especially regarded as all important. The desire for straightness had a tendency to produce knuckling-over, which at one time was countenanced, but in recent years this defect has been eradicated by careful breeding and intelligent adjudication, and one sees very little of this trouble in the best modern foxhounds. The bone cannot be too large, and the feet in all cases should be round and cat-like, with well-developed knuckles and strong horn, which last is of the greatest importance.

COLOR AND COAT: The color and coat are not regarded as very important, so long as the former is good "hound color," and the latter is short, dense, hard, and glossy. Hound colors are black, tan and white, or any combination of these three, also the various "pies" compounded of white and the color of the hare and badger, or yellow, or tan.

SYMMETRY: The symmetry of the foxhound is of the greatest

A pack of English Foxhounds.

importance, and what is known as "quality" is highly regarded by all good judges.

SCALE OF POINTS:

	Points
Head	5
Neck	10
Shoulders	10
Chest and back ribs	10
Back and loin	15
Hind quarters	10
Elbows	5
Legs and feet	20
Color and coat	5
Stern	5
Symmetry	5
TOTAL	100

GREYHOUND

"A GREYHOUNDE shulde be heded like a Snake and necked like a Drake. Foted like a Kat. Tayled like a Rat. Syded lyke a Teme. Chyned like a Beme." This was the description given by Dame Berners in the *Boke of St. Albans* (1486).

Another picturesque description is found in *The Master of Game*, by Edward, Duke of York: "shuldres as a roe buck; the for legges stregth and grete ynow, and nought to hind legges; the feet straight and round as a catte, and great cleas, the boones and the joyntes of the cheyne grete and hard as the cheyne of an hert; the thighs great and squarred as an hare, the houghs streight, and not crompying as an oxe."

There has been much difference of opinion regarding the origin of the name "Greyhound." The dog was held in high esteem in Greece and some early writers thought that the name came from the word Graius (Grecian). Dr. Caius thought that the name indicated rank in the race. Other authorities felt that the name was derived from the Latin *gradus* (degree) because the Greyhound was outstanding among dogs in swiftness.

Some contended that the word "grey" was a corruption of the word, "great," as the dog was associated in early England with "great" people, or people of high degree. Under Number 31 of the Laws of Canute, enacted in 1016, "No mean person may keepe any greyhounds, but freemen may keepe greyhounds (greihounds), so that their knees be cut before the verderors of the forest, and without cutting of their knees also, if he does abide 10 miles from the bounds of the forest."

Whitaker gave what is probably the real origin of the name when he called attention to the ancient

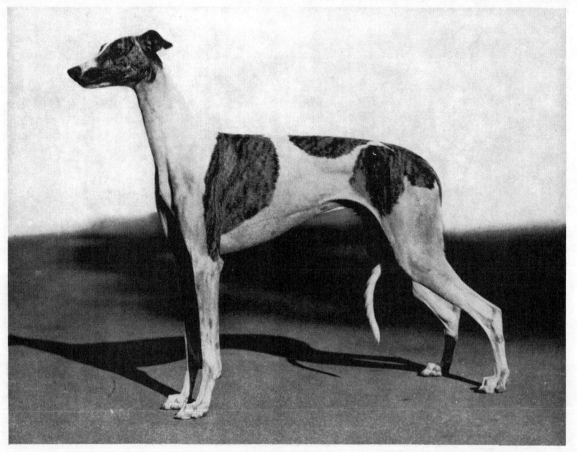

Greyhound.

Greyhounds—note different markings.

British *grech* or *greg*, "a dog." But Mr. Bell wrote that the term very probably applied to the prevailing color of early representatives of the breed. Another conjecture was to the effect that the term may have been a graduation of "gazehound," by which hounds which followed by sight were called at one time, into "grazehound," and thence later into "Greyhound."

No one knows just how old the Greyhound is, nor from whence he originated. Dogs of the Greyhound type are to be seen wherever the earliest records of dogs are found. They appear on the Tombs of Egypt and on Assyrian monuments. The Tomb of Amten, in the Valley of the Nile, contains carvings which show dogs of the Greyhound type in three different scenes. This tomb is said to be of the 4th Dynasty, dating between 3,500 and 4,000 B.C. There are many other instances of ancient carvings of Greyhound-type-dogs, either Greyhounds very similar to those of today or dogs of Saluki appearance, both quite similar. Undoubtedly the Greyhound has altered least of any of the very early breeds, his appearance having shown but little change through the ages.

At least three varieties of Greyhound have been in existence for many, many years. These are the wire-haired, somewhat rough-coated, found mainly in East Russia and Tartary; the silky-haired of Natolia, Persia, and Ancient Egypt; and a rough haired and a smoothhaired breed, the Deerhound and the Greyhound.

The grace and beauty of these dogs have long made them favorites with the artists of many eras. The story of Lelaps, the Greyhound of mythology, is well known.

The important part these dogs have played, and are still playing, in the realm of sport is discussed in another section (*see* Part IX).

Among famous dogs of English racing, other than those mentioned in the text on Coursing and Racing (Part IX), were: Bab at the Bowster, a red-and-fawn bitch weighing only 44 pounds but a frequent winner; Coomassie, the smallest Greyhound to win the Waterloo Cup . . . she weighed a scant 42 pounds; Cerito, three times a Cup winner; Fabulous Fortune, Bit of Fashion, Miss Glendine, Thoughtless Beauty, Lady Lyons, Long Span, and Fullerton.

It was in the early days and in areas of wide open country where it was impossible for the hunter to approach close to his game that the Greyhound made his greatest contribution to Man. His exceedingly keen eyesight and his great speed allowed him to locate and run down his quarry, either killing it outright or bringing it to bay for the arrival of his master.

Wherever the Greyhound went with his master, he excited much interest and attention and was in great demand. When it no longer became necessary to depend on wild game for food, the sport of coursing came into being, and, from that sport, racing, as we know it today, was developed. There are a number of kennels in this country that breed for bench show contenders, but, despite the dog's great beauty and his aristocratic background, comparatively few are kept as companions.

(See also Part IX, this text.)

Description and Standards. The description and standards, by courtesy of AKC follow:

HEAD: Long and narrow, fairly wide between the ears, scarcely perceptible stop, little or no development of nasal sinuses, good length of muzzle, which should be powerful without coarseness. Teeth very strong and even in front.

EARS: Small and fine in texture, thrown back and folded, except when excited, when they are semi-pricked.

EYES: Dark, bright, intelligent, indicating spirit.

NECK: Long, muscular, without throatiness, slightly arched, and widening gradually into the shoulder.

SHOULDERS: Placed as obliquely as possible, muscular without being loaded.

FORE LEGS: Perfectly straight, set well into the shoulders, neither turned in nor out, pasterns strong.

CHEST: Deep, and as wide as consistent with speed, fairly well-sprung ribs.

BACK: Muscular and broad, well arched.

LOINS: Good depth of muscle, well cut up in the flanks.

HIND QUARTERS: Long, very muscular and powerful, wide and well let down, well bent stifles. Hocks well bent and rather close to the ground, wide but straight fore and aft.

FEET: Hard and close, rather more hare than cat feet, well knuckled up with good strong claws.

TAIL: Long, fine and tapering with a slight upward curve.

COAT: Short, smooth and firm in texture.

COLOR: Immaterial.

WEIGHT: Dogs, 65 to 70 pounds; bitches, 60 to 65 pounds.

SCALE OF POINTS:	Points
General Symmetry and Quality	10
Head and Neck	20
Chest and Shoulders	20
Back	10
Quarters	20
Legs and Feet	20
TOTAL	100

HARRIER

THE SPORT of chasing the hare with hounds is very old, older even than stag hunting and had long been enjoyed in a number of countries before fox hunting became a favorite recreation.

Xenophon, the Greek historian, wrote on hare hunting about 400 B.C., but at that time the breed we know as the Harrier was unknown. Yet the pack he maintained probably greatly resembled the Harrier of today.

Many contend that the Harrier is but a small edition of the foxhound, but some authorities have written that the breed came from a cross between the Beagle and St. Hubert Hounds. Stonehenge advanced the theory that the Harrier came from the Southern Hound, with an infusion of a little Greyhound blood. The West Country Harriers, which are colored white, white-and-lemon, badger-pie, and hare-pie, are said to have descended from the heavy, light-colored Staghounds of the Exmoor section.

The rough-coated Beagle is also said to have had a

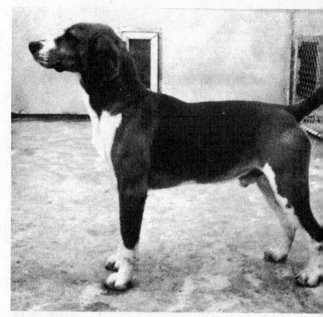

Harrier—Breezewood Coroner of Breezewood Harriers. (Ow Wm. Jones, Concord, N.H.)

Harrier—Dart Vale and Haldon Comrade of Breezewood Harri (Owner: Wm. Jones, Concord, N.H.)

part in the foundation of the breed. Foxhound blood has been introduced into many English packs.

The Association of Masters of Harriers and Beagles was established in England in 1891. The rules observed by the members for admittance of hounds to the Harrier Stud Book were:

The produce on both sides of registered hounds.

The produce of Stud Book hounds with hounds bred from registered parents on one side only.

Hounds bred on one side only from registered parents may be recorded in the yearly Appendix.

Hounds bred on both sides from Hounds so recorded may also be entered in the Appendix.

Hounds bred on one side from registered parents, and on the other side from parents recorded in the Appendix.

The Anglesley Harriers have records which date back to 1744.

Amont the English packs are: the Axe Vale Harriers; the Cotley; the Dart Vale; the Heacham; the Holcombe, where hounds have been kenneled for well over a hundred years; the Mitchelstown, which was the only pack of Black-and-Tan Harriers in existence; the Quarme, and the Weston. The first pack of Harriers in England was the Penistone, which Sir Elias de Midhope established in 1260.

Robert P. Huntington of Staatsburg, N.Y., brought a pack of Harriers over from England in 1911 and hunted them with good sport in this country; Oakleigh Thorne maintained a pack of Harriers at Millbrook, New York, for some years. The breed, however, does not enjoy wide popularity in this country.

Among others who have enjoyed good sport with Harriers in America are Amory L. Haskell, Edward H. Carle and Windsor T. White.

Description and Standards. The description and standards follow.

The points of the modern Harrier are very similar to those of the English Foxhound. The Harrier, however, is smaller than the English Foxhound and the most popular size is 19 to 21 inches.

They should be active, well-balanced and full of strength and quality, with shoulders sloping into the muscles of the back, clean and not loaded on the withers or point.

The back level and muscular, and not dipping behind the withers or arching over the loin.

The elbow's point set well away from the ribs, running parallel with the body and not turning outwards.

Deep, well-sprung ribs running well back, with plenty of head room, and a deep chest.

Good straight legs with plenty of bone running well down to the toes, but not overburdened, inclined to knuckle over very slightly but not exaggerated in the slightest degree.

Round cat-like feet, and close toes turning inwards.

Hind legs and hocks stand square, with a good sweep and muscular thigh to take the weight off the body.

The head should be of a medium size with good bold forehead, and plenty of expression; head must be well set up on a neck of ample length, and not heavy; stern should be set well up, long and well controlled.

IRISH WOLFHOUND

RUGGED, YET graceful, commanding in appearance, yet indicative of great agility, the Irish Wolfhound is the tallest of all dogs. Even with his extraordinary height and harsh, rough coat there is a certain streamline quality about him which denotes sleekness, for the Irish Wolfhound is built along Greyhound lines.

Through historical narration, legend and art, this aristocratic-looking dog is indubitably connected with the period which knew him best, the feudal times of the Middle Ages. His history is deeply colored with romance, and many are the sensational deeds of valor attributed to him.

The Irish Wolfhound was first mentioned A.D. 391 when Quintus Aurelius Symmachus, the Roman

Irish Wolfhound—Heady study. Hank Babbit photo.

Consul, wrote a letter to his brother, Flavianus, thanking him for sending seven Irish Wolfhounds to the Russian circus combats and saying "All Rome viewed them with wonder."

In the Second Century writing of Arrian, dogs of the Irish Wolfhound's description are said to have been brought to Greece in 273 B.C. by the invading Celts.

A fabulous character in Celtic literature was Finn, Master of Hounds of the great kennel of Irish Wolfhounds owned by Cormac, a king of Ireland. In early writings the breed was referred to as "Irish dogs," "big dogs of Ireland," "greyhounds of Ireland," "wolfdogs of Ireland," "the great hounds of Ireland," and "the Irish Wolfhounds." They were widely used in wolf and elk hunting, but also served their masters well as bodyguards and in battle.

With the disappearance of the wolf and elk, the ranks of the breed became greatly diminished and great credit is given Captain G. A. Graham, of Dursley, a Scotch officer in the British Army, who worked for more than 20 years in rehabilitating the breed. His first experiments were made from dogs secured from Sir J. Power, of Kilfane, Mr. Baker, of Ballytobin, and Mr. Mahoney, of Dromore. These were different strains, but none of the individuals were anything as large as the dogs mentioned in early writings. Capt. Graham crossed these dogs with the Great Dane and the Scottish Deerhound, and later used the Russian Wolfhound and one or two other breeds of large dogs.

Using these crosses judiciously, the determined officer attained the size and type he desired, and through his work these characteristics were "set or established. One of his best dogs was Brian, not an especially large dog as he stood just over 30 inches at the shoulder. Other were Banshee and Fintragh, with the bitch, Sheelah, being perhaps the best of his large kennel. The dog which will long be remembered was Champion Cotswold, said to be the best Irish Wolf-

Irish Wolfhound. (For another photo of a good-sized pup of this breed, see Coursing in the U.S.—Part IX.) Photo by Evelyn M. Shafer.

hound ever bred. Cotswold was the property of Mrs. Percy Shewell and stood 34½ inches at the shoulder.

Broadbridge Michael, however, an Irish Wolfhound once owned by Mrs. Mary Beynon of Sutton-at-Hone, Kent, England, stood 39½ inches at the shoulder and is referred to in at least one record book as the world's tallest dog. He was whelped in 1926.

The Irish Wolfhound has found favor among some sportsmen, being used in this country in hunting the timber wolf, other species of wolves, and in the West and Midwest, the coyote. He is also used in other countries on large game. He has great speed and is game to the core, being capable of dispatching a wolf single-handled.

Despite his imposing appearance, the Irish Wolfhound possesses an even temperament, attaching himself to his master with great loyalty and affection. An ancient description read, "Gentle when stroked, fierce when provoked."

Description and Standards. The description and standards, as adopted by AKC follow.

GENERAL APPEARANCE: Of great size and commanding appearance, the Irish Wolfhound is remarkable in combining power and swiftness with keen sight. The largest and tallest of the galloping hounds, in general type he is a rough-coated, Greyhound-like breed; very muscular, strong though gracefully built; movements easy and active; head and neck carried high, the tail carried with an upward sweep with a slight curve towards the extremity. The minimum height and weight of dogs should be 32 inches and 120 pounds; of bitches, 30 inches and 105 pounds; these to apply only to hounds over 18 months of age. Anything below this should be debarred from competition. Great size, including height at shoulder and proportionate length of body, is the desideratum to be aimed at, and it is desired to firmly establish a race that shall average from 32 to 34 inches in dogs, showing the requisite power, activity, courage and symmetry.

HEAD: Long, the frontal bones of the forehead very slightly raised and very little indentation between the eyes. Skull, not too broad. Muzzle, long and moderately pointed. Ears, small and Greyhound-like in carriage.

NECK: Rather long, very strong and muscular, well arched, without dewlap or loose skin about the throat.

CHEST: Very deep. Breast, wide.

BACK: Rather long than short. Loins arched.

TAIL: Long and slightly curved, of moderate thickness, and well covered with hair.

BELLY: Well drawn up.

FOREQUARTERS: Shoulders, muscular, giving breadth of chest, set sloping. Elbows well under, neither turned inwards nor outwards.

LEG: Forearm muscular, and the whole leg strong and quite straight.

HINDQUARTERS: Muscular thighs and second thigh long and strong as in the Greyhound, and hocks well let down and turning neither in nor out.

FEET: Moderately large and round, neither turned inwards nor outwards. Toes, well arched and closed. Nails, very strong and curved.

HAIR: Rough and hard on body, legs and head; especially wiry and long over eyes and underjaw.

COLOR AND MARKINGS: The recognized colors are gray, brindle, red, black, pure white, fawn, or any other color that appears in the Deerhound.

FAULTS: Too light or heavy a head, too highly arched frontal bone; large ears and hanging flat to the face; short neck; full dewlap; too narrow or too broad a chest; sunken or hollow or quite straight back; bent forelegs; overbent fetlocks; twisted feet; spreading toes, too curly a tail; weak hindquarters and a general want of muscle too short in body. Lips or nose liver-colored or lacking pigmentation.

LIST OF POINTS IN ORDER OF MERIT

1. *Typical.* The Irish Wolfhound is a rough-coated Greyhound-like breed, the tallest of the coursing hounds and remarkable in combining power and swiftness. 2. Great size and commanding appearance. 3. Movements easy and active. 4. Head, long and level, carried high. 5. Forelegs, heavily boned, quite straight; elbows well set under. 6. Thighs long and muscular; second thighs, well muscled, stifles nicely bent. 7. Coat, rough and hard, specially wiry and long over eyes and under jaw. 8. Body, long, well ribbed up, with ribs well sprung, and great breadth across hips. 9. Loins arched, belly well drawn up. 10. Ears, small, with Greyhound-like carriage. 11. Feet, moderately large and round; toes, close, well arched. 12. Neck, long, well arched and very strong. 13. Chest, very deep, moderately broad. 14. Shoulders, muscular, set sloping. 15. Tail, long and slightly curved. 16. Eyes, dark.

NOTE: The above in no way alters the "Standard of Excellence," which must in all cases be rigidly adhered to; they simply give the various points in order of merit. If in any case they appear at variance with Standard of Excellence, it is the latter which is correct.

(September 12, 1950)

NORWEGIAN ELKHOUND

THE NORWEGIAN Elkhound is one of the oldest inhabitants of Scandinavia. Long before he became the companion of the Vikings in both sport and conquest, the Elkhound, in much the same form as we find him today, roamed the *saeters* of Norway.

From these early days the Norwegian Elkhound has come down with its original traits unimpaired, a game, fearless hunter and a devoted companion. Four skeletons were discovered in Norway some years ago in a stratum belonging to the Stone Age. Experts pronounced them to be of dogs almost identical with the Norwegian Elkhound of today. Another skeleton was discovered in the Viste Cave at Jaeren, in western Norway, in a stratum which dated from 4,000 to 5,000 B.C. This skeleton was declared that of a dog closely resembling today's Norwegian Elkhound.

The Norwegian Elkhound was apparently no happenstance. He was bred for a particular job in a certain section of the world, and the fact that he has remained essentially the same throughout the years is proof that he did that job well. Especially was he proficient in hunting the elk, from which he gets his name. It is said that through his extraordinary scenting powers, the Norwegian Elkhound could wind an

Norwegian Elkhound—Ch. Crafdal Farms Troll. (Owner: Mrs. Glenna Crafts, Stow, Ohio.)

elk for a distance of three miles. After bringing his quarry to bay, the courageous dog held the animal for his master's arrival, or, with high intelligence, worked the elk in the direction of his master.

He was also used in hunting bears, and later as a gundog and retriever on upland game birds, notably the blackcock.

In Britain, the Norwegian Elkhound was used with success on small ground game, but has been known to kill otter. In this country, it could hardly be classed as a sporting dog, being used mostly as a companion, yet frequently as a farm dog, where he readily takes to working with livestock.

As a breed, the Norwegian Elkhound has been kept remarkably pure. This is evidenced in its high prepotency, for the offspring of any cross-mating will invariably show a strong inheritance of breed characteristics.

In Norway and Sweden the types vary somewhat, that which has been adopted in this country and England being the "Graa Dyrehund" or Grey Elk Dog.

Alert and compact, the breed shows strength and endurance in every line. Such conformation was undoubtedly necessary for the breed to have survived in its original form the vicissitudes of the passing centuries.

The breed is not an old one in this country, nor even in England, for among the first specimens to be imported into England from Norway were those brought back by Sir Alfred Strutt in 1878. Elkhounds were soon imported into England from both Norway and Sweden, and many crosses were made. The variance in type was at first somewhat confusing, but the breed settled into uniformity and has so remained. Champion Gaupa au Giltre, Ch. Rugg au Giltre, Ch. Peik au Giltre, and Ch. Kraus, all from Norway, and Ch. Ialla and Ch. Carros from Sweden, all left their stamp on the breed and influenced the present-day type.

In general appearance the Norwegian Elkhound is a dog fully capable of doing just what he has often

Norwegian Elkhound—Ch. Tryg's Trygger. (Owner: Mrs. Glenna Crafts, Stow, Ohio.)

been called upon to do, hunt day in and day out in rugged country where strength rather than excessive speed is demanded.

Description and Standards. The description and standards, approved by the American Kennel Club follow.

Norwegian Elkhound puppy.

GENERAL DESCRIPTION: The Norwegian Elkhound is a typical Northern dog, of medium size, with a compact, proportionately short body, with a thick and rich, but not bristling, grey coat, with prick ears, and with a tail that is curled and carried over the back. His temperament is bold and energetic.

HEAD: "Dry" (without any loose skin), broad at the ears; the forehead and back of the head only slightly arched; the stop not large, yet clearly defined. The muzzle is of medium length, thickest at the base and, seen from above or from the side, tapers evenly without being pointed. The bridge of the nose is straight; the lips are tightly closed.

EAR: Set high, firm and erect, are higher than they are wide at the base, pointed (not rounded) and very mobile. When the dog is listening, the orifices are turned forward.

EYES: Not protruding, brown in color, preferably dark, lively with a fearless energetic expression.

NECK: Of medium length, "dry" (without any loose skin), strong and well set up.

BODY: Powerful, *compact*, and short, with broad deep chest, well-sprung ribs, straight back, well-developed loins, and stomach very little drawn up.

LEGS: Firm, straight and strong; elbows closely set on; hind legs with little angulation at knees and hocks. Seen from behind, they are straight.

FEET: Comparatively small, somewhat oblong, with tightly closed toes, not turned out. There should be no dewclaws on hind legs.

TAIL: Set high, short, thickly and closely haired, but without brush; tightly curled, not carried too much to one side.

COAT: Thick, rich and hard, but rather smooth-lying. On head and front of legs, short and even; longest on neck and chest, on buttocks, on hindside of fore legs and on underside of tail. It is made up of longer and harder covering hairs, dark at the tips, and of a light, soft, woolly under coat.

COLOR: Grey, with black tips to the long covering hairs; somewhat lighter on chest, stomach, legs, underside of tail, and around anus. The color may be lighter or darker, with a slight shading towards yellow; but a pronounced variation from the grey color disqualifies. Too dark or too light individuals should be avoided; also, yellow markings or uneven coloring. There should be no pronounced white markings.

HEIGHT AT SHOULDER: For dogs about 20.5 inches; for bitches about 18 inches.

OTTERHOUND

INTERESTINGLY unique and individual in appearance and characteristics, the Otterhound is an old breed, yet its origin remains a matter of considerable conjecture.

The Bloodhound, the Southern Hound, the Welsh Harrier, the Bulldog, the old Water Spaniel, the Airedale, and the old Vendee Hound of France are all breeds to whom at least some credit has been given by one authority or another for the development of this, the only water "hound." Some of its characteristic qualities in appearance and its great scenting powers do, indeed, denote Bloodhound influence, and the old Water Spaniel may well have produced the Otterhound's predilection for water work. The Bulldog may have given him his tenacity, the Airedale or Harrier contributed to the roughness of his coat, yet the breed was well established long before many better-known breeds took form. At any rate, not one has yet been able to set finger on a formula for the

Otterhound and definitely say, with positive proof, "This is *it*."

The Otterhound looks very much like a Bloodhound wearing the wrong coat. This coat is rough and extremely thick. There is a deep, oily undercoat which enables the dog to withstand long hours of immersion in cold water. There is no better swimmer among dogs, for its webbed feet aid it greatly in this important phase of its work.

King Henry II of England was the first known Master of Otterhounds. Queen Elizabeth was the first lady Master of Otterhounds. Other Masters of Otterhounds among the reigning English monarchs were

Otterhound.

Kings John, Edward II, Henry VI, Edward IV, Richard III, Henry VII, Henry VIII, and Charles II. Kings Edward I, James I and James VI took legal steps to protect the sport of otterhunting.

The Otterhound is possessed of a remarkably musical bay, and the sound of a well-rounded pack working an otter's "drag" is music of the Gods to the sportsman. The otter, of course, is in its natural element when in the water, is a powerful swimmer and possesses great powers of endurance. It can swim for long stretches under water, but leaves a tell-tale trail of bubbles in its wake and must "vent" or come up to breathe frequently. The scent of an otter is very strong, but nevertheless it requires a dog of great

staying powers, swimming ability, and determination, as well as "nose," to catch and finish off this worthy opponent. Some hunts last an amazingly long time, perhaps the longest on record being 10¾ hours. This was in 1907 by the Carlisle Otterhounds on Eden River. In May, 1908, the Northern Counties Otterhounds ran a "drag" for 23 miles, ending with a kill.

Many lovers of the sport of otterhunting in England prefer to cross their Otterhounds with English or Welsh Foxhounds, rather than hunt the purebred. Such a combination is said to increase stamina, perseverance and "drive" although the unique appearance of the Otterhound is naturally somewhat altered. These dogs do not possess the heavy bay of the pure-bred, but their voices are of sufficient volume and beauty to satisfy most.

The Otterhound must possess a great constitution to withstand such rigorous water work without succumbing to such diseases as pneumonia, and it is only natural that many suffer from rheumatism in later life. But, then, his master is also likely to be similarly afflicted if he takes his hunting too seriously.

The Otterhound has never taken the fancy of the American sportsman. Those that have been imported were brought over mainly for their novelty rather than the utility of the breed in American covers or waters. Otters are seldom hunted in this country.

Otterhounds are sometimes, however, to be seen at bench shows. H. S. Wardner, of New York City, was America's first breeder of Otterhounds. Hartland Mosstrooper and Hartland Statesman, both owned by Mr. Wardner, were the first Otterhounds to be registered with the American Kennel Club.

Description and Standards. The description and standards follow.

In general appearance—always excepting the coat—he much resembles the Bloodhound; he should be perfect in symmetry, strongly built, hard and enduring, with unfailing powers of scent, and a natural antipathy to the game he is bred to pursue. The head should be large, broader in proportion than the Bloodhound's, the forehead high, the muzzle a fair length and the nostrils wide. The ears are long, thin and pendulous, fringed with hair. The neck is not naturally long, and looks shorter than it really is from the abundance of hair on it; the shoulders should slope well, the legs be straight and the feet a good size, but compact; the back strong and wide, the ribs, and particularly the back ribs, well let down; the thighs should be big and firm, and the hocks well let down; the stern well and thickly covered with hair and carried well up, but not curled; the colors are generally grizzle or sandy, with black and tan more or less clearly defined.

Scale of Points:	Points
Skull	10
Jaws	10
Eyes	5
Ears	10
Chest and shoulders	15
Body and loin	15
Legs and feet	10
Coat	10
Stern	5
Symmetry and strength	10
Total	100

RHODESIAN RIDGEBACK

USED EXTENSIVELY in South Africa in hunting the larger beasts of prey, the Rhodesian Ridgeback is peculiarly characterized by a ridge of hair running from set-on of tail to the withers, and growing in opposite direction to the rest of the coat. Only one other breed in all of dogdom is similarly marked. This is the Phu Quoc, a native of the Island of Phu Quoc in the Siamese Gulf, where it was bred by the natives.

Although there are many theories concerning the origin of the Rhodesian Ridgeback, none has been definitely proved, but it is believed that the Phu Quoc was introduced into Africa by Phoenician traders. The two breeds resemble each other to some extent in build, weight and height, as well as the ridge.

This resemblance and the fact that no ridged breeds were found anywhere else in the world substantiates the theory of a close relationship and since there is considerable distance between the island of Phu Quoc and Rhodesia, the journey was undoubtedly made by way of the sea.

There were certainly other breeds which entered into the ancestry of the Ridgeback, however. Great Danes, Mastiffs, Bloodhounds and Greyhounds have been suggested as playing a part in the Ridgeback's history, as many of the Hollanders, Germans and Huguenots who emigrated to South Africa in the 16th and 17th centuries brought dogs with them. But the native dog found among the Hottentots is credited with a strong role. Little is known about this native dog, except that it was a half-wild breed with a crest of reverse hair down its back.

The British authority, Clifford L. Hubbard, believes that the Great Dane and Bloodhound were the most likely European breeds to have been used in developing the Ridgeback. His theory is based on the fact that the term, Bloodhound, was loosely applied in the days when the Ridgeback was becoming known to big-game hunters and generally referred to the type of hound they imported into Africa for hunting big game and which would have included the Schweisshunde. The Great Dane of that period would have been of the early type used for boar hunting in Germany.

In any case, the Boer farmers needed a dog to hunt small game, pull down large game, guard the farm and be a good family dog. The dog would also have to be sturdy enough to withstand the African Bush and the drastic changes from day to night temperatures. Through selective breeding they developed such a dog in the Ridgeback.

History has it that a Reverend Helm introduced two Ridgebacks into Rhodesia in 1877 where big-game hunters, including Cornelius van Rooyen, helped to popularize the breed. They began to breed

Rhodesian Ridgeback—Ch. Kraal's Pungo. (Owner: Dr. Frank Lutman, Philadelphia, Pa.) Photo by Evelyn M. Shafer.

and raise these dogs, the ridge on the back becoming the escutcheon of the breed.

Ridgebacks first appeared in Britain in 1928 where they attracted great attention. Mr. George Gilkey was one of the first to bring specimens to the U.S. By 1950, some outstanding specimens had been imported and there were enough fanciers to found the Rhodesian Ridgeback Club of America. In 1959, the breed was admitted to the American Kennel Club Stud Book.

Description and Standards: The description and standards, by courtesy of AKC, follow.

The peculiarity of this breed is the *ridge* on the back, which is formed by the hair growing in the opposite direction to the rest of the coat. The ridge must be regarded as the characteristic feature of the breed. The ridge should be clearly defined, tapering and symmetrical. It should start immediately behind the shoulders and continue to a point between the prominence of the hips, and should contain two identical crowns opposite each other. The lower edges of the crown should not extend further down the ridge than one third of the ridge.

GENERAL APPEARANCE: The Ridgeback should represent a strong muscular and active dog, symmetrical in outline, and capable of great endurance with a fair amount of speed.

HEAD: Should be of a fair length, the skull flat and rather broad between the ears and should be free from wrinkles when in repose. The stop should be reasonably well defined.

MUZZLE: Should be long, deep and powerful, jaws level and strong with well-developed teeth, especially the canines or molars. The lips clean, closely fitting the jaws.

EYES: Should be moderately well apart, and should be round, bright and sparkling, with intelligent expression, their color harmonizing with the color of the dog.

EARS: Should be set rather high, of medium size, rather wide at base, and tapering to a rounded point. They should be carried close to the head.

NOSE: Should be black, or brown, in keeping with the color of the dog. No other colored nose is permissible. A black nose should be accompanied by dark eyes, a brown nose by amber eyes.

NECK AND SHOULDERS: The neck should be fairly strong and free from throatiness. The shoulders should be sloping, clean and muscular, denoting speed.

BODY, BACK, CHEST AND LOINS: The chest should not be too wide, but very deep and capacious; ribs moderately well sprung, never rounded like barrel hoops (which would indicate lack of speed), the back powerful, the loins strong, muscular and slightly arched.

LEGS AND FEET: The forelegs should be perfectly straight, strong and heavy in bone; elbows close to the body. The feet should be compact, with well-arched toes, round, tough, elastic pads, protected by hair between the toes and pads. In the hind legs the muscles should be clean, well defined, and hocks well down.

TAIL: Should be strong at the insertion, and generally tapering towards the end, free from coarseness. It should not be inserted too high or too low, and should be carried with a slight curve upwards, never curled.

COAT: Should be short and dense, sleek and glossy in appearance, but neither woolly nor silky.

COLOR: Light wheaten to red wheaten. A little white on the chest and toes permissible but excessive white there and any white on the belly or above the toes is undesirable.

SIZE: A mature Ridgeback should be a handsome, upstanding dog; dogs should be of a height of 25 to 27 inches, and bitches 24 to 26 inches.

WEIGHT: (Desirable) Dogs 75 pounds, bitches 65 pounds.

(November, 1955)

SALUKI

"AS OLD as time itself and as fleet as its flying moments," the Saluki is said to be the oldest pure breed in the world. Its antiquity is, indeed, not a figment of the imagination but is readily proved by research into archaeology, art, and literature. Whenever the student approaches the horizon of early civilization, he finds the Saluki firmly established as a definite breed and as firmly entrenched in the affections and daily life of his master.

They are beautifully pictured in old Persian art; they are depicted on the ancient Tombs of Egypt, typical Salukis appearing in a procession on the Tomb of Rehkma-re, the Grand Vizier of Thothmes III, 1400 B.C.; records of them are found at Hierakonpolis as early as 3600 B.C.

It is claimed that the Saluki originally came with the horses from Syria and today whenever Arab chieftains are mentioned, their horses and Salukis immediately come to mind. The Saluki first came to Egypt through trade with the Arabs, so tradition goes, and it is from ancient Egypt that we find some of the earliest records of the breed.

The word *saluki* is classical Arabic, the word *slughi* is colloquial Arabic. To the Arabs the Saluki is known as *el hor,* meaning "The Noble One." He was declared sacred by the Moslems, which gave them the right to eat of the meat brought down by the dog in the chase. The Saluki was the only dog allowed to sleep in the Sheik's tent and to the Saluki the Arab was a slave rather than a master.

Looked upon as sacred, he was never sold but was exchanged among the Arab chiefs and members of nomadic tribes, his value being interpreted in terms of mares, female camels and gennets, according to the dog's ability in the chase. "He is my butcher; he makes me independent of imports and importers," is an old Arabian expression. Salukis have always been looked upon as things of great value.

Perhaps the reason for the long purity of the breed and its freedom from outcrosses is the great expanse of uninhabited land which surround the Arab, allowing him to breed his favorite hound in a world all his own, free from outside encroachment. The Saluki thus remains a symbol of the color and mystery of the ever-changing, yet never-changing, East.

In Arabia the breed is classed into four varieties, the two most distinctive of which are the "Shami" or Syrian, and the "Nejdi." The "Shami" is smooth-coated, with feathered ears and tail and slight feathering on the legs and between the toes, the latter to better allow him to travel over the soft sands. The "Nejdi" is of smooth coat with no feathering.

The Saluki has been called the "Persian Greyhound." The breed is known in Persia as "Tazi," meaning "Arab." This variety is often heavier and larger than the "Shami."

The travels of the nomadic desert tribes took them far and wide and the Saluki's habitat included Egypt, Arabia, Palestine, Syria, Anatolia, Mesopotamia, and Persia. Each tribe specialized in its own particular type of dog, always striving for better animals than those possessed by anyone else. The whelping of a litter was a great occasion. Visitors arrived *en masse,* all hoping to somehow obtain a puppy. Great store was set by all the odd numbers of the litter, the first, third, and fifth being highly prized. If a puppy, upon being removed from its nursing mother, would return to its habitual position each time for seven consecutive days, it became the choice of the master.

Great care was lavished upon the youngsters. Female goats were set aside for their nourishment and camel's milk, thickened with dates and kouskoussou, and sheep's milk often became part of their diet.

The puppies' education began when they were three or four months old, when they were allowed to

Saluki—Am. and Can. Ch. AnaBint of Billa de Esta, CD. (left), and Ch. Yusuf Bin Pasjaa Billa de Esta (right). (Owner: Mrs. William Eltiste, Fallon, Nev.)

catch rats. Shortly afterwards they were often trained with a young falcon, the two starting their hunting careers together. Hares were offered them at six months of age, and later on they were started on young gazelles. When the young Saluki was 15 to 18 months of age, he was allowed to hunt regularly and when two years old, was considered fully qualified for the chase. The gazelle was generally hunted with Saluki and hawk, the dog being trained to pursue the same animal contacted by the hawk. When the hawk struck its prey, the Saluki held it down until the hunters arrived. When hares were hunted in thick undergrowth, the Saluki often set his course entirely by watching the hawk, although the dog has keen scenting abilities. From his use in gazelle hunting, the Saluki is commonly called the "gazelle hound."

It is said that the Arab considers 26 special points in selecting a Saluki. One of these considered important is that the tail, when passed under the thigh, should reach the backbone.

Salukis were first brought into Europe by the Crusaders, it is said. One of these hounds is seen in an early portrait of Duke Henry of Saxony.

The first importations into England were made in 1840, coming from Persia. These were a bitch owned by Sir Hamilton Smith, a dog owned by the Duke of Devonshire at Chatsworth, and a dog in Regents Park Zoological Gardens.

In 1895, W. Jennings-Bramley presented a dog and a bitch puppy to the Hon. Florence Amherst. They came from the Bedawin tribe of Tahawi in Egypt, a district famous for its Syrian stock, La'aman meaning "a flash" or, perhaps, "the swift glance of a lady's eye," and Ayesha, named after the second wife of Mahomet, were of a pure golden color and created much interest. These dogs were said to be of the same breeding as that in the kennels of the Shah of Persia. From their mating, Sama, meaning "the sky," came.

The Hon. Florence Amherst was largely responsible for the popularity of the breed in England, her great

dog Sultan being possessed of remarkable prepotency. Sultan left his stamp very definitely on the breed in England. The Saluki Club was organized in that country in 1912, with the Hon. Florence Amherst as president. To some it may seem ironical to note that the Saluki, dating back nearly 7,000 years, was recognized *as a breed* by the Kennel Club in England in 1922. It was not until 1927 that the breed was officially recognized by the American Kennel Club.

In that year, the Saluki Club of America was organized and the breed has been growing in popularity in this country ever since. The Saluki is a beautifully streamlined dog, every line denoting grace and speed. He is said to be able to travel at the rate of over 43 miles an hour. Arabs generally gave their Salukis names which indicated speed.

In the Hon. Florence Amherst's translation from the *Diwan of Abu Nuwas,* Court Poet and Jester A.D. 800 is found, "It is as though behind the place where his eyelashes meet there are burning coals constantly kindled . . . Like a hawk swooping on sand-grouse, he peels the skin of the earth with four feet. He runs so swift! They do not touch the earth as he runs. In his eagerness his feet have scratched his armpits, and putting and pulling his arms to his sides have cut his ears; in his eagerness the dust is cut from round him."

Description and Standards: The description and standards, by courtesy of AKC follow:

HEAD: Long and narrow, skull moderately wide between the ears, not domed, stop not pronounced, the whole showing great quality. Nose black or liver.

EARS: Long and covered with long silky hair hanging close to the skull and mobile.

EYES: Dark to hazel and bright; large and oval, but not prominent.

TEETH: Strong and level.

NECK: Long, supple and well muscled.

CHEST: Deep and moderately narrow.

FORE QUARTERS: Shoulders sloping and set well back, well muscled without being coarse.

FORE LEGS: Straight and long from the elbow to the knee.

HIND QUARTERS: Strong, hip bones set well apart and stifle moderately bent, hocks low to the ground, showing galloping and jumping power.

LOIN AND BACK: Back fairly broad, muscles slightly arched over loin.

FEET: Of moderate length, toes long and well arched, not splayed out, but at the same time not cat footed; the whole being strong and supple and well feathered between the toes.

TAIL: Long, set on low and carried naturally in a curve, well feathered on the underside with long silky hair, not bushy.

COAT: Smooth and of a soft silky texture, slight feather on the legs, feather at the back of the thighs and sometimes with slight woolly feather on the thigh and shoulder.

COLORS: White, cream, fawn, golden, red, grizzle and tan tricolor (white, black, and tan) and black and tan.

GENERAL APPEARANCE: The whole appearance of this breed should give an impression of grace and symmetry and of great speed and endurance coupled with strength and activity to enable it to kill gazelle or other quarry over deep sand or rocky mountains. The expression should be dignified and gentle with deep, faithful, farseeing eyes. Dogs should average in height from 23 to 28 inches and bitches may be considerably smaller, this being very typical of the breed.

THE SMOOTH VARIETY: In this variety the points should be the same with the exception of the coat which has no feathering.

Saluki—Mazuri Pasjaa of Billa de Esta. (Owner: Mrs. William Eltiste, Fallon, Nev.)

WHIPPET

THERE IS no definite proof of just how the Whippet got its name but the most likely theory is that the dog, in the form of hunting in which he was adept, "whipped-up" his game. This Greyhound in miniature was formerly known as the "Snap Dog," probably for two reasons. He accounted for the rats and rabbits he caught with a quick snap of his powerful jaws, and, in racing, he had a characteristic habit of suddenly turning and snapping at his nearest competitor.

The Whippet is said to have been bred from varied blood. Some authorities wrote that he was the result of Italian Greyhounds crossed with terriers. The terrier breeds mentioned were the Manchester, the old English White Terrier, and the Bedlington Terrier. The terrier blood was supposed to give courage and stamina. It has long since been bred out of the Whippet, however, and he is now definitely established as a Greyhound of the small order.

The Whippet is an exceptionally fast dog, more fleet of foot than any domestic animal of his weight. He is capable of sprinting at the rate of 35 miles an hour. Originally used in coursing rabbits, this streamlined dog has attracted the greatest attention in match races. (Whippet racing is discussed in the section on Coursing and Racing, Part IX.)

In disposition, the Whippet is quiet, dignified, and affectionate. He has none of the "barkiness" of the terrier, but makes a good watchman just the same. Highly decorative, this little dog, which ranges in weight from 10 to 28 pounds, is exceedingly easy to groom; despite his dainty appearance he is easy to care for, and is by no means delicate. For grace, smoothness in action, and beauty in outline, the Whippet ranks high among all breeds.

Cowboy, Collier Lad, and Moley Rat were English dogs with sensational speed records. Probably the greatest early English sire was Tom from Heyside, producer of several world champions.

The Whippet makes an excellent contender in bench shows. Of quiet demeanor, they are generally easy to show and their graceful beauty always attracts attention.

Whippet.

Description and Standards: The description and standards, adopted by the American Whippet Club, and approved by the American Kennel Club follow.

GENERAL APPEARANCE: The Whippet should be a dog of moderate size, very alert, that can cover a maximum of distance with a minimum of lost motion, a true sporting hound. Should be put down in hard condition but with no suggestion of being muscle-bound.

HEAD: Long and lean, fairly wide between the ears, scarcely perceptible stop, good length of muzzle which should be powerful without being coarse. Nose entirely black.

EARS: Small, fine in texture, thrown back and folded. Semipricked when at attention. Gay ears are incorrect and should be severely penalized.

EYES: Large, intelligent, round in shape and dark hazel in color, must be at least as dark as the coat color. Expression should be keen and alert. Light yellow or oblique eyes should be strictly penalized. A sulky expression and lack of alertness to be considered most undesirable.

TEETH: White, strong and even. Teeth of upper jaw should fit closely over the lower. An undershot mouth shall disqualify.

NECK: Long and muscular, well-arched and with no suggestion of throatiness, widening gradually into the shoulders. Must not have any tendency to a "ewe" neck.

SHOULDERS: Long, well-laid back with long, flat muscles. Loaded shoulders are a very serious fault.

BRISKET: Very deep and strong, reaching as nearly as possible to the point of the elbow. Ribs well sprung but with no suggestion of barrel shape. Should fill in the space between the forelegs so that there is no appearance of a hollow between them.

FORELEGS: Straight and rather long, held in line with the shoulders and not set under the body so as to make a forechest. Elbows should turn neither in nor out and move freely with the point of the shoulder. Fair amount of bone, which should carry right down to the feet. Pasterns strong.

FEET: Must be well formed with strong, thick pads and well-knuckled-up paws. A thin, flat, open foot is a serious fault.

HINDQUARTERS: Long and powerful, stifles well bent, hocks well let down and close to the ground. Thighs broad and muscular, the muscles should be long and flat. A steep croup is most undesirable.

BACK: Strong and powerful, rather long with a good, natural arch over the loin creating a definite tuck-up of the underline but covering a lot of ground.

TAIL: Long and tapering, should reach to a hipbone when drawn through between the hind legs. Must not be carried higher than the top of the back when moving.

COAT: Close, smooth and firm in texture.

COLOR: Immaterial.

SIZE: Ideal height for dogs, 19 to 22 inches; for bitches, 18 to 21 inches. These are not intended to be definite limits, only approximate.

GAIT: Low, free moving and smooth, as long as is commensurate with the size of the dog. A short, mincing gait with high knee action should be severely penalized.

Disqualification. Undershot mouth.

(November 9, 1955)

—Group III—Working Dogs—

ALASKAN MALAMUTE

AT THE TOP of the world, in the area bounded by the Arctic Circle, live the Eskimos. They are a people unlike any other, and no man knows truly from whence they came, nor when.

In the lands to the south, the weather is less severe. Trees grow. There is better hunting. And the summers are not so short. But still the Eskimos cling to the land along the Arctic Ocean. It is so now, and it was so when the first white men visited the Arctic.

These people are not split into tribes, as we know them. They speak roughly the same language, and their habits are much the same. So it is with their dogs. The dogs are quite obviously closely related, regardless of the part of the Arctic in which they are found.

Conforming roughly to a classification sometimes called the "wolf-spitz," they are heavily furred, have short, prick ears, and carry their tails over their backs. To this family belong the Alaskan Malamute, the Eskimo, the Siberian Huskie, the Samoyed, and, though not so closely related, the Norwegian Elkhound, Chow Chow, Finnish Spitz, Pomeranian, and Keeshond.

It is probably not correct to call any group of Eskimos a tribe. But living along the Pacific slope of Alaska is a group known as the Mahlemuts, or Malamutes. Many of them live along the shores of Kotzebue Sound, facing Siberia.

These people have developed a fairly distinct type of Arctic dog which is now called the Alaskan Malamute, in honor of the people and land from which it comes.

Both Russian and American writers of the early exploratory days referred to the Malamute people as high type primitives who bred unusually good sled dogs. Some of these writers referred to the dogs as the native Alaskan breed.

Stories by Jack London and other writers cast a glamorous aura about the dogs. This was heightened by the first dogs which came down to the United States, and by the prowess of the dogs in sled races both in Canada and in Alaska.

Then during the period from 1890 to 1918, the white men who went north took southern breeds, which were crossed with the Arctic dogs, including the Malamutes. So-called sportsmen, interested merely in winning the money prizes at sled racing meets, began crossing swift breeds with the sled dogs.

The inevitable result was a decay. The northern lands became populated with mongrels of poor type, intractable dispositions, and no great endurance, either for distance or for weather.

Still, those Eskimos remote from the white man's influence kept to their ages-old breeding lines. American sportsmen, interested in developing the breed in the United States, selected stock from these remote outposts. Thus, the dogs most often seen in the United States are of finest stock.

Between the two World Wars, the Alaskan Malamute Club was founded and received recognition by the American Kennel Club. Pure-bred stock then in the country was registered, and the Stud Book was closed to outside dogs, except as might be imported carrying pedigrees recognized by other recognized Stud Books.

Perhaps the most famous American breeders have been Mr. and Mrs. Milton J. Seeley. Noted sled-dog racers and trainers, they bred and trained many of the dogs which went on the various Antarctic explorations. They also bred and trained dogs for the United States Army during World War II.

Description and Standards. The description and standards as adopted by the Alaskan Malamute Club and approved by the American Kennel Club follow.

GENERAL APPEARANCE AND CHARACTERISTICS: The Alaskan Malamute is a powerful and substantially built dog with deep chest and strong, compact body, not too short coupled, with a thick, coarse guard coat of sufficient length to protect a dense, woolly undercoat, from 1 to 2 inches in depth when dog is in full coat. Stands well over pads, and this stance gives the appearance of much activity, showing interest and curiosity. The head is broad, ears wedge-shaped and erect when alerted. The muzzle is bulky with only slight diminishing in width and depth from root to nose, not pointed or long, but not stubby.

Alaskan Malamute puppy.

The Malamute moves with a proud carriage, head erect and eyes alert. Face markings are a distinguishing feature. These consist of either cap over head and rest of face solid color, usually grayish white, or face marked with the appearance of a mask. Combinations of cap and mask are not unusual. The tail is plumed and carried over the back, not like a fox brush, or tightly curled, more like a plume waving.

Malamutes are of various colors, but are usually wolfish gray or black and white. Their feet are of the "snowshoe" type, tight and deep, with well-cushioned pads, giving a firm and compact appearance. Front legs are straight with big bone. Hind legs are broad and powerful, moderately bent at stifles, and without cowhocks. The back is straight, gently sloping from shoulders to hips. The loin should not be so short or tight as to interfere with easy, tireless movement. Endurance and intelligence are shown in body and expression. They have a "wolflike" appearance by their position, but the expression is soft and indicates an affectionate disposition.

TEMPERAMENT: The Alaskan Malamute is an affectionate, friendly dog, not a "one-man" dog. He is a loyal, devoted companion, playful on invitation, but generally impressive by his dignity after maturity.

HEAD: The head should indicate a high degree of intelligence, and is broad and powerful as compared with other "natural" breeds, but should be in proportion to the size of the dog so as not to make the dog appear clumsy or coarse.

SKULL: The skull should be broad between the ears, gradually narrowing to eyes, moderately rounded between ears, flattening on top as it approaches the eyes, rounding off to cheeks, which should be moderately flat. There should be a slight furrow between the eyes, the topline of skull and topline of the muzzle showing but little break downward from a straight line as they join.

MUZZLE: The muzzle should be large and bulky in proportion to size of skull, diminishing but little in width and depth from junction with skull to nose; lips close fitting; nose black; upper and lower jaws broad with large teeth, front teeth meeting with a scissors grip but never overshot or undershot.

EYES: Brown, almond shaped, moderately large for this shape of eye, set obliquely in skull. Dark eyes preferred.

EARS: The ears should be of medium size, but small in proportion to head. The upper halves of the ears are triangular in shape, slightly rounded at tips, set wide apart on outside back edges of the skull with the lower part of the ear joining the skull on a line with the upper corner of the eye, giving the tips of the ears the appearance, when erect, of standing off from the skull. When erect, the ears point slightly forward, but when the dog is at work the ears are sometimes folded against the skull. High-set ears are a fault.

NECK: The neck should be strong and moderately arched.

Alaskan Malamute—Red Flack Mischief with Gigi DuBuis, Sena-Lak Kennels, Valois, N.Y. Hank Babbitt photo.

Alaskan Malamute—Sena-Lak's Image of Skila. (Owner: Sena-Lak Kennels, Valois, N.Y.)

BODY: The chest should be strong and deep; body should be strong and compactly built but not short coupled. The back should be straight and gently sloping to the hips. The loins should be well muscled and not so short as to interfere with easy, rhythmic movement with powerful drive from the hindquarters. A long loin which weakens the back is also a fault. No excess weight.

SHOULDERS, LEGS AND FEET: Shoulders should be moderately sloping; forelegs heavily boned and muscled, straight to pasterns, which should be short and strong and almost vertical as viewed from the side. The feet should be large and compact, toes tight-fitting and well arched, pads thick and tough, toenails short and strong. There should be a protective growth of hair between toes. Hind legs must be broad and powerfully muscled through thighs; stifles moderately bent, hock joints broad and strong, moderately bent and well let down. As viewed from behind, the hind legs should not appear bowed in bone, but stand and move true in line with movement of the front legs, and not too close or too wide. The legs of the Malamute must indicate unusual strength and tremendous propelling power. Any indication of unsoundness in legs or feet, standing or moving, is to be considered a serious fault. Dewclaws on the hind legs are undesirable and should be removed shortly after pups are whelped.

TAIL: Moderately set and following the line of the spine at the start, well furred and carried over the back when not working—not tightly curled to rest on back—or short furred and carried like a fox brush, a waving plume appearance instead.

COAT: The Malamute should have a thick, coarse guard coat, not long and soft. The under coat is dense, from 1 to 2 inches in depth, oily and woolly. The coarse guard coat stands out, and there is thick fur around the neck. The guard coat varies in length, as does the under coat; however, in general, the coat is moderately short to medium along the sides of the body with the length of the coat increasing somewhat around the shoulders and neck, down the back and over the rump, as well as in the breeching and plume. Malamutes usually have shorter and less dense coats when shed out during the summer months.

COLOR AND MARKINGS: The usual colors range from light gray through the intermediate shadings to black, always with white on underbodies, parts of legs, feet, and part of mask markings. Markings should be either cap-like and/or mask-like on face. A white blaze on forehead and/or collar or spot on nape is attractive and acceptable, but broken color extending over the body in spots or uneven splashings is undesirable. One should distinguish between mantled dogs and splash-coated dogs. The only solid color allowable is the all-white.

SIZE: There is a natural range in size in the breed. The desirable freighting sizes are: *Males:* 25 inches at the shoulders

—85 pounds. *Females:* 23 inches at the shoulders—75 pounds. However, size consideration should not outweigh that of type, proportion, and functional attributes, such as shoulders, chest, legs, feet, and movement. When dogs are judged equal in type, proportion, and functional attributes the dog nearest the desirable freighting size is to be preferred.

Important. In judging Alaskan Malamutes their function as a sledge dog for heavy freighting must be given consideration above all else. The judge must bear in mind that this breed is designed primarily as the working sledge dog of the North for hauling heavy freight, and therefore he should be a heavy-boned, powerfully built, compact dog with sound legs, good feet, deep chest, powerful shoulders, steady, balanced, tireless gait, and the other physical equipment necessary for the efficient performance of his job. He isn't intended as a racing sled dog designed to compete in speed trials with the smaller Northern breeds. The Malamute as a sledge dog for heavy freighting is designed for strength and endurance and any characteristic of the individual specimen, including temperament, which interferes with the accomplishment of this purpose is to be considered the most serious of faults. Faults under this provision would be splayfootedness, any indication of unsoundness or weakness in legs, cowhocks, bad pasterns, straight shoulders, lack of angulation, stilted gait or any gait which isn't balanced, strong, and steady, ranginess, shallowness, ponderousness, lightness of bone, poor over-all proportion, and similar characteristics.

SCALE OF POINTS	*Points*
General Appearance	20
Head	15
Body	20
Legs and Movement	20
Feet	10
Coat and Color	10
Tail	5
TOTAL	100

(April 12, 1960)

BELGIAN SHEEPDOG

THREE VARIETIES of Belgian Sheepdogs are recognized by the American Kennel Club. These are the Groenendael, the Malinois, and the Belgian Tervuren. The second variety, however, is seldom seen. In fact, the predominance of the Groenendael—a long-coated, black dog—has caused most people to think that all Belgians are black. For this reason, many black German Shepherds are mistakenly called Belgian Sheepdogs by the uninformed.

In Belgium, a greater number of varieties are recognized. Besides the three mentioned above, there are the short-coated; wire-coated fawn; wire-coated ash gray; and wire-coated of other colors; the long-coated fawn; and the long-coated of other colors. The Tervuren, or short-coated fawn, was very popular in earlier times.

It is believed that the Groenendael and Malinois differ to some extent in their mental aptitudes. The former is a dog of great initiative, being able to face situations and answer problems which other dogs cannot face. In this respect, G. Horowitz, the noted British authority, believes the Groenendael is superior to the German Shepherd. Apparently in Belgium the dog is now little used with sheep, but is in great demand for obedience contests, and even for police work.

The Malinois is considered a supreme sheepdog, having intense aptitude and love of sheepherding. His coloration is deemed perfect for this, since he is almost invisible at night. The dog has been finely bred for shows, has great beauty, and yet is a star at obedience and guard work as well.

The Groenendael was recognized by the Belgian Kennel Club as far back as 1891. He prospered for many years, not only in Belgium, but in Holland and in France also. In recent years, the breed has been on the decline in both the Netherlands and Belgium, but in France he is still popular. Some effort has been made to popularize him in England, chiefly through the efforts of Mrs. Grant Forbes. The breed is gaining popularity in the United States.

The Malinois probably has the longest official title in dogdom. It is "Chien de Berger Belge Malinoix a poil court fauve charbonne." Fortunately, most countries have shortened it to "Chien de Berger Malinois," or merely to Malinois.

It appears to have originated in the grazing country about Malines, hence its name. It is of more recent recognition than the Groenendael, but it has fairly captured the Belgian fancy, not only because of its beauty, but because of its ability in both sheepdog and police dog trials. In these trials, it has held its own against all competition.

Among its qualities is that of unusual speed, and darting, ground-covering action. It is a tireless dog in the field, and its neutral colors blend into the landscape in a way which does not alarm sheep when being worked or guarded.

On the other hand, as stated, the Malinois has not caught the American fancy to the same extent as has the Groenendael. And yet, the decline of the latter in Belgium has had its effect in the United States, where many really inferior dogs, particularly in temperament, have been seen.

The Groenendael became popular in the United States shortly after World War I. Many American soldiers returned to tell of the remarkable black army dogs owned by the Belgians. Similarly, of course, the German Shepherd reached fame as a "police dog," and during the same period.

Both breeds suffered a decline through the greed of unscrupulous breeders, who set up "puppy factories," and produced scrubs, both physically and mentally, which were sold at high prices.

After the end of World War II, a group of enthusiastic fanciers began working steadily to increase the breed's popularity. The dogs which have been appearing at the shows have been noteworthy for their uniformity, conformation, and character.

Breeders here had one advantage over the Belgians. They had one standard of perfection, and did not have to worry about bringing the Malinois into that standard, since there were so few in the country. For these reasons, a uniform type of Groenendael was established.

All the different types were registered and shown as Belgian Sheepdogs up to July 1, 1959, when the American Kennel Club gave them recognition as three separate breeds. Dogs of the Groenendael type were then registered and shown as Belgian Sheepdogs. The Belgian Tervuren was registered and shown as a separate breed and the Belgian Malinois, although not registrable, was eligible for showing in the Miscellaneous Class. The Malinois had many fanciers, however, and on June 30, 1965, this type met the AKC qualifications for registration and for classes of its own at shows.

The Belgian Tervuren is covered under a separate following main head. The separate descriptions and standards for the Belgian Sheepdog and the Malinois follow.

Description and Standards (Belgian Sheepdog).

PERSONALITY: The Belgian Sheepdog should reflect the qualities of intelligence, courage, alertness, and devotion to master. To his inherent aptitude as guardian of flocks should be added protectiveness of the person and property of his master. He should be watchful, attentive, and always in motion when not under command. In his relationship with humans he should be observant and vigilant with strangers but not apprehensive. He should not show fear or shyness. He should not show viciousness by unwarranted or unprovoked attack. With those he knows well, he is most affectionate and friendly, zealous of their attention, and very possessive.

GENERAL APPEARANCE: The first impression of the Belgian Sheepdog is that of a well-balanced, square dog, elegant in appearance, with an exceedingly proud carriage of the head and neck. He is a strong, agile, well-muscled animal, alert and

Belgian Sheepdog—Ch. Ichim Des Forges Manceux. (Owner: Mrs. Lloyd Rentschler, Woodinville, Wash.) This dog was imported from Belgium.

full of life. His whole conformation gives the impression of depth and solidity without bulkiness. The male dog is usually somewhat more impressive and grand than his female counterpart. The bitch should have a distinctly feminine look.

SIZE AND SUBSTANCE: Males should be 24-26 inches in height and females 22-24 inches, measured at the withers. The length, measured from point of breast bone to point of rump, should equal the height. Bitches may be slightly longer. Bone structure should be moderately heavy in proportion to his height so that he is well balanced throughout and neither spindly or leggy nor cumbersome and bulky.

STANCE: The Belgian Sheepdog should stand squarely on all fours. Side view: the topline, front legs, and back legs should closely approximate a square.

EXPRESSION: Indicates alertness, attention, readiness for activity. Gaze should be intelligent and questioning.

COAT: The guard hairs of the coat must be long, well-fitting, straight, and abundant. They should not be silky or wiry. The texture should be a medium harshness. The under coat should be extremely dense, commensurate, however, with climatic conditions. The Belgian Sheepdog is particularly adaptable to extremes of temperature or climate. The hair is shorter on the head, outside of the ears, and lower part of the legs. The opening of the ear is protected by tufts of hair. Ornamentation: especially long and abundant hair, like a collarette, around the neck; fringe of long hair down the back of the forearm; especially long and abundant hair trimming the hindquarters, the breeches; long, heavy, and abundant hair on the tail.

COLOR: Black. May be completely black or may be black with white, limited as follows: Small to moderate patch or strip on forechest. Between pads of feet. On tips of hind toes. On chin and muzzle (frost—may be white or gray). On tips of front toes—allowable but a fault.

HEAD: Cleancut and strong, overall size should be in proportion to the body.

SKULL: Top flattened rather than rounded. The width approximately the same, but not wider, than the length.

STOP: Moderate.

MUZZLE, JAWS, LIPS: Muzzle moderately pointed, avoiding any tendency to snipiness, and approximately equal in length to that of the topskull. The jaws should be strong and powerful. The lips should be tight and black, with no pink showing on the outside.

EARS: Triangular in shape, stiff, erect, and in proportion to the head in size. Base of the ear should not come below the center of the eye.

EYES: Brown, preferably dark brown. Medium size, slightly almond shaped, not protruding.

NOSE: Black, without spots or discolored areas.

TEETH: A full complement of strong, white teeth, evenly set. Should not be overshot or undershot. Should have either an even bite or a scissors bite.

TORSO, NECK: Round and rather outstretched, tapered from head to body, well muscled, with tight skin.

TOPLINE: The withers are slightly higher and slope into the back which must be level, straight, and firm from withers to hip joints. The loin section, viewed from above, is relatively short, broad and strong, but blending smoothly into the back. The croup is medium long, sloping gradually.

TAIL: Strong at the base, bone to reach hock. At rest the dog holds it low, the tip bent back level with the hock. When in action he raises it and gives it a curl, which is strongest toward the tip, without forming a hook.

CHEST: Not broad, but deep. The lowest point should reach the elbow, forming a smooth ascendant curve to the abdomen.

ABDOMEN: Moderate development. Neither tucked-up nor paunchy.

FOREQUARTERS AND SHOULDER: Long and oblique, laid flat against the body, forming a sharp angle (approximately 90°) with the upper arm.

LEGS: Straight, strong, and parallel to each other. Bone oval rather than round. Development (length and substance) should be well proportioned to the size of the dog. Pastern: medium length, strong, and very slightly sloped.

FEET: Round (cat footed), toes curved close together, well padded. Nails strong and black except that they may be white to match white toe tips.

HINDQUARTERS AND THIGHS: Broad and heavily muscled. The upper and lower thigh bones approximately parallel the shoulder blade and upper arm respectively, forming a relatively sharp angle at stifle joint.

LEGS: Length and substance well proportioned to the size of the dog. Bone oval rather than round. Legs are parallel to each other. The angle at the hock is relatively sharp, although the Belgian Sheepdog does not have extreme angulation. Metatarsus medium length, strong, and slightly sloped. Dewclaws, if any, should be removed.

FEET: Slightly elongated. Toes curved close together, well padded. Nails strong and black except that they may be white to match white toe tips.

GAIT: Motion should be smooth, free and easy, seemingly never tiring, exhibiting facility of movement rather than a hard driving action. He tends to single-track on a fast gait; the legs, both front and rear, converging toward the center line of gravity of the dog. The backline should remain firm and level, parallel to the line of motion with no crabbing. He shows a marked tendency to move in a circle rather than a straight line.

FAULTS: Any deviation from these specifications is a fault. In determining whether a fault is minor, serious, or major, these two factors should be used as a guide: 1. The extent to which it deviates from the Standard. 2. The extent to which such deviation would actually affect the working ability of the dog.

Disqualifications. Viciousness.

COLOR: Any color other than black, except for white in specified areas.

EARS: Hanging (as on a hound).

TAIL: Cropped or stump. Males under 22½ or over 27½ inches in height. Females under 20½ or over 25½ inches in height.

Description and Standards (Malinois).

The Belgian Malinois is a well-balanced square dog, elegant in appearance with an exceedingly proud carriage of the head and neck. The dog is strong, agile, well-muscled, alert and full of life. It stands squarely on all fours and viewed from the side, the top line, forelegs and hind legs closely approximate a square. The whole conformation gives the impression of depth and solidity without bulkiness. The expression indicates alertness, attention and readiness for activity. The gaze is intelligent and questioning. The male is usually somewhat more impressive and grand than its female counterpart, which has a distinctly feminine look.

SIZE AND SUBSTANCE: Males, 24-26 inches in height; females, 22-24 inches measured at the withers. The length, measured from point of breastbone to point of rump should equal the height, but bitches may be slightly longer. Bone structure is moderately heavy in proportion to height so that the dog is well balanced throughout and neither spindly, leggy nor cumbersome and bulky.

COAT: Comparatively short, straight, with dense under coat. Very short hair on the head, ears and lower legs. The hair is somewhat longer around the neck where it forms a collarette, and on the tail and the back of the thighs.

COLOR: Rich fawn to mahogany with black overlay. Black mask and ears. The under parts of the body, tail and breeches are lighter fawn, but washed-out fawn color is a fault. The tips of the toes may be white and a small white spot on the chest is permitted.

HEAD: Cleancut and strong, overall size in proportion to the body. Skull, top flattened rather than rounded, the width approximately the same as the length but no wider. Stop, moderate. Muzzle, jaws and lips; the muzzle moderately pointed, avoiding any tendency to snipiness, and approximately equal in length to that of the topskull. The jaws are strong and powerful. The lips tight and black, with no pink showing on the outside.

EARS: Triangular in shape, stiff, erect and in proportion to the head in size. Base of the ear should not come below the center of the eye. Eyes, brown, preferably dark-brown, medium-size, slightly almond-shaped, not protruding. Nose, black without spots or discolored areas. Teeth; a full complement of strong white teeth, evenly set and meeting in an even bite or a scissors bite, neither overshot nor undershot.

TORSO AND NECK: Round and rather outstretched, tapered from head to body, well-muscled and with tight skin. Topline; the withers are slightly higher and slope into the back which must be level, straight and firm from withers to hip joints. The loin section, viewed from above, is relatively short, broad and strong, but blending smoothly into the back. The croup is medium-long, sloping gradually.

TAIL: Strong at the base, bone to reach hock. At rest it is held low, the tip bent back level with the hock. In action it is raised with a curl, which is strongest towards the tip without forming a hook.

CHEST: Not broad, but deep. The lowest point reaches the elbow, forming a smooth ascendant curve to the abdomen, which is moderately developed, neither tucked-up nor paunchy.

FOREQUARTERS AND SHOULDER: Long and oblique, laid flat against the body, forming a sharp angle (approximately 90°) with the upper arm. Legs straight, strong and paralleled to each other. Length and substance well-proportioned to the size of the dog. Pastern, medium-length, strong and very slightly sloped. Dewclaws may be removed.

FEET: Round (cat-footed) toes curved close together, well padded. Nails strong and black except that they may be white to match white toe tips.

HINDQUARTERS AND THIGHS: Broad and heavily muscled. The upper and lower thigh bones approximately parallel the shoulder blade and upper arm respectively, forming a relatively sharp angle at stifle joint.

LEGS: Length and substance well-proportioned to the size of the dog. Bone oval rather than round. Legs are parallel to each other. The angle at the hock is relatively sharp, although the Belgian Malinois does not have extreme angulation. Metatarsus medium-length, strong, and slightly sloped.

GAIT: Smooth, free and easy, seemingly never tiring, exhibiting facility of movement rather than hard driving action. The dog tends to single-track at a fast gait, the legs both front and rear converging toward the dog's centerline of gravity, while the back line remains firm and level, parallel to the line of motion with no crabbing. The Malinois shows a marked tendency to move in a circle rather than a straight line.

FAULTS: Any deviation from these specifications is a fault, the degree to which a dog is penalized depending on the extent to which the dog deviates from the standard, and the extent to which the particular fault would actually affect the working ability of the dog.

Disqualifications. Ears hanging, as on a hound dog. Tail cropped or stump. Males under 22½ or over 27½ inches in height. Females under 20½ or over 25½ inches in height.

BELGIAN TERVUREN

PREVIOUS TO 1959, the Belgian Tervuren was registered and shown in the U.S. as one of the types of Belgian Sheepdog. That year it was granted registration as a separate breed with separate classification at dog shows. It is practically identical to the Groenendael in conformation, the difference being color. While the Groenendael is black, the Tervuren is fawn-colored up to the age of about eighteen months when the fawn becomes deeper with black tips giving the impression of a coat that has been stroked lightly with charcoal, the black more pronounced on shoulders and back, face, ears and tips of the tail.

Belgian Tervuren—Flair De Fauve Charbonne. (Owner: E. Laurin West, Willington, Conn.) Photo by Evelyn M. Shafer.

In Belgium and France the Tervuren, along with other Belgian types of shepherd dogs, is registered as the Chien de Berger Belge, a term loosely applied to any dog used for herding sheep and all of which have a common origin in the dogs used a hundred or so years ago when sheep herding was a very important part of rural life. Very little attention was paid to the appearance of these dogs. All that mattered to the herdsmen was a dog's strength, ruggedness and herding ability. Breeding for these attributes made the herdsmen oblivious as to whether a dog had short or long hair, was dark-colored or light, and the result was an odd assortment of types, but nevertheless dogs that had the intelligence and trainability that came down in the breeds developed from them.

In the 1880's fences came into use, the menace of wolves preying on herds decreased and growing rail facilities made it possible to ship animals rather than herd them to the city markets. About the same time, dog shows began to be held and with less need for a working dog, breeders began to pay attention to breeding for definite types.

Like the Groenendael and the Malinois, the Tervuren gets its name from the town where it was developed. M. M. F. Corbeel of Tervuren owned a pair of sheepdogs which had long, black-tipped hair. From the mating of these two came a female, Miss, who was acquired by M. Danhieux. Like M. Rose, who was largely responsible for the development of the Groenendael, M. Danhieux was a serious breeder. He bred Miss to the long-haired black Piccard D'Uccle, the same dog used by M. Rose to start his Groenendael strain. Apparently, this dog carried a factor for fawn, for the mating produced Milsart, a blackened fawn dog which in 1907 became the first Tervuren champion.

Although there were Tervurens in the United States in the early 1940's, the first registered Tervuren was imported in 1954. Especially proficient in obedience work, the breed has made a strong impression in that field. In fact, the first American-bred litter, whelped in 1954, had two CD title holders as sire and dam, both of which won their degrees before they were a year of age. D'Jimmy du Clos St. Clair, owned by Betty C. Hinckley of Chicago, in 1958 became the first American champion of the breed.

Description and Standard.

The Belgian Tervuren should reflect the qualities of intelligence, courage, alertness and devotion to master. To his inherent aptitude as guardian of flocks should be added protectiveness of the person and property of his master. He should be watchful, attentive and usually in motion when not under command. In his relationship with humans he should be observant and vigilant with strangers, but not apprehensive. He should not show fear nor shyness. He should not show viciousness by unwarranted or unprovoked attack. With those he knows well, he is most affectionate and friendly, zealous for their attention and very possessive.

GENERAL APPEARANCE: The first impression of Belgian Tervuren is that of a well balanced square dog, elegant in appearance, with proud carriage of head and neck. He is strong, agile, well-muscled, alert and full of life. His whole conformation gives the impression of depth and solidity without bulkiness. The male is usually somewhat more impressive and grand than the female. The female should have a distinctly feminine look. Because of frequent comparisons between the Belgian Tervuren and the German Shepherd Dog, it is to be noted that these two breeds differ considerably in size, substance and structure, the difference being especially noticeable in the formation of the topline and the hindquarters.

SIZE AND SUBSTANCE: Males 24-26 inches in height, and females 22-24. The length measured from point of breastbone to point of rump should equal the height. Bone structure medium in proportion to height so that he is well balanced throughout and neither spindly or leggy nor cumbersome and bulky.

STANCE: He should stand squarely on all fours. Viewed from the side, the topline, ground level, front legs and back legs, should closely approximate a square.

EXPRESSION: Intelligent and questioning, indicating alertness, attention and readiness for action.

COAT: The guard hairs of the coat must be long, well fitting, straight and abundant. They should not be silky or wiry. The texture should be a medium harshness. The under coat should be very dense commensurate, however, with climatic conditions. The hair is shorter on the head, outside the ears and on the lower part of the legs. The opening of the ear is protected by tufts of hair.

ORNAMENTATION: Especially long and abundant hair, like a collarette, around the neck, fringe of long hair down the back of the forearm; especially long and abundant hair trimming the hindquarters—the breeches; long, heavy and abundant hair on the tail.

COLOR: Rich fawn to russet mahogany with black overlay. The coat is characteristically double-pigmented, wherein the tip of each fawn hair is blackened. On mature males, this blackening is especially pronounced on the shoulders, back and rib section. The chest color is a mixture of black and gray. The face has a black mask, and the ears are mostly black. The tail typi-

cally has a darker or black tip. The under parts of the body, tail and breeches are light beige. A small, white patch is permitted on the chest not to extend to the neck or breast. The tips of the toes may be white. White or gray hair (frost) on chin or muzzle is normal. Although some allowance is to be made for dogs under 18 months, when true color is attained, washed-out color or color too black resembling the Belgian Sheepdog is undesirable.

HEAD: Well chiseled, dry, long without exaggeration. Skull and muzzle, measuring from the stop should be of equal length. Overall size should be in proportion to the body. Top of skull flattened rather than rounded, the width approximately the same but not wider than the length. Stop moderate. Muzzle moderately pointed, avoiding any tendency to snipiness. The jaws strong and powerful. The lip should be tight and black, with no pink showing on the outside. Ears are equilateral triangles in shape, well-cupped, stiff, erect, not too large. Set high, the base of the ear should not come below the center of the eye. Eyes brown, preferably dark-brown, medium size, slightly almond-shaped, not protruding. Light or yellow eyes are a fault. Nose black, without spots or discolored areas. Nostrils well defined. There should be a full complement of strong, white teeth evenly set. Either a scissors bite or even bite is acceptable. Should not be overshot or undershot. Teeth broken by accident should not be severely penalized, but worn teeth, especially incisors, are often indicative of the lack of proper bite, although some allowance should be made for age. Discolored (distemper) teeth are not to be penalized.

TORSO: Neck round, muscular, rather outstretched, slightly arched and tapered from head to body. Skin well fitting with no loose folds. Topline horizontal, straight and firm from withers to hip joints. The loin section, viewed from above, is relatively short, broad and strong, but blending smoothly into the back. The croup is medium long, sloping gradually. Tail strong at the base, the last vertebra to reach the hock. At rest the dog holds it low, the tip bent back level with the hock. When in action, he raises it and gives it a curl, which is strongest toward the tip without forming a hook. Tail should not be carried too high nor turned to one side. Chest not broad but deep, the lowest point should reach the elbow, forming a smooth ascendant curve to the abdomen. Abdomen moderately developed, neither tucked up nor paunchy.

FOREQUARTERS: Legs straight, parallel, perpendicular to the ground. Shoulders long and oblique, laid flat against the body, forming a sharp angle (approx. 90°) with the upper arm. Top of the shoulder blades should be roughly a thumb's width apart. Arms should move in a direction exactly parallel to the axis of the body. Forearms long and well muscled. Bone flat rather than round. Pasterns short and strong, slightly sloped. Feet round, toes curved close together, well padded, strong nails. Nail color can vary from black to transparent.

HINDQUARTERS: Legs powerful without heaviness, moving in the same pattern as the limbs of the forequarters. Thighs broad and heavily muscled. Stifles clearly defined, with upper chank at right angles to the hip bones. Bone flat rather than round. Hocks moderately bent. Metatarsi short, perpendicular to the ground, parallel to each other when viewed from the rear. Dewclaws, if any, should be removed. Feet slightly elongated, toes curved close together; heavily-padded, strong nails.

GAIT: Lively and graceful, covering the maximum of ground. Always in motion, seemingly never tiring, he shows facility of movement rather than hard driving action. He tends to single-track at a fast gait, the legs both front and rear converging toward the center line of gravity of the dog. The back line should remain firm and level, parallel to the line of motion with no crabbing. His natural tendency is to move in a circle rather than a straight line.

Disqualifications. Ears hanging, as on a hound. Tail cropped or stump. Color, white markings anywhere except as specified. Teeth, pronounced undershot. Size, males under 22½ or over 27½ inches in height; females under 20½ or over 25½ inches in height.

(May, 1959)

BERNESE MOUNTAIN DOG

SOME 2,000 YEARS ago, Roman armies swept into Helvetia through the pass at Mons Jovis, which we today call St. Bernhard. The Romans eventually went home, but they left their dogs behind. Ever since, these dogs have been called Swiss Mountain Dogs. There are four types of these surviving. One of these, the Bernese Senenhund, Durbachler, or Bernese Mountain Dog, has been brought to the United States in sufficient numbers to receive recognition by the American Kennel Club.

The four breeds, as they are officially known in Switzerland today, are the Appenzell, a short-haired, curled-tailed dog; the Entlebuch, a short-haired, naturally short-tailed dog of smaller size than the former; the Bernese, a long-haired dog of horizontal-tail carriage and larger size than the others; and the Large Mountain Dog, a short-haired dog which is the tallest of all.

These Mountain Dogs share one thing in common. They have shining black coats, with white and brown or rust-colored markings. They are all excellent guard dogs, but some of them have been used as cattle and sheepdogs, while the Bernese has been used only as a draft dog and companion.

The Bernese Mountain Dog is said to be the most popular of all Swiss dogs. Hubbard, in his *The Observer's Book of Dogs,* points out that he is far more popular than the St. Bernard in Switzerland, while being comparatively unknown in other countries.

The breed was popular on both the plains and in the mountains until about 1840, when it began to lose its appeal. In the next 40 years, it was almost entirely supplanted by other breeds, chiefly of foreign importation.

Franz Schertenleib, a cynologist of Berne, is said to have rescued the last of the Bernese stock, which he found in the Durrbach district of Canton Berne. This was in the year 1892. Because he found the dogs at

Bernese Mountain Dog—Ch. Lucki v. Chorrichterhof, C.D. (Owner: Barbara Packard, Los Altos Hills, Calif.) Courtesy Barbara Packard.

Durrbach, they were for a time called Durbachlers.

Schertenleib scoured Switzerland for good specimens, and gradually built the breed back to its original excellence. In 1904 the dogs which resulted from his work were shown at the International Dog Show at Berne.

Professor Albert Heim of Zurich became interested in the breed, and made a special study of it. Upon his conclusions that the Bernese Mountain Dogs actually belonged to a pure breed dating back to Roman times, the breed was admitted to the Stud Book.

Heim, who played a major part in saving and improving all the Mountain Dogs, succeeded in getting a specialty club organized to back the Bernese breed. The club was organized at Burgdorf in 1907, and quickly established branches in other Swiss cities, and in Germany.

By 1936, the breed had spread into England, via Scotland, and the following year it was admitted to the American Kennel Club. Specimens had been brought to America some years earlier, however. Mrs. Egg-Leach, the British sportswoman, is credited with a major part in getting it started in both Great Britain and America.

Description and Standards. The description and standards as adopted by the American Kennel Club follow.

GENERAL APPEARANCE: A well-balanced dog, active and alert; a combination of sagacity, fidelity, and utility.

HEIGHT: Dogs, 23 inches to 27½ inches; bitches, 21 inches to 26 inches at shoulder.

HEAD: Skull flat, defined stop and strong muzzle. Dewlaps very slightly developed, flews not too pendulous, jaw strong with good, strong teeth. Eyes dark, hazel-brown, full of fire. Ears V-shaped, set on high, not too pointed at tips and rather short. When in repose, hanging close to head; when alert, brought slightly forward and raised at base.

BODY: Rather short than too long in back, compact, and well ribbed up. Chest broad with good depth of brisket. Loins strong and muscular.

LEGS AND FEET: Forelegs perfectly straight and muscular, thighs well developed and stifles well bent. Feet round and

Bernese Mountain Dog. Courtesy Barbara Packard.

Bernese Mountain Dog—Ch. Halidom Kela, C.D., by her owners said to be the first female in the U.S. to attain a Championship and the first Champion to also hold an obedience title. (Owners: Mr. and Mrs. A. A. Buchanan, Monroe, New York.) Courtesy Mr. and Mrs. A. A. Buchanan.

compact. Dewclaws should be removed.

TAIL: Of fair thickness and well covered with long hair, but not to form a flag; moderate length. When in repose, should be carried low, upward swirl permissible; when alert, may be carried gaily, but may never curl or be carried over back.

COAT: Soft and silky with bright, natural sheen, long and slightly wavy, but may never curl.

COLOR AND MARKINGS: Jet-black with russet-brown or deep tan markings on all four legs, a spot just above forelegs, each side of white chest markings and spots over eyes, which may never be missing. The brown on the forelegs must always be between the black and white.

Preferable but not a condition, are—white feet, tip of tail, pure white blaze up foreface, a few white hairs on back of neck, and white star-shaped markings on chest. When the latter markings are missing, it is not a disqualification.

Faults—Too massive in head, light or staring eyes, too heavy or long ears, too narrow or snipey muzzle, under or overshot mouth, pendulous dewlaps, too long or Setter-like body, splay or hare feet, tail curled or carried over back, cowhocks and white legs.

SCALE OF POINTS:	Points
General appearance	15
Size and height	5
Head	15
Body	15
Legs and feet	15
Tail	10
Coat	10
Color and markings	15
TOTAL	100

BOUVIER DES FLANDRES

A DOG which has been gaining slowly but steadily in popularity in the United States is the Bouvier des Flandres, or Belgian cattle dog.

The Bouvier des Flandres is a very ancient breed, having existed in several varieties for several hundred years. During this time he had been known under half a dozen names, most of which have referred to his remarkable ability as a cattle drover.

The term "Bouvier" has the meaning of cowherd, or ox driver. Another name once used for this dog was "Chien de Vacher," meaning "cowherd's dog." Still another referred to the harsh coat of one variety, being called "pikhaar," a Flemish term meaning "hair which pricks." The name was discarded because it caused people to connect the dog with a French breed of Picardy shepherd.

The Bouvier des Flandres first came to the attention of breeding experts and show fanciers in 1910. During that year, two Bouviers named Nelly and Even and belonging to M. Poiret of Ghent, were shown at the May International Dog Show at Ghent.

Immediate interest in the breed was aroused. It was then ascertained that at least four varieties of cattle dog existed side by side. There were: (1) the dog we now call the Bouvier des Flandres, a relatively small, fawn or gray dog, having rounded ribs and a rather short head; (2) a somewhat larger dog, usually black, and having a longer head and deeper ribs. This dog was called the Moerman, or Bouvier Pikhaar; (3) a large black, or dark gray dog, having excessive body hair, with the eyes covered, as in the Old English Sheepdog. This breed was called the Bouvier Briarde, and every effort was made to eliminate it; (4) the Bouvier Ardennes, a dog seldom seen at shows, having natural ears, and a rather soft coat.

It was decided that the first type, the Bouvier des Flandres, was really the oldest of the four. And many experts were agreed that the Moerman was obtained by crossing the Bouvier des Flandres with a breed known as the Matin.

The Societe Royale St. Hubert became interested in the breed, and so did Club St. Hubert De Nord. Through its vice president, a Frenchman named M. Fontaine, a standard was set up for the breed in 1912. This followed a meeting of many cattle men at Roulers, West Flanders, in August. Taking part in this meeting were Baron Van Zeiglen, M. Van Her-

Bouvier Des Flandres—A good dog with children. Hank Babb photo.

Bouvier Des Flandres—Ch. Rostan du Clos des Cerbires. Note his lighter-colored coat. (Owner: Miss E. F. Bowles, Collegeville, Pa.)

reweghe, and others of equal importance in the later history of the breed.

The breed caught the fancy of French and Dutch breeders as well. Moreover, the dogs began to perform well at trials, both for cattle driving, defense, and army work. Fanciers became entranced by the dogs, which were good looking, and yet could vie with all other breeds at the trials.

However, World War I nearly caused the extermination of the breed. After the war, breeders began to rebuild on the basis of the stock which had been saved. But for a long time there were at least four standards for the breed, and a dog which might win its championship in Belgium might find itself disqualified in France. This was partly caused by the efforts to bring the Bouvier and the Moerman into the same standard.

Bouviers began to appear in the United States in the late nineteen thirties. Many of these were descendents of the famous Ch. Nic De Sottegem, who belonged to a noted Belgian Army veterinarian, Capt. Darby. Nic's descendents numbered such titans of the breed as Ch. Droya, Ch. Dragon de la Lys. Corshe de Sottegem, Goliath de le Lyt, and others.

World War II cut off Belgian breeding stock, both by making it unavailable for export to the United States, and by reducing the number of dogs actually owned in Belgium. However, there is now sufficient breeding stock in the country to make possible progress in the breed.

Among those responsible for popularity of the breed in the United States have been: Dorothy S. Young, New Canaan, Conn.; Miss E. F. Bowles, Philadelphia, Pa.; and Julius Bliss, New York City.

Description and Standards. The official AKC standard for the Bouvier des Flandres follows.

The Bouvier des Flandres is a rough-coated dog of notably rugged appearance as befitting an erstwhile cattle driver and

farmers' helper of Flandres, and later an ambulance dog and messenger in World War I. He is a compact-bodied, powerfully built dog of upstanding carriage and alert, intelligent expression.

HEAD: The head is medium long, with the skull slightly longer than the muzzle. The skull is almost flat on top, moderately wide between the ears, and sloping slightly toward the muzzle. The brow is noticeably arched over the eyes. The stop is shallow, and the under-eye fill-in good.

EARS: Rough-coated, set high on the head and cropped to a triangular contour. They stand erect and are carried straight up.

EYES: Neither protruding nor sunken, the eyes are set a trifle obliquely in the skull and not too far apart. They are of medium size and very nearly oval. Preferred color, a dark nut-brown. Black eyes, although not considered faulty, are less desirable as contributing to a somber expression. Light-colored eyes, and staring or wild expression are faulty.

MUZZLE: Wide, deep and well filled out, the width narrowing gradually toward the tip of the nose. Cheeks are clean or flat-sided, the jaws powerful, and the lips dry and tight-fitting. A narrow muzzle, suggestive of weakness, is faulty.

TEETH: Strong and white, with the canines set well apart, the teeth meet in a scissors bite.

NOSE: Black and well developed, the nostrils wide open. Across the top the contour is a trifle rounded as opposed to flat. Brown, pink and spotted noses are faulty.

NECK AND SHOULDERS: The neck is well rounded, slightly arched, and carried almost upright, its thickness gradually increasing as it fits gracefully into the shoulders. Clean and dry at the throat. The shoulders are long and sloping.

BODY: The brisket is deep, extending down at least to the point of the elbows, and of moderate width. The back is short, strong and straight. The loins are short, taut, and slightly arched in topline, while the rump is broad and square rather than sloping. Ribs are deep and well sprung. As advantageous for breeding purposes, slightly greater length of loin is permissible in bitches.

TAIL: Set high, carried up, and docked to about 4 inches.

LEGS AND FEET: The leg bones, although only moderate in girth, are made to appear heavy because of their covering with thick, rough hair. Forelegs are straight as viewed from the front or side, with elbows turned neither in nor out. Hindquarters are firm and well muscled, with large, powerful hams. Legs are strong and sturdy, with hocks well let down and wide apart. They are slightly angulated at stifle and hock joints. Viewed from the back, they are absolutely parallel. The feet are round, compact, with toes arched and close. The nails are black, the pads thick and tough.

COAT: Rough, touseled and unkempt in appearance, the coat is capable of withstanding the hardest work in the most inclem-

Bouvier Des Flandres—Ch Bonaparte V. Darling-Astrid. (Owner: Mrs. Fred H. Walsh, Frenchtown, New Jersey.) Photo by Evelyn M. Shafer.

ent weather. The topcoat is harsh, rough and wiry, and so thick that when separated by the hand the skin is hardly visible. The under coat is fine and soft in texture, and thicker in winter. On the skull the hair is shorter and almost smooth. On the brows it is longer, thus forming eyebrows. Longer growth on muzzle and underjaw from mustache and beard. On the legs it is thick and rough, on the feet rather short. Soft, silky or woolly topcoats are faulty.

COLOR: From fawn to black; pepper and salt, gray and brindle. A white star on the chest is allowed. Chocolate brown with white spots is faulty.

HEIGHT: Dogs from 23½ to 27½ inches; bitches, a minimum of 22¾ inches.

SCALE OF POINTS:	Points
Coat	20
Head (eyes, ears, skull, foreface)	20
Shoulders and style	10
Hindquarters (hams and legs)	10
Back, loin, brisket, belly	15
Feet and legs	10
Symmetry, size and character	15
TOTAL	100

(April 14, 1959)

Boxer—Ch. Marquam Hill's Comanche. (Owner: Dr. Robert Bur San Rafael, Calif.) Photo by Evelyn M. Shafer.

BOXER

THE BOXER is one of the most popular breeds in the United States, as he is in his native country of Germany, in France, Australia, Great Britain, Holland, India, and Sweden.

The Boxer is a clean-limbed dog of great strength. And this is matched by sturdy beauty, good nature, good sense, and utter dependability. The Boxer makes an excellent guardian of the home, has been used successfully as a war dog, and is often seen leading the blind.

There are three theories as to the origin of the dog's unusual name. The first is that it is a corruption of the term "beiszer," which beams "biter." Thus, a bullenbeiszer, was a bull biter, or a bull baiter. This fits in with the dog's use, since the ancestors of the Boxer are known to have been used in bull baiting.

Some authorities believe that the term "Boxer" is a corruption of the word "boxl," which was an alternate name given to a now extinct breed called the Brabanter. According to these authorities, the Brabanter was the parent of the Boxer.

The third theory as to the origin of the name is that it was given by an Englishman to the breed in recognition of the fact that many of the dogs appear to spar with their feet in fighting. It is difficult to suppose however, that this single reference by an Englishman to a German breed, already fairly well established, could have stuck.

As with most other breeds, the origin of the Boxer is a matter of conjecture. His ancestors almost certainly were used to fight wild boars and to bait bulls. This has led to the assumption that he is a cross between a Great Dane (sometimes called the German Boar Hound) and the English Bulldog.

His similarity to the English Bulldog, Boston Terrier, and French Bulldog of an earlier period is striking. In fact, Flocki, the first Boxer registered in Germany, could be taken for a Boston Terrier. A picture of Flocki gives no indication of his size. In other respects, Flocki looks as much like a Boston Terrier of 1900 as he does an unrefined Boxer of the same period.

Some students of the breed have noted also a similarity between the early Boxers and the typical "Chiens de Boucher," or "butcher dogs" of France, Belgium, and parts of Germany. Indeed, the Boxer has that sturdiness of body, the strength and nature of the typical butcher dog.

Dr. Dan Gordon, a noted American authority on the breed, held the view that the Boxer, through the Brabanter, is really the ancestor of the English Bulldog. In this, however, he appears to stand alone, since English Bulldogs go back to about 1200 when bull baiting became popular. There is no indication the Boxer, through the Brabanter, has any such history.

The real history of the Boxer begins in that great awakening period for German dogdom—the years just prior to 1900. The Dachshund and Great Dane had been brought to near perfection earlier. But the Boxer, German Shepherd, Doberman Pinscher, and others were chiefly developed in the decade from 1890 to 1900. The success of these breeds brought the improvement of others in the years immediately following.

Three men began to promote the Boxer in Germany in 1894. These were Friedrich Roberth of Munich, Elard Konig, and R. Hopner. As a result of their efforts, a class for Boxers was given at the St. Bernard Club show in Munich in 1895.

The was only one entry. This dog was Flocki, the

number one dog in the Stud Book. Flocki had a blaze face, with white mask. In addition, he had a white collar, chest, and white front legs. There were several spots of white on his hind legs and on one hip. He had a rather long back, his hocks were under him, and he fell away rapidly from the hips to the root of the tail. He was described as being by Dr. Tonissen's Tom, a Bulldog, and Alt Scheckin.

The following year a Boxer Club was formed. On March 29, the first Boxer specialty show was given at the home of Johan Himmelreich. There were 20 entries, and the Himmelreich home was crowded by spectators. The judge was E. Konig.

The top dog of this period was Flock St. Salvator, the fourteenth dog registered. He was owned by A. Kolb. Flock served as a model of the breed, and the first standard was drawn with him in mind. Even so, Boxers, were a varied lot at this time. At the Munich show that year, 25 were shown, but they were entered in three weight classes, a fact which again suggest the English Bulldog and the Boston Terrier. Konig again was the judge.

There followed some 14 years of argument between fanciers of the breed as to the correct standard. Many Boxer clubs had been formed, and the members of these fought with each other until 1910. In that year, a final amalgamation of all the clubs was formed. At the great Mannheim convention in 1911, Dr. Schulein became head of the club, and also editor of the *Boxer-Blatter,* the noted breed magazine which was founded in 1904.

During World War I, the Germans extensively used dogs for Red Cross, messenger, pack, and other services. While German Shepherds predominated in this, some Boxers were used. It is said that the Boxer Club, through its members, gave 60 dogs. These acquitted themselves with distinction.

One of the dogs which went through the war, returned to become one of the great stud forces in the breed's history. He was Rolf von Vogelsberg. He was owned by Mrs. Phillip Stockmann, wife of the man who became editor of the *Boxer Blatter* in 1914. Stockmann continued as editor for almost 30 years.

Some five of the earlier dogs can be said to have laid down the basis for the modern Boxer. These were Flock St. Salvator, 14 (in the Stud Book), Meta von der Passage, 30; Mirzl, Wotan, and Boxco Immergrun. Meta, the "great mother" of the breed, was by Piccolo von Angertor, a brother to Mirzl, out of Ch. Blanka von Angertor, the daughter of a white Bulldog.

Meta was a small dog, of very light color. She was long in body and short of leg. Her head was somewhat coarser than those of modern dogs. Meta was born November 2, 1898. One of her great sons was Ch. Gigerl. Gigerl inherited neither his mother's length of body nor her shortness of leg. He was a brindle, and he did much to further this color.

Flock and Meta produced Schani von der Passage, a fawn who became the mother of Ch. Rigo von Angertor. Rigo created a demand for fawns much as

Gigerl had done for the brindles. Between them, they started the parti-colored Boxers on the way to oblivion.

Perhaps the modern Boxer begins with Rolf von Volgelsberg and Ch. Milo von Eigelstein. Rolf was a brindle and Milo a fawn. They lived about the same time, and each played a tremendous part in the breed. And this, despite the fact that Rolf spent years in war service, and Milo died young.

Both dogs were short backed, and both were fairly tall, which is to say they had reached modern height. Milo was 22 inches at the shoulder and Rolf 23. Milo was said to have had the finest body of any dog up to his time, though his feet were splayed. Rolf was almost perfection in every point, excepting for a slight roach in his back.

Of the more modern "greats" of Germany, most of them have played an equally important part in the United States. Sigurd von Dom was born in 1929, by Iwein von Dom out of Belinde Hassia. He won the Austrian sieger title in 1931, and followed with the German titles in the next two years.

Before coming to the United States, Sigurd sired two famous dogs, Zorn von Dom and Xerxes von Dom. The former was a black brindle and the latter was a golden brindle. They established sire lines of their own in Germany.

Zorn was mated to a daughter of his sire, Sigurd, and produced Lustig von Dom, one of the all-time greats of the breed. Xerxes, in turn, produced Dorian von Marienhof. Lustig took the 1935 sieger title in fawns while Dorian took the title in brindles.

In the United States, sporadic attempts had been made to establish the Boxer as early as 1900. In 1904 the first Boxer was registered in the American Kennel Club Stud Book. This dog was American-bred, but he left no influence on the breed.

In those days, the breed was considered to be something of a Bulldog. It was shown in the nonsporting group with the Boston Terrier, English Bulldog, French Bulldog, etc. Little attention was paid to it.

Herbert L. Lehman, the governor of New York who succeeded Franklin Delano Roosevelt in that office, owned the first American champion. This was the imported Sieger Dampf von Dom, a brindle with white chest markings and white feet. Even so fine a dog as Dampf failed to impress the Americans in 1915. Dampf was a son of Rolf von Vogelsberg.

In the next 17 years, only two more champions were made at American bench shows. One of these was Bluecher von Rosengarten, owned by G. J. Jeuther. The other was Sieger Check von Hunnenstein, who was imported by the Cirrol Kennels.

Then, in 1934, Mrs. Miriam Hostetter Young (later Mrs. William Z. Breed) imported Sigurd von Dom for her Barmore Kennels. Sigurd followed his sensational Austrian and German career by an equally sensational one here. He was 54 times Best of Breed, won eight non-sporting groups, and two Best in Show awards.

Out in Milwaukee, John Phelps Wagner had seen

Boxer—Ch. Terudon's Kiss Me Kate. (Owner: Mr. and Mrs. Theodore Wurmser, Louisville, Ky.) Photo by Evelyn M. Shafer.

the Boxers in the Birkbaum Kennels. A Great Dane breeder, Wagner decided to switch to the then "unwanted and uninteresting Bulldogs," as his friends called them. His friends told him he would not get anywhere with the breed, but Wagner made the change anyway.

Wagner had guessed correctly. Sigurd had caught the imagination of the American public. For his Mazelaine Kennels, Wager imported Sigurd's grandson, Dorian von Marienhof. Dorian came to America in 1936. He followed in the steps of his grandsire, Sigurd, with victory after victory. These were scored in the breed and working group, to which the breed had been removed.

The following year, Dorian's old rival, Lustig von Dom was imported by Erwin O. Fruend of the Tulgey Wood Kennels, Hinsdale, Ill. Wagner added Ch. Utz von Dom, a son of Zorn, to his kennels. Dr. Dan Gordon, author of *The Boxer*, imported Ch. Klaus von der Uhlanshohe, for his Detroit Bladan Kennels.

These dogs, the best Germany had produced, founded a race of dogs in the United States which can compete with the best of their breed anywhere in the world, including Germany.

Among other kennels of that period can be mentioned the Sumbula Kennels of Harold and Lillian Palmedo. Mrs. Palmedo imported Ch. Corso von Uracher, and Ch. Ingo von Heger, etc.

It should be noted that Mrs. Breed of Barmere Kennels owned the first American-bred champion. This was Dodi von der Stoeckersburg. Walter Foster, a Bulldog breeder, who turned to Boxers, and later became a professional handler of all breeds, owned the first American-bred Boxer to win a group. This was Ch. Baldur of Fostoria.

Description and Standards. The description and standards, adopted by the American Boxer Club, and approved by the American Kennel Club follow.

The Boxer is a medium-sized, sturdy dog, of square build, with short back, strong limbs, and short tight-fitting coat. His musculation, well developed, should be clean, hard and appear smooth (not bulgy) under taut skin. His movements should denote energy. The gait although firm is elastic (springy), the stride free and ground-covering, the carriage proud and noble. Developed to serve the multiple purposes of guard, working, and escort-dog, he must combine elegance with substance and ample power, not alone for beauty but to insure the speed, dexterity, and jumping ability essential to arduous hike, riding expedition, police or military duty. Only a body whose individual parts are built to withstand the most strenuous efforts, assembled as a complete and harmonious whole, can respond to these combined demands. Therefore, to be at his highest efficiency he must never be plump or heavy and, while equipped for great speed, he must never be racy.

The head imparts to the Boxer a unique individual stamp peculiar to him alone. It must be in perfect proportion to his body, never small in comparison to the overall picture. His muzzle is his most distinctive feature, and the greatest value is to be placed on its being of correct form and in absolute proper proportion to the skull.

JUDGING: In judging the Boxer, the first thing to be considered is general appearance, then balance; the relation of substance to elegance and of the desired proportions of the individual parts of the body to each other. Consideration is to be given to an attractive color, after which the individual parts are to be examined for their correct constructions and their functions. Special attention is to be devoted to the head.

FAULTS: Head not typical, plump bull-doggy appearance, light bone, lack of balance, bad condition, deficiency in nobility.

HEAD: The beauty of the head depends upon the harmonious proportion between the muzzle and the skull. The muzzle should always appear powerful, never small in its relationship to the skull. The head should be clean, not showing deep wrinkles. Folds will normally appear upon the forehead when the ears are erect, and they are always indicated from the lower edge of the stop running downward on both sides of the muzzle. The dark mask is confined to the muzzle and is in distinct contrast to the color of the head. Any extension of the mask to the skull, other than dark shading around the eyes, creates a somber undesirable expression. The muzzle is powerfully developed in length, width and depth. It is not pointed, narrow, short, or shallow. Its shape is influenced first through the formation of both jawbones, second through the placement of the teeth, and third through the texture of the lips.

The two jawbones do not terminate in the usual scissor-bite; instead the lower jaw protrudes moderately beyond the upper and bends *slightly* upward. The Boxer is normally undershot. The upper jaw is broad where attached to the skull and maintains this breadth except for a very slight tapering to the front. The lower jaw incisor teeth are in a straight line. In the upper jaw they are slightly rounded. The middle incisors should not project. This formation creates frontal width in both jaws and results in the canine teeth being widely separated from each other. The upper corner incisors should fit snugly back of the lower canine teeth, the pre-molars, anterior palliative foramen (a technical term pertaining to the placing of teeth), and molars fitting in the most normal possible manner, creating a sound, powerful bite.

The lips complete the formation of the muzzle. The upper lip is thick and padded, filling out the frontal space formed by the projection of the lower jaw and it is supported by the jaw's fangs. Therefore, these fangs must stand far apart and be of good length so that the front surface of the muzzle shall become broad and squarish and, when viewed from the side, form a rounded angle with the topline of the muzzle. The lower edge of the upper lip rests on the edge of the lower lip. The repandous (bent upward) part of the under-jaw with the lower lip (sometimes called the chin) must not rise above the front of the upper lip, but much less may it disappear under it. It must be perceptible when viewed from the front as well as the side, without protruding and bending upward in the manner of the English Bulldog. The Boxer must not show his teeth or his tongue when his mouth is closed. Excessive flews are not desirable.

The top of the skull is slightly arched, not rotund, or flat, or noticeably broad, and the occiput must not be too pronounced. The forehead forms a distinct stop with the topline of the muzzle, which must not be forced back into the forehead like that of a Bulldog. It should not slant up, or down (down-faced), or be dished. The tip of the nose lies somewhat higher than the root of the muzzle. The forehead shows a suggestion of furrow which, however, must never be too deep, especially between the eyes. Corresponding with the powerful set of teeth, the cheeks are accordingly well developed, without protruding from the head with too bulgy an appearance, preferably they should taper into the muzzle in a slight, graceful curve. The ears are cut rather long, well trimmed, and carried erect. The dark brown eyes, not too small, not protruding or deep-set, disclose an alert and intelligent expression and must never appear gloomy, threatening, or piercing; they should be encircled by dark hair. The nose is broad and black, very slightly turned up; the nostrils are broad with the nasolabial line running between them.

FAULTS: Lack of nobility and expression, somber face, unserviceable bite. Pinscher or Bulldog head, badly trimmed ears, visible conjunctiva (haw), driveling, showing teeth or tongue, light so-called "Bird of Prey" eyes. Sloping top line of muzzle, too pointed or too light a bite (snipy).

NECK: Round, of ample length, not too short; strong and muscular and clean throughout, without dewlap, with a distinctly marked nape and an elegant arch running down to the back. Dewlap is to be faulted.

BODY: Body is square. Measured in profile, a horizontal line from the front of the forechest to the rear projection of the upper thigh should equal a vertical line dropped from the top of the withers to the ground.

CHEST AND FRONT LEG MEASUREMENTS: The brisket is deep, reaching down to the elbows; the depth of the body at the lowest point of the brisket amounts to half the height of the dog at the withers. The ribs, extending far to the rear, are well arched but not barrel-shaped. The loins are short and muscular; the lower stomach line, lightly tucked up, blending into a graceful curve to the rear. The shoulders are long and sloping, close lying, and not excessively covered with muscle. The upper arm is long, closely approaching a right angle to the shoulder blade. The forelegs, when seen from the front, must be straight, stand parallel to each other, and have strong, firmly joined bones. Chest of fair width, and forechest well defined. The elbows must not press too closely to the chest wall or stand off visible from it. The forearm is straight, long, and firmly muscled. The pastern (knee) joint of the foreleg is clearly defined but not distended. The pastern is short, slightly slanting, but standing almost perpendicular to the ground. Feet compact, turning neither in nor out, with tightly arched toes and hard soles (cat's paws).

FAULTS: Too broad and low in front, loose shoulders, chest hanging between the shoulders, hare's feet, hollow flanks, hanging stomach, turned feet, tied-in elbows.

BACK: The withers should be clearly defined, the whole back short, straight, and very muscular.

FAULTS: Roach back, sway back, thin lean back, long narrow loins, weak union with croup.

HINDQUARTERS: In balance with forequarters; strongly muscled. The thighs broad and curved, the breech musculation strongly developed. The croup very slightly sloped, broad. Tail attachment high, rather than low. Tail clipped, carried upward. The pelvis should be long and especially broad in females. Upper and lower thigh long, leg well angulated. In standing position, the leg below the hock joint should be practically perpendicular to the ground (a slight slope is permissible). Viewed from behind the hind legs are straight. The hocks (metatarsus) clean, strong, and short, supported by powerful rear pads with hock joint clean-cut and clearly defined. The rear toes just a little longer than the front toes, but similar in all other respects.

FAULTS: Falling off or too rounded or narrow croup, low-set

tail, higher in back than in front; steep, stiff, or too slightly angulated hindquarters, light thighs, cowhocks, bowlegs and crooked legs, rear dewclaws, soft hocks, narrow heel, tottering, waddling gait, hare feet, hindquarters too far under or too far behind.

HEIGHT: Males—22 inches to 24 inches at the withers. Females—21 inches to 23 inches at the withers. Males should not go under 22 inches and females should not go over 23 inches.

COAT: Short, shiny, lying smooth and tight to the body.

COLOR: The colors are fawn and brindle. Fawn in various shades from light yellow to dark deer red. The brindle variety should have clearly defined black stripes on fawn background. White markings in fawn and brindle dogs are not to be rejected; in fact, they are often very attractive in appearance. The black mark is absolutely required. When white occurs on the muzzle it should be edged by remnants of the black mask. Black toenails are preferred but not essential. Even distribution of head markings is desirable.

CHARACTER: The character of the Boxer is of the greatest importance and demands the most solicitous attention. He should be alert and fearless; willing to make friends, but not necessarily effusive.

FAULTS: Shyness—A dog should be considered shy if he shrinks away from a friendly approach or displays timidity when approached from the rear, or displays cowardice over sudden and unusual noises.

VICIOUSNESS: A dog should be considered vicious that attempts to attack either his handler or the judge. Belligerency toward other dogs should not be considered viciousness.

Disqualifications. Boxers with white or black ground color, or entirely white or black or any color other than fawn or brindle. (White markings are allowed but must not exceed one-third ($\frac{1}{3}$) of the ground color.)

(May 10, 1960)

BRIARD

IN ATTEMPTING to trace the Briard to its origin the researcher is faced with considerable difficulty. While the various authorities agree in basic detail, there remains much that must be left to surmise.

How far back the Briard went in France is unknown. Records dating back to the twelfth century mention Briards bred by Charlemagne. These records mention the dog as the Sheep Dog of Brie, or Berger de Brie. From this it might be assumed that the dog originated in the old Province of Brie and spread to adjoining provinces and, finally, all over France. There is considerable reason to doubt that assumption. Long-haired sheep and cattle dogs have been known for centuries in all of the nations of Europe.

Not in detail, but in basic conformation, size, and coat, the Briard must have come from the same foundation stock as the Bearded Collie, the Hungarian Komondor, Kuvasz, and Puli, the Russian Owtcharka, and the Old English Sheepdog. In detail these dogs vary somewhat in size and in their coloring and quality of coat, but it seems impossible to believe that they did not have common ancestors. Even today the Hungarian Puli appears to be a miniature Briard to such an extent that at one show an experienced judge was quite insistent that an adult Puli standing near the ring be brought into the Briard puppy class.

One surprising point in all this is that the Kerry

Blue Terrier—now rated as belonging to a totally different group—looks like a miniature Briard when not clipped. Some historians claim that within memory of living men there are tales of "big, black dogs, being imported from France" to be bred to native, blue-coated Irish dogs. It is said that even today Kerry Blues are used for herding in Ireland.

It would follow that any attempt to trace the Briard to its origin would become involved with most of the long- or medium-coated working dogs.

Turning to more recent history the Briard was "discovered" by American troops serving in France during World War I. The dogs were the most satisfactory of the breeds used by the French Army. It appears that they had several points of advantage for battle service. Their strength made it possible to wrap machine gun ammunition belts around them and send them up to gun emplacements. The thick coat protected them from the extremes of weather—acting as an insulator in summer and as a protection in winter—their large feet made it possible for them to work over the inevitable muddy ground, and their amazingly acute sense of hearing gave them top billing as guardians against a surprise attack. A further virtue, much extolled by Allied troops, was the uncanny ability of the dog to distinguish between a wounded man who was in desperate need of care and one whose wounds were so severe that help would be of no avail.

Following the war several Briards were brought to the United States. The list of those who claim to have imported the first Briard is a long one, and decidely open to some suspicion. However, there is little doubt that Wallace MacMonnies, son of the famous sculptor, and Miss Francis Hoppin were well up towards the head of the list. Actually none of them can lay claim to the first Briards in the United States, for there are records that the Marquis Lafayette, then living on his estate in America, wrote to one of the DuPonts asking the latter, during a proposed trip to France, to send over several more French sheepdogs to guard the distinguished soldier's flocks. The use of the word "more" would indicate that Lafayette had brought some of the dogs over with him in 1824 when he came here to occupy the estate granted him by the grateful American Congress.

With no desire to again start the argument as to the first importation in modern times, it should be noted that the first registration by the American Kennel Club of a Briard was granted to a dog called Timothy Jacobs, out of Oolala by Marquis, and recorded as having been bred by a B. Danielson in Massachusetts. This dog was registered in the name of Mrs. G. W. Jacobs, Jr., who still maintains some interest in the breed. The date of the registration was

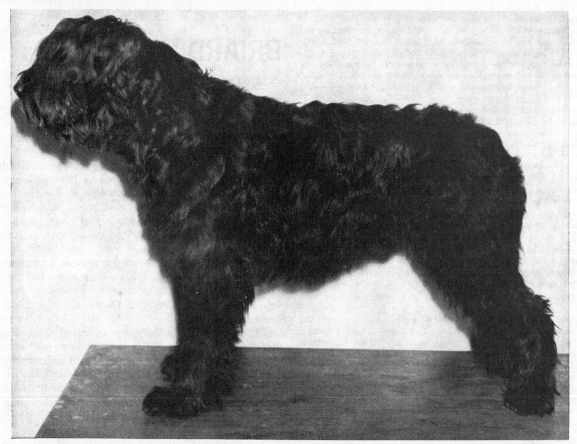

Briard.

1922. Mr. MacMonnies seems to have imported Citronelle de Montjoye in 1923; Miss Hoppin brought over Dauphin de Montjoye in 1925, and the following year Mrs. Harold Ober imported Myrko de Montjoye. It must be pointed out that these records were taken from registrations and there is no proof that previous dogs had not come into this country and had not been registered.

In 1922 a few enthusiasts gathered in New York and formed the Briard Club of America, drawing up the standard almost word for word as a translation of the standard of the French Club, Les Amis du Briard, which had been organized sometime previously. This standard is still substantially the official one.

Those who formed the early club were convinced that the breed should never become popular but should be kept as restricted as possible. Little or nothing was done to stimulate breeding or extensive showing. In spite of this rather reactionary program the breed did grow in popularity; its evident virtues selling the breed in spite of the hesitancy of those behind it to put the dog into the limelight.

During the following 24 years the growth in popularity resulted in some growing pains for the organization and, in 1946, the majority of the enthusiasts who had been in the breed for more than a year or two organized The Briard Fellowship under what were considered rather radical regulations. Among these unorthodox rules was one which specified that all Briards must be registered at birth. Another prohibited the sale of a dog without the delivery of an AKC registration certificate. Still another ruled against the use of professional handlers. Possibly the most widely discussed of all of the Fellowship rules was the one that legislated against the breeding of any Briard bitch unless a Certificate of Approval had been issued by the board of governors after consideration of the quality of the dog. Similar certificates are issued to males but the breeding prohibition does not apply should the male be bred to an unapproved bitch belonging to a non-member.

It was freely predicted that such rigorous control of breeding, sales, and showing would result in the curtailment of breed activity. Exactly the reversal took place. Previous to the activity of The Briard Fellowship there had been three or four litters a year. Many of the puppies had not been registered; there had been considerable inbreeding and each of the handful of breeders had worked along haphazard lines, often limiting all breeding to dogs already owned in that particular kennel. The Fellowship rules proved to be what the breed needed. Breeders were drawn together, stud services exchanged, and an intense but entirely friendly rivalry built up in an effort to produce litters that would merit Certificates of Approval. As these certificates had to be issued by a board composed of rival breeders, it meant that quality in the dogs, as well as adherence to the other regulations, was a necessity.

As one example of the stimulating effect of the regulations, the Fellowship had 56 entries at the first specialty match for the breed ever held in America. This doubled the largest entry ever previously known in the breed. Yet, in the opinion of experienced onlookers, every dog in this record entry was the equal to the best that had been shown during the previous decade.

One of the reasons for the increased demand for Briards is the adaptability of the dog to the varied climatic and family conditions found in America. In few other nations will there be found so wide a variation in climate as, for example, the perpetual summer of our extreme southern states or the eight-month winter of some of the districts along the Canadian border. Yet Briards are kept and bred in both extremes without difficulty. The answer lies in the typical Briard coat.

In fact the Briard really has two coats; the medium-long outer coat which, under normal conditions, does not shed. It is as permanent as the hair on the human head. In the fall a dense, felt-like under coat known as the pelage appears. In the black dogs this is usually a dark gray; in the tawnies, a brownish color. Coupled with the outer coat the pelage acts as a protection against the extreme cold. The outer coat sheds rain and snow, the pelage protects from the bitter winds. In summer the outer coat acts as an insulator against the heat, much on the same principle as the loose garments of desert dwellers.

Some of the best known Briards in America are kept in a section where winter temperatures often go well below zero. Not only are the kennels unheated but they are simply sheds, open entirely to the south. Semi-enclosed sleeping boxes are provided but the dogs refuse to use them. Some of them sleep, by preference, in snow drifts during the bitterest of nights. Yet dogs raised under such Spartan conditions are shipped to Florida and California and experience no difficulty in becoming acclimated to temperatures that seldom go below 50 degrees.

One of the virtues which help to popularize Briards is the fact that the outer coat does not normally shed. The inner coat does loosen in the spring but it does not come out on carpets, clothing, and furniture. The short, dense pelage is caught by the outer hairs and can be combed out. Some Briard owners follow the practice of combing for a minute or two every day while others try to give the dog a grooming once a week. If some attention is not given the coat, especially in the spring, the mats resulting from the loosened pelage will prove stubborn.

Another feature of the Briard is that it should never be bathed. Most of the top-flight Briards in America have never had a soap and water bath from the day of their birth. Thus the dog requires the minimum of attention. There is no clipping, no bathing, and only a minimum of necessary combing.

Temperamentally the Briard is quiet as befits his size. He seldom dashes aimlessly from point to point. Those who like the typical terrier disposition, the constant activity, may readily consider the Briard as too stolid. He is the opposite extreme to the "flea-on-

Briard—A head study.

a-hot-griddle" type. His attitude towards guests is usually one of dignified acceptance. Seldom will he break down to lavish affection or become kittenish except when alone with his intimate family. As a guardian he combines the virtues of acute hearing with a deep and rather frightening bark. Briards can be taught to attack, but they are more inclined to be companions and guardians rather than dogs that spring automatically to the attack.

With his family, and with children, he is apt to forget his dignity in the joy of playfulness, but he hates to be laughed at or to be forced to be a clown. All in all he takes himself quite seriously when strangers are about.

While the standard draws no color lines beyond specifying that there should be no white patches, it does say that dark colors are preferred. In spite of this, a great proportion of the leading show winners are tawnies, or a combination of tawny or gray and black, or tawny with some black trim around the muzzle. There are still many all blacks, but their proportionate number is falling off in view of the more spectacular appearance of the light-colored, or bi-colored dogs.

Description and Standards. The description and standards, by courtesy of AKC follow.

GENERAL APPEARANCE: A strong and substantially built dog, fitted for field work, lithe, muscular, and well proportioned, alert and active.

SIZE: Height at shoulders: dogs, 23 to 27 inches; bitches, 22 to 25½ inches. Young dogs may be below the minimum.

HEAD: Large and rather long. Stop well marked and placed at equal distance from top of head and tip of nose. Forehead very slightly rounded. Line from stop to tip of nose straight.

TEETH: Strong; white and meeting exactly even.

MUZZLE: Neither narrow nor pointed.

NOSE: Rather square than rounded, always black.

HAIR: Heavy and long on top of the head, the ears and around the muzzle, forming eyebrows standing out and not veiling the eyes too much.

EYES: Horizontal, well opened, dark in color and rather large; intelligent and gentle in expression.

EARS: Placed high, alert, may be cropped or left natural. If cropped, the ears are carried erect; if uncut, they should not be too large or carried too flat. There shall be no preference shown to either cropped or uncropped ears.

CONFORMATION: Neck muscular and distinct from the shoulders; chest broad and deep; back straight; rump slightly sloped; legs muscular with heavy bone; hock not too near the ground, making a well marked angle, the leg below the hock being not quite vertical.

TAIL: Uncut, well-feathered, forming a crook at the end, carried low and twisted neither to right nor left. The length of the tail should equal the distance from the root of the tail to the point of the hock.

FEET: Strong, round, with toes close together and hard pads; nails black.

COAT: Long, slightly wavy, stiff and strong.

COLOR: All solid colors are allowed except white. Dark colors are preferable. Usual colors: Black, black with some white hairs, dark and light grey, tawny, and combinations of two of these colors provided there are no marked spots and the transition from one to the other takes place gradually and symmetrically.

DEWCLAWS: Two dewclaws on each hind leg are required. A dog with only one cannot be given a prize.

Faults: Muzzle pointed; eyes small, almond shaped or light in color; rump straight or too sloped; white spot on the breast (a large white spot is very bad); tail too short or carried over the back; white nails.

Disqualifications: Size below the limit; absence of dewclaws; short hair on the head, face or feet; tail lacking or cut; nose light in color or spotted; eyes spotted; hair curled; white hair on feet; spotted colors of the coat.

BULLMASTIFF

AS HIS name suggests, the Bullmastiff is a cross between a Bulldog and a Mastiff. It is therefore not possible to separate his history from that of the other two dogs any more than it is possible to separate those of the Bulldog and the Mastiff themselves. For both of the parents of the Bullmastiff appear to have come from the same parent stock, and both were used for bull and bear baiting.

It would appear that, about 1890, when the huge Mastiff was on the decline, an effort was made to breed a somewhat smaller dog. Mastiffs were at that time used as guard dogs by gamekeepers on the great estates of the British Isles.

One cross which was tried was that of the Mastiff and the Bulldog, thus bringing together two strains which had been quite close together in previous centuries. The result was a dog, smaller than the Mastiff, very heavy, and yet very agile. In addition, the dog proved quiet. That is, when prowling the grounds in search of poachers, he would remain quiet until told to attack.

Gamekeepers over much of Great Britain began to take up the fad of crossing the two breeds. The new breed was called the "Keeper's Night Dogs." As such, the dogs were shown at exhibitions in 1900 and 1901. One famous exhibition took place at a metropolitan dog show, when a W. Burton of Thorneywood Kennels, Nottingham, offered a one pound prize to anyone who could escape from a muzzled dog. The volunteer lost, and *The Field* reported the famous encounter in detail on Aug. 20, 1901.

There followed much agitation to have the breed recognized. But it was not until 1925 that the English Kennel Club gave it recognition as the Bullmastiff. Three years later, challenge certificates were made possible, or in other words, championships were allowed.

A provision in the recognition of the new breed specified that the dogs registered would have to be pure-bred for three generations. Dogs farther back in the pedigrees would have to be half Bulldog and half Mastiff. This ensured that only Bulldog and Mastiff blood entered into the breed, and that consistency of type would be established very early.

According to Hutchinson, the "pillars" of the new breed were Thorneywood Terror and Thorneywood Lion, owned by Mr. Burton, and Osmaston Nell and Osmaston Daisy, owned by J. Biggs. Still another famous early breeder was S. E. Moseley. His noted Farcroft Felton Frajeur became a champion in both England and the United States, and did much for the breed in the latter country.

The Bullmastiff grew steadily in popularity during the nineteen twenties. His more moderate size, quietness, great strength, and agility, made him a success

Bullmastiff—Pocantico Ambassador Sirius. (Owner: E. H. Forsythe, address not listed.) Hank Babbitt photo.

from the start. Also, he showed an aptitude for police work, plus eagerness to learn.

The breed began to make many friends in the United States, so that in October, 1933, the American Kennel Club opened its Stud Book to the breed. About two years later, the Bullmastiff Club of America drew up a standard of the breed, which was then recognized by the American Kennel Club.

The British and American standards differ somewhat. The British feel that the best dogs show 50 percent Bulldog and 50 percent Mastiff in their general conformation. But in America, the dog is supposed to be 60 percent Mastiff and only 40 percent Bulldog. The British standard calls for dogs of 26 inches, as against the American of 25 to 27 inches.

The year 1939 was a great one in American Bullmastiff history. That year many fine dogs were imported. Donald M. MacVicar of Peekskill, N.Y., imported no less than five. These were Beryl's Choice, Chang Felius, Jubilee Boy, Ragger, and Righto. Ruth Ellen Patton brought over Milbrook Murla; Nathan M. Ohrbach imported Sambourne Pongo, and Mary L. Delafield brought in Milbrook Withraed.

The following year, Victor Dane imported Fairhazel Jenny, Great of Harbex, Toby of La Tasyll, and Katrine of Harbex for his kennels at Tarzana. Cal. Bess of the Fenns was another imported at this time, while Trusty Trooper came over in 1941.

The breed gained particular fame about the Hollywood move colony, with Harry M. Warner, Douglas Fairbanks and later, Gen. Elliott Roosevelt, getting Bullmastiffs.

Bullmastiff—Ch. Chit-Image of Hurstacres. (Owner: Hurstacres Kennels, Muncie, Ind.) Photo by Ruth Chin.

Another well-known person who became a fancier and breeder of "Bullmastiffs" was John D. Rockefeller Jr., Tarrytown, N.Y.

Description and Standards. The description and standards as adopted by the Bullmastiff Club of America and approved by the American Kennel Club, follows.

GENERAL APPEARANCE: That of a symmetrical animal, showing great strength; powerfully built but active. The dog is fearless yet docile, has endurance and alertness. The foundation breeding was 60% Mastiff and 40% Bulldog.

HEAD: Skull large, with a fair amount of wrinkle when alert; broad, with cheeks well developed. Forehead flat. Muzzle broad and deep; its length, in comparison with that of the entire head, approximately as 1 is to 3. Lack of foreface with nostrils set on top of muzzle is a reversion to the Bulldog and is very undesirable. Nose black with nostrils large and broad. Flews not too pendulous, stop moderate, and the mouth (bite) preferably level or slightly undershot. Canine teeth large and set wide apart. A dark muzzle is preferable. The eyes are dark and of medium size. The ears are V-shaped and carried close to the cheeks, set on wide and high, level with occiput and cheeks, giving a square appearance to the skull; darker in color than the body and medium in size. The neck is slightly arched, of moderate length, very muscular, and almost equal in circumference to the skull.

BODY: Compact. Chest wide and deep, with ribs well sprung and well set down between the forelegs.

FOREQUARTERS: Shoulders muscular but not loaded, and slightly sloping. Forelegs straight, well boned and set well apart; elbows square. Pasterns straight, feet of medium size, with round toes well arched. Pads thick and tough, nails black.

BACK: Short, giving the impression of a well balanced dog.

LOINS: Wide, muscular and slightly arched, with fair depth of flank.

HINDQUARTERS: Broad and muscular with well developed second thigh denoting power, but not cumbersome. Moderate angulation at hocks. Cowhocks and splay feet are bad faults.

TAIL: Set on high, strong at the root and tapering to the hocks. It may be straight or curved, but never carried hound fashion.

COAT: Short and dense, giving good weather protection. Colors are red, fawn or brindle. Except for a very small white spot on the chest, white marking is considered a fault.

SIZE: Dogs, 25 to 27 inches at the shoulder, and 110 to 130 pounds weight. Bitches, 24 to 26 inches at the shoulder, and 100 to 120 pounds weight. Other things being equal, the heavier dog is favored.

(February 6, 1960)

COLLIE

A WORKING breed for centuries, it is probable that few Collies boasted written records of their lineage prior to about 1860.

This does not, however, mean that the Collie was unknown until this time. His origin has been for years the subject of much discussion and speculation. Some have suggested that his ancestry goes back to Biblical times of about the fifth century B.C. There is evidence that in the Roman civilization one of the three recognized classifications of dogs was the sheepdog. From the earliest days when man became an agronomist, growing his crops, tending his herds, and otherwise comporting himself in such a way that he might be suspected of having in his make-up some of the elements of civilization, man has had sheep and cattle. Wherever man has tended sheep and cattle he has had the companionship of the Collie, or one of his immediate ancestors, to make his task a little easier, his daily work a little more sure and efficient.

It is believed that when the Romans invaded England their sheepdogs came with them and were interbred with the dogs that were at that time native in that area. During the sixteenth, seventeenth and eighteenth centuries sheep raising became increasingly important in the Highlands of Northern Scotland and cattle raising flourished in the County of Northumberland in England. Following the same system of selection and breeding for definite characteristics that today produces our show ring champions, these early users of working dogs slowly developed dogs that had special adaptability for their particular work. The Smooth-Coated Collie gradually became identified as the cattle-driving dog of Northumberland County and the Rough-Coated Collie was evolved for the rigors of the climate and the topography of northern Scotland. There is little doubt that both varieties came from a common ancestor. As early as any breeding records were kept, Collies of both varieties appeared in a single litter. By selective breeding for coat the two distinct varieties were established. But even today Smooth Collies are obtained by breeding a Rough to a Smooth.

By about 1800 the breed had obtained some prominence and there is little question that the Collie, even then, was being held pure in strain, although it is probable that no breeding records were kept. In early Colonial days the settlers brought Collies to America and it is probable that the ordinary "farm Collie" that the general public today calls "the short-nosed kind of Collie" owes his origin to these early American importations from Scotland.

There is speculation about the source of the name of the Collie. In the Scottish Highlands there were sheep that had black legs known as the "Colley" sheep ("Colley" being the Anglo-Saxon term for black). Others hold that these sheep had black faces. But, faces or legs, the dogs that tended the Colley sheep, the dogs that had been trained, selected, and bred for their agility and ingenuity in negotiating the narrow sheep paths of northern Scotland, the dogs that had been developed by the necessity of their owners to have the native wisdom of the mind of the shepherd, the consideration that is necessary to the leading of other animals to the following of their will, the force and drive that were needed in the rough country they had to traverse, and the dogs that provided the invaluable companionship for the lonely shepherd on his hillside, took on the name of the sheep they tended and became known as the "Scot's Colley dog." Often this name was changed to the "Scotch sheepdog" and later it became universally recognized as "the Collie." It is not uncommon today to hear the Collie referred to as the "Scotch" Collie.

With all this to support the origin of the Collie there is little except the fact that the original Collies

Rough Collie. Photo by Evelyn M. Shafer.

were black in color to give credence to the theory that the Collies originated in Wales and were called the "Coallies." It seems much more reasonable to accept the version previously mentioned.

Bearing in mind the work for which the breed was developed we see how wisely man, in the seventeenth and early eighteenth centuries, aided nature in the production of an ideal sheepdog. Essentially the Collie of today is the Collie of the early 1800's except for refinements that have added tremendously to the majesty of his appearance. Then, as now, the Collie had a harsh, straight outer coat and a dense under coat, offering insulation alike to the blazing rays of the summer sun and the driving rains and snows of the winter. Although size has undoubtedly increased, the Collie remains a dog of essentially the same proportions.

Since about 1870, stops have become less pronounced, coloring, shape, and placement of eye have improved, muzzles and heads have been lengthened, more dogs with proper ear carriage have been bred; but fundamentally the lithe, active dog, with no useless timber about him, that worked with the shepherd in the northern hills of Scotland, the sagacious Collie that enabled one man and his dog to do the work of ten men, was essentially the Collie as we know him today . . . "the dog with the keen mind of a man and the winning ways of a woman."

Never a dog to go out of his way to seek trouble, the Collie meets trouble when and as it comes in a most capable manner. Up to a certain point he seems actually to ignore trouble . . . to hold himself above such things. When the end point of a Collie's tolerance is reached, however, he employs all of his age-old sagacity in disposing of his annoyance with the least possible delay. His nature is affectionate, making him an excellent dog for children and with all of his size, he displays grace and consideration, comporting

himself in the presence of children with the same care that is sometimes associated with walking on eggs. Few dogs can be trained as easily as the Collie, provided the trainer displays an average understanding of dogs generally. Although the Collie will give of himself lavishly in doing his master's bidding, it is not usually easy to get him to repeat what he has already done and done well. Collies have been known to go through a handsome repertoire of tricks, one after the other, and to stare unbelievingly at the person who asks them to do again that which they have just accomplished so well. By some this characteristic is mistaken for an evidence of lack of brains, but probably those who believe this have not analyzed the situation to a sufficient degree. The Collie that is asked to repeat, time after time, something that has already been accomplished with canine dispatch and dexterity is undoubtedly amazed, and no doubt his canine reasoning ability is much disturbed by what he seems to recognize as a flaw in his master's brain rather than a discrepancy in his own!

Queen Victoria of England is generally credited with the responsibility of having "discovered" the Collie in the sense that she played an important part in bringing him to the attention of the public. Visiting at Balmoral in Scotland, her fancy was captivated by the handsome Collies in the early 1860's and their introduction to the show ring was inevitable.

The first dog show to provide classes for the "Scotch Sheep Dog" was the show of the Birmingham Dog Society in England in 1860. One of the pillars of the breed in these early days was "Old Cockie" who was born in 1868 and owned by a Mr. White. He was the progenitor of our sable and white Collies and it is unfortunate that no picture of him is known to exist except one taken after the dog had reached the age of ten years which is said to fail to do him justice. He died at the age of twelve and Mr. White never divulged his pedigree, if indeed he knew it. At this early time the most popular Collie color was black. In fact the absence of white was a prized attribute of the earlier show Collies. (Today the novice places a spurious value on white and even markings.)

Other prominent Collies then were Mec, a tricolor born in 1870, Hero, and Marcus in 1876, and Thompson's Bess, owned and shown by W. W. Thomson of Surrey. In 1873 the tricolor Trefoil was born, and he was to exert a powerful influence on the Collies of the future. He won honors not only in the show ring but also by being the sire of Collies with very long frills that practically touched the ground. Litter brothers were Tartan and Tricolor. A well-known tricolor female of 1873 was Ashwin's Lassie, to be followed in 1876 by Wheeler's Old Bess a good working dog that passed on to her puppies her lovely head and expression.

About 1875 or '76 the breeders began to concentrate on show characteristics and among the fanciers at this time were: J. Bissell, M. C. Ashwin, J. Charles, W. H. Charles, A. W. Walker, J. Bagshaw, Hon.

Edward Digby, J. Dean Tomlinson, Dr. W. A. G. James, and A. H. Megson. The latter gentleman contributed strongly to the progress of the Collie from a well-fortified purse, by strategic purchases. Among his purchases were Ch. Chieftan Rutland, Metchley Wonder, Southport Perfection (purchased for £1000), Edgebaston Marvel and, from T. H. Stretch, Ormskirk Emerald, the latter purchase being for £1500.

By 1885 T. H. Stretch had acquired an international reputation for his success with Collies as an exhibitor and breeder, and contemporaries whose Collie careers shone brilliantly were: Hugo Ainscough, Robert Tait, H. E. Packwood, W. E. Mason, W. W. Stanfield, C. H. Wheeler, Fred Robson, and R. H. Lord. In 1895, the "Scotch Sheep Dog" classification of the Birmingham Society was changed to Collies.

In 1902 the famous Collie Anfield Model was whelped. He was by Parbold Piccolo ex Bellfield Beauty, was bred by Hugo Galt and owned by Mr. Mason of the Southport Kennels. He lives in Collie history partially by means of a fortunate photograph that has been said to flatter the dog considerably.

Collies in America were shown for the first time at the 1878 Westminster show, where two Collies appeared "from the royal kennels of Queen Victoria at Balmoral, Scotland." The striking appearance of these beautiful dogs, their keen intelligence, and their winning ways soon captured public fancy and by 1884, when Collies were judged at Westminster by James Mortimer, there were 58 Collies shown.

On September 17, 1884, the American Kennel Club was formed and the Collie Club of America was organized on August 26, 1886, and became one of the oldest of the specialty clubs and one of the earliest of the member parent clubs in the American Kennel Club. Its early fortunes were guided by Jenkins Van Schaick, its first president, and J. D. Shotwell, its first secretary.

During the first decade after the formation of the Collie Club of America, many were attracted to the Collie and among the early supporters of the breed we find Martin Dennis, Edward Beard, W. Atlee Burpee and Company, A. R. Kyle, Messrs. McEwan and Gibson, Dr. J. P. Gray, Thomas H. Terry, H. B. Cromwell, John A. Long, A. D. Lewis, Jas. A. Watson, J. Pierpont Morgan, and Alvin Untermeyer.

At the turn of the twentieth century in America the parent club was very active in the interest of Collies and at its specialty show held at Stamford, Conn., on February 6 and 7, 1903, the judge, Robert A. Murray of Boston, selected Geo. Higgins, Jr.'s Winnetka Ballyarnet Eclipse as Winner's Dog and found his Winner's Bitch in Merry Shield owned by the Balmoral Kennels. Among other fanciers at this time were: R. D. Bokannan, Columbus, Ohio, S. Gano, Madisonville, Ohio, the Vancroft Kennels, Dr. M. D. Macnab, Chicago, Messrs. Black and Hunter, Harrisburg, Pa., M. M. Palmer, Stamford, Conn., John R. Flinn, Johnstown, Pa., T. E. Orr, Pittsburgh, Pa., the

Ard-Na-Clochan Kennels, and L. A. Woodward.

Among the prominent kennels of this time could be found the Cragstone Kennels of J. Pierpont Morgan which introduced many famous names in Collie history. Here we find such well-known winners of the period as Ch. Sefton Hero, Ch. Rufford Ormonde (an imported blue merle of excellent quality), Ch. Wishaw Clinker, and Ch. Parbold Purity, to mention only a few. W. Ormiston Roy, founder of the Coila Kennels, of Montreal, Canada, became very active in the breed and his untiring energy resulted in the Coila Kennels housing many splendid Collies of remarkably good type. Mr. Roy probably attended as many, if not more, of the New York shows of the Westminster Kennel Club than any fancier now living.

H. B. Hungerford, Chicago, Illinois, a man of considerable wealth, established the Mountaineer Kennels and exhibited extensively in the hottest of competition. Among his better-known dogs of the early 1900's were Ch. Parbold Peacock, Ch. Roger Trelawney, and Ch. Mountaineer Magnet. By about 1905 Mrs C. M. Lunt was firmly establishing her Alstead Kennels with judicious importations, selective breeding, and show honors. Located at Rahway, New Jersey, Mrs. Lunt's kennels housed a host of outstanding Collies and her breeding operations formed a framework upon which others carried on to new honors under their own kennel names. Among some of her earlier dogs were: Ch. Alstead Parbold President, Ch. Alstead Parbold Peepshow, Ch. Laund Luminous, Ch. Alstead Seedley Supremacy, Ch. Seedley Queen, Ch. Seedley Victorious, and Ch. Alstead Adjutant.

Samuel Untermeyer of New York owned many well-known Collies under his Greystone Kennel name and, assisted by Joe Burrell, such distinctive Collies as the following were to win laurels in the show ring: Ch. Southport Sculptor, Ch. Greystone Enchantress, Ch. Squire of Tytton, and Ch. Greystone Tyttonian.

About 1909, the name of Dr. O. P. Bennett became famous in the breed and from then, until the time of his death in 1945, his Tazewell Collies became a pillar of the breed and his knowledge of Collies came to universal esteem. To mention a few of his famous Collies, he owned Ch. Seedley Superior, Ch. Parbold Proclamation, Ch. Parbold Picador, Ch. Cock Robin of Arken, Ch. Tazewell Tittle, Ch. Tazewell Tricolor, and Ch. Tazewell Goldfield.

The period between 1910 and 1920 was a productive one for Collie interest. During this time the following people began to attract general attention for their success with Collies: Mrs. May McCurdy, New Brunswick, New Jersey, who had established the Pinewoods Kennels and had purchased Ch. Seedley Stirling: Thos. P. Hunter, Philadelphia, who made the Knocklayde Collies famous in a very short time and who owned, among other splendid Collies, Ch. Knocklayde King Hector, Ch. Knocklayde Queen Prim, and Ch. Knocklayde King Slam. It was during this time that Miss Bullocks of California was very active in the breed with Ch. Imna Select and Ch. Imna Improve.

W. R. Van Dyck was exhibiting some fine specimens as early as 1918, and some 15 or 20 years later was to own one of the great Collies of the middle late Thirties in Ch. Honeybrook Big Parade. Ch. Ormskirk Peaceful, a lovely tricolor, heaped new fame upon the Harswing Kennels of Mr. and Mrs. Wm. H. Schwinger, Ebenezer, N.Y. Still another of the well-known breeders of the decade before 1920, was Edwin L. Pickhardt of the Sterling Kennels at Bridgewater, Conn. In 1919 he imported some of the finest Collies to be found in England. Among his better known Collies were: Ch. Laund Limit, Ch. Sterling Stardust, and Ch. Sterling Silverflash, the latter bitch being America's first white champion. From 1940 to 1949 his most famous Collies were Ch. Sterling Starmist (one of the all-time greats), Ch. Sterling Syndicate, Ch. Sterling Spearhead, and Ch. Sterling Showmaster.

From 1920 to 1930 the following people began to take their places among the nationally-known exhibitors and breeders: Mrs. Florence B. Ilch, who established the Bellhaven Kennels with the capable assistance of Mike Kennedy and who campaigned, among others, such Collie luminaries as Ch. Bellhaven Strongheart, Ch. Bellhaven Seedley Snowdrop, Ch. Laund Lindberg of Bellhaven, Ch. Laund Loyalty of Bellhaven, who won the best in Show award at Westminster in 1929, Ch. Bellhaven Black Lucason, Ch. Braegate Model of Bellhaven and later, the remarkable winner Ch. Laund Liberation of Bellhaven. In 1920 Albert Payson Terhune, whose writing had done so much to bring the Collie to the attention of the public, campaigned Ch. Sunnybank Sigurd, among other good Collies, and exerted a tremendous influence for good within the breed.

Contemporaries were: Mrs. Lillian Miller of Seattle, with her Olympic Collies; D. L. Findley of St. Louis of Lochland fame, a vital force in the production of better whites; and Charles Wernsman, who established the Arken Collies. His foundation bitch was Ch. Halbury Jean who was to produce six champions. Bred by Halbury Kennels, she was by Alstead Aviator by Ch. Seedley Supremacy ex Halbury Expression. Among the Arken Collies were: Ch. El Troubadour of Arken, Ch. El Capitan of Arken, Ch. Future of Arken, Ch. Spirit of Arken, Ch. Mamaron of Arken, Ch. Sir King of Arken, and Ch. Monsieur the Count of Arken. Another of his breeding was Ch. Cock Robin of Arken, later purchased by Dr. O. P. Bennett of Tazewell fame.

The Noranda Kennels of Mr. and Mrs. Wm. H. Long, Jr., began to make their mark felt in the fancy in the late 1920's and they owned such excellent Collies as Ch. Lady Lukeo of Cosalta, Ch. Lady Nan of Noranda, Ch. Master Lukeo of Noranda, Ch. Heidi of Naronda, Ch. Cadet of Noranda, Ch. Ink Spot of Noranda, Ch. Noranda Snow Patch (America's second white champion bitch), and Ch. Hector of Noranda.

Fred L. Kem's Lodestone Kennels achieved nationwide acclaim about 1929 and one of their most famous Collies was Lodestone Landmark, a well-named sire of many champions who was a great factor in the improvement of the breed.

From 1930 on a great many fanciers were to come into the public eye for their achievements in breeding good Collies and exhibiting them extensively.

The Collie Club of America began a period of intensive growth in 1944 and has since become one of the largest specialty clubs in the world. Truly the dog with "the wisdom of a man and the ways of a woman" has entrenched himself firmly in the heart of America. Fortunately his popularity has been achieved without the sacrifice of type that usually accompanies a great increase of registrations in a breed, and our American-bred Collies of today hold their own, without fear or favor, with other Collies bred anywhere in the world. No longer does the "imported dog" over-awe the fancy. It is too easy today to point to an equally good, or often a better dog, on the next bench at any of our larger shows. This is an infallible indication of the quality that is being bred into, and held within, the modern Collie in America.

Dogs over 20 years old are very rare, but a Collie once owned by a Mrs. Cole of Cyrus Street, Clerkenwell, London, England, was reported as age 27 when it died on December 18, 1937.

COLLIE, ROUGH

The rough-coated Collie is a favorite breed in Belgium and Holland and is extremely popular in America, Australia, Great Britain, Denmark, Germany, and New Zealand.

Description and Standards. The description and standards, by courtesy of the Collie Club of America and AKC follow.

GENERAL CHARACTER: The Collie is a lithe, strong, responsive, active dog, carrying no useless timber, standing naturally straight and firm. The deep, moderately wide chest shows strength, the sloping shoulders and well-bent hocks indicate

A pair of Rough Collies. Photo by Evelyn M. Shafer.

speed and grace, and the face shows high intelligence. The Collie presents an impressive, proud picture of true balance, each part being in harmonious proportion to every other part and to the whole. Except for the technical description that is essential to this Standard and without which no Standard for the guidance of breeders and judges is adequate, it could be stated simply that no part of the Collie ever seems to be out of proportion to any other part. Timidity, frailness, sullenness, viciousness, lack of animation, cumbersome appearance and lack of over-all balance impair the general character.

HEAD: The head properties are of great importance. When considered in proportion to the size of the dog the head is inclined to lightness and never appears massive. A heavy-headed dog lacks the necessary bright, alert, full-of-sense look that contributes so greatly to expression. Both in front and profile view the head bears a general resemblance to a well-blunted lean wedge, being smooth and clean in outline and nicely balanced in proportion. On the sides it tapers gradually and smoothly from the ears to the end of the black nose, without being flared out in backskull ("cheeky") or pinched in muzzle ("snipy"). In profile view the top of the backskull and the top of the muzzle lie in two approximately parallel, straight planes of equal length, divided by a very slight but perceptible stop or break. A mid-point between the inside corners of the eyes (which is the center of a correctly placed stop) is the center of balance in length of head.

The end of the smooth, well-rounded muzzle is blunt but not square. The underjaw is strong, clean-cut and the depth of skull from the brow to the under part of the jaw is not excessive. The teeth are of good size, meeting in a scissors bite. Overshot or undershot jaws are undesirable, *the latter* being more severely *penalized*. There is a very slight prominence of the eyebrows. The backskull is flat, without receding either laterally or backward and the occipital bone is not highly peaked. The proper width of backskull necessarily depends upon the combined length of skull and muzzle and the width of the backskull is less than its length. Thus the correct width varies with the individual and is dependent upon the extent to which it is supported by length of muzzle. Because of the importance of the head characteristics, *prominent head faults are very severely penalized.*

EYES: Because of the combination of the flat skull, the arched eyebrows, the slight stop and the rounded muzzle, the foreface must be chiseled to form a receptacle for the eyes and they are necessarily placed obliquely to give them the required forward outlook. Except for the blue merles, they are required to be matched in color. They are almond-shaped, of medium size and never properly appear to be large or prominent. The color is dark and the eye does not show a yellow ring or a sufficiently prominent haw to affect the dog's expression. The eyes have a clear, bright appearance, expressing intelligent inquisitiveness, particularly when the ears are drawn up and the dog is on the alert. In blue merles, dark brown eyes are preferable, but either or both eyes may be merle or china in color without specific penalty. A large, round, full eye seriously detracts from the desired "sweet" expression. *Eye faults are heavily penalized.*

EARS: The ears are in proportion to the size of the head and, if they are carried properly and unquestionably "break" naturally, are seldom too small. Large ears usually cannot be lifted correctly off the head, and even if lifted, they will be out of proportion to the size of the head. When in respose the ears are folded lengthwise and thrown back into the frill. On the alert they are drawn well up on the backskull and are carried about three-quarters erect, with about one-fourth of the ear tipping or "breaking" forward. *A dog with prick ears or low ears cannot show true expression and is penalized accordingly.*

NECK: The neck is firm, clean, muscular, sinewy and heavily frilled. It is fairly long, carried upright with a slight arch at the nape and imparts a proud, upstanding appearance showing off the frill.

BODY: The body is firm, hard and muscular, a trifle long in proportion to the height. The ribs are well-rounded behind the well-sloped shoulders and the chest is deep, extending to the elbows. The back is strong and level, supported by powerful hips and thighs and the croup is sloped to give a well-rounded finish. The loin is powerful and slightly arched. Noticeably fat dogs, or dogs in poor flesh, or with skin disease, or with no under coat are out of condition and are moderately penalized accordingly.

LEGS: The forelegs are straight and muscular, with a fair amount of bone considering the size of the dog. A cumbersome appearance is undesirable. Both narrow and wide placement are penalized. The forearm is moderately fleshy and the pasterns are flexible but without weakness. The hind legs are less fleshy, muscular at the thighs, very sinewy and the hocks and stifles are well bent. A cowhocked dog or a dog with straight stifles is penalized. The comparatively small feet are approximately oval in shape. The soles are well padded and tough, and the toes are well arched and close together. When the Collie is not in motion the legs and feet are judged by allowing the dog to come to a natural stop in a standing position so that both the forelegs and the hind legs are placed well apart, with the feet extending straight forward. Excessive "posing" is undesirable.

GAIT: The gait or movement is distinctly characteristic of the breed. A sound Collie is not out at the elbows but it does, nevertheless, move toward an observer with its front feet tracking comparatively close at the ground. The front legs do not "cross over," nor does the Collie move with a pacing or rolling gait. Viewed from the front, one gains the impression that the dog is capable of changing its direction of travel almost instantaneously, as indeed it is. When viewed from the rear, the hind legs, from the hock joint to the ground, move in comparatively close-together, parallel, vertical planes. The hind legs are powerful and propelling. Viewed from the side, the gait is smooth not choppy. The reasonably long, "reaching" stride is even, easy, light and seemingly effortless.

TAIL: The tail is moderately long, the bone reaching to the hock joint or below. It is carried low when the dog is quiet, the end having an upward twist or "swirl." When gaited or when the dog is excited it is carried gaily but not over the back.

COAT: The well-fitting, proper-textured coat is the crowning glory of the rough variety of Collie. It is abundant except on the head and legs. The outer coat is straight and harsh to the touch. A soft, open outer coat or a curly outer coat, regardless of quantity, is penalized. The under coat, however, is soft, furry and so close together that it is difficult to see the skin when the hair is parted. The coat is very abundant on the mane and frill. The face or mask is smooth. The forelegs are smooth and well feathered in the back of the pasterns. The hind legs are smooth below the hock joints. Any feathering below the hocks is removed for the show ring. The hair on the tail is very profuse and on the hips it is long and bushy. The texture, quantity and the extent to which the coat "fits the dog" are important points.

COLOR: The four recognized colors are sable and white, tri-color, blue merle and white. There is no preference among

Smooth Collie. Photo by H. Hewett.

them. The sable and white is predominantly sable (a fawn sable color of varying shades from light gold to dark mahogany) with white markings usually on the chest, neck, legs, feet and the tip of the tail. A blaze may appear on the foreface or backskull or both. The tri-color is predominantly black, carrying white markings as in a sable and white and has tan shadings on and about the head and legs. The blue merle is a mottled or "marbled" color, predominantly blue-gray and black with white markings as in the sable and white and usually has tan shadings as in the tri-color. The white is predominantly white, preferably with sable or tri-color markings. Blue merle coloring is undesirable in whites.

SIZE: Dogs are from 24 to 26 inches at the shoulder and weigh from 60 to 75 pounds. Bitches are from 22 to 24 inches at the shoulder, weighing from 50 to 65 pounds. *An undersize or an oversize Collie is penalized according to the extent to which the dog appears to be undersize or oversize.*

EXPRESSION: Expression is one of the most important points in considering the relative value of Collies. *Expression*, like the term "character" is difficult to define in words. It is not a fixed point as in color, weight or height and it is something the uninitiated can properly understand only by optical illustration. In general, however, it may be said to be the combined product of the shape and balance of the skull and muzzle, the placement, size, shape and color of the eye and the position, size and carriage of the ears. An expression that shows sullenness or which is suggestive of any other breed is entirely foreign. The Collie cannot be judged properly until its expression has been carefully evaluated.

(March 10, 1959)

COLLIE, SMOOTH

Description and Standards. The Smooth Variety of Collie is judged by the same Standard as the Rough Variety, except that the references to the quantity and the distribution of the coat are not applicable to the Smooth Variety, which has a hard, dense, smooth coat.

(March 10, 1959)

DOBERMAN PINSCHER

THE STORY of the Doberman Pinscher begins about 1890, during that period when sportsmen the world over were beginning to show an intense interest in the development of pure-bred dogs. In the years between 1880 and 1910, many breeds, such as the German Shepherd, Boxer, Giant Schnauzer, and others, were developed and brought to perfection. Among these, and not the least of them, is the Doberman Pinscher.

The breed owes its name to Louis Dobermann of Apolda, in Thueringia. Apparently, Dobermann began experimenting in the breeding of dogs as early as 1870, using as assistants "a grave digger and a bell ringer."

By 1890, Dobermann had decided exactly what he wanted in the way of a dog. His ideal was a giant terrier. That is, a dog built upon terrier lines and owning a terrier's grace and agility, but one with the strength of a typical German working shepherd, or draft dog. The dog he visioned would look much like a five-pound Miniature Pinscher but would be some 15 times heavier.

Dobermann also wanted a dog which would be unusually "sharp," which is an euphonious German way of saying that the dog should be willing to attack man or beast, or even the devil himself. And whatever else they might have been, "Dobermann's Dogs" were "sharp."

An early Swiss pioneer in the breed, Gottfried Liechti, as quoted by Philipp Gruenig, wrote: "They were certainly robust, had absolutely no trace of fear —not of the devil himself—and it required a good deal of courage to own one."

"Dobermann's Dogs" sold like "hot cakes," as another early writer put it. Other early breeders, too, became interested chiefly in color and sharpness, and this interest continued for many years. Thus, Gruenig states that Mars von Simmenau, born in 1927, lived up to his name, and adds: "He was covered with scars, and was the sharpest dog I ever saw."

In 1890, Louis Dobermann, produced the matriarch of the Doberman Pinscher breed, a bitch called Schnupp. When the Dobermann Pinscher Club of Germany was organized in 1912, Schnupp was given number one place in the Stud Book. Of Schnupp and her puppies, Horowitz says there were deplorable to look at, and very ferocious. But they caught the German fancy immediately.

Very little is known about the early dogs which Louis Dobermann and his two assistants used in manufacturing the breed, and there have been various theories concerning this. One belief is that he used the old black and tan German Pinscher extensively. A possible clue to this is that the breed was first called "Dobermann's Dogs," and only later, Dobermann Pinscher. However, it cannot be forgotten that Dobermann had the conception of a giant Pinscher, or terrier, so that he may have been inclined to call the dog a Pinscher, whether or not he used any German Pinscher blood.

There can be no question that Dobermann used some of the native Shepherd strains for which Thueringia was so famous. Even though he used shorthaired Shepherds in the main, some of the early Dobermanns had rather long hair. Moreover, many of the early litters contained bob-tailed dogs in them. These bob-tailed dogs were highly esteemed by early breeders, and at that time, the long-tailed dogs were bobbed, rather than totally docked.

The Rottweiler also served as a pillar of the breed. This dog had remained in a localized area of Germany from the days of the Roman invasions, being a guardian of the army supply dumps. He had survived as a useful draft dog. The resemblance between the two is plain, but the Rottweiler is heavier, and lacks the extraordinary agility which is a hallmark of the modern Doberman Pinscher. The barrel chests of the Rottweiler sometimes showed up in earlier Doberman Pinschers, and were considered a fault.

The influence of both the Shepherds and the Rottweiler remains in the modern Doberman, chiefly in

Doberman Pinscher—Ch. Kay Hill's Paint the Town Red. (Owner: Mrs. Harold Kay, Harrisburg, Pa.) Photo by Evelyn M. Shafer.

certain instincts and hereditary aptitudes. Thus, the Doberman shows, to a remarkable degree, guarding and property instincts and herding and driving aptitudes. The Rottweiler, however, gives the Doberman his great power.

Whether or not Louis Dobermann used crosses of the English Manchester Terrier is not known, but later breeders did. The Manchester Terrier was itself a cross between the Manchester Ratter and the Whippet. From this cross the Doberman gained alertness, refined strength, and great ability.

The cross also greatly gentled the breed. But the Germans corrected this immediately by crossing in certain rather savage Greyhounds, thus bringing the Doberman back to its original "sharpness." Among these Greyhounds was a black bitch, whose daughter, Stella, was whelped in 1908. This Greyhound cross, through Sybelle von Langen, appears in the Blankenberg strain.

Goswin Tischler began his von Groenland Kennels in 1895, naming them after "Greenland Street" in Apolda. Otto Goeller, also of Apolda, founded his von Thueringen Kennels in 1901. Louis Dobermann was by this time dead, and Goeller, perhaps more than anyone else, should be given credit for saving and improving the breed.

Tischler owned a dog called Bosco, whelped in 1893, and a bitch called Caesi. From these he bred the first Doberman sieger, Matzi von Groenland, whelped Aug. 15, 1895. Gruenig describes him as having a coarse body, very long hair, and a light eye.

The Doberman of this time was a short-headed dog with a heavy body. The breeders were using intense inbreeding to establish type, or chiefly color and sharpness. They now added in the Manchester to improve color, to lengthen the head, and finally to get a short, hard coat.

These characteristics were achieved in part in Prinz von Iln-Athen, born in 1899, and Fedor von Aprath,

born in 1906. The latter in particular had the desired longer head. This was further accentuated by the introduction of Greyhound blood between the years 1900 and 1908.

The longer head brought with it a tendency to certain degenerative faults which still appear in the modern dog. These are the absence of teeth, principally the pre-molars, undershot or overshot jaws, and a Roman nose. It is now believed that missing teeth are tied up with temperament faults. A tolerance of a quarter of an inch is allowed, although a scissor bite is considered ideal.

Perhaps the first great stud dog of the breed was Hellegraf von Thueringen, born June 12, 1904, and bred by Otto Goeller. Hellegraf can be considered the patriarch of the breed. He was a brown, and conformed reasonably well to modern ideas of the breed, except perhaps in muzzle.

In 1909, another potent sire, Prinz Modern von Ilm-Athen was born in the kennels of G. Krumbholz of Wickenstedt. He later entered stud duty at Harry Peek's von Jaegerhof Kennels, where he was an outstanding success.

The very next year two litter brothers, Bodo and Bob von Elfenfeld, came to the kennels of E. Toennes of Elberfeld. With these two dogs, the modern Doberman head appears in its full beauty. Bodo and Bob were sons of Moutz von Burgwall, a dog with a good head, though not the equal of those of his sons.

Importations to the United States were sporadic before World War I, and hardly figure in the modern breed. When the great Dobermans began to come, it is ironic that much of the foundation stock came from Holland rather than from Germany.

The first really great importation was Angola von Grammont. A bitch, she was a litter sister of the immortal Ajax. She was born at H. Kloeppel's von Grammont Kennels at Den Haag, The Netherlands, July 15, 1917.

Many considered Angola the most beautiful Doberman bitch whelped up to that time. She came to the White Gate Kennels of H. K. Mohr of Philadelphia, Pa., in the early 1920's, but not before she had given birth to some illustrious offspring in her native Holland. The best of these, including Elfrieda von der Koningstad, born in 1920, and Elisa and Favorit von der Koningstad, born in 1921, themselves came to America.

In addition, Carlo von der Koningstad, a son of Angola's brother, Ajax, came to the United States. Carlo proved one of the great foundation sires in this country.

Perhaps the greatest dog of the World War I period was Lux von der Blankenburg, who was born in 1918 a few months before the end of the war. He was bred by C. Blank of the Blankenburg Kennels in Berlin. Lux was another of those dogs described as "rowdy and vicious."

In 1924, Lux sired Claus von Sigalsburg, and in 1926, Lotte II von Simmenau. Both of these came to the United States, as did Lux himself. Lux sired dogs of excellent class, and his offspring in the United States, at least, were of good nature.

Both Mars von Simmenau, and his brother, Modern, came to the United States. They were born at the kennels of C. Winkler of Mertschnetz in 1927. The temperament of Mars already has been mentioned. Modern appears to have been of a gentler disposition. This, coupled with his unusual beauty, made him a successful sire in this country.

At about this period, Altara von Riga was brought to the United States from Russia. She was mated to Graf von Blankenburg, then on the Pacific Coast. From this mating came Karl von Blankenburg, one of the most successful American-bred dogs of the period. Thus, it can be said that Americans drew upon the bloodlines of the world for their stock.

Of later importations, perhaps the most important were Jockel von Burgund, Troll von Engelsburg, Ferry von Rauhfelsen, and Moriz von Roedeltal. Based upon their American show records, the first three, at least, must be ranked with the all time great of all breeds. All four became American champions, and all sired noted dogs.

Jockel was considered oversize by German standards, and did little winning in his homeland. Ferry was imported by the Giralda Farms of Mrs. Geraldine Dodge, but both Jockel and Ferry ended up at the Randahof Kennels, Van Nuys, Cal.

Troll was a son of Muck von Brunia, the outstanding dog of Germany during his time, and a sieger and American champion. Troll was best of breed at the 1934 and 1935 German sieger shows, winning the title of World Sieger. During the next couple of years, he was at stud in Germany.

Then Willie Schaefer of the Lindenhof Kennels, Golf, Ill., imported Troll, as he had his sire Muck. Troll quickly won American and Canadian titles, and

meawhile, his offspring in Germany were making a sensational record for themselves. Schaefer, incidentally, had imported Jockel.

It was Schaefer who organized the First American Amateur Training Club for Working Dogs, at Chicago in 1933. This organization was the forerunner of the obedience trial movement in the United States. The members were chiefly Doberman Pinscher fanciers, but other owners of working dogs quickly joined.

Schaefer was president and director of training, while John Roberts was secretary-treasurer and chief instructor. The club set up branches in 1944, the first of which was in Cleveland. The Cleveland branch was made up entirely of Doberman fanciers, including Frank L. Grant, Oscar E. Barlow, and Clyde Henderson.

Grant and Henderson played prominent parts in Dogs For Defense, the civilian organization which supplied dogs for war service.

In addition, both collaborated with the Doberman Pinscher Club of America, Forest Hall, of Hallwyre Kennels, Dallas, Texas, and Richard Webster of Marienland Kennels, Baltimore, in getting the U.S. Marine Corps to nominate the Doberman as the official Marine war dog. Henderson became the first man to lead a platoon of combat dogs into battle, and later became senior Marine officer in charge of dog training.

Thus, Doberman Pinscher fanciers can be given major credit for establishing Working Dog, Obedience, and War Dog standards in the United States. They further demonstrate the hold the breed gets upon its fanciers, since most of them were active in the breed 15 years or longer—Schaefer began in Germany in 1919.

Other early breeders include F. F. H. Fleitmann of Far Hills, N.J., breeder of an outstanding dog Ch. Westphalia's Uranus; Glenn S. Staines of the Ponchartrain Kennels, Detroit, who, besides breeding and importing many champions, conducted a guide dog school for many years; and there were many others.

It should be said that the modern Doberman Pinscher, as he is bred in the United States, is temperamentally a far distant dog from the ferocious "Doberman's Dogs." They made not only top war dogs, but many of them have been exceptional guides for the blind. They still are not afraid of the devil himself, but most of them mind their own business and do not pick fights. Their value in the role as police officer companions, especially in crowd control work, is impossible to estimate.

The Doberman is considered the favorite working dog in South Africa.

Description and Standards. The description and standards follow.

1. GENERAL CONFORMATION AND APPEARANCE: The appearance is that of a dog of good middle size, with a body that is square, the height, measured vertically from the ground to the highest point of the withers, equalling the length, measured horizontally, from the forechest to the rear projection of the

Doberman Pinscher—Ch. Borona the Warlock. (Owner: Henry G. rampton, Miami, Fla.) Photo by Evelyn M. Shafer.

upper thigh. Height, at the withers, males 26 to 28 inches, ideal being about 27 inches; bitches, 24 to 26 inches, ideal being about 25½ inches. Compactly built, muscular and powerful, for great endurance and speed. Elegant in appearance, of proud carriage, reflecting great nobility and temperament. Energetic, watchful, determined, alert, fearless, loyal, and obedient.

Faults: Coarseness. Fine Greyhound build. Undersized or oversized. *Disqualifying Faults:* Shyness, viciousness. *Shyness:* A dog shall be judged fundamentally shy if, refusing to stand for examination, it shrinks away from the judge; if it fears an approach from the rear; it shies at sudden and unusual noises, to a marked degree. *Viciousness:* A dog that attacks, or attempts to attack either the judge or its handler is definitely vicious. An aggressive or belligerent attitude towards other dogs shall not be deemed viciousness.

Doberman Pinscher puppies.

Doberman Pinscher—A head study. Photo by Evelyn M. Shafer.

2. HEAD: (Shape, eyes, teeth, ears): *Shape:* Long and dry, resembling a blunt wedge, both frontal and profile views. When seen from the front, the head widens gradually towards the base of the ears in a practically unbroken line. Top of skull flat, turning with slight stop to bridge of muzzle, with muzzle line extending parallel to the top line of the skull. Cheeks flat and muscular. Lips lying close to jaws, and not drooping. Jaws full and powerful, well filled under the eyes. Nose, solid black in black dogs, dark brown in brown ones, and dark grey in blue ones.

Faults: Head out of balance in proportion to body. Ram's dishfaced, cheeky or snipey heads.

EYES: Almond shaped, not round, moderately deep set, not prominent, with vigorous, energetic expression. Iris of uniform color, ranging from medium to darkest brown in black dogs, the darker shade being the more desirable. In reds or blues, the color of the iris should blend with that of the markings, but not be of a lighter hue than that of the markings. *Faults:* Slit eyes. Glassy eyes.

TEETH: Strongly developed and white. Lower incisors upright, and touching inside of upper incisors—a true scissors bite. 42 teeth—(22 in lower jaw, 20 in upper jaw). Distemper teeth should not be penalized.

Disqualifying Faults: Overshot more than $\frac{3}{16}$ inch. Undershot, more than $\frac{1}{8}$ inch.

EARS: Well trimmed, and carried erect. (In all states where ear trimming is prohibited, or where dogs with cropped ears cannot be shown, the foregoing requirements are waived.) The upper attachment of the ear, when held erect, should be on a level with the top of the skull.

3. NECK: Carried upright, well muscled and dry. Well arched, and with nape of neck widening gradually toward body. Length of neck proportioned to body and head.

4. BODY: Back short, firm, of sufficient width, and muscular at the loin extending in a straight line from withers to the slightly rounded croup. Withers pronounced and forming the highest point of body. Brisket full and broad reaching deep to the elbow. Chest broad, and forechest well defined. Spring of ribs pronounced. Belly well tucked up, extending in a curved line from chest. Loins wide and muscled. Hips broad in proportion to body, breadth of hips being approximately breadth of body at rib spring. Tail, docked at approximately second joint, should appear to be the continuation of the spine, without material drop.

5. FORE QUARTERS: Shoulder blade and upper arm should meet at an angle of ninety degrees. Relative length of shoulder and upper arm should be as one to one, excess length of upper arm being much less undesirable than excess length of shoulder blade. Legs, seen from the front and side, perfectly straight and parallel to each other from elbow to pastern; muscled and sinewy, with round, heavy bone. In a normal position, and when gaiting, the elbow should lie close to the brisket. Pasterns firm, with an almost perpendicular position to the ground. Feet well arched, compact, and cat-like, turning neither in nor out.

6. HIND QUARTERS: In balance with fore quarters. Upper shanks long, wide and well muscled on both sides of thigh with clearly defined stifle. Hocks while the dog is at rest, hock to heel should be perpendicular to the ground. Upper shanks, lower shanks, and hocks parallel to each other, and wide enough apart to fit in with a properly built body. The hip bone should fall away from the spinal column at an angle of about thirty degrees. The upper shank should be at right angles to the hip bone. Croup well filled out. Cat-feet, as on front legs, turning neither in nor out.

7. GAIT: The gait should be free, balanced, and vigorous,

with good reach in the fore quarters, and good driving power in the hind quarters. When trotting, there should be a strong rear action drive, with rotary motion of hind quarters. Each rear leg should move in line with the fore leg on the same side. Rear and front legs should be thrown neither in nor out. Back should remain strong, firm and level.

8. COAT, COLOR, MARKINGS: Coat, smoothaired, short, hard, thick, and close-lying. Invisible grey under coat on neck permissible. Allowed colors, black, brown, or blue. Markings, rust red, sharply defined, and appearing above each eye, and on muzzle, throat, and forechest, and on all legs and feet, and below tail. White on chest, not exceeding one-half square inch, permissible.

The foregoing description is that of the ideal Doberman Pinscher. Any deviation from the above-described dog must be penalized in proportion to the extent of the deviation, and in accordance with the appended scale of points.

SCALE OF POINTS: *Points*

1. General Conformation and Appearance
   Proportions   8
   Bone ⎫
   Substance ⎭   8
   Temperament ⎫
   Expression ⎬   8
   Nobility ⎭
   Condition   5
                                                    ──
                                                     29
2. Head
   Shape   6
   Teeth   5
   Eyes   3
   Ears   1
                                                    ──
                                                     15
3. Neck   3
                                                    ──
                                                     3
4. Body
   Backline ⎫
   Withers ⎪
   Loins ⎬   8
   Tail Placement ⎭
   Chest ⎫
   Brisket ⎪
   Rib Spring ⎬   8
   Tuck-up ⎭
   Shape and proportions   4
                                                    ──
                                                     20
5. Fore Quarters
   Shoulders ⎫
   Upper arms ⎪
   Legs ⎬   5
   Pasterns ⎭
   Angulation   4
   Paws   2
                                                    ──
                                                     11
6. Hind Quarters
   Upper thigh ⎫
   Stifle ⎬   5
   Hocks ⎭
   Angulation   4
   Paws   2
                                                    ──
                                                     11
7. Gait   6
                                                    ──
                                                     6
8. Coat ⎫
   Color ⎬   5
   Markings ⎭
                                                    ──
                                                     5
           Total   100 100

Disqualifications. Shyness, viciousness. Overshot more than 3/16 of an inch; undershot more than 1/8 of an inch.

GERMAN SHEPHERD DOG

THE GERMAN Shepherd Dog is one of the world's best known dogs. Made so, perhaps, by the American motion picture, he has maintained his popularity by his great beauty and strength, his superiority as a guide for the blind, in military service, and in obedience contests.

He grew to world-wide popularity immediately after World War I, when the German nation was in disrepute with a major portion of the globe. And then, after a slump which was more or less consonant with the Depression, though not caused by it, he returned to popularity as Hilter's Germany was rising to power. Then, though a second world war devastated the world as nothing like it had before, the German Shepherd maintained, and even increased his popularity.

Today, the German Shepherd stands among the first three in American dogs. Breed clubs promote him intelligently; he is regularly seen in obedience work; and good specimens are to be seen everywhere. Regarded as the favorite working breed in America, Denmark, France, Italy, and Sweden, the German Shepherd is also extremely popular in Great Britain, Germany, India, New Zealand, and South Africa.

Because of German thoroughness in documentation, more is known about the actual origin of the German Shepherd than is the case with almost any other dog. And yet this breed too has been burdened by romantic stories trying to root its origin in ages long gone by. It is now stated as fact that the German Shepherd is a descendant of a Bronze Age race of shepherd dogs.

This appears to have come about through the fantastic, and certainly unscientific book written by Captain Max von Stephanitz, called *The German Shepherd Dog in Word and Picture*. In this book, von Stephanitz tried to prove that the entire race of shepherds came from one ancestral stock. Most of this stock, particularly the German Shepherd, supposedly came down from the Bronze Age, via a dog called Canis Poutiatini, and through a later one called the Hovawart.

Another writer noted a stray line in Tacitus, the Roman historian, which speaks of "the wolf-like dog of the country around the Rhine." This was taken as proof that the German Shepherd had existed in its present form from early Roman times. It was argued too, that the German Shepherd was, in times past, called the "wolf dog."

One writer states that wolves and Collies, the latter popular in Europe at the time, were introduced into the breed. He adds, however, that this was without success. The truth is that the modern German Shepherd does not look particularly like a wolf and that earlier ones looked even less so. In fact, pictures of early members of the breed show merely varying types of shepherd dogs, most of which had erect ears.

It should be understood that, following the Franco-Prussian War, that is, about 1880, Europeans developed an extraordinary interest in dog shows, and at the same time, a passion for sheepdogs. Each small market district had its own variety of sheep, cattle, and drover's dogs.

But the days of their greatest use were coming to an end. The railroad was making cattle driving unnecessary. Ranges were being fenced. The wolves were gone from the mountain slopes. Population pressures were making intensive livestock raising in relatively restricted areas necessary.

The sportsmen of that day were looking for dogs with which they might enter the new sport of dog showing. They looked for the outlandish; for dogs which could be promoted; and finally, for dogs of beauty. But they realized suddenly, too, that the shepherd dog, with his amazing and almost human abilities, was a part of a fast vanishing past.

The Germans began to seek means of perpetuating these sheep and cattle dogs. And they also cast about for a means of utilizing the abilities of the dogs. So the first attempts at training dogs for police and war work began to be made.

This would appear to be the true background of the shepherd dogs of all of Europe. For the Dutch, the Belgians, and the French began to improve and fix the types of their breeds almost at the same time. To a certain extent, so did the Swiss, the Hungarians, Spaniards, Italians, and Austrians. The Germans, in some cases, helped the others, particularly the Kuvasz, Komondor, and Puli.

We can start the first real history of the German Shepherd, as distinct from other shepherds, in 1891. That year, the Phylax Society was founded to sponsor the breed. Two men, Captain Reichelmann-Dunau, and graf von Hahn, were dominant in it. Others were Herr Wachsmuth and Herr Sparwasser, who liked "fancy dogs."

This Society died in 1894. It collapsed because of an argument which has raged in every specialty club devoted to working or sporting dogs which has been founded since. One group wanted to breed exclusively for herding, driving, and protection instincts. The other wanted to fix the type until the German Shepherd would be a thing of beauty unequaled in the world.

In 1896, the European dog fancy was fairly electrified when Dr. Gerland of Hildesheim introduced trained police dogs. Gerland's work had followed that of another Hildesheimer, Captain Schoenherr who, in 1886, had used dogs to clear up disorders which the police had not been able to handle. Capt. Schoenherr later became the head of the Prussian Government Breeding and Instruction School of Service Dogs at Grunheide.

The fact that these rapidly-vanishing shepherd dogs could be at once a thing of beauty and a police or war dog lent point to the efforts of German fanciers to save their shepherd dogs. They went to work with vast enthusiasm.

Now the great shepherd dog areas of Germany were in Wurttemberg, alongside Switzerland and the Alps; Bavaria on the Czech border, and more particularly that part called Swabia; and Thuringia, in Central Germany. The dogs of these areas varied in coat, size—ranging from 21 to 28 inches at the shoulder—tail carriage, ear carriage, etc.

According to von Stephanitz himself, the Thuringian shepherd was used to get erect ears. The Wurttemberg dogs had "lopped ears," but had reliability of tail carriage. Finally, a big Swabian working dog was added.

This brings us to the next important date—1899. In that year the "Der Verein fur Deutsche Schaferhunde" (Society for the Promotion of the Breeding of German Shepherd Dogs) was founded. Captain Max von Stephanitz was its head from April 22, 1899, until July 1, 1935. He was a breeding genius, and he ruled the organization with an iron, if benevolent, hand.

It was von Stephanitz who added in the Swabian dog, Audifax von Grafrath. He was "pitch forked into the breed as an absolute outsider. It was about that time—1902—a necessary attempt to give a broader basis to the breed. A big, mighty fellow, with excellent dorsal muscles and a correspondingly swift gait, Audifax certainly transmitted these good qualities and often, his somewhat over-developed head as well." Those were von Stephanitz's words.

Thus, it might be said that the German Shepherd gets its erect ears and wolf-gray color from the Thuringian; his tail carriage and other colors from the Wurttemburg; and his size, great strength of back, and gait from the Swabian.

Pictures of some of these dogs are still extant. They were a weedy lot, though some of them were beginning to look like German Shepherds. Their mixed origin, however, produced several varieties. Thus, in 1915, Mason reported there were three coat varieties.

He listed them as (1) Smooth; (2) Long-haired, wavy, but hard, with the hair partially covering the eyes; and (3) Wire-haired, with beard and tuft over the eye brows.

According to Elliot Humphrey of The Seeing Eye, there were 450 police stations using dogs in Germany as early as 1910. Most of these dogs were German Shepherds. By the end of World War I, 48,000 dogs were in German Army service, plus countless others in civilian police work. Most of these, too, were German Shepherds, although the war and police service must be given credit for rescuing a number of other breeds from extinction.

Still, the battle between the working German Shepherd owners and the show fanciers continued. Humphrey says that the last whelping to produce both show and work winners was in 1909. After that, the German Shepherd became primarily a show dog until obedience trials made possible the working and showing of the same dog at the same dog show.

German Shepherd—Barinka's Aero. (Owner: Catherine F. Stetka, ite Lake, N.Y.) Photo by William P. Gilbert.

The Germans then began an intensive breeding program to fix type. They created a modern miracle, and yet they sewed the seeds for what later became a disaster to the breed. For from somewhere shyness crept in. It did not appear so often in Germany, at least at first, but it played havoc with foreign breeders who did not understand what they were up against. However, the results of this did not show up until much later.

Some of the dogs which were considered pillars of the breed before 1909 were: Tell von der Kriminalpolizi; Luchs von Kalsmundt-Wetzler; Beowulf; Hettel Uckermark; Roland von Starkenberg; Dewelt Barbarosso; Graf Eberhard von Hohen Esp; Horrand von Grafrath; and Hektor von Schwaben.

The latter was German Grand Champion in 1900 and 1901. There is a good picture of him extant, so that it is possible to compare him with dogs of each of the following decades. In something less than 20 years, the modern German Shepherd was created from dogs such as Hektor.

During the first World War, the Belgians and French were using dogs for war purposes. The English were using Airedales and Irish Terriers for certain war purposes also. It seems reasonable that these breeds would have jumped into world-wide popularity because of their war records. But as it turned out, it was the dog of the enemy which did so, the Airedale excepted.

There are several reasons why the German Shepherd was the one to forge ahead. First, the British had not been blind to the new German dog, and a substantial number had been imported to England before the war. The British breeders, though they hated the Germans, clung to their dogs. The name was merely changed to Alsatian.

Lieut. Col. J. T. C. Moore-Brabazon, who had known the breed before the war, witnessed German dogs, probably captured, in action. He, and others, returned home with the determination to shove the breed ahead in England. Aside from its war work, it

was now further glamorized by naming it the Alsatian Wolf Dog. The Alsatian Wolf Dog Club was formed in 1919, less than a year after the end of the war. The term "Alsatian" has stuck ever since, but the "wolf" was dropped in 1930.

In America, too, the breed was well established before the war. In 1912, Benjamin Throop, Scranton, Pa., and Miss Anne Tracy, Highland Falls, N.Y., entered the breed. The following year, the German Shepherd Dog Club of America was founded. There were 26 members. Mrs. C. Halstead Yates was president, and Mr. Throop, secretary-treasurer.

That year, two champions were crowned. They were Miss Tracy's Luchs, and L. I. DeWinter's Herta von Ehrangrund. Mr. DeWinter lived at Suttenberg, N.J., and called his kennels Winterview.

Then Ch. Apollo von Hunenstein came to America. An amazing dog, whelped February 20, 1912, he held championships in Austria, Belgium, France, and Germany. He came to the United States in 1914.

The following year, with imports cut off, the first specialty show was held at Greenwich, Conn., on June 11. There were 40 dogs benched. At the 1916 specialty show, 96 dogs were entered. Such entries argue a firm foundation for the breed. Miss Tracy, incidentally, judged both shows.

Since prejudice against the Germans was rampant in the United States as well as England, the "German" was dropped from the breed name. But the Americans never would permit a name denoting the wrong origin to be applied as the British did.

Following the war, the breed certainly would have continued its steady development, since some of the greatest German Shepherds which ever lived were imported at this time. But another incident occurred which suddenly skyrocketed the breed into world-wide fame.

A dog called Etzel von Oeringen arrived in the United States in company with Bruno Hoffman. Etzel eventually went to Hollywood, the property of Jane Murfin. She teamed up with Larry Trimble, a dog trainer. And then one day a dog movie star was born. Etzel had become the immortal Strongheart.

The name of Strongheart and the name of the German Shepherd were shortly on the tongue of nearly every movie-goer in the world. And it seemed that every one of them wanted a German Shepherd.

Lawrence Armour of Green Bay Kennels, Chicago, imported Nores von der Kriminalpoletzi, the sire of Strongheart. And everyone who could, bred to the dog. Thousands upon thousands of dogs were bred and sold as brothers or cousins of Strongheart.

And then there appeared another to vie with Strongheart. This was a puppy brought from France and of uncertain pedigree. This dog was Rin Tin Tin.

In the half-dozen years that followed, the German Shepherd became the most popular dog in the world. In a half-dozen countries, he was the leading breed, and usually by overwhelming majorities. Perhaps the Canadian record is the best example, for there the breed appears to have been unknown until after World War I.

In 1920, five dogs were registered as Shepherd Sheepdogs. The following year, the classification was changed to Shepherd Dogs, and three varieties were listed together. These were in approximately equal numbers, German Shepherds, Belgian Groenendaels, and Belgian Malinoix. Perhaps a dozen each.

But, in 1923, German Shepherds were given separate classifications and 84 were registered. This number doubled in 1924, doubled again in 1925, and again in 1926. And while it was topping all breeds in Canada that year, as many as 25,000 were being registered in the United States.

In England, in Canada, in the United States, no one had ever heard of such a thing. German Shepherds were breaking world records in every stud book.

And then came the slump. Starting in 1928—later in Canada—the breed began to drop. It required 20½ pages merely to list all the dogs registered in the Canadian Stud Book in 1928. In 1936 only two pages were used.

Many things had happened. The Germans had unloaded upon us the misfits they themselves might have destroyed. Americans bred to any and everything. Shyness showed up. Many of the dogs were work dogs, misunderstood and aggressive. Their owners couldn't handle them; the neighborhoods couldn't tolerate them.

Every slum had its dozens of mongrel, half-wild "po-leece" dogs. Mongrels and pure-breds were biting people. The newspapers always carried the same story. "German police dog runs berserk . . ." etc. Everybody owned Strongheart's brother, or Rin Tin Tin's sister, or a cross between a German Police Dog and a wolf. And the results were disastrous.

And yet, a group of American breeders stood by their breed. Wealthy and enthusiastic fanciers were added. They kept breeding good ones, and importing more, until in the end, the American dogs became the envy of the world.

Four world-famous sires came to this country. They were Dolf von Dustenbrook, who came in 1920 to P. A. B. Widener, Elkins Park, Pa.; Hamilton Erich von Grafenworth, who went to Hamilton Farms, Gladstone, N.J.; Gerri von Oberklamm, imported jointly by John Gans and a syndicate of others; and Cito Berslust, brought over by Gans in 1922.

These dogs had the best blood in Germany in them, including that of the famous Flora Berkemeyer, greatest bitch in the breed's history. Most of them were descended from a mating between Flora and Apollo before his importation to America. Apollo, by the way, is mounted at the Peabody Museum at Yale.

In 1923, Mrs. Geraldine Rockefeller Dodge started her Giralda Farms Kennels at Madison, N.J., and Marie Leary opened Cosalta Kennels at Greenwich, Conn. Widener, whose Joselle Kennels played so big a part in the breed, died in 1948, but not until he had helped to establish the German Shepherd as a Coast Guard dog supreme.

In 1936, Gans brought Sieger Pfeffer von Bern to the United States. Pfeffer turned out to be a sire of miraculous ability. So did Sieger Odin Von Busecher Schloss, imported in 1938 by Mrs. and Mrs. Sidney Heckert Jr.'s Villa Marina Kennels at Santa Barbara, California.

World War II did not bring a cessation of activity in German Shepherds. In fact, American dog breeding continued to grow throughout the war years. In the case of the German Shepherd, the breed began to make a name for itself as a war dog.

The German Shepherd was selected as the official Navy and Coast Guard dog, and the Widener Estate at Elkins Park, Pa., became a training center for the dogs. World War II was a global affair. And it turned out that the German Shepherd had the coat to take almost any kind of weather better than most any other kind of dog. Thus, a German Shepherd trained at Elkins Park could be ordered to Coast Guard patrol on any coast, from Alaska to Florida, without consideration of climatic conditions.

This is perhaps the place to mention the German Shepherd's other outstanding contribution to man, that of a guide for the sightless. When the Germans began to train guides for the blind in 1917, German Shepherds predominated in the work.

Josef Weber, a German Army war dog trainer, and later a trainer of guide dogs for blind German soldiers, came to America and set up a training kennel in New Jersey. About the same time, The Master Eye, a guide dog training school, was begun in Minnesota. Both used German Shepherds.

Meanwhile, Mrs. Harrison Eustis began her experiments in breeding super-dogs at Vevey, Switzerland in 1924. Her project there was called Fortunate Fields. Elliott Humphrey, Willi Ebeling, and others worked with her. They later established The Seeing Eye at Morristown, N.J. Weber was one of the first trainers there.

German Shepherd puppies. Studer Photo Co.

German Shepherd—All-black coats are not uncommon.

Since then, many thousands of German Shepherds have devoted their lives to leading the blind. Other dogs have done so also, but German Shepherds have predominated, and the public has come to associate the breed with that activity.

World War II, of course, created a chaotic condition in Germany. But many American soldiers brought German Shepherds home with them. The majority of these dogs came with pedigrees, but were technically not registerable because of the collapse of the German Kennel Club.

Perhaps one final example of the world-wide predominance of this breed can be shown in the following fact. A Clevelander named John R. Sharp built a small German Shepherd kennel entirely upon the basis of stock seen and purchased in Japan.

Description and Standards. The description and standards, adopted by the German Shepherd Dog Club of America and approved by the American Kennel Club follow.

GENERAL APPEARANCE: The first impression of a good German Shepherd Dog is that of a strong, agile, well-muscled animal, alert and full of life. It should both be and appear to be well balanced with harmonious development of the fore quarter and hind quarter. The dog should appear to the eye, and actually be, longer than tall; deep-bodied, and presenting an outline of smooth curves rather than corners. It should look substantial and not spindly, giving the impression both at rest and in motion, of muscular fitness and nimbleness without any look of clumsiness or soft living.

The ideal height for dogs is 25 inches, and for bitches 23 inches at the shoulder. This height is established by taking a perpendicular line from the top of the shoulder blade to the ground with the coat parted or so pushed down that this measurement will show only the actual height of the frame or structure of the dog. The working value of dogs above or below the indicated heights is proportionately lessened, although variations of an inch above or below the ideal height are acceptable, while greater variations must be considered as faults. Weights of dogs of desirable size in proper flesh and condition average between 75 to 85 lbs., and of bitches between 60 and 70 lbs.

The Shepherd should be stamped with a look of quality and nobility—difficult to define but unmistakable when present. The good Shepherd Dog never looks common.

The breed has a distinct personality marked by a direct and fearless, but not hostile, expression; self-confidence and a certain aloofness which does not lend itself to immediate and indiscriminate friendships.

Secondary sex characteristics should be strongly marked, and every animal should give a definite impression of masculinity or feminity, according to its sex. Dogs should be definitely masculine in appearance and deportment; bitches unmistakably feminine without weakness of structure or apparent softness of temperament.

The condition of the dog should be that of an athlete in

good condition, the muscles and flesh firm and the coat lustrous.

The Shepherd is normally a dog with a double coat, the amount of under coat varying with the season of the year and the proportion of the time the dog spends out of doors. It should, however, always be present to a sufficient degree to keep out water, to insulate against temperature extremes, and as a protection against insects. The outer coat should be as dense as possible, hair straight, harsh and lying close to the body. A slightly wavy outer coat, often of wiry texture, is equally permissible. The head, including the inner ear, foreface and legs and paws are covered with short hair, and the neck with longer and thicker hair. The rear of fore and hind legs has somewhat longer hair extending to the pastern and hock respectively. Faults in coat include complete lack of any under coat, soft, silky or too long outer coat and curly or open coat.

STRUCTURE: A German Shepherd is a trotting dog and his structure has been developed to best meet the requirements of his work in herding. That is to say a long, effortless trot which shall cover the maximum amount of ground with the minimum number of steps, consistent with the size of the animal. The proper body proportion, firmness of back and muscles and the proper angulation of the fore and hind quarters serve this end. They enable the dog to propel itself forward by a long step of the hind quarter and to compensate for this stride by a long step of the fore quarter. The high withers, the firm back, the strong loin, the properly formed croup, even the tail as balance and rudder, all contribute to this same end.

PROPORTION: The German Shepherd Dog is properly longer than tall with the most desirable proportion as 10 to 8½. We have seen how the height is ascertained; the length is established by a dog standing naturally and four-square, measured on a horizontal line from the point of the prosternum, or breast bone, to the rear edge of the pelvis, the ischium tuberosity, commonly called the sitting bone.

ANGULATION: (a) *Fore quarter:* The shoulder blade should be long, laid on flat against the body with its rounded upper end in a vertical line above the elbow, and sloping well forward to the point where it joins the upper arm. The wither should be high and with shoulder blades meeting closely at the top and the upper arm set on at an angle approaching as nearly as possible a right angle. Such an angulation permits the maximum forward extension of the fore leg without binding or effort. Shoulder faults include too steep or straight a position of either blade or upper arm, too short a blade or upper arm, lack of sufficient angle between these two members, looseness through lack of firm ligamentaion and loaded shoulders with prominent pads of flesh or muscles on the outer side. Construction in which the whole shoulder assembly is pushed too far forward also restricts the stride and is faulty.

(b) *Hind quarter:* The angulation of the hind quarter also consists ideally of a series of sharp angles as far as the relation of the bones to each other is concerned, and the thighbone should parallel the shoulder blade while the stiflebone parallels the upper arm. The whole assembly of the thigh, viewed from the side, should be broad with both thigh and stifle well muscled and of proportionate length, forming as nearly as possible a right angle. The metacarpus (the unit between the hock joint and the foot commonly and erroneously called the hock) is strong, clean and short, the hock joint clean-cut and sharply defined.

HEAD: Clean-cut and strong, the head of the Shepherd is characterized by nobility. It should seem in proportion to the body and should not be clumsy, although a degree of coarseness of head, especially in dogs, is less of a fault than over-refinement. A round or domey skull is a fault. The muzzle is long and strong with the lips firmly fitted, and its top line is usually parallel with an imaginary elongation of the line of the forehead. Seen from the front, the forehead is only moderately arched and the skull slopes into the long wedge-shaped muzzle without abrupt stop. Jaws are strongly developed. Weak and too narrow underjaws, snipy muzzles and no stop are faults.

(a) *Ears:* The ears should be moderately pointed, open toward the front, and are carried erect when at attention, the ideal carriage being one in which the center lines of the ears, viewed from the front, are parallel to each other and perpendicular to the ground. Puppies usually do not permanently raise their ears until the fourth or sixth month, and sometimes not until later. Cropped and hanging ears are to be discarded. The well-placed and well-carried ear of a size in proportion to the skull materially adds to the general appearance of the Shepherd. Neither too large nor too small ears are desirable. Too much stress, however, should not be laid on perfection of carriage, if the ears are fully erect.

(b) *Eyes:* Of medium size, almond shaped, set a little obliquely and not protruding. The color as dark as possible. Eyes of lighter color are sometimes found and are not a serious fault if they harmonize with the general coloration, but a dark brown eye is always to be preferred. The expression should be keen, intelligent and composed.

(c) *Teeth:* The strong teeth, 42 in number—20 upper and 22 lower—are strongly developed and meet in a scissor grip in which part of the inner surface of the upper teeth meets and engages part of the outer surface of the lower teeth. This type of bite gives a more powerful grip than one in which the edges of the teeth meet directly, and is subject to less wear. The dog is overshot when the lower teeth fail to engage the inner surfaces of the upper teeth. This is a serious fault. The reverse condition—an undershot jaw—is a very serious fault. While missing premolars are frequently observed, complete dentition is decidedly to be preferred. So-called distemper teeth and discolored teeth are faults whose seriousness varies with the degree of departure from the desired white, sound coloring. Teeth broken by accident should not be severely penalized but worn teeth, especially the incisors, are often indicative of the lack of a proper scissor bite, although some allowance should be made for age.

NECK: The neck is strong and muscular, clean-cut and relatively long, proportionate in size to the head and without loose folds of skin. When the dog is at attention or excited the head is raised and the neck carried high, otherwise typical carriage of the head is forward rather than up and but little higher than the top of the shoulder, particularly in motion.

TOP LINE: (a) *Withers:* The withers should be higher than and sloping into the level back to enable a proper attachment of the shoulder blades.

(b) *Back:* The back should be straight and very strongly developed without sag or roach, the section from the wither to the croup being relatively short. (The desirable long proportion of the Shepherd Dog is not derived from a long back but from overall length with relation to height, which is achieved by breadth of fore quarter and hind quarter viewed from the side.)

(c) *Loin:* Viewed from the top, broad and strong, blending smoothly into the back without undue length between the last rib and the thigh, when viewed from the side.

(d) *Croup:* Should be long and gradually sloping. Too level or flat a croup prevents proper functioning of the hind quarter which must be able to reach well under the body. A steep croup also limits the action of the hind quarter.

(e) *Tail:* Bushy, with the last vertebra extended at least to the hock joint, and usually below. Set smoothly into the croup and low rather than high, at rest the tail hangs in a slight curve like a sabre. A slight hook—sometimes carried to one side—is faulty only to the extent that it mars general appearance. When the dog is excited or in motion, the curve is accentuated and the tail raised, but it should never be lifted beyond a line at right angles with the line of the back. Docked tails, or those which have been operated upon to prevent curling, disqualify. Tails too short, or with clumpy ends due to the ankylosis or growing together of the vertebrae, are serious faults.

BODY: The whole structure of the body gives an impression of depth and solidity without bulkiness.

(a) *Forechest:* Commencing at the prosternum, should be well-filled and carried well down between the legs with no sense of hollowness.

(b) *Chest:* Deep and capacious with ample room for lungs

and heart. Well carried forward, with the prosternum, or process of the breast bone, showing ahead of the shoulder when the dog is viewed from the side.

(c) *Ribs:* Should be well-sprung and long, neither barrel-shaped nor too flat, and carried down to a breast bone which reaches to the elbow. Correct ribbing allows the elbow to move back freely when the dog is at a trot, while too round a rib causes interference and throws the elbow out. Ribbing should be carried well back so that loin and flank are relatively short.

(d) *Abdomen:* Firmly held and not paunchy. The bottom line of the Shepherd is only moderately tucked up in flank, never like that of a Greyhound.

LEGS: (a) The bone of the legs should be straight, oval rather than round or flat and free from sponginess. Its development should be in proportion to the size of the dog and contribute to the overall impression of substance without grossness. Crooked leg bones and any malformation such as, for example, that caused by rickets, should be penalized.

(b) *Pastern:* Should be of medium length, strong and springy. Much more spring of pastern is desirable in the Shepherd Dog than in many other breeds as it contributes to the ease and elasticity of the trotting gait. The upright terrier pastern is definitely undesirable.

(c) *Metacarpus (The so-called "hock"):* Short, clean, sharply defined and of great strength. This is the fulcrum upon which much of the foreward movement of the dog depends. Cow hocks are a decided fault but before penalizing for cow hocks, it should be definitely determined, with the animal in motion, that the dog has this fault, since many dogs with exceptionally good hind quarter angulation occasionally stand so as to give the appearance of cowhockedness which is not actually present.

(d) *Feet:* Rather short, compact, with toes well-arched, pads thick and hard, nails short and strong. The feet are important to the working qualities of the dog. The ideal foot is extremely strong with good gripping power and plenty of depth of pad. The so-called cat-foot, or Terrier foot, is not desirable. The thin, spread or hare-foot is, however, still more undesirable.

PIGMENT: The German Shepherd Dog differs widely in color and all colors are permissible. Generally speaking, strong rich colors are to be preferred, with definite pigmentation and without the appearance of a washed-out color. White dogs are not desirable, and are to be disqualified if showing albino characteristics.

GAIT: (a) *General Impression:* The gait of the German Shepherd Dog is outreaching, elastic, seemingly without effort, smooth and rhythmic. At a walk it covers a great deal of ground, with long step of both hind and fore leg. At a trot, the dog covers still more ground and moves powerfully but easily with a beautiful coordination of back and limbs so that, in the best examples, the gait appears to be the steady motion of a well-lubricated machine. The feet travel close to the ground, and neither fore nor hind feet should lift high on either forward reach or backward push.

(b) The hind quarter delivers, through the back, a powerful forward thrust which slightly lifts the whole animal and drives the body forward. Reaching far under, and passing the imprint left by the front foot, the strong, arched hind foot takes hold of the ground; then hock, stifle and upper thigh come into play and sweep back, the stroke of the hind leg finishing with the foot still close to the ground in a smooth follow-through. The over-reach of the hind quarter usually necessitates one hind foot passing outside and the other hind foot passing inside the track of the forefeet and such action is not faulty unless the locomotion is crabwise with the dog's body sideways out of the normal straight line.

(c) In order to achieve ideal movement of this kind, there must be full muscular coordination throughout the structure with the action of muscles and ligaments positive, regular and accurate.

(d) *Back transmission:* The typical smooth, flowing gait of the Shepherd Dog cannot be maintained without great strength and firmness (which does not mean stiffness) of back. The whole effort of the hind quarter is transmitted to the fore quarter through the muscular and bony structure of the loin, back, and withers. At full trot, the back must remain firm and level without sway, roll, whip, or roach.

(e) To compensate for the forward motion imparted by the hind quarter, the shoulder should open to its full extent—the desirability of good shoulder angulation now becomes apparent—and the fore legs should reach out in a stride balancing that of the hind quarter. A steep shoulder will cause the dog either to stumble or to raise the forelegs very high in an effort to coordinate with the hind quarter, which is impossible when shoulder structure is faulty. A serious gait fault results when a dog moves too low in front, presenting an unlevel top-line with the wither lower than the hips.

(f) The Shepherd Dog does not track on widely separated parallel lines as does the terrier but brings the feet inward toward the middle line of the body when at trot in order to maintain balance. For this reason a dog, viewed from the front or rear when in motion will often seem to travel close. This is not a fault if the feet do not strike or cross, or if the knees or shoulders are not thrown out, but the feet and hocks should be parallel even if close together.

(g) The excellence of gait must also be evaluated by viewing from the side the effortless, properly coordinated covering of ground.

CHARACTER: As has been noted before, the Shepherd Dog is not one that fawns upon every new acquaintance. At the same time, it should be approachable, quietly standing its ground and showing confidence and a willingness to meet overtures without itself making them. It should be poised, but when the occasion demands, eager and alert, both fit and willing to serve in any capacity as companion, watchdog, blind leader, herding dog or guardian, whichever the circumstances may demand.

The Shepherd Dog must not be timid, shrinking behind its master or handler; nervous, looking about or upward with anxious expression or showing nervous reactions to strange sounds or sights, nor lackadaisical, sluggish or manifestly disinterested in what goes on about him. Lack of confidence under any surroundings is not typical of good character; cases of extreme timidity and nervous unbalance sometimes gives the dog an apparent, but totally unreal courage and it becomes a "fear biter," snapping not for any justifiable reason but because it is apprehensive of the approach of a stranger. This is a serious fault subject to heavy penalty.

In summary: It should never be forgotten that the ideal Shepherd is a working animal, which must have an incorruptible character combined with body and gait suitable for the arduous work which constitutes its primary purpose. All its qualities should be weighed in respect to their contribution to such work, and while no compromise should be permitted with regard to its working potentiality, the dog must nevertheless possess a high degree of beauty and nobility.

EVALUATION OF FAULTS: Note: Faults are important in the order of their group, as per group headings, irrespective of their position in each group.

DISQUALIFYING FAULTS: Albino characteristics; cropped ears; hanging ears (as in a hound) ; docked tails.

VERY SERIOUS FAULTS: Major faults of temperament; undershot lower jaw.

SERIOUS FAULTS: Faults of balance and proportion; poor gait, viewed either from front, rear or side; marked deficiency of substance (bone or body) ; bitchy male dogs; faulty backs; too level or too short croup; long and weak loin; very bad feet; ring tails; tails much too short; rickety condition; more than four missing premolars or any other missing teeth; unless due to accident; lack of nobility; badly washed-out color; badly overshot bite.

FAULTS: Doggy bitches; poorly carried ears; too fine heads; weak muzzles; improper muscular condition; faulty coat, other than temporary condition; badly affected teeth.

MINOR FAULTS: Too coarse heads; hooked tails; too light, round or protruding eyes; discolored teeth; condition of coat, due to season or keeping.

Disqualifications. White, if indicative of albino characteristics. Cropped ears, hanging ears. Docked tail.

GREAT DANE

THE GREAT DANE is a dog of unusual beauty. He has been called "statuesque"—a term which fits him perfectly, for he is of great size and dignity, and is cleanly made throughout. He has nobility of carriage to an unusual degree, and his dignity is not combined with aloofness, but with friendliness. Modern Great Danes range in height from 32 to 36 inches in males.

Because of his size and beauty, the Great Dane is a typical "estate dog." Yet he is one of the few large breeds which have been taken into the city apartment with equal success. This has been a hurdle which few of the larger dogs could negotiate. But the Great Dane, with his short coat, dignity, and easy-keeping qualities, has seemed to thrive in apartment houses about as well as on the large suburban estates.

Perhaps for this reason, one finds Great Dane kennels located in the heart of major cities to a larger extent than is true with most breeds.

Most authorities are agreed that the Great Dane is a descendant of the Molossian dog of Greco-Roman times. Others carry him back as far as 2200 B.C., believing the "tiger dog" of Egypt to be his ancestor.

The reasons for this are several. One is that dogs of immense size have been portrayed since 2200 B.C., and at least one type of these great dogs has been a heavy dog, but neither so heavy as the Mastiff, nor so light as the Greyhound. Another reason is that, wherever artists have tried to portray head anatomy of these dogs in detail, Great Dane type has always been shown.

One cannot, of course, state that a single breed has kept pure since 2200 B.C. But, since that time there has been a dominant type of dog which we can say resembles the Great Dane. Strains developed, and were mingled with other strains, and re-crossed. Strains were given various names. But through it all, a dominant, Dane-like type remained.

In the tombs of Beni-Hassan, the Egyptians left many drawings of their dogs. There are Greyhound types, and there are larger and heavier types. Some of these appear Dane-like, and they also appear to have been Harlequin. One, not a Harlequin, has a lighter body than the usual Dane, but his head structure is reasonably that of a Dane. These tombs date from 2200 to 2000 B.C.

The Cunobeline Coin, a Greek coin which some authorities place at 39 years before Christ and others earlier, is believed to show a Dane-like dog. The dog is immense, for a human is riding it. The ears are erect. The tail is longer than that of any modern dog. The hair is short. Several authorities have said that this is a Dane in every important particular.

Several Greek and Roman bas reliefs show dogs of Dane-like appearance, and one painting on an Athenian Hydria, dated about 400 B.C., shows a dog that conforms rather closely to eighteenth century portraits of Danes. There is also an ornamental Roman pavement which shows a Dane-like dog.

In medieval times there were a number of paintings which showed dogs of startling likeness to modern Danes. Gaston de Fois wrote his immortal *Livre du Chasse* about 1387, and a few years later an English nobleman translated the book and published it in England under his own name. Gaston had sometimes as many as 1000 dogs in his kennels. Probably about 1450, his book was profusely illustrated. Among the dogs shown were some called Alaunts. There can be no doubt that these are Great Danes. They are of large size, with heavy muzzles, cropped ears, and true Dane body. The difference between these dogs and Mastiffs is clearly shown.

Aldrovandus, in 1522, shows some dogs of fair type. But in 1580, Antonius Tempesta of Florence shows dogs of excellent Dane-like appearance. The difference between these Alaunts or Danes, and Mastiffs, is again clearly shown.

Again in 1686, Blome pictures Great Danes being used for boar hunting. Rydinger, about 1740, also shows Great Danes being used to hunt wild boars. In fact, in much of the medieval and later art, Great Danes, Alaunts, or boar hounds, are shown in hunting scenes. Almost always other breeds are shown also, so that a comparison is possible.

Meanwhile, Dalziel, an immortal British dog authority, and a man of great accuracy, pointed out that Great Danes were brought to England before the Norman conquest. Apparently the Saxons brought them in for use in boar hunting.

The breed apparently disappeared in later times in England. One reason given was the extraordinary ferocity of the breed. This appears to have been a characteristic of the Great Dane until quite recently, for Watson tells us that the breed was barred from the New York dog show for a time for this cause.

Another reason may have been that the wild boar and the giant wolf both disappeared fairly early in the British Isles. They could not withstand the onslaught of the increasing population, improved horses and hunting weapons, improved hunting dogs, and the restricted area of the islands.

Great Dane—Colorations vary; this one is tan or tawny.

The modern history of the Great Dane begins about 1800. The name Great Dane already had been established. Buffon describes the breed, and even gives measurements. His book, published in 1798, shows a drawing of "Le Grand Danois." However, Buffon's illustrator was a poor one, not only on Danes but on other breeds too, so that the dog looks less Danish than dogs of 300 years earlier.

Edwards, in his *Cynographia Britannica*, 1803, has a picture titled, "The Danish Dog." Two dogs are shown. Both are true Danes, with one of them being a Harlequin. In *The Sportsmen's Cabinet*, published the same year, the excellent animal artist, Reinagle, shows a dog which he calls a Great Dane, or Irish Greyhound. Reinagle believed the two breeds to be identical, but there is little of the Greyhound about this dog.

In 1807, a pair of "wild boar hounds," was imported from Hesse-Cassel for the Duchess of York. These were named Hannibal and Princess, and they were Great Danes much as we know them today.

At this point, we should discuss the origin of the name. The evidence given so far certainly proves that the dog, regardless of the name used, was known over all of Europe. He could not, however, have been, even if one throws out ancient history, a Danish dog.

The Germans, of course, claim the breed as their own. But neither could he have been of German origin. The Germans themselves disowned the name of German Boar Hound. They called the breed by various names. Or rather, they stated there were various strains, or varieties of the breed, called Boar Hound, Ulmer Dog, German Mastiff, Tiger Dog (for the Harlequins), etc.

Herr Gustav Lang of Stuttgart pointed out, about 1870, that no one could distinguish between these races of dogs. He, and others, decreed that all the other names were to be abolished, and that thereafter the breed would be known as the German Mastiff. The Germans then began to bring the breed to a perfection which gave it a world-wide popularity.

Despite this, the Germans could not make the name stick. The breed was not of German origin, and it was certainly not of Mastiff type. So the rest of the world stuck to just as illogical a name, the Great Dane. That is what it remains to this day.

Much argument has developed as to the size of dogs of the last century. Buffon's measurements would show dogs of 28 inches and weighing about 85 pounds. These were perhaps average figures, and some dogs probably equalled 31 inches. Richardson, in 1848, gave the size as 30 to 32 inches. Lang also reported that 36-inch dogs simply did not exist.

Francis Butler of New York imported a Great Dane from Germany in 1857 which was said to have been 37 inches at the shoulder. Later, the dog was taken to England where he was a sensation. Harrison Weir of the *Illustrated London News* drew an excellent picture of him which is still extant.

However, James Watson stated that the dog was only 34 inches tall. He added that, since the dog was "in a class by himself," so far as height was concerned, this was excellent proof that other Great Danes were nowhere near that size, either in England or America.

Another Dane, imported by a Chicagoan in 1891, was advertised as "the largest dog in the world." However, no actual height was given for this dog. So it can be said that, in general, dogs of the last century were from 28 to 31 inches at the shoulder. Only a few dogs, such as Butler's Prince, exceeded this.

During the years from 1850 to 1890, the Germans were busy perfecting the breed, about as they later did with the German Shepherd. The effects of this can be shown in England and America, where the breed developed along similar lines, and during a similar period.

Great Danes began to appear at British shows as early as 1877, though no classes were offered for them. In 1882, they were shown at Birmingham as Boarhounds, and in 1884 they were admitted to the Stud Book as Great Danes.

That same year, James Watson visited England and was amazed at the quality of the dogs he saw, and at their height. The following year, 1885, a Great Dane show was held at the Ranelagh Club grounds. Men from other breeds were brought in to measure the dogs. The largest—and one which had impressed Watson as the best he saw—was Cedric The Saxon, measuring $33\frac{1}{4}$ inches at the shoulder.

In America, Great Danes began to appear at the shows in 1880. However, in 1881, at a show in the American Institute Building in New York, the dogs were so bad tempered, started so many fights, and caused such a furor, that the show superintendent, a man named Lincoln, barred them thereafter. It was not until after his death, in 1887, that Danes were permitted to return to the shows.

The 1890 show had 34 entries, and before the next show, the German Mastiff, or Great Dane Club of America, was organized. A dog called Melac was the top winner. Two years later, the club changed its name to the Great Dane Club. A dog called Wenzel beat Melac that year in New York, but it was conceded that the best dog of the year was Major McKinley, an Indiana dog.

There are excellent photographs of the dogs of that period. Major McKinley, Thor H. Earl of Wurttemberg, and others, could win championships against modern American dogs. Moreover, entries at shows compared favorably with modern shows. There were 69 individual dogs at the New York show in 1898, judged by J. Blackburn Miller.

Meanwhile, in England in 1896, Mrs. Horsfall imported the famous Ch. Hannibal of Redgrave. He was the first in one of the greatest kennels in modern history. Hannibal is said to have been on the small side, but beauty, soundness, and absolute conformity to ideal type would have made him the sensation today that he was at that time.

It was in 1898 that Charles E. Tilford imported the famous Sandor vom Inn to the United States. Sandor

United States for many years, the Great Dane breed has prospered.

Description and Standards.

The description and standards, adopted by the Great Dane Club of America and approved by the American Kennel Club, follow.

SCALE OF POINTS:		Points
1. General Conformation		30
a. General Appearance	10	
b. Color and Markings	8	
c. Size	5	
d. Condition of Coat	4	
e. Substance	3	
2. Movement		28
a. Gait	10	
b. Rear End (Croup, Legs, Paws)	10	
c. Front End (Shoulders, Legs, Paws)	8	
3. Head		20
a. Head Conformation	12	
b. Teeth	4	
c. Eyes (nose and ears)	4	
4. Torso		20
a. Neck	6	
b. Loin and Back	6	
c. Chest	4	
d. Ribs and Brisket	4	
5. Tail		2
TOTAL		100

1. *General Conformation* .... 30 *points*

a. GENERAL APPEARANCE: 10 points—The Great Dane combines in its distinguished appearance, dignity, strength and elegance with great size and a powerful, well-formed, smoothly-muscled body. He is one of the giant breed, but is unique in that his general conformation must be so well-balanced that he never appears clumsy and is always a unit—the Apollo of dogs. He must be spirited and courageous—never timid. He is friendly and dependable. This physical and mental combination is the characteristic which gives the Great Dane the majesty possessed by no other breed. It is particularly true of this breed that there is an impression of great masculinity in dogs as compared to an impression of femininity in bitches. The male should appear more massive throughout than the bitch, with larger frame and heavier bone. In the ratio between length and height, the Great Dane should appear as square as possible. In bitches, a somewhat longer body is permissible. *Faults:* Lack of unity; timidity; bitchy dogs; poor musculature; poor bone development; out of condition; rickets; doggy bitches.

b. COLOR AND MARKINGS: 8 points (a) *Color*—Brindle Danes. Base color ranging from light golden yellow to deep golden yellow always brindled with strong black cross stripes. The more intensive the base color and the more intensive the brindling, the more attractive will be the color. Small white marks at the chest and toes are not desirable. *Faults:* Brindle with too dark a base color; silver-blue and grayish-blue base color; dull (faded) brindling; white tail tip.

(b) *Fawn Danes*. Golden yellow up to deep golden yellow color with a deep black mask. The golden deep yellow color must always be given the preference. Small white spots at the chest and toes are not desirable. *Faults:* Yellowish-gray, bluish-yellow, grayish-blue, dirty yellow color (drab color), lack of black mask.

(c) *Blue Danes:* The color must be a pure steel-blue as far as possible without any tinge of yellow, black or mouse gray. *Faults:* Any deviation from a pure steel-blue coloration.

(d) *Black Danes*. Glossy black. *Faults:* Yellow black, brown black or blue black. White markings, such as stripes on the chest, speckled chest and markings on the paws are permitted but not desirable.

Great Dane—Ch. Gretchen's Khan of Mountdania. (Owner: Gretchen Wyler, Mountdania Kennels.)

was the best Great Dane at the New York show that year, and he was never beaten. The best dogs which could be imported from Germany were brought in to go against Sandor, but he was invincible. Muss-Arnolt drew an excellent portrait of Sandor at less than two years of age. It shows him to have been a dog of wonderful soundness, and somewhat heavier in body than Hannibal of Redgrave.

Hannibal of Redgrave and Sandor vom Inn represented virtual perfection in Great Danes at a time when most of the great modern breeds were hardly well begun. Since their day, Great Dane type has not changed at all, and if there is any difference, it is chiefly one of size. The modern dogs do tend to be an inch or two above the Danes of the period before 1900.

One other thing should be mentioned about the dogs of 1900. Through some miracle of breeding which will never now be known, breeders had totally eliminated the bad tempers which had characterized the breed for centuries. It was only 20 years before, in 1880, when F. Adcock, the British sportsman owned Satan, a dog known far and wide as being a "perfect terror in temper." And it was only 19 years before that the breed had been barred from New York shows because of bad temper.

But the dogs of 1900, and those since, have been noted for their gentility. Fights among them are no more common than among other dogs, such as Spaniels. And many people state it is far easier to stop them from fighting than it is with other breeds.

Outstanding Great Danes in America during the intervening years have been too numerous to mention. Ever since the earliest days, the Americans have imported the best that could be bought in Germany. With this stock and blood native to Canada and the

(e) *Harlequin Danes.* Base color: pure white with black torn patches irregularly and well-distributed over the entire body; pure white neck preferred. The black patches should never be large enough to give the appearance of a blanket nor so small as to give a stippled or dappled effect. (Eligible but less desirable are a few small gray spots, also pointings where instead of a pure white base with black spots there is a white base with single black hairs showing through which tend to give a salt and pepper or dirty effect.) *Faults:* White base color with a few large spots; bluish-gray pointed background.

c. SIZE: 5 points—The male should be not less than 30 inches at the shoulders but it is preferable that he be 32 inches or more, providing he is well proportioned to his height. The female should not be less than 28 inches at the shoulder, but it is preferable that she be 30 inches or more, providing she is well proportioned to her height.

d. SUBSTANCE: 3 points—Substance is that sufficiency of bone and muscle which rounds out a balance with the frame. *Faults:* Lightweight whippety Danes; coarse, ungainly proportioned Danes; always there should be balance.

e. CONDITION OF COAT: 4 points—The coat should be very short and thick, smooth and glossy. *Faults:* Excessively long hair (stand-off coat); dull hair (indicating malnutrition, worms and negligent care.)

2. *Movement* .... 28 *points*

a. GAIT: 10 points—Long, easy, springy stride with no tossing or rolling of body. The back line should move smoothly, parallel to the ground. The gait of the Great Dane should denote strength and power. The rear legs should have drive. The forelegs should track smoothly and straight. The Dane should track in two parallel straight lines. *Faults:* Short steps. The rear quarters should not pitch. The forelegs should not have a hackney gait (forced or choppy stride). When moving rapidly the Great Dane should not pace for the reason that it causes excessive side-to-side rolling of the body and thus reduces endurance.

b. REAR END (Croup, Legs, Paws): 10 points—The croup must be full, slightly drooping and must continue imperceptibly to the tail root. Hind legs, the first thighs (from hip joint to knee) are broad and muscular. The second thighs (from knee to hock joint) are strong and long. Seen from the side, the angulation of the first thigh with the body, of the second thigh with the first thigh, and the pastern root with the second thigh should be very moderate, neither too straight nor too exaggerated. Seen from the rear, the hock joints appear to be perfectly straight, turned neither towards the inside nor towards the outside. *Faults:* A croup which is too straight; a croup which slopes downward too steeply; and too narrow a croup. Hind legs: soft, flabby, poorly muscled thighs; cowhocks which are the result of the hock joint turning inward and the hock and rear paws turning outward; barrel legs, the result of the hock joints being too far apart; steep rear. As seen from the side, a steep rear is the result of the angles of the rear legs forming almost a straight line; over-angulation is the result of exaggerated angles between the first and second thighs and the hocks and is very conducive to weakness. The rear legs should never be too long in proportion to the front legs.

Paws, round and turned neither towards the inside nor towards the outside. Toes short, highly arched and well closed. Nails short, strong and as dark as possible. *Faults:* Spreading toes (splay foot); bent, long toes (rabbit paws); toes turned towards the outside or towards the inside. Furthermore, the fifth toe on the hind legs appearing at a higher position and with wolf's claw or spur; excessively long nails; light colored nails.

c. FRONT END (Shoulders, Legs, Paws): 8 points—*Shoulders:* The shoulder blades must be strong and sloping and seen from the side; must form as nearly as possible a right angle in its articulation with the humerus (upper arm) to give a long stride. A line from the upper tip of the shoulder to the back of the elbow joint should be as nearly perpendicular as possible. Since all dogs lack a clavicle (collar bone) the ligaments and muscles holding the shoulder blade to the rib cage must

be well developed, firm and secure to prevent loose shoulders. *Faults:* Steep shoulders, which occur if the shoulder blade does not slope sufficiently; over angulation; loose shoulders which occur if the Dane is flabbily muscled, or if the elbow is turned toward the outside; loaded shoulders.

Forelegs: The upper arm should be strong and muscular. Seen from the side or front the strong lower arms run absolutely straight to the pastern joints. Seen from the front, the forelegs and the pastern roots should form perpendicular lines to the ground. Seen from the side, the pastern root should slope only very slightly forward. *Faults:* Elbows turned toward the inside or toward the outside, the former position caused mostly by too narrow or too shallow a chest, bringing the front legs too closely together and at the same time turning the entire lower part of the leg outward; the latter position causes the front legs to spread too far apart, with the pastern roots and paws usually turned inwards. Seen from the side, a considerable bend in the pastern towards the front indicates weakness and is in most cases connected with stretched and spread toes (splay foot); seen from the side a forward bow in the forearm (chair leg); an excessively knotty bulge in the front of the pastern joint.

Paws: Round and turned neither toward the inside nor toward the outside. Toes short, highly arched and well closed. Nails short, strong and as dark as possible. *Faults:* Spreading toes (splay foot), bent, long toes (rabbit paws); toes turned toward the outside or toward the inside; light colored nails.

3. *Head* .... 20 *points*

a. HEAD CONFORMATION: 12 points—Long, narrow distinguished, expressive, finely chiseled, especially the part below the eyes (which means that the skull plane under and to the inner point of the eye must slope without any bony protuberance in a pleasing line to the full square jaw), with strongly pronounced stop. The masculinity of the male is very pronounced in the expression and structure of head (this subtle difference should be evident in the dog's head through massive skull and depth of muzzle), the bitch's head may be more delicately formed. Seen from the side the forehead must be sharply set off from the bridge of the nose. The forehead and the bridge of the nose must be straight and parallel to one another. Seen from the front, the head should appear narrow, the bridge of the nose should be as broad as possible. The cheek muscles must show slightly but under no circumstances should they be too pronounced (cheeky). The muzzle part must have full flews and must be as blunt vertically as possible in the front; the angles of the lip must be quite pronounced. The front part of the head, from the tip of the nose up to the center of the stop should be as long as the rear part of the head from the center of the stop to the only slightly developed occiput. The head should be angular from all sides and should have definite flat planes and its dimensions should be absolutely in proportion to the general appearance of the Dane. *Faults:* Any deviation from

Great Dane—A pair of Harlequins. (Owner: Meistersinger Kennels, Fern Creek, Ky.)

the parallel planes of skull and foreface; too small a stop; a poorly defined stop or none at all; too narrow a nose bridge; the rear of the head spreading laterally in a wedgelike manner (wedge head): an excessively round upper head (apple head); excessively pronounced cheek musculature; pointed muzzle; loose lips hanging over the lower jaw (fluttering lips) which create an illusion of a full deep muzzle. The head should be rather shorter and distinguished than long and expressionless.

b. TEETH: 4 points—Strong, well developed and clean. The incisors of the lower jaw must touch very lightly the bottoms of the inner surface of the upper incisors (scissors bite). If the front teeth of both jaws bite on top of each other, they wear down too rapidly. *Faults:* Even bite; undershot and overshot; incisors out of line; black or brown teeth; missing teeth.

c. EYES: 4 points—Medium size, as dark as possible, with lively, intelligent expression, almond-shaped eyelids, well-developed eyebrows. *Faults:* Light-colored, piercing, amber colored, light blue to a watery blue, red or bleary eyes; eyes of different colors; eyes too far apart; mongolian eyes; eyes with pronounced haws; eyes with excessively drooping lower eyelids. In blue and black Danes, lighter eyes are permitted but are not desirable. In Harlequins, the eyes should be dark. Light colored eyes, two eyes of different color and wall-eyes are permitted but not desirable.

c1. NOSE (no points): The nose must be large and in the case of brindled and "single-colored" Danes, it must always be black. In Harlequins, the nose should be black; a black spotted nose is permitted; a pink colored nose is not desirable.

c2. EARS (no points): Ears should be high, set not too far apart, medium in size, of moderate thickness, drooping forward close to the cheek. Top line of folded ear should be about level with the skull. *Faults:* Hanging on the side as on a Foxhound. Cropped ears; high set; not set too far apart, well pointed but always in proportion to the shape of the head and carried uniformly erect.

4. *Torso* .... 20 *points*

a. NECK: 6 points—The neck should be firm and clean, high set, well arched, long, muscular and sinewy. From the chest to the head, it should be slightly tapering, beautifully formed, with well developed nape. *Faults:* Short, heavy neck, pendulous throat folds (dewlaps).

b. LOIN AND BACK: 6 points—The withers forms the highest part of the back which slopes downward slightly toward the loins, which are imperceptibly arched and strong. The back should be short and tensely set. The belly should be well shaped and tightly muscled, and with the rear part of the thorax, should swing in a pleasing curve (tuck-up). *Faults:* Receding back; sway back; camel or roach back; a back line which is too high at the rear, and excessively long back; poor tuck-up.

c. CHEST: 4 points—Chest deals with that part of the thorax (rib cage) in front of the shoulders and front legs. The chest should be quite broad, deep and well muscled. *Faults:* A narrow and poorly muscled chest; strong protruding sternum (pigeon breast).

d. RIBS AND BRISKET: 4 points—Deals with that part of the thorax back of the shoulders and front legs. Should be broad, with the ribs sprung well out from the spine and flattened at the side to allow proper movement of the shoulders extending down to the elbow joint. *Faults:* narrow (slab-sided) rib cage; round (barrel) rib cage; shallow rib cage not reaching the elbow joint.

5. *Tail* .... 2 *points*

Should start high and fairly broad, terminating slender and thin at the hock joint. At rest, the tail should fall straight. When excited or running, slightly curved (saber like). *Faults:* A too high, or too low set tail (tail set is governed by the slope of the croup); too long or too short a tail; tail bent too far over the back (ring tail); a tail which is curled; a twisted tail (sideways); a tail carried too high over the back (gay tail); a brush tail (hair too long on lower side). Cropping tails to desired length is forbidden.

FAULTS OF THE GREAT DANE

Disqualification Faults: Deaf Danes. Danes under minimum height. Without visible scrotum. Spayed bitches. Monorchids. White Danes without any black marks (albinos). Merles, a solid mouse-gray color or a mouse-gray base with black or white or both color spots or white base with mouse-gray spots. Harlequins and solid-colored Danes in which a large spot extends coat-like over the entire body so that only the legs, neck and the point of the tail are white. Brindle, Fawn Blue and Black Danes with white forehead line, white collars, high white stockings and white bellies. Danes with predominantly blue, gray, yellow or also brindled spots. Docked tails. Split noses.

The faults below are important according to their grouping (very serious, serious, minor) and not according to their sequence as placed in each grouping.

Very serious: Lack of unity. Poor bone development. Poor musculature. Lightweight whippety Danes. Rickets. Timidity. Bitchy dog. Sway back. Roach back. Cowhocks. Pitching gait. Short steps. Undershot teeth.

Serious: Out of condition. Coarseness. Any deviation from the standard on all coloration. Deviation from parallel planes of skull and foreface. Wedgehead. Poorly defined stop. Narrow nose bridge. Snipey muzzle. Any color but dark eyes in fawns and brindles. Mongolian eyes. Missing teeth. Overshot teeth. Heavy neck. Short neck. Dewlaps. Narrow chest. Narrow rib cage. Round rib cage. Shallow rib cage. Loose shoulders. Steep shoulders. Elbows turned inward. Chair legs (front). Knotty bulge in pastern joint (adult dog). Weak pastern roots. Receding back. Too long a back. Back high in rear. In harlequins, a pink nose. Poor tuckup (except in bitches that have been bred). Too straight croup. Too sloping croup. Too narrow croup. Over-angulation. Steep rear. Too long rear legs. Poorly muscled thighs. Barrel legs. Paws turned outward. Rabbit paws. Wolf's claw. Hackney gait.

Minor: Doggy bitches. Small white marks on chest and toes —Blues, Blacks, Brindles and Fawns. Few gray spots and pointings on Harlequins. In Harlequins, black spotted nose. White tipped tail except on Harlequins. Excessively long hair. Excessively dull hair. Apple head. Small top. Fluttering lips. Eyes too far apart. Drooping lower eyelids. Haws. Any color but dark eyes in Blacks, Blue and Harlequins. Discolored teeth. Even bite. Pigeon breast. Loaded shoulders. Elbows turned outward. Paws turned inward. Splay foot. Excessively long toe nails. Light nails (except in Harlequins). Low-set tail. Too long a tail. Too short a tail. Gay tail. Curled tail. Twisted tail. Brush tail.

GREAT PYRENEES

A MEMBER of the Mastiff family, this dog, once known as the Pyrenean Mastiff, most likely was brought into Europe from Asia Minor by two different routes—one by sea, accompanying the Phoenician traders from Cadiz to Spain, whence it became established in the Spanish Pyrenees, thence crossing later onto the French side of the Pyrenees; and one by land, marching westward with the Aryan hordes, leaving its kin in all the prominent mountain valleys of Europe. As a breed the Great Pyrenees thus dates back far into the centuries before Christ, its fossil remains being found in deposits of the Age of Bronze, 1800-1000 B.C.

Once in Europe, the Pyrenean Mastiff developed under climatic conditions similar to those of his native habitat and remained well isolated in the high mountainous areas until medieval times. By 1407 French writers told of the usefulness of these "Great Dogs of the Mountains" as guardians of the Chateau of Lourdes where they were regarded as regular assistant guards to the men on their daily rounds and where provision was made for them in the sentry boxes.

In 1675 they were adopted as the Royal Dog of France by Louis XIV, then the Dauphin, and subsequently became much sought after by the nobility. However, much of their life has been spent in giving useful and devoted service to their French and Spanish peasant shepherd masters, protecting the farms in winter, whence the affectionate term, "Mat Dog"; in summer, guarding the valuable flocks and herds entrusted to their care on the high mountain pasturages. "The Great Dogs of the Mountains" were used to patrol at night and give the alarm of approaching danger. Equipped with a spiked collar, they became such renowned enemies of the bears and wolves that roamed the mountains that they were called "Pyrenean Bearhounds" or "Pyrenean Wolfhounds" in some of the early writings. Highly intelligent and easy to train, they were even used for running contraband goods across mountain passes.

In 1662 Great Pyrenees dogs were carried to Newfoundland by Basque fishermen as companions and also to serve as guardians for the new settlements. Here it was that they became mated with the black Curly-coated Retriever, favorite breed of the English settlers, and, as a result of this mating, the Landseer Newfoundland was born.

In 1870 Pyrenean blood was fused with that of other large breeds akin to the St. Bernard to help bring back that noble dog after his numbers were so greatly depleted by distemper and avalanche.

In 1824 General Lafayette introduced the breed to America by sending over two males to his friend, J. S. Skinner, author of *The Dog and the Sportsman.* Lafayette recommended these dogs from personal experience as of inestimable value to wool-growers in all regions exposed to the depredations of wolves and sheep-killing dogs. From that date until 1931, only a few scattered specimens found their way to the United States. They came as pets, and were brought over by visitors to France who became enamored of the breed in its native land. But in 1931, the first breeding pair was brought in by Mr. and Mrs. Francis V. Crane, of Needham, Mass. to found their famous Basquaerie Kennels.

The original male was Urdos de Soum, who went on to become the first sire and first champion in the breed in America. The original bitch died, necessitating a second bitch importation in 1932. From the mating of Urdos de Soum with the bitch, Blanchette du Givre, came the first litter ever to be born in America, whelped on June 20, 1933. Not only were these kennels the introducers of this grand old breed to this country and the pioneers in promoting its development and spread in the United States, but they were over many years practically the sole importers of stock from Europe, bringing over some 50 specimens altogether, representative of all the best and most outstanding bloodlines of France, Belgium, and

Great Pyrenees—Ch. Brigadier Jerramagne LaRue, CDX, and Ch. Grenadier Alano Leo, C.D. (Owner: Philip and Twila Jones, Hemet, Calif.) Hank Babbitt photo.

Holland. The last importation from the Continent was a bitch, Norah de Bonnefont-Pyrenees, which was smuggled out of France into Italy in 1940 after the outbreak of war. She came to America on the last passage of a U.S. liner from Italy. Even her grandson carried on her blood at stud at Basquaerie.

Basquaerie Kennels not only served as the foundation kennels for the breed in America but exported many specimens to far-distant lands. Prior to World War II, American-bred puppies were shipped to Canada, Mexico, British Northwest Territories, Belgium, Porto Rico, and India. This latter shipment comprised a breeding pair consigned to the Maharajah of Jind. On December 25, 1939, they presented him with the first litter of Great Pyrenees ever to have been born in India. After World War II, Basquaerie Kennels sent a breeding pair to Holland where both attained their Dutch championships and produced puppies; also to England where the male puppy became an English champion, becoming the second imported representative of the breed ever to attain a coveted championship in that country. Cote de Neige Kennels exported puppies to Switzerland and to Venezuela; and La Colina Kennels also exported a puppy to South America. The breed thus continued to spread far afield.

The most famous dog imported by Basquaerie Kennels was the European Tri-International (French, Belgian, and Luxembourg) Champion, and later

American Champion, Estat d'Argeles of Basquaerie, judged the most perfect Great Pyrenees in France in 1936 when he was purchased and brought to America. Estat was responsible for stamping the fine broad type of bear-like Pyrenean head on his resulting descendants. A bronze model of him stands at the American Kennel Club as an example of the accepted standard of the breed.

The Great Pyrenees were accorded official recognition by the American Kennel Club in February, 1933. From that year dates the classes for the breed at all licensed dog shows. Breed registrations started with 13 in 1933, all of which were imported. The interest of the bench show fancy in the breed is reflected in the increasing number of breed entries each year in a growing number of shows.

There have been seven outstanding dogs which played an important part in establishing and popularizing the Great Pyrenees in this country:

Champion Urdos de Soum, Champion Aspe du Pic du Jer, Champion Basquaerie Gui de Noel, Champion Basquaerie Bichon, C.D., Champion K'Eros de Guerveur of Basquaerie, Champion Koranne of Basquaerie, C.D., and Champion Basquaerie Beau Estagel.

An important chapter that can be written about the service of this beautiful and noble breed for man concerns his work in World War II. In France, several specimens were trained and used in service with the Alpine Chasseurs and some met their death in this service of carrying messages and packs for the troops. In America, they were trained exclusively for pack work and were destined for use in an Alaskan campaign, had such become necessary.

Suited only for Arctic service because of their color, they were never trained for guard work because of being such a perfect target. Because of their size, density of coat, and color, they were rejected for Army work. However, on July 9, 1942, Mrs. Francis V. Crane, as secretary of the Great Pyrenees Club of America, cooperated with Harry I. Caesar in charge of procurement for Dogs for Defense in arranging for a trial unit of eight to be sent to Front Royal, Virginia, for training. These original eight dogs worked out so well that they were sent to Camp Rimini in the Rocky Mountains and calls came in for subsequent shipments, all to be sent to that camp. There they were used for pack work, the dogs being trained in tandem fashion in units of three in carrying a 60-lb. dismantled machinegun, pulling a toboggan loaded with Red Cross supplies, and carrying packs of up to 40 pounds of ammunition. The dogs in one unit alternated in these tasks and worked with one man.

The plea for 100 dogs for this training was far more than could be assembled. Fortunately, all ideas of an Alaskan campaign were abandoned and subsequently all dogs trained in this service came home in February 1943. However, a few of the earlier specimens did get out of the country and saw active service with units in the Aleutian Islands, in Labrador, and in Greenland. All dogs were returned with official Army discharges and honorable mention for meritorious service. About 25 Great Pyrenees reached training sites, a unit large enough to prove the value of these dogs in a highly specialized field of service.

It is as a loyal and devoted companion-guard for the country home that the Great Pyrenees actually excels and fits best into the scheme of life in the country of his adoption. Trustworthy in disposition, the Great Pyrenees is an ideal dog for children. They are, also, clean in their habits, quiet in the house, lithe in their movements, and easily kept in condition. Highly intelligent and easily trained, deeply devoted to home and family, not excessively heavy eaters or overly large in size or cumbersome, they make the ideal watchdog for the home. They do not require excessive amounts of exercise to keep in condition nor constant grooming to keep looking fit.

Description and Standards. The description and standards, adopted by the Great Pyrenees Club of America and approved by the American Kennel Club follow.

1. GENERAL APPEARANCE: A dog of immense size, great majesty, keen intelligence, and kindly expression; of unsurpassed beauty and a certain elegance, all white or principally white with markings of badger, grey, or varying shades of tan. In the rolling, ambling gait it shows unmistakably the purpose for which it has been bred, the strenuous work of guarding the flocks in all kinds of weather on the steep mountain slopes of the Pyrenees. Hence soundness is of the greatest importance and absolutely necessary for the proper fulfilment of his centuries' old task.

2. SIZE: The average height at the shoulder is 27 inches to 32 inches for dogs and 25 inches to 29 inches for bitches. The average length from shoulder blades to root of tail should be the same as the height in any given specimen. The average girth is 36 inches to 42 inches for dogs and 32 inches to 36 inches for bitches. The weight for dogs runs from 100 to 125 pounds and 90 to 115 pounds for bitches. A dog heavily boned; with close cupped feet: double dewclaws behind and single dewclaws in front.

3. HEAD: Large and wedge shaped, measuring 10 inches to 11 inches from dome to point of nose, with rounding crown, furrow only slightly developed with no apparent stop.

CHEEKS: Flat.

EARS: V- shaped, but rounded at the tips, of medium size, set parallel with the eyes, carried low and close to the head except when raised at attention.

EYES: Of medium size set slightly oblique, dark rich brown in color with close eyelids, well pigmented.

LIPS: Close fitting, edged with black.

DEWLAPS: Developed but little.

The head is in brief that of a brown bear, but with the ears falling down.

4. NECK: Short, stout, and strongly muscular.

5. BODY: Well-placed shoulders set obliquely, close to the body.

BACK AND LOIN: Well-coupled, straight and broad.

HAUNCHES: Fairly prominent.

RUMP: Sloping slightly.

RIBS: Flatsided.

CHEST: Deep.

TAIL: Of sufficient length to hang below the hocks, well plumed, carried low in repose, and curled high over the back "making the wheel" when alert.

6. COAT: Created to withstand severe weather, with heavy fine

Great Pyrenees—Puppies, eight weeks old. (Owner: Soleil Great
Pyrenees, Sterling, Kansas)

white under coat and long, flat, thick outer coat of coarser
hair, straight or slightly undulating.

7. QUALITIES: In addition to his age-old position in the
scheme of pastoral life as protector of the shepherd and his
flock the Great Pyrenees has been used for centuries as a guard
and watchdog on the large estates of his native France, and for
this he has proven ideal. He is as serious in play as he is in
work, adapting and molding himself to the moods, desires and
even the very life of his human companions, through fair
weather and foul, through leisure hours and hours fraught
with danger, responsibility, and extreme exertion; he is the
exemplification of gentleness and docility with those he knows,
of faithfulness and devotion for his master even to the point of
self-sacrifice; and of courage in the protection of the flock
placed in his care and of the ones he loves.

8. SCALE OF POINTS: *Points*

(a) HEAD: 25 points comprised as follows:
    Shape of skull 5
    Ears 5
    Eyes 5
    Muzzle 5
    Teeth 5

(b) General Conformation: 25 points comprised as follows:
    Neck 5
    Chest 5
    Back 5
    Loins 5
    Feet 5

(c) Coat: 10 points. (d) Size and Soundness: 25 points. (e)
Expression and General Appearance: 15 points. Total number
of points 100.

KOMONDOR

EUROPEAN AUTHORITIES on shepherd dogs say
that the Komondor (for which the plural is Komondorok) is the king of the world's shepherd dogs. They
say he "goes to work before he is trained instead of

afterward." But other writers on the breed, notably
some in America, say the Komondor is less a herd
dog than a guardian of the flock.

But all are agreed that the Komondor and the
Kuvasz are the oldest European canine breeds, allowing perhaps for a slight admixture of other breeds.

Tibet is frequently given as the real ancestral home
of the Komondor. Keller, Roda Roda, and others
believe that Tibetan dogs were used to strengthen
many other European breeds, both because of their
great size and their unusual working aptitudes.

Some say that the Komondor was brought into
Europe by the Magyar invasion, about a thousand
years ago. A few writers, however, state that the Huns
found Komondorok on the steppes of Russia, and
brought them along into Europe. These writers state
that the Komondor is a descendant of a shepherd dog
called the Aftscharka.

Whatever the truth of his origin, the Komondor
has been a distinct type of dog for at least a thousand
years. Shepherds in the Hortobagy area of Hungary,
in particular, appear to have kept the breed pure,
guarding the breed much as the individual dogs
guarded the flocks on the plains and slopes.

Almost from the day of its origin, the Ebtenyestok
Orzagos Egesulete, the most important registering
body in Hungary, has sponsored the breed, and has
opened its stud book to registrations.

The Germans, too, began to sponsor the breed,
using it both for sheep work and for police and
guard work. The famous German fancier, Baron
Zolten von Kenez, was a prime factor in the growth
of the breed in Germany. In 1922, the Komondor
Club of Munich was formed. The breed then spread
into Italy, Belgium, and Holland.

By 1935, a few Komondorok began to appear in
this country, coming chiefly from Germany. However,
a few came from Hungary, and at least one from
Italy. In November, 1937, the American Kennel Club
recognized the breed, and a standard was adopted for
it.

The dogs grow to immense size, with some of them
reaching 30 inches at the shoulder, and weighing in
excess of 100 pounds. Even so, they are believed to be
somewhat smaller than the dogs of a thousand years
ago. They are all white—other colors are barred.

In their native country—on the puszta—the coat
grows over the eyes, and is always long and heavily
matted. The sheep of the area are semi-wild, and the
matted wool of the Komondor is said to act as a dis-
guise.

As are many sheepdogs which spend their lives in
the open, and which are descendants of such dogs,
the Komondorok tend to be distrustful of strangers.
Yet they are loyal friends to those whom they know,
and they have charming dispositions. Thus, they
make ideal guard dogs about country estates and children.

The rise of the Nazis in Europe upset many breeding plans. The Komondor was included. Hitler was
well on his way before the breed was recognized in

this country, so that the Komondor did not get well established before World War II prevented the further importation of breeding stock. For a time thereafter a chaotic situation existed regarding stud books and registration papers.

This undoubtedly hurt the Komondor. But another factor probably has been his ragamuffin appearance. In order to make him attractive to American bench show exhibitors, it has been necessary to comb out the mats and dress the dog up. This, of course, tends slightly to alter his true appearance.

Among the early breeders in this country were Dr. Tibor de Cholnoky, Greenwich, Conn., and Robert H. Burdsell, New York City. For a time, Dr. Cholnoky and Gene Tunney, the onetime world's heavyweight boxing champion, were partners in the ownership of the famous Pannonia Pandur, one of the best known matrons in the Stud Book.

Description and Standards. The description and standards, as adopted by the American Kennel Club follow.

GENERAL APPEARANCE: The Komondor is characterized by imposing strength, courageous demeanor, and pleasing conformation. In general he is a big, muscular dog with plenty of bone and substance.

NATURE AND CHARACTERISTICS: As a house guard as well as a guardian of herds he is, when grown up, an earnest, courageous, and very faithful dog. The young dog, however, is just as playful as any other puppy. He is much devoted to his master and will defend him against attack by any stranger. On account of this trait he is not used for driving the herds, but only for guarding them. His special task is to protect the animals, and he lives during the greater part of the year in the open air without protection against strange dogs and all kinds of beasts of prey.

HEAD: The head of the Komondor is covered all over with long hair, and thus the head looks somewhat short, in comparison to the seemingly wide forehead. If the hair is smoothed it will be seen that the skull is somewhat arched if viewed from the side; the forehead is not wide, but appears, however, wider through the rich growth of hair. The stop is moderate, it is the starting point of the muzzle which is somewhat shorter than the length of the skull. The top line of the muzzle is straight and about parallel with the line of the top of the skull. The muzzle should be fairly square. The lips cover the teeth closely and are black. The muzzle is mostly covered by long hair. The edges of the muzzle are black or steel-blue grey. The jaws are powerful, and the teeth are level and close together evenly.

EARS: The ears are rather low set and hang along the side of the head. They are medium sized, and their surface is covered with long hair.

EYES: The eyes express fidelity. They are medium-sized and almond shaped, not too deeply set and surrounded by rough, unkempt hair. The iris of the eyes is of coffee or darker brown color, light color is not desirable. Blue-white eyes are disqualifying. The edges of the eyelids are slate-grey.

MUZZLE: In comparison to the length given in the head description, the muzzle is wide, coarse, and not pointed. The nostrils are wide. The color of the nose is black. Komondors with flesh-colored noses must absolutely be excluded from breeding. A slate-colored or dark brown nose is undesirable but may, however, be accepted for breeding purposes.

NECK: The neck is covered with long hair, is muscular, of

Komondor.

medium length, moderately arched. The head erect. No dewlap is allowed.

BODY: The body is characterized chiefly by the powerful, deep chest which is muscular and proportionately wide. The height at the top of shoulders is 23½ inches to 31½ inches, the higher, the better. The shoulders slope into the neck without apparent protrusion. The body is moderately long and level. Back and loins are wide. The rump is wide, muscular, moderately sloping towards the root of the tail. The body should be somewhat drawn up at the rear, but not greyhound-like.

TAIL: The tail is as a straight continuation of the rump-line, and reaches down to the hocks slightly curved upwards at its end. It is covered in its full length with long hair, which when the dog is at ease almost touches the ground. When the dog is excited the tail is raised up to the level of the back. The tail should not be docked. Komondorok born with short tails must be excluded even for breeding purposes.

FORELEGS: The forelegs should be straight, well boned, and muscular. Viewed from any side, the legs are like vertical columns. The upper arm joins the body closely, without loose elbows. The legs are covered all around by long, evenly hanging hair.

HIND QUARTERS AND LEGS: The steely, strong bone structure is covered with highly-developed muscles, and the legs are evenly covered with long hair, hanging down in matted clods. The legs should be straight as viewed from the rear. Stifles well bent. Dewclaws must be removed. The body and the legs should about form a rectangle.

FEET: The feet should be strong, rather large and with close, well arched toes. The hind feet are stronger, and all are covered with long hair. The nails are black or slate-grey. The pads are hard, elastic, and black.

COAT: The entire body of the Komondor is covered with a long, soft, woolly, dense hair, of different length on the different parts of the body, with inclination to entanglement and shagginess. If the dog is not taken care of, the hair becomes shaggy on the forelegs, chest, belly, rump and on the sides of the thigh and the tail. The longer and the more ragged, the better, though as above stated the length of the hair varies on the different parts of the body. The longer hair begins on the head and ears and lengthens gradually on the body, being longest on the thighs and the tail. A somewhat shorter, but still long hair is found on the legs, the muzzle and the cheeks. Too-curly hair is undesirable.

COLOR: The color of the hair is white. Any other color is disqualifying.

SIZE: The bigger the Komondor, the better, a minimum height of 25½ inches at top of shoulders for males and 23½ inches for females is required.

FAULTS: Light or flesh-colored nose, albino or blue eyes, highly set and small ears. Short, smooth hair, on the head and legs, strongly curled tail, color—other than white.

KUVASZ

PROBABLY THE best known of all the Hungarian and Balkan dogs is the Kuvasz (plural, Kuvaszok). This breed has been known in Europe for many more centuries than some readers might suppose. Whereas conventional breed histories tend to say "for nearly a thousand years," there is reason to conclude it might more accurately be stated as "for the past seven thousand years."

Until recently, the history of the Hungarian working breeds was mostly a subject of speculation, and their origins placed in vastly separated regions.

By contrast, consider the research and findings of the Hungarian-born kynologist, Sandor Palfalvy, M.D., member of the Alabama Academy of Science

Kuvasz—Ch. Hamralvi Demost Happy Fella. (Owner: Kuvasz Hamralvi Kennels—Dr. and Mrs. Z. M. Alvi, Beverly Hills, Calif.)

and a breeder of the Puli for 47 years—many of these years having been spent in research concerning the Puli history and that of the Hungarian people.

His research included a thorough study of the Sumerian, Sanskrit, Greek and Latin literature and, as well, excavated findings from the Tigris-Euphrates Valley. From these he found the names of the three breeds frequently mentioned in ancient literature, and reason to conclude that the Komondor, the Kuvasz, and the Puli were indeed domesticated and employed by Sumerian herdsmen as far back as seven to eight thousand years ago. These dogs accompanied herdsmen during their travels from Mesopotamia to the region of present-day Hungary.

The word "Kuvasz" is of Sumerian origin, not Turkish, as some have thought. The first letters "KU" are from an old Sumerian word for dog, "Kudda." Modern Hungarian has the word as "Kutya." Then there is another word important in the history of the Kuvasz, the word "Assa." meaning "horse," in Sumerian. Ku-Assa, therefore, means a dog that guarded and ran alongside horses and horsemen.

Step back in history to the year 2250 B.C., when the great Babylonian King Hammurabi inscribed a series of laws on a huge stone which can now be seen at the Louvre Museum in Paris. Included in this Code is mention of the three Hungarian breeds—Kuvasz, Komondor and Puli.

Then, at the site of Akkad in Northern Mesopotamia, a city of the 30th Century, B.C., there was found a clay board containing cuneiform writing and bearing the words KU-ASSA. This piece is now at the Asmolean Museum.

Back even farther, in the 35th Century, B.C., was the city called Ur, by the Euphrates River, also in Mesopotamia—a city mentioned in the Old Testament. Within its ruins two clay boards were found which listed the belongings of two families, Kuth and Bana. Along with a number of horses, cattle and sheep, the listing includes Pulik, Komondorok, and eight KU-ASSA owned by the Kuth family and two by Bana. These boards are at the British Museum, having been acquired through the work of Sir C. Leonard Wooley, archeologist, in a project sponsored by the British Academy of Science.

There are undoubtedly more references, another being from a clay tablet 7,000 years old found in 1931 during explorations of the ruins of the city of Ugarit, also in Mesopotamia, ruins dating back to 5,000 B.C. Under excavations directed by Sir H. J. McDonald, a clay tablet was found on which was inscribed in cuneiform writing the word KU-AS-SA. This tablet is displayed at the London British Museum.

Some have attempted to claim that the name "Kuvasz" is a corruption of the Turkish word "Kawasz," meaning a bodyguard. In some explanations this has even been amplified to mean "armed guard of nobility"! This, however, is a false trail to anyone checking historical facts re the Kuvasz.

You may, of course, look up the word "Kawasz" in Hutchinson's dog encyclopedia and see the following explanation: " 'Kawasz,' in Turkish the word means 'armed guardian of security of the European consuls and ambassadors dressed in an especially picturesque costume.' "

To summarize some salient facts then about the Kuvasz, here are several questions and answers, based on the convictions of those who have gone into the matter at some length.

Q. Is "Kuvasz" taken from a Turkish word?

A. No. It is of Sumerian origin.

Q. Did the Turks bring the Kuvasz breed to Hungary?

A. No; there is evidence that the Kuvasz existed in present-day Hungary for almost 500 years. As a matter of fact, quite likely the presence of the Kuvasz breed in Turkey resulted from some of these dogs being taken from Hungary to Turkey.

Q. Was the Kuvasz dog owned exclusively by royalty in Hungary?

A. No. The Kuvasz was a valuable working dog, badly needed and much used by those trying to eke out a living from the land—the herdsmen and the peasants. This does not mean, of course, that some of the royalty did not also own or keep dogs of the Kuvasz breed.

Q. Did the Kuvasz perhaps originate in Tibet?

A. No. It is more likely the Kuvasz was taken to Tibet from the Tigris-Euphrates Valley during mass migrations caused by the war-like Assyrians. He was also taken to China where Kuvasz dogs may be seen, bred pure white, light or dark brown, depending on the work expected of them. Those guarding livestock are white. Elsewhere, incidentally, some authorities have mentioned the Kuvasz as sometimes black. This is quite rare. At one time, perhaps even before World War II, there was a black Kuvasz at the London Zoo. He was listed as "black Kuvasz, a Tibetan dog." Black suddenly may appear in a litter very occasionally. The same happens with the Komondors, a black one of the latter having been owned in Canada, circa 1950.

A young pair of Kuvasz was brought to the U.S. in the late 1920's by a Hungarian couple who, in the trying circumstances of getting established in this country, found it necessary to part with the dogs. A Miss May E. Marsh of Madison, New Jersey (who later became Mrs. J. Scoffield Rowe), was fascinated with the majestic beauty of the Kuvasz and purchased the male. After much difficulty and expense, she succeeded in importing a bitch and soon became the owner of the first American-bred litter of Kuvaszok, thereupon establishing the Romanse Kennels. In 1934 the breed began to gain acceptance in the U.S. and was thereafter frequently exhibited, several dogs gaining championship ratings.

There is reason to believe that the Rowe's endeavored to form a Kuvasz Club sometime in late 1939 or in 1940, however records as to this are not available. In any case, the Romanse Kennels became inactive in the early 1940's following the death of Mr. Rowe.

In Europe during World War II, the number of Hungarian-owned Kuvaszok declined drastically. During the Revolution of 1956, their numbers likewise diminished. Since that period, however, Hungarian owners have bent every effort to restore quality to the breed.

In 1946, Rike Von Waldfried was imported from Germany by Mr. and Mrs. Frank Zeigler of Manchester, Pennsylvania, and paid for by food packages. This Kuvasz bitch was subsequently bred to Zeigler's dog, Dickens Von Leonardshof, and produced ten puppies.

These dogs were exhibited in such shows as Morris, Essex, and Madison Square Garden, as well as elsewhere, and a championship was won by Rike, thus making her eligible for registration with AKC. The names Dickens and Rike appear on many pedigrees of American-bred Kuvaszok. By the late 1950's, however, the Zeiglers had become inactive in breeding, though they continued to promote the breed until advanced age intervened.

It was not until relatively recently—January, 1966 —that new interest in the Kuvasz became evident in the U.S., this being marked by the appearance of the first issue of a Kuvasz Newsletter, and formation of The Kuvasz Club of America on 30 April, 1966, through the efforts of Dr. and Mrs. Z. M. Alvi of Beverly Hills, and other Californians.

Providing assistance in drafting a standard for the breed was Dr. Zoltan Balassy, one of the authors in the International Standards, an international judge of the Hungarian breeds, and President of the Hungarian Dog Breeders' National Association—Komondor and Kuvasz Division, of Budapest, Hungary.

Interest in the breed and the club continues to grow at a steady pace. More Kuvaszok are being exhibited right along, the club members confident

Kuvaszok—These dogs (referred to in the text) were once owned by Frank V. Zeigler of Manchester, Pa. The first dog (left) is Rike v. Waldfried, imported by Mr. Zeigler from Germany in 1946 and paid for by food packages.

that the magnificent Kuvasz is finally on his way to a secure and promising place in the U.S.

Incidentally, a male Kuvasz—Nagyhazi Betyar—was imported by Mr. Harry Tytle of Walt Disney Studios. This dog became the canine star of the film "101 Problems of Hercules."

What then is the nature of the Kuvasz, a rather large dog standing from 26 to 30 inches tall and weighing from 75 to 125 pounds at maturity, dependent, of course, on sex and individual variations, but invariably all white?

Wholeheartedly devoted and fantastically loyal to his owners, the magnificent Kuvasz quickly earns the respect and love of all those who allow him to share their lives. Possessing high intelligence, courage, fearlessness and ability to act on his own initiative, he is greatly valued as a guardian and protector, as he has ever been over the centuries.

The rugged Kuvasz adjusts to all climates and conditions. Whereas the young Kuvaszok are playful and stay clowns for a long time, the grown dog is usually quiet and dignified, barking only when warning is necessary. The Kuvasz will stand up to any foe. He is strong, willing, alert, and every ready to assume responsibilities. He is able to move with lightning speed if he senses there is a need.

His natural role is that of a guard-companion, whether of a home, of children, or through helping in the management or care of livestock. Given the chance, he seems to prefer the company of children, in which circumstances he is gentle, but ready and willing to play. When he plays, it is without displaying the uncontrollable frenzy sometimes seen in other dogs. Moments after a lively "wrestling about" with older children, the Kuvasz will quietly accept the liberties of a crawling infant. Still, it is important that parents educate small children in the care of their dog and teach them to recognize the animal's feelings

of pain and pleasure, for no dog should be treated with the same carelessness as a stuffed toy.

The Kuvasz is primarily a one-family dog. His big heart is given freely and completely to those he loves, returning to his masters undying fidelity for such affections as are tendered him. Taken away from his home—the family which he has accepted—the mature dog may have difficulty transferring his affection to others. Consequently, some have been known to die of heartbreak.

The Kuvasz treats strangers circumspectly, he will accept them for what they seem to be and be rather cool and aloof, yet he is polite enough to those he does accept. However, he makes friends cautiously. When he does accept someone as a friend, it is usually a lasting understanding so far as the Kuvasz is

Kuvasz—Ch. Hamralvi Amna Dea-Ari. (Owner: Kuvasz Hamralvi Kennels—Dr. and Mrs. Z. M. Alvi, Beverly Hills, Calif.)

concerned. To summarize, the nature of the Kuvasz is very well described in an old Hungarian proverb:

"The friend of his master is his friend—his master's enemy is his enemy."

The Kuvasz moves like a wolf. He shows much agility and freedom of movement. He is light-footed. His gait is powerful, outreaching, graceful and rhythmic. At a fast gallop, the Kuvasz glides along with minimal up and down body movement. Nature indeed has given him superior qualities of strength, speed, and the kind of free movement so indispensable to the working dog—all instantly apparent to anyone spending even a few moments studying him.

A sturdy, hardy fellow, the Kuvasz need not and should not be pampered. He may sleep indoors or outside; most likely he will prefer the outdoors. Where he sleeps in summer is of lesser importance, however with the onset of cold weather his sleeping quarters should be constant, either all-season inside a building, or all-season outside.

The Kuvasz's coat insulates him against heat and cold and should never be cut. It will grow to the thickness necessary to keep him warm, but frequent changes in temperature may cause unseasonal shedding.

A dog such as the Kuvasz should have considerable exercise, and his owner is well-advised to see that he gets it. If possible, he should also have some opportunity to run in areas open enough so that he can really stretch out and go now and then, as such exercise is beneficial and a welcome change from other routine.

This, perhaps, is as good a place as any to consider one of the fallacies sometimes entertained respecting the larger dogs. Some feel that the larger the dog, the greater the space should be for him to roam about or the property where he should be kept from the standpoint of his need for exercise, etc. Having much open space in which to run and exercise undoubtedly may be an advantage to any dog, yet this of itself will not insure that the dog has sufficient exercise.

Many readers undoubtedly have driven through rural areas—places where a dog would seem to have all kinds of space to run and exercise. How many times in such places does one actually see a dog doing that? Sad to say, the dog, if there is one, is probably asleep on the porch or in the yard—about as lazy, some farmers might say, as the hired man! Space alone, then, does not insure a dog's exercise. If there are children with whom the dog may play outdoors, then undoubtedly the dog will get some. But every dog owner should consider his dog's welfare and whatever the environment may be, insure that the dog gets regular exercise as part of his health program.

GROOMING

Observing the pristine whiteness of his coat, one is apt to presume that the Kuvasz needs frequent bathing and expensive grooming. This is not so.

The texture of his coat is such that it resists dirt and the coat is odorless except when wet. Rarely, however, does the Kuvasz need to be bathed, for frequent bathing throws out of balance the natural oil secretions of the dog's skin in any breed.

Just a few minutes attention a day is all that is required to keep him in presentable condition. The coat should be combed with a good quality pin brush, a treatment which most dogs enjoy. Give special attention to the areas behind the ears where the coat is extremely fine, the back of the thighs where the hair is long and very thick, and to the tail. Follow the pin-brush combing for a minute or so of brushing the coat with a pure boar-bristle brush.

The Kuvasz to be exhibited may require a bath a few days before the show—but certainly not the day before the exhibition. Bathing sometimes loosens the dog's hair and may cause excessive shedding. If so, this requires more time to repair its texture. A pine tar soap is inexpensive and does a good bathing job; do not use products intended for human hair when washing any dog.

In warm summer weather there is nothing wrong with bathing a dog outdoors simply through the use of a garden hose. Let him shake most of the water off, himself; you do not need to towel-dry him as he will dry within a short time anyway, but it may be well to walk him for a while on a leash to prevent him from rolling in the grass and getting dirty all over again. But in cold climates and in the wintertime, avoid bathing the dog.

For dog shows, the Kuvasz should be presented in a completely natural but immaculately clean condition. Except for possible straggly hairs on the hocks, his coat is never trimmed nor are his whiskers ever cut off. Long "eye-brows", if any, may be cut at about the half-way point, but only if they tend to curl into the dog's eyes and bother him.

If the dog has regular exercise on rough ground, there should be little problem with his nails or with accumulation of excessive hair at his feet.

Description and Standards. The description and standards, as drafted by the Kuvasz Club of America, follow.

GENERAL CHARACTERISTICS: The Kuvasz is a spirited dog of keen intelligence, determination, courage and curiosity. Very sensitive to praise and blame. Primarily a one-family dog, he is most devoted, gentle and patient without being overly demonstrative. He is ever ready to protect his loved ones, even to the point of self sacrifice. He manifests a particularly strong protective instinct towards children. Towards accepted strangers, however, he is polite but rather suspicious and very discriminating in making new friends. As a guard dog he is unexcelled, possessing ability to act on his own initiative at just the right moment without instruction. He is bold, courageous and fearless. He has good scent, and has been used to hunt large game.

GENERAL APPEARANCE: Being a working dog of the larger size, the Kuvasz is sturdily built and well balanced. A well proportioned white dog, neither lanky, nor cobby. Strong-boned, well-muscled, but not coarse. The slightly inclined croup indicates untiring working ability. The trunk and the limbs form a horizontal rectangle only slightly deviated from the square. He impresses the eye with strength and activity combined with light footedness. He moves freely on strong legs. Any tendency to weakness or lack of substance is a decided fault. Substance being the sufficiency of bone and muscle which creates a balance with the frame. In judging the Kuvasz, the first thing to consider is substance and movement. His hindquarters are particularly well developed to enable the dog to cover rough terrain and obstacles. Any sign of unsound hips, straight stifles or cowhocks should be severely penalized.

MOVEMENT: The movement of the Kuvasz is similar to that of a wolf. It is easy, free and elastic. At a slow walk the Kuvasz paces, i.e., he moves simultaneously both left legs, then both right legs. As the speed of motion increases, his gait becomes powerful, outreaching and rhythmic. Feet travel close to the ground. Hind legs reach far under, meeting, or even passing the imprints of the front legs. Moving towards an observer, the front legs do not travel parallel to each other, but rather close together *at* the ground. When viewed from the rear, the hind legs, from the hock joint down also move close *at* the ground. As speed increases, the legs gradually angle more inward until the pads are falling on a line directly under the longitudinal center of the body, almost single tracking. Unless excited, the head is carried rather low, about at the level of the shoulders. The Kuvasz is capable of trotting 15 to 18 miles without tiring. The desired movement can not be maintained without sufficient angulation and firm slimness of body.

HEIGHT: 28″ to 29½″ for dogs; 26″ to 27½″ for bitches.

WEIGHT: Dogs: 100 lbs. to 120 lbs. approximately; bitches: 75 lbs. to 95 lbs. approximately.

COLOR: White preferred. Ivory-white permissible.

HEAD: The most beautiful part of the Kuvasz. Its proportions are of great importance. The length of the head is 45% of the height of dog at withers. The width of the head is: one-half of the length; 5½″ to 6½″ for dogs, 5″ to 6″ for bitches. The skull is elongated but not pointed. The forehead is long, slightly domed—35° to 40° above the plane of the muzzle. The longitudinal midline of the forehead is pronounced; it widens as it comes down to the top of the muzzle. The stop is not defined. Cheeks flat.

EARS: Medium-sized; V-shaped. Set well back, about half-way between the parallel of the eyes and top of head. Standing slightly away from the head in upper third, then lie close to the head. In alert position should not protrude above the head. Length of ears is about 50% of the length of the head.

EYES: Almond-shaped. Set wide apart, 20 degrees below the plane of the muzzle, somewhat slanted. Dark-brown in color— the darker the better. Should not show any haw. Lids tight.

MUZZLE: The length of muzzle is 40% to 42% of the length of head. 4½″ to 5½″ for dogs, 4″ to 5″ for bitches. The top of muzzle is straight. It is not pointed. The horizontal plane of the bottom of the muzzle falls on the horizontal plane of the back (coat separated). Inside of mouth preferably black. Tongue and gums deep pink.

NOSE: Blunt, black, nostrils well open.

LIPS: Black and not pendulous, closely covering the teeth.

BITE: Scissor bite preferred. Level bite acceptable. Teeth set close together. Jaws powerful.

NECK: Muscular, without dewlap. It is of medium length, but rather on the short side.

FOREQUARTERS: Chest deep but medium wide. Shoulders muscular. In order to permit a maximum forward extension of the forelegs, the scapula and the humerus form a 90° angle. The legs have strong bone, are perfectly straight and well muscled. Elbows neither in, nor out. While standing, the pasterns are at not less than 75° to the horizontal. When viewed from the side, the chest bone protrudes slightly in front of shoulders. The joints are dry, hard. The stand is medium wide.

BODY: The withers are rather long and definitely elevated over the level of the back. The back is of medium length, straight, firm and quite broad. The loin is short and tight. The croup slightly sloping, well muscled, wide. (A heavy coat often makes the croup appear overdeveloped.) The stomach well tucked up.

HINDQUARTERS: Well angulated. The thigh broad and muscular. The metatarsus broad and of great strength as much of the forward drive depends on it. No dewclaws.

FEET: Well padded; pads resilient, black or slate-gray. Feet closed tight forming round "cat feet." The hind paws somewhat longer. Some hair between the toes; the less the better. Dark nails preferred.

TAIL: Set low, Natural length, reaching down at least to the hocks. In repose it hangs down resting on the body, the end but slightly lifted. Ideally, there should not be much difference in the carriage of the tail in state of excitement or in repose. In state of excitement the upper two-thirds of the tail may be elevated to the level of the loin, but no higher. The lower one-third portion may subsequently be raised slightly above the loin.

SKIN: The skin is heavily pigmented. The more slate-gray or black pigmentation, the better.

COAT: The coat of the Kuvasz ranges from quite wavy to straight, but is not too curly. Generally medium-coarse in texture, it will not mat or cord. At the base of the coarser guard hair, there is a fine under coat. The neck has a mane which extends to and covers the chest. Distribution of the coat over the body follows a definite pattern regardless of type. The head, muzzle, ears and paws are covered with short, straight, smooth coat. The coat on the front side of the forelegs up to the elbows and the hind legs below the thighs, is also short and smooth. The backs of front legs are feathered to pasterns with about 2″ to 3″ long hair. The body and sides of thighs are covered with a coat of medium length. The entire tail and back of thighs are covered abundantly by about 4″ to 6″ long hair. The hair on the lower surface of the tail is the longest.

It is natural for the Kuvasz to lose most of the long coat during hot summer months. "Summer coat" should not be penalized. Full, luscious coat comes in by the end of October or in November, depending of regional climatic differences.

FAULTS: Any deviation from the standard. Upper two-thirds of tail carried above the level of the loin. Light eyes. Short, thick muzzle; muzzle too long and narrow. Splay feet. Weak pasterns. Out at elbows. Too long in back. Sway or roach-back. Weak rear assembly. Straight stifles. Lifting of front feet in hackney-like action at the cost of lost energy and speed. Underdeveloped bony arches of the eyes. Pronounced stop. Drooping eyelids. Pendant, loose flews. Ears set too close to the head, too high or too low on the head. Ears casted backwards. Long neck. Too-wide chest. Loose or straight shoulders. Skin lacking pigmentation. Yellowish color on coat, or spot of such color. Loose composition. Overweight. The seriousness of these faults should be determined by the extent to which the deviation would affect the working ability of the dog. Scars on body resulting from work should not penalize the dog in the show ring, unless they interfere with free movement, or utility for work.

Disqualifying Faults. Curled up tail—in repose or in excitement. Undershot bite. Strongly overshot bite. Overly pronounced stop. Matting or cording tendency of the coat. Wiry coat. Massive broad head accompanied by a short heavy muzzle with pendant, drooling flews. Dogs smaller than: 26″; bitches smaller than: 24″.

MASTIFF

PROBABLY MORE confusion exists about the origin of the famous breed known as the Mastiff than most any other. This arises out of the fact that in other centuries the term "mastiff" seems to have represented any very large dog of mongrel origin. At still other periods, size may not have been involved in the term, it then carrying merely the significance of "mongrel house dog."

At the same time, some authorities claim that at least four strains of Mastiff were kept pure-bred for 400 years. Our modern dogs are supposed to descend from these strains, one of which was kept at Lyme Hall from the time of the battle of Agincourt, Oct. 25, 1415. This would also mean that a pure-bred dog existed side by side with mongrels called Mastiffs for 400 years.

Other researchers believe the Mastiff to be a basic type of dog, which has maintained itself, despite occasional cross-breeding, since at least 2200 B.C. A bas relief of this period shows a dog of Mastiff type, according to these researchers.

The Assyrians had a habit of burying terra cotta dogs under their doorsteps to scare away evil spirits. Many of these, dating from the time of Assurbanipal, have been found. Researchers see in these a direct resemblance to the present-day Mastiff.

Still other writers consider that the Mastiff actually had his origin in Tibet, spreading from there to Persia, Assyria, Babylonia, Egypt, and finally into Greece. This would make the more or less legendary Tibetan Mastiff the ancestor of the present dog.

Probably about 400 B.C., an unknown Greek sculptor made a statue of a dog called Molossus, belonging to Olympias, daughter of King Pyrrhus. This dog is recognizable as a type common in Greece, Assyria, and to some extent in Egypt. It was sometimes called the Molossian dog, and it is supposed to be the direct ancestor of the Mastiff. According to this theory, the Great Dane is a cross between the Greyhound and the Mastiff.

But other writers have sternly rejected this origin for the Mastiff and Great Dane. According to them, the Mastiff is really a parent English type which spread about the world, perhaps via Phoenician shipping. One early writer states that Imperial Rome maintained a "Procurator Cynegii" at Winchester. It was this man's job to buy dogs for use in the Roman armies and in the Roman arenas.

By 1400, bull and bear baiting had become common in England. In the time of Henry VIII, it

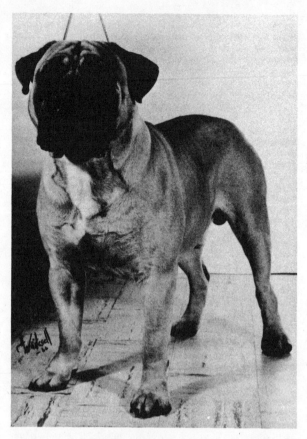

Bullmastiff—for comparison.

was so popular that he appointed a "Master of the Royal Game of Bears and Mastiff Dogs."

Caius, in 1570, in his *Treatise on English Dogges,* mentions three kinds of dogs, the Bandogge, Tydogge, and Mastyne. The three were closely related, and apparently all were used in some kind of baiting sport. The Bulldog is supposed to descend from the Bandogge. According to Caius, the Mastyne was so-called because of the fatness of his body.

In 1600, Camden gives a description of Paris Garden, which was near St. Thomas Hospital. ". . . a place like a theatre for baiting bears and bulls with dogs and kennels of bandogs, which are so strong and bite so hard that three of them are enough to seize a bear, and four a lion."

Many writers believe this bandog was the ancestor of both the Bulldog and the Mastiff. They quote repeatedly the formula that three Mastiffs will kill a bear, and four a lion.

Watson, the great American dog authority of the 1900's, made a careful study of the Mastiff. He was inclined to throw out all of the heroic tales about the Mastiff in favor of the theory that he was merely one form of the smooth-coated Collie.

He points out that in the *Four Bookes of Husbandry,* published in 1586, two types of farm dogs were listed, the "Shepherd's Masty," and the "House Masty." He conceives that the latter was merely an

Mastiff—Ch. Adonis of Sparry. (Owner: Mr. Dan Ostrow, Silver Spring, Md.) Photo by Evelyn M. Shafer.

overly-heavy shepherd dog, used chiefly for guarding property.

In 1871, Richardson decided that the Mastiff was a mixture of Bulldog and Talbot Hound. Ash, a modern authority, apparently believes that the Mastiff belongs to a basic type, which also includes the Bulldog, Pug, and St. Bernard.

Whatever the truth of this may be, there is little doubt that the British developed during the eighteenth century, a huge dog which could be recognized as a true breed. Some of these dogs were 32 and 33 inches at the shoulder, and they had correspondingly heavy bodies. Probably they were the largest dogs in the world at that time. These dogs were called Mastiffs, and there certainly were pure-bred strains of them.

But then, as the nineteenth century began, bull and bear baiting were outlawed forever in England. Almost immediately the huge Mastiffs began to decline. There was no use for such a breed any longer, particularly those among the breed which were ferocious. In the next 30 years, the breed almost disappeared.

By 1830, British sportsmen began to be alarmed about the situation. A concerted effort was made to save the breed. John Crabtree, a gamekeeper for Sir George Armitage, began to breed Mastiffs to serve as gamekeepers' dogs.

T. H. V. Lukey bred the famous Wallace which died in 1840. Lukey introduced the so-called Alpine Mastiffs into his strain. And he also used some stock which he had secured from America. One of his dogs, Governor, born in 1861, was considered the finest Mastiff of his time.

The modern Mastiff is subject to many faults of unsoundness. Students of the breed blame this on Ch. Crown Prince, bred by a Mr. Woolmore, and born in 1880. Crown Prince won a great show victory. He differed in face from other Mastiffs of the time, being of huge skull and short foreface, but in any case he won.

Thereafter, it became the rage to breed to Ch. Crown Prince. Jealous breeders said the dog was straight in stifle, low and too short in body, and a poor mover. He was also said to be of unpleasant color, and to have had an ugly "Dudley," or mottled face. His paternity also was questioned.

Despite this supposedly bad influence, the breed actually did continue to improve. In 1883, the Old English Mastiff Club was formed. Early members of this club were Dr. J. Sidney Turner, W. K. Taunton, Rev. W. J. Mellor, and Dr. Forbes Winslow. Their standard for the breed is very close to the present one.

During World War I, the breed almost disappeared again. This was due partly to lack of sufficient food for such large animals, and partly to the ending of that period of gracious and opulent living which, in England, stopped with World War I. But once again, English fanciers came to the rescue of the breed.

In North America, Mastiffs, or so-called Mastiffs, have been known since earliest times. Columbus reported he saw dogs like Mastiffs on the Florida island of St. Mary. Again, early writers quote a passage from Sir Walter Raleigh which cannot now be found. According to this, the English soldiers cooked up their Mastiffs to ward off starvation.

From then on, there are occasional references to Mastiffs throughout American literature. The dogs were usually imports, and very little effort was made to place the breed on a firm foundation here.

Then in the period between the two World Wars, some of the best British stock was imported to this country. Included were some of the dogs from the famous Hellingly Kennel of England. The Mastiff Club of America was formed, and the present breed standard was approved by the American Kennel Club, July 8, 1941.

Description and Standards. The description and standards as adopted by the Mastiff Club of America, Inc., and approved by the American Kennel Club follow.

GENERAL CHARACTER AND SYMMETRY: Large, massive, symmetrical and well-knit frame. A combination of grandeur and good nature, courage and docility.

GENERAL DESCRIPTION OF HEAD: In general outline giving a massive appearance when viewed from any angle. Breadth greatly to be desired.

SKULL: Broad and somewhat rounded between the ears, forehead slightly curved, showing marked wrinkles which are particularly distinctive when at attention. Brows (superciliary ridges) moderately raised. Muscles of the temples well developed, those of the cheeks extremely powerful. Arch across the skull a flattened curve with a furrow up to the center of the forehead. This extends from between the eyes to halfway up the skull.

EARS: Small, V-shaped, rounded at the tips. Leather moderately thin, set widely apart at the highest points on the sides of the skull continuing the outline across the summit. They should lie close to the cheeks when in repose. Ears dark in color, the blacker the better, conforming to the color of the muzzle.

EYES: Set wide apart, medium in size, never too prominent. Expression alert but kindly. The stop between the eyes well marked but not too abrupt. Color of eyes brown, the darker the better and showing no haw.

FACE AND MUZZLE: Short, broad under the eyes and running nearly equal in width to the end of the nose. Truncated, i.e., blunt and cut off square, thus forming a right angle with the upper line of the face. Of great depth from the point of the nose to under jaw. Under jaw broad to the end and slightly rounded. Canine teeth healthy, powerful and wide apart. Scissor bite preferred but a moderately undershot jaw permissible providing the teeth are not visible when the mouth is closed. Lips diverging at obtuse angles with the septum and sufficiently pendulous so as to show a modified square profile. Nose broad and always dark in color, the blacker the better, with spread flat nostrils (not pointed or turned up) in profile. Muzzle dark in color, the blacker the better. Muzzle should be half the length of the skull, thus dividing the head into three parts—one for the foreface and two for the skull. In other words, the distance from tip of nose to stop is equal to one-half the distance between the stop and the occiput. Circumference of muzzle (measured midway between the eyes and nose) to that of the head (measured before the ears) as 3 is to 5.

NECK: Powerful and very muscular, slightly arched, and of medium length. The neck gradually increases in circumference as it approaches the shoulder. Neck moderately "dry" (not showing an excess of loose skin).

CHEST AND FLANKS: Wide, deep, rounded and well let down

between the forelegs extending at least to the elbow. Forechest should be deep and well defined. Ribs extremely well rounded. False ribs deep and well set back. There should be a reasonable, but not exaggerated, cut-up.

SHOULDER AND ARMS: Slightly sloping, heavy and muscular. No tendency to looseness of shoulders.

FORELEGS AND FEET: Legs straight, strong and set wide apart, heavy boned. Elbows parallel to body. Feet heavy, round and compact with well-arched toes. Pasterns strong and bent only slightly. Black nails preferred.

HIND LEGS: Hind quarters broad, wide and muscular. Second thighs well developed, hocks set back, wide apart and parallel when viewed from the rear.

BACK AND LOINS: Back muscular, powerful and straight. Loins wide and muscular, slightly rounded over the rump.

TAIL: Set on moderately high and reaching to the hocks or a little below. Wide at the root, tapering to the end, hanging straight in repose, forming a slight curve but never over the back when dog is in action.

COAT: Outer coat moderately coarse. Under coat, dense, short and close lying.

COLOR: Apricot, silver fawn or dark fawn-brindle. Fawn-brindle should have fawn as a background color which should be completely covered with very dark stripes. In any case muzzle, ears and nose must be dark in color, the blacker the better, with similar color tone around the orbits, extending upwards between them.

SIZE: Dogs—minimum 30 inches at the shoulder, bitches—minimum 27½ inches at the shoulder.

SCALE OF POINTS:	Points
General character and symmetry	10
Height and substance	10
Skull	10
Face and muzzle	12
Ears	5
Eyes	5
Chest and ribs	10
Forelegs and feet	10
Back, loins and flanks	10
Hind legs and feet	10
Tail	3
Coat and color	5
TOTAL	100

NEWFOUNDLAND

A LONG AND romantic history has been built up around the Newfoundland dog, but in truth, most of it is pure conjecture. The most likely story is that the modern Newfoundland is the result of a cross between native Newfoundland dogs, or wolves, and ships' dogs; with the resultant strains purified and beautified in England.

Early writers do not mention any dog as being found on the island. This omission hardly seems possible if a dog of the size and striking individuality of the Newfoundland was in existence there.

Moreover, if today there are any dogs of this breed on the island, they are descendents of dogs bred in England. This is explained by saying that the demand for the dogs had caused all of them to be exported from Newfoundland to England and other European countries.

In his *Discourse and Discovery of Newfound Land with the reason for a Plantation,* Capt. Richard Whitbourne gives no indication that there were any

kind of dogs on the island. But he does report that his "Mastiffe-dogge" mingled with the wolves on a number of occasions, and was gone nine or ten days on each.

The question immediately arises, could this Mastiff have mated with the wolves to produce the huge Newfoundland dogs? Whitbourne visited Newfoundland in 1615. Other ships' dogs may have mated with wolves, native dogs, or crosses between wolves and Whitbourne's Mastiff, to have produced the breed.

Whatever the truth of this conjecture, the earliest pictures of the Newfoundland show him to have possessed many of the characteristics of the Arctic dogs. The Arctic dogs themselves look suspiciously like wolves, and some of them, like the Arctic wolves, reach a weight well over 100 pounds.

As for these ships' dogs, it has been suggested that they were Abruzzi sheepdogs, or Great Pyrenees. But there actually is no real evidence to support such a claim.

For example, some assert that in 1662 Great Pyrenees dogs were carried to Newfoundland by Basque fishermen to serve as companions and guardians of the new settlements. These dogs then mated with black curly-coated retrievers, these last said to have been a favorite breed with the English settlers. From such matings, the Landseer Newfoundland (any Newfoundland not entirely all black) came about. The origin of the Newfoundland dog still remains a hazy question, but there is no doubt that dogs of a distinctive breed did originate there. It remained, however, for breeders in England later on to refine the breed to size and appearance as seen today.

Lieut. Col. Hamilton, an experienced dog investigator, visited Newfoundland about 1830. He reported that the true Newfoundland dog was black and tan. Also, the Newfoundland at that time did not equal the huge height of present-day dogs. A height of 26 to 27 inches seems to have been normal.

The greater size came in England. The reasons for this would appear to have been better care, a better climate, and the English genius for developing the type of dogs they desired in a very few generations.

Watson, the very hard-headed American authority, made a careful investigation of the Newfoundland. He is more circumspect in his chapter, but in his "Contents" he says: "A Modern English Development from a Mixed Lot of Common Dogs of Various Colours, Coats, and Sizes."

It is probable that we can accept this statement of Watson, and certainly without prejudice to a very noble animal. For the breed has spread over a large portion of the world strictly on the basis of his good looks and his undoubted merits.

At first, the British fancied an all-black dog. Then Sir Edwin Landseer painted a black and white Newfoundland. This color became the rage in England. But the blacks have predominated in the United States, with the so-called Landseer type somewhat less common.

Watson points out that the Newfoundland was a

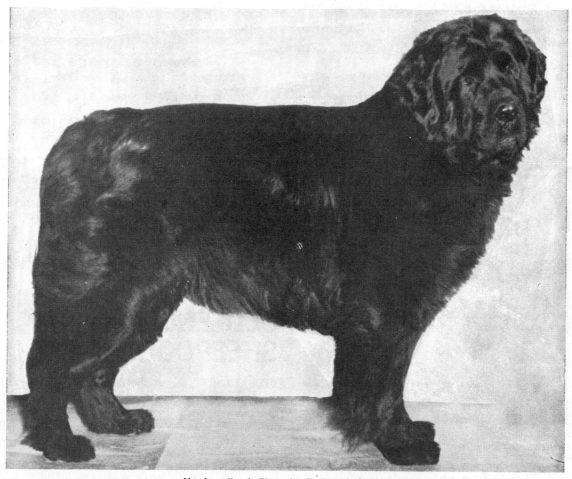

Newfoundland. Photo by Evelyn M. Shafer.

superb water dog. As a result, all large water dogs were called Newfoundlands. He considered that Landseer was merely painting a large water dog, calling it a Newfoundland since, as he says, Landseer's dog is not distinguished by Newfoundland type.

Edward C. Ash quotes many articles and letters from British authorities to show the dog's superior ability in the water. These tell of the dogs being used to rescue objects—and humans—which fell into the water from ships or docks.

In 1929, life-saving trials for Newfoundlands actually were started in England by a Mr. Keeling at Studley Castle. Though successful they were not continued.

Few Newfoundlands were seen in the United States until after World War I. Watson mentions one, which he considered of exceptional quality. It was called Mayor of Bingley, and was brought to this country by a Mr. Mason in 1881. Two later imports which he considered first class were Captain and Black Boy.

The breed suffered in England during both World Wars. But it began a resurgence in America about 1935, and has continued to improve despite World War II. The dogs being shown today are of good type, excellent soundness, and unusually sweet dispositions. They still carry their inherent love of water. Both blacks and black and whites are being shown.

Description and Standards. The description and standards, by courtesy of the Newfoundland Club of America, follow.

SYMMETRY AND GENERAL APPEARANCE: The dog should impress the eye with strength and great activity. He should move freely on his legs with the body swung loosely between them, so that a slight roll in gait should not be objectionable; but at the same time a weak or hollow back, slackness of the loins or cowhocks should be a decided fault.

HEAD: Should be broad and massive, the occipital bone well developed, there should be no decided stop, and the muzzle should be short, clean cut and rather square in shape, and covered with short, fine hair.

COAT: Should be flat and dense, of a coarsish texture and oily nature, and capable of resisting the water. If brushed the wrong way it should fall back into its place naturally.

BODY: Should be well ribbed up with a broad back. A neck, strong, well set on to the shoulders and back, with strong muscular loins.

FORELEGS: Should be perfectly straight, well covered with muscle, elbows in but well let down and feathered all down.

HIND QUARTERS AND LEGS: Should be very strong; the legs should have great freedom of action, and a little feather. Slackness of loins and cowhock are a great defect; dewclaws are objectionable, and should be removed.

CHEST: Should be deep and fairly broad and well covered with hair, but not to such an extent as to form a frill.

BONE: Massive throughout, but not to give a heavy, inactive appearance.

FEET: Should be large and well shaped. Splayed or turned out feet are objectionable.

TAIL: Should be of moderate length, reaching down a little below the hocks, it should be of fair thickness, and well covered with long hair, but not to form a flag. When the dog is standing still, and not excited, it should hang downwards with

Newfoundland—This puppy is a Landseer Newfoundland, Newfoundlands other than all-black being called "Land-seers."

a slight curve at the end; but when the dog is in motion it should be carried a trifle up, and when he is excited straight out with a slight curve at the end. Tails with a kink in them, or curled over the back, are very objectionable.

EARS: Should be small, set well back, square with the skull, lie close to the head, and covered with short hair, and no fringe.

EYES: Should be small, of a dark brown color, rather deeply set but not showing any haw, and they should be set rather widely apart.

COLOR: Dull jet black. A slight tinge of bronze, or a splash of white on chest and toes is not objectionable.

HEIGHT AND WEIGHT: Size and weight are very desirable so long as symmetry is maintained. A fair average height at the shoulders is 28 inches for a dog, and 26 inches for a bitch and a fair average weight is, respectively: dogs, 140 to 150 pounds; bitches, 110 to 120 pounds.

OTHER THAN BLACK (Landseers): Should in all respects follow the black except in color, which may be almost any, so long as it disqualifies for the black class, but the colors most to be encouraged are white and black or bronze. Beauty in markings to be taken greatly into consideration.

Black dogs that have only white toes and white breasts and white tip to tail, should be exhibited in the classes provided for "black."

SCALE OF POINTS:	*Head*	*Points*
Shape of skull		8
Eyes		8
Ears		10
Muzzle		8
Points for head		34

Body	
Neck	4
Chest	6
Shoulders	4
Loin and back	12
Hind quarters and tail	10
Legs and feet	10
Coat	12
Size, height and general appearance	8
Body points	66
TOTAL POINTS	100

Markings of White and Black Dogs	
Head	3
Saddle	5
Rump	2
TOTAL	10

"Definition for Preference"

Black head marked with narrow blaze.

Even marked saddle.

Black rump, extending on to tail.

The ten points above are to be considered in differentiating between "Landseers," not added to standard.

OLD ENGLISH SHEEPDOG

THE ODDEST dog at the dog shows, in the public mind, is the Old English Sheepdog. When he gets into motion, with his queer, shuffling, drover's dog gait, his fantastic coat trailing in the breeze, and his eyes almost totally covered with hair, few in the crowds can resist him.

No claims for great antiquity can be made for him, despite his name of "Old English." Still, his known history goes back to 1835, and there are claims made for him for a century before. The latter, however, are chiefly conjectures.

One camp believes that Gainsborough was painting a "bob-tail" or "bearded collie" when he painted the Duke of Buccleuch and his dog in 1771. Others say the dog portrayed is nothing more than a large, rough-coated terrier of the Dandie Dinmont type. All agree than an 1835 painting by Sidney Cooper shows a true Old English Sheepdog.

One writer, Watson, believes that the breed originated about 1800. He guessed that British breeders crossed a now extinct type of Russian Setter with the smooth Sheepdog, or bandog, and the Turnspit. The resulting dog was then increased in size to present-day standards.

The breed apparently caught the public fancy very early. One Old English was shown at the Agricultural Hall Show at Islington, in 1865. Birmingham provided separate classes for the breed in 1873. After that, the "gorgeous grizzles" were a fixture at all the big shows of England.

It is not known when the breed first appeared in the United States, but they must have been brought in before 1890. Classes were opened up for them at the Westminster Show in New York in 1903, and 56 dogs actually were entered. That would indicate that the breed had had more than a decade in which to get established.

However, some of the dogs were in an imported string belonging to the Tilley brothers of Shepton Mallet, England. These dogs completely eclipsed the American dogs, taking all but one of the first prizes. The best dog was Merry Boy, and the best female, Bouncing Lass.

Among other entries were Stylish Boy and Bilton Bob. Stylish Boy was returned to England when not sold, but he appeared again at the 1904 New York show, and again in 1905. He appears in many pedigrees, including many of that day in Canada.

Champion Wilberforce belongs to that period, as does Ch. Dolly Gray. From pictures of both, they appear no different than top dogs of today, and prove that the breed had been fixed as to type long, long ago. Wilberforce belonged to Mrs. G. S. Thomas of Hamilton, Mass., wife of the internationally famous dog judge. Dolly Gray belonged to the Tilley brothers.

Old English Sheepdogs appeared in Canada shortly after 1900. They were an immediate success there. The Canadian climate is excellent for the Old English, and it is possible to keep them in coat most of the year. Among the early champions were Sir Alex, owned by E. E. Landford, and Snowflake, owned by the Clearbrook Kennels of Mrs. W. H. White. Strangely enough, a dog of this period, bred in England, was called General Wainright.

Since the 1900 period, the Old English Sheepdog has maintained a fairly steady position in both the United States and Canada. Other breeds have risen and fallen in popularity, but the Old English has remained neither a rare dog, nor a common one.

It is said that one reason for his failure to gain great popularity is his heavy, dense coat. In truth, this coat is somewhat difficult to care for if the dog is not to look like a ragamuffin. The dog must be brushed daily and combed several times a week, else mats form. And yet, if combed too much, the dog's coat tends to be less luxuriant than is desired. Once wet to the skin, as when bathed, it requires hours to dry the dog.

Old English Sheepdog.

Old English Sheepdog puppies with their mother.

Still, real Old English enthusiasts do not mind the work. Moreover, they save the combings. These combings are made into yarn, from which homespun garments, sport coats, and gloves are made. These are striking in appearance, very durable, and very warm. It must be added, too, the completed garments are expensive.

There is no doubt that the heavy facial and head coat interferes with the dog's vision. Some Old English fanciers say that the dogs are so accustomed to the little light that gets through the coat, that their eyes ulcerate in the brightness, if the hair is clipped away.

They say further that the dog compensates for this partial blindness by increasing the acuteness of his nose and hearing, somewhat as a human does when blindness approaches. There is no doubt that the Old English does possess very keen hearing and sense of smell. Yet there is no way to prove the point.

Old English Sheepdogs have done well in obedience work. They form an outstanding attraction in the obedience rings, where their unusual looks and charming personalities make them standout crowd pleasers. Mr. and Mrs. E. Herbert Gilg, Pittsburgh, Pa., did excellent work with their Old English in these trials.

At least one Old English Sheepdog entered Army service during World War II. At first, the dogs were barred because of their coats. But it was soon discovered this could be clipped down to the point where the dogs were not so great a care.

Donaldson Davidson of Akron, Ohio, clipped one of his dogs, and it was given preliminary work by Dogs For Defense trainers before entering Army service, where it performed acceptably for the duration of the war. There were no reports that its eyes ulcerated when the hair was clipped away, but Mr. Davidson did tell of its amusing antics brought about by increased vision. "It discovered for the first time that it was a dog, like other dogs," he said.

In the modern history of the breed there was one great breeding triumph which would rank as a major achievement for any breed. This occurred on May 18, 1940, when there was born a litter of Old English Sheepdog puppies which contained six future champions.

Julius Kraft of Shagbourne Kennels, purchased Ch. Mistress Opal of Pastorale. She won several Best in Show awards before being mated to Ch. Merriedip of Pastorale. There were 12 pups in the litter of which six won championships.

Two of these, Black Baron, owned by Mrs. Howard Hickinbotham, San Mateo, Cal., and King's Messenger, owned by Stanley Kraft, but always shown by Julius Kraft, the breeder, between them won over 20 Best in Show awards in All Breed competition. The other champions in the litter were: Lady Love, Lancashire Lass, Jenny Wren, and Lord Peter Whimsey.

Description and Standards. The description and standards, by courtesy of the Old English Sheepdog Club of America, follow.

SKULL: Capacious and rather squarely formed, giving plenty of room for brain power. The parts over the eyes should be well arched and the whole well covered with hair.

JAW: Fairly long, strong, square and truncated. The top should be well defined to avoid a Deerhound face. *(The attention of judges is particularly called to the above properties, as a long, narrow head is a deformity.)*

EYES: Vary according to the color of the dog. Very dark preferred but in the glaucous or blue dogs a pearl, wall or china eye is considered typical. *(A light eye is most objectionable.)*

NOSE: Always black, large and capacious.

TEETH: Strong and large, evenly placed and level in opposition.

EARS: Medium sized, and carried flat to side of head, coated moderately.

LEGS: The forelegs should be dead straight, with plenty of bone, removing the body a medium height from the ground, without approaching legginess, and well coated all around.

FEET: Small, round; toes well arched, and pads thick and hard.

TAIL: It is preferable that there should be none. Should never, however, exceed 1½ or 2 inches in grown dogs. When not natural-born bobtails however, puppies should be docked at the first joint from the body and the operation performed when they are from three to four days old.

NECK AND SHOULDERS: The neck should be fairly long, arched gracefully and well coated with hair. The shoulders sloping and narrow at the points, the dog standing lower at the shoulder than at the loin.

BODY: Rather short and very compact, ribs well sprung and brisket deep and capacious. *Slabsidedness highly undesirable.* The loin should be very stout and gently arched, while the

hind quarters should be round and muscular and with well-let-down hocks, and the hams densely coated with a thick, long jacket in excess of any other part.

COAT: Profuse, but not so excessive as to give the impression of the dog being over-fat and of a good hard texture; not straight but shaggy and free from curl. *Quality and texture of coat to be considered above mere profuseness.* Softness or flatness of coat to be considered a fault. The under coat should be a waterproof pile when not removed by grooming or season.

COLOR: Any shade of grey, grizzle, blue or blue-merled with or without white markings or in reverse. *Any shade of brown or fawn to be considered distinctly objectionable and not to be encouraged.*

SIZE: Twenty-two inches and upwards for dogs and slightly less for bitches. Type, character and symmetry are of the greatest importance and are on no account to be sacrificed to size alone.

GENERAL APPEARANCE AND CHARACTERISTICS: A strong, compact-looking dog of great symmetry, practically the same in measurement from shoulder to stern as in height, absolutely free from legginess or weaselness, very elastic in his gallop, but in walking or trotting he has a characteristic ambling or pacing movement, and his bark should be loud, with a peculiar "pot-casse" ring in it. Taking him all round, he is a profusely, but not *excessively* coated, thick-set, muscular, able-bodied dog with a most intelligent expression, free from all Poodle or Deerhound character. *Soundness should be considered of greatest importance.*

SCALE OF POINTS:	Points
Skull	5
Eyes	5
Ears	5
Teeth	5
Nose	5
Jaw	5
Foreface	5
Neck and shoulders	5
Body and loins	10
Hind quarters	10
Legs	10
Coat (texture, quality and condition)	15
General appearance and movement	15
TOTAL	100

PULI

IN HUNGARY, in the famous sheep grazing lands known as the puszta, there are four main types of sheepdogs. The two larger breeds are called the Komondor and the Kuvasz. The two smaller breeds are the Pumi and the Puli (for which the plural is Pulik). The latter dogs are sometimes lumped together under the general title, Juhasz Kutya, meaning "shepherd's dog."

It is said that, in Hungary, the Pumi is a sort of "town dog," while the Puli still is used on the plains. The city dwellers are said to consider the two breeds as virtually identical. But on the puszta, they are considered separate breeds.

Horowitz, the British sheepdog expert, considers the Puli to be merely a small edition of the Komondor. In truth, the two dogs do appear to be similar. However, the Komondor, because of his great size, is used as much as a guard dog as he is for sheep-herding, whereas the Puli is almost entirely used for herding. An exception is in Germany, where a few Pulik have been trained for police work.

Old English Sheepdog—A head study. (Dog from Win-Sons Old English Sheepdog Kennels, Villa Park, Ill.) Photo by Gillette.

Puli—American-Mexican Ch. Nagykunsagi Csorgo, shown with combed-out coat. (Breeder: Dr. Imre Bordacs, Budapest, Hungary. Owner: Bob and Anne Kennedy, San Bernardino, Calif.) Photo by Ludwig.

Some writers, notably Mehely, have said that the Puli is really of Nordic origin, being descended from Iceland and Lapland dogs. There would appear to be no real basis of fact in this, other than the general statement which can be made that probably all shepherd dogs originated in the northern countries.

Other writers have asserted that the Puli is the Hungarian water dog, mentioned by Heppe, in a book written in 1751. According to this view, the Puli is a rabbit and duck dog, as well as a sheepdog.

In the decade beginning in 1930, Pulik began to appear in America. They were brought here at about the same time as the Komondor, Kuvasz, and other types of European shepherd dogs. They attracted immediate attention, not only because of their good

Puli—Eight-weeks-old puppy.

looks, but because they proved to be alert and easily trained.

A standard for the breed was first approved by the American Kennel Club, September 15, 1936. During the next four years, a fair amount of bloodstock was imported from Hungary and Germany, so that the breed had a good start before World War II shut off imports.

With a groomed coat rather than his natural corded and somewhat unkempt-appearing coat, the Puli is admired by many. But with either coat he has his followers and quite probably there are many, many more Pulik owned in America today than ever before.

Description and Standards. The description and standards as listed by the American Kennel Club, follow.

GENERAL APPEARANCE: A dog of medium size, vigorous, alert, and extremely active. By nature affectionate, he is a devoted and home-loving companion, sensibly suspicious of strangers and therefore an excellent guard. Striking and highly characteristic is the shaggy coat which centuries .ago fitted him for the strenuous work of herding the flocks on the plains of Hungary.

HEAD: Of medium size, in proportion to the body. The skull is slightly domed and not too broad. Stop clearly defined but not abrupt, neither dished nor downfaced, with strong muzzle of medium length ending in a nose of good size. Teeth are strong and comparatively large, and the bite may be either level or scissors. Flews tight. The ears hanging and set fairly high, medium size, and V-shaped. The eyes deep-set and rather large, should be dark brown, but lighter color is not a serious fault.

NECK AND SHOULDERS: Neck strong and muscular, of medium length, and free of throatiness. Shoulders clean-cut and sloping, with elbows close.

BODY: The chest is deep and fairly broad with ribs well sprung. Back of medium length, straight and level, the rump sloping moderately. Fairly broad across the loins and well tucked up. Occasionally born bobtail, which is acceptable, but the tail is never cut. The tail is carried curled over the back when alert, carried low with the end curled up when at rest. Forelegs straight, strong, and well boned. Feet round and compact with thick-cushioned pads and strong nails. Hindquarters well developed, moderately broad through the stifle which is well bent and muscular. Dewclaws, if any, may be removed from both forelegs and hind legs.

Puli—American-Mexican International Champion Cinkotai Csibesz. (Owner: Hunnia Puli Kennels, Tarzana, Calif.) Photo by Ludwig.

COAT: Characteristic of the breed is the dense, weather-resisting double coat. The outer coat, long and of medium texture, is never silky. It may be straight, wavy, or slightly curly, the more curly coat appearing to be somewhat shorter. The undercoat is soft, woolly, and dense. The coat mats easily, the hair tending to cling together in bunches, giving a somewhat corded appearance even when groomed. The hair is profuse on the head, ears, face, stifles, and tail, and the feet are well haired between the toes. Usually shown combed, but may also be shown uncombed with the coat hanging in tight, even cords.

COLOR: Solid colors, black, rusty-black, various shades of gray, and white. The black usually appears weathered and rusty or slightly gray. The intermixture of hair of different colors is acceptable and is usually present in the grays, but must be uniform throughout the coat so that the over-all appearance of a solid color is maintained. Nose, flews, and eyelids are black.

HEIGHT: Males about 17 inches, and should not exceed 19 inches. Females about 16 inches, and should not exceed 18 inches.

SERIOUS FAULTS: Overshot or undershot. Lack of undercoat, short or sparse coat. White markings such as white paws or spot on chest. Flesh color on nose, flews, or eyelids. Coat with areas of two or more colors at the skin.

(April 12, 1960)

ROTTWEILER

IN THE LATTER years of the "Golden Age" of sports, which ended about 1932, international dog salesmen began to bring in large numbers of Middle European dogs, chiefly of the working or shepherd dog type. Among these was the Rottweiler, a dog which had been "rescued" in Germany about 1900 when that country's own interest in working dogs suddenly expanded.

Dogs such as the German Shepherd and Doberman Pinscher have their origin in the mixture of various breeds, including shepherds, in the drive to fix a certain type. The Rottweiler served as one of the ancestral pillars for the Doberman Pinscher, and has lived to see his descendant become one of the most popular dogs in the world.

This is strange enough, considering that the Rottweiler is a very ancient type of dog. It is considered that he was originally a cattle drover and guard for the supply dumps of the Roman armies. It was the custom of the Roman armies to carry their food with them "on the hoof." This they did by employing dogs to drive their sheep and cattle.

The area about the town of Rottweil, which is on the Neckar River, in Wurttemburg, South Germany, was conquered by Rome some 1900 years ago. And the story has it that the Roman dogs were left there, where the breed has been kept ever since, and from whence it gets its name.

It is said by others that the Romans did not customarily eat beef, having the same prejudice against it as Americans have against horse meat (since they user their cattle as draft animals). But in any case, the Rottweiler was traditionally the Roman camp dog, and he does fit the descriptions of these dogs fairly well.

During the Middle Ages, Rottweil was a livestock center. Butchers from Rottweil used to have to leave the walled town in order to go on buying expeditions through the countryside. Robbers were likely to be lying in wait in the forests, and the butchers had to have cash for their purchases.

So it became the custom for the butchers to tie their money belts about the necks of their Rottweilers. They were then unmolested on the trip out. On the trip back, the dogs were used as drovers. For this reason, the dogs were often called Metzgerhunds.

Toward 1900, cattle driving in Germany was outlawed. The breed then might have gone out of existence had it not been selected as one suitable for army and police service. It was stated that, in 1905, only one Rottweiler bitch was still alive in Rottweil.

However, there were more in other parts of Germany. These were carefully gotten together, and a definite program to save and improve the breed was undertaken. A specialty club for the breed was established and this, together with the dog's success in army and police work, ensured its continued existence.

The resemblance of the Rottweiler to his relative, the Doberman Pinscher, is obvious. However, he is a heavier, slower dog than the Doberman, and less volatile. He is a dog of great power, steady disposition, and great self-reliance. While he lacks the Doberman's lithe, trim beauty, he makes up for it by his own appearance of power and his great dignity.

Very few of the dogs have come to the United States, but those which have come have been excellent specimens. The breed was recognized by the American Kennel Club on April 9, 1935. Despite World War II, it was able to hold on. Recruits for the breed since the war were in sufficient numbers to assure steady progress.

Description and Standards. The description and standards, courtesy of Reichsverband für das

Rottweiler—Ch. Jaro vom Schleidenplatz. (Owner: Charles McKelvey, Chalfont, Pa.) Photo by Evelyn M. Shafer.

Deutsche Hundewesen, and adopted by the American Kennel Club follow.

GENERAL APPEARANCE AND CHARACTER: The Rottweiler is a good sized, strongly-built active dog. He is affectionate, intelligent, easily trained to work, naturally obedient, and extremely faithful. While not quarrelsome, he possesses great courage and makes a splendid guard. His demeanor is dignified and he is not excitable.

HEAD: Is of medium length, the skull broad between the ears. Stop well pronounced as is also the occiput. Muzzle is not very long. It should not be longer than the distance from the stop to the occiput. Nose is well developed, with relatively large nostrils and is always black. Flews which should not be too pronounced are also black. Jaws should be strong and muscular; teeth strong—incisors of lower jaw must touch the inner surface of the upper incisors. Eyes are of medium size, dark brown in color and should express faithfulness, good humor, and confidence. The ears are comparatively small, set high and wide and hang over about on a level with top of head. The skin on head should not be loose. The neck should be of fair length, strong, round and very muscular, slightly arched and free from throatiness.

FORE QUARTERS: Shoulders should be well placed, long and sloping, elbows well let down, but not loose. Legs muscular and with plenty of bone and substance, pasterns straight and strong. Feet strong, round and close, with toes well arched. Soles very hard, toe nails dark, short and strong.

BODY: The chest is roomy, broad, and deep. Ribs well sprung. Back straight, strong, and rather short. Loins strong and deep, and flanks should not be tucked up. Croup short, broad, but not sloping.

HIND QUARTERS: Upper thigh is short, broad and very muscular. Lower thigh very muscular at top and strong and sinewy at the bottom. Stifles fairly well bent, hocks strong. The hind feet are somewhat longer than the front ones, but should be close and strong with toes well arched. There should be no dewclaws. Tail should be short, placed high (on level with back) and carried horizontally. Dogs are frequently born with a short stump tail and when tail is too long it must be docked close to body.

COAT: Hair should be short, coarse, and flat. The under coat which is absolutely required on neck and thighs should not show through outer coat. The hair should be a little longer on the back of front and hind legs and on tail.

COLOR: Black, with clearly defined markings on cheeks, muzzle, chest and legs, as well as over both eyes. Color of markings: Tan to mahogany brown. A small spot of white on chest and belly is permissible but not desirable.

HEIGHT: Shoulder height for males is 23¾ to 27 inches, for females 21¾ to 25¾ inches, but height should always be considered in relation to the general appearance and conformation of the dog.

FAULTS: Too lightly built or too heavily built, sway back, roach back, too long body, lack of spring of ribs. Head too long and narrow or too short and plump. Lack of occiput, snipey muzzle, cheekiness, top line of muzzle not straight, light or flesh colored nose, hanging flews, overshot or undershot, loose skin on head, ears set too low, or ears too heavy, long or narrow or rose ear, or ears uneven in size. Light, small or slanting eyes or lack of expression, neck too long, thin or weak, or very noticeable throatiness. Lack of bone and muscle, short or straight shoulders, front legs too close together or not straight, weak pasterns, splay feet, light nails, weak toes. Flat ribs, sloping croup. Too heavy or plump body. Flanks drawn up. Flat thighs, cowhocks or weak hocks, dewclaws. Tail set too high or too low or that is too long or too thin. Soft, too short, too long or too open coat, wavy coat or lack of under coat. White markings on toes, legs, or other parts of body, markings not well defined or smudgy. The one-color tan Rottweiler with either black or light mask or with black streak on back as well as other colors such as brown or blue are not recognized and are believed to be cross-bred, as is also a long-haired Rottweiler. Timid or stupid appearing animals are to be positively rejected.

SAMOYED

IN GORGEOUS beauty, the Samoyed, the most glamorous of all work dogs, with a heritage of centuries of service to and companionship with mankind, came before the English public in the very early 1900's as something different in the canine world.

In the very early days men with their herds roved the plateau of Iran and lived from the land. Property ownership did not exist; the land belonged to all in the beginning, and then later to the swift and the strong. As mankind increased and separated off into families, tribes of kinsmen with the ever-increasing need of more and more grazing land for their herds, then reindeer, drifted off, or were forced off, to farther pastures.

Through the centuries this process continued across Mongolia, then the center of the world's culture. Farther and farther north went the tiny nomadic tribe we now call the Samoyede people, until at long last they reached the farthest reaches of northern Siberia, between the Yenisei River in Siberia westward to the Petchora River in Russia. Here was a haven, fortressed by Nature's own walls of ice and snow. And here the Samoyede people with their dogs and herds remained for centuries since long before the Christian era.

Here was peace and plenty. Moss for the reindeer, fish, Arctic bear, foxes, walrus for the nomads, milk and meat and clothing from the reindeer, and natural shepherds in their natural dogs. Never were a primitive people more happily situated. Here with them their dogs shared their ice-walled "chooms," slept in their master's bed, shared his table, feasted and starved, alternately even as he did. They joyfully joined with them in the hunt for walrus or other game, and frequently "dug in" in the snow, burying themselves with only their noses sticking out, and those noses carefully protected by the tips of their tails, the long hair of which served as a natural air filter. Long centuries of Arctic suns bleached the original yellow coat to purest white, and gave an icy sheen to the tips of the hair. The dogs were also provided with a second and warm under coat of purest wool to provide warmth in winter and to be shed for summer comfort, leaving still the glorious outer coat of hair to maintain the beauty which always has been and always will be the Samoyed's birthright. Intelligence grew with the constant companionship with man, fleetness came in herding the reindeer, gentleness came likewise in this work—a shepherd is a protector—never a killer.

Then into this primitive peace came the inroads of civilization. The world then had one field of adventure for the young—Arctic and Antarctic expeditions were the rage. In 1870 stories leaked to the outer world of the peaceful Samoyede people and of their dogs—hidden, like the diamond, for so long from the world at large. More and more frequently came the visiting explorers from the outer world, and in 1889, Ernest Kilburn Scott purchased from the natives a

Samoyed—Ch. Silver Cloud of Maple Shade. (Owner: Mrs. Peg Morgan, West Richfield, Ohio.) Photo by Norton of Kent.

"fat pup" as a gift for his wife, Clara Kilburn Scott. This dog, Sabarka, a deep biscuit-colored dog, was soon joined by a cream-colored mate from North Russia, Whirtay Petchora (widely known as Whitey Petchora).

In 1897 the Nansen and Jackson-Harmsworth expeditions returned together in the ship Windward and from the Jackson-Harmsworth Expedition eight dogs went to the Kilburn Scotts. Major Frederick Jackson presented the pure white Jacko, a lead dog of the expedition, to Queen Alexandra. Kvik, born on the ship, came to England. Russ, bought in Tobolsk by the dog dealer Trondjhem for the Duke of Abruzzi, also came to England on the Polar Star. Then one by one, the "giants" of the breed were born—dogs who appear in almost every pedigree. Pearlene, born in 1902, Russolene in 1903, Ivanoff in 1908, Nansen, son of Musti and Whitey, 1901, Olgalene, the same year, Neva, born in the 1800's, daughter of Sabarka and Whitey, and herself dam, with Musti as sire, of Olaf Oussa—these are names which can never be forgotten among Samoyed fanciers. Then came Houdin, one of the Abruzzi expedition dogs, who sired the great bitch Hecla (by Pearlene). This is the handful of dogs from whom all of the present-day Samoyeds have sprung. Jacko, pure white, was much used at stud. In America, by December, 1906, the Russian champion Moustan had been registered, and with a few kennel mates was to start the breed here. Gift of the Czar's brother to the Belgian Countess who was also Princess de Montyglyon, Moustan kept up the breed's tradition in civilization of the patronage of nobility.

Then in 1908 the Kilburn Scotts brought back to England from Sydney, the great dog Antarctic Buck whose sons, South Pole, Southern Cross, Fang, Mez-

enit, Kaifas and his daughter Kirche, were to become "foundation stones" of the even better Samoyed of today, together with the progeny of Miss Puxley's Sam out of her Keena, and the progeny of Ayesha, brought in from Russia in 1910 by F. Gordon Colman, to later become the property of Mrs. Cammack and later of Mrs. Grey-Landsberg. In a very few pedigrees is found the name of Olaf, litter brother of Southern Cross, who went out to the Pole with Captain Scott and into the forever unknown.

But in America one import followed another—slowly at first, until Miss Ruth Nichols brought in the bitch, Wiemur, in 1914, to be bred to descendants of Moustan. Mrs. Frank Romer brought in Tobolsk and Draga. Tobolsk, one of the greatest Samoyeds of all times, disappeared and his passing is unrecorded. Then came Barin and Yukon Mit. American Samoyed dogs were practically all from these three great dogs—Tobolsk, Barin, and Mit. The Harry Reids who, owning a great son of Tobolsk, Ch. Toby of Yurak II, began to import and brought in the English Ch. Tiger Boy, and followed this importation by many more before they gave up breeding in 1937.

About a year after Tiger Boy's coming, Miss Elizabeth Hudson brought in Storm Cloud, and by strange coincidence, the descendants of Storm Cloud in England, through Peter of Kobe, bred to descendants of Kara Sea, and the descendants of Storm Cloud in America, through Vida of Snowland, bred to Siberian Nansen of Farnigham of Snowland, were long to dominate the American scene. While in England the great kennels of Mrs. Dorothy L. Perry, Mrs. Edwards, and Miss Marion Keyte-Perry were keeping the breed going actively, here in America Mrs. Helen S. Harris, of Philadelphia, with her Snowland Kennels, was sending throughout America Samoyeds with a sparkle and lilt of spirit heretofore unknown. Miss Martha Humphriss of Westerly, Rhode Island, had had many fine importations, of whom not the least were the beautiful Stara of Farningham and the English Ch. Barena of Farningham, and had owned the dog whose influence is perhaps greater on this breed than any other American-bred dog—Icy King—sire of well over 100 outstanding puppies—and most noted as sire of the great Prince Kofksi.

In the years from 1936 to about 1943, Mrs. Harris, following importation with importation, with a hand gifted at careful breeding, and Monsignor Keegan, who seemed able to bring out a good new dog each year, dominated the Eastern show scene, but the breed was now nationwide, and on the West Coast, Mrs. A. E. Mason was bringing in imports, White Way of Kobe, son of the famous White Fang and Silver Spark of the Arctic, to have great influence on the coast dogs. Mrs. Ashley brought in Nova Sonia of Kobe—and many an average show dog came from either Mrs. Harris' or Mrs. Mason's stock; descended from Nova Sonia, or came down from Icy King.

Then came the war years and in England a new kennel arose, to stand with the great—Mrs. Westcott's Snowland Kennels, with Christina Mariee and Taz as her foundation dogs. Following World War II the first imports here came from Mrs. Westcott's breeding, Ch. Martingale Snowland Taz, owned by Dr. Ivens of Philadelphia, and Ch. Snowland Stara, owned by Mrs. L. L. Miller of Albuquerque, New Mexico. These dogs were shortly joined by a host of other imports, and the Samoyed breed today is firmly entrenched in this country. Nor—as some breeders discontinued—has their work ceased or their strain disappeared. The Snow Crest Kennels in Roselle, N.J., owned by Mrs. E. C. Grillo, carried on perhaps the purest American Snowland strain, while the Breezewood Kennels in Indianapolis continued the Nova Sonia of Kobe line combined with Snowland. The Sammar Kennels, owned by J. J. Marshall of Chicago, also continued the Snowland bloodlines.

Known as the dog that "carries the spirit of Christmas in its heart and face the whole year through," the Samoyed has served mankind in many ways other than as helper to the reindeer herdsman. His work as a sled dog has been outstanding. Samoyeds were used in the Arctic and Antarctic expeditions of Borchgrevink, Scott, Shackleton, Nansen, Abruzzi, Fiala, and Baldwin. All of these explorers had highest praise for the breed.

The Samoyed is a hardy dog in any climate, withstanding the coldest of weather in the winter, yet apparently being fairly comfortable in summertime. The dog has no doggy odor. In disposition he is naturally well-mannered, makes a fine companion for children, is affectionate but never fawning, courageous but not quarrelsome.

Proclaimed as the most beautiful of all dogs, the Samoyed was originally called the Samoyede, but the last "e" was officially dropped from the spelling in 1947.

Description and Standards. The description and standards, as adopted by the Samoyed Club of America, follow.

GENERAL CONFORMATION: The Samoyed, being essentially a working dog, should present a picture of beauty, alertness and strength, with agility, dignity and grace. As his work lies in cold climates, his coat should be heavy and weather resistant, well groomed, and of good quality rather than quantity. The male carries more of a "ruff" than the female. He should not be long in the back as a weak back would make him practically useless for his legitimate work, but at the same time, a close-coupled body would also place him at a great disadvantage as a draft dog. Breeders should aim for the happy medium, a body not long but muscular, allowing liberty, with a deep chest and well-sprung ribs, strong neck, straight front and especially strong loins. Males should be masculine in appearance and deportment without unwarranted aggressiveness; bitches feminine without weakness of structure or apparent softness of temperament. Bitches may be slightly longer in back than males. They should both give the appearance of being capable of great endurance but be free from coarseness. Because of the depth of chest required, the legs should be moderately long. A very short-legged dog is to be deprecated. Hindquarters should be particularly well developed, stifles well bent and any suggestion of unsound stifles or cowhocks severely penalized. General appearance should include movement and general conformation, indicating balance and good substance.

SUBSTANCE: Substance is that sufficiency of bone and muscle which rounds out a balance with the frame. The bone is heav-

ier than would be expected in a dog of this size but not so massive as to prevent the speed and agility most desirable in a Samoyed. In all builds, bone should be in proportion to body size. The Samoyed should never be so heavy as to appear clumsy nor so light as to appear racy. The weight should be in proportion to the height.

HEIGHT: Males—21 to 23½ inches; females—19 to 21 inches at the withers. An oversized or undersized Samoyed is to be penalized according to the extent of the deviation.

COAT (Texture & Condition): The Samoyed is a double-coated dog. The body should be well-covered with an under coat of soft, short, thick, close wool with longer and harsh hair growing through it to form the outer coat, which stands straight out from the body and should be free from curl. The coat should form a ruff around the neck and shoulders, framing the head (more on males than on females). Quality of coat should be weather resistant and considered more than quantity. A droopy coat is undesirable. The coat should glisten with a silver sheen. The female does not usually carry as long a coat as most males and it is softer in texture.

COLOR: Samoyeds should be pure white, white and biscuit, cream, or all biscuit. Any other colors disqualify.

MOVEMENT: The Samoyed should trot, not pace. He should move with a quick agile stride that is well timed. The gait should be free, balanced and vigorous, with good reach in the forequarters and good driving power in the hindquarters. When trotting, there should be a strong rear action drive. Moving at a slow walk or trot, they will not single track, but as speed increases the legs gradually angle inward until the pads are finally falling on a line directly under the longitudinal center of the body. As the pad marks converge the forelegs and hind legs are carried straight forward in traveling, the stifles not turned in nor out. The back should remain strong, firm and level. A choppy or stilted gait should be penalized.

REAR END: Upper thighs should be well developed. Stifles well bent—approximately 45 degrees to the ground. Hocks should be well developed, sharply defined and set at approximately 30 per cent of hip height. The hind legs should be parallel when viewed from the rear in a natural stance, strong, well developed, turning neither in nor out. Straight stifles are objectionable. Double jointedness or cowhocks are a fault. Cowhocks should only be determined if the dog has had an opportunity to move properly.

FRONT END: Legs should be parallel and straight to the pasterns. The pasterns should be strong, sturdy and straight, but flexible with some spring for proper let-down of feet. Because of depth of chest, legs should be moderately long. Length of leg from the ground to the elbow should be approximately 55

Samoyed—Puppies, six weeks old. Hank Babbit photo.

percent of the total height at the withers—a very short-legged dog is to be deprecated. Shoulders should be long and sloping, with a layback of 45 degrees and be firmly set. Out at the shoulders or out at the elbow should be penalized. The withers separation should be approximately 1-1½ inches.

FEET: Large, long, flattish—a hare-foot, slightly spread but not splayed; toes arched; pads thick and tough, with protective growth of hair betwen the toes. Feet should turn neither in nor out in a natural stance but may turn in slightly in the act of pulling. Turning out, pigeon-toed, round or cat-footed or splayed are faults. Feathers on feet are not too essential but are more profuse on females than on males.

HEAD: Skull is wedge-shaped, broad, slightly crowned, not round or apple-headed, and should form an equilateral triangle on lines between the inner base of the ears and the center point of the stop. Muzzle of medium length and medium width, neither coarse nor snipy; should taper toward the nose and be in proportion to the size of the dog and the width of skull. The muzzle must have depth. The stop is not too abrupt, nevertheless well defined. The lips should be black for preference and slightly curved up at the corners of the mouth, giving the "Samoyed smile." Lip lines should not have the appearance of being coarse nor should the flews drop predominately at corners of the mouth.

EARS: Strong and thick, erect, triangular and slightly rounded at the tips; should not be large or pointed, nor should they be small and "bear-eared." Ears should conform to head size and the size of the dog; they should be set well apart but be within the border of the outer edge of the head; they should be mobile and well covered inside with hair; hair full and stand-off before the ears. Length of ear should be the same measurement as the distance from inner base of ear to outer corner of eye.

EYES: Should be dark for preference; should be placed well apart and deep-set; almond shaped with lower lid slanting toward an imaginary point approximating the base of ears. Dark eye rims for preference. Round or protruding eyes penalized. Blue eyes disqualifying.

NOSE: Black for preference but brown, liver, or Dudley nose not penalized. Color of nose sometimes changes with age and weather.

JAWS AND TEETH: Strong, well set teeth, snugly overlapping with scissors bite. Undershot or overshot should be penalized.

EXPRESSION: The expression, referred to as "Samoyed expression," is very important and is indicated by sparkle of the eyes, animation and lighting up of the face when alert or intent on anything. Expression is made up of a combination of eyes, ears and mouth. The ears should be erect when alert; the mouth should be slightly curved up at the corners to form the "Samoyed smile."

NECK: Strong, well muscled, carried proudly erect, set on sloping shoulders to carry head with dignity when at attention. Neck should blend into shoulders with a graceful arch.

CHEST: Should be deep, with ribs well sprung out from the spine and flattened at the sides to allow proper movement of the shoulders and freedom for the front legs. Should not be barrel-chested. Perfect depth of chest approximates the point of elbows, and the deepest part of the chest should be back of the forelegs—near the ninth rib. Heart and lung room are secured more by body depth than width.

LOIN AND BACK: The withers forms the highest part of the back. Loins strong and slightly arched. The back should be straight to the loin, medium in length, very muscular and neither long nor short-coupled. The dog should be "just off square"—the length being approximately 5 percent more than the height. Females allowed to be slightly longer than males. The belly should be well shaped and tightly muscled and, with the rear of the thorax, should swing up in a pleasing curve (tuck-up). Croup must be full, slightly sloping, and must continue imperceptibly to the tail root.

TAIL: The tail should be moderately long with the tail bone terminating approximately at the hock when down. It should be profusely covered with long hair and carried forward over the back or side when alert, but sometimes dropped when at rest. It should not be high or low set and should be mobile and loose—not tight over the back. A double hook is a fault. A judge should see the tail over the back once when judging.

DISPOSITION: Intelligent, gentle, loyal, adaptable, alert, full of action, eager to serve, friendly but conservative, not distrustful or shy, not overly aggressive. Unprovoked aggressiveness to be severely penalized.

Disqualifications. Any color other than pure white, cream, biscuit, or white and biscuit. Blue eyes.

(April 9, 1963)

GIANT SCHNAUZER

THE GIANT SCHNAUZER, or Riesenschnauzer, is a strikingly beautiful dog. Ranging up to 25 inches or more in height, he has the build of a terrier, but the strength and agility of the finest working dogs. He is the largest of the Schnauzer family, but in other respects conforms fairly close to the standard and miniature varieties.

As is the case with most of the cattle and sheep dogs of Germany, the Giant Schnauzer had his origin in southern Germany, in Wurttemberg, and to a larger degree, in Bavaria. For many years, the breed was called the Munchener, a name which would indicate its place of origin as the area about Munich.

It would appear that the Giant Schnauzer was primarily a cattle drover. How much actual Schnauzer blood is in his ancestry is a matter of doubt. The Germans were perfectly capable of crossing various breeds to get a type which had virtually been laid out on a drawing board in advance.

In the case of the Giant Schnauzer, it is possible that Standard Schnauzers were used to get the wire coat and pepper and salt colors. Thuringian shepherd dogs may have been used to get erect ear carriage, or at least, ears which would stay erect when cropped. It is supposed that Great Danes, not so large then as now, were used to obtain size and the black color.

The similarity of the Giant Schnauzer and the Bouvier des Flandres has caused many students to believe that the two are closely related. But there is

Giant Schnauzer. Photo by Evelyn M. Shafer.

no real evidence for this contention. It appears more probable that the Bavarians merely used available dogs in the rich shepherd country in which they lived.

As cattle driving disappeared, there became no use for the big dogs on the farms of Swabia and Bavaria. He seems then to have been taken over by the butchers and brewers of the towns. He was a favorite at Munich, and as the Munchener dog, he was kept a pure breed for years.

Naturally, a dog of his striking appearance came to the attention of German show fanciers in the period between 1900 and 1910. Even so, the breed might have died out, had not it been selected as suitable for police and war service training. Dogs of this breed then began to appear at training exhibitions.

A few of the dogs were brought to America before World War I, though no real attempt was made to establish the breed here. After the war, more dogs were brought over, but they could not withstand the competition of the German Shepherd, then skyrocketing to world-wide fame. Yet a few discriminating breeders held onto their stock, and though still rare, the breed is well established here.

Description and Standards. The description and standards, courtesy of Reichsverband für das Deutsche Hundewesen, follow.

GENERAL IMPRESSION: The Giant Schnauzer is a robust, sinewy, more heavy-set than slender dog, of somewhat rectangular build. His nature combines high-spirited temperament with extreme reliability.

HEAD: Strong and elongated, gradually narrowing from the ears to the eyes and thence towards the tip of the nose, in proportion to the size of the body. Its total length (tip of nose to occiput) should compare approximately to one-third the length of the back (withers—first dorsal vertebra—to the beginning of the tail). Upper part of the head (occiput to the base of the forehead) broad between the ears—its width should not be more than two-thirds of the length—with flat, creaseless forehead and well-muscled but not too strongly developed cheeks. Ears, small and V-shaped of moderate thickness, set well on the head and dropping forward closely to the cheek, or cropped, with ears evenly cut, placed high and carried erect in excitement. Eyes medium-sized, dark, oval turned forward, brows arched and wiry.

The powerful ferreting snout formed by the upper and lower jaws (base of forehead to the tip of nose) should be in proportion to the upper head and should end in a moderately blunt manner, with heavy stubby whiskers. Ridge of the nose straight, and running almost parallel to the extension of the forehead. The tip of the nose is black and full. Lips tight and not overlapping, with strongly developed fangs, healthy and pure white.

NECK: Not too short with skin close-fitting at the throat. Nape strong and slightly arched.

FORE QUARTERS: Shoulders slanting and flat, but strongly muscled. Forelegs (upper and under arm) seen from all sides are vertical without any curve.

CHEST: Moderately broad with visible strong breast bone and reaching at least to the height of the elbow and slowly extending backwards. Back strong and straight with well-developed short thighs. The length of back equal to shoulder height (from withers vertical to floor) built squarely, belly well drawn up towards the back.

TAIL: Carried high and cut down to three joints.

HIND QUARTERS: Thighs slanting and flat, but strongly muscled. Hind legs (upper and lower thighs) at first vertical to the

Giant Schnauzer—Camoli's Borgia of the East. (Owner: K. Dea Stuart and James H. Rosenberger, address not listed.)

knee, from knee to hock in line with the extension of the upper neckline, from hock vertical to ground.

PAWS: Short, round, extremely compact paws, with close arched toes (cat's paws) dark nails and hard soles.

HAIR: Close, strong, hard and wiry, on the back seen against the grain, unruly—that is, neither short, nor smooth; shorter on ears, forehead, legs and paws.

HEIGHT: From 21½ to 25½ inches shoulder height.

COLOR: All pepper and salt colored or similar equal mixtures, pure black or black with tan.

FAULTS: Too plump, or too light, low or high-legged build, too heavy around head, creased forehead, sticking-out or badly carried ears, light eye (with yellow or light-grey rings) strongly protruding cheek bones, flabby throat skin; undershot or overshot jaw. Teeth too pointed, too small or too long, sunken or roached back, chest with barrel ribs (tubby) slanting crupper, elbows turned out, heels turned in, hind part overbuilt, too steep, spread open toes, long and flat (hare) paws, too short, sleek, too long, soft, silky, curled, rolled, shaggy hair, all white, spotty, tigered, red and reddish colors.

Small white breast spot, or marking on the breast is not a fault.

STANDARD SCHNAUZER

FEW BREEDS can boast three sizes from which to choose. But this is true of the Schnauzer, a German breed which comes in Giant, Standard, and Miniature sizes. Here we are concerned with the Standard Schnauzer, oldest of the three types.

The breed is a very old one. A Stuttgart statue, dated 1620, is supposed to show a watchman and his Schnauzer dog. Though there is some doubt as to this, there is little question that Albrecht Durer owned a dog which conforms closely to present-day Schnauzers. He painted his dog a number of times between 1490 and 1504. At about the same time, Lucas Cranach, the Elder, placed a Schnauzer-type dog in a tapestry which is still extant.

Most authorities state that the dog was never a terrier, but was always a cattle dog and a ratter. And it is true that he comes from the great shepherd dog countries of Germany, Wurttemberg and Bavaria. Also, the breed came to the attention of show dog fanciers rather early in the period when Germany was becoming interested in shepherd dogs.

Still, one of the few guesses as to the exact origin of the breed states that it was developed from crosses of the black "pudel," or Poodle, and the gray Wolf-spitz, that is, the breed conforming in the Pomeranian and Keeshhond. The soft under coat was supposed to have come from the Poodle and the harsh pepper and salt gray from the Wolf-spitz.

At least one English student of the breed feels that the Schnauzer was developed entirely from Shepherd blood. This author states that the dog was never considered a terrier, and never called a Schnauzer Terrier.

It is true that the typical Schnauzer is rather heavier throughout than a true terrier. Neither is his gait typical of the modern terrier. Yet he was originally shown as the Wire-haired Pinscher, and the word pinscher has the meaning of terrier.

The first recorded importation into the United States was of a dog called Fingal, brought to Rochester, N.Y., in 1905, by a Mrs. Leisching. From that time until July 10, 1945, the dog was officially classified in the United States as a terrier. He then was placed in the Working Group.

Standard Schnauzer. Photo by Ken Smith.

Similarly, in Canada, Doberman Pinschers and Schnauzers were imported at about the same time. The Canadians listed them as Pinschers, Doberman, and Pinschers, Schnauzer.

The dog's extraordinary ability as a ratter would seem to make him more of a terrier than a working dog. Ratting trials are still held in Europe for the breed, so that this terrier characteristic is still being fostered.

Schnauzers were first shown at the Third International Dog Show at Hanover, in 1879. The winning dog was named "Schnauzer," and he came from the Wurttemberg Kennels of Burger Leonburg. This is, of course, shepherd dog country, and one type of Shepherd from this area is called the Leon-burger. Another early kennel of this period was called Plavia, and was owned by Max Hartenstein.

In 1880, a standard for the breed was published. Ten years later, the first specialty show for the breed was held, and drew an entry of 93 dogs. This indicates that the Germans already had fixed the type, and that interest in this breed was already widespread, at a time when the German Shepherd, Doberman, and others, were just getting started.

The Bavarian Schnauzer Club was formed at Munich in 1907. But an even earlier club, called a Pinscher Club, was formed at Cologne in 1895. In 1918, the two clubs united, and became the official representatives of the breed in the German Kennel Club. It was, incidentally, called the Pinscher Schnauzer Club.

The breed appears to have developed out of two main lines, but with both going back to Schnauzer, and to a dog called Seppel. The Germans rather heavily inbred to establish and hold type, and this developed the two powerful sire lines. Representatives of Schnauzer and Seppel were the two champions (siegers) Rex van Den Gunthersburg, and Rigo Schnauzerlust, his son. These two dogs are the "pillars" of the breed.

Rex von Egelsee, a little brother to Rigo, was heavily used also. The Egelsee kennel name is world famous.

Schnauzer activity began shortly after World War I in the United States. The noted Swiss female, Resy Patricia, became the first champion. The great Sieger Holm von Egelsee was the first sieger to be imported, and the first male to win an American championship. Mrs. Maurice Newton then bred Ch. Fracas Franconia, a daughter of Resy Patricia.

The Schnauzer Club of America was founded in 1925. However, the large number of imports of both Standards and Miniatures brought the need for separate parent clubs. Therefore, in 1933, the American Miniature Schnauzer Club was organized, and the older club began a new existence as the Standard Schnauzer Club of America.

In Canada, the Schnauzers arrived a year or two after heavy importations to the United States began. A dog called Cortlandt Curacco was one of the first official importations. He was from the line of Rigo

Schnauzerlust, and was born June 21, 1926. The breed has prospered in both countries, but has not enjoyed the popularity of the Miniature.

Description and Standards. The description and standards, as adopted by the Standard Schnauzer Club of America and approved by the American Kennel Club follow.

The Standard Schnauzer is a robust, sinewy, heavy-set dog of the Terrier type, sturdily built, square in the proportion of body length to height, with good muscle and plenty of bone. His nature combines high spirited temperament with extreme reliability. His rugged build and dense, harsh coat are accentuated by arched eyebrows, bristly mustache and luxurious whiskers.

HEIGHT: At withers, from 18 to 20 inches for males, and from 17 to 19 inches for females. *Faults*—Animals under or over these measurements.

HEAD: Strong and rectangular, diminishing slightly from the ear to the eyes, and again to the tip of the nose. Total length about one-third and the length of the back, measuring from the withers to the beginning of the tail.

SKULL: Moderately broad between the ears, width not exceeding two-thirds the length. *Faults*—Too narrow or pronounced.

FOREHEAD: Flat and unwrinkled.

CHEEKS: Well muscled, but not too strongly developed. *Faults*—Protruding cheek bones.

MUZZLE: Strong and in proportion to the skull, ending in moderately blunt manner, with wiry whiskers accenting the rectangular shape of the head. *Faults*—Too long or too short, pointed or lacking whiskers; dish-faced or down-faced.

NOSE: Powerful, black and full, with ridge running almost parallel to the extension of the forehead. Lips tight and not overlapping.

EARS: Evenly shaped, set high and carried erect when cropped. If uncropped, they should be small and V-shaped, of moderate thickness and carried rather high and close to the head. *Faults*—Low-set, houndy ears and badly cut ears.

EYES: Medium size, dark brown, oval and turned forward.

Standard Schnauzer—A pair of young pups. Photo by Dale Smith.

Vision should not be obstructed from the front or profile by too long an eyebrow. The brow should be arched and wiry. *Faults*—Too large, round, or protruding, light or yellow-ringed eyes.

JAW: Level, powerful and square. *Faults*—Overshot or undershot.

TEETH: Sound, strong and white, with canines meeting in scissors bite. *Faults*—Pointed or irregular.

NECK: Nape should be strong, slightly arched and set cleanly on the shoulders. Skin should be tight, fitting closely to the throat. *Faults*—Too short, thick, long and throaty.

SHOULDERS: Somewhat sloping, strongly muscled. *Faults*—Loose, straight or low shoulders or steep-set front.

CHEST: Moderately broad, with the breast-bone plainly discernible and reaching at least to the height of the elbows extending slowly backwards. Belly well drawn up towards the back, but no tuck-up. *Faults*—Too broad or too narrow, shallow or false chest.

BACK: Strong, stiff, straight and short, with a well-developed short loin section, the ribs well sprung. Length of the back from the withers to the set-on of tail should approximate the height at withers. *Faults*—Too long, sunken or roached.

FORELEGS: Straight and vertical when seen from all sides, bone carried well down to the feet, elbows set close to body and pointing directly backward. *Faults*—Legs too high, low thin, or weak, elbows turned out or in. Pasterns sunken or any weakness of joint, bone or muscular development.

FEET: Small and compact; round with thick pads, strong nails. Toes well arched and pointing straight ahead. *Faults*—Toed-in or toed-out and long or spreading feet.

HIND QUARTERS: Strongly muscled, with thighs slanting and flat, never appearing overbuilt or higher than the shoulders. *Faults*—Hocks let down, cowhocks or any weakness of joint.

Standard Schnauzer—Taking the jump at a trial. Photo by Percy T. Jones.

BODY: Compact, strong, short coupled and substantial so as to permit great flexibility.

TAIL: Set moderately high and carried erect. Cut down to two joints and should not be longer than two inches. *Faults*—Too steep, level or too long a croup.

COAT: Hard and wiry, standing up on the back and, when seen against the course of the hair, neither short nor lying flat. The outer coat should be harsh, the under coat soft. It should be trimmed only to accent the body outline and should not be more than an inch long except on the ears and skull. *Faults*—Soft, smooth, curly; too long or short; too closely trimmed, dyed or excessively powdered.

COLOR: Pepper and salt or similar equal mixtures, light or dark including pure black. *Faults*—Solid colors other than black, also very light or whitish, spotted or tiger colors. A small white spot on the breast is not a fault.

ACTION: The gait should be sound, strong, quick, free, true and level.

Disqualifications. Shy, savage or highly nervous dogs and dogs which are in excess of or less than the standard in height.

SHETLAND SHEEPDOG

Shetland Sheepdog.

THE SHETLAND Sheepdog, as the name implies, came originally from the Shetland Islands, a land unique for the diminutive breeds of domestic animals which it has given to the world. From very ancient times Shetland ponies have been bred on the Islands along with the comparably small Shetland cattle and Shetland sheep. Working sheepdogs of small stature are known to have been used for generations in the hills of Shetland as sheepdrivers, and similar types of small dogs are found in the neighboring Orkney Islands and in the Outer Hebrides.

Like the diminutive dogs that guard the flocks, the Shetland sheep are very small, being only about half the size of the Scotch black-faced sheep. Because of their size it is never necessary to have so large a dog to herd them and keep them in bounds as it is in the Highlands of Scotland. The crofter prefers the smaller dogs for tending the flock, because they serve his purpose better than the larger dogs.

The origin of the Shetland Sheepdog is difficult to fathom for lack of authentic records. The Shelties are sometimes called Toonie dogs by the Shetlanders—after the Toon or township; and the older inhabitants are wont to boast that their particular Toonie dog was the direct forebear of the breed. As many different theories are offered to account for their origin as there are separate types.

In times past the dogs were selected and bred solely for their working ability and the crofters took no particular pains to produce animals of good appearance and uniform type as long as they were capable of performing the duties expected of them. From the scant information obtainable it is believed that the forebears of the breed first found their way to the Islands through the travels of the fishing fleets from Scandinavia, Scotland, and Holland which stopped at Shetland in the summer time. There seems to be but little doubt that the beginning of the breed dated from the time of the arrival at the Islands of a black-and-tan King Charles Spaniel detained from a yacht that touched there.

The early Greenland whalers, stopping at the Shetlands to land members of their crews, brought with them their Yakki dogs, so named after the natives of Greenland, who were known as Yaks. The Yakkis were crossed with the Shetland dogs, and distinct traces of this cross can be seen in the large, erect ears, heavy brush, height of 14 to 17 inches, and the characteristic black muzzle. There is likewise little doubt about some connection between the Icelandic dogs and those of the Shetlands, either through crossbreeding or similarity of origin.

That the modern Collie and the Shetland Sheepdog possess a common ancestor in the old-time Hill Collie is a certainty, although cross-breeding and evolution have so far removed each from its common forebear that they can no longer be regarded as belonging to the same breed. The Shetlanders often brought over from Scotland good working Collies of somewhat smaller stature than the exhibition Collies, and these were frequently crossed with the Toonie dogs. Thus the present-day Shetland breed is a combination of the older native types of the Islands with Collies selected for their small size and working capacity.

The earliest historical record in connection with the Shetland Sheepdog, bearing the date of 1840, is an old engraving of the town of Lerwick, capital of the Islands, showing a Shetland pony in the background, and a small, Collie-like dog in the foreground, indicating that the Shetland dogs had been commonly known there for perhaps a century or longer. The next recorded date is 1844, when an article written by a traveler to the Islands described the dogs as living in the house, playing by the fire, and sleeping on the couch.

Up to 1850, according to Dr. Bowie, a resident of Shetland and an authority on the breed, there were no large-sized dogs in the land. At this time, however, numbers of crofts were turned into large sheep-runs and the old Shetland Collie was replaced by the larger Collies that were required for the larger flocks. Yet it was not until nearly 60 years later that the

Shetland Collie Club, upon its founding in 1908, acted to safeguard the breeding of the Sheltie, which otherwise soon would have become extinct.

The general appearance of the original Shetland dogs may be learned from a description published in 1906. The average type was described as Collie in miniature, but there were several points of divergence, notably the ears, which were set very close together like a pair of fluffy wings. The body was long, set low on sturdy, well-feathered short legs, and the usual weight varied from 6 to 10 lbs. The prettier dogs were white or white with gold markings, although the black-and-tan or all black were more commonplace. The long, silky coat was rare, the half-long soft coat being most in evidence. The eyes were soft, round, and in good proportion to size.

The early dogs have also been described as resembling the Butterfly dog or Papillon of today. They have also been likened to the long-haired Chihuahua, originally known as the Mexican Toy Shepherd, with its heavier muzzle, coarser and larger frame, and coat like silk floss with the fringed effect of the Papillon.

The original Shetland Sheepdog was neither sufficiently pure-bred nor of enough real merit upon which to found a show breed without outside help. Reared in the rigorous northern climate, the dogs had lived and worked for many generations under conditions that begot unusual stamina, sturdy build, and a high degree of intelligence in the breed. Owing to environmental forces, however, the Shetland dogs that were sent out from the Islands in the beginning were very uneven in type, although they did possess great stamina and fine muscular development.

The first attempt to develop a standard type with a view to introducing the Shetlands for exhibition and show-breeding has been credited to an Islander, a Mr. Loggie, who utilized the show Collie to cross with the Shetlands. But it was not until 1906 that specimens of the Shetland dogs were shown for the first time at Crufts in London, where they drew very favorable comment. Two years later, the Shetland Collie Club was founded at Lerwick, where the dogs had been exhibited for 12 years or more.

Requests for recognition of the breed by the English Kennel Club were unavailing at that time and, as a consequence, the Scottish Shetland Collie Club was formed in 1909 by a few enthusiastic fanciers who published their own Stud Book and registered all the Collie miniatures older than 12 months. A year later, at the Crufts show of 1910, a separate classification was provided for the breed for the first time, and drew a very good entry from both Scotch and English exhibitors. Shortly thereafter the Ladies Kennel Association established classes for the Shetlands and was rewarded with an entry equal to that in the regular Collie classes.

Shetland dogs were introduced in America for the first time at the 1911 shows following a series of notable exhibitions abroad. At the Crufts show this same year there had been another excellent entry, although dogs of entirely different build had been benched, some of them standing low to the ground with relatively long backs and without the Collie appearance which is an essential characteristic of the true Sheltie. The diversity of sizes and types precipitated anew the controversy over height and build that had flared up intermittently.

Reverberations of the controversy continued to be heard on both sides of the Atlantic for many years. In America the problem of size caused considerably more agitation than it did abroad, mainly because Shetlands carrying Collie crosses had been exported to the United States and the succeeding generations bred from them had thrown back in size to their larger forebears.

In 1914, the English Sheepdog Club came into existence, and threw its weight in support of the miniature Collie by adopting a standard which described "the general appearance of the Shetland Collie as approximately that of a show Collie in miniature, ideal height, 12 inches." Later in the year the English Kennel Club, in conformance with the combined action of the Scotch and English Shetland Clubs, granted separate classification in its register. In effect, this meant that the Shetland finally had been recognized as being a breed in its own right and not merely a miniature of the Collie.

The breed nearly disappeared in England during the four years of World War I, and might have been lost entirely except for the fact that one breeder introduced a Collie cross to prevent the Collie type from vanishing. Thanks to this cross, the Shetland dogs began to show more uniformity of type, becoming sturdy, well-boned animals between 13 and 14 inches tall.

After much dissension and controversy the description of height was fixed by the leading clubs at "from 12 to 15 inches, the ideal being half way." As late as 1929, however, two distinct types of dogs were still competing with one another, but a turning point in the development of the Sheltie was now close at hand. The year 1929 marked the founding of the American Shetland Sheepdog Association at the Westminster Show in February, with its Description borrowed from the British Breeders Association; and it was in that same year that one of the most significant steps in the history of the breed was taken by both the English and Scottish Clubs in a resolution to the effect that the Shetland Sheepdog should be described as "resembling a Collie (rough) in miniature." There were still differences of opinion over size, but the Collie type predominated at last.

While the Shetland Sheepdog is primarily a working dog, the innate traits of character that have been developed in the breed through many generations of herding and guarding experience make them the best of companions. By their selection of dogs which would work, the crofters succeeded in conserving all the sagacity, alertness, and stamina of the sheepdog's Collie ancestry. The very origin and evolution of the breed tended to establish the permanence of their mental make-up and character traits even though it

Shetland Sheepdog. Photo by Wm. Brown.

failed to fix the physical points.

The temperament of the Sheltie is directly traceable to the influence of his native environment. His beauty of form and feature with his instinctive intelligence for herding and driving come from the Collie. His affection for human beings, his love of family life, and his devotion to his owners is the direct result of his close association with the crofters, while his docility, sweetness of disposition, and love of the outdoors is a heritage from his Spaniel ancestry. His hardiness comes from the rigors of the climate, and his natural watchdog attitude is the outgrowth of his training as a guard and protector of the croft.

The Sheltie has won a place for himself in America both in the role of a companion and as a working dog. Sheepgrowers in the western states of Montana, Colorado, Utah, Idaho, and Oregon have found the Shetlands well-suited to the duties required of them. Because of their light gait the dogs cover a great deal of ground without getting footsore, and it enables them to stay on top of deep snow where bigger dogs would break through. They are also less rough with the ewes at lambing time than some of the heavier types of Collies.

Description and Standards. The description and standards, by courtesy of the AKC follow.

The Shetland Sheepdog, like the Collie, traces to the Border Collie of Scotland, which, transported to the Shetland Islands and crossed with small, intelligent, longhaired breeds, was reduced to miniature proportions. Subsequently crosses were made from time to time with Collies. This breed now bears the same relationship in size and general appearance to the Rough Collie as the Shetland Pony does to some of the larger breeds of horses. Although the resemblance between the Shetland Sheepdog and the Rough Collie is marked, there are differences which may be noted.

GENERAL DESCRIPTION: The Shetland Sheepdog is a small, alert, rough-coated, longhaired working dog. He must be sound, agile and sturdy. The outline should be so symmetrical that no part appears out of proportion to the whole. Dogs should appear masculine; bitches feminine.

SIZE: The Shetland Sheepdog should stand between 13 and 16 inches at the shoulder. *Note:* Height is determined by a line perpendicular to the ground from the top of the shoulder blades, the dog standing naturally, with forelegs parallel to line of measurement. Heights below or above the desired size range are to be disqualified from the show ring.

COAT: The coat should be double, the outer coat consisting of long, straight, harsh hair; the under coat short, furry, and so dense as to give the entire coat its "stand-off" quality. The hair on face, tips of ears and feet should be smooth. Mane and frill should be abundant, and particularly impressive in males. The forelegs well feathered, the hind legs heavily so, but smooth below the hock joint. Hair on tail profuse. *Note:* Excess hair on ears, feet, and on hocks may be trimmed for the show ring. *Faults:* Coat short or flat, in whole or in part; wavy, curly, soft or silky. Lack of undercoat. Smooth-coated specimens.

COLOR: Black, blue merle, and sable (ranging from golden through mahogany); marked with varying amounts of white and/or tan. *Faults:* Rustiness in a black or a blue coat. Washed out or degenerate colors, such as pale sable and faded blue. Self-color in the case of blue merle, that is, without any merling or mottling and generally appearing as a faded or dilute tricolor. Conspicuous white body spots. Specimens with more than 50 percent white shall be so severely penalized as to effectively eliminate them from competition. *Disqualification:* Brindle.

TEMPERAMENT: The Shetland Sheepdog is intensely loyal, affectionate, and responsive to his owner. However, he may be reserved toward strangers but not to the point of showing fear or cringing in the ring. *Faults:* Shyness, timidity, or nervousness. Stubbornness, snappiness, or ill temper.

HEAD: The head should be refined and its shape, when viewed from top or side, be a long, blunt wedge tapering slightly from ears to nose, which must be black. Top of skull should be flat, showing no prominence at nuchal crest (the top of the occiput). Cheeks should be flat and should merge smoothly into a well-rounded muzzle. Skull and muzzle should be of equal length, balance point being inner corner of eye. In profile the top line of skull should parallel the top line of muzzle, but on a higher plane due to the presence of a slight but definite stop. Jaws clean and powerful. The deep, well-developed underjaw, rounded at chin, should extend to base of nostril. Lips tight. Upper and lower lips must meet and fit smoothly together all the way around. Teeth level and evenly spaced. Scissors bite. *Faults:* Two-angled head. Too prominent stop, or no stop. Overfill below, between, or above eyes. Prominent nuchal crest. Domed skull. Prominent cheekbones. Snipy muzzle. Short, receding, or shallow under-jaw, lacking breadth and depth. Overshot or undershot, missing or crooked teeth. Teeth visible when mouth is closed.

EYES: Medium size with dark, almond-shaped rims, set somewhat obliquely in skull. Color must be dark, with blue or merle eyes permissible in blue merles only. *Faults:* Light, round, large or too small. Prominent haws.

EARS: Small and flexible, placed high, carried three-fourths erect, with tips breaking forward. When in repose the ears fold lengthwise and are thrown back into the frill. *Faults:* Set too low. Hound, prick, bat, twisted ears. Leather too thick or too thin.

EXPRESSION: Contours and chiseling of the head, the shape, set and use of ears, the placement, shape and color of the eyes, combine to produce expression. Normally the expression should be alert, gentle, intelligent and questioning. Toward strangers the eyes should show watchfulness and reserve, but no fear. Neck should be muscular, arched, and of sufficient length to carry the head proudly. *Faults:* Too short and thick.

BODY: In over-all appearance the body should appear moderately long as measured from shoulder joint to ischium (rearmost extremity of the pelvic bone), but much of this length is actually due to the proper angulation and breadth of the shoulder and hindquarter, as the back itself should be comparatively short. Back should be level and strongly muscled. Chest should be deep, the brisket reaching to point of elbow. The ribs should be well sprung, but flattened at their lower half to allow free play of the foreleg and shoulder. Abdomen moderately tucked up. *Faults:* Back too long, too short, swayed or roached. Barrel ribs. Slab side. Chest narrow and/or too shallow.

FOREQUARTERS: From the withers the shoulder blades should slope at a 45-degree angle forward and downward to the shoulder joints. At the withers they are separated only by the vertebra, but they must slope outward sufficiently to accommodate the desired spring of rib. The upper arm should join the shoulder blade at as nearly as possible a right angle. Elbow joint should be equidistant from the ground or from the withers. Forelegs straight viewed from all angles, muscular and clean, and of strong bone. Pasterns very strong, sinewy and flexible. Dewclaws may be removed. *Faults:* Insufficient angulation between shoulder and upper arm. Upper arm too short. Lack of outward slope of shoulders. Loose shoulders. Turning in or out of elbows. Crooked legs. Light bone.

FEET *(front and hind):* Feet should be oval and compact with the toes well arched and fitting tightly together. Pads deep and tough, nails hard and strong. *Faults:* Feet turning in or out. Splay-feet. Hare-feet. Cat-feet.

HINDQUARTERS: There should be a slight arch at the loins, and the croup should slope gradually to the rear. The hipbone (pelvis) should be set at a 30-degree angle to the spine. The thigh should be broad and muscular. The thighbone should be set into the pelvis at a right angle corresponding to the angle of the shoulder blade and upper arm. Stifle bones join the thighbone and should be distinctly angled at the stifle joint. The overall length of the stifle should at least equal the length of the thighbone, and preferably should slightly exceed it. Hock joint should be clean-cut, angular, sinewy, with good bone and strong ligamentation. The hock (metatarsus) should be short and straight viewed from all angles. Dewclaws should be removed. Feet *(see Forequarters)*. *Faults:* Croup higher than withers. Croup too straight or too steep. Narrow thighs. Cowhocks. Hocks turning out. Poorly defined hock joint. Feet *(see* Forequarters).

TAIL: The tail should be sufficiently long so that when it is laid along the back edge of the hind legs the last vertebra will reach the hock joint. Carriage of tail at rest is straight down or in a slight upward curve. When the dog is alert the tail is normally lifted, but it should not be curved forward over the back. *Faults:* Too short. Twisted at end.

GAIT: The trotting gait of the Shetland Sheepdog should denote effortless speed and smoothness. There should be no jerkiness, nor stiff, stilted, up-and-down movement. The drive should be from the rear, true and straight, dependent upon correct angulation, musculation, and ligamentation of the entire hindquarter, thus allowing the dog to reach well under his body with his hind foot and propel himself forward. Reach of stride of the foreleg is dependent upon correct angulation, musculation and ligamentation of the forequarters, together with correct width of chest and construction of rib cage. The foot should be lifted only enough to clear the ground as the leg swings forward. Viewed from the front, both forelegs and hind legs should move forward almost perpendicular to ground at the walk, slanting a little inward at a slow trot, until at a swift trot the feet are brought so far inward toward center line of body that the tracks left show two parallel lines of footprints actually touching a center line at their inner edges. There should be no crossing of the feet nor throwing of the weight from side to side. *Faults:* Stiff, short steps, with a choppy, jerky movement. Mincing steps, with a hopping up and down, or a balancing of weight from side to side (often erroneously admired as a "dancing gait" but permissible in young puppies). Lifting of front feet in hackneylike action, resulting in loss of speed and energy. Pacing gait.

SCALE OF POINTS:		*Points*
GENERAL APPEARANCE		
Symmetry	10	
Temperament	10	
Coat	5	25

HEAD		
Skull and stop	5	
Muzzle	5	
Eyes, ears and expression	10	20
BODY		
Neck and back	5	
Chest, ribs and brisket	10	
Loin, croup, and tail	5	20
FOREQUARTERS		
Shoulder	10	
Forelegs and feet	5	15
HINDQUARTERS		
Hip, thigh and stifle	10	
Hocks and feet	5	15
GAIT		
Gait—smoothness and lack of waste motion when trotting		5
TOTAL		100

Disqualifications. Heights below or above the desired range, i.e. 13-16 inches. Brindle color.

(May 12, 1959)

SIBERIAN HUSKY

THE SIBERIAN HUSKY belongs to the family of Arctic sled dogs which also includes the Eskimo, Alaskan Malamute, and Samoyed. Next to the Samoyed, he is the most popular among Americans. He is smaller and more refined in build and appearance than either the Alaskan Malamute or the Eskimo, and it is probable that, pound for pound, he is the toughest draft dog that lives.

The origin of the Siberian Husky is obscure, as with the other Arctic dogs. It is tied in with the origin of the Arctic peoples themselves, and this, too, is still somewhat a mystery.

One theory—this held by Dr. Edward M. Weyer, Jr.—is that the Eskimo migrated from Siberia to Alaska, and from thence across the Arctic Circle to Greenland, at least 2,000 years ago. They took with them their dogs, the ancestors of the Malamute and the Eskimo.

Filling in behind the migrating Eskimos were the Chuchis, an Eskimo-like people who settled around the basin of the Kolyma River, and along the foothills of the Cherski Mountains. These people developed the dog which we call the Siberian Husky, but which might more properly be called the Siberian Chuchi.

It is impossible to distinguish this breed from other Arctic dogs in the accounts of early explorers. Baron Wrangell, and others, mention sled dogs as coming from Kamchatka, the Bering Peninsula, and all the way to Baffin Land and Greenland, but the accounts are not sufficiently explicit to give a researcher in breeds any real clues.

Yet even the early explorers were specific about the work the dogs did. They praised them as sled dogs, marveled at their endurance and their extraordinary ability to find a trail.

One account tells of relay stations in Siberia where it was possible to exchange sled dogs for the continuation of a journey. This would indicate that Arctic Siberia had an intricate transportation system, via dogs, many decades ago.

Among other distinctive features, it was reported that the dogs have no body odor; that they howl rather than bark; and that, while killers of other dogs and other animals, they are gentle with humans.

In this latter respect, the Siberian Husky appears to have a better reputation than either the Malamute or the Eskimo. This could be from a difference in living habits. The Chuchis and the Samoyedes, that is, the Asiatic Arctic peoples, keep their dogs with them in their dwellings. But the North American Eskimos quite generally do not. The dogs live out in the snow and get only a very minimum of human companionship. This tends to make them wilder and more intractable than their Siberian cousins.

The origin of the name "Husky" is rather unusual. It is said to have been a term given the Eskimos by the early North American explorers. In recent years, it has come to mean any northern dog which is used for sled work, whether or not he is pure-bred. The Siberian Husky is the only breed in which the term has become part of the proper name.

Shortly after 1900, Americans in Alaska began to hear fabulous accounts of a superior race of sled dogs lying about a thousand miles beyond Alaska, in Siberia. Several teams of these dogs, Siberian Huskies, made their appearance in Alaskan sled races in 1909 and 1910. Thereafter, great numbers of the dogs were imported. They have won a large proportion of sled races since, where mere speed under mild weather and trail conditions were not the only factors.

Tales about the dogs and their prowess and gentleness began to reach the United States. By 1930, fair numbers of them were being brought into the country for breeding purposes. Because of this, and because of the remoteness of the original breeding stock, the breed has not suffered from mongrel crosses to the extent the Malamute and Eskimo have.

The breed's gentleness has helped him to increasing popularity, too, although it must be admitted he has suffered from suspicion engendered by the actions of other Arctic dogs. His smaller size and great beauty also have combined to make him more popular than other Arctic breeds, save only the Samoyed.

Among those responsible for the popularity here of the Siberian Husky were Mr. and Mrs. Milton Seeley of the Chinook Kennels, Wonalancet, N.H. They were master breeders and trainers, and specialized in training Siberians and Eskimos for Arctic exploration and for war work.

Description and Standards: The description and standards, adopted by the Siberian Husky Club and approved by the American Kennel Club follow.

GENERAL APPEARANCE: The Siberian Husky is a medium-sized working dog of powerful but graceful build. His moderately compact and well-furred body, erect ears, and brush tail curved over the back suggest the northern heritage of the capable sled dog. His characteristic gait is free and effortless but unbelievably strong when called upon to pull. And the keen and friendly expression in his slightly oblique eyes indicates the amenable disposition of the good companion.

HEAD: The skull is of medium size, in proportion to the body; a trifle rounded on top and tapering gradually to the eyes, the width between the ears medium to narrow. Muzzle medium long, that is, the distance from nose to stop is about equal to the distance from stop to occiput. Skull and muzzle are finely chiseled. Lips dark and close-fitting, the jaws strong, and the teeth meeting in a scissors bite. *Faults:* Head too heavy; skull too wide; the muzzle either bulky, snipy, or coarse. The ears are medium in size, set high, and carried erect. When at attention, they are practically parallel to each other. They are moderately rounded at the tips and well furred on the inner side. *Faults:* Too large, too low-set, and not strongly erect. The eyes are set a trifle obliquely, their expression keen but friendly, interested, and even mischievous. Color may be either brown or blue, one brown eye and one blue eye being permissible but not desirable. *Faults:* Eyes set too obliquely.

NOSE: Preferably black, with brown allowed in specimens of reddish-colored coats; and flesh-colored nose and eye rims allowed in white dogs. The nose that is temporarily pink-streaked in winter is permissible but not desirable.

NECK: Strong, arched, and fairly short.

BODY: Moderately compact but never cobby. Chest deep and strong but not too broad, the ribs well sprung and deep. Shoulders powerful and well laid back. Back of medium length and strong, the back line level. Loins taut, lean, and very slightly arched. *Faults:* Weak or slack back; roach back.

LEGS AND FEET: The legs are straight and well muscled, with bone substantial but not heavy. Hindquarters powerful with good angulation. Well bent at stifles. Dewclaws on the rear legs, if any, are to be removed. The feet are oval in shape, medium in size; compact and well furred between the toes. Pads tough and deeply cushioned. In short, a typical snowshoe foot, somewhat webbed between the toes. *Faults:* Bone too light or too heavy; insufficient bend at stifles; weak pasterns; feet soft and/or splayed.

TAIL: A well-furred brush carried over the back in a sickle curve when the dog runs or stands at attention, and trailing out behind when working or in repose. When carried up, the typical tail does not curl to either side of the body, nor does it snap flat to the back. The tail hair is usually of medium

Siberian Husky—Ch. S.K.Mo's Charney Korsar. (Owner: Mrs. Lou I. Richardson, Riverside, Calif.) Photo by Ludwig.

Siberian Huskies—The team owned by Mrs. Lorna Demidoff, Monadnock Kennels, Fitzwilliam, New Hampshire. Photo by Evelyn M. Shafer.

length, although length varies somewhat with over-all coat length.

COAT: Double. The under coat is dense, soft and downy, and should be of sufficient length and density to support the outer coat. The outer coat is very thick, smooth-textured and soft, giving a smooth, full-furred appearance and a clean-cut outline. It is usually medium in length; a longer coat is allowed so long as the texture is soft and remains the same in any length. *Faults:* Harsh texture, or a rough look which obscures the clean-cut outline of the dog; absence of under coat, except while actually shedding.

COLOR: All colors and white, and all markings are allowed. The various shades of wolf and the silver grays, tan and black with white points are most usual. A variety of markings, especially on the head, are common to the breed, these including many striking and unusual patterns not found in other breeds. The cap-like mask and spectacles are typical.

SIZE. Both height and weight are very important. Dogs, from 21 to 23½ inches at the shoulder; bitches, from 20 to 22 inches. Dogs, from 45 to 60 pounds; bitches, from 35 to 50 pounds. Dogs over 23½ inches and bitches over 22 inches are to be disqualified.

SUMMARY: Most important of the Siberian Husky's characteristics are medium size and moderate bone, soft coat, high-set ears, ease and freedom of action, and good disposition. A gait, or a general appearance in any way clumsy, heavy, or unwieldy is to be penalized. In addition to the faults already noted, obvious structural faults common to all breeds, such as cow-hocks, for instance, are as undesirable in the Siberian Husky as in any other breed, even though they are not specifically mentioned therein.

Disqualification. Height over 23½ inches in dogs; over 22 inches in bitches.

(March 12, 1963)

ST. BERNARD

PERHAPS NO breed of dog has the world-wide reputation enjoyed by the St. Bernard. But this breed is relatively rare as compared to some of the terriers and sporting dogs, and even some other Swiss dogs. His origins are shrouded with as much mystery as cloaks many other breeds. And yet, in his present form, he is really one of our oldest breeds.

It is supposed that the breed takes its name from the noted Monk, Bernard de Menthon, but it is more correct to say that the dogs were named from the Hospice at the St. Bernard Pass, in the Swiss Alps. There is no evidence to show that dogs were used at

the time of St. Bernard, the first reference to them in the Hospice records being in 1774.

What the early dogs were, or even what they looked like, is a matter of conjecture. But it is said that the monks did not breed dogs at the Hospice, but farmed out the bitches at farms in the valley. Only males were used in the work at the Pass. Performance, rather than looks, counted. And in the earlier days, at least, there is no evidence that the monks bred for anything else. The dogs, therefore, could have come from very mixed stock.

It was Sir Edwin Landseer, the painter, who was responsible for the popular conception of the St. Bernard as a dog going through the snowdrifts with a small cask of wine or rum tied to his neck. In this picture, two dogs are standing over a fallen traveler. One appears to be baying to attract attention. The dog with the wine cask licks the fallen man's bare hand and wrist.

According to Watson, Landseer was 17 when he painted this picture in 1819. These dogs were said to be Cora and Caeser, the property of a Mrs. Boodie. Landseer drew the sire of these dogs, Lion, as early as 1815, and his brother, Thomas, made an engraving of it. Lion was called an Alpine Mastiff, but Landseer named the later painting "Dogs of St. Gothard."

It appears doubtful that the dogs at the Hospice actually took much part in rescue work of the type pictured by Landseer. Others, who visited the Hospice, stated that the dogs were used chiefly as guides over the treacherous last five miles of the trail over the crest. Their job was to find the trail, and to warn of dangerous footing. One such account was published in the *English Stockkeeper*, Aug. 27, 1887. It was written from the Hospice by a W. O. Hughes-Hughes, at that time prominent among English St. Bernard breeders.

Nevertheless, it is a widely held belief that the way the dogs were used evolved from the experience of the monks who discovered their dogs were excellent pathfinders, especially when wind-driven snow obliterated the trail or made it otherwise impossible to go more than a few feet beyond the doors of the Hospice without losing all sense of direction. The dogs were also found to have such an excellent sense of smell that they could locate helpless persons overcome by storms.

Not given any special training, the young dogs were merely allowed to run with older dogs on patrols, there usually being three or four dogs forming a patrol during and following storms. If they came upon a storm victim, two dogs would lie down close by the victim to warm him. One of them would lick the victim's face to restore consciousness. Another dog, in the meantime would have started back for the Hospice to alarm the monks and guide them to the scene. The dogs were also said to have an uncanny sense of impending avalanche, changing positions in some cases just seconds before an avalanche swept over the spot where they had been standing.

One of the most noted of the early dogs at the Hospice was called Barry. After his death, before 1815, Barry was stuffed and mounted, and placed in a Berne museum. He appears to have been a medium-sized, short-coated dog, with a heavy body. It is now assumed, though on no good authority, that Barry was typical of the first and true St. Bernards. Idstone, an unreliable reporter, stated that Barry saved 42 lives. Rev. J. C. Macdona, one of the first great British breeders, raised this figure to 75.

The kennels at the St. Bernard Hospice appear to have been badly depleted in 1815, and again in 1830, once by distemper and once by an avalanche. According to Herr Schumacher, who wrote a history of the breed covering the years 1815 to 1880, the monks then used Newfoundland and Great Dane stock to bring up the size and vigor of the remaining dogs. Other writers say that Mastiffs and Pyrenean Sheepdogs were used also.

Whatever the truth of these statements, it would appear that the monks were not any more interested in size and strength than they were in type. Also, there is positive evidence that short-coated dogs were preferred. Finally, the evidence is strong to show that there was a true Alpine Mastiff in existence in Switzerland at that time. This dog, perhaps a cast-off from the Hospice, may have been used in reconstituting the St. Bernard breed, and in getting the long coat.

The Schumacher account seems most probable, since Schumacher himself was a heavy donor. He noted that the long-coated dogs were given away. He described the cast-offs as being red and white, with black face and neck, double dewclaws, and great height. So it is possible that our modern St. Bernards actually do come from these cast-offs. That would make them Swiss farm dogs.

Rev. J. C. Macdona was the first great British breeder. It can be said that but for him we might not have a St. Bernard dog today. He had a flair for getting publicity, and he kept the breed in the limelight at the shows from 1870 to 1880. The head painting of his dog, Bayard, was perhaps the best known dog picture of the time in England.

We owe the modern St. Bernard to Macdona and other British breeders of that period. They fixed the type, color, and coat, and increased the size to the present standard. For that reason, one can examine the pictures of St. Bernards of the period from 1880 to 1900 without using imagination as a means of guessing the breed.

Watson, the American dog authority, and himself a St. Bernard fancier and judge, believed that the first St. Bernards to be brought to America were sent by General Lafayette to J. F. Skinner in 1828. Skinner was a one-time Assistant Postmaster General, and was editor of the *American Farmer* and the *Sporting Magazine*.

Gen. Lafayette sent Skinner two "French sheepdogs," and later two dogs which Skinner himself described as "Pyrenean or St. Bernard." Skinner was interested in European sheepdogs, but he tells of the use of the dogs at the St. Bernard Hospice, so it seems evident they did come from there. Whether they were actually St. Bernards, or Great Pyrenees, or crosses arising out of the 1815 disaster, cannot be known.

St. Bernards were shown at the first New York dog show in 1879. There were classes for both roughs and smooths. A dog which Watson described as "one of Dan Foster's picked-up dogs," was a winner in smooths. Two pups, which finished second and third were Miss Pearsol's Fino and Mr. Haines' Don. Fino came from the Hospice.

Two others in the beaten field were Barclay Jermain's Chamonix and Burdett Loomis's Alpe. Both were from Switzerland.

Importations from Prince Albert Solm's kennels led the roughs, but Watson describes them as "ordinary." He says the first good rough in this country was Mr. Hearn's Monk, which won the champion's prize in 1882, but died a few weeks later. Another good one of the time, according to Watson, was Bonivard, which came from the kennel of William Graham of Belfast, Ireland.

Mason, who brought the world famous "Dogs of all Nations" exhibit to the San Francisco International Exposition in 1915, gives us an excellent picture of the dogs of that period. According to him, the typical dogs of the period were about 30 inches tall and weighed around 200 pounds. He pictures a much stronger back than is seen today.

Croxton-Smith, and other writers, both English and American, have pointed out that increasing the size and weight of the breed has tended to bring a heavy proportion of dogs faulty in back and in hind quarters. While not necessarily unsound, the dogs have had a lumbering gait, which has put them at a disadvantage in variety group competition at the dog show. Cow hocks have been a common fault for many years.

The dogs have, as a rule, a placid disposition being gentle with children. However, due to their great size and weight, they are extremely dangerous if bad tempered, or when aroused. A bite from a

St. Bernard. Photo by Evelyn M. Shafer.

Cocker Spaniel and one by a St. Bernard are decidedly different things.

Record books, incidentally, show as the largest dog in the world a St. Bernard named "Brandy," that died in Oxfordshire, England at a weight of 259 pounds.

In some years, the breed has received bad publicity because of its bites. One incident involved a dog from the Hospice itself. On the other hand, several dogs have received widespread publicity because of their gentleness. Thus, world-wide attention was drawn to a Cleveland dog, named Rebecca of Ridgewood, which in several occasions brought in baby birds and rabbits unharmed. The same dog was widely used as a demonstrator and recruiter for Dogs For Defense during the war.

While a great companion, the St. Bernard's size and appetite have prevented him from becoming as common as his fame should dictate. Still, the breed is thoroughly established in the United States, and dogs of unusual soundness and gait have been appearing.

This soundness has paid off in the show ring where St. Bernards have been winning group and Best in Show honors.

Description and Standards: The description and standards, by courtesy of the St. Bernard Club of America, follow.

SHORTHAIRED

GENERAL: Powerful, proportionately tall figure, strong and muscular in every part, with powerful head and most intelligent expression. In dogs with a dark mask the expression appears more stern, but never ill-natured.

HEAD: Like the whole body, very powerful and imposing. The massive skull is wide, slightly arched and the sides slope in a gentle curve into the very strongly developed, high cheek bones. Occiput only moderately developed. The supra-orbital ridge is very strongly developed and forms nearly a right angle with the horizontal axis of the head. Deeply imbedded between the eyes and starting at the root of the muzzle, a furrow runs over the whole skull. It is strongly marked in the first half, gradually disappearing toward the base of the occiput. The lines at the sides of the head diverge considerably from the outer corner of the eyes toward the back of the head. The skin of the forehead, above the eyes, forms rather noticeable wrinkles, more or less pronounced, which converge toward the furrow. Especially when the dog is in action, the wrinkles are more visible without in the least giving the impression of morosity. Too strongly developed wrinkles are not desired. The slope from the skull to the muzzle is sudden and rather steep.

The muzzle is short, does not taper, and the vertical depth at the root of the muzzle must be greater than the length of the muzzle. The bridge of the muzzle is not arched, but straight; in some dogs, occasionally, slightly broken. A rather wide, well-marked, shallow furrow runs from the root of the muzzle over the entire bridge of the muzzle to the nose. The flews of the upper jaw are strongly developed, not sharply cut, but turning in a beautiful curve into the lower edge, and slightly overhanging. The flews of the lower jaw must not be deeply pendant. The teeth should be sound and strong and should meet in either a scissors or an even bite; the scissors bite being preferable. The undershot bite, although sometimes found with good specimens, is not desirable. The overshot bite is a fault. A black roof to the mouth is desirable.

NOSE (Schwamm): Very substantial, broad, with wide open nostrils, and, like the lips, always black.

EARS: Of medium size, rather high set, with very strongly developed burr (Muschel) at the base. They stand slightly away from the head at the base, then drop with a sharp bend to the side and cling to the head without a turn. The flap is tender and forms a rounded triangle, slightly elongated toward the point, the front edge lying firmly to the head, whereas the back edge may stand somewhat away from the head, especially when the dog is at attention. Lightly set ears, which at the base immediately cling to the head, give it an oval and too little marked exterior, whereas a strongly developed base gives the skull a squarer, broader and much more expressive appearance.

EYES: Set more to the front than the sides, are of medium size, dark brown, with intelligent, friendly expression, set moderately deep. The lower eyelids, as a rule, do not close completely and, if that is the case, form an angular wrinkle toward the inner corner of the eye. Eyelids which are too deeply pendant and show conspicuously the lachrymal glands, or a very red, thick haw, and eyes that are too light, are objectionable.

NECK: Set high, very strong and in action is carried erect. Otherwise horizontally or slightly downward. The junction of head and neck is distinctly marked by an indentation. The nape of the neck is very muscular and rounded at the sides which makes the neck appear rather short. The dewlap of throat and neck is well-pronounced: too strong development, however, is not desirable.

SHOULDERS: Sloping and broad, very muscular and powerful. The withers are strongly pronounced.

CHEST: Very well arched, moderately deep, not reaching below the elbows.

BACK: Very broad, perfectly straight as far as the haunches, from there gently sloping to the rump, and merging imperceptibly into the root of the tail.

HINDQUARTERS: Well-developed. Legs very muscular.

BELLY: Distinctly set off from the very powerful loin section, only little drawn up.

TAIL: Starting broad and powerful directly from the rump is long, very heavy, ending in a powerful tip. In repose it hangs

St. Bernard. Photo by Evelyn M. Shafer.

St. Bernard—A head study. Photo by Evelyn M. Shafer.

straight down, turning gently upward in the lower third only, which is not considered a fault. In a great many specimens the tail is carried with the edge slightly bent and therefore hangs down in the shape of an f. In action all dogs carry the tail more or less turned upward. However it may not be carried too erect or by any means rolled over the back. A slight curling of the tip is sooner admissible.

FOREARMS: Very powerful and extraordinarily muscular.

FORELEGS: Straight, strong.

HIND LEGS: Hocks of moderate angulation. Dewclaws are not desired; if present, they must not obstruct gait.

FEET: Broad, with strong toes, moderately closed, and with rather high knuckles. The so-called dewclaws which sometimes occur on the inside of the hind legs are imperfectly developed toes. They are of no use to the dog and are not taken into consideration in judging. They may be removed by surgery.

COAT: Very dense, short-haired (stockhaarig), lying smooth, tough, without however feeling rough to the touch. The thighs are slightly bushy. The tail at the root has longer and denser hair which gradually becomes shorter toward the tip. The tail appears bushy, not forming a flag.

COLOR: White with red or red with white, the red in its various shades; brindle patches with white markings. The colors red and brown-yellow are of entirely equal value. Necessary markings are: white chest, feet and tip of tail, nose band, collar or spot on the nape; the latter and blaze are very desirable. Never of one color or without white. Faulty are all other colors, except the favorite dark shadings on the head (mask) and ears. One distinguishes between mantle dogs and splash-coated dogs.

HEIGHT AT SHOULDER: Of the dog should be 27½ inches minimum, of the bitch 25½ inches. Female animals are of finer and more delicate build.

Considered as faults are all deviations from the standard, as for instance a sway-back and a disproportionately long back, hocks too much bent, straight hindquarters, upward growing

hair in spaces between the toes, out at elbows, cowhocks and weak pasterns.

LONGHAIRED

The longhaired type completely resembles the shorthaired type except for the coat which is not shorthaired (stockhaarig) but of medium length plain to slightly wavy, never rolled or curly and not shaggy either. Usually, on the back, especially from the region of the haunches to the rump, the hair is more wavy, a condition, by the way, that is slightly indicated in the shorthaired dogs. The tail is bushy with dense hair of moderate length. Rolled or curly hair on the tail is not desirable. A tail with parted hair, or a flag tail, is faulty. Face and ears are covered with short and soft hair; longer hair at the base of the ear is permissible. Forelegs only slightly feathered; thighs very bushy.

(May 12, 1959)

WELSH CORGI (Cardigan)

OF THE two types of Welsh Corgis, the dog from Cardiganshire is said to be the oldest in point of pure breeding. Yet he has lagged behind his close relative from Pembrokeshire in both England and the United States.

The usually accredited history of the Cardigan Corgi was written by a Welsh fancier, W. Lloyd-Thomas of Mabws Hall, Llanrhystyd, Cardiganshire, South Wales.

According to Lloyd-Thomas, the dog belonged to the Central Europe Celts who invaded Wales around 1200 B.C. He was used, perhaps by them but later on, at least, by their followers as a cattle dog, biting at the heels of the cattle, and then dropping to the ground to avoid their kicks.

The dog's chief function is better comprehended by realizing that in the period of his greatest usefulness —later on, but still several hundred years ago—the Crown owned practically all the land, but permitted the tenant farmers, or crofters, to fence off only very small patches surrounding their own dooryards, though they were permitted, on the other hand, to graze their cattle on the Crown-owned "open land," or open range out beyond these small settlements. Consequently, they needed a dog which would move the cattle out to the open range and, once there, drive the cattle even farther out to graze. This was most important, hence the Corgi was a cattle-driving dog rather than a herding dog. By whistle signals the little dogs received their orders—whether to move the cattle farther out, etc., or to bring them back. These small dogs, in other words, were most appropriate for this kind of work.

The original type of Corgi, found about Bronant in the heart of the Celtic Wales country, virtually disappeared after the division of the Crown Lands and the fencing of the ranges. To save the stock, crosses apparently were made with both the red and the brindle herding dogs. The former crosses were said not to be successful.

The dog was said originally to have been a

Welsh Corgi Cardigan.

member of the Dachshund family, whereas Pembroke-shire fanciers claim the Wolf-spitz family as the origin of their variety. However, some writers freely admit that crosses were made between the two varie-ties, and that these account for the similarity of the two.

The Cardigan dog has a long tail, and he differs in color and texture of coat from the Pembroke. Collie crosses may account for this.

The two varieties were introduced into the United States in approximately equal numbers. But the dog from Cardiganshire has failed to catch on, so that he is still relatively rare here.

Description and Standards: The description and standards, by courtesy of the Cardigan Welsh Corgi Club, follow.

GENERAL APPEARANCE: Low set, sturdily built, with heavy bone and deep chest. Overall silhouette long in proportion to height, culminating in low tail and fox-like brush. Expression alert and foxy, watchful yet friendly. General impression: a handsome, powerful small dog, capable of both speed and endurance, intelligent, sturdy but not coarse.

HEAD AND SKULL: Skull moderately wide and flat between the ears, with definite though moderate, stop. Muzzle to measure about three inches in length, or in proportion to the skull as three to five. Muzzle medium, i.e., neither too pointed nor too blunt but somewhat less fine than a Pembroke. Nose black. Nostrils of moderate size. Underjaw cleancut and strong.

EYES: Medium to large, and rather widely set, with distinct corners. Color dark to dark amber, but clear. Blue eyes, or one dark and one blue eye permissible in blue merles.

MOUTH: Teeth strong and regular, neither overshot nor undershot. Pincer (level) bite permissible but scissor bite pre-ferred, e.g., the inner side of the front teeth resting closely over the front of the lower front teeth.

EARS: Large and prominent in proportion to size of dog. Slightly rounded at the tips, moderately wide at the base and carried erect, set well apart and well back, sloping forward when erect. Flop ears a serious fault.

NECK: Muscular, well developed, especially in males, and in proportion to dog's build; fitting into strong, well-shaped shoul-ders.

FOREQUARTERS: Chest broad, deep, and well let down between forelegs. Forelegs short, strong and slightly bowed around chest, and with distinct but not exaggerated crook below the carpus. Elbows close to side. A straight terrier-like front is a fault.

BODY: Long and strong, with deep brisket, well-sprung ribs with moderate tuck-up of loin.

Welsh Corgi Cardigan.

Topline level except for slight slope of spine above tail.

HINDQUARTERS: Strong, with muscular thighs. Legs short and well-boned.

FEET: Round and well padded. Hind dewclaws, if any, should be removed. Front dewclaws may be removed.

TAIL: Long to moderately long resembling a fox brush. Should be set fairly low when standing or moving slowly, streaming out when at a dead run, lifted when tracking or excited, but never curled under the back. A rat-tail or a whip tail are faults.

COAT: Medium length but dense. Slightly harsh texture, but neither wiry nor silky. Weather-resistant. Any overly short coat or a long and silky and/or curly coat are faults. Normal grooming and trimming of whiskers is permitted. Any trimming that alters the natural length of the coat is not permitted and is a serious fault. A distinctly long coat is a disqualification.

SIZE: Height approximately 12 inches at the highest point of the shoulder blades. Length usually between 36 and 44 inches from nose to tip of tail. In considering the height, weight and length of a dog, overall balance is a prime factor.

COLORS: Red, sable, red-brindle, black-brindle, black, tri-color, blue merle. Usually with white flashings on chest, neck, feet, face or tip of tail. No preferences among these colors. A dog predominantly white in color should be seriously faulted. Pure white is a disqualification.

(March, 1967)

WELSH CORGI (Pembroke)

AMONG THE late-comers on the American dog scene is the Welsh Corgi, of which there are two types. Here we deal with the type which comes from Pembrokeshire, in South Wales. It is a short-legged, often tailless, bright-eyed dog, whose droll appearance and good spirits have won him many friends.

The dog is sometimes called the Ci Sawdl, or simply, the Welsh heeler. This latter describes his work, for he is used as a cattle driver and for rounding up the famous Welsh ponies.

It is said that the name Corgi comes from "cor" meaning dwarf, and "gi" meaning dog. Another explanation is that the name derives from "cur," meaning to "watch over" something. But there is perhaps a better explanation told the writer by a noted philologist.

Only three or four words have come down to us from the Celtic language, that is, which have become a part of our own language. Whiskey is one, and corgi is another. Corgi, in Celtic, meant simply "dog." But when the Norman Conquest of England came, the Normans brought in their own blooded dogs. The peasants were forbidden to own these blooded dogs, and the Normans dismissed the local dogs as simply mongrels.

The native word "corgi," or "curgi," took on the meaning of "mongrel dog," "cur," or "mut." But the name survived in Wales as a term for a cattle dog.

Pembrokeshire fanciers state that their breed dates back at least to A.D. 920, when King Howell Dda codified the Welsh laws, and mentioned therein the Welsh cattle dogs. According to these fanciers, Welsh

Welsh Corgi Pembroke.

Corgis have existed about as they are today ever since.

However, it was not until 1928 that the breed was admitted to the English Kennel Club Register. Three years before a Welsh Corgi Club had been organized. When members were unable to get along with Cardigan fanciers, and all efforts to bring the two varieties together failed, a Cardigan club was formed in 1934.

Shortly after its admittance to the English Register, the dog began to appear in America. At that time a pamphlet was issued which gave a quite different origin for the modern breed. This pamphlet stated that the original and ancient dog had disappeared. In order to develop a breed which, it was assumed, looked like this extinct dog, Smooth Collies, Dachshunds, and other breeds were crossed.

This history has disappeared in favor of more romantic ones, but it may explain why such odd-looking dogs appeared in some of the earlier litters in the 1920 to 1930 period.

Another thing which plagued British fanciers was the dog's tail. Some dogs were born tailless, others with merely a stump, and still others with a rather longer tail than would be graceful in a dog so short. However, the rules prohibited docking these long tails.

So a judge might find himself with a class of dogs with tails of all length, or no tails. As one British writer puts it, he might not know whether he had some very poor Pembrokeshire Corgis in front of him, or some very good Cardiganshires. In America, this problem does not arise, since the long-tailed Pembrokeshire dogs are docked at birth.

The Pembroke is higher, shorter in body than the Cardigan, his legs are straighter and lighter-boned and his coat is of a finer texture. Pembroke ears are pointed at the tip and stand erect whereas the Cardigan's are rounded. The Pembroke is, of course, short-tailed whereas the Cardigan has a long tail. Compared with the Cardigan, the Pembroke is said to be

Welsh Corgi Pembroke.

more restless, more easily excited.

In England, the breed was given a tremendous boost when King George bought some dogs for his two daughters. The present Queen is still a Corgi fan.

Description and Standards: The description and standards, by courtesy of the Welsh Corgis Club, follow.

GENERAL APPEARANCE: Low-set, strong, sturdily built, alert and active, giving an impression of substance and stamina in a small space; outlook bold, expression intelligent and workmanlike. The movement should be free and active, elbows fitting closely to the sides, neither loose nor tied. Forelegs should move well forward, without too much lift, in unison with thrusting action of hind legs.

HEAD AND SKULL: Head to be foxy in shape and appearance, with alert and intelligent expression, skull to be fairly wide and flat between the ears; moderate amount of stop. Length of foreface to be in proportion to the skull as three is to five. Muzzle slightly tapering. Nose black.

EYES: Well set, medium size, hazel in color and blending with color of coat.

EARS: Pricked, medium-sized, slightly pointed. A line drawn from the tip of the nose through the eye should, if extended, pass through, or close to, the tip of the ear.

MOUTH: Teeth level, or with the inner side of the upper front teeth resting closely on the front of the under ones.

NECK: Fairly long.

FOREQUARTERS: Legs short and as straight as possible. "Straight as possible" means straight as soundness and deep broad chest will permit. It does not mean terrier-straight. Ample bone carried right down to the feet. Elbows should fit closely to the sides, neither loose nor tied. Forearm should curve slightly round the chest.

BODY: Of medium length, with well-sprung ribs. Not short-coupled or terrierlike. Level top line. Chest broad and deep, well let down between the forelegs.

HINDQUARTERS: Strong and flexible, slightly tapering. Legs short. Ample bone carried right down to the feet. Hocks straight when viewed from behind.

FEET: Oval, the two center toes slightly in advance of two outer toes, pads strong and well arched. Nails short.

TAIL: Short, preferably natural.

COAT: Of medium length and dense; not wiry. Self colors in red, sable, fawn, black and tan, or with white markings on legs, chest and neck. Some white on head and foreface is permissible.

WEIGHT AND SIZE: Dogs, 20 to 24 pounds; bitches, 18 to 22 pounds. Height, from 10 to 12 inches at shoulder.

(February 10, 1952)

—Group IV—Terriers—

AIREDALE TERRIER

LITTLE IS known of the Airedale Terrier prior to 1850. Although the origin of the breed, like the origin of all species, is somewhat uncertain, there is enough known to trace it back to the Brokenhaired or Old English Terrier or Working Terrier. Antique art has revealed that there were English dogs which bore a distinct resemblance to the terriers from which all these breeds were produced. The coloring of the Airedale is one of the oldest in the history of the dog group. The black and tan coloring is mentioned in the earliest printed books about dogs and it is interesting to note that the arrangements of the two colors was similar in scheme to that of the Airedale as it is today. The extinct Black and Tan Old English Terrier is believed by many authorities to have been the common ancestor, not only of the Airedale, but of the Fox, Welsh, and Irish Terriers as well.

The Airedale Terrier has come through a variety of names. Known early as the "broken-haired" or "working" terrier, the names Waterside Terrier and Bingley Terrier were given to the breed and, finally, it was called the Airedale.

The name, Airedale, is said to have originated in a novel manner. These terriers, under all their then various names, were shown in increasing numbers at all the local agricultural shows at the time when dog shows were in their infancy. An extremely large entry of "Waterside Terriers" appeared at a show held at Bingley, Yorkshire, England, and the judge, impressed by the number, remarked that so popular and important a breed ought to have a better name than they possessed. As this was known as the Airedale show, that name was given to the breed.

Even then there were arguments for and against the names Airedale, or Bingley. Some authorities insisted that it should be Bingley Terrier (Corsincon in *British Dogs* [Dalziel] 1889) and it was described as a "sort of relation to the Dandie Dinmont and the Bedlington. His weight to be 35 to 45 lb. and to be very strongly built, the ribs rounder, the haunches wider and more muscular than the Bedlington, and much longer than the Dandie. The head large, ears falling close to the cheeks, but rather wider and shorter in comparison to the Dandie or Bedlington. The neck strong and the dog finished off by a thick, coarshish tail, docked to about 6 inches." The prevailing color was stated as being grizzle of various shades with tan about the face, with hair on top of head lighter and softer than on the body. And, "he has a lot of hound blood in him."

The mild disposition of the Airedale is said to have probably been inherited from hound blood. It was the early sportsmen of Yorkshire who developed the crossing that eventuated in the Airedale. The varying types of the Black and Tan Terrier were used by these sportsmen for hunting the fox, badger, weasel, otter, water rats, and small game around the rivers Colne, Calder, Warfe, and Aire. These terriers, also used as guardians, were exceedingly agile, possessed excellent eyesight and tremendous courage, but they lacked the keen nose and swimming power of the rough-coated Otterhound. A constructive attempt to produce the virtues of both in a better breed of larger and stronger terriers brought about the crossing of these breeds and produced the then "Waterside" Terrier.

The "Waterside" Terrier, on which the Airedale was founded, had a reputation of being able to lead a hard and rugged life. They were usually good vermin destroyers and excellent water dogs, able to swim against strong river currents, and had the ability to hunt in the manner of spaniels if necessary. But, on the whole, they were a somewhat carelessly-bred lot. Little of the "Waterside" Terrier has been carried over into the present-day handsome and well-built Airedale. Even as early as 1890, the change and progress was evident. In Shaw's *Dog Book,* the writer remarks that many of his readers who were acquainted with the old Yorkshire "Waterside" Terrier would probably fail to recognize him under this new designation the "Airedale Terrier."

In the late '90's the generally accepted description of the breed held that it was developed from a cross between one of the old rough-coated Scotch Terriers

and Bull Terriers, the Scotch Terrier weighing 12 to 22 pounds with a bluish-grey back and tan legs and a hard, rough coat. Otterhound was then used and this produced a large, ungainly creature with big, falling ears and a soft coat. Crossed and recrossed, first with a Scotch Terrier and then with a Bull Terrier, better feet and good ears were obtained. The Otterhound again was used, and with further crosses of Bull Terrier the original Airedale was developed.

However, some authorities of that time believed that a shorter road in breeding would have produced the same type. Thunder, a noted dog of that period, was of very weak type and better type might have been obtained if the Fox Terrier, or the then Irish Terrier and the Manchester had been used.

At one time Airedale classes presented representatives of the breed that differed nearly as widely as his various names, not only in size and shape, but in colors and points. The breed had to face a hard, long road before a standard was finally established. After a battle with wrong colors, wrong shades, soft coats, smooth coats, long ears and wrongly-placed markings, a list of disqualifications was given by the Committee of the Airedale Terrier Club in 1889. These were then: A Dudley nose; white on throat face, or feet (white on any other part of the body, objectionable).

A small white blaze on the chest is not objectionable by today's standards of the breed and occurs in some strains.

There was vast improvement in the Airedale from 1889 to 1894, the latter year the breed gaining real popularity in the United States, Holland, and Germany. In 1886 the breed was entered in the Kennel Club Stud Book with 24 entries, nearly all with pedigrees.

In 1902, owners began to demand more size which eventuated in a report by the Airedale Terrier Club which read, ". . . size is one, if not the most important characteristic of the breed . . . and judges shall consider undersized specimens of the breed as severely handicapped when competing with dogs of standard weight (at that time, 40-45 lbs. dog) . . . and that any of the Club's judges who, in the opinion of the Committee, shall give prizes or otherwise push to the front dogs of small type, shall be at once struck from the list of specialized specialist judges."

Also, "Judges ought to be particularly careful in not giving prizes to animals too small in size and which are likely to resemble in appearance the Irish or Welsh Terrier."

This last is particularly interesting because in 1889 a picture of New-bred Jack, illustrating the Airedale, greatly resembled a Welsh Terrier. The weight in 1889 is stated to have been 40 to 45 pounds, but back in 1879 some of the dogs were much larger, one weighing 53 pounds at a year old and another 52 pounds at 16 months.

It was in 1879 that classes were first provided for Airedale Terriers at the Airedale Agricultural Society's show held at Bingley, Yorkshire. The towns· of Skipton, Bradford, Keighley, and Otley followed with

Airedale Terrier. Photo by Evelyn M. Shafer.

classifications. In 1883 a public exhibition of an Airedale against a badger was staged at the Wolverhampton show. That same year a class under the title of "Airedale" or "Waterside Terrier" was provided at the Birmingham National Dog Show in England. Two years later the name "Waterside" was dropped, the breed being simply classified as "Airedale."

Champion Master Briar (1897-1906) is accepted as the first great sire and forerunner of the breed as it is known today. One of his famous sons, Champion Clonmel Monarch, was exported to Philadelphia where American fanciers were shaping the breed.

It is conceded that the ancestry of the present-day top-notchers of the breed in most of the countries which breed, exhibit, and support the breed with Airedale Terrier clubs is traced to Champion Warland Ditto (1919-1927), the Cragsman King family, and the Warland Kennels which bred their foundation bitches to Ch. Rhosddu Royalist.

His daughter, the International Champion Warland Strategy, produced the key sire who, when bred to her sister, produced the great sire Ch. Warland Whatnot. He in turn, sired Clonmel Monarque, whose sons, Ch. Clee Courtier and Clee Brigand, produced a number of champions during the years 1928-1935 when bred to bitches by the record sire, Ch. Flornell Mixer. Mixer was a Warland Ditto grandson. Warland Ditto, his sire, Cragsman Dictator, his dam Ch. Warland Strategy, and her sire Ch. Rhosddu Royalist were all exported to the United States.

The Airedale is considered the favorite terrier in Germany. Airedale Terriers have been used on large game in Africa, in India, and in Canada. They are also widely used in this country on small game and have been included in a number of well-known bear, wolf, and mountain lion packs. At one time the Airedale Terrier was widely acclaimed in this country as

Airedale Terrier—A head study. Photo by Evelyn M. Shafer.

"the dog that can do anything any other dog can do —and then lick the other dog." His versatility is unquestioned but it is hardly that wide. Airedales have also been used successfully for police duty in Great Britain and in Germany, but, like all breeds, their greatest appeal for their owners is their companionship and faithful attachment as pets.

Description and Standards. The description and standards, adopted by the Airedale Terrier Club of America and approved by the American Kennel Club follow.

HEAD: Should be well balanced with little apparent difference between the length of skull and foreface.

SKULL: Should be long and flat, not too broad between the ears and narrowing very slightly to the eyes. Scalp should be free from wrinkles—stop hardly visible and checks level and free from fullness.

EARS: Should be V-shaped with carriage rather to the side of the head, not pointing to the eyes, small but not out of proportion to the size of the dog. The top line of the folded ear should be above the level of the skull.

FOREFACE: Should be deep, powerful, strong and muscular, should be well filled up before the eyes.

EYES: Should be dark, small, not prominent, full of Terrier expression, keenness and intelligence.

LIPS: Should be tight.

NOSE: Should be black and not too small.

TEETH: Should be strong and white, free from discoloration or defect. Bite either level or vise-like. A slightly overlapping or scissor bite is permissible without preference.

NECK: Should be of moderate length and thickness gradually widening towards the shoulders. Skin tight, not loose.

SHOULDERS AND CHEST: Shoulders long and sloping well into the back. Shoulder blades flat. From the front, chest deep but not broad. The depth of the chest should be approximately on a level with the elbows.

BODY: Back should be strong, short, and level. Ribs well sprung. Loins muscular and of good width. There should be but little space between the last rib and the hip-joint.

HIND QUARTERS: Should be strong and muscular with no droop.

Airedale Terrier puppies. Photo by Evelyn M. Shafer.

TAIL: The root of the tail should be set well up on the back. It should be carried gaily but not curled over the back. It should be of good strength and substance and of fair length.

LEGS: Forelegs should be perfectly straight, with plenty of muscle and bone.

ELBOWS: Should be perpendicular to the body, working free of sides.

THIGHS: Should be long and powerful with muscular second thigh stifles well bent, not turned either in or out, hocks well let down parallel with each other when viewed from behind.

FEET: Should be small, round, and compact with a good depth of pad well cushioned; the toes moderately arched, not turned either in or out.

COAT: Should be hard, dense, and wiry, lying straight and close, covering the dog well over the body and legs. Some of the hardest are crinkling or slightly waved. At the base of the hard, very stiff hair should be a shorter growth of softer hair termed the under coat.

COLOR: The head and ears should be tan, the ears being of a darker shade than the rest. Dark markings on either side of the skull are permissible. The legs up to the thighs and elbows and the under part of the body and chest are also tan and the tan frequently runs into the shoulder. The sides and upper parts of the body should be black or dark grizzle. A red mixture is often found in the black and is not to be considered objectionable. A small white blaze on the chest is a characteristic of certain strains of the breed.

SIZE: Dogs should measure approximately 23 inches in height at the shoulder; bitches slightly less. Both sexes should be sturdy, well muscled and boned.

MOVEMENT: Movement or action is the crucial test of conformation. Movement should be free. As seen from the front the forelegs should swing perpendicular from the body free from the sides, the feet the same distance apart as the elbows. As seen from the rear the hind legs should be parallel with each other, neither too close nor too far apart, but so placed as to give a strong, well-balanced stance and movement. The toes should not be turned either in or out.

Yellow eyes, hound ears, white feet, soft coat, being much over or much under the size limit, being under-shot or over-shot, having poor movement, are faults which should be severely penalized.

SCALE OF POINTS:

	Points
Head	10
Neck, Shoulders and Chest	10
Body	10
Hind Quarters and Tail	10
Legs and Feet	10
Coat	10
Color	5
Size	10
Movement	10
General Characteristics and Expression	15
TOTAL	100

AUSTRALIAN TERRIER

AS ITS name denotes, the Australian Terrier is a native of Down-Under, dating from 1885 when it was first exhibited in Melbourne as the Australian Rough. "Rough" applied to the coat, not temperament, for this sturdy small terrier, although keen enough when aroused is essentially a docile homebody.

Its present name was acquired in 1889 when the first Australian Terrier Club was formed in Melbourne. A few specimens were exported to Great Brit-

ain about this same period and in 1933, a separate registry was granted to the breed by the Kennel Club of England. About 12 years later Aussies made their first appearance in the United States but they remained practically unknown until 1957 when the groundwork laid by fanciers of the breed made possible the formation of the Australian Club of America. The following year, nine Aussies were entered in the Miscellaneous Class of the Westminster Kennel Club show in New York. In 1959, Westminster's Miscellaneous Class had its largest entry on record when 44 Australian Terriers made their appearance. In 1960 the broke their own record with an entry of 58. The Aussie had arrived! That same year the Australian Terrier became the 114th breed to be admitted to registry by the American Kennel Club. At the time there were 10 champions from Australia, England and New Zealand being shown and nine Aussies had gained titles in obedience competition.

Nell N. and Milton Fox, owners of the Pleasant Pastures Kennels, Point Pleasant, N.J., can probably be credited with the initial work of promoting the breed in America. Mrs. Fox, a native of New Zealand, was familiar with the Aussie in her homeland and in Australia and England, and imported a number of champions.

The first American champion of the breed was Ch. Cooees Straleon Aussie, a blue-tan male, born July 1, 1957, bred and owned by Mr. and Mrs. Fox. Their Ch. Pinedales Tambo, a red bitch, was third in the Top Ten Terriers in breed competition through February, 1963. The first three Aussies to place in the Terrier Group were: Ch. Sydnum Solitare, an imported bitch, Ch. Tinee Town Traveller, an imported dog, and Ch. Wingspan Wallaby an American-bred.

Other outstanding sponsors of the breed have been: Mrs. Malcom Brush, Los Altos Hills, Calif.; Mr. and Mrs. A. W. Bartholomew, Thornoaks Kennels, Harvard, Ill.; Mrs. Jane Henderson, Stockton,

Australian Terrier—Ch. Cooles Stralian Aussie of Pleasant Pastures. First Australian Terrier to win an AKC Championship. (Owner: Pleasant Pastures Kennels, Mt. Pleasant, N.Y.)

Australian Terrier—Head study of Ch. Pleasant Pastures Sugar Candy. (Owner: Mr. and Mrs. Alan M. Binlosky, Novelty, Ohio)

N.J.; Mr. and Mrs. W. M. Tompkins, Jr., Stonebrae Kennels, Woodbury, Ga.; Mrs. Rebecca McDonald, Armac Kennels, San Jose, Calif.; and Mrs. G. S. Lund, Tammikin Kennels, Bellingham, Wash.

In 1963 there were about 125 members of the Australian Club of America and registrations with the AKC approaching 900. American champions to date number about 50 and more than 18 Aussies have obedience titles.

Although the Aussie is not an old breed as the history of breeds is reckoned, it existed long before 1885 in that far-flung root of so many terrier breeds, the broken-hair or rough-coated terrier which was known in Australia as well as in the British Isles.

For improvement and setting the type that eventually became the Australian Terrier, crosses were resorted to with various British sporting terriers. The Cairn, the Dandie Dinmont, the Irish Terrier and the prick-eared Skye Terrier have all been credited with playing a part in the molding of the Aussie.

Long used in the Australian bushland as guardians of mines and herders of sheep, these small terriers with a twinkle in their eyes and alert expression, have an inherited sense of responsibility and are adaptable to a city apartment or country home. They have a weather-resistant coat about two inches in length that requires little grooming and no clipping or plucking.

Two distinguishing characteristics are a soft, silvery top-knot and a ruff at the neck, the latter said to be a protection when they tangle with rats or snakes on Australian farms.

"Neither snappy nor yappy", say the fond admirers of this breed, "dog that enjoys fun and family life, but that can be courageous and aggressive when aroused."

Description and Standards. The description and standards approved by AKC follow.

GENERAL APPEARANCE: A small, sturdy, rough-coated terrier of spirited action and self-assured manner.

HEAD: Long, flat-skulled, and full between the eyes, with the stop moderate. The muzzle is longer than the distance from the eyes to the occiput. Jaws long and powerful, teeth of good size meeting in a scissors bite, although a level bite is acceptable. Nose black. Ears set straight, high on the skull and well apart. They are small and pricked, the leather either pointed or slightly rounded and free from long hairs. Eyes small, dark, and keen in expression; not prominent. Light-colored and protruding eyes are faulty.

NECK: Inclined to be long, and tapering into sloping shoulders; well furnished with hair which forms a protective ruff.

BODY: Low-set and slightly longer from the withers to the root of the tail than from the withers to the ground. Chest medium-wide, and deep, with ribs well sprung but not round. Topline level. Tail set on high and carried erect but not too gay; docked leaving two-fifths. Forelegs straight and slightly feathered to the carpus or so-called knee; they are set well under the body with elbows close and pasterns strong. Hindquarters strong and well muscled, but not heavy; legs moderately angulated at stifles and hocks, with hocks well let down. Bone, medium in size. Feet are small, clean and cat-like, the toes arched and compact, nicely padded and free from long hair. Nails strong and black.

COAT: Outer coat harsh and straight, and about two and one-half inches all over the body. Under coat, short and soft. The top-knot, which covers only the top of the skull, is of finer texture and lighter color than the body coat.

COLOR: May be blue-black or silver-black, with rich tan markings on head and legs. The blue-black is bluish at the roots and dark at the tips. In the silver-blacks each hair carries black and silver, alternating with black at the tips. The tan is rich and deep, the richer the better. Also, sandy color and clear red are permissible but not as desirable, other things being equal, as the blue and tan. In the sandies, any suggestion of shading or smuttiness is undesirable.

GAIT: Straight and true; sprightly, indicating spirit and assurance.

TEMPERAMENT: That of a hard-bitten terrier, with the aggressiveness of the natural ratter and hedge-hunter, but as a companion, friendly, affectionate and biddable.

SIZE: Shoulder height, about 10 inches. Average weight, 12 to 14 pounds.

(September 13, 1960)

BEDLINGTON TERRIER

THE BEDLINGTON TERRIER, like the Dandie Dinmont, came originally from the eastern end of the Border districts in England. There are many reasons to believe that the one strain had a good deal to do with the other. They are both credited with having been developed, with various crosses, from the old Border Sleuth Hound or short-legged, rough-haired terrier of the Border dales. The distinguishing characteristics of both breeds, not found in other terriers, are the long ears and the top-knots.

Many authorities credit the Bedlington Terrier with a longer lineage of traceable pedigrees than any other terrier, in fact, longer than any breed with the exception of the Greyhound and a few packs of English Foxhounds. There are, of course, no photographs of the first so-called Bedlington or it might be seen that he looked nothing like the Bedlington of today.

The famed progenitor of the breed was a dog named Old Flint, whelped in 1782 and owned by Squire Trevelyan. Originally the breed was known as the Rothbury or Rodbery Terrier. This name derived from a famous bitch brought from Staffordshire by a company of nailmakers who settled in Rothbury. The terriers of this section were used to go to earth and worked with packs of foxhounds kept there at the time.

From the very nature of the inhabitants of these mining districts from whence came the Bedlington, one can surmise the kind of a dog that would appeal to them. It would have to be able to hold its own when pitted against other dogs in match fights, fast enough to catch a rabbit in the open, and game enough to tackle anything from badger to fox. It would have to be a first-rate water dog. The Bedlington was all these. He was particularly well known as a fighter to the death when set upon.

Somewhere along the road in the development of the breed there must have been a long-legged terrier cross, and it is firmly believed that there was a Whippet cross, for the miners and nailers were fond of coursing and naturally put speed into their terriers. These game terriers were kept by nomadic tinkers and gypsies who traveled the country in search of work or sport, or a wager. It may well be surmised that the rough, tough ancestors of the present-day Bedlington were often employed as pit fighters, badger and rat terriers as well as assistants to hounds in fox hunting.

In the *Live Stock Journal* as late as 1875, the Bedlington was given no other name than a "northern counties Fox Terrier," and this by Thomas John Pickett who is given credit for having a great part in elevating the variety into the station of a recognized breed. Pickett was known also as the Duke of Bedlington and it was the mining town of that name from which the breed derived its name.

Young Piper, a dog whelped in 1825, and belonging to Joseph Ainsley, a stone mason, was apparently the first of the breed to be known as a Bedlington. The dam of Young Piper was Christopher Dixon's Phoebe, a bitch with a "black body, brindled legs and a tuft of hair on her head" (top-knot). She was 13 inches in height. There are diverse opinions as to whether this same Phoebe or another bitch was subsequently brought from Bedlington and given to Andrew Riddle of Framlington or whether it was Coate's Phoebe, named for the vicar of that name. In any event Phoebe was mated to James Anderson's Piper, described as a slender, liver-colored dog weighing about 15 pounds. Andrew Riddle's Wasp was the dam of Coate's Phoebe and she traced back to Old Flint. W. Clark's Scamp, almost a century later, also traced back to Old Flint.

Anderson's Piper was sired by a dog named

Bedlington Terrier—Ch. Boriska Tressa of Terrylor. (Owner: Lloyd N. Fein, Livingston, New Jersey) Photo by Evelyn M. Shafer.

Peachem. And here is an interesting tie-in with the Dandie Dinmont, for Peachem is mentioned as both a Bedlington and a Dandie Dinmont. Peachem was owned by two hawkers, Robert and Paul Scott of Jedburgh, noted Terrier breeders and, as a Dandie Dinmont, he won at the Crystal Palace show in 1872.

The first show to have a Bedlington class was at Bedlington in 1871. In 1875 the Bedlington Terrier Club was established.

Ainsley's Young Piper is credited with giving the long-ear characteristic to the breed but that is largely conjecture. He is famous for many other reasons. He lived to be 15 years old and at 14, toothless and almost blind, drew a badger at which other terriers had failed. All his long life he was at work on foxes, badgers, and otters and was noted for his killing prowess. In 1835, he saved Mrs. Ainsley's 14-months-old baby from an enraged sow. It can, therefore, be determined that as early as that date he was a tractable pet, his courageous heart and lovable qualities gradually endearing him to his owners as a house dog.

His baby lamb-like appearance is deceiving. The characteristics of gameness and hardihood are still retained. In fact, not too many years ago, when a commission was sent to England for a "thoroughly game Fox Terrier" and one was sent, there was an accompanying message that if he was not game enough, then no Fox Terrier would do and the buyer would have to get a Bull Terrier or a Bedlington.

According to an article published some years ago in the *English Field,* the origin of the breed could be traced no farther back than the first quarter of the nineteenth century. If this is taken as authority the starting point of the breed was the mating of two terriers owned by E. Donkin, Master of the Flotterton Hounds.

The long-legged, 15-16 inch dog is a little less than

Bedlington Terrier puppies.

a century old. The credited Whippet influence began to be seen in 1879 when Dr. Lamond Heming's Geordie was exhibited at Bristol. Geordie was 15 inches in height and weighed 24 pounds.

Although there are certain outward characteristics in the Bedlington that indicate a strong relationship to the Dandie Dinmont, there are also wide divergencies. The Bedlington in point of build and color stands alone. It is well described as a lathy dog and the lines on which it is built shows that it is speedy. There are two distinct colors, liver and blue. It is only a question of fancy which is preferred. In early days the liver was much in evidence and many of the best dogs were that color. Lately the blue has become more fashionable.

The Bedlington enjoyed a notable popularity in the early shows in England, but then seemed to be supplanted by the growing popularity of the Airedale. The breed also suffered from the craze for extra long heads and this influence began to be seen in the less rounded character of the head in the vicinity of the occiput. It must be said that it is now an entirely different looking dog. In the early days "trimming" was not resorted to. There was plenty of grooming but that was all. In other respects he was shown as Nature intended rather than as man saw fit.

The breed took a tremendous boost, both in standards of perfection and popularity, in 1947 when Anthony Neary, breeder of Greenwich, Conn., and manager for Mr. and Mrs. William Rockefeller's Rock Ridge Kennels, piloted their Rock Ridge Night Rocket to Best in Show at the famed Morris and Essex Kennel Club Show at Madison, N. J. This young dog was a virtual dark horse. Then, the following winter, in 1948, Champion Night Rocket easily went Best of Breed, won the Group, and took Best in Show over a 2,540 dog all-breed entry at the Westminster Show at Madison Square Garden, New York, the first of his breed to win that honor.

Description and Standards. The description and standards, adopted by the Bedlington Terrier Club of America and approved by the American Kennel Club follow.

SKULL: Narrow, but deep and rounded, high at the occiput, wedge-shaped, covered with profuse top-knot, which should be nearly white, and when trimmed, should give a Roman nose appearance.

JAWS: Long and tapering. There must be no "stop" and the line from occiput to nose end straight and unbroken. Well filled up beneath the eye. Close fitting lips, no flew.

TEETH: Level or pincer-jawed. The teeth should be large and strong.

NOSE: The nostrils must be large and well defined. Blues and blue and tans have black noses, livers, sandies, etc., have brown noses.

EYES: Small, bright and well sunk. The ideal eyes have the appearance of being triangular. Blue should have a dark eye; blue and tans have light eyes with amber lights; liver and sandies have a light hazel eye.

EARS: Moderate sized, filbert shaped, set on low and hanging flat to the cheek. They should be covered with short, fine hair, with a fringe of silky hair at the tip.

LEGS AND FEET: Muscular and moderate length. The hind legs, by reason of the roach back and arched loin, have the appearance of being longer than the forelegs. The forelegs should be straight, with a moderately wide chest and hare feet.

BODY: Muscular, yet markedly flexible. Flat ribbed and deep through the brisket, well ribbed up. The chest should be deep and fairly broad. The back should be roached and the loin markedly arched. Light, muscular, galloping quarters which are also fine and graceful.

NECK: Long, tapering, arched neck, deep at the base. The neck should spring well from the shoulders, which should be flat, and head should be carried high.

COAT: The coat is very distinctive and unlike that of any other terrier, in that it should be thick and linty (not wiry) and when in show condition should not exceed one inch in length. It should be brushed on the body and back from the root of the tail toward the head, and should not lie flat against the body. There should be an absence of hair on the ears except at the tip, where the *fringe* should be from one-half to one inch long. The hair on the legs should be slightly longer and straighter than that of the body. The top-knot should be highest at the occiput and taper gradually to just in back of the nose. It (the top-knot) should be rounded from side to side from an imaginary line drawn from the outer corner of the eye to the top of the ear on one side to a like line on the opposite side.

TAIL: Of moderate length, thick at the root, tapering to a point and gracefully curved, slightly feathered, nine to eleven inches long, scimitar shaped, carried elevated but not over the back.

COLOR: Blue, blue and tan, liver, liver and tan, sandy, sandy and tan.

HEIGHT: About 15 or 16 inches.

WEIGHT: Dogs, about 24 pounds; bitches, about 22 pounds.

ACTION: Very distinctive. Rather mincing, light and springy, must gallop like a Greyhound, with the whole body.

GENERAL: A graceful, lithe but not shelly, muscular dog, with no sign of coarseness or weakness. The whole head should be pear-shaped or wedge-shaped. The expression in repose is mild and gentle. When roused, the eyes should sparkle, and the dog look full of temper and courage.

SCALE OF POINTS:	*Points*
Head	20
Size	10
Teeth	10
Color	5
Legs and Feet	10
Ears	5
Eyes	5
Nose	5
Body	15
Coat	10
Tail	5
TOTAL	100

BORDER TERRIER

ALTHOUGH THE Border Terrier was not given recognition by the English Kennel Club until 1920 it had been exhibited in large numbers at the many Agricultural Society shows in the Border country previous to that date.

Purely a working terrier, the strain had been carefully preserved by farmers and shepherds of the Cheviot Hills Border country where a "dead game" terrier was greatly needed to hunt and kill the powerful hill foxes which could prey easily on the stock in this sparsely inhabited country. These dogs had to have length of leg to get over the ground swiftly and yet be small enough to follow the fox to earth.

The ancestry of the Border goes back to a type known about the end of the seventeenth century, an excellent working dog confined to this district, and probably closely related to the forerunner of the Lakeland, the Bedlington, and the Dandie Dinmont.

A picture of 1826 shows one of these small dogs with "Old Yeddie Jackson," the Hunter King of North Tyne. It has been established that the type was

Border Terrier—A head study.

known in the Border country well over a hundred years ago, where it was used to hunt badger and otter as well as the fox. These dogs had to be active and strong for the work required of them. Their harsh, dense coat was necessary to protect them from the rains and mists of the hills in prolonged exposure. Although little is known of the actual ancestry of the breed, it has been said that dogs of this breed had been traced back to Flint, which may or may not have been Squire Trevelyan's Old Flint, the Bedlington whelped in 1782. As mentioned previously, many of the popular names of that period were given to terriers of different breeds.

At an early state in its career, the breed was known as the Reedwater Terrier, and is believed to have been related in its early history to the Patterdale Terriers.

Following recognition by the English Kennel Club and the formation of the Border Terrier Club in 1920, many of the breed have been exhibited at the shows in Great Britain but, outside of the leading shows, not too many are yet seen in competition in the United States.

Description and Standards. The description and standards of the Border Terrier follow.

Since the Border Terrier is a working terrier of a size to go to ground and able, within reason, to follow a horse, his conformation should be such that he be ideally built to do his job. No deviations from this ideal conformation should be permitted, which would impair his usefulness in running his quarry to earth and in bolting it therefrom. For this work he must be alert, active and agile, and capable of squeezing through narrow apertures and rapidly traversing any kind of terrain. His head, "like that of an otter," is distinctive, and his temperament ideally exemplifies that of a terrier. By nature he is good-tempered, affectionate, obedient, and easily trained. In the field he is hard as nails, "game as they come" and driving in attack. It should be the aim of Border Terrier breeders to avoid such over-emphasis of any point in the Standard as might lead to unbalanced exaggeration.

GENERAL APPEARANCE: He is an active terrier of medium bone, strongly put together, suggesting endurance and agility, but rather narrow in shoulder, body and quarter. The body is covered with a somewhat broken though closefitting and intensely wiry jacket. The characteristic "otter" head with its keen eye, combined with a body poise which is "at the alert," gives a look of fearless and implacable determination characteristic of the breed. The proportions should be that the height at the withers is slightly greater than the distance from the withers to the tail, i.e., by possibly 1-1½ inches in a 14-pound dog.

WEIGHT: Dogs, 13-15½ pounds, bitches, 11½-14 pounds, are appropriate weights for Border Terriers in hard-working condition.

HEAD: Similar to that of an otter. Moderately broad and flat in skull with plenty of width between the eyes and between the ears. A slight, moderately broad curve at the stop rather than a pronounced indentation. Cheeks slightly full.

EARS: Small, V-shaped and of moderate thickness, dark preferred. Not set high on the head but somewhat on the side, and dropping forward close to the cheeks. They should not break above the level of the skull.

EYES: Dark hazel and full of fire and intelligence. Moderate in size, neither prominent nor small and beady.

MUZZLE: Short and "well filled." A dark muzzle is characteristic and desirable. A few short whiskers are natural to the breed. The teeth should be strong, with a scissors bite, large in proportion to size of dog. Black nose and of a good size.

NECK: Clean, muscular and only long enough to give a well-balanced appearance. It should gradually widen into the shoulder.

SHOULDERS: Well laid back and of good length, the blades converging to the withers gradually from a brisket not excessively deep or narrow.

FORELEGS: Straight and not too heavy in bone and placed slightly wider than in a Fox Terrier.

FEET: Small and compact. Toes should point forward and be moderately arched with thick pads.

BODY: Deep, fairly narrow and of sufficient length to avoid any suggestion of lack of range and agility. Deep ribs carried well back and not oversprung in view of the desired depth and narrowness of the body. The body should be capable of being spanned by a man's hands behind the shoulders. Back strong but laterally supple, with no suspicion of a dip behind the shoulder. Loin strong and the under-line fairly straight.

TAIL: Moderately short, thick at the base, then tapering. Not set on too high. Carried gaily when at the alert, but not over the back. When at ease, a Border may drop his stern.

HINDQUARTERS: Muscular and racy, with thighs long and nicely molded. Stifles well bent and hocks well let down.

COAT: A short and dense under coat covered with a very wiry and somewhat broken top coat which should lie closely, but it must not show any tendency to curl or wave. With such a coat a Border should be able to be exhibited almost in his natural state, nothing more in the way of trimming being needed than

Border Terrier. Photo by Evelyn M. Shafer.

a tidying-up of the head, neck and feet. The hide should be very thick and loose fitting.

MOVEMENT: Straight and rhythmical before and behind, with good length of stride and flexing of stifle and hock. The dog should respond to his handler with a gait which is free, agile and quick.

COLOR: Red, grizzle and tan, blue and tan, or wheaten. A small amount of white may be allowed on the chest, but white on the feet should be penalized.

SCALE OF POINTS: | | Points
|---|---:|
Head, ears, neck and teeth .... | 20
Legs and feet .... | 15
Coat and skin .... | 10
Shoulders and chest .... | 10
Eyes and expression .... | 10
Back and loin .... | 10
Hindquarters .... | 10
Tail .... | 5
General appearance .... | 10
TOTAL .... | 100

(March 14, 1950)

BULL TERRIER

THERE ARE two varieties of Bull Terrier, the orginal white variety, in which markings behind the set-on of head constitute a disqualification, and the recently developed colored variety, in which brindle is the preferred color.

In appearance, the Bull Terrier presents a combination of balanced power, grace, and agility with no hint of coarseness or awkwardness. Pound for pound, he is the strongest of all dogs and possesses the most powerful muzzle of any of the terriers.

The Bull Terrier was developed in the early eighteen fifties by James Hinks of Birmingham, England, a breeder and dealer in dogs. His son, Carleton Hinks, gives what is probably the most authentic account as to exactly how the breed was developed. Writing for the *Bullterrier Handbook,* published about 1927, Carleton Hinks says:

The forefathers of these dogs we know today could truly be called ugly, having short, thick heads with a certain amount of layback, blunt muzzles, thick-set bodies and bow legs, whilst in color they varied from black and tans, brindle reds, fawns, fallows, etc. They were then known as Bull-and-terriers, owing to the fact of their being a cross between a Bulldog and a Terrier, the latter being chiefly the large smooth black and tan Terrier or any Terrier which showed gameness and a nose for rats. These dogs were neither Bulldogs nor Terriers, but mongrels in appearance. However, they served the purpose which they were bred for, i.e., fighting, ratting, badger and bull baiting.

These dogs proved an ideal cross for the work, as the strength, courage and stamina of the Bulldog was united with the intelligence and quickness of the Terrier. The Bulldog appearance was predominant and although they were noted for their gameness and devotion, their appearance was deadly against them.

It would be in the early fifties when a great change came about. Mr. James Hinks of Birmingham bred a strain of all white dogs which he called Bullterriers, and as Bullterriers they became duly recognized. Mr. Hinks had previously owned some of the gamest old stock and by using an outcross again with the White English Terrier and Dalmatian, thus getting still further from the Bulldog, he was at last rewarded with the

apple of his eye, this after careful and patient breeding, including many disappointments. The results from these crossings were usually piebald and snowbald in color, and the puppy with the most white in each litter was kept, and these in turn were mated to each other until at last Hinks was able to produce an all-white puppy, with many more to follow. These Birmingham dogs showed a refinement and grace, absence of the bow legs and colored patches. The Bulldog appearance being minus, they were longer and cleaner in head, stronger in muzzle with more of a Roman finish at the end of the nose, also longer in neck, free from lippiness and throatiness and perhaps more active. This change that came about brought the Bullterrier many admirers and the milk white dog became the fashion. He could now be described as a handsome dog, and with his extra strength and length of muzzle became more deadly for his work in the pit, and pure white became the accepted color.

Owing to the fact of the then known fighting dogs being colored, these sterling white Terriers were at first challenged as to their gameness, but Hinks had been careful with his breeding stock and only the very gamest were bred from. He was always ready to back his dog's courage with a match in the pit. Probably one match that took place in London worthy of mention was the match between Hinks' bitch Puss of Brum weighing 40 pounds, and Mr. Tupper's colored bitch weighing 60 pounds. An uneven match by all appearances but in the end Puss killed her opponent, returned to the Dog Show at Holborn, London, caught the judge's eye and annexed the red.

Harry Preston, a famous Bull Terrier breeder during England's development of the breed and who may be regarded as an eye witness, agrees with Carleton Hinks that the breed originated by crossing the Bull-and-terrier with the White English Terrier (a dog whose maximum weight is given as 20 pounds) but says that at various times Pointers, Greyhounds, Whippets, and Dalmatians touched the strain.

In the earlier days, weights usually ran between ten and 38 pounds, and classes were generally divided as under and above 16 pounds. Probably the best of the earlier dogs was Ch. Tarquin, which was imported to the United States in 1880.

About 1895 cropping was forbidden in England, and the breed received a serious set-back. In seeking to develop erect ears, these were often bred for at the expense of other qualities, and crooked fronts, weak pasterns, and other faults became more prevalent. In the United States where cropping was allowed, the first Bull Terrier with natural erect ears to reach its championship was Blodwen of Voewood, in the Twenties.

The dog rapidly developed more along terrier than Bulldog lines, despite differences of opinion as to what the type should be. Later, however, England began to favor a lower, broader dog, often with a wider skull and shorter muzzle. The United States preferred the terrier type, these dogs being leggier and having depth of chest rather than breadth, with a head brick-shaped rather than egg-shaped.

Probably the best compromise of the qualities of both types was reached with Ch. Coolyn North Wind, bred by Mrs. Z. Platt Bennett, president of the Bull Terrier Club of America. This 40-pound pure white dog won 50 Best of Breeds, a record not touched by any other Bull Terrier. He was a son of Ch. Coolyn Bailfire, the greatest sire of his generation, known especially for his ability to pass on head quality.

A great daughter of Ch. Coolyn Bailfire was Ch. Coolyn Quicksilver, who finished her championship in four shows in eight days—probably an all-time record. She was Best of Breed 22 times, probably a record for bitches. Quicksilver was one of the famous Silver litter, all of which went to their championships—the dogs Coolyn Silversuit and Coolyn Silverspot, and the bitch Coolyn Silverheels. The dam of this litter was the famous Ch. Brendon Bluestocking, a 38-pound bitch. A later mating of Bailfire and Bluestocking produced another litter of four of which three finished their championships.

The next great sire in this country was likewise owned by Mrs. Bennett. This was Int. Ch. Raydium Brigadier, who has sired at least eight champions in this country and who is in the pedigree of countless champions. Brigadier, in his prime, weighed about 50 pounds. His head had such a tremendous fill that when first shown in this country, many people termed him a freak. But gradually his egg-shaped type of head has begun to prevail as more acceptable than the longer, narrower and flatter head which had been preferred in the United States.

Brigadier's most famous son was undoubtedly the 58-pound Ch. Heir Apparent to Monty-Ayr, better known as Bat, owned and bred by Dr. E. S. Montgomery, author of *The Bullterrier*. Bat had what is probably the most interesting record of achievements of any Bull Terrier that ever lived. He was the first of two American-Bred Bull Terriers to go Best in Show (Albion Kennel Show, Michigan 1946, under A. W. Brockway). American Kennel Club records show that up to his retirement in 1946 he was Best of Variety 32 times, won the Group eight times, placed in the group 12 times. He scored 97.6 points the only time he appeared in an obedience ring. In 1944 and 1945 he won the Isis Vabo trophy offered for the best show Bull Terrier. He was selected to participate in the Parade of Champions at Rockefeller Plaza, New York during National Dog Week in 1944, and is the only Bull Terrier to have won the International Diploma of Honor presented by *Dog World* for outstanding achievements.

In addition to his bench show record, Bat had unusual field abilities. He won the Open Class in the Cabot Field Trials at Marwood, Pa., in the fall of 1945, defeating an entry which included 16 Beagles or cross-bred Beagles and one Kerry Blue Terrier. He also won second in the Ohio Valley Field Trial, an unusual accomplishment for a Bull Terrier.

The youngest champion in this country was White Queen of Monty-Ayr, at 7½ months. The youngest to win best of opposite sex at a five point show was Ch. Elsie Dinsmore of Ernicor (1947 Specialty), age six months, 9 days; a runner up to this record was Elsie's daughter, Ch. Madame Pompadour of Ernicor, Best of Winners and Best of Opposite Sex at Devon 1948, age six months, 10 days (win cancelled by the AKC because date of birth was not given on entry blank). Counting this show, Pompadour was probably the

youngest Bull Terrier to have won three five-point shows in a row by the age of ten months. At her next show, age twelve months, she won another five points to complete her championship, being the first Bull Terrier in many years to compete in consecutive five-point shows (Devon, Specialty, Westminster, Lackawanna). The cancellation of her first win started discussion in the American Kennel Club to clarify their rules concerning the omission of data on entry blanks.

In Canada, Buxton Baron was the first importation, in 1891. Canada's greatest Bull Terrier undoubtedly, was Ch. Haymarket Faultless, owned and bred by Humphrey Elliot, which was the only Bull Terrier ever to go Best in Show at Westminster (1918).

Canada's most important Bull Terrier some twenty years ago undoubtedly was Ch. Bricktops Spitfire, imported by W. W. Rooney, who bred many champions. The dog's granddaughter, Charlwood Dream Girl, was the only international champion bred in Canada. Spitfire's descendants have been a dominant factor in building the Monty-Ayr strain, as were those of Int. Ch. Tithing Tidbit of Snug Harbor, imported by Daniel J. Bowen about 1933.

In the Midwest, W. J. McCortney exercised a considerable influence on the breed through his importations of dogs such as Ch. Gardenia Juno, imported in 1934 in whelp to the Regent trophy winner, Ch. Gardenia Guardsman. Juno provided the impetus which led to Tanark Queen mother, the dam of Ch. Heir Apparent to Monty-Ayr, and is prominent in the pedigree of the dogs from Mr. and Mrs. E. L. Lomax of the Coast and of many other breeders. Mr. McCortney also imported Gardenia Duke of Tanark, a dog with a head of somewhat the shape and size of a football, and Ch. Gardenia Stop Press, which was later acquired by Mr. and Mrs. A. L. Detwiler. Stop Press, a half-brother of Int. Ch. Raydium Brigadier, proved to be an important sire.

Perhaps the most famous Coast Bull Terrier was the undefeated Ch. Flying Snow, bred by Frank Babcock who owned his first Bull Terrier in 1879.

Bull Terrier—Ch. Ormandy's Burson's Bounty. (Owner: Lewisfiel Kennels, Charlottesville, Va.) Photo by Thomas Fall, Ltd.

Undoubtedly the leading breeder in New England, and one of the best known of all Bull Terrier breeders was Mrs. Drury L. Sheraton, whose Queen Anne kennels became internationally famous. Mrs. Sheraton bred many champions, including the two in one litter which she sold to William E. Schratwieser, veteran judge and vice-president of the Bull Terrier Club of America; these were Punch Son of Judy and Lady East Rockaway, both of which Mr. Schratwieser quickly took through to their championships. Mrs. Sheraton bred many champions and did much judging.

In England, the breed received somewhat of a setback during World War II although it acquired considerable prestige for its achievements. According to Colonel James Y. Baldwin, Commandant of the War Dogs Training Establishment, Bull Terriers ranked third among the most suitable breeds.

In breeding, the English have shown quite a competitive spirit and many are the trophies offered for special purposes. The most famous is the Regent Trophy, offered for the best dog or bitch owned by a member of the Bull Terrier Club of England and first exhibited during that year.

The Bull Terrier was originally a sporting dog, bred for fighting—hence the emphasis on strength, agility, and balance. All his senses are unusually keen —his hearing, sight, and sense of smell, His remarkable versatility has made him popular in the cold climate of Canada and in the torrid heat of India; he is being used for herding sheep, for hunting, has been an actor on the stage and on the screen, won honors in war work, and placed high in obedience work. As the breed developed, more amd more emphasis was laid on disposition and less and less on the desire to fight. In fact, the English standard states, "Full of fire, but of sweet disposition amenable to discipline." As a consequence, today the Bull Terrier is not at all a quarrelsome dog—in fact like men conscious of their physical superiority, he generally seeks to avoid trouble. J. V. McAree tells how Toronto's most famous fighting dog, the immortal Slick, used to frolic on the streets around his master and would even flee for his home if pursued by another dog. He would fight only when breasted in the pit. Bull Terriers, not trained for obedience work, have been known to stand in the Terrier Group without a leash, with adjacent dogs snarling and growling.

One unusual by-product of the Bull Terriers sporting past, and which perhaps explains his capability for affection, is that a dog had to be developed which was not only unusually strong, fast, thoroughly game, and able to think for himself in an emergency, but which at the same time would not lose its head when fighting and bite its master no matter how badly it might be hurt. This latter characteristic makes the breed unusually reliable with children, whose often unmerciful mauling would cause a less friendly dog to snap. When the Bull Terrier's patience is tried beyond bounds, his reaction is to get up and move. Ch. Rebel of Blighty, owned by Cabot Briggs, once

Bull Terrier—Lewisfield Ransom of Lewisfield Kennels, Charlottesville, Virginia.

losing patience with a Pekingese which insisted on fighting, picked the small dog up and dropped it unharmed in a waste basket.

The most notable mental characteristics of the Bull Terrier are desire for human companionship, longing for affection, unusual intelligence and an apparent sense of humor. His sensitive spirit requires that he should be led rather than forced, praised when he does right rather than scolded when he does wrong.

With so great a wealth of loveable friendliness inherent in a properly-bred Bull Terrier, it is a pity that in many quarters he should have such an undeserved reputation for being quarrelsome and vicious.

The Bull Terrier should not be confused with what is popularly called the "American Bull Terrier" or "Pit Bull," which was the dog sometimes used for fighting in this country. These dogs had a shorter, squarer head, with more stop, and were of a mixed type. These fights, though illegal, were held under recognized rules and officiated over by regular judges. After a pit dog wins three fights he becomes a "champion."

The remarkable personality of the Bull Terrier has made it the favored companion of people who have learned to appreciate what this breed has to give in unfailing measure. President Theodore Roosevelt had a Bull Terrier when he was in the White House. General Patton had Willie as his constant companion during his European campaign. John G. Winant, once governor of New Hampshire and ambassador to Great Britain, was a breeder and exhibitor of Bull Terriers, as was F. Freeland Kendrick, a mayor of Philadelphia. One of Mr. Kendrick's famous champions, Queensbury Potentate, was stolen by the New Jersey sporting crowd and used for nearly a year to fight in the pit without having been defeated before he was recovered.

The Bull Terrier Club of England was started in 1887, ten years before the Bull Terrier Club of America. The Colored Bull Terrier Club of England was started in 1937.

The Bull Terrier is considered the favorite terrier in India and South Africa.

Description and Standards. The description and standards, as amended by the Bull Terrier Club of America, and approved by the American Kennel Club follow.

WHITE

The Bull Terrier must be strongly built, muscular, symmetrical and active, with a keen determined and intelligent expression, full of fire but of sweet disposition and amenable to discipline.

HEAD: Should be long, strong and deep right to the end of the muzzle, but not coarse. Full face it should be oval in outline and be filled completely up giving the impression of fullness with a surface devoid of hollows or indentations, *i.e.*, egg shaped. In profile it should curve gently downwards from the top of the skull to the tip of the nose. The forehead should be flat across from ear to ear. The distance from the tip of the nose to the eyes should be perceptibly greater than that from the eyes to the top of the skull. The underjaw should be deep and well defined. The lips should be clean and tight. The teeth should meet in either a level or in a scissors bite. In the scissors bite the upper teeth should fit in front of and closely against the lower teeth, and they should be sound, strong and perfectly regular. The ears should be small, thin and placed close together. They should be capable of being held stiffly erect, when they should point upwards. The eyes should be well sunken and as dark as possible, with a piercing glint and they should be small, triangular and obliquely placed; set near together and high up on the dog's head. The nose should be black, with well developed nostrils bent downwards at the tip.

NECK: Should be very muscular, long, arched and clean, tapering from the shoulders to the head and it should be free from loose skin. The chest should be broad when viewed from in front, and there should be great depth from withers to brisket, so that the latter is nearer the ground than the belly.

BODY: Should be well rounded with marked spring of rib, the back should be short and strong. The back ribs deep. Slightly arched over the loin. The shoulders should be strong and muscular but without heaviness. The shoulder blades should be wide and flat and there should be a very pronounced backward slope from the bottom edge of the blade to the top edge. Behind the shoulders there should be no slackness or dip at the withers. The underline from the brisket to the belly should form a graceful upward curve.

LEGS: Should be big-boned but not to the point of coarseness; the forelegs should be of moderate length, perfectly straight, and the dog must stand firmly upon them. The elbows must turn neither in nor out, and the pasterns should be strong and upright. The hind legs should be parallel viewed from behind. The thighs very muscular with hocks well let down. Hind pasterns short and upright. The stifle joint should be well bent with a well developed second thigh. The feet, round and compact with well arched toes like a cat.

TAIL: Should be short, set on low, fine, and ideally should be carried horizontally. It should be thick where it joins the body, and should taper to a fine point.

COAT: Should be short, flat, harsh to the touch and with a fine gloss. The dog's skin should fit tightly. The color should be pure white, though markings on the head are permissible. Any markings elsewhere on the coat shall disqualify.

MOVEMENT: The dog shall move smoothly, covering the ground with free, easy strides, fore and hind legs should move parallel each to each when viewed from in front or behind.

The forelegs reaching out well and the hind legs moving smoothly at the hip and flexing well at the stifle and hock. The dog should move compactly and in one piece but with a typical jaunty air that suggests agility and power.

FAULTS: Any departure from the foregoing points shall be considered a fault, and the seriousness of the fault shall be in exact proportion to its degree, *i.e.* a very crooked front is a very bad fault; a rather crooked front is a rather bad fault; and a slightly crooked front is a slight fault.

Disqualification. Color, any markings other than on the head shall disqualify.

COLORED

The Standard for the Colored Variety is the same as for the White except for the sub-head "Color" which reads: *Color.* Any color other than white, or any color with white markings. Preferred color, brindle. A dog which is predominately white shall be disqualified.

Disqualification. Color, any dog which is predominantly white shall be disqualified.

(December 11, 1956)

CAIRN TERRIER

THE CAIRN TERRIER, originally known as the "Short-haired Skye Terrier," is one of, if not the oldest, true British terrier. There is some doubt as to whether the first Cairns came from the mainland of Scotland or the Isle of Skye, but most opinion leans toward the "Misty Isle." As far back as Sixteenth Century writings, reference may be found to dogs which must surely have been the progenitors of present-day Cairns.

At least four Scottish terrier breeds may be considered descended from the Cairn—namely, the Scottish, West Highland White, long-haired Skye, and the Kyle, the latter now extinct. The Waternish and Drynoch strains from the Isle of Skye and the Harris strain from the Isle of Harris were the basis of the early British Cairns. Mrs. Alastair Campbell, a pioneer of the breed in Britain, was instrumental in gaining recognition of the breed by the Kennel Club there in 1910.

These hardy little dogs were maintained in packs by the Scottish lairds for use in routing fox, badger, and other fur-bearing vermin from their hiding places in the rocky terrain. They were also used extensively for otter hunting, proving themselves as capable as the spaniels in the water. The crofter usually kept one or two as house pets, proof of the versatility and adaptability of this breed.

The Cairn is the smallest of the working terriers. It is a hardy, active dog with a gameness which is unsurpassed. Its compact size makes it extremely desirable as a house dog, its spirit and alertness being ideal characteristics for those seeking a watchdog. Although very affectionate with "his own," he may show a certain aloofness with others. His gaiety and intense interest in everything new makes him an excellent and amusing companion.

The Cairn is a longer-bodied dog than the Scottish

Cairn Terrier.

or West Highland White Terrier but not so long as the Dandie Dinmont in relation to body-length and height from the ground. However, a weedy Cairn is not to be desired any more than one with a too-short back. The Cairn's activity is one of its most distinctive features and, although good bone and general substance are demanded, this does not mean a clumsy build. Cairns adapt themselves readily to the habits of their masters and will thrive on little or much exercise. However, those owners planning to take their dogs into the show ring should provide regular exercise to keep feet and legs in hard condition and body flesh firm. Because of their double coats they may be kenneled in either heated or unheated quarters. Being so completely beguiling in their natural shagginess, their owners have never submitted to the whims of doggy fashion. Even for the show ring, the Cairn requires only a little "tidying-up" around ears, feet, and tail to present an appearance as smart as the most trimmed and dressed-up dog in the show. The winning Cairn is the result of careful breeding rather than careful barbering.

The Cairn Terrier is regarded as the favorite terrier in Great Britain. The first Cairn Terriers were imported by Mrs. Harriet L. Price of the Robinscroft Kennels in 1913. These were a dog and a bitch from the "Out of the West" Kennels and were shown at Danbury, Connecticut, in October, 1913, in the miscellaneous class, taking first and third. In 1914, classes were provided for Cairns at Danbury for the first time in the United States. The first litter registered by the American Kennel Club was bred by Mrs. Price and born in 1914.

Fortunately for the breed, the Cairn has never been over-commercialized. This has tended to limit his popularity more than with some other small breeds. However, he continues to enjoy steadily increasing

approval and popularity both in the show ring and with the general public. His infectious charm and personality cannot be disregarded, and it has yet to be disproved that once one has owned a Cairn, no other breed ever quite takes its place.

Description and Standards. The description and standards, as adopted by the Cairn Terrier Club of America follow.

GENERAL APPEARANCE: That of an active, game, hardy, small working Terrier of the short-legged class; very free in its movements, strongly but not heavily built, standing well forward on its fore legs, deep in the ribs, well-coupled with strong hind quarters and presenting a well-proportioned build with a medium length of back, having a hard weather-resisting coat; head shorter and wider than any other Terrier and well furnished with hair giving a general foxy expression.

SKULL: Broad in proportion to length with a decided stop and well furnished with hair on the top of the head, which may be somewhat softer than the body coat.

MUZZLE: Strong but not too long or heavy. Teeth large—mouth neither over nor undershot. Nose black.

EYES: Set wide apart, rather sunken, with shaggy eyebrows, medium in size, hazel or dark hazel in color depending on body color with a keen Terrier expression.

EARS: Small, pointed, well carried erectly, set wide apart on the side of the head. Free from long hairs.

TAIL: In proportion to head, well furnished with hair but not feathery. Carried gaily but must not curl over back. Set on at back level.

BODY: Well-muscled, strong, active body with well-sprung deep ribs, coupled to strong hind quarters with a level back of medium length, giving an impression of strength and activity without heaviness.

SHOULDERS, LEGS, AND FEET: A sloping shoulder, medium length of leg, good but not too heavy bone; forelegs should not be out at elbows, and be perfectly straight, but fore feet may be slightly turned out. Fore feet larger than hind feet. Legs must be covered with hard hair. Pads should be thick and strong and dog should stand well up on its feet.

COAT: Hard and weather-resistant. Must be double coated with profuse harsh outer coat with short, soft, close furry under coat.

COLOR: May be any color except white. Dark ears, muzzle and tail tip are desirable.

IDEAL SIZE: Involves the weight, the height at the withers and the length of body. Weight for bitches 13 pounds; for dogs 14 pounds. Height at the withers—bitches 9½ inches; dogs 10 inches. Length of body from 14¼ inches to 15 inches from the

Cairn Terrier puppies.

front of the chest to back of hind quarters. The dog must be of balanced proportions and appear neither leggy nor too low to the ground; and neither too short nor too long in body. Weignt and measurements are for matured dogs at two years of age. Older dogs may weigh slightly in excess and growing dogs under these weights and measurements.

CONDITION: Dogs should be shown in good, hard flesh, well muscled and neither too fat or thin. Should be in full, good coat with plenty of head furnishing, be clean, combed, brushed, and tidied up on ears, tail, feet, and general outline. Should move freely and easily on a loose lead, should not cringe on being handled, should stand up on their toes and show with marked terrier characteristics.

Faults

SKULL: Too narrow in skull.

MUZZLE: Too long and heavy a foreface—mouth over or undershot.

EYES: Too large, prominent, yellow, ringed, are all objectionable.

EARS: Too large, round at points, set too close together, set too high on the head; heavily covered with hair.

LEGS AND FEET: Too light or too heavy bone. Crooked forelegs or out at elbow. Thin ferrety feet; feet let down on the heel or too open and spread. Too high or too low on the leg.

BODY: Too short back and compact a body, hampering quickness of movement and turning ability. Too long, weedy and snaky a body, giving an impression of weakness. Tail set on too low. Back not level.

COAT: Open coats, blousy coats, too short or dead coats, lack of sufficient under coat, lack of head furnishings, lack of hard hair on the legs. Silkiness or curliness. A slight wave is permissible.

NOSE: Flesh or light-colored nose.

COLOR: White on chest, feet or other parts of body.

SCALE OF POINTS	*Points*
General Appearance (Size and Coat)	30
Skull	5
Muzzle	10
Eyes	5
Ears	5
Body, Neck and Chest	20
Shoulders, Legs and Feet	20
Tail	5
TOTAL	100

DISQUALIFICATIONS: Flesh-colored nose.

DANDIE DINMONT TERRIER

LIKE MOST of the Border and Scottish breeds, the origin of the Dandie Dinmont is somewhat obscure. It is fairly evident that the Dandie and the Bedlington must have had much in common in their early development. It is certain that the names Phoebe and Peachem are prominent in both ancestries. But this fact alone need not be the basis for taking it as incontrovertible proof that both were on the same family tree as these were popular names, possibly because of the fame of each of the dogs.

Stonehenge (J. M. Walsh) wrote that the Dandie Dinmont was the result of crossing the Otterhound and the old and now extinct Scottish Terrier (a breeding often attributed to have played a part in

producing many of the terriers of the north). However, other early authorities have adhered to the now quite universal theory that the Dandie Dinmont was bred from selected specimens of the native rough-haired terrier of the Border in the Cheviot Hills between England and Scotland. The old Scottish Terrier did not mean the all-black dog of today but a longer-bodied, supple type. This suppleness was developed in the Dandie by careful breeding to make him more adaptable for going to ground in the hunting of everything from rats to badger and fox.

It was not until 1814 that the fame of the breed extended beyond the Border, but it was first recorded as a distinct type about 1700. In Gainsborough's portrait of Henry, third Duke of Buccleuch, a Dandie appears, and although this portrait was painted in 1770, the dog is identical to the Dandie type of today.

The type now known as the Dandie Dinmont traces back to one Piper Allen in 1704. This dog belonged to a tribe of gypsies who wandered about the country with their bagpipes. They became equally as famous for their terriers as their piping. It is to the Allen family that the dogs named Phoebe and Peachem are also credited.

The names given to the breed locally were Charlie's Hope Terrier and Mustard and Pepper Terrier. In 1814 Sir Walter Scott's novel, *Guy Mannering*, was published and in the book there appeared the charming character of Dandie Dinmont, burly tenant farmer of Charlieshope with his exceptional race of terriers, Auld Pepper, Young Pepper, Young Mustard, Little Pepper, and Little Mustard. The character of Dandie Dinmont was a composite of all the yeomen of the Cheviot dales which Scott greatly admired but it fitted so well one James Davidson of Hindlee that between the time of the publication of the book and Davidson's death in 1820, his mustard- and pepper-colored dogs had gained the name of Dandie Dinmont Terriers.

The present-day Dandie still retains many of the characteristics that impressed Scott and inspired him to write of them, "I had them a'regularly entered, first wi' rottens—then wi' stots or weasels—and then wi' the tods and brocks—and now they fear naething that ever cam wi' a hairy skin on 't."

Today the hunting prowess of the Dandie is not often required. He is credited with being more serene than most of the terriers and his good disposition and amiable nature has made him an excellent house pet. There is a great deal of wisdom in that large, domed head.

The Dandie, unlike other terriers, has no straight lines. He is long and made up of curves. There are two distinct colors, Pepper and Mustard, the Pepper color ranging from a dark bluish black to a light silvery grey. Mustards vary from a reddish brown to a pale fawn. The intermediate shades of both are desirable.

In the coat of a puppy and the coat of a grown dog there is a vast difference, the puppy having a coat quite short and soft, but it gradually takes on

Dandie Dinmont Terrier.

the correct texture of crispness, a mixture of hardish and soft hair.

The top-knot and points of the ears are of light, silky, white hair which, when fluffed up, forms one of the characteristic features of the "show" Dandie. In England the Dandies are shown in their natural state with a minimum of plucking and clipping, and the practice is growing increasingly popular in the United States. Usually a Dandie can be kept in show shape by a daily brushing and combing.

The height should be from eight to eleven inches at the shoulder, the length of back about 15-16 inches, and a full-grown Dandie in good working condition should weigh between 14 and 24 pounds.

Description and Standards. The description and standards, by courtesy of the Dandie Dinmont Terrier Club of America, follow.

HEAD: Strongly made and large, not out of proportion to the dog's size, the muscles showing extraordinary development, more especially the maxillary. *Skull* broad between the ears, getting gradually less towards the eyes, and measuring about the same from the inner corner of the eye to back of skull as it does from ear to ear. The forehead well domed. The head is *covered* with a very soft silky hair, which should not be confined to a mere top-knot and the lighter in color and silkier it is the better. The *Cheeks*, starting from the ears proportionately with the skull have a gradual taper towards the muzzle, which is deep and strongly made, and measures about three inches in length or in proportion to skull as three is to five. The *Muzzle* is covered with hair of a little darker shade than the top-knot, and of the same texture as the feather of the fore-

legs. The top of the muzzle is generally bare for about an inch from the back part of the nose, the bareness coming to a point towards the eye, and being about one inch broad at the nose. The nose and inside of *Mouth* black or dark colored. The *Teeth* very strong, especially the canine, which are of extraordinary size for such a small dog. The canines fit well into each other, so as to give the greatest available holding and punishing power, and the teeth are level in front, the upper ones very slightly overlapping the under ones. (Many of the finest specimens have a "swine mouth," which is very objectionable, but it is not so great an objection as the protrusion of the under jaw.)

EYES: Set wide apart, large, full round, bright, expressive of great determination, intelligence and dignity; set low and prominent in front of the head; color, a rich dark hazel.

EARS: Pendulous, set well back, wide apart, and low on the skull, hanging close to the cheek, with a very slight projection at the base, broad at the junction of the head and tapering almost to a point, the fore part of the ear tapering very little—the tapering being mostly on the back part, the fore part of the ear coming almost straight down from its junction with the head to the tip. They should harmonize in color with the body color. In the case of a Pepper dog they are covered with a soft, straight, brownish hair (in some cases almost black). In the case of a Mustard dog the hair should be mustard in color, a shade darker than the body, but not black. All should have a thin feather or light hair starting about two inches from the tip, and of nearly the same color and texture as the topknot, which often gives the ear the appearance of a *distinct point*. The animal is often one or two years old before the feather is shown. The cartilage and skin of the ear should not be thick, but rather thin. Length of ear from three to four inches.

NECK: Very muscular, well-developed and strong, showing great power of resistance, being well set into the shoulders.

BODY: Long, strong, and flexible; ribs well sprung and round, chest well developed and let well down between the forelegs; the back rather low at the shoulder, having a slight downward curve and a corresponding arch over the loins, with a very slight gradual drop from top of loins to root of tail; both sides of backbone well supplied with muscle.

TAIL: Rather short, say from eight inches to ten inches, and covered on the upper side with wiry hair of darker color than that of the body, the hair on the under side being lighter in color and not so wiry, with nice feather about two inches long, getting shorter as it nears the tip; rather thick at the root, getting thicker for about four inches, then tapering off to a point. It should not be twisted or curled in any way, but should come up with a curve like a scimitar, the tip, when excited being in a perpendicular line with the root of the tail. It should neither be set on too high nor too low. When not excited it is carried gaily, and a little above the level of the body.

LEGS: The forelegs short, with immense muscular development and bone, set wide apart, the chest coming well down between them. The feet well formed and *not flat*, with very strong brown or dark-colored claws. Bandy legs and flat feet are objectionable. The hair on the forelegs and feet of a Pepper dog should be tan, varying according to the body color from a rich tan to a pale fawn; of a Mustard dog they are of a darker shade than its head, which is a creamy white. In both colors there is a nice feather, about two inches long, rather lighter in color than the hair on the fore part of the leg. The hind legs are a little longer than the fore ones and are set rather wide apart but not spread out in an unnatural manner, while the feet are much smaller; the thighs are well developed, and the hair of the same color and texture as the forelegs, but having no feather or dewclaws; the whole claws should be dark; but the claws of all vary in shade according to the color of the dog's body.

COAT: This is a very important point; the hair should be about two inches long; that from skull to root of tail, a mixture of hardish and soft hair, which gives a sort of crisp feel to the hand. The hair should not be wiry; the coat is what is termed piley or pencilled. The hair on the under part of the body is lighter in color and softer than on the top. The skin on the belly accords with the color of dog.

COLOR: The color is Pepper or Mustard. The Pepper ranges from a dark bluish black to a light silvery grey, the intermediate shades being preferred, the body color coming well down the shoulder and hips, gradually merging into the leg color. The Mustards vary from a reddish brown to a pale fawn, the head being a creamy white, the legs and feet of a shade darker than the head. The claws are dark as in other colors. (Nearly all Dandie Dinmont Terriers have some white on the chest, and some have also white claws.)

SIZE: The height should be from eight to eleven inches at the top of the shoulder. Length from top of shoulder to root of tail should not be more than twice the dog's height, but preferably one or two inches less.

WEIGHT: The preferred weight from 18 to 24 pounds. These weights are for dogs in good working condition.

The relative value of the several points in the standard are apportioned as follows:

SCALE OF POINTS	Points
Head	10
Eyes	10
Ears	10
Neck	5
Body	20
Tail	5
Legs and Feet	10
Coat	15
Color	5
Size and weight	5
General Appearance	5
TOTAL	100

FOX TERRIER

THE SMOOTH Fox Terrier was receiving the distinction of a classification at shows more than a decade before a similar privilege was accorded to the Wire-Haired. Because of his work in driving the fox from holes, and of his keen sight and nose, the Fox Terrier was first classified among the sporting breeds.

In 1862 at the Birmingham show, there was a class for "White and Other Smooth-Haired English Terriers except Black and Black-and Tans." The next year, a distinct class was given at Birmingham. There were very few entries, but in 1868 the classes for Fox Terriers were the best filled in the Nottingham show, having 62 exhibited.

During these years, it must be admitted that practically every type of dog with a terrier aspect and a docked tail was shown in this class. However, some of the better breeders were steadfastly maintaining the highest terrier standards and by 1876, since the terriers shown by these breeders were the consistent winners, an ideal was set.

Colonel Thornton's Pitch, in a painting made in 1790, is considered the first record of a Fox Terrier nearest to the type of the ultimate refinement of the breed. Pitch was a white smooth-coated terrier with markings. The ancient background of the Smooth is conceded to be widely separated from that of the rough-coated black and tan working terrier that produced the Wire-Haired Terrier. The more important ancestors of the Smooth were the smooth-coated Black and Tan, the Bull Terrier, Beagle, and Greyhound. Such a variety of antecedents hardly seems possible in the eventual development of today's smart-looking autocrat of the terrier group. Early breeders such as the Rev. Jack Russell, Captain Percy Williams, and Jack Morgan kept certain strains of terriers, and apart from their fox-hunting attributes, became interested in the variety and bred and showed them.

Jack Morgan, huntsman to Lord Galway, was chiefly instrumental in bringing the Grove Terriers to the perfection they attained. Old Jock and Grove Nettle were famous terriers. Ben Morgan, huntsman to Lord Middleton, had acquired Nettle from his brother. She was the first of the Morgan strain without "red ears" and is described as a "pretty shaped tan headed bitch with a black mark on her side" whose "only fault" was the difficulty to keep her above ground! She was sold at a high price at the age of 7½ years. Old Jock, winner of 33 first prizes and eight championships, was by a black and tan dog (believed to have been from a strain developed by the Duke of Rutland who used his black and tan terriers to cross with the Belvoir Terriers and thus obtain the desired colored head). Old Jock is said to have marked his progeny with the colored head as did another well-known terrier, Old Trap. Both were used extensively in breeding, many and varied types of Fox Terrier bitches being sent to them.

Belvoir Joe, bred by W. Cooper, huntsman to the

Fox Terrier—Smooth-haired. Int. Ch. Canadian Ambassador.
Owner: Charles Berlin, Aliber Kennels, Great Neck, New York)

The original Fox Terrier standard, as drawn in 1876 by the Fox Terrier Club of England, has been little changed except for reducing the weight of a male dog in show condition from 20 to 18 pounds, indicating that early breeders knew very well what they desired. The same standard was adopted by the American Fox Terrier Club, and later enlarged upon to include measurements.

James M. Austin glorified the Smooth in this country when he brought over the illustrious Nornay Saddler, a dog that was to make history as an example of perfection of the breed. He not only completed a remarkable show record but during the 12-year period, 1934-1946, sired more American Smooth-Haired champions than did any other sire.

Mr. Austin also brought over Avon Peddlar and Bowden Night Reveller, two of England's top Smooths. Mrs. Charles Henry Fallass imported Avon Bondette, Oneway Storm, and Buckland of Andely. The latter was England's most successful show Smooth, and the only one to compare in show and stud record with the celebrated Saddler.

The Smooth-Haired Fox Terrier is quite popular in this country, being a favorite in city, town, or country. His many good qualities are certain to keep him high in popular favor.

The Smooth Fox Terrier is regarded as the favorite terrier in Sweden.

The Wire-Haired Fox Terrier is considered the favorite terrier in Belgium, Canada, Holland, and Italy.

It is generally conceded that the Wire-Haired Fox Terrier is an older variety than the Smooth, although the latter was the first to be known to the show ring. The Wire-Haired Fox Terrier was originally known as the Rough-Haired Terrier but later became the Wire-Haired Terrier. Fox Terrier was added to the Wire-Haired variety's name at a later date, the smooth-haired variety being called "Fox Terrier" first.

That the Wire-Haired Fox Terrier is an older variety is given support in various ways. The broken-haired or wire terrier was a favorite vermin dog, later becoming identified with foxhound packs where they were used to go to ground for foxes. Turberville, in 1611, in his *The Noble Arts of Venerie or Hunting* alluded to terriers of two kinds, stating that in his opinion, one sort came out of Flanders or the Low Countries and that "they have crooked legges and short heared" but that there was also another kind "shaggy and straight legged," He then went on to explain that the short-legged kind were better for getting down the holes and the long-legged ones were better for hunting above ground but "also would go down holes."

About 1748 a Dutch painting, executed by Hamilton, son of a Scotsman, was a still life of flowers and fruit with a Wire-Haired Terrier in the foreground which was quite similar in type to the breed as it was in the early 1900's.

Terriers were extremely popular at a very early

Belvoir, ranks high in fame. He was by Trimmer out of a "grand looking" bitch, Trinket, and it was said that his pedigree could be traced back for 40 years. During those 40 years, Mr. Cooper had very carefully kept the strain free from Bull Terrier.

Other packs had excellent strains. They were used by the Quorn Hunt in cubbing season but seldom at other times. In Shropshire there was a strain developed known as the Shropshire or Cheshire breeds. These were said to have had too much "bull" used in their development so that the type became too much that way in appearance. There were famous old terriers from this pack, however, among them being Old Tartar, who had a brilliant career and sired Typke, a great winner in North Country shows.

Many stories are related about the pluckiness and fortitude of these early-day Fox Terriers. A dog called Old Jim, at 11 months of age, is said to have tackled a pet monkey which had a savage disposition and was very strong. He had bedeviled the terrier and when no one was around one day, Jim decided to take up the matter. The monkey was discovered dead in his cage. Jim was alive but somewhat the worse for wear.

A terrific breed boom started in 1869 when nearly one-tenth of the dogs shown at Islington were Fox Terriers. Every year the numbers gained, at one time reaching 270 entries at the Nottingham show. This rage resulted for a time in some indiscriminate breeding and faking, but there were always sincere and honest breeders who kept zealously to type.

Francis Redmond, noted English breeder, exhibitor, and judge of the Smooth, is popularly acclaimed as having been the foremost breeder and authority in establishing the type as it is today. He bred, among others, the celebrated Trap. He judged the first specialty show of the American Fox Terrier Club in 1886 where there was the remarkable entry of 75 Smooths and 4 Wires.

date. They gained notoriety for their intelligence, bravery, and devotion. The Wire-Haired Terriers were widely produced in North Durham and Yorkshire, England, where, for the most part, they were developed by the huntsmen of the foxhound packs.

The Rev. Jack Russell of Dennington, North Devon, England, is given credit for having made the badger-digging, rough-haired white terrier popular. The parson's wire terrier breeding activities extended from 1812 to 1870, and it is believed that the breed might have died out if it had not been for his studied breeding methods. He kept the strain pure from 1815 on, only using an outside cross once: Old Jock, a famous Smooth. The Smooth-Haired Fox Terriers were used in a substantial way in the later improvement of the Wire. Up to 1915, the Smooth-Haired Fox Terriers were far from numerous.

The Jack Russell strain became famous for their pluck and keenness. The white ones, moreover, were very popular. A white terrier had been somewhat of a rarity. In 1803 it was considered unusual enough to have it mentioned that the mother of a wonderful litter of seven puppies, sold at the Running Horse livery stables in Piccadilly for one and twenty guineas, was a white-pied.

The distinct varieties up to about that time had been generally black with tanned legs and muzzles, a spot of the same color over each eye.

The white color became increasingly popular as it could be easily seen and distinguished from the fox or badger. The reddish-colored varieties were often mistaken for the fox by the inexperienced. Terriers of the best blood and most determined ferocity became very fashionable. No foxhound's establishment was complete without a brace of well-bred terriers with one of these terriers larger and stronger than the other. From the moment of throwing into covert these terriers were indefatigable in their efforts to be up with or near the pack. The hard, dense jacket of the Wire-Haired was considered desirable by many as being more suitable for standing the wear and tear of a day's hard hunting.

In 1858, a hunting article appeared in *The Field*, describing a kennel in Cheshire where there was a "pack of seven couples of beautiful white terriers, whose pedigrees had been registered with as much care and precision as those of any pack of foxhounds. In symmetry they are perfect and their legs and feet quite models for Masters of Hounds and huntsmen to study."

In the course of the Rough-Haired Terrier's development and use with foxhounds, an occasional cross between the breeds very likely occurred. In a sporting publication dated about 1794, it was written that a terrier had run a mile in two minutes, the second mile in four minutes, the third in six minutes, the fourth in eight minutes, and so on. Afterwards this terrier ran the same distance, six miles, in 32 minutes. The writer intimated that the "terrier" was half hound.

Rough-Haired Terriers received their first show classification at Darlington, England, in 1869. Wire-Haired Terriers were listed at the Birmingham show in 1879. Three years later, the English Kennel Club Stud Book changed the classification to Wire-Haired Fox Terriers.

The first Wire of completely authentic record was Kendal's Old Tip, a kennel dog of the Grimmington Hounds. Old Tip, whelped in 1866, came from a strain of Wire-Haired Terriers, tan with a black stripe down the back, which had been developed by Mr. Thornton, a Yorkshire squire. One of these terriers was crossed with a Smooth-Haired Fox Terrier to produce the desirable strain.

William Carrick's Venture, one of the best Wire-Haired Terriers of that period, came from Old Tip as did another well-known dog, Hayward Field's Tussle. Venture, a white dog with one marked ear, 16 pounds in weight, was shown at Birmingham in 1872, and took second prize. The first prize was withheld for "want of Merit."

The following year at the Crystal Palace and Manchester Shows, the team of Venture, Tip, and Turpin were shown and took several prizes. Venture subsequently won first prizes, one under the same judge at Birmingham in 1874.

A breed standard had not yet been adopted. In 1876 the standard was drawn by the Fox Terrier Club of England, the second oldest single breed club in existence. (The English Bulldog Club was organized the same year.)

The American Fox Terrier Club was organized in 1885 and adopted the English standard for the breed. In 1913, a group of English fanciers organized the Wire Fox Terrier Association and in 1944, the Wire Fox Terrier Club in the United States was organized at a meeting at Madison Square Garden, New York.

Tyke, an importation, sent to the Hon. John E. I. Granger by Mr. Carrick, was the winner of the first Wire-Haired variety in the New York show of 1883.

Mr. Carrick's Tack, whelped in 1884, was one of the earlier dogs of importance in shows in England.

Fox Terrier—Wirehaired. Ch. Hallwyre Head Coach. (Owner: Hallwyre Kennels, Dallas, Texas)

Two famous Wires were Briggs, purchased by T. Wootton for Lord Lonsdale in 1883 for £200, and Miggs, bought for £105.

The Hon. George Steadman Thomas' Endcliffe Kennels was the first important establishment in the United States to produce Wire-Haired Fox Terriers. Mr. Thomas became renowned as a breeder of champions and an outstanding judge. Rowsley's Kennels began importing good Wires in 1907. The famous Wildoaks Kennels of Mrs. Richard Bondy was established in 1924. The Hallwyre Kennels of Forest N. Hall in Texas was an early Wire establishment. Probably none, however, achieved any more fame than the Ohio Hetherington Kennels of Mr. and Mrs. T. H. Carruthers, III.

Description and Standards. The description and scale of points follow.

SMOOTH

The following shall be the standard of the Fox Terrier amplified in part in order that a more complete description of the Fox Terriers may be presented.

HEAD: The skull should be flat and moderately narrow, gradually decreasing in width to the eyes. Not much stop should be apparent, but there should be more dip in the profile between the forehead and the top jaw then is seen in the case of a Greyhound. The cheeks must not be full. The ears should be V-shaped and small, of moderate thickness, and drooping forward close to the cheek, not hanging by the side of the head like a Foxhound. *The topline of the folded ear should be well above the level of the skull.* The jaws, upper and lower, should be strong and muscular and of fair punishing strength, but not so as in any way to resemble the Greyhound or modern English Terrier. There should not be much falling away below the eyes. This part of the head should, however, be moderately chiseled out, so as not to go down in a straight slope like a wedge. The nose, toward which the muzzle must gradually taper, should be black. *It should be noticed that although the foreface should gradually taper from eye to muzzle and should tip slightly at its juncture with the forehead, it should not "dish" or fall away quickly below the eyes, where it should be full and well made up, but relieved from "wedginess" by a little delicate chiseling.* The eyes and the rims should be dark in color, *moderately* small and rather deep-set, full of fire, life and intelligence and as nearly as possible circular in shape. *Anything approaching a yellow eye is most objectionable.* The teeth should be as nearly as possible together, i.e. *the points of the upper (incisors) teeth on the outside of or slightly overlapping the lower teeth. There should be apparent little difference in length between the skull and foreface of a well-balanced head.*

NECK: Should be clean and muscular, without throatiness, of fair length, and gradually widening to the shoulders.

SHOULDERS: Should be long and sloping, well laid back, fine at the points, and clearly cut at the withers.

CHEST: Deep and not broad.

BACK: Should be short, straight (i.e. level), and strong, with no appearance of slackness. *Brisket should be deep, yet not exaggerated.*

LOIN: Should be very powerful, *muscular* and very slightly arched. The foreribs should be moderately arched, the back ribs deep *and well sprung,* and the dog should be well ribbed up.

HINDQUARTERS: Should be strong and muscular, quite free from droop or crouch; the thighs long and powerful; *stifles well curved and turned neither in nor out; hocks well bent and near the ground should be perfectly upright and parallel each with the other when viewed from behind,* the dog standing well up on them like a Foxhound, and not straight in the stifle. *The worst possible form of hindquarters consists of a short second thigh and a straight stifle.*

STERN: Should be set on rather high and carried gaily, but not over the back or curled. It should be of good strength, anything approaching a "pipe-stopper" tail being especially objectionable.

LEGS: The forelegs viewed from any direction must be straight with bone strong right down to the feet, showing little or no appearance of ankle in front, and being short and straight in pasterns. Both forelegs and hind legs should be carried straight forward in traveling, the stifles not turning outward. The elbows should hang perpendicularly to the body, working free of the sides.

FEET: Should be round, compact and not large; the soles hard and tough; the toes moderately arched and turned neither in nor out.

COAT: Should be smooth, flat, but hard, dense and abundant. The belly and under side of the thighs should not be bare.

COLOR: White should predominate; brindle, red, or liver markings are objectionable. Otherwise this point is of little or no importance.

SYMMETRY, SIZE AND CHARACTER: The dog must present a generally gay, lively and active appearance; bone and strength in a small compass are essentials, but this must not be taken to mean that a Fox Terrier should be cloddy, or in any way coarse—speed and endurance must be looked to as well as power, and the symmetry of the Foxhound taken as a model. The terrier, like the hound, must on no account be leggy, nor must he be too short in the leg. He should stand like a cleverly made hunter, covering a lot of ground, yet with a short back, as before stated. He will then attain the highest degree of propelling power, together with the greatest length of stride that is compatible with the length of his body. Weight is not a certain criterion of a terrier's fitness for his work—general shape, size and contour are the main points; and if a dog can gallop and stay, and follow his fox up a drain, it matters little what his weight is to a pound or so. *According to present-day requirements, a full-sized, well-balanced dog should not exceed 15½ inches at the withers, the bitch being proportionately lower —nor should the length of back from withers to root of tail exceed 12 inches, while, to maintain the relative proportions, the head should not exceed 7¼ inches or be less than 7 inches. A dog with these measurements should scale 18 pounds in show condition—a bitch weighing some 2 pounds less—with a margin of 1 pound either way.*

BALANCE: This may be defined as the correct proportions of a certain point, or points, when considered in relation to a certain other point or points. It is the keystone of the terrier's anatomy. The chief points for consideration are the relative proportions of skull and foreface; head and back; height at withers and length of body from shoulder-point to buttock—the ideal of proportion being reached when the last two measurements are the same. It should be added that, although the head measurements can be taken with absolute accuracy, the height at withers and length of back and coat are approximate, and are inserted for the information of breeders and exhibitors rather than as a hard and fast rule.

MOVEMENT: Movement, or action, is the crucial test of conformation. The terrier's legs should be carried straight forward while traveling, the forelegs hanging perpendicular and swinging parallel with the sides, like the pendulum of a clock. The principal propulsive power is furnished by the hind legs, perfection of action being found in the terrier possessing long thighs and muscular second thighs well bent at the stifles, which admit of a strong forward thrust or "snatch" of the hocks. When approaching, the forelegs should form a continuation of the straight line of the front, the feet being the same distance apart at the elbows. When stationary, it is often difficult to determine whether a dog is slightly out at shoulder, but, directly he moves, the defect—if it exists—becomes more apparent, the forefeet having a tendency to cross, "weave," or "dish." When, on the contrary, the dog is tied at the shoulder, the tendency of the feet is to move wider apart, with a sort of paddling action. When the hocks are turned in—cowhock—the stifles and feet are turned outwards, resulting in a serious loss of propulsive power. When the hocks are turned outwards the tendency of the hind feet is to cross, resulting in an ungainly waddle.

N.B.—Old scars or injuries, the result of work or accident, should not be allowed to prejudice a terrier's chance in the show ring, unless they interfere with its movement or with its utility for work or stud.

WIRE

This variety of the breed should resemble the smooth sort in every respect except the coat, which should be broken. The harder and more wiry the texture of the coat is, the better. On no account should the dog look or feel woolly; and there should be no silky hair about the poll or elsewhere. The coat should not be too long, so as to give the dog a shaggy appearance, but, at the same time, it should show a marked and distinct difference all over from the smooth species.

SCALE OF POINTS:	*Points*
Head and ears	15
Neck	5
Shoulders and chest	10
Back and loin	10
Hindquarters	15
Stern	5
Legs and feet	15
Coat	15
Symmetry, size and character	10
TOTAL	100

Disqualifications. Nose—White, cherry or spotted to a considerable extent with either of these colors. Ears—Prick, tulip or rose. Mouth—Much undershot, or much overshot.

IRISH TERRIER

THERE WAS a time when it was thought that the Irish Terrier was a breed peculiar to the Emerald Isle. There is ample proof, however, that, like the Scottish and Welsh Terriers, it goes back to that good old ancestor of most terriers, the wirehaired black and tan sporting dog of the Great Britain which existed over 200 years ago. The Irish Terrier's relationship to the Welsh Terrier is certain, but the fact remains that it was developed and kept in Ireland for many generations. Old Irish manuscripts refer to the Irish Sporting Terrier, where it was described as the poor man's sentinel, the farmer's friend, and the gentleman's favorite.

Early Irish Terriers were bred, like all the early terriers, for their working qualities and hunting ability, rather than for appearance. The color range was wide and varied . . . black and tan, grey and brindle, wheaten of all shades, red being predominant. Size, too, did not matter if the dog was game and sturdy. In 1872, 1873, and 1874, when the Irish Terrier first gained attention, type was still a matter of opinion. At the Dublin Show in 1874, prizes were offered for Irish Terriers under 9 lbs. weight and over 9 lbs. weight. At the 1875 show a pure-bred "white" Irish Terrier won the class.

Mr. R. G. Ridgway of Waterford, writing in the *Livestock Journal* (1875), admitted that the Irish Terriers at the Dublin Show were a mixed lot but

Irish Terrier—Ch. Nut Brown Susan. (Owner: Rudolph Jensen, Chicago, Ill.) Photo by Frasie Studio.

maintained that there was still to be found in Ireland a strain of terrier that had not been crossed by any of the foreign breeds and which justly deserved to be considered a distinct and "pure" breed, by name "the Irish Terrier." This was no doubt in reference to the large strain kept in County Cork that were mostly *wheaten,* or to a breed found in Ballymena and the north of Ireland which were more like the type of today, being racy with long, punishing jaws, wheaten in color but softer and more open in coat.

Mr. Ridgway, in his *Dogs of the British Islands* (1878), wrote that the breed had been pure in Ireland and "remembered" 50 or 60 years before, and was peculiarly adapted to Irish conditions. They were, he wrote, hardy, able to stand wet, cold, and hard work without showing fatigue, and their coats, because they were hard and wiry, allowed them to hunt the thickest gorse without inconvenience.

F. M. Jowett, an ardent fancier of the breed at a later date, further attests to their ability as sporting companions when he wrote that "they take to water as easily as young ducks, soon learn to love a gun, and are easily trained to fetch and carry and retrieve, both on land and in water." Their sporting proclivities were directed primarily to vermin killing and they were said to be unsurpassed at swimming and killing water rats, but Mr. Jowett also had dogs that were "thoroughly broken to ferrets which would mark rabbits, either in burrow, hedge or loose stone walls. When the ferret was put in, the dogs would stand back and wait until the rabbit was bolted, and then retrieve it to hand when it was shot." Others were used to work stubble fields for partridge which they would handle and retrieve "as well as any Spaniels."

Many stories are related to the prowess of the breed in badger hunting. One C. W. Chabrel of Cardiff, had a bitch, Crow Gill Fury, which won a first prize of a gold medal in a contest in 1894 for running the trail of a badger true until very near the end when she "got on to rabbits, which were plentiful about that part." Two of Fury's puppies drew a badger when only eight months old, and another daughter of hers drew a 30 lb. badger, twice, for a wager of five pounds.

In 1879 the Irish Terrier Club was formed. The first meetings were held in Dublin in March; rules were drafted, amended, and passed, and afterwards submitted to the English section of the club at a London meeting on April 28 of the same year. One of the then existing fashions for the breed was cropped ears, which was strongly opposed by the majority of members. At the first general meeting of the club in 1880, there was a regular discussion on the "cropping" question which led, eventually, to the first attempt to introduce uncropped Irish Terriers at the Crystal Palace Show, June 2, that year. It was resolved "that at all shows where the Challenge Cup is offered, the Committee also offer at least one prize for the best uncropped Irish Terrier Puppy exhibited." That was the first step.

Later this became a more drastic move when, at the Kennel Club Show in 1887, it was resolved that "no club specials, money or cups shall be awarded to any Irish Terrier born after July, 1887, if cropped." There were objections to this, however, as it meant debarring many good Irish Terriers from Challenge Cup competition for Best Irish Terrier. As time went on, however, cropping became more and more unpopular, and in 1889 it was abolished altogether when the Kennel Club made the rule "that any Irish Terrier whelped after Dec. 31, 1889, if cropped, will not be eligible to compete at any Kennel Club show."

William Graham of Belfast is credited with having done more to produce the modern show type of Irish Terrier than any other single exhibitor of his day. It was he who bought as a puppy Champion Erin, called the mother of the breed. She, he claimed, was the best Irish Terrier bitch he ever saw, and others agreed. When bred to Killiney Boy, owned by Mr. Burke of Dublin, she produced a famous litter. Erin was mated to other dogs of the time and happened to be one of those bitches so predominantly rich in type that whatever might be the sire, her litters turned out well. Killiney Boy's dam was of Welsh Terrier type, a rough black and tan, and it is supportive evidence of the relationship between the Irish and Welsh Terriers that black and tan puppies frequently appeared in subsequent litters of his progeny.

Erin's first litter from Killiney Boy produced Playboy, a strong favorite on the bench, and whose ears were so small and well carried that they were allowed to remain on instead of cropped (the fashion at his time). He, in turn, produced another great show dog, Bogie Rattler, which, when mated to Biddy II, sired two pups which are said to have laid the foundation for the modern drop-eared type. These were Champion Bachelor and his litter brother, Benedict, who became a pillar of the breed. From Erin also came the dam of Brick Pat, the winner of the Irish Terrier Club's Challenge Trophy twelve times.

The points of the breed were first given in the *Fancier's Gazette* (March 25, 1875), as drawn up by one "Shamrock." The authentic standards of the breed drawn by the Irish Terrier Club in 1879 stood until 1897 when they were revised and as such made the standard as it is today. The standard revised and officially adopted by the Irish Terrier Club of America in 1929 is practically identical to the English Standard for 1897.

One of the proud boasts of the Irish Terrier fanciers is that the breed proved very successful as war dogs during both World Wars. Serving as messengers and sentinels with a spirit and disregard for danger that was outstanding, they attained fame and high praise for their work. Their following today is small but sincere.

Description and Standards. The description and standards, revised and officially adopted by the Irish Terrier Club of America follow.

HEAD: Long, but in nice proportion to the rest of the body; the skull flat, rather narrow between the ears, and narrowing slightly towards the eyes; free from wrinkle; with the stop hardly noticeable except in profile. The jaws must be strong and muscular, but not too full in the cheek, and of good punishing length. The foreface must not fall away appreciably between or below the eyes; instead, the modeling should be delicate and in contradistinction, for example, to the fullness of the foreface of the Greyhound. An exaggerated foreface, which is out of proportion to the length of the skull from the occiput to the stop, disturbs the proper balance of the head, and is not desirable. Also, the head of exaggerated length usually accompanies oversize or disproportionate length of body, or both, and such conformation is not typical. On the other hand, the foreface should not be noticeably shorter than is the skull from occiput to stop. Excessive muscular development of the cheeks,

Irish Terrier—Ch. Solidarity Tim. (Owner: Rudolph Jensen, Chicago, Ill.) Photo by Frasie Studio.

Irish Terrier puppies.

or bony development of the temples, conditions which are described by the fancier as "cheeky," or "strong in head," or "thick in skull," are objectionable. The "bumpy" or "alligator" head, sometimes described as the "taneous" head, in which the skull presents two lumps of bony structure with or without indentations above the eyes, is unsightly and to be faulted. The hair on the upper and the lower jaws should be similar in quality and texture to that on the body, and only of sufficient length to present an appearance of additional strength and finish to the foreface. The profuse, goatlike beard is unsightly and undesirable and almost invariably it betokens the objectionable linty and silken hair in the coat.

TEETH: Should be strong and even, white and sound; and neither overshot nor undershot.

LIPS: Should be close and well-fitting, almost black in color.

NOSE: Must be black.

EYES: Dark hazel in color; small not prominent, full of life, fire and intelligence. The light or yellow eye is most objectionable.

EARS: Small and V-shaped; of moderate thickness; set well on the head, and dropping forward closely to the cheek. The ear must be free of fringe, and the hair much shorter and somewhat darker in color than on the body. A "dead" ear, houndlike in appearance, must be severely penalized. It is not characteristic of the Irish Terrier. An ear which is too slightly erect is undesirable.

NECK: Should be of fair length and gradually widening towards the shoulders; well and proudly carried, and free from throatiness. Generally there is a slight frill in the hair at each side of the neck, extending almost to the corner of the ear.

SHOULDERS AND CHEST: Shoulders must be fine, long, and sloping well into the back. The chest should be deep and muscular, but neither full nor wide.

BACK AND LOIN: The body should be moderately long—neither too long nor too short. The short back, so coveted and so appealing in the Fox Terrier is *not* characteristic of the Irish Terrier. It is objectionable. The back must be symmetrical, strong and straight, and free from an appearance of slackness or "dip" behind the shoulders. The loin strong and muscular, and slightly arched. The ribs fairly sprung, deep rather than round, with a well-ribbed back. The bitch may be slightly longer in appearance than the dog.

HIND QUARTERS: Should be strong and muscular; powerful thighs; hocks near the ground; stifles moderately bent.

STERN: Should be docked, and set on rather high, but not curled. It should be of good strength and substance; of fair length and well covered with harsh, rough hair, and free from fringe or feather. The three-quarters dock is about right.

FEET AND LEGS: The feet should be strong, tolerably round, and moderately small; toes arched and turned neither out nor in, with black toe-nails. The pads should be deep, not hard, but with a pleasing velvety quality, and perfectly sound; they must be entirely free from cracks or horny excrescences. Corny feet, so-called, are to be regarded as an abominable blemish; as a taint which must be shunned. Cracked pads frequently accompany corny growths, and these conditions are more pronounced in hot and dry weather. In damp weather and in winter such pads may improve temporarily, but these imperfections inevitably reappear and the result is unsound feet, a deplorable fault which must be heavily penalized. There seems to be no permanent cure for this condition, and even if a temporary cure were possible the disease is seldom, if ever, eradicated and undoubtedly it is transmitted in breeding. The one sure way to avoid corny and otherwise unsound feet is to avoid breeding from dogs or bitches which are not entirely free from this taint. Legs, moderately long, well set from the shoulders, perfectly straight, with plenty of bone and muscle, the elbows working clear of the sides; pasterns short, straight, and hardly noticeable. Both fore and hind legs should move straight forward when traveling; the stifles should not turn outwards. "Cowhocks"—that is, where the hocks are turned in, and the stifles and feet are turned out, are intolerable. The legs should be free from feather, and covered, like the head, with hair of similar texture to that on the body, but not so long.

COAT: Should be dense and wiry in texture, rich in quality having a broken appearance, but still lying fairly close to the body, the hairs growing so closely and strongly together that when parted with the fingers the skin is hardly visible; free of softness or silkiness, and not so long as to alter the outline of the body, particularly in the hind quarters. At the base of the stiff outer coat there should be a growth of finer and softer hair, differing in color, termed the under coat. Single coats, which are without any under coat, and wavy coats, are undesirable; the curly coat is most objectionable. On the sides of the body the coat is never as harsh as on the back and the quarters, but it should be plentiful and of good texture.

COLOR: Should be whole-colored; the bright red, red wheaten, or golden red colors are preferable. A small patch of white on the chest, frequently encountered in all whole-colored breeds, is permissible but not desirable. White on any other part of the body is most objectionable.

SIZE AND SYMMETRY: The most desirable weight in show condition is 27 pounds for the dog and 25 pounds for the bitch. The height at the shoulder should be approximately 18 inches. This terrier must be active, lithe, and wiry in movement, with great animation, sturdy and strong in substance and bone-structure, but at the same time free from clumsiness, for speed, power, and endurance are most essential. The Irish Terrier must be neither "cobby" nor "cloddy" but should be built on lines of speed, with a graceful, racing outline.

The weights herein mentioned are ideal and serve as a guide to both breeder and judge. In the show ring, however, the informed judge readily identifies the over-sized or under-sized Irish Terrier by its conformation and general appearance. The weights named should be regarded as limit weights, as a rule, but it must be considered that a comparatively small, heavily-built and "cloddy" dog—which is most undesirable, and not at all typical—may easily be of standard weight, or over it, whereas another terrier which is long in leg, lacking in substance and built somewhat upon the lines of a Whippet—also undesirable and not at all typical—may be of the exact weight, or under it; therefore, although the standard weights must be borne well in mind, weight is not the last word in judgment. It is of the greatest importance to select, in so far as possible, Terriers of moderate and generally accepted size, possessing the other various necessary characteristics.

TEMPERAMENT: The Irish Terrier is game and asks no quarter. He is of good temper, most affectionate, and absolutely loyal to mankind. Tender and forbearing with those he loves, this rugged, stout-hearted terrier will guard his master, his mistress, children in his charge, or their possessions, with unflinching courage and with utter contempt of danger or hurt. His life is one continuous and eager offering of loyal and faithful companionship, and devoted, loving service. He is ever on guard, and stands between his house and all that threatens.

Negative Points

White nails, toes and feet, minus	10
Much white on chest	10
Dark shadings on face	5
Mouth undershot or cankered	10
Coat shaggy, curly or soft	10
Uneven in color	5
TOTAL	50

Disqualifying Points

Nose: Any other color than black. *Mouth:* Much undershot or overshot. *Ears:* Cropped ears. *Color:* Any other color than red, golden red, or red wheaten. A small patch of white on the chest is permissible; othewise parti-colored coats disqualify.

KERRY BLUE TERRIER

IN ANY discussion of treatise written on this true dog of Eire, color strikes the important note. Gameness, of course, as in all the terrier breeds, was uppermost, but even in the early days of the Kerry, color ranked a close second. As an indication of pigmentation, old Kerry men insisted on a black roof of the mouth and black gums.

The highly distinguishing characteristic color in the Kerry Blue has been zealously guarded. So meticulous are present-day Kerry fanciers in preserving the true blue coloring that in 1947 a new standard was devised to forestall any deviation into lilacs, violet blues, purples or greenish blues that might have qualified under the existing standard of "a shade of blue."

The breed first came into prominence in County Kerry in Ireland, in the rugged mountain regions. Here, it is quite firmly established, they had been pure-bred for a hundred years. The late Dr. George J. Pierce of the Bushmont Kennels, Ballyduff, Tralee, County Kerry, wrote in the late 1920's that he had traced the breed back 150 years through conversations in his youth with old fanciers whose fathers had talked to older fanciers. But the Kerry did not emerge into the competitive show ring until June, 1913, when five "Irish Terriers (Blue)" were judged at an Irish show.

The Kerry had been an all-purpose dog in the homes of the County Kerry folks. They were used to tend cows and sheep, destroy vermin, and acted as guardians for the home and children. Moreover, they were indispensable in the important sports of early days, ratting and drawing badgers. They were also used for hunting small game and birds to some extent and were good retrievers. No thought was ever given to their bench show possibilities until the breed was adopted as the national dog of the Irish Republic.

English fanciers first took an interest in the Kerry Blue at the Killarney Show, September 16, 1913, where there was an entry of twenty "Irish Blue Terriers (Working)." The breed was first introduced officially in England at Cruft's in February, 1922, when Bracehill of Bailey was Best of Breed. The first English Challenge certificates were awarded at the Great Joint Terrier show in 1922, and won by Matrell's Sapphire Beauty, which became the first English champion. Two that later became champions took second and third, Joe of Leysfield and Nofa Jacobin. The enthusiastic reception accorded the breed in England naturally drew the attention of fanciers in the United States.

In the same year, 1922, four Kerry Blue Terriers were shown at the Westminster Show in New York, entered in the miscellaneous class. For two years after this first appearance, the Kerry Blues remained under the miscellaneous classification, but in 1924 they were officially admitted by the American Kennel Club as a recognized breed and given an official championship rating.

It is believed that the first to import a Kerry Blue Terrier was Tommy Grisdale who returned from a trip to England with a "dark, straggly looking specimen, that resembled nothing in terrier competition at the time" (early 1920's).

Subsequently, Mrs. William Randolph Hearst imported a brace and when Gene Tunney was world heavyweight champion, he imported three of the breed.

B. E. Watson, Jr., is credited with having performed wonders in improvement of the breed in type and quality. It was he who figured out the mating

Kerry Blue Terrier—Ch. Donagayl's King Essler. (Owner: Don Plumb, Des Moines, Iowa) Photo by William P. Gilbert.

that produced Rackety Packety Killsmenkeg, a bitch that, mated to Ch. Ben Edar Bawcock, produced four champions in her first litter and in a second litter of the same breeding produced three champions.

Mrs. C. H. Jackson, Jr., of Santa Barbara, California, imported the great English champion, Leinster Leader, in 1928, the first Kerry to go Best in Show at an all-breed show in the country. Later, in 1930, Mrs. Jackson brought over English Ch. Black Prince of the Chevin, the first Kerry to go Best in Show in an all-breed championship show in England.

In Ireland the standard of the breed calls for them to be shown in the rough. The Irish will not permit the trimming of coat. In England, coats must be trimmed and, with a few minor exceptions, the standard is identical with the old American standard.

In the revised color requirement, the essentials are contained in the following: (A) Up to 12 months solid black is not a disqualification, but thereafter it is. (B) Up to 18 months, the dark blue, and brown in various shades and mixtures with grey and blue, are all permissible. (C) At 18 months and over the exceptions to the shades listed above should be kept out of the ring until they have turned to the mature natural color as defined in the standard.

Description and Standards. The revised description and standards, adopted by the U.S. Kerry Blue Terrier Club and approved by the American Kennel Club follow.

HEAD: Long, but not exaggerated and in good proportion to the rest of the body. Well balanced with little apparent difference between the length of the skull and foreface. (20 points)

SKULL: Flat, with very slight stop, of but moderate breadth between the ears, and narrowing very slightly to the eyes.

Kerry Blue Terrier—Ch. Donagayl's Brigadoon Gal. (Owner: Mr. and Mrs. Donald W. Hutton, Charleston, Ill.) Photo by Ritter.

CHEEKS: Clean and level, free from bumpiness.

EARS: V-shaped, small, but not out of proportion to the size of the dog, of moderate thickness, carried forward close to the cheeks with the top of the folded ear slightly above the level of the skull. A "dead" ear houndlike in appearance is very undesirable.

FOREFACE: Jaws deep, strong, and muscular. Foreface full and well made up, not falling away appreciably below the eyes but moderately chiseled out to relieve the foreface from wedginess.

NOSE: Black, nostrils, large and wide.

TEETH: Strong, white and either level or with the upper (incisors) teeth slightly overlapping the lower teeth. An undershot mouth should be strictly penalized.

EYES: Dark, small, not prominent, well placed and with a keen Terrier expression. Anything approaching a yellow eye is very undesirable.

NECK: Clean and moderately long, gradually widening to the shoulders upon which it should be well set and carried proudly. (5 points)

SHOULDERS AND CHEST: Shoulders fine, long and sloping, well laid back and well knit. Chest deep and of but moderate breadth. (10 points)

LEGS AND FEET: Legs moderately long with plenty of bone and muscle. The forelegs should be straight from both front and side view, with the elbows hanging perpendicularly to the body and working clear of the sides in movement, the pasterns short, straight, and hardly noticeable, both fore and hind legs should move straight forward when traveling, the stifles turning neither in nor out. (10 points)

Feet should be strong, compact, fairly round and moderately small, with good depth of pad free from cracks, the toes arched, turned neither in nor out, with black toenails.

BODY: Back short, strong, and straight (i.e., level) with no appearance of slackness. Loin short and powerful with a slight tuck-up, the ribs fairly well sprung, deep rather than round. (10 points)

HIND QUARTERS AND STERN: Hind quarters strong and muscular with full freedom of action, free from droop or crouch, the thighs long and powerful, stifles well bent and turned neither in nor out, hocks near the ground and, when viewed from behind, upright and parallel with each other, the dog standing well up on them. Tail should be set on high, or moderate length and carried gaily erect, the straighter the tail the better. (10 points)

COLOR: The correct mature color is any shade of blue gray or gray blue from deep slate to light blue gray, of a fairly uniform color throughout except that distinctly darker to black parts may appear on the muzzle, head, ears, tail, and feet. (10 points)

Kerry color, in its process of "clearing" from an apparent black at birth to the mature gray blue or blue gray, passes through one or more transitions—involving a very dark blue (darker than deep slate), shades or tinges of brown, and mixtures of these, together with a progressive infiltration of the correct mature color.

Up to 18 months such deviations from the correct mature color are permissible without preference and without regard for uniformity. Thereafter, deviation from it to any significant extent must be severely penalized.

Solid black is never permissible in the show ring. Up to 18 months any doubt as to whether a dog is black or a very dark blue should be resolved in favor of the dog, particularly in the case of a puppy. Black on the muzzle, head, ears, tail, and feet is permissible at any age.

COAT: Soft, dense, and wavy. A harsh, wire or bristle coat should be severely penalized. In show trim the body should be well covered but tidy, with the head (except for the whiskers), and the ears and cheeks clear. (15 points)

GENERAL CONFORMATION AND CHARACTER: The typical Kerry Blue Terrier should be upstanding, well knit and in good balance, showing a well-developed and muscular body with definite terrier style and character throughout. A low-slung Kerry is not typical. (10 points)

HEIGHT: The ideal Kerry should be 18½ inches at the withers for a dog, slightly less for a bitch.

In judging Kerries a height of 18-19½ inches for a dog and 17½-19 inches for a bitch should be given primary preference. Only where the comparative superiority of a specimen outside of the ranges noted clearly justifies it, should greater latitude be taken. In no case should it extend to a dog over 20 inches or under 17½ inches or to a bitch over 19½ inches or under 17 inches.

The minimum limits do not apply to puppies.

WEIGHT: The most desirable weight for a fully-developed dog is from 33-40 pounds, bitches weighing proportionately less.

DISQUALIFICATIONS: Solid black. Dewclaws on hind legs.

LAKELAND TERRIER

MANY VARIETIES of terriers were found in the northern countries of England in the early 1800's. Each took the name of the locality where the breed was found in greatest numbers. Many old names were lost when breeds gained recognition, and there were many cases where the same breed came through a variety of names before one was finally agreed upon by breeders.

The Lakeland Terrier did not get his present name until around 1925. Previous to that year, he had been known variously as the Patterdale Terrier, the Colored Working Terrier, and the local name of Fell Terrier.

Cumberland, in the northern Border country of England, was the birthplace of the Lakeland. Here, in the Lake districts of England, it was bred and raised and worked, with "working" qualities of premier importance. The ancestors of the Lakeland, way back, are closely related, if not merely the same, as the progenitors of the Border Terrier and hence also related to the Bedlington and Dandie Dinmont and being, of course, a descendant of the Old English Black and Tan Terrier.

Farmers and sportsmen in the Lake district kept these terriers to hunt with hounds. Not only was it sport, but it was dire necessity to hunt down and destroy the foxes that raided the flocks of sheep and other stock in this country. The main requisite of a dog was gameness, and the Lakeland used in hunts of the Fell districts were trained to attack the fox in his lair and not merely draw it. A dog in this kind of work had to be nimble and quick, the slim torso of the Lakeland allowed it to squeeze into the fastnesses of the rocks, and it had to have unbounded courage.

Every pack of hounds in the lake district had its accompanying game terriers. Those that were outstanding in showing courage were used as breeding stock and their puppies were given away among followers of the hunt, who in turn retained the best workers to keep the strain dominant in gameness.

A story is told of a native Lakeland Terrier owned by Lord Lonsdale, which, in 1871, crawled 23 feet under rock after an otter. After three days' work of blasting and digging, the dog was reached, none the worse for his experience. Still other stories are related

Lakeland Terrier—Ch. Edgemoor Emerald. (Owner: Mr. and Mrs. Donald J. Riter, Chardon, Ohio). Photo by Paul Toppelstein.

of dogs locked underground for 10 or 12 days that were taken out alive.

At the Agricultural Shows in the Lake district, classes for the best looking terrier, suitable for fox or otter, were held as early as 1896. Later these classes were divided as to color; for white working terriers and colored working terriers.

The first efforts to promote the Lakeland (or Cumberland County breed) took place at the Kersurck Show in 1912. World War I then caused an interruption of activities and the movement died out until 1921. In 1921 a meeting of fanciers was called at Whitehaven in Cumberland. It was at this meeting that the standard was drawn up and the name Lakeland adopted. Shortly afterwards the breed was made eligible for registration in the Kennel Club Stud Book of England.

Description and Standards. The description and standards, adopted by the Lakeland Terrier Club and approved by the American Kennel Club follow.

GENERAL APPEARANCE: The Lakeland Terrier is a small, workman-like dog of square, sturdy build and gay, friendly, self-confident demeanor. He stands on his toes as if ready to go, and he moves, lithe and graceful, with a straight-ahead, free stride of good length. His head is rectangular in contour, ears V-shaped, and wiry coat finished off with fairly long furnishings on muzzle and legs.

HEAD: Well balanced, rectangular, the length of skull equaling the length of the muzzle when measured from occiput to stop, and from stop to nose-tip. The skull is flat on top and moderately broad, the cheeks almost straight-sided, and the stop barely perceptible. The muzzle is broad with straight nose bridge and good fill-in beneath the eyes. The nose is black, except that liver-colored noses shall be permissible on liver-coated dogs. Jaws are powerful. The teeth, which are comparatively large, may meet in either a level, edge-to-edge bite, or a slightly overlapping scissors bite. Specimens with teeth overshot or undershot are to be disqualified. The ears are small, V-shaped, their fold just above the top of the skull, the inner edge close to the cheeks, and the flap pointed down. The eyes, moderately small and somewhat oval in outline, are set squarely in the skull, fairly wide apart. Their normally dark color may be a warm brown or black. The expression depends upon the dog's mood of the moment; although typically alert, it may be intense and determined, or gay and even impish.

NECK: Reachy and of good length; refined but strong; clean at the throat, slightly arched, and widening gradually into the shoulders. The withers, that point at the back of the neck where neck and body meet, are noticeably higher than the level of the back.

BODY: In over-all length-to-height proportion, the dog is approximately square. The moderately narrow chest is deep; it extends to elbows which are held close to the body. Shoulder blades are sloping, that is, well laid back, their musculature lean and almost flat in outline. The ribs are well sprung and moderately rounded. The back is short and level in topline. Loins are taut and short, although they may be a trifle longer in bitches than in dogs. Quarters are strong, broad, and muscular.

LEGS AND FEET: Forelegs are strongly boned, clean, and absolutely straight as viewed from the front or side, and devoid of appreciable bend at the pasterns. Hind legs too are strong and sturdy, the second thighs long and nicely angulated at the stifles and the hocks. Hocks are well let down, with the bone from hock to toes straight and parallel to each other. The small feet are round, the toes compact and well padded, the nails strong. Dewclaws, if any, are to be removed.

TAIL: Set high on the body, the tail is customarily docked so that when the dog is set up in show position, the tip of the docked tail is on an approximate level with the skull. In carriage it is gay or upright, although a slight curve in the direction of the head is considered desirable. The tail curled over the back is faulty.

COAT AND COLOR: Two-ply or double, the outer coat is hard and wiry in texture, the undercoat soft. Furnishings on muzzle and legs are plentiful as opposed to profuse. The color may be blue, black, liver, black and tan, blue and tan, red, red grizzle, grizzle and tan, or wheaten. Tan, as desirable in the Lakeland Terrier, is a light wheaten or straw color, with rich red or mahogany tan to be penalized. Otherwise, colors, as specified, are equally acceptable. Dark-saddled specimens (whether black grizzle or blue) are nearly solid black at birth, with tan points on muzzle and feet. The black recedes and usually turns grayish or grizzle at maturity, while the tan also lightens.

SIZE: The ideal height of the mature dog is 14½ inches from the withers to the ground, with up to a ½-inch deviation either way permissible. Bitches may measure as much as one inch less than dogs. The weight of the well-balanced, mature specimen in hard, show condition, averages approximately 17 pounds, those of other heights proportionately more or less.

Size is to be considered of lesser importance than other qualities, that is, when judging dogs of equal merit, the one nearest the ideal size is to be preferred. Symmetry and proportion, however, are paramount in the appraisal, since all qualities together must be considered in visualizing the ideal.

MOVEMENT: Straight and free, with good length of stride. Paddling, moving close, and toeing-in are faulty.

TEMPERAMENT: The typical Lakeland Terrier is bold, gay, and friendly, with a self-confident, cock-of-the-walk attitude. Shyness, especially shy-sharpness, in the mature specimen is to be heavily penalized.

SCALE OF POINTS: *Points*

Head	15
Eyes, ears, expression	15
Neck	5
Body	10
Coat	15
Legs and feet	10
Size and symmetry	10
Movement	10
Temperament	10
TOTAL	100

Disqualification. The front teeth overshot or undershot.

(May 14, 1963)

MANCHESTER TERRIER

THE RACY, sleek Manchester Terrier had been in existence for many, many years before the advent of dog shows. In Edward's *Cynographic Britannica* of 1800, a print is shown of a group of "terriers" and the black and tan depicted is considerably like the present-day type Manchester, except that the arrangement of colors is not like that of present standards. It has, however, much of the breedy, "classy" appearance so characteristic of the breed today.

It is generally conceded that the early, old broken-haired Black and Tan Terriers of the north of England held a major part in the ancestry of the Manchester. These were the accomplished rat killers, coarser, far less graceful dogs, but nevertheless much in demand for their gameness. The Manchester district was a famous sporting center where rat killing and rabbit coursing, the "poor man's sport", were popular diversions. It was here that a fancier by the name of John Hulme is said to have produced a breed adept at both these kinds of contests by mating a Whippet bitch to a famous rat-killing, dark-brown cross-bred terrier. The results of this cross proved so successful that other fanciers took to breeding them, working on a refinement of line purity of color. The breed was originally called Black and Tan Terrier, but a Sam Handley of Manchester accomplished so much in making the breed popular and promoted it so enthusiastically, that the name was changed to Manchester in order to honor him.

As they gained in popularity, breeding became more widespread with many good dogs being produced in Derbyshire and Warwickshire, England, and in the United States, so that the name Manchester was considered too restricted a designation. So breeders went back to the name Black and Tan, and in 1884 the Black and Tan Terrier Club was formed in Great Britain. Thus it was known until 1923.

When the anti-cropping edict went into effect in England some 37 years ago, breeders found it difficult to produce the Manchester with the small button ear desired and many became discouraged. Consequently, a great many ceased breeding them and the Manchester went out of fashion.

There were those, however, who never lost their devotion to this active, quick-moving type of terrier, and they persisted in their efforts to keep the breed going. It is due to these diehards that the foundation was laid for the fine specimens being produced today. Popular interest in the breed had waned, but in an attempt to bring the Manchester back to its former high status, fanciers in America grouped together in 1923 and established the Manchester Terrier Club of America. This not only spurred the old breeders to continued efforts but brought many new ones into the ranks. New blood lines were established by importing dogs from England, added impetus was given the breed and, by the sustained work of the

Manchester Terriers.

club, entries have been steadily increasing at leading shows.

Description and Standards. The description and standards follow.

HEAD: Long, narrow, tight-skinned, almost flat, with a slight indentation up the forehead; slightly wedge-shaped, tapering to the nose, with no visible cheek muscles, and well filled up under the eyes; tight-lipped jaws, level in mouth, and function-ally level teeth, or the incisors of the upper jaw may make a close, slightly overlapping contact with the incisors of the lower jaw. Eyes are small, bright, sparkling and as near black as pos-sible; set moderately close together; oblong in shape, slanting upwards on the outside; they should neither protrude nor sink in the skull. Nose, black.

EARS *(Toy Variety)*: Of moderate size; set well up on the skull and rather close together; thin, moderately narrow at base; with pointed tips; naturally erect carriage. Wide, flaring, blunt-tipped or "bell" ears are a serious fault; cropped or cut ears shall disqualify.

EARS *(Standard Variety)*: Erect, or button, small and thin; smaller at the root and set as close together as possible at the top of the head. If cropped, to a point, long and carried erect.

NECK AND SHOULDERS: The neck should be a moderate length, slim and graceful; gradually becoming larger as it approaches, and blend smoothly with the sloping shoulders; free from throatiness; slightly arched from the occiput.

CHEST: Narrow between the legs; deep in the brisket.

BODY: Moderately short, with robust loins; ribs well sprung out behind the shoulders; back slightly arched at the loin, and falling again to the tail to the same height as the shoulder. Forelegs straight, of proportionate length, and well under body.

Hind legs should not turn in or out as viewed from the rear; carried back; hocks well let down. Compact, well arched feet, with jet black nails; the two middle toes in the front feet rather longer than the others; the hind feet shaped like those of a cat. Moderately short tail, set on where the arch of the back ends; thick where it joins the body, tapering to a point, not carried higher than the back.

COAT: Smooth, short, thick, dense, close and glossy; not soft.

COLOR: Jet black and rich mahogany tan, which should not run or blend into each other but abruptly forming clear, well-defined lines of color division. A small tan spot over each eye; a very small tan spot on each cheek; the lips of the upper and lower jaws should be tanned, extending under the throat, ending in the shape of the letter V; the inside of the ears partly tanned. Tan spots, called rosettes, on each side of the chest above the front legs, more pronounced in puppies than in adults. There should be a black "thumb mark" patch on the front of each foreleg between the pastern and the knee. There should be a distinct black "pencil mark" line running length-wise on the top of each toe on all four feet. The remainder of the forelegs to be tan to the knee. Tan on the hind legs should continue from the penciling on the feet up the inside of the legs to a little below the stifle joint; the outside of the hind legs to be black. There should be tan under the tail, and on the vent, but only of such size as to be covered by the tail. White in any part of the coat is a serious fault, and shall dis-qualify whenever the white shall form a patch or stripe meas-uring as much as one-half inch in its longest dimension.

WEIGHT *(Toy Variety)*: Not exceeding 12 pounds. It is sug-gested that clubs consider dividing the American-bred and open classes by weight as follows: 7 pounds and under, over 7 pounds and not exceeding 12 pounds.

WEIGHT *(Standard Variety)*: Over 12 pounds and not exceeding 22 pounds. Dogs weighing over 22 pounds shall be disqualified. It is suggested that clubs consider dividing the American-bred and open classes by weight as follows: over 12 pounds and not exceeding 16 pounds, over 16 pounds and not exceeding 22 pounds.

Disqualifications. White in any part of the coat, forming a patch or stripe measuring as much as ½ inch in its longest dimension. Over 22 pounds, in Standard varieties. Cropped or cut ears, in Toy varieties.

(June 12, 1962)

(*See also* Toy Manchester Terrier, Group V.)

NORWICH TERRIER

THE NORWICH TERRIER is not an old breed. Less than 100 years ago a few British sportsmen set about producing a small, working terrier that would be game to the core, robust in constitution, and reasonably active for its size. At that time there were no Cairns, Sealyhams, or West Highland White Terriers before the public and sportsmen felt that it was necessary to have a "small" terrier.

That it is a by-product of the Irish Terrier is all that is known of the origin of the Norwich Terrier. Small Irish Terriers were crossed with some English or Scottish "earth dogs." These may have been Border Terriers, and it is claimed by some authorities that the Staffordshire, Bull Terrier, and Bedlington shared in the ancestry of the breed. It was thought that the soft coats that occasionally appeared in the Norwich were the result of the Bedlington influence, but accoring to other experts this could have come from the small Irish or Glen of Imaal Terriers.

Most of the early breeders seem to have worked independently in the study and development of the Norwich, but it might be assumed that in later times they learned of each other, got together and bred dogs together. The originator of the breed is usually given as a Mr. Nichols of Wymondham, of Norfolk, England, who aimed at a small terrier, red in color, and called his strain Norwich Terriers. The strain was taken up and promoted by F. Low, a veterinary surgeon who was well known in the hunting field. J. E. Cooke, onetime Master of the Norwich Staghounds, is also credited with having extended and aided in the development of the breed as is R. J. Reed, who took them up in 1909.

Charles Lawrence of Trumpington supplied many of the undergraduates at Cambridge with terriers. These became a fad, so much so that many fanciers believed that the breed should be known as the "Cantab" because of its collegiate beginnings. However that may be, they were known around the campus at Cambridge as "Trumpington Terriers" in the 1880's. Richard Hoare, who was at Cambridge at that time, obtained terriers bred by Lawrence from "very small Irish Terriers," and continued to own the breed for many years afterward.

All these terriers had the reputation of being exceedingly game and to spell certain death to rats and rabbits. Mrs. Phyllis Fagan of Outwood, one of the most prominent breeders of this plucky little dog, had a bitch named Brownie that was said to point pheasant or grouse and retrieve from land or water. Another story told of Brownie is that she was lost from the London Hotel where Mrs. Fagan was staying during the first World War and three weeks later was found at Ealing, presumably trying to get to her home at Windsor.

Mrs. Fagan had secured her first Norwich Terrier in 1914 from a man named Jones who handled hunters in shows for Mr. Stokes of Market Harborough.

The breed was first introduced into the United States shortly after World War I when the same Mr. Jones sold several dogs to the various hunt clubs here. They were very popular with the Masters of Foxhounds and became known as "Jones Terriers" in honor of their breeder. The Cheshire Hunt Club maintained a small kennel of Norwich Terriers for many years.

Mrs. Fagan and Mrs. D. Normandy Rodwell were largely responsible for achieving recognition for the breed by the English Kennel Club in 1932. In 1936, the breed was recognized by the American Kennel Club.

For a while a chief point of dispute in the standard concerned the color, some maintaining stoutly that nothing but red should be recognized, but today black and tan or grizzle as well as red and red-wheaten are fully acceptable.

Description and Standards. The revised description and standards, adopted by the Norwich Terrier Club and approved by the American Kennel Club follow.

HEAD: Skull wide, slightly rounded with good width between the ears. Muzzle strong but not long or heavy, with slightly "foxy" appearance. Length about one-third less than the measurement from the occiput to the bottom of the stop, which should be well defined. *Faults*—A long narrow head; over square muzzle; highly rounded dome. *Ears*—Prick or drop. If pricked, small, pointed, erect and set well apart. If dropped, neat, small, with break just above the skull line, front edge close to cheek, and not falling lower than the outer corner of the eye. *Faults*—Oversize; poor carriage. *Eyes*—Very bright, dark and keen. Full of expression. *Faults*—Light or protruding eyes. *Jaw*—Clean, strong, tight lipped, with strong, large, closely-fitting teeth; scissors bite. *Faults*—A mouth badly over- or undershot. *Neck*—Short and strong, well set on clean shoulders.

BODY: Moderately short, compact and deep with level topline, ribs well sprung. *Faults*—Long weak back, loaded shoulders.

LEGS: Short and powerful and as straight as is consistent with the short legs for which we aim. Sound bone, round feet, thick pads. *Faults*—Out at elbow, badly bowed, knuckled over. Too light in bone.

QUARTERS: Strong, rounded, with great powers of propulsion. *Faults*—Cowhocks.

TAIL: Medium docked, carriage not excessively gay.

COLOR: Red (including red-wheaten), black and tan or grizzle. White markings on the chest, though allowable, are not desirable. *Faults*—White markings elsewhere or to any great extent on the chest.

COAT: As hard and wiry as possible, lying close to the body, with a definite under-coat. Top coat absolutely straight; in full coat longer and rougher forming almost a mane on shoulders and neck. Hair on head, ears and muzzle, except for slight eyebrows and slight whiskers, is absolutely short and smooth. These dogs should be shown with as nearly a natural coat as

Norwich Terrier—Photo by Evelyn M. Shafer.

possible. A minimum amount of tidying is permissible but excessive trimming, shaping and clipping shall be heavily penalized by the judge. *Faults*—Silky or curly coat.

WEIGHT: Ideal, 11 to 12 pounds.

HEIGHT: Ideal, 10 inches at the withers.

GENERAL APPEARANCE: A small, low rugged terrier, tremendously active. A perfect demon yet not quarrelsome and of a lovable disposition, and a very hardy constitution. Honorable scars from fair wear and tear shall not count against.

Disqualification. Cropped ears shall disqualify.

(May 9, 1961)

MINIATURE SCHNAUZER

THE MINIATURE SCHNAUZER (or Zwergschnauzer) is identical with the Standard or medium-sized Schnauzer, except for difference in size and a slightly more variation in color. They are not the result, however, of matings of medium-sized Schnauzers but of an outcross of Schnauzers to Affenpinschers.

The Standard Schnauzers are, for the most part, pepper and salt in color. Among the Miniatures pepper and salt prevails, but black coats appear frequently. The black sometimes has a tendency to be soft, a quality that breeders endeavor to correct and consider as having come from the black German Poodle, far back in Schnauzer ancestry.

The well-proportioned compactness of the Miniature probably has as much to do with the popularity of the breed, although many fanciers will say that it is his excessively gay disposition and adaptability as a house pet. The Miniature still remains in the terrier group, although the Standard Schnauzer, at the request of the Standard Schnauzer Club of America, was transferred from the terrier to the working group in July, 1945. The Miniature remains in the terrier group in America, but is not so classed in Germany or England.

The origin of the Schnauzer is considered as being a cross between the "dog of Bologne" and the Spitz.

The oldest German kennel club was founded in 1878. The following year at the Third German International Show in Hanover, with about 900 dogs, wire-haired Pinschers of German breeding were exhibited for the first time. A dog "Schnauzer" won first prize, exhibited by the Wurtemberg Kennel of Burger-Leonberg.

Previous to any show debut, however, the Schnauzer had a long history. There is no question of its being a breed of great antiquity. Albrecht Durer depicted a Schnauzer in a water color "Madonna With the Many Animals" executed in 1492. In a tapestry made about 1501 a representation of a Schnauzer appears.

The Schnauzer (the breed with a beard on the muzzle, the German word for muzzle being *schnauze*) was used extensively in Germany as a drover's dog, used to pull carts with produce from the farms to the towns, and guard them while there. He was used as well in working with sheep, cattle, and hogs and, in fact, doing all the duties of the regulation farm dog. He was also used as a rat catcher, and even in modern times German Schnauzer Clubs hold periodical "ratting" trials in order to keep the Schnauzer a "working" breed, and not merely a show dog. The Miniature is an especially good ratter.

The small Schnauzer may have been developed entirely by chance, often the main reason for a new breed. In any case, it has taken its niche in life, both as a show dog and a desirable pet. They have been bred for over 40 years and were exhibited as a distinct breed as early as 1899. Miniatures have been bred in the United States since 1925 and the American Miniature Schnauzer Club was formed in August, 1933.

Description and Standards. The description and standards, adopted by the American Miniature Schnauzer Club and approved by the American Kennel Club follow.

GENERAL APPEARANCE: The Miniature Schnauzer is a robust, active dog of terrier type, resembling his larger cousin, the Standard Schnauzer, in general appearance, and of an alert, active disposition. He is sturdily built, nearly square in proportion of body length to height, with plenty of bone, and without any suggestion of toyishness.

HEAD: Strong and rectangular, its width diminishing slightly from ears to eyes, and again to the tip of the nose. The forehead is unwrinkled. The topskull is flat and fairly long. The foreface is parallel to the topskull, with a slight stop, and is at least as long as the topskull. The muzzle is strong in proportion to the skull; it ends in a moderately blunt manner, with thick whiskers which accentuate the rectangular shape of the head. The teeth meet in a scissors bite. That is, the upper front teeth overlap the lower front teeth in such a manner that the inner surface of the upper incisors barely touches the outer surface of the lower incisors when the mouth is closed. The eyes are small, dark brown and deep-set. They are oval in appearance and keen in expression. When cropped the ears are identical in shape and length, with pointed tips. They are in balance with the head and not exaggerated in length. They are set high on the skull and carried perpendicularly at the inner edges, with as little bell as possible along the outer edges. When uncropped, the ears are small and V-shaped, folding close to the skull.

NECK: Strong and well arched, blending into the shoulders, and with the skin fitting tightly at the throat.

BODY: Short and deep, with the brisket extending at least to the elbows. Ribs are well sprung and deep, extending well back to a short loin. The underbody does not present a tucked-up appearance at the flank. The topline is straight; it declines slightly from the withers to the base of the tail. The overall length from chest to stern bone equals the height at the withers.

FOREQUARTERS: The forequarters have flat, somewhat sloping shoulders and high withers. Forelegs are straight and parallel when viewed from all sides. They have strong pasterns and good bone. They are separated by a fairly deep brisket which precludes a pinched front. The elbows are close, and the ribs spread gradually from the first rib so as to allow space for the elbows to move close to the body.

HINDQUARTERS: The hindquarters have strong-muscled, slanting thighs: they are well bent at the stifles and straight from hock to so-called heel. There is sufficient angulation so that, in stance, the hocks extend beyond the tail. The hindquarters never appear overbuilt or higher than the shoulders.

FEET: Short and round (cat-feet) with thick, black pads. The toes are arched and compact.

ACTION: The trot is the gait at which movement is judged. The dog must gait in a straight line. Coming on, the forelegs are parallel, with the elbows close to the body. The feet turn neither inward nor outward. Going away, the hind legs are parallel from the hocks down, and travel wide. Viewed from the side, the forelegs have a good reach, while the hind legs have a strong drive with good pick-up of hocks.

TAIL: Set high and carried erect. It is docked only long enough to be clearly visible over the topline of the body when the dog is in proper length of coat.

COAT: Double, with a hard, wiry outer coat and a close under coat. The body coat should be plucked. When in show condition, the proper length is not less than three-quarters of an inch except on neck, ears and skull. Furnishings are fairly thick but not silky.

SIZE: From 12 to 14 inches. Ideal size 13½ inches. *(See disqualifications.)*

COLOR: The recognized colors are salt and pepper, black and silver, and solid black. The typical color is salt and pepper in shades of gray; tan shading is permissible. The salt and pepper mixture fades out to light gray or silver white in the eybrows, whiskers, cheeks, under throat, across chest, under tail, leg furnishings under body, and inside legs. The light under-body hair is not to rise higher on the sides of the body than the front elbows.

The black and silvers follow the same pattern as the salt and peppers. The entire salt-and-pepper section must be black.

Black is the only solid color allowed. It must be a true black with no gray hairs and no brown tinge except where the whis-

Miniature Schnauzer—Ch. Jonaire Pocono Rock 'N Roll. (Owner: Jonaire Kennels, Mt. Pocono, Pa.)

Miniature Schnauzer—A head study. American and Canadian Ch. Wildwood's Showboat. (Owner: Paul E. Miley, Cleveland, Ohio)

kers may have become discolored. A small white spot on the chest is permitted.

FAULTS: *Type*—Toyishness, raciness, or coarseness. *Structure*—Head coarse and cheeky. Chest too broad or shallow in brisket. Tail set low. Sway or roach back. Bowed or cowhocked hindquarters. Loose elbows. *Action*—Sidegaiting. Paddling in front, or high hackney knee action. Weak hind action. *Coat*—Too soft or too smooth and slick in appearance. *Temperament*—Shyness or viciousness. *Bite*—Undershot or overshot jaw. Level bite. *Eyes*—Light and/or large and prominent in appearance.

Disqualifications. Dogs or bitches under 12 inches or over 14 inches. Color solid white or white patches on the body.

(May 13, 1958)

SCOTTISH TERRIER

THERE IS NO recorded history of the Scottish Terrior prior to 1879. That year they were exhibited as a distinct breed, and the following year the dogs known in the present-day pedigrees were firmly entrenched as true show Scottish Terriers. The fact that J. A. Adamson of Aberdeen was a successful breeder at that time, and that many other residents of that district were breeding and showing the same variety, no doubt accounts for the name "Aberdeen" being applied to the Scottie, a term that was destined to cling for over half a century.

The antiquity of the ancestry of the breed is unassailable as it is certain that the Scottish Terrier owes its origin to the Highland Terrier, from which came the various Scotch breeds, the Skye, the Cairn, West Highland White Terrier, and even the Yorkshire.

Long before shows were thought of, the terriers in different parts of the Highlands had developed into distinct variations. The type that produced the Scottish Terrier is generally conceded to have been found in the Blackmount region of Perthshire, Moor of Rannoch, and surrounding districts. It is highly improbable that there was no cross breeding among the terriers of the Highlands. Pedigrees were considered of little account as long as the dogs showed plenty of capacity for work, gameness, and resembled the indigenous breed in appearance.

Captain Mackie in an account of a tour made about 1880, and recounted in Thomson Gray's monograph on the breed in 1887, tells of visiting various fox and tod hunters who had possessed the same strain for 60 years. He bought dogs on this tour which became the foundation of a strong kennel of Scottish Terriers in the early days of their show history.

Prior to the 1897 show at the Alexandria Palace, London, there had been considerable controversy as to what constituted a Scottish Terrier, whether it was the Skye or the Cairn or the Dandie that should receive the appellation.

In Stonehenge's *The Dogs of the British Isles* (1867) no mention is made of Scottish Terriers, but the illustration facing Chapter Five, "terriers not being Skyes, Dandies, Fox or Toys," shows a picture of Mr. Radclyffe's dog Rough, seated on a barrel, holding a rat in his mouth. Rough bears a remarkable resemblance to the modern Scottish Terrier, but is given no breed name. He is described as a good, rough-and-ready dog, rough headed, lion hearted, never to die in debt, and equivalent to about two dozen rat traps!

Rough was shown, unsuccessfully, however, in 1865. It must be remembered that there were no distinct classification at that time. In a variety class for rough-haired terriers in 1877, there was such a variety of types, coats, sizes, and colors that the judge, who had been interested enough to offer the prizes for the class, was unable to decide on the merits of the entries and the prizes were withheld. However, it was there that the "new variety," the Aberdeen, appeared —a prick-eared, hard-coated terrier that immediately caught the public fancy.

At the 1879 show where the Scottish Terrier emerged as a distinct breed, there was an entry of 13. The judge, J. B. Morrison, awarded first and second in both dogs and bitches to Paynton Pigott's entries. At the end of July in the same year, classes were given at Perth and Mr. Adamson got first and second in bitches. The following year it was the latter's Roger Rough and Mr. Piggott's Tartan and Syringa that rose, not only as great winners, but as the beginning of pedigree history. It was then that the modern history of the Scottish Terrier began.

The essentials of the standard as drwn up by J. B. Morrison in 1880 have been retained in all the later standards, with only minor changes being introduced. In 1882, the Scottish Terrier Club was organized,

Scottish Terrier—Ch. Lynnscot Enchantress. (Owner: Mr. and Mrs. R. J. McLaughlin, Allendale, New Jersey)

with joint officers for England and Scotland. Separate clubs were eventually formed, due to growing interest in the breed, and the Morrison standard was revised in 1933. The present American standard was adopted in 1925. In practically all details, the English and American standards are the same; the major differences being in weight requirements.

As early as 1883, Scottish Terriers were brought to the United States when John Naylor imported a dog and a bitch "Tam Glen" and "Bonnie Belle." Mr. Naylor showed extensively and later brought over many more importations. The first Scottish Terrier registered in America was Dake, a brindle dog whelped in 1884 and bred by O. P. Chandler of Kokomo, Indiana. Dake was sired by Naylor's imported and celebrated Glenlyon.

Description and Standards. The revised description and standards, adopted by the Scottish Terrier Club of America and approved by the American Kennel Club follow.

SKULL: (5 Points) Long, of medium width, slightly domed and covered with short hard hair. It should not be quite flat, as there should be a slight stop or drop between the eyes.

(1) MUZZLE: (5 Points) In proportion to the length of skull, with not too much taper toward the nose. Nose should be black and of good size. The jaws should be level and square. The nose projects somewhat over the mouth, giving the impression that the upper jaw is longer than the lower. The teeth should be evenly placed, having a scissors or level bite, with the former being preferable.

EYES: (5 Points) Set wide apart, small and of almond shape, not round. Color to be dark brown or nearly black. To be bright, piercing and set well under the brow.

EARS: (10 Points) Small, prick, set well up on the skull, rather pointed but not cut. The hair on them should be short and velvety.

NECK: (5 Points) Moderately short, thick and muscular, strongly set on sloping shoulders, but not so short as to appear clumsy.

CHEST: (5 Points) Broad and very deep. well let down between the fore legs.

BODY: (15 Points) Moderately short and well ribbed up with strong loin, deep flanks and very muscular hind quarters.

(2) LEGS AND FEET: (10 Points) Both fore and hind legs should be short and very heavy in bone in proportion to the size of the dog. Forelegs straight or slightly bent with elbows close to the body. Scottish Terriers should not be out at the elbows. Stifles should be well bent and legs straight from hock to heel. Thighs very muscular. Feet round and thick with strong nails, fore feet larger than the hind feet. *Note:* The gait of the Scottish Terrier is peculiarly its own and is very characteristic of the breed. It is not the square trot or walk that is desirable in the long-legged breeds. The forelegs do not move in exact parallel planes—rather in reaching out incline slightly inward. This is due to the shortness of leg and width of chest. The action of the rear legs should be square and true and at the trot both the hocks and stifles should be flexed with a vigorous motion.

TAIL: (2½ Points) Never cut and about seven inches long, carried with a slight curve but not over the back.

COAT: (15 Points) Rather short, about two inches, dense under coat with outer coat intensely hard and wiry.

(3) SIZE AND WEIGHT: (10 Points) Equal consideration must be given to height, length of back and weight. Height at shoulder for either sex, should be about 10 inches. Generally, a well balanced Scottish Terrier dog of correct size should weigh from 19 to 22 lbs. and a bitch from 18 to 21 lbs. The principal objective must be symmetry and balance.

COLOR: -(2½ Points) Steel or iron grey, brindled or grizzled, black, sandy or wheaten. White markings are objectionable and can be allowed only on the chest and that to a slight extent only.

GENERAL APPEARANCE: (10 Points) The face should wear a keen, sharp and active expression. Both head and tail should be carried well up. The dog should look very compact, well muscled and powerful, giving the impression of immense power in a small size.

(4) PENALTIES: Soft coat, round or very light eye, over or undershot jaw, obviously over or under size, shyness, timidity or failure to show with head and tail up are faults to be penalized. No judge should put to Winners or Best of Breed any Scottish Terrier not showing real terrier character in the ring.

SCALE OF POINTS:	Points
Skull	5
Muzzle	5
Eyes	5
Ears	10
Neck	5
Chest	5
Body	15
Legs and feet	10
Tail	2½
Coat	15
Size	10
Color	2½
General appearance	10
TOTAL	100

SEALYHAM TERRIER

ALTHOUGH THE show influence had a great deal to do with the eventual refinements and improvements that occurred in the Sealyham, the breed was developed for a first, last and always working terrier.

It was Captain John Edwardes who originated the breed and whose country place in Pembrokeshire bore the name given to his terriers. Considered somewhat of an eccentric old sportsman, Captain Edwardes seems to have devoted the latter part of his life to the hunting of fox, badgers, otters, rats, rabbits, and even polecats that abounded on his acreage. It became an obsession with him to develop a terrier that would be a size to go into earth and that would fearlessly tackle any of these creatures and fight to the death, if necessary.

The country was rich in terriers but those in Captain Edwardes' territory are said to have been a sort of mongrel type with which he was quite dissatisfied, so he proceeded to "make" his own breed. That a dog as true and beautiful as the Sealyham emerged from the Captain's various experiments hardly seems possible in the light of all the many "ingredients" attributed to the process. It must be added that the Captain, besides following a strong line of survival of the fittest, must have done a considerable amount of studied and careful breeding.

Some authorities claim that the "Corgi", the cattle dog on the farms of Pembrokeshire, took the eye of the old sportsman as likely foundation stock. Then he began to reach out and it is reasonable to believe, with many others, that he introduced the Dandie Dinmont, not only for the short legs, but because of its reputation for pluck. The West Highland White Terrier is believed to have been used to some extent and it is fairly definite that contribution was made by the Bull Terrier. Early observers of the breed thought that a resemblance to the Wire Fox Terrier was evident. Students of the breed trace the Dandie in the slightly domed skull, wide eye and hint of topknot, while the long punishing jaw reveals the Bull Terrier.

Whatever the mixture, Captain Edwardes succeeded remarkably well in attaining his desire. He did not live to see the breed recognized by the Kennel Club, nor to know how popular it became as a show dog, as he passed away in the 1870's. But it would probably have been of little moment to the rugged old gentleman as his only aim, and that of other early breeders, was to evolve a short-legged, smart-looking, brainy, and workman-like terrier.

He carried out a rigid regime in his breeding program and, from all accounts, he deviated only once from his fast rule of destroying all pups that showed the slightest timidity. Pups were started early in a training curriculum and by the time they were a year old, they had had considerable experience in ratting. Then, at that age, they were given the acid test. Polecats were plentiful in the forests near Sealyham, and its was the Captain's aim to have his terriers as adept on them as on other game. A trail was laid by dragging a polecat across a field, then securing it in a pit, with only a small opening. The animal was tied but in such a way that he could put up a fair fight. Then the dog was set on the trail which, as can be imagined by the odoriferous nature of the polecat, it had no trouble in following. If, when the pit was reached, the dog showed reluctance to dig in and fight, if he minced about or shirked, he was considered too cowardly to be kept at Sealyham, and was dispatched.

A story is told about one dog that was a fine hunter in every other respect, but when it came to the polecat test, he refused to go in. Every inducement was given but the dog hedged, so his doom was sealed. However, the man who took care of him was so attached to the dog that he begged the Captain to allow him to keep him because he was such a good ratter, and the Captain finally consented. Before the dog was two years old he became one of the gamest dogs on the place and achieved such fame that the Captain eventually bought him back from the farmer.

Although the Sealyham had many ardent adherents who carried on a careful breeding program to keep the strain pure long after the Captain's demise, it was some time before the breed was seen at a Kennel Club show. They had been entered at local shows and undoubtedly were brought before the public in contests held by badger-digging clubs. Weasels were hunted with small packs and sportsmen were very

Sealyham Terrier.

much aware of the breed's merits. They were given their first special class at the Kennel Club Show in October, 1910. Even then Fred W. Lewis had to personally guarantee the four classes. The result was an entry of about six dogs in each class. The breed was given recognition in 1911 and the Kennel Club offered the first Challenge Certificates for Sealyhams at the Great Joint Terrier Show, London, that year.

Some of the earlier dogs from which the moderns have sprung exceeded the present weight standard considerably. Peer Gynt, bred by J. H. Merton, is said to have weighed as much as 27 pounds and Fred Lewis' Huntsman weighed about 24 pounds.

In 1911 Sealyhams were imported to the United States. The American Kennel Club immediately recognized the breed and they made their show debut the same year at San Mateo, California.

They attained great popularity from the very first. The American Sealyham Terrier Club was founded on May 15, 1913. A revised standard of points was adopted in 1935.

The club holds an annual specialty show for American-bred Sealyham Terriers at which its annual futurity stakes are judged. The club also awards Working

Certificates on recommendation by a committee or by Masters of Foxhounds.

Description and Standards. The description and standards, adopted by the American Sealyham Terrier Club and approved by the American Kennel Club follow.

The Sealyham should be the embodiment of power and determination, ever keen and alert, of extraordinary substance, yet free from clumsiness.

HEIGHT: At withers about 10½ inches. Weight: 21 pounds for dogs, and 20 pounds for bitches. It should be borne in mind that size is more important than weight.

HEAD: Long, broad and powerful, without coarseness. It should, however, be in perfect balance with the body, joining neck smoothly. Length of head roughly three-quarters height at withers or about an inch longer than neck. Breadth between ears a little less than one-half length of head.

SKULL: Very slightly domed, with a shallow indentation running down between the brows, and joining the muzzle with a moderate stop.

CHEEKS: Smoothly formed and flat, without heavy jowls.

JAWS: Level, powerful, and square. Overshot or undershot bad faults.

TEETH: Sound, strong and white, with canines fitting closely together.

NOSE: Black, with large nostrils. White, cherry or butterfly bad faults.

EYES: Very dark, deeply set and fairly wide apart, of medium size, oval in shape with keen terrier expression. Light, large or protruding eye bad faults.

EARS: Folded level with top of head, with forward edge close to cheek. Well rounded at tip, and of length to reach outer corner of eye. Thin, not leathery, and sufficient thickness to avoid creases. Prick, tulip, rose or hound ears bad faults.

NECK: Length slightly less than two-thirds of height of dog at withers. Muscular without coarseness, with good reach, refinement at throat, and set firmly on shoulders.

SHOULDERS: Well laid back and powerful but not overmuscled. Sufficiently wide to permit freedom of action. Upright or straight shoulder placement highly undesirable.

LEGS: Forelegs strong, with good bone; and as straight as is consistent with chest being well let down between them. Down on pasterns, knuckled over, bound, and out at elbow, bad faults. Hind legs, longer than forelegs and not so heavily boned.

FEET: Large but compact, round with thick pads, strong nails. Toes well arched and pointing straight ahead. Fore feet larger, though not quite so long as hind feet. Thin, spread or flat feet bad faults.

BODY: Strong, short coupled and substantial, so as to permit great flexibility. Brisket deep and well let down between fore legs. Ribs well sprung.

BACK: Length from withers to set on of tail should approximate height at withers, or 10½ inches. Top line level, neither roached or swayed. Any deviations from these measurements undesirable.

HIND QUARTER: Very powerful, and protruding well behind the set on tail. Strong second thighs, stifles well bent, and hocks well let down. Capped or cowhocks bad faults.

TAIL: Docked and carried upright. Set on far enough forward so that spine does not slope down to it.

COAT: Weather-resisting, comprised of soft, dense under coat and hard, wiry top coat. Silky or curly coat bad fault.

COLOR: All white, or with lemon, tan or badger markings on head and ears. Heavy body markings and excessive ticking should be discouraged.

ACTION: Sound, strong, quick, free, true and level.

Note: The measurements were taken with calipers.

SCALE OF POINTS:		*Points*
General Character, Balance and Size		15
Head	5	
Eyes	5	
Mouth	5	
Ears	5	
Neck	5	
	—	25
Shoulders and Brisket	10	
Body, Ribs and Loin	10	
Hind Quarters	10	
Legs and Feet	10	
Coat	10	
	—	50
Tail	5	
Color (Body Marking and Ticking)	5	
	—	10
TOTAL		100

SKYE TERRIER

" . . . brought out of barbarous borders fro' the uttermost countryes

northward . . . which, by reason of the length of heare, makes showe neither of face nor of body."

SO WROTE Dr. John Caius describing the Skye Terrier in his historic volume *Englishe Dogges*, the first book devoted solely to dogs. This quotation from a book written in the sixteenth century, establishes the antiquity of the Skye as a breed. At that time the Skye was a newcomer to England from his native highlands and, though Dr. Caius' words "length of heare" could still be applied today, he differed in appearance from the present-day "beauty."

For beautiful indeed is this terrier with his smooth cascades of shining groomed coat, the tender softness of eyes obscured by a thick veil of hair . . . attributes which earned him the name of the "Heavenly breed" as a tribute from admirers.

This purely Scottish breed had its early home in the mist-shrouded island of Skye, but it was also found in other islands of the Hebrides as well as on the mainland of Scotland. It is said that Dr. Johnson, returning from a visit to the Islands with Boswell in 1773, remarked that otters and weasels were plentiful on the island of Skye and that the foxes were numerous and were hunted by small dogs.

The earliest descriptions of the breed present a terrier much smaller in size than the type of today, a size more adapted to burrowing and taking to water. It had a profuse, hard coat, with short legs, a body long in proportion to its height, and with ears that were neither erect nor drooping, but half erect and raised to alertness when aroused. In the early days the Highlander cared far less for beauty than for the sporting ability of his dogs, and although it seems difficult to credit the languishing-beauty appearance of the Skye of today with bloodthirsty tendencies, the breed was originally used and developed for hunting among the rough rocks and crevices of his native shores. He needed the face fringe to protect his eyes,

Skye Terrier—Ch. Major Ben of Iradell. (Owner: Mrs. N. Clarkson Earl, Jr., Ridgefield, Conn.)

his lithe, long body for agility in getting into burrows and dens.

When the Skye first made his appearance in England, it was taken up by the nobility, than which nothing could do more to make it fashionable. Queen Victoria greatly admired the breed and always owned several Skyes from 1842 on. In 1896, a Skye was presented to the then Princess of Wales who later became Queen Alexandria. Sir Edwin Landseer's paintings in which the Skye was introduced helped to draw public attention. It was still considerably smaller in size than today's type. Mr. Pratt of Paddington, London, had Skyes around 1885, and one dog, Sandy, weighed about 16 pounds, considered an ideal weight at that time.

There is no question about when the Skye was accepted by the Kennel Club, for the breed was included in the first volume of the Kennel Club Stud Book. A bitter dispute started in 1874 and continued for five years concerning the distinctions of the Scottish breeds of terriers. Finally, the Kennel Club was approached to settle the controversy. It centered upon those which were claimed to be pure Skyes, a dog described as Scotch, and a third which was called Aberdeen. The differences were plain but an issue was made over which had the right to be Scottish!

The Skye has been surpassed in popularity by many of the more modern breeds of terriers, but it is unrivalled in length of time of popularity because it has existed over a period of long duration. Before the turn of the century, it was an important breed in American dog shows. It retains great popularity in Scotland and England.

Two varieties of Skye Terrier are recognized, the prick-eared and the drop-eared (pendant). In other respects both are identically the same in all points.

Description and Standards. The description and standards adopted by the Skye Terrier Club of America and adopted by the American Kennel Club follow.

GENERAL APPEARANCE: The Skye Terrier is a dog of style, elegance, and dignity; agile and strong with sturdy bone and hard muscle. Long, low, and lank—he is twice as long as he is high

—he is covered with a profuse coat that falls straight down either side of the body over oval-shaped ribs. The hair well feathered on the head veils forehead and eyes to serve as protection from brush and briar as well as amid serious encounters with other animals. He stands with head high and long tail hanging, and moves with a seemingly effortless gait. Of suitable size for his hunting work, strong in body, quarters, and jaw.

TEMPERAMENT: That of the typical working terrier capable of overtaking game and going to ground, displaying stamina, courage, strength, and agility. Fearless, good-tempered, loyal, and canny, he is friendly and gay with those he knows and reserved and cautious with strangers.

HEAD: Long and powerful, strength being deemed more important than extreme length. Moderate width at the back of the skull tapers gradually to a strong muzzle. The stop is slight. The dark muzzle is just moderately full as opposed to snipy, and the nose is always black. Powerful and absolutely true jaws and mouth with the incisor teeth closing level, or with the upper teeth slightly overlapping the lower.

EYES: Brown, preferably dark brown, medium in size, close-set, and alight with life and intelligence.

EARS: Symmetrical and gracefully feathered. They may be carried prick or drop. When prick, they are medium in size, placed high on the skull, erect at their outer edges, and slightly wider at the peak than at the skull. Drop ears, somewhat larger in size and set lower, hang flat against the skull.

NECK: Long and gracefully arched, carried high and proudly.

BODY: Preeminently long and low. The backline is level, the chest deep, with oval-shaped ribs. The sides appear flattish due to the straight falling and profuse coat.

FOREQUARTERS: Legs short, muscular, and straight as possible. "Straight as possible" means straight as soundness and chest will permit; it does not mean "terrier straight." Shoulders well laid back, with tight placement of shoulder blades at the withers, and elbows should fit closely to the sides and be neither loose nor tied. Forearm should curve slightly around the chest.

HINDQUARTERS: Strong, full, well developed, and well angulated. Legs short, muscular, and straight when viewed from behind.

FEET: Large harefeet preferably pointing forward, the pads thick and nails strong and preferably black.

MOVEMENT: The legs proceed straight forward when traveling. When approaching, the forelegs form a continuation of the straight line of the front, the feet being the same distance apart as the elbows. The principal propelling power is furnished by the hind legs, which travel straight forward. Forelegs should move well forward, without too much lift. The whole movement may be termed free, active, and effortless and give a more or less fluid picture.

TAIL: Long and well feathered. When hanging, its upper section is pendulous, following the line of the rump, its lower section thrown back in a moderate arc without twist or curl. When raised, its height makes it appear a prolongation of the backline. Though not to be preferred, the tail is sometimes carried high when the dog is excited or angry. When such carriage arises from emotion only, it is permissible. But the tail should not be constantly carried above the level of the back nor hang limp.

COAT: Double. Under coat short, close, soft, and woolly. Outer coat hard, straight, and flat, 5½ inches long without extra credit granted for greater length. The body coat hangs straight down each side, parting from head to tail. The head hair, which may be shorter and softer, veils forehead and eyes and forms a moderate beard and apron. The long feathering on the ears falls straight down from the tips and outer edges, surrounding the ears like a fringe and outlining their shape. The ends of the hair should mingle with the coat at the sides of the neck.

COLOR: The coat must be of one over-all color at the skin but may be of varying shades of the same color in the full coat, which may be black, blue, dark or light gray, silver, platinum, fawn, or cream. The dog must have no distinctive markings except for the desirable black points of ears, muzzle, and tip of tail, all of which points are preferably dark even to

Skye Terriers—A family, with Junior at right. Hank Babbitt photo.

black. The shade of head and legs should approximate that of the body. There must be no trace of pattern, design, or clear-cut color variations, with the exception of the breed's only permissible white which occasionally exists on the chest not exceeding 2 inches in diameter.

The puppy coat may be very different in color from the adult coat. As it is growing and clearing, wide variations of color may occur; consequently this is permissible in dogs under 18 months of age. However, even in puppies there must be no trace of pattern, design, or clear-cut variations with the exception of the black band of varying width frequently seen encircling the body coat of the cream-colored dog, and the only permissible white which, as in the adult dog, occasionally exists on the chest not exceeding 2 inches in diameter.

SIZE: Dogs: Shoulder height, 10 inches. Length, chest bone over tail at rump, 20 inches. Head, 8½ inches. Tail, 9 inches. Bitches: Shoulder height, 9½ inches. Length, chest bone over tail at rump, 19 inches. Head, 8 inches. Tail, 8½ inches. A slightly higher or lower dog of either sex is acceptable, providing body, head, and tail dimensions are proportionately longer or shorter. The ideal ratio of body length to shoulder height is 2 to 1, which is considered the correct proportion.

Measurements are taken with the Skye standing in natural position with feet well under. A box caliper is used vertically and horizontally. For the height, the top bar should rest on the withers. The head is measured from the tip of the nose to the back of the occipital bone, and the tail from the root to tip. Dogs 8 inches or less at the withers and bitches 7½ inches or less at the withers are to be penalized.

(February 8, 1964)

STAFFORDSHIRE TERRIER

THE ANCESTORS of the Staffordshire were true fighting dogs, known as Bull-and-Terriers, and a lighter type of Bulldog. In many respects the Bulldog of the 1800's resembled the Staffordshire of today, for it was entirely unlike the present short "sour mug" Bulldog. The early Bulldog stood straighter on his legs and was, of necessity, more agile for the uses to which it was put, that of fighting and baiting.

Around 1800 to 1820, the Bulldog was crossed with the Old English Terrier to produce the Staffordshire, as a type more adapted to fighting in the pit. The Bulldog, used for bull and bear baiting, ranking high among the most fashionable sports from the middle of the sixteenth century to the seventeenth, was large and heavy, a type which had come down from the large mastiff-type fighting dog of England called the "Alaunt," a direct descendant from the "Pugnaces."

As bull and bear baiting gradually went out of fashion, matching dog against dog became a popular sport and to combine the gameness and agility of the terrier with the tenacity and courage of the Bulldog, the cross was made in an effort to produce a dog unmatched for pit fighting. The Staffordshire name, however, was not given to the breed until after it had come through a variety of nomenclatures. Originally known as the "Bull-and-Terrier dog," or "Half and Half," it gradually became referred to as "Pit Dog" or "Pit Bull Terrier." When they were brought to America in 1870, they were known as "Pit Bull Terriers," later as "American Bull Terriers" or "Yankee Terriers."

Specialized dog breeding, which began to take on a serious aspect during the late 1800's, rather ignored the Staffordshire with its dark past of barbarous "blood sports," bear and bull baiting, dog fighting, and even matches between man and dog.

His past gave him a disreputable character, but the miners in Staffordshire and other near localities preserved the breed, keeping all the qualities of gameness and intelligence.

The Staffordshire did not invade the show ring until 1935, the same year that the Staffordshire Bull-terrier Club was formed. Joe Dunn of Cradley Heath is credited with instigating the move for forming a club in order to protect the interests of the variety. After many meetings and discussions the club was formally organized, with Jack Barnard of Chesterton as the first president.

The present American strain goes back to Pilot,

Staffordshire Terrier—Anson's Sir Boss. (Owner: Jack L. Anson, Oxford, Ohio.)

Staffordshire Terrier—A head study.

gether dog, muscular, but agile and graceful, keenly alive to his surroundings. He should be stocky, not long-legged or racy in outline. His courage is proverbial.

HEAD: Medium length, deep through, broad skull, very pronounced cheek muscles, distinct stop; and ears are set high.

EARS: Cropped or uncropped, the latter preferred. Uncropped ears should be short and held half rose or prick. Full drop to be penalized.

EYES: Dark and round, low down in skull and set far apart. No pink eyelids.

MUZZLE: Medium length, rounded on upper side to fall away abruptly below eyes. Jaws well-defined. Under jaw to be strong and have biting power. Lips close and even, no looseness. Upper teeth to meet tightly outside lower teeth in front. Nose definitely black.

NECK: Heavy, slightly arched, tapering from shoulders to back of skull. No looseness of skin. Medium length.

SHOULDERS: Strong and muscular with blades wide and sloping.

BACK: Fairly short. Slight sloping from withers to rump with gentle short slope at rump to base of tail. Loins slightly tucked.

BODY: Well sprung ribs, deep in rear. All ribs close together. Fore legs set rather wide apart to permit of chest development. Chest deep and broad.

TAIL: Short in comparison to size, low set, tapering to a fine point; not curled or held over back. Not docked.

LEGS: The front legs should be straight, large or round bones, pastern upright. No resemblance of bend in front. Hind quarters well-muscled, let down at hocks, turning neither in nor out. Feet of moderate size, well-arched and compact. Gait must be springy but without roll or pace.

COAT: Short, close, stiff to the touch, and glossy.

COLOR: Any color, solid, parti, or patched is permissible, but all white, more than 80 percent white, black and tan, and liver not to be encouraged.

SIZE: Height and weight should be in proportion. A height of about 18 to 19 inches at shoulders for the male and 17 to 18 inches for the female is to be considered preferable.

FAULTS: Faults to be penalized are Dudley nose, light or pink eyes, tail too long or badly carried, undershot or overshot mouths.

Paddy, and other "Pit Bull Terriers" imported by "Cockney" Charlie Lloyd soon after the Civil War. The transplanted English stock flourished in America, but was not given recognition by the American Kennel Club until 1935 and gained the name of Staffordshire Bull Terriers.

There have always been differences of opinion about the distinctions between the English and American branches of the Staffordshire Terrier family. The fact that gameness and working qualities were more important to fanciers than purity of conformation naturally brought this about. The English branch has been more variable as to conformation while the American branch has striven to follow more closely the bench show type. Breeders in this country have developed a type that averages a good ten pounds heavier than the modern Staffordshire of England.

Although gameness is an attribute of the Staffordshire, the use to which it has been put because man has used this courage for his own sport in pit fighting should not be held against a dog that has many other endearing qualities. Around children they are affectionate and safe, and are of a docile and tractable nature in general.

Description and Standards. The description and standards, adopted by the Staffordshire Terrier Club of America and approved by the American Kennel Club follow.

GENERAL IMPRESSION: The Staffordshire Terrier should give the impression of: great strength for his size; a well put-to-

WELSH TERRIER

JUST AS the Welsh people are the purest of British lineage, so is the Welsh Terrier of the oldest type of British Terrier. Crab, an early Welsh Terrier, was said to have had a note attached to his name that he and some others were brought to Harlech in 1854. Cymru O'Gymru was a dog of remarkable stamp even at that date and was described as being a great improvement on the old Welsh Terrier stock.

The rough-haired black and tan terrier is found in many old prints and paintings of even earlier days and the type commonly known as the "Old English Terrier" or "Black and Tan Wire-Haired Terrier" was one and the same with the Welsh, although the latter came to be bred on slightly longer legs and a larger head was desired rather than the short, stumpy head considered correct at an earlier period. The color of the Welsh, however, is as it was a hundred years ago.

As late as 1886, only one class was allotted by the Kennel Club Stud Book for "Welsh or Old English Wire-haired Black and Tan Terriers" which bears out the fact that they were the same. In 1888 the class in the Kennel Club Stud Book was altered to

Welsh Terrier, and though an attempt was made to form an Old English Terrier Club, it failed and the name of the breed, as such, was eliminated from combination with Welsh.

However, the similarity was still so marked that in the Darlington Show in 1893, Dick Turpin, a well-known show dog, was entered in two classes, both as a Welsh Terrier and Old English Terrier, winning first prize in the former and reserve in the latter. He continued his dual role until 1896 and then emerged as third in the Old English Terriers!

In 1885 a show of Welsh Terriers was held at Carnavon where 21 entries were made. The classes were called "local classes." In 1886, the Welsh Terrier Club was formed and that year, at Carnavon, there were Ch. Topsy, one of the best bitches of that time, and Ch. Bob Bethesda, described as "a lovely little terrier, with the best bodies, coat, legs and feet." His head, however, was considered as being too short. He was used with Otterhounds as were many of the dogs of that day. These also went to ground in fox and badger hunting, and were used extensively by the sporting fraternity.

Longer-headed dogs began to appear. One of these was Mawddy Nonsuch, purchased by a Mr. Buckley for £200. This dog became a famous winner. At Barn Elms in 1887, Bob Bethesda won over Mawddy, however. A remarkably good dog was Contention which, it was found, had been bred by crossing a Fox Terrier with an Airedale, a breeding that produced a Welsh Terrier-type of quite good stamp. It was Contention that caused the Welsh Terrier Club to decide that none of its specials should go to cross-bred dogs.

The first Welsh Terriers brought to the United States were imported by Prescott Lawrence in 1888. He imported a dog and a bitch named T'Other and Which, and showed them at the old Madison Square Garden Show in the miscellaneous class. No other Welsh Terriers were imported for some time until Ch. Red Palm made his debut. The first classification offered for the Welsh was at Westminster in 1901, and four or five dogs were shown.

Welsh Terriers should stand about 15 inches and weigh about 20 pounds. The head should be broader than that of the Fox Terrier but the skull should be very flat and the eyes set fairly far apart to give the characteristic and unmistakable Welsh expression so different from other terriers.

Description and Standards: The description and standards, by courtesy of the Welsh Terrier Club of America, follow.

HEAD: The skull should be flat, and rather wider between the ears than the Wire-haired Fox Terrier. The jaw should be powerful, clean-cut, rather deeper, and more punishing—giving the head a more masculine appearance than that usually seen on a Fox Terrier. Stop not too defined, fair length from stop to end of nose, the latter being of a black color.

EARS: The ear should be V-shaped, small, but not too thin, set on fairly high, carried forward and close to the cheek.

EYES: The eye should be small, not being too deeply set in or protruding out of skull, of a dark hazel color, expressive and indicating abundant pluck.

Welsh Terrier. Photo by Evelyn M. Shafer.

NECK: The neck should be of moderate length and thickness, slightly arched and sloping gracefully into the shoulders.

BODY: The back should be short, and well-ribbed up, the loin strong, good depth, and moderate width of chest. The shoulders should be long, sloping, and well set back. The hind quarters should be strong, thighs muscular and of good length, with the hocks moderately straight, well let down, and fair amount of bone. The stern should be set on moderately high, but not too gaily carried.

LEGS AND FEET: The legs should be straight and muscular, possessing fair amount of bone, with upright and powerful pasterns. The feet should be small, round and catlike.

COAT: The coat should be wiry, hard, very close and abundant.

COLOR: The color should be black and tan, or black grizzle and tan, free from black penciling on toes.

SIZE: The height at shoulder should be 15 inches for dogs, bitches proportionately less. Twenty pounds shall be considered a fair average weight in working condition, but this may vary a pound or so either way.

SCALE OF POINTS:	Points
Head and jaws	10
Ears	5
Eyes	5
Neck and shoulders	10
Body	10
Loins and hind quarters	10
Legs and feet	10
Coat	15
Color	5
Stern	5
General appearance	15
TOTAL	100

Disqualifying Points

(1) Nose: white, cherry or spotted to a considerable extent with either of these colors. (2) Ears: prick, tulip or rose. (3) Undershot jaw or pig-jawed mouth. (4) Black below hocks or white to an appreciable extent.

WEST HIGHLAND WHITE TERRIER

FOR THE ancestors of the West Highland White Terrier, one must turn back to the same stock that produced the Scottish Terriers, Cairns, and Dandie Dinmonts. In litters of the old-fashioned Cairn Terriers, the ancestors of the type now known as the Scottish, white puppies were not welcome and most breeders did away with them. Once in a while, however, a white puppie was kept, another collected from a different source, and as other whites were collected and bred together, any other color than white was given away or destroyed. This breeding for color and type soon developed a distinct variety.

The Malcolm family of Poltalloch, Scotland, kept the breed pure for many generations. They were originally known as the Poltalloch Terrior and sometimes as the Roseneath, the latter name taken from the Duke of Argylle's estate in Dumbartonshire, Scotland. The lineage of the West Highland is said to go back to the time of James I, who wanted some "earthdogges" out of Argyleshire.

As the breed began to claim attention as a variety, they were named the Roseneath Poltalloch, or, sometimes, the Cairn or White Scottish Terrier. Finally the name West Highland White was suggested and adopted.

Captain Mackie's description of his journey in search of terriers with "Charlie" as mentioned in the chapter on Scottish Terriers in Mr. Gray's book, *Dogs of Scotland* (1887), is the first published material on the Poltalloch Terriers. Captain Mackie, on visiting Poltalloch, found the terriers to weigh from 16 to 20 lbs., a determined vermin-destroying look about them, "well knit together" and "linty white in color" with hair "hard and bristly", the body of medium size, "between the cobby and long, but very deep." He wrote further that they "stood on short bony legs, the fore ones nearly straight" and "I have had the breed and hope to have it again. I know exactly what those dogs are fit for and may add that no water was ever too cold and that no earth was ever too deep for them."

After the breed emerged into notoriety, it underwent the usual attempts at so-called improving. Fortunately the old-fashioned type remained popular, and all fads of making it something different failed. In one of the fads, the straight front with lowness to the ground grew to such a desirability that it was said that the sight of the little creatures paddling along with their legs right under them, with their "littye marys" bumping the ground, was too much for the risibilities of the fancy, and this brought the fad to an end.

In breed history, some famous dogs were Ch. Morven, which weighed 17 pounds and Ch. Kiltie. The latter was brought to the United States by Robert Goelet and for which he reputedly paid £400. Mr. Goelet, the first to import the West Highland White Terrier to this country, also brought over Rumpus Glenmohr. Glenmohr Model, a son of a famous dog, Atholl, was brought to America as was another well-known dog, Dazzler Sands, sired by Balloch Bhan, a producer of first-class dogs and bitches. These laid the foundation stock from which the present-day fanciers in America started their strains.

The hardy little West Highlander is a rugged outdoor dog, yet by size and his merry, lighthearted ways has come to be an ideal house pet. Adherents of the breed lay claim that it is not difficult to keep their white coats clean as the Highlander has a dry skin with a lack of doggy odor, and that having a hard, stiff coat, a thorough brushing is all that is required to keep him sleek.

The West Highland White Terrier Club of America was admitted to membership in the American Kennel Club in 1909.

Description and Standards. The revised description and standards, adopted by the West Highland White Terrier Club of America and approved by the American Kennel Club follow.

GENERAL APPEARANCE of the West Highland White Terrier is that of a small, game, hardy-looking terrier exhibiting good showmanship, possessed with no small amount of self-esteem, with varminty appearance strongly built, deep in chest and back ribs, straight back and powerful hindquarters on muscular legs, and exhibiting in a marked degree a great combination of strength and activity. The coat should be about 2 inches long, white in color, hard, with plenty of soft under coat, and no tendency to wave or curl. The tail should be as straight as possible and carried not too gaily, and covered with hard hair, but not bushy. The skull should be not too broad, being in proportion to the terribly powerful jaws. The ears shall be as small and sharp-pointed as possible and carried tightly up, and must be absolutely erect. The eyes of moderate size, as dark as possible, widely placed with a sharp, bright, intelligent expression. The muzzle should not be too long, powerful and gradually tapering toward the nose; the roof of mouth and pads of feet are usually black in color. The dog should be tidied up. Con-

West Highland White Terrier. Photo by Evelyn M. Shafer.

siderable hair should be left around the head to act as a frame for the face to yield a typical Westie expression.

COLOR: Pure white; any other color objectionable.

COAT: Very important, and seldom seen to perfection; must be double-coated. The outer coat consists of hard hair, about 2 inches long, and free from any curl. The under coat, which resembles fur, is short, soft and close. Open coats are objectionable.

SIZE: Dogs should measure about 11 inches at the withers, bitches, about one inch less.

SKULL: Should not be too narrow, being in proportion to his powerful jaw, not too long, slightly domed, and gradually tapering to the eyes, between which there should be a slight indentation or stop, eyebrows heavy. There should be little apparent difference in length between the muzzle and the skull.

EYES: Widely set apart, medium in size, as dark as possible in color, slightly sunk in the head, sharp and intelligent, which, looking from under the heavy eyebrows give a piercing look. Full eyes and also light-colored eyes are very objectionable.

MUZZLE: Should be nearly equal in length to the rest of the skull, powerful and gradually tapering toward the nose, which should be fairly wide. The nose itself should be black in color. The jaws level and powerful, the teeth square or evenly met, well set and large for the size of the dog. Teeth much overshot or much undershot should be heavily penalized. Muzzles longer than the skull and not in proportion thereto are objectionable.

EARS: Small, carried tightly erect and never dropped, set wide apart and terminating in a sharp point. The hair on them should be short, smooth and velvety and they should never be cut. The ears should be free from fringe at the top. Round-pointed, broad and large ears are very objectionable as are ears set too closely together or heavily covered with hair.

NECK: Muscular and nicely set on sloping shoulders.

CHEST: Very deep, with breadth in proportion to the size of the dog.

BODY: Compact, straight back, ribs deep and well arched in the upper half of rib, presenting a flattish side appearance, loins broad and strong, hindquarters strong, muscular and wide across the top.

LEGS AND FEET: Both fore- and hind legs should be short and muscular. The shoulder blades should be comparatively broad, and well sloped backwards. The points of the shoulder blades should be closely knitted into the backbone, so that very little movement of them should be noticeable when the dog is walking. The elbow should be close into the body both when moving or standing, thus causing the foreleg to be well placed in under the shoulder. The forelegs should be straight and thickly covered with short hard hair. The hind legs should be short and sinewy. The thighs very muscular and not too wide apart. The hocks bent and well set in under the body, so as to be fairly close to each other either when standing, walking, or trotting. The forefeet are larger than the hind feet; are round, proportionate in size, strong, thickly padded, and covered with short hard hair. The hind feet are smaller and thickly padded. Cowhocks detract from the general appearance. Straight or weak hocks, both kinds, are undesirable, and should be guarded against.

TAIL: Five or 6 inches long, covered with hard hairs, no feather, as straight as possible, carried gaily but not curled over back. Tails longer than 6 inches are objectionable.

MOVEMENT: Should be free, straight and easy all round. In front the leg should be freely extended forward by the shoulder. The hind movement should be free, strong and close. The hocks should be freely flexed and drawn close in under the body, so that when moving off on the foot the body is thrown or pushed forward with some force. Stiff, stilty movement behind is very objectionable.

Attention of Judges. Under no consideration should a West Highland White Terrier be judged or trimmed as a Scottish Terrier. They are a distinct breed differing in head, body, hindquarters, movement and general over-all type. They are *not* white Scottish Terriers.

SCALE OF POINTS	Points
General appearance	15
Color	7½
Coat	10
Size	7½
Skull	5
Eyes	5
Muzzle	5
Ears	5
Neck	5
Chest	5
Body	10
Legs and feet	7½
Tail	5
Movement	7½
TOTAL	100

FAULTS: *Coat*—Any silkiness, wave or tendency to curl is a serious blemish as is an open coat, single coat or one having black, gray or wheaten hairs therein. *Size*—Any specimens under the minimum or over the maximum height limits are objectionable. *Eyes*—Full or light-colored. *Ears*—Round-pointed, poorly placed, drop, semierect or overly large. *Muzzle*—Overly long forefaces, teeth too much overshot or too much undershot or defective teeth.

(September 15, 1959)

—Group V - Toys—

AFFENPINSCHER

THE AFFENPINSCHER is a charming little dog which, in appearance, rather lives up to his other name, the Monkey Pinscher, or simply the Monkey Dog. He has surprising intelligence, and is a game, durable little fellow weighing, on an average, about seven pounds.

He gets his name of "Monkey Dog" from his prominent chin hair tuft and mustache. He has bushy eyebrows and cropper ears which are, however, partially covered by wiry hair.

Some German writers state that the breed is an old one, being well known as early as the seventeenth century. While there is little available evidence to support this, the breed had reached its present point of perfection by 1900. This indicates that the breed had been well established for some time.

While his origins are not clear, it has been suggested that the Affenpinscher is a close relative of the Miniature Pinscher. The wire coat is thought to have come from crosses with other German wire-haired breeds, or from the Skye Terrier.

As with so many other European dogs, the Affenpinscher did not make his appearance in the United

Affenpinscher. Photo by Evelyn M. Shafer.

States until the decade of 1930 to 1940. The start of World War II then interfered with further importation of bloodstock.

The breed got its biggest stimulus in the United States with the importation of Osko von der Franziskusklause in 1936, by Mrs. Bessie Mally, Cicero, Ill. On September 15, 1936, the American Kennel Club gave the breed a place in its Stud Book, adopted the present standard of the breed, and reserved classes for it at dog shows.

In the next three or four years it began to make its appearance at shows in the New York and Chicago areas. Breeders of other toy dogs became interested immediately. Among these were Mrs. Henrietta Proctor Donnell, the internationally-known toy dog expert of New York.

She purchased several dogs sired by Osko from Mrs. Malley, but later showed the imported dog, Everl von

der Franziskusklause, and Nolli von Anwander, by Prinz von der Franziskusklause.

One of the first American champions of the breed was Ch. Duke of Wolf II, owned by Thelma D. Wolf.

The Affenpinscher is generally considered to have been one of the progenitors of the much better-known Brussells Griffon.

Description and Standards. The description and standards adopted by the American Kennel Club, follow.

As in most Toys, general appearance is one of, if not the most important single point in the Affenpinscher. Details are of secondary importance, and anatomical variations are of small concern.

GENERAL APPEARANCE: Small, but rather sturdy in build and not delicate in any way. He carries himself with comical seriousness and he is generally quiet and a very devoted pal. He can get vehemently excited, however, when attacked and is fearless toward any aggressor.

COAT: A very important factor. It is short and dense in certain parts and shaggy and longer in others, but should be hard and wiry. It is longer and more loose and shaggy on the legs and around the eyes, nose and chin, giving the typical monkey-like appearance from whence comes his name. The best color is black matching his eyes and fiery temperament. However, black with tan markings, red, grey, and other mixtures are permissible. Very light colors and white markings are a fault.

HEAD: Should be round and not too heavy, with well-domed forehead.

EYES: Should be round, of good size, black, and very brilliant.

EARS: Rather small, set high, pointed and erect, usually clipped to a point.

MUZZLE: Must be short and rather pointed with a black nose. The upper jaw is a trifle shorter than the lower jaw; while the teeth should close together, a slight undershot condition is not material. The teeth, however, should not show.

NECK: Short and straight.

BODY: The back should be straight with its length about equal to the height at the shoulder. Chest should be reasonably deep and the body should show only a slight tuck up at the loin.

LEGS: Front legs should be straight as possible. Hind legs without much bend at the hocks and set well under the body.

FEET: Should be round, small, and compact. Turned neither in nor out, with prefereably black pads and nails.

TAIL: Cut short, set and carried high.

SIZE: The smaller dog, if of characteristic type, is more valuable and the shoulder height should not exceed 10¼ inches in any case.

CHIHUAHUA

THE CHIHUAHUA is generally credited with being the world's smallest breed of dog. Individuals weighing as little as one pound have been known, though weights of from two to four pounds are considered ideal. The Chihuahua is also one of the most popular of breeds in the United States, where it ranks with the first dozen breeds in registrations.

There are many glamorous stories about the origin and history of the Chihuahua. But independent scientists, who have studied all available data in Mexico itself, have determined that these stories are pure fiction. However, it is necessary to mention them in order that the truth may be known.

Both European and American sources credit the Chihuahua with being the oldest breed of dog indigenous to the North American continent. According to them, the Toltecs, as early as the year 900, owned the ancestors of this dog. Both the Toltecs and the Aztecs are supposed to have used the dogs in their religious ceremonies.

As usually given, the Chihuahua is descended from the Techichi, or is a cross between Aztec dogs and the native wild dog of Chihuahua, the Tepetzcuintli. The Aztecs supposedly used another name for the breed, on occasion, this being "Alco."

The truth does considerable violence to these old stories. First of all, archaeologists and paleontologists are agreed that no dogs of any kind existed in Mexico before the coming of the Spaniards. The Techichi is a prairie dog, which is not a dog at all, but a rodent. The Tepetzcuintli of the Aztecs may

Chihuahua, long-haired. Photo by James T. Manion.

now be extinct, but the modern animal of that name is the Aguti. Lastly, "Alco," is not an Aztec word, but a Peruvian.

Dr. Isaac Ochoterena, one of the greatest of living paleontologists and biologists in Latin America, has written several books on the animals indigenous to Mexico. He wrote:

No dog fossils have ever been discovered in Mexico, either in graves or other parts. I declare that I am totally ignorant as to the origin of the story of the Chihuahua dog being a native of Chihuahua, and furthermore, that it can be found wild in that state.

It all has sprung perhaps from confusion arising from the fact that Chihuahua has a lot of prairie dogs, but these, as you know, are rodents and not dogs.

One of the greates of the archeologists of the last, century was Manuel Orozco Y Berra, who was born in Mexico City in 1816. He wrote:

The Aztecs had only three domesticated quadrupeds, all of which carried as root, the word "itzcuintli," which the Spaniards translated as "dog," but the real meaning of the word is unknown today. It appears that these pets were abandoned by the Aztecs after their defeat by the Spaniards, and are now totally extinguished, but they deserve a description, because they were the only pets the natives had.

The Aztecs, in other words, did not have dogs. Neither did they have horses, pigs, cattle or sheep. In the State of Vera Cruz there is a living animal carrying one of the three names mentioned above by Manuel Orozco Y Berra. This is the Tepetzcuintli. But this animal is the Aguti, and is not a dog.

Current American histories of the Chihuahua mention writings by Cortes, Columbus, and others. But in these cases, faulty translations have changed the original meaning.

In Cortes' Letter No. II appears the passage: "You can see for sale, chickens, quails, rabbits, hares, deer, and something like small dogs that they raise, castrate and eat." The translation leaves out the "something like," and thus makes it appear the Aztecs had dogs.

Bernal Diaz Del Castello, who accompanied Cortes, and who wrote the best book of the period on the New World, also was careful of his language. He writes ". . . Several caciques came to greet us very kindly and they brought gold gifts and four diadems, and two little animals like dogs . . ."

Friar Juan de Torquemada, wrote: "The Aztecs ate partridge, quail, rabbits, hares and something like little dogs that they fattened, just as we do our pigs." Again he writes: ". . . something like little dogs, that looked like gophers or small rabbits, and live in holes in the ground like moles."

One American writer says that Columbus found Chihuahua dogs in the West Indies. But Columbus' biographer, Bartolome de Las Casas had this to say:

On Saturday the 17th of November, 1492, we took a boat, left the ship and landed on the islands. We saw very large nuts and a lot of great big rats that the natives called "guanimiqui-najes" and the same kind of animals we described in Chapter 46, saying that they looked like dogs, but they don't bark, they issue a shrilling sound.

And again:

Four footed animals we did not see, only those creatures that look like dogs and that they are very good to eat, better than rabbits and hares.

Later, in telling about how Columbus had set his "mastiffs" upon the natives, he writes:

. . . they would bite the Indians so fast that each dog could tear a hundred Indians in one hour, because as these Indians wore no clothes and they did not know what dogs were, the ferocious animals had a good grip on their flesh and would tear them to pieces, and they killed these Indians faster than they could kill boars and deer in Europe.

Joseph De Acosta, most acute and diligent observer of the first white men to reach America—he went to Peru in 1571—wrote:

There are no real dogs here, and these that roam wild are descendants of the ones brought by the Spaniards. The animals

the Indians have as pets they call them "Alco" and they are so fond of them they would go without eating in order to feed their pets.

One American writer speaks of the forerunner of the Chihuahua as being the Tepanchichi. But the correct translation of this word is "wall rodent," or mouse. Similarly, the translation of Techichi is "rock rodent," or gopher, or prairie dog.

The State of Chihuahua is the coldest of all the Mexican states, and during nearly six months of the year there is freezing temperature and ice at night. Obviously, this is hardly the climate in which the Chihuahua dog could live in that wild state. But in this State, the wild prairie dog is called the Perro Chihuahueno, which could be translated "Chihuahua dog."

These facts should serve to discredit the story of Rosina Casselli, who toured Europe in 1903 and 1904 with a troupe of Chihuahua dogs. She reported that the dogs lived in the wild state in Chihuahua State.

It might be added here that the Aztecs never lived in Chihuahua, which was populated by the most primitive Indians of the hunting and fishing culture. Nor was there any trade with the Aztecs at that period, since there were no roads and high mountains intervened.

The best available evidence, from the Mexican standpoint at least, is that the ancestors of the modern Chihuahua came from the Orient in fairly recent times. For hundreds of years it has been an oriental sport to dwarf various species of animals and plants. The Chinese especially have dwarfed many types of plants, fish, and even dogs.

The Spaniards established a trade route from China to the Philippine Islands, to Acapulco, across Mexico, and thence to Spain. Hairless dogs and Chihuahuas, the latter merely dwarfs of some oriental species, could have come in in this way. There is a record of a pair of dwarfed dogs being brought from the Orient to Mexico City where they were displayed as curiosities in 1785.

The offspring of these dogs might have been taken to the State of Chihuahua and there propagated their kind. But this is pure speculation, for there is no evidence of this having happened.

About 1895 Chihuahuas began to appear at some of the wealthy homes in Mexico City. And at about the same time they began to appear in homes along the northern side of the Mexican border. It is again speculation, but Chinese emigrants to the region about El Paso, Texas, might have brought their dwarfed dogs with them.

Today, it is certain that all the Chihuahuas in Mexico come from the United States. There is no standard for the breed in Mexico, and there is no kennel which raises them, or ever has raised them to any extent in Mexico. There are, perhaps, not more than 1,000 Chihuahuas in Mexico, and many other breeds are far more popular in that country.

James Watson, the famous American dog judge, writer, and investigator, bought at least one Chi-

Chihuahua, smooth. Photo by Evelyn M. Shafer.

Chihuahua, smooth—puppies. Photo by Evelyn M. Shafer.

huahua in the El Paso area. But the first one to be registered by the American Kennel Club was Midget owned by H. Rayner of El Paso. Midget was whelped July 18, 1903. Rayner registered three more in 1905, and J. M. Lee of Los Angeles, Cal., registered another which was bred by Rayner.

As people in the colder areas of the United States discovered that the dogs could be kept successfully in Northern homes, interest in the breed grew. In 1928, Ch. Empress Carlotto was bought by a Canadian, and now hundreds of these dogs are bred and raised yearly in Canada.

The Chihuahua Club of America was founded in 1923. It has done an excellent job in promoting the breed. The Chihuahua appears at virtually all the dog shows, but to a lesser degree that would be supposed. Though delicacy of the dog during travel is one factor, the chief reason is that the vast majority of the dogs are sold as house pets and their owners do not subject them to the dog shows.

The smooth Chihuahua is considered the favorite toy breed in America and is extremely popular in South Africa.

Description and Standards. The description and standards, adopted by the Chihuahua Club of America and approved by the American Kennel Club, follow.

CHIHUAHUA—SMOOTH COAT

HEAD: A well-rounded-apple, dome skull, with or without molera. Cheeks and jaws lean. Nose moderately short, slightly pointed (self-colored, in blond types, or black). In moles, blues, and chocolate, they are self-colored. In blond types, pink nose permissible.

EARS: Large, held erect when alert, but flaring at the sides at about an angle of 45 degrees when in repose. This gives breadth between the ears.

EYES: Full, but not protruding, balanced, set well apart—dark, ruby, or luminous. (Light eyes in blond types, permissible.)

TEETH: Level.

NECK AND SHOULDERS: Slightly arched, gracefully sloping into

lean shoulders, may be smooth in the very short types, or with ruff about neck preferred. Shoulders lean, sloping into a slightly broadening support above straight forelegs that are set well under, giving a free play at the elbows. Shoulders should be well up, giving balance and soundesss, sloping into a level back. (Never down or low.) This gives a chestiness, and strength of forequarters, yet not of the "Bulldog" chest; plenty of brisket.

BACK AND BODY: Level back, slightly longer than height. Shorter backs desired in males. Ribs rounded (but not too much "barrel-shaped").

HINDQUARTERS: Muscular, with hocks well apart, neither out or in, well let down, with firm sturdy action.

TAIL: Moderately long, carried cycle either up or out, or in a loop over the back, with tip just touching the back. (Never tucked under.) Hair on tail in harmony with the coat of the body, preferred furry. A natural bobtail or tailless permissible, if so born, and not against a good dog.

FEET: Small, with toes well split up, but not spread, pads cushioned, with fine pasterns. (Neither the hare nor the cat-foot.) A dainty, small foot with nails moderately long.

COAT: In the smooth, the coat should be soft texture, close and glossy. (Heavier coats with under coats permissible.) Coat placed well over body with ruff on neck, and more scanty on head and ears.

COLOR: Any color—solid, marked or splashed.

WEIGHT: One to 6 pounds, with 2 to 4 pounds preferable, if 2 dogs are equally good in type, the more diminutive is preferred.

GENERAL APPEARANCE: A graceful, alert, swift-moving little dog with saucy expression. Compact, and with terrierlike qualities.

SCALE OF POINTS	Points
Head, including ears	20
Body	20
Coat	10
Tail	5
Color	5
Legs	15
Weight	10
General appearance and action	15
TOTAL	100

Disqualifications. Cropped tail, broken down or cropped ears.

LONG COAT

The long-coated variety of the Chihuahua is judged by the same standard as the smooth-coated variety, except for the following.

COAT: In the Long Coats, the coat should be of a soft texture, either flat or slightly curly, with under coat preferred. Ears fringed (heavily fringed ears may be tipped slightly, never down), feathering on feet and legs, and pants on hind legs. Large ruff on neck desired and preferred. Tail full and long (as a plume).

Disqualifications. Too thin coat, that resembles bareness.

SCALE OF POINTS:	Points
Head, including ears	20
Body	20
Coat	20
Tail	5
Color	5
Legs	10
Weight	5
General appearance and action	15
TOTAL	100

Disqualifications. Cropped tail, broken down or cropped ears, too thin coat that resembles bareness.

(January 12, 1954)

ENGLISH TOY SPANIEL

EVEN THOUGH the English Toy Spaniel comprises one of England's oldest group of pure breeds, considerable confusion exists about it. This arises out of the fact that there are four varieties, divided by color and name. Moreover, in England, all four varieties are officially registered under the name for one variety, while Canada and the United States lump all four under the general name, English Toy Spaniels.

The varieties, as finally settled upon by the Toy Spaniel Club of England in 1885, are: King Charles, a black and tan; Ruby, a red; Prince Charles, a tricolor; and Blenheim, a red and white. Since 1923, in England, all four varieties are now listed as King Charles Spaniels. (The Cavalier King Charles Spaniel is *not* an AKC breed classified under the English Toy Spaniel heading. For Cavalier King Charles Spaniel, *see* Little-Known Dogs, Part XVII.)

Strangely enough, there would appear to have been no very good reason why they should have been called King Charles Spaniels in the first place. King Charles I died in 1649, but Toy Spaniels were known in England at least 100 years earlier. Charles II also favored spaniels, as did King James, and some early writers referred to the breed as the King James Spaniel.

Baroness Wentworth, perhaps the greatest authority on the breed, states that the English Toy Spaniels, excepting the Blenheim variety, are descendants of dwarf spaniels of France, and to a lesser extent, from similar dogs of Holland and Italy. She has the opinion that the dogs were much larger than the modern version. This would appear true of the dogs pictured by painters of the period of King Charles I.

There is some evidence that the King Charles as a black-and-tan actually was developed by the Duke of Norfolk, and in much later times. This Duke of Norfolk gave his name, and probably erroneously, to the early Springers.

Thus, Craven reports in the *Young Sportsman's Manual*: "The Spaniel tribe is a numerous one, and variously designated, from the beautiful little creature known as Charles The Second's, or the Duke of Norfolk's breed, to the handsome Springer."

Southey also reported: "Our Marlborough and King James Spaniels are unrivalled in beauty. The latter breed, that are black and tan, with hair almost approximating to silk in fineness, were solely in the possession of the Duke of Norfolk."

This Duke of Norfolk prized his dogs so highly that he refused to sell or give them away. Unwanted pups were fed to his eagles. He did, however, give one to the Duchess of York on condition that she would not breed from the dog in direct line. This was reported by Colonel Hamilton, who also noted the black and tan color of the dogs.

Some writers have pointed out that both Charles I and Charles II had a passionate love of all spaniels, with many of his dogs being described as black and white, or black, rather than black and tan. But in any case, the name became associated with the two kings and stuck.

In proof of the early use of the name, there is the advertisement quoted by Mrs. Raymond Mallock from the *Daily Courant* of Jan. 9, 1720:

Whereas a little black and white Spaniel of King Charles Spaniel breed, about six months old (the white on her neck had been lately burned) broke loose out of Mr. Nash's shop in Bishopgate St. on Thu. last about 8 o'clock in the morning with a piece of red worsted garter about her neck. Whoever has taken up the bitch and will bring her to the Sign of St. Martins in York Buildings shall have 5/- for their pains.

Many writers have suggested that the similarity of the English Toys to the Japanese Spaniel and other oriental types indicates a strong relationship. Accordingly to these writers, the Japanese Spaniel, the Pug, and perhaps the Maltese, have been used in the ancestry of the English Toys. There is, however, little beyond the speculative to give evidence of this.

At the same time, very much is known of the origin or the Blenheim or Marlborough variety. This red and white dog was originally called a Cocker, or Cocking Spaniel. Many writers testified to his gaminess. But he was the smallest of the spaniel family to be used in hunting, and he tired rather quickly. He was given the name Blenheim as early as 1700.

During the last century, beginning about 1835, breeders began to shorten the muzzle of the three varieties. Eventually, the Blenheim was crossed with the others, until today, the four varieties are undistinguishable except as to color.

Prior to 1885, only two types were recognized, the Blenheim and the King Charles. But in that year, breeders began to clamor for recognition of the red and tri-color. These were first registered separately in 1892. It had apparently been the intention to call the Prince Charles, the Prince Charlie, after Bonnie Prince Charlie, but through an error, the former name was given.

The breed was well known in the United States throughout the nineteenth century. While never among the very popular breeds, there was a sufficient demand to keep a number of so-called "professional" breeders busy supplying the market with puppies.

When American dog shows became popular, after the foundation of the American Kennel Club in 1885, the dogs began to appear in fair numbers at the shows. Many pictures of the dogs of that period are extant. They show animals of a beauty hardly to be improved upon today.

A Mrs. Senn of New York City had three famous black and tan champions called Perseverance, Square Face, and Romeo. Mrs. Raymond Mallock imported the famous English Ch. Rollo about 1900, and this dog quickly made his American championship as well.

Description and Standards. The description and standards, by courtesy of the Toy Spaniel Club of America, follow:

Note: Under the ruling of the American Kennel Club, passed December 16, 1902, Prince Charles, King Charles, Ruby, and Blenheim Spaniels are classed together as English Toy Spaniels.

HEAD: Should be well domed, and in good specimens is absolutely semi-globular, sometimes even extending beyond the half-circle, and absolutely projecting over the eyes, so as nearly to meet the upturned nose.

EYES: The eyes are set wide apart, with the eyelids square to the line of the face—not oblique or fox-like. The eyes themselves are large and dark as possible, so as to be generally considered black, their enormous pupils, which are absolutely of that color, increasing the description.

STOP: The "stop," or hollow between the eyes, is well marked, as in the Bulldog, or even more so; some good specimens exhibit a hollow deep enough to bury a small marble in it.

NOSE: The nose must be short and well turned up between the eyes, and without any indication of artificial displacement afforded by a deviation to either side. The color of the end should be black, and it should be both deep and wide with open nostrils. A light-colored nose is objectionable, but shall not disqualify.

JAW: The muzzle must be square and deep, and the lower jaw wide between the branches, leaving plenty of space for the tongue, and for the attachment of the lower lips, which should completely conceal the teeth. It should also be turned up or "finished" so as to allow of its meeting the end of the upper jaw, turned up in a similar way as above described. A protruding tongue is objectionable, but does not disqualify.

EARS: The ears must be long, so as to approach the ground. In an average-sized dog they measure 20 inches from tip to tip, and some reach 22 inches or even a trifle more. They should be set low down on the head and hang flat to the sides of the cheeks, and be heavy feathered.

SIZE: The most desirable size is from 9 pounds to 12 pounds.

SHAPE: In compactness of shape, these Spaniels almost rival the Pug, but the length of coat adds greatly to the apparent bulk, as the body, when the coat is wetted, looks small in comparison with that dog. Still, it ought to be decidedly "cobby," with strong stout legs, short broad back, and wide chest.

COAT: The coat should be long, silky, soft, and wavy, but not curly. There should be a profuse mane, extending well down in the front of the chest. The feather should be well displayed on the ears and feet, and in the latter case so thickly as to give the appearance of being webbed. It is also carried well up the backs of the legs. In the Black and Tan the feather on the ears is very long and profuse, exceeding that of the Blenheim by an inch or more. The feather on the tail (which is cut to the length of about 1½ inches) should be silky, and from 3 to 4 inches in length, constituting a marked "flag" of a square shape, and not carried above the level of the back.

COLORS, KING CHARLES AND RUBY: The King Charles and Ruby types which comprise one show variety are solid-colored dogs. The King Charles are black and tan (considered a solid color), the black rich and glossy with deep mahogany tan markings over the eyes and on the muzzle, chest and legs. The presence of a few white hairs intermixed with the black on the chest is to be faulted, but a white patch on the chest or white appearing elsewhere disqualifies. The Ruby is a rich chestnut red and is whole-colored. The presence of a few white hairs intermixed with the red on the chest is to be faulted but a white patch on the chest or white appearing elsewhere disqualifies.

COLORS, BLENHEIM AND PRINCE CHARLES: The Blenheim and Prince Charles types which comprise the other show variety are broken-colored dogs. The Blenheim is red and white. The ground color is a pearly white which has bright red chestnut or ruby red markings evenly distributed in large patches. The ears and cheeks should be red, with a blaze of white extending from the nose up the forehead and ending between the ears in a crescentic curve. In the center of the blaze at the top of the forehead, there should be a clear "spot" of red, the size of a dime. The Prince Charles, a tri-colored dog, is white, black and tan. The ground color is a pearly white. The black consists of markings which should be evenly distributed in large patches. The tan appears as spots over the eyes, on the muzzle, chest and legs; the ears and vent should also be lined with tan. The Prince Charles has no "spot," that being a particular feature of the Blenheim.

SCALE OF POINTS: Points

King Charles, or Black and Tan. Prince Charles, White, with Black and Tan Markings. Ruby, or Red

Symmetry, condition, size and soundness of limb	20
Head	15
Stop	5
Muzzle	10
Eyes	10
Ears	15
Coat and feathering	15
Color	10
TOTAL	**100**

Blenheim or White with Red Markings

	Points
Symmetry, condition, size and soundness of limb	15
Head	15
Stop	5
Muzzle	10
Eyes	10
Ears	10
Coat and feathering	15
Color and markings	15
Spot	5
TOTAL	**100**

Disqualifications. King Charles and Ruby: A white patch on the chest, or white on any other part.

BRUSSELS GRIFFON

IN THE United States, the name Brussels Griffons is used generally to cover three varieties of Toy dogs. These are the Brussels Griffon, which is distinguishable from the Belgian Griffon (Griffon Belge) by color, and the Brabancon (Petite Brabancon), which is smooth-coated.

The true Brussels Griffon is a sturdy, reddish brown dog, with cropped ears, and a dense, wiry coat.

Klipspindle Blizzard, a Cavalier King Charles Spaniel. (Owner: Mr. and Mrs. Raymond Evans, Mentor, Ohio)

Brussels Griffon.

His whiskers and expression give him a strange, almost human expression.

The Belgian Griffon differs from the Brussels only in color. He can be black and reddish brown; all black; or black with reddish brown markings. The Brabancon, or smooth-coated dog is either reddish brown, or black with reddish brown markings.

The term "griffon" means thickly-haired. It thus hardly applies to the Brabancon, or smooth-coated dog. This inconsistency was noted in Belgium itself. The smooth-coated dog appeared in litters born of a cross between Griffons and the Pug. At first, these pups were destroyed. Later they were allowed to live, and the name Petite Brabancon was given to them.

There are half a dozen theories as to the origin of the Brussels Griffon. An opinion held by many of the early Belgian breeders was that the breed developed from crossing small terriers with the Pug, and perhaps the Toy spaniels. Others have felt that the Barbet and the Hollandsche Smoushound have had a share in the ancestry of the breed.

It would appear probable that, whatever crosses were used, the Toy-dog-sized Griffon (minus the snub nose) is an ancient Belgian "arch-type" of dog.

One reason for this statement is Jan Van Eyck's painting of Arnolfini and his Wife. Van Eyck painted this picture in 1434. In the clearest possible fashion, he shows a Griffon, with its rough, wiry coat, sharp eyes, and pricked, cropped ears. Even the size of the

dog would correspond to that of modern Brussels Griffons.

Handley Spicer, the English authority and breeder of nearly 50 years ago, points to other "unmistakable" Brussels Griffons in paintings by Jacopo du Empoli, between 1554 and 1640. These pictures would indicate that Henry III of France had forebears of the modern Brussels Griffon.

In the period following 1870, the breed became immensely popular in Belgium, partly because it was the favorite dog of Queen Henrietta Maria. Later, Queen Astrid continued to royal patronage. By 1880, the breed had reached its present peak of perfection.

The British dog authority, Hubbard, states that a dog which had been best in show at Brussels in 1880, was then imported to England where it founded the English strain. He does not, however, name the dog. Most other British writers speak guardedly on the subject, saying that "to the best of their knowledge" the first Brussels Griffons were imported about 1894, though there are "traditions" of imports 20 years earlier.

However that may be, by 1908 the quality of the British dogs was such that a noted Belgian judge stated that the British champions, Glenartney Sport and Copthorne Treasure, were the two most perfect specimens in existence.

This is interesting to note because of the importation during 1948 by E. J. Weist of three dogs from England. These are Lalarookh Tit Willow, Lalarookh Susanne, and Lalarookh Snookie.

Importations to the United States began about 1900, and have continued fairly steady ever since. In Canada, the Brabancons appear to have gotten a start somewhat ahead of the wire-coated dogs. Miss Constant Van Camp showed four of these dogs at Canadian shows in 1913. She also imported a number of Brussels Griffons.

From the earliest times, writers have noted with surprise the intelligence and ease of training the Brussels Griffons. While not seen so often in American obedience contests, they have competed sensationally well in European events, where their precision has given them top records, even against such dogs as German Shepherds.

Description and Standards. The description and standards follow.

GENERAL APPEARANCE: A toy dog, intelligent, alert, sturdy, with a thick-set short body, a smart carriage and set-up, attracting attention by an almost human expression.

HEAD: *Skull*—Large and round, with a domed forehead. *Ears* —Small and set rather high on the head. May be shown cropped or natural. If natural they are carried semi-erect. *Eyes* —Should be set well apart, very large, black, prominent, and well open. The eyelashes long and black. Eyelids edged with black. *Nose*—Very black, extremely short, its tip being set back deeply between the eyes so as to form a lay-back. The nostrils large, the stop deep. *Lips*—Edged with black, not pendulous but well brought together, giving a clean finish to the mouth. *Jaws*—Chin must be undershot, prominent, and large with an upward sweep. The incisors of the lower jaw should protrude over the upper incisors, and the lower jaw should be rather broad. Neither teeth nor tongue should show when the mouth is closed. A wry mouth is serious fault.

BODY AND LEGS: Brisket should be broad and deep, ribs well sprung, back level and short. *Neck*—Medium length, gracefully arched. *Tail*—Set and held high, docked to about one third. *Forelegs*—Of medium length, straight in bone, well muscled, set moderately wide apart and straight from the point of the shoulders as viewed from the front. Pasterns short and strong. *Hind legs*—Set true, thighs strong and well muscled, stifles bent, hocks well let down, turning neither in nor out. *Feet*—Round, small, and compact, turned neither in nor out. Toes well arched. Black pads and toenails preferred.

Brussels Griffon—Puppies. Note contrast in types, the smooth at left, the rough at right.

COAT: There are two distinct types of coat—rough and smooth. The rough coat should be wiry and dense, the harder and more wiry the better. On no account should the dog look or feel woolly, and there should be no silky hair anywhere. The coat should not be so long as to give a shaggy appearance, but should still be distinctly different all over from the smooth coat. The head should be covered with wiry hair slightly longer around the eyes, nose, cheeks, and chin, thus forming a fringe. The Smooth coat is similar to that of the Boston Terrier or English Bulldog, with no trace of wire hair.

COLOR: In the rough-coated type, coat is either 1. reddish brown, with a little black at the whiskers and chin allowable, or 2. black and reddish brown mixed, usually, with black mask and whiskers, or 3. black with uniform reddish brown markings, usually appearing under the chin, on the legs, over the eyebrows, around the edges of the ears and around the vent, or 4. solid black. The colors of the smooth-coated type are the same as those of the rough-coated type except that solid black is not allowable. Any white hairs in either the rough or smooth coat are a serious fault, except for "frost" on the black muzzle of a mature dog, which is natural.

WEIGHT: Usually 8 to 10 pounds, and should not exceed 12 pounds. Type and quality are of greater importance than weight, and a smaller dog that is sturdy and well proportioned should not be penalized.

SCALE OF POINTS: *Points*

HEAD

Skull	5
Nose and stop	10
Eyes	5
Chin and jaws	10
Ears	5 35

COAT

Color	12	
Texture	13	25
Body (brisket and rib)	15	
Legs	10	
Feet	5	
General Appearance (neck, topline, and tail carriage)	10	40
TOTAL		100

Disqualifications. Dudley or butterfly nose, white spot or blaze anywhere on coat, hanging tongue, jaw overshot, solid black coat in the smooth type.

(February 6, 1960)

ITALIAN GREYHOUND

THE ITALIAN Greyhound is a rare but ancient breed of dog. Except in its native land, it has never been extremely popular in numbers. Yet the grace, beauty, and easy-keeping qualities of this smallest member of the Greyhound family have ensured a steady supply of good breeding stock in many of the countries of the world.

As to the origin of the breed, there is no question. It comes from Italy, where it is called the Piccoli Levrieri Italiani. And it is a miniature of the large Greyhound which has been man's sporting companion longer than any other breed.

When the breed was dwarfed to its present size is not known for certain. One British writer states that a mummy of a miniature Greyhound has been found in the tomb of one of the Pharaohs of Egypt. He does not, however, name either the Pharaoh or the location of the tomb. Yet thousand of mummies of dogs and cats have been found in Egypt, notably at Abydos.

Claims have been advanced that the Italian Greyhound is a prominent figure in canine art of the Roman period. But other writers have stated that these claims are not well supported. All agree, of course, that it would be strange if the Romans, with their love of breeding fancy animals for their ladies, had not bred miniatures of the Greyhound.

By Renaissance times, however, the Italian Greyhound was well established. He was the darling of the great court ladies, and he appears to have been bred with no other thought than to supply a lady's lap dog.

In 1790 Bewick wrote: "The small Italian Greyhound is not above half the size (of the Greyhound) but perfectly similar in form. In shape it is exquisitely beautiful and delicate. It is not common in this country (England), the climate being too rigorous for the extreme delicacy of its constitution."

Thirteen years later, Taplin wrote: "No plausible or satisfactory suggestions as to the origin of the breed" has been found, which breed "seems only calculated to soothe the vanity and indulge the frivolities of antiquated ladies."

The breed had indeed become the darling of royal ladies. Anne of Denmark, consort of James I of England, owned an Italian Greyhound. So did Mary Beatrice D'Easte, consort of James II. As an Italian, she brought her dog from Italy.

Paul Veronese, the painter, has left an excellent likeness of this dog. He was very coarse as compared to later dogs, for instance, the lovely Eos owned by Queen Victoria. But it is not possible to generalize from this. Beatrice may simply have owned an inordinate affection for an inferior dog.

Other royal fanciers of this breed were Mary Queen of Scots and Frederick The Great of Prussia. Lord Lytton, Sir Percey Shelley, son of the poet, and others of British nobility, have owned Italian Greyhounds. Shelley's Linda is said to have been a perfect miniature Greyhound weighing eight and a half pounds.

Strangely enough, the breed in England appears to have prospered in the North, and in Scotland, despite the comparatively severe weather in those areas. Several judges after 1860 have reported on the excellence of dogs seen in, and around, Edinburgh, Scotland.

The British crossed the Italian Greyhounds with certain small terriers. The reason for this is not known, but the experiment was a failure. The dogs became very coarse, and it took many years to bring them back to the true type. However, the breed still maintains a terrier's love of ratting.

In his 1859 edition, Stonehenge pictures the noted dog, Gowan's Billy. This dog was of Italian lineage, and about as inbred as it is possible to be. But he was a dog of superlative beauty, and apparently would have been the equal of any dogs shown today.

Italian Greyhounds appear to have enjoyed a reasonable popularity in the United States between 1875 and 1900. But by the time Watson wrote his famous *The Dog Book,* he reported that only Dr. F. H. Hoyt of Sharon, Pa., was then still breeding them. The New York show had withdrawn classes for the breed, and Watson remarked that this did not happen until a breed was about extinct.

Yet the breed did not die out, whereas in England, World War I almost brought the extinction of the Italian Greyhound there. Strangely enough, when a British committee began to revive the breed, it turned to the United States for help. The British are not accustomed to coming to America for bloodstock, and perhaps no other breed can boast of this.

Two bitches were exported from the world-famous Aira Vana Kennels to England, where they successfully survived the six months' quarantine, and duly contributed to the great breed revival which set in. These two dogs were Isola Princess and Isola Daphne.

Rigorous weather conditions in Canada have not injured the Italian Greyhound. It is as popular in that country as in the United States, if not more so. Among the early Canadian breeders were Ed. Beaupre of Winnipeg, Manitoba, and Mrs. T. W.

Italian Greyhound—Ch. Russo's Little Bennato di Xena. (Owner: Louis F. Russo and Jerry Dwyer, Hollywood, Calif.) Photo by Alfred Stillman.

Edwards, Ontario, whose Prince Ivanovich became the first champion of the breed when it was campaigned during 1912 and 1913.

Despite their apparent fragility, Italian Greyhounds are strong and active, and are no more susceptible to injury than are other Toy breeds. In some cases they are less so. They almost never require baths. Their coat does not change so that shedding is imperceptible. They are probably more likely to chill in transit to and from dog shows, but they are as hardy as other dogs in their daily life about the house. Their bark is very deep for their size, but Italian Greyhounds are not "yappers," and are easily controlled in this, as in other respects.

Description and Standards. The description and standards, by courtesy of the Italian Greyhound Club, England, follow.

GENERAL APPEARANCE: A miniature English Greyhound, more slender in all proportions, and of ideal elegance and grace in shape, symmetry and action.

HEAD: Skull, long, flat and narrow. Muzzle, very fine, nose dark, teeth level. Ears, rose shaped, placed well back, soft and delicate. Eyes, rather large, bright and full of expression.

BODY: Neck, long and gracefully arched. Shoulders, long and sloping. Chest, deep and narrow. Back, curved and drooping at the hind quarters.

LEGS AND FEET: Forelegs, straight, set well under the shoulders, fine pasterns, small delicate bones. Hind legs, hocks well let down, thighs muscular. Feet, the long "hare foot."

TAIL: Rather long, fine and with low carriage.

COAT: Skin fine and supple, hair thin and glossy like satin.

COLOR: All shades of fawn, red, mouse, blue, cream and white are recognized, black and tan terrier markings not allowed.

ACTION: High stepping and free.

SIZE: Two classes, one of eight pounds and under and one over eight pounds. A good small dog is preferable to an equally good large one but a good larger dog is preferable to a poor smaller one.

SCALE OF POINTS:	Points
Skull	6
Muzzle	8
Ears	8
Eyes	5
Neck	8
Shoulders	5
Chest	5
Back	8
Fore legs	8
Hind legs	8
Feet	8
Tail	8
Coat	4
Color	3
Action	8
TOTAL	**100**

JAPANESE SPANIEL

IT IS NOW almost 100 years since the first Japanese Spaniels, or Japanese Chins, were brought to the United States. Since that time, the breed has prospered here, in England, and in many other countries. Its enduring popularity among the lovers of Toy dogs has been built on the breed's charm, alertness, and easy-keeping qualities. Even World War II, with the bitterness it engendered against Japan, has not injured the breed's popularity.

Most dog authorities agree that Pekingese, Pug, and Japanese Chin are ancient Oriental types which probably were closely related at one time. It is supposed, for instance, that the pure-bred dog is not native to Japan, and that he therefore came from China or Korea.

There are two theories as to how he arrived. The first is that royal embassies from China and Korea brought dogs as presents to the emperor of Japan. In support of this, Collier, in his *Dogs of China and Japan*, quotes an old text, which is briefed as follows:

A Korean prince sent a mission to Japan about the year 732. He included a "Ssuchan Pai" dog, as well as a hunting dog. The former was a lap dog with such a charming disposition that all the court ladies of Japan wanted one. Accordingly, the price of small dogs went up.

The second theory as to the arrival of the toy dog in Japan is that he was brought in by Buddhist teachers. If this was so, it places the date as sometime after A.D. 520, the year generally given for the arrival of Zen Buddhism to China.

Many writers have noted that the Chinese regarded the Pekingese dog with great awe, as being a protector of the Buddhist faith, that is, one of Buddha's lions. When Buddha stretched forth his hand, his fingers were supposed to change into lions, whose roars subjected the enemy.

There is extant a Japanese painting which shows the transmission of the law through the great patri-archs of Zen Buddhism. One of the patriarchs holds a dog-like animal in his lap. But, in reality, the animal looks more like a fox than a dog. If a dog, he would be closer to Pomeranian type, though with a long brush or tail.

In the famous *Sketch Book* of the Lady Sei Shona-gon, there is an appealing story of the imperial cat and the court dog, Okinamaru. Lady Sei Shonagon was a lady-in-waiting to the Empress, and she wrote her diary between A.D. 991 and 1000.

In this story, the cat had been en-nobled. The dog attacked the cat and was banished, or exiled, to "Dog's Island." He escaped and returned, was badly beaten, but was finally forgiven. There is no evidence that the dog had been given any royal rank. But that there was an island to exile dogs, even as for royal political outcasts, is significant.

Kaempfer, in his *History of Japan*, tells us that about 1727, he saw a reward posted for "20 shuits of silver . . . to be given as a reward to anybody that would discover the accomplices of a murder lately committed upon a dog."

Kaempfer also noted that, even in Nagasaki, which was far from the Imperial court, no one dared harm a dog. These lay in the streets, giving way to neither man nor horse, and huts had been built in every street to house the aged and infirm dogs.

Kaempfer declares that in the Japan of that period, more dogs were bred than in any nation on earth. But he did not ascribe this to Buddhism, but rather to the fact that the Emperor had been born under the Japanese astrological sign of the dog. Moreover, it should be noted that Shinto was the official religion of Japan.

Commodore Perry opened Japan to the Occident in 1853. In the book, *Commodore Perry's Expedition to Japan*, it is observed:

The Commodore upon subsequent enquiry learned that there are three articles which in Japan, as he understood, always form part of an Imperial present. These are rice, dried fish, and dogs . . . Why these should have been selected, or what they particularly symbolize he did not learn . . . and four small dogs of a rare breed were sent to the President as part of the Emperor's gift. We have observed also in the public prints that two were put aboard of Admiral Sterling's ship for her Majesty of England.

The writer noted that these dogs resembled English Toy Spaniels. He speculated that, in 1613, when Capt. Saris returned to England from Japan, he might have brought back some of these dogs, and that these, mixed with the English Toys, accounted for the pushed-back nose of the English dogs. It is from this pure speculation that the tradition has grown up that the Japanese Chin is the ancestor of the English Toy Spaniel.

One further quotation from this source is, however, fruitful. "The species sent as a present by the Emperor is by no means common in Japan. It is never seen running about the streets, or following its master in his walks, and the Commodore was informed that dogs of this kind are costly."

If Queen Victoria's pair of Japanese Spaniels

Japanese Spaniel.

reached her, there is no evidence of it in chronicles of that time or later. James Watson received permission from William Speiden, who was with Perry, to quote from his diary on the subject of the others:

Among the President's presents were four dogs of the pug character, but with beautiful long hair, black and white in colour. The Commodore gave two of these dogs to Admiral Stirling of the British Navy to take to the Queen of England.

The other two were named Master Sam Spooner and Madame Yeddo, and were put aboard the steam frigate *Mississippi*, together with some Japanese cats. Quite a pretty little dog was given me, which I named Simoda, that being the town where I received it shortly before sailing on Oct. 1, 1854 for home. In January of the following year, and just before we reached Valparaiso, Sam Spooner died, and in February, Madame Yeddo also died. My pet survived them about a month. All three were buried at sea in sailor fashion, being put in shotted canvas bags. These dogs were all of the most delicate build and had to be handled carefully.

Two other dogs came home on another ship and were sent by the Commodore for his daughter, Mrs. August Belmont. We were given to understand that the dogs were very rare in Japan and very valuable. They were never allowed to run the streets, but were carried in beautiful straw baskets when taken out of doors. Many had really attractive faces, almost human, especially the females.

The Belmont dogs, named Yiddo and Jap, died without issue, so it remained for later importations to establish the breed. These imports, brought in almost by the hundreds, were a varied lot, so that dogs ranged in weight from two pounds to ten times that much.

The New York show of 1882 had nine entries. A tenth was entered in the miscellaneous class, being called a "Pekingese (China) Spaniel." The three judges of the show, Grant (who had judged the Japanese breed), Wise, and Watson, gave this dog, Chico, a special prize. They considered it the best of the bunch.

A Japanese Spaniel Club was organized at about this time, but it became inactive in later years. The present Japanese Spaniel Club of America was founded in 1912, and has been active ever since.

Among the early dogs were the champions in the kennels of Mrs. Senn of New York City. Watson considered her Ch. Senn Senn the greatest of the breed he had seen. Others of her champions were Ch. Senn-Sation and Ch. Crestwood Oyama. Another early champion was O'Kasan, owned by Dr. R. T. Harrison, New York City.

The Japanese Spaniel became popular in Canada about 1900, and remained popular until World War I. The war period brought an end to breeding for a time, but interest in the breed later revived, and today many of the larger shows have excellent classes of entries.

Description and Standards. The description and standards, by courtesy of the Japanese Spaniel Club of America, follow:

GENERAL APPEARANCE: That of a lively, high-bred little dog with dainty appearance, smart, compact carriage and profuse coat. These dogs should be essentially stylish in movement, lifting the feet high when in action, carrying the tail (which is heavily feathered, proudly curved or plumed) over the back. In size they vary considerably, but the smaller they are the better, provided type and quality are not sacrificed. When divided by weight, classes should be under and over seven pounds.

HEAD: Should be large for the size of the dog, with broad skull, rounded in front.

EYES: Large, dark, lustrous, rather prominent and set wide apart.

EARS: Small and V-shaped, nicely feathered, set wide apart and high on the head and carried slightly forward.

NOSE: Very short in the muzzle part. The end or nose proper should be wide with open nostrils, and must be the color of the dog's markings, i.e., black in black-marked dogs, and red or deep flesh color in red or lemon-marked dogs. It shall be a disqualification for a Black and White Japanese Spaniel to have a nose any other color than black.

NECK: Should be short and moderately thick.

BODY: Should be squarely and compactly built, wide in chest, "cobby" in shape. The length of the dog's body should be about its height.

TAIL: Must be well twisted to either right or left from root and carried up over back and flow on opposite side; it should be profusely covered with long hair (ring tails not desirable).

LEGS: The bones of the legs should be small, giving them a slender appearance, and they should be well feathered.

FEET: Small and shaped somewhat long; the dog stands up on its toes somewhat. If feathered, the tufts should never increase the width of the foot, but only its length a trifle.

COAT: Profuse, long, straight, rather silky. It should be absolutely free from wave or curl, and not lie too flat, but have a tendency to stand out, especially at the neck, so as to give a thick mane or ruff, which with profuse feathering on thighs and tail gives a very showy appearance.

COLOR: The dogs should be either black and white or red and white, i.e., parti-colored. The term red includes all shades of sable, brindle, lemon and orange, but the brighter and clearer the red the better. The white should be clear white, and the color, whether black or red, should be evenly distributed, patches over the body, cheek and ears.

SCALE OF POINTS:	Points
Head and neck	10
Eyes	10
Ears	5
Muzzle	10
Nose	5
Body	15
Tail	10
Feet and legs	5
Coat and markings	15
Action	5
Size	10
TOTAL	100

Disqualification. In black and whites, a nose any other color than black.

MALTESE DOG

THE ORIGIN of few dogs is so puzzling as that of the Maltese, a name which has been famous in dogdom for perhaps 3000 years. No one can be certain that the darling of the Roman and Greek ladies before the time of Christ was the same delightful Toy dog which today owns the name.

The Maltese Dog of today is a pure white dog weighing from 2½ to 7 pounds, with hair which completely covers the frame, hanging in an even part from the nose to the tail. Did "Ye Ancient Dogge of

Maltese Dog—Ch. Aennchen's Poona Dancer. (Owner: Frank Oaer star and Larry Ward, Euclid, Ohio). Photo by William E. Kelly.

Malta" fit this description?

No one knows. But research by Baroness Wentworth and others would make it appear that the ancient dog was more of a Pomeranian type.

One section of the famous *Greek Anthology* was devoted to 748 epitaphs, some imaginary and some real, covering the whole range of Greek history. Ash gives a translation of one of these as follows: "The stone on this spot commemorates the swift-footed Maltese, who was the faithful guardian of Eumelos." This dog was called "Bull."

While this sepulchral poem specifically calls the dog a Maltese, it is difficult to imagine a dog, such as the modern Maltese, being described as "swift-footed." Moreover, "Bull" is a most unlikely name for a lady's lap dog.

Pliny Secundus, who was a contemporary of Jesus, quotes Callimachus, as saying that the island of Melita has given its name to a species of small dogs, named Melitae. Was this island the island of Malta?

Strabo, 60 B.C., the most quoted Roman on the subject, would seem to answer this in the negative. As quoted by Topsell, writing in 1607, the passage reads:

There is a towne in Pachynus, a promontory of Sicily called Melita, from whence are transported many fine little Dogs called Melitei canes. They were accounted the jewels of women, but now the said towne is possessed by fishermen, and there is no such reckoning made of those tender little dogs, for these are not bigger than common Ferrets or Weasils, yet are they not small in understanding, nor mutable in their love to men; for which cause they are also nourished tenderly for pleasure; whereupon came the proverbe "Melitea Catella" for one nourished for pleasure, and "Canis Digno Throno," because princes hold them in their hands sitting upon their estate.

Ash relates that, in an effort to solve the puzzle, he examined every work on Malta contained in the British Museum. He states that he could not find a single reference to the Maltese Dog in any of them. He could not say from this, whether visitors to the island simply were not interested in dogs, or whether the breed was no longer kept there.

Perhaps the earliest evidence of the Maltese Dog, as we know him today, comes in Sir Joshua Reynolds' noted painting of Nellie O'Brien. She has a dog of distinct Maltese type in her lap. This picture was painted in 1763.

Whatever the dog's origin, it became quite popular in various parts of Europe and in England after 1800. By that time the dog was known under various other names. Buffon had called him "Chien de Malte," or "Bichon." He appears to have preferred the latter. Still another name was "Shock Dog," apparently derived from the dog's shock of hair.

Richardson, in 1847, gives a good description of the modern dog, about in the terms of a present-day uninitiated dog lover. That is, he describes it as a "small poodle, with silky hair instead of wool, and the short, turned-up nose of the pug."

To add to the puzzle, Richardson traces the pedigree of a famous bitch of the time, Psyche, owned by one Miss Gibbs of Morden. This dog was the offspring of two dogs, Cupid and Psyche, which were bought in Manila, in the Philippines, and not in Malta.

They were shipped from Manila in 1841, as presents for the Queen, but the voyage took eight months and the dogs were in so disreputable a shape upon their arrival in England that the presentation could not be made. The dogs had been imported by Capt. Lukey of the East India Co., and he gave them to his brother, a Mastiff breeder.

Richardson personally studied Psyche. She weighed 3¼ pounds, and her hair measured 15 inches in length "across the shoulders." In a later book, Richardson stated that the dogs should not exceed five pounds in weight, although he reports seeing good ones weighing as much as 6½ pounds. In his 1859 edition, Stonehenge gives a picture of Psyche, which shows her to have been a "modern" dog in most respects.

Commenting on the fact that Psyche's parents came from Manila, Idstone reported that he had seen several excellent Maltese which came from the West Indies.

The first dog show class for Maltese was given in London at the Agricultural Hall in 1862. After that, the breed increased its popularity until about 1880. It held its own until World War I, and then began to die out in England.

Miss Van Oppen of Harlingen, Barnet, led the move to revive the breed. She went directly to Malta to replenish her stock, but could find no Maltese there. "Inquiries resulted in dogs nearly as big as Sheepdogs being offered," she wrote. She eventually purchased stock in Holland and Germany.

When James Watson wrote his famous *The Dog Book* in 1909, he commented that "such a thing as a good Maltese dog is all but unknown in this country, and few seem to care about taking up the fancy . . ."

Yet the breed was already strongly established in Canada. By 1913, there were fair classes of them at widely-spread shows, some even being shown at Victoria City. The most powerful kennel of the period, however, belonged to Mrs. H. E. Short of London, Ontario. First Canadian champion of the breed was Highbury Snow Ball, born June 8, 1908, and imported to Canada from England by Raymond W. Gard of Toronto. Snow Ball won his championship in 1915.

Maltese dogs are strong and, as a rule, very healthy. At various times they have been called Spaniels and Terriers, with the latter name predominating in the United States and Canada. However, because it is obvious that a three-pound dog can hardly be used for sporting purposes, the majority of governing bodies in dogdom now limit the name to Maltese Dog.

Description and Standards. The description and standards, by courtesy of AKC follow:

GENERAL APPEARANCE: The Maltese is a toy dog covered from head to foot with a mantle of long, silky, white hair. He is gentle-mannered and affectionate, eager and sprightly in action, and, despite his size, possessed of the vigor needed for the satisfactory companion.

HEAD: Of medium length and in proportion to the size of the dog. The skull is slightly rounded on top, the stop moderate. The drop ears are rather low set and heavily feathered with long hair that hangs close to the head. Eyes are set not too far apart; they are very dark and round, their black rims enhancing the gentle yet alert expression. The muzzle is of medium length, fine and tapered but not snipy. The nose is black. The teeth meet in an even, edge-to-edge bite, or in a scissors bite.

NECK: Sufficient length of neck is desirable as promoting a high carriage of the head.

BODY: Compact, the height from the withers to the ground equaling the length from the withers to the root of the tail. Shoulder blades are sloping, the elbows well knit and held close to the body. The back is level in topline, the ribs well sprung. The chest is fairly deep, the loins taut, strong, and just slightly tucked up underneath.

TAIL: A long-haired plume carried gracefully over the back, its tip lying to the side over the quarter.

LEGS AND FEET: Legs are fine-boned and nicely feathered.

Maltese Dog—An adult pair imported some years ago from Europe by Dr. and Mrs. Vincenzo Calvares of Concord, Mass. These dogs are not terriers, but of the spaniel family. Acme News Photo.

Forelegs are straight, their pastern joints well knit and devoid of appreciable bend. Hind legs are strong and moderately angulated at stifles and hocks. The feet are small and round, with toe pads black. Scraggly hairs on the feet may be trimmed to give a neater appearance.

COAT AND COLOR: The coat is single, that is, without undercoat. It hangs long, flat, and silky over the sides of the body almost, if not quite, to the ground. The long head-hair may be tied up in a knot or it may be left hanging. Any suggestion of kinkiness, curliness, or woolly texture is objectionable. Color, pure white. Light tan or lemon on the ears is permissible, but not desirable.

SIZE: Weight under 7 pounds, with from 4 to 6 pounds preferred. Over-all quality is to be favored over size.

GAIT: The Maltese moves with a jaunty, smooth, flowing gait. Viewed from the side, he gives an impression of rapid movement, size considered. In the stride, the forelegs reach straight and free from the shoulders, with elbows close. Hind legs to move in a straight line. Cowhocks or any suggestion of hind leg toeing in or out are faults.

TEMPERAMENT: For all his diminutive size, the Maltese seems to be without fear. His trust and affectionate responsiveness are very appealing. He is among the gentlest mannered of all little dogs, yet he is lively and playful as well as vigorous.

(November 12, 1963)

PAPILLON

WHEN A typical Papillon has his ears erect, they have the appearance of butterfly wings attached to the head. And it is from this that the dog gets his name of Papillon, meaning butterfly. In France, however, the breed is sometimes called Le Chien Ecureuil, or Squirrel Dog, this having reference to the dog's beautiful tail.

The breed is supposed to have developed from a mutation in the Belgian Spaniel, called Epagneul Nain. The mutation brought about the outspread, or butterfly ears. The hanging ear is, however, common, and both types may appear in the same litter. There is no discrimination against the hanging ear in the judging ring.

The breed is believed to be quite old. One account states that a Bologna dog dealer, Giovani Filliponi, introduced the breed to France, by selling one to Louis XIV. Paintings dating from one in 1688 by Abraham Van Du Temple of Antwerp, show dogs presumably of this type.

Some writers have noted the similarity of the breed to the Chihuahua, and have suggested that the dog originated in Latin America. But there is no real evidence to show any connection.

The breed was granted recognition in England in 1923. Though the dogs appeared in this country much earlier, a parent club was not organized for the breed until the formation of the Papillon Club of America in 1935. This club adopted the standard of the Southern Counties Papillon Society of England, and the American Kennel Club, in turn, approved this standard.

Description and Standards.

GENERAL APPEARANCE: The Papillon is a small, friendly, elegant toy dog of fine-boned structure, light, dainty and of lively action; distinguished from other breeds by its beautiful, butterfly-like ears.

HEAD: Small. The skull of medium width, and slightly rounded between the ears. A well-defined stop is formed where the muzzle joins the skull. The muzzle is fine, abruptly thinner than the head, tapering to the nose. The length of the muzzle from the tip of nose to stop is approximately one-third the length of the head from tip of nose to occiput.

NOSE: Black, small, rounded, and slightly flat on top. *Disqualification:* Pink, spotted or liver-colored.

EYES: Dark, round, not bulging, of medium size and alert in expression. The inner corner of the eye is on a line with the stop. Eye rims black.

MOUTH: Lips are tight, thin, and black. Teeth meet in a scissor bite. Tongue must not be visible when jaws are closed. *Fault:* Overshot or undershot.

EARS: The ears of either the erect or drop type should be large with rounded tips and set on the sides and towards the back of the head. (1) Ears of the erect type are carried obliquely and move like the spread wings of a butterfly. When alert, each ear forms an angle of approximately 45 degrees to the head. The leather should be of sufficient strength to maintain the erect position. (2) Ears of the drop type, known as Phalene, are similar to the erect type, but are carried drooping and must be completely down. *Fault:* Ears small, pointed, set too high, one ear up or ears partly down.

NECK: Of medium length.

BODY: Must be slightly longer than the height at the withers. It is not a cobby dog. Topline straight and level. The chest is a medium depth with well-sprung ribs. The belly is tucked up. Forequarters—shoulders well developed and laid back to allow freedom of movement. Forelegs—slender, fine-boned and must be straight. Removal of dewclaws on forelegs optional. Hindquarters—well developed and well angulated. Hocks inclined neither in nor out. The hind legs are slender, fine-boned and parallel when viewed from behind. Dewclaws, if any, must be removed from hind legs. Feet—thin and elongated (harelike), pointing neither in nor out.

TAIL: Long, set high and carried well arched over the body. The plume may hang to either side of the body. *Fault:* Low-set tail, one not arched over back or too short.

COAT: Abundant, long, fine, silky, flowing, straight with resilient quality, flat on back and sides of body. A profuse frill on chest. There is no undercoat. Hair short and close on skull, muzzle, front of forelegs and from hind feet to hocks. Ears well fringed with the inside covered with silken hair of medium length. Backs of the forelegs are covered with feathers diminishing to the pasterns. Hind legs are covered to the hocks with abundant breeches (culottes). Tail is covered with a long, flowing plume. Hair on feet is short, but fine tufts may appear over toes and grow beyond them forming a point.

SIZE: Height at highest point of shoulder blades 8 to 11 inches. Weight is in proportion to height. *Fault:* Over 11 inches. Over 12 inches disqualifies.

GAIT: Free, quick, easy, graceful, not paddle-footed, nor stiff in hip movements.

COLOR: White predominates, with patches which may be any color except liver. Also tri-colored (black and white with tan spots over the eyes, on the cheeks, in the ears and under the tail). Color must cover both ears and extend over both eyes. A clearly defined white blaze and noseband together with symmetrical head markings are preferable but not essential. The size, shape and placement of the patches on the body are without importance. A saddle is permissible. Among the allowable colors there is no preference. *Disqualification:* Liver color, coat of solid color, all white or one with no white, white patches on ears or around eyes. *Disqualifications:* Pink, spotted or liver-colored.

HEIGHT: Over 12 inches.

COLOR: Liver color, coat of solid color, all white, or one with no white, white patches on ears or around eyes.

(June 8, 1965)

Puppy, left, sits beside her Papillon mother. Acme Photo.

PEKINGESE

IN ALL the dog kingdom no breed owns a more romantic history than the Pekingese. The palace dogs of the ancient Chinese emperors were not the same as the Pekingese we know today, for they were undoubtedly much larger. Yet the same distinctive Lion dog type is known to have been well established many, many years ago. The type can be identified in Korean bronze of 2000 B.C.

There have never been any lions in China, yet for centuries the dog we know as the Pekingese has been called the little Lion Dog of Peking. China embraced Buddhism in the first century, during the reign of Emperor Ming-ti. It was natural that the lion of Buddha should become the nation's sacred symbol.

But there were no lions in China and the provision of models for Chinese artists presented a problem. In the belief that the Chinese tigers and the lion were related, artists devised the curious tiger-lion which appears in the work of that period. Visitors from other Buddha-worshipping countries, however, called attention to the fact that there was considerable similarity in the appearance of the Emperor's palace dogs and the Buddhist symbols . . . and the problem of the artists was solved. The Emperor's dogs became the models, were forthwith called Lion Dogs, and played an important part in the Chinese Buddhist art of the next 2000 years.

The little Lion Dog became a sacred symbol. He was surrounded by royal restrictions and his breeding was strictly confined to the environs of the Court under the supervision of the Chief Eunuchs. He was treated with the greatest of care, all puppies being brought to the Emperor for personal selection.

The Emperor's dogs lived in the sacred temple and it is said that the puppies were often nursed by slave girls whose unwanted girl babies were killed at birth.

Four dogs were personally selected by the Emperor as his own bodyguard. Highest officials paid them honor. They preceded the Emperor to the Chamber of Ceremonials on occasions of state, two of them announcing his approach at correct intervals with short, piercing barks. The other two daintily held the hem of the royal robes in their mouths. Theft of, or damage to, a royal dog was punishable by a torturous death. The efficaciousness of the stringent restrictions placed around them is proved by the complete lack of evidence that any of the sacred dogs strayed beyond the province of the palaces for many centuries.

The looting of the Imperial Palace at Peking by the British in 1860 brought about the first introduction of the Pekingese into the western world. Rather than face the enemy troops in defeat, the aunt of the Chinese Emperor committed suicide and four Pekingese were found guarding her body. Throughout the castle bodies of these little dogs were found, the Chinese preferring to kill them rather than let them fall into the hands of the British. One of the dogs of the Emperor's aunt was brought to England by a Lieutenant Dunne and was presented to Queen Victoria, who gave it the appropriate name of "Looty." This dog was fawn and white in color. The others were appropriated by Admiral John Hay, and taken to Goodwood Castle, becoming the foundation stock of the Goodwood strain.

Towards the end of the nineteenth century, the Dowager Empress T'Zŭ Hsi, then acting as Regent for her infant son, became quite friendly with the American people, showing her favor by making gifts of some of these dogs. Among the recipients were the then Alice Roosevelt and the late J. P. Morgan. Few of these dogs were used for breeding purposes after they came to America and most of the American breeding stock came from England.

The following poem, from which the present standard is said to have been evolved, is attributed to the Empress T'Zŭ Hsi and was translated by the distinguished English writer, Mrs. Coath Dixey, author of *Lion Dog of Peking:*

Let the Lion Dog be small, let it wear the swelling cape of dignity around its neck, let it display the billowing standard of pomp over its back.

Let its face be black, let its forefront be shaggy, let its forehead be straight and low, like unto the brow of an Imperial harmony boxer.

For its colour let it be that of the lion, a golden sable, to be carried in the sleeve of a yellow robe, or the colour of a red bear, or striped like a dragon, so that there may be dogs appropriate to every costume in the Imperial wardrobe.

Whose fitness to appear at public ceremonies and functions shall be judged by their colour, and by their artistic contrast with the Imperial robes.

Let it venerate its ancestors and deposit offerings in the Canine Cemetery of the Forbidden City on each new moon.

Let it be taught to refrain from gadding about, let it comfort itself with the dignity of a Duchess.

Let it learn to instantly bite the foreign devils!

Let it wash its face like a cat with its paws, let it be dainty in its food, that it shall be known for a Royal and Imperial dog by its fastidiousness.

Let its eyes be large and luminous, let its ears be set like the sails of a war junk, let its nose be like that of the Monkey God of the Hindu.

Let its forelegs be bent so that it shall not desire to wander far or leave the Imperial precincts.

Let its body be shaped like that of a hunting lion spying for its prey.

Let its feet be tufted with plentiful hair that its footfalls may be noiseless, and for its standard of pomp, let it rival the whisk of the Tibetan yak, which is flourished to protect the Imperial litter from the attacks of flying insects.

Let it be lively that it may afford entertainment by its gambols, let it be wary that it may not involve itself in danger, let it be sociable in its habits, that it may live in amity with the other beasts, fishes or birds that find protection in the Imperial Palace.

Sharks' fins and curlews' livers and the breasts of quails, on these may it be fed, and for drink give it the tea that is brewed from the Spring buds of the bush that groweth in the province of Han Kon, or the milk of the antelopes that pasture in the Imperial parks, or broth made from the nests of sea swallows.

Thus shall it preserve its integrity and self respect, and in the day of sickness let it be anointed with the clarified fat of the leg of a sacred leopard and give it to drink a throstle's egg shell—full of the juice of the custard apple in which has been dissolved three pinches of shredded rhinocerous horn—and apply to it piebald leaches.

So shall it remain, but if it die, remember that thou, too, art mortal . . .

The Ladies' Kennel Association made room for the breed in the bench show activities in England, establishing a Pekingese classification in 1898. The breed caught on rapidly and six years later the Pekingese Club was formed. Ah Cum and Mimosa, two reds belonging to Mrs. Douglas Murray, did much to strengthen the breed in England.

The Pekingese is regarded as a favorite toy breed in Australia, Germany, South Africa, and Sweden; the breed is also extremely popular in America and Great Britain.

The breed is exceedingly popular in this country and now occupies a commanding position in America's dog world. The Pekingese is noted for his courage and seldom shows any fear of anything. On the world in general he apparently looks with a condescending attitude, although in the privacy of the home of his family he seems to like to drop his dignity for the pleasures of a rollicking romp.

Description and Standards. The description and standards, adopted by the Pekingese Club of America and approved by the American Kennel Club follow.

EXPRESSION: Must suggest the Chinese origin of the Pekingese in its quaintness and individuality resemblance to the lion in directness and independence and should imply courage, boldness, self-esteem and combativeness rather than prettiness, daintiness or delicacy.

Pekingese—A rare black one. Photo by A. C. Bauer.

SKULL: Massive, broad, wide and flat between the ears (not dome shaped) wide between the eyes.

NOSE: Black, broad, very short and flat.

EYES: Large, dark, prominent, round, lustrous.

STOP: Deep.

EARS: Heart shaped, not set too high, leather never long enough to come below the muzzle, nor carried erect, but rather drooping, long feather.

MUZZLE: Wrinkled, very short and broad, not overshot nor pointed. Strong, broad under jaw, teeth not to show.

SHAPE OF BODY: Heavy in front, well sprung ribs, broad chest, falling away lighter behind, lion-like. Back level, not too long in body; allowance made for longer body in bitch.

LEGS: Short fore legs, bones of forearm bowed, firm at shoulder; hind legs lighter but firm and well shaped.

FEET: Flat, toes turned out, not round, should stand well up on feet, not on ankles.

ACTION: Fearless, free and strong, with slight roll.

COAT, FEATHER, AND CONDITION: Long, with thick under coat, straight and flat, not curly nor wavy, rather coarse, but soft; feather on thighs, legs, tail and toes long and profuse.

MANE: Profuse, extending beyond the shoulder blades, forming ruff or frill round the neck.

COLOR: All colors are allowable. Red, fawn, black, black and tan, sable, brindle, white and parti-color well defined; black masks and spectacles around the eyes, with lines to ears are desirable.

DEFINITION OF A PARTI-COLOR PEKINGESE: The coloring of a parti-colored dog must be broken on the body. No large portion of any one color should exist. White should be shown on the saddle. A dog of any solid color with white feet and chest is *not* a parti-color.

TAIL: Set high, lying well over back to either side; long, profuse, straight feather.

SIZE: Being a toy dog, medium size preferred, providing type and points are not sacrificed; extreme limit 14 pounds.

SCALE OF POINTS:	*Points*
Expression	5
Skull	10
Nose	5
Eyes	5
Stop	5
Ears	5
Muzzle	5
Shape of body	15
Legs and feet	15
Coat, feather and condition	15
Tail	5
Action	10
TOTAL	100

PENALIZATIONS: Protruding tongue, badly blemished eye, overshot, wry mouth.

DISQUALIFICATIONS: Weight—over 14 pounds; Dudley nose.

MINIATURE PINSCHER

THE CONSTANT desire to improve species of livestock has resulted in the development of a number of "manufactured" breeds in the dog family. Most of these experiments have been carefully planned toward a certain goal and most of them have eventually proved satisfactory. Once a breed has been established there has been an occasional desire to increase or decrease its size. Usually this desire has been on the part of breeders who fancy Toy dogs.

The Doberman Pinscher may well be termed a "manufactured" breed. And the Miniature Pinscher is the result of the desire of some Doberman Pinscher fanciers to produce a small edition of their favorite breed. Almost as soon as the Doberman came into being as an established breed, fanciers of the small type of dog began their efforts to "breed down" and create a separate breed that would retain the Doberman's general characteristics and appearance and yet mature into much smaller dogs in height and weight. Their efforts were quickly rewarded, and the Miniature Pinscher made its appearance as a breed which ran true to type even before the Doberman Pinscher was "officially" recognized as a distinct breed.

The Miniature Pinscher was first recognized by what is now called the Pinscher Schnauzer Klub, originally organized in Germany in 1895 as the Pinscher Klub. Ten years later the small dog began to attract much attention, and this interest maintained until World War I interfered with serious dog breeding activities all over Europe. Soon after hostilities ceased, breeding activities were resumed and several of these little fellows were imported to this country.

A few were exhibited in the miscellaneous class during the next ten years, and in 1929 the Miniature Pinscher Club of America was organized, bringing about an upswing in breeding activities. The breed now enjoys considerable popularity in this country.

The Miniature Pinscher is ideal for the fancier who wants a lively, alert, bold little house dog that always presents a neat, clean appearance and possesses an affectionate disposition, particularly toward its master or the family.

The Miniature Pinscher is regarded as the favorite toy breed in Denmark, Holland, and Italy.

Description and Standards. The description and standards adopted by the Miniature Pinscher Club of America, Inc., and approved by the American Kennel Club, follow.

GENERAL APPEARANCE: The Miniature Pinscher was originated in Germany and named the "Reh Pinscher" due to his resemblance in structure and animation to a very small specie of deer found in the forests. This breed is structurally a well-balanced, sturdy, compact, short-coupled, smooth-coated toy dog. He is naturally well groomed, proud, vigorous and alert. The natural characteristic traits which identify him from other toy dogs are his precise Hackney gait, his fearless animation, complete self-possession, and his spirited presence.

Faults—Structurally lacking in balance, too long- or short-coupled, too coarse or too refined (lacking in bone development causing poor feet and legs), too large or too small, lethargic, timid or dull, shy or vicious, low in tail placement and poor in action (action not typical of the breed requirements). Knotty overdeveloped muscles.

HEAD: In correct proportion with the body. *From Top:* Tapering, narrow with well-fitted but not too prominent foreface which should balance with the skull. No indication of coarseness. *From Front:* Skull appears flat, tapering forward toward the muzzle. Muzzle itself strong rather than fine and delicate, and in proportion to the head as a whole; cheeks and lips small, taut and closely adherent to each other. Teeth in perfect alignment and apposition. *From Side:* Well-balanced with only a slight drop to the muzzle, which should be parallel to the top of the skull.

EYES: Full, slightly oval, almost round, clear, bright and dark even to a true black; set wide apart and fitted well into the sockets.

EARS: Well-set and firmly placed, upstanding (when cropped, pointed and carried erect in balance with the head).

NOSE: Black only (with the exception of chocolates, which may have a self-colored nose).

Faults—Too large or too small for the body, too coarse or too refined, pinched and weak in foreface, domed in skull, too flat and lacking in chiseling, giving a vapid expression. Jaws and teeth overshot or undershot. Eyes too round and full, too large, bulging, too deep-set or set too far apart; or too small, set too close (pig eyes). Light-colored eyes not desirable. Ears poorly placed, low-set hanging ears (lacking in cartilage) which detract from head conformation. (Poorly cropped ears if set on the head properly and having sufficient cartilage should not detract from head points, as this would be a man-made fault and automatically would detract from general appearance.) Nose any color other than black (with the exception of chocolates which may have a self-colored nose).

NECK: Proportioned to head and body. Slightly arched, gracefully curved, clean and firm, blending into shoulders, length well-balanced, muscular and free from a suggestion of dewlap or throatiness. *Faults*—Too straight or too curved; too thick or too thin; too long or short; knotty muscles; loose, flabby or wrinkled skin.

BODY: *From Top:* Compact, slightly wedge-shaped, muscular with well-sprung ribs. *From Side:* Depth of brisket, the base line of which is level with the points of the elbows; short and strong in loin with belly moderately tucked up to denote grace in structural form. Back level or slightly sloping toward the rear. Length of males equals height at withers. Females may be slightly longer. *From Rear:* High tail-set; strong, sturdy upper shanks, with croup slope at about 30 degrees; vent opening not barreled.

FOREQUARTERS: Forechest well-developed and full, moderately broad, shoulders clean, sloping with moderate angulation, co-ordinated to permit the true action of the Hackney pony.

HINDQUARTERS: Well-knit muscular quarters set wide enough apart to fit into a properly balanced body.

Faults—*From top*—too long, too short, too barreled, lacking in body development. *From side*—too long, too short, too thin or too fat, hips higher or considerably lower than the withers, lacking depth of chest, too full in loin, sway back, roach back or wry back. *From rear*—quarters too wide or too close to each other, overdeveloped, barreled vent, underdeveloped vent, too sloping croup, tail set low. *Forequarters*—forechest and spring of rib too narrow (or too shallow and underdeveloped), shoulders too straight, too loose, or too short and overloaded with muscles. *Hindquarters*—too narrow, undermuscled or overmuscled, too steep in croup.

LEGS AND FEET: Strong bone development and small clean joints; feet catlike, toes strong, well-arched and closely knit with deep pads and thick, blunt nails.

FORELEGS AND FEET: As viewed from the front straight and upstanding, elbows close to body, well-knit, flexible yet strong with perpendicular pasterns.

HIND LEGS: All adjacent bones should appear well-angulated with well-muscled thighs or upper shanks, with clearly well-defined stifles, hocks short, set well apart turning neither in or out, while at rest should stand perpendicular to the ground and upper shanks, lower shanks and hocks parallel to each other. *Faults*—Too thick or thin bone development, large joints, spreading flat feet. Forelegs and Feet—bowed or crooked, weak pasterns, feet turning in or out, loose elbows. Hind legs—thin undeveloped stifles, large or crooked hocks, loose stifle joints.

TAIL: Set high, held erect, docked to ½ to 1 inch. *Faults*—Set too low, too thin, drooping, hanging or poorly docked.

COAT: Smooth, hard and short, straight and lustrous, closely adhering to and uniformly covering the body. *Faults*—Thin, too long, dull; upstanding; curly; dry, area of various thickness or bald spots.

COLOR: 1. Solid red or stag red. 2. Lustrous black with sharply defined tan, rust-red markings on cheeks, lips, lower jaw, throat, twin spots above eyes and chest, lower half of forelegs, inside of hind legs and vent region, lower portion of hocks and feet. Black pencil stripes on toes. 3. Solid brown or chocolate with rust or yellow markings. *Faults*—Any color other than listed; very dark or sooty spots.

DISQUALIFICATIONS: Thumb marks or any area of white on feet or forechest exceeding one-half (½) inch in its longest dimension.

SIZE: Desired height 11 inches to 11½ inches at the withers. A dog of either sex measuring under 10 inches or over 12½ inches shall be disqualified. *Faults*—Oversize; undersize; too fat; too lean.

SCALE OF POINTS:

	Points
General appearance and movement —*(very important)*	30
Skull	5
Muzzle	5
Mouth	5
Eyes	5
Ears	5
Neck	5
Body	15
Feet	5
Legs	5

Miniature Pinscher.

Color	5
Coat	5
Tail	5
TOTAL	100

Disqualifications. Color—Thumb marks or any area of white on feet or forechest exceeding one-half (½) inch in its longest dimension. *Size*—A dog of either sex measuring under 10 or over 12½ inches.

(May 13, 1958)

POMERANIAN

NOW RUNNING in weight slightly over or less than seven pounds, the Pomeranian originally was a rather large dog weighing upwards of 30 pounds. It is generally accepted that its ancestors was the large white Spitz dog bred down from the Iceland and Lapland sledge-dogs. The sharp and foxy muzzle, small, erect, and pointed ears, fluffy coat and curling plumed tail are all characteristics of the dogs of the Spitz group.

The breed derives its name from Pomerania, yet some authorities claim that the dog existed before the country, and, very much in its present form, was a favorite of the ladies of Rome and Greece. Practically all of the old descriptions refer to the Pomerian as the wolf and sheep dog of its native country, which is sufficient evidence that some of the breed, at least, must have been dogs large enough to do the hard work required. Almost invariably the Keeshond is comparatively mentioned whenever the Pomeranian's origin is discussed. Certainly the breed, in its original form, was not confined to the northern part of Germany, for somewhat similar dogs were found in many parts of the world.

Queen Victoria brought a small dog of this type from Florence in 1888, where she had gone to spend a winter, and it was her favorite for a number of years. This marked the beginning of the breed's popularity in England, for the first importations met with considerable indifference, if not downright prejudice. Queen Victoria founded a kennel and was a frequent exhibitor of Pomeranians.

In the early part of the nineteenth century, the Pomeranians in England were dogs weighing around 30 pounds. Occasionally one or two puppies in a litter would be unusually small. At first these were destroyed. Later it was found that they would fully mature, yet were of much smaller size than their parents. The same luxuriant growth of coat maintained and these small dogs began to attract much attention, particularly when shown with normal-size members of their own breed. These smaller dogs weighed around 16 pounds and its was quite unusual to find one which weighed as little as 12 pounds.

Despite this change in type, the breed failed to catch the fancy of the English until Queen Victoria's interest gave it a terrific boost. Breeders found that they could produce smaller dogs without sacrificing coat or character. Also other colors could be brought

Pomeranian—Ch. Sunaold's Gay Cavalier. (Owner: Mrs. Edna E. Girardot, Scotia, New York) Photo by Evelyn M. Shafer.

in. These features of smaller and brilliant colors in various shades made the breed much more fashionable. The sable color was developed and became the rage, dogs of this color bringing high prices and being much in demand. Many of these small dogs were exported to other countries and so the breed's popularity spread. Although the fanciers of the larger dogs continued breeding, the smaller type went far ahead of the original stock in numbers and popularity. Finally the larger type all but disappeared, and Pomeranians weighing four and five pounds were not at all uncommon.

Pomeranians first appeared in this country in 1899. This charming little fellow, with his prideful, vivacious manner, never fails to attract attention in the show ring. He possesses an alert spirit which makes him an excellent watchdog, and while he is quite bold, his temper is even.

Description and Standards. The description and standards, by courtesy of the American Pomeranian Club, follow.

APPEARANCE: The Pomeranian in build and appearance should be a compact, short-coupled dog, well-knit in frame. He should exhibit great intelligence in his expression, docility in his disposition, and activity and buoyancy in his deportment, and be sound in action.

HEAD: The head should be wedge-shaped, somewhat foxy in outline, the skull being slightly flat, large in proportion to the muzzle. In its profile it has a little stop which must not be too pronounced, and the hair on the head and face must be smooth or short-coated. The muzzle should finish rather fine. The teeth should meet in a scissors grip, in which part of the inner surface of the upper teeth meets and engages part of the outer surface of the lower teeth. This type of bite gives a firmer grip than one in which the edges of the teeth meet directly, and is subject to less wear. The mouth is considered *overshot* when the lower teeth fail to engage the inner surfaces of the upper teeth. The mouth is *undershot* when the lower teeth protrude beyond the upper teeth. One tooth out of line does not mean an undershot or overshot mouth. *Eyes*—The eyes should be medium in size, rather oblique in shape, not set too wide apart, or too close together, bright and dark in color. The eye rims of the blues and browns are self-colored. In all other colors the eye rims must be black. *Ears*—The ears should be small, not set too far apart or too low down, and carried perfectly erect, and should be covered with soft, short hair. Trimming unruly hairs on edges of ears permissible. *Nose*—Should be self-colored in blues and browns. In all other colors should be black.

NECK AND SHOULDERS: The neck rather short, well set in, and lionlike, covered with a profuse mane and frill of long, straight hair sweeping from the underjaw and covering the whole of the front part of the shoulders and chest as well as the top part of the shoulders. The shoulders must be clean and laid well back.

BODY: The back must be short and level, and the body compact, being well ribbed up and rounded. The chest must be fairly deep.

LEGS: The forelegs must be well feathered and perfectly straight, of medium length and strength in due proportion to a well-balanced frame. The feet small, compact in shape, standing well up on toes. The hind legs and thighs must be well feathered down to the hocks, and must be fine in bone and free in action. Trimming around the edges of the toes and up the back of the legs to the first joint is permissible.

TAIL: The tail is characteristic of the breed, and should be turned over the back and carried flat, set high. It is profusely covered with long, spreading hair.

COAT: There should be two coats, an under- and an over coat; the first a soft, fluffy undercoat, and the other a long, perfectly straight and glistening coat covering the whole body, being very abundant around the neck and forepart of the shoulders and chest where it should form a frill of profuse, standing-off, straight hair extending over the shoulders. The hindquarters should be clad with long hair or feathering from top of rump to the hocks. The texture of the guard hairs must be harsh to the touch.

COLOR: Twelve colors, or color combinations, are permissible and recognized, namely, black, brown, chocolate, beaver, red, orange, cream, orange-sable, wolf-sable, blue, white, and parti-color. The beaver color is a dark beige. A parti-color dog is white with orange or black color distributed in even patches on the body, with white blaze on head desirable. Where whole-colored and parti-colored Pomeranians compete together, the preference should, other points being equal, be given to the whole-colored specimen. Sable-colored dogs must be shaded throughout as uniformly as possible, with no self-colored patches. In orange-sable, the undercoat must be a light tan with deeper orange guard hairs ending in black tippings. In wolf-sable, the undercoat is light gray with a deeper shade of steel-gray guard hairs ending in black tippings. A shaded muzzle on the sables is permissible, but a black mask on sables is a minor fault. Orange Pomeranians must be self-colored throughout, with light shadings of the same tone (not white) on breechings permitted. A black mask on an orange Pomeranian is a major fault. White chest, white foot, or white leg on whole-colored dogs are major faults. White hairs on black, brown, blue or sable Pomeranians are objectionable. Tinges of lemon or any other color on white dogs are objectionable. The above colors, as described, are the only allowable colors or combination of colors for Pomeranians.

SIZE: The weight of a Pomeranian for exhibition is 3 pounds to 7 pounds. The ideal size for show specimens is from 4 to 5 pounds.

CLASSIFICATION: The classes for Pomeranians may be divided by color in open classes as follows: Black and brown; red, orange or cream; sable. Any other allowable color.

FAULTS

Major—Round, domey skull. Too large ears. Undershot. Pink eye rims. Light or Dudley nose. Out at elbows or shoulders. Flat-sided dogs. Down in pasterns. Cowhock. Soft, flat, open coat. Whole-colored dogs with white chest, or white foot or leg. Black mask on an orange. *Objectionable*—Overshot. Large,

round or light eyes. High or low on legs. Long toes. Too wide in hind legs. Trimming too close to show date. Tail set too low on rump. Black, brown, blue, and sable should be free from white hairs. Whites should be free from lemon or any other color. Black and tan. Underweight or overweight. *Minor*—Must be free from lippiness, wide chest. Tail should not curl back. Black mask on sable. White shadings on orange.

(April 12, 1960)

SILKY TERRIER

DURING THE comparatively short span of time this appealing Toy breed has been known it has gathered three different names. Founded in the Sydney Area of New South Wales, it was first called the Sydney Silky Terrier and first exhibited as such in Australia in 1907. Two years later, along with the formation of the Victorian Silky and Yorkshire Terrier Club, a Standard was drawn up, and about the same period exports were made to India and to Great Britain. In 1955, their name became the Australian Silky Terrier, and officially carried by all Australian Kennel Clubs. Regarded as a distinct breed in its homeland for more than 25 years, stud book records were maintained by both the Royal Agricultural Society Kennel Club and the Kennel Control Council. American sponsors of the breed adopted the name, Silky Terrier, and under that name it became admitted to the American Kennel Club stud book in 1959.

Early Australian breeders created the Silky mainly from crosses between the Australian Terrier and the Yorkshire Terrier, whether deliberately or accidentally is not known. In any case, eventual development by patient selection and skill produced a dog of eight to ten pounds with silky-textured hair of blue and tan and a character and conformation all its own. Designed as a companion pet, the Silky was never a working dog in the bushland like most Australian breeds. Nevertheless, its forceful terrier quality made its valuable to cottage dwellers who claimed the Silky helped control rats and even snakes on poultry farms.

As far back as 1947 American fanciers had given

Silky Terrier—Ch. Milan Miss Sandra of Iradell. (Owner: Iradell Kennels, Ridgefield, Conn.) Photo by Evelyn M. Shafer.

thought to founding a breed club in the United States and during the summer and fall of 1954 several Silky owners and breeders in the Bay Area of San Francisco began to pool their lists of owners to further that goal. This group included Mrs. Margaret Citrino of Mill Valley, Mrs. Florence Dahlstrom of Sausalito, Thomas J. Fromm of Berkeley, and Robert E. Garrett and Howard A. Jensen of San Francisco. Col. and Mrs. N. Clarkson Earl, Jr. became pioneers of the breed in the East, importing foundation stock for their Iradell Kennels in Ridgefield, Conn. starting in 1957. Their Milan Chips of Iradell, imported in 1958, became the first American champion of the breed.

Lightly built and rather low set, there is pronounced terrier spirit in this small toy dog, a quality considered so important by the Silky breed's fanciers that it is written in the Standard. Also included in the Standard is reference to maintaining size so as to avoid accentuating "toyishness as opposed to definite terrier character."

Description and Standards. The Silky Terrier is a lightly built, moderately low-set toy dog of pronounced terrier character and spirited action.

HEAD: The head is strong, wedge-shaped, and moderately long. The skull is a trifle longer than the muzzle, in proportion about three-fifths for the skull, two-fifths for the muzzle; it is flat, and not too wide between the ears. The stop is shallow.

EARS: Small-V-shaped and pricked. They are set high and carried erect without any tendency to flare obliquely off the skull.

EYES: Small, dark in color, and piercingly keen in expression. Light eyes are a fault.

TEETH: Strong and well-aligned, scissors bite. A bite markedly undershot or overshot is a serious fault.

NOSE: The nose is black.

NECK AND SHOULDERS: The neck fits gracefully into sloping shoulders. It is medium long, fine and to some degree crested along its top line.

BODY: Low-set, about one-fifth longer than the dog's height at the withers. A too-short body is a fault. The back line is straight, with just a perceptible rounding over the loins. Brisket medium-wide, and deep enough to extend down to the elbows.

TAIL: The tail is set high and carried erect or semi-erect but not over-gay. It is docked and well coated but devoid of plume.

FOREQUARTERS: Well laid back shoulders, together with good angulation at the upper arm, set the forelegs nicely under the body. Forelegs are strong, straight, and rather fine-boned.

HINDQUARTERS: Thighs well muscled and strong, but not so developed as to appear heavy. Legs moderately angulated at stifle and hocks, with the hocks low and equidistant from the hock joints to the ground.

FEET: Small, cat-like, round, compact. Pads are thick and springy while the nails are strong and dark-colored. White or flesh-colored nails are a fault. The feet point straight ahead, with no turning in or out. Dewclaws, if any, are removed.

COAT: Flat, in texture fine, glossy, silky; on matured specimens the desired length of coat from behind the ears to the set-on of tail is from five to six inches. On the top of the head the hair is so profuse as to form a topknot, but long hair on face and ears is objectionable. Legs from knee and hock joint to feet should be free from long hair. The hair is parted on the head and down over the back to the root of the tail.

COLOR: Blue and tan. The blue may be silver-blue, pigeon-blue or slate-blue, the tan deep and rich. The blue extends from the base of the skull to the tip of the tail, down the forelegs to the pasterns, and down the thighs to the hocks. On the tail the blue should be very dark. Tan appears on muzzle and cheeks, around the base of the ears, below the pasterns and hocks, and around the vent. There is a tan spot over each eye. The topknot should be silver or fawn.

TEMPERAMENT: The keenly alert air of the terrier is characteristic, with shyness or excessive nervousness to be faulted. The manner is quick, friendly, responsive.

MOVEMENT: Should be free, light footed, lively and straightforward. Hindquarters should have strong propelling power. Toeing in or out is to be faulted.

SIZE: Weight ranges from eight to ten pounds. Shoulder height from nine to ten inches. Pronounced diminutivess (such as a height of 8 inches) is not desired; it accentuates the quality of toyishness as opposed to the breed's definite terrier character.

(April 14, 1959)

TOY POODLE

THE SMALLEST of the Poodle varieties, known as the Toy Poodle, is generally conceded to be descended directly from the Standard and Miniature Poodles, a "bred down" breed, so to speak. This "breeding down," or diminishing in size, undoubtedly required much selective breeding, but the little fellow apparently possesses all the tendencies and high intelligence of his larger brothers.

At one time a Toy breed called the "White Cuban" was quite popular in England. These dogs were a bit larger to the ground. They were called "sleeve dogs" and were favorites of society. The breed is said to have originated in Cuba, and some authorities believed it was the result of crosses between the German or French white corded Poodles and the Maltese. It was first seen in England in about 1700 and shortly afterwards the Toy Poodle made its appearance. The "White Cuban" is said to have been brought to England from Spain. The present-day type of Toy Poodle, however, is not believed to be related to the "White Cuban."

Toy Poodle—Ch. Harmo Divot. (Owner: Harmo Kennels, Amherst, New Hampshire) Photo by Evelyn M. Shafer.

In fact, Toy Poodles were known to exist in Germany many years before the "White Cuban" appeared in England. They are pictured in the line drawings of the German artist, Dürer. That they were popular in Spain is proved by the paintings of Goya in the latter part of the eighteenth century. How long they had been in Spain before Goya pictured them is not known. The Toy Poodle was also a favorite of members of the court of Louis XVI of France.

Description and Standards. The Standard for the poodle (Toy variety) is the same as for the Standard and the Miniature varieties, except as regards height. (*See also* Poodle, Group VI.)

PUG

THERE HAS long been considerable speculation about the place of origin of the Pug. As he is sometimes called the "Dutch Dog," it is natural for many to assume that Holland was his first home. True, the dog was extremely popular in that country, but the preponderance of the evidence points to China as his birthplace. In fact, most of the Toy dogs with short noses and large heads and tails curled over their backs originated in that country.

Dutch traders did a lively business in China, and the breed was introduced into England from Holland. Yet most of the best English dogs of the late nineteenth century and American dogs of the early twentieth century traced back to Click, a dog of pure Chinese breeding. While the Pug was popular in Holland, it is notable that little attention was paid to him by the painters of that nation, many of whom used dogs of various breeds in their best works.

Among the early fanciers in England were Lord and Lady Willoughby D'Eresby, Charles Morrison, and Mrs. Laura Mayhew. Mrs. Mayhew owned Click, an apricot fawn dog that became the outstanding sire of the earliest days. He was sired by Lamb, a dog from Pekin, and his dam was Moss, said to belong to Lord Willoughby. This noted fancier is said to have obtained his original stock from a tight-rope walker billed as the female Blondin, who brought her dogs from Russia. There were silver fawn, somewhat smutty, in color. They had better wrinkling than the dogs from Holland but had pinched faces and small eyes. Click is said to have been the cross needed for these dogs to produce the desired type. Reginald F. Mayhew, Mrs. Mayhew's son, stated that Moss, the dam of Click, was definitely of Chinese breeding, although rumor had it that Click's parents were lemon and white Japanese Spaniels.

Mr. Morrison's dogs were a bright golden color. His dogs became particularly well known as he operated a well-patronized hostelry and many guests saw them. Color was the distinguishing difference between these strains and they were freely interbred.

Pug—American, Canadian, Cuban and Bermudian Ch. Pugville' Mighty Jim. (Owner: Mrs. F. Doherty, Pugsville Kennels, Bernards ville, New Jersey)

The first black Pug to be exhibited in England was one belonging to Lady Brasey, who exhibited it at the Maidstone show in about 1866. It is said that the black Pug came from an infusion of blood from the Japanese Pug. This breed was white or black or white and black. Some black Pugs of today have a tendency to show a bit of white on the chest and feet.

Among the earliest American fanciers were Drs. Cryer and Ivy. Dr. Cryer's Roderick is said to have been the first Pug of quality to be shown in this country. Roderick had his faults, however, as his hind legs were straight to the extent of being double-jointed.

The Pug enjoyed a long period of popularity in this country, but the importation of other Toy dogs, such as the Pomeranian and Japanese Spaniels, sent them on the down grade and for a time but few were to be seen at dog shows.

The Pug is an affable little fellow, full of spunk and needing far less care than other members of the Toy group. He is essentially a house dog and needs the warmth and comfort of the interior. In recent years he has gained back much of his lost popularity. The Pug is regarded as a favorite toy breed in New Zealand.

Description and Standards. The description and standards, by courtesy of the Pug Dog Club, England, follow:

SYMMETRY: Symmetry and general appearance, decidedly square and cobby. A lean, leggy Pug and a dog with short legs and a long body are equally objectionable.

SIZE AND CONDITION: The Pug should be *multum in parvo*, but this condensation (if the word may be used) should be shown by compactness of form, well-knit proportions, and hardness of developed muscle. Weight from 14 to 18 pounds (dog or bitch) desirable.

BODY: Short and cobby, wide in chest and well ribbed-up.

LEGS: Very strong, straight, of moderate length, and well under.

FEET: Neither so long as the foot of the hare, nor so round as that of the cat; well split-up toes, and the nails black.

MUZZLE: Short, blunt, square, but not upfaced.

HEAD: Large, massive, round—not apple-headed, with no indentation of the skull.

EYES: Dark in color, very large, bold and prominent, globular in shape, soft and solicitous in expression, very lustrous, and, when excited, full of fire.

EARS: Thin, small, soft, like black velvet. There are two kinds —the "Rose" and "Button." Preference is given to the latter.

MARKINGS: Clearly defined. The muzzle or mask ears, moles on cheeks, thumb-mark or diamond on forehead, back-trace should be as black as possible.

MASK: The mask should be black. The more intense and well defined it is the better.

WRINKLES: Large and deep.

TRACE: A black line extending from the occiput to the tail.

TAIL: Curled tightly as possible over the hip. The double curl is perfection.

COAT: Fine, smooth, soft, short and glossy, neither hard nor woolly.

COLOR: Silver or apricot-fawn. Each should be decided to make the contrast complete between the color and the trace and the mask. Black.

SCALE OF POINTS:	Fawn	Black
Symmetry	10	10
Size	5	10
Condition	5	5
Body	10	10
Legs and feet	5	5
Head	5	5
Muzzle	10	10
Ears	5	5
Eyes	10	10
Mask	5	...
Wrinkles	5	5
Tail	10	10
Trace	5	...
Coat	5	5
Color	5	10
TOTAL	100	100

Pugs—Pugville's Mighty Jim with three of his offspring.

TOY MANCHESTER TERRIER

THE TOY Manchester Terrier is the result of selective breeding, designed to produce a diminutive dog that retained the good qualities of the foundation stock. At one time the craze for tininess was so great and inbreeding so prevalent that a number of Toy breeds suffered greatly from lack of stamina. This was true with the Toy Manchester Terrier. The breed developed a reputation for being hard to raise, delicate, and unable to withstand anything but extremely careful treatment.

This, naturally, caused the breed to lose in popularity, and fanciers returned to saner breeding practices, the weight average now being about seven pounds without any specific limit. Since that time the breed has been regaining its lost popularity.

Size and the natural ear carriage are the only essential differences between the Manchester Terrier and his small brother. The larger dog weighs about 20 pounds and his ears are naturally semi-erect. The Toy's natural ear carriage is erect. When cropped, the ears are similar in carriage.

It is said that crosses with the Italian Greyhound were made in an effort to bring down the size, but these crosses were unsatisfactory.

Description and Standards. The Standard for the Manchester Terrier (Toy variety) is the same as for the Manchester Terrier except as regards weight and ears. (*See* Manchester Terrier, Group IV.)

SHIH TZU

THE LITTLE Shih Tzu was one of the exotic gift dogs of the Dalai Lamas of Tibet. They gave them to the Emperors of China who back as far as the sixteenth century crossed the beautifully-coated Shih Tzu with the more hardy Pekingese. The Shih Tzu is presumed to be a descendant of the Lhasa Apso, another favorite of the Chinese court. The Tibetan Terrier, Shih Tzu and Pekingese were all known in their early days as Lion Dog and although the Shih Tzu seems to have declined at one time, it is possible that the little gift dog continued under the name Tibetan Terrier, which it closely resembled.

It wasn't until 1930 that the Shih Tzu attracted interest in England and several European countries, and in 1957 The Shih Tzu Club of America was formed. The shaggy little dogs were recognized by the American Kennel Club in 1969.

At maturity the Shih Tzu weighs between 12 and 16 pounds and is about 11 inches tall, the body is longer than it is tall with an upcurled, plumed tail. The head is broad with a square muzzle and the eyes are large and dark. The drop ears of the Shih Tzu

Shih Tzu—Hey Boy of Sangchen. (Owner: Turn Again Lane Kennels, Tryon, North Carolina)

are heavily fringed and the head is covered with hair including a fall over the eyes, a beard, whiskers, and upstanding hair growth on the nose. The legs are short and heavy-boned with large feet nicely haired between the toes. Shih Tzus have long, thick coats that may be any color or combination of colors.

According to one recent newspaper account, the Shih Tzu breed has increased in America from some estimated 300 dogs eight years ago to approximately 3,000 today.

Description and Standards. The following description and standards have been approved by the American Shih Tzu Club Inc. and the AKC.

GENERAL APPEARANCE: Very active, lively and alert, with a distinctly arrogant carriage. The Shih Tzu is proud of bearing as befits his noble ancestry, and walks with head well up and tail carried gaily over the back.

HEAD: Broad and round, wide between the eyes. Muzzle square and short, but not wrinkled, about one inch from tip of nose to stop. Definite stop. *Eyes:* Large, dark and round but not prominent, placed well apart. Eyes should show warm

Shih Tzu puppies. (Owner: Bill-Ora Shih Tzu Kennels, Dallas, Texas) Photo by Will C. Mooney.

expression. *Ears:* Large, with long leathers, and carried drooping; set slightly below the crown of the skull; so heavily coated that they appear to blend with the hair of the neck. *Teeth:* Level or slightly undershot bite.

FOREQUARTERS: Legs short, straight, well boned, muscular, and heavily coated. Legs and feet look massive on account of the wealth of hair.

BODY: Body between the withers and the root of the tail is somewhat longer than the height at the withers; well coupled and sturdy. Chest broad and deep, shoulders firm, back level.

HINDQUARTERS: Legs short, well boned and muscular, are straight when viewed from the rear. Thighs well rounded and muscular. Legs look massive on account of wealth of hair.

FEET: Of good size, firm, well padded, with hair between the pads. Dewclaws, if any, on the hind legs are generally removed. Dewclaws on the forelegs may be removed.

TAIL: Heavily plumed and curved well over the back; carried gaily, set on high.

COAT: A luxurious, long, dense coat. May be slightly wavy but not curly. Good woolly undercoat. The hair on top of the head may be tied up.

COLOR: All colors permissible. Nose and eye rims black, except that dogs with liver markings may have liver noses and slightly lighter eyes.

GAIT: Slightly rolling, smooth and flowing, with strong rear action.

SIZE: Height at withers—9 to 10½ inches—should be no more than 11 inches nor less than 8 inches. Weight of mature dogs—12 to 15 pounds—should be no more than 18 pounds nor less than 9 pounds. However, type and breed characteristics are of the greatest importance.

Faults: Narrow head, overshot bite, snipiness, pink on nose or eye rims, small or light eyes, legginess, sparse coat, lack of definite stop.

(September 1, 1969)

YORKSHIRE TERRIER

CONSIDERABLY less than a hundred years old, the Yorkshire Terrier is definitely a "man-made" breed. Yet the real source of its origin still remains in doubt. In Yorkshire, where the breed was developed and from which it gains its name, the residents kept many Terriers and Toy dogs as companions and undoubtedly many crosses were made among them. This same district also produced the Airedale, the largest of the Terriers, and some authorities have held that the two breeds came from common parentage. The fact that both are born black and tan and change their coat color later adds authority to the premise.

The first dogs to be prominently mentioned in connection with the Yorkshire Terrier's origin are Swift's Old Crab and Kershaw's Old Kitty. The former was a black and tan Terrier from Manchester and the latter was a Terrier of the drop-ear Skye type. Old Kitty was blue in color. The mating between these two was made about 1850. Huddersfield Ben, perhaps the first pillar of the breed, traced back to Old Crab and Old Kitty, but it is very probable that the Manchester, Maltese, Skye, Dandie Dinmont, and Paisley all contributed to the establishment of the Yorkshire breed.

These little dogs were not always known as Yorkshire Terriers. They were first shown in England under the classification of "Broken-haired Scotch or

Yorkshire Terrier. Photo by Evelyn M. Shafer.

Yorkshire Terriers." Along about 1870, Mozart, a son of Huddersfield Ben, won a first prize in the Variety Class at the Westmoreland show. Angus Sutherland, of Accrington, was the reporter who covered the show for *The Field* and his written comment read, "They ought no longer to be called Scotch Terriers but Yorkshire Terriers." The name caught on and was adopted.

Originally the Yorkshire was by no means a Toy. His weight ran from 12 to 14 pounds. It was through selective breeding that the breed has been dwarfed. Some of this diminishing in size was accomplished within 20 years of the time the Yorkshire first became "recognized" as a breed. For some time, however, the breed did not run true to type, so far as weight was concerned, as specimens ranged from 2¾ pounds to 13 pounds in the show ring.

The Yorkshire's coat, also, went through an evolution. Writing in 1857, in the third edition of his book, Stonehenge said:

Since the first edition of this book was published, a considerable change has taken place in the type of several of the Terrier family. At that time the Yorkshire Terrier was represented by an animal only slightly differing from the old Scotch dog, his shape being nearly or exactly the same, and his coat differing simply in being more silky. Such an animal was Mr. Spink's Bounce and by comparing his portrait with that of Mrs. Foster's Huddersfield Ben it will readily be seen that a great development of coat has been accomplished in the latter.

Huddersfield Ben was a very potent sire and transmitted his good qualities to his progeny in marked degree. During his career at stud he was considered the greatest stud dog in England. Many of his sons and daughters carried on and his "family" was largely responsible for the establishment of the breed.

The coat and color of the Yorkshire are the breed's outstanding characteristics. Carefully tended, the coat

often sweeps the ground, but some fanciers choose to keep it slightly shorter. No matter what its length, the coat must be perfectly straight and of a fine silky texture. The keeping of a Yorkshire Terrier in "show shape" requires constant care, but breed fanciers feel that the distinctive appearance it presents makes this care worth while.

In color the Yorkshire is a dark steel blue from the occiput to the root of the tail, a rich, golden tan on the head, and a bright tan on the chest.

The Yorkshire Terrier is regarded as a favorite toy breed in Great Britian. It is an alert active little dog, and, if allowed would be as frolicsome as any of the Terrier family.

Perhaps no history of the Yorkshire Terrier would be complete without including the story of Smokey. Smokey, an obviously pure-bred Yorkshire, was found in a shell hole after an American charge into Japanese lines in the New Guinea jungle, near Nadzab. She became the possession of William Wynne of Cleveland.

Wynne took Smokey to a Japanese prisoner of war camp, but the Japanese prisoners said they had never seen her. Tests were made, but Smokey did not appear to understand either English or Japanese. So the mystery of her origin will never be known.

Traveling in a soldier's pack, Smokey went through 150 air raids, flew 12 air-sea rescue missions, and went through a typhoon at Okinawa. Thus, she went through all the island-hopping of the Pacific war. In the meantime, Wynne, who had no previous training experience, taught her to waltz, walk a tight rope, and jump through hoops, among other things.

At Lingayen, the Signal Corps had to lay a telegraph wire through an eight-inch pipe under an air strip. Smokey crawled 70 feet through the pipe, dragging a tow line to which was attached the wire.

The 26th Photo Reconnaissance Squadron, Fifth Air Force, made a special parachute for the dog, and she learned to make jumps from a 30-foot tower. She

Yorkshire Terrier—Ch. Gleno Playboy. (Owner: Mrs. Leslie S. Gordon, Jr. and Miss Janet E. Bennett, Glenview, Ill.) Photo by Glenview Studio.

ate C-Rations, Spam, took soldier's vitamin pills, and got her bath in Wynne's helmet.

Various outfits from Australia to Japan decorated her, and the medals were placed on her green blanket, which was made from the cloth of a card table. *Yank* magazine gave her the title of "Mascot of the South Pacific."

Smokey and Wynne entertained at dozens of Army and Navy hospitals over half of the world, and not only during the latter part of the war, but long after it was over.

Description and Standards.

GENERAL APPEARANCE: That of a long-haired Toy Terrier whose blue and tan coat is parted on the face and from the base of the skull to the end of the tail and hangs evenly and quite straight down each side of the body. The body is neat, compact and well proportioned. The dog's high head carriage and confident manner should give the appearance of vigor and self-importance.

HEAD: Small and rather flat on top, the skull not too prominent or round, the muzzle not too long, with the bite neither undershot nor overshot and teeth sound. Either scissors bite or level bite is acceptable. The nose is black. Eyes are medium in size and not too prominent, dark in color and sparkling with a sharp, intelligent expression. Eye rims are dark. Ears are small, V-shaped, carried erect and set not too far apart.

BODY: Well proportioned and very compact. The back is rather short, and the back line level, with height at shoulder the same as at the rump.

LEGS AND FEET: Forelegs should be straight, elbows neither in nor out. Hind legs straight when viewed from behind, but sti-

fles are moderately bent when viewed from the sides. Feet are round with black toenails. Dewclaws, if any, are generally removed from the hind legs. Dewclaws on the forelegs may be removed.

TAIL: Docked to a medium length and carried slightly higher than the level of the back.

COAT: Quality, texture and quantity of coat are of prime importance. Hair is glossy, fine and silky in texture. Coat on the body is moderately long and perfectly straight (not wavy). It may be trimmed to floor length to give ease of movement and a neater appearance, if desired. The fall on the head is long, tied with one bow in center of head or parted in the middle and tied with two bows. Hair on muzzle is very long. Hair should be trimmed short on tips of ears and may be trimmed on feet to give them a neat appearance.

COLORS: Puppies are born black and tan and are normally darker in body color, showing an intermingling of black hair in the tan until they are matured. Color of hair on body and richness of tan on head and legs are of prime importance in adult dogs to which the following color requirements apply:

Blue: Is a dark steel-blue, not a silvery-blue and not mingled with fawn, bronze or black hairs.

Tan: All tan hair is darker at the roots than in the middle, shading to still lighter tan at the tips. There should be no sooty or black hair intermingled with any of the tan.

COLOR ON BODY: The blue extends over the body from back of neck to root of tail. Hair on tail is a darker blue, especially at end of tail.

HEADFALL: A rich, golden-tan, deeper in color at sides off head, at ear roots and on the muzzle, with ears a deep rich tan. Tan color should not extend down on back of neck.

CHEST AND LEGS: A bright rich tan, not extending above the elbow on the forelegs nor above the stifle on the hind legs.

WEIGHT: Must not exceed seven pounds.

(May, 1966)

—Group VI - Non-Sporting Dogs—

BOSTON TERRIER

ORIGINALLY a pit Terrier, used for fighting, once called the "round-headed bull," and the "American Bull Terrier," subject to much wrangling as to type, size, and color, the Boston Terrier is one of the very few breeds to be developed in this country. Despite the stormy stages of his development, this handsome little dog quickly found favor with a great many Americans and now, with type well established, is firmly entrenched in many countries throughout the world.

The foundation-stone of the breed was a dog known as Hooper's Judge, owned by Robert C. Hooper, of Boston, and purchased from William O'Brien of that city in the late '60s or early '70s Judge was supposedly imported from England, and was described as "half English Bulldog and half English Terrier." He is said to have been a dark brindle dog, with a blazed face, standing well up on his legs and weighing slightly over 30 pounds. Judge was mated with a bitch names Gyp, of equally unknown pedigree, and owned by Edward Burnett of Southboro, Mass. Gyp was said to look very much like a

Bulldog. From this mating came a dark brindle dog, with an evenly-marked white face, which resembled his dam in type, being low on the legs. Known as Wells' Eph, this dog weighed about 28 pounds. He was bred to a bitch named Tobin's Kate, again of unknown breeding. She was a rich golden brindle and weighed only about 20 pounds. One of the puppies from his mating was Barnard's Tom, later owned by J. P. Barnard and recognized as the first pillar of the Boston Terrier breed. Another dog from this mating was Atkinson's Toby, which was not such a success at stud as his brother.

Other dogs which figured in the formation of the breed were those known as the Jack Reed dog, the Perry dog, O'Brien's Ben, and Kellem's Brick. All were of unknown breeding, and all were probably imported from England. One might wonder why these dogs were unpedigreed, but it must be remembered that they were all bred for pit fighting and little record of breeding was kept in this sport. The Reed dog weighted about 12 pounds and was reddish brindle in color with a somewhat rough coat. The Perry dog was blue and white and was said to have been brought over from Scotland. Kellem's Brick, from England, was a small black spotted dog, weigh-

Boston Terrier.

ing about 18 pounds, with a reputation as a determined fighter. O'Brien's Ben was a white and brindle dog.

There was not much uniformity of type in these early dogs. They had not yet become known as Boston Terriers, but were shown in the general category of "Bull Terriers." As their numbers increased, along with the desire for exhibiting, the Boston show committee opened classes for "Round-headed Bull and Terriers, any colour." This brought increased interest, and Messrs. Boutelle and Bicknell of Providence, R.I., established the Round Head Kennels in keeping with the name.

The Boston fanciers organized a club and in 1891, under the name "American Bull Terrier Club," filed application for membership in the American Kennel Club. It was suggested by James Watson, noted writer and authority, that the dog was not a Bull Terrier and, as it was bred only at Boston and vicinity, a better name would be "Boston Terrier." The name of the club was changed to Boston Terrier Club and it was admitted to membership in the American Kennel Club in 1893.

After the breed had become established, the opinions of many of the leading fanciers differed and this resulted in a variance of type. These differences, however, never went so far as to establish definite strains or families. Four dogs of the early days stand out for their remarkable prepotency. These were Buster, owned by Alexander L. Goode, of Boston; Tony Boy, owned by Franklin C. Bixby of Boston; Sullivan's Punch, and Cracksman.

Buster was not a typical Boston Terrier, his show record was unimpressive, but his list of winning progeny and their get is nothing short of phenomenal. Among the many good ones sired by Buster were:

Champion Monte, one of the greatest show dogs of this breed, Champion Stephen's Rex, Spottswood Banker, Maxine's Boy, Broker, Squantum Criterion, Dazzler, Pat G., and Rattler II. Cracksman was a great-grandson.

Tony Boy's get excelled in color. They were rather small in size, possessed the desired tail properties, and exerted much influence on the breed.

Sullivan's Punch was a white dog with brindle head markings, but despite this handicap proved to be a truly great sire.

Dogs of the Cracksman line were somewhat light in color running into golden brindles. They possessed exceedingly appealing eyes and excelled in expression.

Members of the Boston Terrier fancy are now legion. At one time the Boston was probably the most popular show dog in America and he still ranks fairly high in public affection. Among those whose breeding activities contributed much to the success of the breed were:

Dr. Walter G. Kendall; Mr. and Mrs. Charles H. Annable, Danvers, Mass.; Mrs. Madeline C. McGlone, New York City; Dan Haggerty, Boston, Mass.; Mr. and Mrs. H. C. Hayhurst, Dallas, Texas; Mrs. A. L. Barrett, New York City; Mr. and Mrs. J. J. Middleton, Cleveland, Ohio; Droll and Rosenbloom, New York City; and H. N. Bulger, Lawrence, Mass.

The weight classifications have long been the subject of much discussion among Boston Terrier fanciers. The three divisions, lightweight, middleweight, and heavyweight, now call for lighter dogs than they did originally.

Description and Standards. The amended description and standards, adopted by the Boston Terrier Club of America and approved by the American Kennel Club, follow.

GENERAL APPEARANCE: The general appearance of the Boston Terrier should be that of a lively, highly intelligent, smooth-coated, short-headed, compactly-built, short-tailed, well-balanced dog of medium station, of brindle color and evenly marked with white. The head should indicate a high degree of intelligence and should be in proportion to the size of the dog; the body rather short and well knit, the limbs strong and neatly turned; tail short; and no feature be so prominent that the dog appears badly proportioned.

The dog should convey an impression of determination, strength, and activity, with style of a high order; carriage easy and graceful.

A proportionate combination of "Color" and "Ideal Markings" is a particularly distinctive feature of a representative specimen, and a dog with a preponderance of white on body, or without the proper proportion of brindle and white on head, should possess sufficient merit otherwise to counteract its deficiencies in these respects.

The ideal "Boston Terrier Expression" as indicating "a high degree of intelligence," is also an important characteristic of the breed.

"Color and Markings" and "Expression" should be given particular consideration in determining the relative value of "General Appearance" to other points.

SKULL: Square, flat on top, free from wrinkles; cheeks flat; brow abrupt, stop well defined.

EYES: Wide apart, large and round, dark in color, expression alert but kind and intelligent. The eyes should set square in the skull, and the outside corners should be on a line with the cheeks as viewed from the front.

MUZZLE: Short, square, wide and deep, and in proportion to

Boston Terrier—Doing his stuff at an obedience trial. Photo by James N. Keen.

skull; free from wrinkles; shorter in length than in width and depth; not exceeding in length approximately one-third of length of skull; width and depth carried out well to end; the muzzle from stop to end of nose on a line parallel to the top of the skull; nose black and wide, with well-defined line between nostrils. The jaws broad and square, with short, regular teeth. Bite even or sufficiently undershot to square muzzle. The chops of good depth but not pendulous, completely covering the teeth when mouth is closed.

EARS: Carried erect, either cropped to conform to shape of head or natural hat, situated as near corners of skull as possible.

Head Faults: Skull "domed" or inclined; furrowed by a medial line; skull too long for breadth, or *vice versa;* stop too shallow; brow and skull too slanting. Eyes small or sunken; too prominent; light color or wall eye; showing too much white or haw. Muzzle wedge-shaped or lacking depth; down-faced; too much cut out below the eyes; pinched or wide nostrils; butterfly nose; protruding teeth; weak lower jaw; showing "turn up," layback or wrinkled. Ears poorly carried or in size out of proportion to head.

NECK: Of fair length; slightly arched and carrying the head gracefully; setting neatly into shoulders.

Neck Faults: Ewe-necked; throatiness; short and thick.

BODY: Deep with good width of chest; shoulders sloping; back short; ribs deep and well sprung, carried well back to loins; loins short and muscular; rump curving slightly to set-on of tail; flank very slightly cut up. The body should appear short but not chunky.

Body Faults: Flat sides; narrow chest; long or slack loins; roach back; sway back; too much cut up in flank.

ELBOWS: Standing neither in nor out.

FORE LEGS: Set moderately wide apart and on a line with the point of the shoulders; straight in bone and well muscled; pasterns short and strong.

HIND LEGS: Set true; bent at stifles; short from hocks to feet; hocks turning neither in nor out; thighs strong and well muscled.

FEET: Round, small and compact and turned neither in nor out; toes well arched.

LEGS AND FEET FAULTS: Loose shoulders or elbows; hind legs too straight at stifles; hocks too prominent; long or weak pasterns; splay feet.

GAIT: The gait of the Boston Terrier is that of a sure-footed, straight-gaited dog, fore legs and hind legs moving straight ahead in line with perfect rhythm, each step indicating grace and power.

Gait Faults: There shall be no rolling, paddling or weaving when gaited and any crossing movement, either front or rear, is a serious fault.

TAIL: Set-on low; short, fine and tapering; straight; or screw; devoid of fringe or coarse hair, and not carried above horizontal.

Tail Faults: A long or gaily-carried tail; extremely gnarled or curled against body. (*Note*—The preferred tail should not exceed in length approximately half the distance from set-on to hock.)

IDEAL COLOR: Brindle with white markings. The brindle to be evenly distributed and distinct. Black with white markings permissible but brindle with white markings preferred.

IDEAL MARKINGS: White muzzle, even white blaze over head, collar, breast, part or whole of fore legs, and hind legs below hocks.

Color and Markings Faults: All white; absence of white marking; preponderance of white on body; without the proper proportion of brindle and white on head; or any variations detracting from the general appearance.

COAT: Short, smooth, bright and fine in texture.

COAT FAULTS: Long or coarse; lacking lustre.

WEIGHT: Not exceeding 25 pounds, divided by classes as follows: Lightweight: under 15 pounds. Middleweight: 15 and under 20 pounds. Heavyweight: 20 and not exceeding 25 pounds.

Disqualifications: Solid black; black and tan; liver or mouse colors. Dudley nose. Docked tail or any artificial means used to deceive the judge.

SCALE OF POINTS:	*Points*
General Appearance	10
Skull	10
Eyes	5
Muzzle	10
Ears	2
Neck	3
Body	15
Elbows	4
Fore Legs	5
Hind Legs	5
Gait	10
Feet	5
Tail	5
Color	4
Ideal Markings	5
Coat	2
TOTAL	100

BULLDOG

GENERALLY ACCEPTED as a symbol of British pluck and endurance, the Bulldog is considered to be a breed of purely British origin. In its background is very probably found the large, strong and broad-mouthed war dogs of the early Britons. The first description to be found in literature was that of W. Wulcher who, in 1500, referred to them as the Bondogge. Under Dr. Johannes Caius' grouping in 1570 we find the breed referred to as the Mastine or Bandogge, among the sundry names for which was the "Butchers Dogge." It was not until the early 1630's that the breed was referred to in literature as the "Bulldog."

There has always been much argument concerning the origin of the breed, particularly among fanciers of the Bulldog and the Mastiff, both claiming their favorite breed to be the ancestor of the other. Perhaps both were descended from the "alauntes" mentioned in the *Master of Game,* by Edward, the second Duke of York, practically a translation of Gaston de Foix's *Livre de Chasse,* and written about 1406-1413. Edward interpolated a description of his own when he stated that the Alaunt of the butcher was good for baiting the bull. It is very probable that the Alaunts of that period were more like Great Danes than anything else, and certainly larger than the low-slung Bulldog. The Bulldog of the present is a far different dog than the first to bear that name.

There is little doubt that the Bulldog derived his name from the so-called "sport" of bull-baiting, once quite popular in England. In *The Survey of Stamford,* the following reference is made to what was the probable origin of the "sport":

William Earl Warren, Lord of this town in the reign of King John, (1209), standing upon the walls of his castle at Stamford saw two bulls fighting for a cow in the castle meadow, till all the butchers' dogs pursued one of the bulls, which was maddened by the noise and multitude, through the town. This so pleased the Earl that he gave the castle meadow where the bulls combat began, for a common to the butchers of the town after the first grass was mowed, on condition that they should find a "mad bull" on a day six weeks before Christmas for the continuance of that sport forever.

According to Dr. Caius, the bull was caught by the ear when baited. Only a large and exceedingly strong dog could hold a bull that way, but as the sport grew in popularity and dogs were bred for their exceptional courage and ferociousness, it is likely that some smaller and daring dog pinned a bull by the nose. The effectiveness of this hold was at once apparent and dogs were taught to try for it. This hold also probably brought about the development of dogs which were low on the legs, yet possessed of great strength. Rules of bull-baiting varied. At one time and in one section of England it was generally understood that the dog had to pull the bull backward once around the ring. In another section the rules were that the dog had to pin and throw the bull.

Dog-fighting was a natural outgrowth of bull-baiting, particularly after that dubious "sport" declined. And for a long time the cruel "sport" of dog-fighting was carried on in London and the Midlands. Dogs used for this purpose were quite different from the present-day Bulldog. They were higher on the leg, lighter in bone, smaller in skull, longer in muzzle, and not nearly so wide in front. They were generally cropped to lessen the chances of their opponent's getting a hold on their ears. That they were extremely courageous and capable of withstanding great punishment goes without saying, for many of these fights were to the death.

Dog fighting became illegal by legislation in 1835, and, while it was carried on under cover for some time, the practice gradually died out. And with its passing went the major interest in Bulldogs. The breed almost became extinct, for it required some years to lose the stigma of the "sport."

"Bill" George, a legitimate dealer in dogs whose establishment was called "Canine Castle", is credited with playing a considerable part in the revival of interest in the breed. One of his well-known dogs was Bill George's Dan.

The first show classes for the breed were held at Birmingham in 1860, and they appeared at the London shows a year or so later. Old King Dick was probably the outstanding dog of that time and the name of Champion Crib, one of his descendants, can be found far back in the pedigrees of some of the dogs of today. Monarch and Gamester, bred by J. W. Berrie, were sons of Crib out of the same litter. Monarch became a prominent sire. Among the early breeders were: F. G. W. Crayer, J. S. Pybus Sellon, F. W. Crowther, W. H. Sprague, and A. E. Vicary. The Bulldog Club was founded in 1874 and one year later became the Bulldog Club, Inc.

The first dog truly representative of the breed to be shown in this country was Donald, a lightweight which had done considerable winning in England. He was sent over for the New York Show in 1880 by the Irish fancier, Sir William Verner. He was by no means as low on the leg as our present-day dogs, although he possessed a good head. John P. Barnard, of Boston, was an early exhibitor in the Bulldog classes, and some of his stock played a part in the formation of the Boston Terrier. Col. John E. Thayer took up the breed and imported some good ones, winning numerous prizes until 1890, when he severed his connection with the breed.

The Bulldog Club of America was formed in 1890. Some of the early members were: John H. Matthews, New York City; R. B. Sawyer, Milwaukee, Wisc.; Retnor Kennels, New York City; E. Sheffield Porter, New Haven, Conn.; and C. G. Cugle, Hartford, Conn.

There is none of the old fighting, bull-baiting dog in the present-day Bulldog. Formidable in appearance with the look of great strength and courage, the Bulldog is docile in manner and affectionate by nature. He has long since lived down the stigma of the

Bulldog—Ch. Gordon's Sir Winston. (Owner: Mr. and Mrs. Gordon Schiletz, Parma, Ohio) Photo by Paul Toppelstein.

"sport" from which he gained his name. The breed is now well established in this country and had many admirers.

The breeding of Bulldogs is no task for the amateur. Due to their physical make-up, whelping is often difficult and Caesarean operations are sometimes necessary. Sterility in bitches occurs in a degree of considerable magnitude. A good bitch, able to bear and raise her young, is quite a valuable animal.

Description and Standards. The description and standards, by courtesy of the Bulldog Club of America, follow.

GENERAL APPEARANCE, ATTITUDE, EXPRESSION, ETC.: The perfect Bulldog must be of medium size and smooth coat; with heavy, thick-set, low-swung body, massive short-faced head, wide shoulders and sturdy limbs.

The general appearance and attitude should suggest great stability, vigor and strength.

The disposition should be equable and kind, resolute and courageous (not vicious or aggressive), and demeanor should be pacific and dignified.

These attributes should be countenanced by the expression and behavior.

GAIT: The style and carriage are peculiar, his gait being a loose-jointed, shuffling, sidewise motion, giving the characteristic "roll." The action must, however, be unrestrained, free and vigorous.

PROPORTION AND SYMMETRY: The "points" should be well distributed and bear good relation one to the other, no feature being in such prominence from either excess or lack of quality that the animal appears deformed or illy proportioned.

INFLUENCE OF SEX: In comparison of specimens of different sex, due allowance should be made in favor of the bitches, which do not bear the characteristics of the breed to the same degree of perfection and grandeur as do the dogs.

SIZE: The size for mature dogs is about 50 pounds; for mature bitches about 40 pounds.

COAT: The coat should be straight, short, flat, close, of fine texture, smooth and glossy. (No fringe, feather or curl.)

COLOR OF COAT: The color of coat should be uniform, pure of its kind and brilliant. The various colors found in the breed are to be preferred in the following order: (1) Red brindle, (2) all other brindles, (3) solid white, (4) solid red, fawn or fallow, (5) piebald, (6) inferior qualities of all the foregoing.

Note: A perfect piebald is preferable to a muddy brindle or defective solid color.

Solid black is very undesirable, but not so objectionable, if occurring to a moderate degree in piebald patches. The brindles to be perfect should have a fine, even and equal distribution of the composite colors.

In brindles and solid colors a small white patch on the chest is not considered detrimental. In piebalds the color patches should be well defined, of pure color and symmetrically distributed.

SKIN: The skin should be soft and loose, especially at the head, neck and shoulders.

WRINKLES AND DEWLAP: The head and face should be covered with heavy wrinkles, and at the throat, from jaw to chest, there should be two loose pendulous folds, forming the dewlap.

SKULL: The skull should be very large, and in circumference, in front of the ears, should measure at least the height of the dog at the shoulders.

Viewed from the front, it should appear very high from the corner of the lower jaw to the apex of the skull and also very broad and square.

Viewed at the side, the head should appear very high, and very short from the point of the nose to occiput.

The forehead should be flat (not rounded or "domed"), neither too prominent nor overhanging the face.

CHEEKS: The cheeks should be well rounded, protruding sideways and outward beyond the eyes.

Bulldog—Ch. Rawburn Bayside Bayberry. (Owner: Cyril Bernfeld, Allendale, New Jersey) Photo by Evelyn M. Shafer.

BRISKET AND BODY: The brisket and body should be very capacious with full sides, well-rounded ribs, and very deep from the shoulders down to its lowest part, where it joins the chest. It should be well let down between the shoulders and fore legs, giving the dog a broad, low, short-legged appearance.

The body should be well ribbed up behind with the belly tucked up and not rotund.

BACK: The back should be short and strong, very broad at the shoulders and comparatively narrow at the loins. There should be a slight fall in the back, close behind the shoulders (its lowest part), whence the spine should rise to the loins (the top of which should be higher than the top of the shoulders), thence curving again more suddenly to the tail, forming an arch (a very distinctive feature of the breed), termed "roach-back" or, more correctly, "wheel-back."

FORE LEGS: The fore legs should be short, very stout, straight and muscular, set wide apart, with well-developed calves, presenting a bowed outline, but the bones of the legs should not be curved or bandy, nor the feet brought too close together.

STOP: The temples or frontal bones should be very well defined, broad, square and high, causing a hollow or groove between the eyes. This indentation, or "stop," should be both broad and deep and extend up the middle of the forehead, dividing the head vertically, being traceable to the top of the skull.

EYES AND EYELIDS: The eyes, seen from the front, should be situated low down in the skull, as far from the ears as possible and their corners should be in a straight line at right angles with the stop. They should be quite in front of the head, as wide apart as possible, provided their outer corners are within the outline of the cheeks when viewed from the front.

They should be quite round in form, of moderate size, neither sunken nor bulging, and in color should be very dark.

The lids should cover the white of the eyeball, when the dog is looking directly forward, and the lid should show no "haw."

EARS: The ears should be set high in the head, the front inner edge of each ear joining the outline of the skull at the top back corner of skull, so as to place them as wide apart, and as high and as far from the eyes as possible.

In size they should be small and thin. The shape termed "rose ear" is the most desirable. The "rose ear" folds inward at its back lower edge, the upper front edge curving over, outwards and backwards, showing part of the inside of the burr. (The ears should not be carried erect or "prick-eared" or "buttoned" and should never be cropped.)

FACE: The face, measured from the front of the cheek bone to the tip of the nose, should be extremely short, the muzzle being very short, broad, turned upwards and very deep from the corner of the eye to the corner of the mouth.

Nose: The nose should be large, broad and black, its tip being set back deeply between the eyes.

The distance from bottom of stop, between the eyes, to the tip of nose should be as short as possible, and not exceed the length from the tip of nose to the edge of under lip.

The nostrils should be wide, large and black, with a well-defined line between them. Any nose other than black is objectionable and "Dudley" or flesh-colored nose absolutely disqualified from competition.

Chops: The chops or "flews" should be thick, broad, pendant and very deep, completely overhanging the lower jaw at each side. They join the under lip in front and almost or quite cover the teeth, which should be scarcely noticeable when the mouth is closed.

Jaws: The jaws should be massive, very broad, square and "undershot", the lower jaw projecting considerably in front of the upper jaw and turning up.

Teeth: The teeth should be large and strong, with the canine teeth or tusks wide apart, and the six small teeth in front, between the canines, in an even, level row.

Neck: The neck should be short, very thick, deep and strong and well arched at the back.

Shoulders: The shoulders should be muscular, very heavy, wide-spread and slanting outward, giving stability and great power.

Chest: The chest should be very broad, deep and full.

Elbows: The elbows should be low and stand well out and loose from the body.

Hind Legs: The hind legs should be strong and muscular and longer than the fore legs, so as to elevate the loins above the shoulders.

Hocks should be slightly bent and well let down, so as to give length and strength from loins to hock.

The lower leg should be short, straight, and strong, with the stifles turned slightly outward and away from the body. The hocks are thereby made to approach each other, and the hind feet to turn outward.

Feet: The feet should be moderate in size, compact and firmly set. Toes compact, well split up, with high knuckles and with short, stubby nails.

The front feet may be straight or slightly out-turned, but the hind feet should be pointed well outward.

Tail: The tail may be either straight or "screwed" (but never curved or curly), and in any case must be short, hung low, with decided downward carriage, thick root and fine tip.

If straight, the tail should be cylindrical and of uniform taper.

If "screwed" the bends or kinks should be well defined and they may be abrupt and even knotty, but no portion of the member should be elevated above the base or root.

Scale of Points: Points

Proportion and symmetry	5
Attitude	3
Expression	2
Gait	3
Size	3
Coat	2
Color of coat	4
General properties	22
Skull	5
Cheeks	2
Stop	4
Eyes and eyelids	3
Ears	5
Wrinkle	5
Nose	6
Chops	2
Jaws	5
Teeth	2
Total, head	39

Neck	3
Dewlap	2
Shoulders	5
Chest	3
Ribs	3
Brisket	2
Belly	2
Back	5
Fore legs and elbows	4
Hind legs	3
Feet	3
Tail	4
Total, body, legs, etc.	39
Grand Total	100

Disqualification. Dudley or flesh-colored nose.

CHOW CHOW

POSSESSED OF an air of aloofness, which, if the term could properly be applied to a dog, amounts to downright snobbishness, the Chow Chow might well be termed the national dog of China. True, the Pekingese has his claim on that distinction, but the Chow Chow is the only Chinese breed which can be used for the various purposes in which an average-size dog is employed.

It has been said that the Chow is the common mongrel of China, but no one seems to know where that idea originated. That it is a false conception is proved by the fact that, while China, indeed, has its mongrel dogs, the Chow has been an established breed for many years. The theory has been advanced that his breed descended from an ancestor other than that of the Western dogs, perhaps the bear. Like that animal, the Chow is remarkably sure-footed. In some respects there is a slight resemblance to the bear, but students have never given very serious consideration to the theory.

Another theory attributes the origin of the Chow

Chow Chow—Ch. Charmar Canton Lu. (Owner: Mr. and Mrs. C. H. Evans, Grand Rapids, Mich.)

Chow Chow puppies.

to a cross between the old Mastiff of Tibet and the Samoyed. But the question arises: "Where did the Chow get his blue-black tongue?" It is the only breed with that characteristic. Another theory is in contraposition, holding that the Chow is one of the basic breeds and perhaps the ancestor himself of the Samoyed, the Eskimo, the Norwegian Elkhound, the Keeshond, and the Pomeranian, all of a somewhat similar type.

The breed's name has no particular significance as to loyalty or use and is said to have been taken from the pidgin English term for articles, including bric-a-brac, ivory, and porcelain curios, brought from the Orient during the latter part of the eighteenth century. Rather than minutely describe the small items of his cargo, the master of a sailing vessel entered them as "chow chow," which, in time, came to include the dog.

The Chow Chow is used, to some extent, as a hunting dog in China, although his main duties entail the guarding of his master's property. In this country, he is used as a pet and guard dog.

While devoted to the family that owns him, the Chow has no use for strangers. As a breed, these dogs are rather high strung and sensitive, although they seldom show any shyness in the show ring. They are not generally of a trusting nature, but look upon friendly advances with some suspicion.

Among the dogs which did much to establish the breed in England were Ch. Lemming, Ch. Akbar, and try was Takya, owned by Miss A. C. Derby, and Ch. Rochow Dragoon.

The first of the breed to be exhibited in this country was Takya, owned by Miss A. C. Derby, and shown at the Westminster Kennel Club in New York.

Description and Standards. The description and standards, adopted by the Chow Chow Club and approved by the American Kennel Club follow.

GENERAL APPEARANCE: A massive, cobby, powerful dog, active and alert, with strong, muscular development, and perfect balance. Body squares with height of leg at shoulder; head, broad and flat, with short, broad, and deep muzzle, accentuated by a ruff; the whole supported by straight, strong legs. Clothed in a shining off-standing coat, the Chow is a masterpiece of beauty, dignity, and untouched naturalness.

HEAD: Large and massive in proportion to size of dog, with broad, flat skull; well filled under the eyes; moderate stop; and proudly carried.

EXPRESSION: Essentially dignified, lordly, scowling, discerning, sober, and snobbish—one of independence.

MUZZLE: Short in comparison to length of skull; broad from eye to end of nose, and of equal depth. The lips somewhat full and overhanging.

TEETH: Strong and level, with scissors bite; should neither be overshot, nor undershot.

NOSE: Large, broad, and black in color. *Disqualification*—nose spotted or distinctly other color than black, except in blue Chows, which may have solid blue or slate noses.

TONGUE: A blue-black. The tissues of the mouth should approximate black. *Disqualification*—tongue red, pink, or obviously spotted with red or pink.

EYES: Dark, deep-set of moderate size, and almond-shaped.

EARS: Small, slightly rounded at tip, stiffly carried. They should be placed wide apart, on top of the skull, and set with a slight, forward tilt. *Disqualification*—drop ear or ears. A drop is one which is not stiffly carried or stiffly erect, but which breaks over at any point from its base to its tip.

BODY: Short, compact, with well-sprung ribs, and let down in the flank.

NECK: Strong, full, set well on the shoulders.

SHOULDERS: Muscular, slightly sloping.

CHEST: Broad, deep and muscular. A narrow chest is a serious fault.

BACK: Short, straight, and strong.

LOINS: Broad, deep, and powerful.

TAIL: Set well up and carried closely to the back, following line of spine at start.

FORE LEGS: Perfectly straight, with heavy bone and upright pasterns.

HIND LEGS: Straight hocked, muscular, and heavy boned.

FEET: Compact, round, cat-like, with thick pads.

GAIT: Completely individual. Short and stilted because of straight hocks.

COAT: Abundant, dense, straight, and off-standing; rather coarse in texture with a soft, woolly under coat. It may be any clear color, solid throughout, with lighter shadings on ruff.

Disqualifications. Nose spotted or distinctly other color than black, except in blue Chows, which may have solid blue or slate noses. Tongue red, pink or obviously spotted with red or pink. Drop ear or ears.

DALMATIAN

THE SPOTTED dog figuring so prominently in the art of ancient Egypt and Greece may or may not have been the ancestor of the Dalmatian, but we do know that the breed stems back to very early times. He has passed through many evolutions in type during the centuries, but, in all, has about as straight a record as any dog.

It is known that he was found in many sections, perhaps because he was a favorite with the Romany gypsies whose endless wanderings carried them to far places. His first proved home was Dalmatia, a province of Austria on the Eastern shore of the coast of Venice, and it was from this section that he received his "official" name.

Many have been the names applied to this versatile dog. Count Buffon, for some strange reason, called him the Bengal Harrier. The noted writer, Youatt, claimed that he was of the same stock as the Danish dog, now the Great Dane, differing only in size. The English had a number of nicknames for the breed, among them being "English Coach Dog," "Carriage Dog," "Plum Pudding Dog," "Fire House Dog," and

"Spotted Dick." He was also called the "Talbot," which supported the theory that he was descended from the Old English hounds.

The Dalmatian, as we know him today, is definitely not a hound, as we know hounds today, but James Watson, in his *The Dog Book*, pointed out that even in the early days the interpretation of the term "hound" had wide latitude. Yet the Dalmatian has been used as a sporting dog in practically every manner in which sporting dogs are employed. He is still a good tracker, a better than fair retriever, and, given a reasonable amount of proper training, can generally be developed into a gun dog of no mean ability, as many of them are easily taught to point. His great versatility goes beyond the sport of hunting, for the Dalmatian has been used in practically every role assigned to useful dogs. He has been a draft dog and a shepherd, a sentry and a guard. He has even occupied the spotlight of the stage and circus, and has acquitted himself with credit in every task presented. He played a prominent part in the various aspects of war work during World War II, and his record in Obedience trials is outstanding.

As a "coach-dog" the Dalmatian stands pre-eminent. Early Egyptian art pictures him following a chariot. His love for accompanying horses on the road is an inbred instinct, developed over hundreds of years. And in the days of coaching he lent dress, distinction, and dignity to any equipage, whether he trotted under the rear axle, under the front axle, or assumed a difficult position under the pole between the wheelers and leaders. As an affectionate and faithful companion, of extremely clean appearance and habits, the Dalmatian has won the respect of all dog lovers.

In the early days of coaching, the old fashion of cropping the ears close to the head was followed and the trade-mark of the Dalmatian was a padlocked brass collar. The practice of cropping the ears has, to the betterment of the welfare of the dog and the improvement of his looks, long since been abandoned.

The Dalmatian is one of the most unusual and distinctive of all dogs in appearance. Clean-limbed, with his clearly defined round spots of back or liver standing out boldly against a pure white background, he makes an imposing sight whether alert or in repose.

The puppies are born pure white, but the spots develop quickly. Much attention is paid to the markings nowadays. Heavy tickings are not to be desired, nor are solid-colored ears. Patches are definitely frowned upon.

The dog is bred for road work, and for this he is admirably equipped. His lines denote extreme endurance. He has a happy disposition, makes friends readily, but his true affection and real loyalty belongs to his master or his master's family. The Dalmatian is not a noisy, quarrelsome dog, but is rather one of quiet dignity, ready to meet friendly advances halfway, yet always remembering his responsibility for guarding the person and property of his owner.

The Dalmatian has been prominent in Obedience trials since that activity was introduced into this country. Whiteside Sioux Lad was the first registered male Dalmatian to achieve a C.D. degree, and his litter mate, Whiteside Sioux Bright Spot, both owned by Mrs. Wilbur E. Dewell, Fairfield, Conn., also won her C.D. degree in 1940. Lad went on to annex the degree of C.D.X.

The first degree of U.D.T. awarded to a Dalmatian was won by Io, a ten-year-old bitch, owned by Mr. and Mrs. Harland W. Meistrell of Westbury, Long Island, N.Y. This performance encouraged many Dalmatian owners to work their dogs for Obedience trial competition. Tally-Ho Blackeyed Susan, also owned by the Meistrells, was the first bench show champion Dalmatian to achieve a C.D. title.

On November 14, 1948, the first Dalmatian road trials to be held in this country under the sponsorship of the Dalmatian Club of America were inaugurated. The interest evidenced indicates that his activity, designed to perpetuate the breed's primary usefulness in the old days, working with horses, is destined to grow.

Among the early pillars of the breed in England were Ch. Silverden King of Coldharbour, Ch. Snow Leopard, Ch. Best of Cards, and Ch. Winning Trick.

Some of the early breeders in this country were:

Sergeant Price, Philadelphia; Dr. Lougest, the well-known Mastiff and Bloodhound breeder, and the Windy Valley Kennels, owned in partnership by J. B. Thomas, Jr., and H. T. Peters.

Description and Standards. The description and standards, by courtesy of the Dalmatian Club of America, follow.

The Dalmatian should represent a strong, muscular, and active dog; poised and alert; free of shyness; intelligent in expression; symmetrical in outline; and free from coarseness and lumber. He should be capable of great endurance, combined with a fair amount of speed.

Dalmatian—Ch. Barney Oldfield in the Valley. (Owner: Lois Meistrell, Great Neck N.Y.) Photo by Evelyn M. Shafer.

HEAD: Should be of a fair length, the skull flat proportionately broad between the ears, and moderately well defined at the temples, and not in one straight line from the nose to the occiput bone as required in a Bull Terrier. It should be entirely free from wrinkle. *Muzzle*—Should be long and powerful—the lips clean. The mouth should have a scissors bite. Never undershot or overshot. It is permissible to trim whiskers. *Eyes*—Should be set moderately well apart, and of medium size, round, bright, and sparkling, with an intelligent expression; their color greatly depending on the markings of the dog. In the black-spotted variety the eyes should be dark (black or brown or blue). In the liver-spotted variety they should be lighter than in the black-spotted variety (golden or light brown or blue). The rim around the eyes in the black-spotted variety should be black; in the liver-spotted variety, brown. Never flesh-colored in either. Lack of pigment a major fault.

EARS: Should be set rather high, of moderate size, rather wide at the base, and gradually tapering to a rounded point. They should be carried close to the head, be thin and fine in texture, and preferably spotted. Nose—in the black-spotted variety should always be black; in the liver-spotted variety, always brown. A butterfly or flesh-colored nose is a major fault.

NECK AND SHOULDERS: The neck should be fairly long, nicely arched, light and tapering, and entirely free from throatiness. The shoulders should be oblique, clean, and muscular, denoting speed.

BODY, BACK, CHEST, AND LOINS: The chest should not be too wide, but very deep and capacious, ribs well sprung but never rounded like barrel hoops (which would indicate want of speed). Back powerful; loin strong, muscular and slightly arched. *Legs and Feet*—Of great importance. The forelegs should be straight, strong, and heavy in bone; elbows close to the body; feet compact, well-arched toes, and tough, elastic pads. In the hind legs the muscles should be clean, though well defined; the hocks well let down. Dewclaws may be removed from legs. *Nails*—In the black-spotted variety, black or white; or a nail may be both black and white. In the liver-spotted variety, brown or white; or a nail may be both brown and white.

GAIT: Length of stride should be in proportion to the size of the dog, steady in rhythm of 1, 2, 3, 4 as in the cadence count in military drill. Front legs should not paddle, nor should there be a straddling appearance. Hind legs should neither cross nor weave; judges should be able to see each leg move with no interference of another leg. Drive and reach are most desirable. Cowhocks are a major fault.

TAIL: Should ideally reach the hock joint, strong at the insertion, and tapering toward the end, free from coarseness. It should not be inserted too low down, but carried with a slight curve upwards, and never curled.

COAT: Should be short, hard, dense, and fine, sleek and glossy in appearance, but neither woolly nor silky.

COLOR AND MARKINGS: Are most important points. The ground color in both varieties should be pure white, very decided, and not intermixed. The color of the spots in the black-spotted variety should be dense black; in the liver-spotted variety they should be liver brown. The spots should not intermingle, but be as round and well defined as possible, the more distinct the better. In size they should be from that of a dime to a half-dollar. The spots on the face, head, ears, legs, and tail to be smaller than those on the body. Patches, tri-colors, and any color markings other than black or liver constitute a disqualification. A true patch is a solid, sharply defined mass of black or liver that is appreciably larger than any of the markings on the dog. Several spots that are so adjacent that they actually touch one another at their edges do not constitute a patch.

SIZE: The desirable height of dogs and bitches is between 19 and 23 inches at the withers, and any dog or bitch over 24 inches at the withers is to be disqualified.

Major faults. Butterfly or flesh-colored nose. Cowhocks. Flat feet. Lack of pigment in eye rims. Shyness. Trichiasis (abnormal position or direction of the eye-lashes).

Faults. Ring or low-set tail. Undersize or oversize.

Dalmatian—A head study. Ch. Penny of Watseka. (Owner: Robert and Gail Sbarge, Racine, Wisc.)

SCALE OF POINTS:	*Points*
Body, back, chest and loins	10
Coat	5
Color and markings	25
Ears	5
Gait	10
Head and eyes	10
Legs and feet	10
Neck and shoulders	10
Size, symmetry, etc.	10
Tail	5
TOTAL	100

Disqualifications. Any color markings other than black or liver. Any size over 24 inches at the withers. Patches. Tri-colors. Undershot or overshot bite.

(December 11, 1962)

FRENCH BULLDOG

A BAT-EARED dog of intriguing appearance, the French Bulldog has been called a misnomer by some authorities. These writers maintain that the proper name, Boule-Douge Francais, should never have been translated into English, but it must be admitted that in general appearance the breed looks much like a miniature English Bulldog.

In fact, many hold that the Boule-Dogue Francais, or French Bulldog, found its origin in the Toy Bulldog of England which was never in high favor with British fanciers. Many of these small dogs were exported to France and these, doubtless, crossed with some of the breeds of that country.

There was much argument among the early promoters of the breed concerning the proper type of ear, some favoring the rose ear of the English Bulldog and others holding for the erect bat type. The latter was finally adopted as proper and is perhaps the outstanding feature of the breed, for no other dog's ear had the well-rounded top like that of the French Bulldog.

There has also been considerable difference of opinion among French, English, and American fanciers as to proper weight standards, but the French Bulldog Club of America has seen fit to make its own regulations in this regard.

The French Bulldog has none of the dour expression of the English Bulldog, but rather has an alert appearance as one ever ready for a romp, which is exactly in keeping with the character of the breed.

Some maintain that the French Bulldog has played a far more important part in the formation of the Boston Terrier that the promoters of that breed care to admit. Be that as it may, it is certain that the breed had a warm reception when its was introduced into this country and still has many admirers.

The controversy over the type of ear led to the formation of the French Bulldog Club of America, the first organization devoted to the interests of the breed, and this organization set the type and did much to give the breed a fine start in this country. In 1898, the club staged a specialty show in the Waldorf-Astoria Hotel, New York, on a scale never seen before. The outstanding success of the affair, with its attendant publicity, made the attractive little dog a favorite of society, and he has enjoyed considerable popularity ever since.

Ch. Nellcote Gamin, imported in 1904 by Mr. and Mrs. Samuel Goldenberg, proved a boon to the breed, and the name of this famous sire can be found in the pedigree of almost every French Bulldog in this country today.

Primarily kept as pets and companions, the Frenchie is a good watchdog of much intelligence. Never noisy or boisterous, he is always ready for a frolic. The smooth, short coat is easily kept clean and no special primping is necessary for an appearance in the show ring.

Description and Standards. The description and standards by courtesy of the French Bulldog Club of America, follow.

GENERAL APPEARANCE: The French Bulldog should have the appearance of an active, intelligent, muscular dog, of heavy bone, smooth coat, compactly built, and of medium or small stature.

PROPORTION AND SYMMETRY: The points should be well distributed and bear good relation one to the other, no feature being in such prominence from either excess or lack of quality that the animal appears deformed or poorly proportioned.

INFLUENCE OF SEX: In comparison of specimens of different sex, due allowance should be made in favor of the bitches, which do not bear the characteristics of the breed to the same marked degree as do the dogs.

WEIGHT: A lightweight class under 22 pounds; heavyweight class, 22 pounds, and not over 28 pounds.

HEAD: The head should be large and square. The top of the skull should be flat between the ears; the forehead should not be flat but slightly rounded. The stop should be well defined causing a hollow or groove between the eyes. The muzzle should be broad, deep and well laid back; the muscles of the cheeks well developed. The nose should be extremely short; nostrils broad with well-defined line between them. The nose and flews should be black except in the case of lighter dogs,

French Bulldog.

where a lighter nose color is acceptable. The flews should be thick and broad, hanging over the lower jaw at the sides, meeting the underlip in front and covering the teeth which should not be seen when the mouth is closed. The underjaw should be deep, square, broad, undershot and well turned up.

EYES: The eyes should be wide apart, set low down in the skull, as far from the ears as possible, round in form, of moderate size, neither sunken nor bulging, and in color dark. No haw and no white of the eye showing when looking forward.

NECK: The neck should be thick and well arched, with loose skin at throat.

EARS: The ears shall hereafter be known as the bat ear, broad at the base, elongated, with round top, set high in the head, but not too close together, and carried erect with the orifice to the front. The leather of the ear fine and soft.

BODY: The body should be short and well rounded. The chest, broad, deep and full, well-ribbed with the belly tucked up. The back should be a roach back, with a slight fall close behind the shoulders. It should be strong and short, broad at the shoulders and narrowing at the loins.

LEGS: The fore legs should be short, stout, straight and muscular, set wide apart. The hind legs should be strong and mus-

French Bulldog.

cular, longer than the fore legs, so as to elevate the loins above the shoulders. Hocks well let down.

FEET: The feet should be moderate in size, compact and firmly set. Toes compact, well split up, with high knuckles and short, stubby nails, hind feet slightly longer than fore feet.

TAIL: The tail should be either straight or screwed (but not curly), short, hung low, thick root and fine tip; carried low in repose.

COLOR, SKIN AND COAT: Acceptable colors are: all brindle, fawn, white, brindle and white, and any color except those which constitute disqualification. The skin should be soft and loose, especially at head and shoulders, forming wrinkles. Coat moderately fine, brilliant, short and smooth.

Disqualifications: Other than bat ears; black and white, black and tan, liver, mouse, or solid black (black means black without any trace of brindle, eyes of different color; nose other than black except in the case of lighter dogs, where a lighter color nose is acceptable; hare lip; any mutilation; over 28 pounds in weight.

SCALE OF POINTS:	Points
Proportion and symmetry	5
Expression	5
Gait	4
Color	4
Coat	2
Total, general properties	20
Skull	6
Cheeks and chops	2
Stop	5
Ears	8
Eyes	4
Wrinkles	4
Nose	3
Jaws	6
Teeth	2
Total, head	40
Shoulders	5
Back	5
Neck	4
Chest	3
Ribs	4
Brisket	3
Belly	2
Fore legs	4
Hind legs	3
Feet	3
Tail	4
Total, body, legs, etc.	40
GRAND TOTAL	100

KEESHOND

ONCE THE symbol of a political party in Holland, the Keeshond is an interesting little dog which, through sheer personality and beauty, has found a place in the hearts of American dog lovers. Subject of considerable controversy concerning color and type, the breed has now settled into a definite type, and while solid blacks and solid whites sometimes occur, the accepted color is silver grey with black tipped hair.

Known to be an old breed in its native Holland, the Keeshond was introduced into England in 1900 as a "Dutch Barge Dog" and registered as such by the Kennel Club. A number of years later, Miss Hamil-

ton Fletcher (later Mrs. Wingfield Digby) brought back a number of dogs from a yachting trip on the Dutch canals and showed two of them (Breda and Saani) at the National Dog Show at Birmingham. A specialist club was formed in 1925, with Mrs. Digby as president and honorary secretary. The name was "officially" changed to Keeshond in 1926.

The breed began to find favor among British fanciers. This revived interest in Holland, where the breed had, for some time, been neglected, and Keeshond breeding activities on the native soil of the breed took on increased vigor.

Many years before, these little dogs were to be seen on the decks of practically every barge in the Dutch canals, and they were also quite prevalent on the farms of the country. There has been, through the intervening years, a considerable change in type, to such an extent that at one time two different standards were considered. Nevertheless, the Keeshond continues, in general, to reflect the fine characteristics of the old barge dogs.

The story of the origin of the Keeshond's name has a varied flavor. The name is said to be taken from that of Cornelis de Gyselaer, a leader of the political party called "The Patriots" during the time of Holland's internal strife in the middle of the eighteenth century. "Kees" is short for the Dutch Christian name "Cornelis." Another version has it that de Gyselaer was a dog lover and had a little dog named "Kees." This dog was his constant companion and struck the fancy of his followers, who adopted it as their symbol, in opposition to the Pug, which was the mascot of the opposing party led by the Prince of Orange. When the "Orangists" came into power, the breed had become so closely identified with "The Patriots" party that many members of that organization were somewhat fearful of owning them and dis-

Keeshond—Ch. Ruttkay Roem. (Owner: Ruttkay Keeshond Kennels, Royersford, Pa.)

posed of their dogs. Only the steadfast maintained the breed.

The name "Keeshond" has been ridiculed by some who gave it the pronunciation "Cheese hond"! This was entirely unfair, as the proper pronunciation is "Case Hond" or "Case" for short.

It has, also, been argued that the name had no connection whatever with de Gyselaer or his dog, "Kees," and the dogs were called Keeshonden long before the patriot leader came into the political limelight.

At one time the breed was known as "Foxdog" and, for a while, "Overweight Pomeranian." There is little doubt that the dog came from the same strains that produced the Samoyed, the Norwegian Elkhound, the Chow Chow, the Finnish Spitz, and the Pomeranian. Some authorities have held that the Keeshond is the direct ancestor of the Pomeranian.

While the dog has always been used mainly as a companion and guard, it is said to be a keen ratter and rabbiter if the owner chooses to point its energies in that direction. The Keeshond is noted for its adaptability and can be easily trained to many uses.

One of its main attractions is its magnificent coat, which is waterproof, does not mat, and requires little grooming. It was once the custom in Holland to shave a Keeshond in the fashion of a Poodle, but that practice has been discontinued.

It is a reliable dog with children, although extremely sensitive and, if not properly handled, is inclined to become somewhat timid.

Description and Standards. The description and standards, adopted by the Keeshond Club, and approved by the American Kennel Club follow.

GENERAL APPEARANCE AND CONFORMATION: The Keeshond is a handsome dog, of well-balanced, short-coupled body, attracting attention not only by his alert carriage and intelligent expression, but also by his luxurious coat, his richly plumed tail, well curled over his back, and by his foxlike face and head with small pointed ears. His coat is very thick round the neck, fore part of the shoulders and chest, forming a lionlike mane. His rump and hind legs, down to the hocks, are also thickly coated forming the characteristic "trousers." His head, ears and lower legs are covered with thick short hair. The ideal height of fully matured dogs (over 2 years old), measured from top of withers to the ground, is: for males, 18 inches; bitches, 17 inches. However, size consideration should not outweigh that of type. When dogs are judged equal in type, the dog nearest the ideal height is to be preferred. Length of back from withers to rump should equal height as measured above.

HEAD: Expression is largely dependent on the distinctive characteristic called "spectacles"—a delicately penciled line slanting slightly upward from the outer corner of each eye to the lower corner of the ear, coupled with distinct markings and shadings forming short but expressive eyebrows. Markings (or shadings) on face and head must present a pleasing appearance, imparting to the dog an alert and intelligent expression. *Fault*—Absence of "spectacles." *Skull*—The head should be well proportioned to the body, wedge-shaped when viewed from above. Not only in muzzle, but the whole head should give this impression when the ears are drawn back by covering the nape of the neck and the ears with one hand. Head in profile should exhibit a definite stop. *Fault*—Apple head, or absence of stop.

MUZZLE: The muzzle should be dark in color and of medium length, neither coarse nor snipy, and well proportioned to the skull. *Mouth*—The mouth should be neither overshot nor undershot. Lips should be black and closely meeting, not thick, coarse or sagging; and with no wrinkle at the corner of the mouth. *Fault*—Overshot or undershot. *Teeth*—The teeth should be white, sound and strong (but discoloration from distemper not to penalize severely); upper teeth should just overlap the lower teeth. *Eyes*—Eyes should be dark brown in color, of medium size, rather oblique in shape and not set too wide apart. *Fault*—Protruding round eyes or eyes light of color.

EARS: Ears should be small, triangular in shape, mounted high on head and carried erect; dark in color and covered with thick, velvety, short hair. Size should be proportionate to the head—length approximating the distance from outer corner of the eye to the nearest edge of the ear. *Fault*—Ears not carried erect when at attention.

BODY: The neck should be moderately long, well shaped and well set on shoulders; covered with a profuse mane, sweeping from under the jaw and covering the whole of the front part of the shoulders and chest, as well as the top part of the shoulders. *Chest, Back and Loin*—The body should be compact with a short straight back sloping slightly downward toward the hindquarters; well ribbed, barrel well rounded, belly moderately tucked up, deep and strong of chest. *Legs*—Forelegs should be straight seen from any angle, and well feathered. Hind legs should be profusely feathered down to the hocks—not below, with hocks only slightly bent. Legs must be of good bone and cream in color. *Fault*—Black markings below the knee, penciling excepted. *Feet*—The feet should be compact, well rounded, catlike, and cream in color. Toes are nicely arched, with black nails. *Fault*—White foot or feet.

TAIL—The tail should be set on high, moderately long, and well feathered, tightly curled over back. It should lie flat and close to the body with a very light gray plume on top where curled, but the tip of the tail should be black. The tail should form a part of the "silhouette" of the dog's body, rather than give the appearance of an appendage. *Fault*—Tail not lying close to the back. *Action*—Dogs should show boldly and keep tails curled over the back. They should move cleanly and briskly; and the movement should be straight and sharp (not lope like a German Shepherd). *Fault*—Tail not carried over back when moving.

COAT: The body should be abundantly covered with long, straight, harsh hair; standing well out from a thick, downy undercoat. The hair on the legs should be smooth and short, except for a feathering on the front legs and "trousers," as previously described, on the hind legs. The hair on the tail should be profuse, forming a rich plume. Head, including muzzle, skull and ears, should be covered with smooth, soft, short hair—velvety in texture on the ears. Coat must not part down the back. *Fault*—Silky, wavy or curly coats. Part in coat down the back.

COLOR AND MARKINGS: A mixture of gray and black. The undercoat should be very pale gray or cream (not tawny). The hair of the outer coat is black tipped, the length of the black tips producing the characteristic shading of color. The color may vary from light to dark, but any pronounced deviation from the gray color is not permissible. The plume of the tail should be very light gray when curled on back, and the tip of the tail should be black. Legs and feet should be cream. Ears should be very dark—almost black. Shoulder line markings (light gray) should be well defined. The color of the ruff and "trousers" is generally lighter than that of the body. "Spectacles" and shadings, as previously described, are characteristic of the breed and must be present to some degree. There should be no pronounced white markings.

Very Serious Fault—Entirely black or white or any other solid color; any pronounced deviation from the gray color.

SCALE OF POINTS:		Points
General conformation and appearance		20
Head:		
Shape	6	
Eyes	5	
Ears	5	
Teeth	4	20

Body:
            Chest, back and loin 10
            Tail 10
            Neck and shoulders 8
            Legs 4
            Feet 3   35
Coat 15
Color and markings 10

            TOTAL 100

LHASA APSO

SINCE THE beginning of the Manchu Dynasty in 1583 and until as late as 1908, it was the custom for the Dalai Lama of Tibet to make presentation of one of the special breed of dogs native to the sacred Lama villages to members of the Imperial families of China and other dignitaries. It was considered a great honor to receive one of these dog gifts and, moreover, it supposedly brought good fortune to the recipient. This dog was the Lhasa Apso.

In the mysterious land of Tibet beyond the northern boundary of India, the Lhasa Apso has been in existence for probably some 800 years. Travel has ever been rare in that wild and mountainous country and visitors to these lands had no opportunity to see these dogs as they were kept within the sanctity of the homes of the mighty in the villages around the sacred city of Apso. Hence, they were never mentioned by early travelers.

The Lhasa Apso is purely Tibetan, known in his homeland as "Abso Seng Kye" which means "Bark Sentinel Lion Dog." When it first made its appearance in England it was known as the Talisman Dog and Sheng Trou and then, for a time, a few were called Lhassa Terriers; others were called Apsos. About 1934, the Tibetan Breeds Association was formed and a strong movement started to get the breed and type according to a standard. It was then that the present name was established.

The coat is profuse, heavy, and inclined to be shaggy, possibly the reason for the "apso" in the name which is from the Tibetan "rapso" meaning goat-like. This dense coat is characteristic of the four breeds native to Tibet, which is understandable in a country of intense cold at certain times of the year. All of the breeds also carry their tails curled up over their backs. These are the Tibetan Terrier, raised everywhere in the country, the toy Tibetan Spaniel, and the large, powerful Tibetan Mastiff. The huge Mastiffs are used in Tibet as the outside guard dogs but, within, it is the Lhasa Apso who is used as a sentinel. Generations of breeding and training as a watch dog have made one of their chief characteristics a propensity for being bright, hardy, and alert and having a keenly-developed instinct for detecting friends from strangers. They are extremely responsive to affection and are devoted companions to their owners.

It is said that the crude manner of breeding among the Tibetans is the reason for the fact that colors are not fixed. The first two brought to the United States were a black and white male, Taikoo, and a female the color of raw silk, Dinkie. From them came offspring in colors of black and white, grizzle and white, golden, honey-colored, and brown and white.

It has been suggested that the Lhasa Apso has a place in the religion of Tibet but evidence for this belief has never been brought forth from the mysterious land where Mount Everest reaches skyward.

Description and Standards. The description and standards, adopted by The American Kennel Club, April 9, 1935, follow.

CHARACTER: Gay and assertive, but chary of strangers.

SIZE: Variable, but about 10 inches or 11 inches at shoulders for dogs, bitches slightly smaller.

COLOR: Golden, sandy, honey, dark grizzle, slate, smoke particolor, black, white or brown. This being the true Tibetan Lion Dog, golden or lion-like colors are preferred. Other colors in order as above. Dark tips to ears and beard are an asset.

BODY SHAPE: The length from point to shoulders to point of buttocks longer than height at withers, well ribbed up, strong loin, well developed quarters and thighs.

COAT: Heavy, straight, hard, not woolly nor silky, of good length and very dense.

MOUTH AND MUZZLE: Mouth level, otherwise slightly undershot preferable. Muzzle of medium length; a square muzzle is objectionable.

HEAD: Heavy head furnishings with good fall over eyes, good whiskers and beard; skull narrow, falling away behind the eyes in a marked degree, not quite flat, but not domed or apple shaped; straight foreface of fair length. Nose black, about 1½ inches long, or the length from the tip of nose to eye to be roughly about one-third of the total length from nose to back of skull.

EYES: Dark brown, neither very large and full, nor very small and sunk.

EARS: Pendant, heavily feathered.

LEGS: Fore legs straight, both fore and hind legs heavily furnished with hair.

FEET: Well feathered, should be round and cat-like, with good pads.

TAIL AND CARRIAGE: Well feathered, should be carried well over back in a screw, there may be a kink at the end. A low carriage of stern is a serious fault.

Lhasa Apso—Ch. Drax Ka-u. (Owner: Drax Kennels, Hialeah, Fla.)

POODLE

THE STANDARD Poodle is considered a favorite breed in America, Canada, Denmark, France, and Sweden and the favorite non-sporting breed in Australia, Germany and Italy.

Acclaimed by those who have had experience with the breed as the most intelligent of all breeds, the Poodle is, indeed, a dog of great versatility. In fact, students of the canine kingdom would be confronted with a mammoth task if they attempted to find a dog which, as a breed, possesses more intelligence, for the Poodle does have some almost human characteristics.

Owners of other breeds who attempt to argue the question with Poodle fanciers generally despair of making progress or leave with some doubt in their minds as to the soundness of their own position.

One who looks upon a clipped Poodle for the first time is inclined to feel that this old custom is a form of expressing the personal vanity of the owner. Nevertheless, it does have its practical side. The Poodle was originally a sporting dog, used extensively in France for retrieving. He is still a splendid worker in this respect, although his main use in this country is as a pet and companion. The Poodle's coat is extremely heavy and the custom of clipping grew out of the fact that his coat impeded the dog's progress in the water. Shaving from the ribs to the stern increased his efficiency as a water worker.

In French, the Poodle's generic name is "Caniche," derived from "duck-canard," the same source from which "Chien Canne" came. The dog has long been called "Chien Canne" in France.

Known for many years as the national dog of France, the Poodle is really of German origin, troops from that country having brought the first specimens of the breed into France. There it soon became a national favorite. The profuse coat lent itself to fashioning into fanciful designs and became the accepted custom. These "styles" of clipping have now narrowed down, as a general rule, to two: the Continental where the hind quarters are bare with rosettes on the hips and hocks, and the English saddle clip in which the hips are covered by a short clipped blanket of hair. Either fashion really enhances the appearance of the dog for they better reveal his beautiful outline and elegance. The natural qualities of the dog—vitality, dignity, and alertness—are rather enhanced by the custom.

That the custom of clipping Poodles is an old one is proved through art of some antiquity. Bernardine Pinturiccio, in 1490, depicted a well-trimmed Poodle of the Toy variety in his series of paintings, "Patient Grizelda." Martin de Vaux pictured a clipped Poodle in his famous sixteenth century painting "Tobit and his Dog." One of the drawings of Albert Durer (1471-1528) shows a dog of this breed clipped in the fashion of the day.

In regard to the intelligence of the Poodle, Stone-

Standard Poodle. Ch. Puttencove Privateer. (Owner: Mrs. George Putnam, Manchester, Mass.) Photo by Evelyn M. Shafer.

henge, in his *Dogs of the British Isles*, quoted L. Clement as follows:

> Scientists have told us that the Poodle's cerebral cavity is more capacious than in other dogs, and that the frontal sinuses are fully developed, also that the general foundation of the head and skull exhibit every indication of extraordinary intelligence.

Domini was a Poodle that had a reputation in England for remarkable intelligence, it being claimed that he could tell time by the clock and even play a good game of dominoes! For many years the breed has figured prominently in vaudeville and circus acts. In recent years, Poodles have had great success in Obedience trials in this country and England.

In olden times, these dogs were used to considerable extent in hunting for truffles. Often they were used in combination with a Dachshund, the Poodle locating the edible underground fungus and the Dachshund digging it out. At one time truffle hunting was quite an industry in the rural districts of England. Most of the dogs used were Poodles or Poodle-crosses.

Where size is concerned the Poodle has shown great elasticity in bending to the whims of man's breeding activities, so much so that three sizes are recognized. These are the Standard, Miniature, and Toy. (*See also* Toy Poodle, Group V.) All three classifications breed generally true to type.

The Miniature Poodle is an extremely popular dog in Australia, Great Britain, and South Africa and is considered a favorite non-sporting breed in New Zealand.

There are two types of Poodles, the curly and the corded. Efforts have been made to separate the "varieties" in official classification, but authorities have contended that both types are of the same breed and the difference lies only in the treatment of the coat. If allowed to grow indefinitely without brushing and

Miniature Poodle—Ch. Lawnfield's Presentation. (Owner: Marguerite H. Crosby, Lockport, New York) Photo by Evelyn M. Shafer.

oiling to prevent breaking, the coat will form thin round mats which become, with length, a mass of ropelike cords. Then the Curly Poodle becomes the Corded Poodle.

It is extremely difficult to keep a Corded Poodle in proper condition, for the long, tightly twisted cords often reach the ground. This interferes with his exercise and also prevents him from engaging in his natural activities. Consequently this type is seldom seen nowadays.

It has been said that the Poodle is the ancestor of the Irish Water Spaniel and the Curly-coated Retriever. Indeed, with the exception of the tail and muzzle, the Poodle looks very much like the Irish Water Spaniel.

The first Poodle Club was established in 1886. In England there is also the Curly Poodle Club, the Miniature Poodle Club, and the International Poodle Club.

Miss Jane Lane's prefix, "Nunsoe," was long associated with Poodle activities in England and a number of fine dogs of this breeding were brought to America, meeting with great success in the show-ring.

Description and Standards. The description and standards adopted by the Poodle Club of America and approved by the American Kennel Club follow.

GENERAL APPEARANCE, CARRIAGE AND CONDITION: That of a very active, intelligent and elegant-looking dog, squarely built, well-proportioned, moving soundly and carrying himself proudly. Properly clipped in the traditional fashion and carefully groomed, the Poodle has about him an air of distinction and dignity peculiar to himself.

HEAD AND EXPRESSION: (a) *Skull:* moderately rounded, with a slight but definite stop. Cheek-bones and muscles flat. *Muzzle:* long, straight and fine, with slight chiseling under the eyes. Strong without lippiness. The chin definite enough to preclude snipiness. Teeth white, strong and with a scissors bite. Nose sharp with well-defined nostrils. (b) *Eyes:* set far apart, very dark, full of fire and intelligence, oval in appearance. (c) *Ears:* set low and hanging close to the head. The leather should be long, wide and heavily feathered.

NECK AND SHOULDERS: Neck well proportioned, strong and long to admit of the head being carried high and with dignity. Skin snug at throat. The neck should rise from strong muscular shoulders which slope back from their point of angulation at the upper foreleg to the withers.

BODY: The chest deep and moderately wide. The ribs well sprung and braced up. The back short, strong and slightly hollowed, the loins short, broad and muscular. (Bitches may be slightly longer in back than dogs.)

TAIL: Straight, set on rather high, docked, but of sufficient length to insure a balanced outline. It should be carried up and in a gay manner.

LEGS: The forelegs straight from the shoulder, parallel and with bone muscle in proportion to size of dog. The pasterns should be strong. The hind legs very muscular, stifles well bent and hocks well let down. The thigh should be well developed, muscular and showing width in the region of the stifle to insure strong and graceful action. The four feet should turn neither in nor out. *Feet*—Rather small and oval in shape. Toes arched, close and cushioned on thick, hard pads.

COAT: Quality: very profuse, of harsh texture and dense throughout.

CLIP: A Poodle may be shown in the "Puppy" Clip or in the traditional "Continental" Clip or the "English Saddle" Clip. A Poodle under a year old may be shown in the "Puppy" Clip with the coat long except the face, feet and base of tail, which should be shaved. Dogs one year old or older must be shown in either the "Continental" Clip or "English Saddle" Clip.

In the "Continental" Clip the hindquarters are shaved with pompons on hips (optional). The face, feet, legs and tail are shaved leaving bracelets on the hind legs, puffs on the forelegs and a pompon at the end of the tail. The rest of the body must be left in full coat.

In the "English Saddle" Clip the hindquarters are covered with a short blanket of hair except for a curved shaved area on the flank and two shaved bands on each hind leg. The face, feet, forelegs and tail are shaved leaving puffs on the forelegs and a pompon at the end of the tail. The rest of the body must be left in full coat.

COLOR: The coat must be an even and solid color at the skin. In blues, grays, silvers, browns, cafe-au-laits, apricots and creams the coats may show varying shades of the same color. This is frequently present in the somewhat darker feathering of the ears and in the tipping of the ruff. While clear colors are definitely preferred such natural variation in the shading of the coat is not to be considered a fault. Brown and cafe-au-lait Poodles have liver-colored noses, eye-rims and lips, dark toenails and dark amber eyes. Black, blue, gray, silver, apricot, cream and white Poodles have black noses, eye-rims and lips, black or self-colored toenails and very dark eyes. In the apricots while black is preferred, liver-colored noses, eye-rims and lips, self-colored toenails and amber eyes are permitted but are not desirable.

GAIT: A straightforward trot with light springy action. Head and tail carried high. Forelegs and hind legs should move parallel turning neither in nor out. Sound movement is essential.

SIZE: The Standard Poodle is over 15 inches at the withers. Any Poodle which is 15 inches or less in height shall be disqualified from competition as a Standard Poodle.

The Miniature Poodle is 15 inches or under at the withers, with a minimum height in excess of 10 inches. Any Poodle which is over 15 inches, or 10 inches or less at the withers shall be disqualified from competition as a Miniature Poodle.

The toy Poodle is 10 inches or under at the withers. Any Poodle which is more than 10 inches at the withers shall be disqualified from competition as a Toy Poodle.

VALUE OF POINTS:	Points
General appearance, carriage and condition	20
Head, ears, eyes and expression	20
Neck and shoulders	10
Body and tail	15
Legs and feet	15
Coat—color and texture	10
Gait	10
TOTAL	100

Major Faults. Eyes: round in appearance, protruding, large or very light. Jaws: undershot, overshot or wry mouth. Cowhocks. Feet: flat or spread. Tail: set low, curled or carried over the back. Shyness.

Disqualifications. Parti-colors: The coat of a parti-colored dog is not an even solid color at the skin but is variegated in patches of two or more colors. Any type of clip other than those listed in section on coat.

Any size over or under the limits specified in section on size.

(July 14, 1959)

SCHIPPERKE

SOMETIMES ERRONEOUSLY called a Dutch dog, the Schipperke is a dog of Belgian origin. He came from the Flemish provinces of that country and has long been associated with the barges of that section. Perhaps this association is, in some measure, the cause of the confusion concerning the locale of his origin; Belgium and Holland were at times united in the early days.

The name Schipperke is Flemish for "Little Captain" and is properly pronounced "skeep-er-ker" (the last r almost silent). The names Spits and Spitske were discarded and Schipperke chosen as a compliment to a Mr. Renssens, who was largely responsible for the recognition of the breed and was known as "the father of the Schipperke." Mr. Renssens was the owner of a barge line which plied between Brussels and Antwerp, and many of these little dogs were used as guards on these boats.

Often born tailless (no more than an inch of tail is allowable under the standard), the Schipperke was not always without a caudal appendage. The practice of short docking is said to have started with a shoemaker, who, angered by the continued theft of his neighbor's dog, cut off its tail, improving the appearance so much that other owners followed the practice, which soon became the accepted custom.

Although the breed was called the Spits and Spitske, and often compared with the Pomeranian, it is said to have descended from the black sheepdog called the "Leauvenaar," common in the Flemish provinces. Some authorities are equally positive it is a "spitz" breed.

The breed makes a splendid house dog, being affectionate and alert, ever ready to signal the approach of strangers. In appearance it is quite distinctive, resembling no other breed very closely. Its foxlike head and keen expression attracts much attention wherever it is shown.

Walter J. Comstock, of Providence, R.I., is said to have brought the first Schipperke to America in 1888. Frank Dole, well-known authority and writer, was among the very early exhibitors in this country.

Description and Standards. The description and standards, adopted by the Schipperke Club of America and approved by the American Kennel Club follow.

The name Schipperke is Flemish for Little Captain and is correctly pronounced Skeeper-ker (last r almost silent). This standard is an interpretation of the standard of the country of the Schipperke's origin—Belgium.

APPEARANCE AND GENERAL CHARACTERISTICS: Excellent and faithful little watchdog, suspicious of strangers. Active, agile, indefatigable, continually occupied with what is going on about him, careful of things that are given him to guard, very kind with children, knows the ways of the household; always curious to know what is going on behind any closed door or about any object that has been moved, betraying his impressions by his sharp bark and outstanding ruff, seeking the company of horses, a hunter of moles and other vermin; can be used to hunt, a good rabbit dog.

HEAD: Fox-like, fairly wide, narrowing at the eyes, seen in profile slightly rounded, tapering muzzle not too elongated nor too blunt, not too much stop.

NOSE: Small and black.

EYES: Dark brown, small, oval rather than round, neither sunken nor prominent.

EXPRESSION: Should have a questioning expression: sharp and lively, not mean or wild.

EARS: Very erect, small, triangular, placed high, strong enough not to be capable of being lowered except in line with the body.

TEETH: Meeting evenly. A tight scissors bite is acceptable.

NECK: Strong and full, slightly arched, rather short.

SHOULDERS: Muscular and sloping.

CHEST: Broad and deep in brisket.

BODY: Short, thick set and cobby. Broad behind the shoulders, seeming higher in front because of the ruff. Back strong, short, straight and level or slightly sloping down toward rump. Ribs well sprung.

LOINS: Muscular and well drawn up from the brisket but not

Schipperke—Ch. Donrho's Stargitt. (Owner: Donrho Kennels, Valparaiso, Ind.) Don Petrulis Photography.

to such an extent as to cause a weak and leggy appearance of the hind quarters.

FORE LEGS: Straight under the body, with bone in proportion, but not coarse.

HIND QUARTERS: Somewhat lighter than the foreparts, but muscular, powerful, with rump well rounded, tail docked to no more than one inch in length.

FEET: Small, round and tight (not splayed) nails straight, strong and short.

COAT: Abundant and slightly harsh to the touch, short on the ears and on the front of legs and on the hocks, fairly short on the body, but longer around neck beginning back of the ears, and forming a ruff and a cape; a jabot extending down between the front legs, also longer on rear where it forms a culotte the points turning inward. Under coat dense and short on body, very dense around neck making ruff stand out. Culotte should be as long as the ruff.

COLOR: Solid black.

WEIGHT: Up to 18 pounds.

Faults: Light eyes, large round prominent eyes, ears too long or too rounded, narrow head and elongated muzzle, too blunt muzzle, domed skull, smooth, short coat with short ruff and culotte, lack of under coat, curly or silky coat, body coat more than three inches long, slightly over or undershot, swayback, Bullterrier shaped head, straight hocks. Straight stifles and shoulders, cow hocks, feet turning in or out, legs not straight when viewed from front. Lack of distinction between length of coat, ruff and culotte.

Disqualifications. Any color other than solid black. Drop or semi-erect ears. Badly over-shot or under-shot.

Part XX

THE HUMANE MOVEMENT

The first dog who hunted with and fought beside his friend, Man, in prehistoric times, probably started the Humane Movement. After the kill, the hunter-warrior likely rubbed bear grease or its Stone Age equivalent on his own wounds and the wounds of his canine companion. The dog licked his master's hand in gratitude. This was, and still is, the oldest alliance in the animal kingdom.

KINDNESS TOWARD ANIMALS —MAN'S EARLY DISPOSITION

CONTEMPORARY writers are inclined to date the Humane Movement as originating in England late in the 18th Century. However, many ancient civilizations taught and enforced respect for the rights of dogs and other animals.

Among the peoples sharing in humane beliefs in ancient times were the Egyptians, the Babylonians, the Persians, some of the African tribes, and to some extent the Chinese and the Hebrews (see Your Dog and the Law—Part I).

Many of the world's great religions for thousands of years have taught kindliness toward all animals. In the Old Testament, animals are mentioned with sympathy and admiration over two hundred times. Plutarch records that followers of the Greek philosopher Pythagoras (582-500 B.C.) ". . . made a practice of kindness to animals." Aristotle (384-322 B.C.) wrote sympathetically of ". . . the sagacity of the noble dog."

Buddha (563-483 B.C.) preached pity. Confucius (550-479 B.C.) believed in fairness toward animals.

Genesis VIII, 1, tells how God ordained that two of each species of animals should enter the Ark at the time of the Flood, to insure their survival. The solicitude of the Almighty extended to dogs, as well as to other animals.

David, the Psalmist, expressed God's wish for the sustenance of all of life: "You open your hand and satisfy the desire of every living thing." (Psalm 144, 16.)

Nineveh was saved not only for the sake of its human inhabitants, but also for the sake of the animals that lived there. (Jonas IV, 11.) The teachings of Jesus speak of God's benevolence toward both human beings and lesser creatures: "Look at the birds of the air; they do not sow or reap . . . yet your heavenly Father feeds them." (Matthew VI, 26; Luke XII, 24.)

Love and kindliness for dogs are exemplified in the lives of many of the Christian saints and the writings of prominent Protestant and Catholic theologians and humanitarians, as well as the Bible, itself.

St. Bernard (923-1008 A.D.) wrote: "Every creature is at man's service in order to better bring man to God's service." The founder of the great and little St. Bernard hospices, from which the famed dogs set out to rescue travelers, practiced what he preached.

The love of St. Francis of Assisi (1182-1226) for animals also is well-known.

The church, in medieval times, functioned in lieu of the modern humane societies. Many of the Popes have had their beloved dogs—for example, Paul V (reigned 1605-21), Paul IX (1846-78) and Leo XIII (1878-1903).

Treatises or sermons against cruelty to animals were not always understood. In post-Reformation England, the first sermon on record on this topic was preached in 1772 by an Anglican vicar. The Rev. James Granger shocked and ". . . gave almost universal disgust to two considerable congregations," according to accounts of the sermons. "Mentions of dogs and horses from the pulpit were considered a prostitution of the dignity . . ." of the clergy.

But sentiment had been slowly accumulating against the brutality to dogs involved in bull baiting. An article by an anonymous writer published in an English magazine in 1749 criticized cock fighting and bull baiting.

Bull Baiting Outlawed In England. In 1800, Sir William Pulteney introduced in Parliament a bill to outlaw bull baiting, but it was defeated. A second attempt, two years later, also failed.

Lord Erskine persuaded the House of Lords to pass, in 1809, a bill ". . . for preventing wanton and malicious cruelty to animals," but the measure later was defeated in the House of Commons. However, in 1822, Richard Martin of Galway persuaded Parliament to pass a law recognizing the rights of dumb animals and compelling their humane care. King George IV, a personal friend of the M.P. from Ireland, dubbed him "Humanity" Martin.

SOCIETIES FORM AGAINST CRUELTY TO ANIMALS

Two years after the passage of Martin's law, the Society for the Prevention of Cruelty to Animals was organized in London. Although Martin was widely credited with founding the Society, he himself cited the Rev. Arthur Broome as the originator.

Royalty took an increasing interest in humane work. Princess Victoria, at the age of 16, expressed devotion to humanitarian principles. On her ascension to the throne in 1837 she befriended the Humane Society, and in 1840 granted it the right to use the "Royal" prefix.

"Humanity" Martin died in 1834, at the age of 80. A year after his death Parliament passed a law providing protection for all domestic animals. The Royal Society for the Prevention of Cruelty to Animals continued to grow and sponsor the educational work which is the basis of all humane society programs.

The idea was beginning to take hold that the teaching of kindness to dogs and other animals to children and young adults was an important step toward the prevention of crimes of violence in later life. One of the first to assert this thesis was an English jurist, Jeremy Bentham (1748-1832), who believed that there was a solid link between the rights of animals and human morality.

Soon societies for the protection of dogs and other animals were formed in all the countries of Europe. The doctrine of the SPCA spread to America, where hunting dogs and watchdogs always had been highly prized and, for the most part, well-treated.

The colonists in both the North and the South had dogs. Two dogs accompanied the Pilgrims in the Mayflower. Dogs saved many a pioneer from a surprise attack by Indians and were correspondingly rewarded.

George Washington and most men of his generation loved dogs. A sturdy Newfoundland accompanied explorers Meriwether Lewis and William Clark from St. Louis to the Pacific Northwest and back (1804-06). Even in the grimmest and hungriest crises, when the snow was so deep that game could not be found and many members of the expedition had to subsist on Indian dog meat, Lewis sternly vetoed all suggestions that the Newfoundland be added to the larder.

ASPCA FORMED

Young Abraham Lincoln once jumped into a river to save a dog. When Lincoln became President he happened to include, among many other diplomatic appointments, a new secretary for the American Legation in Russia. The choice fell on Henry Bergh, son of a wealthy New York shipbuilder. Bergh had spent his youth writing plays and poetry and traveling widely about Europe.

During his travels Bergh saw many instances of dogs stoned, circus horses abused and other animal cruelties. One day, after taking his post at St. Petersburg, he saw a Russian droshky driver beating a horse . . . and the course of history changed.

At the age of 50 the dilettante poet Bergh suddenly became a crusader for the humane treatment of animals. Daily he went through the streets of the Russian capital, endeavoring to teach peasants and noblemen not to abuse their horses and dogs. Finally, discouraged over the Russian attitude, he resigned his post and returned to New York where he organized the American Society for the Prevention of Cruelty to Animals. Bergh wore spats and carried a cane, but he was no lightweight; the SPCA carried a "big stick."

Among the charter members were many of Bergh's wealthy friends, August Belmont, James J. Roosevelt, John Jacob Astor, Jr., Hamilton Fish, Horace Greeley, Peter Cooper and Mayor John T. Hoffman. The New York State Legislature granted a charter to the new organization on April 10, 1866. Backed by the prestige of his group, Bergh in nine days lobbied through the Legislature an act making cruelty to animals a misdemeanor and giving the young society certain powers to enforce the law.

Certain interests called Bergh "the great meddler" and tried to block his work, but it spread across the nation. The second American SPCA was formed in Philadelphia as a result of the work of Col. M. Richard Muckel and Mrs. Caroline Earle White.

HUMANE EDUCATIONAL PROGRAM STARTED IN AMERICA

George Thorndike Angell, a Boston attorney, interested himself in activities against cruelty to animals long before he ever heard of a SPCA. He fathered the American humane education movement. Two years before the formation of Bergh's society in New York, Angell drew up a will setting aside a considerable portion of his property for use in circulating information ". . . calculated to prevent cruelty to animals."

In 1868, Angell and a group of other prominent Bostonians sponsored a meeting which organized the Massachusetts SPCA. The first board of directors included John Quincy Adams, Henry Saltonstall, George Tyler Bigelow, George Noyes, Russell Sturgis Jr., and William Appleton. Mrs. Appleton was one of the guiding spirits behind the Society, but in an era

Tiny Yorkshire pup. Hank Babbit photo.

when it was still considered improper for a lady to take part in civic activities, her role was in her husband's name.

At Angell's instigation, the Society started the first American publication devoted to humane work: *Our Dumb Animals*. The first edition appeared on June 2, 1868 and was distributed by members of the Boston police force.

The next year Angell visited England and persuaded the Royal SPCA to sponsor a humane-topic essay contest among school children. The contest was so successful that Angell spread the idea in the United States upon his return home in 1870.

Meanwhile, he attended in Zurich, Switzerland on August 3-6, 1869 the first International Congress of humane societies. Humane activities continued to thrive in Europe.

Cardinal Zigliari, an Italina theologian (1833-1893) wrote: "Cruelty to animals is a sin because it inspires acts that are contrary to the ends and the order designed by the Creator." The Catholic Archbishop of Westminster, Cardinal Manning, wrote in 1891: "We owe to God the duty of treating all His creatures according to His own perfections of love and mercy. 'The righteous man is merciful to his beast.'"

Societies Spread and Grow. The work in America went on rapidly. The San Francisco SPCA was orga-

nized on April 8, 1868, the fourth such society in the nation.

Boston crusader Angell traveled through many states, organizing or inspiring the organization of humane societies. The Illinois Humane Society was formed in 1870. In May, 1871, in the Church of the Unity at Boston, Angell delivered what was probably the first sermon given by a layman, certainly in the United States and likely in the world, on the subject of cruelty to animals.

Angell delivered at Dartmouth on Oct. 4, 1875, what was believed to be the first such lecture ever given at any college in North America. He also spoke at Harvard, Amherst and other schools.

In November, 1878, Angell undertook a Southern tour. In Baltimore, he made friends with the noted evangelist, the Rev. D. L. Moody, spoke at a revival meeting attended by thousands, and passed out 2,000 humane educational pamphlets. A few days later Angell addressed the National Grange at its convention in Richmond, Va., and through Grange delegates sent humane pamphlets to every state in the Union.

In 1879, Angell spoke in Detroit, Milwaukee and Minneapolis. A Hartford, Conn., schoolgirl asked and obtained his help in forming a humane society in that state. His work extended to New Orleans.

Catharine Smithies, who established the first Bands of Mercy in England in collaboration with the Rev. Thomas Timmins, credited Angell with inspiring her work. Angell and his fellow crusaders formed Bands of Mercy in many states. He helped Father Patrick Strain organize the first Catholic Band of Mercy in the parochial schools of Lynn, Mass. in 1882.

By 1884 membership in the Bands of Mercy in the nation exceeded 234,000, including, for example, 30,000 Cincinnati school children.

By the time that Henry Bergh died on the day of the great blizzard of 1888, twenty-two years after founding the ASPCA, his idea that animals should be protected from cruelty had reached out and touched the heart and conscience of the nation. Humane societies had become established in 37 of the 38 states then in the Union and more and more states were enacting anti-cruelty laws.

In 1889 Angell established the American Humane Education Society, one of his greatest achievements. He died in 1909. Dr. William O. Stillman, president of the American Humane Association, delivered a tribute at the Association's annual meeting: "Mr. Angell was a giant in this cause. He, more than anyone, perhaps, who has recently lived, has given impetus to the Humane Movement."

The Massachusetts SPCA elected as Angell's successor in the Society's presidency Dr. Francis H. Rowley, pastor of the First Baptist Church of Boston. Dr. Rowley inspired the building of the Angell Memorial Animal Hospital, the first of its kind in New England. At the dedication, in 1915, Dr. A. Lawrence Lowell, president of Harvard University, said: "The degree of civilization can be measured by the width of human sympathy."

Easily fitting into a lady's basket purse—three Chihuahuas.
Photo by Nachod.

Dr. Stillman, an Albany, N.Y., physician, became interested in humane work and was elected a vice-president of the American Humane Association in 1895. He was elevated to the AHA presidency in 1904 when the incumbent, Dr. Albert Leffingwell, was sent on a diplomatic mission to Russia. Dr. Stillman was reelected to the Association's presidency until his death in 1924. He was fond of dogs and kept a number at his country home. In 1912 he established the Association's magazine, *The National Humane Review.*

In 1910, over thirty nations sent representatives to an International Humane Conference held at Washington, D.C. In 1923, another world conference, at New York, drew delegates from all over the world. The International Society for the Protection of Animals was incorporated in 1959 by the Royal SPCA and the American Humane Assn.

In the United States, there were by 1967 more than 800 humane organizations of varying names and areas of work, but all with a common goal: kindness to dogs, cats and other animals. The societies ranged numerically from 85 in California to three in Alaska.

There was at least one statewide organization (sometimes several) in every state. For example: Arizona SPCA, Arizona Humane Society, Animal Crusaders of Arizona, Inc.; Alabama Association of Humane Societies, Alabama League Against Animal Suffering, and Alabama Federation of Humane Societies.

Local societies have such assorted names as: Tailwagger Federation, Beverly Hills, Calif.; Mercy Crusade, Inc., and Pet Aid League, Burbank, Calif.; Dog Haven, Granby, Conn.; Playground Humane Society, Ft. Walton Beach, Fla.; Orphans of the Storm, Lake

Bluff, Ill.; The Sanctuary, Martinsville, Ind.; Helping Hand Humane Society, Topeka, Kans.; Animal Defenders' League, Portland, Ore.; Six Flags Humane Society, Victoria, Tex.; Downeast Animal Welfare, Inc., Southwest Harbor, Maine; Bide-A-Wee Home, New York City, and the Performing & Caged Animals Protection League, Vancouver, British Columbia.

The Good Shepherd Federation for Animal Birth Control, of Monte Bello, Calif., the Humane Society of the Virgin Islands, the New York Women's League for Animals, the Home for Friendless Animals of Noblesville Ind., and the Animal Crusaders of Everett, Wash., all are working for the same cause, each in its own way.

So are the Animal Anti-Cruelty Association Of Arizona And The Southwest, the Western Humane Education Society (San Francisco), the Pet Assistance Foundation (Los Angeles), the Latham Foundation for Promotion of Humane Education (Oakland, Calif.), and many other regional or national organizations or foundations.

AMERICAN HUMANE ASSOCIATION ACTIVITIES

The American Humane Association is a loose federation composed for the most part of state and local societies, working largely toward common ideals, but not bound or governed by the AHA. Working mostly through charitable donations, and only occasionally subsidized by city, county or state dog-tag revenues, the local societies carry on important educational campaigns. Thousands of dogs are cared for, rehabilitated and placed in homes where possible, or spared from further suffering through merciful anesthesia deaths, through this work.

For instance, the SPCA in New York City, which has 300 employees, has cared for 20,000,000 animals in the first century of its operations. Each year this Society's adoption service places an average of 21,000 animals for adoption. The Society's hospital was the scene of the first open-heart surgery to save a dog's life. The hospital, opened in 1912, is currently doing research on glaucoma—an eye disease, and on malignant lymphoma, a now-incurable form of cancer.

This SPCA hospital is the nation's largest user of veterinary medicines, giving 13,000 anti-distemper vaccine doses in the average year, as well as thousands of other inoculations. The hospital sends radio-guided ambulances to the scenes of accidents, fires and other emergencies, to save dogs and other endangered animals.

In the educational field the New York SPCA sets a good example with its broad educational program. A traveling zoo, stocked with dogs, cats, monkeys, rabbits and birds, takes the message of kindness to animals to children in schools, playgrounds and hospitals. Other programs teach the prevention of cruelty to employees of pet shops, circuses and other places where dogs and other animals are kept.

The ASPCA Animalport at the Kennedy International Airport caters exclusively to animal air travelers with a stop-over in New York. Since it opened in 1958, the Animalport has played host to more than 600,000 animals of 138 species, including dogs, race horses, zoo animals, pets owned by men of the U.S. armed services, cattle for food or breeding purposes flown to needy countries, etc.

The broad work of education and lobbying for national legislation protecting dogs and other animals necessarily had to be carried on by national organizations.

Concern For Animals As Experimental Subjects. The National Society for Medical Research was founded soon after World War II. The late Dr. Robert Gesell, chairman of the Department of Physiology at the University of Michigan, assisted the organization at its start but urged that scientists act to prevent the abuse of dogs and other experimental animals.

"Nothing was done, either by the National Society for Medical Research or the American Humane Association," says Mrs. Roger Stevens, Dr. Gesell's daughter.

"My husband and I offered a gift of $10,000 to the Association to study and act on matters of treatment and procurement of experimental animals, but the gift was declined because the field was so controversial," Mrs. Stevens records.

"The field was unpopular alike with the medical profession and with anti-vivisectionists who, at that time, were the only persons offering criticisms of any kind of the treatment of animals in laboratories."

Deciding that it was "impossible to get action from existing groups," Roger and Christine Stevens in 1951 founded the Animal Welfare Institute, of which Mrs. Stevens became president. The institute has dedicated itself to studies which provide laboratories with free manuals and other information on the proper care and treatment of dogs and other animals used in medical and other scientific experiments.

At the suggestion of prominent attorney, the late Abe Fortas, the Institute and its friends also founded the Society for Animal Protective Legislation which was registered under Federal law and qualified to lobby for remedial laws in the field.

Efforts in this field went back to the 1876 act of the British Parliament providing for the humane treatment of animals used in research. Based upon recommendations made by a Royal Commission, the act required licenses for the performance of experiments painful to animals. Famed scientists Charles Darwin and Thomas Huxley helped get the law passed.

The law stipulated that ". . . the experiment must be for the advancement by new discovery of physiological knowledge or knowledge which will be useful for saving or prolonging life or alleviating suffering in man or animals." Some ten conditions were attached to all licenses, including the provision: "If an animal at any time during any of the said experiments is found to be suffering severe pain which is likely to endure, such animal shall forthwith be painlessly killed."

British scientists found that the legislation to assure humane treatment for experimental animals did not interfere with legitimate research. In the year 1937 the British Home Office, administrator of the act, licensed 918,960 experiments involving dogs or other animals.

In 1960 the total number of experiments licensed in Great Britain rose to 3,701,187. Of this total, 355,720 (fewer than 10 percent) were surgical. Most of the others involved experiments with new drugs or foods and/or vitamins or mineral supplements, and the like.

Of the surgical total, 51,560 were experiments under anaesthesia without recovery of consciousness. Surgical procedures under anaesthesia with subsequent recovery of consciousness numbered 304,160. In addition, there were 4,335 lecture experiments on anaesthetized animals which were killed before recovery of consciousness.

Most significantly, from the viewpoint of the humanitarians, there were no experiments on conscious animals illustrating lectures to students, according to the report from Major C. W. Hume, secretary-general of the Universities Federation for Animal Welfare.

Two years later the late Lord Brain, a past president of the Royal College of Physicians, commented: "A very large volume of animal experiments is carried out in the United Kingdom. The existence of the restrictions and inspections imposed by law, in my experience, works extremely well and prevents the infliction of unnecessary pain on experimental animals without in any way restricting the activities of genuine scientific research."

Sir Arthur Porritt, surgeon to Queen Elizabeth II and president of the Royal College of Surgeons, agreed.

"I have never heard of any genuine surgical research being hampered by our present regulations for preventing the infliction of unnecessary pain on laboratory animals," Sir Arthur wrote in 1962.

Meanwhile, experiments in the United States had grown to immense proportions. There were no figures available because laboratory use of experimental animals was unregulated. However, by 1950 it was estimated that millions of animals were used yearly in American laboratories—including hundreds of thousands of dogs.

In 1962, the late Fred Myers, then executive director of the Humane Society of the United States, testified before a Congressional committee that some 300,000,000 animals were being used yearly in this country.

The immense use of animals meant that many of them were not housed or cared for under suitable conditions. In 1961, Dr. Mark L. Morris, president of the American Veterinary Medical Association, warned: "Research conducted on malnourished, diseased and parasite-ridden laboratory animals will only continue to add misinformation to our medical literature, invalidate research results, increase the cost of research and interfere with production."

With all kinds of experiments being conducted, and no law for uniform standards of animal care or merciful death, differences of opinion naturally arose as to what sort of regulations should be sought.

The Animal Welfare Institute, founded by Mr. and Mrs. Stevens, took the lead in studying legislation on the subject. The Institute advocated a Federal law patterned after the British Act of 1876 and engaged in a broad program of humane education for research scientists and the general public. The Society for Animal Protective Legislation worked unswervingly for regulatory legislation.

WARDS Founded. The year 1953 witnessed the founding of WARDS: Welfare of Animals Used for Research in Drugs and Surgery.

"WARDS is the only civilian (laymen's) organization devoted exclusively to the scientific handling of research animals," said Mrs. Peyton Hawes Dunn, secretary of the organization.

"The failure to provide the basic needs of these dogs and other animals has caused the brutal and unscientific conditions of which the public is becoming aware.

"WARDS wants these animals to be supervised locally and nationally by veterinarians, which would in no way interfere with research or medicine."

The Humane Society of the United States Formed. Meanwhile, the National Society for Medical Research sought to persuade or in some instances to compel Humane Society shelters to provide dogs and cats for experimentation. Because the NSMR offered no specified limitation on pain in such experimentation, most humane organizations fought all attempts at such legislation.

In some states and localities the NSMR was successful in enacting legislation to compel the supply of animals for experiments; in others, not.

"The NSMR worked hard to undermine organized animal protective groups," Mrs. Stevens charged. "So successful was this pressure that the editor of *The National Humane Review,* organ of the American Humane Association, who had been writing hard-hitting, factual articles, was told that he could no longer use the words, 'National Society for Medical Research' in any article for publication in The Review. He resigned and the AHA's educational director and field director resigned with him.

"They formed a new organization, the National Humane Society, whose name was later changed (after they were sued by the AHA because of the similarity of names) the Humane Society of the United States."

The new organization, the Humane Society of the United States, was incorporated on November 22, 1954. It was felt "that the American Humane Movement would be strengthened by a new type of national society," a statement from the organization's service director, Patrick Parkes, explained. "The Society opposes and seeks to prevent all use or exploitation of animals that cause pain, suffering or fear."

"The HSUS maintains an education department, an affiliates department, a field service department and is building a National Humane Education Center," Mr. Parkes stated. "The Society has been particularly active in pressing for humane slaughter legislation, a Federal law to protect laboratory animals, and amendments to state, municipal and county laws concerning cruelty to animals or the regulation of animals."

National Catholic Society for Animal Welfare Formed. The American Humane Association's former educational director, Miss Helen Jones, founded the National Catholic Society for Animal Welfare in 1959, after having been associated for a time with the Humane Society of the United States.

"The NCSAW was founded to fill two needs: to overcome the indifference of Catholics to the suffering of animals and to fill the vacuum caused by the lack of any organized religious support for the protection of animals," Miss Jones wrote.

"From the first, the Society's membership has included people of all creeds who recognize that mercy and compassion for all life, including God's animal world, are basic to all religion."

In 1961 the organization received the Apostolic blessing of Pope John XXIII, who granted an audience to two of its officers.

"The Society is a lay organization and is not controlled or supported by the hierarchy," Miss Jones wrote.

Half a dozen hearings were held by Congressional committees as a result of campaigns conducted by the various humane societies. Demands for action were spurred by articles written by a Washington newspaperwoman, Mrs. Ann Cottrell Free, who discovered that dogs were being mistreated in a government laboratory.

Testifying in 1962 at a hearing conducted by Representative Kenneth Roberts (D., Ala.,) then chairman of the House Commerce Committee's Subcommittee on Health and Safety, Mrs. Free said:

"I could not believe it when a troubled Food and Drug Administration scientist told me in October, 1959, that deep in the sub-basement of the South Agriculture Building dogs were kept in cages for life. Only seeing would be believing. I obtained permission to see these animals.

"In those windowless, sub-basement rooms hundreds of dogs flung themselves against the bars of their cages, piled tier on tier. They were barking, screaming, whining. A few were mute and drooped their heads in the dark corners. Others circled ceaselessly in their cages. The steel grids beneath their feet showed their pathetic, circular paths. . ."

The Nation's press began to demand action. An editorial in *The New York Times* on October 26, 1962 noted that ". . . the thirst for scientific knowledge, combined with human carelessness, may sometimes result in laboratory conditions and procedures

In memory of Old Drum and Senator Vest's famous tribute to a dog, delivered during a Missouri law suit involving the killing of a dog. This bronze statue, executed by Reno Gastaldi of St. Louis, stands on the lawn of the present courthouse in Warrensburg, Missouri. (See also Text, page 343.) Courtesy of Warrensburg Chamber of Commerce.

which do not meet the highest standards of medical research. Bills introduced in the Senate and House during the past session were patterned on legislation enacted in England 86 years ago. The British example, which has not hampered fruitful medical research, should be followed here."

Nevertheless, there were contrary opinions from part of the medical profession and from some of the veterinarians. However, as the *Times*' editorial said: "Many of the great achievements of modern medical research would not have been possible without experimentation on animals. Researchers must remain free to avail themselves of this invaluable technique; but all freedoms bear inherent responsibilities."

Several organizations changed their positions during hearings held in 1965 and 1966 by the Senate Commerce Committee and the House Agricultural Committee. Some groups were accused of advocating bills which critics said were so severe they had no chance of passage. Antivivisectionists, for the most part, opposed all bills on the grounds that to enact any regulatory legislation would condone surgical experiments to which some humanitarians objected.

Opinions were so divided that for a time it appeared that no legislation at all would be enacted: a result familiar for decades. At this point, Barry Bingham, editor and publisher of The Louisville (Ky.) *Courier-Journal*, sounded a call to all humane organizations to cease their skirmishing and unite behind a bill that could be passed.

Recent U.S. Laws On Pre-Experimental Animal Care. Although all the societies did not support the developing legislation, enough did so that Congress passed Public Law 89-544 (August 22, 1966). It is an Act authorizing the Secretary of Agriculture to regulate the transportation, sale and handling of dogs, cats and certain other animals intended to be used for purposes of research or experimentation (for main provisions, see Your Dog and The Law—Part I.)

In signing the bill into law, President Lyndon B. Johnson had made these pointed comments:

"Science and research do not compel us to tolerate the kind of inhumanity which has been involved in the careless and callous handling of animals in some of our laboratories. This will put an end to such conditions."

Most American presidents have been fond of dogs and many have helped the Humane Movement. The Animal Welfare Institute presented its 1966 Albert Schweitzer Award jointly to two United States Senators chiefly instrumental in the passage of the law: Warren Magnuson (D., Wash., who as Chairman of the Senate Commerce Committee called the vital hearing held in 1966, and A.S. Mike Monroney (D., Okla.), who obtained adoption of the Monroney Amendment, extending provisions for dog care into the laboratories.

Although the Humane Society of the United States did not support the Monroney Amendment and some other organizations were silent, the Act received decisive support from the Animal Welfare Institute, the Society for Animal Protective Legislation, WARDS, the Massachusetts Society for the Prevention of Cruelty to Animals (the Nation's largest such state organization) and the Virginia Federation of Humane Societies.

The law regulates only pre-experiment care. Some humane societies are working for an act which would regulate experimental conditions.

HUMANE ANIMAL TREATMENT —OF ONGOING CONCERN

Meanwhile, the World Federation for the Protection of Animals held its Fifth World Congress in October 1966 in Barcelona, Spain, and voted in favor of a program: "to provide every policeman in every village with a place as a temporary refuge for strayed animals and the means of humane destruction for aged and sick animals, under veterinary advice; to support all efforts to encourage research not involving the use of living animals, and to investigate the alternatives to vivisection."

The Humane Movement, foreshadowed in the writings of Pliny (23-79 A.D.) and advanced by scholars, philosophers and saints, goes on. There probably will always be divided opinions on how to proceed on certain details, but there are many common goals.

APPENDICES

Dog Publications

The *"American Field"*

Table—States, Dog Shipment Requirements

Stud Books and Registers

Addresses Abroad—Dog Organizations, Clubs

Glossaries—Where Found

    Bird Dog Field Trial Terms

    Coursing Terms

    Dog Show Terms

    Foxhunting Terms

    General Glossary

    Greyhound Racing Terms

    Obedience Trial Terms

    Sheepdog Working Terms

——Dog Publications——

THE WIDESPREAD interest in dogs, dog breeding, and dog topics is nowhere better demonstrated than in the numerous publications devoted to these subjects. The periodicals listed below are representative.

The American Cooner (Monthly) 116 E. Franklin, Sesser, Illinois 62884

American Field (Weekly newspaper) (F.D.S.B.) 222 West Adams St., Chicago, Illinois 60606

American Kennel Gazette (Monthly) (AKC) 51 Madison Ave., New York, New York 10010

Bloodlines Journal (UKC) 321 W. Cedar St., Kalamazoo, Michigan 49007

The Chase (Monthly) 152 Walnut St., Lexington, Kentucky 40501

Dog News (Monthly) 406 Elm St., Cincinnati, Ohio 45238

Dog World (Monthly) 469 East Ohio St., Chicago, Illinois 60611

Dogs In Canada 200 Davenport Road, Toronto, Canada

Full Cry (Monthly) Box 190, Sedalia, Missouri 65301

Hounds and Hunting (Monthly) 142 W. Washington St., Bradford, Pennsylvania 16701

The Hunter's Horn (Monthly) Sand Springs, Oklahoma 74063

Hunting Dog 827 No. Fourth St., Greenfield, Ohio 45123

National Stock Dog (etc.) *Magazine*, Route 1, Butler, Indiana 46721

Popular Dogs (Monthly) 2009 Ranstead St., Philadelphia, Pennsylvania 19103

Western Kennel World (Monthly) 20 Sycamore St., San Francisco, California 94110

There are a number of periodicals devoted to specific breeds, some being published or sponsored by various club organizations. To ascertain whether or not a periodical is available regarding a particular breed, inquire of the appropriate national club organization (see clubs listed elsewhere in this volume).

The following periodicals are *examples* of such special interest or specific breed publications.

The American Brittany (Monthly) Route 3, Box 14, Sherwood, Oregon 97140

The American Dachshund (Monthly) 1016 Cypress Way, San Diego, California 92103

The Boxer Review (Monthly) 819 Santee St., Los Angeles, California 90014

The Cocker Spaniel Visitor, 819 Santee St., Los Angeles, California 90014

Collie and Shetland Sheep Dog, 819 Santee St., Los Angeles, California 90014

The German Shepherd Dog Review (Monthly) P.O. Box 1221, Lancaster, Pennsylvania 17604

German Shorthaired Pointer (Monthly) 124 East Plum St., Box 395, Saint Paris, Ohio 43072

Pekingese Parade (Monthly) 218 E. 48th St., Savannah, Georgia 31405

The Poodle Review (Monthly) 26 Commerce St., New York, New York 10014

The Weimaraner Magazine (Monthly) Box 531, Madison, Wisconsin 53701

Some samples of magazines devoted to dogs.

──The "American Field"──

WITH ITS columns devoted almost entirely to bird dog and bird dog activities, the *American Field*, with editorial and publication offices at 222 West Adams Street, Chicago, Illinois, is America's oldest sporting journal. Established in 1874 as the *Chicago Field*, the name was changed to the present title in 1881 without a break in publication.

The first editor was Luther Shinn, one of the first active editorialists to warn the nation against the depletion of wild life resources in the west. Succeeding him were C. W. and W. W. Marsh, brothers, of Sycamore, Illinois. Dr. Nicholas Rowe assumed control in 1881 and remained as the head of the paper until his death in 1896. His widow carried on until her death in 1920, when the controlling interest of the paper passed to Stewart J. Walpole.

The *American Field* made great strides under the management of Dr. Rowe and still greater progress under the direction of Mr. Walpole. With its coterie of brilliant field trial reporters, among whom were numbered: Major J. M. Taylor, Dr. William A. Bruette, Charles P. Richards, Claudius Conant, Freeman Lloyd, James Isgrigg, Fred Pond, David H. Eaton, C. B. Whitford, Ed Banks, and Albert F. Hochwalt, the *American Field* soon became the bird dog fancier's "bible," as it is today.

The present editor and publisher is William F. Brown, who succeeded the late Frank M. Young. Most of the American and Canadian bird dog field trials are now regularly reported in the *American Field* and no other publication devotes so much space to bird dog affairs.

Among its editorial staff members are: George M. Rogers, Jack Downs, John S. O'Neall, Sr. & Jr., William F. McCarty, Evelyn Monte, Albert J. Pilon, David H. Fletcher, Dr. Earl E. Bradley, Henry P. Davis, C. F. Fogg, W. F. Brown, et. al.

The *American Field* became a weekly six months after its establishment, and there have been but minor changes in its format since that time.

THE FIELD DOG STUD BOOK

In 1876, the *American Field* opened a free kennel registry for all dogs used in field sports, thereby setting in motion the first machinery for the keeping of an authentic registry for dogs in the United States. This was to supplement the work initiated by Arnold Burges in his book, *American Kennel and Sporting Field*. An imported English Setter named Adonis was the first registration in Mr. Burges' record. Numbers 1 to 177, inclusive, were given to imported English, Irish, and Gordon Setters, while from 178 to 242 became a division for "native Setters," so called because they were derived from strains bred in Amer-

ica, although the foundation stock was imported. The next division, numbering 45, consisted of Cross-Bred Setters.

The *American Field* began to publish, free of charge, registrations for the *National American Kennel Club Register*. In 1877 it was announced that a total of 656 registrations had been made, but it was not until 1879 that Volume I of the *Register* was published and six years passed before Volume II appeared. Dr. Rowe decided to donate these records to the American Kennel Club, then headed by Major J. M. Taylor, and public acknowledgment of the gift was made in Volume IV, published in 1887.

The Field Dog Stud Book came into existence in 1900, under the sponsorship of the *American Field*, and since has specialized in sporting dog breeds, principally utility field dogs. It is, however, an all breed registry. Its registrations have averaged over 20,000 a year, mainly pointers, setters, Brittany Spaniels, German Shorthaired Pointers, retrievers, and some spaniels. By far the great majority of pointers and setters recorded in the United States are registered in the Field Dog Stud Book. Individual registration fee is three dollars.

The *American Field*, a publication devoted to bird dogs and bird dog activities.

REQUIREMENTS FOR TRAVELING IN THE 50 STATES OF THE U.S.A.

State	Health certificate	Rabies inoculation	Within this time	Puppies	Other
Alabama	*	*	6 mo.	3 mo.	3, 6
Alaska	*	*	6 mo.		6
Arizona	*	*	1 yr. kv / 3 yr. mlv	4 mo.	2
Arkansas	*	*	1 yr.		2, 6, 7
California	*	*	2 yr. cev / 1 yr. ntv	4 mo.	
Colorado	*	*	1 yr.	3 mo.	6, 7
Connecticut	*	*	6 mo.		1, 2, 6
Delaware	*	*		4 mo.	2
Florida	*	*	6 mo.		
Georgia	*	*	6 mo.		2, 6
Hawaii	120-day quarantine. $5 registration fee, plus daily fee of $1 for dogs and 70¢ for cats.				
Idaho	*	*	6 mo. ntv / 2 yr. cev	4 mo.	2, 6, 10
Illinois	*	*	6 mo. kv / 1 yr. mlv	16 wks.	
Indiana	*	*	mlv or equal duration	4 mo.	7
Iowa	*	*	2 yr. cev / 1 yr. kv	4 mo.	1, 7
Kansas	*	*	1 yr.	3 mo.	
Kentucky	*	*	1 yr. kv / 2 yr. mlv	4 mo.	1, 2, 6, 7
Louisiana	*	*	2 yr. cev / 1 yr. ntv	2 mo.	
Maine	*				
Maryland	*	*	1 yr.	4 mo.	2, 6
Massachusetts	*	*	1 yr.		1
Michigan	*	*	6 mo. kv	6 mo.	1, 4, 7
Minnesota	*	*	1 yr. kv / 2 yr. mlv	6 mo.	1, 6
Mississippi	*	*	6 mo.	3 mo.	2, 7
Missouri	*	*	3 yr. mlv / 1 yr. kv	4 mo.	
Montana	*	*	2 yr. mlv	3 mo.	5
Nebraska	*	*	2 yr. mlv / 1 yr. kv	4 mo.	
Nevada	*	*	2 yr. cev / 1 yr. ntv	4 mo.	1, 2, 6
New Hampshire	*	*	3 yr. cev / 1 yr. kv	3 mo.	2, 6
New Jersey	*				2, 6
New Mexico	*	*	1 yr.	3 mo.	
New York					
North Carolina	*	*	1 yr.	4 mo.	1, 5
North Dakota	*	*	3 yr. mlv	3 mo.	1, 2, 6, 8
Ohio	*	*	3 yr. cev / 1 yr. other	6 mo.	
Oklahoma	*	*	1 yr.		2, 6
Oregon	*	*	2 yr. mlv / 6 mo. kv	4 mo.	5
Pennsylvania					9
Rhode Island	*	*	6 mo. kv / 2 yr. mlv	6 mo. All Dogs	2, 6
South Carolina	*	*	1 yr.		2, 6
South Dakota	*	*	1 yr.		
Tennessee	*	*	1 yr.		2, 6
Texas	*	*	6 mo.		
Utah	*	*		4 mo.	7
Vermont	*	*	1 yr. mlv	4 mo.	2, 7
Virginia	*	*	1 yr.	4 mo.	2, 6, 7
Washington	*	*	2 yr. mlv / 6 mo. kv	4 mo.	5, 7
West Virginia	*	*	1 yr.		1, 2, 6, 7
Wisconsin	*	*	3 yr. cev / 1 yr. other	6 mo.	
Wyoming	*	*	2 yr. cev / 1 yr. tcv	4 mo.	2, 6

Courtesy of ASPCA

Code definition

* — Health certificate or rabies inoculation required
Time — rabies inoculation must be given within the time listed
MLV — modified live virus vaccine
KV — killed virus vaccine
CEV — chick embryo vaccine
NTV — nerve tissue vaccine
Puppies — are exempt from rabies vaccination requirement up to age listed

Other
1 — show dogs exempt
2 — dogs from rabies quarantine area not admitted
3 — dogs with screwworms not admitted
4 — may be quarantined 60 days if from rabies area
5 — dogs from rabies quarantine area may enter with written permit
6 — not admitted if exposed to rabies or from an area where rabies exists
7 — cats require health certificate and rabies vaccination
8 — hunting dogs must receive rabies vaccination within 30 days of entry
9 — proof of ownership required
10 — puppies under 4 months from a quarantine area need a permit from Bureau of Animal Industry

—Stud Books and Registers—

LISTED below are the publications and organizations in the United States maintaining stud books for the registration of pure-bred dogs. Full information concerning the requirements for registration, fees, nominations of litters, etc., may be obtained by writing these organizations direct.

American Kennel Club (All breeds) 51 Madison Ave., New York, N. Y., 10010.

American Field Publishing Company (Field Dog Stud Book, All Breeds, but mainly Sporting) 222 West Adams St., Chicago, Ill. 60606.

United Kennel Club, 321 W. Cedar St., Kalamazoo, Mich. 49007.

The Chase Publishing Company (International Foxhunters Stud Book), 152 Walnut St., Lexington, Ky. 40501.

Hunter's Horn (Standard Foxhound Stud Book), Sand Springs, Okla. 74063.

Full Cry Kennel Club, (Coonhounds), Box 190, Sedalia, Mo. 65301.

National Stock Dog Registry, Rt. 1, Butler, Ind. 46721.

The National Coursing Association, 300 North Cedar St., Abilene, Kansas 67410. (Inquire re greyhounds/coursing hounds.)

Addresses Abroad
—Dog Organizations, Clubs—

THE ADDRESSES of some of the more prominent dog organizations outside the U.S.A. are included for reference, but the reader is reminded that these addresses may change from time to time.

Canadian Kennel Club, Inc.—1173 Bay St., Toronto, Ontario, Canada.

The Kennel Club—1, Clarges St., Piccadilly, London, W.1 England. (This is for the British Kennel Clubs).

International Federation of Kennel Clubs (F.C.I.)—36 Grand Rue, Thuin (Hainaut), Belgium. (This organization also has another address at #12 Rue Leopold II, also in Thuin, Belgium.)

Verband fur das Deutsche Hundewesen—46 Dortmund, Germany, Schwanen Str. #30.

Svenska Kennelklubben—Kungsgatan No. 51, 11 Stockholm, Sweden.

Real Sociedad Canina de Espana, Madrazo 20, Madrid, Spain.

Bermuda Dog Shows—Mrs. Edward Flieger, Show Secretary, Son Cy Cottage, Pembrook, Bermuda.

In most countries the chief kennel club organization is named on lines corresponding with the American pattern, i.e., The Norwegian Kennel Club, etc. To secure the current address for such a country's club, write to its nearest consulate offices or tourist bureau. The addresses of such offices are obtainable from telephone directories such as for Washington, D.C. or New York City, usually available for reference in libraries.

—Glossaries—Where Found—

—General Glossary—

ALMOND EYES: The eye set in surrounding tissue of almond shape.

ANGULATION: The angles formed by a meeting of the bones; mainly, the shoulder, upper arm, stifle, and hock.

APPLE-HEADED: With skull round instead of flat on top.

APRON: The frill or long hair below the neck on long-coated dogs, such as the Collie.

B., OR b.: Abbreviation for bitch, as described on show catalogs, racing cards.

BABBLER: The hound that barks when not on the trail.

BALANCED: A consistent whole; symmetrical, typically proportioned as a whole or as regards its separate parts; i.e., balance of head, balance of body, or balance of head and body.

BANDOG: A dog tied by day, released at night. Tiedog.

BARREL: Rounded rib section.

BAT-EARED: Ears held erect like those of a bat, as those of the French Bulldog.

BAY: The voice of a trailing hound while hunting or when the quarry is brought to a stand.

BEARD: The profuse, bushy whiskers of a Brussels Griffon, not the whiskers of a Terrier.

BEAUTY SPOT: A distinct spot, usually round, of colored hair, surrounded by the white of the blaze, on the topskull between the ears. (Blenheim Spaniel, Boston Terrier.)

BEEFY: Overheavy development of the hindquarters.

BELTON: The blue and white or orange and white mingling color of Setters. The colors so closely intermingle as to make a distinct color, known as blue belton or orange belton. "Belton" was derived from the name of a Northumberland village.

BENCH SHOW: A dog show at which the dogs competing for prizes are "benched" or leashed on benches.

BEST IN SHOW: A dog-show award to the dog adjudged best of all breeds.

BEVY: A flock of birds.

BILATERAL CRYPTORCHID: *See* Cryptorchid.

BIRD DOG: A sporting dog trained to hunt birds.

BITCH: A female dog.

BITE: The relative position of the upper and lower teeth when the mouth is closed. *See* Level bite, Scissors bite, Undershot, Overshot.

BLAZE: A white mark running up the face and between the eyes.

BLINKER: A dog that points a bird and then leaves it, or upon finding a bird, avoids making a definite point.

BLOCKY: Square or cubelike formation of the head.

BLOODED: A dog of good breeding; pedigreed.

BLOOM: Glossiness of coat.

BLUE MERLE: Blue and gray mixed with black. Marbled.

BOARD: To feed, house, and care for a dog for a fee.

BOBTAIL: A naturally tailless dog or a dog with a tail docked very short. Often used as a name for the Old English Sheepdog.

BOLT: To drive or "start" an animal out of its earth or burrow.

BONE: Describing conformation. A well-boned dog denotes strength.

BOSSY: Overdevelopment of the shoulder muscles.

BRACE: Two dogs.

BREECHING: The tan colored hair on the thighs of Manchester Terriers and other breeds.

BREED: Pure-bred dogs more or less uniform in size and structure, as produced and maintained by man.

BREEDING PARTICULARS: Sire, dam, date of birth, sex, color, etc.

BRINDLE: A mixture of light and dark hairs, generally with grey or brown as the main color.

BRISKET: The part of the body in front of the chest and between the fore legs.

BROCK: A badger.

BROKEN COLOR: A self-colored dog with the main color broken by white.

BROKEN-HAIRED: A roughed-up wire coat.

BROKEN-UP FACE: A receding nose, together with a deep stop, wrinkle, and undershot jaw. (Bulldog, Pekingese.)

BROOD BITCH: A female kept for breeding purposes.

BRUSH: A tail heavily covered with hair, such as that of the Collie.

BULL BAITING: An ancient sport in which the dog baited or tormented the bull.

BURR: The inside of the ear.

BUTTERFLY-NOSE: A spotted nose.

BUTTOCKS: The rump or hips.

BUTTON-EAR: One that drops over in front, as that of the Fox and Irish Terriers.

BYE: At field trials, an odd dog remaining after the dogs entered in a stake have been paired in braces by drawing.

CANINE: A group of animals—dogs, foxes, wolves, jackals.

CANINES: The two upper and two lower sharp-pointed teeth next to the incisors. Fangs.

CASTRATE: To remove the testicles of the male dog.

CAT FOOT: Compact, round foot, like that of a cat.

CATCH DOG: A dog used to catch and hold a hunted animal, so the huntsman can take it alive.

CHAMPION: A dog that has been recorded a Champion by AKC as a result of defeating a specified number of dogs in specified competition at a series of dog shows. A *Field Champion* is determined in the same way as a result of competition at field trials.

CHARACTER: Expression, individuality, and general appearance and deportment as considered typical of a breed.

CHEEKY: Full, thick cheeks.

CHEST: The part of the body or trunk that is enclosed by the ribs.

CHINA EYE: A blue wall eye.

CHISELED: Clean-cut in head, particularly beneath the eyes.

CHOKE COLLAR: A leather or chain collar fitted to the dog's neck in such a manner that the degree of tension exerted by the hand tightens or loosens it.

CHOPS: Jowls or pendulous flesh of the lips and jaw. (Bulldog.)

CHOREA: A nervous jerking caused by involuntary contraction of the muscles, usually affecting the face or legs.

CLIP: The method of trimming the coat in some breeds, notably the Poodle.

CLODDY: Low, thickset, comparatively heavy.

CLOSE-COUPLED: Comparatively short from withers to hipbones.

COAT: The hair covering a dog's body.

COBBY: Short and compact.

COLLAR: The marking around the neck, usually white. Also a leather or chain for restraining or leading the dog, when the leash is attached.

COMPANION DOG (C.D.); COMPANION DOG EXCELLENT (C.D.X.); UTILITY DOG (U.D.); TRACKING DOG (T.D.): Titles awarded and recorded by AKC to dogs that have attained certain minimum scores at a specified number of licensed or member AKC obedience trials or that have passed an AKC tracking test.

CONDITION: General health, coat and appearance.

CONFORMATION: The form and structure, make and shape; arrangement of the parts in conformance with breed-standard demands.

CORKY: Active, lively, alert.

COUPLE: Two hounds.

COUPLING: The part of the body between the ribs and pelvis; the loin.

COURSING: The sport of chasing the hare by Greyhounds. Also the sport of running to earth predators such as coyotes or wolves by use of Greyhounds and other large coursing hounds.

COW-HOCKED: Hocks that turn inward.

CRANK-STERN: A screw-tail.

CRANK TAIL: A tail carried down and resembling a crank in shape.

CREST: Top part of the arch of a dog's neck, particularly applied to Sporting dogs.

CROPPING: The practice of cutting a dog's ears to make them stand erect and pointed.

CROSSBRED: A dog whose sire and dam are representatives of two different breeds.

CROUP: Portion of body directly behind the set-on or root of tail.

CROWN: The highest part of the head; the topskull.

CRY: The baying or "music" of the hounds.

CRYPTORCHID: The adult whose testicles are abnormally retained in the abdominal cavity. Bilateral cryptorchidism involves both sides; that is, neither testicle has descended into the scrotum. Unilateral cryptorchidism involves one side only; that is, one testicle is retained or hidden, and one descended.

CULOTTE: The feathery hair on the back of the fore legs of Pekingese, Pomeranians, and Schipperkes.

CUR: A mongrel.

CUSHION: Fullness or thickness of the upper lips. (Pekingese.)

D. OR d.: Abbreviation for male dog, as described on show catalogs, racing cards.

DAM: The female parent.

DAPPLED: Mottled marking of different colors, no one predominating.

DEADGRASS: Tan or dull straw color.

DERBY: Field-trial competition for young, novice sporting dogs usually between one and two years of age.

DEWCLAW: The extra toe or claw occasionally found on the inside of the hind legs of some dogs.

DEWLAP: Loose skin under a dog's chin.

DIEHARD: Nickname of the Scottish Terrier.

DISH-FACED: When a depression in the nasal bone makes the nose higher at the tip than at the stop.

DISQUALIFICATION: A decision made by a judge or by a bench-show committee following a determination that a dog has a condition that makes it ineligible for any further competition under the dog-show rules or under the standard for its breed.

DISTEMPER TEETH: Teeth discolored or pitted as a result of distemper or other enervating disease or deficiency.

DOCKING: Shortening the dog's tail by cutting.

DOG: A male dog; also used collectively to designate both male and female.

DOG SHOW: A competitive exhibition for dogs at which the dogs are judged in accordance with an established standard of perfection for each breed.

DOMED: Evenly rounded in topskull; convex instead of flat. Domy.

DOUBLE COAT: An outer coat resistant to weather and protective against brush and brambles, together with an undercoat of softer hair for warmth and waterproofing.

DOWN-FACED: Opposite to Dish-faced. When the nasal bone inclines downward toward the tip of the nose.

DOWN IN PASTERN: Weak or faulty pastern (metacarpus) set at a pronounced angle from the vertical.

DRAG: A trail prepared by dragging along the ground a bag impregnated usually with animal scent.

DRAWING: Selection by lot of dogs to be run, and in which pairs, in a field-trial stake.

DROP-EAR: Ears hanging close and flat to the side of the cheeks.

DROPPER: A cross between a Pointer and a Setter.

DRY NECK: The skin taut, neither loose nor wrinkled.

DUAL CHAMPION: A dog that has won both a bench-show and a field-trial championship.

DUDLEY NOSE: A flesh colored nose.

ELBOW: The joint at the top of the fore leg, next to the body.

ELBOWS-OUT: Elbows not close to the body, as those of the Bulldog. A fault in most other breeds.

EWE NECK: Concave curvature of the top neckline.

EXPRESSION: The general appearance of all features of the head as viewed from the front and as typical of the breed.

EYETEETH: The upper canines.

FAKING: To change the appearance of a dog by artificial means with the object of deceiving the onlooker as to its real merit.

FALL: The long hair overhanging the face of Yorkshire and Skye Terriers.

FANCIER: A person especially interested and usually active in some phase of the sport of pure-bred dogs.

FANGS: See Canines.

FEATHER, FEATHERING: The long hair fringe on the back of the legs of some breeds.

FEET EAST AND WEST: The toes turned out.

FETCH: The retrieve of game by the dog; also the command to do so.

FIDDLE FRONT: Forelegs out at elbows, pasterns close, and feet turned out. French front.

FIDDLE-HEADED: A long, wolfish head.

FIELD TRIAL: A competition for certain Hound or Sporting Breeds in which dogs are judged on ability and style in finding or retrieving game or following a game trail.

FLAG: Long-haired tail.

FLANK: The side of the body between the last rib and the hip.

FLARE: A blaze that widens as it approaches the topskull.

FLAT BONE: The leg bone whose girth is elliptical rather than round.

FLAT-SIDED: Ribs insufficiently rounded as they approach the sternum or breastbone.

FLEWS: The pendulous inner corners of the lips of the upper jaw.

FLUSH: To drive birds from cover, to force them to take flight. To spring.

FLYING EARS: Any characteristic drop ears or semi-prick ears that stand or "fly."

FOREARM: The bone of the foreleg between the elbow and the pastern.

FOREFACE: The front part of the head, before the eyes. Muzzle.

FOSTER MOTHER: A bitch or other animal, such as a cat, used to nurse whelps not her own.

FOUL COLOR: A color or marking not characteristic.

FRILL: The hair under the neck and on the chest, as in the Collie.

FRINGES: See Feathering.

FROG-FACE: Non-receding nose on a Bulldog.

FRONT: The forepart of the body as viewed head on; i.e., forelegs, chest, brisket, and shoulder line.

FURROW: A slight indentation or median line down the center of the skull to the stop.

FUTURITY STAKE: A class at dog shows or field trials for young dogs which have been nominated at or before birth.

GAIT: The manner in which a dog walks, trots, or runs.

GAME: Hunted wild birds or animals.

GAY: A tail which is carried well up. Proper in some breeds, a fault in others.

GAZEHOUND: Greyhound or other sight-hunting hound.

GELD: See Castrate.

GENEALOGY: Recorded family descent.

GOOSE-RUMPED: A sloping rump with the tail set on too low.

GRIZZLE: Bluish-gray.

GROOM: To brush, comb, trim, or otherwise make the coat neat.

GROUPS: The breeds as grouped in six divisions to facilitate judging.

GUN DOG: A dog trained to work with its master in finding live game and retrieving game that has been shot.

GUNS: Sportsmen who do the shooting at field trials.

GUN-SHY: A dog which is fearful at the sight of a gun or at its report.

HACKLES: Hair on neck and back raised involuntarily in fright or anger.

HAM: Muscular development of the hind leg just above the stifle.

HANDLER: A person who handles a dog in the show ring or at a field trial. *Also see* Professional Handler.

HARD-MOUTHED: When a retrieving dog bites or damages the bird or animal being retrieved he is said to be hard-mouthed.

HARE-FOOT: A long narrow foot.

HARLEQUIN: Mottled or pied in color as some Great Danes.

HARNESS: A leather strap shaped around the shoulders and chest, with a ring at its top over the withers.

HAW: An inner eyelid more developed in some breeds than in others, generally red in color.

HEAT: Common term for season or oestrum.

HEEL: *See* Hock; also a command to the dog to keep close beside its handler.

HEIGHT: Vertical measurement from the withers to the ground; referred to usually as shoulder height. *See* Withers.

HIE ON: A command to urge the dog on; used in hunting or in field trials.

HOCK: The tarsus or collection of bones of the hind leg forming the joint between the second thigh and the metatarsus; the dog's true heel.

HOLT: The lair of the fox or other animal in tree roots, banks, drains or similar hideouts. Lodge.

HONORABLE SCARS: Scars from injuries suffered as a result of work.

HOUND: A dog commonly used for hunting by scent or sight.

HOUND-MARKED: A coloration composed of white, tan, and black. The ground color, usually white, may be marked with tan and/or black patches on the head, back, legs, and tail. The extent and the exact location of such markings, however, differ in breeds and individuals.

HOUND JOG: The usual pace of the hound.

HUCKLE-BONES: The top of the hip joints.

IN-BREEDING: The mating of very closely related dogs.

INCISORS: The upper and lower front teeth between the canines.

INTERBREEDING: The breeding together of dogs of different varieties.

ISABELLA: Fawn or light bay color.

JUDGE: The arbiter in the dog-show ring, obedience trial, or field trial.

KENNEL: Building in which dogs are housed.

KINK-TAIL: A tail with a break or kink in it.

KISS MARKS: Tan spots on the cheeks and over the eyes.

KNUCKLING OVER: Faulty structure of carpus (wrist) joint allowing it to double forward under the weight of the standing dog; double-jointed wrist, often with slight swelling of the bones.

LAYBACK: The receding nose of a Pug, Toy Spaniel or Bulldog.

LEAD: A strap, cord, or chain attached to the collar or harness for the purpose of restraining or leading the dog. Leash.

LEASH: A thong by which dogs are held. Three Greyhounds (obsolete term).

LEATHER: The skin of the external ear.

LEVEL BITE: When the front teeth (incisors) of the upper and lower jaws meet exactly edge to edge. Pincer bite.

LEVEL-JAWED: Teeth meeting evenly; jaw neither overshot nor undershot.

LIAM: Leash.

LICENSE: Formal permission granted by AKC to non-member club to hold a dog show, obedience trial, or field trial; or to a person to handle dogs in the show ring for pay.

LINE-BREEDING: The mating of dogs of similar strains not too closely related.

LIPPY: Having excessively hanging lips.

LITTER: Collective term for the puppies born to a bitch at the same whelping.

LIVER: A color; i.e., deep, reddish brown.

LOADED SHOULDERS: When the shoulder blades are shoved out from the body by overdevelopment of the muscles.

LOIN: Region of the body on either side of the vertebral column between the last ribs and the hindquarters.

LOWER THIGH: *See* Second thigh.

LUMBER: Superfluous flesh.

LUMBERING: An awkward gait.

LURCHER: A crossbred hound.

LYMER: A hound of ancient times led by a liam.

MAD DOG: A rabid dog.

MANE: Thick hair on neck.

MANTEL: Dark-shaded portion of the coat on shoulders, back, and sides. (St. Bernard.)

MASK: The dark muzzle of some breeds.

MATCH SHOW: Usually an informal dog show at which no championship points are awarded.

MATE: To breed a dog and bitch.

MEDIAN LINE: *See* Furrow.

MERLE: Bluish-gray color marbled with black.

MISCELLANEOUS CLASS: A competitive class at dog shows for dogs of certain specified breeds for which no regular dog show classification is provided.

MOLERA: Incomplete, imperfect or abnormal ossification of the skull.

MONGREL: A dog whose parents are of mixed-breed origin.

MONORCHID: A unilateral cryptorchid. *See* Cryptorchid.

MUSIC: The baying of the hounds.

MUTE: To run mute, to be silent on the trail; i.e., to trail without baying or barking.

MUZZLE: The head in front of the eyes—nasal bone, nostrils, and jaws. Foreface. Also, a strap or wire cage attached to the foreface to prevent the dog from biting or from picking up food.

MUZZLE BAND: White marking around the muzzle. (Boston Terrier.)

NON-SLIP RETRIEVER: The dog that walks at heel, marks the fall, and retrieves game on command; not expected to find or flush.

NOSE: Organ of smell; also, the ability to detect by means of scent.

OCCIPITAL PROTUBERANCE: A prominently raised occiput characteristic of some gun-dog breeds.

OCCIPUT: The prominent bone at the top of the skull.

OESTRUM: The periods during which a bitch is ready to accept a dog for mating.

OPEN BITCH: A bitch that can be bred.

OPEN CLASS: A class at dog shows in which all dogs of a breed, champions and imported dogs included, may compete.

ORANGE BELTON: *See* Belton.

ORGANIZED COMPETITION: Competition governed by the rules of a club or society, such as the AKC, organized to promote the interests of pure-bred dogs.

OTTER-TAIL: A thick tapering tail similar to that of the otter, such as in the Labrador Retriever.

OUT AT ELBOWS: Elbows turning out from the body as opposed to being held close.

OUT AT WALK: To lease or lend a puppy to someone for raising.

OUTCROSS: The mating of unrelated dogs or those of an entirely different strain.

OVERHANG: A heavy or pronounced brow. (Pekingese.)

OVERSHOT: The front teeth of the upper jaw protrude over those of the lower jaw.

PACE: A gait which tends to promote a rolling motion of the body. The left foreleg and left hind leg advance in unison, then the right foreleg and right hind leg.

PACK: A number of hounds kept together in the same kennel.

PAD: Sole of the foot.

PADDLING: Moving with forefeet wide.

PAPER FOOT: A flat foot with thin pads.

PARTICOLOR: A coat of two colors in equal proportions.

PASTERN: Leg below the knee of the front leg or below the hock of the hind leg.

PEAK: The pointed top of the skull in such breeds as the Bloodhound and Basset hound.

PEDIGREE: A table of genealogy, giving the names of the dog's ancestors.

PENCILING: Dark lines divided by streaks of tan on the toes of a Manchester Terrier.

PIED: Comparatively large patches of two or more colors. Piebald, parti-colored.

PIGEON BREAST: A chest with a short protruding breast bone.

PIG JAW: See Overshot.

PILE: Dense undercoat of soft hair.

PILEY: A coat which contains both soft and hard hair, as in the Dandie Dinmont.

PINCER BITE: See Level bite.

PLUME: Feathery tail carried over the back, as in the Pomeranian.

POACH: When hunting, to trespass on private property.

POINT: The immovable stance of the hunting dog taken to indicate the presence and position of game.

POINTS: Color on face, ears, legs, and tail when correlated—usually white, black or tan.

POLICE DOG: Any dog trained for police work.

POMPON: A rounded tuft of hair left on the end of the tail when the coat is clipped. (Poodle.)

PREMIUM LIST: An advance-notice brochure sent to prospective exhibitors and containing details regarding a forthcoming show.

PRICK-EARS: Those standing erect.

PRICK EAR: Carried erect and usually pointed at the tip.

PROFESSIONAL HANDLER: A person licensed by the AKC to show dogs for their owners, for a fee.

PUT DOWN: To prepare a dog for the show ring; also used to denote a dog unplaced in competition.

PUPPY: A dog under twelve months of age.

PURE-BRED: A dog whose sire and dam belong to the same breed, and are themselves of unmixed descent since recognition of the breed.

QUALITY: Refinement, fineness.

RACY: Slight in build and long in legs.

RAT TAIL: The root thick and covered with soft curls; at the tip devoid of hair, or having the appearance of being clipped. (Irish Water Spaniel.)

REGISTER: To record a dog's breeding particulars.

RETRIEVER: A hunting term. The act of bringing back shot game to the handler.

RINGER: A substitute for; a dog closely resembling another dog.

RING STERN: A curled tail.

RING TAIL: Carried up and around almost in a circle.

ROACH BACK: A back arched convexly along the spine, especially towards the hind quarters, as in the Greyhound.

ROAN: A close mixture of any color with white.

ROMAN NOSE: A nose whose bridge is so comparatively high as to form a slight convex line from forehead to nose tip. Ram's nose.

ROSE EAR: One folding backwards, as in the Bulldog.

ROUNDING: Cutting or trimming the ends of the ear leather. (English Foxhounds.)

RUDDER: The tail.

RUFF: The frill or apron of long hair around the neck of certain breeds, as in the Chow Chow.

SABLE: A lacing of black hairs over a lighter ground color. In Collies and Shetland Sheepdogs, a brown color ranging from golden to mahogany.

SADDLE: A rectangular marking of black on the back extending to the upper flanks.

SCENT: The odor left by an animal on the trail (ground scent), or wafted through the air (air-borne scent).

SCISSORS BITE: A bite in which the outer side of the lower incisors touches the inner side of the upper incisors.

SCREW TAIL: A naturally short tail twisted in more or less spiral formation.

SECOND THIGH: That part of the hindquarter from the stifle to the hock, corresponding to the human shin and calf. Lower thigh.

SEDGE: See Deadgrass.

SEEING EYE DOG: A dog trained by the institution, The Seeing Eye, as guide for the blind.

SELF COLOR: One color or whole color except for lighter shadings.

SELF-MARKED: A dog that is of a whole color, with faint shadings on chest, feet and tail.

SEMI-PRICK EARS: Ears carried erect with just the tips leaning forward.

SEPTUM: Bone between the nostrils.

SHELLY: A narrow, weedy body.

SHOULDER: The top of the shoulder blade.

SHOULDER-HEIGHT: Height of dog's body as measured from the withers to the ground. See Withers.

SICKLE TAIL: One with an upward curve above the level of the back.

SIRE: The male parent.

SLED DOGS: Dogs worked usually in teams to draw sleds.

SLOPING SHOULDER: The shoulder blade set obliquely or "laid back."

SMOOTH COAT: Short hair, close-lying.

SNIPY: A pointed, weak muzzle.

SOUNDNESS: The state of mental and physical health when all organs and faculties are complete and functioning normally, each in its rightful relation to the other.

SPAY: To perform a surgical operation on the bitch's reproductive organs to prevent conception.

SPEAK: To bark.

SPECTACLES: Shadings or dark markings over or around the eyes or from eyes to ears.

SPLASHED: Irregularly patched, color on white or white on color.

SPLAYFOOT: A flat foot with toes spreading. Open foot, open-toed.

SPREAD: Width between the forelegs when accentuated (Bulldog.)

SPRING: See Flush.

SPRING OF RIBS: Curvature of ribs for heart and lung capacity.

SQUIRREL TAIL: Carried up and curving more or less forward.

STAKE: Designation of a class, used in field-trial competition.

STANCE: Manner of standing.

STANDARD: A description of the ideal of each recognized breed, to serve as a word pattern by which dogs are judged at shows.

STANDOFF COAT: A long or heavy coat that stands off from the body.

STARING COAT: The hair dry, harsh, and sometimes curling at the tips.

STATION: Comparative height from the ground, as high-stationed, low-stationed.

STERN: The tail of a Sporting dog, particularly Foxhound.

STERNUM: Breastbone.

STIFLE: The joint in the dog's hind leg equivalent to the knee in man.

STILTED: The choppy, up-and-down gait of the straight-hocked dog.

STOP: The depression at the junction of the nose and skull between the eyes.

STRAIGHT-HOCKED: Lacking appreciable angulation at the hock joints. Straight behind.

STRAIGHT SHOULDERS: The shoulder blades rather straight up and down, as opposed to sloping or "well laid back."

STUD BOOK: A record of the breeding particulars of dogs of recognized breeds.

STUD DOG: A dog used for breeding purposes.

SUBSTANCE: Bone.

SUPERCILIARY ARCHES: The ridge, projection, or prominence of the frontal bone of the skull over the eye; the brow.

SWAYBACK: Concave curvature of the back line between the withers and the hipbones.

TEAM: Three or more dogs of one breed.

TERRIER: A group of dogs used originally for hunting vermin.

THIGH: The hindquarter from hip to stifle.

THROATINESS: Loose skin about the throat where none should be present.

THUMB MARKS: Black spots on the fore legs of a Manchester Terrier.

TICKED: Small, isolated areas of black or colored hairs on a white ground.

TIMBER: Bone, especially of the legs.

TONGUE: The voice of a hound when on scent.

TOPKNOT: The long, fluffy hair on the top of the head of some breeds.

TOY DOG: One of a group of dogs characterized by very small size.

TRACE: The dark mark down the back of a Pug.

TRAIL: To hunt by following ground scent.

TRIANGULAR EYE: The eye set in surrounding tissue of triangular shape; three cornered eye.

TRICOLOR: A dog of three different colors, generally black, white, and tan.

TRIM: To groom the coat by plucking or clipping.

TROUSERS: The hair on the hind quarters of the Afghan.

TRUMPET: The slight depression or hollow on either side of the skull just behind the orbit or eye socket, the region comparable with the temple in man.

TUCKED UP: Characterized by markedly shallower body depth at the loin. Small-waisted.

TULIP-EAR: An upright ear.

TURN-UP: The projecting turned-up chin of the Bulldog.

UNDERSHOT: The lower teeth projecting beyond the upper.

UNILATERAL CRYPTORCHID: *See* Cryptorchid.

UPPER ARM: The humerus or bone of the foreleg, between the shoulder blade and the forearm.

VARMINTY: A keen, very bright or piercing expression.

VENT: Tan-colored hair under the tail of some breeds.

WALL-EYE: Parti-colored blue and white eye.

WEAVING: When in motion, the crossing of the forefeet or the hind feet. Traveling "in and out."

WEEDY: Too lightly formed.

WELL-SPRUNG: Well formed, rounded ribs.

WHEATEN: A pale yellowish color.

WHEEL BACK: The back line arched markedly over the loin. Roached.

WHELPING: The act of giving birth to puppies.

WHELPS: Unweaned puppies.

WHIP TAIL: Carried out stiffly straight, and pointed.

WHISKER: Longer hairs on muzzle sides and underjaw.

WIND: To catch the scent of game.

WINNERS: An award given at dog shows to the best dog (winners dogs) and best bitch (winners bitches) competing in regular classes.

WIRE-HAIRED: A harsh, crisp coat.

WITHERS: The highest point of the shoulders, immediately behind the neck.

WRINKLE: The loosely folded skin on the forehead and sides of the face in some breeds such as the Bloodhound and Bulldog.